Ex Líbrís

SMITHSONIAN'S®
GREAT BATTLES
& BATTLEFIELDS
OF THE CIVIL WAR

OTHER BOOKS BY EDWIN C. BEARSS

Rebel Victory at Vicksburg

Hardluck Ironclad

Forrest at Brices' Cross Roads

Fort Smith: Little Gibraltar on the Arkansas

The Campaign for Vicksburg, Volume I: Vicksburg Is the Key

The Campaign for Vicksburg, Volume II: Grant Strikes a Fatal Blow

The Campaign for Vicksburg, Volume III: Unvexed to the Sea

National Museum of American History

SMITHSONIAN'S®
GREAT BATTLES
& BATTLEFIELDS
OF THE CIVILWAR

A Definitive Field Guide

Based on the Award-Winning Television Series by MasterVision®

Jay Wertz and Edwin C. Bearss

Foreword by James M. McPherson

William Morrow and Company, Inc.
New York

Book typography by Cindy Kendrick
Maps created by Michael Morgan
Based on maps designed by David E. Streib and Jay Wertz
and created by David E. Streib
from *Smithsonian's*® *Great Battles of the Civil War*
Video Series Copyright 1993 MasterVision®

It is the policy of William Morrow and Company, Inc., and its imprints and affiliates, recognizing the importance of preserving what has been written, to print the books we publish on acid-free paper, and we exert our best efforts to that end.

Wertz, Jay.
    Smithsonian's great battles & battlefields of the Civil War : a definitive guide based on the award-winning television series by MasterVision / Jay Wertz and Edwin C. Bearss ; introduction by James M. McPherson.
        p.   cm.
    At head of title: National Museum of American History
    ISBN 0-688-13549-8
    1. United States—History—Civil War, 1861–1865—Battlefields—Guidebooks.
2. Historic sites—United States—Guidebooks.   3. United States—Guidebooks.
4. United States—History—Civil War, 1861–1865—Campaigns. I. Bearss, Edwin C.   II. Title.
III. Title: Smithsonian's great battles and battlefields of the Civil War.   IV. Title: Great battles & battlefields of the Civil War.
E641.W48   1997
917.304'929—DC20   96–1481
                                                                          CIP

Printed in the United States of America

First Edition

1 2 3 4 5 6 7 8 9 10

BOOK DESIGNED BY CINDY KENDRICK

Dedicated to the memory of Edward C. Ezell

Foreword

The explosion of interest in the American Civil War during the past decade has produced a vast increase in visiting of Civil War sites. Hundreds of group tours of battlefields are sponsored annually by Civil War roundtables, tour operators, preservation groups, educational institutions such as the Smithsonian, elderhostels, and the like. The United States Army and Marine Corps organize "staff rides" of Civil War battlefields to teach timeless lessons of strategy and tactics to modern officers.

But most visitors to Civil War battlefields are individuals on their own or in small family groups. They are eager to learn more about the epic events that forever changed and shaped the destiny of the United States. The annual number of visitors to Gettysburg National Military Park approaches two million, while several other national and state Civil War battlefield parks count their annual visitors in the hundreds or scores of thousands. The National Park Service and the counterpart agencies of several state parks have done a good job with limited resources to offer tourists maps and self-guided driving tours. Private guides are available for some battlefields.

Many important battlefields and hundreds of other Civil War sites, however, are not part of any park system. Some of the war's most crucial battles were fought in Virginia's Shenandoah Valley, around Atlanta, and on the south side of Nashville. Not one of these battlefields is preserved in public ownership; most traces of all of them have disappeared wherever cities have spread their commercial and residential tentacles over once hallowed ground. Only small fractions of the dozens of separate battle sites around Richmond and Petersburg are preserved in the two national battlefield parks near these cities. Visitors who want to trace and visit surviving portions of these campaigns and battles whose sites are not preserved in public ownership are often frustrated by inadequate or inaccurate maps, hard-to-find historical markers, or the total absence of any markers at all. And sometimes even the self-guiding tours in national or state parks are confusing or skimpy.

To meet a growing demand for help in finding and understanding these sites, several Civil War battlefield guidebooks have been published in recent years. Some cover most or all of the principal campaigns and battles; others specialize in detailed maps, narratives, and driving tours for a single campaign or a single state. But no guidebook has combined comprehensive coverage of *all* Civil War sites with an intensive focus on each campaign or battle—until now. *Smithsonian's Great Battles and Battlefields of the Civil War* fills a crying need for a single volume that students of the war can take with them to Civil War sites *everywhere*—even abroad, for part of the American Civil War took place in the ports and capitals of foreign countries. *Smithsonian's* is a guide to more than battlefields; many important surviving sites associated with political, economic, or social developments in the war are also included.

Two of the most knowledgeable experts on the Civil War have combined their talents to produce this guidebook. Jay Wertz is the writer and producer of the video series *Smithsonian's Great Battles of the Civil War*, the best television documentary of the great campaigns on land and water that left

620,000 dead in America's bloodiest war. Edwin C. Bearss, chief historian emeritus of the National Park Service, is the foremost guide to Civil War battlefields. His encyclopedic knowledge and photographic memory for details and terrain as well as the larger picture are legendary. Wertz and Bearss have packaged their expertise, along with clear and easy-to-follow maps and directions for driving and walking tours, into this comprehensive and handy volume. Its narratives of campaigns and battles are concise and masterful; the organization by states and regions, with cross-references to related areas and operations, are clear and logical.

I have been to many of the battlefields and other sites covered in this book. But now I must go back, with the book in hand, to see the things I missed the first and even the fourth and fifth times. And as soon as I can, I intend to rack my bicycle on the car and head to some of the many sites I have never before visited. The only guide I will need to take with me is *Smithsonian's Great Battles and Battlefields of the Civil War*. It is truly the bible for Civil War tourism.

JAMES M. MCPHERSON

Preface

The American Civil War is thought by many historians to be the fundamental event shaping the character of the United States of America. The ideas of liberty, democracy, and individual freedom were forged in a war that formed this country from the passions of individuals yearning to be free of the tyranny of a great colonial power. On the battlefields of the Revolutionary War, men bled and died so that the ideals set forth in the Declaration of Independence would flourish. But the nation had to endure more hardships and blood before those ideals were shaped into the blueprint for a society where all would be truly free. The Civil War provided the ultimate test of the ability of the country to resolve its impassioned regional and cultural differences and emerge a stronger entity capable of surviving and growing within a framework of unity.

The personal connection people feel with the events, places, and personalities of the war, through family history, proximity of its locations, and the impact of the war, continues to make the Civil War the most studied and fascinating part of America's history.

The Smithsonian Institution has long recognized the need to take the study of America's history beyond the storied treasure of artifacts deposited in its collections. With the commissioning, in 1991, of the video series *Smithsonian's Great Battles of the Civil War,* and later, the television series of the same name, the Smithsonian sought to bring together not only the artifacts of its and other collections, but also the impressions of modern historians, locales where the history was made, and fascinating battle re-creations by dedicated reenactors. The approach was a comprehensive chronological study with modern visual and audio techniques of the people, places, and events of the war linked by cause and result, to enhance the awareness and study of the period. With this book, the Smithsonian Institution seeks to add to the resources of those who study the Civil War, and to bring to new audiences a comprehensive look at the battles and the places they were fought so that many might be enriched by the experience of learning and walking the "hallowed ground," in the footsteps of history.

There is a variety of works in the vast archive of Civil War volumes available to people who want to tour Civil War regions or major battlefields. This book, based on the 1993 Civil War Sites Advisory Commission's *Report on the Nation's Civil War Battlefields,* places in a single volume virtually all the battles and engagements that constituted the four-year conflict. In addition to describing the actions and their causal associations with battles, campaigns, strategies, and policies, the battles and the people engaged in them are linked to places where visitors may see and experience the traces of their history. Great effort has been made to provide specific directions and/or contacts for travelers who set off to explore the historical areas where decisions were made and men fell in defense of the principles they held dear.

Arranged by states and regions, this guide is organized to make touring as organized, smooth, and pleasurable as possible. Within the text and at the end of major sections, cross-references are given to help travelers or readers follow the progress of campaigns and chronological events, and will give them an integrated description of notable Civil War personalities. The identification of specific units and their leaders will aid the reader or traveler interested in tracking the accomplishments of the participants from place to place, and perhaps add to understanding the adventures of a specific regiment or ancestor. Though these are not in-depth identifications, they may inspire interest to dig further. And because touring Civil War battlefields and sites provides an enriching and entertaining outing or vacation to boot, information is given for visitor facilities, related recreational opportunities, bed and breakfasts, and so forth.

Much of the credit for information on specific sites goes to people who live in nearby communities, and to those whose work, both remunerative and voluntary, is to conserve and maintain these sites—whatever compensation they receive is exceeded by the hard work and enthusiasm they share for preserving these elements of our national heritage. Increasing awareness of the importance of the preservation of Civil War battlefields has yielded a number of new locations where the events of the war may be studied and appreciated. Many of these sites are receiving additional interpretive features to enhance their value to visitors. We hope that this book will encourage and aid more people to tour Civil War battlefields, sites, and related structures, to enrich their own understanding and appreciation of this most important period in American history.

JAY WERTZ and EDWIN C. BEARSS

Acknowledgments

A production of this magnitude required the cooperation of many people, who gave of their time and talents primarily because of their belief in this project as a significant and valuable aid in the enrichment and understanding of the Civil War and its place in American history. Clearly, my personal thanks are directed most importantly to my co-writer, Ed Bearss. An author of many works on his own, Ed is experienced in giving acknowledgment to many people and organizations. It is difficult, he told me, to measure the contribution of specific sources, and to specify certain people or groups. Naturally, being a rookie book writer, I always yield to his greater experience and knowledge—except in this one instance. I feel compelled to give some specific acknowledgment to those who were of great help to me in my work on this book.

To the many people around the country and abroad who provided information on various specific battlefields and points of interest, you have my heartfelt thanks. Some information, through no fault of the sources, arrived too late for inclusion; however, future editions will include expanded and updated site information which I will continue to gather. My thanks to Oliver J. Keller for introducing me to a number of people who provided me information on the Georgia chapter. William R. Scaife gave me a personal tour of the Johnston River Line and reviewed the Georgia chapter. My thanks also to Mark Christ, Bob Bradley, Dr. Stephen R. Wise, Brian L. Polk, Larry Ludwig, and Norman A. Nicolson for reviewing portions of the manuscript. Milton Bagley provided information on Streight's Raid tour sites. Susan Laccetti of *The Atlanta Journal* suggested including information on bike trails. My great thanks also to Jim McPherson for graciously consenting to write the Foreword.

The production staff was outstanding. My personal thanks to William Morrow & Company, Inc.'s editor in chief, Will Schwalbe, and Doris Cooper, Linda Kocur, and Tom Nau of the editorial and production departments. Thanks to Hannah Runge Mullin, acting director, and James E. Lewis, Jr., product manager of the Smithsonian Office of Product Development & Licensing, for their assistance in coordinating this project. A very special thanks to all the photographers listed in the picture credits; to Alexander Verbitsky for adapting the cover design from *Smithsonian's Great Battles of the Civil War* video series; to Virginia W. Wilson for accounting services; to TeleVu San Diego for a great office environment in which to write; to Kelly Greene and Hope Sinatra for assisting with the layout; and to Elizabeth Royte, Peter Kreutzer, Victor Sitkowski, Judy Hartman, Celia Kelly, and Aaron Ledger for assistance in copyediting the manuscript. I also want to thank Margie Bearss for helping me maintain constant communication with Ed, who was frequently on the road giving lectures and leading tours of Civil War battlefields.

Three individuals worked tirelessly to assist me with the production: Cindy Tiano, who provided much assistance with the word processing, Michael Morgan, who created the maps, and Cindy Kendrick, who created the design of the book and did the layout and typesetting. They are all outstanding professionals in their fields. I also want to express my sincere appreciation and thanks to my fiancée, Belem Contreras, for her support during the long hours of research, writing, and production. Finally, this project would not have been possible without the vision and efforts of Richard Stadin of MasterVision®, Inc., who, together with Will Schwalbe, had the idea and provided the means and impetus to see it through to its conclusion. Again, my heartfelt thanks to all of you.

JAY WERTZ

Contents

List of Maps xxv
Introduction—How to Use This Guide xxvii

ALABAMA 1
BRIDGEPORT   1
ATHENS   2
DECATUR   4
DAY'S GAP AND STREIGHT'S RAID   5
SELMA   8
MONTGOMERY   11
MOBILE AREA   13
  Battle of Mobile Bay   14
  Spanish Fort   23
  Fort Blakeley   24
  Citronelle   26

ARKANSAS 29
PEA RIDGE   30
PRAIRIE GROVE   34
ARKANSAS POST   38
HELENA   40
LITTLE ROCK   42
CAMDEN CAMPAIGN   45
CHALK BLUFF   49

THE DISTRICT OF COLUMBIA 51
THE UNITED STATES CAPITOL   52
THE WHITE HOUSE   54
THE TREASURY BUILDING   57
THE SMITHSONIAN INSTITUTION   58
THE DEFENSE OF WASHINGTON   62
  The Washington Arsenal   62
  The Washington Navy Yard   63
  The Washington Forts   64
  Fort Stevens   66

WASHINGTON'S BRIDGES 69
FORD'S THEATRE AND THE PETERSEN HOUSE 70

THE FAR WEST 75
ARIZONA 76
  Picacho Pass 77
  Apache Pass 78
CALIFORNIA 80
NEW MEXICO 83
  Fort Fillmore and San Augustin Spring 84
  Fort Craig and Valverde 85
  Glorieta 89
  Peralta 96

FLORIDA 101
PENSACOLA AREA 102
MARIANNA 107
APALACHICOLA 107
ST. MARKS 108
NATURAL BRIDGE 110
CEDAR KEY 111
TAMPA AREA 112
  Bayport 112
  Tampa 112
KEY WEST AND THE DRY TORTUGAS 113
JACKSONVILLE AREA 116
  Fernandina 116
  St. Augustine 118
  Jacksonville 120
  Olustee 124

GEORGIA 129
KENNESAW (BIG SHANTY) 131
CHICKAMAUGA 133
  Longstreet's Rail Journey 135
RINGGOLD 142
SHERMAN'S 1864 ATLANTA CAMPAIGN 144
  Tunnel Hill 147
  Rocky Face Ridge 148
  Dalton 150

Dug Gap   151
Resaca   152
Rome Cross Roads   156
Rome   157
Cassville   158
Allatoona Pass   161
New Hope Church   164
Pickett's Mill   165
Dallas   166
Lost-Pine-Brushy Mountain Line   169
Kennesaw Mountain and Kolb's Farm   170
Marietta   175
ATLANTA AREA   177
Smyrna Line–Ruff's Mill   177
Johnston's River Line   178
Roswell   182
Chattahoochee River   183
THE BATTLES FOR ATLANTA   184
Peachtree Creek   186
The Battle of Atlanta   190
New Manchester   198
Ezra Church   199
Utoy Creek   201
JONESBORO AND THE FALL OF ATLANTA   202
Battle of Jonesboro   203
Lovejoy's Station   204
Federal Occupation of Atlanta   205
PALMETTO   210
WEST POINT   212
COLUMBUS   213
ANDERSONVILLE   215
IRWINVILLE   220
SUNSHINE CHURCH   221
THE MARCH TO THE SEA   223
Macon   224
Griswoldville   226
Milledgeville   228
Madison   229
Washington   230
Augusta   230
Waynesboro   232

Ebenezer Creek   233
SAVANNAH AREA   **234**
Fort Pulaski   234
Fort McAllister   237
Savannah   239
Darien   242

INTERNATIONAL 245

Naval Action on the World's Oceans   248
The *Trent* Affair   249
Blockade-runners   250
Confederate Cruisers   251

KENTUCKY 259

COLUMBUS   **260**
PADUCAH   **262**
MIDDLE CREEK   **263**
MILL SPRINGS   **264**
CONFEDERATE 1862 KENTUCKY CAMPAIGN   **266**
Richmond   267
Perryville   268
CYNTHIANA   **273**
FRANKFORT   **274**
LOUISVILLE   **276**
MUNFORDVILLE   **278**
KENTUCKY CAVALRY RAIDS AND RAIDERS   **280**
John Hunt Morgan   280
Nathan Bedford Forrest   282
William C. Quantrill   282

LOUISIANA 285

NEW ORLEANS   **286**
BATON ROUGE   **293**
BAYOU COUNTRY   **295**
GRAND COTEAU   **298**
PORT HUDSON   **299**
ALEXANDRIA   **304**
RED RIVER CAMPAIGN   **307**
SHREVEPORT   **313**
VICKSBURG AREA   **314**

Lake Providence   314
Delta Area—The Canal Projects   315
Milliken's Bend   316

MARYLAND 319

WESTMINSTER   320
BALTIMORE   321
ANNAPOLIS JUNCTION   323
ANNAPOLIS   324
POINT LOOKOUT   325
WASHINGTON, D.C., AREA   326
Rockville   328
FREDERICK   329
MONOCACY   330
SOUTH MOUNTAIN   333
ANTIETAM   334
WILLIAMSPORT-HAGERSTOWN   340

THE MIDWEST 343

ILLINOIS   344
Cairo   344
Springfield   345
Galena   346
INDIANA   348
Corydon   349
OHIO   349
Cincinnati   350
Buffington Island   350
Salineville   351

MISSISSIPPI 353

CORINTH-IUKA   354
GRANT'S FIRST VICKSBURG CAMPAIGN   358
Holly Springs   358
BRICES' CROSS ROADS   359
TUPELO   361
OKOLONA   362
GRENADA   363
GRANT'S SECOND VICKSBURG CAMPAIGN   364
Yazoo Pass Expedition   365

Greenville   366
Yazoo City   366
Steele's Bayou Expedition   367
VICKSBURG AREA   **368**
Chickasaw Bayou   368
NAVAL OPERATIONS AT VICKSBURG   **370**
Farragut's Expedition   370
Porter's Operations   371
THE STRATEGY CHANGES IN GRANT'S SECOND VICKSBURG
CAMPAIGN   **372**
Grand Gulf   376
Port Gibson   377
Natchez   381
Raymond   382
Jackson   382
Champion Hill   385
Big Black River   386
VICKSBURG BATTLES   **387**
May 19 Assault   387
May 22 Assault   388
Vicksburg Siege   388
GRIERSON'S RAID   **394**
MERIDIAN CAMPAIGN   **396**
BILOXI–SHIP ISLAND   **397**

MISSOURI 399
NEW MADRID   **401**
BELMONT   **402**
CAPE GIRARDEAU   **403**
STERLING PRICE'S 1864 MISSOURI RAID   **404**
Fort Davidson   405
St. Louis   406
CENTRALIA MASSACRE   **408**
BOONVILLE   **408**
GLASGOW   **409**
LEXINGTON   **410**
INDEPENDENCE   **411**
BYRAM'S FORD   **411**
WESTPORT   **412**
MARMITON   **413**

NEWTONIA   413
CARTHAGE   414
WILSON'S CREEK   415

NORTH CAROLINA 419

HATTERAS INLET   419
ROANOKE ISLAND   420
PLYMOUTH   422
KINSTON   425
NEW BERN   426
FORT MACON   427
WILMINGTON   428
FORT FISHER   430
FAYETTEVILLE–MONROE'S CROSS ROADS   435
AVERASBORO   436
BENTONVILLE   437
BENNETT PLACE   440

THE NORTHEAST 443

DELAWARE   443
Fort Delaware   443
NEW YORK   444
VERMONT   446
St. Albans   446

THE NORTHWEST 449

COLORADO   450
Sand Creek Massacre   451
IDAHO   452
Bear River Massacre   452
KANSAS   453
Lawrence Massacre   454
Sterling Price's 1864 Raid   456
Marais des Cygnes–Mine Creek (Mound City)   456
Baxter Springs Massacre   458
MINNESOTA   459
Fort Ridgely   459
New Ulm and Birch Coulee   460
Wood Lake   460

NORTH DAKOTA   462
  Big Mound   462
  Dead Buffalo Lake   463
  Whitestone Hill   463
  Killdeer Mountain   464

OKLAHOMA 467
  ROUND MOUNTAIN   468
  CHUSTO-TALASAH   468
  CHUSTENALAH   469
  OLD FORT WAYNE   470
  FIRST CABIN CREEK   470
  HONEY SPRINGS   471
  MIDDLE BOGGY DEPOT   471
  SECOND CABIN CREEK   472
  DOAKSVILLE   472

PENNSYLVANIA 477
  CHAMBERSBURG   478
  LEE'S 1863 INVASION OF THE NORTH
    (GETTYSBURG CAMPAIGN)   480
    Carlisle   482
    York   483
    Hanover   484
    Gettysburg   485

SOUTH CAROLINA 503
  CHARLESTON AREA   503
    Fort Sumter   504
    Fort Moultrie   507
    Sullivan's Island   509
    Charleston Harbor   511
    Castle Pinckney   514
    Charleston   515
    Secessionville, James and Folly Islands, and Vicinity   518
    Morris Island   521
  BEAUFORT AREA   524
    Port Royal   524
    Hilton Head   527
    Beaufort   527
    Pocotaligo   528

Honey Hill   528
SHERMAN'S MARCH THROUGH SOUTH CAROLINA   530
Rivers Bridge   531
Columbia   532

TENNESSEE 537

FORT HENRY   538
FORT DONELSON   540
JOHNSONVILLE   543
ISLAND NUMBER 10   545
FORT PILLOW–PLUM POINT BEND   548
MEMPHIS   551
HATCHIE BRIDGE   554
SHILOH   555
JACKSON–PARKER'S CROSS ROADS   559
MURFREESBORO   561
STONES RIVER   562
HOOVER'S GAP–LIBERTY GAP   567
CHATTANOOGA AREA   569
Chattanooga   569
Brown's Ferry and Wauhatchie   572
Orchard Knob–Lookout Mountain   573
Missionary Ridge   575
KNOXVILLE AREA   580
Campbell's Station   580
Knoxville   581
Fort Sanders   583
MOSSY CREEK   585
DANDRIDGE   586
FAIR GARDEN   586
BLUE SPRINGS   587
BULL'S GAP   588
GREENEVILLE   589
BLOUNTVILLE   590
BEAN'S STATION   591
CUMBERLAND GAP   592
COLUMBIA   595
SPRING HILL   597
FRANKLIN   599
NASHVILLE   602

TEXAS 609

SABINE PASS   610
GALVESTON   613
CORPUS CHRISTI   615
PALMITO RANCH   617

VIRGINIA 621

WASHINGTON, D.C., AREA   622
  Arlington   622
  Alexandria   623
  Dranesville   624
  Fairfax   624
  Chantilly   625
FIRST MANASSAS   626
SECOND MANASSAS   630
BRISTOE STATION   632
LOUDOUN AND FAUQUIER COUNTIES   633
  Ball's Bluff   633
  Loudoun Valley   634
  Thoroughfare Gap   636
  Buckland   636
LOWER SHENANDOAH VALLEY AREA   637
  First Kernstown   637
  Second Kernstown   638
JACKSON'S VALLEY CAMPAIGN   640
  Battles of Front Royal and First Winchester   640
  Second Winchester   641
SHERIDAN'S 1864–65 SHENANDOAH VALLEY CAMPAIGN   641
  Third Winchester (Opequon)   643
  Fisher's Hill   645
  Cedar Creek   646
NEW MARKET   649
HARRISONBURG   652
CROSS KEYS   653
PORT REPUBLIC   653
PIEDMONT   654
McDOWELL   655
WAYNESBORO   656
CULPEPER AND ORANGE COUNTIES   657
  Cedar Mountain   657

Kelly's Ford   658

Brandy Station   659

Rappahannock Station   663

Mine Run   664

Stoneman's Raid   665

FREDERICKSBURG AREA   **666**

Fredericksburg   666

Chancellorsville   672

GRANT'S SPRING 1864 VIRGINIA CAMPAIGN   **679**

The Wilderness   680

Spotsylvania   684

North Anna River   688

Trevilian Station   690

RICHMOND AREA   **691**

Yellow Tavern   691

Kilpatrick's Raid   692

FEDERAL 1862 CAMPAIGN AGAINST RICHMOND
(PENINSULA CAMPAIGN)   **694**

Stuart's June 1862 Ride Around McClellan   697

THE SEVEN DAYS' BATTLES   **699**

Oak Grove   699

Beaver Dam Creek   700

Gaines's Mill   700

Totopotomy Creek–Cold Harbor   702

Seven Pines   705

Savage's Station–White Oak Swamp–Glendale   707

Malvern Hill   708

Chaffin's Farm–New Market Heights   710

Bermuda Hundred   712

Drewry's Bluff   714

PETERSBURG AREA   **716**

Petersburg   716

The Crater   719

Globe Tavern   721

Ream's Station   721

Peeble's Farm   721

Boydton Plank Road–Burgess's Mill   722

Hatcher's Run   724

Fort Stedman   724

Five Forks   727

Petersburg Assault   729

City Point   732
RICHMOND   **734**
THE FALL OF RICHMOND   **736**
THE ROAD TO APPOMATTOX   **739**
Amelia Court House   739
Jetersville   740
Sailor's Creek   741
High Bridge–Farmville   744
Appomattox Court House   746
SOUTHEASTERN VIRGINIA   **751**
Naval Action at Hampton Roads   751
Fort Monroe   755
Battle of Big Bethel   758
Yorktown   759
Williamsburg   761
Suffolk   762
WESTERN AND SOUTHWESTERN VIRGINIA   **763**
Lynchburg   763
Lexington   765
Hanging Rock   767
Cloyd's Mountain   767
Saltville-Marion   768

WEST VIRGINIA 771
CARNIFAX FERRY   **772**
PRINCETON-LEWISBURG   **773**
DROOP MOUNTAIN   **775**
PHILIPPI   **776**
RICH MOUNTAIN–LAUREL HILL   **777**
CHEAT MOUNTAIN   **778**
GREENBRIER RIVER   **779**
CAMP ALLEGHENY   **779**
MOOREFIELD   **780**
HARPERS FERRY   **781**
SHEPHERDSTOWN   **784**

APPENDICES 787
Appendix A: Washington, D.C., Area Forts   787
Appendix B: Locations of Selected Civil War Movies and
Television Programs   787

BIBLIOGRAPHY 790
PICTURE CREDITS 793
INDEX 797

LIST OF MAPS

Alabama Tour Map   xxxii
Battle of Mobile Bay   15
Arkansas Tour Map   28
Battle of Pea Ridge   34
District of Columbia Tour Map   50
Washington, D.C., Defenses   62
Far West Tour Map   74
Battles of Glorieta and Apache Canyon   91
Florida Tour Map   100
Battle of Olustee   124
Georgia Tour Map   128
Atlanta Area Tour Map   130
Battle of Chickamauga–Day One   136
Battle of Chickamauga–Day Two   138
William T. Sherman's Atlanta Campaign   145
Battle of Kennesaw Mountain   173
Battle of Peachtree Creek   187
Battle of Atlanta   190
Cruises of the CSS Alabama   252
Kentucky Tour Map   258
Battle of Perryville   270
Louisiana Tour Map   284
Battle of Port Hudson   301
Battles of Mansfield and Pleasant Hill   308
Maryland Tour Map   318
Battle of Antietam   335
Midwest Tour Map   342
Mississippi Tour Map   352
Grant's Second Vicksburg Campaign   378
May 22, 1863, Federal Assault on Vicksburg   389
Missouri Tour Map   398
Sterling Price's 1864 Missouri Raid   404
North Carolina Tour Map   418
Federal Assaults on Fort Fisher   431

Battle of Bentonville   438
Northeast Tour Map   442
Northwest Tour Map   448
Oklahoma Tour Map   466
Pennsylvania Tour Map   476
Battle of Gettysburg—Day One   487
Battle of Gettysburg—Day Two   490
Battle of Gettysburg—Day Three   496
South Carolina Tour Map   502
Charleston Area Battles and Assaults   516
July 18, 1863, Assault on Fort Wagner   520
Tennessee Tour Map   536
Battle of Shiloh   556
Battle of Stones River   564
Battles of Orchard Knob, Lookout
    Mountain, and Missionary Ridge   574
Battle of Franklin   599
Texas Tour Map   608
Virginia Tour Map   618
Eastern Virginia Tour Map   619
Arlington—Alexandria Area, Fredericksburg
    Area, and Richmond—Petersburg Area
    Tour Maps   620
Battle of First Manassas   627
Battle of Cedar Creek   647
Battle of Brandy Station   660
December 13, 1862, Battle of
    Fredericksburg   667
Battle of Chancellorsville, May 2–4,
    1863 (two maps)   674
The Wilderness, May 5–7, 1864   681
Spotsylvania, May 8–21, 1864   685
Petersburg Battles and Assaults   717
West Virginia Tour Map   770

Introduction
How to Use This Guide

This Civil War history and field guide is organized by states. When, as in the case of the Northeast chapter, no single state contains a sufficient number of entries to warrant a single chapter, the states are included in an easy-to-tour region. The five regions, which with the individual state listings cover the continental United States and actions abroad, are: the Far West, International, the Midwest, the Northeast, and the Northwest. All regions and states are listed together in alphabetical order.

A unique feature of this guide is that at the end of each listed region, site, or historical commentary, there are cross-references to guide readers to the continuation of a campaign, for example, or chronological events covered in other chapters. A suggested tour route, including directions, is given for each chapter; there are hints on how to tie together a tour of several states and tips on the best times to travel in particular regions.

Travel symbols are given at the end of the entry to each significant site with visitor accommodations. The key to these symbols is given below.

🚲	Bicycling	🚤	Boating
🚌	Bus Transportation	⛺	Campground
⛪	Church	⛴	Ferry
🐟	Fishing	🏵	Gift Shop
♿	Handicap Accessible Facilities	🚶	Hiking Trails
🐎	Horseback Riding	❓	Information
🏛	Museum	Ⓡ	No Parking at Site
P	Parking	🪑	Picnic Facilities
🍴	Restaurant	🚻	Rest Rooms
〰	Swimming	⛷	Winter Recreational Facilities
$	Admission $3 or under per person		
$$	Admission $3 to $8 per person		
$$$	Admission $8 or more per person		

A few suggestions for touring Civil War battlefields are in order for the traveler who has not spent a great deal of time in the past exploring battlefields. Common sense and a respect for hallowed ground and its enjoyment by others are necessities when driving or walking through Civil War battlefields. Therefore, rather than spending time on general travel reminders, such as wearing comfortable shoes, or bringing a camera and insect repellent with you, the focus here will be for the maximum appreciation by and safety of you, your family or touring group, and the site.

Where parking is not provided, park completely and carefully off the highway, respecting the conditions of what are sometimes delicate ground features and, of course, avoiding private property. Take maximum safety precautions day or night in urban areas. Most developed sites have trails, but unmarked and expansive areas can be explored with caution. Be especially careful of earthworks—they are always fragile and sensitive to wear. Nearly all public and private sites post rules on pets, off-road vehicles, hunting, etc.—please familiarize yourself with the regulations and follow them. Report any signs of vandalism to park personnel or to phone numbers listed in this guide. Wanton, unexplained destruction of property at Civil War sites is on the rise. Never use metal detectors to hunt for relics. Anything worth finding at these sites has already been discovered and taken away. You run the risk of destroying earthworks or groundcover by digging up what will probably be nothing more than a bottle cap or automobile part.

The battle maps accompanying each chapter are keyed to the legend listed below. The following symbols are used on the battle maps in all chapters. Red symbols indicate Confederate military; blue symbols indicated Federal military. Relief features range from low elevations (light green) to high elevations (dark brown). Roads are tan; railroads are black. Unless otherwise indicated, north is at the top of the map.

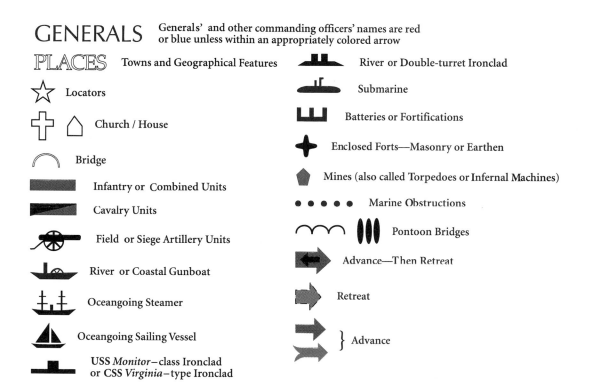

GENERALS   Generals' and other commanding officers' names are red or blue unless within an appropriately colored arrow

PLACES   Towns and Geographical Features

☆   Locators

✝ ⌂   Church / House

⌒   Bridge

Infantry or Combined Units

Cavalry Units

Field or Siege Artillery Units

River or Coastal Gunboat

Oceangoing Steamer

Oceangoing Sailing Vessel

USS *Monitor*–class Ironclad or CSS *Virginia*–type Ironclad

River or Double-turret Ironclad

Submarine

Batteries or Fortifications

Enclosed Forts—Masonry or Earthen

Mines (also called Torpedoes or Infernal Machines)

• • • • •   Marine Obstructions

Pontoon Bridges

Advance—Then Retreat

Retreat

Advance

SMITHSONIAN'S® GREAT BATTLES & BATTLEFIELDS OF THE CIVIL WAR

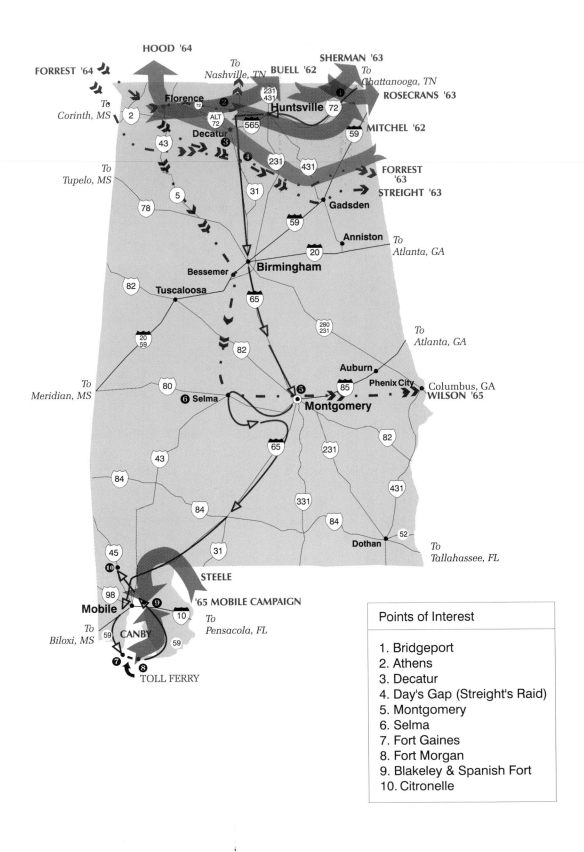

HOOD '64

FORREST '64

To Nashville, TN

BUELL '62

SHERMAN '63

To Chattanooga, TN

ROSECRANS '63

To Corinth, MS

Florence

Huntsville

MITCHEL '62

Decatur

To Tupelo, MS

FORREST '63

STREIGHT '63

Gadsden

Anniston

To Atlanta, GA

Bessemer

Birmingham

Tuscaloosa

To Atlanta, GA

To Meridian, MS

Selma

Auburn

Phenix City

Columbus, GA

WILSON '65

Montgomery

Dothan

To Tallahassee, FL

STEELE

'65 MOBILE CAMPAIGN

Mobile

To Pensacola, FL

To Biloxi, MS

CANBY

TOLL FERRY

Points of Interest
1. Bridgeport
2. Athens
3. Decatur
4. Day's Gap (Streight's Raid)
5. Montgomery
6. Selma
7. Fort Gaines
8. Fort Morgan
9. Blakeley & Spanish Fort
10. Citronelle

Alabama

Alabama has the distinction of being one of the least-fought-over Confederate states east of the Mississippi River. But it was the site of the first capital of the CSA, and loans from the Alabama state government financed early war efforts. From as early as the spring of 1862, Federal campaigns were launched against it; but none succeeded in penetrating deep into the state for long. Though it was blockaded with success, Alabama's largest antebellum city, Mobile, was not taken until war's end. Except for a brief cavalry raid in July 1864—part of William T. Sherman's campaign to destroy the railroads leading to Atlanta—the capital, Montgomery, and the central part of the state escaped Federal attention until Brig. Gen. James H. Wilson's cavalry raid in March and April of 1865. Instead, Alabama became a thoroughfare for troops of both sides heading to battles in Mississippi, Georgia, and Tennessee, as well as a source of manpower and mineral, agricultural, and industrial war supplies.

BRIDGEPORT

Important as a rail depot, Bridgeport was where the Memphis & Charleston Railroad from the west crossed the Tennessee River before winding around Lookout Mountain and entering Chattanooga. Bridgeport and nearby Stevenson, Alabama—at the junction of the Nashville & Chattanooga Railroad and the Memphis & Charleston Railroad—were early targets of Federal operations. On April 11, 1862, a division of Maj. Gen. Don Carlos Buell's Army of the Ohio that did not make the march to Savannah, Tennessee, entered northern Alabama under Brig. Gen. Ormsby Mitchel. His troops seized the Memphis & Charleston Railroad at Huntsville, and action in the state began. It was Mitchel's force that was then to march east and take Chattanooga after the Andrews Raiders had disrupted railroad communications from Atlanta (see **Big Shanty, Georgia**). But with the failure of the Andrews raid, the campaign fizzled. Four and a half months later, the area was again contested during the advance of General Buell's army on Chattanooga, though Gen. Braxton Bragg's Confederate Army of the Mississippi arrived first in the "Gateway City" (as it was called then), frustrating the Union plans (see **Chattanooga, Tennessee**). The Federals had first occupied Stevenson and Bridgeport, the latter after a savage skirmish on April 29, 1862. Stevenson was reoccupied by the Rebels on August 30, 1862, by troops led by Brig. Gen. Samuel Bell Maxey in cooperation with Bragg's march north from Chattanooga that led to his invasion of Kentucky. Bridgeport was also retaken, and the Confederates then rebuilt the rail line between the two towns, which had been destroyed by evacuating Union troops.

Points of Interest

Bridgeport is located on US72, 3 miles south of the Tennessee state line. Stevenson is just north of US72 on AL117, 9 miles southwest of Bridgeport. Little is left to indicate the busy thoroughfare for troop movements through the area in 1862–64 except modern rail lines that generally follow the Civil War tracks. One point of interest is the depot in Stevenson, which is the Civil War–era station.

DRIVING TOUR—*Proceed to Athens*
READING—*Chattanooga Campaign: Chattanooga, Tennessee*

ATHENS

In September 1864 Maj. Gen. Nathan Bedford Forrest launched his first raid on Sherman's supply line from Nashville to Atlanta at the suggestion of new department commander Lt. Gen. Richard Taylor. Forrest set out from northeast Mississippi with 3,500 troopers, picking up 1,000 more near Florence, Alabama. Athens was a Union stronghold on the Central Alabama Railroad, sometimes known as the Nashville & Decatur Railroad, running south from Nashville, not far north of its junction with the Memphis & Charleston Railroad. The Federals had fortified the town with a redoubt (earthen defensive enclosure) garrisoned by 600 soldiers. Forrest shelled the redoubt on September 24 and offered to accept surrender, but the Northerners refused. Forrest then turned to a clever strategy that he would employ several times during the war: holding a parley with the Federal officers while maneuvering his men to convey the idea that his force was much larger than it was. The charade resulted in the Union surrender and the Rebels' capture of the redoubt garrison, two railroad blockhouses, and a number of bluecoats from a relief column sent from Decatur by Brig. Gen. Robert Granger to relieve Athens. After appropriating what supplies he needed and putting the torch to the rest, Forrest sent the prisoners back to Florence and headed for the Tennessee border.

On September 25 Forrest attacked another protected railroad facility—the trestle at Sulphur Branch, nine miles north of Athens. The fort and railroad blockhouses were pummeled into surrender by Forrest's horse artillery. The action netted 1,000 more prisoners and more equipment than Forrest could carry forward with him.

Points of Interest

From I-65, take exit 351 to US72, westbound. Proceed 1.9 miles after passing under a railroad trestle to Jefferson Street (AL127). Turn right on Jefferson. The battle in which the Federal relief column from Decatur fought its way north through Forrest's dismounted troopers occurred on South Jefferson Street between US72 and Forrest Street. This bloody encounter, in which the Union commander, Lt. Col. Jonas D. Elliot, was killed and Forrest's brother, Lt. Col. Jesse Forrest, was wounded, was fought in close quarters. The Federal force surrendered after Elliot was mortally wounded and the fort was in possession of the Confederates. Proceed north on Jefferson Street and turn left on Green Street for one block, then left on Brown's Ferry. At .05 mile is Trinity Congregational Church. The fort was located behind the church.

There are many antebellum buildings in Athens. One is the home of the nineteenth century senator Luke Pryor at the intersection of Jefferson and Pryor streets and another is Founder's Hall at Athens State College. It is at East Pryor and South Beatty streets. Return to Jefferson Street and proceed 9 miles north to Fort Hampton Road. Turn right (east) and proceed .08 mile to the Elkmont Depot. This is the area where the Battle of Sulphur Creek Trestle was fought.

In the battle of Sulphur Creek Trestle, the Federal garrison was, as in Athens, made up primarily of African-American units—ex-slaves recruited in the area. During the battle the Federal commander was killed and Maj. Eli Lilly stepped in to lead the soldiers. Lilly later established a pharmaceutical company that bears his name and founded the Lincoln Library in Indianapolis. Today the old rail depot is the visitors center for Rails to Trails, a walking trail that extends from Athens to the Tennessee Line, along the trace of the old Central Alabama Railroad. The casemate that replaced the trestle burned by the Confederates, and remains of the earthen fort that protected it, can still be seen by walking the trail. Proceed 1.1 miles south on the trail to the historical markers.

From Elkmont, take Sandlin Road 4.4 miles east to rejoin I-65 at exit 361. Proceed south to Decatur. 🚲 🖼 ♿ 👫 🐎 ❓ 🏛 P 🚂 🍴 🚻

DRIVING TOUR—*Proceed to Decatur*
READING—*Forrest's Campaign*—*Tullahoma, Tennessee*

DECATUR

Decatur was a strategic location for military operations in Alabama, Mississippi, and Tennessee. At this point, the Memphis & Charleston Railroad crossed the Tennessee River and connected with the Central Alabama Railroad, just north of the river. Twice, large Federal armies passed through this area. The first time, in July 1862, elements of Maj. Gen. Don Carlos Buell's Army of the Ohio marched east from Corinth, Mississippi, in a race to beat Braxton Bragg's army to Chattanooga (see **Corinth, Mississippi,** and **Tupelo, Mississippi**). Though Bragg's rail route was roundabout, Rebel destruction of the Memphis & Charleston and Buell's need to rebuild it enabled Bragg to win the race to Chattanooga. After fighting a skirmish at Courtland on July 25, Buell's force was compelled to redirect its march north to interpose itself between Bragg's columns and Federal-held Nashville.

In October 1863, four divisions of the Army of the Tennessee under Maj. Gen. William T. Sherman, marching eastward from Memphis in relief of Chattanooga, crossed the Tennessee River here. Leaving soldiers under Brig. Gen. Grenville M. Dodge in this vicinity to repair the Central Alabama Railroad, Sherman and his force continued eastward to Bridgeport.

At Trinity, six miles southwest of Decatur, on August 22, 1862, Confederate cavalry under Col. Philip D. Roddey clashed with the 7th Illinois Cavalry. The Confederates captured a derailed Federal supply train.

Forty-two miles west of Decatur, the Tennessee River town of Tuscumbia saw units from both sides march through town often. A skirmish on December 13, 1862, between the

52nd Illinois under Col. Thomas Sweeny, of postwar Fenian fame (see **International**), and Roddey's cavalry resulted in the Rebels falling back from the town and burning the bridge over Little Bear Creek.

Points of Interest

Little survives of Civil War Decatur, but the Old Decatur District between Lee Street and the Tennessee River is the site of the wartime town. The Old State Bank in the Bank Street Commercial District is a restored 1833 structure open for tours. The Hinds-McEntire House at 120 Sycamore Street served at various times as a headquarters for both Federal and Confederate forces occupying the town.

Depending on your exact route and timetable, you may also want to visit the Tannehill State Historic Site, 24 miles southwest of Birmingham (which is 80 miles south of Decatur), just off I-20. The iron furnace there supplied the mills of Selma with pig iron. The furnace restoration is exemplary. You may want to visit this site in connection with your visit to Day's Gap or en route to Selma. TANNEHILL STATE HISTORIC SITE, 12632 Confederate Parkway, McCalla, Alabama 35111; 205-477-5711.
🚲 ⛺ 🏠 🛶 🏕 ♿ 🚶 🐎 ❓ 🏛 P ⊟ 🍴 🚻 $

DRIVING TOUR— *Proceed to Day's Gap*
READING— *1862: Murfreesboro, Tennessee; 1863: Bridgeport, Alabama*

DAY'S GAP AND STREIGHT'S RAID

In the spring of 1863, while Maj. Gen. William S. Rosecrans's Union Army of the Cumberland faced Gen. Braxton Bragg's Confederate Army of Tennessee in Middle Tennessee after the Federal victory at Stones River, cavalry actions broke the pattern of sluggish inaction on the part of these two major armies. Most of these sorties were raids by gutsy Rebel horsemen under dashing leaders—Maj. Gens. Earl Van Dorn and Joseph Wheeler, and Nathan Bedford Forrest, then a brigadier general. Vexed by these raids, Rosecrans welcomed a suggestion by Col. Abel D. Streight of his command for a Federal raid into the Deep South to cut Bragg's supply line, the Western & Atlantic Railroad. Rosecrans approved the plan for Streight to mount 2,000 infantrymen for the long campaign, but forced Streight to use mostly mules for the mounts because of a shortage of horses. The number and condition of the mules, and the inexperience of the riders, delayed and frustrated the start of the raid, but Streight eventually left Eastport, in northeast Mississippi, after redeploying from Nashville. He crossed Bear Creek into northwest Alabama on the morning of April 22.

Southern forces were at first unaware of Streight's mission. On April 24, at Leighton, Alabama, a Union force under Brig. Gen. Grenville M. Dodge, summoned eastward from Corinth, Mississippi, engaged and forced back Confederate troops in an effort to screen Streight's raid. Later, Dodge encountered Forrest's cavalry, ordered south by Bragg from Spring Hill, Tennessee, in a skirmish on Town Creek, near Courtland. Streight, after resting two days at Tuscumbia and losing 500 men deemed unfit for the operation, set out on April 26 and for three days, guided by units in his force made up of North Alabama Unionists, made measured but steady progress in rainstorms. On April 29, the weather

cleared and Streight rode up onto Sand Mountain into the mountains and hollows of north Alabama. His first objective was the manufacturing town of Rome, Georgia. That night he camped at Day's Gap, and continuing the ride east along the Old Corn Road the next morning, he was surprised by Confederates coming up behind him.

Forrest, having learned about Streight's march in the course of his Town Creek skirmish with Dodge, had taken most of his force and set out to intercept the bluecoated riders. During the next three days the fight continued, Streight laying ambushes for Forrest while the "Wizard of the Saddle" kept up a running fight day and night. Clashes occurred at Day's Gap, Hog Mountain, Blountsville, the Locust Fork of the Black Warrior River, and Blount's Plantation. At Turkeytown, Streight took advantage of a Confederate repulse to send 200 of his best riders racing ahead to Rome to seize the Oostanaula River bridge. He hoped to use that natural barrier to slow Forrest.

Nathan Bedford Forrest rose from a childhood of poverty in Tennessee to become a self-made millionaire. He also rose from the rank of private in the Confederate army to become a lieutenant general by war's end and one of the Confederacy's best cavalry commanders.

At this point efforts of two local civilians aided Forrest, adding one hero and one hero-ine to Southern lore. Sixteen year old Emma Sansom showed Forrest a little known ford across Black Creek near Gadsden, cutting the Rebel pursuit time and gaining her a signed note of thanks from "Old Bedford." John Wisdom performed a Civil War version of Paul Revere's ride by galloping through northeast Alabama from Gadsden to Rome. Wisdom's warning gave Rome citizens time to rally resistance to Streight's 200-man flying column.

Forrest continued his unrelenting pursuit the night of May 2. Streight, his men tired, horses and mules fatigued, and ammunition damp, pressed on in the night. Near Gaylesville, Alabama, the Federals burned the Round Mountain Iron Work, their only permanently successful demolition during the raid. His command exhausted, Streight halted for rest and food at nine A.M. on May 3, east of Cedar Bluff, some five miles from the Georgia border and twenty from Rome. Forrest, thanks to Emma Sansom's shortcut and driving his reinforced command hard, attacked the Federals, interrupting their breakfast. Once again employing his clever stratagem, Forrest advanced a flag of truce and called for Northern surrender. When this was refused, he asked Streight for a parley. The two met between the lines while Forrest employed the terrain and guile to give the Federal colonel the idea that the Confederates had more cannons and men than reality proved. This charade, the exhaustion of his troops, along with a message from the Rome contingent that the Confederate home guard held the bridge and town, caused Streight to surrender his remaining 1,050 raiders. Added to this number were the 200 mounted soldiers in Streight's flying column snared by Forrest on the way to Rome. With his force never numbering more than 600, Forrest destroyed Streight's proud command of more than twice that. The Rebel horsemen, with their prisoners, rode into Rome to a hero's welcome (see **Rome, Georgia**).

Points of Interest

To get to Day's Gap, proceed southward from Decatur on I-65 or US31 for 31 miles. At the intersection of either route with AL157, take AL157 north 6 miles to West Point. Proceeding northwest toward Moulton, notice the point where the road begins to climb up to the Cumberland Plateau. At the top of the first rise are markers describing the actions at Day's Gap and Hog Mountain. The area is rugged and scenic and gives an impression not far different from that viewed by the mule-riding men of Streight's command as they began their running battle out of the mountains.

Backtracking toward Cullman on AL157, take US278 east. The portion of the highway to the intersection of US231 follows the route of the running battle. Blountsville, site of a skirmish during the raid, is 7 miles south on US231. Continuing east another 15 miles, you will enter Walnut Grove. The spring along the highway just east of town was the location of a camp where Forrest gave a portion of his command a brief nighttime rest. Another 18 miles east is Gadsden. On Meigham Boulevard in the city, a marker indicates the site of Emma Sansom's house, and a fenced burial plot in the median strip nearby contains the graves of three Sansoms.

The other significant point of interest is the surrender site monument at Cedar Bluff. This is most easily reached during a tour of northwest Georgia. However, you can also reach it by continuing east from Gadsden on US411 to Centre, then taking AL9 north to Cedar Bluff. Four miles east of Cedar Bluff, a monument on the north side of the road marks the site of the surrender. The ridge to the north is where Forrest staged his noisy troop movements to the confused and awed Streight.

<hr>

DRIVING TOUR—*Proceed to Selma*
READING—*Rosecrans's Advance on Chattanooga: Chattanooga, Tennessee*

<hr>

SELMA

The most important manufacturing area for Confederate cannons and heavy war matériel southwest of Richmond was Selma, Alabama. Rich in natural resources for iron production and located on the Alabama River, the ironworks here were responsible for the manufacture of cannon tubes (barrels)—including the largest and most powerful produced in the South—and naval armament. Here, in 1863, construction of the ironclad CSS *Tennessee* (see **Mobile Bay**) began. The ship was towed to Mobile for outfitting and eventual combat. Munitions factories here turned out bullets and cartridges, and a large arsenal was located in the town.

In the winter of 1865, in conjunction with an advance on Mobile by forces under Maj. Gen. Edward R. S. Canby and a cavalry raid from East Tennessee into western North Carolina and Virginia led by Maj. Gen. George Stoneman, Lt. Gen. Ulysses S. Grant directed that his young protégé, Brig. Gen. James H. Wilson, lead a powerful mounted column in a strike southward from the Tennessee River. Grant's purpose for these operations was to ensure the destruction of the Confederate war effort in the Deep South while he and Sherman defeated the armies of Gens. Robert E. Lee and Joseph E. Johnston in the East.

Wilson had been Grant's topographical engineer at Vicksburg. Later, he led a cavalry division under Maj. Gen. Philip H. Sheridan in Grant's spring and summer 1864 campaign in Virginia, as well as during November and December 1864 in Middle Tennessee and at Nashville under Maj. Gen. George Thomas. Wilson assembled a force of 13,500 troopers, well supplied and most armed with Spencer seven-shot repeating carbines. The expedition started late due to weather and supply problems, but by March 22, 1865, it was riding through northwestern Alabama. Wilson knew that Nathan Bedford Forrest, recently promoted to lieutenant general, had in the area his cavalry corps that had challenged Wilson during Gen. John Bell Hood's Middle Tennessee Campaign. But with his force and armament, Wilson invited confrontation with Forrest.

On March 31, Wilson's advance drove a force of Forrest's cavalry from Montevallo, fifty-five miles north of Selma. The principal forces in this engagement were Federal cavalry under Brig. Gen. Emory Upton (see **Spotsylvania, Virginia**) and Confederate cavalry commanded by Brig. Gen. Philip D. Roddey, plus Col. Edward Crossland's Kentucky brigade. On April 1, at Ebenezer Church, midway to Selma, Upton's cavalry, along with that of Brig. Gen. Eli Long, defeated Forrest's troopers in close combat. Forrest himself engaged in a saber-and-pistol duel with a young Indiana captain. Though Forrest's arm was badly slashed, he shot the Federal officer with his revolver, killing him. The Federal officer became Forrest's thirtieth victim in hand-to-hand combat.

After the victory at Ebenezer Church, Wilson's force burst into Selma on April 2 after a twenty-five-minute assault on the Rebel works guarding the northern and eastern approaches to the town. Although Forrest cut his way out, 2,700 prisoners were taken, including 150 officers. The destruction of the town's industrial facilities and captured munitions was completed. A number of homes were looted and several were burned by Union stragglers. Wilson, on April 7, pressed eastward for Montgomery.

Points of Interest

A tour of Selma should begin on Main Street (US80), the principal thoroughfare through Selma. Just before crossing the Edmund Pettus Bridge, a landmark in the March 1965 Selma-to-Montgomery civil rights march, turn right (north) on Water Street one block to the brick plaza. A circular route will bring you back on US80 east, where you will cross the bridge and continue toward Montgomery. Selma is an excellent location for bicycle tours because the city is charming and relatively small with moderate street traffic. You may also want to visit sights associated with Selma's Civil Rights Movement history.

At the plaza, park and walk toward the Alabama River. A kiosk in the plaza has information on all of Selma's historic sights, including information on one of the largest Civil War reenactment events, held here annually. You will pass the St. James Hotel, which housed Confederate officers supervising the work in Selma's munitions factories, and later, officers of Wilson's Federal cavalry. At water's edge, view the river and imagine the commerce that plied this waterway, looking in the 1860s much as it does today. You can drive or walk 5 blocks north to the Old Depot Museum. This was not the railroad depot during the Civil War. Rather, it was the site of the Confederate Naval Foundry, which built the CSS *Tennessee* and many other implements of war. On the lawn of the museum is a UDC (United Daughters of the Confederacy) monument to the Confederate Iron Works and several artifacts that were constructed during the war at the foundry. The UDC is a post-war ladies organization which, among other things, has local chapters which were responsible for the placement of many monuments to Southern soldiers and the Confederate war effort.

Backtracking, by vehicle, south on Water Street past US80 (Main Street) you dead-end into Church Street. One block north, two lighted columns locate the entrance to the Confederate arsenal at Selma, now gone. Another block north and west leads to Union Street and the Smitherman Historical Building. This impressive antebellum structure was used as a hospital by the Confederates. Driving a few blocks north on Union brings you to Fair Oaks. This Greek Revival mansion, named for its splendid foliated lawn, was used as a hospital by Wilson's Federal cavalry when they occupied the town. Proceeding north again, you will come to Sturdivant Hall (McLeod Street) and White-Force Cottage (Fortress Street), the latter the home of a half-sister of Mary Todd Lincoln, who was often critical of the North and her brother-in-law, the president.

As you drive back toward Main Street you pass the Mabry-Jones House, where Capt. Catesby ap Roger Jones, CSN, lived with his wife and wife's parents. The former executive officer of the ironclad CSS *Virginia* (known in the North as the *Merrimack*) and her captain in the epic March 9, 1862, duel with the USS *Monitor* (see **Hampton Roads, Virginia**) assumed command of the Selma Iron Works in 1863 and turned it into the Confederate Naval Foundry. Jones was killed in Selma in 1877 by a neighbor with whom he was quarreling. Jones is buried in Selma's Live Oak Cemetery, as is Confederate Lt. Gen. William J. Hardee and several other notable Civil War personalities.

Return to Main Street and Water Street to conclude your Selma tour. You may wish to spend the night here in one of Selma's lovely bed-and-breakfast establishments before proceeding south over the bridge and taking US80 east to Montgomery.

DRIVING TOUR—*Proceed to Montgomery*
READING—*Wilson's Campaign: Montgomery*

MONTGOMERY

The third capital of Alabama, incorporated from two small towns in 1819 and chosen as the site for the capital in January 1846, lies on the Alabama River near the center of the state. Here, in 1861, the Confederate government was created. The Provisional Confederate Congress met in the city in early February to form the Confederate States of America, unanimously electing Jefferson Finis Davis provisional president on February 9. Davis was not at the convention—he had returned to Mississippi after resigning his U.S. Senate seat in January, to lead the forces of his home state of Mississippi in the war he saw on the horizon. But Davis, a moderate on the question of secession in early 1861, assumed the post and began conducting the business of government out of a red brick cotton warehouse before the end of the month. On May 20, 1861, the Confederate capital was moved to Richmond, Virginia, and Montgomery's role in the war diminished.

Period lithograph of Jefferson Davis's inauguration at the Alabama State Capitol, February 18, 1861

Montgomery continued as a transportation, supply, and hospital center during the war. A mid-July 1864 Federal cavalry raid damaged the railroad east of the city. On April 12, 1865, Brig. Gen. James Wilson's cavalry occupied the city. A partial destruction of the city was ordered, but the beautiful Greek Revival State Capitol was spared.

Points of Interest

Proceed east on US80 from Selma, avoiding the Interstate junctions, and enter the city center. US80 becomes Madison Avenue. At Court Street, turn north and drive two blocks to the Civic Center. There, the remains of the office building used by the Confederates to run the government stood. Interpretive signs indicate the site and describe the various Confederate national flags. Return south on Court Street to Dexter Avenue; on the southeast corner is the Winter Building. An interpretive marker here describes this site where on April 11, 1861, the order was telegraphed to Brig. Gen. P.G.T. Beauregard which resulted in the firing on Fort Sumter (see **Charleston, South Carolina**).

Continue east on Dexter to the Alabama State Capitol. Here Jefferson Davis gave his inaugural address from the west portico on February 18, 1861. There is a statue of Davis on the Capitol grounds. Nearby an interpretive marker describes Wilson's arrival at Montgomery in mid-April 1865. The Alabama Department of Archives and History, located opposite the Capitol on Washington Avenue, contains exhibits relating to the formation of the Confederate government, the inauguration of Jefferson Davis, and Alabama's role during the Civil War.

While Montgomery has several fine antebellum residences, the most noteworthy in Civil War history is the first Confederate executive mansion. Now located one block southwest of the Capitol at 644 Washington Avenue, it was moved from another location. Tours are given daily.

DRIVING TOUR—*Proceed to Mobile*
READING—*Wilson's Campaign: Columbus, Georgia*

MOBILE AREA

Mobile was Alabama's largest city during the Civil War. The bustling port and commerce center did not fall to Union forces until April 12, 1865, three days after General Lee's surrender at Appomattox Court House. Long an objective of Federal army and navy commanders, especially Ulysses S. Grant and David G. Farragut, priorities and circumstances led to the postponement of decisive action against Mobile until late summer 1864. In the meantime, Mobile continued to receive cargo through the blockade, one of only four large Confederate ports—along with Charleston, South Carolina; Galveston, Texas; and Wilmington, North Carolina—to do so after mid-1862. Among the more than 200 Confederate vessels to slip into and out of Mobile Bay during the blockade was the famous Southern commerce raider CSS *Florida* (see **Confederate Cruisers** in **International**). The entrance to Mobile's thirty-mile-long bay which had been protected by three forts and numerous natural and man-made obstructions was closed by Farragut's August 1864 victory in the Battle of Mobile Bay. But the city still had formidable defenses. Earthworks ringed Mobile's western side; the earthworks of Fort Blakeley (spelled Blakely during the Civil War) and Spanish Fort were constructed to protect Mobile's eastern approach after the Federal naval victory. Artillery batteries on marsh islands guarded the head of the Bay and the Mobile River. Gen. Joseph E. Johnston called Mobile the most strongly fortified city in the Confederacy.

Points of Interest

Mobile is a city of cosmopolitan charm, much like New Orleans. Mobile, however, in addition to the French influence, shows influences from its periods of Spanish and British rule. Among the antebellum buildings in the city that have Civil War connections are City Hall, Barton Academy, and Christ Episcopal Church, where Confederate Lt. Gen. Leonidas Polk, an Episcopal bishop, once presided. At the Grand Hotel evidence of a cannonball impact from 1865 can be seen.

Magnolia Cemetery contains the remains of Gen. Braxton Bragg and five other Confederate generals. In a square reserved for the Mobile National Cemetery are the interred dead from Fort Blakeley and Spanish Fort. There is a prominent monument to the 76th Illinois Infantry. Nearby in a square designated as the "Confederate Rest" are buried the remains of those Confederate soldiers who died in the Mobile area, including those lost at Spanish Fort and Fort Blakeley. Adm. Raphael Semmes (see **Confederate Cruisers** in

International) and Father Abram Ryan, the poet priest of the Confederacy, are buried in Mobile's Catholic Cemetery. Downtown Mobile has statues of Ryan and Semmes.

Mobile was surrounded by three lines of earthworks on its western side. A lunette (a type of earthen fort) is on the grounds of the Mobile Infirmary on St. Stephen's Road. Fort McIntosh is on a small island—Oyster Shell Reef—and its remains are visible at low tide.

City of Mobile Visitor and Welcome Center—Along the waterfront, Fort Conde, a reconstructed French fort from the 1720s (not extant during the Civil War) serves as the free informational center for the city, including historical attractions. It is open from 8:00 A.M. to 5:00 P.M. daily except on Christmas and during Mardi Gras. In the waterfront park across from the center (Battleship Park, admission charged), in addition to the powerful warship from a more recent period (USS *Alabama,* BB60, which is open for touring), is Alabama Cruises. This 90-minute boat tour of Mobile Bay and Mobile River takes you to the site of two forts that protected Mobile harbor, Fort (Battery) McIntosh and Battery Gladden. ALABAMA CRUISES, INC., P.O. Box 101, Mobile, AL 36601; 205-433-6101.
♿ P ⛱ 👫 🎣 🛥 $

DRIVING TOUR—*Proceed to Fort Gaines*
READING—*Battle of Mobile Bay*

Battle of Mobile Bay

Although R. Adm. David G. Farragut had wanted to capture Mobile shortly after taking New Orleans in April 1862, and in similar fashion to that successful campaign, it was not until August of 1864 that he was able to defeat Confederate naval forces in Mobile Bay and capture the three forts guarding the entrance to the bay in cooperation with Federal land forces. The delays resulted from several factors. The first was Lincoln's desire to have Farragut dash his fleet against the bastion at Vicksburg (see **Vicksburg, Mississippi**). The result of this campaign was running the Vicksburg gauntlet with most of his deepwater squadron, only to have the ships return downstream again having had little impact on the imposing Southern batteries. The Vicksburg problem was destined to require the services of river ironclads and a skilled army led by a resourceful commander.

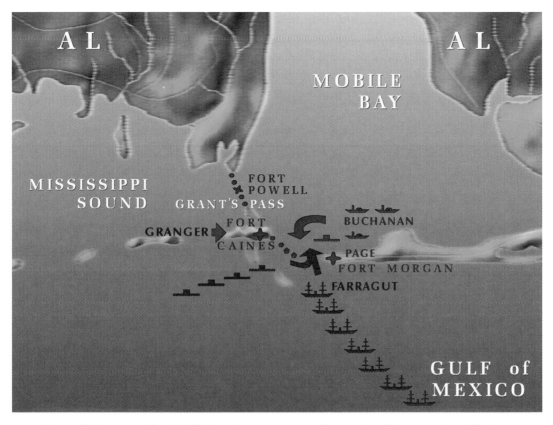

Farragut's force moved into Mobile Bay from two passes on the morning of August 5, 1864. The iron-clads preceded the wooden ships past Fort Morgan and through the torpedo (mine) field just west of the narrow channel. Inside Mobile Bay they were challenged by four Confederate vessels including the CSS Tennessee. At the same time, Maj. Gen. Gordon Granger's infantry was approaching Fort Gaines on Dauphin Island from the west.

The latter part of 1862 was spent waiting for the addition of ironclad vessels to join the fleet, but they would be tied up in the futile Federal effort to challenge the forts in Charleston harbor through the summer of 1863 (see **Charleston, South Carolina**). During that time, Farragut was again called up the Mississippi River. His fleet assisted Maj. Gen. Nathaniel Banks in the Port Hudson campaign (see **Port Hudson, Louisiana**).

After a five-month convalescent leave, Farragut returned to the West Gulf Blockading Squadron in January 1864. The Lincoln administration was still not terribly interested in challenging the Mobile defenses, what with so many other priorities in mind. One of these other priorities, the Red River Campaign, with General Banks in charge, would utilize the troops Farragut needed to assist with his project (see **Red River, Louisiana**).

In the meantime, the Confederates had stiffened the defenses of Mobile. Veteran sailor Adm. Franklin Buchanan, appointed as naval commander at Mobile in August 1862, laid out formidable obstacles. Fort Powell was built across Grant's Pass, the back door to Mobile Bay. The two forts commanding the main channel, Forts Morgan and Gaines, were strengthened and their garrisons reinforced. Obstructions were positioned in the channels. The most effective Confederate naval weapon perfected during the war was the torpedo, or, as the North called them, "infernal machines." These were submerged mines, each bearing a massive charge and one of a variety of mechanisms available for setting it off. Those laid in the channel at Mobile, some 200 torpedoes in the main channel alone, used impact detonators—triggered by contact with a large floating body, such as a Federal warship. The torpedoes were distributed such that the usable channel was reduced to the two hundred yards on the east side, directly under the big guns of Fort Morgan.

That wasn't all Buchanan planned. If the Federals ran that gauntlet, a naval force would be waiting inside the bay. Warships were being assembled not only in the thirty-mile-long bay itself, but in Selma, too, which was turning out the most formidable ship of all the ironclad ram CSS *Tennessee*. The CSS *Tennessee*, constructed under Buchanan's close supervision, was towed downriver to Mobile for outfitting, securing her armor plate and mounting big guns at facilities southeast of the city. But only three other gunboats, the *Selma*, the *Morgan*, and the *Gaines*, were available to Buchanan in August of 1864. These were lightly armored and carrying only 16 guns among the trio.

Even so, that was enough to convince Farragut—who in late May had slipped into the bay to get a good look at the *Tennessee*—to wait for reinforcement, namely, Union ironclads that had earlier been promised him. The *Tennessee*, with her six-inch armor plate and 6 large Brooke rifled guns, 2 on pivots capable of firing in three directions, posed a challenge, particularly to Farragut's wooden ships.

There were weaknesses in the construction of the *Tennessee*, particularly in the engines available to power her. Farragut hoped that the ironclad would venture out of the harbor to challenge his fleet in open water, where she would be at a disadvantage. Buchanan considered the possibility—like Farragut he was impatient for some action—but decided against it.

Farragut spent his time waiting for the arrival of the ironclads by planning every detail of his attack. He had the carpenter aboard his flagship, the USS *Hartford*, fashion small wooden blocks shaped like boats which the admiral used in studying the ships and conditions of maneuver on a tabletop.

On July 20, the first of the four promised ironclads, the USS *Manhattan*, arrived. This single-turreted monitor was followed by two double-turreted river monitors, the *Chickasaw* and the *Winnebago*, from the Mississippi River. But the *Manhattan*'s sister ship, USS *Tecumseh*, was still en route from the Atlantic Ocean harbor at Hampton Roads.

By August 2, 1,500 to 3,000 soldiers—fewer than Farragut had asked for but all that division commander Maj. Gen. Edward R. S. Canby could spare—arrived from New Orleans under the command of Maj. Gen. Gordon Granger. They landed on the west end of Dauphin Island the next afternoon to advance on and invest the smaller of the two masonry forts guarding the channel, Fort Gaines. Farragut also sent gunboats to bombard Fort Powell from Grant's Pass. He still hesitated in commencing his bold dash into Mobile Bay. He anxiously awaited arrival of the *Tecumseh*, then being towed from Pensacola Bay, Florida, by one of Farragut's big oceangoing warships, the USS *Richmond*.

Farragut always worked with as much information as he could possibly get. For this reason he climbed up in the rigging of the USS Hartford *to see above the smoke from the deck guns. Capt. Drayton had a quartermaster pass a rope around Farragut as a safety precaution to prevent him from falling to the deck if he was wounded. The 1864 newspapers dramatized the incident in word and picture. This lithograph presents a bit more realistic rendering.*

Finally, with the arrival of the *Tecumseh* on the afternoon of August 4, all was ready. The hour for the run into the bay was set for daybreak the next day, August 5, to take advantage of the flood tide. Farragut ordered his ships into two battle columns—the ironclads would make the first approach, entering the channel from the southwest. Seven wooden warships, each with a gunboat lashed to her port side providing a symbiotic relationship, would follow through the main channel from the south. The gunboat engines would provide extra power to the warships. The larger sloops-of-war would offer protection to their consorts from Fort Morgan's big guns.

By 5:45 A.M. all the ships were aligned, and the columns headed for the bay. Each warship tandem was to follow slightly to the right rear of the previous, to maximize firepower. The monitors ranged ahead of the warship column, and the first shot was fired by one of the fifteen-inch guns of the *Tecumseh*, in the van, at 6:20 A.M. Then at 7:07 A.M., as the monitors bore down on Fort Morgan, the Confederate batteries answered, and within twenty minutes the firing became general—the monitors and warships pounding Fort Morgan and her water battery; the Rebel guns blasting back.

No major damage to either side was sustained in this gunplay, and the problem now became one of maneuverability in the narrow channel. The lead warship, the USS *Brooklyn*, slowed down behind the slower monitors and was stalled in front of the fort's blistering fire. Then the *Brooklyn* started to drift backwards, blocking the channel. The cause of this confusion—then unknown to Farragut, lashed in the rigging of the USS *Hartford* for a better view of the action—was that the *Tecumseh* had met with disaster.

Alerted to the Federal attack, Admiral Buchanan had the four Confederate vessels under way shortly after dawn. He deployed his force west of the channel, behind the torpedo (mine) field. Upon seeing the *Tennessee*, Capt. Tunis A. M. Craven, commander of the *Tecumseh,* conned the ironclad monitor directly toward the Rebel ironclad. The *Tecumseh* hit a mine two hundred yards from the *Tennessee*, and within minutes she disappeared beneath the sur-

The last fighting moments of the CSS Tennessee, *in this engraving from* Harper's Weekly, *as the USS* Chickasaw *and other Federal ships close in on her. After her capture, the ram was recommissioned the USS* Tennessee *and was part of the Federal navy.*

face with Craven and most of the crew. Seeing this, the commander of the *Brooklyn* backed his ship away from what he thought was the minefield, blocking the only safe part of the channel.

It was then that Farragut made a quick and daring decision that resulted in saving his fleet and giving posterity one of the most quoted phrases of the war. Praying for guidance from his lofty position high above the deck of the *Hartford,* he heard a voice inside telling him to "go on." He ordered the column to follow the sunken *Tecumseh*'s route into the minefield. "Damn the torpedoes, full speed ahead!" is the remembered version of a series of orders Farragut gave. The result was the column of warships and their consorts, led by the *Hartford,* headed into the area where the torpedoes were positioned. The ships' crews tensed as they heard the torpedoes bouncing against the ships' hulls. But all passed the minefield, including the *Brooklyn,* which re-joined the column.

The general failure of the torpedoes came as no surprise to Farragut and his top commanders. Farragut had reasoned that the torpedoes were full of damp powder and waterlogged fuses. Several clandestine torpedo recoveries by the Federals before the attack had confirmed this. But as Fort Morgan was dropping out of range of the Union ships in the bay, the *Tennessee* and her three consorts were dead ahead.

Broadside to the oncoming Federal ships, Buchanan's small fleet unleashed a galling fire, which damaged the *Hartford.* But then the gunboats lashed to Farragut's flagship and the USS *Richmond* cast off and chased the three Southern gunboats. The *Gaines* got shot up and was thereafter beached and burned by her crew. The *Metacomet,* the *Hartford*'s former consort, chased down the *Selma* and forced her surrender in a shallow part of Mobile Bay. Only the CSS *Morgan* survived to fight another day. She took cover under the guns of her namesake fort, then escaped up the bay after dark.

Brig. Gen. Richard Page, commander of Fort Morgan, had thirty-seven years of service in the U.S. Navy when the Civil War began. He lived into the twentieth century and died in Pennsylvania at age ninty-four.

Ruins of Fort Morgan after its surrender

That left "Old Buck" Buchanan in his ironclad to continue the battle. He tried twice to ram the *Hartford* with the slow-moving *Tennessee.* Unsuccessful both times, he then ran the line of Union warships following the *Hartford.* Although he inflicted some damage on the six Federal ships, none of it was consequential. In turn, the Federals' shot bounded off the *Tennessee.* When Buchanan next charged the Federal monitors, the experience of rebounding shot was shared by both Yankee and Rebel sailors.

With this last hurrah, the *Tennessee* retired to the shelter of Fort Morgan. The Federal warships rendezvoused and anchored about four miles inside Mobile Bay and, while crews attended to postbattle damage control and care of the wounded, the cooks started the morning meal, only about thirty minutes later than Farragut's promise to "pipe all hands to breakfast in Mobile Bay" at eight o'clock. As this was happening, Capt. Percival Drayton, commander of the *Hartford,* expressed his concern to Farragut about the danger the *Tennessee* posed still afloat. Not fifteen minutes after the admiral assured Drayton that pursuit of the Rebel ironclad would begin right after breakfast, he was spared the trouble. The *Tennessee* was spied by lookouts heading full speed for the anchored Union ships.

Farragut designated the USS *Monongahela* and the USS *Lackawanna,* with false iron prows, to run down and ram the *Tennessee,* but their initial effort failed, and the *Tennessee* continued her run toward the *Hartford.* The two flagships locked in mortal combat like two great savage animals, and *Hartford* sustained serious blows. At one point in the melee, the *Lackawanna*, having only damaged herself in trying to ram the *Tennessee*, nearly rammed the *Hartford*. Frustrated by the confusion of the moment, Farragut turned to the *Hartford*'s signal officer. "Can you say 'For God's sake' by signal?" "Yes sir" was the reply. "Then say to the *Lackawanna*, 'For God's sake, get out of our way and anchor.' "

In the end it was another ironclad that did in the *Tennessee*. The double-turreted *Chickasaw* maneuvered astern of the *Tennessee* and shot away in rapid succession her smokestack, gunport shutters, and steering chains. One witness described the intensity of the attack, noting that the *Chickasaw* was "firing the two 11-inch guns in her forward turret like pocket pistols." By ten o'clock, with the *Tennessee* disabled and Buchanan wounded, the great ironclad ram surrendered.

The casualties in the naval battle were in proportion to the size of the respective crews. Federal dead and wounded totaled 342, including 92 lost in the sinking of the USS *Tecumseh*. Confederate casualties were 12 killed and 20 wounded; however, 243 Rebel sailors were also captured aboard the CSS *Selma* and the CSS *Tennessee*. Later that night, as Farragut was describing the victory in a letter to his wife, an explosion was heard from across Mobile Bay. It was the Confederates blowing up Fort Powell after evacuating it. The Federal monitors had pounded the small fort unmercifully during the afternoon.

On August 6, the Federal fleet hammered Fort Gaines, while Granger's soldiers pressed against the fort's landward front. This siege continued through the night until the fort capitulated early the next day. The unconditional surrender yielded another 818 Confederate prisoners.

Fort Morgan, though surrounded by devastation and an enemy force, refused to yield. The craggy and stolid ex-U.S. and C.S. sailor, Brig. Gen. Richard L. Page, a cousin of Robert E. Lee, had no intention of surrendering. For two weeks following the landing of Granger's soldiers on Mobile Point east of the fort on August 9, an unrelenting shelling from land and water tore apart Fort Morgan's ramparts. But the garrison held out. On August 22, 3,000 rounds were fired, including those from the guns of the captured *Tennessee*. Fires raged throughout the fort and all but 2 of the guns were knocked out. The following morning at six o'clock, the fort surrendered. The Battle of Mobile Bay was over.

Points of Interest

Mobile Bay is an exciting and beautiful location; it is worth spending a full day or more to explore the two forts and enjoy the scenery and activities of this wondrous seaside area.

The recommended route is to proceed south from Mobile on AL163 past Cedar Point, above the former location of Fort Powell, then cross the causeway to Fort Gaines on Dauphin Island. From Fort Gaines, cross the bay where the two fleets did battle on the toll car ferry to Fort Morgan. From Fort Morgan take AL180 cast, then proceed north on AL59 or AL59/US98 to Spanish Fort.

Fort Gaines—For more than three centuries, European colonists and their descendants have inhabited strategic Dauphin Island. The French explored the island first, and a wooden fort was built on the site of Fort Gaines. The area and island were alternately occupied by the forces of Britain and France, and after 1780, by Spain. In April 1812 the area—known as West Florida—was formally incorporated into the United States. Like Fort Morgan, the present fort is a Third System fort. With its imposing brick scarps, casemated guns, and dry moat, Fort Gaines was a typical Third System fort. These forts were designed and supervised by a board of military engineers headed from 1816 to 1834 by a Frenchman, Brt. Brig. Gen. Simon Bernard. Fort Gaines was planned and surveyed in 1821, but was not completed until the late 1850s. The pentagonal structure is in excellent condition, with walls (scarps) 22.5 feet in height and many gun casemates and buildings well preserved. One of the most exciting architectural aspects of Fort Gaines is the long bombproof galleries (tunnels) that connect the casemates, which are at the bastioned angles of the pentagonal fort, with the parade ground.

Fort Gaines has many fine artifacts, including two Parrott rifled guns used in the siege, as well as the anchor and chain from the USS *Hartford*. The fort has a museum, a gift shop, and an excellent brochure that describes an in-depth walking tour of the fort. Take the brochure on the ferry across the bay because it will explain and orient, in relation to the fort, many sites of the naval action.

Finally, Fort Gaines has excellent recreation facilities nearby operated by the fort's owner and managing entity—the Dauphin Island Park and Beach Board. These include a full-service campground, fishing pier, public boat launch and trails to the Gulf of Mexico, and a bird sanctuary.

The fort is open seven days a week, 8:30 A.M. to 5:00 P.M. Liability is not assumed, and children must be accompanied by an adult. For more information, including camping information and rates, contact FORT GAINES HISTORIC SITE, P.O. Box 97, Dauphin Island, AL 36528; 205-861-6992.

Fort Morgan—Like Fort Gaines, Fort Morgan was a Third System fort. With its full complement of 40 guns, hot-shot furnaces, and double scarp, Fort Morgan was designed to be impregnable to naval attack. The folly of this thinking was borne out by the events of the Civil War. But despite the pounding it took for more than two weeks in August 1864, this landmark operated by the Alabama Historical Commission is intact and fascinating to visit. From its impressive 1833 cornerstone above the sally port (entrance), to its barbette (top) level gun emplacements and chapel with inlaid cross, Fort Morgan is a delight to explore. There is a museum with exhibits on the naval battle and siege outside the fort, and there are interpretive signs throughout the park. The fort is open daily from 8:00 A.M. to 6:00 P.M. (or dark), with the museum opening an hour later and closing an hour earlier. Other facilities include beach access, a fishing pier, and picnic facilities. A nominal admission fee is charged. Group rates are available. If you enter from the east (land) side, a per-car fee is charged to enter the park's grounds. FORT MORGAN, 51 Highway 180 West, Gulf Shores, AL 36542; 334-540-7125. 🚲 🛥 🐟 🎇 ♿ 👫 ❓ 🏛 〰 🚻 💲

DRIVING TOUR—*Proceed to Spanish Fort*
READING *(Chronological)*— *Sheridan's 1864–65 Shenandoah Valley Campaign: Virginia; or Sherman's 1864 Atlanta Campaign: Georgia*

Spanish Fort

Spanish Fort and Fort Blakeley constituted the two key Confederate defensive positions guarding the eastern approaches to Mobile. Although Mobile was downgraded as a Federal objective after the Battle of Mobile Bay shut off the port operations to blockade-running, Northern interest in taking the city was rekindled in early 1865. This was part of a plan by Lt. Gen. U. S. Grant (the other parts being cavalry raids by Generals James H. Wilson and George Stoneman) to smash the military capabilities of the forces in the Deep South and divert Confederate attention from William T. Sherman's relentless march north from Savannah, Georgia, into the Carolinas (see **Sherman's March Through South Carolina**). The task of taking Mobile fell to Maj. Gen. Edward R. S. Canby, then commanding the Military Division of west Mississippi. Canby assembled two reinforced corps. The larger force, led by Maj. Gens. Gordon Granger and A. J. Smith from their staging areas on Mobile Point and Dauphin Island, was to move up the east shore of Mobile Bay and take Spanish Fort. The smaller force, Maj. Gen. Frederick Steele's column, departed Pensacola on March 20 and was to take Fort Blakeley. Union monitors and gunboats commanded by R. Adm. Henry K. Thatcher, Farragut's successor, supported the operation. Much to Grant's frustration, Canby dragged his feet due to logistical concerns. By the time the campaign got under way in mid-March, Sherman had left Fayetteville, North Carolina, and one of the campaign's important objectives had been lost. Nevertheless, Canby's 45,000-man army by April 1 had both Spanish Fort and Fort Blakeley under attack. The defenses were manned by troops from Maj. Gen. Dabney H. Maury's command.

Prior to the arrival of Federal troops in front of Spanish Fort, Union naval operations had been checkmated in the lower bay by the mud shoals of Dog River bar, several floating batteries salvaged from unfinished ironclads, and torpedoes. Following the army's approach, Thatcher sent several gunboats over the bar to cut communication between Spanish Fort, Fort Blakeley, and Mobile. Though the Federal navy had "swept" the eastern side of the bay for mines, the "infernal machines" sank two Union ironclads on successive days—the USS *Milwaukee* on March 28 and the USS *Osage* on March 29. On April 1, the steamer *Randolph* struck a mine and sank while trying to salvage the *Milwaukee*.

Siege operations directed against Spanish Fort began March 28. Though the Confederate garrisons were aided by fire from the CSS *Morgan,* the Rebel vessel that had escaped from the Battle of Mobile Bay, and the CSS *Nashville,* an unfinished ironclad even larger than the *Tennessee,* Federal firepower eventually prevailed. Spanish Fort was evacuated by its Confederate defenders on April 8.

Fort Blakeley

Fort Blakeley had been invested by Steele's command beginning on April 1. The Federals established three lines of works, each day inching closer to the Rebel works, which lay to the west. The Confederate line was a strong and well-planned series of redoubts, trenches, and rifle pits on commanding ground less than a mile east of the town of Blakeley. The garrison was comprised of 3,400 men—a Missouri brigade led by Brig. Gen. Francis M. Cockrell and a Mississippi brigade, both formerly part of the Army of Tennessee; and a small brigade of young Alabama reserves. Steele's force included Brig. Gen. John P. Hawkins's division of United States Colored Troops (for details and background on USCT, see **Milliken's Bend, Louisiana**), a division of the XVI Corps and two divisions of the XIII Corps. Union artillery hammered the Rebels round-the-clock.

On April 9, just hours after Gens. Robert E. Lee and U. S. Grant signed the document surrendering the Army of Northern Virginia at Appomattox Court House, a total of 16,000 Federal troops began an echeloned attack from south to north. At the center of the assault were Confederate Redoubts Nos. 3 and 4, defended by elite soldiers of the 1st Missouri Brigade. The works were engulfed by the charging Federals in less than thirty minutes. In all, more than 3,200 Confederates were captured; some escaped the disaster by swimming across the Blakeley River.

Points of Interest

Spanish Fort and Fort Blakeley offer two extreme comparisons in preservation of Civil War sites. Blakeley, diligently protected, has some of the best existing Union and Confederate earthworks, a delight for even veteran battlefield explorers. Spanish Fort has nearly been obliterated by the suburbanization of the Mobile area. There are, however, important landmarks visible at both battlefields.

Spanish Fort—Although the Spanish Fort battlefield is fragmented and developed, there are several areas in which interpretive markers and earthworks give a picture of the siege. Along US98 heading west toward Mobile, there is a historical marker at Confederate Drive indicating the site of Fort McDermott. Continuing north on US98 (or taking AL59 north to US98 if you continued north on that highway from Fort Morgan), cross I-10 and go up the hill until you arrive at the intersection with US31. Across US31 is the entrance to Spanish Fort Estates. The first of several Alabama State historical markers is at the entrance. Continue into the development on the main street, called Spanish Main, and hold to the right. In this

Redoubt No. 4 was a key position in the Confederate defenses of Fort Blakeley. This position was a focal point of the Federal assault on April 9, 1865. Preservation efforts have paid off—the Confederate and Union earthworks at Historic Blakeley State Park are among the finest original works in existence.

area of the subdivision there are streets named Southern Way, General Canby Drive, and Pirate's Cove, which feature historical markers describing the location of various batteries and actions.

Exiting the development again via Spanish Main, turn left onto US31, go to the next traffic light, and make a half left onto AL225. Approximately 1.5 miles north there is an elementary school on the east side of the road. Continue 0.1 mile to the bottom of the hill and park in the apartment complex on the left. Walk back up the hill to the woods just opposite the school. A short distance from the highway are the remains of some of the Spanish Fort earthworks. If you look closely you can see where the Federal earthworks crossed the Confederate trenches after the Southerners withdrew to a shorter interior line.

Historic Blakeley—This beautiful location is a 3,800-acre National Register Site and an Alabama State Park. It is on AL255 about 4.5 miles north of Spanish Fort. The entrance to the 2,000-acre state park is well marked. In addition to the extensive preserved earthen works and rifle pits (including Redoubts 3 to 9), there are other markers and remains of the former town and a scenic view of historic Blakeley River. Facilities include a large picnic area, 10.5 miles of nature and bike trails, a pavilion available for group events, a forty-unit primitive campground, tours by park naturalists, and special annual events. Check with the park for scheduled Civil War reenactments and demonstrations. The park is open 9:00 to 6:30 daily (opening and closing one-half hour earlier in the winter) except Christmas Eve and Christmas Day. HISTORIC BLAKELEY, 33707 State Highway 225, Spanish Fort, AL 36527; 334-626-0798.

🚲 🛶 ⛺ 🎣 🚶 🐎 ❓ P 🏕 🚻 $

DRIVING TOUR—*Proceed to Citronelle*
READING *(chronological)*— *Ford's Theatre and the Petersen House: The District of Columbia*

Citronelle

On May 4, 1865, Lt. Gen. Richard Taylor, CSA, met with Maj. Gen. Edward R. S. Canby, USA, here. The result of the meeting between the two department commanders was the surrender of all remaining Confederate land forces east of the Mississippi River. Five days after Taylor's surrender, Nathan Bedford Forrest, after rejecting the idea of leading his troopers across the Mississippi River to join the forces of Gen. Edmund Kirby Smith's Trans-Mississippi Department, surrendered his cavalry corps at Gainesville, Alabama, 125 miles north of Citronelle.

Citronelle, a quaint small town, does not currently have any historical markers commemorating the surrender.

DRIVING TOUR—*Proceed to Mississippi, Florida, or Georgia*
READING *(chronological)*—*Palmito Ranch, Texas*

To
Neosho, MO

Pea Ridge NMP

Chalk
Bluff Park

Mammoth Spring

62

65

62

62

Rogers

62

Harrison

Mountain Home

62

Walnut Ridge

Prairie
Grove
BSP

Fayetteville

Blytheville

62

167

Jonesboro

71

65

Batesville

67

Newport

55

Clinton

63

40

Fort Smith

Russellville

Bald Knob

64

71

Conway

W. Memphis

To
Memphis, TN

40

67

40

Forrest City

Little Rock

40

Brinkley

270

Hot Springs

Bayou Fourche

49

Helena

Mena

Jenkins'
Ferry

Pine Bluff

De Witt

71

70

Arkadelphia

165

De
Queen

67

65

Arkansas Post NM

Washington

Elkin's Ferry

Marks'
Mills MSP

McGehee

Prairie D'Ane

167

53

79

71

4

Poison
Spring
MSP

165

30

Hope

Camden

To
Dallas, TX

Texarkana

82

To
Greenville, MS

71

El Dorado

82

Crossett

To
Shreveport, LA

To
Lake Providence, LA

Arkansas

Arkansas, particularly northwest Arkansas, like its neighbor Missouri to the north and the Indian Territory (today's Oklahoma) to the west, experienced partisan warfare, with its grim and horrible aspects. Although a staunch slave state with plantation agriculture in its south and east regions, Arkansas was not in the first wave of seven states to secede from the Union. However, following on the heels of the Fort Sumter bombardment and surrender and Lincoln's subsequent call for volunteers, the state severed its ties with the North on May 6, 1861. On that date the vote for secession was 69–1 in the state legislature. The one dissenting vote came from the Ozark region in the northwestern part of the state, where many fiercely independent mountaineers looked upon the Confederacy with the same disdain as they did the United States government. Ironically, it was in northwest Arkansas that the first large-scale Civil War actions in the state began, in 1862, and were decisively concluded in favor of the North.

By 1865, however, Federal and Confederate forces campaigned in nearly every part of the state, from the early battles in the northwest—Pea Ridge and Prairie Grove—to the struggle for the Mississippi River and its Arkansas tributaries, and later, the occupation of Little Rock and the Union campaigns through the state toward Louisiana and into the Indian Territory. You will want to include Arkansas on your tour of Civil War battlefields because of the pristine condition of its well-preserved battlefields. From Pea Ridge and Prairie Grove in the Ozarks to Arkansas Post, Marks' Mills, Jenkins' Ferry, and Poison Spring in the southern part of the state, few of the state's battlefields have been victimized by urban sprawl.

Your tour of Arkansas will take from three to four days, traveling from northwest to south. Suggested overnight stops are in Fayetteville, Fort Smith, Little Rock, and Camden. You will delight in the handsome scenery, friendly people, and pleasant, relaxed atmosphere of the state while enjoying the history. Travel Arkansas in early April to late October for maximum enjoyment. The autumn color season in north-west Arkansas is magnificent. You can also combine visiting Arkansas sites with travel in the adjoining states of Mississippi, Louisiana, Oklahoma, Tennessee, or Missouri. See the tour map for details.

PEA RIDGE

The Telegraph Road from Springfield, Missouri, to Fayetteville, Arkansas, was a well-traveled route by the time the soldiers in blue and gray began to march and camp in the much contested Ozarks. At the beginning of March 1862, the route had most recently been traversed by the command of Maj. Gen. Sterling Price, the former Missouri governor and Mexican War hero who laid claim to victory at Wilson's Creek and other Confederate victories in his home state in August and September 1861 (see **Wilson's Creek** and **Lexington, Missouri**). But this time, however, having evacuated his Springfield, Missouri, base in mid-February, he was withdrawing to the south in the face of an advance from Rolla by Brig. Gen. Samuel R. Curtis's Army of the Southwest, charged with driving the Rebels out of southwest Missouri.

On Little Sugar Creek in northwest Arkansas, Price's Missourians rendezvoused with Brig. Gen. Benjamin McCulloch's Confederate division on February 17. The combined Rebel force of 15,000 withdrew down the Telegraph Road and into the fastness of the Boston Mountains near Fayetteville. Here on March 2, they were joined by Maj. Gen. Earl Van Dorn, whom President Jefferson Davis had recently put in charge of the Trans-Mississippi District which encompassed Missouri, Arkansas, the Indian Territory, and northern Louisiana. Van Dorn, like his president a Mississippi native, was a dashing and daring hero of the Mexican and Indian wars who, while in command in Texas in the spring of 1861, had seized Federal assets and driven Northern soldiers from the Lone Star State. The ambitious Van Dorn, with plans of capturing St. Louis and possessing Missouri for the South, was faced with Curtis's force already in Arkansas and blocking his way into Missouri. One other force was at his disposal—some 800 Cherokees and Texans led into Arkansas by Brig. Gen. Albert Pike. Van Dorn consolidated his forces and moved out on March 4, with Pike's Indians and Texans, to join the force at Bentonville.

Curtis's army had halted its pursuit near present-day Rogers, Arkansas, and Curtis dispersed his command. Two of his divisions, under the former Baden army officer

Brig. Gen. Franz Sigel, hero to the nation's German Americans, camped west of Bentonville. Another division was commanded by Col. Jefferson C. Davis, a West Pointer who was an officer at Fort Sumter when the war began (see **Fort Sumter, South Carolina**). Davis's men occupied the high ground overlooking Little Sugar Creek, a scant four miles south of the Missouri border. Between them, at the original stopping point at Cross Hollows, Curtis maintained his headquarters with the division of Col. Eugene A. Carr.

Alerted to the Confederate advance as Van Dorn's columns passed north of Fayetteville, Curtis hastened to concentrate his 10,500-man army behind Little Sugar Creek. Sigel successfully re-joined Curtis and the other two divisions on March 6, after fighting his way through Confederate roadblocks north of Bentonville. The Little Sugar Creek line, partially entrenched, was a formidable position against an attack from the south. A long narrow mountain ridge, Pea Ridge, was at the Federal rear. As Curtis watched Rebel campfires begin appearing to the southwest, he was fully aware that he was outnumbered, but he felt confident he could more than hold his own.

Van Dorn was concerned about the strong Union position, and felt a frontal attack would be suicidal. However, General McCulloch, familiar with the area, knew a detour—a road that passed to the west of the hamlet of Leetown, north of Pea Ridge and re-joined the Telegraph Road north of Elkhorn Tavern. Van Dorn decided to make a night march to gain this advantage, planning to destroy Curtis's army, and then it would be "Hazza for St. Louis!" It was a bold stroke, and everything would need to proceed perfectly.

After stoking the fires and leaving a strong force behind to confuse the Federals, Van Dorn and Price marched the Missourians of Price's command around Pea Ridge, their vanguard reaching the Telegraph Road in the Federals' rear at eight-thirty A.M. on March 7. McCulloch's Texas, Louisiana, and Arkansas troops—McCulloch was a former Texas Ranger—

Federal artillery was massed at this position along Telegraph Road on the morning of March 8, 1862, to drive the Confederates from their positions around Elkhorn Tavern.

marched north with Price, but a change in plans caused them to turn east with the intention of passing the south face of Pea Ridge en route to a rendezvous with Price at Elkhorn Tavern. Pike's Cherokees and Texans, who had finally arrived from the Indian Territory, followed McCulloch.

Another commander might have retreated or surrendered, but Curtis, a methodical former engineer, lawyer, and politician, did not panic. He turned his lines around and moved them into position to face the enemy. Keeping one division in reserve, Curtis first sent cavalry, then Col. Peter J. Osterhaus's task force, and finally infantry and artillery from Davis's division to engage McCulloch. Col. Eugene A. Carr, a hard-fighting former U.S. Army regular, faced Price and Van Dorn. Carr fought a skillful holding action, making use of rugged ground east and west of the Telegraph Road, the center axis of the Confederate attack. For most of the afternoon, the fighting ebbed and flowed near the Elkhorn Tavern, a telegraph office and traveler's stop. Van Dorn's "double envelopment" might have triumphed in spite of stiff Northern resistance had it not been for bad luck and breakdowns in Confederate communication.

The Rebels were tired and hungry from their all-night march. Although they made steady gains against Carr's grim midwesterners north of the Elkhorn Tavern, they could not rout the smaller Federal force in the six-hour fight. North of Leetown, Rebel cavalry and the Cherokee units routed the initial line of Federal horse soldiers, but Pike's people celebrated the victory too long and could not be brought forward to help McCulloch's hard-pressed units. The Cherokees resisted formations that would subject them to artillery fire, which they greatly feared. However, Cherokee leader Col. Stand Watie and his regiment performed admirably throughout this and later conflicts. A crisis developed in the Leetown battle for the Confederates. McCulloch was killed while going forward to reconnoiter, and Brig. Gen. James McIntosh, his successor, was soon dead as well. Col. Louis Hébert, the leader of McCulloch's infantry, was captured, leaving Pike, who lacked credibility and military experience, in charge. The Confederate attack in this sector halted. The weary Federals did not pursue their advantage.

Carr's stubborn resistance and late reinforcement forestalled a Southern victory south of Elkhorn Tavern. The Southerners lacked ammunition to enable them to rout Carr's badly mauled troops before dark. That night, Pike brought the remnants of his and McCulloch's command to Van Dorn at Elkhorn Tavern. A Confederate ordnance train was en route via the Bentonville detour, but turned back. Van Dorn, who was ill and commanding from an ambulance, anxiously awaited morning to see what the Federals would do.

When dawn came on March 8, the Federals were in a better position, with reinforced lines. Sigel and his two divisions were on Curtis's left, facing north and east toward Elkhorn Tavern, while Curtis's two divisions held the ground southwest of the tavern, with Davis's division straddling the Telegraph Road. Although withdrawal was advised by several of his subordinates in a council of war the night before, Curtis decided to hold his ground. The Confederates had artillery unlimbered southwest of Elkhorn Tavern; Watie and his Cherokees held Pea Ridge. The Rebel cannoneers were desperately short of ammunition.

Curtis was not intimidated. He ordered Sigel to start a cannonade, which the former minister of war of the German revolutionary government executed with precision. The Rebel firepower reduced, Sigel's two divisions then advanced toward the ridge and tavern, rolling up the Southern line. Their surge forward was soon joined by Carr's and Davis's divisions. Both wings of the Federal army relentlessly converged on Elkhorn Tavern. The Southern force was driven from the field. Van Dorn's scattered units took a week to reassemble near Van Buren, south of their Boston Mountains starting point.

The Battle of Pea Ridge put an end to the Confederate plans to recover Missouri, and Curtis's army soon left the region on a difficult march that brought them to Helena, Arkansas, in mid-July (see **Helena**). Van Dorn planned another invasion of Missouri farther east, but it was canceled by higher authority. Pike returned to the Indian Territory with his Cherokees and Texans. Van Dorn and most of his troops were sent east of the Mississippi to oppose the Union threat to northern Mississippi (see **Corinth, Mississippi**).

Points of Interest

Samuel Curtis wrote shortly after the Battle of Pea Ridge (or Elkhorn Tavern, as the South called it) that the granite mountain would serve as a memorial to the men who had fallen at its base. His statement was affirmed in July 1956, when President Dwight D. Eisenhower signed the legislation authorizing establishment of Pea Ridge National Military Park.

Pea Ridge National Military Park—This spectacular 4,300-acre park, the largest Civil War national park west of the Mississippi River, is 27 miles north of Fayetteville and 4 miles south of the Missouri state line on US62. Just west of the highway is the entrance to the park and visitor center. At the visitor center, see the exhibits and the audiovisual interpretive program, then pick up an official map and brochure. The park is toured by a one-way road that starts at the Leetown battlefield and circles east over Pea Ridge and to the Elkhorn Tavern area. Among the facilities at the park are bike and horse trails, picnic facilities, interpretive maps, and recorded accounts of the action. 🚲 ♿ 🚶 🐎 ❓ 🏛 P 🪑

DRIVING TOUR—*Proceed to Prairie Grove*
READING *(chronological)*—*Glorieta, New Mexico (The Far West)*

Prairie Grove

In the late autumn of 1862, the northwest corner of Arkansas again erupted with the thunder and lightning of battle. The return of the conflict to this arena was caused by

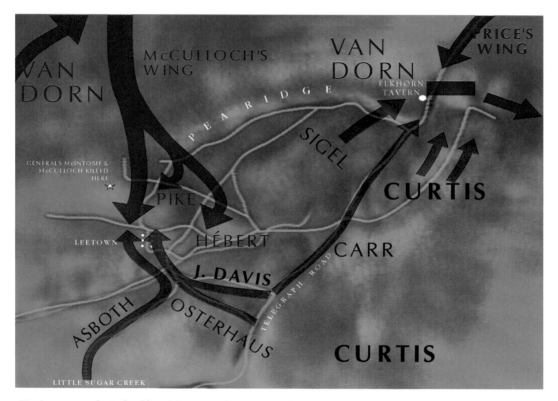

Hoping to turn the Federals' position on Little Sugar Creek, Van Dorn's Confederates marched to the west of the Federal position and attacked on March 7 from the north. Federal commander Curtis turned his forces around and met the Rebel assaults. By March 8, the fighting was over in Leetown and the battle centered on Elkhorn Tavern. After the Federals overwhelmed the Confederates at the tavern, the Southerners retreated to the east.

an ambitious Southern officer and his desire to drive the Yankees from his home state. Maj. Gen. Thomas C. Hindman, a slightly-built lawyer and ex–U.S. congressman from Helena who distinguished himself at Shiloh, was given command of Confederate forces in Arkansas in late May 1862, replacing Earl Van Dorn. By this time Samuel Curtis, promoted to major general after the Battle of Pea Ridge, was making new inroads in the state. After occupying Batesville and threatening Little Rock, Curtis marched his army to Helena. There he rendezvoused with the U.S. Navy. Union gunboats had followed up their June 6, 1862, victory at Memphis (see **Memphis, Tennessee**) with the White River expedition, resulting in the capture of a Confederate battery at St. Charles on June 17, although at the cost of heavy damage to and loss of 105 lives aboard the ironclad gunboat USS *Mound City*. A drop in water level prevented the Federals from holding St. Charles and Des Arc. The navy's withdrawal from White River compelled Curtis to establish a fortified enclave at Helena in order to provision his army.

To counter these incursions, Hindman performed a miracle in logistics by raising an army through rigorous enforcement of the conscription laws, and equipping it by establishing new factories and foundries in the state. Hindman drew up an ambitious plan, as Van Dorn had done, for carrying the war into southwest Missouri and southeast Kansas as well as routing Union forces in the Cherokee Nation (see **Oklahoma**). And though his harsh tactics resulted in some loss of power in August, when Maj. Gen. Theophilus Holmes arrived in Little Rock to replace him in command of what was redesignated as the Trans-Mississippi Department, Hindman succeeded in having Holmes endorse his move into Missouri. The first step in this plan, however, was unsuccessful.

Hindman's force—Texans, Arkansans, Missourians, and Native Americans—took the field in early September, cleared the Federals out of the Indian Territory, and advanced into the lead-mining district of southwest Missouri, centering on Granby. However, while Hindman was conferring with Holmes in Little Rock, the Federal Army of the Frontier engaged his force and beat it back into northwest Arkansas (see **Newtonia, Missouri,** and **Fort Wayne, Oklahoma**). Hindman was not discouraged by the Old Fort Wayne defeat, thinking that he could trap the Federals, now pursuing the fleeing Rebel cavalry in northwest Arkansas and the Indian Territory. The Union commander, Brig. Gen. John M. Schofield, believing the fighting in the region to be over for the winter, in mid-November returned with two of his three divisions to Springfield, Missouri, leaving the largest division under the command of Brig. Gen. James G. Blunt, in the vicinity of Maysville.

The advance of Hindman's cavalry under Brig. Gen. John S. Marmaduke north from Van Buren across the Boston Mountains to Canehill (now called Cane Hill) in late November drew a vigorous response from the aggressive Blunt. Taking the field, he attacked and defeated the Rebel horsemen in a running fight on November 28 at Canehill.

Then Hindman received some disturbing news from General Holmes in Little Rock. He was ordered to bring his troops to the state capital in preparation to reinforcing the Vicksburg Confederates. The order was initiated at the highest levels in Richmond. Shocked by this turn of events and knowing that desertion would be high as his volunteers and conscripts—particularly those from west Arkansas—marched away from a Federal force invading their homeland, Hindman wrote a reply to Holmes stating that he would comply with the order once he had driven the Northerners back into Missouri. He then headed north from Van Buren, near Fort Smith, with 11,500 infantry and 22 guns on a cold December 3.

Blunt was still at Canehill southwest of Fayetteville when he heard of Hindman's advance. With only 7,000 men he was outnumbered, but the pugnacious Maine-born Kansas abolitionist had no thought of retreat. Instead, he called for reinforcements. The only Federal units in the area were Schofield's other two divisions, 6,000 men under Brig. Gen. Francis J. Herron. Schofield had gone to St. Louis on sick leave. Inspired by Herron's leadership, the Union soldiers marched ninety miles from their camps on the Wilson's Creek battlefield (see **Wilson's Creek, Missouri**), past Elkhorn Tavern, arriving at Fayetteville at midnight on December 6, less than four days after their call to arms.

As Herron's force began the last leg of their journey to Canehill, Hindman had completed his much slower wintry march through the rugged Boston Mountains. But Hindman did not stop at Canehill to challenge Blunt. Instead, hearing of Herron's approach, he bypassed Blunt to attack the reinforcements first, planning to defeat the Federal force in detail (first interposing between and then fighting separated units one at a time). Nine miles from Fayetteville, after brushing aside Rebel cavalry, Herron encountered the Confederates in a line drawn along a ridge overlooking the broad Illinois Creek bottom near the village of Prairie Grove.

Though Herron's men were exhausted from their grueling march, they formed a line of battle fronting the high ground from which Confederate smoothbore artillery dueled with long-range Union guns. Some of the Northern soldiers fell asleep while shells burst around them. From midday until past dark, the battle was contested without either side gaining a distinct advantage. Blunt, hearing the battle, marched his division first to Rhea's Mill, then southeast to assail Hindman's left flank. Herron's force sustained most of the action and Union casualties in the battle. With the coming of the early twilight, the firing sputtered to a stop.

The morning of December 8, the Federals awakened to an empty field. Realizing that he had lost the advantage of numbers and surprise, Hindman withdrew his force during the night, using blankets to muffle the rumbling wheels of the artillery and wagons. Exhausted and battle-weary, the Yanks did not pursue Hindman as he retreated first to Fort Smith then turned his corps toward Little Rock in compliance with General Holmes's order. Once again, the Federals forestalled a Confederate drive into Missouri and tightened their grip on the northwest corner of Arkansas.

Points of Interest

Prairie Grove Battlefield State Park—The site of part of the battle is preserved in this Arkansas state park on US62 at Prairie Grove, 10 miles southwest of Fayetteville. Most of the adjacent lands, which remain in private hands, are as pastoral as they were in 1862. Available for day use every day of the year, Prairie Grove Battlefield State Park features a visitor center that has books for sale and information on tours and special programs at the park. A self-guided battlefield trail gives an excellent opportunity to walk the battlefield over a 1-mile-long foot trail. Among the sights on the trail is the Borden House, a key landmark in the battle. The house was destroyed during the Civil War, and the current structure was built on the footprint of that structure in the late 1860s. PRAIRIE GROVE BATTLEFIELD STATE PARK, P.O. Box 306, Prairie Grove, AR 72753; 501-846-2990. ♿ 🚶 ❓ P 🏘

Canehill—The running fight between Blunt's force and Marmaduke's cavalry occurred in a 12-mile area beginning in the town of Cane Hill and traversing the mountainous region south to Cove Creek. Historical markers in the town of Cane Hill interpret the action. The Cane Hill Cemetery (south of County Highway 13) contains the graves of some of Cane Hill's Civil War fatalities. Cane Hill is on AR45, 7 miles southwest of Prairie Grove.

Fort Smith National Historic Site—Fort Smith is most famous for its role in the settlement of the Indian Territory before and after the war; however, the second fort (1838–71) was seized by the Confederates on April 23, 1861. In September 1863, the Federals regained control of Fort Smith and used it as a base for operations in Arkansas and the Indian Territory. Located on the Arkansas River, there is a visitor center with a

Rebuilt Borden House, seen in the distance, and Orchard Site on Prairie Grove Battlefield. Two Federal assaults in this area were turned back.

museum containing exhibits, a video program, and a bookstore. There are brochures for touring the fort and wayside exhibits. Interpretive tours, demonstrations, and other programs are held, primarily in the summer. Check with the park for further information. Admission is charged; the fee is waived for seniors with a Golden Age Passport and school groups. The site is open from 9:00 A.M. to 5:00 P.M. every day. You can reach Fort Smith from I-40 west by taking I-540 to Rogers Avenue. Take Rogers Avenue west until it ends in downtown Fort Smith. From I-40 eastbound, take exit 64B, travel east for 6 miles and take the first right after crossing the Arkansas River bridge. FORT SMITH NATIONAL HISTORIC SITE, P.O. Box 1406, Fort Smith, AR 72902; 501-783-3961. 🏕 ♿ ❓ 🏛 P $

DRIVING TOUR—*Proceed Through Little Rock to Arkansas Post*
READING (*chronological*)—*Fredericksburg, Virginia*

ARKANSAS POST

In January 1863, the Federals in the west needed a victory. Other than the Battle of Prairie Grove, recent events in Texas, Louisiana, and Mississippi had turned sour for the North. Maj. Gen. Earl Van Dorn's Holly Springs and Nathan Bedford Forrest's West Tennessee raids had frustrated U. S. Grant's advance down the Mississippi Central Railroad (see **Holly Springs, Mississippi**). Maj. Gen. William T. Sherman's attack on Chickasaw Bayou had ended in disaster (see **Chickasaw Bayou, Mississippi**). Sherman, smarting from the recent defeat, consulted with Maj. Gen. John A. McClernand, his immediate superior, and R. Adm. David Dixon Porter, commander of the Mississippi Squadron. Sherman's idea, endorsed by McClernand, was a combined army-navy assault on Arkansas Post and its reinforced earthwork, which had been built at a strategic bend of the Arkansas River in the latter half of 1862. Fort Hindman, named for the former Confederate district commander and Battle of Prairie Grove leader, was fifty river miles above the confluence of the Arkansas and Mississippi rivers. Not only did the fort protect the river approach to Little Rock, but its commander, Brig. Gen. Thomas J. Churchill, employed Arkansas Post as a base from which to stage raids on Federal shipping on the Mississippi. This last reason was the official one, but Sherman and McClernand saw it as a morale boost for the Army of the Mississippi, which was the designation McClernand gave to his command. The 30,000-man expedition embarked on 60 transports, with both generals aboard. Convoyed by three ironclads and other gunboats from Porter's fleet, the expedition departed Milliken's Bend, Louisiana, on January 5. On the ninth, the first Federal troops disembarked below the fort and the gunboats steamed ahead. The Confederates anticipated the attack, but not the size of it. Nevertheless, General Churchill was determined to hold the fort.

On January 10, the gunboats began a bombardment of Fort Hindman. The fort's 11 cannons were outgunned. At the same time, Union infantry seized outlying rifle pits downstream from Fort Hindman. The next day, the bombardment continued and silenced the fort's big guns, while the Federal troops pressed the Confederates holding the fort and those posted in rifle pits extending from the fort to Post Bayou. By four o'clock white flags were raised. Yankee soldiers raced to be the first to occupy the fort while other infantry mopped up Rebel resistance in the rifle pits. Total casualties for the battle were 1,201, not counting the 4,791 Confederate prisoners, a not insignificant number of the Southern combat force remaining in Arkansas. Among the forces engaged were two with unusual and colorful names—the Chicago Mercantile Artillery and Johnson's Texas Spy Company.

There was jubilation over the victory among the Federal troops who took part in the operation and throughout the North. An exception was General Grant, who saw the movement of the Union forces north from Milliken's Bend and up the Arkansas River as a "wild goose chase" by his rival McClernand and a wasteful distraction from the main goal of his western army—Vicksburg. After learning that the expedition had been proposed by his friend, Sherman, and not McClernand, Grant's concern was relieved. But, as he outranked McClernand, Grant soon ordered the Army of the Mississippi to return to Milliken's

The Bombardment and Capture of Fort Hindman,
Arkansas Post, Arkansas, January 11, 1863—*a Currier
and Ives lithograph*

Bend for redesignation and a new assignment in the Vicksburg campaign (see **Grant's Second Vicksburg Campaign, Mississippi**).

Points of Interest

Arkansas Post National Memorial—Not only is Arkansas Post a Civil War battle site, it is also the site of the first European settlement in the lower Mississippi Valley. But the town was damaged by the battle and erased by changes in the Arkansas River channel in the more than 130 years since the fight. The river also destroyed Fort Hindman. Nevertheless, visiting Arkansas Post is a rewarding experience. Paths and interpretive signs trace the battle's events. Confederate rifle pits can be viewed. The visitor center provides audiovisual presentations, interpretive panels, and artifacts. Another exhibit tells the story of Arkansas's only Revolutionary War battle. To get to Arkansas Post take US65 south from Little Rock to Dumas. Turn north onto US165 and proceed for approximately 10 miles across the Arkansas River then east on AR169 to the park. The visitor center is open from 8:00 A.M. to 5:00 P.M. except Christmas, and there are picnic facilities in the park. ARKANSAS POST NATIONAL MEMORIAL, Route 1, Box 16, Gillett, AR 72055; 501-548-2207.
🏕 ♿ 🚶 ❓ 🏛 P

DRIVING TOUR—*Proceed to Helena*
READING (*chronological*)—*Porter's operations:
Naval Operations at Vicksburg, Mississippi*

HELENA

The Mississippi River town of Helena was first occupied by Federal troops in July 1862 and served as a vital link in the Federal supply line between Cairo, Illinois, and the Union-held enclaves that served as springboards for U. S. Grant's campaigns that resulted in the capture of Vicksburg. The first Union army commander at Helena, Maj. Gen. Samuel Curtis, occupied as his headquarters the mansion belonging to Confederate general Thomas Hindman, further infuriating the five-foot-four-inch Arkansan. For almost a year the Federal occupation was conducted without challenge. Then, in mid-June 1863, Richmond nudged Theophilus Holmes, then commander of the District of Arkansas, to move against Helena to help relieve the siege of Vicksburg (see **Vicksburg, Mississippi**) by interdicting the Union's Mississippi River supply line.

Union spies got word of the impending attack to Helena's then commander, Maj. Gen. Benjamin Prentiss. A hero of the Battle of Shiloh, Prentiss was initially skeptical of the assault. This would make little difference, as his predecessors had had the Federal troops and black work gangs fortify the land approaches to the town. The most important of these works were four redoubts (enclosed earthworks), Batteries A, B, C, and D, as well as Fort Curtis. Admiral Porter promised three gunboats to come to Prentiss's aid, but only the veteran USS *Tyler*—a timberclad gunboat—arrived before the battle. On July 4, 1863, unaware of events taking place at Vicksburg and Gettysburg, the Confederates, under Holmes but with Maj. Gen. Sterling Price in field command, launched an early-morning attack. Although the Federals were prepared, the Rebels stormed Battery C on Graveyard Hill in the center of the Federal line. The Federals withdrew after spiking (disabling) their guns, yet before the Southerners could use the advantageous position to hammer Fort Curtis or another part of the Union line, Prentiss called the guns of the *Tyler* into play. The more than 400 shells fired at the Confederates by the *Tyler* along with bitter resistance by Union soldiers posted in Battery D on Rightor's Hill, turned the tide. Holmes called off the assault by ten-thirty A.M., and the Confederates pulled back into the Arkansas foliage. Prentiss's failure to follow up soon cost him his job. This was the last major Rebel attack on Union strongholds in northeastern Arkansas.

A month later, the Helena enclave was the starting point for Maj. Gen. Frederick Steele's campaign to Little Rock. Also, several regiments of USCT were organized and based in Helena.

Points of Interest

Helena can be reached from US49. On the US49 bypass south of the city, there is a tourist information center that provides additional information on Helena's Civil War role. Within the city, Estevan Hall, at 653 Biscoe Street, was occupied by the U.S. Army during the war. The 1826 house has been remodeled but retains its character. Farther along Biscoe Street, at the corner of Arkansas Street, is a historical marker identifying the site of Confederate general Thomas Hindman's house, which, as noted earlier, was also Federal general Curtis's headquarters when he commanded the Helena enclave.

Continuing west on Arkansas Street, drive up a steep hill to Military Road. Here, on Crowley's Ridge, is a historical marker locating the Battery D redoubt, one of the major Federal works involved in the battle. The defenses are on private property, but you can check with the tourist information center about access to the redoubt, the dry ditch, and an excellent view of the Mississippi River. Returning to Biscoe Street, which becomes Columbia as you travel farther west, turn west on York to Beech Street. At 323 Beech, a house that was occupied by Federal soldiers still has pockmarks from the battle. Behind the house is Graveyard Hill, site of Battery C, the center of the Federal line. A marker describes the fight for Battery C.

Finally, visit Maple Hill Cemetery, opened after the war to replace the one on Graveyard Hill. Maj. Gen. Thomas C. Hindman and other Southern soldiers are buried there. Likewise, nearby Confederate Cemetery contains the grave of Helena resident and Confederate hero Maj. Gen. Patrick Cleburne.

DRIVING TOUR—*Proceed to Little Rock*
READING *(chronological)*—*Port Hudson, Louisiana*

LITTLE ROCK

In the summer of 1863, with a renewed confidence wrought by the surrenders of Vicksburg and Port Hudson (see **Vicksburg, Mississippi,** and **Port Hudson, Louisiana**), and the repulse of the Confederate attack on Helena, Maj. Gen. Ulysses S. Grant planned to again carry the war to the Confederates in Arkansas. The garrison of the Helena enclave was bolstered by the arrival of Maj. Gen. Frederick Steele with a XVI Corps division, flushed with victories gained in the Vicksburg campaign. Upon Steele's arrival, Maj. Gen. Benjamin Prentiss resigned and Steele assumed command of the Federal forces at Helena. A plan was drawn up in which Steele's two divisions, some 6,000 strong, would cross the eastern part of the state with the capital, Little Rock, as the objective. At the same time a smaller force, seven regiments under Brig. Gen. James G. Blunt, fresh from victories over Confederate forces in the Indian Territory (see **Honey Springs, Oklahoma**), occupied Fort Smith, Arkansas, on September 1. Blunt would be available, if needed, to close on Little Rock from the west.

Steele began his march on August 10. At Clarendon he was reinforced by a large division of cavalry, 6,000 horse soldiers led by Brig. Gen. John W. "Black Jack" Davidson, who had recently rendezvoused with Union gunboats on the White River. Confederate forces guarding the eastern approaches to Little Rock were led by Maj. Gen. Sterling Price, a familiar name in Arkansas, who had taken over command of the District of Arkansas when Lt. Gen. Theophilus Holmes took ill. Price positioned his 8,000 men north of the Arkansas River, across the river and downstream from the capital. Price had few troops to oppose the Federals' eastward march from Fort Smith; but that force, a cavalry column under Col. William F. Cloud, had a much greater distance to travel than Steele, so Price hoped to first lure Steele into a costly assault on his forces, who had entrenched.

By August 23, Steele had established his base of operations at DeVall's Bluff, on the White River, forty-five miles east of Little Rock. Davidson's cavalry on August 25 beat the Confederate horse soldiers and forced the Rebels to retire into their works at Bayou Meto. Price held this line until September 7, when Steele outflanked him by reaching the Arkansas River at Ashley's Mill, downstream from Little Rock.

On the night of September 9, Union pioneers (soldiers working on military engineering projects), bridged the Arkansas River, and, covered by artillery fire from the river's north bank and a demonstration downstream, Davidson's troopers crossed the river by eleven A.M. on September 10. The first serious opposition to Davidson's advance was encountered at Bayou Fourche, five miles southeast of Little Rock. Aided by Steele's artillery on the far side of the Arkansas, Davidson's bold attack forced the Rebels confronting him to give way. Steele's and Davidson's columns then advanced nearly abreast.

Price evacuated Little Rock and withdrew his force to Arkadelphia. Governor Harris Flanigan and the state legislature moved the capital to Washington, Arkansas, leaving the mayor to surrender Little Rock to General Steele. With the arrival of Colonel

Cloud's column in Little Rock on September 18, the Federals exercised a loose control over the part of the state north of the Arkansas River, as well as maintaining the enclaves in Little Rock, Fort Smith, and Pine Bluff, all on the river. Bitter partisan warfare and Confederate raids by Brig. Gen. Joseph Orville "Jo" Shelby and others, however, ensured that there would be no peace in the state north of the Arkansas River until the end of Reconstruction.

Points of Interest

The Old State Capitol, the Little Rock Arsenal, and the Quapaw Quarter—In Little Rock there are two sites with significance to the Civil War period. The Old State House, 300 West Markham Street, was the state capitol from 1836 to 1911. Here in 1861, Arkansas' secessionist convention was held. In 1863 the Confederate government evacuated the capitol in advance of Maj. Gen. Frederick Steele's occupation of the city. He used the building as his headquarters during the occupation. The Old State House has a history museum, a gift shop and a brochure for self-guided tours. Group tours guided by a volunteer can be arranged with prior reservation. The site is open weekdays and Saturday and Sunday afternoon; there is a small admission charge. For more information, call 501-324-9685. 🏵 ❓ 🏛 $

The Little Rock Arsenal, now the Arkansas Museum of Science and History, is located in MacArthur Park. MacArthur Park (one block west of I-30 at East Ninth Street) was once the site of more than twenty structures at the arsenal. The U.S. arsenal was surrendered to state authorities before Arkansas seceded and was held by the Confederates for two years. The structure housing the current museum was built in 1840–42. A brochure describes the building's history and an exhibit is being constructed. A slide presentation is available upon request. There is also a plaque describing the city's Quapaw Quarter. There is a small admission charge to

Federal troops marching into Little Rock in September 1863

the museum which is open every day including Sunday afternoon. For more information, call 501-324-9231.   🛇 🏛 💲

DRIVING TOUR—*Proceed to Washington or Poison Spring State Park*
READING *(chronological)—Chickamauga, Georgia;*
Trans-Mississippi Campaigns—Baxter Springs Massacre, Kansas (The Northwest)

CAMDEN CAMPAIGN

Through the early months of 1864, the Federal campaign up Louisiana's Red River began to affect Federal control of most of Louisiana and threatened to carry the war deep into the heart of East Texas (see **Red River Campaign, Louisiana**). In conjunction with the advance up the river by Maj. Gen. Nathaniel Banks's army and R. Adm. David D. Porter's naval squadron, Maj. Gen. Frederick Steele was to proceed southwest from his Little Rock base and march on Shreveport, Louisiana, the headquarters since the previous year of Lt. Gen. Edmund Kirby Smith's Trans-Mississippi Department. There they would rendezvous with Banks's army.

Steele departed Little Rock on March 23 and headed southwest, toward Arkadelphia, with a force of 8,000. A 4,000-man column from the Army of the Frontier, an aggregation of black and white units led by Brig. Gen. John M. Thayer, was to proceed southeast from Fort Smith to unite with Steele at Arkadelphia. Another 2,000 Federal cavalry and mounted infantry, operating out of Pine Bluff, were to cooperate with Steele and harass the Confederates in southeast Arkansas. The first week of marching was not strenuous, Steele's troops shaking out the lethargy induced by six months of uneventful garrison duty. The swollen waterways and muddy roads of springtime slowed the Federal column. Crossing the Ouachita River and arriving at Arkadelphia on March 29, Steele was concerned that nothing had been heard from Thayer's column, then threading its way across the Ouachita Mountains. Scouts could not locate it.

Because of the distance to be covered and the difficulty in foraging (obtaining supplies from off the country) in the area they were marching through, Steele's men were put on short rations. The lack of supplies was the controlling factor in Steele's timetable to reach Shreveport. By April 1, he decided he could no longer wait for Thayer at the designated meeting point and moved forward without him. That same day, Steele's column encountered its first Confederate resistance—a skirmish with Rebel cavalry.

These Southerners belonged to Maj. Gen. Sterling Price, District of Arkansas commander. Price's infantry were en route to Shreveport to reinforce the army Kirby Smith was assembling to oppose Banks's advance. To oppose the march and buy time, Price had called in his cavalry from points as far as off as Columbus and Camden. These grim fighters were organized into two divisions, one led by Brig. Gen. James F. Fagan and the other by Brig. Gen. John S. Marmaduke. Better known were brigade commanders Jo Shelby and William "Old Tige" Cabell.

There were daily skirmishes, involving both the front and the rear of the Union column, from the time the Federals left Arkadelphia until they were overtaken by Thayer's column on April 9, on the south bank of the Little Missouri River. The most serious fighting with the Rebel cavalry was at Okolona on April 3, involving the rear of Steele's column, and at Elkin's Ferry, at the Little Missouri River crossing, on April 3–4.

Thayer had been delayed by bad roads in his march from Fort Smith. Although he arrived with wagons of supplies plundered along the way, there was very little food; the arrival of Thayer's men would overburden Steele's already thin stores. Four days of continuous fighting on Prairie DeAnn (also spelled Prairie D'Ane) and at Moscow involved Steele's and Price's forces on April 10–13.

Short of sufficient supplies to subsist his troops and livestock for the march to Shreveport, Steele, after bluffing an attack on Washington—where the Confederates had relocated the state capital after fleeing Little Rock—turned his army east and headed for Camden. He planned to post troops in the forts and earthworks erected by the Confederates, communicate with General Banks in Louisiana, and look toward Pine Bluff and the U.S. Navy for supplies before resuming his march on Shreveport. Arriving at Camden on April 15, Steele's soldiers took possession of the town and its defenses. Price had been recently reinforced by Maj. Gen. Samuel Bell Maxey and two brigades—one white and one Native American—from the Indian Territory.

On April 17, Steele sent a heavily guarded train of wagons west to forage. They were attacked by Maxey's and Marmaduke's horse soldiers on April 18 at Poison Spring. The Rebels, including Choctaw Indians, overwhelmed the escort—the 1st Kansas Colored Infantry and white units from Kansas, Iowa, and Indiana—and captured or destroyed all the wagons and teams. It was "war to the knife and the knife to the hilt."

Many of the Federal soldiers were killed or captured and most of the blacks did not make it back to Camden. Some wounded, especially those of the 1st Kansas, reportedly were killed and scalped by the Indians in retaliation for Union plundering in the territory.

In addition to this disaster, Steele had just received word of the failure of the Red River campaign. The impact on his situation was that immediately following the Battle of Pleasant Hill on April 9 (see **Red River Campaign, Louisiana**), Price's two infantry divisions that had been rushed to Louisiana were, along with Maj. Gen. John G. Walker's Texas division ("Walker's Greyhounds"), sent north and were nearing Camden after a hard march.

Upon the arrival of department commander Kirby Smith and these additional troops, the Confederates sealed the western approaches to Camden. The Rebels, now outnumbering their foe, started to maneuver around the Northerners. Rebel cavalry under General Fagan was ordered to cross the Ouachita to intercept a wagon train endeavoring to supply Steele from Pine Bluff. On April 25 at Marks' Mills near the Saline River, Fagan attacked a wagon train returning to Pine Bluff after delivering supplies to Camden. The Rebels captured more than 300 wagons and 4 cannons. Only 300 of the 2,000 Union soldiers guarding the train escaped.

Word of the Marks' Mills disaster reached Camden on the evening of April 25 and precipitated a crisis for the beleaguered Federals. Steele responded to the emergency with alacrity. By daybreak on April 26, the Federals had evacuated Camden, crossed the Ouachita, and started up the military road heading for Little Rock. It was sunrise on April 28 before the Confederates were across the swollen rivers and in pursuit of the Yanks.

Late on April 29 the Rebel vanguard overtook Steele's rear guard as the Union army was preparing to cross the Saline River at Jenkins' Ferry. The next day there was bitter fighting across the flooded bottom as Kirby Smith committed his divisions piecemeal in a futile effort to crush Steele's force. The Federals pulled up their pontoon bridge and escaped to the north. Kirby Smith did not pursue, and Steele's tattered columns returned to Little Rock on May 3, ending the six-week campaign.

Steele suffered almost 2,800 casualties on his march through southwest Arkansas; the Confederates 2,300. The Federals also lost 9 cannons, more than 600 wagons, and thousands of horses and mules to the Confederates. The campaign, as Steele had predicted before starting out, was a Union disaster.

Points of Interest

The first actions in the Camden campaign occurred at Elkins' Ferry, Prairie D'Ane, and Moscow. These sites are along AR53 between the Little Missouri River and Bluff City. From Little Rock, travel southeast on I-30 to Arkadelphia, then on US67 to AR53. On the way, but not on the tour route, is Washington. From Washington you can rejoin AR53 north of Bluff City from AR24, then proceed southeast to Poison Spring Monument State Park. From there, take AR53 southeast to Camden.

Old Washington Historic State Park—Located 9 miles north of I-30 on AR4, the park is a nineteenth-century museum village with buildings, grounds, and a cemetery. Included in the park is the building that served as the capitol of Confederate Arkansas from mid-September 1863 to the end of the war. Demonstrations are given in two of the museums, the print shop, and the blacksmith shop. The weapons museum has a fine collection of Civil War firearms. The park features walking and guided tours, and a calendar of special events, including an annual Civil War reenactment in September. Camping is available during special events. Open every day from 8:00 A.M. to 5:00 P.M. Admission is charged; special rates for students, seniors, and groups. OLD WASHINGTON HISTORIC STATE PARK, P.O. Box 98, Washington, AR 71862; 501-983-2684.   🍴 🖼 ♿ ❓ 🏛 P $$

Poison Spring Monument State Park—This site contains trails and an outdoor exhibit of six panels that describes the action that took place there. At nearby White Oak Lake State Park a two-day reenactment of the battle is held annually in March. Poison Spring is open from 6:00 A.M. to 10:00 P.M. every day. POISON SPRING MONUMENT STATE PARK, c/o White Oak Lake State Park, Route 2, P.O. Box 28, Bluff City, AR 71722; 501-685-2748.   🚶 ❓

Camden—Camden has a number of sites including homes that survived the war. Among the guests at the McCollum-Chidester House were Confederate general Price and Union general Steele. The Neo-Classical house, which is at 926 Washington Street and now a museum, retains many of its original furnishings. A small admission is charged.

Two examples of earthworks are extant in the town. One is Fort Lookout, off Gravel Pit Road. The rifle pits and cannon emplacements guarded the town along the Ouachita River. The other is Fort Southerland in Fort Southerland Park, on Bradley Ferry Road, two blocks west of US79. This site, also on the Ouachita River, has interpretive signs. The two forts were constructed by the Confederates in 1864 in anticipation of a Federal attack from the north.

Camden also has a Confederate cemetery at Adams Avenue and Pearl Street. There are many fine accommodations in Camden, including bed-and-breakfast establishments. From Camden, take US79 northeast to AR8, then east to Marks' Mills Battleground Historic Monument State Park.

Marks' Mills Battleground Historic Monument State Park—The small site has a pavilion, picnic tables, and an interpretive sign detailing the battle. Each April a special commemorative event is held. The park is open daylight hours. MARKS' MILLS BATTLEGROUND HISTORIC MONUMENT STATE PARK, c/o Moro Bay State Park, 6071 Highway 15 South, Jersey, AR 71651; 501-463-8555.   ❷ P 🪑

From Marks' Mills, return west to US79 at Fordyce and follow US167 or AR229 north to US270. Jenkins' Ferry Monument State Park is located off AR46 near AR291, 5 miles south of Prattsville.

Jenkins' Ferry Monument State Park—This site has interpretive signs, picnic tables, and recreational water activities on the adjacent river. For more information, contact the superintendent of Catherine State Park in Hot Springs: 501-844-4176.

CHALK BLUFF

Although not part of the Camden campaign, a county park commemorates an action in the extreme northeast part of the state. On May 2, 1863, two Federal commands pursued the cavalry of Brig. Gen. John S. Marmaduke which was returning from an unsuccessful raid into southeast Missouri. The Confederates were crossing back into the state across the St. Francis River when the Federals caught up with them. The battle was fought across the river as the last of Marmaduke's command forded the waterway. Part of Marmaduke's force was the Missouri cavalry of Jo Shelby, and Jeff Thompson, the "Swamp Fox of the Confederacy," assisted in the crossing. The Federals under Brig. Gens. John McNeil and William Vandever did not pursue the force into Arkansas.

Points of Interest

Chalk Bluff Park—A visit to this park can be included in a tour of New Madrid and Cape Girardeau, Missouri (see **Missouri**). It is located off US62 just west of the town of St. Francis, Arkansas. The site features self-guided walking tours and is open every day from 8:00 A.M. to 5:00 P.M. For more information, call 501-598-2667.   ⛺ ♿ 🚶 ❷ 🚻

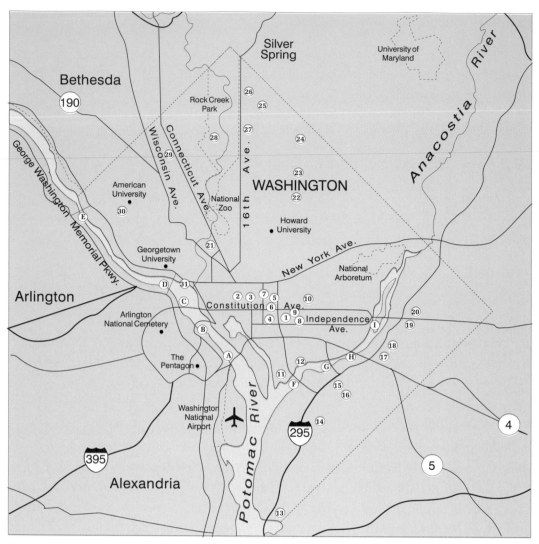

1. U.S. Capitol
2. The White House (Executive Mansion)
3. The Treasury Building
4. Smithsonian Institution (original building)
5. National Portrait Gallery (old Patent Office)
6. National Archives Building (post–Civil War building)
7. Ford's Theatre National Historic Site
8. Library of Congress (Adams Building)
9. Supreme Court Building (site of Old Capitol Prison)
10. Union Station Plaza (site of B&O Railroad Station)
11. Fort McNair (site of Washington Arsenal)
12. Washington Navy Yard
13. Fort Greble Park (Washington Defense Fort—WDF)
14. St. Elizabeths Hospital
15. Frederick Douglass National Historic Site
16. Fort Stanton Park (WDF)
17. Fort Davis Park (WDF)
18. Fort Du Pont Park (WDF)
19. Fort Chaplin Park (WDF)
20. Fort Mahan Park (WDF)
21. Oak Hill Cemetery
22. Soldiers' and Airmen's Home (Anderson Cottage)
23. Fort Totten Park (WDF)
24. Fort Slocum Park (WDF)
25. Battleground Cemetery
26. Walter Reed Army Medical Center
27. Fort Stevens Park (WDF)
28. Fort De Russey–Rock Creek Park (WDF)
29. Fort Reno Park (WDF)
30. Battery Kemble (WDF)
31. Chesapeake & Ohio Canal National Historical Park (Georgetown Visitor Center)

A. Mason (Long) Bridge
B. Arlington Memorial Bridge
C. Theodore Roosevelt Bridge
D. Francis Scott Key Bridge
E. Chain Bridge
F. Douglass Bridge
G. Eleventh Street Bridge
H. Sousa Bridge
I. Whitney Young Bridge

The District of Columbia

W ashington, D.C., was designed to be the stately, elegant capital of a great nation, but as the Civil War began it was a city in transition. Just sixty years old, with a population of more than sixty thousand, it had seen other American cities grow more quickly and assume more stability. And as the Civil War dragged on, the District became a sprawling military base, the Union's primary point of assembly for men, matériel, communications, and command.

The principal Federal buildings of the time reflected the city's status as a work in progress. The Executive Mansion and the Treasury Department building were magnificent structures, while three-story buildings housed the War and Navy departments on Seventeenth Street, NW, the site of what today is the Executive Office Building. The State Department, a smaller three-story building, was just north of the Treasury Department. Diagonally across from one another, at the intersection of Seventh and F streets, NW, were the granite edifices of the General Post Office and the Patent Office. The Capitol, however, presented a shabby exterior to foreign visitors used to the ornate palaces of Europe, and in 1861 the dome and other additions were under construction. On the Mall, a dismal landscape surrounded the Smithsonian Institution's red-spired castle. To the west, the Washington Monument, its ambitious construction stalled at 156 feet by a lack of funding, presented a curious sight. Many governmental functions operated from converted houses and commercial buildings scattered throughout the area.

The main thoroughfare of Washington, then as now, was Pennsylvania Avenue. It was designed with a clear sight line between the Capitol and the Executive Mansion, interrupted only by the Treasury building. Up and down the avenue the business of government, the lifeblood of the city, flowed. Hotels lined the north side, most notably Willards' at Fourteenth Street, where Republicans went to see and be seen. On the south side, the Central Market shared the thoroughfare with countless small businesses, grog shops, and brothels.

Civil and infrastructure problems plagued Washington. Managed by an inefficient local government at the mercy of Congress for appropriations, the city was considered the "stepchild of the nation." Streets were rutted and unsafe, and the police force was considered a farce. Sewage clogged City Canal, and an extraordinary number of bars, brothels, and gambling establishments emptied the pockets of government clerks and legislators who called Washington their part-time home. Yet Washington also had a high society. Public culture was limited, but for the wealthy and influential, parties were the vogue. Prominent Southern politicians and their society-conscious ladies hosted some of the grandest, but as the tensions in the country heightened and disunion loomed, such events became increasingly partisan. Washington's number one product, after all, was politics.

On the eve of the Civil War the military presence in Washington was slight. Tangible facilities included, in Southeast, the Navy Yard and the Marine Barracks; the U.S. Arsenal in Southwest; and the Naval Observatory in Northwest. In the last weeks of 1860, President James Buchanan brought General-in-Chief Winfield Scott, the septuagenarian hero of two American wars, back from his headquarters in New York City. From his office in the Winder Building on Seventeenth Street, across from the War Department, Scott prepared for the conflict the possible Southern secession would bring. Starting with the threat to Federal installations in Southern states and the violence that Abraham Lincoln's inauguration might spark, Scott mapped the North's war strategy.

With the exception of the battle at Fort Stevens, which is covered below, no battles were fought in the District of Columbia during the war, but significant political, strategic, and social events and decisions did take place here. Washington is divided into quadrants, with the northwest containing most of the sites covered.

THE UNITED STATES CAPITOL

The congressional activities in the Capitol during the war did not differ much from those that preceded it. And there was the ongoing construction of two new wings—the Senate and House chambers—and the new dome, but the most noteworthy events staged at the Capitol during the period were President Lincoln's first and second inaugurations. The first, on March 4, 1861, took place amid the breakup of the Union, with the country on the brink of war. The second, on March 4, 1865, occurred when most Northerners felt the war would soon end. At both these crossroads Lincoln's addresses reflected the mood of the times, but in particular stressed conciliation and the hope for unity.

Threats against Lincoln followed him daily on his February journey east from Illinois, on up to the inauguration. A plainclothes detective force under the direction of Allan Pinkerton infiltrated the groups of clandestine antagonists scattered throughout the region. A military force under the command of Charles P. Stone kept careful watch over the ceremony, but Lincoln was accessible. He rode in an open carriage with outgoing president Buchanan, and spoke on the Capitol steps, protected by only a wooden canopy. Lincoln's address clearly articulated the tenets of the Republican platform, but he also held out an olive branch to his Southern

An unknown artist painted this dramatic march of Federal soldiers down Washington, D.C.'s Pennsylvania Avenue from an 1861 Thomas Nast sketch. The leading units sport the colorful Zouave uniforms popular in the early-war period. The unfinished dome of the U.S. Capitol looms in the background.

brethren. "We are not enemies but friends," he said. "We must not be enemies. Though passion may have strained, it must not break our bonds of affection."

The event went off without incident. A young Patent Office clerk, Clara Barton, wrote: "The 4th of March has come and gone, and we have a live Republican President and, what is perhaps singular, during the whole day we saw no one who appeared to manifest the least dislike to his living."

Lincoln's second inauguration was not as grand in scale or as heavily guarded as the first. With the end of the war seemingly in sight, the president had switched his running mate to a Tennessean, Andrew Johnson. In ill health, the vice president–elect was reluctant to attend the ceremony, and then, giving his speech in the Senate chamber, he raised eyebrows with slurred words and hyperbole. Onlookers thought he was drunk. Lincoln's address, given just before he was sworn in on the Capitol steps by the former cabinet member and new chief justice Salmon P. Chase, was scholarly and forward-looking, "with malice toward none and charity for all."

After four years of a hectic military presence in the city and with an improved District police force, the protection of the president and other dignitaries was well in hand. Still,

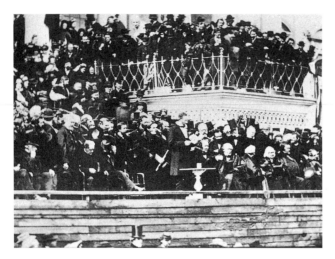

Abraham Lincoln's second presidential inauguration on March 4, 1865, photographed by Washington's Alexander Gardner. Two men in this photograph, one with some minor fame, the other unknown, would within six weeks enter the ranks of history's most notorious individuals. John Wilkes Booth is standing on the railed balcony to the left of the flag, and Lewis Powell, wearing a wide-brimmed hat, is standing directly below the president's lectern.

one man managed to charge the presidential party as it moved from the Rotunda to the east Capitol steps. Officers quickly subdued him. But a popular actor, sitting on the inaugural platform at the invitation of his girlfriend's father, would five weeks later have another encounter with President Lincoln. His name was John Wilkes Booth.

Points of Interest

The U.S. Capitol is open to the public when Congress is not in session and may be visited on a limited basis when the Senate and House of Representatives are meeting. For chamber passes, contact the office of your local congressional representative. Daily passes to areas other than the chambers are available from a booth at the Capitol's main steps. At the western foot of Capitol Hill at the edge of the Capitol Reflecting Pool is the Grant Memorial, featuring Henry Shrady's sculpture of U. S. Grant astride his favorite horse, Cincinnati.

THE WHITE HOUSE

Known as the Executive Mansion during the Civil War, the White House was home to one of history's most skilled and beloved leaders, and the nerve center of his extraordinary four-year, thirty-day administration. Here Abraham Lincoln served tirelessly as commander in chief and made some of the most epochal decisions in United States history, issuing the Emancipation Proclamation, the Homestead Act of 1862, and the Proclamation on Amnesty and Reconstruction. During the first four years of the war Lincoln seldom left the White House grounds, except to visit the Capitol or the War Department. Occasionally he would go to the theater or on a Sunday carriage ride, and during the hot summers, he and

*The first reading of the preliminary Emancipation Proclamation on September 22, 1862, painted by
Francis B. Carpenter, who visited with Lincoln a number of times before starting the work. Pictured with
Lincoln (left to right) are Secretary of War Edwin M. Stanton, Secretary of the Treasury Salmon P. Chase, Secretary
of the Navy Gideon Welles, Secretary of the Interior Caleb B. Smith, Secretary of State William H. Seward,
Postmaster General Montgomery Blair, and Attorney General Edward Bates.*

his family would sometimes stay in the Anderson Cottage at the Soldiers' Home, where he
would meet with the leaders of the Army of the Potomac.

As the secession crisis climaxed, Lincoln was besieged by thousands of prospective office
seekers. They camped out in the corridors and public rooms of the Executive Mansion,
even in the hallway separating the family living quarters from Lincoln's East Wing office.
Some critics charged that he spent more time dealing with the applicants than he did the
explosive situations brewing in Charleston, Pensacola, and Virginia, but the war troubled
the president deeply, and in the early days of his administration he suffered many sleep-
less nights.

In foreign affairs, Lincoln was little challenged, but when a crisis arose (see
International and **Texas**), he and Secretary William Henry Seward handled it with
skill. Lincoln's cabinet—which included, out of political necessity, the three candidates

he had bested in the 1860 Republican primary—was both a help and a hindrance to him in the prosecution of the war. In addition to Seward, the cabinet members most closely tied to Civil War history were Edwin M. Stanton, the second secretary of war; Gideon Welles, the secretary of the navy; and Salmon Portland Chase, the secretary of the treasury.

It was Seward who wisely advised Lincoln to withhold the issuance of the Emancipation Proclamation until it was supported by Federal victories. Welles, one of the most loyal cabinet members, pushed for the modernization of the U.S. Navy and the introduction of ironclads. And Stanton, though he irritated nearly everyone with whom he conducted business, skillfully placed the resources of the North into the hands of the generals who would eventually turn the tide of the war. Salmon Chase, as secretary of the treasury for most of the war, ensured that the Republic's enormous bills would be paid, but he—and his beautiful and ambitious daughter, Kate Chase Sprague—also never forgot that Lincoln had foiled his chance to be president. It was Chase who would instigate Lincoln's most difficult political crisis.

The winter of 1862–63 was a bleak time at the Executive Mansion. The North had suffered serious setbacks, the most important of these being the Federal army's defeat at Fredericksburg, Virginia (see **Fredericksburg, Virginia**). The stinging reverse at the hands of Gen. Robert E. Lee was crushing to the Oval Office. Secretary Chase, backed by Radical Republicans—who felt Lincoln was not proceeding fast enough to achieve emancipation—accused the moderate Seward of having undue influence on Lincoln. The disgruntled Republican senators passed a resolution limiting executive privilege and mandating congressional approval of a new cabinet, whose vote on policy issues the president would be bound by.

The resolution would not have passed a constitutional test, but Lincoln used his acute political skills to avoid an ugly and drawn-out affair. Seward submitted his resignation, but the president held it while he summoned the Radical Republicans to his office to air their grievances. The senators were accompanied by Chase, but after they were seated, the remainder of Lincoln's cabinet, except Seward, entered the room. When the cabinet members refuted the charges, Chase was in no position to disagree and further crisis was averted. After the meeting Chase submitted his resignation, but Lincoln refused to accept it and refused Seward's as well, thus keeping two more than able men in their posts.

Points of Interest

Start your visit to the White House and Presidential Park at the White House Visitor Center, 1450 Pennsylvania Avenue NW, located on the ground floor of the Old Post Office. Here you can view exhibits on the history of the Executive Mansion and vie for the limited number of tour tickets available each day. The center is open every day from 7:30 A.M. to 4:00 P.M., and usually all tickets are distributed by 10:00 A.M. For recorded visitor information, call 202-456-7041 or call 202-208-1631 to speak with park personnel.

Interior—During the early days of the conflict, the "Grim Chieftain," Jim Lane, and his Frontier Guards camped in the East Room.

Exterior—During the Lincoln presidency, the south lawn of the White House was a forested wilderness that extended to the Potomac. The general public crossed the north lawn without restriction, and the bustle of wartime activity brought soldiers and clerks in great numbers onto the grounds of the Executive Mansion.

At the north corner of the Ellipse, west of the intersection of Fifteenth Street and Pennsylvania Avenue, stands an equestrian statue of Maj. Gen. William T. Sherman.

THE TREASURY BUILDING

After Fort Sumter's surrender, on April 13, 1861, Washington was in turmoil. Southerners, including resigned army and navy officers, crowded Long Bridge on their way into Virginia. Women and children fled to the protection of the loyal Northern states. Lincoln's call for 75,000 volunteer soldiers awakened patriotism in most parts of the North, but the troops to defend the city did not arrive immediately. Washington was isolated, cut off to the south by Virginia, which withdrew from the Union on April 17, and to the north by Maryland, where secessionist thugs in control of Baltimore cut rail and telegraph lines to the U.S. capital.

Rumors of a force marching from Virginia to seize the capital spread throughout the city. The government settled on the imposing U.S. Treasury building as the final Federal bastion. Workers boarded and sandbagged the Capitol, the Patent Office, and other Federal buildings, but the expansive Treasury was the focus of their efforts. The department's clerks formed a militia unit and made preparations for the president and senior officials to manage the government from the basement. Volunteer units arrived in the city before Rebel banners appeared on the far Potomac shore and the Treasury building never became a fortress. Today it is a Washington landmark.

Points of Interest

Tours of the Treasury building are given on Saturday mornings and only with advanced reservation. To arrange a ninety-minute tour of the building, including the 1864 vault, call 202-622-2000 and follow the prompts. Tours for groups, those with disabilities, and tours of the Bureau of Engraving can also be arranged by calling this number.

THE SMITHSONIAN INSTITUTION

The Smithsonian Institution was founded in 1846 with a grant to the United States from the British immigrant scientist James Smithson. The oldest building, the red stone structure with many towers known today as the Castle, was designed by James Renwick, Jr., and built on the partially developed Capitol (now National) Mall. It was completed in 1855.

The building contained exhibits, a library, and offices devoted to the study of scientific, historical, and cultural subjects. The gardens were planned by famed horticulturist Andrew J. Downing, who also designed the gardens of the Executive Mansion and Capitol.

In December 1861, as Republicans in Congress clamored to abolish slavery in the District of Columbia, the Smithsonian hosted a series of lectures by abolitionists Wendell Phillips, Henry Ward Beecher, and Horace Greeley, among others. On the Mall on June 18, 1861, at the invi-

The original building of the Smithsonian Institution and the Washington Mall photographed in 1862. The mall was still under development at the time and an unsightly canal flowed nearby. Despite the rigors of war and rapid growth, the area managed to blossom into the treasured location of gardens, museums, and monuments of today.

tation of the Smithsonian's director, a twenty-nine-year-old inventor and aeronaut named Thaddeus S. C. Lowe, demonstrated the gas-filled balloons he had developed for military observation, impressing Lincoln and the secretary of war. Later, Maj. Gen.

George B. McClellan employed Lowe and his balloons extensively in the Peninsula and other early campaigns (see **Richmond Area, Virginia**).

Points of Interest

The Smithsonian Institution has grown from the single Civil War–era building to a two-city museum complex covering all aspects of science, technology, history, art, education, and culture. Of principal interest to Civil War enthusiasts are four of the Washington museums, three of them on the National Mall, and one, the National Portrait Gallery, located in the former Patent Office, at Eighth and F streets, NW. For an information packet, write to SMITHSONIAN INFORMATION, Washington, D.C. 20560; or call 202-357-2700 (TDD for hearing-impaired visitors, 202-357-1729) between 9:00 A.M. and 5:00 P.M. Eastern Time.   🚌 🏣 ♿ ❓ 🏛 🍽 🚻

The National Museum of History and Technology—The National Museum of History and Technolgy is the premier trustee of artifacts from our nation's past. Hundreds of objects and exhibits fill the halls, ranging from the Era of Exploration and initial contact by Europeans and Africans with Native Americans to the Space Age. The Armed Forces history section is on the second floor. The Civil War memorabilia on display at any given time represent just a fraction of the permanent collection. Among the exhibits always on display are Federal and Confederate uniforms, battle flags, Gatling guns, Maj. Gen. Philip H. Sheridan's war horse, and a bullet-riddled tree trunk from the Battle of Spotsylvania's Bloody Angle.

The National Air and Space Museum—The National Air and Space Museum features exhibits on the Civil War's importance in the development of flight for military purposes. In addition to artifacts and exhibits of Lowe's and others' balloons, the museum has silk panels from the Confederate balloon that was captured by the Federal navy on Virginia's James River on July 4, 1862.

Smithsonian Institution Building—The Castle, as it is known, is a landmark of Civil War Washington architecture. Of interest to visitors in the building is the Smithsonian Information Center, with a variety of exhibits, two orientation films, and electronic information centers. The building also houses the Woodrow Wilson International Center for Scholars. Later a U.S. president, Wilson, as a boy, watched some of the events of the Civil War pass by his Georgia and South Carolina homes.

The National Portrait Gallery—The second floor of the National Portrait Gallery has a permanent exhibit on the Civil War. Included are paintings, drawings, broadsides, and other artifacts from the period. On the staircase wall between the first and second floors hangs a large painting that depicts a gathering of U. S. Grant and other Federal generals. Although these officers were never actually together in this grouping, the painting represents a form of illustration common during the last century. An exhibit of presidential portraits also hangs on the first floor.

Other Civil War Sites—Many of the buildings and sites associated with the Civil War are in or near the "Federal Triangle," an area extending from the U.S. Capitol to the White House, between the National Mall and Pennsylvania Avenue. Most of these sites are within walking distance of the Federal Triangle Metro station. A short distance away is Gallery Place, also a Metro stop. Use this station to reach the National Portrait Gallery; the site of the Civil War–era Post Office and the National Museum of American Art, where Lincoln's Second Inaugural Ball took place. Also nearby are Ford's Theatre and the Petersen House, opposite each other on Tenth Street. Both are discussed in detail at the end of this chapter.

The Willard Hotel, at Fourteenth and E streets, stands on the site of the Willards' Hotel of Civil War fame.

The National Archives building, constructed in the 1930s, houses some of America's most important official documents, including the Constitution and the Declaration of Independence, which are on display daily. Open from 10:00 A.M. to 9:00 P.M. from April 1 to Labor Day; 10:00 A.M. to 5:30 P.M. otherwise.

It is difficult to visit Washington, D.C., without thinking of the Civil War. Squares, circles, and Metro stops take the names of Federal heroes. At Farragut Square, Logan Circle, McPherson Square, and Thomas Circle, to name just a few, stand statues—most of them equestrian—of these and other Union Civil War heroes. A detailed map of Washington will show the location of all these statues. (A similar statuary array of Confederate leaders can be found on Monument Avenue in Richmond—see **Richmond, Virginia.**) Only one Confederate general, Albert Pike, has an outdoor statue in Washington, located at the southeast corner of Third and D streets next to the D.C. Municipal Center. Pike led Native American Rebels at the Battle of Pea Ridge and is depicted here in his Masonic regalia.

At Seventeenth and F streets is the Winder Building, a former U.S. Army headquarters that through the war's early days served as the command post of Gen. Winfield Scott, then as the office of Maj. Gens. George B. McClellan and Henry W. Halleck, and Lt. Gen. U. S. Grant. In 1859, New York congressman Daniel E. Sickles lived at 722 Jackson Place, on the west side of Lafayette Park. The building there today is a 1960s reconstruction. Sickles killed his wife's lover, the son of Francis Scott Key, in Lafayette Park.

Near the intersection of Louisiana and New Jersey avenues is the site of the Baltimore & Ohio (Branch) Railroad station. The Supreme Court Building, on First Street, faces the east side of the U.S. Capitol. During the Civil War the Old Capitol Prison stood here. Among those imprisoned for their Confederate sympathies was the Washington socialite Rose O'Neal Greenhow. In 1861, she lived on the corner of Sixteenth and H streets, now the Hay-Adams Hotel. Greenhow was a partisan hostess to and confidante of Washington politicians. Also imprisoned here were Louisa Buckner, the niece of Montgomery Blair, Lincoln's postmaster general, who was caught smuggling quinine to Confederate forces, and Henry Wirz, commandant of prisoners at Andersonville, who was hanged on the Old Capitol Prison grounds on November 10, 1865 (see **Andersonville, Georgia**).

A number of cemeteries with Civil War significance lie within southeast Washington. Congressional Cemetery, near present-day Robert F. Kennedy Stadium, at 1801 E Street, SE, is the final resting place of Mathew Brady and the Lincoln conspirator David Herold. Mount Olivet Cemetery, on Bladensburg Road, contains the gravesite of Mrs. Mary Surratt. Buried in Oak Hall Cemetery, at 3001 R Street NW, are Surgeon General Joseph K. Barnes, Joseph Henry, Robert T. Merrick, John Nicolay, Maj. Gen. Jesse Reno, Edwin M. Stanton, Joseph Willard, Judge Andrew Wylie, and Adjutant General Lorenzo Thomas.

Founded in 1852, St. Elizabeths Hospital, 2700 Martin Luther King Jr. Avenue, SE, is the Federal government's first mental hospital designed for military personnel. The first medical superintendent, Dr. Charles H. Nichols, collaborated with social reformer Dorothea Dix, who was similarly active during the war, to establish a model institution. Several of the buildings, including the Center Building, are original and there is a Civil War cemetery.

Also in the southeast, at Cedar Hill (1900 Anacostia Drive, SE), is the Frederick Douglass House National Historic Site. Douglass, a mulatto slave who escaped to the North and became an outspoken abolitionist, settled here in 1877. Douglass was a vocal advocate of Abraham Lincoln, and two of his sons fought with the 54th Massachusetts Infantry, an African-American regiment (see **Fort Wagner, South Carolina**). After the war, Douglass worked in U. S. Grant's 1868 and 1872 presidential campaigns and served as the U.S. Marshal for the District of Columbia. The visitor center has exhibits and audiovisual programs. The house and visitor center are open daily except Christmas, Thanksgiving, and New Year's Day, and there is parking available. FREDERICK DOUGLASS NATIONAL HISTORIC SITE, c/o NATIONAL CAPITAL PARKS–EAST, 1900 Anacostia Drive, SE Washington, DC 20020; 202-426-5960 or 202-426-5961.

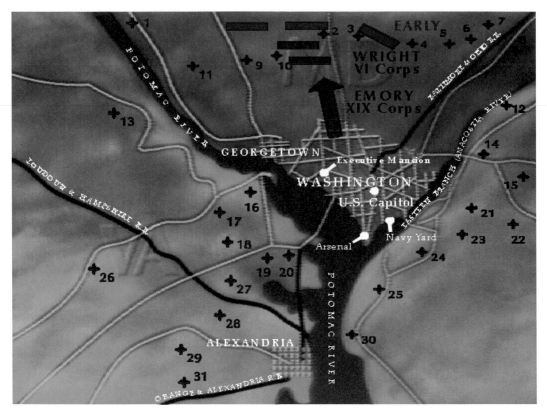

*The forts that made up the defense of Washington in the Civil War (listed by their numbers in Appendix A).
Protecting Washington from the north, Forts De Russy (10), Stevens (2), Slocum (3), and Totten (4) came under fire
from forces under Lt. Gen. Jubal Early on July 11–12, 1864. The Federal army's VI Corps, followed
by the XIX Corps, joined militia and other units in the city to finally drive Early from the capital's gates.*

THE DEFENSE OF WASHINGTON

In 1861, Washington was the site of two major Federal defense installations: the Navy Yard and the Arsenal. With the outbreak of hostilities, hundreds of support facilities—hospitals, barracks, depots, even a military bakery in the basement of the Capitol—sprang up in the District to support the war effort.

The Washington Arsenal

The Army Ordnance Department used the bustling Washington Arsenal, on the site of present-day Fort McNair, to store and distribute arms throughout the war. During the first hectic days of the Lincoln administration the Arsenal was in such turmoil that the president, strolling south one day from the Executive Mansion, found its gates left wide open—a potentially disastrous oversight. In May and June 1865, the Lincoln assassination trial took place here, across Second Avenue from the Fort McNair Officers' Club, in a building adjacent to what are now the tennis courts. Few of the leftover armaments and artifacts from the Civil War remain here.

The Washington Navy Yard

The Washington Navy Yard became a locus of activity at the start of the war. Its commandant was Franklin Buchanan, the first superintendent of the U.S. Naval Academy at Annapolis and a veteran of two wars. Buchanan was also a Marylander who cast his lot with the South (see **Hampton Roads, Virginia**) and was replaced by John A. Dahlgren, a friend of Abraham Lincoln's and an ordnance expert. During Dahlgren's tenure at the yard he designed a powerful naval shell gun, known as the Dahlgren gun, that was used on most Union warships.

During the war, the Washington Navy Yard served as a supply depot and communications hub only; it was too small to accommodate large forces. The nearby U.S. Marine Barracks housed the Marines who protected the navy yard, and the Marine Battalion that fought at First Manassas was organized and staged out of the barracks here. At war's end, most of the conspirators in the Lincoln assassination (see **Ford's Theatre**) were for a short time imprisoned on monitors anchored here.

Points of Interest

Visitors to the Navy Yard, on Eighth Street, SW, can park on the base, or use the Eastern Market stop of the Metro. A guard at the yard's main gate can direct you to the museum, which should be your first stop.

The modern Navy Memorial Museum is devoted to all periods of U.S. Navy history, with excellent exhibits on the Federal and Confederate navies. Artifacts include items from the USS *Monitor,* the USS *Hartford,* the USS *Kearsarge,* the USS *Cairo,* the USS *Tecumseh,* the blockade-runner *Modern Greece,* and items recovered from the sunken Confederate raider, CSS *Alabama* (see **International**). Other Civil War exhibits include displays of Medals of Honor and other Civil War medals and an iron plate used as a target to test the Dahlgren gun, developed at the navy yard. The museum also has the *Intelligent Whale* in its annex, a

Union submarine designed during the Civil War and built just after the war's end. The museum is open seven days a week from 9:00 A.M. to 5:00 P.M.

Outside the museum and beginning on Dahlgren Avenue, at Leutze Park, is Willard Park, better known as the "Walk of Cannons." The park features thirty-three cannon tubes, many from the Civil War era, rifled Brooke guns from the CSS *Tennessee,* and a British Blakely rifled gun from the commerce raider CSS *Florida.*

A guide pamphlet available in the museum describes the historic buildings at the Washington Navy Yard. The ground floor of the Latrobe Gate, the oldest continually manned U.S. Marine post in the nation, was built when the yard was established. Building number one, the New Commandant's Quarters, is now the office of the early history branch. Lincoln visited here many times when John A. Dahlgren was commandant of the navy yard. The slip and marine railway for the eastern ship house are extant; they were used in the repair of navy ships. For more information, contact the Navy Memorial Museum, Washington Navy Yard, 20374; 202-433-4882.

The Washington Forts

Having had to scramble to protect the city after the Battle of First Manassas (Bull Run), Federal officials commissioned John G. Barnard, chief engineer of the Department of Washington, to survey and construct a ring of forts around the District and adjacent counties in Maryland and Virginia. The masonry structures of previous fortifications, made obsolete by rifled artillery, gave way to new earthen forts, redoubts, redans, lunettes, and rifle pits. A 37-mile line of works—including 68 forts and 93 batteries mounting more than 800 cannons and 93 mortars—eventually surrounded the city. Traces of these fortifications remain in national, county or city parks, and are featured in the appropriate chapters. The District forts included within the National Park System are listed immediately below. Those District forts which are now parks and under the supervision of National Capital Parks–East are in Washington NE, SE, and SW. They are listed from north to south with locations and relevant features.

Fort Mahan—Benning Road and Forty-second Street, NE; retains part of the original earthwork.

Fort Chaplin—Texas Avenue and C Street, SE, across from the Mary Plummer Elementary School; the earthen fort is nearly intact.

Fort DuPont—Alabama Avenue between Massachusetts and Minnesota SE; retains overgrown pieces of the original earthwork. It is the largest park in the Southeast.

Fort Davis—Alabama and Pennsylvania avenues, SE; retains overgrown pieces of the original earthwork.

Fort Ricketts—Bruce Place and Fort Place, SE; retains pieces of earthworks and what is believed to be part of an artillery redoubt.

Fort Stanton—Erie and Evans roads, SE; part of the original fort is now a churchyard, the rest is in the park with only portions of earthworks extant.

Fort Carroll—Near 3720 Nicholas Avenue, SW; has outerworks and part of a battery extant.

Fort Greble—At Elmira Street and Nicholas Avenue, SW; retains pieces of the original carthwork.

The following fortifications are administered by the National Park Service and are part of Rock Creek Park beginning near the Potomac River, in the Northwest, from west to east (excluding Fort Stevens, treated separately):

Battery Kemble—Nebraska Avenue and Chain Bridge Road, NW; retains some of the form of the original work.

Fort Bayard—River Road and Western Avenue, NW; a small park with no traces of the fort.

Fort Reno—Belt Road and Chesapeake Street, NW; now little more than a large field, used primarily for concerts; however, the strategic location is obvious from the rise it is located on. It was named for Maj. Gen. Jesse L. Reno, the Federal IX Corps commander killed at the Battle of South Mountain (see **South Mountain, Maryland**). Nearby, on Massachusetts Avenue, is the Naval Observatory, which during the Civil War, was located on the hill now occupied by the Navy's Bureau of Medicine, west of Twenty-third Street and north of Constitution Avenue.

Only traces remain of Fort De Russy, which is in a wilderness area. It came under Confederate attack on July 11–12, 1864 (see **Fort Stevens**). From Military Road, take Oregon Avenue north and park where convenient. On the east side of the street you'll find trail markings that lead about a half mile through the woods to a plaque on a large boulder and the remains of the earthworks.

Fort Slocum—Kansas Avenue and Madison, NW was involved in the defense of Washington during Early's Raid, July 11–12, 1864. Some rifle pits and portions of a battery remain. The location of the fort on high ground gives indication of its defensive value.

Fort Totten—Riggs Road near North Capitol Street, NE, along with Fort Stevens, is the best preserved of the forts that faced Early's attack. Much of the earthworks and part of the trench fronting the works remain.

Fort Bunker Hill—Sargent Road NE is heavily wooded with some traces of earthworks.

Fort Lincoln Park—Just outside the District on Bladensburg Road, this fort guarded that important Civil War thoroughfare. No traces of the Civil War earthworks remain; however, part of an 1812 battery and a Dahlgren gun are in the park. Fort Lincoln is best known for its adjoining, nonmilitary cemetery.

All these parks have interpretive markers describing the forts located there and their position in the network of Washington defenses.

Fort Stevens

Originally called Fort Massachusetts, Fort Stevens was renamed for fallen Union brigadier general Isaac Stevens, who was killed at the Battle of Chantilly, Virginia, on September 1, 1862. Fort Stevens, near Fort De Russy, was the northernmost fort in the Washington wartime defenses. It protected the Seventh Street Pike, one of the main roads from Maryland into the city. The main action here took place in mid-July, 1864, when Lt. Gen. Jubal A. Early's army mounted the only serious Rebel threat to the District of Columbia.

After defeating a smaller Federal force at Monocacy, Maryland, on July 9, Early's veteran command marched southeastward, intent on diverting Federal troops from Petersburg, where Union armies were confronting the entrenched Confederates. But the heat, dust, and strain of the previous day's battle slowed the Rebels' advance (see **Monocacy, Maryland**), and Early's troops arrived at the Washington defenses on Monday afternoon, July 11, facing Forts Slocum, Stevens, and De Russy. Earlier in the day, Brig. Gen. John McCausland's Confederate cavalry, advancing along the Georgetown Pike, had closed to within sight of Fort Reno.

The Union War Department had spent Sunday cobbling together all available units, including old soldiers from the nearby Soldiers' Home, members of the Invalid Corps, the Quartermaster Corps teamsters, Navy Yard mechanics, and Treasury clerks, all of whom joined the 100-Day Men, the untrained volunteers and dismounted cavalry officers upon whom the defense of the capital momentarily rested. This motley army was led by no fewer than four major generals—Christopher C. Augur, Alexander McCook, Quincy A. Gillmore, and Quartermaster General Montgomery Meigs.

The Confederates moved in force down the Silver Spring Road, skirmishing with Federal cavalry. Upon reaching the defenses, Confederates unleashed a telling fire, intent on gaining intelligence about the strength and composition of Federal units. One of these units was a depleted veteran regiment, the 25th New York Cavalry, fighting dismounted. Apparently, their appearance on the line gave Early pause. He countermanded the general attack and continued reconnaissance skirmishing. If Early thought veteran reinforcements had been rushed to oppose him, he was correct. After learning the scope of Early's expedition, Lt. Gen. Ulysses S. Grant had ordered two divisions of the Army of the Potomac VI Corps, under Maj. Gen. Horatio Wright, to dock at the Navy Yard and march north through the city. Another force, the XIX Corps from the Gulf Coast, en route to Petersburg, was also ordered to land at the Washington wharves.

On Tuesday morning, the VI Corps moved into the Fort Stevens works, relieving those who had stood tall the previous day. Early ordered his skirmishers forward on July 12, but by then the Army of the Potomac was occupying trenches to the fort's left and right. Early again called off the assault and resumed skirmishing. Gray-clad sharpshooters and snipers took aim from trees and houses in the rolling fields to the north. The Union response was heavy artillery.

Lincoln visited Fort Stevens on July 12, accompanied by Mrs. Lincoln and political officials. At one point, General Wright ordered a VI Corps brigade to assault two houses where Rebel sharpshooters hid. As the firefight worsened, Wright tried to shepherd his civilian visitors to safety, but the sharp crack of musketry and the boom of cannons were a new experience for the president. Standing atop a firing step to observe the Federal charge, he placed his head and upper chest above the protective walls of the parapets. Before Wright could move the president to a safer position, a staff officer standing next to the president was wounded. Seeing the danger, an exasperated aide, a young officer named Oliver Wendell Holmes, Jr., yelled to the president, whom he did not recognize, "Get down, you damn fool!" Later a thrice-wounded veteran, Holmes would become a justice of the United States Supreme Court.

With such a strong and determined force deployed against them, the Confederates abandoned their positions during the night of July 12–13 and backtracked into the Shenandoah Valley. At the time, Early remarked to an aide, "Major, we haven't taken Washington, but we've scared Abe Lincoln like hell!"

Points of Interest

Fort Stevens is at Thirteenth and Quackenbos streets, a block west of Georgia Avenue and two blocks north of Military Road in northwest Washington. As part of Rock Creek Park, the fort is administered by the National Park Service. The partially reconstructed fort contains several pieces of heavy artillery, the exterior of a powder magazine, and a monument commemorating Lincoln's visit. Even today, visitors who peer over the parapets and look downhill to the north may understand the logic of a defense line that was once tested but never penetrated.

As with the rest of Rock Creek Park, Fort Stevens is open during daylight hours for touring and picnicking. Pets must be leashed and fires are permitted only in grills or standing fireplaces. The park headquarters and information center is on Beach Drive, south of Military Road. For voice and TDD information, call 202-426-6832.   🚌 ♿ ❓ P ⛱

Four other sites in the Fort Stevens area are notable. Fort Slocum Park, on Third Street, lies on the grounds of the third fort that Early attacked. The Anderson Cottage is at the U.S. Soldiers' and Airmen's Home, at Park Place and Rock Creek Church Road. Battleground National Cemetery, located at 6625 Georgia Avenue, contains the graves of 41 Federal dead from the engagement at Fort Stevens, and monuments to Company K, the 150th Ohio National Guard, the 122nd New York Infantry, the 98th Pennsylvania Infantry, and the 25th New York Cavalry.

Heavy artillery pieces such as this one in Fort Stevens were the mainstay of the forts in Washington's defenses. The guns answered the probing Confederate attacks of Lt. Gen. Jubal Early's Army of the Valley on July 11–12, 1864, while infantry and dismounted cavalry soldiers manned rifle pits and works adjoining the artillery positions.

Finally, the National Museum of Health and Medicine, at Walter Reed Army Medical Center, is the antecedent of the Army Medical Museum, which was established in 1862. While neither the present building nor the vaulted pavilion built just after the war are Civil War sites, the extensive·collections warrant attention for their standing exhibits on the Lincoln assassination and Civil War medical and health care. Among the unusual artifacts are surgical instruments, tissue samples, models, and the tibia of Union major general Daniel E. Sickles, whose lower right leg was amputated on the battlefield after the second day of fighting at Gettysburg. Also on the grounds is a plaque marking the spot where the sharpshooter who fired at President Lincoln during the attack on Fort Stevens stood. NATIONAL MUSEUM OF HEALTH AND MEDICINE, Armed Forces Institute of Pathology, Walter Reed Army Medical Center, 16th Street NW, Washington, DC 20306-6000; 202-782-2200. 🚌 ♿ ❷ P 🪑

READING—*Second Kernstown, Virginia*

WASHINGTON'S BRIDGES

Because of their strategic importance, Washington's bridges to Virginia were heavily guarded. None of them remain in their original form. Long Bridge, connecting to Alexandria, is now a railroad bridge, the Aqueduct Bridge from Georgetown was replaced by the present-day Francis Scott Key Bridge, and the Chain Bridge, connecting with the Leesburg Pike, retains only its original name.

Paralleling the Potomac's north bank is the Chesapeake and Ohio Canal, which saw heavy use during the Civil War and was a frequent target of Confederate demolition efforts. In 1862, mules towed boatloads of Federal troops along the canal on their way to the Shenandoah Valley. The canal is now a National Historical Park with a visitor center in Georgetown. For more information on historical features of the canal and recreational opportunities, visit the canal information center at the Foundry Mall between Thirtieth and Thomas Jefferson streets or call 202-653-5844. 🚌 ♿ ❷ 🪑 🍴 🚻

FORD'S THEATRE AND THE PETERSEN HOUSE

Of the many events that grieved the nation during the Civil War, none was more tragic than the assassination of Abraham Lincoln. The loss shattered the president's family and saddened the larger family of politicians, government officials, and military personnel who worked so closely with him to achieve victory. The loss to the nation can never be measured: Not content with the end of active hostilities, Lincoln was at the time of his death already planning how he would heal the nation's wounds. John Wilkes Booth's bullet changed all that; snuffing out a merciful president's leadership and replacing it with the vengeful hatred of a thousand disjointed voices. For the former Confederate states in particular, the impact of Reconstruction would be felt for many generations to come.

While Lincoln was still in Virginia with the Federal armies, news reached Washington of the capture of Petersburg and Richmond, the once-proud Confederate capital (see **Richmond, Virginia**). The capital broke into a week of wild celebration. Cannons boomed, bands played, fireworks exploded, and nearly every building in the city produced some sort of lighted tribute. People thronged the streets, and only the rowdiest of offenses raised the ire of the District police.

Only the president was missing. In the evening of April 9, Lincoln returned from City Point, Virginia, by steamer, and while on his way to the White House received word of Lee's surrender (see **Appomattox Court House, Virginia**). If the revelers were pleased, they wanted most to see their heroic president and crowded the Executive Mansion grounds. Trumpets blared and cheers were raised, but the president made only two brief appearances on the portico that day and the next, promising the crowd that he would deliver a speech from the Executive Mansion balcony on Tuesday evening, April 11.

Concern for Lincoln's safety was expressed by Secretary of War Stanton and others, though the president gave the warnings little regard. Lincoln spoke that Tuesday evening, but to the crowd's surprise he spent little time lauding the accomplishments of his administration and the military. Instead, he focused on the peaceful reincorporation of the Confederate states into the Union, and on various reforms, including the suggestion of limited voting rights for African Americans.

John Wilkes Booth, the handsome and popular actor from a Maryland family with a rich theatrical heritage, was in the crowd. He had professional success, a comfortable income, and an ease with the ladies, but he also had a strong allegiance to the South and a maniacal hatred of the Republican government's policies. The focus of his contempt was Abraham Lincoln. For months, he had been planning to kidnap the president in order to ransom Confederate prisoners and win concessions for the South. Now, with the war all but over, Booth changed his tack. He turned to Lewis Powell, a confidant with him at the White House, and said, ". . . that is the last speech he will ever make." It may have been Booth's first thought of assassination, and left open only the questions of where and when.

Washington's newspapers regularly published the president's comings and goings, but Booth's kidnap plans had been frustrated by Lincoln's last-minute cancellations. Booth and his associates had once lain in ambush for the president on a suburban road. On April 14, Good Friday, the Lincolns decided to attend the Ford's Theatre production of *Our American Cousin,* a comedy starring Laura Keene. Booth was a regular performer at the theater, which was one of several well-known private playhouses in the city that vied for presidential visits, and he was familiar to the proprietor, John T. Ford, and other theater employees. He moved through the theater at will, even using it as a mail drop. It was about noon on Friday, while calling for his mail, that he learned of the Lincolns' evening plans.

Booth quickly rounded up his cohorts, most of whom had lost their enthusiasm for the intrigue and were not prepared for murder. Compounding the tragedy, a Federal clerk who boarded at Mary Surratt's H Street rooming house had a month earlier reported Booth and his band of conspirators to the War Department, but the report had slipped through bureaucratic cracks and Booth was never questioned.

The president had invited Lt. Gen. Ulysses S. Grant, who had arrived in Washington on April 13, and Mrs. Grant, to accompany him and his wife to the performance. But Grant, a humble, unpretentious man, wanted to avoid the attention thrust upon him as the conquering hero. And Mrs. Grant, who had recently been shunned and embarrassed by the temperamental Mary Todd Lincoln, wanted no part of an evening with her. Despite some consternation, the Grants explained that they were anxious to join their children in New Jersey and declined the invitation, unwittingly increasing Booth's chances for success.

A series of coincidences and security oversights allowed Booth to shoot the president. On Good Friday afternoon, Booth observed the Grants en route to the depot and even rode beside their carriage to ensure they would not be attending the theater that night. Without the general in attendance, no military escort accompanied the party to the theater, and the president had with him only a bodyguard, his valet, and two guests, the unarmed U.S. Army major Henry Rathbone and his fiancée, Miss Clara Harris.

Booth's plan also called for the simultaneous assassinations of Vice President Andrew Johnson and the secretary of state, William H. Seward, who was confined to his bed with a broken jaw and arm. But George Atzerodt, an unreliable conspirator, lost his nerve and never made the attempt on Johnson's life. A dim-witted but physically powerful Confederate deserter, Lewis Powell, alias Lewis T. Paine, slashed his way through Seward's house, wounding several servants, a male nurse, two of Seward's sons, and the secretary. Powell then escaped into the Washington night. Seward survived the attack.

In Ford's Theatre about 10:15 P.M., during a monologue by one of the play's comic actors, Booth entered the presidential box, which Lincoln's bodyguard had left unattended. Booth aimed a derringer at the back of the president's head and fired a single shot. Lincoln slumped forward. After slashing Major Rathbone with a hunting knife, the acrobatic Booth leaped twelve feet to the stage, catching a spur on the flag that draped the front of the presidential box, and consequently may have broken his left leg upon landing. He stumbled across the stage and out the door to his waiting horse, escaping from the city over the Navy Yard Bridge.

Those at Ford's Theatre were stunned. Minutes ticked away before the news finally reached Federal government officials, who were already reacting to the knifing of Secretary Seward. Two physicians rushed to Lincoln and carried him across the street to the house of William Petersen, a tailor. On a bed in a rear bedroom, Lincoln, surrounded by doctors, by most of his cabinet, and by military officers, succumbed to his wound at 7:22 A.M. on April 15, 1865.

Shock waves reverberated through the city and the nation. In tribute to a man whose power and patience, intellect and virtue had led the country through its most difficult time, Washington draped its buildings in shrouds of mourning. People wept openly in the streets. On April 18, thousands of mourners filed past the coffin in the White House East Room, prior to a state funeral. A large procession then accompanied the president's coffin to the Capitol, where several more days of viewing and a service took place. On April 21, the draped casket was loaded aboard a special funeral train, which slowly made its way to Illinois, stopping to let more than seven million people at crowded depots and stations view the coffin. The train arrived in Springfield, Lincoln's final resting place, on May 3 (see **Springfield, Illinois**).

Booth and another conspirator, David Herold, were eventually cornered in a Virginia tobacco barn (see **Fredericksburg, Virginia**), and Federal agents rounded up the others implicated in the crime: Powell, Atzerodt, Edman Spangler, Mary Surratt, Booth's school friends Samuel Arnold and Michael O'Laughlin, and Dr. Samuel Mudd, who had set Booth's broken leg (see **Washington, D.C., Area, Maryland**).

Points of Interest

Ford's Theatre National Historic Site—Though just twenty-six months old, Ford's Theatre was shuttered after the assassination. In 1866 the Federal government, which had acquired the building, converted it to offices. Tragedy struck at Ford's again on June 9, 1893, when the floors collapsed and killed twenty-two people. The building was used as a storage facility until 1932, when it became the home of the Lincoln Museum. It was restored, in the 1960s, to its 1865 appearance.

The theater is now open for historical touring and live theater productions. The lavishly decorated presidential box looks largely as it did on the night of April 14, 1865: the original portrait of George Washington—carefully placed by Henry Clay Ford, John Ford's younger brother—hangs where it did that night.

The Lincoln Museum fills the basement of the theater. It began with Osborn Oldroyd's collection of Lincolniana and has been expanded to include such artifacts as the murder weapon and other of John Wilkes Booth's personal possessions.

The three ground-floor rooms of the Petersen House, directly across 10th Street, have been restored to their appearance of April 14–15, 1865. Mary Todd Lincoln wept in the front parlor on that night, comforted by her son, Capt. Robert Todd Lincoln. In the back parlor, Edwin M. Stanton issued orders and interviewed witnesses to the assassination. The back bedroom depicts the scene as witnessed by the officials and physicians who attempted to make Lincoln's last moments as comfortable as possible. The pillow on display, with its blood-stained pillowcase, is original.

The Petersen House is open from 9:00 A.M. to 5:00 P.M. every day except Christmas. Park rangers offer tours. Ford's Theatre is closed when rehearsals and matinee performances are in progress, usually Thursdays, Saturdays, and Sundays. Admission to the site is free. Performance information for the theater is available at the box office and throughout Washington. FORD'S THEATRE NATIONAL HISTORIC SITE, 511 and 516 Tenth Street, NW, Washington, D.C. Direct written inquiries to National Capitol Parks–Central, 900 Ohio Drive SW, Washington, DC 20242; 202-426-6924, TDD 202-426-1749.

DRIVING TOUR—*Proceed to Rockville, Maryland, or Arlington, Virginia*

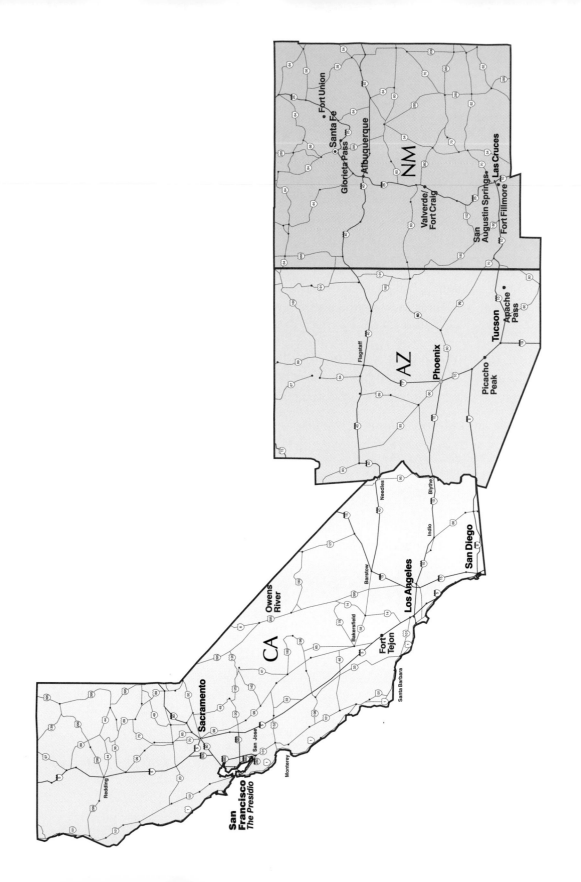

The Far West

T hough physically removed from the immediate tensions that sparked the Civil War, the Far West did not escape the conflict's ravages. The West's white settlers, in general, were more concerned with local problems than with those of the states, but they were profoundly affected by the South's secession. In addition to territory and people, the region also had ore—particularly gold and silver—and cultivated products that were coveted by North and South alike.

Partisan alignment in the West ran roughly along geographic lines. The territory of New Mexico south of the 34th parallel, including what today is Arizona, was generally pro-Confederate, while north of that line sentiments tilted toward the Union. Hispanics, numerous in the territory, generally opposed the South and slavery (as did, incidentally, the Mexican government, though the governors of several of Mexico's northern states were sympathetic to the Confederates). Utah Territory, the Mormon stronghold, remained loyal to the Federals despite its problems with the U.S. government. Oregon and its northern neighbor, Washington Territory, also favored the Union.

California, mineral rich, prosperous and growing, was a member of the Union, having been admitted as a free state in the Compromise of 1850. But Southern sentiment there ran strong, particularly downstate. There were also many Southerners in the Nevada Territory's mining camps, which led to spirited but generally harmless wrangling among neighbors. Despite decreasing resources during the war years, the U.S. Army command in California was charged with safeguarding the region's political integrity, and its gold and silver deposits.

It will take five days to tour the Far West sites of these little-known but fascinating Civil War battles and engagements. Whether you start from the east (recommended if practical) or the west, suggested stops are in Albuquerque and/or Santa Fe (two nights), Phoenix, and the northern part of Greater Los Angeles.

ARIZONA

Until 1863, the present-day area of Arizona was part of the New Mexico Territory, which comprised the future states of Arizona and New Mexico. Though this section discusses sites and actions in what is now the state of Arizona, it is interesting to note that, from the 1861 Southern perspective, "Arizona" was considered that portion of New Mexico Territory south of the 34th parallel. So said a March 1861 convention of the territory's pro-Confederate citizens held in Mesilla, New Mexico. On August 1 that same year, Lt. Col. John R. Baylor, victor of the first Rebel campaign in the territory (see **Fort Fillmore, New Mexico**), proclaimed the establishment of the territory of Arizona, with Mesilla as its capital and himself as governor.

The first action between forces of the North and South in what is now Arizona would really be better called an inaction. Four companies of U.S. Army regulars abandoned Forts Buchanan and Breckinridge, south and north of Tucson, respectively. While en route to Fort Fillmore, Baylor sent a force under Capt. Isaiah Moore, to intercept them. Learning that the Southerners had captured Fort Fillmore, the Federal force marched instead to Fort Craig, near Socorro, New Mexico, eluding Baylor's army. The Federal evacuation of the two southern Arizona forts increased Indian attacks around Tucson and helped solidify Confederate support in the area.

On January 27, 1862, as part of Brig. Gen. Henry Hopkins Sibley's campaign in the territory (see **New Mexico**), Capt. Sherod Hunter was sent with a company of cavalry—about 60 troopers—to Tucson, where they were well received by residents. On February 28, the Confederate flag was raised there.

On March 3, 1862, Col. James Reily led a detachment of 20 Texan soldiers and a lieutenant to Sonora, Mexico. Reily offered the Sonoran governor a pact of cooperation with the Confederacy. Although Sibley hoped to ally the north Mexican states with the CSA, the agreement they made allowed the Rebels to purchase supplies only with gold or silver, and not Confederate paper currency.

Meanwhile, Hunter's force ventured across Arizona, confiscating supplies, livestock, and a few Northern-owned mines, and guarding the territory against attacks by Apache Indians. The separate, rapid sorties gave some Union leaders the impression that Hunter's force was larger than it was. Early in March some of Hunter's soldiers, having ridden westward down the Gila River to the Pima Indian villages at Stanwix Station, confiscated from the U.S. purchasing agent—who was taken prisoner—supplies meant for Federal forces. While in this area the Rebels would have their first confrontation with the California Column.

Picacho Pass

The California Column, under Col. James H. Carleton, was formed in the San Francisco area from units originally designated to guard the overland mail route from Salt Lake City. In the fall of 1861, in response to threats by Southern sympathizers (see **California**), the column marched to southern California. The appearance of Sibley's expedition on the Texas–New Mexico border in the winter of 1861–62 broadened the column's role considerably. Over a period of months the units were marched in staggered formation across the desolate southern California deserts, to Fort Yuma in the Arizona portion of New Mexico Territory. (Arizona Territory was formed in 1863.)

Carleton, still in Los Angeles, ordered a detachment of the 1st California Cavalry, under the pretext of fighting the Tonto Indians, to recapture Tucson from Hunter's Rebels. Capt. William McCleave, the commander of the expedition, took a handful of men to the house of A. M. White, Federal purchasing agent, near the Pima Indian villages (present-day Phoenix). To their surprise, Hunter was masquerading as the previously captured purchasing agent; White, and McCleave and his men were taken prisoner.

In late March 1862, another detachment of California infantry and cavalry, with a battery of two mountain howitzers, left Fort Yuma under Capt. William Calloway. When the vanguard reached Gila River Bend (present-day Gila Bend), they were fired on by some Texas troopers destroying Federal hay caches. The Rebels were pursued but not caught.

At the Pima villages, Captain Calloway discovered that the last detachment of Texans, under Lt. Jack Swilling, had pulled out and were en route to Tuscon to join Hunter's main force. Calloway dispatched Lt. James Barrett with twelve troopers to sweep wide and hit the Texans on their flank, while his main column attacked them head-on. On April 15, Barrett overtook the 16-man Rebel detachment at Picacho Pass, forty-five miles northwest of Tucson. As Barrett's men fought the Texans in the chaparral below Picacho Peak, Calloway charged. Barrett and 2 Union cavalrymen were killed, 3 Federals and 2 Texans were wounded. Three Texans were taken prisoner and the rest escaped. That night the Federals bivouacked on the battlefield and buried the dead. The next day, Calloway, over the protest of his officers, retreated to Stanwix Station. Had he pursued the Rebels, his larger force would probably have driven Hunter from Tucson and beyond.

Points of Interest

The Picacho Pass Battle area is part of Picacho Peak State Park, located 71 miles southeast of Phoenix at Picacho, off exit 112 of I-10. The graves of Barrett and the two other Federal soldiers are reportedly twenty feet from the Southern Pacific Railroad tracks at Picacho Pass. The park has a campground.   ▲ ⫰⫯ ❓ P ⫯⫯

DRIVING TOUR—*Proceed to Apache Pass or Southern California*
READING— *Peralta, New Mexico*

Apache Pass

Calloway's detachment was reinforced by a major element of the California Column from Fort Yuma, under Lt. Col. Joseph R. West. At the Pima villages they established a temporary fort named Fort Barrett, in honor of the Federal lieutenant killed at Picacho Pass. On May 14, West's force left for Tucson, stopping on the way at old Fort Breckinridge, which was named for the former U.S. vice president John C. Breckinridge, then a Confederate general. The fort was eventually garrisoned and its name changed to Fort Stanford, in honor of California's governor, Leland Stanford. When West reached Tucson, on May 20, he found it abandoned. Hunter's troopers had evacuated on May 4 and, after some trouble with the Apaches, re-joined the withdrawing Confederates of Sibley's Expedition on the Rio Grande.

By this time Carleton was bringing the rest of the column from Fort Yuma to the Pima villages. He ordered West to continue his advance southeastward to old Fort Buchanan. Arriving in Tucson on June 7, Carleton set up a military and provisional territorial government to protect the town's citizens and conduct military operations. On June 15, he sent three couriers to New Mexico, to let Brig. Gen. Edward R. S. Canby—who had been promoted on May 31, 1862—know of the column's progress.

Apache Pass, in the southernmost extension of the U.S. Rockies, is long and narrow, rising to 5,115 feet, and has the only free-flowing spring in the area. On June 18 Carleton's couriers—an infantry sergeant, a civilian express rider, and a guide—were attacked by Apaches east of the pass. The sergeant and guide were killed, but the express rider escaped, fighting off the Indians until he reached Mesilla, New Mexico, 170 miles away. Although he was captured by the Confederates there, he did manage to get word to Canby, through sympathizers, of the California Column's approach. But the Rebels learned of the column, too.

Carleton, not knowing the fate of the couriers, sent a detachment of soldiers to New Mexico from Tucson. On June 25, Lt. Col. Edward E. Eyre and troopers of the 1st California Cavalry, while watering their horses at the spring in Apache Pass, were approached by the Apache chieftain Cochise and about 100 well-armed and mounted Apache warriors carrying a white flag. Food and tobacco were distributed and the Indians promised not to attack the soldiers, but later that day three soldiers who had left the camp were found dead. Two had been scalped. That night, shots rang through the Federal camp which was located about two miles east of the pass, wounding a surgeon. Eyre's detachment continued on to New Mexico without further incident. On June 29 they met a scouting party from Fort Craig, sent by Col. John M. Chivington, uniting for the first time Colorado and New Mexico volunteers with the California Column. On July 4, Eyre's detachment reached the Rio Grande near Fort Thorn. For the first time in almost a year the Stars and Stripes flew over southern New Mexico Territory.

On July 10, a second detachment, under Capt. Thomas L. Roberts, left Tucson for the Rio Grande. They were attacked five days later, near the abandoned Butterfield Stage station in Apache Pass. One soldier was killed. Roberts sent infantry up into the rocks as skirmishers on both sides of the canyon, but the Apaches, led in this battle by both Cochise and Mangas Coloradas, fired down on the soldiers from positions on the hillsides. Six troopers were sent to warn the cavalry guarding the supply wagon train, farther back, while Roberts unlimbered his two mountain howitzers, eventually dislodging the Apaches with shells. The Federals gained control of the spring at four P.M., then withdrew to the abandoned station with the wagon train. The next day, the supply train met Roberts's force at the stagecoach station, and the battle was renewed. The spring was retaken and held by the Californians until they departed for the Rio Grande the next morning.

The Battle of Apache Pass, on July 15–16, 1862, was the largest Federal army action fought with the Apaches in Arizona, and called attention to the strategic value of Apache Pass. Nine Apaches were killed in the battle, compared to two U.S. Army soldiers.

Points of Interest

Apache Pass is within the Fort Bowie National Historic Site. Fort Bowie was begun as a permanent military camp by Brig. Gen. James H. Carleton, to control the spring and secure the route to California. Other forts were also established by Carleton during the Civil War period in response to Indian attacks.

Fort Bowie National Historic Site—This rustic and scenic park contains the sites associated with the battles between the Apaches and the California column in the pass. The old military road has been turned into a 1.5-mile walking trail which leads to the sites associated with the actions and the visitor center. The trailhead, which has parking, rest rooms, and a picnic area, can be reached from I-10 by exiting at Willcox and traveling 22 miles south on AZ186. The trail, which is open from sunrise to sunset, takes you past the ruins of the Butterfield Stage station, the Chiricahua Apache Indian Agency Building, the ruins of the first and second forts, the post cemetery, and Apache Springs, the source of water which was of major importance for travelers in the pass. The visitor center is open every day from 8:00 A.M. to 5:00 P.M. except December 25 and is manned by uniformed rangers. Take precautions for the weather conditions (extreme heat and sudden storms are a possibility) when hiking the trail. For more information and access for persons with disabilities, contact the park. FORT BOWIE NATIONAL HISTORIC SITE, Dos Cabezas Route, P.O. Box 6500, Willcox, AZ 85643-9737; 520-847-2500.   ♿ 👫 ❷ P ⛱ 🚻

DRIVING TOUR—*Proceed to Picacho Pass or Fort Fillmore, New Mexico*
READING—*Indian Actions: Minnesota (The Northwest)*

CALIFORNIA

The Golden State, young but growing in the 1860s, has many ties to the Civil War. Because of hostile Indians and the uncertain loyalty of the many Hispanic settlers, a significant U.S. Army presence was maintained there after the Mexican War. Garrisons and supply facilities were established in San Francisco, Los Angeles, and San Diego, and at strategic points in between and all the way north to the Oregon border. Albert Sidney Johnston, Lewis Armistead, Richard S. Garnett, and Braxton Bragg were future Confederate generals who served in California in the antebellum period. On the Federal side, before the war, Henry W. Halleck, Edwin V. Sumner, Winfield Scott Hancock, William T. Sherman, and Ulysses S. Grant all served in California.

During the Civil War years conflicts between whites and Indians that dated to the 1850s were exacerbated, causing such disruption that California volunteers and the few U.S. Regulars still on the Pacific coast were called out. Although no Confederates were involved, these actions—principally in northwest California on the Klamath, Trinity, Eel, and Salmon rivers, and in the Owens River valley—were a drain on Federal resources and affected the nation's war effort. Elsewhere in California, Confederates and their sympathizers organized clandestine activities and passed intelligence along to the Rebel leadership. In late 1861, an armed group of sympathizers, led by California Assembly speaker Daniel Showalter, was captured near San Diego (on the present-day Mesa Grande Indian Reservation) en route to Arizona to join Southern forces.

California's most significant contribution to the Federal war effort were the soldiers it sent into action outside the state. A total of 15,725 Californians joined the Union army during the war. The "California Column," organized and led by Col. (later Brig. Gen.) James H. Carleton, marched east from Fort Yuma in mid-March of 1862 in response to the Confederate invasion of New Mexico. The column was put together from volunteer units raised and trained in the San Francisco Bay Area and formed into two regiments of infantry—the 1st and 5th California—plus five companies of the 1st California Cavalry and one of the 2nd California Cavalry. They were joined by a company of the 3rd U.S. Artillery. The column's strength was 2,350 men. Although its vanguard engaged Capt. Sherod Hunter's Confederates in what is now Arizona, it was July 4 before the column reached the Rio Grande, near Fort Thorn. By then Sibley's Rebels were on their way back to Texas. Parts of the column ventured as far east as Fort Davis, Texas (see **Texas**). Carleton and the column occupied New Mexico Territory, and waged war against Indians, enabling the Colorado Volunteers to do the same in their home territory, and allowing most U.S. Regulars from the territories to join the fight against the Confederates in the east.

After the war, Union general William S. Rosecrans became a rancher near today's Redondo Beach and was later elected to Congress. Other officers and men from both sides settled in the state and worked in the growing railroad, mining, and agricultural industries. In nearby Nevada, Union soldiers established a town and named it after Maj. Gen.

Jesse L. Reno, who was killed in the Battle of South Mountain. Civil War noncombatant Samuel L. Clemens, who left Missouri after—by his account—one day in the militia, wrote stories about California lore under the nom de plume Mark Twain while working as a Virginia City, Nevada, journalist.

The Civil War battlefields of California are too separated and obscure to warrant a trip to the state for that reason alone. California, however, has a rich historical heritage, and its rapid economic growth and strategic location have made the Golden State a place of many firsts. Combining visits to such places as Fort Tejon, Fort Point, Alcatraz, the San Francisco Presidio, and the Owens River valley with other historical sights will give the traveler a much different view of California than that of theme parks and movie stars. Speaking of movies, nearly every early motion picture with a Civil War theme—*Gone With the Wind*, *Birth of a Nation*, and *They Died with Their Boots On*, to name a few—was filmed in southern California, and the locations of these film shoots are worth a visit. See the appendix for further reading on this subject.

Points of Interest

Drum Barracks—Located at Wilmington, south of Los Angeles, Drum Barracks was a Civil War boot camp for the training of California Volunteers. Today it is a California State Historic Site.

Fort Tejon State Historic Park—This California state park, located 71 miles north of downtown Los Angeles just off I-5 at the Frazier Park exit, is in rugged terrain. Fort Tejon was situated to guard the road from Los Angeles to San Francisco as it passes through the mountains that separate the Central Valley from the Los Angeles foothills. It was a major outpost for U.S. Army operations in the area. Future Union Maj. Gen. Winfield Scott Hancock and Confederate Brig. Gen. Lewis A. Armistead became close friends while serving at the post, though that friendship came to an end with Armistead's death at Gettysburg. In early 1862 cavalry forces were dispatched from the fort to put down trouble in the Owens River valley.

The facilities at the park include a picnic area, trails, and some reconstructed fort buildings. On the third Sunday of each month, from May through October, Civil War demonstrations are held, including skirmishing by reenactment units.   ♿ ⚆ ❓ P ⛉ ⚇

San Francisco—The Presidio, no longer active, is part of Golden Gate National Recreation Area. Two other units of the recreation area, Fort Mason and Alcatraz, were fortified to guard against Confederate invasion of the harbor. Fort Point, now Fort Point National Historic Site, was also fortified. On March 15, 1863, Federal authorities in San Francisco broke up a Confederate operation by seizing the *J. M. Chapman*, a merchant vessel. Rebel subversives purchased the ship with the intent of disrupting commerce and transporting arms and men to the Confederacy through Mexico. The leaders were imprisoned for a time at Alcatraz. For more information, contact the GOLDEN GATE NATIONAL RECREATION AREA at 415-556-2920 and the FORT POINT NATIONAL HISTORIC SITE at 415-556-1693.

NEW MEXICO

The area that is now the state of New Mexico was the first in the Far West to be directly involved in the Civil War. This area was at the time part of New Mexico Territory, which included present-day Arizona, New Mexico, and that part of Nevada south of the 37th parallel. As with California and the territories of Utah and Colorado, there was a large U.S. Army presence here between the Mexican War and the election of Abraham Lincoln. Eight forts were scattered throughout the area, along with a garrison at Santa Fe. Before the war, military units were primarily concerned with guarding against Indian attacks, thwarting raiding parties from Mexico, guarding roads and trails, and escorting surveyors and explorers.

The military commander in charge of the territory in 1861 was Col. William W. Loring, who was appointed by John B. Floyd, the Virginian who was secretary of war under President James Buchanan. Floyd had done what he could in the weeks between Lincoln's election and his own resignation to support the South. Loring and Lt. Col. George B. Crittenden resigned and would later become CSA generals. They used their influence to encourage officers in their commands to join the Southern forces. After the secession of their home states, many officers followed Loring and Crittenden and submitted their resignations, including Joseph Wheeler, James Longstreet, Richard S. Ewell, Cadmus M. Wilcox, Carter L. Stevenson, and Henry H. Sibley. The latter had seen much service in the territory, and would soon return to New Mexico as a CSA brigadier general. Before leaving, Loring placed Lt. Col. Edward R. S. Canby in charge of the Department of New Mexico.

The first indications that the Confederates would try to establish a military presence in New Mexico came early. In Texas, using surrendered U.S. military supplies, Lt. Col. John

R. Baylor, CSA, formed the 2nd Texas Mounted Rifles. The rugged men he recruited first secured Fort Bliss, then carried the war into present-day New Mexico, considered the gateway to a Confederate conquest of the West.

Meanwhile, Canby scrambled to fortify his department against continued Indian attacks, as well as any threat that might come from across the Texas border. He decided to strengthen five key forts—Union, Craig, Stanton, Fillmore, and Garland (across the border in Colorado Territory)—and abandon the others. By the end of June 1861, as soldiers stationed in the mountain territories were sent to Fort Leavenworth, Kansas, for assignment to the war theaters in the East, Canby's force had dwindled to fewer than 2,500. He made urgent pleas to the territorial governors of New Mexico and Colorado for volunteers.

Later, once the Confederate threat to the territory was removed, Federal attention focused on the problems caused by the Indians. Canby sought and was granted reassignment farther east and was replaced by Brig. Gen. James H. Carleton, who organized and led the California Column (see **California**). Carleton waged an unrelenting and effective campaign against Native Americans of the Navajo, Kiowa, and other Apache tribes, killing and disarming many, while driving others onto reservation lands on the Bosque Redondo in the Pecos River valley, where he established Fort Sumner.

Fort Fillmore and San Augustin Spring

Colonel Baylor and his battalion of 2nd Regiment, Texas Mounted Rifles left Fort Bliss, Texas, and entered New Mexico on July 23, 1861. Their first objective was Fort Fillmore, protecting the town of Mesilla, thirty-eight miles up the Rio Grande. Baylor's force camped near the fort the evening of July 24, with a surprise attack on the garrison planned for the morning. A Rebel picket on duty that night, a former U. S. Army soldier, warned the Federals of the impending attack. Baylor learned of the betrayal and the attack was abandoned. The Confederates instead crossed to the west bank of the Rio Grande and occupied Mesilla.

That afternoon, fifty-five-year-old Maj. Isaac Lynde—in command of Fort Fillmore—with nine of his ten companies, ventured to Mesilla to demand the Texans' surrender. An inconclusive skirmish between Lynde's 380 men and the 300 Texans erupted, with some casualties, and Lynde eventually withdrew.

At one A.M. on July 27, Lynde ordered the evacuation of the fort. After destroying what could not be hauled, the column, with wives and children, started the difficult march northeast for Fort Stanton. Baylor sent a detachment to occupy Fort Fillmore and with the rest of his force gave pursuit. The next day, at San Augustin Spring, the Texans caught up with the Northerners and Baylor demanded surrender. Without firing a shot or destroying his supplies, and against the advice of his staff, Lynde surrendered his force of more than 500. Included in the Texans' rich haul was $17,000 in money drafts. The paroled Federals were forced to march with limited supplies across the Jornada del Muerto ("Day's Journey of the Dead Man") to Fort Craig, and the lucky ones eventually made it to Fort Leavenworth, via Santa Fe and Fort Union. The hapless Lynde was dismissed from the army.

Points of Interest

Fort Fillmore no longer exists, but the downtown area of Mesilla, now a suburb of Las Cruces called La Mesilla Plaza, has many buildings that were standing during the Civil War. Take exit 140 from I-10 south on NM28 (Calle de El Paso) to La Mesilla Plaza. On US70, 17 miles north of I-25 exit 6, is San Augustin Pass, the location of the confrontation there.

DRIVING TOUR and READING—*Proceed to Fort Craig and Valverde*

Fort Craig and Valverde

On December 28, when Colonel Canby moved his headquarters another 160 miles down the Rio Grande, from Santa Fe to Fort Craig, the situation in the territory had changed significantly. On August 2, 1861, after Fort Fillmore fell, Lt. Col. Benjamin S. Roberts destroyed all the supplies his units could not carry, and Fort Stanton was evacuated. The Confederates occupied the fort, but soon abandoned it. In response to Canby's request for help, two companies of the 2nd Colorado Volunteer Infantry marched south; Capt. Theodore H. Dodd's Company A reported to Fort Craig, while Capt. James H. Ford's Company B stopped at Fort Union in northeastern New Mexico.

In July 1861, General Sibley had met with Jefferson Davis in Richmond and advocated an invasion and conquest of New Mexico Territory. He found a willing audience for his recitation of the advantages of such a campaign—the gathering of large quantities of pre-

For more than twenty years after their days together at West Point, Maj. Gen. Edward R. S. Canby had been a friend of Henry Sibley, his Rebel antagonist in New Mexico. Although Canby was overly cautious in confronting the enemy, he achieved success as a department commander throughout the war.

war U.S. military stores, an expansion of slave territory, the seizure of mineral riches, the establishment of a Confederate port on the Pacific coast, and ultimately, a conquest of northwestern Mexico. Sibley raised three regiments of hardy troopers, designated the 4th, 5th, and 7th Texas Mounted Rifles, along with two batteries, each armed with four twelve-pounder mountain howitzers.

Beginning in October 1861, the "Walking Whiskey Keg," as Sibley was known to his men, sent his 3,000 soldiers on staggered marches across the parched West Texas landscape. Baylor had heard rumors of Federal plans to retake Fort Bliss, using troops under Brig. Gen. Edwin V. Sumner who would land at Guaymas, in Sonora, Mexico. Baylor urged Sibley to hurry his marchers. The rumors were in fact true, the expedition having been promoted by Californian businessmen worried about a successful Rebel invasion of New Mexico and beyond. On January 3, Sibley sent his troops up the Rio Grande to establish a forward staging area near Fort Thorn, and proclaimed the people of New Mexico "liberated" by the Confederate forces. Sumner's expedition was canceled.

Sibley was anxious to replenish his supplies—diminished by the long march across West Texas—from the Federal magazines and depots in New Mexico. On February 7 his army departed Fort Thorn, and by February 16 the Texans were within one and a half miles of Fort Craig, where the prudent Canby—a friend of Sibley's since their careers had first crossed at West Point, more than twenty years before—had kept his units to check a Rebel advance up either the Rio Grande or the Pecos River. Canby consolidated his force—a grab-bag garrison of 3,810 U.S. Regulars, New Mexico Volunteers, and militia, plus

Dodd's company of Colorado Volunteers—within the adobe fort on the west side of the Rio Grande. Sibley considered the fort too strong to assault, and hoped to lure the Federals to battle outside, but Canby did not bite. On February 19, the Texans marched seven miles south of Fort Craig and crossed to the east side of the river, where they camped on high ground. The next night, in a brief skirmish, the Rebels beat back a Federal detachment sent by Canby.

The night of February 20, a Union spy company headed by Capt. James "Paddy" Graydon ventured from Fort Craig and attempted to send two old mules, carrying packs of explosive twenty-four-pound howitzer shells, into the Confederate camp. True to the beasts' contrary nature, they turned tail and followed their Union handlers. The explosion harmed no one, except the mules, but alerted the Texans. That night there was also an unrelated stampede of 200 Rebel horses, which resulted in a shortage of mounts that would plague the Southerners for the rest of the campaign.

The next morning, Sibley's vanguard headed toward a river crossing at Valverde, six miles north. In an attempt to pin the garrison in place, a detachment was left behind to demonstrate against Fort Craig, but the Federals became aware of Sibley's move. With their supply line north to Socorro threatened, Graydon and several mounted New Mexico militia units crossed the river to the vicinity of the Rebel camp, while a larger mounted force under Lt. Col. Benjamin S. Roberts—soon followed by 6 cannons and an infantry battalion—rode north to intercept the Confederate column. When the Federals arrived at the Rio Grande, they found Maj. Charles S. Pyron's battalion of the 2nd Texas Mounted Rifles, and the Battle of Valverde began.

Union artillery kept the Rebels at bay while first Union cavalry, followed by infantry, crossed the river. Lt. Col. William R. Scurry, with his 4th Texas Mounted Rifles and several mountain howitzers, took a position on Pyron's right. Under the cover of cottonwoods and a sand ridge, the Texans were able to maneuver, while the Federals were for the most part exposed in the open terrain east of the river. With the Confederates trying to cross the river, a fierce artillery and musket duel developed. The 5th Texas, with Col. Tom Green in command, was called up, and with Sibley claiming illness—most say he was drunk — Green took command of the Confederates.

Canby dispatched more units, concentrating all his efforts at Valverde. The Federal center was in a grove of cottonwoods on the east riverbank, from which the Texans had been driven early in the battle. The Federal reinforcements, U.S. Regulars, Colorado Volunteers, and the 1st Regiment of New Mexico Volunteers under famed frontiersman Lt. Col. Christopher "Kit" Carson, moved to the left and right of the grove. Then Company B of the 5th Texas Mounted Rifles, armed with nine-foot lances tipped by three-by-twelve-inch steel blades, charged the Federal left, but they were no match for Dodd's Colorado volunteers. Only 3 of the 40 lancers escaped harm, but their bravery was recognized by both sides. Confederate Col. Tom Green later described it as "one of the most gallant and furious charges ever witnessed in the annals of battle."

The failure of the lancers' charge prompted Colonel Roberts to order Capt. Alexander McRae's six-gun battery to the east bank of the river. When additional Confederate artillery arrived at one P.M., under Capt. Travanion T. Teel, the cannon duel was renewed. Though several assaults on Lt. Robert H. Hall's howitzers and their supporting force on the south end of the Union line were repulsed, a desperate Confederate charge led by Maj. Samuel A. Lockridge overwhelmed McRae's guns on the Federal left. The Southerners poured shot from their guns and the captured cannon into the weakened Union line, and Canby ordered all forces back to Fort Craig, with the 5th U.S. Infantry covering the retreat.

For the number of engaged, casualties ran high: Canby listed Union losses as 68 dead, 160 wounded, and 35 missing; Green reported 36 Confederate dead, 150 wounded, and 1 missing. For the next two days the wounded were removed under flags of truce. Of the 6 cannons captured by the Confederates, five eventually found their way to Maj. Gen. Richard Taylor's command in Louisiana. The other, its carriage broken, was buried in El Paso, only to be unearthed and used in the Mexican Revolution of 1911.

After defeating Canby at Valverde the Confederates were flush with victory, while the Federals distributed the blame. Canby cited the poor showing and failure to follow orders by the New Mexico Volunteers, excepting the majority of Carson's regiment. Others blamed command mismanagement. One Federal officer suggested that if Canby had remained at the fort and Roberts had commanded the field for the entire battle, the day would have belonged to the Union.

Points of Interest

To get to Fort Craig, take exit 124 from I-25. Make a left at the end of the ramp and continue to the intersection with NM1. Turn right (south) on NM1 and at 6.2 miles there will be a sign indicating a left turn to Fort Craig. The fort is 4.5 miles down this road. Fort Craig is in ruins, having suffered nearly a century of vandalism before attempts were made to preserve it. It is on public lands and is administered by the Bureau of Land Management. An archaeological dig is under way, and visitor features are limited. There is a self-guided-tour pamphlet, some interpretive trails, and a parking lot.

The Valverde battlefield can be reached by returning north to I-25 exit 124. Instead of reentering the freeway, turn right, then immediately to the left. There is a historical marker indicating the battlefield. Most of the action took place on the east and west riverbanks of the Rio Grande. The river's present conveyance channel is some 60 yards west of the 1862 channel. South of the battlefield is Mesa del Contadera, a battlefield landmark also known as Black Mesa, which rises some 300 feet above the countryside and delineates the battlefield's southern edge. Hall's Federal battery, which successfully withstood Confederate charges, was positioned just to the north.

<hr />

DRIVING TOUR—*Proceed to Albuquerque*
READING—*Glorieta*

<hr />

Glorieta

Even with their victory, the Texans were in a precarious position. The garrison at Fort Craig remained in Federal hands and blocked the road back to Texas. With their only source of supply to the north, they resumed their march toward Albuquerque. On February 25, the 2nd New Mexico Regiment surrendered the town of Socorro without a fight and, after taking oaths of neutrality, were permitted to return to their homes. When the Texans reached Albuquerque, they did not find the anticipated cache of U.S. supplies, which had been moved to Santa Fe by the Federal quartermaster. General Sibley sent Major Pyron and his command on to Santa Fe, but again the quartermaster's quick action frustrated the Rebels. On March 4, after the Federals had destroyed all the supply depots in the city, a 120-wagon train escorted by the Santa Fe garrison left for Fort Union, and the territorial government of Henry Connelly found it prudent to relocate to nearby Las Vegas, New Mexico.

The "Brigands" spearheading the Confederate advance entered Santa Fe on March 10, and three days later Pyron's command bivouacked in the plaza. The Confederates set up their own government, aided by sympathetic civilians, some of whom had traveled with Sibley's Expedition up the Rio Grande. The Confederates, deviating from Sibley's December 20 pre-invasion proclamation, seized civilian property. Most of the populace, especially the Hispanics, were hostile toward the Texans. Sibley knew his expedition would founder if he didn't push on to Fort Union and capture its arsenal and supplies. He thought that if he continued to forge rapidly onward, an opposing force could not rise quickly enough to stop him.

The two companies of Colorado volunteers that arrived in New Mexico in early 1862 were the vanguard of a larger force intent on beating back the Confederate threat to the mountain territories. The early-war period saw a surge of volunteerism among the hearty miners and frontiersmen of the Colorado Territory, who in the fall of 1861 trained in camps near Denver (see **Colorado, The Northwest**). On February 22, as the Valverde combatants were picking up wounded from the previous day's battle, the main force of the 1st Colorado Volunteers left Denver, led by Col. John P. Slough, a thirty-three-year-old lawyer. Also with them was Maj. John M. Chivington, presiding elder of the Methodist church in Denver, who had declined the force's chaplaincy and was given a combat command instead.

When they reached Pueblo, Colorado, Slough learned of the Confederate victory at Valverde, and asked his troops to quicken their pace to forty miles a day. On March 8, after learning of the fall of Albuquerque and Santa Fe, the Coloradans stripped their packs to just a blanket and their weapons, and scrambled across the rugged mountains. They reached Fort Union three days later, having marched four hundred miles in thirteen days.

At Fort Union, Slough and Col. Gabriel R. Paul disagreed about their mission. Paul wanted to stay put and defend the fort, but Slough thought a more aggressive tack would be preferable. His interpretation of Canby's orders allowed him to harass the enemy, obstruct their movements, and, if possible, cut their supply line. On March 22, Slough pulled rank on Paul and left him with a small garrison at the fort, while he set out for Bernal Springs, fifty miles to the southwest. Under his command were the 1st Colorado Volunteers, several companies of U.S. infantry and cavalry, one company of 4th New Mexico Volunteers, James H. Ford's 2nd Colorado company, and two batteries of artillery with four guns each, for a total of 1,342 men, of whom 75 percent were Coloradans.

Sibley, who planned to descend on Fort Union, was unaware of the Colorado troops in the territory. Major Pyron left Santa Fe first, with his battalion of the 2nd Texas Mounted Rifles, four companies of the 5th Texas Mounted Rifles, three locally recruited spy companies, and two six-pounder cannons, totaling 400 men in all. Colonel Scurry took the 4th

Texas Mounted Rifles and part of the 7th Texas toward Galisteo from Albuquerque. The two wings were to unite later on the road to Fort Union. Because it had proved impossible to replace all the horses lost in the Fort Craig stampede, most of the 5th Texas Mounted Rifles and Col. Tom Green, its commander, remained at Albuquerque.

The pass at Glorieta, on the way from Fort Union to Santa Fe—which had been known since the 1820s as the Santa Fe Trail—was the apex of the climb through the Sangre de Cristo Range of the Rockies. Before the conquistadors, padres, and American frontiersmen, it had been used by Indians for thousands of years. The road for the most part followed Galisteo Creek through Apache Canyon, and this was the only feasible route over the mountains. Arriving at Bernal Springs, the Federals camped and Slough prepared an

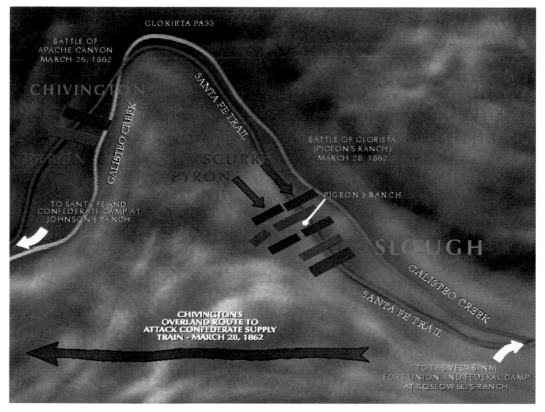

Fought in the rugged mountains of northern New Mexico, the Battle of Glorieta pitted soldier against soldier on some of the most grueling terrain of any Civil War battlefield.

advance force to locate the Texans. On March 25 a mixed infantry and cavalry force of 418 under Major Chivington's command left Bernal Springs. They camped that night at Kozlowski's Ranch, east of the pass.

The next day, after passing Glorieta and descending down the western slope, the expedition captured 32 Confederate scouts. Learning that the Rebels were indeed moving toward Fort Union, Chivington led the force quickly but cautiously into an area known as Apache Canyon, where they came upon Pyron's command. The Northerners had no cannon and took cover among the rugged bluffs flanking the trail. Rebel artillery blasted the canyon, but Chivington, with a pistol in each hand and one or two under each arm, directed an advance that drove the Texans back into a natural rock fortress—after which they destroyed a bridge over an arroyo that separated them from the Federals. The Union troops scaled the cliffs and fired down on the Confederates, but it was a charge by the 1st Colorado's Company F, in which 103 horses leapt the bridgeless arroyo, that dislodged the Texans and forced their retreat.

Chivington's command gathered up the Union dead and the wounded of both sides and withdrew to Pigeon's Ranch, east of Glorieta Pass, leaving a rear guard to resist a Confederate advance. At Pigeon's Ranch the ranch house was converted to a field hospital. A cache of Confederate flour, left behind earlier, was discovered, allowing the hungry Union soldiers to eat, though a lack of water compelled most of them to return to Kozlowski's Ranch.

An overnight truce allowed the Rebels to remove their wounded and bury their dead, and also request speedy reinforcement from Scurry in Galisteo. Slough, with the remainder of his command, arrived that night at Kozlowski's Ranch. A few hours later, Scurry's Texans joined Pyron at Johnson's Ranch after a march over the mountains. The Rebels anticipated another attack in the morning, but none came. Leaving his wagon train with a small guard at Johnson's Ranch, Scurry, on March 28, marched the consolidated force of about 1,200 to a position a mile west of Pigeon's Ranch and formed a line of battle.

Union spies reported that the Texans planned to advance through Apache Canyon, and Slough and Chivington devised a daring plan. Chivington, with 490 men, would march over the mountains and strike the Rebels in the rear, while Slough, with the remaining force of 850, would head through the pass to face the Confederate front. Chivington left Kozlowski's Ranch with a guide at eight-thirty in the morning, and Slough formed a line at Pigeon's Ranch opposite the Rebels, who were just eight hundred yards to the west.

With the first report of the Confederate guns, at eleven A.M., the Battle of Glorieta began. The Rebel line extended from one craggy slope of the narrow gorge to partway up the other. The Federals unlimbered their artillery and returned fire. Slough sent companies of Colorado volunteers to the left and to the right, up the sides of the canyon, protected by the cover of boulders, outcroppings, juniper, and scrub pine. The Union artillery at the center of the line, on a slight elevation of the Santa Fe Trail, drew the concentrated fire of the Texans.

If the Confederate leader Scurry had known the size of the force facing him, he might have reacted differently. But the topography and ground cover caused uncertainty, and that, along with the Texans' experience in the Battle of Apache Canyon two days previous, made them cautious. Company I, 1st Colorado, on Slough's right pressed forward toward the Confederate guns on the Rebel left, but reinforcements were rushed to the sector by Scurry. Hand-to-hand combat followed, it was "root hog or die," and the Coloradans were checked. On the opposite flank, Pyron attacked the Colorado infantry skirmishing on the hillside. Though they were reinforced, the Pikes Peakers had to give way, albeit stubbornly.

The Federals pulled back eight hundred yards and re-formed their line just west of Pigeon's Ranch. Slough's artillery dueled with a Rebel cannon, and for the next three hours musket and artillery fire was exchanged. Colorado volunteers silenced Confederate batteries by picking off Texas gunners. Union skirmishers climbed "Sharpshooters Ridge," on Slough's right flank, to protect the artillery and keep the Texans from outflanking the line.

Scurry called up reinforcements and then ordered a coordinated, three-pronged attack against Slough's flanks and center, hoping to repeat the Valverde success by capturing the Union artillery. The attacks met stubborn resistance on the Union left and center, but north of the Santa Fe Trail Texans led by Major Pyron seized "Sharpshooters Ridge." In the bitter fighting some of the Union gunners were shot, but the cannons were withdrawn to a safer position, just forty yards from the supply train. The Confederates made a last, desperate attempt to take the guns, but were repulsed. At five P.M., after six hours of fighting, Slough withdrew to Kozlowski's Ranch. He was satisfied he had achieved his mission and harassed the enemy. Some of the Federal troops were reluctant to leave, feeling they could drive the Confederates back, but soldiers on both sides were too exhausted to have continued the contest.

Slough, it turned out, knew only part of the story. As his men were beginning their withdrawal, the Confederates sent a messenger under a white flag to ask for a truce, ostensibly to take care of the dead and wounded. Slough agreed to a cessation of hostilities until noon the next day, unaware—unlike Scurry—that the Confederate supply train had been destroyed.

Chivington's command had worked its way up and across rough terrain for five hours before finally arriving, near the mouth of Apache Canyon, at a thousand-foot bluff that overlooked the Confederate camp at Johnson's Ranch. Below, approximately 75 wagons were guarded by some 200 Texans. The guard had been larger, but some of the Texans headed for the front on their own to join the fight. Chivington determined to overwhelm the guard with an all-out attack. On a signal, Federal troops using ropes scrambled down the escarpment, and within minutes were in the camp, rounding up the surprised soldiers and teamsters. Some Rebels escaped, including the messenger who delivered the news of the disaster to Scurry. Only 1 Federal soldier was wounded, and 5 captured early in the battle were reunited with their comrades.

With no practical way to transport the captured supplies, the Union soldiers set about destroying the wagons and their contents of ammunition, food, medical supplies, and other materials. A cannon was spiked and its carriage smashed. A number of horses and mules were slaughtered, which further limited the Texans' mobility. Chivington, not wishing to risk an encounter with another Confederate force, decided to return to camp over the mountain again. A Catholic padre, known to the Federal guide, led the expedition on a different route in the darkness. The tired, thirsty soldiers arrived back at the Federal camp at ten P.M. and were welcomed in victory by their comrades.

The Battle of Glorieta was a hard and desperate fight. Most of the soldiers fought six hours at close quarters without rest or refreshment. Among those killed and wounded were many officers. The records as to casualties are unclear, with the Confederates having 121 men killed, wounded, or captured. The Federal casualties were 31 killed, more than 50 wounded, and 30 missing. Though both sides claimed victory, the advantage was with the Federals. After less than two days' rest at Pigeon's Ranch, with little food or water, the Texans returned to Santa Fe, where their stay would be brief. The march down the Rio Grande Valley would prove to be full of hardship. Called the "Gettysburg of the West" by some, the two fights at Glorieta and the raid on Johnson's Ranch turned the tide of the war in the Far West. Sibley's subsequent retreat to Texas would end the Rebels' dream of a Confederacy that spanned from the Atlantic Ocean to the Pacific.

Points of Interest

Albuquerque—In the late 1800s a former Confederate major, T. T. Teel, led a group of curious citizens to a site 500 feet north of San Felipe Church, and unearthed eight cannons buried by the Confederates prior to their evacuation of the city. The recovered guns were given to the city of Albuquerque and the Colorado Historical Society. The church is located at the Historic Old Town Plaza, at San Felipe and Romero streets, in South Plaza. Nearby is the Albuquerque Museum and Casa de Armijo, which served as a headquarters for Union officers. Several miles west of Albuquerque is Old Cienega village, which has the original adobe mill building from Fort Union. Also, fifteen miles south of Albuquerque is Peralta, which is covered later in this chapter.

Santa Fe—The center city of Santa Fe is steeped in Hispanic heritage. The old plaza is located in the heart of the city off US84/285. The Palace of the Governors was used by military commanders, including those of the Texans during their occupation of Sante Fe. The Sante Fe National Cemetery on North Guadalupe Street contains the graves of Union and Confederate soldiers killed at Valverde and Glorieta.

To reach Glorieta sites, take I-25 north from Santa Fe. At exit 294, get off the freeway and look at the knoll to the west, which was the site of Johnson's Ranch. Return to the freeway and get off at exit 297. The walls of the canyon will be on either side of you. Nearby is the arroyo the Colorado cavalry jumped their horses over. It is on private property. Return to the freeway and continue east.

Pecos National Historical Park—Portions of the Glorieta battlefield have recently become part of the new Pecos National Historical Park. The park visitor center is located off I-25 exit 307, then north on NM63. Near the visitor center is one of the buildings of Kozlowski's Ranch, the Federal camp. The landscape has changed little since the battle. The rocky outcroppings in the gorge, and the juniper and scrub pine, make it easy to visualize Confederate Texans and Union soldiers moving from rock to tree, taking deadly aim at anything in front that moved. The Cañoncito Unit of the park preserves the Battle of Apache Canyon.

The Glorieta Unit of the park is on NM50 northwest of the visitor center. Here are Sharpshooters Ridge and the restored Pigeon's Ranch. Some information on the battle is available at the ranch. Across the road, in a deep gully near Galisteo Creek, a blood-red granite United Daughters of the Confederacy monument honors the men of the Sibley Expedition, and nearby, a monument commemorates the soldiers of the 1st Colorado.

Due to the progressive state of development of the park, the superintendent requests that those visitors interested in touring the sites associated with the Battle of Glorieta contact the park to arrange a guided tour. PECOS NATIONAL HISTORICAL PARK, P.O. BOX 418, PECOS, NM 87552–0418; 505-757-6032.   ❷ ♿ ⚑ 🏛 P ⚥

Fort Union National Monument—This adobe fort was typical of those built in the Southwest before and for some time after the Civil War. It protected the military supply line into the New Mexico Territory from Fort Leavenworth, Kansas, and the flow of pioneer and commercial traffic along the adjacent Santa Fe Trail. In 1862, Fort Union became the focal point of General Sibley's Confederate expedition. Sibley was stationed at the post before the war and supervised the construction of some of its buildings. At the height of his campaign, in late February and early March 1862, Fort Union, along with Fort Garland, Colorado, was the last outpost between Sibley and the mines of Colorado.

Fort Union was the launching point for Col. John P. Slough's march against the Confederates, which culminated in the Battle of Glorieta. During Slough's twelve-day stay at the fort before marching out to battle, his army of rowdy Pikes Peakers succeeded in getting into all kinds of trouble. After the Confederates were forced from the territory, Fort Union became the base for Colorado Volunteers and other units assigned to keep peace on the frontier, guard the Santa Fe Trail, and campaign against Indians.

Fort Union National Monument is located just off I-25, 67 miles northwest of Pecos National Historical Park. At exit 366, turn left (north) on NM161 for approximately 8 miles. The road dead-ends into the park. Facilities include an interpretive museum, exhibits, and a video program. FORT UNION NATIONAL MONUMENT, P.O. Box 127, Watrous, NM; 505-425-8025.   ▦ ♿ ⚑ ❷ 🏛 P ⛱ ⚥ $

———————————————

DRIVING TOUR—*Proceed to Colorado or Texas*
READING—*Picacho Pass*

———————————————

Peralta

After the devastating losses to their transportation corps and stores of supplies, suffered at Glorieta and Johnson's Ranch, Sibley's force began its long journey back to Texas.

Scurry's command straggled into Santa Fe on March 29 and were joined there by General Sibley, Colonel Green, and the six companies of the 5th Texas Mounted Rifles that had been at Albuquerque. Slough was ready to pursue the Rebels, but a messenger from Fort Craig arrived with orders from Colonel Canby directing the Coloradans back to Fort Union to aid in its protection. When Slough and his men arrived at the fort and discovered that it was not in any danger, Slough resigned his command in disgust. He later traveled east, gained a commission as a brigadier general, and served as military governor of Alexandria, Virginia. He returned to New Mexico after the war as chief justice of New Mexico Territory, and was killed in December 1867 in a shootout in the billiard room of the La Fonda in Santa Fe.

With Rebels north and south of him, Canby was isolated from resupply. Upon learning of the activities to the north, he left Fort Craig on April 1, leaving behind New Mexico Volunteers with Kit Carson in command. Marching up the road that paralleled the west bank of the Rio Grande, Canby sent orders to Fort Union to have a force march west to meet him. Although irritated at having to countermarch twice in response to Canby's vacillating dispatches, the command nevertheless left Fort Union on April 6, under Colonel Paul and Major Chivington. On the heels of the withdrawing Texans, Governor Connelly had returned to Santa Fe and reestablished the Federal territorial government.

Sibley consolidated his position at Albuquerque. On April 8, Canby's force arrived within one mile of the town and demonstrated. Union cannon pounded the city briefly, but when the Confederates refused to evacuate the women and children, Canby halted the bombardment. On the night of the ninth, Canby marched his force to Tijeras—fifteen miles to the northeast—and waited for Paul's Fort Union force, which arrived late on April 13. Chivington was elevated to the rank of colonel and assigned to lead the Colorado Volunteers in place of the departed Slough.

With the convergence of the Federal columns, the Confederate position in Albuquerque was tenuous, and Sibley ordered the town evacuated on April 12. At Peralta, twenty-two miles to the south, the Confederates stopped to wait for Colonel Green's unit, the last Texans to leave Albuquerque. When Green's unit arrived, they took over Governor Connelly's ranch near Peralta and ransacked it. Unknown to the Texans, on the evening of the fourteenth the Federals made camp about a mile north of their position. Chivington called for a night attack, but Canby denied the request. The next morning, Paddy Graydon's spy company was dispatched to ascertain the Confederates' strength and position.

Green's 5th Texas Mounted Rifles were on the east side of the river, isolated from Sibley's force. The Federals moved forward in two columns, one under Chivington, one under Paul, driving the Rebels from the ranch toward the river and opening the Peralta battle. Sibley moved his entire force east of the river to join Green. Opposing lines were drawn and an artillery duel ensued. Despite requests from Chivington and Paul to drive Green's Confederates into the Rio Grande, Canby maintained a defensive posture. The one Federal success before a blinding sandstorm swept in and stopped the battle was the capture of a Rebel supply train on its way from Albuquerque. That night, Green's force crossed to the west bank of the Rio Grande and marched five miles downriver.

The Confederates left many sick and wounded soldiers at their Peralta camp. Because of his failure to seize the opportunity to bag the Confederate force, Canby was subjected to recriminations by his troops, particularly the Colorado soldiers. Still, he maintained the same caution shadowing the Rebel retreat down the Rio Grande. Encouraged by his subordinates to bypass Fort Craig, Sibley abandoned his cumbersome wagons and sent his army into the mountains west of the Rio Grande. A Confederate officer who had been in the territory since Baylor's 1861 incursion led the group through the Magdalena Mountains. The Texans, with little more than the clothes on their backs, suffered greatly during this desperate march.

After a ten-day march of more than one hundred difficult miles, on April 25 Sibley's command again arrived at the Rio Grande, forty miles south of Fort Craig. From there, Sibley and the head of the column continued southward, arriving at Fort Bliss, Texas, in the first week of May. Some Texans remained in New Mexico until July 8 when, with the approach of the California Column, the last units withdrew. Sibley at first reported to Richmond that the campaign was a success, but later changed his assessment, stating, "the Territory of New Mexico is not worth a quarter of the blood and treasure expended in its conquest." Many of his soldiers placed the campaign's failure directly on Sibley's shoulders.

The Federals, themselves on short rations during the latter part of their march, arrived at Fort Craig on April 22. Canby's subordinates wanted to pursue the Rebels through the mountains, or intercept them when they regained the Rio Grande, but he resisted these entreaties. Graydon's spy company did follow the Rebels for a time, picking up abandoned equipment and those sick and wounded Texans who had not died from the elements or been killed by Apaches or Mexican bandits.

At camps in and around Fort Craig and Valverde, the Federal command was reorganized. Canby soon returned to his Santa Fe headquarters, and for a time Chivington took command of the District of Southern New Mexico. On July 4, Chivington and his regiment left Fort Craig and returned to Colorado and a heroes' welcome.

Points of Interest

Peralta—On NM47, about 15 miles south of Albuquerque, is the town of Peralta. The fight here took place at what is now the intersection of Bosque Farms Boulevard and Abo Road.

DRIVING TOUR—*Proceed to Santa Fe*
READING—*Far West: Apache Pass, Arizona*

Florida

A lthough as the least populous Confederate state Florida contributed the fewest soldiers to the cause, the state was by no means lacking in spirit or action. As a percentage of its population, Florida sent the most men of all the Southern states to the Confederate services. With the exception of its northeastern coastal areas, Florida was relatively removed from and undisturbed during most of the conflict. Its primary role was as breadbasket, supplying the Rebel army with agricultural goods, cattle, and salt. The rich cotton-growing land in northeast Florida was an essential Southern asset, and the earliest Confederate strategies called for many of Florida's volunteers to remain there and guard against Northern incursions. Most of the cotton that left Florida during the war was transported overland; the Florida coast-line was not especially conducive to blockade-running, and most of the state's key ports—Pensacola, Cedar Key, Tampa, Apalachicola, and St. Marks on the Gulf coast; Jacksonville, St. Augustine, and Fernandina on the Atlantic—were effectively blockaded or occupied by the Federals for much of the war.

Pensacola, a pre-war U.S. Navy shipyard protected by three Third System forts and additional batteries on the seacoast, was never fully controlled by the Confederates. Fort Pickens, near Pensacola, and two forts in the Florida Keys withstood pre–Fort Sumter insurgent actions, and were the only masonry forts in the Confederacy to remain in Federal hands through the entire war. (On the other hand, Tallahassee and far-off Austin, Texas, were the only Confederate capitals not taken by the Federals during the war.)

Touring Civil War battlefields in the Sunshine State is enormously rewarding. In most cases the sites are rustic and unsullied, giving the feeling of what they were in the

1860s. The forts are by and large well preserved. And Florida, after all, is Florida. A tour combining the state's Civil War sites with other historical sites, and its beaches and other natural and man-made attractions, makes it enjoyable for both Civil War enthusiasts and people with a casual interest.

PENSACOLA AREA

Pensacola and its harbor have been an important connection to the sea since the Spaniards first explored the area in the 1540s. In 1559, the Spanish made Pensacola one of the first European settlements in the New World. It was a strategic center during the European wars of the eighteenth and nineteenth centuries, and in 1821, when Spain ceded Florida to the United States, the U.S. military quickly established a presence there. A navy yard was established in Warrington, south of Grande Bar, and beginning in 1829 three masonry forts and a large masonry redoubt were constructed.

Fort Pickens, a Third System coastal fortification, was built on the western tip of Santa Rosa Island. A pentagonal structure, it was designed to mount more than 200 guns in casemate and barbette tiers. On the west side of the channel and nearly opposite Fort Pickens, on Foster's Bank, was Fort McRee, a circular work with a water battery designed to emplace 125 cannons. It was completed in the 1840s. On the north side of the bay, west of the navy yard, Fort Barrancas was built on top of the old Spanish Fort San Carlos, and Bateria San Antonio, erected in 1797 by the Spanish, became its water battery. Together they could mount 44 guns. The Advanced Redoubt, eight hundred yards north of Fort Barrancas, guarded the land approaches to the navy yard. Together, the three forts provided a triangular field of fire protecting the harbor.

Pensacola's importance was recognized by both the North and South, but during the tense days just after Abraham Lincoln's election, the two ranking Federal army officers at Pensacola were allowed to go on leave. The officer left in charge, 1st Lt. Adam Slemmer, on his own initiative, moved his artillery company from the barracks into Fort Barrancas, and when orders finally arrived from Washington for him and Cmdr. James Armstrong, in charge of the navy yard, to protect Federal property, Pensacola was already secure. On January 8, 1861, shots were fired at Fort Barrancas, and Slemmer, wanting to take the most defensible position with his small command, moved his company and some marines to Fort Pickens. While marines and sailors remained on the mainland to guard the navy yard, Armstrong yielded to threats from Alabama state troops and surrendered the facility on January 12, for which he was later convicted following a court-martial.

Slemmer declined to surrender. Although there were approximately 800 Florida and Alabama militia troops in and around Pensacola, he put his 80 soldiers, sailors, and marines to work remounting cannons at Fort Barrancas, which as a matter of government policy had been allowed to fall into a state of disrepair. No attack was forthcoming, however, because the Buchanan administration had worked out an agreement with former Florida U.S. senator and future C.S. secretary of the navy Stephen Mallory: As long as the fort was not reinforced, it would not be attacked. When reinforcements did arrive on the USS *Brooklyn,* they at first remained aboard the ship. Finally, on April 7, Lt. John L. Worden, future commander of the USS *Monitor* (see **Hampton Roads, Virginia**), hand-carried a message from Lincoln's navy secretary Gideon Welles, ordering the captain of the *Brooklyn* to land the troops.

Meanwhile, William H. Seward, Lincoln's secretary of state, was trying to divert attention from the serious problems at home by instigating a crisis with Spain over its presence in the Caribbean. Troops were loaded aboard the steamship USS *Atlantic,* which, escorted by the warship USS *Powhatan,* steamed for Florida. The conflict with Spain didn't develop, but the secession crisis did, coming to a head with the firing on Fort Sumter. Between April 12 and 16 Federal reinforcements—from the *Brooklyn* and then from the *Atlantic*—landed at Fort Pickens, and Lt. David Dixon Porter, the ambitious and self-confident commander of the *Powhatan,* had to be restrained from attacking Forts McRee and Barrancas.

The Pensacola region was by then part of a Confederate military district commanded by the acerbic Brig. Gen. Braxton Bragg, who despite personal reluctance to—and even after Fort Pickens was reinforced—continued to honor Mallory's agreement. On September 2, 1861, at the navy yard, a detachment from Fort Pickens destroyed a submerged floating dry dock that the Rebels were trying to raise and use, but still Bragg maintained his restraint. When another Federal raiding party burned the schooner *Judah,* however, which the Confederates were refitting for use as a privateer, Bragg ordered Brig. Gen. Richard H. Anderson—with 1,000 men—to launch a surprise attack on Union camps east of Fort Pickens on Santa Rosa Island. Anderson's men landed on the island on October 8 and easily overwhelmed the 6th New York, the regiment guarding the fort's land approaches, but then Federal resistance stiffened and the soldiers rallied under the fort's guns.

The Confederates were driven back to their boats by the reinforced Northern infantry, but not before they had looted the Federal camp. Fewer than twenty had been killed on each side. The Federals, in retaliation, began a two-day bombardment of the Rebel mainland fortifications. In this and another artillery duel on January 1, 1862, the Yankee artillerists maintained the upper hand. Late in March, a Federal expedition to Santa Rosa Island's east end destroyed a mainland Rebel camp and shelled a Confederate schooner.

Ulysses S. Grant's successful campaign against Forts Henry and Donelson in Tennessee (see **Fort Henry** and **Fort Donelson, Tennessee**) triggered a manpower crisis in the Confederacy. General Bragg and his Pensacola troops, with others, were rushed to Corinth, Mississippi. On May 7 the last of the Rebels in Pensacola started on their way to Mobile, Alabama, to be sent up the Mississippi River to meet other threats, most particularly at Vicksburg and Fort Pillow. Two nights later, fires in the navy yard prompted a bombardment from Fort Pickens. On May 10, Federal army Lt. Richard Jackson received the city's formal surrender from the mayor of Pensacola.

For the next two years Pensacola served as a supply center and blockading squadron port. Then, in the spring of 1864, the port saw a buildup in preparation for Adm. David G. Farragut's campaign against Mobile, Alabama (see **Battle of Mobile Bay, Alabama**). An intended Confederate navy raid on Fort Pickens never materialized, though the raiders did succeed in capturing a small U.S. vessel, the sloop *Creole.*

Points of Interest

Most of Pensacola's Civil War sites are within Gulf Islands National Seashore, including Santa Rosa Island and Fort Pickens. The Advanced Redoubt and Fort Barrancas are on the Pensacola Naval Air Station. Although Forts Pickens and Barrancas are separated by a mile of water, it requires a drive of 30 miles around the bay to get from one to the other. There are many hotels and motels in Pensacola, while the Gulf Islands National Seashore facilities include camping, beach, and other recreational activities. When planning your visits to the sites, take into account your overnight plans.

Downtown Pensacola is 6 miles south of I-10 via the I-110 connector. All the sites can be reached from the end of the I-110 freeway. To get to Fort Barrancas and the Advanced

Redoubt, take Garden Street west until it turns into Navy Boulevard (FL295). Navy Boulevard leads directly to the Pensacola Naval Air Station main gate, where you may obtain a daily pass to visit the sites. To get to Santa Rosa Island and Fort Pickens, take Chase Street east to the intersection with US98. Follow US98 over the Pensacola Bay Bridge to Pensacola Beach Road (FL399). This road turns to the west and becomes Fort Pickens Road, which leads into the park.

Before leaving downtown you may want to visit the Pensacola Historic Museum, which occupies the oldest Protestant church building in Florida. During the Civil War it was used as a hospital and barracks by Federal forces. It now has exhibits and a library, including an extensive collection of photographs, maps, and illustrations. PENSACOLA HISTORIC MUSEUM, 405 South Adams Street, Pensacola, FL 32501; 904-433-1559.

Fort Barrancas—Completed in 1844 on the site of the Spanish Fort San Carlos, Fort Barrancas incorporates as its water battery Bateria San Antonio, one of four Spanish-built fortifications extant east of the Mississippi. The fort and water battery were stabilized and rehabilitated by the Park Service from 1978 to 1980. Nearby is a 0.5 mile woodland nature trail. The Advanced Redoubt, which is nearly the size of Fort Barrancas and took fifteen years to build, was also stabilized by the Park Service. It is located 0.5 mile north of Fort Barrancas on Fort Road. A covered way connected these two sites during the Civil War. The site has its own parking lot. Check with the Fort Barrancas visitor center for hours of operation.

Fort Barrancas has its own parking lot and is open daily from 9:30 A.M. to 5:00 P.M. The fortifications close at sunset. Guided tours are conducted at 11:00 A.M. and 2:00 P.M. The visitor center has special programs, exhibits, a slide show, and a gift shop. For information, phone 904-455-5167.   ♿ ❶ P ⌜ ⏣

West of Fort Barrancas, the National Museum of Naval Aviation provides an in-depth look at the history and technology that helped doom the masonry coastal forts in the 1940s.

Navy Yard—The former U.S. Navy docks, where the CSS *Judah* was destroyed and Federal blockading ships were resupplied, are also on the Pensacola Naval Air Station. The site of the old docks is at Radford Boulevard and East Avenue, 1.5 miles east of Fort Barrancas. The entrance gate to the navy yard and a portion of the original wall still stand.

Fort Pickens and Santa Rosa Island—The Battle of Santa Rosa Island was fought near Battery Cooper, a reinforced concrete artillery emplacement within the Fort Pickens

Fort Pickens viewed from the northwest. The location of Bastion D is on the right side of the picture—it was destroyed in an 1899 powder magazine explosion. The five corners, or bastions, projected out and allowed artillery mounted there to sweep the areas outside the fort's walls during an attack.

unit of Gulf Islands National Seashore. You should first go to Fort Pickens and the visitor center, where there is a gift shop and interpretive walks and guided tours are available. The museum and auditorium, housed in a former army post building, have interpretive exhibits and special programs, including lectures and audiovisual presentations. Be sure to see the former officers' quarters, where the Apache chieftain Geronimo and his followers were imprisoned from 1886 to 1888.

The recreational facilities at Fort Pickens are marvelous. There is a two-hundred-site campground on the beach, available on a first-come first-served basis, with a camp store and laundry. There are beach areas with outdoor showers on both the bay and gulf sides of the island. There is fishing, from a fishing pier and other nonswimming areas, in accordance with state laws. There is hiking on the Blackbird Marsh Nature Trail, but check with a park ranger about hiking trails through the dunes, which are subject to changing conditions. There is also an amphitheater, where park events are held, and there is an excellent bike trail as well. For information, phone 904-934-2635.

For more information, contact GULF ISLANDS NATIONAL SEASHORE, 1801 Gulf Breeze Parkway, Gulf Breeze FL 32561; 904-934-2600. Radio information at 1630 AM.

🚴 ⛺ ⛵ 🏕 ♿ 🚶 ❓ 🏛 P ⛽ 🍴 🚻 🌊 $

DRIVING TOUR—*Proceed to Marianna*
READING—*Key West and the Dry Tortugas*

MARIANNA

On September 27, 1864, under the Hungarian revolutionary and Pea Ridge hero Brig. Gen. Alexander Asboth, a Federal force of 700—including the mounted infantry of the 2nd Maine Cavalry, selected companies of mounted infantry from the 82nd and 86th U.S. Colored Troops, and a battalion of the 1st Florida Cavalry (Union)—was defeated here by home guard soldiers. Asboth was wounded during the fight and his left arm had to be amputated.

Points of Interest

On the Jackson County Courthouse lawn there is an historical marker describing the Marianna engagement. Two blocks west of the courthouse, at the new St. Luke's Church, is a United Daughters of the Confederacy marker indicating the site of the original church, which was burned by the Federals.

DRIVING TOUR—*Proceed to Apalachicola*
READING *(chronological)*—*New Market, Virginia*

APALACHICOLA

At the time of the Civil War, Apalachicola, located at the mouth of the Apalachicola River, was considered Florida's most important cotton-exporting port. No attempt was made by the Federals to land and permanently control the port, though the town was briefly occupied by Union sailors in early April 1862. It was finally back under Union control in late April 1865. Because the Confederate navy posed no significant threat, throughout the war the Federals intercepted blockade-runners and confiscated cotton from boats in the harbor. Cotton was a particularly valuable commodity and this and other confiscated goods could be resold with the proceeds divided among the crew.

There was one U.S. Navy sortie to Apalachicola in response to a Rebel threat. Early in May 1864, rumors of an attack by Confederate sailors from the gunboat CSS *Chattahoochee,* advancing in small boats on the blockader USS *Adela* caused launches carrying Yankee tars to be sent ashore. The Confederates, seeing the Yankees approaching, abandoned their mission (for more about the CSS *Chattahoochee,* see Confederate Naval Museum, **Columbus, Georgia**).

Points of Interest

The harbor and town of present-day Apalachicola (58 miles southeast of Panama City on US98) make it easy to picture the bustling activity of Florida's largest import/export center in the 1860s. For a military picture of the area at that time, visit Fort Gadsden State Historic Park (10 miles east on US98/319, then north 15 miles on FL65). The fort was used for recruiting blacks and Indians during the War of 1812, and was reconstructed in 1818 under the supervision of Lt. James Gadsden, for whom it was named. (As minister to Mexico, in 1853 he negotiated the Gadsden Purchase.) The fort was abandoned until the Confederates garrisoned the earthwork in 1862. There is an interpretive trail, fort models, a picnic and playground, and a boat ramp. It is open from 8:00 A.M. to sundown daily; there is no admission charge. FORT GADSDEN STATE HISTORIC SITE, P.O. Box 157, Sumatra, FL 32334; 904-670-8988.

DRIVING TOUR and READING—*Proceed to St. Marks*

ST. MARKS

East of Apalachicola, the harbor town of St. Marks on Apalachee Bay—at the confluence of the Wakulla and St. Marks rivers—saw naval action and the landing of Federal troops. The Confederates built a battery, Fort William, near the lighthouse. On June 15, 1862, two Union warships bombarded the fort and the defenders withdrew. Union sailors then landed and destroyed the battery and buildings.

In mid-July 1863, Lt. Cmdr. Alexander Crosman led a force of 130 sailors up the St. Marks River. Their goal was the capture of the Confederate steamer *Spray* and a schooner loaded with cotton that accompanied it. Before the nighttime expedition passed St. Marks lighthouse, however, a Rebel sentry challenged the party and shore batteries fired on the boats, forcing Crosman and his men to turn back.

The next expedition up the St. Marks River was intended as a diversion to accompany Union operations in northeast Florida in February 1864, but when the Federals were dealt a sharp blow at Olustee (see **Olustee**), East Gulf Blockading Squadron commander R. Adm. Theodorus Bailey canceled the plan.

The final Federal expedition in the area, in March 1865, was a combined army-navy operation with the objective of occupying Tallahassee. When they saw 16 U.S. Navy ships anchored off St. Marks, the Confederates mined the lighthouse and retreated. On March 3, 300 Federal sailors seized the East River Bridge, four miles north of the lighthouse, but the next day the Union gunboats were grounded in the river's shallow waters. Seeking a crossing farther north, the army landed on the east side of the river, under veteran Maj. Gen. John Newton. Their search upriver led to the Battle of Natural Bridge.

Points of Interest

St. Marks is 18 miles southeast of Tallahassee. From Apalachicola, continue east on US98 to St. Marks. From Tallahassee, take FL263 or US27 to FL363 and go south for 15 miles to the town. San Marcos de Apalache State Historic Site contains remnants of the old Spanish fort, Confederate works, and a military cemetery. The visitor center is built on the foundations of the Marine Hospital, where yellow fever victims were treated. It is open from 9:00 A.M. to 5:00 P.M. Thursday through Monday, except for Thanksgiving, Christmas, and New Year's Day. SAN MARCOS DE APALACHE STATE HISTORIC SITE, P.O. Box 27, St. Marks, FL 32355; 904-925-6216. ▣ ⴜ ❷ ⛪ P ⏚ ⚥ $

One mile east at Newport, take FL59 south for 9 miles to the St. Marks Lighthouse; the site of Confederate Fort Williams can be found in the St. Marks National Wildlife Refuge.

DRIVING TOUR and READING—*Proceed to Natural Bridge*

This monument to the Confederate soldiers who fought in the Battle of Natural Bridge is located just west of the Confederate breastworks, portions of which are still visible.

NATURAL BRIDGE

General Newton's Federal column, which included several African-American units, marched toward Tallahassee from the Gulf of Mexico on March 5, 1865, looking for a place to cross to the west bank of the St. Marks River. Florida cavalry blocked the bridge at Newport, so Newton left a diversionary force there and continued upstream. A natural bridge spanned the river near Woodville. Anticipating a crossing there, the Confederate commander Brig. Gen. William Miller ordered Lt. Col. George Scott to move his force to the bridge and block the Federal advance.

Some 600 Rebels, including walking wounded, men as old as seventy, teenagers, and cadets from the West Florida Seminary (now Florida State University) in Tallahassee, dug in behind previously constructed earthworks on the west bank of the river. In the foggy pre-dawn hours of March 6, the Federal force initiated the contest, but three major charges and ten hours of fighting did not gain the Yankees an inch of ground. Lacking naval support and reinforcements, Newton ordered a withdrawal. The Federals suffered 21 killed and 127 wounded or captured—to the Rebels' 3 killed and 22 wounded—and by sunset of the next day they had returned to the protection of the fleet downriver. This was a rare victory, small but decisive, the South enjoyed in the closing months of the war.

Points of Interest

Natural Bridge State Historic Site is a small scenic park on the battlefield site. From Tallahassee or St. Marks, follow FL363 to Woodville and look for the brown signs, which mark the turnoff onto Natural Bridge Road to the east, which leads to the park. The St. Marks railroad bicycle path begins at the intersection of FL363 and US319, and follows the roadbed of the Civil War–era railroad that connected the state capital with the

Gulf of Mexico port. Except for a few scattered homes and the man-made bridge that replaces the natural bridge that was there, the pine forest looks much as it did when Union veterans battled the hastily assembled Rebel force. The park contains a large monument and interpretive battlefield signs, and there are traces of the Confederate earthworks. Each March on the weekend nearest the battle's anniversary, there is a reenactment of the Battle of Natural Bridge, as well as Union and Confederate living-history camps. The park is open daily from 8:00 A.M. until sundown. There is parking and a picnic area. NATURAL BRIDGE STATE HISTORIC SITE, c/o San Marcos de Apalache State Historic Site, P.O. Box 27, St. Marks, FL 32355; 904-925-6216. ❷ P ⛱ ♁

DRIVING TOUR—*Proceed to Cedar Key and Tampa Area*
READING—*Averasboro, North Carolina*

CEDAR KEY

The small town of Cedar Key was the western terminus of Florida's only Civil War–era coast-to-coast railroad, which was completed in 1861. On January 16, 1862, Union naval forces descended on the harbor and village and burned seven small blockade-runners and coastal vessels, but the port remained open. In the fall of 1862, landing parties from U.S. Navy gunboats destroyed saltworks in the area. On February 8, 1865, Maj. Edmund C. Weeks, USA, led his Federal command up the Florida Railroad from Cedar Keys. Confederate militia and irregulars under Capt. John Dickison—the "Forrest of Florida"—attacked the column on February 13 and in a running fight forced the Yanks back to the Gulf. As a result, Weeks's force failed to reinforce Maj. Gen. John Newton's march up the St. Marks River toward Tallahassee, which ended in Federal defeat at Natural Bridge. Cedar Key is an island 21 miles southwest of US19 on FL24. The small town has two museums that feature exhibits on the Civil War, including the battle between Weeks and Dickison.

DRIVING TOUR—*Proceed to Tampa Area*
READING—*Jacksonville and Olustee*

Tampa Area

Bayport

Like Cedar Key, the small town of Bayport was a favorite of blockade-runners. In early April 1863, an expedition of U.S. Navy sailors and marines landed briefly and destroyed a Rebel battery and a cargo ship. Other raids in July 1864 captured some cotton and resulted in the burning of the town's custom house. As late as the spring of 1865, blockade-runners operated out of the port, and some were captured by the East Gulf Blockading Squadron.

Tampa

Blockade-runners operated out of Tampa's fine harbor, and the area also had a heavy concentration of saltworks. The requirements for this cottage industry, to collect the residue from boiling seawater, were simple—a boiling pot and firewood. Since salt's use as a preservative was vital to military food supplies, the saltworks on Florida's Gulf coast became targets of U.S. Navy raids.

In Tampa Bay on June 30 and July 1, 1862, after the Confederates refused to surrender the town, shots were exchanged between a Federal gunboat and shore batteries. The Rebel artillerists were inexperienced (most of Florida's soldiers had been moved to Tennessee) but they performed admirably. On October 16, 1863, 2 Union warships bombarded Fort Brooke, while a land force marched fourteen miles to the Hillsborough River and attacked several steamers there. The Rebels destroyed 1 vessel to preclude her capture, but the Federals took 2 others.

Early in May 1864, a combined army-navy expedition landed and captured Tampa in three days, taking 40 prisoners. Destruction of the saltworks continued through the year. Only once, on November 12, was a Federal sortie unsuccessful, when a combined army-navy expedition was turned back by Rebel cavalry. Although small saltworks flourished up and down the Gulf coast, the hostile Federal incursions on them drove the price of salt up 6,000 percent over the war's four years.

Points of Interest

Fort De Soto Park on Mullet Bay is in the area of the Confederate battery known as Fort Brooke. Fort Brooke is now a parking lot. Fort De Soto still has some of its original Spanish-American War–era artillery pieces on display. The park has facilities for camping, fishing, and swimming. From I-175, take FL682 west over the toll bridge to the Pinellas Bayway Toll Road (FL679), which dead ends into Fort De Soto.

The Gamble Plantation—One of the few antebellum plantation houses remaining in Florida, the Gamble Plantation was purchased by the United Daughters of the Confederacy as a memorial to Confederate secretary of state Judah P. Benjamin, the only Jewish member of Jefferson Davis's cabinet. Benjamin stayed at the Gamble Plantation in May 1865 while fleeing Federal authorities. A brilliant lawyer and politician before serving the Confederacy as attorney general, secretary of war, and finally secretary of state, Benjamin soon left Tampa for the West Indies. Eventually he made his way to London and became one of Britain's most sought-after barristers.

The Gamble Plantation is just off I-75 exit 43 at Ellenton. It has an interpretive center, and scheduled tours are given Thursday through Monday. Demonstrations of sugar-cane processing are conducted the third weekend in March. It is open 8:00 A.M. to sunset every day. GAMBLE PLANTATION STATE HISTORIC SITE, 3708 Patten Avenue, Ellenton, FL 34222; 813-723-4536.   🗺 ♿ ❓ 🏛 P 🚻 👫 💲

DRIVING TOUR—*(optional): Proceed to Key West, or to Orlando and Jacksonville*
READING—*Apalachicola and St. Marks*

KEY WEST AND THE DRY TORTUGAS

No Civil War battles were fought in the Florida Keys, but the two Third System forts there played an important role. Fort Zachary Taylor in Key West and Fort Jefferson in Dry Tortugas were begun in the 1840s, though at the start of the Civil War the latter was not yet completed. Recognizing the Straits of Florida's importance to Union naval operations, at the start of the war Federal authorities quickly manned the forts, ensuring the safety of the deepwater anchorage at Key West and continuing passage of Federal ships between the Atlantic Ocean and the Gulf of Mexico throughout the war years.

In the tense days of December 1860, Lt. Thomas A. Craven, USN, informed Washington that he would defend the two forts from "any bands of lawless men" in the area. On the eve of Florida's secession, army Capt. John Brannan and 45 men arrived at Fort

Taylor and no Southern attempt was made thereafter to commandeer the fort and its eight-inch smoothbore guns. Fort Jefferson, commanded by Capt. Montgomery Meigs, was without armament until January 19, when Maj. L. G. Arnold arrived from Boston with reinforcements and cannons. On January 22, a well-armed Florida schooner arrived and demanded the surrender of the fort, but Arnold refused and threatened action. The Southern vessel backed down, even though the Federal artillerists were still in the process of mounting the fort's first gun. In a few months 68 artillery pieces were in place.

The real problem for the soldiers and sailors stationed at the two forts was not Rebel attacks or sabotage, but tropical disease. Nevertheless, the port of Key West remained open, servicing the Federal blockading vessels. And long after the Civil War, Fort Zachary Taylor remained a part of the nation's defense system; during the Cuban missile crisis in 1962, it was armed with radar and 4 missile batteries.

Points of Interest

Key West—The town of Key West is an excellent place for strolling and bicycle riding, and its historic sites are close to downtown. Fort Zachary Taylor State Historic Site is located at the end of Southard Street, which is the southern terminus of US1. The fort was modernized in the late 1890s and for more than sixty-five years little of the Third System masonry could be seen. Restoration started in 1968 is returning the fort to its Civil War appearance. A rich cache of guns, ammunition, and other artifacts unearthed during the restoration are now on display at the fort and in its museum. There is also a model of the fort as it appeared in the 1860s. Guided tours are given daily at 2:00 P.M.

The park is open daily from 8:00 A.M. to sundown. Facilities include a beach with showers and changing rooms, and a picnic area with barbecue grills. FORT ZACHARY TAYLOR STATE HISTORIC SITE, P.O. Box 289, Key West, FL 33040; 305-292-6713. 🚲 ⛴ ♿ ❓ P 🍴 🍽 🚻 〰 $

During the war construction was begun in Key West on two Martello towers overlooking the harbor, of the type employed in Europe since the Middle Ages to spot an approaching enemy. Although neither was completed, they were manned during the war and batteries were established nearby. Both towers are privately owned but available for touring. The Key West Garden Club takes care of the remains of West Martello and maintains a garden there. WEST MARTELLO TOWER, JOE ALLEN GARDEN CENTER, Atlantic Boulevard, Key West, FL 33040. An art gallery and cultural museum in

East Martello contain items from Key West's history. EAST MARTELLO MUSEUM, 3501 South Roosevelt Boulevard, Key West, FL 33040; 305-296-3913.

The Key West Lighthouse Museum, built in 1846, features a museum in the keeper's quarters. In the collection is a sword lost at Fredericksburg by Maj. Gen. George G. Meade, USA, who oversaw the construction and repair of lighthouses in the Keys in the 1850s. KEY WEST LIGHTHOUSE MUSEUM, 938 Whitehead Street, Key West, FL 33040; 305-294-0012.

Dry Tortugas National Park—This is one of the least-visited sites in the national park system, only because it is not accessible by private automobile or public transit. The Dry Tortugas Islands are located seventy miles west of Key West, and may be reached only by air or boat charter, or private boat. A visit to the islands, and the coral reef that all but encloses them, is enjoyable for scuba and snorkel divers, bird watchers, and history enthusiasts. For history enthusiasts, Fort Jefferson on Garden Key is of particular interest. The huge three-tier fort has survived the ravages of time and hurricanes intact, and stabilization efforts, which began in 1988, have made it easier for visitors to see the fort as it was: the guardian of the Straits of Florida, the eighty-mile passage between Florida and Cuba through which the Gulf Stream surges.

Although it never came under fire during the Civil War, Fort Jefferson is an excellent example of a Third System fort. For almost a decade beginning in 1861, it was a military prison. Its best-known prisoner was Dr. Samuel Mudd, who set John Wilkes Booth's broken right fibula after the assassin's flight from Ford's Theatre (see **The District of Columbia**). When the post doctor, among many others, died during an outbreak of yellow fever in the late summer of 1867, Mudd volunteered and helped squelch it. In recognition of his courageous efforts, President Andrew Johnson commuted his life sentence.

Besides a boat dock and fishing facilities, the park has a visitor center, camping, a shaded picnic area, and secluded beach. There is no food for sale on Garden Key. Information on seaplane access may be obtained in Key West. For more information on getting to the island, contact the superintendent of Everglades National Park, P.O. Box 279, Homestead, FL 33030.

DRIVING TOUR—*Proceed to Miami and Jacksonville*

JACKSONVILLE AREA

The most bitterly contested region of Florida during the Civil War was in the northeast, where rail links and sea-lanes provided the way for Florida's livestock, naval stores, and agricultural products to be shipped to other states of the Confederacy. The Federals took an early interest in the area, sending in an expedition in February 1862. With the exception of several coastal enclaves, little more than temporary occupation was accomplished. The Jacksonville area, like most of Florida, remained, except on several brief occasions, in the control of the Confederates for the entire war.

Jacksonville is Florida's largest city, and your tour can start in a northeasterly, southerly or westerly direction. There are ample overnight accommodations, including camping, in all areas except at Olustee, where the nearest lodging is in Lake City, twenty miles west.

Fernandina

After Flag Officer Samuel Du Pont's warships successfully engaged the Confederate forts guarding Port Royal, South Carolina (see **Port Royal, South Carolina**), and Union forces occupied Hilton Head and Beaufort, the Federal navy went in search of a coaling port to service the South Atlantic Blockading Squadron.

On February 28, 1862, Du Pont sailed with 26 ships from Port Royal for Cumberland Sound and Fernandina. The town was the eastern terminus of the Atlantic and Gulf Central Railroad, which ran from Cedar Key on the Gulf of Mexico across northern Florida. Gen. Robert E. Lee, then in charge of the Southeastern defenses, ordered the Amelia Island garrison to dismantle its batteries. On March 3, the Rebels evacuated the island without the loss of a man, carrying with them 18 of the 33 cannons.

Aware of the withdrawal, Du Pont had kept his warships outside the bar while dispatching gunboats, under the command of Percival Drayton, to reconnoiter Cumberland Sound west of Amelia Island. On March 4, a landing party raised the Stars and Stripes over Fort Clinch, the first seized U.S. fort in the South to be repossessed. As Drayton's forces continued down Cumberland Sound to Amelia River, they engaged in an unusual running battle. When the last Confederate forces were leaving aboard a train pulled by two locomotives, Drayton's soldiers and marines fired on them from their boats. The Rebels returned fire from their railway cars.

Du Pont landed at Fort Clinch later in the day and declared it battle-ready, but there was little powder for the remaining Confederate guns. Brig. Gen. Horatio G. Wright landed at Fernandina with his army brigade on March 5 and Du Pont prepared to continue down the coast to St. Augustine, his next target. Fernandina was used as a naval coaling station throughout the war and served as a base of operations for later campaigns in the area. Fort Clinch was unfinished when Federal soldiers retook it, and the 1st New York Volunteer Engineers were responsible for much of its completion.

Points of Interest

Fernandina—To reach Fernandina (now named Fernandina Beach) and Fort Clinch, take I-95 north from Jacksonville to exit 129. Turn east toward Yulee on FLA1A for 13 miles to Amelia Island and Fernandina Beach. The fort is north of town on Atlantic Avenue.

Fort Clinch State Park includes the fort and a 1,086-acre park with recreation facilities. Since the fort saw no combat and no later construction changed its appearance, it looks much as it did in March 1862, when a Federal landing party found it abandoned. A number of mounted artillery pieces are on display, and a barracks has been restored.

Recreational facilities include a beach with bathhouse, picnic and fishing areas, and a nature trail. There is an interpretive center and gift shop. A booklet is available that offers historical information and a detailed diagram of the fort. The park is open from 8:00 A.M. to

Castillo de San Marcos, built by the Spanish in the late 1600s, differs in construction from the Third System masonry forts of the Civil War, which were primarily built with clay-formed bricks. This fort was built from a unique sedimentary rock called coquina which is strong but susceptible to wear.

sunset year-round. The fort is open daily 9:00 A.M. to 5:00 P.M. FORT CLINCH STATE PARK, 2601 Atlantic Avenue, Fernandina Beach, FL 32034; 904-261-4212.

➤ ▦ ♿ ⚧ ❷ P ⚺ $

In the town of Fernandina Beach, on Atlantic Avenue, is the Amelia Island Lighthouse, built in 1838. It is a good architectural example of a pre–Civil War lighthouse, but is not open to the public. There are also many antebellum buildings and homes in the town, particularly along Centre Street. The First Presbyterian Church, on North Sixth Street, was built in 1859 and was used as a Federal barracks.

DRIVING TOUR and READING—*Proceed to St. Augustine*

St. Augustine

The oldest continually inhabited community established (in 1564) by Europeans in the United States is St. Augustine, Florida. As Spain struggled to maintain her presence in east Florida, in fear of her European rivals, this area was contested numerous times. In 1672 construction was begun on a fort, Castillo de San Marcos, that was completed by 1695 and replaced a succession of wooden fortifications. When Florida was ceded to the United States in 1821 the fort was renamed Fort Marion, after Revolutionary War hero Francis Marion.

The St. Augustine Blues, a Florida militia unit, seized the fort from a U.S. Army ordnance sergeant on January 7, 1861. Two companies of the 3rd Florida Infantry garrisoned the fort. On March 11, 1862, the USS *Wabash,* Flag Officer Du Pont's flagship, anchored off the St. Augustine bar. When no armed resistance arose, he sent C.R.P. Rodgers ashore under a flag of truce and a white flag was raised over the fort. The mayor of St. Augustine informed Rodgers that the Confederate garrison had departed the night before. The Federals occupied the fort and repositioned 1 of its 2 remaining eight-inch seacoast howitzers at the main road entering the city from the north.

Although the Confederate leadership gave up St. Augustine without a fight, the civilians, particularly the women, were hostile to the Yankee soldiers. Over the months of occupation, several Federal parties ventured outside of St. Augustine and skirmished with Florida cavalry.

On March 23, 1862, a bloody little encounter took place near Smyrna, on Mosquito Inlet, fifty-one miles down the coast from St. Augustine. Two Union gunboats anchored near present-day Canaveral National Seashore to guard a shipment of live oak being prepared for the trip north. Eight sailors from a landing boat were killed by the Confederates. The rest escaped in the night to the ships waiting offshore.

On March 22, 1864, Union troops were ambushed at the town of New Smyrna Beach, sixty-seven miles south of St. Augustine, while on their way to destroy the sugar mill there. Forty-two Federals were killed. On July 26, Union reprisals leveled the town.

Points of Interest

St. Augustine, 38 miles south of Jacksonville on I-95, has a number of sites and attractions related to its rich history. Castillo de San Marcos National Monument is a treasure trove of more than four centuries' military and civilian life in the area, and the first such site to receive historic preservation funding appropriated by the U.S. Congress for restoration, in 1884. There are exhibits on and artifacts from the periods of Spanish and British rule, from occupation by U.S. and Confederate forces, and from the time it was a place of confinement for Seminoles and other Native Americans. Among the cannons, mounted and unmounted, exhibited on the barbette tier of the four-bastioned coquina fort, is one Civil War–era rifled gun.

Castillo de San Marcos has guided tours and special programs; interpretive exhibits within the casemates feature the different periods in the fort's history. There is also a gift shop. The fort is open from 9:00 A.M. to 7:45 P.M. April through October, and until 5:15 P.M. November through March. CASTILLO DE SAN MARCOS NATIONAL MONUMENT, 1 Castillo Drive, St. Augustine, FL 32085; 904-829-6505.   🖼 ♿ 🚶 ❷ P 🚻 $

Other Civil War sites in St. Augustine include the St. Francis Barracks, on the corner of Marine and St. Francis streets, where Union soldiers were housed. Today it is the headquarters for the Florida National Guard. Across St. Francis Street is the Oldest House, a national historic landmark, and the adjacent Museum of Florida's Army, which is in a house once occupied by Union army officer Brig. Gen. Martin D. Hardin. Nearby is the national cemetery, which has a mass grave and monument for U.S. soldiers, sailors, and marines who lost their lives in the First, Second, and Third Seminole Wars. Government House on St. George Street was the guardhouse for the Federal Provost Guard (military police) during Union occupation. In Plaza de la Constitution, across the street, is the Confederate War Memorial. For information on all these sites and other attractions, stop at the Visitor Information Center on San Marcos Avenue at Castillo Drive.

DRIVING TOUR—*Proceed to Jacksonville*
READING—*Atlantic seacoast actions: New Bern, North Carolina*

Jacksonville

While awaiting a tide favorable for landing at St. Augustine, Flag Officer Du Pont dispatched gunboats north to cross the bar and enter the St. Johns River. This began a three-year campaign by the Federals to control Florida's major river and restrict the shipment of agricultural produce and timber from the state's interior to Confederate forces. By the time the side-wheeler USS *Ellen* crossed the bar and entered the river, the Confederates on Talbot Island and at Fort Steele had abandoned the earthworks that guarded the river approach to Jacksonville. Sailors raised the Union flag over the lighthouse at Mayport Mills and, on March 10, 1862, six companies of the 4th New Hampshire landed. The next night, withdrawing Rebels put the torch to the railroad depot, two foundries, seven sawmills, a warship under construction, and other war matériel. At noon the next day Federal soldiers marched into Jacksonville without incident, and the first of four occupations of Jacksonville by Union forces began.

Brig. Gen. Horatio G. Wright arrived to command the occupation forces, and local Unionists set about to form a loyal state government. But on April 9, the day before a convention to form the government was to be held, the Federals withdrew from Jacksonville and returned to Fernandina. Union gunboats continued to patrol the St. Johns River, and the commander of Confederate forces in northeast Florida, Brig. Gen. Joseph Finegan, ordered construction of two new batteries at St. Johns Bluff, upstream from present-day Fort Caroline National Memorial.

These artillery emplacements threatened Federal gunboats patrolling the St. Johns, and forced the Union to take action. On September 30, 1862, a Union force under Brig. Gen. John M. Brannan left Hilton Head, South Carolina, and landed at Mayport Mills the following day. By October 3 they occupied the St. Johns Bluff battery, which the Confederates had hastily abandoned. Leaving behind a detachment to dismantle the heavy Confederate guns and load them onto transports, Brannan marched his command forward through the jungle-like terrain. He discovered the battery at Yellow Bluff similarly abandoned and, arriving in Jacksonville on October 5, found it deserted except for a few civilians. The next day another detachment, accompanied by gunboats, went upriver to the vicinity of present-day Orlando in search of Confederate steamers. They returned on October 9 with the CSS *Governor Milton* in tow.

On October 11, the Federals began their withdrawal from Jacksonville, their mission— to break up the Confederate shore batteries—accomplished. The last troops departed the area on October 12, leaving the navy to patrol the St. Johns.

The third occupation of Jacksonville began in March 1863. Two features made this expedition distinctive. First, Federal African-American regiments set foot on Florida soil for the first time. Two regiments, organized in Hilton Head and designated the 1st and 2nd South Carolina, landed in Jacksonville on March 10. The troops began to construct two forts in the city, Higginson and Montgomery, named after the regiments' white commanders. Second, fearing that the appearance of the former slaves in blue uniforms would trigger a general slave uprising, Confederate Brig. Gen. Joseph Finegan employed a rifled thirty-two-pounder cannon, mounted on a railroad flatcar and pushed by a locomotive to one and a half miles of Jacksonville on the Atlantic & Gulf Central Railroad.

On March 25, the railroad gun fired on the Jacksonville garrison, but after seven shots Union gunboats on the river found their range and the Confederate piece was withdrawn. The next day the Federals mounted a ten-pounder Parrott rifled gun on a car, and accompanied by infantry, a locomotive pushed it four miles west of Jacksonville. The infantry drove in the Confederate pickets. Two Federal soldiers were killed in this war's first railroad-car-to-railroad-car artillery duel and the Northerners were compelled to retreat to their earthworks. On March 31, the Federal force withdrew, after destroying the buildings with any military value that were still standing in the city.

The final occupation of Jacksonville began in February 1864 and lasted until the end of the war. This expedition, conceived and led by Maj. Gen. Quincy A. Gillmore, had four objectives. All but the fourth were characteristic of most of the Federal operations in Florida. They were to acquire war materials such as timber and turpentine, cut off the source of Confederate commissary supplies, recruit for black units among the state's ex-slaves, and create a new state government enabling Florida's quick return to the Union.

1864 was an election year. Lincoln's December 1863 Proclamation of Amnesty and Reconstruction called for the creation of new state governments and congressional representation in Confederate states in which 10 percent of the eligible voters signed oaths of allegiance to the United States. It was assumed that in the November general election Abraham Lincoln would receive Florida's electoral votes. Because of its political objectives, Gillmore's proposed invasion of northeast Florida had been heartily endorsed by the Lincoln administration. Upon learning of the plan, Lincoln sent his twenty-five-year-old private secretary, John Hay, to assist Gillmore in his mission to implement a reconstruction policy in Florida, while Gillmore was still at his headquarters at Hilton Head, South Carolina, biding his time during the siege of Charleston (see **Charleston, South Carolina**).

On February 6, a division 8,000 strong, composed primarily of New England, New York, U.S. Regular and black units, with 2 mounted units and 4 companies of artillery, departed from Hilton Head. The next day, two gunboats escorted the expedition to the Jacksonville docks, where the troops landed unopposed. While Hay began to administer oaths of allegiance, starting with Rebel prisoners, the two gunboats and accompanying troops steamed south and trained their guns on two river towns, Picolata and Palatka. The towns were occupied and garrisoned, and the troops there and downriver ensured Union control of the navigable regions of the St. Johns River for the remainder of the war.

The Union division, led by Brig. Gen. Truman Seymour, marched west, while Hay, having accomplished all he could in Jacksonville, waited for the army to consolidate its gains. It would be a wait for naught. The stunning defeat of the Federal force at Olustee (see **Olustee**) ended the campaign and the Federals did not again venture beyond their coastal enclaves.

After the Confederate victory Hay was compelled to give up the plan to establish a new government. Following the retreat from Olustee, the Union army fortified Jacksonville. A line of breastworks with 7 batteries protected the land approaches to the city. Gunboats prowled the waterways, and signal stations were set up at the former Rebel strongholds of Yellow Bluff and St. Johns Bluff. Twelve thousand reinforcements were brought in, though most were soon withdrawn. After the spring of 1864, what remained were mostly African-American units. Perhaps because of the presence of these units, race problems in Jacksonville during Reconstruction were minimal. The burgeoning free-black and reconstructed-white population created a melting pot community relatively free of the postwar problems that plagued many of the South's cities and towns.

Points of Interest

Although there is little remaining evidence of the Federal presence in the city of Jacksonville, the batteries the Confederates constructed along the St. Johns River are still there. Yellow Bluff Fort has become a state memorial, and it contains the remains of earthworks. The park has picnic facilities and is open from 8:00 A.M. to sunset. To reach Yellow Bluff Fort State Memorial, take I-95 north or US90 east to the intersection with FL9A. Go south or north, respectively, on FL9A to the New Berlin Road exit, and head toward New Berlin. The park is 0.5 mile south of FL9A and 0.5 mile east of New Berlin Road.

The St. Johns River Lighthouse, built in 1859, is located on the Mayport Naval Station and is open to the public on weekends. During the war the lighthouse's lantern was disabled by its keeper to prevent its use by the Federal navy. To get there from FL9A, take FL105 east to the naval station.

In Jacksonville, the site of the 1863 Federal Fort Higginson is at the intersection of Broad and Bay streets, near the old railroad terminal. The Federal earthworks constructed after the Battle of Olustee ran from Hogan's Creek to Union and Beaver streets, then to Davis Street and south to McCoys Creek.

The Jacksonville Maritime Museum, at Jacksonville Landing, features the hull of the USS *Columbine,* a Federal gunboat captured in 1864. The Museum of Science and History features artifacts from a cargo ship, the USS *Maple Leaf,* that was sunk by an "infernal machine" (torpedo). The ship was carrying the armament and supplies for four Union regiments that were part of Gillmore's expeditionary force. JACKSONVILLE MUSEUM OF SCIENCE AND HISTORY, 1025 Museum Circle, Jacksonville, FL 32207-9053; 904-396-7062. 🖼 ♿ 🚶 ❓ P 🚻 $

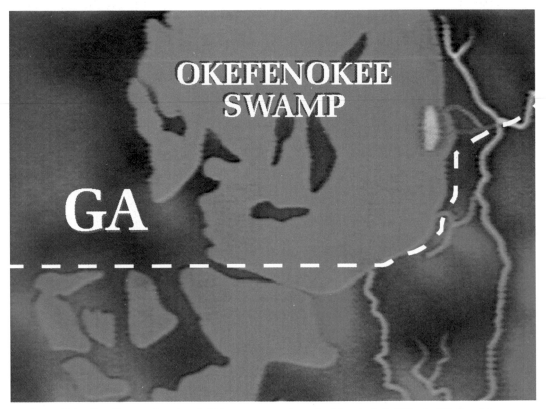

When Brig. Gen. Truman Seymour led his troops west along the Atlantic & Gulf Central Railroad, he was preceded by his cavalry under Col. Guy V. Henry. Henry reported the buildup of Confederate forces at Ocean Pond, but they were assumed to be only home guards. In fact, Brig. Gen. Joseph Finegan assembled a command nearly equal to the Federal force, including veterans from Charleston, and picked a defensive position that blocked the Federals' advance and forced them to assault him head-on in the Battle of Olustee.

DRIVING TOUR and READING—*Proceed to Olustee*

Olustee

By February 9, 1864, the vanguard of Quincy A. Gillmore's expedition was at Baldwin, the intersection of two of Florida's major railroads. The cavalry, under Col. Guy V. Henry, rode ahead toward Lake City—Gillmore's objective—but upon learning that large numbers of militia were gathering they turned back at Olustee. When they returned to

*The podium at the entrance to the battlefield trail, just to the west of this monument to Confederate
soldiers at Olustee, gives a seven-minute audio recording describing the battle from
a Southern soldier's point of view.*

Sanderson they discovered the infantry had already pulled back and taken position at Barber's Landing. While Gillmore had received reports about the increasing strength of Rebel forces, his chief concern was logistics. He had not brought teams and wagons and was reliant on the railroad, but the only available locomotive had broken down.

To solve his logistical problems, Gillmore turned over the command of the expedition to the division commander, Brig. Gen. Truman Seymour, and returned to Hilton Head. Seymour was a graduate of West Point's celebrated class of 1846 and a veteran commander. He had been an artillery captain at Fort Sumter when it was first fired upon. During the war he had held command in a series of major actions, without the distinction that leads to promotion and higher command.

Gillmore left strict orders for Seymour to hold the South Fork of the St. Marys River and protect Jacksonville from Confederate attack. He was not to venture west. But by February 19, Seymour could no longer resist the opportunity to score a quick and decisive victory in his chief's absence. Having received reports that the Rebels were tearing up the rails of the Atlantic & Gulf Central, he prepared to march west. With his force reduced to 5,500 and 16 cannons, due to the loss of soldiers detailed for garrison duty, Seymour hoped to seize the advantage through initiative and careful planning. Leaving Barber's Landing at dawn on February 20, Seymour's troops slogged through Sanderson, marching in three columns for better speed and protection.

Brig. Gen. Joseph Finegan's command, charged with the defense of East Florida, was marching east and reinforced by Brig. Gen. Alfred Colquitt, whose Georgia Brigade was rushed down from the Charleston area. After organizing the 5,000 men into three brigades, Finegan selected a good defensive position at Olustee. The troops entrenched, anchoring their left on Ocean Pond and their right on a swamp, and awaited the Yankees' advance.

Once past Sanderson, the cavalry screening Seymour's march encountered Confederate horse soldiers. The Federals pushed ahead, and Seymour and Finegan reinforced their cavalries with infantry. The Yankee foot soldiers—the 7th Connecticut—were armed with seven-shot repeating rifles. Some three miles east of the entrenched Confederates, his cavalry stalled, Seymour called up more infantry. The 7th New Hampshire, a battalion armed with Spencers, filed into position on the right, and the 8th U.S. Colored troops moved into position on the left. Finegan, meanwhile, boldly seized the initiative and advanced to meet the foe.

Colquitt, with four regiments of Georgians, carried the fight to the bluecoats. First, the 7th Connecticut pulled back to regroup, and then the 7th New Hampshire broke ranks and fled. Seymour called up the New York Brigade and the soldiers hastened forward. But the New Yorkers were wearied by their ten-mile march, and the Confederates, who were close by, were fresh and eager. In the desperate struggle the Confederates slowly gained the upper hand.

Seymour now brought up his last reserves, two African-American regiments, including the 54th Massachusetts, heroes of Fort Wagner, but they were too late. By dusk Seymour had seen enough and a retreat was ordered. The withdrawal was so rapid and disorganized that the Federals abandoned 6 cannons, which were claimed by the Confederates as victory trophies.

Federal casualties were 1,861, one third of their total engaged, while the Confederate number was 946, mostly wounded. On the retreat back to Jacksonville, the Federal casualty list rose. There were few ambulances and wagons and many of the wounded had to be carried on crude litters. After the Federals began returning on February 22, churches and homes in Jacksonville filled up with wounded and dying soldiers. One participant described the first part of the retreat: "Ten miles we wended or crawled along, the wounded filling the night air with lamentations, the crippled horses neighing in pain, and the full moon kissing the cold, clammy lips of the dying."

Points of Interest

Olustee Battlefield State Historic Site—The site is 42 miles west of Jacksonville on US90. To get there, take the US90 exit from I-10. It is an excellent location to get the geographical feel of a Civil War battle. The pine forest and palmetto thickets are much as they were then, which perhaps explains why Civil War reenactors travel from all around the country every February (on the weekend closest to its February 20 anniversary) to re-create this battle.

The park features monuments, an interpretive center, a seven-minute audio presentation of the battle from a Confederate soldier's perspective, and other exhibits. The battlefield trail has signs indicating unit placement and other information. The site is open Thursday through Monday, from 9:00 A.M. to 5:00 P.M. and admission is free. OLUSTEE BATTLEFIELD STATE HISTORIC SITE, P.O. Box 40, Olustee, FL 32072; 904-752-3866.
♿ 🚶 ❓ P 🚿

DRIVING TOUR—*Proceed to Georgia*
READING *(chronological)—Dalton, Georgia*

① Big Shanty
② Chickamauga
③ LaFayette
④ Ringgold
⑤ Tunnel Hill
⑥ Rocky Face Ridge–Dalton
⑦ Dug Gap
⑧ Resaca
⑨ Rome Cross Roads
⑩ Rome
⑪ Cassville
⑫ Kingston
⑬ Allatoona
⑭ New Hope Church
⑮ Pickett's Mill
⑯ Dallas
⑰ Lost–Pine–Brushy Mountain

⑱ Kennesaw Mountain–
Kolb's Farm–Marietta
⑲ Smyrna–Ruff's Mill
⑳ River Line
㉑ Roswell
㉒ Chattahoochee River
㉓ Peachtree Creek
㉔ Battle of Atlanta–Decatur
㉕ Stone Mountain
㉖ Sweetwater Creek
㉗ Ezra Church–Utoy Church–Atlanta
㉘ Jonesboro
㉙ Lovejoy Station
㉚ Palmetto
㉛ West Point
㉜ Columbus
㉝ Andersonville

㉞ Irwinville
㉟ Sunshine Church
㊱ Macon
㊲ Griswoldville
㊳ Milledgeville
㊴ Madison
㊵ Crawfordville
㊶ Washington
㊷ Augusta
㊸ Waynesboro
㊹ Ebenezer Creek
㊺ Savannah
㊻ Fort Pulaski
㊼ Fort McAllister
㊽ Darien

Georgia

Georgia, except for the Sea Islands, did not become a battleground until relatively late, but the Peach State was thoroughly involved in the war effort. More than 100,000 Georgians fought in the Confederate army, and significant leaders such as Alexander H. Stephens, Howell Cobb, Robert Toombs, James Longstreet, John B. Gordon, William J. Hardee, Lafayette McLaws, and Joseph Wheeler called it home. The state's major contribution, beyond manpower, however, was in transportation, war matériel, and food. Its plantations and factories sent forth timber, cotton, corn, hogs, uniforms, and munitions for the army and navy, while its extensive network of railroads delivered them throughout the South. Later in the war, Georgia's heartland provided sites for prisoner of war camps.

The war first came to Georgia in 1862, in the form of raids and coastal operations, but not until mid-September 1863, with the Battle of Chickamauga, did large-scale action occur there. The Federal campaign to sear the state, with the manufacturing and railroad city of Atlanta the chief objective, began May 7, 1864, under Maj. Gen. William T. Sherman.

Georgia features the most entries in this guide after Virginia. The destruction of many parts of the state during the Atlanta Campaign, Sherman's March to the Sea, and James H. Wilson's raid caused much bitterness among Georgians, while the post–World War II economic boom saw little regard paid to the preservation of Civil War sites. But that is now changing; there are many current efforts to enhance and protect Georgia's wonderful heritage of Civil War sites and structures.

This tour begins in Atlanta, Georgia's capital, largest city, and center of commerce and tourism. An alternate tour start is Savannah, where the state's earliest combat action in the Civil War occurred. Plan to spend a week to thoroughly tour Georgia's rich Civil War heritage.

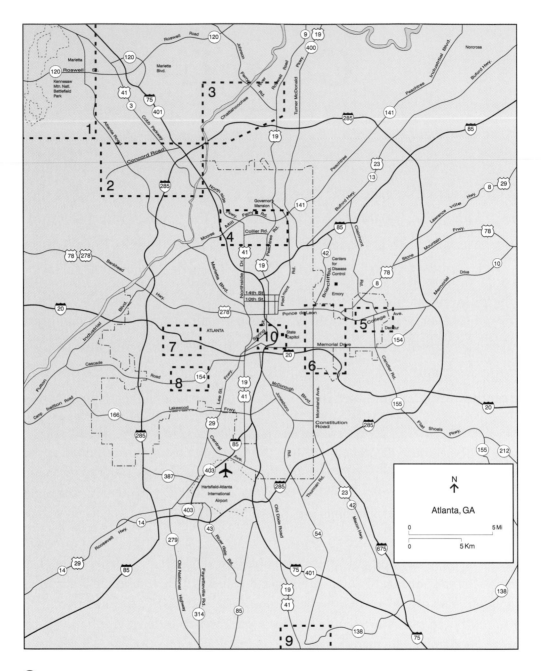

1. Kennesaw Mountain–Kolb's Farm–Marietta
2. Smyrna–Ruff's Mill–River Line
3. Chattahoochee River
4. Peachtree Creek
5. Decatur
6. Battle of Atlanta–Grant Park–Oakland Cemetery
7. Ezra Church–Westview Cemetery
8. Utoy Creek–Cascade Springs
9. Jonesboro
10. Downtown Atlanta

To start the tour in Atlanta, take I-75 north twenty-five miles to exit 118, then follow the road west until it becomes Cherokee Street or follow signs for the Kennesaw Civil War Museum. For the other tour start, see **Savannah**.

KENNESAW (BIG SHANTY)

The action that began in this small town on a spring morning in 1862 brought the war to Georgia in shocking fashion. Called Andrews' Raid or "the Great Locomotive Chase," this raid by the North—orchestrated by James J. Andrews, a Virginia-born civilian with Union patriotism—had all the elements of a terrific drama. It was originally Brig. Gen. Don Carlos Buell's idea to sabotage the railroad bridges between Atlanta and Chattanooga during the Federal drive on Middle Tennessee in the winter of 1862, when Andrews spied for Buell. But Andrews called off the all-civilian raid believing conditions were not right. In April, Brig. Gen. Ormsby Mitchel asked Andrews to carry out a similar raid on the Western & Atlantic Railroad to disrupt Southern communications with Chattanooga, as Mitchel planned a move on the "Gateway City" from the west. This time the other raiders were soldier volunteers, who brought their skills and courage to the plan.

On the night of April 11, Andrews and the 24 volunteer soldiers met at the Kennesaw House Hotel in Marietta, Georgia (see **Marietta**). The next morning, at dawn, they boarded a northbound train as passengers. When the train stopped at Big Shanty, the passengers and crew debarked for breakfast, and Andrews and his people went to work.

Andrews did not know that the Confederates had recently established a base at Big Shanty and that several hundred Rebel soldiers were camped near the depot. His men uncoupled all but the first three boxcars, fired up the powerful locomotive, the General, and with a lurch they roared off. William A. Fuller, a conductor, abandoned his breakfast in the Lacy Hotel and started after the General, first on foot, then by commandeering, in turn, a hand car, a switching engine, the Yonah, and later, the William R. Smith, a freight engine. Along the way he was joined by Georgia militiamen.

At Kingston, the General was delayed an hour on a siding by a southbound train and Fuller drew closer. Although the raiders cut telegraph wires at several stops, none of the proposed bridge burnings was executed. Between Calhoun and Tunnel Hill, Fuller and 10 militia soldiers boarded the Texas, a southbound locomotive that they ran in reverse. Andrews's men dropped the three boxcars of their train, but the Southerners pushed them in front of their successive locomotives, the last one intercepted and pushed through the railroad tunnel at Tunnel Hill. The raiders also dropped cross ties, but to no avail; the Texas continued to close the gap.

In one of a series of paintings on the "Great Locomotive Chase" by Wilbur Kurtz, the General, having exhausted its fuel north of Ringgold, Georgia, sits idle on the track of the Atlantic & Western Railroad as Andrews' raiders flee into the surrounding hills. In the background, the Texas closes in with conductor William Fuller leading the chase to recover the engine which was taken from his northbound train.

Two miles north of Ringgold, the General's fuel was exhausted, and Andrews gave the order to scatter (see **Ringgold**). The raiders tried to disappear into the hills, but most were captured within a week. Andrews and 7 raiders, chosen at random, were hanged; the rest escaped prison or were exchanged in March 1863. Many of the raiders received Medals of Honor, the first recipients of the prestigious military award.

Big Shanty was noteworthy also in 1864. After Sherman shifted his "army group" eastward from Dallas (see **Dallas**), his troops again faced Joseph Johnston's Army of Tennessee. Sherman set up his headquarters along the Western & Atlantic Railroad at Big Shanty during June as the Federals challenged Johnston's Lost-Pine-Brushy Mountain and Kennesaw Mountain lines (see **Kennesaw Mountain**). In October 1864, Gen. John Bell Hood led the Army of Tennessee north to disrupt Federal operations. On October 4, 1864, Hood's troops captured Union garrisons protecting the railroad at Big Shanty and nearby Acworth.

Points of Interest

The Kennesaw Civil War Museum—This attractive nonprofit museum, operated under the auspices of the city of Kennesaw, features the General, which was brought to Kennesaw as a permanent exhibit in 1972 and is fully restored and well maintained. Other exhibits focus on the Great Locomotive Chase, movies about the event (including Buster Keaton's *The General*) and related Civil War subjects. Also in the museum are mementos of the twentieth-century Civil War artist Wilbur Kurtz, a relative of William Fuller by marriage. There is a gift shop in the museum. A restored caboose and Civil War cannon are out in front of the museum. Across a small road and adjacent to the museum's auxiliary parking lot is a restored depot building. The museum is open from 9:30 to 5:30 Monday–Saturday, 12:00 to 5:30 Sunday, and there is a nominal admission charge. THE KENNESAW CIVIL WAR MUSEUM, 2829 Cherokee Street, Kennesaw, GA 30144; 770-427-2117. 🗺 ♿ ❷ 🏛 P 👫 $$

Near the museum, on GA293, is a monument to the General, as well as several state historical markers detailing the chase and the role of Big Shanty in Sherman's 1864 Atlanta campaign. Proceed north on GA293, reenter I-75 at exit 120, drive 72 miles north to exit 141 to Chickamauga.

DRIVING TOUR—*Proceed to Chickamauga*
READING—*the Great Locomotive Chase: Allatoona Pass*

CHICKAMAUGA

The most significant single Civil War battle west of the Appalachian Mountains in terms of casualties was Chickamauga, fought September 19–20, 1863, with 34,624 total casualties. The campaign for Chattanooga until mid-September had gone well for Maj. Gen. William Starke Rosecrans's Army of the Cumberland. A series of Federal feints and flanking moves to the south compelled Gen. Braxton Bragg's Army of Tennessee to abandon the Gateway City (see **Chattanooga, Tennessee**) and protect his supply lines in northwest Georgia. Not content to stay and fortify Chattanooga, Rosecrans moved on the heels of what he thought was a fleeing Rebel army. Three of Rosecrans's four corps—Maj. Gen. Alexander McCook's XX Corps on the right, Maj. Gen. George H. Thomas's XIV Corps in the center, and Maj. Gen. Thomas Crittenden's XXI Corps on the left—forged ahead on a broad front.

Bragg, an intense, brooding man often at odds with his subordinates over many matters, was finally putting the brakes on his long southward flight that, except for the weeks preceding the Battle of Stones River (see **Stones River, Tennessee**), started almost a year earlier after the Battle of Perryville, Kentucky (see **Perryville, Kentucky**). Through erroneous reports planted among civilians and deserters, Bragg created a counter-intelligence scam designed to give the Federals the idea that his army was scattered and demoralized. Instead, the were regrouping in LaFayette and awaiting reinforcements from Mississippi, Virginia, and elsewhere just as two of Rosecrans's corps were crossing Lookout Mountain in northwest Georgia: McCook's near Alpine in the south and Thomas's at Stevens's Gap in the center, while Crittenden, after occupying Chattanooga, passed Missionary Ridge through Rossville Gap, occupying Ringgold and Lee and Gordon's Mill.

By the second week in September Rosecrans was beginning to notice what Bragg had in mind—to defeat the separated parts of the Army of the Cumberland in detail, that is, one at a time. At

Maj. Gen. William Starke Rosecrans was a brilliant strategist and organizer who brought his Army of the Cumberland within inches of annihilating the Confederate Army of Tennessee as he pursued them into northwest Georgia. However, after Rosecrans's army retreated into Chattanooga following his stunning defeat at Chickamauga, President Lincoln described him as "stunned and confused, like a duck hit on the head."

Davis's Cross Roads on September 10 and 11, General Bragg missed a golden opportunity to defeat in detail General Thomas's XIV Corps. On September 9, Brig. Gen. James Negley's division, passing through Stevens's Gap, entered McLemore's Cove, seizing Davis's Cross Roads. Bragg prepared to strike Negley's isolated division. Maj. Gen. Patrick Cleburne's Confederate division took position at Dug Gap east of the cross-roads while Maj. Gen. Thomas Hindman's division was positioned several miles north of the crossroads. A lack of initiative on the part of Hindman frustrated Bragg's plans of September 10. By the next morning, Brig. Gen. Absalom Baird's division reinforced Negley, but the Confederate force in the area grew larger as well. However, once again the Rebel command failed to strike a swift blow and the commencement of skirmishing caused Thomas to order his two divisions to pull back from Davis's Cross Roads, frustrating Bragg's opportunity to severely cripple and possibly begin to defeat in detail Rosecrans's army.

Gen. Braxton Bragg, CSA, an intense and rigid leader, had few friends among the Confederate leadership. One of them, however, was President Jefferson Davis, who relied on Bragg's leadership and advice throughout the war. As commander of the Army of Tennessee, Bragg withdrew from the field after his soldiers had severely crippled the enemy.

On September 12–13, an attack against Crittenden, whose corps was concentrating on Lee and Gordon's Mill, was also scrapped when Polk protested that Crittenden had consolidated his scattered divisions. Rosecrans moved, when it was almost too late, to pull back McCook and Thomas and close on Crittenden's corps anchored on Lee and Gordon's Mill. By the night of September 17, Crittenden's corps, the army's left wing, was at the mill, Thomas was at Pond Spring, and McCook held the Federal right at Stevens's Gap. Rosecrans continued to edge his army northward the next day and evening, September 18, as the Yankees bought time in disputing the Confederate crossings of the Chickamauga. The battle opened with these cavalry-infantry engagements at Alexander's Bridge and Reed's Bridge, frustrating Bragg's plan to turn Rosecrans's left and cut him off from Chattanooga.

Longstreet's Rail Journey

Because Maj. Gen. Ambrose Burnside's Army of the Ohio occupied Knoxville after Buckner's evacuation of the East Tennessee city, crucial miles of the Virginia & Tennessee Railroad, the most direct railway between Virginia's Piedmont and Chattanooga, were in Federal hands. Therefore, when two divisions of Longstreet's corps received the assignment to transfer to Bragg's command, they were forced to take a roundabout route through the Carolinas and Atlanta, finally disembarking the cars at Catoosa Station near Ringgold. After more than two years of war, the South's crazy quilt railroad system was in terrible shape. Adding to the problems of varying gauges of track and private ownership, the war had taken its toll on locomotives, rolling stock, bridges, and rights-of-way. Longstreet's 15,000 veterans used sixteen different rail lines for the seven-hundred-mile trip from Gordonsville, Virginia, to Catoosa Station. Mary Boykin Chesnut, the wife of South Carolina politician James Chesnut and an astute observer of the

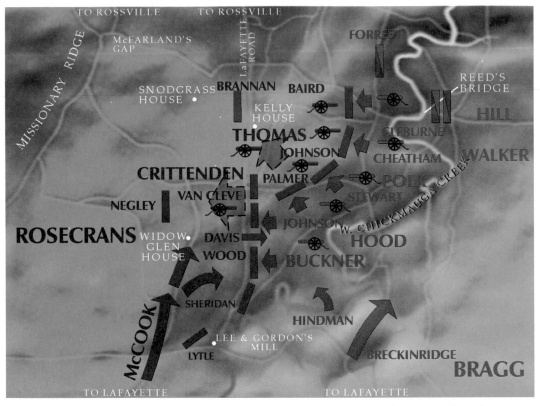

The Battle of Chickamauga opened on the evening of September 18 with cavalry-infantry skirmishes at Reed's Bridge and Alexander's Bridge as the Federals sought to delay the Confederate crossing of the creek. By the next morning, September 19, these lines were formed. Attacks planned by Bragg on the Confederate right did not begin as scheduled and elements of Thomas's corps pushed Forrest's cavalry back before Polk's infantry began a concerted assault on the Federal left. Throughout the day, fighting broke out all along the front. Brig. Gen. Jefferson Davis's division scored a momentary breakthrough across the LaFayette Road, but was driven back by the first brigades of the Army of Northern Virginia that had arrived on the field under Hood. By the end of the day, Thomas's corps had been severely hammered and pulled back to the Rossville Road. The Federal line, though bloodied, held.

wartime conditions in the South, had the opportunity to observe Longstreet's force en route. She described the scene in her diary: ". . . what seemed miles of platform cars, and soldiers rolled in their blankets lying in rows with their heads all covered, fast asleep. In their gray blankets . . . they looked like swathed mummies."

Also on September 18, brigades of Lt. Gen. James Longstreet's Army of Northern Virginia corps began to arrive on the field, adding to the reinforcements Bragg had already received. Bragg had formed five infantry corps under Lt. Gens. Leonidas Polk and Daniel

H. Hill and Maj. Gens. Simon Buckner, William H. T. Walker, and John B. Hood. Bragg had hoped to deliver a punishing blow to the Federal left, now held by Thomas's four divisions, east of the LaFayette Road, with Walker's and Polk's corps early on September 19. But the attack started late and by the time Polk's men crossed Chickamauga Creek, Thomas had launched a preemptory attack that beat back Forrest's dismounted cavalry near Jay's Mill until "Shot Pouch" Walker's infantry came to their aid. By the time the Rebels returned the courtesy, reinforcements from Crittenden and McCook stemmed an overrun of the Federal left.

Fierce fighting erupted all along the four-mile front of wooded areas occasionally dotted with small fields on September 19. Three major Confederate assaults—by Maj. Gen. Alexander Stewart's and Bushrod R. Johnson's divisions of Buckner's corps in the center; John Bell Hood's division on the Rebel left; and a dusk attack by Maj. Gen. Patrick Cleburne's division of Hill's corps on the right—all punished, but failed to shatter, the Federal lines. Union reinforcements, arriving in timely fashion, stemmed Bragg's sledgehammer-like blows. Though ruptured momentarily by A. P. Stewart's "Little Giant" division, the Federal lines stood firm at the end of the day.

On September 20, Bragg ordered Polk to renew his attack on Thomas's advancing *en echelon*, while Longstreet looked for an opening in the center. Although Polk's attacks on the Federal left began late at 9:30 A.M., they were vicious. From his headquarters near the Widow Glenn House, Rosecrans received a report of a gap in his line on Thomas's right near the Brotherton Cabin. Actually, the units were in place, but were concealed by the tree line. Brig. Gen. Thomas Wood's two-brigade division was ordered to move into the phantom gap, which created a real rupture in the Federal line. The timing was disastrous. Longstreet, unaware of the windfall, by chance launched an assault that propelled eight brigades of Rebel veterans into the gap. The flood waters of Confederate infantry flowed unstoppably across the LaFayette Road, past the Brotherton Cabin and directly toward Rosecrans's headquarters. Col. John Wilder's 2,000-man brigade, armed with Spencer seven-shot repeating rifles, in position near the Widow Glenn House, tried to slow the Rebel onslaught, but could not turn back Longstreet's determined veterans. Rosecrans, his headquarters staff, McCook, and Crittenden and thousands of their soldiers left the field hurriedly as Longstreet's men surged northward.

Meanwhile, George Thomas's units were holding their own against the bludgeoning of Polk's wing. But now a new problem confronted the stout general. Longstreet's force was

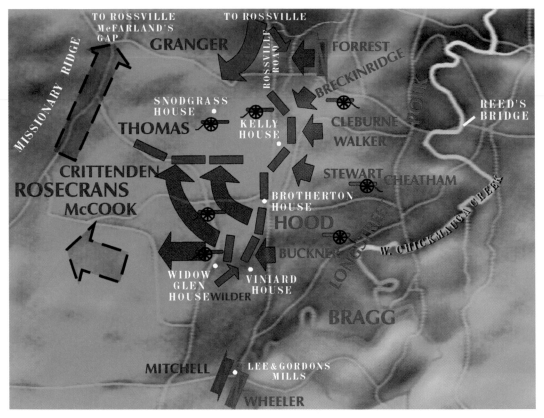

The second day of the Battle of Chickamauga, September 20, began as the first; scheduled attacks on the Federal left did not start on time. When they did, led by Breckinridge's division, they were successful in continuing to hammer the Federal units already weakened by the previous day's fighting. As Rosecrans shifted units to meet the attacks, a mistake developed when Wood's division was moved out of position in the center. As a result, forces commanded by Longstreet found a gap in the Federal line and marched through. The advance caused a rout to begin on the Federal right which drove most of Crittenden's and McCook's men from the field, along with Rosecrans and his staff. The rout was stemmed when Thomas, already severely challenged on his front, established a line along Horseshoe Ridge to meet the assault on his flank. Aided by two brigades from the reserve corps sent down the Rossville Road by Maj. Gen. Gordon Granger, Thomas held off numerous assaults by Longstreet's wing until an orderly withdrawal was executed.

rolling northward toward Snodgrass Hill, which was perpendicular to Thomas's breastworks east of the LaFayette Road. Cool as the chill that greeted him that September morning was Thomas, as he formed a new line along Snodgrass Hill and Horseshoe Ridge to the west. Thomas's resistance to Longstreet's slashing attacks was enormously aided by the arrival of two reserve brigades sent from south of Rossville Gap led by Maj. Gen. Gordon Granger on his own initiative. The line held against repeated attacks by Longstreet's wing.

Maj. Gen. George H. Thomas, CSA, served throughout the Civil War in Kentucky, Tennessee, and Georgia, where he continually proved to be a reliable and successful commander. He was unshakable in battle, though he often moved slowly—a frustration to quick-acting Generals Grant and Sherman. Thomas's soldiers, however, never were routed from a field of battle.

By evening, Thomas executed an orderly withdrawal north through McFarland's Gap and joined the rest of the Army of the Cumberland on its way to Chattanooga. His heroic stand earned him the nom de guerre the "Rock of Chickamauga."

Rosecrans lost his command and did not lead an army into combat for the remainder of the war. Although both McCook and Crittenden were acquitted of wrongdoing in Courts of Inquiry, McCook never had another field command except briefly while serving in Washington during Jubal Early's July 1864 raid and Crittenden resigned in December 1864, after serving as a divisional commander in the Army of the Potomac. Braxton Bragg's greatest victory soon lost its luster as he again began feuding with his generals. Though he drove the Union army from the field of battle, he was appalled by the 18,454 Confederate casualties—2,000 more than the Federals, who listed more than 3,000 as missing—and despite the urging of his subordinates, he refused to follow up by attacking the Federals before they made Chattanooga. In the end, the decision led to Bragg's downfall.

Points of Interest

Chickamauga and Chattanooga National Military Park, Chickamauga Unit—The largest and one of the most beautiful Civil War battlefield parks in the National Park System, this battlefield park was the first of the four original national military parks—Gettysburg, Shiloh, and Vicksburg being the other three—to receive congressional approval and funding. Two veterans of the battle, Gens. H. V. Boynton and Ferdinand Van Derveer, were largely responsible for championing the park. It was dedicated in 1895 on the battle's thirty-second anniversary.

Most of the Chickamauga Unit's 6 square miles consists of pristine landscapes that, except for the well-placed tour park roads and hundreds of monuments, appear much as they did in 1863. The one exception is US27, a busy two-lane north-south highway that is superimposed over the old LaFayette Road, though this highway is being rerouted to bypass the park. The park's roads follow the battle, and they are frequently one-way. The Chickamauga Unit is located 6 miles west of I-75, exit 141 via GA2

Snodgrass Hill, now part of Chickamauga and Chattanooga National Military Park, was the center of the stand made by Maj. Gen. George H. Thomas to save the Federal Army of the Cumberland from complete destruction on September 20, 1863. Thomas made his headquarters near this log cabin reconstructed on the site of the Snodgrass House.

at Fort Oglethorpe. From Chattanooga, take US 27 for 3 miles south to Rossville, then another 3 miles south to Fort Oglethorpe. Stop first at the visitor center, on US27 at the north end of the park, to view the exhibits and pick up a brochure and map.

The visitor center has a multimedia program, the Fuller firearms collection, an artillery park featuring the battle's various types of field artillery, and a library-research facility. There is also an outstanding bookstore. An audiotape tour of the battlefield is available for rental. The seven-mile battlefield driving tour includes wayside exhibits featuring most of the important landmarks. Most of the states that supplied volunteer troops have monuments. Along the park roads cast-iron placards, red for Confederate, blue for Union, designate troop positions and describe their movements. Artillery pieces—original tubes mounted on replica carriages—are positioned at battery locations.

Of particular interest in the park are three cabins. The Snodgrass and Kelly cabins are reconstructions; the Brotherton Cabin on the LaFayette Road (US27) is the original. This cabin was at the center of the September 20 Confederate breakthrough of Longstreet's left wing. Wilder Tower is adjacent to the site of Rosecrans's September 19 headquarters.

Wilder's brigade attempted to resist the September 20 breakthrough here. A platform at the top of the tower provides an excellent view of the battlefield. CHICKAMAUGA AND CHATTANOOGA NATIONAL MILITARY PARK, P.O. Box 2128, Fort Oglethorpe, GA 30742; 706-866-9241. 🚲 🖼 ♿ 🚶 🐴 ❓ 🏛 P 🚻

Two points of interest are outside the national military park. Reed's Bridge, just east of the park on Reed's Bridge Road, is where one of the opening cavalry engagements occurred. Lee and Gordon's Mill, 0.5 mile south of the park and just east of US27, occupies the site of the original 1836 building. The mill was the location of Maj. Gen. Thomas Crittenden's headquarters in September 1863. It is privately held and is undergoing restoration by its owner.

Gordon-Lee Mansion—This Greek revival mansion, completed in 1847, was built by and for James Gordon, a wealthy businessman whose mill was a landmark. On September 16, Rosecrans and his staff occupied the house and used it as a headquarters for two days, until moving to the Widow Glenn Cabin nearer the fighting. The mansion and its grounds then served as the main Federal field hospital. A National Register property, it is today a bed-and-breakfast inn and used for special functions. It is located in the town of Chickamauga, just south of the national military park, on GA341. GORDON-LEE MANSION, 217 Cove Road, Chickamauga, GA 30707; 706-375-4728.

Lee and Gordon's Mill was a landmark on the Chickamauga Creek when Maj. Gen. Thomas Crittenden's corps arrived in the area under orders to pursue the Confederate Army of Tennessee, which Rosecrans incorrectly supposed was in wild retreat. When Bragg chose to stand his ground in northwest Georgia, Rosecrans hurriedly consolidated the separate corps of his army here to avoid having one or more of them cut off and defeated. The mill is undergoing restoration.

Rossville—The Iowa Reservation, on US27 at Rossville, is a small outpost of Chickamauga and Chattanooga National Military Park, where a monument and plaques describe the role of Iowa units in the Battle of Chattanooga (see **Chattanooga, Tennessee**).

Davis's Cross Roads—The site of Bragg's attempt to trap Thomas's lead division in McLemore's Cove is located at the intersection of GA193 and GA341 between Chickamauga and LaFayette. The site maintains an integrity true to the time of the battle. If possible visit the site before your extensive tour of the Chickamauga battlefield to see how the failure of the Confederates to trap one or more Federal divisions in this cul de sac prevented an even more devastating blow to Rosecrans's army than that resulting from the Battle of Chickamauga.

LaFayette—Eighteen miles south of Chickamauga on US27, LaFayette was the scene of a June 24, 1864, engagement between a Federal occupation force, under Col. Louis D. Watkins, and controversial Confederate Brig. Gen. Gideon J. Pillow (see **Fort Donelson, Tennessee**). Pillow withdrew after Watkins was reinforced. John B. Gordon Hall, built in 1836, was renamed for the Confederate general who was a student here. Gen. Braxton Bragg maintained his headquarters at John B. Gordon Hall September 8–17, 1863.

DRIVING TOUR—*Proceed to Ringgold*
READING—*Chattanooga, Tennessee*

RINGGOLD

In November 1863, after the Confederate Army of Tennessee's defeat at the Battle of Chattanooga (see **Chattanooga, Tennessee**), a significant delaying action at Ringgold Gap saved its wagon trains from destruction. Gen. Braxton Bragg tagged Maj. Gen. Patrick Cleburne and his division, constituting the Rebel rear guard, to delay the Federals and give the Confederates time to move wagons, artillery, and the army along the muddy road to a defensible position at Dalton, Georgia, centering on Rocky Face Ridge.

The day after the frantic retreat from Missionary Ridge, while his troops were sleeping west of Ringgold, Cleburne conducted a night reconnaissance to the east and discovered a defensible position in a deep gorge bounded on the south by Taylor's Ridge and on the north by White Oak Mountain. Early on the morning of November 27, 1863, Cleburne placed his 4,100 men and 2 cannons, concealed by woods and brush, along the ridge and in the gorge. By eight A.M. the Federal skirmishers were driving the Confederate cavalry toward Taylor's Ridge, and soon after the head of Maj. Gen. "Fighting Joe" Hooker's 12,000-man column emerged from Ringgold.

Maj. Gen. Patrick R. Cleburne, CSA, was an Irish immigrant who served three years in Her Majesty's 41st Regiment of Foot and joined the Confederate army as a private. He quickly rose through the ranks in the west and became one of the most talented and respected Confederate generals. His charm and intelligence earned the unflagging respect of his men.

At the last possible moment, Cleburne's people unleashed a vicious fire that scattered the blue skirmishers in front. Several hours of probing the Confederate line did not break it, and Hooker decided to wait for his artillery, which had been delayed by bridgeless streams and muddy roads. By afternoon, Cleburne left the field with just half the casualties of those of his foe, his mission accomplished beyond the expectations of his superiors, who deemed it sacrificial. Maj. Gen. Ulysses S. Grant, in command in Chattanooga, was disappointed but not surprised. Forty-eight hours earlier, Cleburne had also effectively hamstrung Maj. Gen. William T. Sherman's part in the Chattanooga battle. Hooker was ordered not to advance in order to protect Sherman's march north to relieve the Confederate siege of Maj. Gen. Ambrose Burnside's force at Knoxville (see **Knoxville, Tennessee**).

Points of Interest

Ringgold is a charming little town off the beaten path in the mountainous area of northwest Georgia. Take US27 north of the Chickamauga battlefield. At the traffic light, turn right (east) on GA2 and follow it 6 miles to the intersection of US41. Ringgold is 2 miles south on US41. Monuments and markers dot the Catoosa County courthouse lawn. Several describe Ringgold's role as an important Southern hospital center. The Whitman-Anderson House at 309 Tennessee Street was used by U. S. Grant after the Battle of Ringgold Gap as a headquarters.

The most significant landmark in the town is the railroad depot, built in 1850. On US41 at the southeastern edge of town, the stone depot still shows signs of the battle—lighter-colored stone pieces replace those originals battered in 1863. One-half mile farther east on the right (west) side of the highway is a wayside, one of five of the Atlanta Campaign funded and built in the mid-1930s by the U.S. government. Although the wayside is in need of repairs, this is an important stop—you are in the middle of the gorge defended by Cleburne and his men. Interpretive signs describe the Battle of Ringgold Gap and the launch of Maj. Gen. William T. Sherman's 1864 Atlanta Campaign from this area.

Other points of interest include a monument on the Ooltewah-Ringgold Road, 2 miles north of Ringgold, marking the end of the Great Locomotive Chase.

At the intersection of GA2 East and US41, 1.8 miles south of the wayside, is the Old Stone Church. Blood stains are visible on the wood floor, dramatically illustrating its wartime role as a hospital following the Battle of Ringgold Gap.

Continue east on GA2 for 4 miles to Varnell, in Crow Valley. Called Varnell's Station during the war, cavalry of Maj. Gen. John A. Schofield's column of Sherman's "army group" first clashed with Confederate cavalry and infantry here in Crow Valley on May 7, 1864. Prater's Mill was a landmark at the time. Varnell House was used as a hospital and headquarters in May 1864.

Return to US41 on GA2. As you pass through the Cherokee Valley, you may note a private road heading north. It goes to Catoosa Springs, an antebellum mineral resort used as a Confederate hospital, among whose patients were Braxton Bragg and his wife. Maj. Gen. O. O. Howard's Union corps camped there on the eve of the Atlanta Campaign. No wartime structures exist and the area is presently closed to the public. Continue south on US41 to Tunnel Hill.

DRIVING TOUR—*Proceed to Tunnel Hill*
READING—*Knoxville, Tennessee; Sherman's 1864 Atlanta Campaign: Tunnel Hill*

SHERMAN'S 1864 ATLANTA CAMPAIGN

Early in May 1864, Maj. Gen. William T. Sherman launched his campaign through northwest Georgia. More than eight months later, he and his "army group" swept through Georgia and the Carolinas in an action that, in concert with U. S. Grant's "army group's" campaign against the Army of Northern Virginia, ended in the defeat of the principal Confederate forces. Most of the battles waged on Peach State soil were fought during Sherman's Atlanta Campaign and his March to the Sea.

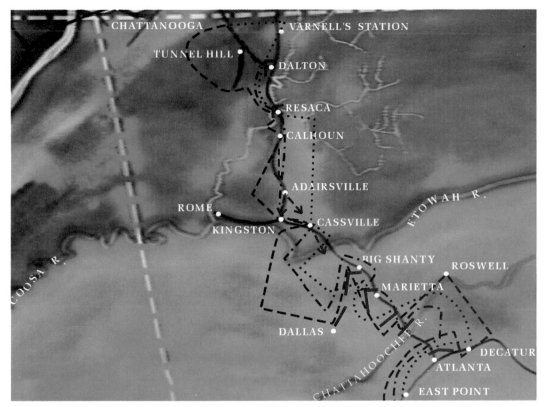

Maj. Gen. William T. Sherman's "army group" marched through northwest Georgia in three columns that operated in mutual support of one another. The Army of the Cumberland (dash and dot), the largest, marched primarily on a central access along the Atlantic & Western Railroad, moving ponderously but steadily forward, while the Army of the Tennessee (dashes) and the Army of the Ohio (dots) executed flanking maneuvers to get between the Confederate Army of Tennessee's fortified positions (red lines) and its base of supplies in Atlanta. As the campaign progressed, General Johnston withdrew (red arrows) from one prepared position to another to avoid being cut off from Atlanta while he looked for an opportunity to slow down or halt Sherman's advance.

Sherman's strategy of total war, engagement with the means and spirit of the people as well as its armed forces, was endorsed by the Washington government and General-in-Chief Grant. The rule of the day in the Georgia campaigns was to throw the superior weight of the Federal war machine against smaller, less well-equipped Southern forces. Both belligerents used solid strategies and well-planned tactics, and both exhibited quality leadership and individual bravery. In the end it was the force of numbers and superior material management that proved to be the decisive factors for the Federals.

Sherman's primary objective, at first, was the destruction of the Confederate Army of Tennessee, led by Gen. Joseph E. Johnston, rather than the capture of Atlanta. Johnston's leadership had reinvigorated his army at its winter camp in Dalton, Georgia, but relations between Johnston and the Richmond leadership were strained. It was expected of Johnston that he recover much of Tennessee, which should have been unthinkable given the Federal forces then occupying the state. To add to Johnston's woes, during the early part of the campaign, his requests for reinforcements and supplies were often downgraded or delayed.

In contrast, Sherman not only enjoyed a numerical superiority of nearly two to one, he enjoyed the confidence of General Grant and President Lincoln. After Grant was appointed commander of all Federal armies on March 9, 1864, he laid out a coordinated plan by all the armies in the field. The second major component of the strategy, after the destruction of Gen. Robert E. Lee's Army of Northern Virginia, was Sherman's assignment in Georgia. Beyond overall strategy, the details of the campaign were left to Sherman.

Maj. Gen. William Tecumseh Sherman, USA, served as an officer in the Federal army from First Manassas until the end of the war. His first few months were rocky, but after he began serving under U. S. Grant as a commander in the Army of the Tennessee at Shiloh, he displayed skill and determination in battle. The lasting relationship he developed with Grant led to the two directing the campaigns that finally meant victory for the North.

Relations between the two generals, who were also friends, had never been better. Sherman later wrote, perhaps referring sarcastically to earlier, much publicized allegations about the two before success brought them universal admiration in the North: "We were as brothers, I the older in years, he the higher in rank. He stood by me when I was crazy and I stood by him when he was drunk; and now we stand by each other always." In the postwar years Sherman gained another close friend of high rank, Confederate general Joseph E. Johnston. But on May 1, 1864, as he assessed the ranks of his "army group," his mind was on the destruction of Johnston's army and the cause it was fighting for.

NOTE: The driving tour and reading for the Atlanta Campaign is continuous from Tunnel Hill through Atlanta.

Tunnel Hill

On May 7, 1864, Sherman's "army group" marched from its camps in northwest Georgia. The force, in excess of 98,000 men, was divided into the Army of the Cumberland, 60,773 strong under Maj. Gen. George H. Thomas; the Army of the Tennessee, with 24,465 men led by Maj. Gen. James B. McPherson; and the Army of the Ohio, with 13,559 soldiers under Maj. Gen. John M. Schofield. Combined, the armies had 254 guns and a cavalry corps. Sherman's plan was simple—Thomas's large army would march in the center, opposing the principal Confederate force entrenched north and west of Dalton, while McPherson and Schofield would seek advantages on the flanks.

To test the strategy, Sherman assigned Thomas to move against the Confederate fortifications and the two passes that opened through Rocky Face Ridge–Mill Creek Gap and Dug Gap. Schofield would support Thomas by marching south along the East Tennessee Railroad via Varnell's Station. Sherman hoped these operations would divert the Rebels, while McPherson took the Army of the Tennessee on a roundabout march from Lee and Gordon's Mill through Snake Creek Gap. Traversing this mountain gap, discovered by scouts during Thomas's mid-February 1864 offensive (see **Dalton**), would place McPherson in the Rebel rear fourteen miles south, astride the railroad at Resaca.

At eleven A.M. on Saturday, May 7, Federal guns fired the opening shots of the campaign at Tunnel Hill, which took its name from the 1,477-foot railroad tunnel that ran through Chetoogeta Ridge. Opposing Maj. Gen. John M. Palmer's XIV Corps of the Army of the Cumberland was the dismounted cavalry of the Army of Tennessee under Maj. Gen. Joseph Wheeler. The Confederate cavalry was protecting the ridge and the valley that separated it from Rocky Face Ridge, and until the Federals were reinforced, provided stubborn resistance to Palmer's infantry and artillery.

Although Johnston wanted to plug the tunnel, it was ultimately abandoned intact by the Confederates when orders from Richmond to proceed with the operation were not received in time. Sherman's "army group" pressed it into service as a link in its vital supply line by rail from Chattanooga as the force thrust deeper into Georgia.

Points of Interest

The major points of interest for the engagement are located just southeast of the small community of Tunnel Hill, 6 miles south of Ringgold on US41. From US 41, turn left on Oak Street and go to Clisby Austin Drive. Or, from I-75, take exit 138 and proceed south on GA201 to Main Street, turn right, then immediately left over the railroad tracks to Clisby Austin Drive. Here are Georgia historical markers that describe the engagement, the tunnel, and the Clisby Austin House.

At the eastern end of Clisby Austin Drive, you can park and view the tunnel's western portal. It is to the right of a larger tunnel, which was built in the 1920s and is used by the modern railroad. A restoration of the tunnel and a historical park are planned, but currently the entrance is on railroad property. The General passed through the tunnel during the Great Locomotive Chase, pursued closely by the Texas running in reverse. On the ridge above the two railroad tunnels are Confederate earthworks and gun emplacements.

The open fields to the south were part of the battleground. The brick Clisby Austin House, or Meadowlawn, was built in 1848 and used as a summer resort. Confederate general John Bell Hood was treated here after being wounded and having his right leg amputated at the hip during the Battle of Chickamauga. Sherman made the Clisby Austin House his headquarters from May 7 to 12. Today the restored house is open for tours and in September an annual reenactment of the Battle of Tunnel Hill is held. For more information on the house, tunnel, battlefield, and future plans, contact THE TUNNEL HILL HISTORICAL FOUNDATION, P.O. Box 114, Tunnel Hill, GA 30755; 706-673-5152. ❓ P

DRIVING TOUR and READING—*Proceed to Rocky Face Ridge*

Rocky Face Ridge

After Thomas's army forced Wheeler's cavalry from Tunnel Hill, Sherman and his staff got their first close look at Rocky Face Ridge, the "Georgia Gibraltar." Extending more than ten miles from north to south, rising in places to fifteen hundred feet, the ridge was the bulwark of Johnston's defensive line, though he later bemoaned its weakness. Lt. Gen. William Hardee's corps manned the ridge north and west of Dalton while Hood's guarded Crow Valley, creating a virtual wall of firepower. Pioneers from Maj. Gen. Alexander Stewart's division impounded the waters of Mill Creek. Above, in Buzzard's Roost, artillery emplacements loomed, commanding the approaches to Mill Creek Gap. These were the obstacles facing the Federals converging on Rocky Face Ridge.

Schofield, after pushing elements of Wheeler's cavalry through Varnell's Station, joined Thomas marching from Tunnel Hill and their four corps formed a wide arc confronting the Confederate positions. On May 8, Federal demonstrations against Rocky Face Ridge began. At Poplar Springs, Brig. Gen. Edward M. McCook's cavalry battled mounted and dismounted troopers from Wheeler's cavalry. North of Dalton, Schofield launched five sorties against the entrenchments. While these assaults, by design, didn't dislodge the Rebels, they kept them pinned in position. To Schofield's right, Brig. Gen. John M. Newton's division of Howard's corps advanced south down the crest of Rocky Face against stubborn resistance. The terrain equalized the Union's superior numbers and no significant advantage was gained.

The heaviest fighting in the northern sector came when Brig. Gen. Jefferson C. Davis's division of Palmer's corps pressed forward in Mill Creek Gap, south of the wagon road. Here, also, Confederate forces turned back the Federal advance. Three attempts by the 34th Illinois to break the dam flooding Mill Creek Gap failed.

Points of Interest

From Tunnel Hill, proceed south on US41. Before crossing under I-75, you will enter Mill Creek Gap. On the south side of US41 is the second 1930s Georgia Campaign wayside. It describes the action in the area of Rocky Face Ridge. From this vantage point you can see the rugged mountain escarpment known as Buzzard's Roost, where Confederate artillery frowned on the men of Palmer's corps. A trail on the east side of Mill Creek leads to a flume, where Brig. Gen. James D. Morgan's Federal brigade made the strongest attack on the ridge. Traces of the old wagon road are just past the Mill Creek bridge. GHC markers describe the action in this area. Although many Rebel earthworks still exist on Rocky Face Ridge, they are on private property and inaccessible without an experienced local guide. Proceed south on US41 to the town of Dalton.

Dalton

Dalton was the center of the Confederate Army of Tennessee's 1863–64 winter encampment, the site of Johnston's headquarters during the fighting on Rocky Face Ridge, and the scene of other earlier and later actions.

In February 1864, Lt. Gen. George Thomas, under orders from Maj. Gen. Ulysses S. Grant, demonstrated against the Confederate Rocky Face fortifications covering Dalton. Grant acted on information, which was true, that two divisions of Lt. Gen. William Hardee's corps had been rushed to central Alabama in response to Sherman's raid on Meridian, Mississippi (see **Meridian, Mississippi**). In view of a week's delay in starting a "formidable reconnaissance" from Ringgold, Hardee's divisions were already returning to Dalton, and some of his people were manning the works as Thomas's army probed Rebel defenses at Tunnel Hill, Rocky Face Ridge, and Dug Gap. The presence of Joseph Wheeler's cavalry at Tunnel Hill delayed the first Federal attack a day and when Maj. Gen. John M. Palmer's corps appeared before Tunnel Hill on February 24, the Rebel horsemen fell back to Mill Creek Gap. The next day the 36th Indiana Mounted Infantry scaled and occupied Dug Gap. However, on the morning of February 26, soldiers from Patrick Cleburne's division drove the Hoosiers from Dug Gap and Palmer's coordinated attack found Hardee's corps in force. Thomas recalled his columns. Federal casualties during the six days, February 22–27, were 345, more than twice those of the Army of Tennessee. The principal gain of Thomas's demonstration was the valuable information garnered on the terrain and Confederate defenses that the Union forces applied in their advance ten weeks later.

Later in 1864, Union garrisons at Dalton came under attack. On August 14, Joseph Wheeler's cavalry launched a three-day cavalry raid into northwest Georgia and eastern Tennessee to break up Sherman's supply line. This was followed, on October 13, by the arrival of Gen. John B. Hood's Army of Tennessee in front of the town after the Confederates wrecked the railroad northward from Resaca. The entire 1,000-man Federal garrison when called to surrender laid down their arms. Hood hounded by Sherman's pursuing columns, after failing to destroy the railroad tunnel at Chetoogeta Ridge, turned southwest and marched into Alabama (see **Palmetto** and **Allatoona Pass** and **Franklin, Tennessee**).

Points of Interest

Now known primarily for its carpet mills, before and during the Civil War Dalton was a railroad center. The Western & Atlantic depot, built in 1852, saw the pursuit of the General by the Texas in 1862, the arrival of Longstreet's Army of Northern Virginia corps in 1863, and the provisioning of the Confederate Army of Tennessee in the first months of 1864. Near the railroad is the only statue to be found in the south of Confederate general Joseph E. Johnston. The Blunt House on Thorton Avenue (US41/GA3), built in 1848, was temporarily used as a Federal hospital. The Hamilton House, on the corner of Chattanooga Avenue and Matilda Street, was the headquarters of Orphan Brigade commander Brig. Gen. Joseph H. Lewis.

The Confederate cemetery, at West View Cemetery on Emory Street, contains the remains of 425 Southern soldiers. Four Federal soldiers are buried beneath a memorial statue in the middle of the cemetery. East of the railroad is Fort Hill, where the Federal blockhouse that was attacked by Hood's force in October 1864 was located. The tourist information center on Walton Avenue, near I-75, can provide more information on Dalton's excellent cultural resources and attractions.

Dug Gap

Along with its May 8, 1864, feints on Rocky Face Ridge, General Hooker's XX Corps effectively screened the Army of the Tennessee's march from Lee and Gordon's Mill via Villanow. Hooker's effort was focused on Dug Gap—the middle pass through Rocky Face Ridge, midway between Mill and Snake creeks—and was assigned to Brig. Gen. John W. Geary's division, principally former Army of the Potomac soldiers. Geary dispatched one brigade to Villanow to cover the march of McPherson's corps, while the other two brigades crossed Mill Creek and approached Dug Gap.

The Federal attack on Dug Gap was one of the diversions assigned to the Federal Army of the Cumberland by Maj. Gen. William T. Sherman in the opening phase of the Atlanta Campaign. The Federal soldiers found difficult going in scaling the precipitous face of Rocky Face Ridge as the Rebels fired shots and rolled boulders from the crest. The attack was called off after only a few Union soldiers made it to the top, but the attack succeeded in helping to mask Maj. Gen. James B. McPherson's flanking march.

By mid-afternoon Geary's men had driven Rebel skirmishers,

the 9th Kentucky Regiment of the Orphan Brigade, from the Babb House at the base of the ridge. Rifled artillery was set up to fire on the two regiments of Arkansas Mounted Rifles, and their reinforcements, in Dug Gap. While the Federals, advancing by files, struggled to gain a foothold, the Confederates shot from behind the natural rock palisades at the crest of the ridge, and rolled huge boulders down on the advancing soldiers. A few Federals gained the summit and fought hand-to-hand with defenders, but the attack withered away. Geary followed with an assault on both flanks, but these too were successfully repulsed and at dusk the effort was suspended. Geary's force sustained 357 casualties, the most costly of the Rocky Face Ridge diversions.

Points of Interest

Dug Gap Battlefield Park is a small well maintained area, little changed since the battle. The rock palisades are breathtaking in their natural beauty and can be readily understood as invaluable to the Dug Gap defenders. Remnants of Confederate breastworks are also visible. The park is maintained by the Whitfield-Murray Historical Society, an extension of the local Civil War Roundtable. The park is normally open weekends and limited parking is available.

Resaca

In the first seventy-two hours of the Atlanta Campaign, when Maj. Gen. James B. McPherson and his Army of the Tennessee failed to occupy Resaca (named for the U.S. victory in the Mexican War, Resaca de la Palma), and block the withdrawal of Joseph E. Johnston's army from Dalton, William T. Sherman, reportedly said, "Well, Mac, you have missed the opportunity of a lifetime." It is easy to see why Sherman was disappointed. The chance to place a large Federal force on the Confederate Army of Tennessee's lifeline railroad, blocking its retreat with a numerically superior force following behind, seemed like the perfect plan. But several factors intervened to help explain McPherson's lack of determination in taking Resaca.

The force left Lee and Gordon's Mill on May 7, traveled via Rock Spring, and arrived that night at Ship's Gap, east of LaFayette. Confederate cavalry was absent in the area and the marchers continued undetected the next day through Villanow. The night of May 8, they camped on the western side of Snake Creek Gap. Once aware of the column, Col. Warren Grigsby's Rebel cavalry, which had fought that day at Dug Gap, and Daniel

Lt. Gen. Leonidas Polk, CSA, was a West Point friend of Jefferson Davis before he became interested in the ministry and was ordained an Episcopal bishop. When the war broke out, the soldier-clergyman felt the call of duty and joined the Confederate army. Davis assigned him a command in Kentucky and Polk served for more than three years in the west until he was killed at Pine Mountain during the Atlanta Campaign.

Reynolds's Arkansas brigade, the lead element of Lt. Gen. Leonidas Polk's Army of Mississippi, were rushed to aid Brig. Gen. James Cantey's brigade, which was guarding the railroad at Resaca.

Grigsby's cavalry pushed back McPherson's vanguard, the 9th Illinois Mounted Infantry, advancing to Sugar Valley on the morning of May 9, and Union battle lines were formed. Brig. Gen. Thomas Sweeny's XVI Corps division soon drove the cavalry from Bald Hill, across Camp Creek and into entrenchments west of the railroad. McPherson then ordered the 9th Illinois, his only mounted troops, to reconnoiter north of Resaca. The horse soldiers returned, having cut telegraph wires but failing to destroy any track or find a more advantageous position. At four P.M., McPherson ordered an assault on the Rebel works. Cadets from the Georgia Military Academy in Marietta formed a skirmish line, fired one volley at the attackers, and retired into the earthworks. The Federal infantry advanced, but McPherson, observing the action from Bald Hill with his corps commanders, lost his nerve and ordered the force to retire. The Army of the Tennessee recrossed Camp Creek and sat down for the night at Snake Creek Gap.

McPherson's concern was that Rebel reinforcements moving south from Dalton down the railroad might cut him off. Without cavalry, he told Sherman, he was unable to ascertain what was happening elsewhere. Sherman ordered most of his remaining "army group" south to Snake Creek Gap, and finally, on the night of May 12–13, Johnston swiftly and quietly moved his army into the entrenchments at Resaca.

By dawn the Confederates were occupying the Resaca works. Lt. Gen. Leonidas Polk, who was in command at Resaca until Johnston arrived, took charge of the Rebel left which anchored on the Oostanaula River and extended northward between Camp Creek and the railroad. North of Polk's position, Lt. Gen. William Hardee's corps extended the line north then east, where it joined Lt. Gen. John B. Hood's corps. Hood bent his right flank south and vested on the Conasauga River, creating a front of more than four and one half miles. Cannons were placed at two salient angles where the lines bent. Wheeler's cavalry patrolled the east bank of the Conasauga, and Johnston sent Maj. Gen. William H. T. Walker's infantry division and cavalry south to Calhoun to await developments.

Sherman ordered his four corps, then arriving through Snake Creek Gap, to take post opposite the Confederate entrenchments and on the left of McPherson's army, as it again advanced east from Snake Creek Gap. Hooker's XX Corps formed on McPherson's left, then Palmer's XVI Corps and Schofield's Army of the Ohio extended the line north and east. Howard's IV Corps, marching south from Mill Creek Gap, took position on Schofield's left. Attacks would be launched from these positions on May 14, but first Brig. Gen. Judson Kilpatrick's cavalry drove in Confederate pickets, and Maj. Gen. John A. Logan's XV Corps retook Bald Hill.

On May 14, McPherson's two corps advanced across Camp Creek and compelled Polk to re-form his line closer to Resaca while Federal artillery used the position gained to shell the railroad bridge. Hooker's corps was ordered to march to the left of the line to reinforce Howard's unsupported corps. Palmer's corps and Schofield's army launched attacks on the Confederate salient that gained ground before being checked by Hardee's infantry and Maj. Thomas Hotchkiss's artillery battalion. Late in the afternoon, Hood attacked Howard's exposed left flank, but Hooker's reinforcements arrived in time to contain Hood's assault. Satisfied with Hood's progress, Johnston ordered this attack resumed in the morning.

To the south, Brig. Gen. Thomas Sweeny's XVI Corps division sought to establish an Oostanaula River bridgehead at Lay's Ferry. Several units crossed the river in boats, with only cavalry opposing them, and in response, Walker's division marched west from Calhoun. Upon receiving reports that the Confederates were crossing upriver, and fearing he would be cut off, Sweeny recalled his force. Walker's division, in reaction to this news, returned to Calhoun.

On May 15, Palmer's corps and most of McPherson's two corps held their ground; Howard struck the salient angle where Hotchkiss's guns were posted; Hooker's XX Corps attacked the right of the Confederate line, and Sweeny retried laying the pontoon bridge.

Hooker's eleven-thirty A.M. attack began the heaviest fighting of the day. John Geary's division attacked down the wagon road, and seized the small earthen fort defended by Capt. Max Van Den Corput's four guns, but withering rifle fire drove the Yankees out of the fort and the cannon remained abandoned and mute between the lines until after dark. Hood's offensive was launched against the Union left in the afternoon, but word that Sweeny's bluecoats had crossed the Oostanaula led to its cancellation, though Stewart's division had engaged Hooker's corps.

Sweeny's lead units at Lay's Ferry crossed the river on an abandoned flatboat. Despite fire from Walker's division, Sweeny successfully reinforced his bridgehead and positioned his pontoons. Johnston, learning of Sweeny's success, decided to continue his retrograde movement. During the night, Geary's men retrieved Van Den Corput's abandoned guns, but it was the only prize of the day for the Federals. The Confederate army evacuated the Resaca defenses during the night, burned the railroad bridge, took up the pontoon bridge they had laid farther east, and their rear guard silently withdrew. Sweeny's bridgehead enabled Sherman to resume his southward advance on May 16.

Points of Interest

From the north there are two ways to enter Resaca. From Dalton on I-75 or US41, turn right at exit 134 and take the road to Carbondale. Seven miles from exit 134, turn left onto GA136. This route follows the last part of the Federal march through Snake Creek Gap. A more direct route is to follow US41 south to Resaca. Start the tour of the battlefield on GA136 west of town. Near the I-75 crossing, a rise overlooks Camp Creek. This was the part of the Confederate line held by Leonidas Polk on May 14. Looking to the west, you can see McPherson's positions, Snake Creek Gap, and what is left of Bald Hill, much of it obliterated by grading several years ago. The lines extended north, parallel to the interstate. Returning east on GA136, proceed north on US41 for 2.25 miles. Turn right onto Chitwood Road. The wooded ridge on the left was Hood's Confederate line. Houses have been built on the former earthworks. Each May, on a weekend close to the fight's anniversary, a reenactment of the Battle of Resaca is held near here. Returning to US41, proceed another 0.5 mile to the Whitfield County line. This is where Geary's attack began. The fort occupied by Van Den Corput's Cherokee Artillery was in the woods east of the highway. Georgia historical markers along US41 describe this advance and other details of the battle.

From the Whitfield County line, drive 1 mile south. The third Atlanta Campaign wayside, on the east side of the road, features a relief map of the battle. Take the paved road just north of the wayside to the east. It ends at the Resaca Confederate Cemetery where many of those killed in the Battle of Resaca are buried.

Proceed south on US41 through Resaca to Calhoun. Lay's Ferry is no longer accessible but by taking GA156 west to Grogan Road, then going north to Leg Road, you can view the area where the Federals put down the pontoon bridge to flank Johnston's position.

Rome Cross Roads

Johnston withdrew across gently rolling, open fields which afforded little natural protection. Starting his main force to Adairsville, he detached Hardee's corps to delay the Federal advance. On May 16, the XVI Corps crossing the Oostanaula River first at Lay's Ferry spearheaded the Army of the Tennessee. Part of the IV and XIV corps remained at Resaca to repair bridges destroyed by the Rebels. Sweeny's XVI Corps division advanced southward on the Sugar Valley–Adairsville Road, while Federal artillery was posted on the heights north of the intersection at Rome Cross Roads.

As the Federal vanguard approached the crossroads, two of Hardee's divisions emerged from the trees. The vicious surprise attack drove back the Federal column and Hardee held the crossroads until one A.M. on May 17, when he withdrew to rejoin the rest of Johnston's army. Johnston used this maneuver—moving his main force along all available roads while employing a rear guard to force the pursuing Federals to deploy and give battle—successfully several times in the campaign.

Points of Interest

From the intersection of US41 and GA53 in downtown Calhoun, proceed west on GA53 for 1.2 miles, across Oothkalooga Creek to a secondary road that leads off to the right. This is Rome Cross Roads. Hardee's corps started its attack from the hills east of GA53 and his artillery was posted there. Sweeny's division came down the secondary road on the right. Federal artillery was posted on the rise west of GA53. Proceed southwest on GA53 for 21 miles to the city of Rome.

Rome

Rome, an important manufacturing town at the confluence of the Oostanaula River and Etowah River (which becomes the Coosa), supplied the Confederate army with such items as cannon tubes, cartridge boxes, and haversacks. The town twice became the focus of Federal operations. Rome and the bridge over the Oostanaula was one of the major objectives of Col. Abel D. Streight's April–May 1863 raid through northern Alabama and northwest Georgia. A mounted detachment sent ahead by Streight turned back after finding Rome stoutly defended, only to be captured along with Streight's entire force, by Nathan Bedford Forrest's pursuing cavalry. On the afternoon of May 3, Forrest paraded the captured Federals through Rome's streets.

A year and a fortnight later, Rome was threatened by a much larger Federal column. On May 16, Brig. Gen. Jefferson C. Davis, under instruction from Sherman, marched his division down the west bank of the Oostanaula River, seeking a crossing to cut the railroad line between Rome and Kingston. When it was reported that no bridge exited east of Rome, Davis marched on the town.

In the meantime, several brigades of the Confederate Army of Mississippi, under Maj. Gen. Samuel G. French, arrived in Rome from Alabama. Two brigades of infantry and one of cavalry were posted north of the town, while artillery and home guards were posted on two hills overlooking the rivers, at Fort Jackson and Fort Stovall. Davis arrived on the afternoon of May 17 and deployed his troops across the wagon road, two miles to the north. On the morning of May 18, preparations were made for an assault. During the night, French received orders from Johnston to evacuate Rome and all Confederate units were transported east on the railroad. Two Rebel cottonclads escaped down the Coosa River, despite being shelled by the Federal artillery. The Union force marched into town and established a small garrison, and the Confederates lost important manufacturing facilities, most of which were burned when the Federals pulled out of the town on November 10, 1864.

Points of Interest

The people of Rome are proud of the small but important role their town played in the Civil War. The visitor center, which is at the site of Fort Jackson, where Confederate artillery was positioned to oppose the Federal advance, is just off GA53 as you enter town. Then proceed to the center of town and north on US27. At Hospital Drive a Georgia historical marker identifies DeSoto Hill, where Davis formed his line of battle. Davis left Rome for Dallas via the road which is now GA101. Follow US27 south to its junction with GA101 and US411. Turn left on US411 and drive to Myrtle Grove Cemetery. Fort Stovall was located here on Myrtle Hill. In Myrtle Grove Cemetery is the grave of John Wisdom, Georgia's Paul Revere (see **Day's Gap and Streight's Raid, Alabama**). If you did not visit the site of Streight's surrender to Forrest in Cedar Bluff, Alabama, it is 25 miles west of Rome on GA20/AL9. Otherwise, take the Rome bypass 3 miles north to GA293 and proceed to Kingston.

Cassville

As he led his army in retreat from Resaca, Gen. Joseph E. Johnston was uncomfortable with the terrain south of the Oostanaula River. The landscape was no longer mountainous; instead gently rolling hills were dotted with fields and streams. After rejecting a position at Calhoun, Johnston finally took position near the village of Cassville, where a ridge gave him his first opportunity to take the offensive against the larger Federal force. It was also there that the tension between Johnston and two of his three corps commanders, John Bell Hood and Leonidas Polk, particularly the former, escalated.

Sherman thought it unlikely that Johnston would dig his heels in on the gently rolling hills, but he looked to the Allatoona Hills, south of the Etowah River, as his next likely position. By marching Hardee's corps and the trains south to Kingston, Johnston had left Sherman evidence that most of his army was headed that way. Sherman divided his army into three parts for the march south. On the far right, McPherson's army marched via Barnsley Gardens. Thomas's Army of the Cumberland pursued the Rebel force on the road from Adairsville to Kingston, and Schofield, with Hooker following at a distance, headed to the southeast, toward Cassville and two of Johnston's three corps. Sherman was not completely deceived by Johnston's trap, and he cautioned his commanders to be prepared for a fight at any time.

As Schofield's army marched toward Cassville, Johnston placed Polk's corps across the road on Schofield's front, while Hood was dispatched to the north, to take him in the flank. Johnston personally accompanied Hood to the field and showed him the area from which he wanted him to launch his flank attack. But then the cavalry division of Brig. Gen. Edward M. McCook approached Hood's from the rear. To meet McCook's threat Hood was compelled to redeploy A. P. Stewart's division. McCook retreated, but Johnston's plan was ruined. Johnston abandoned his offensive and positioned his armies for a stand just east of Cassville, on a formidable ridge. Hardee's corps joined Polk's and Hood's corps in a continuous line running from north to south. Schofield, Hooker, and Howard drew up on high ground west of the valley, and Federal artillery was placed on knolls that enfiladed Polk's front.

But no attack was forthcoming. That night, Johnston, Hood, and Polk—joined later by Hardee—met, and Polk and Hood expressed concerns about their position. Johnston reluctantly ordered a withdrawal to the Allatoona Hills, and by dawn on May 20, the Army of Tennessee was gone.

Points of Interest

Kingston—To make a short side trip to Barnsley Gardens, once an extensive plantation, turn north from GA293 onto Barnsley Church Road. Just before GA106 (0.7 mile) is Barnsley Church, the only extant structure on the 1850s estate of Godfrey B. Barnsley, the former English consul in Savannah. Then continue north to GA106 and turn right. At 0.6 mile east of Rock Face Road is a GHC marker pointing out the ruins of other Barnsley Gardens structures. Confederate Col. R. G. Earle was killed in a cavalry skirmish and buried there. McPherson's Army of the Tennessee headquartered at Barnsley Gardens on May 18, on the way to Dallas. To complete this side trip, continue east on GA106 to Hall Station Road and turn right for Kingston.

During the Atlanta Campaign, Kingston was occupied by Federal troops from time to time. From May 19 to May 23, while his soldiers rested, Sherman occupied the Thomas V. B. Hargis House and developed his flanking strategy against Johnston. Sherman returned to Kingston in early November, after pursuing Hood's forces to Alabama, and made the final decisions there for his March to the Sea.

When Sherman ordered Kingston burned, the only house of worship to survive was the Kingston Methodist Church (Church Street). In the park across the street from the railroad, on May 12, 1865, Brig. Gen. William T. Wofford surrendered Georgia's last soldiers to Brig. Gen. Henry M. Judah. In the Confederate cemetery (Johnston Street), 250 Confederate soldiers, mostly unknowns, and 2 Union soldiers are buried. The Confederate Decoration Day, or Memorial Day, has been held in Kingston each April since 1865.

The Price House, on US411 southeast of Kingston, was the home of Col. Hawkins F. Price, a member of the Georgia Secession Convention, and in May 1864 it was a headquarters for Union generals Daniel Butterfield and Joseph Hooker. Continue east on US411 or GA293 to Cassville.

Cassville—Cassville is located just off US41/GA3, where it intersects GA293 (at this point called Spur 293-C). On US41 are GHC markers that describe the action on May 18, 1864, and the location of the local women's college, which was used briefly by Confederate skirmishers. Cross US41 on the Spur 293-C to the Cassville-White Road. It is just southwest of I-75 exit 127. Perhaps the best opportunity to defeat the Federal "army group" in detail was lost on May 18, when John Bell Hood did not follow through with the attack on Schofield's army, north of town. At the spur and Cassville-White Road is the fourth Atlanta Campaign wayside, which at the time of this writing is in disrepair.

Continuing east on the Cassville-White Road you will come to the three churches that, along with three houses used to keep the sick, survived the town's November 5, 1864, burning by Federal soldiers. The reason this prosperous, culturally rich town was torched remained a mystery for more than a century, until a Federal officer's diary revealed that in late 1864 the area hosted guerrilla activity and a Federal patrol had been found murdered nearby. Sherman ordered every structure within a five-mile radius of the murder scene razed, but the churches were spared. The Baptist church was later rebuilt, while the Methodist and Presbyterian churches are the original structures. Turn right on Church Street for the Methodist church. Another 0.4 mile past it is the old Cassville cemetery. The Confederate section contains the graves of more than 300 unknown soldiers, those who were cared for in eight large hospitals here. The grave of Georgia native Brig. Gen. William T. Wofford, of the Army of Northern Virginia, is also here. The second Confederate line Johnston established skirted the cemetery.

Returning to the Cassville-White Road via Chann-Facin Road, a monument and park mark the site of the old courthouse. The Federal line on May 18 was on the ridge northwest of here. On May 24, Wheeler's cavalry captured a Federal supply train here. At Cass Station, 0.1 mile from GA293, the depot and a store were standing at the time of the Great Locomotive Chase. GHC markers on the road between Cassville and Cass Station mark the May 19 Confederate line and Polk's headquarters.

Continue south on US41 or return to I-75 and continue south across the Etowah River to Allatoona.

Allatoona Pass

Johnston's strong natural fortress at Allatoona Pass was well known to William T. Sherman. As a junior officer in the early 1840s he'd remembered the terrain and mountainous railroad pass, though the Confederates had fortified it when they arrived on May 20. While he planned a flanking strategy, Sherman gave his soldiers a few days' rest.

Allatoona Pass played a significant part in two other northwest Georgia events: Gen. John Bell Hood's fall 1864 campaign to Alabama and Tennessee and the Great Locomotive Chase. When the General roared through, Andrews did not disable a small yard engine on a siding, the Yonah, which allowed William Fuller to later switch to it from his handcar. Andrews also failed to destroy or block the bridge over the Etowah River, just to the northwest, which would have forestalled his pursuers.

While in the Dallas–New Hope Church area Sherman sent Federal cavalry to occupy Allatoona Pass and ordered that strong fortifications be built there. A 1,000-man garrison was assigned to the post and during the latter stages of the Atlanta Campaign it became Sherman's main supply depot. The first objective of Hood's September 1864 offensive was to destroy Sherman's supply line, but Sherman learned of the campaign from spies and Southern newspapers.

Sherman dispatched a division of Howard's Army of the Tennessee to Rome, under the command of Brig. Gen. John M. Corse. Hood had units from A. P. Stewart's corps descend on the railroad near Big Shanty and Acworth, where they captured the Federal garrisons, cut telegraph lines, and tore up eight miles of track. Sherman ordered Corse to Allatoona Pass to reinforce the garrison. Hood thought that Allatoona was lightly protected and sent a single division, under the command of Maj. Gen. Samuel G. French, with instructions to "fill in" the railroad cut and destroy the railroad bridge over the Etowah River.

Still, the garrison—with just over 2,000 men—was outnumbered, but the Federals had two fortifications—the Star Fort and the Eastern Redoubt—on the high ground above the Federal depot, and trenches, rifle pits, and another fortified position, Rowett's Redoubt, farther down grade. Via signal flags Sherman told the Allatoona garrison commander, and later Corse, to hold out until reinforcements arrived. Sherman's messages were later paraphrased by war correspondents as "Hold the fort, I am coming," and the slogan was soon turned into a revival hymn by Phillip P. Bliss. Corse's force arrived at one A.M. on October 5, and there was little time for sleep. Unaware that the garrison had been reinforced, French marched his force through the night, though the dark wooded terrain precluded final deployment until daylight. With dawn came an artillery duel between French's massed battery south of the pass and the Federal guns in the two forts.

Under a truce flag French issued a surrender demand, but received no reply. At ten-twenty A.M., while one brigade of his division was getting

This photograph by George Barnard, who accompanied William T. Sherman's "army group" during its advance to Atlanta, looks north toward Allatoona Pass. Federal warehouses sit to the right of the tracks; a depot and the Clayton House are to the left. The Star Fort was located on the bluff to the left of the pass and the eastern redoubt was to the right of the pass.

into position to the north, he launched two brigades from the west. The Rebel attack first fell on the Union soldiers in Rowett's Redoubt, and fierce hand-to-hand fighting did not end until the Rebels overran the earthwork. A few survivors made it into the Star Fort. The Eastern Redoubt then came under a concerted attack from Brig. Gen. Claudius Sears's Mississippi brigade, but their strong position frustrated the Confederate advance. Cross-fire from artillery and infantry pinned the Yankees in the fortification until Corse ordered it evacuated.

Efforts then focused on the Star Fort, into which nearly the entire Federal force crowded. Concentrated small arms fire and canister kept French's men at bay, and three Confederate assaults were repulsed. Casualties mounted and Corse was wounded in the face. By early afternoon the fighting had settled into fitful skirmishing, and French received word from his cavalry that Federal reinforcements were arriving. With difficulty, French decided to withdraw, and by one-thirty P.M. the exhausted Southern forces began their march to New Hope Church. Along the way they captured the Federal blockhouse that guarded the railroad at Allatoona Creek, but failed to destroy the Federal stores in warehouses at Allatoona Pass.

With 1,603 killed, wounded, and captured out of a total 5,301 engaged on both sides, the Battle of Allatoona Pass resulted in the highest percentage of casualties of any battle in the war except the Battle of Gettysburg. The Confederates gained nothing from the action and though the Federals avoided the loss of the important rail depot and the Etowah bridge, other posts on the Western & Atlantic line fell to Hood's raids. On October 6, French's command joined the Confederate army near New Hope Church, and Hood marched north to Resaca with Sherman on his heels.

Points of Interest

There are three sites to visit near the large Allatoona Lake Recreational Area, including Allatoona Pass. Leave I-75 at exit 123 and take the access road 0.5 mile west to US41, then turn north across the Etowah River bridge. Just east of the highway you can see the old piers of the Etowah River railroad bridge. An exit north of the present bridge will lead you to River Road, where you can park for a closer look. When Johnston evacuated Allatoona Pass, the Confederates burned this bridge. The Federals later rebuilt it, but Sherman had it dismantled before his March to the Sea. A half mile north of the river is an old section of track on the Western & Atlantic line.

If you continue north on the River Road for 2.4 miles, you will come to Cooper's Furnace Historic Site, which has a picnic area and a playground. Mark Anthony Cooper's Furnace was once the Etowah Iron Works, which employed 600 people and milled iron and supplied other goods—including flour—for the Confederacy. Schofield's corps, pursuing Johnston from Cassville, skirmished with the Rebels there on May 21, 1864. The Federals then destroyed the ironworks, whose furnace is there in the park.

To get to Allatoona Pass, take I-75 south from exit 123 to exit 122, Emerson-Allatoona Road and drive east for 1.5 miles. Across the road from the two-story Clayton-Mooney House is an Army Corps of Engineers parking lot. The railroad cut it to the north of the lot. Trail head markers indicate walking tours to the eastern redoubt, trench lines, and, on a more rugged trail, the Star Fort. For more information on Allatoona sites contact the Etowah Valley Historical Society, P.O. Box 1886, Cartersville, GA 30120; 770-606-8862. 👫 ❷ P

The Clayton-Mooney House, known as the Clayton House during the battle, was used as a hospital after the battle. Bloodstains still can be seen on the upstairs floors. In the yard of the house is a small memorial to the Confederate soldiers killed in the battle. To arrange a tour of the house, contact Diane Mooney, 620 Old Allatoona Road S.E., Cartersville, GA 30121.

Just past the village of Allatoona, where the present railroad crosses the highway, a small iron-fenced plot contains the grave of an unidentified Confederate soldier killed in the Battle of Allatoona. The gravesite was moved from another location so that railroad crews could maintain it. Return to I-75, turn left on US41 just beyond the interstate, and drive south on US41 to GA92, then continue south to the Pickett's Mill–New Hope–Dallas area.

READING— *the Great Locomotive Chase: Cassville and Kingston; Hood's 1864 Tennessee Campaign: Resaca; Atlanta Campaign: New Hope Church*

New Hope Church

To bypass the Allatoona Hills, General Sherman decided to flank to the right. His objective was Dallas, a small crossroads county seat about fifteen miles south of Allatoona and the same distance west of Marietta, his next objective. Sherman ordered twenty days' rations for his troops, but predicted they would be at the Chattahoochee River in a few days. He was wrong. Determined Confederates kept him from the river for more than a month.

A photograph of portions of the Confederate defense line at New Hope Church taken shortly after the battle. The entrenched Confederates held off the attack of Maj. Gen. Joseph Hooker's XX Corps on May 25, 1864.

Anticipating Sherman's flanking strategy, Johnston had Wheeler's cavalry scout the area west of the railroad. The Federal march began on May 23, and as Sherman's three armies headed toward Dallas, Johnston had three of his corps in motion to checkmate the move. When Thomas's Army of the Cumberland, with Hooker's XX Corps in the lead, crossed Pumpkinvine Creek, Confederate cavalry pickets fired on the vanguard. Brig. Gen. John Geary's division drove back the cavalry attempting to burn the bridge, but at New Hope Church they found Hood's corps defending the crossroads.

For the Federals, who were unable to fully deploy in the tangled underbrush, the fighting at New Hope Church was difficult. Hood's corps had already cut logs for breastworks and were lightly entrenched. Geary then had his men stop their advance and prepare for battle. At four P.M., with a thunderstorm threatening, the Federals resumed their offensive. Federal casualties quickly mounted and Hooker stopped the assault, but while he waited for help, torrential rain and growing darkness delayed Howard's corps. There were nearly 1,600 Federal casualties, and the soaked ground had added to the distress of the wounded. The next day the two opposing armies skirmished, but no assaults were attempted.

Pickett's Mill

On May 27, Sherman decided to outflank Johnston's New Hope–Dallas line. In an attempt to turn the line, O. O. Howard led two Army of the Cumberland divisions and a brigade from Schofield's XXIII Corps to the extreme left of the Union line, but Johnston shifted Hood's corps farther right, and with Polk in the center and Hardee covering the Rebel left, he sent Cleburne's elite division to the extreme right of the Rebel infantry line at Pickett's Mill. Cutting through the underbrush with difficulty, Howard's troops arrived near Pickett's Mill in the afternoon. In a thickly wooded area between two creeks, three brigades under Confederate generals Mark P. Lowrey, Daniel Govan, and Hiram Granbury set up a defensive line. One brigade was kept in reserve and John H. Kelly's cavalry covered Cleburne's flank.

At four-thirty P.M., Howard launched an attack with two divisions. Brig. Gen. William B. Hazen's brigade was in the vanguard. Hazen's men drove in the pickets, but as they mounted the slope on the far side of a deep ravine they were fired upon by artillery and Granbury's Texans. The Federal advance melted. Trying to get out of the ravine, Union soldiers turned east into a cornfield, but they were met there by Lowrey's brigade reinforced by one of Govan's Arkansas regiments. Other Federal units engaged, but the assault did not break Cleburne's defensive line.

At ten P.M., the Federal attacks winding down, Cleburne ordered his troops to clear the line. The Rebels advanced through the pitch-black wilderness, bayonets fixed and then, with a Texan-Indian yell, they charged. In the end, 232 Yankees were captured at Pickett's Mill, with 1,732 casualties—1,284 more than Confederate casualties. Cleburne later wrote, "The enemy advanced in numerous and constantly reinforced lines. His men displayed a courage worthy of an honorable cause, pressing in steady throngs within a few paces of our men. Granbury's men . . . were awaiting them, and throughout awaited them with calm determination, and as they appeared upon the slope, slaughtered them with deliberate aim."

Dallas

After the debacle at Pickett's Mill, Sherman did not again attempt to break the Confederate line. He sent the cavalry of George Stoneman and Kenner Garrard ahead to seize and hold Allatoona Pass while he prepared his forces to return east, back to the railroad line. Johnston also anticipated this move, but did not immediately withdraw from Dallas in case he was wrong. On May 28, acting on reconnaissance, he ordered an assault against the Federal line. Brig. Gen. William Bate planned an enveloping maneuver, sending cavalry under Brig. Gen. William H. "Red" Jackson to turn the Federal flank while infantry assaulted the Yankee entrenchments.

At three forty-five in the afternoon, Frank Armstrong's brigade of Jackson's cavalry surged into and across the no-man's land separating the two lines. The troopers met a strongly entrenched and determined division of the XV Corps some of whose soldiers were armed with repeating rifles. Bate's infantry awaited a signal from the cavalry to advance, but when the commander of the Orphan Brigade thought he heard the signal, he sent his men forward prematurely. The Florida brigade joined in the attack, which met stout resistance, and the Orphan Brigade sustained more than 50-percent casualties.

Johnston thought Hood's plan to hold the Federals in position with a flank attack near Pickett's Mill had promise, but Hood canceled the action—concerned the enemy was stronger than reported—and the general's frustration mounted. Johnston launched night attacks May 29–31, but Sherman disengaged his forces and moved them northeast toward the railroad. By June 4, Johnston was compelled to withdraw to the east,

*A portion of the Confederate fortifications at New Hope Church
as they appear today. The battlefield here is largely developed;
however, this section of trenches, a small
Confederate cemetery, and memorial remain.*

where he established a new defensive line a dozen miles southeast of Allatoona Pass and anchored on Lost, Pine, and Brushy mountains.

Points of Interest

Although it requires some backtracking it is worthwhile exploring the three actions in chronological order. They are easily covered in less than a day, even if you linger at the wonderfully rustic and virtually intact Pickett's Mill State Historic Site. From Allatoona, return to US41 and head south until you reach GA92. When it intersects with GA381, bear right and proceed southwest on GA381, which generally follows the New Hope–Dallas line of entrenchments, to New Hope Church.

New Hope Church—The area is now a rural village with a few traces of the long lines of entrenchments both armies threw up. Directly south of the crossroads, where GA381 intersects with GA120C, is a brick church, which was built on the site of the log structure that gave New Hope Church its name. A small plot of land behind the church contains the last of the five former NPS waysides. A GHC marker points out Lost Mountain. Across GA120C is a section of the Confederate earthworks, today maintained by the state, from which the Rebels resisted the Army of the Cumberland's assault on May 25. A monument with a Confederate flag and the grave of Lt. Col. John Herrod, Mississippi infantry, can be found there. A monument in front of the New Hope Baptist Church (1886) is dedicated to all the soldiers who fought in the battle.

Pickett's Mill—Take GA381 north and turn right (southeast) onto Mount Tabor Church Road to get to Pickett's Mill State Historic Site, one of the nation's best-preserved Civil War battlefields. Check in at the visitor center and view the exhibits, including a seventeen-minute film and an interactive game that simulates the battle.

Outside, a two-mile trail will take you to all the battle's major locations, where many of the earthworks are visible. For those who do not wish to hike around the battlefield, an observation platform behind the visitor center allows for viewing Pat Cleburne's line. The site is open from 9:00 A.M. to 5:00 P.M. Tuesday to Saturday, and from 12:00 noon to 5:00 P.M. Sunday. It is also open on all holidays except Thanksgiving and Christmas Day.

These entrenchments thrown up by Maj. Gen. Patrick Cleburne's division are a portion of the extensive earthworks extant at Pickett's Mill State Historic Site, and are among the best in the nation. The rustic site vividly tells the story of the battle fought here.

Except for some trails the park is handicap accessible. Fishing, hunting, and, of course, relic collecting are not allowed. PICKETT'S MILL STATE HISTORIC SITE, 2640 Mount Tabor Road, Dallas, GA 30132; 770-443-7850.

Dallas—From Pickett's Mill, return to GA381 and drive southwest to Dallas. There is little left to indicate the bloody repulse of Bate's division here on May 28. There are two GHC markers at the intersection of GA381 and GA6 (Memorial and Merchant roads). Another marker on GA Business 6 south of town describes the role of the Orphan Brigade. There is a marker on GA61 south of Dallas and another 2 miles farther south, indicating battle positions. Preservation efforts are now under way to save the remains of some earthworks that are currently inaccessible.

From Dallas, take US278/GA6 southeast for 4 miles to its intersection with GA120. Turn left and proceed to GA92. Turn left again and travel north. You will pass several more GHC markers that track the routes of the two armies to and from the Dallas area and locate the headquarters of Hardee, Hood, and Johnston. None of the houses used as headquarters remains. At Cross Roads Church, 1 mile west of Burnt Hickory on the Dallas-Acworth Road, a marker identifies the May 24–25 marches of Hardee and Hood, the June 2 march of the XXIII Army Corps, and the June 5 march of the XV and XVI Army corps. Turn right on the Dallas-Acworth Road and continue east to US41, then south on US41 to Stilesboro Road to begin your tour of the Lost-Pine-Brushy mountain line.

Lost-Pine-Brushy Mountain Line

Through most of June heavy rains turned Georgia red clay into a quagmire. The Federal march back to the Western & Atlantic was arduous, and Sherman established his headquarters at Acworth and Big Shanty (see **Big Shanty**). On June 11, he sent his cavalry south to locate Johnston's army, which they found entrenched along a ten-mile front stretching from Brushy Mountain, past Pine Mountain, to Lost Mountain. Hood's corps, screened by Wheeler's cavalry, held the northern (right) flank, Polk's corps the middle, and Hardee's corps extended southward, to where Red Jackson's cavalry maintained a thin line on Lost Mountain.

Bate's division was positioned forward of the rest of the line on Pine Mountain. On the morning of June 14, Johnston, Polk, and Hardee surveyed the threats to the position. The Federals had established their line north and west of Johnston's, and the 5th Indiana Battery, positioned less than a mile away, began to fire. The first shell sent the senior officers for cover, but the second hit Polk in the chest, killing him instantly. Polk, Missionary Bishop of the Southwest, was universally admired in the South as a spiritual and moral leader. Later that day, three Federal divisions closed on Pine Mountain and Bate's division was withdrawn. Federal soldiers found a note there, pinned to the ground with a broken ramrod: "You damned Yankee sons of bitches has killed our old Gen. Polk."

Federal assaults continued on June 15. Thomas advanced in the center with Schofield on his right, while Stoneman's cavalry took on the Rebel troops guarding Lost Mountain. Two of Hooker's divisions attacked Cleburne's men at Gilgal Church, southwest of Pine Mountain, but were repulsed. The next day, Brig. Gen. Milo Hascall's division of Schofield's corps forced the Rebel cavalry from Lost Mountain. Johnston folded his left flank back to Mud Creek. The salient of the Confederate line was at the Latimer House, held by Maj. Gen. Samuel G. French's division. On June 17, three Federal divisions attacked Cleburne's new position on Mud Creek. The following day, three divisions of the Army of the Cumberland attacked French and exposed his division to enfilading fire. That night, June 18, Johnston moved his army south so they could prepare positions on the Kennesaw Mountain Line.

Points of Interest

From US41, take Stilesboro Road south to Beaumont Drive. Turn right and climb the steep hill 1.25 miles to the crest of Pine Mountain. A GHC marker describes the salient that was here. The marble monument that marks the spot where General Polk died, is on a residential property. Return to Stilesboro Road and turn right, then proceed 2 miles to New Salem Road. Turn right again and proceed 0.8 mile to Kirk Lane. Near this intersection, on June 18, the salient angle of Loring's corps on Latimer's Farm was attacked by Absalom Baird's division of the Federal XIV Corps.

Continue west on New Salem Road to Burnt Hickory Road and turn right. At 3 miles you will come to Due West Road (CAUTION: There are several roads in this area with the words "Due West" in the name; this one is the Old Sandtown Road). Turn right and in a few hundred yards you will come to Kennesaw–Due West Road. Turn right and several hundred yards ahead on the north side of the road, pull off the highway into the gravel lot. Gilgal Church is gone and a small schoolhouse is on its site. In front of the building is a mock up of a Civil War entrenchment of the type constructed during the Atlanta Campaign. A monument on the slight rise to the left of the parking lot describes the fight.

From Gilgal Church, return to the intersection and turn left (south) on Acworth–Due West Road. Follow it to the Dallas Road (GA120) and turn left (east). In a short distance you will come to a GHC marker describing the action on June 17–18 at Mud Creek. Continue east on the Dallas Road and in the distance you get a good view of the twin peaks of Kennesaw. Turn left (north) on Mount Calvary Road, go to Burnt Hickory Road, and turn right. On the north side of the highway, just before entering the Kennesaw National Battlefield Park, is the Hardage House, which was Leonidas Polk's headquarters, June 10–14. The bishop-general conducted church services here just before his death. Continue east on Burnt Hickory Road to Kennesaw National Battlefield Park, turning north on Old Mountain Road to the visitor center.

Kennesaw Mountain and Kolb's Farm

The twin peaks, Big and Little Kennesaw mountain, are area landmarks, as they were during the Civil War. Big Kennesaw is the highest peak in a continuous ridge that also includes Little Kennesaw, Pigeon Hill, and Cheatham Hill. After the Confederates moved their artillery pieces to the crests of these hills, by hand and tow ropes, Johnston's guns commanded the railroad and a level area separating Kennesaw from Pine and Lost mountains. Hood occupied the northern slopes, nearest the railroad and beyond; Polk's former corps, now under Maj. Gen. William W. Loring, had the center; and Hardee's corps occupied the southern flank.

On June 19, the Federals' marched to within artillery range of the Kennesaw line, establishing their line in much the same fashion as at Brushy, Pine, and Lost mountains. Sherman wanted to flank the Rebels' strong position, and he ordered the XX and XXIII corps to march south around the Confederate left flank and secure the road to Marietta. From there, Sherman thought, an enfilading fire could roll up Johnston's army. Johnston saw opportunity as well. On the night of June 21, he ordered Hood to block the Powder Springs Road to Marietta. When the Federals arrived there on June 22, they found Hood's determined force in their front. With heavy artillery support they formed a defensive line on a brushy, wooded ridge overlooking fields and ravines. Along the road was the farm and house of the widow of Valentine Kolb, from which the battle derived its name.

Late in the day, without authority, Hood launched a poorly planned attack on the Federals with two of his three divisions. After struggling through dense underbrush to reach the Federal works, the Confederates suffered casualties and failed to take them. This resulted in negative reports for the senior officers involved. Sherman reprimanded Hooker for overestimating the enemy and criticizing his brother officers, which had caused him to entrench his corps. Johnston admonished Hood for attacking when a defensive stance was mandated.

On June 25, for the first time in the campaign, Sherman planned an all-out frontal assault. Whether he did this because the rains precluded him from continuing the rapid flanking moves that had thus far proven so successful; or he wanted to avoid a stalemate, which might free Johnston's armies to help Lee in Virginia; or because he was mindful of Northern newspaper editors, who were questioning whether he was a "fighting general," Sherman took on what was one of Johnston's most sturdy defensive positions. Whatever his final reasons, he ordered the assault for eight A.M. on June 27, 1864.

From left to right, all parts of the line would participate. A diversionary attack was ordered on the north slope of Kennesaw Mountain, to be carried out by the XVII Corps of the Army of the Tennessee and Sweeny's XVI Corps division. Logan's XV Corps was ordered to move against Little Kennesaw Mountain and Pigeon Hill, while to the south the Army of the Cumberland would assail the ridge held by Cheatham's and Cleburne's divisions. Meanwhile, on the extreme Federal right, Hooker's and Schofield's armies were to hold Hood's corps in place and probe his flank.

Following a one-hour cannonade by more than 200 Federal guns, the June 27 attack commenced on schedule. Shortly before nine A.M. the blue regiments marched east, first in the relative security of wooded terrain, but then in the open fields that provided a clear view of the rocky hills. Rebels' pickets scattered before them. Confederate General French later wrote of what he saw: "A bird's-eye view of one of the most magnificent sights ever allotted to man, to look down upon a hundred and fifty thousand men arrayed in the strife of battle below. 'Twere worth ten years of peaceful life, one glance at their array!'"

Three brigades of Logan's corps tried to ascend the slopes of Little Kennesaw and Pigeon Hill against French's command, only to falter under the return fire, described by French as "a roar as constant as Niagara and as sharp as the crash of thunder with lightning in the eye." Although they came as close as thirty feet to the main Rebel line, the advance halted and the Federals found what cover they could. Only slightly more successful was the attack on Cheatham's division by an even larger force of the Army of the Cumberland—two divisions under Brig. Gen. Jefferson C. Davis and Brig. Gen. John Newton. In the massed infantry assault up "Cheatham Hill," toward a salient known after the battle as the "Dead Angle," row after row of the attackers breasted the defensive fire from the hill's crest. But Cheatham received help from Cleburne's nearby division and the tide turned. After two hours, Thomas ordered those who were able to withdraw, with the rest of the survivors to come in once darkness provided cover.

McPherson and Thomas had been stopped cold, but against Hood, Schofield exploited his toehold south of Olley's Creek to secure ground overlooking the Nickajack Creek Valley. In the afternoon, when Sherman wired Thomas in hopes that the largest of his armies could continue the assault, the "Rock of Chickamauga" replied, "We have already lost heavily today without gaining any material advantage. One or two more such assaults would use up this army." Assessing the assault at Kennesaw later, corps commander O. O. Howard concluded, "We realized now, as never before, the futility of direct assault upon entrenched lines already well prepared and well manned."

The focus turned to the horrendous Federal casualties. Underbrush ignited on one part of the field and a Confederate colonel arranged a temporary truce, calling out to the Yankees, "Come and remove your wounded; they are burning to death; we won't fire a gun till you get them away. Be quick!" Federal casualties for the day were 3,000. Confederate casualties were 552.

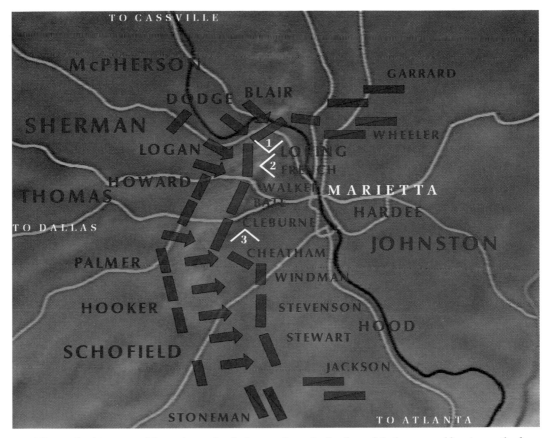

The Battle of Kennesaw Mountain was fought in rugged terrain that formed the last natural barrier north of the Chattahoochee River. After holding off an ill-planned offensive by Lt. Gen. John B. Hood at Kolb's Farm, and thinking Gen. Joseph E. Johnston may have weakened his center to bolster his flanks, Maj. Gen. William T. Sherman launched an attack on the Confederate center on June 27, 1864. Three corps of the Army of the Cumberland assaulted the center, supported by attacks on both flanks. The Army of the Tennessee XVII Corps demonstrated against Big Kennesaw Mountain (1), the XVI Corps attacked Little Kennesaw Mountain (top of 2), while the XV Corps launched a concerted attack against Pigeon Hill (bottom of 2). The hill in the center of the line—actually a ridge—since the battle has been known as Cheatham Hill (3) for one of the Rebel division commanders holding it. The two Army of the Cumberland corps attacking there were soundly beaten; however, Maj. Gen. John Schofield's XXIII Corps, in demonstrating on the right, opened an opportunity for Sherman to turn his opponent's flank and march closer to Atlanta.

Schofield's corps in the following days inched ahead to gain the Sandtown Road west of Smyrna, and Sherman renewed his flanking strategy. On June 30 a truce was called to allow for the burial of the dead, which was done without regard to rank, and sometimes identification. Sherman had McPherson pass behind the Army of the Cumberland and join Schofield. On the morning of July 3, pickets advanced to the crests of the Kennesaw peaks. The Rebels had quietly left the night before. By noon, Sherman was in Marietta. He assumed Johnston had taken his command beyond the Chattahoochee River, but he soon discovered two more obstacles to a river bridgehead.

Points of Interest

Kennesaw Mountain National Battlefield Park—Though it may seem out of the way, travel north from Burnt Hickory Road on Old Mountain Road to Stilesboro Road. Turn right and shortly you will see the visitor center entrance at the foot of Big Kennesaw Mountain. The center has exhibits, an audiovisual program, rest rooms, and a bookstore. There are park rangers and guides to answer any questions. The Mountain Road, off the parking lot, features a monument to Georgia soldiers and at its crest is a scenic view of Marietta and beyond. Two long trails, excellent for hardy bicyclists and hikers, completely traverse the park from north to south.

These entrenchments are a part of the line drawn on what is now known as Cheatham Hill on the Kennesaw Mountain National Battlefield. Here, Confederates from the divisions of Maj. Gens. Benjamin F. Cheatham and Patrick R. Cleburne held off the determined uphill charge of Federal soldiers from the Army of the Cumberland's IV and XIV corps.

To begin your driving tour, retrace your route back to Dallas Road and turn left. Travel a short way east to John Ward Road and turn right. Cheatham Hill Road branches to the left. Follow it south to Powder Springs Road and park in the lot at Kolb's Farm. NPS and GHC markers describe the Battle of Kolb's Farm and the 1836 Kolb House, which has been restored. The Federal line was on the ridge to the west.

Drive north on Cheatham Hill Road to the John Ward Road. GHC markers identify the different Federal positions before the June 27 attack. Continue north to the Dallas

Road and turn right. You will soon come to the road leading to Cheatham Hill. Drive to the parking area. At Cheatham Hill there are cannon emplacements, Confederate and Federal earthworks, and a large monument to Illinois soldiers, who made up much of "Fighting Dan" McCook's brigade of Jefferson Davis's division. Four hundred and eight Illinois soldiers died in the June 27 assault. There are also the remains of a tunnel begun by Federal soldiers, though it was left unfinished when the position was abandoned. Denuded of brush and trees to represent an 1864 cornfield, the large grassy field gives an idea of the grade and distance the Federals had to traverse in their assault on the hill.

From Cheatham Hill, continue east on Dallas Road, then turn west on Burnt Hickory Road. When you reach Old Mountain Road, park in the designated area. There are numerous markers indicating the positions of various divisions and corps. A short steep trail north of Burnt Hickory Road takes you to the Confederate works and boulder-studded ridge occupied by Frank Cockrell's Missouri brigade. To climb Little Kennesaw, continue on the trail north.

Continue east on Burnt Hickory Road. When it merges with Dallas Road in Marietta it becomes Whitlock Avenue. Kennesaw Mountain National Battlefield Park is open every day; the visitor center is open from 9:00 A.M. to 5:00 P.M.; the trails and roads during daylight hours. Picnicking is permitted in designated areas and pets are permitted if leashed. KENNESAW MOUNTAIN NATIONAL BATTLEFIELD PARK, 900 Kennesaw Mountain Drive, Kennesaw, GA 30144; 770-427-4686.   🚲 🎫 ♿ 🚶 ❓ 🏛 P 🪑 🚻

DRIVING TOUR—*Proceed to Marietta*
READING—*Atlanta Area*

Marietta

In the 1860s Marietta, Georgia, was a major stop on the Western & Atlantic Railroad. During the Civil War it did not see any combat action and served as a supply and command center, playing a significant role in a number of events, from Andrews' Raid to Sherman's Atlanta Campaign.

On April 11, 1862, Andrews' Federal Raiders met in the evening at Kennesaw House, the town's leading hotel, and the next morning they boarded the train that took them to Big Shanty and the General. On July 3, 1864, as Thomas's Army of the Cumberland pursued the Confederate Army of Tennessee, Sherman and his staff established temporary headquarters at Kennesaw House. The Federals made Marietta one of their supply depots.

Kennesaw House, the historic old hotel that played a part in the "Great Locomotive Chase" and was occupied at various times by other Civil War personalities, is now an elegant dining establishment serving old-fashioned Southern dishes such as might have been enjoyed by the guests in the 1860s. It is located in the middle of a restored district of Marietta around the old railroad depot.

Yankee repair gangs made quick work of Rebel railroad destruction and Federal supply trains soon chuffed into Marietta in support of Sherman's advance to the Chattahoochee.

Points of Interest

From Kennesaw Mountain National Battlefield Park, drive east on Burnt Hickory Road, which in Marietta becomes Whitlock Avenue. Just before the center of the city, you will cross modern railroad tracks. Park in the lot, north of Whitlock and west of the tracks, at the Marietta Welcome Center, which has information on historical walking and driving tours. This is where Andrews and his raiders boarded the train that took them to Big Shanty. Directly across the tracks is Kennesaw House, built in 1850 as a summer resort hotel. The hotel burned shortly after the war but was rebuilt. It was used by Southern wounded and refugees until July 1864, when Sherman made Kennesaw House a headquarters on July 3. Today it is a family restaurant with a lovely Victorian ambiance. A short walk to the east takes you to the center of Marietta. The town square contains several monuments commemorating the development of the railroad.

Driving again, from the depot parking lot, you may want to take Kennesaw Avenue north. Several antebellum houses on Kennesaw Street have Civil War significance. The

Archibald Howell House at 303 Kennesaw Avenue was the headquarters of Federal Brig. Gen. Henry M. Judah during the occupation period. Fair Oaks at 505 Kennesaw Avenue was Gen. Joseph E. Johnston's headquarters during the Kennesaw Mountain phase of the Atlanta Campaign. Oakton at 581 Kennesaw Avenue was the headquarters of Confederate General Loring during the same period. Just off Kennesaw Avenue, on Church Street, is the First Presbyterian Church, built in 1854 and used as a Federal hospital.

Return to the center of Marietta and drive south on Powder Springs Road. At West Atlanta Street is the Confederate cemetery, established in 1863. The graves of 3,000 soldiers are marked by marble slabs. There is also a bronze cannon, which accompanied cadets from the Georgia Military Institute when they were called into action during Sherman's March to the Sea. South of the cemetery, on Powder Springs Road, is the site of the Georgia Military Institute, which served as a large Southern hospital until Marietta fell into Federal hands. A country club is there now. The Bostwick-Fraser House at 325 Atlanta Street was also a Federal hospital.

Return north to GA120 and go east on Washington Street, which turns into Roswell Road. You will soon come to the entrance to Marietta National Cemetery, which is the final resting place for 10,300 Federal soldiers killed or who died in the Atlanta Campaign. Forty-four hundred Federal soldiers were killed in the Georgia actions; 23,000 were wounded and 4,500 were reported captured or missing. Today, the cemetery is operated by the Veterans Administration. From the national cemetery, take Fairground Street south to South Cobb Drive. The Planters restaurant on Pearl Street is on the site of the Glover House, the scene of skirmishing on July 3. Continue on South Cobb Drive to Concord Road in Smyrna.

READING—*the Great Locomotive Chase*: *Kennesaw (Big Shanty)*

ATLANTA AREA

Smyrna Line–Ruff's Mill

When Johnston pulled back from his Kennesaw line, he took up a line protecting the railroad between Rottenwood and Nickajack creeks near Smyrna Camp Ground. The southern flank of this line was held by the Georgia militia. These 3,000 soldiers, mostly those too young or old to join the regular ranks, were on conditional loan from Georgia's recalcitrant governor Joseph Brown and under the command of Maj. Gen. Gustavus W. Smith. Although the militia, which Brown had the option of recalling at any time, had joined Johnston's army on June 1, it did not see any significant action until Smyrna. Smith was a once highly regarded officer who had floundered upon assuming command of the Southern armies opposing Maj. Gen. George B. McClellan after Johnston was wounded at the Battle of Seven Pines on May 31, 1862 (see **Richmond, Virginia**). Not being able to handle the pressure of that command, he gave way to Robert E. Lee. In small actions at Smyrna, however, Smith and his inexperienced troops proved their worth.

Anxious to catch Johnston on the north side of the Chattahoochee, Sherman pushed his army commanders into action on July 4. The Smyrna line was not a strong line— Johnston meant only to delay Sherman there to allow his wagons time to cross the Chattahoochee—but once again the Federals were repulsed in attacks on the dug-in Rebels. A brigade from Howard's corps attacked near the railroad but was repulsed by troops of Pat Cleburne's division in what was known as the Battle of Smyrna.

At Nickajack Creek, soldiers from Dodge's XVI Corps, Army of the Tennessee, at six P.M. assaulted the salient angle where Hood's corps joined Hardee's at Ruff's Mill. Carter Stevenson's gray-clad skirmishers were driven back to the main line, but the assault could not penetrate it, despite heavy Federal casualties. However, Maj. Gen. Francis Blair's XVII Corps penetrated far to the south, placing it between the Chattahoochee and the Confederate main line, so in the early-morning hours of July 5, Johnston abandoned the Smyrna line.

Johnston's River Line

Army of Tennessee chief of artillery Francis Asbury Shoup began in mid-June to discuss with Johnston establishing a unique aboveground line of fortifications on the near bank of the Chattahoochee River for the protection of the railroad and wagon road bridges to Atlanta. Johnston ordered a special locomotive to take Shoup to Atlanta to arrange for the construction of what later became known as Johnston's River Line. Slaves from nearby plantations were organized into work gangs and under Shoup's direction a four-mile crescent-shaped line of fortifications was constructed. The key provision was a diamond-shaped compressed earth fortification, walled on the interior and exterior with horizontal logs. Connecting these infantry enclosures were traverses, stockades of vertical logs sharpened to a point, which were further intersected by artillery redoubts. The system allowed for the artillery and infantry enclosures, nicknamed "Shoupades," to be mutually supporting in establishing a cross-fire, as well as a line of fire to the front.

Upon arriving at the line on July 5, many Confederate soldiers were confused by the strange-looking line of fortifications. Some even started dismantling them or digging trenches without orders. Some officers, John Bell Hood included, urged Johnston to bypass the line and cross the Chattahoochee River. Others, like Pat Cleburne, realized the advantages of the design and he offered impromptu instructions on how to defend them to some of his men. The Shoupades and the rest of the line were occupied by the Army of Tennessee on July 5.

The dim view of the system of fortifications expressed by some Confederates was not shared by Johnston's chief adversary. Sherman later wrote about the River Line, "I confess I had not learned beforehand of the existence of this strong place . . . which proved one of the strongest pieces of field fortifications I ever saw." Federal brigades began taking up positions opposite the River Line on July 5, driving cavalry and the Georgia militia before them. As they approached the River Line, four corps, Blair's, Logan's, Hooker's, and Palmer's, drew up in front of the fortifications. Howard's corps probed the river above the line while to the south Dodge's corps also advanced to the river. At Vining's Station, units of Absalom Baird's division pursued a Confederate wagon train attempting to cross the Chattahoochee at Pace's Ferry. The pursuit was taken up by William Hazen's brigade of Howard's corps, and though the wagons got across the river, the Rebel cavalry was unable to cut the moorings of the pontoon bridge from the south bank. It was later captured and used by the Federals.

Close on the heels of Baird's division were Generals Sherman and Thomas. On Vining's Hill, overlooking the Chattahoochee River, Sherman and Thomas had their first view of the spires of Atlanta, eight miles away.

With the city in sight, in his mind Sherman cemented his intention, undoubtedly considered after the defeat at Kennesaw, of making the capture of Atlanta, rather than the destruction of Johnston's army, his primary objective. He studied the alternatives available to him. Quickly, he dispatched his cavalry on far-reaching reconnaissance to the north and south. Kenner Garrard was sent north; his objective was Roswell, a manufacturing town and river crossing ten miles upstream (see **Roswell**). George Stoneman's cavalry division was sent south to look for river crossings downstream. They came upon the manufacturing town of New Manchester, whose textile factory was churning out Confederate cloth (see **New Manchester**).

In bypassing the River Line, Sherman digressed from his usual pattern of marching around Johnston to the south and west. Concerns for the safety of his supply line and that Confederate reinforcements might then be rushed from Virginia by rail through the Carolinas prompted Sherman to decide to approach Atlanta from the north and east. He sent Schofield's corps, which had remained in the vicinity of Smyrna, to look for a suitable point to cross the Chattahoochee River between Pace's Ferry and Roswell while the rest of his force remained in front of the Confederate works. These developments caused Johnston to evacuate the River Line on July 9.

Points of Interest

In the Smyrna area, at the intersection of South Cobb Drive and Concord Road, turn right on Concord Road. Concord Road follows the Smyrna line. The area to the east, where Cleburne was attacked, has a GHC marker but is totally developed. Drive southwest for 2.5 miles to a covered bridge at the intersection of Concord Road and Covered Bridge Road. You will be in the middle of a scenic woodland, designated both nationally and locally as the Concord Covered Bridge Historic District. Parking is difficult but it is worth trying to find so you can explore this area for a few minutes, where Fuller's XVI Corps brigade attacked Stevenson's Division north of Nickajack Creek.

The wooded area and creek look very much as they did when Fuller's men drove the skirmishers of Hood's corps from the area of Ruff's Mill. Though on private property, Ruff's Mill, a gristmill, and the miller's house are visible from the road. Both were standing at the time of the battle. The covered bridge was rebuilt after the war. The bridge, the gristmill and a woolen mill, which made Confederate uniforms (visible about 0.5 mile northeast on Concord Road to the right when the leaves are off the trees), were burned by Federal troops. Several other historic houses and sites are in the district. Plans are under way to increase the preservation of and access to the area, which is threatened by the construction of a high-volume highway.

Return to South Cobb Drive and proceed south to the intersection of King's Spring Road. Just south of the intersection is the Alexander Eaton house which was John Bell Hood's headquarters from July 3 to July 5. Continue on South Cobb Drive to Ridge Road to tour Johnston's River Line.

Gen. Joseph Eggleston Johnston, CSA, was a brilliant tactician who commanded the respect and admiration of his troops. He was, however, often at odds with President Jefferson Davis, who ignored Johnston's prewar military seniority when he ranked three other generals above him.

The "Shoupades" are unique examples of military engineering, and the preservation of Johnston's River Line has been of great concern to Atlanta Campaign preservationists. At this time several parts of the line exist but are all on private property. (Efforts are under way with civic authorities for the establishment of a county park that encompasses the extreme southern end of the line, the River Line extension.) However, one Shoupade can be viewed from a distance of about 100 feet at Ridge Road. More extensive touring of at least two Shoupades and one artillery redan is possible with advanced permission and an experienced guide. For further information, please contact CIVIL WAR TOURS, 2684 Canna Ridge Circle NE, Atlanta, GA 30345-1410; 404-908-8410.

Vinings Hill GA23 (Mount Wilkinson), from which Sherman first observed Atlanta on July 5, after the two-month campaign through northwest Georgia, is located on Paces Ferry Road in Vinings. Take Ridge Road east a short distance to Atlanta Road, turn left (north) to Paces Ferry Road. The hill is partially developed; however, a small family cemetery dating to the nineteenth century occupies the crest. Continuing east on Paces Ferry Road to the Chattahoochee River, you will see the area where Wheeler's cavalry battled Federal infantry while protecting a wagon train crossing. Later, part of the Army of the Cumberland crossed here on pontoon bridges. Johnston's principal crossing was over the railroad bridge and old wagon road 0.5 mile north where US41 crosses the river. These bridges were then burned by the Confederates.

To reach US41 from Paces Ferry Road, take Mill Road a short distance north. There are several GHC markers between the river and I-285, which you will enter to travel north to Roswell. Or return west a short distance on Paces Ferry Road and enter I-285 north to GA9 north, Roswell Road, and travel 8 miles north to Roswell.

Roswell

Brig. Gen. Kenner Garrard's cavalry arrived in Roswell, eighteen miles north of Atlanta, on July 5. Wheeler's cavalry skirmished with the advancing cavalry and burned the covered wagon road bridge across the Chattahoochee. The bluecoated cavalry quickly seized the crossing. Then they made an interesting discovery. On Vickery Creek, north of the Chattahoochee, a woolen mill was in full operation, turning out fabric for the Confederate army. Farther upstream on the creek, two cotton mills were also turning out cloth. The head weaver at the woolen mill, Theopholie Roche, who had been born in France, had raised the French flag over the mill. Insisting to Garrard that the facility was thus a neutral, he kept the spindles turning. Garrard rejected this line of reasoning and ordered the workers out of the mill and burned it and the two cotton mills.

Garrard reported the incident to Sherman, who not only approved of the cavalryman's decision but went a step further, ordering the workers charged with treason and suggesting that Roche could be hanged at Garrard's discretion. Although Garrard spared the head weaver, four hundred men, women, and children were arrested, transported by wagon under guard to the Western & Atlantic Railroad, and sent on cars to a detention camp north of Louisville, Kentucky. They never came to trial for the crime of treason and after the war few returned to Roswell.

On July 9, John Wilder's Lightning Brigade of Garrard's cavalry forded the river at Shallow Ford a half mile west of the Roswell bridge under the protection of the horse artillery of the Chicago Board of Trade. The crossing was secured without casualties. From July 13 to July 17, McPherson's Army of the Tennessee crossed on pontoon bridges at Roswell en route to the Georgia Railroad at Decatur and Stone Mountain. Roswell was occupied by Federal troops during the remainder of 1864.

Points of Interest

Roswell has a rich and well-preserved history including some areas that were significant in the Atlanta Campaign and subsequent Federal occupation. Although the mills were burned, Federal soldiers were under orders not to destroy private property, so many of Roswell's antebellum homes are extant. Whether you enter the city via GA9 or GA120, stop first at the Roswell visitor center, 617 Atlanta Street (GA9). A self-guided tour pamphlet gives information on all the historic points of interest and suggestions for hiking trails.

Among those points of interest particularly associated with Civil War events are the Old Bricks, on Sloan Street, built for the factory workers at the mills who were taken away and incarcerated. The 1839 structure is considered the nation's oldest extant apartment building. From nearby Mill Street, you can peer down into Vickery Creek where two of the three mills were located. Brick ruins of the old machine shop identify the site of one of the cotton mills that was torched. North on Mimosa Boulevard is the 1840 Roswell Presbyterian Church which was used as a hospital by the Federals. On Bulloch Avenue (GA120) west of town is Bulloch Hall, the antebellum residence of Confederate naval agent James Bulloch (who was also Theodore Roosevelt's grandfather), which Union soldiers used as a barracks during the occupation. At the Chattahoochee River crossing of GA9 is the site of the woolen mill and the covered bridge the Rebels burned. Just west of the highway is the site of Wilder's crossing on July 9.

From Roswell, return via route I-75, Windy Hill exit north to Powers Ferry Road and enter the Chattahoochee River National Recreation Area.

Chattahoochee River

Schofield's search for a river crossing led him to the mouth of Sope Creek, six miles upstream from Pace's Ferry. While his pontooners prepared their boats on Sope Creek in a position screened from the river by high bluffs, a brigade of Maj. Gen. Jacob D. Cox's division discovered a rock dam upriver and crossed it, earning the honor, on July 8, of being the first Federal troops to cross the Chattahoochee. Shortly after that, the 12th Kentucky Infantry Regiment, manning the pontoon boats, swept down the rapids of Sope Creek and crossed the river. They quickly overwhelmed the small cavalry guard on the river's south bank. A pontoon bridge was laid at Isom's Ferry, the south bank was fortified and Schofield sent brigade after brigade across the river.

One of the most humorous events of the campaign was the crossing of a detachment of the 1st Tennessee Regiment Cavalry (Union) under Col. James Brownlow, who crossed the Chattahoochee at Cochran's Ford, one-half mile downriver from Sope Creek on July 9. The event was described by their division commander Edward McCook. "It was deep and he [Brownlow] took them over naked, nothing but guns, cartridge boxes and hats. They drove the enemy out of their rifle pits, captured a non-commissioned officer, three men and two boats on the other side. They would have got more, but the Rebels had the advantage in running through the bushes with clothes on. It was certainly one of the funniest sights of the war, and a very successful raid for naked men to make."

Points of Interest

After Schofield's forces established a bridgehead in this area, his corps and the IV Corps crossed the Chattahoochee River here. Chattahoochee River National Recreation Area is divided into several units and is an ideal location for a number of recreational activities. Within the boundaries of the Palisades Unit is the crossing site of the IV Corps at Powers Ferry. The Cochran Shoals Unit is the location of the river crossing of Brownlow's nude cavalry. Just a bit upriver on Paper Mill Road is the mouth of Sope Creek, and a short distance upriver from that is the site of the old rock dam. The overlook to Sope Creek can be reached by taking a short hike along a trail from a Chattahoochee NRA parking lot off Paper Mill Road. On the overlook are the ruins of the Marietta Paper Mill, which was also burned by Garrard's cavalry.

On GA27 From the Chattahoochee NRA, return to I-75 and proceed south across the river to the West Paces Ferry Road exit in Atlanta. CHATTAHOOCHEE RIVER NATIONAL RECREATION AREA, 1978 Island Ford Parkway, Dunwoody, GA 30350; 404-399-8070.

Activities vary by location; fees for some activities; check official guide or call for specific information.

THE BATTLES FOR ATLANTA

With the River Line successfully bypassed by Sherman's soldiers, the Confederates completed their withdrawal from north of the Chattahoochee on July 9, burning all the bridges across the river. They temporarily occupied prepared works on the river's south bank. But later the same day, Johnston withdrew his forces to the outer line of defenses on Peachtree Creek, one and a half miles north of Atlanta's main fortifications. Stoneman's successful sortie to the south left Johnston unsure of Sherman's next move. Another development that had been brewing for some time would have a major impact on the Atlanta Campaign.

As the Federal armies were crossing the river, Johnston planned to isolate the Army of the Cumberland. McPherson's army was many miles to the east, marching west along the

Georgia Railroad from northeast of Decatur. Schofield's army moved from the Sope Creek bridgehead into DeKalb County, through today's Druid Hills, to the town of Decatur to continue railroad destruction and then turn west toward Atlanta (see **The Battle of Atlanta**). Thomas's army was therefore alone in confronting the main Confederate force after crossing on pontoons from Paces Ferry north to Powers Ferry. Johnston's plan was to attack the isolated Army of the Cumberland from east to west, hurling it back against unfordable stretches of the Chattahoochee.

Johnston delivered the plan to his army in a published address to his troops on July 17. Unfortunately for him, he did not communicate the details of his strategy adequately to Richmond, or to President Jefferson Davis's special military adviser, Gen. Braxton Bragg, then in Atlanta to confer with Johnston on Davis's behalf. That night, a telegram was delivered to Johnston's headquarters informing him that he was relieved of his command and that John Bell Hood, elevated to the rank of general, had been assigned to replace him as commander of the army.

The decision had been slow in coming, but had not been without warning. Previous efforts to encourage Johnston to stand and give battle, rather than to fall back to prepared defenses had gone unheeded. Johnston's vague communications with Richmond about his plans and numerous requests for reinforcements had placed the entire Confederate cabinet in favor of his removal—even those who previously supported him. Ironically, it was Davis who held out the longest, no doubt realizing the dangers in changing a commander at that critical time. When the decision was reached, the choices for replacement were few—William Hardee, who had refused command of the army before; Alexander Stewart, who had only recently been named to replace William Loring as commander of Leonidas Polk's former corps; and Hood. In seeking advice from Robert E. Lee on his former subordinate, Davis received only the response that Hood was "a fighter."

The announcement was received by much of the army with shock and sadness. Many soldiers and officers of the Army of Tennessee loved and respected Johnston. They looked forward to Johnston's planned offensive as the opportunity to defeat the Yankees. Hood, himself, opposed the change. He wired Richmond stating his feeling on the change of command, but Davis immediately wired Hood personally that the order must stand. On July 18, the change of command was officially rendered and Johnston left the army immediately.

Newspaper reports of the change quickly reached the Federal side and there was much jubilation. McPherson and Schofield, for example, were West Point classmates of Hood—Schofield had tutored the Kentuckian in mathematics—and knew of his aggressive and reckless tendencies. One report offered by a Federal officer was that before the war Hood bet $2,500 with "nary a pair in his hand." Sherman, who maintained much respect for Johnston and knew his army did as well, said later of the change of command, "At this critical moment the Confederate government rendered us most valuable service."

Peachtree Creek

That same day, July 18, Thomas's army was advancing on Peachtree Creek from the north; Palmer's corps on the right, Hooker's in the center and Howard's on the left, moving down the present-day Powers Ferry Road. Wheeler's cavalry skirmished with the advancing columns, then burned the bridges over Peachtree Creek and rode east to attend to the developing crisis along the Georgia Railroad. Palmer's crossing of Peachtree Creek was opposed by elements of Stewart's corps near Howell's Mills for most of the day on July 19.

Hood operating from headquarters in Atlanta was unsure of the location of all his units in the confusion that accompanied the change of command. Cavalry, artillery, and infantry moved about in haste and with unproductive efforts. Hood's former corps, assigned to Benjamin Cheatham, was on the right flank. Hardee's men were in the center, and Stewart on the left, posted along the line of defenses north of Atlanta. Hood formulated a battle plan for July 20, an assault on Thomas's army. But rather than ordering a counterclockwise attack which would have the potential of driving the Federals back toward the unfordable section of the Chattahoochee, Hood ordered an attack in the opposite direction—an attack *en echelon,* in which the right flank units would begin the attack to be followed in succession from right to left. Should the Federals retreat, they would have roads and no natural water obstacle at their backs, except Peachtree Creek which they were then crossing.

By the evening of July 19, the Federal units of Palmer's, Hooker's, and Howard's corps had crossed Peachtree Creek and established a line on high ground a quarter mile south of the creek. The Federals found high ground south of Peachtree Creek and took advantage of this and the fact that most of the terrain in front of them consisted of under-

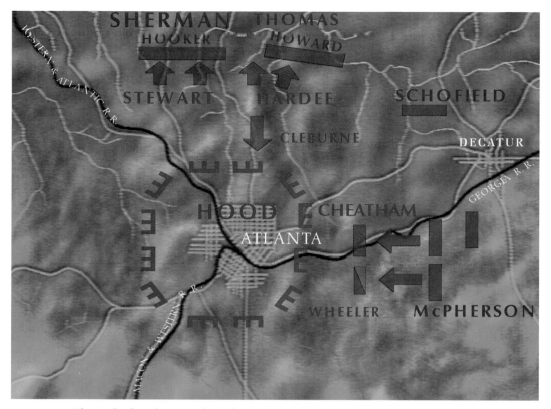

The Battle of Peachtree Creek was fought in the hills north of what was then north of and beyond the limits of Atlanta. Missing the opportunity to catch Maj. Gen. George H. Thomas's Army of the Cumberland as it crossed the creek, the Confederate corps of Hardee and Stewart attacked and hit the Federal divisions of Williams, Geary, Ward, and Newton after they had deployed on high ground south of the creek. The attacks, uncoordinated and against good defensive positions, sent the Rebels into retreat after desperate fighting. Compounding their problems was the threat from the east by the Federal armies of Schofield and McPherson. Hood ordered Hardee to send Maj. Gen. Patrick Cleburne's division to help Wheeler's cavalry meet the threat on that front.

brush-filled ravines. The Confederate attack was planned for one P.M., but by then Hood had discovered that Cheatham's corps needed to move farther east to address the threat coming from that direction and a large gap was developing between his and Hardee's corps. After adjustments were made the gap still existed and was more than two miles wide, placing the attacking units in unfamiliar terrain and giving the Federals sufficient time to steady their lines.

The first Rebel unit, Bate's division, moved forward at four P.M. As the troops moved through the tangled underbrush, they were fired upon by John Newton's division of Howard's corps, holding the commanding ground along present-day Brighton Street. Bate's division scarcely became involved in the battle. To Bate's left, William H. T. Walker's division met heavy resistance from a forward bulge in the Federal line and was turned back. Maney's division, to Walker's left, then faltered, exposing the right flank of Stewart's corps. Loring's division took up the advance.

Loring's two brigades made the most forward progress. They advanced across ground on either side of Tanyard Branch of Peachtree Creek, Brig. Gen. Winfield Featherston's brigade on the right and Brig. Gen. Thomas Scott's brigade on the left. Featherston reached the vicinity of Collier's Mill, but William T. Ward's brigade of Hooker's corps arrived to check Featherston's forward progress and force the Rebels back. Central to this effort was Ward's 79th Indiana regiment commanded by future U.S. President Benjamin Harrison. Scott's brigade overran the forward position of the 33rd New Jersey and captured their flag. But as they crossed Tanyard Branch in a low-lying gully, Scott's people were hammered by Brig. Gen. John Geary's massed artillery posted on the bluffs above, and, unsupported, they were driven back.

Stewart's other two divisions, under Walthall and French, made little headway. Edward Walthall's division had the disadvantage of operating out of a deep ravine and stalled under the fire of Williams's and Geary's XX Corps divisions. Though French on the extreme left of the Confederate line attacked on more favorable ground and met light resistance from Palmer's corps, his isolated effort could not be sustained and he pulled back.

As afternoon shadows lengthened into those of evening, Hardee was about to send Maney's relatively fresh division and Cleburne's division, which had been held in reserve, to attack again, when he received an urgent request from Hood to rush a division to the extreme right of Cheatham's corps, which was being threatened by the other two Federal armies. Cleburne's division was ordered on a forced march to the east of Atlanta. This set the stage for the next chapter: The Battle of Atlanta.

Points of Interest

In the vicinity of West Paces Ferry Road, there are numerous GHC markers tracing the routes of the advancing corps of the Army of the Cumberland. Of particular interest is a

Gen. John Bell Hood, CSA, was promoted to full general and given command of the Army of Tennessee because Jefferson Davis and the Richmond leadership were unhappy with the defensive tactics and gradual withdrawal of Gen. Joseph E. Johnston in front of Maj. Gen. William T. Sherman's advance. Hood, known for his aggressive style, immediately attacked Sherman's forces advancing on Atlanta, but the three attacks failed and Atlanta was soon lost to the Union forces.

monument on the grounds of an industrial plant at 950 West Marietta Street (US41) where the change of Confederate command took place. Johnston's last headquarters was up the street at 1030 West Marietta Street, the site of the Dexter Niles House. West of I-75 off West Paces Ferry at 3101 Andrews Drive is the Atlanta History Center, which has numerous artifacts and exhibits pertaining to the campaign, special events, and a research library. Of historical interest on the grounds is the 1840 Tullie Smith House (moved to this site), one of the few structures in Atlanta to survive the war.

The Peachtree line generally followed present-day Collier Road. There are numerous GHC markers pertaining to the battle but traffic patterns and limited parking make stopping difficult. There is a monument on the grounds of Piedmont Hospital, Peachtree at Brighton Road, and GHC markers where Bate's attack jumped off. Other GHC markers with easy access are at the entrance of Bobby Jones Golf Course and Atlanta Memorial Park.

The best point from which to appreciate the battle is Tanyard Branch Park, on Collier Road 0.5 mile west of Peachtree. Here there is parking and a meadow through which the Tanyard Branch of Peachtree Creek runs. Interpretive plaques describe the action in this area which was the site of Scott's brigade's deepest penetration of the Federal line. On Collier Road just above the park are the millstones from the Old Collier Mill which was located on the creek.

Return to I-75 and proceed north to I-285 east, exit at US78 east for a short drive to Stone Mountain.

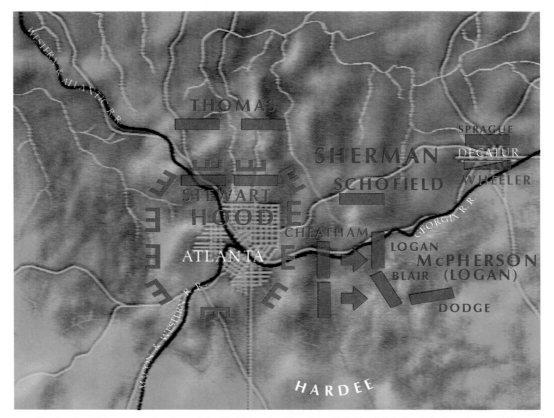

The Battle of Atlanta was fought on July 22, 1864, after Gen. John Bell Hood failed to halt the advance of the Federal Army of the Cumberland as it approached Atlanta from the north. Hoping to defeat the Army of the Tennessee approaching from the east, Hood designed a broad flanking maneuver, force-marching Hardee's corps from the north, through Atlanta, and to the southeast, in order to get to the rear of Maj. Gen. James B. McPherson's army. At the same time, Stewart's corps was ordered back to Atlanta's main line of fortifications on the north. Hardee's exhausted soldiers marched all night, but logistical problems delayed the attack until after noon. By that time, McPherson had placed the XVI Corps on the left flank and Hardee's attack met with stout resistance. Hood did not order the planned supporting attack of Cheatham's corps until mid-afternoon and although the Confederates achieved a breakthrough in front of the XV Corps, it was not sustained. Wheeler's cavalry, ordered to destroy Federal wagon trains in Decatur, was challenged by infantry and did not achieve the objective. Hood's "second sortie" as it is sometimes called failed decisively.

The Battle of Atlanta

While the Army of the Cumberland was advancing on Atlanta from the north, Sherman's other two armies marched southeast from their Chattahoochee River crossings. Schofield's Army of the Ohio approached Decatur from the northwest while McPherson's Army of the Tennessee swung farther east, finally converging on Decatur from the

Maj. Gen. John A. Logan, USA, was a political general who did not always have the full confidence of his West Point–trained comrades. But he was ever a brave and loyal commander and skillfully led a brigade, a division, and finally a corps in the Army of the Tennessee. Except for taking leave to help Lincoln in the 1864 presidential election, Logan served with Sherman's "army group" through the surrender of Confederate armies in April 1865.

north and northeast. It was of paramount importance to Sherman to ensure that no reinforcements from Virginia would be allowed to fill Johnston's ranks. Therefore, he ordered Garrard's cavalry to Stone Mountain to destroy portions of the Georgia Railroad. On July 18, Garrard's cavalry and Brig. Gen. Joseph Lightburn's brigade of the XV Corps, driving Joseph Wheeler's Rebel cavalry before them, arrived at Stone Mountain and destroyed two miles of track and supporting facilities at the Stone Mountain depot. Garrard was subsequently ordered, on July 20, to Covington, where late on July 21, he destroyed Georgia Railroad track and bridges between Lithonia and Alcovy. He returned to Decatur on July 24.

At the same time, the rest of the Army of the Tennessee and Schofield's XXIII Corps were marching on Decatur. Schofield's corps stopped short of the town, camping in the vicinity of present-day Emory University on July 19. That same day, the three corps of the Army of the Tennessee occupied Decatur. From there, they began marching west along the line of the Georgia Railroad, tearing up the track and destroying railroad property.

By this time, John Bell Hood, having assumed command of the Confederate forces, was attempting to align his units for the defense of Atlanta. His defense was to attack, the expectation of his superiors in Richmond. Less than two days into his new command he, in the process of launching his Peachtree attack on Thomas's army, was compelled by the advance of McPherson and Schofield to move his former corps, now commanded by Maj. Gen. Benjamin F. Cheatham, farther east. This resulted in the shift of Hardee's corps east that delayed the start of the July 20 assault on Thomas. The threat east of

Atlanta was loudly announced at one P.M. on July 20 by the report of Capt. Francis De Gress's Company H, 1st Illinois Artillery's twenty-pounder Parrotts. Three shells dropped into Atlanta from De Gress's battery on a hill north of the Georgia Railroad.

Maj. Gen. John Logan's XV Corps occupied the front astride the Georgia Railroad while Maj. Gen. Frank Blair's XVII Corps pushed south,

The Atlanta Cyclorama tells the story of the Battle of Atlanta and was created in 1885–86 by William Wehner and a team of eleven artists. Maj. Gen. John "Black Jack" Logan was a major sponsor of the cyclorama and is seen prominently in it, riding his black horse at the head of a column of soldiers coming to the aid of their comrades near the Troup Hurt House.

along present-day Moreland Avenue, opposed by Wheeler's cavalry. Wheeler's cavalry took a defensive stance on Bald Hill (near I-20 and Moreland Avenue). The XVII Corps attacked the position, necessitating Hood to send an urgent message to Hardee to rush units intended for the attack on Thomas to reinforce Wheeler. Pat Cleburne's division arrived at Bald Hill at midnight after a forced march from the Peachtree Creek line. The next day, Bald Hill was attacked by two divisions of Blair's corps and taken by Brig. Gen. Mortimer Leggett's 3rd Division, giving rise to the Federal designation of Bald Hill as Leggett's Hill. The Rebel trenches taken over by the Yanks were refaced and preparations made to train artillery on Atlanta.

That evening, July 21, Hood readied a plan for another assault on the Federals. Wheeler had reported that Blair's left flank was "in the air," that is, unprotected and open to attack on the flank. Hood, inspired by the Robert E. Lee–Stonewall Jackson maneuver that gave the South victory at Chancellorsville (see **Chancellorsville, Virginia**), ordered Hardee's corps to evacuate its position north of Atlanta and march through the night to the southeast, to launch an attack on the exposed flank of the Army of the Tennessee. But Hood underestimated the time needed for the more-than-fifteen-mile march on narrow roads,

Maj. Gen. James Birdseye McPherson, USA, was a promising officer, well liked by both Grant and Sherman. He was an invaluable leader for the Army of the Tennessee in Sherman's Atlanta Campaign. McPherson was anxious to conclude the campaign for Atlanta so he could take leave in order to go to Baltimore and marry his fiancée.

down Peachtree Road through the streets of Atlanta, and back up the Fayetteville Road. To complicate matters, Cleburne's division, part of Hardee's corps, had trouble disengaging from the Leggett's Hill battle to join the march. Three other points of the plan, which Hood explained in person to his senior commanders, were a frontal assault on Logan and Blair by Cheatham's corps and a raid by Wheeler's cavalry on McPherson's large wagon train approaching Decatur from the north. Alexander Stewart's corps, the only Rebel force remaining north of Atlanta, would withdraw during the night to the city's main line of defense.

Exhausted Confederate soldiers of Hardee's corps did not arrive at the jump-off positions until noon on July 22. As the troops of Maj. Gen. William H. T. Walker and Maj. Gen. William B. Bate struggled through the last underbrush-laden pine woods to a clearing, they looked upon the largest obstacle to Hood's plan—the XVI Corps to their front. The previous day, McPherson had ordered Grenville Dodge's corps, held in reserve, to take position to the east to protect Blair's flank against the kind of attack Hood had in mind. The arrival of Thomas W. Sweeny's division and a brigade of John Fuller's with artillery support was timely.

The fiery "Shot Pouch" Walker, at the head of his division, ordered the Rebels forward at twelve-fifteen P.M., along with Bate's division. Walker was struck down and killed by a Federal sharpshooter. After some confusion resulting from Walker's death, the attack drove ahead, but the Federal position, with artillery advantageously located on a hill, was too strong and the assault stalled. Thirty minutes later, Cleburne's division moved forward and struck Blair's corps in the flank, driving those Federals not captured or shot down to Leggett's Hill.

General McPherson, hearing the sound of gunfire while lunching with his staff north of Dodge's position, mounted his horse and with several officers rode south to where Dodge's corps was posted. Satisfied with the ability of that force to hold off the attack, he dispatched another officer to issue some orders, then rode south to check on the condition of Blair's corps with two officers and an orderly. Brig. Gen. Giles A. Smith's division having already been routed, the group rode down a road and

When Gone With the Wind *premiered in Atlanta in 1939, Mayor Hartsfield invited the picture's stars, Clark Gable and Vivian Leigh, to visit the Atlanta Cyclorama. They were quite impressed with it and Gable with his inimitable sense of humor remarked that the only thing missing was him. A short time later, his face was put on one of the three-dimensional soldiers which were added in a diorama at the base of the painting.*

into Confederate skirmishers of Cleburne's division. McPherson turned his horse to flee and was fatally shot through the back by a Rebel corporal. The others were captured; one of the Union officers had his watch broken when his horse slammed into a tree during the melee, fixing the time of McPherson's death at 2:02 P.M. When the captain of the Confederate contingent inquired as to the identity of the dead major general, one of the Federal officers, Col. Robert K. Scott, replied tearfully, "Sir, it is General McPherson. You have just killed the best man in our army!"

Reinforced, Blair's corps held Cleburne at bay from Leggett's Hill. The focus of the battle then shifted north to the area north and south of the Georgia Railroad, defended by John Logan's corps. Logan assumed temporary command of the Army of the Tennessee upon McPherson's death. Hood did not launch the frontal assault by Cheatham's corps until three P.M., but did order Maney's division of Hardee's corps and the Georgia militia under G. W. Smith to attack south of Cheatham's corps. The assault started at three-thirty P.M. with Maney on the right and continued northward, with the greatest success coming from Arthur M. Manigault's brigade north of the Georgia Railroad. They drove a wedge into the Federal line and flanked the Federals to the north, capturing De Gress's battery near the two-story brick Troup Hurt House. Other brigades fanned south, flanking other Federal units.

A repeat of Longstreet's Chickamauga rout seemed to be in the making. Sherman, observing the action from his headquarters three quarters of a mile to the northwest, ordered Schofield to mass artillery on the hill there and train it on the Southern advance. General Logan exhibited skill and energy in bringing up reinforcements from Dodge's corps and reforming the broken lines of the XV Corps. (This is the time frame and battlefield vividly portrayed in the *Battle of Atlanta* Cyclorama painting [see **Points of Interest**].) By late afternoon, Cheatham also received an order to withdraw the division which broke through the line. General Manigault later wrote, "There was nothing left for us to do but obey, and I never saw men obey an order so unwillingly."

Concurrent with the *Battle of Atlanta*, Wheeler's cavalry was staging a running battle through the streets of Decatur with the brigade sent by McPherson to protect the Federal wagon train. The train was diverted west to safety and Wheeler broke off the contest in the afternoon when ordered to support General Hardee. Except for the massed artillery, Sherman sent no reinforcements to aid the Army of the Tennessee in the restoration of their lines and fight to avenge their fallen leader's death. Sherman later wrote his reasoning, "I knew that the attacking force could only be part of Hood's army, and that if assistance were rendered by either of the other armies, the Army of the Tennessee would be jealous."

Among those saddened by the news of McPherson's death was John Bell Hood, who grieved for his fallen West Point classmate at the same time as he grieved for "Shot Pouch" Walker. Sherman, to whose headquarters McPherson's body was brought after Federal soldiers recovered it, wept for the man he saw as his successor. Tragically, McPherson had been anxious to conclude the campaign for Atlanta to apply for leave in order to travel to Baltimore, Maryland, and marry his fiancée. Sherman wrote to the young woman shortly after the battle, "I yield to no one but yourself the right to exceed me in lamentations for our dead hero."

Points of Interest

On US78 in the village of Stone Mountain there are two GHC markers. One along the railroad describes the action here involving Garrard's cavalry. On the hill above, the other indicates the burial in the cemetery there of 150 unknown Confederate dead. Stone

Mountain Park, which has the large sculpture of Confederate leaders carved in its face, was probably part of the battlefield here. The park annually holds Civil War encampments and events. Follow US78 west to Decatur.

From Decatur, McPherson's Army of the Tennessee started its march west along the Georgia Railroad. The July 22 battle between Joseph Wheeler's cavalry and Col. John W. Sprague's infantry brigade moved north from the present-day campus of Agnes Scott College to the courthouse square. There are markers at both locations. The Swanton house at 240 Atlanta Street was briefly the headquarters of Federal Brig. Gen. Thomas Sweeny. From Decatur, follow Dekalb Avenue south to Atlanta, the route of the XV Corps's march.

At Oakdale Road, turn south then west on Memorial Drive to Clifton Street. This was the extreme left of the Federal line where Sweeny's division was posted to cover the left flank of

This monument was erected at the spot where Maj. Gen. James B. McPherson was killed during the Battle of Atlanta on July 22, 1864. A similar monument stands at the location of Maj. Gen. William H. T. Walker's death.

Blair's corps. Federal artillery occupied the present-day grounds of Murphy High School. The attack started here at twelve-fifteen P.M. on July 22. Nearby at Glenwood Avenue and Wilkinson Drive is a monument to fallen Confederate General Walker, at the site where he was killed. General McPherson was killed in mid-afternoon while riding to the site of the action along Glenwood Avenue to the west. His memorial cannon is at the intersection of McPherson Avenue and McPherson Monument Place.

From Glenwood Avenue, proceed north on Moreland Avenue across I-20 to the intersection of Memorial Drive. Leggett's (Bald) Hill is just south of here but the construction of I-20 greatly altered the hill's profile. As you proceed north on Moreland you are following the front of Logan's line which continued northward to Little Five Points. North of Dekalb Avenue and east of Moreland is DeGress Avenue. There are numerous GHC markers in the area but the only two where parking is possible is the site of the capture of DeGress's battery at the end of the block and the Troup Hurt House site, midblock. A

Oakland Cemetery in Atlanta. Many of the Confederate soldiers who heroically fought in the battles for Atlanta are buried here along with Confederate leaders, including John Brown Gordon.

former church building now occupies the site.

Follow the signs off North Highland Avenue west of Moreland to the Jimmy Carter Presidential Library. This was the site of the Augustus Hurt House, where Sherman maintained a command post on July 22. Schofield's artillery posted on this hill enfiladed the Confederate line attacking Logan's corps. Proceed east to Boulevard Avenue, then south to Grant Park.

Grant Park is the home of several attractions including the Atlanta Zoo. It was named for Col. Lemuel P. Grant, a prominent citizen who also laid out Atlanta's ring of fortifications for the Confederate defense. Though restored, Grant's 1854 home, nearby at 327 St. Paul Avenue, is one of the few extant structures dating to the Civil War.

At the extreme southwest corner of the park are the remains of Fort Walker, the southeast salient of Grant's Atlanta Line of Fortifications. Although part of the fort is a playground now, it is one of the few examples of Confederate works in the city available for public viewing. There is a marvelous view of Atlanta here. In the center of Grant Park is the *Battle of Atlanta* Cyclorama. America's largest painting (several feet taller than the *Battle of Gettysburg* Cyclorama in Pennsylvania), it was painted in Atlanta by German artists in 1885–86. A diorama was added later and the work has been restored. Also in the cyclorama is the engine Texas, which completed the chase of the General in the Great Locomotive Chase. The City of Atlanta facility also has Civil War exhibits, a film and a bookstore. ATLANTA CYCLORAMA, 800 Cherokee Avenue SE, Atlanta, GA 30315; 404-624-1071.   🚌 ❂ ♿ ❷ 🏛 👫

Travel north out of the park on Cherokee Avenue to Martin Luther King Drive. Oakland Cemetery is the location of the graves of many Confederate soldiers including Maj. Gen. John B. Gordon. There is the Confederate monument, the *Lion of Atlanta*, a sculpture dedicated to unknown civilians killed in the city's siege, and a plaque indicating the hanging nearby of seven Andrews' Raiders. James J. Andrews was hanged at Third and Juniper streets in downtown Atlanta. Across the street from the cemetery is the site of Fulton Industries, a major producer of rolled iron for Confederate warships.

From Oakland Cemetery, take Boulevard Avenue south a short distance to I-20 and travel west through Atlanta to exit 11, then south to Sweetwater Creek State Park.

DRIVING TOUR—*Proceed to Sweetwater Creek (New Manchester)*
or downtown Atlanta
READING—*Atlanta Campaign: To Ezra Church*

New Manchester

As Sherman sought to maneuver around Johnston's River Line in early July he sent Maj. Gen. George Stoneman's cavalry south to confuse the Confederates about where his "army group" might cross the Chattahoochee River. On July 2, Stoneman's cavalry happened on the manufacturing village of New Manchester, a series of mills on Sweetwater Creek southeast of Atlanta, patterned after those at Roswell. In much the same manner as Garrard's cavalry would do at Roswell, on July 9 Stoneman had Lt. Col. Silas Adams's cavalry brigade dismantle the mills, which were producing cloth for the Confederacy. The operatives, mostly women and children, were sent under guard to Marietta, where, all the while denying their services to the Confederacy, they were put on northbound trains.

These decaying brick walls are all that remain of a wool mill in the town of New Manchester in Sweetwater Creek State Park. A creekside trail leads to the mill; other structures and features of the town, no longer extant, are described by interpretive markers and pamphlets. The ruins and the park's rustic beauty make it well worth a visit.

The shutdown of the New Manchester mills and the dispatching of the population were so devastating that the town was never resettled.

Points of Interest

What little remains of the antebellum town of New Manchester and the area along Sweetwater Creek has been turned into a recreational park by the state of Georgia. Secluded trails lead to the traces of the town and the most prominent ruins in the park—a mill. The trail to the ruins is about 1.2 miles in length and a brochure is available in the parking areas of the park.

Return to Atlanta via I-20 east and exit at Martin Luther King Drive.

Ezra Church

After the Battle of Atlanta, Sherman was faced with some difficult decisions. The fortifications of Atlanta were deemed by his chief engineer to be exceedingly strong. But before making his next tactical move, he was faced with an important command decision. To replace the fallen McPherson, Maj. Gen. Joseph Hooker was the logical choice. He was the senior corps commander in the army. However, after consulting with George Thomas and others, Sherman selected Maj. Gen. Oliver O. Howard, IV Corps commander. Hooker was not only incensed at having had his seniority passed over, he strongly disliked Howard, whom he felt bore much responsibility for the Army of the Potomac's defeat at Chancellorsville (see **Chancellorsville, Virginia**). Hooker immediately requested to be relieved as leader of the XX Corps and did not hold a field command for the rest of the war. Ironically, another former Army of the Potomac general whom Hooker held in no favor was summoned from Vicksburg to replace Hooker as commander of the XX Corps, Maj. Gen. Henry Slocum. General Logan, a non–West Pointer, was also incensed by Sherman's choice and saw it as an example of U.S. Military Academy elitism.

John Bell Hood also had command decisions to make after the two disastrous offensives at the gates of Atlanta. William Hardee tendered his resignation, but was persuaded by Jefferson Davis to stay on. Stephen Dill Lee was elevated to the rank of lieutenant general and brought from Mississippi to take command of Hood's former corps. Benjamin Cheatham was returned to division command.

Ruling out a siege or costly attacks on the Confederates holed up in Atlanta, Sherman decided to go after the two railroads that still linked Atlanta with the outside world. The

Atlanta & West Point and Macon & Western railroads converged to approach Atlanta from the southeast and southwest at East Point over the tracks of the latter. This was Sherman's objective as, on July 27, he ordered Howard to march the Army of the Tennessee behind the positions of the other two Federal armies to approach those railroads from west of Atlanta.

Simultaneously, Sherman set in motion a three-division cavalry operation, the largest of the campaign, to move on the Macon & Western Railroad at Lovejoy Station. Two columns of cavalry began a southward ride that same day—one under Edward McCook riding west of Atlanta and the other Maj. Gen. George Stoneman's division with Kenner Garrard's division striking south and passing well east of Atlanta. Stoneman convinced Sherman to allow him to then ride farther south with his division to liberate imprisoned Federal officers from Camp Oglethorpe in Macon and the more than 30,000 enlisted prisoners at Camp Sumter, better known as Andersonville Prison (see **Macon** and **Andersonville**). But Stoneman's failure to rendezvous first with McCook at Lovejoy Station and determined opposition from Maj. Gen. Joseph Wheeler's Rebel cavalry turned the cavalry operation into one of the few Confederate successes during the Atlanta Campaign (see **Palmetto** and **Sunshine Church**).

Riding along with the Army of the Tennessee's columns, the one-armed Maine-born general remarked to Sherman that he thought Hood would attack the army before they reached their destination. Determined resistance by Red Jackson's Rebel cavalry, which the Union soldiers pushed before them, told Howard that Hood was planning an attack. That night, Howard had his army halt on a ridge near Ezra Church, a small Methodist meetinghouse west of Atlanta.

Howard was correct. Hood ordered S. D. Lee's corps to march from Atlanta out Lickskillet Road to check the Army of the Tennessee. Alexander Stewart's corps was given orders to march on Lee's left and maneuver behind Howard's column. Lee formed a line of battle opposite the Federals, with subordinates and men he had known for only a few days. Nevertheless, his orders were precise and well executed against superior numbers of Union soldiers who were fortified. One brigade of Federals, holding a position on open ground, used benches from Ezra Church and their knapsacks as barricades. The twelve-thirty P.M. initial attack by Lee's two divisions started well but the Union force then counterattacked and Lee's corps was driven back under the withering fire.

Stewart's corps, which did not get the opportunity to march around the Federal flank, was ordered in against the XV and XVII corps, attacking over the ground from which Lee had withdrawn. The Yankee fire was no less damaging to Stewart's corps. Stewart was slightly wounded in the action and it was his replacement who called retreat at four P.M.

The Battle of Ezra Church was Hood's third defeat in a week, costing many Confederate casualties in a war of attrition which if continued spelled disaster. For Sherman, it completed the third of his three-sided box around Atlanta, and moved men of his "army group" into a better position from which to better continue their fight to cut the last railroad into Atlanta.

Utoy Creek

With little to show in the way of positive results in the cavalry expeditions, Sherman settled into a siege of Atlanta with day and night bombardments of the city. He started the shelling with a regular and deliberate pace from four P.M. to dark. Gradually it increased in intensity. He also continued to maneuver his infantry forces to close in on the railroads. Sherman ordered Schofield's Army of the Ohio to advance to East Point.

Sherman expected the advance to get under way on the afternoon of August 4, but only light skirmishing occurred that day and the next because of the wilderness conditions along Utoy Creek and the refusal of Maj. Gen. John M. Palmer to cooperate with Schofield. Palmer, like Logan, a citizen soldier, resigned and the Federal units were aligned for attack on August 6. But by then Hood had entrenched on high ground overlooking the north branch of Utoy Creek.

The Battle of Utoy Creek started the morning of August 6 with two Kentucky regiments—one for the North and the other Confederate—facing off against each other. One of Schofield's divisions attacked but made no progress against Hardee's corps. Another of Schofield's divisions got into position. At four P.M. Palmer's corps, now led by Brig. Gen. Richard W. Johnson, launched an assault which quickly disintegrated. That evening Hood ordered Hardee to pull back if he were in danger of being cut off, and on the morning of August 7 the Federals discovered the area along Utoy Creek abandoned and theirs for the taking. The battle pointed out to Sherman the difficulty inherent in attempting to close off Atlanta's last railroad.

Points of Interest

Atlanta's Moseley Park, on Martin Luther King Drive north of I-20 exit 17, is the site of Ezra Church. The low rise northwest of the park is the apex of the Federal line, the salient angle held by Col. Hugo Wangelin's brigade. The Confederate attack was across the grassy expanse of the park from the south and west of the park. A monument and GHC markers in the park describe the battle. South of the freeway, on Gordon Road, is West-view Cemetery. The gatehouse is at the location where Atlanta's Alms House stood. This was a rallying point for the Confederates forming for the attack. A map of the cemetery available during business hours at the gatehouse identifies the location of Confederate graves, the Ezra Church Battle monument, and a section of Confederate earthworks. The Confederate monument, on a hill, is visible from the entrance.

The Cascade Springs Nature Preserve on Cascade Road is a City of Atlanta park which has only been open a few years. A short trail is marked that leads to rifle pits and earthworks near the quarry that once occupied the site. A Confederate gun emplacement is above the spring and pumphouse. The attacks of the Army of the Ohio's Jacob Cox and Milo Hascall against the Orphan Brigade took place within this preserve. To the southeast of the preserve, near the corner of Centra Villa and Venetian Drives, is Utoy Church, used as a Confederate hospital. There are Confederate graves in the small cemetery behind the church and remains of a Rebel trench.

JONESBORO AND THE FALL OF ATLANTA

Through the month of August Maj. Gen. William T. Sherman stepped up the rate of fire of his cannons in the siege of Atlanta. Eight four-and-a-half-inch heavy-rifled siege guns were transported from Chattanooga, and these guns, firing at the rate of one shell every twenty minutes, struck into the heart of the city—commercial buildings, churches, residences were all in the firing line. Gen. John Bell Hood protested that Atlanta was filled with noncombatants a mile from the Confederate trenches, but Sherman countered that Atlanta was a military arsenal and continued the shelling. On August 18, Brig. Gen. Judson Kilpatrick, returning to the army after recovering from a wound received at Resaca, began a cavalry raid around Atlanta from west to east, but did little damage to the remaining two railroads that supplied Atlanta and sustained Hood's army.

By August 23 Sherman decided to abandon the siege of Atlanta and concentrate his infantry forces to cut the Macon & Western and Atlanta & West Point railroads. With Joseph Wheeler's Confederate cavalry away on a raid in northwest Georgia and deep into Tennessee to break up Sherman's supply line—a raid that ranged north to Strawberry Plains near Knoxville, northwest to the Nashville approaches, and as far west as Tuscumbia, Alabama, but which did no appreciable damage to Sherman's rail communications with his bases in Tennessee—Hood at first did not discern the Federal plan. Maj.

Gen. Henry Slocum's XX Corps withdrew north to the banks of the Chattahoochee River to protect the Northern supply lines, while the rest of Sherman's "army group" were concentrated southwest of Atlanta to march to the vicinity of Jonesboro to cut the Macon & Western. Hood interpreted these maneuvers as a general Federal withdrawal. Even when Red Jackson's cavalry brought Hood reports of the Federal march to Jonesboro, Hood felt this action was merely a raid by one Federal corps. He sent two corps under the leadership of Lt. Gen. William Hardee south to Jonesboro with orders to attack that force.

Battle of Jonesboro

Hardee arrived at Jonesboro by rail on August 31 with his former corps, then led by Maj. Gen. Patrick R. Cleburne, and Lt. Gen. S. D. Lee's corps, a day after one of Maj. Gen. Oliver O. Howard's Army of the Tennessee corps crossed the Flint River and camped west of Jonesboro. At the same time, the command of Maj. Gen. John Schofield—his Army of the Ohio and the Army of the Cumberland's IV Corps—was marching to cut the railroad at Rough and Ready (near present-day Hartsfield-Atlanta International Airport), while Maj. Gen. George Thomas with the Army of the Cumberland's XIV Corps was in a similar southeast march midway between Rough and Ready and Jonesboro. Hearing the trains carrying Rebel troops to Jonesboro in the early-morning hours of August 31, Howard prepared a line of defense with two of his three corps east of the Flint River forming a right angle.

Hardee's plan was to have Cleburne attack the right of the Federal force, where Maj. Gen. Thomas Ransom's XVI Corps was entrenched and angled back to the river, followed by a frontal attack by Lee's corps against Maj. Gen. John A. Logan's XV Corps. The attack did not get under way until late afternoon and the first Confederate troops engaged, Cleburne's former division under the "Fighting Preacher," Brig. Gen. Mark P. Lowrey, drove Kilpatrick's cavalry back across the river. But the division was separated from the rest of the corps and Lee launched his frontal attack far ahead of schedule. Brig. Gen. John M. Corse's division held off attacks by the rest of Hardee's corps across a deep ravine while the Federal XV Corps stiffened against the premature attack of Lee's corps. The Confederate assault was repulsed. That same day Schofield's army cut the Macon & Western after skirmishing with Rebel horsemen at Rough and Ready. This caused Hood to recall Lee's tired, battle-worn corps to Atlanta, an order that was implemented with alacrity. Hardee, resuming command of his corps, remained at Jonesboro, and virtually assured the success of the Federal operation then in progress.

Hardee formed a tighter defense line in the town of Jonesboro, with his left flank running parallel to the railroad in a north-south direction, and, from a salient angle formed northwest of the town, his right flank ran along a shorter east-west front near the Warren House. On September 1, Howard launched an assault on the line with Black Jack Logan's corps, supported by Blair's, advancing from the west while two Army of the Cumberland corps attacked from the north. The attack began at four P.M. and while Logan assaulted the left flank, Brig. Gen. Jefferson C. Davis's XIV Corps attacked the salient angle and captured two batteries of Confederate guns and more than 800 prisoners, including Brig. Gen. Dan Govan. Hardee put a brigade in to close the breach in the center of his line and held off any further Federal gains. Maj. Gen. David Stanley's Federal IV Corps, attacking down the railroad, was slowed by an elaborate abatis that the Rebels from States Rights Gist's brigade had cut and woven from trees with their pocketknives earlier in the day. This only postponed the inevitable, and during the night of September 1–2, Hardee evacuated Jonesboro and withdrew down the railroad to Lovejoy's Station.

Lovejoy's Station

With news of the defeat at Jonesboro, General Hood realized that his army confronted disaster if it remained in Atlanta. He ordered the corps remaining in Atlanta, Lt. Gen. Alexander Stewart's, to evacuate the city. Stewart's men took the McDonough Road south to avoid Sherman's armies astride the Macon & Western Railroad north of Jonesboro and at Rough and Ready. They proceeded south to Lovejoy's Station on the night of September 1 to join the remnants of Hardee's corps, which had retreated to that position after the Battle of Jonesboro. S. D. Lee's corps, having countermarched north to East Point after the first day's fight at Jonesboro, met Hood and Stewart's corps there. Lee was ordered to march briefly toward Atlanta as if to oppose the Federals, then countermarch south to Lovejoy's.

There, the Army of Tennessee threw up earthworks (which are lost today), and remained for nearly three weeks. Sherman advanced to Lovejoy's Station with Howard in the lead, but, upon launching a late-afternoon probe against the entrenched Rebels, decided to wait for word from General Slocum, then advancing cautiously toward Atlanta. When word reached Sherman that Slocum had occupied the city on the morning of September 2 after Hood's evacuation, Sherman ordered his entire force to Atlanta, perhaps missing an opportunity to deliver a punishing blow to the Confederate forces gathering at Lovejoy's Station. In Atlanta, Sherman allowed the hard-campaigning Federals to rest and refit.

Lovejoy's Station reentered the picture in November. After Hood took the Army of Tennessee north, the area was evacuated. But in October 1864 part of the Georgia militia, under the command of Maj. Gen. Gustavus W. Smith rendezvoused in this area. On November 16, 1864, Howard's wing of Sherman's command moved through this area at the beginning of the March to the Sea. Judson Kilpatrick's cavalry, screening the right flank of Howard's wing, skirmished with Brig. Gen. Alfred Iverson's Rebel horsemen at Lovejoy's and drove them back southeast toward Griffin.

Federal Occupation of Atlanta

Shortly after midnight on September 1–2, the Federal "army group" positioned both north and south of Atlanta knew something eventful was occurring in the city when booming sounds filled the air. Sherman, at Jonesboro, feared Hood might have turned on Slocum and engaged him in battle. The real reason for the commotion was the destruction of ordnance trains of eighty-one cars and seven locomotives. The last Confederate forces to leave the city exploded the trains, trapped by Federal control of the railroads leaving the city in relays to prevent its capture. The next morning, September 2, the lead elements of the Federal XX Corps encountered a group of civilians northwest of the city. Mayor James M. Calhoun surrendered Atlanta to the XX Corps's Brig. Gen. John T. Ward and asked for protection for civilians and private property. Sherman, arriving in Atlanta on September 3, wired to General Halleck in Washington, "Atlanta is ours and fairly taken." The news of victory counterbalanced the difficult summer of reverses in the East that had jeopardized the chances of Lincoln's reelection, only two months off.

The Federal occupation of Atlanta continued through mid-November. Sherman, in September, called for the evacuation of all civilians from the city, prompting an exchange of letters with Mayor Calhoun and General Hood. From this exchange of communications, in which Sherman lectured on the culpability of civilians engaged in or supporting the cause of those who were in violation of the laws of the United States, meaning the Confederates, the ideas he developed were turned into a paraphrase that Sherman later used and which is the most famous quote attributed to him—"War is hell!"

By mid-November, when Sherman had returned to Atlanta after giving up the pursuit of Hood's Army of Tennessee, then at Florence, Alabama, bracing for its march into Middle Tennessee (see **Spring Hill, Tennessee**), he had successfully lobbied Grant for permission to break loose from his line of communications and begin a destructive march to the coast. On November 14, Federal engineers began to knock down key rail and manufacturing facilities. Fires accompanied this destruction and swept through the city. Only the city hall, five churches—saved after an appeal from a Catholic priest—one hotel, the Masonic Temple, and 400 residences remained. The smoldering ruins were still in evidence the next morning as the first units stepped off in their eastward journey from Atlanta, the historic march to the sea.

After the September 2, 1864, fall of Atlanta, Federal soldiers quickly occupied key locations in the city. The 2nd Massachusetts, the Provost Guard of Sherman's "army group," occupied the park in front of the Atlanta City Hall. The site is now the location of Georgia's State Capitol.

Points of Interest

Downtown Atlanta—In downtown Atlanta there are several sites associated with the siege and capture of the city. Starting in the north part of the city, there is one noteworthy GHC marker at Marietta Street and Northside Drive Expressway. Here, Mayor James M. Calhoun met the advance of the Federal XX Corps on September 2, to surrender the city and seek Union army protection for the community. Nearby was Fort Hood, the northwest salient of the Confederate fortifications of Atlanta. The line ran through the campus of the Georgia Institute of Technology east of here. The Federal siege line was parallel to the Rebel line, a few present-day blocks north. Portions of the Federal works are preserved on private land, but are currently inaccessible. A rise just west of I-75 at 14th Street was part of the Federal line.

In the center of Atlanta, you can walk to sites that were important to the siege and occupation as well as to the lifeblood of the city. The sites are within walking distance of the famous Underground Atlanta between Pryor Street and Central Avenue just southeast of Five Points, the Civil War–era commercial center of Atlanta. Alabama Street, in Underground Atlanta, was an important commercial street during the Civil War as well and was adjacent to the railroad, which the modern streets that have created Underground Atlanta pass over. Within the Underground are exhibits depicting Atlanta's past, inter-

On the night of September 1–2, the Federal forces in Jonesboro heard loud explosions coming from the north. The sound was from the destruction of these Confederate ordnance trains, eighty-one cars and seven locomotives, which were detonated to prevent the ammunition and rolling stock from being captured by the Federals after the Rebel withdrawal that night from Atlanta. The trains were exploded near the site of Fulton Industries, a rolling mill that supplied the Confederates with war goods.

mingled with numerous shops and restaurants. Of particular interest to the Civil War Atlanta are a gas lamppost, with a hole in its base reported to be the result of Federal shelling, and a marker locating the car shed—the railroad depot that appears in many Civil War photographs and in a climactic scene of *Gone With the Wind*.

A block and a half southeast of the Underground at Martin Luther King Drive and Washington Street is the Georgia state capitol. The capitol is on the site of Atlanta's Civil War–era city hall. The capitol grounds contain interpretive markers and statues, including an equestrian monument of John B. Gordon. In 1886, Jefferson Davis made one of his last public appearances here along with James Longstreet and Gordon at the dedication of a statue to Davis's friend and Confederate politician Benjamin Hill. Inside the capitol's Georgia Museum of Industry and Trade there are Civil War exhibits and flags. The nearby Georgia Department of Archives and History has a large collection of documents. Across Washington Street from the capitol at the current Atlanta City Hall, part of which occupies the site of the John Neal House, Sherman's headquarters in Atlanta, is a monument to Father Thomas Patrick O'Reilly, who convinced the Federals to spare the destruction of five downtown churches and the city hall.

From downtown Atlanta, proceed south on I-75/85 to the Lakewood Freeway (GA154/166).

East Point–Red Oak—There are a few scattered sites relating to the movement of Sherman's forces around the southwest front of Atlanta's fortifications from East Point, west and south to Red Oak. Most are identified only by GHC markers but a few buildings from the period, rare in Fulton County, remain. On Campbellton Road, at Adams Park, just northwest of the Delowe Drive exit from the Lakewood Freeway (GA154/166) there are some Confederate earthworks remaining from the southwest extension constructed to protect the railroad junction at East Point. Farther west on Campbellton Road at Union Road is Rock Owl Church, founded in 1828, where the two sides skirmished during Sherman's march on the railroads south of Atlanta. GHC markers on Fairburn Road south of Ben Hill at Mount Gilead Methodist Church, which was used as a hospital by both sides, describe the movements of Schofield's and Thomas's armies on August 27–29 as they marched toward Jonesboro. A skirmish took place here on August 28. Other GHC markers along GA139 and GA85 indicate the extension of the Confederate line of earthworks and the movements of the Federal forces to Rough and Ready and Jonesboro. The current army base Fort McPherson was a prewar militia camp and Confederate training facility. Barracks and a cartridge factory there were burned by the Rebels evacuating Atlanta. After the war, Generals George Meade and John Pope served at the post as commanding officers of the Third Military District.

Rough and Ready—Rough and Ready (present-day Mountain View) is on GA3 just east of Hartsfield-Atlanta International Airport. There are three GHC markers that indicate the position occupied here by Hardee's corps on August 30, prior to his being ordered to Jonesboro. Rough and Ready was also used as a transfer point from which civilians, ordered by Sherman to leave Atlanta in early September, were turned over to Confederate escorts by the Federals who accompanied them south from Atlanta.

Jonesboro—Jonesboro is on US41/19 south of Atlanta, exit 77 from I-75. A preferred route south from Atlanta, East Point, or the airport area is to use I-75 exit 78 and travel south on GA85. The Thames House at Thames and Clark Howell roads just west of GA85 stood during the march south by the Federal IV and XXIII corps. A GHC marker on Thames Road identifies the earthworks dug here in August by Hardee's corps to oppose the Federal advance on the railroad at Rough and Ready. At GA138, turn left. You are now traveling east toward Atlanta on the route the Federal Army of the Tennessee used to approach Jonesboro from the west. As you cross the Flint River, you see the several GHC markers that detail the deployment of Howard's army on August 30, 1864.

The August 31 attack on Howard's Army of the Tennessee took place in the area on both sides of GA138 between the Flint River and US41/19. This area is almost entirely com-

The Warren House, built in 1840, is one of the few remaining landmarks of the Battle of Jonesboro. The battle on September 1, 1864, raged just to the north and west of the house. After the Federals drove the Confederates from the area, the house was used as a hospital and a headquarters by the 52nd Illinois Regiment. Visible evidence of the fighting remained for many years and the house still has a few battle scars.

mercial now. A better indication of the terrain conditions then is given by the ravine where Cleburne's attack against the XVI Corps was repulsed. This is in a residential area southwest of the intersection and can be reached by taking any of the paved roads south of GA138 and west of US41/19. Note your entrance point as many of the roads wind about and some end in cul-de-sacs.

The town of Jonesboro is several blocks east and the main street is GA3. The railroad, which follows the Civil War–era roadbed, runs through the middle of the town. The courthouse, jail, and depot were built in 1869 to replace those destroyed in Kilpatrick's August 1864 cavalry raid. A few blocks north of the depot on the east side of the railroad is the Patrick Cleburne Confederate Cemetery, where many of the Southern soldiers killed in the Battle of Jonesboro are buried. At Mimosa Drive, 0.2 mile north of the cemetery, is the Warren House, near the salient angle where Daniel Govan's Arkansas Brigade received the punishing blows of the Federal attack. The house, which still has battle scars, was used as a hospital by the Federals after the battle. It is not open for tours. However, two Jonesboro antebellum mansions, Ashley Oaks Mansion and Stately Oaks Plantation, may be toured. For more information on tours and special events, including the Tara Ball in September, the Fall Festival and Battle Reenactment in October, and the Tour of Homes and Dessert Sampler, all at Stately Oaks, contact the Clayton County Convention and Visitors Bureau, 8712 Tara Boulevard, Jonesboro, GA; 770-478-4800 or 1-800-662-STAY.

Lovejoy's Station—On US41 at Hastings, north of Lovejoy's Station, a GHC marker describes the November 16, 1864, cavalry action between Judson Kilpatrick's Union cavalry and Alfred Iverson's cavalry. Kilpatrick drove Iverson south to Bear Creek Station (Hampton), where a GHC marker on US41 south of Lovejoy's describes the skirmish there in which Kilpatrick sent Iverson skedaddling south toward Griffin. A GHC marker at Lovejoy's Station on US41 at Talmadge Road describes the formation of a Georgia militia force under Maj. Gen. G. W. Smith and its march to the area to oppose Federal forces. No remains of the earthworks from the September occupation of the area by the Army of Tennessee or the later militia occupation exist. The Crawford-Talmadge Plantation, Talmadge Road, stood when the Confederates assembled here after the evacuation of Atlanta. Reportedly, the mansion was the inspiration for Twelve Oaks in Margaret Mitchell's *Gone With the Wind*.

PALMETTO

On September 19, Hood began moving the 35,000-man Army of Tennessee from Lovejoy's Station to this stop on the Atlanta & West Point Railroad. Six days later, on September 25, President Jefferson Davis arrived at the Rebels camps for a council of war, wherein Hood laid out his plans for an invasion of Tennessee.

Davis, as much trying to ascertain the leadership difficulties in the Army of Tennessee as anything, sat for three days with Hood, then implemented a plan to take care of some of the problems. William Hardee, whom Hood blamed for most of the failure in the fall of Atlanta and whom Hardee countercharged with incompetence, was assigned to head the Department of Georgia, Florida, and South Carolina. Hood was to remain in command of the Army of Tennessee; however, Davis placed P.G.T. Beauregard in charge of an entirely new Division of the West, larger than that which Gen. Joseph E. Johnston had been assigned to command nearly two years earlier. While it was primarily an advisory, rather than a fighting position, Beauregard did have veto power over any action of Hood, and of Lt. Gen. Richard Taylor, who commanded in Alabama, Mississippi, and east Louisiana. Davis departed Palmetto on September 27, while Hood prepared for his march across the Chattahoochee River and into northwest Georgia which began the next day.

In July, as part of what was deemed the "Great Cavalry Raid," Brig. Gen. Edward M. McCook proceeded southwest across the Chattahoochee River with the objective of linking up with a cavalry force riding around the east flank of the Confederate force in Atlanta under Maj. Gen. George Stoneman. United, the plan was for the force to break the Macon & Western Railroad at Lovejoy's Station. After crossing the Chattahoochee twelve miles downstream from Campbellsville on the morning of July 28 and tearing up track on the Atlanta & West Point Railroad at Palmetto, McCook arrived at Lovejoy's Station early on July 29. However, after Stoneman's force did not arrive and McCook learned of the presence of the Confederate cavalry under Maj. Gen. Joseph Wheeler, he backtracked, intending to recross the Chattahoochee River via Newnan.

Wheeler's force pursued McCook's cavalry and caught up with the rear unit at Line Creek. The Federal troopers were slowed by exhaustion and misdirected by Confederate prisoners they had taken earlier. By the time McCook's main force reached Newnan on July 30, dismounted troopers under Brig. Gen. Philip D. Roddey, who were en route to Atlanta, had formed a battle line in town and skirmished with McCook's lead regiment. McCook then diverted his column farther south, but the relentless Wheeler divided his force and battled the scattered units of McCook's command in detail. After this series of actions, collectively known as the Battle of Brown's Mill, McCook and his surviving troopers, in groups and some individually, recrossed the Chattahoochee River to safety. McCook lost 68 percent of his command, most captured, and only when he returned to Marietta on August 5 did he learn that Stoneman had failed to communicate his intention to ride first to Macon and Andersonville to liberate Federal prisoners and had met disaster at Sunshine Church (see **Sunshine Church**).

Points of Interest

On US29 in the center of Palmetto is a small park and memorial to the Confederate Army of Tennessee. Situated 3 miles north of the town near the railroad were the entrenchments and camp of Hood's army from September 19–29. Southeast of Palmetto on Line Creek the rear guard of Edward McCook's cavalry battled part of Wheeler's cavalry on July 29. Proceed south on US29 to Newnan.

A GHC marker on the courthouse lawn in Newnan describes the Battle of Brown's Mill, which took place 3 miles south of the town. Newnan, like many other towns in this region, contained Confederate hospitals. Dr. Samuel H. Stout, medical director of the Army of Tennessee, supervised seven hospitals here. In Oak Hill Cemetery are the graves of 268 Confederate soldiers who died while convalescing here. Only 2 graves are unidentified.

From the courthouse, proceed south on US29 for 1.4 miles to Corinth Road. Turn right and travel 1 mile to the Millard Farmer Road, then drive 2.5 miles on this road to the Old Corinth Road. In this area, Col. Henry Ashby's Confederate cavalry attacked the head of

McCook's column. There is a UDC marker, the Wheeler Monument, to the left of the intersection. Return to I-85 at exit 8 and proceed southwest to West Point.

WEST POINT

The western terminus of the Atlanta & West Point Railroad, where the Chattahoochee River curves south to form the Alabama-Georgia border, was an important transportation center for the South. But when Sherman's "army group" cut off this railroad from Atlanta after the Battle of Jonesboro, its significance was reduced. Consequently, West Point was one of the last strategic points in Georgia to be occupied by the Federals. It was not until April 16, 1865, one week after Lee's surrender at Appomattox, that the town fell to one of Brig. Gen. James H. Wilson's cavalry columns led by Col. Oscar LaGrange, proceeding northeast from Tuskegee, Alabama.

The town was garrisoned by Georgia militia and extra-duty men under Brig. Gen. Robert C. Tyler, a veteran commander in western battles since Belmont, Missouri. Wounded while a colonel at Missionary Ridge and suffering the amputation of a leg, Tyler was placed in charge of the garrison at West Point in 1864. A fort was built and named Fort Tyler.

On that Easter Sunday, 1865, Wilson's troopers placed the fort under siege for eight hours, culminating in the capitulation of the garrison and the death of Tyler. Later, the Federal cavalry destroyed 19 Confederate engines and 340 cars loaded with commissary and other supplies, and burned the wagon and railroad bridges over the Chattahoochee. Then they resumed their eastward march to Macon.

Points of Interest

There are three areas of interest in West Point. Take GA18 west 1.4 miles to Avenue E and turn north one block to East Eleventh Street. On the corner are historical markers indicating the graves of 76 Union and Confederate soldiers killed or mortally wounded in the Battle of West Point. Among the graves in the plot, of which only 19 are identified, are those of Tyler and his second-in-command.

Proceed south to GA18 and west for 0.5 mile to the downtown area. On the corner of GA18/US29 and West Eighth Street is a historical marker describing the battle. This is also an opportunity to see the railroad terminus, although all buildings and tracks are postwar. Fort Tyler is gone but if you proceed west on Eighth and follow it to the left behind the U.S. Post Office, you come to the base of a hill on North Fourteenth Street. Proceed up the hill to the corner of North Fourth Avenue. In this small residential area was the approximate location of Fort Tyler.

COLUMBUS

This city on the Chattahoochee River, 120 miles southwest of Atlanta, was known for its manufacturing capabilities and as a transportation center. It was the farthest northern port on the Chattahoochee River; the falls just north of the city made the river unnavigable for any shipping north of Columbus. Two railroads, a line extending west in Alabama toward Montgomery, and a spur running south from West Point, linked the city with its most important civic neighbors. In the antebellum period, the cotton was brought to the river in large quantities, then shipped downriver to the Florida panhandle and on to the Gulf of Mexico.

The most noteworthy of Columbus's manufacturing in what was Georgia's fourth largest city at that time was its riverfront rolling mill. It was from this mill that the materials were taken to construct the Chattahoochee River fleet of Confederate gunboats and an ironclad, named the CSS *Jackson* when she was completed late in the war in 1865. Cannon barrels, railroad rails, and plating armor for other Rebel ships were also fabricated here.

The gunboat CSS *Chattahoochee* and others were launched on the river but saw only limited duty because the Federals never mounted a campaign on the Chattahoochee. The ironclad ram CSS *Jackson* was barely completed by war's end and was cut adrift and sunk to avoid capture.

Columbus avoided the horrors of battle until after the surrender of the Army of Northern Virginia at Appomattox Court House, although Confederate troops passed through the city in late January and early February 1865 when units of the Army of Tennessee numbering in the hundreds rather than the thousands came through en route east to challenge Sherman's northeastward march from Savannah. Then on April 16, 1865, Brig. Gen. James H. Wilson arrived west of the city intent on destruction of its manufacturing facilities. Columbus was a target on Sherman's list to Wilson as he and his 10,000 troopers rode east from Montgomery, Alabama, to destroy the last vestiges of Deep South war goods supply to the Confederate armies. A rare night attack ensued, though the Georgia militia there was no match for Wilson's powerful columns and the city was in Union hands by midnight that same day.

Points of Interest

Confederate Naval Museum—Although the Confederate Naval Museum, located on the Chattahoochee River, is not itself historical, its collection is. Most important, it contains major remains from two Confederate gunboats, discovered buried in the mud of the river that, like that of the USS *Cairo* in Vicksburg, Mississippi, and the CSS *Neuse* in Kinston, North Carolina, provides haunting glimpses of the vessels of the riverine navies. The two vessels here are the CSS *Chattahoochee*, a wooden screw-driven river gunboat, and the CSS *Jackson*, a river ironclad originally named the *Muscogee*. The remains of the hulls that were excavated in 1961–64 are on display, reassembled to give an idea of the ships' size and construction. Other artifacts recovered from the vessels, including armor, machinery, and armament, are displayed alongside the hulls or in the museum.

The museum has a fine collection of paintings, models, uniforms, weapons, and other artifacts that shed light on the role of naval operations in the Confederacy and noteworthy naval battles such as Hampton Roads and Mobile Bay. It also has exhibits that unfold the stories of the notorious and successful Confederate commerce raiders including the *Alabama*, the *Florida*, and the *Shenandoah*.

The museum is located at 202 Fourth Street and is open Tuesday to Friday, 9:00 A.M. to 5:00 P.M., and 1:00 P.M. to 5:00 P.M. Saturday and Sunday; it is closed Monday. There is no admission charge but donations are encouraged. 🖼 ♿ ❓ 🏛 🚻

Along Columbus's revitalized riverfront, besides an excellent view of the river vital to commerce in the Civil War era is the site of the rolling mills so important to the Confederate war effort. Historical markers indicate the site of the old river commerce wharf and the rolling mills. The present structure was built on the site in the 1870s to replace the one destroyed by Wilson's cavalry. It has been added to several times.

Columbus has many fine examples of restored antebellum dwellings in the downtown area. Several of the houses have Civil War significance. The Mott House, in its original location, currently on the property of the Fieldcrest Spinning Mills, was Federal Brig. Gen. James H. Wilson's headquarters during his occupation of Columbus in mid-April 1865. On Second Avenue between Ninth and Tenth streets are several homes extant during the Federal occupation of the city. One, moved from the outlying countryside, was the summer home of Confederate Capt. John S. Pemberton, the pharmacist credited with creating the original Coca-Cola formula.

On Tenth Street, across from the 1870s-era Springer Opera House, are several historical markers that describe the interesting stories of Columbus regiments and some of the weapons produced here. Just around the corner on Third Avenue, a marker in front of the police station locates the Columbus arsenal. At Fourth Avenue and Fourteenth Street, a monument and historical marker commemorate Columbus's role in the Civil War.

Just across the Chattahoochee in Phenix City, Alabama, is Fort Gilmer, an earthen fortification built in 1863 to protect Columbus from an attack from the west. A pentagonal earthen fort with 30-foot-high ramparts and adjoining trenches, it is the best remaining example of the extensive defensive system thrown up to protect the city. Fort Gilmer was not manned during Wilson's raid because of a lack of manpower. To get to Fort Gilmer, take US80 west across the bridge into Phenix City, then go north on US280 for 3 miles. Pull into the shopping center on the left and park. Walk up the hill on the rim of the new construction and find the path that leads to the fort.

ANDERSONVILLE

As the Civil War approached the end of its third year, the problem of handling prisoners of war became a serious matter for the Confederates, for several reasons. One was the increasing prison population which occurred because of the Lincoln administration policy of discouraging the parole and exchange of soldiers who could then fight again for the South and because of the Confederates' refusal to exchange black prisoners or treat their white officers the same as other as prisoners of war. Another was that the decreasing resources of the South resulted in shortages of food and supplies for the Rebel army, making these necessities even scarcer for prisoners of war. Finally, as the Federals captured more Southern territory, the likelihood of Union raids to free their prisoners increased.

This last reason was on the mind of Gen. John Bell Hood in September 1864 as he prepared to launch a campaign against Maj. Gen. William T. Sherman's lines of communications north of Atlanta. Hood ordered all prisoners moved from Andersonville, Georgia, to other facilities in preparation for changing his base to Palmetto from Lovejoy's Station. In doing so, he was leaving the line of the Macon & Western Railroad unprotected and Andersonville was on a spur of that railroad. Indeed, a Federal cavalry raid in July had the liberation of Andersonville as one of its objectives, but the defeat of Maj. Gen. George A. Stoneman in this raid sent many of his troopers to Andersonville as prisoners (see **Sunshine Church**).

The South's most notorious prison lasted a mere fourteen months. While other prison pens such as Belle Isle in Richmond were in operation longer, Andersonville, known officially as Camp Sumter because it was in Sumter County, was not only the largest Civil War prison, but had the reputation of being the worst. Evidence of this is the death rate of 28.7 percent or 12,912 of the 45,000 prisoners who spent time at Andersonville. Two other large prisons, Elmira, New York, a Federal prison, and Salisbury, North Carolina, a Confederate prison, had the next highest mortality rates with just under 25 percent. The size of Andersonville's population and the resulting overcrowding also contributed to the deadly conditions. But to understand the tragedy of Andersonville, it is first important to understand the reasons behind it.

Being a prisoner of war is one of the most trying experiences a human being can have. Besides the environmental hardships, having to endure the deprivation of necessities, harsh treatment by their captors, boredom, and lack of hope can have devastating physical, mental, and emotional effects on prisoners of war. In the Civil War more American soldiers were in captivity than in any other period of the nation's history. More Federal soldiers were captured in the Civil War than were American soldiers in all the twentieth-century conflicts combined. Many, particularly the Confederates who surrendered at the end of the war, were soon on parole. But many others endured months and sometimes years in prison camps.

Andersonville was beset by problems from the beginning. Even the selection of the site was difficult as residents of several areas of southwest Georgia found ways to avoid having the prison located near them. But by 1864 the Confederate government knew it was necessary to build a large prison for enlisted men in an area far from the theaters of conflict and where food would be more plentiful. Construction was started on the site in January 1864 and the design—a stockade surrounding an open field—was of the type then deemed necessary for large numbers of captives. A prison population of 10,000 was planned for. Materials, tools, and even manpower were in short supply, though slaves were impressed from the area to provide most of the construction labor. Transportation on the inadequate railroads caused delays and shortages in bringing lumber, medicine, and food to the site. Nevertheless, the first group of captives from Richmond arrived on February 25, 1864, to an as yet unfinished stockade.

While those in charge of the prison did intend to provide prisoners with the basic necessities—food, shelter, and clothing—and to create a secure facility, they fell short in all these. The design of the prison itself was faulty. The hospital was originally located inside the stockade; the bakery, cookhouse, and guard camps were located upstream from the only source of water leading into the stockade; barracks were not constructed until September, when the prison population was greatly reduced. Resources in 1864 were scarce in the South. Supplies that were not needed for the Confederate army and designated for Andersonville often ended up with speculators or stranded by inadequate transportation. Lack of experience and bureaucratic squabbling among officers of the prison and in Richmond and the state capital led to more shortages and a guard detail of inexperienced Georgia Reserves—mostly old men and boys—replacing regular Confederate forces within a few months. On several occasions in the first months of the prison's operation, officers from Richmond were sent to investigate the conditions and the reports they filed accurately described the appalling conditions. But little was done to alleviate the problems.

By August 1864, the prison held more than 32,000 men. Though the stockade was expanded, it was still too small. In very tight quarters, with only their self-made improvised shelter "shebangs" to shield them from the elements, tattered clothes, deplorable sanitary conditions, food that was often uncooked, spoiled, and in short supply, disease rampant, and deaths occurring daily, the prisoners often became desperate. Those of low character and sometimes those who were just stronger preyed on their weak, sick, and dying comrades. Some gave up hope and chose to end their misery by crossing the "dead line," a nineteen-foot no-man's-land between the enclosure occupied by the prisoners and the inside of the stockade wall. Others tried to escape—while on work details outside the stockade or by digging tunnels under the wall. Nearly all were recaptured and punished severely. Other prisoners, however, sought to make the best of their desperate situation by finding solutions for their own survival by assisting their less innovative or less fortunate comrades.

Most of the deaths occurred because of the inadequate medical care provided for the prisoners. Steps were taken to control the most familiar diseases that were brought into the camp and exacerbated by the filthy conditions, but those epidemics accounted for only a small percentage of the deaths. Overcrowding and unsanitary conditions in both the hospital and the camp itself led to killer conditions—gangrene, dysentery, and infections were much in evidence. And these afflictions were very often fatal not only because of the general lack of medical knowledge at the time but because of the lack of staff, supplies, and hospital facilities. Contrary to the intent of prison officials and surgeons to provide adequate care, the reality of these shortages combined with mismanagement, lack of caring, and even exploitation by those overseeing prisoners led to increasing numbers of deaths.

After Hood's change of base to Palmetto in September, many of the prisoners were moved to other camps in coastal Georgia and neighboring South Carolina. The prisoners that remained at Andersonville were mostly those too sick to move. By April 1865, with the end of the Confederacy in sight, the remaining prisoners were started to Florida, returned to Andersonville, and then sent to Camp Fisk, four miles east of Vicksburg, where they were paroled. Many of these men while en route up the Mississippi lost their lives in late April when the transport *Sultana* exploded and sank. The end of Camp Sumter at Andersonville officially came in early May when cavalry from Brig. Gen. James H. Wilson's command arrived there. Capt. Henry E. Noyes arrested Capt. Henrich "Henry" Wirz, a Swiss émigré who had acted as commandant of prisoners since shortly after the facility had opened, except when he had been too ill to attend to his duties for five weeks in the summer of 1864. Since Wirz was in charge of everything within the interior of the prison, he was held responsible for the conditions of the prison, and the many deaths of the prisoners of war at Andersonville.

Wirz was taken to Washington, where he was charged with conspiring to destroy the health and lives of Federal prisoners of war at Andersonville and with murder. He was tried by a military tribunal, sentenced to death, and hanged on November 10, 1865 (see **The District of Columbia**). There is no evidence that Wirz ever murdered or ordered a prisoner to be killed, but he along with the others named as conspirators, including Jefferson Davis, were held responsible by a Northern population—inflamed by months of newspaper and other accounts, often embellished, about the terrible conditions at the prison—bent on vengeance for the prisoners' deaths. Only Wirz was tried; of the others named among the most culpable was Brig. Gen. John H. Winder, post commander for three months at Andersonville, who died of a heart attack on February 6, 1865.

Wirz's abrasive personality, made worse by a painful broken right wrist that never healed, made him an easy target as a monster. In fact, although he had done some positive things for the prisoners, especially cracking down on the organized bands of "raiders," prisoners who formed gangs to prey on other prisoners, the conditions were what they were and situation was what it was in Andersonville. In the end, Wirz was a scapegoat—not innocent but not entirely guilty, a player in a system that was not equipped to handle and did not place the proper importance on the fair and humane treatment of prisoners of war.

Points of Interest

Andersonville National Historic Site—Today, the former Camp Sumter and the Andersonville National Cemetery serve as a memorial and legacy not just to the Federal prisoners of war who suffered and died there but to American prisoners of war in all wars and conflicts. The main entrance to the site, which is reached from GA49, 10 miles northeast of Americus, Georgia, leads you first to the visitor center. There uniformed Park Service interpreters are available to provide information and answer questions. The visitor center features exhibits on Andersonville and the cemetery as well as Civil War prisons in general and the systems of parole and exchange. There is a slide program and relief maps of Andersonville in 1864–65 and today.

The park tour route guides you through the national cemetery which contains the graves of the prisoners who died at Andersonville, other Civil War soldiers, and more recent veterans. Thanks to the efforts of a July 1865 mission headed by Clara Barton, nearly all the prisoners who died at Andersonville have been identified and their graves marked. The tour road continues to the site of the stockade and other parts of the prison. A POW museum featuring exhibits on prisoners of all wars has been established at the north end of the stockade. Other features include monuments placed by various states and groups, some of the wells and tunnel shafts dug by prisoners, earthworks that protected the camp, and markers for camp buildings.

On the west side of the stockade, a portion of the stockade, one of two stockade entrances, and several "shebangs" have been reconstructed. The stockade "pigeon roosts" (guard towers) and dead line at the northeast corner of the prison pen have also been reconstructed. Another feature is the Providence Spring House. On August 9, 1864, during a rainstorm, a new spring welled up out of the ground, providing much-needed fresh water for the prisoners who attributed its appearance to Divine Providence. ANDERSONVILLE NATIONAL HISTORIC SITE, Route 1, P.O. Box 85, Andersonville, Georgia 31711; 912-924-0343. 🗺 ♿ ❓ 🏛 P ⛱ 🚻

In the small town of Andersonville across GA49 from the park, there is a monument to Captain Wirz, erected in 1909 by the Georgia Division of the UDC. From Andersonville, proceed north on GA49, then east on GA26 to I-75. From there you can proceed south to Irwinville, which is recommended, or north to Macon.

DRIVING TOUR—*Proceed to Irwinville*
READING—*prisons: Point Lookout, Maryland*

IRWINVILLE

Near Irwinville in south central Georgia, on May 10, 1865, Jefferson Davis was captured, ending his five-week flight from Richmond. Davis was on his way to the Trans-Mississippi Confederacy to link up with Gen. Edmund Kirby Smith and other Confederates, having traveled by horseback in a southwesterly direction through Washington and Sandersville, Georgia. His family joined him near Dublin on May 7. Still traveling with Davis was cabinet member John H. Reagan and an escort of three officers and ten volunteer cavalrymen. Ten thousand dollars in gold coins, the remnants of the Confederate treasury, most of which had been sent elsewhere, was carried with them in saddlebags. On the evening of May 9 the Davis party made camp near Irwinville.

The 4th Michigan Cavalry under Lt. Col. Benjamin D. Pritchard was in pursuit of other Confederate officials but received a tip on the evening of May 9 that Davis's party was in the area. The troopers approached the camp in the early-morning hours. Simultaneously, the 1st Wisconsin Cavalry under Lt. Col. Henry Harraden, which was assigned to pursue Davis, arrived. The two commands were unaware of each other's presence, having arrived by different routes.

On the morning of May 10, both units surrounded Davis's camp. In the smattering of gunfire which followed, two members of the 4th Michigan—John Rupert and John Hines—were accidentally shot and killed by troopers from the 1st Wisconsin and four Federals were wounded. Davis, believing the commotion to be caused by Rebel marauders, left his tent but discovered his error. When he returned, his wife, Varina, implored him to escape alone and threw her shawl on her husband's head to disguise him. He was soon accosted by a mounted Federal, who hoped to topple him from his horse, but was restrained by Varina when the trooper leveled a carbine at him. The rest of the party was captured without injury. One officer, John Ward, former captain of the raider CSS *Tallahassee,* escaped by bribing a trooper. The rest were taken to Brig. Gen. James H. Wilson's headquarters in Macon and from there by train to a steamer waiting in Augusta.

Points of Interest

Jefferson Davis Memorial Park—The park is on GA32, 1.1 miles north of Irwinville, which is 13 miles east of I-75. The park has a museum, built by the WPA in 1939–40, a playground, rest rooms, picnic tables, and a pavilion. The park is open 9:00 A.M. to 6:00 P.M. daily. The museum is open 9:00 A.M. to 5:00 P.M. except between noon and 1:00 P.M. Tuesday through Saturday. Sunday hours are 1:00 P.M. to 5:00 P.M. Admission is charged for parking and the museum. ♿ ❓ 🏛 P ⛱ 🚻 💲

DRIVING TOUR—*Proceed to Sunshine Church*
READING—*Palmito Ranch, Texas*

SUNSHINE CHURCH

As an arm of the "Great Cavalry Raid" at the end of July 1864, Maj. Gen. George Stoneman led 5,000 Federal troopers of his and Brig. Gen. Kenner Garrard's divisions southeast from Decatur. In a plan approved by Sherman, Stoneman was given permission to take his three brigades of cavalry south to Macon and Andersonville to liberate the Union prisoners of war at those camps after joining Edward McCook's cavalry column at Lovejoy's Station—the combined force then to break the Macon & Western Railroad between Lovejoy's Station and Macon. But, after departing from Decatur on July 27, Stoneman, with zealous dreams of the heroic liberation of prisoners, changed his mission. Garrard proceeded independently from east of Atlanta to Flat Rock, where he was to wait for Stoneman. Stoneman, riding far to the southeast, arrived east of Macon on July 29 and proceeded to destroy railroad and other property along the Georgia Central Railroad west of Gordon.

Stoneman then doubled back to Macon. But east of the city, on July 30, he encountered the entrenched Georgia militia under Maj. Gen. Howell Cobb. After Federal artillery unlimbered and fired a few harmless shots at the militia and into the city, Stoneman, receiving reports that a large cavalry force was heading for his flank from the south, remounted his troopers and rode north. The reports, from captured Georgia pickets, were false; Cobb had fabricated the story in order to drive Stoneman into a trap set by part of Maj. Gen. Joseph Wheeler's cavalry.

Wheeler had divided his smaller force after learning of the Federal raid. Part of it was sent to harass Garrard, Wheeler and a portion of his command went after McCook, and Brig. Gen. Alfred Iverson, a native of the Macon area, placed his brigade in the path of Stoneman's force at Sunshine Church, eighteen miles north of Macon. Iverson's defense line, in the shape of an inverted V, was very effective. While dismounted cavalry and artillery held Stoneman in check from the front, part of Iverson's force rode behind the Federals, giving the impression of being the larger force Stoneman had received earlier reports about. About four P.M. on July 31, Stoneman met with his brigade leaders and ordered two brigades to escape while he held off the Rebel force with the other.

About that time Iverson launched a frontal attack and overran the position of Stoneman's dismounted troopers. The two brigades barely escaped and Stoneman surrendered with about 600 men to a force that was smaller than his original force of three brigades. Stoneman and his officers were sent to Camp Oglethorpe in Macon; his captured troopers were sent to Andersonville. The two brigades that got away and proceeded east toward Athens were challenged by militia and turned back toward the Federal lines. Col. Horace Capron's brigade was intercepted by Col. William C. P. Breckinridge's brigade and routed along King Tanyard Creek on August 3. Only Garrard's force escaped relatively unscathed after remaining in the vicinity of Flat Rock, skirmishing ineffectually with the Confederate cavalry, then returning to Decatur ending the "Great Cavalry Raid."

Points of Interest

The Sunshine Church Battlefield is on GA11, 10 miles north of US129 at Round Oak, which is 26 miles northeast of Macon. Several GHC markers south of the village describe the battle, the location of Iverson's line of defense, at the present-day intersection with Pippin Road, and Stoneman Hill, just to the north of GA11 about 2 miles southeast of Round Oak, where the general and his force were captured. The location of the original Sunshine Church is marked; it was burned by Sherman's Federals in the March to the Sea.

Maj. Gen. William T. Sherman and key officers of his march through Georgia and the Carolinas pose in this studio portrait. They are (left to right) Maj. Gens. Oliver O. Howard, Right Wing commander, and John A. Logan, XV Corps commander; Brig. Gen. (later major general) William B. Hazen, XV Corps division commander; General Sherman; Bvt. Maj. Gen. Jefferson C. Davis, XIV Corps commander; Maj. Gens. Henry D. Slocum, Left Wing commander; Joseph A. Mower, XVII Corps division commander; and Francis P. Blair, XVII Corps commander.

THE MARCH TO THE SEA

Beginning in late September 1864, William T. Sherman began to formulate a new strategy for the disposition of his "army group." With Atlanta in hand and the Confederate Army of Tennessee threatening his line of communications extending north into Tennessee, he lobbied Grant to break free of his base and begin a march across Georgia to another strategic target on the Alabama Gulf coast or a port on the South Atlantic coast— Savannah or Charleston. When Hood's army slipped from Sherman's grasp and into north Alabama, Sherman pressed his case to Grant, " I propose that we break up the railroad from Chattanooga [to Atlanta] and strike with our wagons to Milledgeville, Millen and Savannah. By attempting to hold the [rail]roads we will lose 1,000 men monthly, and will gain no results. I can make the march and make Georgia howl."

In the meantime, Maj. Gen. John Schofield had returned to his department in East Tennessee and Sherman sent Maj. Gen. George Thomas with two divisions to Nashville to check raids by Nathan Bedford Forrest on Federal supply depots in north Alabama and Middle Tennessee (see **Athens**, **Alabama**, and **Johnsonville, Tennessee**) and to keep an eye on Hood's army. By November 2, Grant allowed Sherman to proceed with his plan to abandon Atlanta and march to another location, probably Savannah, feeding his army off the land and breaking the spirit and means to make war by destroying farms, mills, and rail facilities in the rich areas of Georgia through which his army would pass.

Sherman's remaining force of more than 62,000 men was divided into two wings of two corps each. The left wing was composed of the XIV and XX corps under the command of Maj. Gen. Henry Slocum. The right wing, under the command of Maj. Gen. Oliver O. Howard, included the Army of the Tennessee's XV and XVII corps. A cavalry division under Brig. Gen. H. Judson Kilpatrick was to operate independently but in support of the two wings. The lead elements of the force left Atlanta on November 15, 1864, amid the destruction of the city. The general direction of the two columns was east and south, toward Macon, Milledgeville, the state capital, Augusta, and Savannah.

The only two forces left in Georgia to oppose Sherman were the cavalry corps of Maj. Gen. Joseph Wheeler and various state troops and militia units, most of which were commanded by Maj. Gen. Gustavus W. Smith. The opposition to Sherman's march was provided primarily by Wheeler's cavalry due to the small size and lack of experience on the part of the militia and the difficulty in transporting them to places where they could intercept Sherman's fast-moving columns. Ironically, the one important victory scored by the Georgia militia during the campaign was outside the state (see **Honey Hill, South Carolina**).

Sherman's left wing under Slocum initially marched along the line of the Georgia Railroad toward Augusta and then southeast to Milledgeville, the point designated for rendezvous with the right wing. Their most challenging obstacles during this march were bridges destroyed by the Confederates, which the Federal soldiers would repair or replace with pontoons while they inflicted their own destruction on the railroad and other targets. The right wing proceeded southeast from Atlanta in the direction of Macon, to threaten that city. The XV Corps encountered light resistance from Rebel cavalry while marching toward Jonesboro, while Kilpatrick, riding in the same general direction at the outset, beat back Iverson's cavalry from Lovejoy's Station (see **Lovejoy's Station**). As the XV Corps passed northeast of Macon, bypassing the city, they encountered the first major resistance of the march in what would prove to be the largest engagement of the campaign at Griswoldville (see **Griswoldville**).

Macon

Although it was Georgia's third largest city during the Civil War, Macon escaped the destructive elements of battle and occupation that other Southern cities endured until April 20, 1865, when Brig. Gen. James H. Wilson culminated his late-war raid through

Alabama and Georgia and made the city his headquarters for a time. Other Federal cavalry had visited the area before: Maj. Gen. George Stoneman had shelled the city and threatened the Georgia militia holding it on July 30, 1864, until he met disaster at the Battle of Sunshine Church, and Brig. Gen. Judson Kilpatrick's troopers had battled elements of Joseph Wheeler's cavalry corps on November 20, driving the Rebels across Walnut Creek and into the fortifications of East Macon. But no armed Federal soldier had entered Macon before Wilson's bloodless capture of the city, except as a prisoner. George Stoneman was one of those prisoners, held with other Federal officers at Camp Oglethorpe until exchanged in September 1864 for Confederate general Daniel Govan.

As Sherman's left wing approached Milledgeville in the third week of November 1864, the state government of Joseph E. Brown evacuated the capital and moved the seat of government to Macon.

Points of Interest

Spared devastation during Sherman's March to the Sea and not a scene of intense fighting, Macon has preserved much of its antebellum architecture. The City Hall, 511 First Street, was built in 1863 and served as the state capitol after the government of Joseph E. Brown fled Milledgeville in November 1864 on the approach of Sherman's "army group." Other historic buildings served as hospitals and a prison for Federal officers. Rose Hill Cemetery on Riverside Drive was established in 1840 and contains the graves of Union and Confederate soldiers in the Confederate Square section.

Among numerous antebellum homes in Macon are the Lanier Cottage, where Confederate officer, lawyer, and renowned poet Sidney C. Lanier was born; the Italian Renaissance Revival Hay House, an opulent mansion built in 1855–59; the Greek Revival Woodruff House, which served as Brig. Gen. James H. Wilson's headquarters when his force occupied Macon; and the Old Cannonball House and Confederate Museum, which shows evidence of Maj. Gen. George Stoneman's July 30, 1864, shelling of Macon. All of these homes are open for touring with admission charged. The 1842 Inn, 355 College Street, is an 1842 home which is now a bed and breakfast. For information on all these sites and more of Macon's rich past, contact the Macon Downtown Welcome Center at Terminal Station, 200 Cherry Street, Macon, GA 31201; 912-743-3401.

Griswoldville

On November 22, 1864, one of three significant battles during Sherman's March to the Sea—the only one on the line of march—occurred just east of the small manufacturing community of Griswoldville, east of Macon. The action resulted from the planned attack on Col. Eli Murray's Federal cavalry brigade of Kilpatrick's cavalry division by Maj. Gen. Joseph Wheeler's cavalry, and the unplanned collision of Georgia State Troops with XV Corps infantry from the division of Brig. Gen. Charles R. Wood.

The previous day, the 9th Michigan Cavalry Regiment had raided Griswoldville, destroying manufacturing and rail facilities, including a factory manufacturing Confederate brass-frame navy revolvers, and most of the town's buildings. Early on the cool morning of November 22, Wheeler attacked Murray's brigade, which was not involved in the raid on the town but was camped two miles east of Griswoldville. Brig. Gen. Charles C. Walcutt's XV Corps brigade, camped four and a half miles northeast of Griswoldville, was on the extreme right of the infantry in Howard's right wing. Together, Walcutt and Murray drove the Rebel cavalry west through Griswoldville, then retired and entrenched on a ridge one mile east of the town. Their right was anchored on the Georgia Central Railroad and the left on a branch of Big Sandy Creek. The Federals barricaded their line with fence posts and rails from the Duncan farm, which their position occupied.

The Georgia troops, under the overall command of Maj. Gen. G. W. Smith, consisted of Smith's Georgia Militia, Georgia State Troops under Lt. Col. Beverly D. Evans, the Athens and Augusta Local Defense Battalions under Maj. Ferdinand Cook, and a battery of light artillery. Smith was under orders to transport these soldiers to Augusta, the city that department commander Lt. Gen. William J. Hardee concluded to be Sherman's destination. Smith remained in Macon to attend to the movement of the trains and supplies and sent the force forward along the railroad under senior brigadier Pleasant J. Philips, with orders not to seriously engage any enemy encountered.

As Philips's force, which left Macon at eight A.M. on November 22, approached Griswoldville, he discovered the Georgia State Troops formed in line of battle west of Griswoldville. When it was ascertained that the Federals (Walcutt's brigade) had withdrawn from the town, the Georgia State Troops proceeded east on the railroad as previously ordered, Philips following with the rest of the force not far behind. Soon, Cook's battalions came face-to-face with the entrenched Yankees. Philips, who was said to be drinking heavily, ordered a line of battle formed and at two-thirty P.M. launched an all-out attack on the Federal force, which was superior in number, partially armed with seven-shot Spencer repeating rifles, barricaded, and made up of veterans. Aided by cavalry and Col. Milo Smith's XV Corps brigade that was dispatched to the scene, Walcutt's brigade turned back the poorly equipped Georgians, most of whom were older men and boys.

Though the fighting lasted to dusk, the Federal position was not seriously threatened during this battle. The Confederates in seven attacks sustained 523 casualties, compared to 92 for the Federals, and retreated to the defenses on the east side of Macon. Among the Union wounded was General Walcutt. Walcutt's brigade, Milo Smith's brigade, most of which was held in reserve, and the cavalry regiments that were engaged joined their respective units as Sherman prepared to undertake the second phase of his march, from the Milledgeville area, where his four corps and cavalry were now camped, to converge again at Millen, a town on the Georgia Central Railroad, near where the Confederates had built a prison pen to hold thousands of the Andersonville prisoners.

Points of Interest

Griswoldville is located 10 miles east of Macon and can be approached from two directions. Take US129 east for 3.7 miles, then turn right on SR49, which is Griswoldville Road. Follow SR49 east for 4.1 miles to the corner of Henderson Road. At this intersection, where the railroad crosses the road, was the town of Griswoldville. An alternative route is to take US80 east for 3 miles, then bear left on GA57 for 3.5 miles to Ridge Road (unmarked at the intersection), and turn left and travel north to the railroad. All that remains in evidence of the town is the millpond northeast of the intersection. Continue east parallel to and south of the railroad on a secondary paved road.

Two GHC markers along this paved road indicate the deployment and assault of the Georgia State Troops and the site of the cavalry skirmish. A short distance past the cavalry skirmish marker is another road which intersects the road and goes north. At the top of this rise was the center of Walcutt's line on the Duncan Farm. The Confederate assaults, failing to flank the Federal line on either end, funneled into an attack on this strong position at Walcutt's center. All of these sites other than the roads themselves and 25 acres embracing much of the Duncan Farm are on private property, but preservation efforts are under way at Griswoldville. At Clinton, 12 miles north of SR49 on US129, the McCarthy-Pope House, restored from 1809, and several other historical buildings stand. For more information, contact the Old Clinton Historical Society, Inc., Clinton, Georgia.

DRIVING TOUR and READING—*Proceed to Milledgeville*

Milledgeville

The lead elements of the Federal XX Corps entered Milledgeville, the state capital, without opposition on November 22. The state legislature had adjourned earlier and fled to Macon, accompanied by the Georgia Militia which had remained there. Sherman arrived the next day with the rest of Henry Slocum's left wing. Federal soldiers looted the State House and State Library; the State Arsenal and railroad depot were burned and the powder magazine blown up. Some of the Federal officers held a mock legislature in the Hall of Representatives and debated and repealed Georgia's Ordnance of Secession. While Sherman, who was not present enjoyed the joke, he was more inclined to focus his attention on the next leg of the march—from Milledgeville to Millen. In addition to the continued destruction of the Georgia Central Railroad during the next phase of the march, Sherman also hoped to release the Federal prisoners, many of whom were formerly at Andersonville, then incarcerated in a new prison six miles north of Millen at Magnolia Spring. By November 24, the left wing had departed Milledgeville and the right wing started east from its camps near Gordon.

Points of Interest

Milledgeville (US441) has a number of historic buildings and homes, most located in the central area. The Baldwin County Convention and Visitors Bureau offers a brochure and tours of the historic district. The visitor bureau is located at 200 West Hancock Street, Milledgeville, GA 31601. For more information, call 800-653-1804 or 912-452-4687. Among the historic buildings featured are the 1807 Old State Capitol, 201 East Greene Street; the 1838 Old Governor's Mansion, 120 South Clark Street; and St. Stephen's Episcopal Church, 220 South Wayne Street. The Governor's Mansion, which Sherman occupied during his brief stay in Milledgeville, can be toured. A fee is charged. For more information, call 912-453-4545.

———◆◆◆———

DRIVING TOUR and READING—*Proceed to Madison*

———◆◆◆———

Madison

On the March to the Sea, the Federal XX Corps passed through Madison on November 20 after destroying sixteen miles of railroad track between Social Circle and this town. The day before, Brig. Gen. John Ward's XX Corps division had destroyed railroad cars, support facilities, and Confederate army supplies here. Lt. Col. Silas Adams's brigade of Stoneman's cavalry, after leaving their chief at Sunshine Church, destroyed supplies here on August 1, 1864 (see **Sunshine Church**). At Madison, the three divisions of the XX Corps divided, with Brig. Gen. John Geary's 2nd Division continuing east along the railroad while the other two divisions turned south.

Points of Interest

Madison, on US278 a few miles north of I-20 exit 51, is a lovely little town full of historical structures and shade trees. Among the antebellum homes here is that of Joshua Hill, a Georgia politician during the war and Reconstruction. The city cemetery contains the graves of Confederate soldiers, most unknown, and a black hospital attendant, who died in an area hospital.

While the town of Crawfordville, 37 miles east of Madison (I-20 exit 55) was not on the route of Sherman's march, the town is famous as the home of the Confederate vice president. Alexander H. Stephens Historic Site is a memorial to the Georgia statesman. His restored home, Liberty Hall, and grave are here amid large trees and beautiful grounds. Tours of the mansion are given and there is a small Confederate museum in one of the outbuildings. Camping, boating, fishing, and hiking are available at nearby A. H. Stephens State Park.

———◆◆◆———

DRIVING TOUR and READING—*Proceed to Washington*

———◆◆◆———

Washington

Washington was also bypassed by the Federals in Sherman's March to the Sea. However, the town was home to powerful prewar U.S. and Confederate planter, politician, and general Robert A. Toombs. Toombs, who served briefly as the Confederacy's first secretary of state, and Jefferson Davis were political enemies for much of the conflict. Nevertheless, Toombs offered his home and services to Davis during his May 1865 flight through the state. Davis, who held his last meeting here with several cabinet members, arrived after his family had already left for Abbeville, Georgia. He sent a message thanking Toombs but stayed elsewhere for the one night (May 3–4) he spent here.

Points of Interest

Washington has a number of lovely antebellum frame homes on tree-lined streets, a definite stop for those interested in the architecture of the Old South. Among them are the home of Robert A. Toombs, now a state historic site on GA10. The Washington-Wilkes Historical Museum, in a restored antebellum home at 308 East Robert Toombs Avenue, has Jefferson Davis artifacts in its collection. The Gilbert-Alexander House, Alexander Drive, was home to Brig. Gen. E. Porter Alexander, General Longstreet's artillery commander.

DRIVING TOUR and READING—*Proceed to Augusta*

Augusta

Augusta was a large manufacturing and rail city on the Savannah River. Here in January 1861 the U.S. Arsenal was seized by the state militia under orders from Gov. Joseph E. Brown. Col. Josiah Gorgas, Confederate chief of ordnance, quickly expanded the facility to turn out cartridges and artillery ammunition, and store firearms. The need for raw materials, especially gunpowder, prompted an inventive Confederate engineer, Col. George W. Rains, to start construction in September 1861 of the Augusta Powder Works, on the Augusta Canal, near the Savannah River northwest of the city.

The Augusta Powder Works was a two-mile-long complex of factory components and offices, which together created an assembly-line process that turned out as much as five thousand pounds of gunpowder daily. The complex began production in May 1861 and

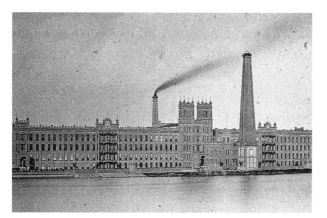

The Augusta Powder Works was a two-mile-long complex of buildings along the Augusta Canal. It turned out as much as five thousand pounds of gunpowder daily, supplying nearly all the Confederate armies in the field with the powder necessary to sustain their fighting power. The brick chimney seen in this nineteenth-century photograph remains today in a complex of postwar manufacturing buildings.

continued operation until April 18, 1865. Despite Rains's excellent design and emphasis on safety, four explosions occurred during the life of the facility.

Returning from his trip to the Confederate camp at Palmetto in October 1864, Jefferson Davis gave a public address in Augusta, accompanied on the platform by Gen. P.G.T. Beauregard and Lt. Gen. William Hardee, both on the way to accept their new assignments after the fall of Atlanta (see **Palmetto**).

The Federal army, during Sherman's March to the Sea, did not pass through Augusta. Kilpatrick's cavalry, during the march between Milledgeville and Millen, feinted toward Augusta but never rode into the city; they were intercepted by Joseph Wheeler's cavalry and battled the Confederate horsemen at Waynesboro and Buckhead Creek (see **Waynesboro**). During Sherman's march through South Carolina, Kilpatrick again demonstrated toward Augusta, raiding Aiken, South Carolina, on February 11, 1865.

Points of Interest

The brick chimney is all that remains of the gunpowder factory that at that time was second only to the Du Pont facility in Wilmington, Delaware, in size in the world. The facility's main building was the largest permanent structure built during the war by the Confederate government. The brick obelisk chimney (the nation's tallest Confederate monument), currently surrounded by a series of postwar brick factory buildings, is on Broad Street at Goodrich Street. Take Washington Road (GA28) several miles southeast of I-20 exit 65 until it forks into Broad Street (to the left) and John C. Calhoun. The Augusta Arsenal is located at Walton Way and Katharine Street. It was in continuous use for 128 years until closed by the U.S. Army in 1955. GHC markers in Augusta also locate the Georgia Railroad and Banking Company (Eighth Street at the railroad shops), the starting point of Georgia's first railroad; the Old Richmond Academy Building and First Presbyterian Church (500 block of Telfair Street), which both served as hospitals during the war; and the birthplace of Joseph Wheeler, Wheeler and Aumond roads, 1 mile northwest of Augusta.

DRIVING TOUR and READING—*Proceed to Waynesboro*

Waynesboro

On November 23, 1864, Sherman ordered Judson Kilpatrick's cavalry to the left of the "army group," to head northeastward toward Augusta to indicate that Sherman's columns were headed there, destroy the railroad, burn the Briar Creek trestle and then to ride to Magnolia Springs and liberate Federal prisoners held at Camp Lawton since October. Confederate General Wheeler, hoodwinked, massed his horse soldiers on the Augusta approaches. Kilpatrick reached the Georgia Railroad north of Waynesboro on November 26, but the tail of his column was attacked in its camp that night at Sylvan Grove by Wheeler's cavalrymen who, realizing their mistake, were in hot pursuit. The next day Kilpatrick, learning that the prisoners had been removed from Camp Lawton, turned south through Waynesboro, setting fire to the town, though the pursuing Rebel troopers brought the fires under control.

On the night of November 27, the Federals camped near Buckhead Creek. Kilpatrick, pitching his tent far from his troops, was nearly captured when Wheeler's people attacked the camp early the next morning. The Federal rear guard held off the Rebels at the creek and formed a barricaded line farther south on the Reynolds Plantation. After turning back two Confederate charges, the Federal cavalry rode south to Louisville.

Sherman now ordered Kilpatrick to go after Wheeler again and sent Brig. Gen. Absalom Baird's division of the XIV Corps to support him. The combined Federal force drove Wheeler's cavalry from Rocky Creek on December 2; then, after Wheeler shot up Federal infantry breaking up the Georgia Railroad the next day, Kilpatrick launched a cavalry attack on Wheeler's barricaded position across the railroad south of Waynesboro on December 4. An assault by infantry and horse artillery broke the first line south of the town; then a mounted charge drove the Confederates from their second line in Waynesboro. Wheeler retreated to Brier Creek. Kilpatrick returned to the Federal camps in preparation for his next mission during the third and final leg of Sherman's march from Millen to Savannah.

Points of Interest

Several GHC markers near Waynesboro describe the various actions in the area. At US25 and GA24, south of Waynesboro, the cavalry actions on November 26 and December 4 south of and in the town are described. At Brier Creek and GA56, 4 miles northeast, the November 27 Federal bridge-burning attempt and cavalry skirmish are detailed. The GHC marker for the December 2 action at Rocky Creek Church is on GA24 at Rocky Creek, 5 miles southwest of Waynesboro, and 4 miles south on US25 in Idlewood, the December 3 attack on Baird's and Kilpatrick's railroad wreckers by Wheeler at Thomas's Station is described. Bellevue Plantation, 3 miles west of US25 near Perkins on Old Buckhead Church Road, was a temporary burial site for soldiers killed in the November 28 Confederate attacks. The battle also was fought in the churchyard of the 1845 Old Buckhead Church, which is on a dirt road leading west from US25, 4 miles west of Perkins. The church and battle are also sited as being 4.3 miles west of a GHC marker on US25 which is 2 miles south of Perkins.

Four miles north of Millen on US25 is Magnolia Spring State Park, the site of the Camp Lawton prison pen. The park features a visitor center and interpretive kiosk with exhibits describing the facility, Confederate earthworks, and camping facilities.

DRIVING TOUR and READING—*Proceed to Ebenezer Creek*

Ebenezer Creek

During the final leg of the March to the Sea, as his four corps moved in roughly parallel columns preparatory to besieging Savannah, an incident occurred that over the years has raised passions and fostered debate. The Federal XIV Corps arrived at the bridge over

Ebenezer Creek, near Springfield, twenty-five miles northwest of Savannah on December 7. Confederates, retreating toward Savannah, burned the bridge, but Federal pontoniers, working through the next day, spanned the creek and by daylight on the December 9, the last of trigger-tempered Brig. Gen. Jefferson C. Davis's XIV Corps units were across. Pressed hotly by Wheeler's cavalry, Davis ordered the pontoon bridge dismantled stranding hundreds of ex-slaves, who were following the column. Some drowned trying to cross the bridgeless creek. Wheeler reported capturing nearly 2,000 during the march to the sea, who were returned to their owners.

Points of Interest

There is not a historical marker in the vicinity. To reach the site of the Ebenezer Creek disaster take the county road leading east from Springfield 2 miles to Stillwell, turn south on the paved road that intersects GA275. Halfway between Stillwell and the intersection is the Ebenezer Creek crossing, a haunting site, well worth a visit.

DRIVING TOUR—*Proceed to Fort Pulaski*
READING—*Fort McAllister*

SAVANNAH AREA

Fort Pulaski

Fort Pulaski, on Cockspur Island, protecting the navigable channels at the mouth of the Savannah River eighteen miles downstream from the city, was a Third System masonry fort begun in 1829 and completed in 1847 at this strategic location. This was the third fort on the island and it was named for the Polish general fighting on the side of the Americans in the Revolutionary War who was killed in the 1779 siege of Savannah, Count Casimir Pulaski. Seized by Georgia state militia on January 3, 1861, it was manned by the Confederates and its armament was increased to forty-eight guns. The fort was pentagonal in shape with walls seven and a half feet thick and thirty-five feet high. A wet moat surrounded the fort and the western land front was protected by large earthen work.

This dramatic color lithograph illustrates the bombardment of Fort Pulaski by the Federal guns on Tybee Island, April 10–11, 1862. Though the artists of the period tended to overdo the smoke and fire of battle, the bombardment was intense and severely damaged the fort's southeast angle, threatening the main powder magazine. The surrender of the fort prevented a powder magazine explosion that would have destroyed larger portions of the masonry fort.

The Federals took an early interest in the position as a strategic entry into Georgia. Shortly after the Federal victory at Port Royal in November 1861 (see **Port Royal, South Carolina**) an expedition under Brig. Gen. Thomas A. Sherman landed on nearby Tybee Island, which the Confederates abandoned on November 10. Capt. Quincy Adams Gillmore, a brilliant engineering officer, was put in charge of the siege of Fort Pulaski.

The Federals established eleven batteries on Tybee Island at distances ranging from one to two miles from the fort beginning in February 1862. The work was tedious and difficult, especially dragging the large siege cannons, including 10 rifled guns, over the marshy surface of Tybee Island. During the last mile of the approach, the guns were moved at night to avoid detection by the Confederates in the fort, 385 men under Col. Charles H. Olmstead.

At eight-ten A.M. on April 10, 1862, the Federal bombardment began. Heartened by the accuracy of 10 rifled guns, the 36 Federal cannons and mortars concentrated their fire on the southeast angle of the fort, nearest to Tybee Island. The Confederates responded, but with only 1 rifled gun, their fire was limited and many of the Rebel guns were dismounted during the first hours of the bombardment. By nightfall, serious damage appeared in the southeast angle. The Federal fire continued in the morning and soon two gaping holes in the scarp allowed Union shells to pass through and land close to the fort's main powder magazine in the northwest bastion. At two-thirty P.M. on April 11, the fort surrendered. Only one soldier on each side was killed during the thirty-hour bombardment and there were no seriously wounded. The Federals did not expand their gains beyond the immediate area of Cockspur and Tybee islands. Savannah remained securely in Confederate hands until taken by Maj. Gen. William T. Sherman's "army group" in December 1864.

Points of Interest

Fort Pulaski National Monument—Fort Pulaski, Cockspur Island, is located 20 miles east of Savannah on US80. Today, Fort Pulaski remains an excellent example of a Third System fort; however, its irregular dimensions give it a different footprint than other pentagonal forts of the Third System, such as Fort Sumter. The national monument, occupying Cockspur Island, has faithfully preserved the fort, the damage to which Federal troops from the 48th New York began repairing within six weeks of the devastating thirty-hour bombardment. Restoration began in the 1930s and today the fort and the surrounding area are scenic and spacious. The wet moat, earthen and masonry demilune, a variety of mounted artillery pieces, as well as the shell-battered walls can be viewed by walking the grounds. Uniformed rangers give talks and audio stations describe various points of interest in the casemates, including a prison and refurbished officers' quarters, the powder magazine, barbette tier, and parade ground.

The visitor center features exhibits on Fort Pulaski in the Civil War, coastal artillery, and Count Pulaski and the Revolutionary War siege of Savannah, and an audiovisual presentation. Fort Pulaski is open daily except December 25 and January 1. FORT PULASKI NATIONAL MONUMENT, P.O. Box 30785, Savannah, GA 31410-0785; 912-786-5787. 🔲 ♿ 🚶 ❓ 🏛 P 🪑 🚻

Just east of Fort Pulaski on US80 is Tybee Island, location of the Federal batteries that pummeled the fort on April 10–11, 1862. Two GHC markers in the park at Savannah Beach on the island describe the bombardment of the fort and the batteries. Tybee Island Lighthouse is Georgia's oldest. Information on the lighthouse and the Tybee Museum at Fort Screven on Tybee Island can be obtained by calling 912-786-5801.

DRIVING TOUR—*Proceed to Savannah*
READING *(chronological)*—*Kennesaw (Big Shanty)*

Fort McAllister

When the four corps of Maj. Gen. William T. Sherman's "army group" arrived in front of Savannah's fortifications in the second week of December 1864, Sherman ordered Brig. Gen. Judson Kilpatrick's cavalry to reconnoiter Fort McAllister, on the Ogeechee River fifteen miles southwest of Savannah. Fort McAllister had come to the attention of the Federals earlier. During 1862 and early 1863, the U.S. Navy bombarded the sand fort on a bluff south of a bend in the river near where it flows into Ossabaw Sound, but had no success in seriously damaging the fort's parapets or guns. On January 27, 1863, R. Adm. Samuel F. Du Pont dispatched one of his new ironclad monitors, the USS *Montauk,* under the command of Cmdr. John L. Worden, with four supporting gunboats, to test the effect of the monitors against shore batteries prior to launching a naval attack on Charleston harbor (see **Charleston, South Carolina**).

On February 28 the *Montauk* destroyed a Confederate blockade runner, the *Nashville,* grounded near the fort. The *Montauk* hit an "infernal machine" later in the day, but the damage was repaired. Three other monitors were sent against Fort McAllister by Du Pont on March 3, but had no better success than the *Montauk.* Thereafter, the Federal navy allowed Fort McAllister to continue its defense of the river when Federal priorities shifted elsewhere.

Kilpatrick had planned to assault Fort McAllister with his cavalry, but Sherman countermanded the order and ordered Kilpatrick to make contact with the Federal fleet off the Atlantic Coast. Several of Kilpatrick's troopers rowed out in two canoes and made contact with the USS *Fernandina,* returning to shore with a navy officer who conferred with the Federal cavalry chief. Another three-man team sent by Maj. Gen. Oliver O. Howard also made contact with the navy. The contact with the fleet was imperative to the successful conclusion of the drive because the swampy lowlands around Savannah did not provide the forage and rations necessary to sustain Sherman's army. The key to establishing a water supply line was opening the Ogeechee River to Sherman's forces west of Savannah and to accomplish that, Fort McAllister must be taken.

The 2nd Division of the XV Corps, Sherman's former command, was assigned the task. Sherman personally instructed division commander Brig. Gen. William B. Hazen to assault the fort early on December 13. The previous day Francis De Gress's Illinois battery had established a position across the river from the fort and an artillery duel commenced. An observation platform established at Cheves' Rice Mill enabled Sherman to view the fort's assault.

Hazen's division started early, marching down the south bank of the river. A captured Rebel picket-turned-defector informed the Federal commander of the strength of the Fort McAllister garrison, about 230 defenders, mostly older men and boys, untested in combat, under Maj. George W. Anderson. The informant also warned of torpedoes (land mines) planted on the vulnerable land approaches to the

Fort McAllister on the Ogeechee River proved impenetrable to the fire of U.S. Navy guns for nearly two years. The fort was finally captured when a division of the Federal XV Corps overran it on December 13, 1864, during Maj. Gen. William T. Sherman's March to the Sea. Today, much of the fort is preserved in a beautiful Georgia state park.

fort. Much of the afternoon of December 13 was spent positioning Hazen's three brigades to enable them to converge on the fort's land fronts. Just before five P.M., prodded by an impatient Sherman, Hazen launched an all-out assault. Moving through the minefield and abatis, the Federals surged up and over the parapets and pursued the defenders man by man as they retreated into the fort's bombproofs. Within fifteen minutes, the fort was stormed and the Stars and Stripes planted on the fort's parapet. The Federals lost 24 killed and 110 wounded, many by stepping on torpedoes; the Confederates, 16 killed, 54 wounded and the rest of the garrison and armament captured. That evening, Sherman made contact with a Federal tug, the *Dandelion,* and later met Department of the South commander, Maj. Gen. John C. Foster, offshore. By noon the next day he was on board R. Adm. John A. Dahlgren's flagship *Harvest Moon* conferring with the admiral, and a few days later, the Federal navy was landing supplies at an Ogeechee River wharf.

Points of Interest

Fort McAllister Historic Park—Fort McAllister, a Georgia state park, is located about 12 miles southwest of Savannah, but cannot be reached directly from the city. Take I-95 south from Savannah to exits 14 or 15, Richmond Hill, and proceed east on GA144, taking Spur 144 when the main road bears to the right, for a total of 10 miles. Along the way, GHC markers indicate the movements of Sherman's right wing and Kilpatrick's cavalry. The five-sided fort is excellently preserved and the park contains a museum, audiovisual theater, and other exhibits, including machinery from the sunken CSS *Nashville*. The fort itself can be toured with a self-guided tour pamphlet and park rangers are available to answer questions. Within the fort are several mounted guns, the hot-shot furnace, magazine, bombproof, parade ground, and reconstructed sally-port and parapets featuring abatis.

A trail can be followed to the mortar battery and exterior of the fort. Interpretive signs indicate naval actions and the land assault, including the northwest angle where the 47th Ohio scaled the fort's river face but was driven back, and the southwest angle where the breakthrough first occurred. FORT McALLISTER HISTORIC PARK, Route 2, P.O. Box 394-A, Richmond Hill, GA 31324; 912-727-2339.   🗺 🏃 ❓ 🏛 P 🚻 ⛽ 💲

DRIVING TOUR—*Proceed to Darien*
READING—*Savannah*

Savannah

Savannah, a planned city with a rich colonial and antebellum heritage, was undisturbed by the ravages of war for three and a half years. The capture of Fort Pulaski and an effective blockade by the U.S. Navy greatly reduced its effectiveness as a Confederate port beginning in early 1862, but the city's strong line of defense kept it from being targeted by Federal inland incursions. When Sherman departed from Atlanta in mid-November 1864, a defense line was constructed to augment outposts on the land approaches and a series of water batteries that had kept the Federals from venturing inland from the coast. Lt. Gen. William Hardee, in command of 10,000 soldiers, had already received permission from overall commander Gen. P.G.T. Beauregard to evacuate Savannah to preserve the integrity of his command when Sherman's "army group" began arriving west and northwest of the city on December 9.

One success for the Federals at Savannah in the quiet period between the April 11, 1862, surrender of Fort Pulaski and Sherman's approach to the city came on June 17, 1863. The iron-screw steamer *Fingal* was being converted to an ironclad in Savannah. A deserter brought information to the Federal Army of the South that the ironclad CSS *Atlanta* was about to venture down Savannah's Wilmington River in search of prey among Savannah's blockaders. Warned by the army, Admiral Du Pont sent the ironclad monitors *Weehawken* and *Nahant* in search of the *Atlanta*. At four-fifty-five P.M., the *Atlanta*, having entered Warsaw Sound, fired the first shot at the lead *Weehawken*, commanded by Capt. John Rodgers, which returned fire twenty minutes later. Four of the *Weehawken's* five shots scored hits. By five-thirty P.M., the formidable Rebel ironclad struck her colors before the *Nahant* could get in on the action. The *Atlanta*, which had fired only four rounds, was taken intact and, rechristened as the USS *Atlanta*, was eventually sent north to serve the U.S. Navy on Virginia's James River.

Sherman was content to place Savannah under siege, deeming the defenses too strong to stage a direct attack, even with his superior force of 62,000. The Federals dug in and for ten days engaged in long-range shelling as they awaited the arrival of siege guns from the coast. Sherman was unwilling to commit a large force to cross the Savannah River and cut off the Rebels' retreat through South Carolina. On December 19 three regiments crossed the river and engaged Confederate cavalry. Instead, after issuing a demand for surrender on December 17, which was promptly refused by Hardee, Sherman left for Hilton Head, South Carolina, to discuss plans with General Foster for a coordinated advance from there against Hardee's line of retreat, and to sever the Savannah & Charleston Railroad.

Hardee did not wait for Sherman's plans to unfold. Constructing makeshift pontoon bridges from skiffs, barges, and dismantled wharves, the Confederates spanned two islands and, after scuttling and burning naval vessels, including the ironclad CSS *Georgia*, spiking guns, and dumping ammunition into the river, the soldiers began to evacuate the city on the night of December 20. By three A.M. on December 21, the rear guard of Georgia Militia was over the river and marching toward Hardeeville, South Carolina; from there, the railroad was operating to Charleston.

When the Confederates failed to return skirmishing fire at three A.M., the Federals cautiously moved forward and discovered the trenches abandoned and the city open. Brig. Gen. John W. Geary, whose forces marched into Savannah first, was met at four-thirty A.M. on December 21 by Savannah's mayor and city officials. Geary accepted a letter addressed to Sherman surrendering the city and seeking the protection of the Federal army. Sherman was still making his way back from Hilton Head by boat but bad weather and low tides caused the vessel to run aground below Savannah and by the time Sherman arrived at his headquarters, Union troops were in the streets of Savannah. The next day, December 22, Sherman established headquarters in the city and sent a message to President Lincoln: "I beg to present to you as a Christmas-gift, the city of Savannah, with one-hundred fifty heavy guns and plenty of ammunition, and also about twenty-five thousand bales of cotton."

Points of Interest

Savannah's downtown streets, tree-lined, punctuated by parks and squares, and large numbers of historic structures, embody the traditional charm for which the city is known. A good starting point for a tour of Savannah is the Savannah Visitors Center in the restored Civil War–era Georgia Central Railroad terminal, 303 Martin Luther King, Jr. Boulevard. The terminal houses the visitor information center and the Savannah History Museum, which touches all periods of Savannah history. Companies offering sightseeing tours of the city operate from here. Pamphlets offering self-guided walking and driving tours are also offered.

Numerous city buildings were present when Confederate and then Federal troops occupied the city. Others witnessed the siege of Savannah in the Revolutionary War. Factors Walk runs along the river and was the center of Savannah's busy port facility. Nineteenth-century cotton factors' buildings still dot the waterfront and the 1852 U.S. Customs House is across East Bay Street. General Sherman used the Green-Meldrim House, Madison Square, as his headquarters. The National Historic Landmark was built in the 1850s in the Greek Revival style. It is currently the Parish House of St. John's Episcopal Church and is available for touring with a small donation. For more information, call 912-233-3845.

GHC markers identify other historic buildings in the city and the location of several of the Confederates' defense batteries. Remains of Fort Boggs are near the entrance to the Savannah Country Club. Old Fort Jackson, built in the early nineteenth century, was a fort garrisoned by the Confederates on the river that never came under direct fire. It can be reached by taking President Street east from Savannah and turning left on Woodcock Road to the river. Fort Jackson and Battery Lee, one of a series of earthen river batteries located nearby, can be toured. Fort Jackson has exhibits, an audiovisual program, and gift shop. The fortifications and the sunken ironclad CSS *Georgia* are under the supervision of the Coastal Heritage Society. For more information, call 912-232-3945.

US17ALT, which crosses the Savannah River north of the city, approximates the route used by Hardee's forces as they evacuated Savannah. A GHC marker on US17 near Onslow Island describes the December 12, 1864, action between Federal XX Corps artillery and two Confederate gunboats—CSS *Sampson* and CSS *Macon*—a rare battle between Federal field guns and the Confederate navy.

DRIVING TOUR—*Proceed to Fort McAllister*
READING—*Sherman's March Through South Carolina*

Darien

Darien was an antebellum port and the town attracted the attention of the Federal navy blockading the Georgia coast. The port town of Brunswick was briefly occupied on March 10, 1862, by sailors from the USS *Pocahontas*, USS *Mohican*, and USS *Potomska*. Citizens burned the wharves in Brunswick prior to the Federals' return and Brunswick was abandoned. The Federals first landed on St. Simons Island on March 9, 1862, and returned that summer to occupy it and build Fort Brown. Raids were made on area plantations. On June 11, 1863, Federal black troops, including the 54th Massachusetts, landed at Darien and burned the town. This amphibious raid will be remembered by those who saw the popular movie *Glory*. These soldiers returned in August 1864 and defeated cavalry and home guards defending the town. In mid-December 1864, elements of Kilpatrick's cavalry reached Nahunta, twenty-five miles west of Darien, and destroyed the railroad there.

Points of Interest

Darien is located 60 miles south of Savannah just off I-95. Historical markers on US17, which parallels the interstate, detail Federal amphibious raids into the coastal counties south of Savannah, including Kilpatrick's cavalry forays during Sherman's approach to and siege of Savannah. Among the GHC markers on US17 is one describing the failed Federal attempt to destroy the long railroad bridge, stoutly defended by the Rebels, over the Altamaha River. Other GHC markers in Darien, St. Simons and Jekyll islands, and St. Marys (at the Florida border) locate former Confederate batteries and describe events associated with Union raids made by naval landing parties or troops based on the "Golden Isles." John McIntosh Kell, executive officer of the CSS *Alabama*, was born in Darien. Jekyll Island, Georgia's premier seaside resort, has a historic district. St. Mary's Methodist Church, extant, was used as a quartermaster's depot during the 1862 Federal occupation of the town.

DRIVING TOUR and READING— *Proceed to Jacksonville Area, Florida*

International

I n the late twentieth century, prominent civil wars tend to receive the attention of one or more international organizations—such as the United Nations or NATO—that try to contain the conflict. Sometimes these organizations even intervene to stop the fighting and bring about a negotiated settlement. In the nineteenth century, however, no such international organizations existed, and foreign governments tended to view a civil war in another country as an opportunity to forward their own interests. If a foreign government did intervene, it was usually a matter of either choosing sides or attempting to make the war worse. While direct foreign intervention in the American Civil War was staved off largely by the adroit actions of the Lincoln administration, several incidents had the potential to internationalize the war.

No land conflicts of the Civil War occurred outside the boundaries of the contiguous United States. However, groups of Confederate secret agents were based in Canada (see **St. Albans, Vermont, The Northeast**) and Federal troops patrolled portions of the Rio Grande border in Texas in a show of force during French occupation of Mexico (see **Texas**). So the Civil War's impact on the international scene was primarily in the form of naval actions and political-diplomatic-economic maneuverings. Often these areas were linked.

With the announcement of a naval blockade of the Confederacy by the Lincoln administration in April 1861 and its establishment by the U.S. Navy, the Federal government brought the conflict to the notice of the world. International law affected blockades, as the United States clearly pointed out to the two large colonial and naval powers, Great Britain and France, which were belligerents earlier in the century when Napoleon Bonaparte was conquering most of Europe. During the Civil War these two powers, particularly Great Britain with its close economic ties to the North and even closer ties to the South, were at the forefront of the nations looking on as war flared in the former British and Spanish colonies. Some of the incidents described here nearly resulted in British intervention on the side of the South. In general, the government of Lord Palmerston, during the reign of Queen Victoria, tilted toward the Confederacy as did the French government of Bonaparte's nephew Napoleon III.

On the other hand, the majority of the British and French people, despite losing thousands of jobs in the textile industries as Southern imports of cotton diminished drastically, supported the free-labor policies of the Lincoln administration, particularly after the announcement of the Emancipation Proclamation. One prominent German writer based in England, Karl Marx, described Lincoln as "the single-minded son of the working class." And while most of the rest of Europe remained neutral, Russia came out in support of the North, at one point sending a fleet of warships to New York and other eastern harbors, as well as San Francisco. So Confederate efforts at recognition and aid and Federal countermeasures focused on the governments in London and Paris.

"King Cotton" diplomacy was the basis for early Southern strategy in gaining European recognition for the Confederate States of America. European countries, however, had been stockpiling cotton in the pre-war years as the sectional crisis was building in America. And in 1860 there had been a bumper crop of cotton, which during the early months of the war glutted the world market. Alternative sources of cotton, such as Egypt and India, were also beginning to put an end to the South's monopoly on the production of raw cotton. An early-war embargo by the South did more to deny needed revenue to the Confederacy than it did to affect European diplomatic efforts. Though a trade rival to Britain, the North was still a force to be reckoned with for the European powers; they had no interest in military conflict with the country they recognized as a growing world power. Consequently, Britain remained officially neutral, and efforts to mediate a peaceful solution to the Civil War were increasingly tied to Confederate success on the battlefield. France, with designs on Mexico, had self-interest in mind in supporting the South's war aims, but would not act without Britain. After the Union victory at Gettysburg, even Napoleon III lost interest in recognition of the Confederacy.

The pen was also a war weapon in Europe. Propagandists from the South worked in Europe and attempted to sway public opinion in the face of published Northern accounts of war events. European journalists traveled abroad to report on the war firsthand, and reporters and artists sent back vivid accounts and sketches of battlefield activities from both sides of the battle lines. The *London Illustrated News* rivaled American newspapers such as *Harper's Weekly* and *Leslie's* with engraved images—some delivered through the blockade by British artists working within the Confederate lines.

A number of Europeans joined the ranks of the Union and Confederate armies as participants— adventure seekers, idealists, and sometimes paid soldiers fought at Shiloh, Gettysburg, and elsewhere. Maj. Gen. George B. McClellan had two French princes on his staff. Officers were sent from European armies to observe and study the war in progress.

Confederate officers from the Trans-Mississippi Department, including John B. Magruder (standing, left), Sterling Price (seated, center), and Thomas C. Hindman (seated right), fled to Mexico, where this picture was taken and where they vowed to continue the fight. The effort never materialized.

Some of them would write and publish vivid impressions of the Civil War and its personalities after the war.

Also after the war, some soldiers North and South, particularly officers, sought military adventure elsewhere. A number joined the Egyptian army. Brig. Gen. Thomas Sweeny led the ill-fated Fenian raid on Canada in 1868, a misguided Irish plot to wrest control of the United States' northern neighbor from Great Britain in return for home rule for the "Emerald Isle." Confederate officers from the Trans-Mississippi, including Sterling Price, John B. Magruder, and Thomas C. Hindman, fled to Mexico, where they vowed to continue the fight, though the effort never materialized.

Confederate cavalryman Jo Shelby led a portion of his "Iron Brigade" of Missourians to Mexico and offered his services to Emperor Maximilian, who was leading the French-backed government that had briefly seized power from the democratic government of Mexico. Maximilian declined Shelby's services but offered some land to Shelby and his followers. In May 1865, Maj. Gen. Philip H. Sheridan was sent with 100,000 men to Texas in a show of force to counter the French imperialistic designs. The rightful government of Benito Juárez finally regained control of Mexico, the French withdrew, and Maximilian was executed with two of his Mexican generals by a firing squad. Many of Shelby's band drifted back into the United States, but Shelby and a few followers remained in Mexico for several years.

Naval Action on the World's Oceans

The Confederacy needed a navy and looked to Europe to provide the shipbuilding capabilities the South lacked. James Bulloch—Theodore Roosevelt's grandfather—was sent to Great Britain to buy vessels and offer shipbuilding contracts. His efforts were primarily focused on the Birkenhead shipyards near Liverpool, England. Commodore Matthew Fontaine Maury of the C.S. Navy also purchased two ships for the Confederacy, and another agent ordered a frigate constructed in Scotland. British law forbade arming or supplying ammunition for warships of belligerent nations; however, Bulloch was able to order "merchant" ships built to his specifications by John Laird & Sons and Fawcett, Preston & Co. of Liverpool. Once launched, these ships were outfitted and commissioned elsewhere. Two of these ships—the CSS *Florida* and the CSS *Alabama*—became dreaded Confederate cruisers. They were needed because the Confederate attempt at authorizing privateers to disrupt the merchant fleet of the United States, second in size only to Britain's at that time, was not working effectively.

Bulloch's efforts in procuring vessels abroad were countered by Federal secret agents and diplomats, who gathered information and turned it over to Britain's government to thwart delivery of the ships. Though the two aforementioned ships, along with the CSS *Shenandoah*, were commissioned for Confederate service, along with a number of the others that became blockade-runners and a few cruisers, Bulloch's attempts to have two ironclad warships built for the South were successfully opposed through the efforts of U.S. minister to Great Britain Charles Francis Adams. Bulloch then turned to France, which built two ironclads. One, the cumbersome CSS *Stonewall*, was launched from France, but did not arrive on the other side of the Atlantic until the war was all but over.

The *Trent* Affair

In late 1861, an incident nearly exploded the Civil War well beyond the borders of the United States. Two *envoys* of the Confederate government to Great Britain and France, respected former U.S. senators James M. Mason of Virginia and John Slidell of Louisiana, boarded the British mail steamer *Trent* in Habana after running the blockade through Charleston. Learning of the presence of the South's commissioners on the ship, Capt. Charles Wilkes of the USS *San Jacinto* stopped the *Trent* in international waters, and took the two Southerners into custody. They were then taken aboard the *San Jacinto* to Boston and imprisoned. The outrage was tremendous in Great Britain, while the North hailed Wilkes as a hero for his contention that the commissioners could be treated as contraband of war.

Wilkes had acted on his own, without the prior knowledge or assent of the Lincoln administration. The formal British protest was quick, forceful, and quite justified, yet to cave in to it would have political implications at home. In the end Secretary of State William H. Seward masterfully worked out a compromise that was acceptable to all parties: Mason and Slidell were released and eventually found their way to Europe, and the United States apologized to Great Britain without admitting wrongdoing. Helping to defuse the outcry was the two weeks it took for transatlantic communications—the transatlantic telegraph cable, laid a few years before, had been unsuccessful—and the efforts of Charles Francis Adams, whose frontline diplomacy helped to soothe injured British pride.

St. George, Bermuda, enjoyed a wartime boom as sleek blockade-runners joined oceangoing steamers and sailing vessels for the exchange of cotton, war matériel, and luxury goods.

Blockade-runners

As the war progressed and the Federal blockade of Southern ports tightened, a new type of ship appeared in the waters off the Southern coasts. Low, sleek steamers, some under the ensign of the Confederacy, some under foreign flags, made the runs from the coast to island ports in the Atlantic and the Caribbean. Occasionally, small remote inlets in the South served these blockade-runners; however, difficulties in transporting goods to and from these locations compelled most runners to use the principal port cities with rail lines leading into the hinterland.

As combined Federal operations forced blockade-runners out of more and more ports, the choice dwindled to four—Galveston, Texas, and Mobile, Alabama, on the Gulf; Charleston, South Carolina, and Wilmington, North Carolina, on the Atlantic. As the Federal blockading fleet increased in number and quality of ships, the number of runners intercepted and seized increased dramatically, but some always got through. Running primarily at night with no lights and with muffled engines, civilian captains and crews took their chances because the financial rewards were huge.

Raphael Semmes was promoted to rear admiral by the Confederate government after returning to the South from Cherbourg, France, via England. A detailed and intriguing account of the adventures of the Confederacy's most famous naval commander is in his book, Memoirs of Service Afloat During the War Between the States.

The rewards were great for Union skippers and crews as well, who received a share of the prize money for confiscated cargoes. Some blockade-runners were refitted to work as U.S. Navy blockade ships. As the blockade squadrons grew, other Federal warships were available to operate on the high seas and in foreign ports, checking the documentation of suspected blockade-runners.

Most blockade-runners were bound for Habana, Cuba, Nassau in the Bahamas, and St. George in Bermuda. There and at other, smaller off-shore ports, their cargoes of cotton and other Southern staples were transferred to merchant ships that in exchange offered war goods and other supplies. Toward the end of the war, when most blockade-runners operated only on the link between Wilmington and the Bahamas, luxury goods, which commanded high prices in the South, were exchanged for cash. Thus the principal Confederate strategic aim of employing blockade-runners to supply the armies of the South was in part compromised at a time when military supplies were most desperately needed.

Confederate Cruisers

A number of Confederate cruisers cruised the seas in search of merchant ships flying the ensign of the United States. The CSS *Sumter* was the first raider under the command of the South's most famous sailor, Raphael Semmes. The CSS *Tallahassee,* a converted cruiser that sailed from Wilmington with an all-volunteer Southern crew, did significant damage to Northern shipping off the coast of New England. In a three-week period in August 1864, the *Tallahassee* sunk twenty-six merchant and fishing vessels and bonded another seven.

The fear of capture by Confederate cruisers led many shipowners to change the registry of their American-flagged vessels to other countries. The Confederate cruisers were responsible for destroying more than 250 U.S. vessels, with dozens more bonded and released for payment of their value to the Confederacy later. After the war, claims for destruction wrought by Confederate cruisers were tied up in international courts for years. The damage caused by the CSS *Alabama* and other British-built cruisers wasn't settled until 1872. But the impact of the Confederate cruisers on the United States merchant fleet lasted well beyond that, as the trend to register ships in other countries continued, and the United States never returned to its position as one of the top two merchant marine powers in the world.

One of two Confederate cruisers ordered by James Bulloch in 1861 and built under the guise of another purpose in Liverpool was launched on March 22, 1862. Thirty-seven days later she arrived in the Bahamas, and after rendezvousing on isolated Green Cay with a schooner loaded with military supplies, including six 6-inch rifled guns, she put out to sea again as the CSS *Florida*. Her captain was John Newland Maffitt, who commanded the cruiser for seven months in 1862, taking twenty-four prizes. Maffitt contracted yellow fever and Lt. Charles Morris took command. On subsequent cruises the *Florida* took another thirteen prizes. In addition, Maffitt turned some of the prizes into commerce raiders as well, and these vessels added to the total destructive reputation of the *Florida*.

In the autumn of 1864, CSS *Florida* under Captain Morris put in at Bahía, Brazil, for rest and refitting. Morris received the assurance that the ship would be safe from the

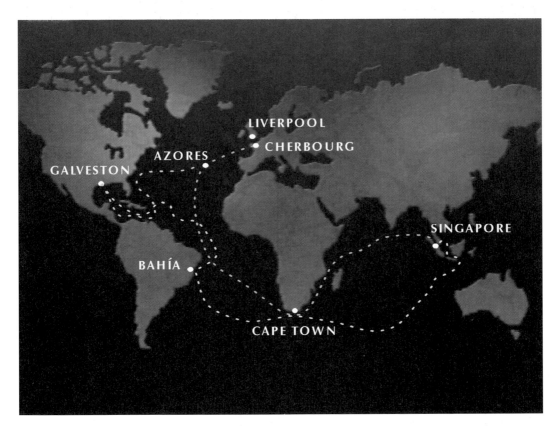

The cruises of the CSS Alabama *included the 1862 segment (white), from the Azores Islands where she was outfitted, to Galveston, Texas, where she sank a Federal warship; the 1863 segment (yellow) included the taking of Yankee prizes in the Atlantic, off South Africa, and in the Orient; and the 1864 segment (blue) which saw the decline of Semmes's health, the stability of the crew, and the soundness of the vessel, which forced Semmes to dock for repairs at Cherbourg, France, on June 11, 1864.*

U.S. consul there. On October 7, however, the consul persuaded Cmdr. Napoleon Collins of the USS *Wachusett*, a steam sloop anchored in the harbor, to defy international law and go after the *Florida*. The *Wachusett* rammed the *Florida* that night while Morris and most of the crew were ashore. The *Florida* took a hard glancing blow but did not sink. Collins had her boarded and her crew seized. The *Florida* was towed to Hampton Roads, Virginia, while Brazil and the European powers forced Washington to issue an apology. Plans were under way to return the *Florida* to Brazil, when she collided with a Federal army transport at Newport News on November 28, 1864, and sank.

The most successful Confederate cruiser was the CSS *Alabama*, the second commerce raider commanded by the brilliant and dashing Raphael Semmes, who would become a Confederate admiral before the conflict ended. Like the CSS *Florida*, the *Alabama* was built at Birkenhead by the Lairds under specifications supplied by Confederate naval agent Bulloch. The ship was delivered to the Azores on August 20, and four days later, off the coast of these islands, Semmes commissioned the CSS *Alabama*.

Semmes was a U.S. Navy veteran who had enlisted as a midshipman at age sixteen and had fought in the Mexican War. After that war, he established a successful law practice in Mobile, but was recalled to naval service in 1856 and was well known to then Secretary of War Jefferson Davis. Resigning his commission in February 1861, he offered his services to the fledgling Confederate navy, and with Davis's full confidence, embarked upon his service as a commerce raider in command of the CSS *Sumter*.

The CSS *Alabama*'s first prey were United States whaling ships off the Azores Islands. That same October 1862, he crossed the Atlantic to attack American shipping off eastern Canada. By then, stories of his reputation, destructive but never brutal, were making headlines in the North. From there his cruise took him to the Caribbean, to the Gulf of Mexico, where he destroyed a Federal warship—the USS *Hatteras*—off the Texas coast (see **Galveston, Texas**), and to Brazil. From there, he sailed to South Africa and into the Indian Ocean and on to Indonesia. In total, the *Alabama* navigated more than 75,000 miles of sea.

As 1864 opened, the *Alabama* was returning to the Atlantic, her machinery wearing out after twenty-two months at sea. By this time the Lincoln administration, under pressure from shipping interests to do something about the Confederate raiders, dispatched warships from the growing U.S. Navy fleet to search out and destroy the raiders. Semmes put in at the harbor at Cherbourg, France, on June 10. Crowds quickly gathered to witness the famed sailors and their ship. Word of the *Alabama*'s arrival reached the U.S. consul, who telegraphed the captain of the USS *Kearsarge*, in a Dutch port three hundred miles away. Sailing hard, Capt. John Winslow had the *Kearsarge* anchored off Cherbourg by June 14. Ironically, Winslow had been a shipmate of Semmes in the U.S. Navy and Semmes had been blockaded at Gibraltar by the *Kearsarge* while in command of the CSS *Sumter,* leading to that ship's internment.

The ships were similar in size and trim, the captains both intelligent and experienced seamen. But the similarities ended there. The *Kearsarge* was ship-shape, and had a well-trained crew, good armament, and reliable ammunition. The *Alabama* lacked in all these areas. Nevertheless, after discussing the matter with his trusted second-in-command, 1st Lt. John M. Kell, Semmes issued a challenge through official channels to and harbor of Cherbourg were crowded with curious spectators, some of whom had even traveled from Paris. Among them was French Impressionist painter Édouard Manet, who would later depict the battle.

At nine forty-five A.M. the *Alabama* weighed anchor and was under way from the harbor. The *Kearsarge* waited well outside the three-mile limit to avoid either ship's having the advantage of seeking protected waters easily. The *Alabama* fired the first shot, and the contest proceeded with thundering broadsides as the ships rounded in six parallel circles. Borrowing from the success of Farragut and others, Winslow *had* heavy anchor chain draped over the sides of the *Kearsarge* for added protection. The *Ala-*

The CSS Alabama *(foreground) battling the USS* Kearsarge *off Cherbourg, France, in this period lithograph. As the* Alabama *began to sink by the stern, the crew abandoned ship. One boat from the* Alabama, *two from the* Kearsarge, *and a passing yacht rescued the officers and crew.*

bama, slower, less maneuverable, armed with lighter guns and less reliable ammunition, started feeling the impact of her foe. After checking stations, Kell informed Semmes that the ship would not last ten minutes. Semmes, concerned for the safety of the wounded, had the colors struck and a boat of wounded was sent to the *Kearsarge* to request aid.

The *Alabama* started sinking. Winslow, having only two boats left undamaged, requested aid from a nearby British steamer, the *Deerhound*. Semmes, casting his sword into the water in a final act of defiance, jumped into the water along with his remaining crew. He and Kell were among those plucked from the water by the *Deerhound* as the *Alabama* disappeared beneath the waves. The *Alabama* suffered 43 casualties, about half killed or drowned; the *Kearsarge*, 3 wounded, 1 mortally.

Hidden from U.S. Navy authorities on the *Deerhound,* Semmes, Kell, and others were taken to England. Semmes eventually made his way back to the South, where he commanded the James River Squadron as the war raged around Richmond and Petersburg, Virginia. Winslow journeyed to Paris shortly after the battle, and Americans in the City of Light received him as a hero. He gained a promotion and the thanks of Lincoln and Congress for his victory over one of history's most famous commerce raiders.

Upon the sinking of the CSS *Alabama,* James Bulloch searched for another potential commerce raider. In October 1864, a merchant steamer, the *Sea King,* was purchased and outfitted near the Azores' island of Madeira. Commissioned the CSS *Shenandoah,* she carried eight guns and was commanded by former U.S. Navy lieutenant James I. Waddell. Waddell was ordered to an area as yet undisturbed by Southern raiders, the Northern Pacific. The area was teeming with fifty-eight Yankee whalers and few Federal warships. On the way, he seized a dozen merchant ships in the South Atlantic, then, sailing via the Indian Ocean and pulling in at Melbourne, Australia, arrived the following spring in the western Pacific. He took four whaling ships on April 1 in the Caroline Islands and continued the campaign in June against a dozen more ships off the coast of Siberia. One vessel had a newspaper on board dated April 14, which told of Lee's surrender at Appomattox.

Refusing to believe that the war was indeed over, Waddell continued his campaign until icy waters forced him south. His prize count had reached thirty-eight. Thinking he then might sail into San Francisco bay and hold the city hostage, he headed southeast. On the way, he overtook a British merchant ship and the story of the war's end was confirmed. Fearing trial as a pirate should he surrender to U.S. authorities, Waddell changed his course to the Indian Ocean and arrived in Liverpool on November 6, 1865, after more than a year at sea. He surrendered CSS *Shenandoah* to British authorities, and the last Confederate ensign was lowered.

Points of Interest

Should you find yourself abroad in one of the places mentioned, you may want to set your mind back to a time when Americans of the North and South braved the sea, as well as shot and shell, in defense of their flags.

The Bahamas—There are no direct points of interest related to the Civil War. In Nassau are the ruins of the Royal Victoria Hotel, built in 1859–61. Undoubtedly, many blockade-running sailors stayed there. The Government House was built in the early nineteenth century, and Vendue House held slave auctions in the early part of the century.

Bermuda—St. George, the former capital of Bermuda, welcomed the business blockade-running brought to the harbor. After the capital was moved to Hamilton, the trade brought a needed economic stimulus to the port. The Confederate Museum, containing exhibits relating to the period, is housed in a building dating from 1700. It housed the office of Confederate agent Maj. Norman Walker, is owned and operated by the Bermuda National Trust, and is open from 9:30 A.M. to 4:30 P.M. in the summer, with slightly shorter hours in the winter. Admission is charged. Fort St. Catherine protected the harbor and was extant during the Civil War. It is two miles from St. George.

Sandy's Parish, on the other end of the island, is home to the Royal Navy Dockyard, on which construction was begun in 1809. The fascinating array of buildings probably witnessed blockade-runners arriving at the port there.

Bahía, Brazil—While nothing remains from the ramming incident and capture of the CSS *Florida*, the beautiful harbor can allow one to visualize the busy port used by warships, merchantmen, and commerce raiders alike.

Cherbourg, Normandy, France—A monument along the quay commemorates the June 19, 1864, battle. Many of the buildings to which spectators flocked to view the battle from windows and roofs are extant.

Artifacts from the USS *Kearsarge* and the CSS *Alabama,* including the sternpost of the *Kearsarge* with a dud shot from the *Alabama* imbedded in it, which Captain Winslow presented to President Lincoln, can be seen at the Navy Museum at Washington Navy Yard (see **The District of Columbia**). Many artifacts brought up from the sunken *Alabama* are also in the collection, while others are on exhibit in France. For information on the location of the CSS *Alabama* artifacts exhibited in France, contact Dr. Ulane Bonnel, President, CSS *Alabama* Commission, 28 Rue d'Artois, Paris, France 75008.

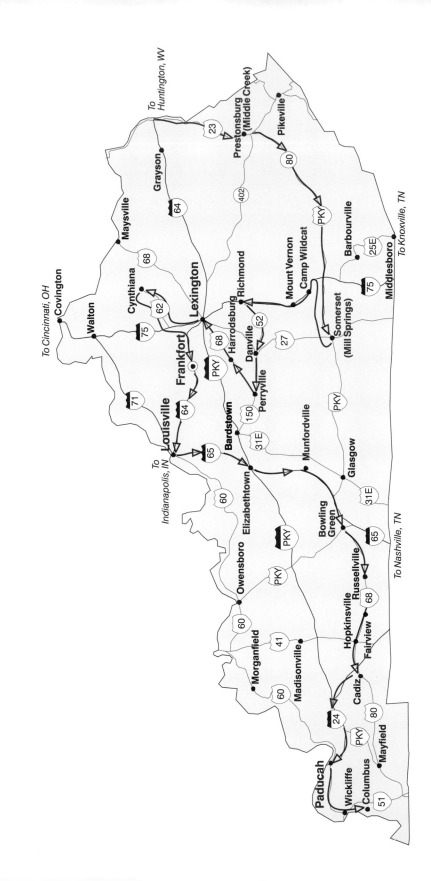

Kentucky

The Bluegrass State, more than its border-state neighbors Missouri and Maryland, embodied the essence of the familiar Civil War "Brother against brother." Regions, communities, even families were torn apart, as men marched in opposite directions to join the ranks of the Union and the Confederacy. More than 75,000 Kentuckians joined the Federal ranks, while 25,000 cast their lot with the Confederacy. U.S. Senator John J. Crittenden, who worked tirelessly in Washington just prior to the inauguration of Abraham Lincoln as sixteenth president for compromise, saw one son, George Bibb, become a Confederate general while another, Thomas Leonidas, became a Union general.

Governor Beriah Magoffin issued a proclamation of neutrality on May 20, 1861, but it was a short-lived policy. On September 3, 1861, Confederate forces under Brig. Gen. Gideon Pillow, on orders from Maj. Gen. Leonidas Polk, occupied Columbus on the Mississippi River. On September 6, Union forces under Brig. Gen. Ulysses S. Grant responded by landing at Paducah, a strategic city at the confluence of the Ohio and Tennessee rivers, trumpeting Polk's move. By late September, Confederates held a line across Kentucky, its left anchored at Columbus, the center at Bowling Green, and the right at Cumberland Gap. Albert Sidney Johnston, the South's second highest-ranking general and friend of President Davis, commanded the vast Department No. 2 from his Bowling Green headquarters. His efforts to hold Kentucky were doomed before the winter ice thawed in mid-January 1862. Defeats at Middle Creek and Mill Springs in eastern Kentucky threatened the Rebels' hold on Cumberland Gap, the gateway to East Tennessee. More serious was the advance of an amphibious force commanded by Grant first up the Tennessee to capture Fort Henry and next against Fort Donelson on the Cumberland (see **Fort Henry** and **Fort Donelson, Tennessee**). By early March, Johnston was compelled to abandon all of Kentucky except for Cumberland Gap to prevent the entrapment of his Bowling Green and Columbus armies.

Kentucky experienced only one major campaign thereafter—the late summer 1862 invasion by Maj. Gen. Edmund Kirby Smith's Army of Kentucky based in Knoxville, Tennessee, and Gen. Braxton Bragg's Army of the Mississippi starting in Chattanooga and surging deep into the Bluegrass region. The Confederate invasion that had threatened Cincinnati and Louisville ended at the Battle of Perryville. After that campaign, battle actions in the state were limited to engagements and skirmishes associated with Confederate cavalry raids under Kentuckian Brig. Gen. John Hunt Morgan and others (see **Cavalry Raids**).

Kentucky, the birth state of Lincoln and Davis, has retained much of its rustic rural beauty to this day. While any time of year will result in a pleasant visit to Kentucky, the state is especially attractive in autumn, when the bright colors of turning leaves add to the overall beauty. A tour of Kentucky sites can be accomplished in several days. Columbus and Paducah in the Jackson Purchase are far removed from the other sites and are more easily accommodated in a tour of eastern Missouri or West Tennessee. They are included here in order of chronology. A variety of cities and towns can be chosen for an overnight stop depending on which direction you are headed and what other states you intend to tour before and after your Kentucky visit.

COLUMBUS

The declared neutrality of Kentucky was broken by events which unfolded in early September 1861 focusing on Columbus, a strategically located town at the foot of a bluff fronting the Mississippi River where the north-south Mobile & Ohio Railroad terminated. Robert Anderson, the Federal commander at Fort Sumter, South Carolina, when the war began (see **Charleston, South Carolina**), was promoted to brigadier general and on August 13, 1861, was named to command the Department of the Cumberland which included Kentucky, his native state. Anderson, until his frail physical condition compelled him to retire from active service, maintained his headquarters in Cincinnati, Ohio. There he oversaw recruiting of Kentuckians for Union service but respecting the state's declared neutrality.

Anderson's diplomatic ways were not shared by the general in charge of the Department of Missouri across the river from Columbus. Maj. Gen. John C. Frémont saw Confederates massed below the Kentucky border in Tennessee as a potential threat to affairs in his department (see **St. Louis, Missouri**). On August 28, he ordered Brig. Gen. U. S. Grant to command of the District of Southeast Missouri with headquarters at Cairo, Illinois. Grant's mission was to clear southeast Missouri of Rebel forces and occupy Columbus.

The Confederates were indeed massing below the Kentucky border, and their commander, Maj. Gen. Leonidas Polk, urged on by General Pillow, decided he had the justification needed to violate Kentucky's neutrality. On September 3, before Grant settled into his new command Confederate soldiers occupied Columbus, to the delight of the town's pro-Southern citizenry. Grant countered the Confederates on September 6, when with two regiments he landed and seized Paducah, thirty-five miles northeast of Columbus (see **Paducah**). Polk spent the next six months fortifying Columbus, including placing heavy guns in batteries commanding the river and covering the land approaches in this, their northernmost position on the Mississippi. At one time, the stronghold, known as the "Gibraltar of the West," emplaced 140 cannons. A huge chain, "Pillow's Folly," was anchored on the Columbus shore and supported by rafts stretched across the river.

These guns would come into play on several occasions against Federal timberclad gunboats operating on the Mississippi. The most notable of these instances was on November 7, 1861, when a feint ordered against Columbus became instead a battle at Belmont, Missouri, directly across the river (see **Belmont, Missouri**). The Confederate cannons shelled troops under U. S. Grant across the river and dueled with two gunboats on the river. On February 23, Federal gunboats exchanged iron with the batteries but by this time preparations were already being made to evacuate. Polk, though he wanted to hold Columbus, was ordered to abandon the stronghold by Gen. P.G.T. Beauregard, Albert Sidney Johnston's second-in-command. Although the position was strong, the deep Federal incursions into Middle Tennessee following the Forts Henry and Donelson disasters necessitated the large Columbus garrison be withdrawn and redeployed elsewhere. Much of the heavy artillery and part of the garrison was withdrawn downriver to Island Number 10, Tennessee (see **Island Number 10, Tennessee**). By March 2, the Confederates had removed most everything of value and evacuated Columbus. The next day Illinois cavalry discovered the fort on the bluffs abandoned and raised the Stars and Stripes. Federal gunboats tied up at Columbus on March 4.

Points of Interest

Columbus-Belmont Battlefield State Park—Located 0.5 mile west of the intersection of KY123 and KY58 at Columbus (KY80, 28 miles west of Purchase Parkway exit 22), the Columbus-Belmont State Park is on the site of the artillery emplacements and for-tifications thrown up by the Confederates to guard the land approaches to Fort De Russy. The water and bluff batteries have eroded into the river. A building used as an infirmary during the occupation houses a museum with an audiovisual program about the Battle of Belmont and the Columbus stronghold's role in it. In addition to the extant earthworks, the anchor sections of chain from "Pillow's Folly" and frag-ments from the huge 128-pounder "Lady Polk," which burst on November 9, 1861, are on the grounds. The park also features a campground, hiking trails, a gift shop, and a snack bar.   ▲ 🗺 ♿ 🚶 ❓ 🏛 P 🏕 🍴 $

DRIVING TOUR—*Proceed to Cairo, Illinois; Belmont, Missouri;*
or Island Number 10, Tennessee
READING—*Paducah*

PADUCAH

When Ulysses S. Grant's orders to occupy Columbus were preempted by Confederate occupation of the town on September 3, 1861, Grant landed at Paducah, Kentucky, on September 6, thirty-five miles northeast of Columbus at the confluence of the Ohio and Tennessee rivers. The town was fortified and garrisoned. With the occupation of Padu-cah, the mouths of the Tennessee River and the Cumberland River, several miles upstream, at Smithland, were held by the Yankees, giving Federal gunboats and steam-boats the opportunity to carry the war deep into the Confederate heartland.

Garrison duty was routine at Paducah until the spring of 1864 when Maj. Gen. Nathan Bedford Forrest, looking for recruits and horses, arrived with his cavalry force shortly after noon on March 25. The Confederates had ridden one hundred miles in fifty hours. Forrest's men had the run of the town, but the Federal garrison occupied Fort Anderson on the river in the town's west end and refused to surrender. The Federals, supported by two tinclad gunboats, raked the town with artillery fire and repulsed an attempt against orders to storm the fort by a Forrest subordinate, Col. Albert Thompson who lost his life. Forrest's men evacuated the town the same day, carrying off much booty, horses, and a few Federal prisoners.

The determined stand by the Federals at Fort Anderson under Col. Stephen G. Hicks was heralded in Northern newspapers, which also pointed out that 140 excellent army horses had been hidden from the raiders. Hearing the account, Forrest subordinate Brig. Gen. Abraham Buford returned on April 14 with a contingent of Kentucky cavalrymen. The Federals again manned the fort, but Buford's troopers made off with the coveted horses.

Points of Interest

Paducah is located just off I-24 exits 3 through 7. Historical markers in Paducah indicate the site of Grant's September 6, 1861, landing (First and Broadway on the wharf); the site of Fort Anderson, a fortification built during Grant's occupation (Trimble Street between Fourth and Fifth), and the headquarters of Brig. Gen. Lew Wallace when he was commander here (Clark Street at Sixth). There is a statue of Confederate officer Brig. Gen. Lloyd Tilghman, who was killed at the Battle of Champion Hill. Tilghman lived at Seventh Street and Kentucky Avenue. The statue is at Seventeenth and Madison streets.

From Paducah, take I-24 east to the Purchase Parkway south, exit 22, to get to Columbus. Or follow the river route via US60 and US51.

DRIVING TOUR—*Proceed to Columbus*
READING—*Forrest's Raid: Fort Pillow–Plum Point Bend, Tennessee*

MIDDLE CREEK

In the autumn of 1861 Confederate authorities were enlisting recruits in the mountainous regions of eastern Kentucky. Orders went out from Federal department commander Brig. Gen. Don Carlos Buell—commanding the Department of the Ohio—to drive the Rebels from that part of the state. Brig. Gen. William Nelson, a huge Kentuckian the size of an all-pro linebacker, advanced into Pikeville and, in an engagement at Ivy Mountain on November 8, sent the Confederates skedaddling back into Virginia.

A month later, Confederate recruiters returned and gathered recruits in camps near Paintsville. Again, Federal soldiers were sent out to drive the Confederates back into Virginia. This time, Col. James A. Garfield, the future U.S. president, led a force against the Rebels. On January 10, 1862, the opposing sides met on Middle Creek. With more firepower and reinforcements, the Federals prevailed and the Southerners, under Brig. Gen. Humphrey Marshall, broke off the engagement. By January 24 Marshall's force was ordered to return to Virginia by way of Pound Gap. Casualties were light in both these engagements.

Points of Interest

If you follow the suggested tour route and enter Kentucky via I-64 from West Virginia, the sites of the Battles of Ivy Mountain and Middle Creek can be reached by taking the first exit in Kentucky, exit 191, and traveling south on US23 to Prestonsburg. The area is attractive; the battle sites retain their historic character; and there is a state recreational park nearby.

Twelve miles west of Prestonsburg on KY114 is a historical marker for the Battle of Ivy Mountain. Closer to town is a historical marker for the Battle of Middle Creek. A building in Prestonsburg just off Main Street was used as a headquarters by Col. James A. Garfield during his campaigning here. There is a historical marker at that location as well. From Prestonsburg, continue south on US23 a short distance to KY80. Go west on KY80, which becomes Daniel Boone Parkway, crossing I-75 to Somerset, then follow US27 and KY90 south to Mill Springs.

DRIVING TOUR and READING—*Proceed to Mill Springs*

MILL SPRINGS

In the latter part of 1861, the Confederates attempted to protect Cumberland Gap, the gateway to East Tennessee, by advancing a force into Kentucky. Brig. Gen. Felix Zollicoffer, a newspaper editor with no military experience but plenty of zeal for combat, was ordered to march his brigade of 2,000 men to a position behind the Cumberland River at Mill Springs, about seventy miles northwest of the Cumberland Gap. But Zollicoffer crossed the Cumberland and bivouacked his men in an entrenched camp at Beech Grove on the north side of the Cumberland. There he was reinforced by a second brigade. When the Confederate general in charge of East Tennessee, Maj. Gen. George B. Crittenden, visited the camp at Beech Grove, he was alarmed by the forward position, with a rapidly rushing river at its rear.

His alarm was caused by the southward march from Lebanon of a division of the Army of the Ohio, 8,000 men under the command of Brig. Gen. George H. Thomas. Thomas, a Virginian, would prove his loyalty and military skill many times in the war as one of the North's most reliable generals. Now he was marching his column for a rendezvous with Albin Schoepf's brigade posted at Somerset, prepatory to attacking Crittenden. Heavy rains and muddy roads slowed Thomas's march to a crawl.

Though the Confederates' position was tenuous, Crittenden decided the best defense was to undertake a preemptory attack on Thomas's troops encamped at Logan's Cross Roads awaiting the arrival of units bogged down on the march from Columbia. The Confederates also believed, mistakenly, that high water in Fishing Creek would prevent Schoepf from coming to Thomas's aid. In a plan that the aggressive Zollicoffer readily agreed to, Crittenden ordered the Confederates forward on a night march in the early hours of January 19, 1862. But rather than surprising Thomas as he had expected, Crittenden found several Federal units ready for his attack. Thomas already had sent his cavalry forward to picket in the direction of the Rebel camp. Fighting began between the two forces in the continuing rainstorm, and the Confederates drove the 10th Indiana back. Zollicoffer was in the middle of the action, but became disoriented. Suffering from myopia, he rode up to Col. Speed Fry of the 4th Kentucky (Union), mistaking him for a Confederate officer. Fry shot and killed him. Zollicoffer was much admired by his men, and his death caused concern among those Rebels who first learned of it. The Southerners attacked again but were repulsed. Union reinforcements arrived, and Yankee counterattacks against the Confederates' right and left gained ground.

Many of the Confederates had flintlock muskets, which failed to work properly in the rain, adding to their problems. The Rebels now broke off the struggle and abandoned the field. Most made it across the river on a steamboat, but victory at Mill Springs was decisive for the Federals. The Confederates in their retreat that only ended at Murfreesboro, Tennessee, abandoned their artillery, wagons, and much of their equipment. The continued bad weather prevented Thomas from adding to his gains by moving on the Cumberland Gap, but this, one of the first big Union victories, boosted morale in the North. Mill Springs victories would be followed within four weeks by Federal victories at Forts Henry and Donelson.

Points of Interest

Some 25 acres, the core of the battlefield, is preserved and interpreted with a trail and waysides by the Mill Springs Battlefield Association. The preserved area, 1 mile south of Nancy on KY235, also includes the mass grave of 106 Confederates killed in the battle and 2 Union dead, and a monument marking the site of General Zollicoffer's death. At Nancy is the national cemetery where you can begin your driving tour of the area that follows KY235, the Old Mill Springs Road, to the Confederate entrenchment camp at Beech Grove. From Somerset return east on KY80 then north on I-75 to Richmond. On US25 at Livingston, 8 miles south of I-75 exit 59, is the access road to the trail leading to Camp Wildcat Battle Monument. Here on October 21, 1861, Confederates under General Zollicoffer attacked a force under Brig. Gen. Albin Schoepf and were repulsed. The trail is steep in places and local inquiry is advised.

DRIVING TOUR—*Proceed to Richmond*
READING—*Fort Henry, Tennessee*

CONFEDERATE 1862 KENTUCKY CAMPAIGN

In mid-August of 1862, flushed by victories over George B. McClellan's Army of the Potomac and John Pope's Army of Virginia in Virginia, and the withdrawal of Federal naval squadrons from Vicksburg, the Confederates launched a two-pronged offensive into the border states of Maryland and Kentucky. In addition to bringing recruits and supplies to their ranks, the campaigns were designed to enhance the chances of European recognition of the Confederacy and possible intervention by Great Britain and France on the side of the South. Both these campaigns would fail, as would supporting Confederate offensives in northeast Mississippi (see **Iuka** and **Corinth, Mississippi**) and into southwest Missouri (see **Newtonia, Missouri**). These campaigns resulted in little more than heavy bloodshed—which the Confederates could not afford in a war of attrition, which the conflict was becoming—and, following Antietam, in Lincoln's preliminary Emancipation Proclamation. Lee's withdrawal to Virginia after the Battle of Antietam (see **Antietam, Maryland**) and Bragg's retrograde movement back into Tennessee after the Battle of Perryville ended the best hopes the Confederates had of winning the war.

Richmond

First to move forward in what would be a well-timed converging advance by the Confederacy's heartland armies were Maj. Gen. Edmund Kirby Smith's columns. Leaving Knoxville on August 14, Kirby Smith bypassed to the west side of the Union-held Cumberland Gap (see **Cumberland Gap, Tennessee**) and thrust deep into eastern Kentucky. By August 29 he was approaching Richmond, a gateway to the Bluegrass region, thirty miles southeast of Lexington. In the van was Col. John S. Scott's cavalry, trailed by Brig. Gen. Patrick R. Cleburne's infantry division. During the day Scott's horse soldiers, as they approached to within three miles of Richmond, encountered Union infantry and, in heavy skirmishing, retreated to beyond Rogersville.

Early the next morning Cleburne advanced on the Federal infantry south of Mount Zion Church. As he would consistently demonstrate throughout many western campaigns, Cleburne showed inspired leadership as he boldly carried the fight until forced to relinquish his command when shot in the face. By this time, General Kirby Smith and units from Brig. Gen. Thomas Churchill's division were on the field. The Confederates pressed forward and by ten-thirty A.M. broke the Union line. The Federals pulled back, rallied, and took position at White's Farm. Here the fighting resumed at noon, with the Federals grimly holding their own until Col. T. H. McCray's Texas brigade enveloped their right. Despite an attempt by Federal commander Maj. Gen. William Nelson, who arrived at two P.M. from Lexington to save the day, the battle became a rout. Nelson rallied 2,500 soldiers on Cemetery Hill south of Richmond, but for the third and last time the line broke and Nelson was wounded. Federal losses were more than 5,194, with 4,100 missing; most of these were captured. The Confederates lost fewer than 500. August 30 was a bleak day for the Lincoln administration; coupled with the Richmond disaster was the Union defeat at Second Manassas. Kirby Smith's army pushed ahead and on September 2 occupied Lexington, then fanned out occupying

Frankfort and threatening Louisville and Cincinnati while awaiting the arrival of Braxton Bragg's Army of the Mississippi.

Points of Interest

Richmond is on US421 at I-75 exit 87. The axis of the Battle of Richmond was US421 from Big Hill north to Richmond. There are historical markers at Mount Zion Church, White's Farm, and the Richmond cemetery battle focal points. Woodlawn was occupied by troops of both sides. Also in Richmond is the house and grave, at Richmond cemetery, of Cassius M. Clay—abolitionist, U.S. minister to Russia, and Lincoln confidant. Clay lived in White Hall. White Hall is now a Kentucky state park, off US25, 6 miles north of Richmond. The beautiful mansion is open for tours on a seasonal basis. WHITE HALL STATE HISTORIC SITE, 500 White Hall Shrine Road, Richmond, KY 40475; 606-623-9178.

From Richmond, a country drive on KY52 west for 31 miles will take you to Danville. From Danville, take US150 west for 10 miles to Perryville. Though other routes are possible, this is the most direct.

DRIVING TOUR—*Proceed to Perryville*
READING—*Munfordville*

Perryville

Confederate Gens. Braxton Bragg's and Kirby Smith's autumn 1862 invasion of Kentucky had reached the outskirts of Louisville and Cincinnati, but Bragg was forced to retreat and regroup. On October 7, the Federal army of Maj. Gen. Don Carlos Buell, numbering nearly 55,000, converged on the small crossroads town of Perryville, Kentucky, in three columns: Maj. Gen. Alexander McCook's corps on the left, acting Maj. Gen. Charles Gilbert's corps in the center, and Maj. Gen. Thomas L. Crittenden's corps on the right. Maj. Gen. George Thomas, acting as Buell's second-in-command, accompanied Crittenden's columns. On September 24, the Lincoln administration, disenchanted with Buell's leadership, ordered his command turned over to Thomas. The order was not hand-delivered to Buell until September 29. But

Maj. Gen. Don Carlos Buell, USA, was a brevetted hero of the Mexican War and friend of Maj. Gen. George B. McClellan. But his bravery and military talent did not sustain his role as a Civil War commander when his overcautious approach and lackluster personality wore thin with the Washington leadership. Removed from command in October 1862 and mustered out of the army in May 1864, he settled in Kentucky after the war.

Thomas, believing a change in command unwise in the midst of the crisis in Kentucky, urged the War Department to allow Buell to continue to lead the Army of the Ohio, and the Lincoln administration acquiesced. When the army left Louisville on October 1 to seek out and beat the Rebels, Buell was in command.

Buell's columns converged on Perryville, near where Doctors Fork emptied into the Chaplin River. The search for water in the region, blighted by a summer-long drought, became almost as important as the search for the Confederate army. Buell's two divisions under Brig. Gen. Joshua Sill that carried out the diversion at Frankfort were preparing to march south to join the other Federal corps. Maj. Gen. William Hardee's corps at Perryville was ordered by Bragg on October 7 to delay the Federal advance. Bragg, deceived as to the whereabouts of Buell's three corps, ordered Maj. Gen. Leonidas Polk to take one division to Perryville, while the other division was ordered to join Kirby Smith's army at Versailles. Col. Joseph Wheeler's Confederate cavalry skirmished with advancing Federals approaching on the Springfield Pike as they neared Doctors Creek west of Perryville on October 7. The Federals sought to secure some of the pools of water in the creek for themselves, but were driven back by Rebel snipers on Peters Hill east of Doctors Fork. After dark, the Northerners withdrew and camped west of the creek.

The Battle of Perryville opened in the predawn hours of October 8, when Buell ordered General Gilbert to throw forward skirmishers to find water. They were from

Brig. Gen. Philip H. Sheridan's division. Sheridan, a short, thin, pugnacious West Pointer, had recently been promoted after demonstrating leadership as a cavalry commander in Mississippi. Sheridan wasted no time in advancing his troops and driving Arkansas Confederates from Peters Hill. After Sheridan's advance there was a lull in the battle. McCook's corps, marching via the Mackville Road, and Crittenden's on the Lebanon Road, were separated from Gilbert's as they converged on Perryville by several miles of hills and hollows. By this time, the division under Polk arrived and both overall commanders were at Perryville, though Buell was unaware

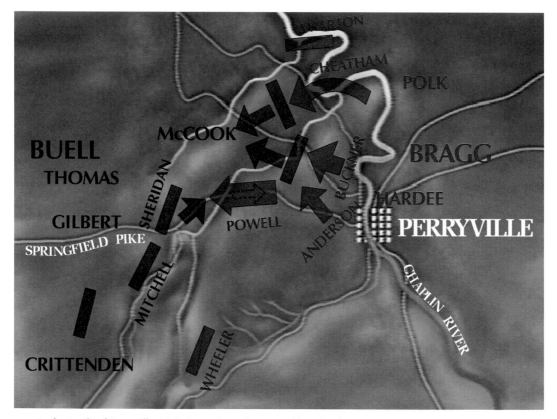

In the Battle of Perryville, Maj. Gen. Alexander McCook's Federal corps took the brunt of the Confederate attack by the corps of Maj. Gens. William J. Hardee and Leonidas Polk. Brig. Gen. Philip H. Sheridan's division started the battle in a predawn search for water by his skirmishers. They established a forward position but were too far advanced to aid McCook's defense with more than a scattering of artillery fire. At 4:15 P.M. Col. Samuel Powell's brigade attacked Sheridan's position, but the attack was repulsed and the Federals drove Powell's men through the streets of Perryville.

of the progress of the battle until four P.M. A phenomenon known as acoustic shadow, a combination of wind and topography, shielded his headquarters from the sounds of battle and he was not informed until a messenger brought in a report that McCook's corps had been terribly mauled, and, unless reinforced, faced disaster.

At two P.M., Bragg ordered Maj. Gen. Benjamin F. Cheatham's division to attack. The attack fell on McCook's corps. The Yanks, many of them "seeing the elephant" for the first time, fought stubbornly, but gave ground as Hardee threw in brigade after brigade on Cheatham's left and hammered McCook's right. Sheridan, from his position on Peters Hill, muffed an opportunity to assail the flank and rear of Dan Adams's Louisiana Brigade as they swept across Doctors Fork to roll up Col. William H. Lytle's brigade, anchoring McCook's right. McCook's forces were driven from the intersection of the Mackville and Benton roads about the time Buell learned of the threatened disaster. Sheridan was then attacked by Col. Samuel Powell's brigade, but he repulsed the assault and, together with Col. William P. Carlin's brigade of Brig. Gen. Robert B. Mitchell's division, drove Powell's Rebels through the streets of Perryville. Crittenden's corps over on the Lebanon Road had not been involved in the fight, but when a delayed message to move forward arrived after sundown, General Thomas decided it was too late in the day for an attack. He assured Buell the corps would attack in the morning.

That would not happen. Bragg, although he had carried the fight to the foe and had severely punished McCook's corps, now realized that he had been outmaneuvered and faced overwhelming numbers. Short of men and munitions, the Confederates withdrew during the night to Harrodsburg, where they rendezvoused with Kirby Smith's troops. Buell, taking cognizance of his heavy casualties and realizing that many of his troops were recruits, was not anxious to test the united Rebel force. What happened next was unexpected. Bragg, after pausing at Harrodsburg, resumed his retrograde by way of Cumberland Gap into East Tennessee.

Lack of substantial Confederate support in the state—manifested by few recruits—harsh conditions, and knowledge of Lee's retreat from Maryland following Antietam, coupled with Confederate defeats at Iuka and Corinth, Mississippi, made Bragg feel that he had accomplished all he could in the Bluegrass State. With little to show, other than captured and requisitioned supplies, for a campaign that had once promised so much, and over the loud protest of Kirby Smith and other senior generals, Bragg's "army group" returned to Tennessee. Bragg retained his command for another fourteen months, in spite of the harsh criticism leveled against him after his withdrawal from Kentucky, but Buell did not. His failure to vigorously pursue Bragg across the Cumberland Mountain barrens led to his sacking by Washington, and the appointment of Maj. Gen. William S. Rosecrans—the victor of Rich Mountain and Corinth—to succeed him.

The Battle of Perryville inflicted heavy casualties for the numbers engaged. The Confederates, with 16,000 combatants, sustained 3,145 casualties or 20 percent of those engaged. The Federals numbered 36,940 and experienced a loss of 4,211 who were either killed, wounded, or missing in action.

Points of Interest

Perryville Battlefield State Historic Park—The park is 2 miles northwest of Perryville on US68. The cultural landscape, both within the park which is expanding its acreage and in the neighborhood, is a gem, comparable with Antietam. The park is open daily and features the Confederate cemetery, memorials, interpretive waysides, hiking trails, and a driving tour, visitor center with exhibits, gift shop, and picnic facilities. PERRYVILLE BATTLEFIELD STATE HISTORIC SITE, P.O. Box 296, 1825 Battlefield Road, Perryville KY 40468; 606-332-8631; FAX 606- 332-2440; e-mail KHOLMAN@sear-net.com. ▣ ♿ 👫 ❷ 🏛 P ⛱ 🚻 $

Other Perryville sites include the Crawford House, which served as Bragg's headquarters the day of the battle, on US68 northeast of Perryville. Crawford Spring, behind the

A portion of the Perryville battlefield in a photograph taken shortly after the battle

house, was used for water by Confederate troops. The town is an antiquarian's dream and has an aura of the 1860s. The Elmwood Inn, in the town, witnessed the battle and is now a bed and-breakfast inn. In Harrodsburg, on US68, 10 miles north of Perryville, are several structures—including St. Phillips Episcopal Church and the Presbyterian Church—identified with the Confederate presence in the town.

Lexington—From Perryville, continue north on US68 through Harrodsburg to Lexington. The US60 Bypass west around the city connects with I-75/64 at the Newtown Pike. You may want to stop in Lexington and tour some sites associated with Civil War personalities from Lexington, including John C. Breckinridge and Mary Todd Lincoln. The Hunt Morgan House and the Mary Todd Lincoln House have been restored and refurnished and are open to the public. There are admission fees. John Hunt Morgan, Gordon Granger, and several other Civil War personalities are buried in Lexington Cemetery, 833 West Main Street. Continue north on I-75 to exit 126, then north on US62 for 20 miles to Cynthiana.

***

DRIVING TOUR—*Proceed to Cynthiana*
READING—*Kentucky Cavalry Raids and Raiders;*
(chronological)—Pocotaligo, South Carolina

***

CYNTHIANA

On July 17, 1862, during Morgan's first Kentucky raid, a skirmish was fought at Cynthiana, northeast of Lexington. Federal units—Kentucky volunteers and home guards—opposed Morgan's crossing of the Licking River covered bridge. Union pickets were forced back into the town when Morgan's men either forded the river or charged the bridge. Fighting continued in the town but Morgan prevailed, capturing the garrison and seizing or destroying supplies.

On his last Kentucky raid in June 1864, Morgan returned to Cynthiana at dawn on June 11. Col. Conrad Garis, with the 168th Regiment Ohio Volunteer Infantry and some home guard troops—300 men altogether—constituted the Union forces at Cynthiana. Morgan divided his men into three columns, surrounded the town, and attacked at the covered bridge, driving the Union forces back toward the depot and north along the railroad. The Rebels set fire to the town, destroying many buildings. As the fighting flared in Cynthiana, another Union force, about 750 men of the 171st Ohio National Guard under the command of Brig. Gen. Edward Hobson, arrived by train a mile north of Cynthiana at Keller's Bridge. Morgan trapped this new Union force in a meander of the Licking River. After some fighting, Morgan forced Hobson to surrender. Altogether, Morgan had about 1,300 Union prisoners of war camping with him overnight in line of battle. Brig. Gen. Stephen Gano Burbridge with 2,400 men attacked Morgan at dawn on June 12. The Union forces drove back the Rebels, causing them to flee into town where many were captured or killed.

Escaping with less than half his force, Morgan returned to Virginia by the end of July. On September 4, 1865, Morgan was hunted down and killed in Tennessee (see **Greeneville, Tennessee**).

Points of Interest

Historical markers on US27 and at the courthouse square describe the engagements fought here in 1862 and 1864 between Morgan's cavalry and Federal troops. Battle Grove Cemetery on Millersburg Road, south of the town, was the site of the June 12, 1864, engagement. A Confederate monument is in the cemetery. Return south on US62 past I-75 and enter I-64 west to Frankfort.

DRIVING TOUR—*Proceed to Frankfort*
READING—*Morgan's Raids 1862: Nashville, Tennessee;*
1864: Greeneville, Tennessee

FRANKFORT

The Kentucky state capital was the scene of exciting events during the Confederates' 1862 Kentucky Campaign. On October 4, as Edmund Kirby Smith's troops occupied the capital, a ceremony was held to inaugurate Richard Hawes, as governor of the state. The ceremony was attended by Kirby Smith and Braxton Bragg, who left Leonidas Polk in charge of four divisions of the Army of the Mississippi camped at Bardstown.

Aware the Federals were on the move, Bragg ordered Polk to evacuate Bardstown and march east to Harrodsburg where he would be joined by Smith's army. But Bragg was mistaken in believing Buell's main thrust was toward Frankfort. It was toward Bardstown, as Polk informed his chief. On the morning of the inauguration, Polk's columns pulled out of Bardstown and headed east; Polk's corps took the Springfield Pike and Hardee's the Glenville Road. Bragg's confusion was enhanced when the inauguration ceremony was interrupted at one P.M. on October 4 by Federal cannon fire booming on the western outskirts of the capital. By four P.M. Bragg had departed Frankfort en route to Harrodsburg. Hawes followed Bragg—the Confederate government in Frankfort had lasted less than eight hours.

Points of Interest

Frankfort is north of I-64 exit 58 on US60. As you enter the capital on US60 you will pass the Frankfort State Arsenal. It was constructed in 1850 on the grounds of the Old State House, which burned in 1836. It was seized by the Confederates during the 1862 campaign, and a small skirmish occurred here in 1864. The building was gutted in a 1933 fire, but the walls are original. The Kentucky Military History Museum, housed in the building, features Civil War exhibits among its collections. For more information, call 502-564-3261.

Downtown and near the State Capitol on Capitol Avenue are many antebellum buildings. On Washington Street near the state capitol are the homes of John J. Crittenden and Thomas L. Crittenden. A marker on the capitol grounds indicates the site where on November 2, 1864, four Confederate prisoners were shot under orders from Brig. Gen. Stephen Burbridge, one of several reprisal killings ordered by Burbridge. Frankfort Cemetery, East Main Street, features a monument honoring soldiers of all wars. Theodore O'Hara, soldier in the Mexican War and Confederate staff officer, author of "The Bivouac of the Dead," is interred here. "The Bivouac of the Dead" is featured on iron plaques in many of the nation's national cemeteries for Civil War dead. Old State House, Broadway and St. Clair Street, houses the museum and offices of the Kentucky Historical Society. Among documents and manuscripts are private and official papers of Jefferson Davis and Abraham Lincoln. The Confederate Room has artifacts from the Civil War. It was here that Confederate governor Richard Hawes's inaugural ceremonies were rudely interrupted on October 4, 1862, by the rapid advance east from Louisville by one of Maj. Gen. Don Carlos

Buell's four Union columns. From Frankfort, take US60 west a short distance to reenter I-64 west at exit 53. Proceed west to downtown Louisville.

DRIVING TOUR—*Proceed to Louisville*
READING—*Perryville*

LOUISVILLE

When Bragg's army moved from Munfordville to Bardstown, Buell's Army of the Ohio took advantage of the strategic blunder by Gen. Braxton Bragg of leaving the route to Louisville open by marching via Elizabethtown and West Point to Kentucky's largest city, uncontested by the Rebels. Louisville was already a huge Federal supply and command center. From Louisville on October 1, 1862, Buell marched his reinforced and reorganized army to find and battle Bragg's and Kirby Smith's Confederates.

Louisville continued as a major Federal base throughout the war. With its docks on the Ohio River and a railroad to Nashville, Louisville became a distribution point for war matériel gathered from many points in the North and funneled to Federal armies as they advanced deep into Tennessee and Georgia. Hospitals and prison camps were established on both sides of the Ohio River to accommodate wounded and sick Union and captured Rebel soldiers (and some civilians) netted in campaigns farther South.

A tragic occurrence in Louisville on the eve of Perryville was the murder of one Union general by a brother officer. Trigger-tempered Brig. Gen. Jefferson C. Davis had been sent to Louisville on September 23 to assist Maj. Gen. William Nelson in organizing soldiers, many just mustered, to meet the Confederate threat to Kentucky. Davis, a veteran of Fort Sumter and Pea Ridge, did not get along with the physically formidable Nelson, who could be called a bully. Davis was humiliated when Nelson relieved him from command and ordered him from the department. Recalled to Louisville upon Buell's arrival, Davis encountered Nelson at the Federal headquarters in the Gault House and the two argued. Moments later, Davis shot Nelson point-blank in the heart with a borrowed pistol in front of many witnesses at the hotel. Though Davis was immediately arrested, he escaped justice in both military and civil courts, thanks to the impending military crisis and the influence of his friend, Indiana governor Oliver P. Morton. Davis went on to command a division and later a corps in Maj. Gen. William T. Sherman's Georgia and Carolina campaigns, and was the officer present in Sitka to represent the United States in 1867 when the nation took formal possession of Alaska.

Points of Interest

Louisville is now a large modern city but does retain some of its antebellum buildings and certainly the charm from earlier times. The Civil War–era Gault House, used as a Federal headquarters by William T. Sherman, William Nelson, and Don Carlos Buell, is no more, but its site at Second and Main streets is identified by a historical marker. General Nelson was killed in the hotel's parlor on September 29, 1862, when the hotel served as General Buell's headquarters. Louisville was surrounded by a 10-mile ring of twelve Federal forts. There are markers at some of the locations of forts along the line, which were named for Union officers killed or mortally wounded in battle.

From Louisville, take I-65 south toward Munfordville. At Elizabethtown, exit 93, there are several interesting sites. A building on the public square has a cannonball lodged in one of its brick walls from the December 1862 shelling of the town by John Hunt Morgan's forces. The house of Confederate Brig. Gen. Ben Hardin Helm is in Elizabethtown. He was the brother-in-law of Mary Todd Lincoln and was killed at the Battle of Chickamauga, Georgia, on September 20, 1863. Fourteen miles southeast of Elizabethtown on US31E is Hodgenville. The Hodgenville Courthouse was burned on February 22, 1865, by Capt. William C. Quantrill and his raiders during their rampage through the state, after Quantrill and a few of his men had shifted their field of operations to Kentucky from the Trans-Mississippi. On US30E, 6 miles north of Hodgenville, is Knob Creek Farm—Abraham Lincoln's boyhood home. The Abraham Lincoln Birthplace National Historic Site is 3 miles south of Hodgenville on US31E. ABRAHAM LINCOLN NATIONAL HISTORIC SITE, 2995 Lincoln Farm Road, Hodgenville, KY 42748; 502-358-3137. ♿ ♟ ❷ P ⛉ ♟

DRIVING TOUR—*Proceed to Munfordville*
READING—*Frankfort*

MUNFORDVILLE

Gen. Braxton Bragg left Chattanooga on August 27, 1862, with 30,000 men organized into two infantry wings. His Army of the Mississippi, employing the "iron horse," had been redeployed from Tupelo, Mississippi, to Chattanooga, beating Maj. Gen. Don Carlos Buell's Army of the Ohio, bogged down in rebuilding the Memphis & Charleston Railroad to the "Gateway City." By September 12, Buell had finally left Nashville, but by then Bragg had entered Kentucky and occupied Glasgow, twenty miles north of the Tennessee line.

The first serious resistance Bragg encountered was from the Federal garrison posted south of Green River at Munfordville. The Federal soldiers—Indianians, Ohioans, and Kentuckians under Col. John T. Wilder—occupied two blockhouses, a redoubt (Fort Craig), and entrenchments protecting the Louisville & Nashville Railroad bridge across the river. A Rebel brigade led by Brig. Gen. James R. Chalmers sent forward on September 14 was repulsed with heavy losses to the attackers after the Federals refused surrender demands. The Union garrison, reinforced to more than 4,000 later that day, held out as Bragg, concerned about the advance of Buell's army to Bowling Green, brought his entire army forward to Munfordville.

One of the human interest stories engendered by the Civil War and its cast of characters that has made its legacy so popular with the American public now occurred. Cultured Confederate Maj. Gen. Simon B. Buckner, a native of Hart County, in which Munfordville is located, dissuaded Bragg from attacking the town for fear of inflicting casualties among his civilian friends and relatives. Instead, Bragg surrounded the Federal garrison. On September 16, Wilder, on recommendation of the locals, secured an interview with Buckner under a flag of truce to ask his advice on what to do. Buckner, who himself had been cordially treated by Brig. Gen. U. S. Grant after the surrender of Fort Donelson (see **Fort Donelson, Tennessee**), was amused by the Indianian's naïveté. Nevertheless, he conducted Wilder on a tour of the Confederate positions. Convinced by what he saw, Wilder said sadly, "I believe I'll surrender." On the morning of September 17, Wilder formally surrendered his 4,000 soldiers, who were disarmed and paroled. Wilder would return as leader of the "Lightning Brigade" to fight many engagements against the Confederate Army of Tennessee, as the Army of the Mississippi was redesignated in November 1862. Bragg's army, after awaiting an attack by Buell until September 20, continued its march north.

Points of Interest

Munfordville is off I-65 just south of exit 65 on US31W. On the south side of the Green River Bridge is Fort Craig, a well-preserved earthwork and key Union stronghold in the September 14–17 battle. Title to Fort Craig and the adjacent battlefield west to the Louisville & Nashville Railroad, and the Col. R. A. Smith monument, is vested in the Hart County Historical Society. The site is accessed from the old Woodsonville Road. Two buildings in the town display historical markers relative to the battle. One, a tavern, still stands and the other, likewise extant, was used to house nurses who cared for the wounded. Historical markers on the Hart County Courthouse Square describe the battle. The Hart County Historical Society maintains an excellent museum opposite the courthouse. One mile south of Green River, on US31W, is a historical marker for the December 17, 1861, Rowlett's Station engagement.

On KY55, 9 miles south of Campbellsville at the Green River crossing, is Tebbs Bend. Here there is a scenic historic driving tour and a memorial commemorating the July 4, 1863, Battle in which, at the beginning of the raid north of the Ohio River, Morgan's cavalry suffered heavy losses in an unsuccessful attempt to rout the 25th Michigan Infantry from their entrenchments. For a guide to the Morgan-Moore Trail, which features sites associated with the Battle of Tebbs Bend, stop first at the interpretive center at nearby Green River Lake State Park. For more information, call 502-465-8255.

From Munfordville, continue south on I-65 into Tennessee or use exit 20 at Bowling Green to take the Green River Parkway north and then I-24 west to visit sites in western Kentucky, Missouri, and Cairo, Illinois. In Bowling Green on the campus of Western Kentucky University are markers and a museum relative to the brief period when the town was headquarters of the Confederate Western Department and Kentucky's Confederate state capital. On US68 at Fairview is the Jefferson Davis State Historic Site. An impressive monument, an obelisk two thirds of the size of the Washington Monument, museum, and reconstructed cabin commemorate the birthplace of the Confederate president. The park is open from May through October. JEFFERSON DAVIS STATE HISTORIC SITE, Highway 68 West, Fairview, KY 42221; 502-886-1765.

DRIVING TOUR—*Proceed to Western Kentucky or Tennessee*
READING—*Louisville*

KENTUCKY CAVALRY RAIDS AND RAIDERS

Three Confederate cavalry leaders raided deep into Kentucky during the war. A fourth cavalry chief, Joseph Wheeler, operated in the state, but his actions were tied to the Confederates' Kentucky 1862 invasion by Braxton Bragg's and Kirby Smith's armies. The three leaders operating independently were cunning, hard hitting, and fearless while invoking fear among their enemies. Two, John Hunt Morgan and Nathan Bedford Forrest, were respected by friend and foe alike. The other, William C. Quantrill, was an outlaw and respected by few beyond his small band of followers. The raids are briefly described here. The most important points of interest are included with other entries.

John Hunt Morgan

Morgan, although born in Alabama, spent most of his life in Kentucky's Bluegrass region. He was not a professional soldier although he served as a volunteer in the Mexican War.

He organized his own militia company in 1857. On September 28, 1861, Morgan and his command, the die having been cast, left Lexington and reported to Brig. Gen. Simon Buckner near Bowling Green. He was mustered into the Confederate Army as a captain on October 27, 1861, and led attacks on Federal patrols and camps in Kentucky in the late fall and winter of 1861–62. He participated in the Battle of Shiloh, was promoted to colonel, and sent to operate deep behind the enemy lines. On July 4, 1862, he left Knoxville, Tennessee, on his first Kentucky raid, a twenty-four-day, one-thousand-mile raid, seizing Federal supplies, destroying railroad property, and capturing and paroling Federal garrisons and pursuers and gaining recruits. This set the example for Morgan's successful

Brig. Gen. John Hunt Morgan, CSA, was over six feet tall, dressed impeccably, and rode the finest horses. His innate leadership ability combined with his dash, flair, and sense of adventure produced a series of daring cavalry raids beneficial to the South, his native state of Kentucky, and beyond.

guerrilla tactics. Among the reasons for his success was that he took with him George Ellsworth, a telegraphic operator, who tapped into Federal wires, garnered intelligence, and sent confusing and sometimes ironic messages to Federal commanders.

He next led a raid into Middle Tennessee and so damaged the "Big South" tunnel north of Gallatin that it closed the Louisville & Nashville Railroad to through traffic for ninety-eight days, brought Buell's advance on Chattanooga to a stop, and handed General Bragg the initiative.

Morgan and his unit participated in the Confederate invasion of Kentucky with Bragg's columns and, upon the Confederate retrograde, he convinced his immediate superior, Maj. Gen. Edmund Kirby Smith, to allow him to stage another raid. Leaving Richmond, Kentucky, on October 17, Morgan raided to the north and west for twelve days, battling some garrisons and destroying railroad property. He returned to Middle Tennessee and, on November 5, from his temporary base at Gallatin (see **Nashville, Tennessee**) attacked the railroad marshaling yards near Nashville.

On December 22, under orders from Braxton Bragg to again disrupt traffic over the Louisville & Nashville Railroad—"Big South" having been reopened—during the advance south from Nashville of Maj. Gen. William S. Rosecrans's Army of the Cumberland (see **Murfreesboro, Tennessee**), Morgan again crossed into Kentucky and raided the railroad, the main Federal supply line for Rosecrans's army. The chief objective was the trestles at Muldraugh's Hill near Elizabethtown, which he destroyed along with other railroad property and supplies. He also captured more than 1,800 prisoners during his "Christmas" raid. With Federal pursuers closing in, Morgan's command hurried south, crossing the Cumberland River at Burkesville on January 2, 1863.

Morgan's next raid through Kentucky was in July 1863. In this operation, Kentucky was a stepping-stone to a larger goal—a raid through Union states north of the Ohio River (see **Ohio** and **Indiana** in **The Midwest**). After crossing into Kentucky on July 1, he fought a series of skirmishes with pursuers and engagements at Tebbs Bend, on Green River, July 4, and Lebanon, Kentucky, July 5. On July 8, he crossed the Ohio River at Brandenburg, Kentucky, and entered Indiana.

Morgan's last raid into Kentucky was an unhappy affair for him and his command. On duty in southwestern Virginia to protect the valuable saltworks and lead mines there from Federal cavalry raids (see **Saltville-Marion, Virginia**), his proposal for a raid back into the Bluegrass State to disrupt William T. Sherman's supply line was vetoed by the

Richmond authorities, who preferred to keep him where he was. But under the pretext of going after Federal commands being organized in Kentucky—by heavy-handed and ruthless Brig. Gen. Stephen G. Burbridge, recently named to command the District of Kentucky—to march on the saltworks, Morgan left Virginia on May 30 with 2,700 men and rode into Kentucky. He struck Mount Sterling on June 8 and captured a garrison, then headed for Lexington, to procure Federal supplies for some of his command who lacked mounts. In both places his force, with many new, undisciplined recruits, engaged in looting and robbery. But a more serious problem for Morgan was the two Federal commands—Brig. Gen. Edward H. Hobson's and Burbridge's—then pursuing him closely. He rode to Cynthiana, determined to do battle. In two days of fighting he captured Hobson's command and was soundly defeated by Burbridge's, barely escaping with a handful of troopers back into Virginia (see **Cynthiana**).

Nathan Bedford Forrest

The "Wizard of the Saddle," as he was called, was a native of Tennessee. Most of his raiding occurred in the Volunteer State and, in addition to operations in Mississippi, Alabama, and Georgia, his command also fought battles alongside other Confederate units. On December 28, 1861, Forrest skirmished with and defeated a command under Maj. Eli H. Murray at Sacramento, Kentucky. Then, in early February 1862, he led his command to Fort Donelson when Gen. Albert Sidney Johnston committed major forces under incompetent leadership to the failed defense of that Cumberland River bastion. Forrest's major raid deep into Kentucky came in March 1864 and was an extension of a thrust deep into West Tennessee to recruit men and collect mounts for his corps. Seeing an opportunity to further his mission and extend the area in which the threat of his presence might panic Federal commanders, he took the Kentucky Brigade to Paducah on the Ohio River (see **Paducah**).

William C. Quantrill

Having already gained a reputation in the Trans-Mississippi as a notorious guerrilla in charge of a band of cutthroats and renegades (see **Lawrence** and **Baxter Springs, Kansas** in **The Northwest**), Capt. William C. Quantrill late in the war took his marauding ways across the Mississippi River. On New Year's Day, 1865, he crossed the Mississippi River near Memphis with about two dozen blue-clad horsemen including Frank James and Jim Younger, disguising the group with a counterfeit name—the 4th Missouri Cavalry. His plan was to ride through Kentucky and Maryland to Washington, D.C., and keep Confederate hopes alive by assassinating President Abraham Lincoln. But Quantrill was still in Kentucky on April 14 when John Wilkes Booth assassinated the president. On May 10, he was severely wounded in a skirmish with Union irregulars near Taylorsville, thirty miles southeast of Louisville. Quantrill died of his wounds in Louisville on June 6.

READING—*Cynthiana*

Louisiana

In the Civil War, the militarily most important state located west of the Mississippi River was Louisiana. For the South, control of the lower Mississippi and of the South's premier antebellum port, New Orleans, was essential. For the same reasons, the North saw capture of New Orleans and control of the lower Mississippi and its system of feeder rivers as a vital element of General-in-Chief Winfield Scott's plan to choke the lifeblood from the South. As early Federal war aims became focused in the west, Louisiana commanded high interest.

As important as river commerce was, Louisiana, with its rich, moist soil, based much of its prosperity on a vibrant agricultural economy. Large crops of cotton, sugar, and rice were planted, harvested, and transported to market along the bayous. Slavery was a key element for all these labor-intensive crops. Louisiana consequently was at the forefront of Deep South secessionist sentiments. One of the first seven states to secede, it continued to resist Federal control over much of its land area for the entire war. High on the list of reasons for this phenomenon was the ability of Confederate general Richard Taylor to stymie the efforts of Maj. Gen. Nathaniel P. Banks. Federal amphibious campaigns beginning in the spring of 1862 succeeded in controlling or effectively patrolling most of the state's key waterways, especially the Mississippi River, and garrisoning towns and controlling land area was less important to the North in Louisiana than elsewhere in the Deep South throughout the first three years of the war.

While the climate of Louisiana is extremely pleasant in the spring and autumn, midsummer can be quite muggy. Nevertheless, any time of year is guaranteed to provide much enjoyment to the visitor because of the friendly people, the sumptuous cuisine, and the characteristic beauty of the state. Thanks to the interstate highway system, a visit to Louisiana is easily combined with tours of the surrounding states of Mississippi, Texas, and Arkansas. Naturally, no visit to Louisiana is complete without a stop in New Orleans, and the Crescent City makes an excellent base from which to tour Fort Jackson, the bayou country, and Baton Rouge. A minimum of a two-day stay is recommended.

Farragut's ships passing Fort Jackson (left) and Fort St. Philip (right) in this period lithograph. Confederate gunboats, fire rafts propelled by tugs, and the CSS Louisiana, *anchored as a floating battery near Fort St. Philip, were obstacles added to the fire from the forts.*

In the French Quarter, several hotels are in buildings that saw much history, including the eight months of Benjamin F. Butler's "reign of terror," as the inhabitants at the time labeled the first Federal occupation.

Moving northward through the state, Alexandria and Shreveport are also excellent cities with ample hostelries and much history. Another two to three days is recommended to tour the sites of the Red River Campaign and the sites of 1863 actions, including Port Hudson. Milliken's Bend and the other sites in the northeast part of the state are best toured in conjunction with your visit to Vicksburg, Mississippi, and relate closely to the Vicksburg Campaign. See the tour map for suggested routes.

NEW ORLEANS

New Orleans, the Crescent City, was the largest and most prosperous and cosmopolitan city in the South at the time of the Civil War. Surrendered with no resistance beyond threats and vocal protests, it was occupied by Federal soldiers and sailors beginning in May 1862. The struggle to capture New Orleans was primarily focused on the two forts guarding the Mississippi River seventy river miles below the city. Before the Federals could get warships close to the two forts, Jackson and St. Philip, the Confederates scored an early-war victory at Head of Passes—one of the few naval contests won by the South.

In September 1861, Federal warships, then maintaining a loose blockade of the Mississippi River, which terminated in a long, narrow arm through which the river discharged into the Gulf of Mexico by three principal passes, ventured up to Head of

Passes. The four-vessel squadron, including the steam sloop USS *Richmond,* and the sailing sloop USS *Vincennes,* first tried entry into Northeast Pass, but finding the water too shallow, moved to Southwest Pass. At Head of Passes, they sealed off the Mississippi River to blockade-runners. But, on October 12, they were surprised by Confederate gunboats, including an ironclad ram, CSS *Manassas,* a cigar-shaped vessel with one gun. The *Manassas* rammed the *Richmond* which went aground, as did the *Vincennes;* Confederate tugs came downriver with burning fire rafts, but the embarrassed Yankee sailors worked their ships free and, abandoning Head of Passes, escaped out to the sea.

It was not until six months later that the Federals launched an all-out attack up the Mississippi. By that time, Navy Department plans for the operation were well developed. But army cooperation was essential, and when Maj. Gen. George B. McClellan became general-in-chief, he assigned troops then being raised by Maj. Gen. Benjamin F. Butler to cooperate in the plan devised by Assistant Navy Secretary Gustavus Fox and endorsed by Secretary of the Navy Gideon Welles. The U.S. Navy in September had occupied Ship Island, Mississippi, which would serve as the base of operations (see **Biloxi–Ship Island, Mississippi**). Cmdr. David D. Porter, a colorful and ambitious navy officer who had recently returned from the Gulf, submitted a plan to use thirteen-inch seacoast mortars, mounted on seagoing schooners, to bombard the Confederate forts from a position out of range of the two forts' big guns. Gideon Welles selected an officer far down the seniority list for overall naval commander, Capt. David Glasgow Farragut. Farragut, then sixty-one years of age, was born in the South but had served in the U.S. Navy for forty years, beginning as a midshipman in the War of 1812 under David D. Porter's father, Com. David Porter, who became Farragut's foster father. Farragut had held routine commands during the Mexican War, but was well thought of despite never having held a major command. His opinion of the secessionist movement proved his loyalty to the Union: "You fellows will catch the devil before you get through with this business!" was his warning to Southerners. He was assigned to command the newly constituted West Gulf Blockading Squadron.

In January 1862, Farragut received orders for the New Orleans operation, orders that were kept in much secrecy. At Ship Island in late February, Farragut assembled a fleet of seventeen warships and gunboats, including the screw sloops USS *Richmond,* USS *Brooklyn,* USS *Pensacola,* and USS *Hartford,* his flagship. Added to these were twenty mortar schooners and six shallow-draft gunboats under Porter's command. More than 10,000 soldiers under Butler had arrived at Ship Island and were loaded onto transports for a landing above the two forts. Farragut's vessels had problems negotiating the bars in Southwest Pass; however, they assembled at Head of Passes by April 15 for the twenty-mile journey upstream to the forts.

The Confederates had made formidable defensive arrangements. Fort Jackson on the west bank and Fort St. Philip on the east were located on a strategic bend in the river. Fort St. Philip was an old Spanish masonry fort that had held off the British in 1815. The larger Fort Jackson, a Third System masonry fort, emplaced 62 guns. Together the forts and their water batteries mounted 109 guns, most of them smoothbore. Between the two forts an obstacle of anchored ship hulks was held in place by heavy chains. The Rebels had four vessels of the Confederate navy, of which two, the CSS *Manassas* and the CSS *Louisiana,* were ironclads. The Louisiana State Navy had two ships, and there were six craft in the River Defense Squadron. The CSS *Louisiana* and another ironclad, the CSS *Mississippi,* unfinished at the time of the battle, were mammoth vessels, designed for 16 guns. The *Louisiana* lacked engines strong enough for propulsion, so she was anchored as a floating battery upriver from Fort St. Philip.

The forts were manned by experienced artillerists, but the Confederate commander in charge of New Orleans, Maj. Gen. Mansfield Lovell, lacked a sizable army force, as troops had been withdrawn from New Orleans for the defense of West Tennessee and northeast Mississippi and had fought valiantly at Shiloh (April 6–7). The forts, the navy, and the water batteries would be the principal means of defense. Cooperation between the Confederate navy and the army was minimal.

By April 18 Farragut's fleet and Porter's mortar schooners were at anchor below the forts. Porter's mortar schooners, their masts camouflaged to look like tall trees, began to find the range of the forts. For two days, the 218-pound projectiles of the mortar fleet landed in or near the forts, but Farragut was dismayed to learn that they caused no significant damage. The pounding continued for three more days, while Farragut began preparations to run his ships by the forts at night. The major remaining obstacle was how to break the barrier of floating hulks.

Volunteers in two gunboats, on the night of April 20, steamed into the area fronting the forts without initially arousing suspicion. They tried different ways to break the chain, but were unsuccessful until the bluejackets in the gunboat *Itasca* crashed over it with a full head of steam. The commotion aroused the forts' garrisons, but the *Itasca* and her sister *Pinola* escaped without major damage.

As mortar fire slackened on April 23, the Confederate leadership prepared for the naval attack they felt would come at any moment. At the prearranged time of two A.M. on April 24, the single column of Federal ships in three flotillas got under way. By three-thirty A.M. the forts began firing on the first column, and the warships returned the fire as they passed, in some confusion as the smoke of battle broke up the line. Just upriver from the forts, the Rebel ships attacked the squadron. The USS *Hartford* ran aground and a fire raft was pushed against her; however, Farragut's flagship sunk the tug holding the raft against the flagship and broke free, the crew controlled the fire, and she was under way again. The CSS *Manassas* rammed the *Brooklyn* with no apparent effect, but then the *Manassas* wandered into the range of the forts and eventually sank. The anchored *Louisiana* and the Federal ships exchanged fire as the Federal columns began to outrange the forts.

Of Farragut's 24 vessels, 3 had problems early on and returned below the forts, where Porter remained with his gunboats and bombers. Upriver the USS *Varuna*, a screw corvette, tangled with the *Governor Moore*, a Louisiana State Navy vessel.

David G. Farragut moved to the North with his wife from Norfolk, Virginia, in April 1861. After being called to service in December 1861, he served in four major campaigns and was with the U.S. Navy on the James River in 1865. He was made a full admiral after the war and continued to serve in the peacetime navy.

The *Varuna* was intentionally run aground to avoid being sunk and was then abandoned by her crew, who were picked up by another Federal vessel. Miraculously, in the more than two hours of deadly fire exchanged, only 37 Federal tars were killed and 146 wounded. Fort Jackson, target of the majority of the more than 7,500 rounds thrown up by the mortars and fire from the ships, had only 9 killed and 33 wounded in the two-week bombardment.

Farragut's squadron stopped upriver to send word to Porter and Butler of the successful run past the forts. Two gunboats were left behind to guard the landing of Butler's troops on Breton Sound. The next day, Farragut's squadron, after exchanging shots with and disposing of the Rebel batteries at Chalmette on the old War of 1812 battlefield, arrived adjacent to the city's waterfront. The wharves of New Orleans were ablaze with burning cotton and other materials denied to the Federals. Angry mobs ranged the shore and tracked and threatened Capt. Theodorus Bailey and another officer sent ashore by Farragut to demand surrender of the city. Although they were stymied by the mayor, leading to Farragut's threat to bombard the city, the cool demeanor displayed by Bailey and Lt. George H. Perkins on their walk through the streets of New Orleans impressed even those in the mob. A young observer wrote later, "It was one of the bravest deeds I ever saw done."

With New Orleans cowed by the guns of Farragut's deep-water ships, the forts were isolated, and Porter sent a demand for surrender. After several refusals and a resumption of the mortar bombardment, the forts' commanders, following a mutiny by the Fort Jackson garrison, agreed to Porter's terms. At the same time, the Confederate naval commander sent the *Louisiana* downstream ablaze and she exploded, enraging Porter. The Rebel naval officers were taken into custody. Butler's troops arrived to occupy the forts and New Orleans, where they relieved Farragut's sailors and marines on May 1. Farragut and Porter then moved on to other assignments.

New Orleans became a Federal command center and supply base. Butler's strict martial law and charges of black market dealings led to his removal in December 1862. Maj. Gen. Nathaniel P. Banks replaced him and used New Orleans as a base for launching what would, except for the seizure and capture of Port Hudson, prove to be generally ineffectual military campaigns for the North. The city also was the organizational center for Federal political experiments designed to bring the Pelican State back into the Union.

Points of Interest

Fort Jackson—From New Orleans, take US90 across the Mississippi River to Algiers and exit on LA23, the Belle-Chasse Highway. Travel 66 miles southeast to Fort Jackson, near Triumph. Fort Jackson (named for U.S. president and hero of the 1815 Battle of Chalmette Andrew Jackson) is a park and recreation area maintained by Plaquemines Parish, which began restoring the fort in 1961. The park is open year-round during daylight hours. A museum and gift shop are located inside one of the casemates, open from 9:00 A.M. to 4:00 P.M. daily. A pamphlet is available which features a walking tour of the fort. FORT JACKSON, Plaquemines Parish, Route 1, Box 640, Port Sulphur, LA 70083; 504-392-6692.

Chalmette—Returning to New Orleans, the Chalmette Unit of Jean Lafitte National Historical Park is a short drive southeast on LA46. The exhibits and museum at the site deal primarily with the 1815 Battle of New Orleans, but Confederate batteries occupied the same area. The Beauregard House on the battlefield, built in 1833, was named for its last owner, Judge René Beauregard, son of Confederate general P.G.T. Beauregard. The nearby national cemetery has graves of Civil War soldiers and sailors and servicemen and women of other wars, including the War of 1812. A picnic area and museum are located at the site, and there is camping at a nearby state park. CHALMETTE, St. Bernard Highway, Chalmette, LA 70043; 504-342-8111.

One mile toward New Orleans on St. Bernard Highway where it turns into St. Claude Avenue is the Louisiana National Guard Military History and State Weapons Museum. It is housed in the restored 1837 powder magazine for Jackson Barracks, a post where such

Jackson Square, New Orleans, during the Civil War. St. Louis Cathedral is still a prominent landmark on the square.

Civil War heroes as Robert E. Lee, Ulysses S. Grant, Jefferson Davis, Braxton Bragg, and William T. Sherman paused at one time or another. The museum has an excellent display of Civil War weapons and is open Monday through Friday, 8:00 A.M. to 4:00 P.M. except holidays. Admission is free. LOUISIANA NATIONAL GUARD MILITARY HISTORY AND STATE WEAPONS MUSEUM, 6400 St. Claude Avenue, New Orleans, LA 70146-0330; 504-278-6242.

New Orleans—There are a number of historic buildings in New Orleans, a city where, in the French Quarter, history is found at every street corner. Among them are buildings which played a part in the drama that unfolded when Farragut's fleet arrived off the docks and Federal soldiers set foot in the city. The U.S. Mint at the corner of Esplanade Avenue and Decatur Street is where Confederate citizen William Mumford tore down the U.S. flag and was hanged for the act. The building is now the Louisiana State Museum. It is open from 10:00 A.M. to 5:00 P.M., Wednesday through Sunday. Admission is charged. Nearby Jackson Square has an equestrian statue of Andrew Jackson, which was there during the war, and the St. Louis Cathedral, subject of several wartime photographs.

The U.S. Customs House at Decatur and Canal streets was used by General Butler as a prison and headquarters. At City Hall, 543 St. Charles, Farragut's sailors lowered the state flag and raised the Stars and Stripes. In the Garden District, Confederate general Leonidas Polk, the former Episcopal bishop of Louisiana, is buried at Christ Church Cathedral, 2919 St. Charles. Confederate secretary of state Judah Benjamin, Commissioner to France John Slidell, Gen. John Bell Hood, and Gen. P.G.T. Beauregard lived in houses that still stand in the Garden District and French Quarter. The Historic New Orleans Collection, 533 Royal Street, is housed in the Merieult House, built in the late 1700s. The collection contains many manuscripts and paintings relating to the Civil War. The Confederate Museum at 929 Camp Street has one of the nation's best collections of Confederate memorabilia.

At Metairie Cemetery, 5100 Pontchartrain Boulevard, are the graves of 2,500 Confederate soldiers buried in the mausoleum, along with Gen. P.G.T. Beauregard. Among other tombs in the cemetery are those of Confederate generals John Bell Hood and Richard Taylor. The cemetery on North Dufrocq Street contains the graves of 2,000 Union soldiers. If you are coming to or leaving from New Orleans via I-10 east, you may want instead to take US90 east for 23 miles to Fort Pike State Commemorative Area. The masonry fort was taken over by state troops in 1861. There are indoor and outdoor exhibits and a picnic area. Otherwise, from New Orleans, take I-10 west to Baton Rouge. There are a number of antebellum plantations near state roads between the two cities. Or you may first want to visit the bayou country southwest of New Orleans. Take US90 west 89 miles to Morgan City.

DRIVING TOUR—*Proceed to Baton Rouge or Bayou Country*
READING—*Farragut's campaign: Baton Rouge;*
(chronological)—Fort Macon, North Carolina

BATON ROUGE

Immediately after the army took over responsibility for New Orleans, Farragut set his sights upriver to carry out the Lincoln administration's mandate to continue up the Mississippi and rendezvous with the Mississippi squadron, then checkmated above Fort Pillow, Tennessee. On May 3, he dispatched four warships upstream to take possession of Baton Rouge. The flotilla reached Baton Rouge on May 5. Three days later, Union sailors and marines from the USS *Iroquois*, under Cmdr. J. S. Palmer, landed at Baton Rouge, took possession of the U.S. Arsenal, and compelled surrender of the city. The naval force then continued upstream, continuing to overawe key points along the river (see **Natchez, Mississippi**).

The Federals lost control of Baton Rouge to Confederate partisans when Farragut's corvettes and gunboats proceeded upriver. After a brief visit to the Vicksburg area and a reconnaissance of the city's river defenses, Farragut returned to New Orleans and stopped briefly at Baton Rouge, reasserting Union authority. Farragut ascended the Mississippi a second time late in June, and the Confederates again resumed control of the city. Returning downriver after the frustration of not being able to take Vicksburg in July 1862, Farragut put ashore at Baton Rouge the brigade of Benjamin Butler's soldiers under Brig. Gen. Thomas Williams, which had accompanied him to Vicksburg.

All would not remain quiet in the former Louisiana capital city for long. On August 5, 1862, the Confederates under Maj. Gen. John C. Breckinridge, well-known Kentucky politician-general and former vice president, attacked the city. Williams was killed while leading his soldiers against Breckinridge's force. The Union infantry, although giving ground, with the help of three of Farragut's gunboats and the ironclad *Essex,* drove off the attackers. The Confederate ironclad ram CSS *Arkansas,* which had already baffled and dismayed the Federal squadrons on the Mississippi (see **Vicksburg, Mississippi**), was to have supported the Rebel attack but developed engine trouble just north of Baton Rouge. The USS *Essex,* under the command of Cmdr. William D. "Dirty Bill" Porter, David D. Porter's half-brother, and two gunboats tracked down the *Arkansas* the next day. The *Arkansas* was set ablaze by her crew and her magazine exploded as the Federal gunboats closed in.

Fearful of a Confederate attack on New Orleans, Butler ordered Baton Rouge evacuated ten days after the Confederate attack was repulsed. Nathaniel Banks, at the suggestion of Farragut, had the city reoccupied without incident as one of his first acts after assuming Butler's command. As of December 17, 1862, the Federals occupied Baton Rouge for the remainder of the war. On May 2, 1863, Col. Benjamin H. Grierson rode into Baton Rouge at the conclusion of his cavalry raid through Mississippi, and he and his troopers received a hero's welcome (see **Jackson's Valley Campaign, Virginia**).

Points of Interest

In Baton Rouge, take exit 1C from I-110 and head west toward the river. The State Capitol is at the north end of Fifth Street. The Pentagon Barracks, next to the current state capitol, was built in 1819–22. Many well-known Civil War officers pulled duty at the barracks. Grant, Custer, Sherman, and Davis all served there. The buildings are still in use and one has a small museum with Civil War exhibits. On the other side of the capitol is the Old Arsenal Museum. Built in 1838, it was the one seized by Louisiana citizens in the tense moments nine weeks after Abraham Lincoln won the 1860 presidential election. After the seizure, William T. Sherman, the first president of Louisiana Seminary in Pineville, which later became Louisiana State University in Baton Rouge, resigned his position and headed north.

The August 5, 1862, battle took place in the city itself. The Battle of Baton Rouge State Monument at 330 South Nineteenth Street identifies the site of the battle. Another marker at Dufrocq and Spain streets marks the site where Col. Henry W. Allen, later Louisiana's Confederate governor, was wounded in the battle. The old State Capitol, North and Lafayette streets, had a fire on December 28, 1862, while Federal troops used it as a barracks. The inside of the castlelike structure was gutted and has been rebuilt, but the exterior remains as it was before and during the war.

DRIVING TOUR—*Proceed to Bayou Country or Port Hudson*
READING—*Farragut's campaign: Natchez, Mississippi;*
(chronological)—Cedar Mountain, Virginia

BAYOU COUNTRY

Along with Sterling Price, John Magruder, and Theophilus Holmes, Maj. Gen. Richard Taylor was assigned a command in the vast Trans-Mississippi Department under the overall command of Gen. Edmund Kirby Smith, given that awesome responsibility in March 1863. Taylor was given his west Louisiana command in July 1862 and arrived in August.

Richard Taylor was neither a West Point graduate nor a professional soldier, yet he brought impressive credentials to the post. He was the son of Mexican War hero and former U.S. President Zachary Taylor (who during his short term in office did enough to thwart Southern expansion of slavery that his body was recently exhumed to determine if his untimely death was the result of deliberate poisoning—it was ascertained that this story was untrue). He was the brother of Jefferson Davis's first wife,

Lt. Gen. Richard Taylor, CSA, often covered the vast area of his west Louisiana department by sleeping at night in an ambulance drawn by fast horses from one town to another.

who had died in 1835, some three months after they were wed. Most important, he had served under Stonewall Jackson in the Shenandoah Valley in 1862 and was an extremely effective commander in that brilliant military campaign (see **Shenandoah Valley, Virginia**). Louisiana was also Taylor's home, and he welcomed his difficult new position.

It was difficult because Taylor lacked the men, matériel, and money to guard the large and remote western Louisiana territory in his charge. But he set about making the most of the situation in order to achieve his objective of driving the Federals from Louisiana. By late October 1862, the Federals had already made inroads into the bayou country west of New Orleans. Donaldsonville was occupied by troops under Brig. Gen. Godfrey Weitzel, Ben Butler's young protégé. Weitzel's troops also advanced down Bayou Lafourche and drove the command of Confederate Brig. Gen. Alfred Mouton back to Brashear City.

In November 1862, the Confederates scored some minor successes and, with the help of the gunboat *Cotton*, stopped the Federals from advancing up Bayou Teche and from capturing a rock-salt quarry near New Iberia. In January 1863, the Federals under Weitzel's command again sought to ascend the Teche but were discouraged by Confederate resistance. The Confederates continued to hold the Teche until early April, when General Banks established a headquarters at Brashear City with a force of 18,000. Taylor personally took charge of the effort to oppose Banks, and at the Battle of Irish Bend on April 13, he held the far larger Federal force at bay on two fronts until he could get his army to safety.

On April 20, 1863, Federal gunboats and troop transports, which had steamed up the Atchafalaya River, captured *Butte-à-la-Rose*. Taylor's army continued its retreat up the Red River to Natchitoches shortly thereafter and Union gunboats of the Mississippi Squadron under R. Adm. David D. Porter that had assisted Grant in the Second Vicksburg Campaign (see **Vicksburg, Mississippi**), ascended the Red River and on May 6 arrived at Alexandria ahead of Banks's army. Banks soon evacuated Alexandria, abandoning the pursuit of Taylor to invest Port Hudson. Taylor was not finished, however. A contingent of Banks's force left at Opelousas moved south again after raiding the bayou country, and returned to Brashear City. There on June 23, Taylor launched a surprise amphibious assault and captured the 1,200-man garrison—which outnumbered the Rebels two to one. Confederate Brig. Gen. Tom Green, one of the few heroes of the Sibley Expedition (see **New Mexico** in **The Far West**), attacked Donaldsonville on June 28. In a rare night engagement, Federal gunboats, cooperating with the garrison, drove off the attackers. The Confederates thus regained all the lost territory in the bayou country except Donaldsonville; but the July surrenders of Port Hudson and Vicksburg blunted these gains and the threat to New Orleans.

Points of Interest

The bayou country can be reached by taking US90 west from New Orleans or I-10 to Lafayette and then US90 east. The first stop in the bayou country is Morgan City, which during the war was Brashear City. The only remnants of the Federal occupation and its use as a base is a portion of one of the earthen defenses built by the Federals, Fort Star. One of the fort's bastions is located on the front lawn of Atkinson Memorial Presbyterian Church, on Fourth Street

Maj. Gen. Nathaniel P. Banks, USA, was a self-made man who lacked the military skill and judgment to gain victories in the field. He was an accomplished and astute politician, however, and served the Union more capably as a military administrator in Louisiana.

in Morgan City. Camp Bisland, the site of the Confederate defensive position on April 12, 1863, has been lost. For information on its location and other sites in Morgan City, contact the Morgan City Archives, 220 Everett Street, Morgan City, LA 70381; 504-380-4621.

Three other sites have significance in the area. Oaklawn Manor, an antebellum estate on LA28 just off LA182, was in Taylor's line of retreat during the Battle of Irish Bend. Also near the battle site, in the town of Franklin, is the Grevemberg House, an 1851 Greek Revival home. It is located just off LA182 on LA233. The house is now a museum and includes Civil War relics. The museum is open Tuesday through Sunday. Call 318-828-2092 for information.

Finally, Shadows-on-the-Teche is a beautiful manor house in New Iberia which was Nathaniel Banks's headquarters when he was campaigning against Taylor in 1863. The house is available for touring every day except Christmas, Thanksgiving, and New Year's Day. Admission is charged. SHADOWS-ON-THE-TECHE, 317 East Main Street, New Iberia, LA 70560; 318-369-6446. Also in New Iberia, at 301 West Main Street is Church of the Epiphany, which was used as a military hospital.

GRAND COTEAU

By July 9, 1863, the Trans-Mississippi Department was effectively cut off from the rest of the Confederacy. Campaigns in Arkansas and Indian Territory threatened to further pare that vast region. The eyes of Washington were on Texas, for both military reasons and political reasons, including sending a warning signal to the French interventionists in Mexico. General-in-Chief Henry W. Halleck pushed General Banks to make an incursion into Texas. Banks favored a coastal approach, but after the Federal defeat at Sabine Pass in September (see **Sabine Pass, Texas**), an inland route through Louisiana seemed inviting. In charge of a sizable force, made up troops that had successfully participated in the Vicksburg and Port Hudson campaigns, was Maj. Gen. William B. Franklin, number one in the West Point class of 1843 in which U. S. Grant had stood twenty-first. Franklin had been sent west after he exchanged blame and criticism with Maj. Gen. Ambrose E. Burnside for the Federal disaster at Fredericksburg in December 1862.

The buildup of Federal troops was of concern to Richard Taylor, who had been maintaining his small mobile force between Alexandria and Bayou Teche. Deciding to test the strength of the Federal columns, he launched a lightning attack on September 29, 1863, at Stirling's Plantation, near Morganza, the northernmost outpost of the Federal army at Brashear City. He killed, wounded, or captured 515 Federals along with their equipment, including artillery.

The Federal column began their advance from Brashear City on October 3, marching to New Iberia. Fitful skirmishing took place with Taylor's mostly mounted units; as the Yanks forged ahead to hoist the U.S. flag over Opelousas again on October 21. The Union columns were strung out, as food and forage was scarce in this area trampled before by opposing armies. Taylor saw a chance to strike a blow at Franklin's force, the division of Brig. Gen. Stephen G. Burbridge, then camped on Carron Crow Bayou. On November 2, Rebel infantry and cavalry advanced upon Burbridge and drove his force back to Bayou Bourbeau, near Grand Coteau. The next day the Federals were hammered again, leaving behind 250 casualties, equipment, and prisoners. This defeat aborted Banks's Teche campaign and started the bluecoats back to New Iberia, where Franklin ordered entrenchments thrown up and had his force go into winter quarters.

Points of Interest

There is little remaining in the Cajun country between Lafayette and Opelousas to identify the actions that characterized this contested region. Some highway markers in Opelousas (I-49) and Grand Coteau (1 mile east of I-49 on LA93, 9 miles south of Opelousas) describe battle actions. There was much destruction in this area as units from both sides sought food and forage during the difficult and fruitless 1863 campaigns.

To leave the bayou country and proceed to Port Hudson, there are two options. From New Iberia, take US90 north to Lafayette, then I-10 east to Baton Rouge. If you have ended your bayou tour in Morgan City and have the time for a longer route, LA70 will carry you through the still-remote Atchafalaya Basin for 33 miles. At the intersection with LA1, go north to Donaldsonville. Along the waterfront in Donaldsonville, where Bayou Lafourche empties into the Mississippi River, was located Fort Butler, where on June 28, the Federal garrison aided by gunboats turned back General Green's Confederate attack. A ditch along the river near the present-day waterworks was part of the fort's moat. From Donaldsonville, tale LA1 north to Baton Rouge, then proceed north on US61 to Port Hudson.

DRIVING TOUR—*Proceed to Baton Rouge and Port Hudson*
READING— *Taylor's 1862 and April 1863 campaigns: Vicksburg Area, Mississippi*
(chronological)—After Bayou Country: Honey Springs, Oklahoma;
after Grand Coteau: Droop Mountain, West Virginia

PORT HUDSON

When Farragut's squadron sailed upriver in late spring of 1862, the Confederates had little in the way of defense on the Mississippi River between New Orleans and Vicksburg. When Farragut abandoned the attempt to take Vicksburg in the fourth week of July he withdrew to New Orleans all but a few gunboats. The Confederates, following Breckin-ridge's August 5 Baton Rouge defeat, fortified the strategic bend in the Mississippi River at Port Hudson. The three bastions (Vicksburg and Grand Gulf, Mississippi, and Port Hudson) gave the Rebels a command of 240 miles of the Mississippi, and denied the Yankees through passage on the river. Via the Red River, the Confederates had an avenue to ship Trans-Mississippi supplies and manpower into the Confederate heartland. Herds of Texas longhorn cattle swam the river above Port Hudson. Located on bluffs at a right angle bend in the river, Port Hudson had steep ravines on its land approaches from the north and south as well, making the site highly defensible. The Port Hudson fortifica-tions were extensive and mounted heavy guns, although only 13 cannons were initially available to be positioned to command the river.

On September 7, 1862, the Federal navy tested the position for the first time as "Dirty Bill" Porter, in the USS *Essex,* ran the batteries from north to south. The *Essex* was badly beaten about by Rebel guns, including some manned by former crewman of the CSS *Arkansas,* whose disabled ironclad had been scuttled four weeks earlier on the *Essex*'s approach.

The real test of the Port Hudson fortifications by the U.S. Navy came in March 1863. R. Adm. David G. Farragut, in cooperation with Banks's land force, planned to steam upriver to blockade supplies coming down to Port Hudson from the Red River and establish contact with R. Adm. David Porter's Missis-sippi Squadron near Vicksburg. Banks's concept was to starve out the garrison. Shunning a siege, he opted for going after the sources of supplies—a goal of his subsequent April campaign through

This color period lithograph dramatizes the ships of R. Adm. David G. Farragut as they ran the Port Hudson batteries on March 14, 1863. The vessel on fire is the USS Mississippi.

the bayou country. On March 14, Federal mortar boats began to bombard Port Hudson in the morning. At eleven-twenty P.M., Farragut's four ship squadron—including the *Hartford*, the *Richmond*, the *Monongahela*; and the side-wheeler *Mississippi*; and gunboats acting as consorts for the first three—got under way and held a course near the east bank of the river, closest to the fort. They surprised the garrison, but soon the fire rafts on the opposite bank were lit and the shells began to fly. The *Hartford* and her consort the *Albatross* made it past the batteries, but the *Richmond* took a hit in the boiler and returned downriver, the *Monongahela* backed down in the current, and the *Mississippi* ran aground, was abandoned, and eventually exploded south of the fort after drifting free.

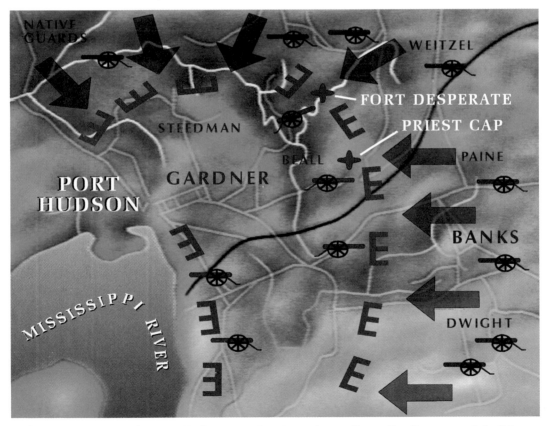

The May 27, 1863, assault on Port Hudson centered on the northeast salient at Fort Desperate and the Priest Cap. African Americans from Louisiana in a Federal unit designated the Native Guards attacked the northwest salient near the river.

Heavy Federal artillery emplaced during the siege of Port Hudson.
Fond of documenting his exploits, General Banks had numerous
photographs such as this one made at Port Hudson after its capture.

Banks's army, although massed on the southeast approaches to Port Hudson, did little to attract the Confederates' attention on what was an exciting March 14–15 night on the river. Farragut continued upriver with the *Hartford* and the *Albatross* and conferred with Grant, then resupplied, and returned downstream to block the mouth of the Red River until relieved by Porter's gunboats. Eventually, Farragut discovered a roundabout route for himself back to New Orleans through the Union-controlled Atchafalaya River enabling the *Hartford* to return to a position north of Port Hudson.

The commander of the Port Hudson garrison, Maj. Gen. Franklin Gardner, was a classmate of Grant's at West Point. He resisted orders by the overall Confederate commander in the west, Gen. Joseph E. Johnston, to evacuate the position. On May 22, Union troops converged from Baton Rouge and Alexandria by way of Bayou Sara to invest Port Hudson, and enable General Banks to begin siege operations. On May 27, costly assaults on the northern and eastern fronts of the four-and-a-half-mile landward perimeter of the works were beaten back. Two black regiments, the first to be engaged in major combat, gallantly charged the Hogback Spur held by the 39th Mississippi and were repulsed with frightful casualties. Other Union attacks were defeated in detail as Rebel troops marched from one threatened area to another. After the May 27 assault, parallels were dug and Federal artillery inched closer. These efforts were supported by Federal naval bombardment, as were the attacks of May 27 and June 14.

Banks launched another all-out attack on June 14 against a sector of the Port Hudson fortifications dubbed the Priest Cap, and was supported by bombardment and a thrust against the Citadel—the stronghold anchoring the Confederate right flank on the Mississippi—but no permanent breach in the line was achieved. Siege operations continued. During the June 14 attack, the Federals encountered fields planted with shells fused to explode when stepped on. This was one of the first uses of "land mines" in military history. Other novel weapons employed by the Confederates at Port Hud-

The Alabama-Arkansas Redoubt, a portion of the excellent Confederate earthworks preserved at Port Hudson State Commemorative Area

son were telescopic rifle sights, a railcar-mounted cannon, two breech-loading artillery pieces, and calcium searchlights.

With the surrender of Vicksburg on July 4, 1863 (see **Vicksburg, Mississippi**), Port Hudson's strategic significance was lost. Nearly starved out by the longest sustained siege in American military history, the Port Hudson Confederates surrendered and stacked arms on July 9. One thousand Rebels of the 7,500-man garrison became casualties through battle or disease, leaving 6,500 to surrender. Of the nearly 40,000 Union soldiers engaged, a fourth were on the killed, wounded, or felled by sickness and sunstroke lists. On July 16, the unarmed merchant vessel *Imperial,* out of St. Louis, arrived at New Orleans after a trip down the Mississippi past Vicksburg and Port Hudson. Lincoln would later write of the result of the two surrenders, "The Father of Waters again goes unvexed to the Sea."

Points of Interest

Port Hudson State Commemorative Area—The extensive Confederate earthworks at Port Hudson are well preserved, with more than half of those involved in the attacks of May 27 and June 14 preserved in the more than 750-acre Port Hudson State Commemorative Area. Unfortunately, the Mississippi River changed its course here after the war, so it is difficult to picture the strategic command the Port Hudson river batteries held over the river, but the lush natural setting, undisturbed fortifications, and interpretive exhibits of the park make a visit to Port Hudson extremely worthwhile.

Your visit to the park should start in the large interpretive center. Well-designed and enlightening exhibits and an auditorium are located here. Printed guides to the 6 miles of battlefield trails are available. Outside the interpretive center is an artillery display and picnic area. Some of the trails are paved and lead to an observation tower, for an overview of a portion of the line and boardwalks with interpretive displays. Other trails are more rustic and require some climbing. No matter what combination of walking trails you choose, your visit will be rewarding. Fort Desperate, Commissary Hill, and the Alabama-Arkansas Redoubt were the scenes of heavy fighting.

The park also offers living-history programs and other periodically scheduled events. For further information, contact the park. PORT HUDSON STATE COMMEMORATIVE AREA, 756 West Plains–Port Hudson Road, Zachary, LA 70791; 504-654-3775.
 ♿ 👫 ❓ 🏛 P 🌲 🚻

South of the state commemorative area, a country road parallels the former river bluff, where additional earthworks on private property may be seen. The road continues to the Port Hudson National Cemetery, located near the southeastern edge of the Port Hudson perimeter. Nearby, on property owned by Georgia-Pacific, is a peace monument erected by that corporation and located where an excavation discovered a Union and a Confederate officer buried side by side. From the cemetery, you can reenter US61 and return to Baton Rouge to continue your tour to Alexandria.

DRIVING TOUR—*Proceed to Alexandria*
READING *(chronological)—Morris Island, South Carolina*

ALEXANDRIA

One of the most significant accomplishments of Maj. Gen. Nathaniel Banks's campaign through the bayou country was the march northward to Alexandria, on the Red River. David D. Porter's gunboat squadron, in early May 1863, with Grant's army ensconced in its Mississippi beachhead twenty-five miles south of Vicksburg and flexing its muscles preparatory to its march inland, sailed down the Mississippi and up Red River to Alexandria and demanded and received surrender of the city on May 6. Banks's army columns arrived on the long march up from the bayou country the next afternoon.

On the way back to the Mississippi as the water level dropped, Porter's gunboats damaged Fort De Russy on the Red River, and on May 11–12, having ascended the Black and Quachita rivers, were checked and turned back by Fort Beauregard, guardian of the lower reaches of the latter river. The Federal river tars would become too familiar with the reaches of Red River from its mouth to above Alexandria. They would return in less than eleven

The ironclads and gunboats of R. Adm. David D. Farragut's Mississippi River Squadron passing through Bailey's dams, as painted by a U.S. Navy officer who was a witness to the event

months in support of another campaign up the Red River (see **Red River Campaign**). When Banks marched against Port Hudson, Alexandria was evacuated by the Yanks and reoccupied by the Confederates on May 24.

Alexandria next became a magnet for Federal activity during the Red River Campaign in March–May of 1864. A 10,000-man column under Brig. Gen. A. J. "Whiskey" Smith, having sailed from Vicksburg, landed at Simmesport on the Red River, and marched against Fort De Russy, which the Confederates had reoccupied and strengthened, stormed it March 14. Marching into Alexandria without further resistance, they rendezvoused with the ironclads and gunboats of R. Adm. David D. Porter's Mississippi Squadron, and the combined force waited the arrival of 15,000 men under Maj. Gen. William B. Franklin from the bayou country. The entire force under Maj. Gen. Nathaniel P. Banks then headed northwest up Red River.

Following a defeat at Mansfield, and loss of nerve after a tactical victory at Pleasant Hill, Banks's force returned to Alexandria and fortified the city. Unseasonably low water on the Red in late April threatened Porter's squadron with disaster. The gunboats were in acute danger of being stranded at the Alexandria rapids but a plan was devised by a Wisconsin lieutenant colonel, Joseph Bailey. Union pioneers felled trees, quarried rocks, and tore down many of Alexandria's buildings to construct a series of wing dams. Like the locks of a canal, the dams increased the level of water successfully in stages and the gunboats, despite serious losses, navigated the rapids and made their way back to the Mississippi. The Federal vessels had to dump their cargoes of confiscated cotton to make good their escape. After the squadron's departure on May 13, Banks's forces burned what was left of Alexandria and marched out. Bailey's dams are one of the war's engineering marvels.

Points of Interest

From Baton Rouge, Alexandria may be reached by two routes. Driving I-10 west to I-49 north is the fastest route. But taking US190 17 miles west to LA1 north will take you along the river to sites at Simmesport, Mansura, and Marksville. Simmesport was the landing site for A. J. Smith's corps loaned by General Sherman to Banks for the Red River campaign and was the point of departure for the Federal forces leaving the region after the failure of the campaign. West of Simmesport along LA1 is a historical marker for the action at Yellow Bayou, May 18, and another roadside marker at Mansura, just south of LA1 on LA107, describes the May 16 action there. North of Marksville on LA452 adjacent to Red River is Fort De Russy. The site has been recently acquired by preservationists.

Much of antebellum Alexandria was dismantled to build "Bailey's dams" or was burned when the Federals evacuated the city. Well-preserved Confederate earthworks remain on the grounds of the Central Louisiana State Hospital. For information on Civil War sites in Alexandria contact the Alexandria-Pineville Convention and Tourist Bureau, P.O. Box 8110, Alexandria, LA 71301; 318-443-7049. The organization offers a brochure on Civil War sites. Just across the Red River in Pineville at the O. K. Allen Bridge on LA165 is the site of the rapids or falls where "Bailey's dams" were built. During periods of low water, before recent navigational improvements, surviving remains of the dams were visible. Historical markers in this area describe Forts Buhlow and Randolph, fortifications built by the Rebels after Banks's departure in case the Yankees returned. They did not.

Pineville was also destroyed during the Red River Campaign; however, Mount Olivet Church on Main Street survives. It was used as a Union barracks. The Pineville National Cemetery is on Shamrock Street. Interestingly, many of the Federals buried here were reinterred after being moved from graves in Brownsville, Texas, at the beginning of the twentieth century.

From Alexandria, travel north on I-49, then west on US84 for 8 miles to Mansfield. If you desire to visit Natchitoches, you can exit I-49 at LA6 east a short distance from the city. Then proceed north on US84 to Mansfield.

DRIVING TOUR—*Proceed to Mansfield*
READING—*Red River Campaign*

RED RIVER CAMPAIGN

When Ulysses S. Grant was appointed general-in-chief of all Federal armies on March 9, 1864, one of the tasks he inherited was the Red River Campaign, scheduled to begin within a week. Grant wanted the large army under Maj. Gen. Nathaniel P. Banks to march against Mobile and capture the largest Confederate port remaining open on the Gulf of Mexico, but that mission must wait until the Red River Campaign was concluded. The initial military objective of the campaign was the capture of Shreveport, command center of the Confederate Trans-Mississippi Department. But the real missions of the campaign were political, economic, and diplomatic.

The often-attempted, never-achieved objective of control of Texas was one of the Federals' principal aims. The economic interests, New England cotton mills, still eyeballed the vast acreage of East Texas as prime land for increasing cotton production for the North and establishing new looms in the South. The Lincoln administration saw Louisiana and Texas as prime states for establishing local governments to be elected by 10 percent of the population under Lincoln's December 1863 Proclamation of Amnesty and Reconstruction and whose electoral votes would be invaluable in the 1864 presidential elections. Banks was to hold elections in New Orleans and

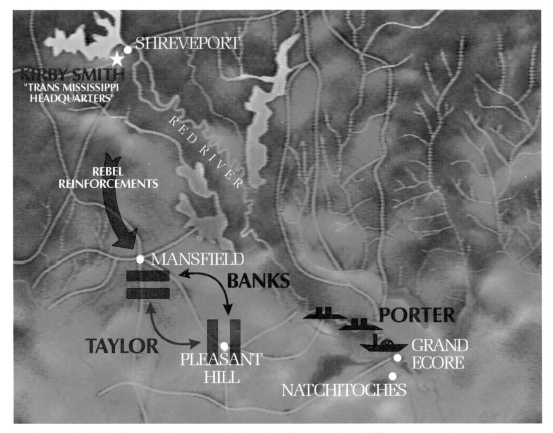

On April 8, 1864, after traveling on an inland road to Shreveport, Banks's force was savagely attacked by Confederates at Mansfield. Taylor's Rebels dogged Banks's retreat to Pleasant Hill and launched an attack the following day. However, weakened by the withdrawal of units that had reinforced him at Mansfield, Taylor could not score a decisive blow on Banks's army. The Federal army rendezvoused with Admiral Porter's squadron and the combined force began a destructive withdrawal to Alexandria.

communities along the march. Thousands of bales of cotton were stockpiled in the Red River basin since the Federals gained control of the Mississippi. These could be seized, transported, and condemned by prize courts giving Federal sailors and tag-along cotton speculators big profits. Finally, a major Union army in Texas would send a signal to the French to curb their ardor for their Mexican adventure.

A second Federal column under Maj. Gen. Frederick Steele was set in motion toward Shreveport, departing Little Rock, Arkansas, on March 23 (see **Camden Campaign, Arkansas**). Maj. Gen. William T. Sherman loaned 10,000 men under "Whiskey" Smith to

Banks for the campaign, under the stipulation that they be returned to Sherman's command by April 15 at the latest. As noted, Smith's corps landed at Simmesport, captured Fort De Russy, and marched to Alexandria. The combined army-navy force left Alexandria on March 26, after Banks encouraged Porter to pass above the Red River rapids with his gunboats. The column's cavalry arrived at Natchitoches on March 31. Most of Banks's infantry and Porter's gunboats had reached Grand Ecore by nightfall April 3.

In March, Maj. Gen. Richard Taylor, in view of the formidable character of the Union advance, had withdrawn his forces northward, except for a cavalry regiment captured by a Federal sortie north of Alexandria at Henderson's Hill on March 21. Taylor fired off request after request to department commander Kirby Smith for reinforcements. Not until April 6 was he joined by Tom Green's Texan Cavalry Division. An infantry division sent down from Arkansas was held at Shreveport as Kirby Smith waited to determine whether the major threat would be in Arkansas or Louisiana.

Taylor could not wait. When information reached him that Banks was marching on the road that ran west then north from Natchitoches to Shreveport through Pleasant Hill and Mansfield, he decided to take a stand and give battle. The Federals would be fifteen miles west of the river at Mansfield, a town thirty miles south of Shreveport. The terrain south of that community, in a pine woods, was suitable for defense, and the Union soldiers would be without gunboat support. Taylor formed a line of battle four miles south of Mansfield on Honeycutt Hill near Sabine Cross Roads, where a cleared area was flanked on the north and south by forests.

The Federal column advanced along the narrow stage road through Pleasant Hill with Brig. Gen. Albert Lee's cavalry division in the lead, followed by the cavalry wagon train and Franklin's infantry with Smith's infantry bringing up the rear. At the same time, Porter with six gunboats steamed north from Grand Ecore with one infantry division on transports. On the afternoon of April 7, Lee's cavalry clashed with Confederate cavalry at Wilson's Farm above Pleasant Hill. The Federal troopers drove off the Rebel horsemen in a two-hour fight, but Lee was disturbed by the presence of the Southern force. His concern was not shared by Banks or Franklin, who did not expect Taylor to give battle south of Shreveport. An infantry brigade was sent forward to support Lee's mounted force. As they advanced on April 8, Lee's cavalry

Federal artillery occupied the center of a line formed on Honeycutt Hill, along the Old Stage Road, now part of the Mansfield battlefield preserved in the Mansfield State Commemorative Area.

again encountered Rebel skirmishers. At two P.M., Lee's vanguard came out of the woods and entered a large clearing 800 yards across to confront Taylor's army in battle array. The Federal cavalry dismounted, and the infantry and cannon were called up to form a line of battle along a rail fence and a ridge called Honeycutt Hill. This began the Battle of Mansfield.

At four P.M. Taylor, sensing that the Federal line was in disarray, ordered an attack by Brig. Gen. Alfred Mouton's division. Federal artillery savaged the Rebel ranks, killing Mouton, and the Federal line held. Taylor, undismayed, ordered a follow-up flank attack, by John G. Walker's Texas Division, which broke the Union line. The Northern soldiers retreated and became entangled in the wagon train blocking the road behind them while the Rebels surged ahead. A Federal infantry division in line two miles farther south deployed in battle line and, after a brief fight, gave way. Another Federal division under Brig.

The Dog Trot House is the only surviving structure of the village of Pleasant Hill, site of the April 9, 1864, battle.

Gen. William H. Emory was deployed a mile farther south at Chapman's Bayou. Emory's line steadied the rout and, though attacked by Taylor at six P.M., stemmed the Confederate advance. After dark, Emory and the rest of the Federal army retreated to Pleasant Hill.

A victory for the South, the Battle of Mansfield, or Sabine Cross Roads as the North called it, cost Banks 2,235 casualties, including 1,500 taken prisoner. Taylor lost 1,000; however, with reinforcements, Brig. Gen. Thomas Churchill's division, reaching him after a long march from Shreveport, he marched early the next day intent on following up his victory. At five P.M., April 9, Taylor attacked the divisions of William Emory and A. J. Smith on a ridge fronting Pleasant Hill. Banks had sent many of the troops engaged the day before and the trains back toward Natchitoches so the Confederates had a slight numerical advantage. Fatigue from marching or fighting the day before, along with confusing terrain, dulled Taylor's two-prong attack, and none of its elements achieved great success. Darkness halted the fighting, with counterattacking Federals—"Whiskey" Smith's "gorrillas"—on the Union left hammering and hurling by Churchill's division.

During the night, Banks lost his nerve and withdrew from Pleasant Hill. The fight cost the Yanks 1,369 casualties and the Rebels 1,626. Banks retreated to Grand Ecore, constructing fortifications. His forces awaited the return of Porter's squadron and its supporting infantry division, which were making their way back down Red River after encountering record low water levels and numerous obstacles, including the huge steamboat *New Falls City*, which the Confederates had sunk to block the river. Constantly under attack from Rebel sharpshooters and a few batteries on shore, including the April 12 fight at Blair's Landing, where the gallant old Confederate hero Tom Green was killed, the squadron and troop transports returned in a battered condition to Grand Ecore.

Richard Taylor contemplated the destruction of Banks's army, but Kirby Smith, immediately after the Battle of Pleasant Hill, ordered Churchill's reinforcements that had been sent to Taylor on the eve of that battle, along with Walker's "greyhounds," to Arkansas. In his weakened condition, Taylor could do little more than skirmish and harass.

Troubles continued for the Federal navy. The largest ironclad, the *Eastport*, struck a torpedo below Grand Ecore, was repaired, but ran aground later when the squadron continued downriver to Alexandria on April 21. She was eventually abandoned and sunk by her crew. After the departure of the navy, Banks abandoned his fortified camp at Grand Ecore, passed through Natchitoches, and began a scorched-earth policy on his route back to Alexandria.

The Federals lost several gunboats and transports to Confederate shore fire but arrived at Alexandria, where they encountered the formidable obstacle of passing the rapids (see **Alexandria**). When Union vessels and soldiers cleared the smoldering ruins of Alexandria on May 13, Taylor lost his last opportunity to destroy Banks's army and Porter's squadron. Two engagements on May 16 at Mansura and May 18 at Yellow Bayou with Texan cavalry now led by Brig. Gen. John A. Wharton, who replaced Tom Green, and Mouton's infantry, commanded by the popular French soldier Prince Camille Polignac, called "Prince Polecat" by the Texans, did not slow down the Union retreat. By May 19 they were across the Atchafalaya at Simmesport and the Mississippi Squadron was back in its namesake river. Taylor was frustrated, but was promoted to lieutenant general and ordered to command of the Department of Alabama, Mississippi, and East Louisiana and given the thanks of the Confederate Congress for his victory over the forces of Nathaniel Banks, who was removed from field command for the final time after the campaign's conclusion.

Points of Interest

Mansfield State Commemorative Area—A stunning Confederate victory in the Trans-Mississippi occurred April 8, 1864, at Mansfield (Sabine Cross Roads). Today, a 178-acre state commemorative area occupies the site on Honeycutt Hill where Confederate forces under General Taylor surprised and turned back the head of Nathaniel Banks's column marching toward Shreveport. The rolling fields separating the initial lines, and the pine woods that concealed the Confederate infantry, are easily distinguishable.

The park features an interpretive center with a gift shop and bookstore, excellent museum, and an audiovisual presentation. Among the exhibits are several dioramas of the Red River Campaign events and pieces of Bailey's dams. An interpretive trail guides you along key points on the battle lines. Monuments and cannons are featured. MANSFIELD STATE COMMEMORATIVE AREA, Route 2, Box 459, Mansfield, LA 71052; 318-872-1474. ♿ ⚥ ❓ 🏛 P ⛱ 🚻

Mansfield Area—In the town of Mansfield, 4 miles north, numerous homes and buildings are extant which served as hospitals during the Red River campaign. Check with personnel at the state commemorative area for specific information on wartime buildings in Mansfield.

Pleasant Hill—From Mansfield State Commemorative Area, travel south on LA175. Historical markers along the highway locate the second and third Federal lines on April 8 as well as the opening cavalry action on April 7 at Wilson's Farm. Continue south on LA175 for about 12 miles. Along the highway, you will see a series of low, granite markers. These monuments describe phases of the Battle of Pleasant Hill (April 9) and were sited by Dr. C. E. Poimboef, and placed by living-history Confederate and Union reenactors who relived the marches, camps, and battles of the Red River campaign from Pleasant Hill to Mansfield during its 130th anniversary in 1994. At the intersection of LA175 and LA174 in Pleasant Hill, a small park contains monuments and additional descriptions of the battle. From Pleasant Hill, take LA174 north to I-49 toward Shreveport.

DRIVING TOUR—*Proceed to Shreveport*
READING—*Camden Campaign, Arkansas*

SHREVEPORT

Confederate headquarters for Gen. Edmund Kirby Smith's Trans-Mississippi Department were in Shreveport. It was also the seat of the Confederate government of Louisiana after Federal occupations forced it from first Baton Rouge, then Opelousas. Though never seriously threatened again following the failure of the Federals' 1864 Red River Campaign, Shreveport was the site of one of the final surrenders of Confederate troops. On May 26, 1865, under terms worked out in New Orleans between Federal general Peter J. Osterhaus representing Maj. Gen. Edward R. S. Canby and Confederate general Simon B. Buckner on behalf of General Kirby Smith, troops of the Trans-Mississippi Department were surrendered at Shreveport. Edmund Kirby Smith and more than 2,000 other unreconstructed Confederates fled to Mexico.

Points of Interest

Cane-Bennett Bluff, located near LA1 downtown, was the site of Gen. Edmund Kirby Smith's headquarters. Fort Humbug Memorial Park, on Clyde Fant Memorial Parkway along the Red River, downtown, features a fort constructed by the Confederates in 1864, when the city was threatened by Banks's and Frederick Steele's converging columns. From Shreveport, continue your tour of Civil War battlefields by traveling west to Texas and Oklahoma, north to Arkansas, or east on I-20 to the Vicksburg-area sites.

DRIVING TOUR—*Proceed to Delta Area (Vicksburg Area), Texas, Oklahoma, or Arkansas*
READING—*surrenders: Palmito Ranch, Texas*

VICKSBURG AREA

In conjunction with Maj. Gen. Ulysses S. Grant's second campaign against Vicksburg, the river parishes of northeastern Louisiana became a Federal staging area. Early in 1863, the 30,000 men of Maj. Gen. John A. McClernand's XIII Corps and Maj. Gen. William T. Sherman's XV Corps occupied camps at Milliken's Bend and Young's Point on the Louisiana shore upstream from Vicksburg. Several canal projects in the area attempted to bypass the Vicksburg batteries. When Federal troops departed the area in April and May to march south, garrisons were left to guard the supply depots at the former camps.

Lake Providence

An oxbow-shaped former bend in the Mississippi River, Lake Providence is located just south of the Arkansas line in northeast Louisiana. One of Grant's proposals in early 1863 was to use Lake Providence to bridge the gap between the Mississippi and bayous feeding Red River. Access to Red River as a route back to the Mississippi had enormous potential for naval support and troop transportation in operating against the Confederate bastions of Vicksburg and Port Hudson. Soldiers from Maj. Gen. James B. McPherson's XVII Corps were put to work reopening an old passage from the flood-swollen Mississippi into the lake. A small river steamboat passed through this waterway into Lake Providence and reconnoitered various waterways draining from the lake, but could find none large enough to admit her. The Lake Providence route was abandoned in March, but like the other canal projects, it kept the soldiers of Grant's army busy when idle time would have brought on increased disease, dissension, and desertion.

Delta Area—The Canal Projects

The narrow spit of land at De Soto Point in Louisiana opposite Vicksburg and bordering a horseshoe-shaped bend in the Mississippi River which, along with the railroad, made the Hill City a key strategic defensive position was of great importance to the Federals beginning in 1862. From Farragut's first June 28 run past the city's guns, when they were far less formidable than seven months later when Grant's campaign against the city began, the idea of bypassing the Mississippi's flow away from the Vicksburg bluffs surfaced.

The canal was begun by soldiers under Brig. Gen. Thomas Williams who accompanied Farragut's squadron to Vicksburg in June 1862. By this time progress was being made by the Federal river squadron on the upper Mississippi, and following a victory in the naval Battle of Memphis on June 6, 1862, a juncture of the two squadrons occurred above Vicksburg on July 1 (see **Memphis, Tennessee**). Disease took its toll on the soldiers during the hot and humid days of July, and when Farragut withdrew downriver on July 24 the canal was abandoned.

Sherman's command, armed with picks, shovels, and some machinery, resumed work on the canal in February 1863. However, in March, a rapid rise in the level of the Mississippi breached the levees, flooding the countryside and stopping work on the canal. The Confederates, having heard of the project, placed new batteries south of Vicksburg where the canal was to have opened into the Mississippi. The project known as "Grant's Canal"—although he had little faith in the project as other than an activity to cure soldiers' boredom—was abandoned in late March.

Sherman's men then started work on the Duckport Canal, a canal project that was several miles northwest, and would connect the Mississippi with first Walnut and then Roundaway Bayou and eventually reconnect with the Mississippi near New Carthage. This project was discontinued when a rapid drop in the level of the river caused Grant to abandon the project after a tug and a number of barges had entered Roundaway Bayou.

Milliken's Bend

After the Federal camp at Milliken's Bend was abandoned in preparation for the overland march of Grant's forces, the area was retained as a Federal supply depot. In an attempt to disrupt Grant's siege of Vicksburg, Maj. Gen. Richard Taylor ordered Brig. Gen. Henry E. McCulloch's Texas Brigade to attack the garrison there. The attack was initially successful, but the ironclad gunboat *Choctaw* and the timberclad *Lexington* came to the aid of the Federal garrison and the Texans were compelled to withdraw.

This was the first action in which black units designated as United States Colored Troops (USCT) saw combat action. Prior battles involving black volunteers organized into state regiments occurred at Port Hudson and elsewhere, but after mid-1863 the United States Colored Troops designation was used for all new units being organized. USCT units, because of discrimination, usually garrisoned forts, supply depots and other facilities; however, they also fought for the North with distinction in major battles such as Brices' Cross Roads, Petersburg, The Crater, Fort Harrison, Nashville and Fort Blakeley (see **Fort Blakeley, Alabama; Brices' Cross Roads, Mississippi; Nashville, Tennessee; Richmond** and **Petersburg, Virginia**).

Points of Interest

There are several fascinating points of interest in northeastern Louisiana relevant to the Vicksburg campaign. While the number of sites in Mississippi and Louisiana associated with the campaign may seem overwhelming, here are a few suggestions should you desire to tour some of these more obscure but very worthwhile sites.

Grant's Canal, the De Soto Point project, is at Delta, a hamlet off I-20 at exit 186. A portion of the canal remains and a historical marker is on-site. Information on and directions to Grant's Canal (a unit of Vicksburg National Military Park) can be obtained at the park visitor center. Grant's Canal, and many other sites mentioned here, are described in a pamphlet, *Grant's March Through Louisiana—A Tour*, published by the Louisiana Civil War Centennial Commission and available through Louisiana libraries.

Three miles east of Newellton (US65 exit from I-20, 26 miles south, then east on LA4), is Winter Quarters State Commemorative Area. The 7-acre site includes an 1850 plantation house used by U. S. Grant as a headquarters in the fourth week of April 1863 as his army prepared to cross the Mississippi first at Hard Times Landing and then Disharoon's plantation. For more information on this site, contact the Louisiana Office of State Parks, P.O. Box 44426, Baton Rouge, LA 70804; 504-342-8111.

DRIVING TOUR—*Proceed to Vicksburg Circle Tour*
READING—*Grant's Second Vicksburg Campaign, Mississippi*

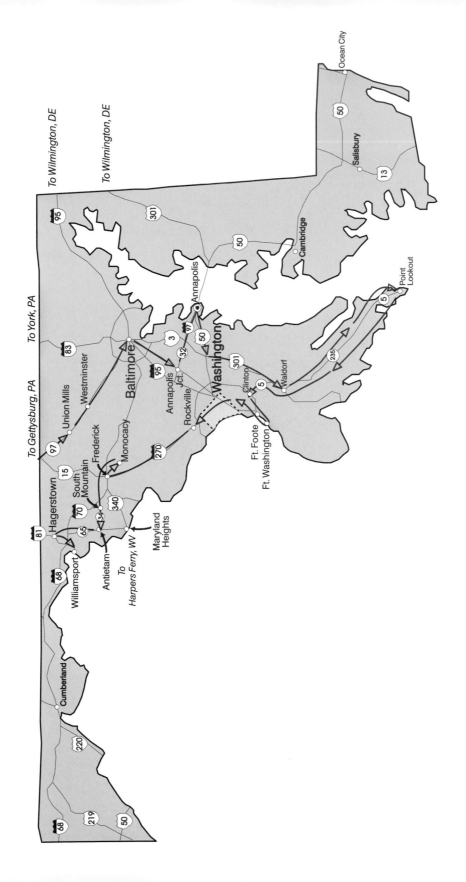

Maryland

"Maryland, My Maryland" was adopted as the Maryland state song in 1939. It was a poem written by James Ryder Randall, a witness to the April 1861 Baltimore riots. Set to the music of the Christmas carol "O Tannenbaum," it was popular as a marching song for Confederate soldiers. The song represented the patriotic spirit of Marylanders, who were geographically split in their allegiance to the Union or the Confederacy and preferred neutrality—putting Maryland first above other allegiances. The eastern shore and counties east and southeast of the District of Columbia, with many large slavery plantations, were sympathetic to the South. The northern and western counties, with small independent-minded farmers and tradesmen, preferred to remain in the Union. Baltimore, the largest city and major seaport, leaned toward the South, especially the city's elite.

The secessionist elements in Maryland sought, unsuccessfully, to interfere with President-elect Lincoln's inaugural trip to Washington. Immediately after the firing on Fort Sumter, they placed a land blockade on the city of Washington. Not until arriving Northern militia units had pushed their way through a Baltimore mob and shortly thereafter occupied Baltimore and Annapolis, did the United States capital's land link to the North return to normal. Manipulating those state government officials who were Unionist, the Federal government, once military control was established, denied some officials' constitutional rights to ensure the state would not secede.

Ironically, both of Gen. Robert E. Lee's invasions of the North and Lt. Gen. Jubal Early's 1864 raid campaigned through the region of the state that was Unionist, across the Potomac River from the Shenandoah Valley and northeastern Virginia. By contrast, John Wilkes Booth, in his flight south from Washington after his assassination of Abraham Lincoln, made use of the pro-Confederate hideouts and courier routes in the country southeast of Washington. Booth crossed the Potomac River from Maryland into Virginia near Port Tobacco, a favored location for Confederate smugglers.

Both Union and Confederate armies, particularly the former, had large numbers of Marylanders in their ranks. Marylanders in command positions included the South's Adms. Franklin Buchanan and Raphael Semmes, Maj. Gen. Isaac R. Trimble, and Brig. Gen. George H. "Maryland" Steuart. The Union army's Maj. Gens. William H. Emory, Edward O. C. Ord and Brig. Gens. Samuel S. Carroll and Robert C. Buchanan were from Maryland.

A tour of Maryland will require from two to three days, longer if a visit to Point Lookout, which has numerous opportunities for recreational activities in addition to its historical interest, is planned. For reasons of historical chronology and geography as well, a trip to Maryland can be combined with visits to Washington, D.C., Pennsylvania, northern Virginia, and West Virginia. The recommended route on the tour map begins in Gettysburg, Pennsylvania, and ends in Harpers Ferry, West Virginia, to link with the routes given in those states' chapters.

WESTMINSTER

During Maj. Gen. J.E.B. Stuart's northward ride to locate the Army of Northern Virginia before the Battle of Gettysburg, he encountered Federal cavalry and infantry in Westminster in Carroll County. A detachment of the 1st Delaware Cavalry, sent to guard the railhead there, were having their mounts reshod on the afternoon of June 29, 1863, at a town blacksmith shop when Westminster citizens spread the alarm of the approaching Rebel cavalry. The Federals quickly mounted their

This hotel in the small community of Emmitsburg, Maryland, saw the passing of the armies to and from Gettysburg—the Army of the Potomac's left wing on its way north and Stuart's Rebel cavalry, after the bloody three-day battle ended. Alexander Gardner's photography crew, on its way to Gettysburg on July 5, were briefly detained here by the Confederate horsemen.

horses and, led by Capt. Charles Corbit, formed along the Washington Road on which the Confederate troopers approached the town. Not realizing they were facing Stuart's entire column, the Federals with sabers charged. They were beaten back, fighting stubbornly, through Westminster's streets. Eventually Stuart surrounded the bluecoats and took most of them prisoner. Most of the Confederates then continued north to spend the night at Union Mills before riding toward Pennsylvania the next morning.

Points of Interest

Residents of the Shellman House at 206 East Main Street witnessed the brief action at Westminster. Young Mary Shellman called J.E.B. Stuart a "Jonny Red Coat," when he stopped briefly at the house after the skirmish. After exchanging jibs, the Virginian gave her a kiss as a punishment for her misguided loyalties. The house is now occupied by the Historical Society of Carroll County. Two young officers of Stuart's cavalry were buried in the churchyard of the Ascension Episcopal Church on Court Street. The body of Lt. William M. Murray of the 4th Virginia remains while the body of Lt. St. Pierre Gibson was reinterred in Virginia.

In Union Mills, 7 miles north of Westminster, the Confederate cavalry spent the night on the property of the Shriver brothers, owner-operators of nearby trade shops. The Rebels were enthusiastically greeted at the home of William Shriver, who was pro-South with sons in the Confederate army. Across the road, food was begrudgingly handed out by Unionist Andrew Shriver, who unlike his brother owned slaves. The tables were turned when Union forces visited the Shriver homesteads the next day. The homesteads and a restored mill are on MD97.

DRIVING TOUR —*Proceed to Baltimore*
READING—*Hanover, Pennsylvania*

BALTIMORE

Baltimore's mayor and chief of police were suspected to be secessionists. For this reason among others, officials in Washington called on the services of private detective Allan Pinkerton to make security arrangements for Abraham Lincoln to travel secretly to the city by rail, cross unnoticed through the downtown area in disguise to the Camden Street

The April 19, 1861, attack on soldiers of the 6th Massachusetts Regiment as they marched from Baltimore's President Street Station to Camden Street Station, is dramatically portrayed in this woodcut. The Federal troops were at the ready as they marched through the hostile secessionist mob. Shots were fired when the soldiers were hit by brickbats in the two-hour fracas.

Station, which served the only rail line to Washington, and continue his journey to the nation's capital. This ruse was successful. Two months later, the 6th Massachusetts Infantry Regiment, the first Northern troops to travel to Washington in response to Lincoln's call for 75,000 volunteers, could not be concealed so easily. The regiment was attacked by a Baltimore mob on April 19, 1861, while traveling along Pratt Street on horse-drawn railcars from the President Street Station to the Camden Street Station. Four soldiers and nine rioters were killed despite efforts of the Baltimore police to maintain order and the rioting continued for several days. The regiment did complete their rail journey to Washington. As a result of the riot, Lincoln dispatched the 6th Massachusetts and 8th New York Infantry and a section of artillery to Baltimore under Maj. Gen. Benjamin Butler. On May 13, Butler seized and occupied Federal Hill, which commands the harbor. Baltimore was hereafter under close scrutiny by Federal authorities and in many ways treated as an occupied city.

Points of Interest

Baltimore had numerous forts, encampments, and hospitals serving the Federal army during the Civil War. Among the most important positions was Federal Hill (Battery Street and Key Highway), where a fort was built by the 5th New York (Duryee's Zouaves) overlooking the harbor. The Baltimore riots took place in an area between the President Street Station (President and Canton streets) and the Camden Street Station (Camden and Howard streets). The area on Pratt Street near Gay Street is where soldiers of the 6th Massachusetts were first attacked. The President Street Station is being restored and exhibits will focus on the Underground Railroad, the Pratt Street Riot and

Civil War Baltimore. Walking tours of the area are currently given. For more information, contact Friends of the President Street Station at 410-332-8134.

There are also numerous Civil War monuments in Baltimore, including the Lee-Jackson Memorial, the Monument to the Confederate Dead and the Maryland Monument to Union Soldiers and Sailors in the Wyman Park–Baltimore Museum of Art area; and the Monument to Confederate Women of Maryland at Charles Street and University Parkway, as well as several Civil War cemeteries. Among these is Green Mount Cemetery (Greenmount and Oliver streets) where Gen. Joseph E. Johnston, Maj. Gens. Arnold Elzey, Isaac R. Trimble, Benjamin Huger and other Confederate leaders are buried. John Wilkes Booth is buried in the cemetery's Booth lot in an unmarked grave.

In Baltimore harbor is Fort McHenry National Monument and Historic Shrine. The 1794 fort is principally known for its role in the War of 1812 and its inspiration in the creation of "The Star-Spangled Banner" by Francis Scott Key. During the Civil War it was used as a Federal prison, incarcerating, among others, Baltimore officials and citizens suspected of being secessionists, including the son and grandson of Francis Scott Key, and Confederate prisoners of war. Also in Baltimore harbor is the USS *Constellation*. The *Constellation*, which is undergoing extensive rebuilding, saw limited sea duty during the Civil War and now houses a maritime museum.

DRIVING TOUR—*Proceed to Annapolis Junction*
READING *(chronological)—Annapolis Junction and Annapolis*

ANNAPOLIS JUNCTION

One of the key locations in Maryland seized by General Butler's forces on May 5, 1861, was Annapolis Junction, between Washington and Baltimore. Here the Baltimore & Ohio Railroad split into the main line, running to Harpers Ferry, through western Virginia and into Ohio, and into the Washington spur. Both links were crucial in bringing men and supplies from the east. After the 6th Massachusetts volunteers seized key points in Maryland in May 1861, subversive activities by Maryland secessionists to disrupt the Federal war effort were minimal.

Points of Interest

Annapolis Junction is located near US1, southwest of Baltimore. It is now in the center of a modern railroad yard. Northwest of Annapolis Junction is the Thomas Viaduct, built in 1835 to carry the tracks of the Baltimore & Ohio Railroad across the Patapsco River. The magnificent 60-foot arches, which can still be seen, were guarded against Rebel raiders by Federal forces during the war.

DRIVING TOUR —*Proceed to Annapolis*
READING—*Annapolis and Washington, D.C., Area*

ANNAPOLIS

The United States Naval Academy, established in 1846 in Annapolis to train future officers of the U.S. Navy in educational and practical naval subjects, was moved to Newport, Rhode Island, in May 1861 for security. The venerable USS *Constitution* ("Old Ironsides"), used for training at the academy, and another ship transferred the midshipmen and instructors to Newport, where the academy remained until the end of the war. Academy buildings were used by the Federal army during the war; for example, units were assembled there for Maj. Gen. Ambrose Burnside's January 1862 expedition to the North Carolina sounds.

In May 1861, forces under Maj. Gen. Benjamin Butler

Federal warships standing at the wharves of the U.S. Naval Academy at Annapolis. After the midshipmen and faculty were relocated to Newport, Rhode Island, the academy served for a time as a landing and departure point for Federal forces traveling to and from Washington and for early operations on the Atlantic coast.

repaired the railroad line from Annapolis to Washington, enabling forces arriving in the capital to bypass the dangerous rail route through Baltimore. Annapolis, as the capital of Maryland, witnessed stormy clashes of state politicians struggling to gain control of the state for the North or South. Nineteen members of the state legislature were arrested on charges of subversive activity and imprisoned by the Federal government.

Points of Interest

The U.S. Naval Academy has several buildings dating to the Civil War. The Naval Academy Museum, in a building built long after the war, has important Civil War exhibits and artifacts. The Maryland State House in the center of Annapolis was the scene of debate over the question of secession. That debate ended when the United States government took control of the 1861 elections to establish a Union-friendly state government. St. John's College, near the State House, was used as a Federal hospital and camp during the war. For more information, please call 410-293-2108.

On Forest Drive in a nearby community of Parole is a marker for Camp Parole. This facility was established for the exchange of prisoners between the two sides after the capture of Harpers Ferry by Stonewall Jackson resulted in more than 12,000 Federals being taken prisoner (see **Harpers Ferry, West Virginia**).

DRIVING TOUR—*Proceed to Point Lookout*
READING *(chronological)—Washington, D.C., Area; Burnside's North*
Carolina Campaign: Roanoke Island, North Carolina

POINT LOOKOUT

A Federal prison for Confederate enlisted men was established at Point Lookout, on barren, swampy land, where the Potomac River flows into the Chesapeake Bay, in July 1863. Because of tension engendered by interpretation of the Dix-Hill cartel of July 1862 for the parole and exchange of prisoners, the number of prisoners of war held in prisons in the North and South had started to increase. Point Lookout eventually held nearly 20,000 prisoners of whom more than 3,300 died.

The stockade was located a few feet above sea level and was subject to tides and flooding. The prisoners lived in tents, and food, shelter, and firewood during the winters were in short supply. Although a school was established for the inmates and medical attention was better than at some other facilities, it is difficult to make distinctions between conditions at Point Lookout and the South's Andersonville, Georgia, prison.

During Lt. Gen. Jubal Early's July 1864 raid to the gates of Washington, he planned to have Bradley Johnson's cavalry brigade, in cooperation with the Confederate navy, raid the prison and free the Confederates held there, but the plan was abandoned.

Points of Interest

Point Lookout State Park, in Scotland, Maryland, has two monuments commemorating the more than 3,300 Confederates who died while held at the prison pen. One of the prison buildings has been reconstructed. Fort Lincoln was a fortification built in 1865 to deter Rebel raids. Special events including living-history demonstrations are provided as scheduled.

Point Lookout State Park has a number of recreational facilities for swimming, boating, and camping. POINT LOOKOUT STATE PARK, P.O. Box 41, Scotland, MD 20687 301-872-5688. 🚲 🛶 ⛺ 🎣 ♿ ❓ P ⛱ 🏊 🚻

DRIVING TOUR—*Proceed to Waldorf (Mudd House)*
READING—*prisons: Fort Delaware, Delaware (The Northeast); or Andersonville, Georgia*

WASHINGTON, D.C., AREA

Several forts built to protect Washington, D.C., are located in Prince Georges County, south and east of Washington. Among these, Fort Foote, located south of Washington, with Battery Rodgers on the Virginia side, commanded the river approach to Washington.

Fort Washington, a few miles south of Fort Foote, was a Third System fort built near the site of its predecessor—Fort Warburton, blown up and its cannons spiked on the approach of a British naval squadron that ascended the Potomac River to Alexandria in August 1814. During the crisis following the secession of South Carolina, Fort Washington was manned by 40 marines from the Washington Navy Yard barracks, replaced later by soldiers. In the first weeks of the war, it was the only fortification protecting Washington. Upon construction of the 66 earthen forts guarding the approaches to the nation's capital, the masonry Fort Washington became less important, and, after the construction of Fort Foote in 1863–64, it no longer constituted a major part of the Washington defense system.

Points of Interest

Fort Foote is off MD414 south of Washington. Administered by the National Park Service, it is an excellent example of the earthen forts of the Washington defense system and mounts two 15-inch Rodman guns.

Fort Washington is located on Fort Washington Road, off MD210 in Prince Georges County; take I-95 exit 3. It is also part of the National Park System. The fort features exhibits of coastal artillery and army life from the early nineteenth through the early twentieth century. There is a visitor center and a bookstore. There is a walking tour of the fort and living-history demonstrations are given seasonally on weekends. Recreational activities include hiking and picnicking in the park and fishing in the Potomac River. Admission is charged to enter the site. For more information, contact Superintendent, National Capital Parks-East, 1900 Anacostia Drive, SE, Washington, D.C. 20020; 310-763-4600. ☚ 🖼 ♿ 👫 ❓ 🏛 P ⛱ 👫

Two sites in Maryland pertain to John Wilkes Booth's flight after his April 14, 1865, assassination of President Abraham Lincoln. The Surratt Tavern, 9118 Brandywine Road, in Clinton, was the former home of Mary Surratt. Booth stopped briefly at the tavern several hours after the assassination to pick up a Spencer carbine and binoculars. For her part in the kidnap plot and aiding Booth, Mrs. Surratt was tried and convicted. Sentenced to die, she was the first woman hanged by the U.S. government (see **Ford's Theatre** in **The District of Columbia**). The house and adjacent visitor center are open for touring. There is a fee. 301-868-1121.

The Dr. Samuel A. Mudd House is on MD232 near Bryantown in Charles County. When Booth, who had met Mudd previously, arrived at the Mudd plantation, the doctor set his broken leg. Arrested, tried, and convicted of conspiracy, Dr. Mudd was sentenced to life imprisonment. While confined at Fort Jefferson, Florida (see **Key West and the Dry Tortugas, Florida**), Dr. Mudd risked his life in 1867 to treat victims of a deadly yellow fever outbreak. President Andrew Johnson commuted Mudd's life sentence in 1869, and Mudd returned to his Charles County home, where he died in 1883. The Mudd house is open for touring. A fee is charged and there is a bookstore and gift shop. 301-934-8464.

DRIVING TOUR—*Proceed to Rockville*
READING—*The Washington Forts, The District of Columbia*

Rockville

Rockville, in suburban Washington's Montgomery County, saw the clash of arms on June 28, 1863. Maj. Gen. J.E.B. Stuart, during his raid around the Army of the Potomac well to the east of Lee's infantry and artillery columns marching toward Pennsylvania, crossed the Potomac on the night of June 27–28 at Rowsers Ford, and rode his cavalry into Rockville. Between there and Tennallytown the Rebels captured a 125-wagon train headed northwest to Frederick with forage for the Army of the Potomac camped there. Stuart's troopers also raided the town, picking up additional supplies and horses. The wagon train became part of Stuart's column and impeded his progress as he rode north searching for Lee's army.

Points of Interest

Rockville has a Confederate monument opposite the old red-brick courthouse on MD355. Some of the city's older homes were the residences of pro-Union or pro-Southern inhabitants. The local population was divided in its loyalties.

DRIVING TOUR —*Proceed to Frederick*
READING— *To Westminster*

FREDERICK

Frederick, a colonial city called Frederick City during the Civil War, was located at the intersection of roads from Washington and Baltimore to West Virginia, Virginia, and Pennsylvania. The Baltimore & Ohio Railroad crossed the Monocacy River near Frederick. The city streets felt the tread of marching columns of soldiers during the three major campaigns that brought the Civil War into Maryland in 1862, 1863, and 1864.

In September 1862, the forces of Robert E. Lee's Army of Northern Virginia passed through Frederick and camped there on their way to Harpers Ferry, Hagerstown, and Boonsboro and the projected invasion of Pennsylvania. Thinking that Federal pursuit was unlikely to be swift or well organized, Lee dispatched three columns—Stonewall Jackson's corps, Lafayette McLaws's two divisions, and John G. Walker's division—to force the surrender of Harpers Ferry while the rest of the army camped west of South Mountain, the extension into Maryland of Virginia's Blue Ridge, between Boonsboro and Hagerstown.

Lee, however, incorrectly believed that the soldiers of the Army of the Potomac were demoralized. They were not. Employing his administrative skills, Maj. Gen. George B. McClellan quickly reorganized the troops and marched them out of the Washington defenses and into Maryland on Lee's heels. The Federal forces, by September 12–13, had arrived in the Frederick area. Then McClellan, not known for his gambling instinct, hit a jackpot. A Union soldier poking around an abandoned Rebel camp at either Best's Grove or the Araby Farm near Frederick found three cigars wrapped in paper. The paper was a copy of Special Order No. 191, Lee's plan for the disposition of his units to ensure the capture of Harpers Ferry. Knowing that most of Lee's army had been sent against Harpers Ferry, McClellan confidently planned to defeat Lee's army by detail.

Unfortunately for McClellan, a pro-Confederate civilian was part of a group being entertained by McClellan when the order was brought to him. Word of the discovery got back to Lee. He force-marched James Longstreet with two divisions back from Hagerstown to South Mountain. The Federals needed to cross South Mountain via three gaps to challenge the Confederate army and Lee hoped to delay McClellan's advance while he consolidated his forces.

In June 1863, the Army of the Potomac again camped in and around Frederick, in pursuit of Lee's Army of Northern Virginia, then invading Pennsylvania (see **Lee's 1863 Invasion of the North, Pennsylvania**). While he was camped at Frederick, Maj. Gen. George Gor-

Maj. Gen. Lewis Wallace, USA, was a political general who drew criticism from U. S. Grant after the Battle of Shiloh. However, his delaying action at Monocacy saved Grant, who had been transferring Washington area troops to Petersburg, the embarrassing disaster of having Jubal Early march into Washington ahead of the troops Grant was leading to defend the city. Wallace is best known for his postwar novel Ben Hur.

don Meade was roused from his sleep early on June 28, 1863, to learn that he had been named to command the Army of the Potomac. Unlike many other officers, Meade did not actively pursue higher command, but when the opportunity came he was equal to the responsibility. He retained the post for the rest of the war.

As Jubal Early's army marched east through Frederick, on their 1864 raid into Maryland that carried it to the gates of Washington D. C., Early on July 9 demanded a payment of ransom to spare the city from his army's retribution for the spring 1864 depredations of Federal Maj. Gen. David Hunter's army in the Shenandoah Valley (see **Lexington, Virginia**). The $200,000 was paid at the old city hall.

MONOCACY

In June 1864, Robert E. Lee sent his Second Corps under Lt. Gen. Jubal Early, to reinforce units defending Lynchburg against Maj. Gen. David Hunter's army that had marched up the Shenandoah Valley sweeping all before it and had crossed to the east of Blue Ridge. Hunter now lost his nerve, retreated into West Virginia, and Early's army advanced down the Shenandoah Valley and threatened Washington and Baltimore. The large-scale raid, Lee hoped, would compel Lt. Gen. U. S. Grant to rush troops from Petersburg's front to defend the Federal capital. Early's 14,000-man army forced the small Federal forces in the lower Shenandoah Valley to take shelter in their fortified enclave on Maryland Heights commanding Harpers Ferry, and the Confederates crossed the Potomac River at Shepherdstown, West Virginia, and headed for Frederick.

Maj. Gen. Lew Wallace was in command of the Federal forces in Maryland in July 1864. His force, numbered only 5,800—home guards and the division of Brig. Gen. James B. Ricketts, which was rushed by boat from City Point, Virginia, near Petersburg to Baltimore after Early crossed the Potomac. Knowing that he was outnumbered, but unsure of the size of the Rebel force, Wallace only hoped to determine whether Early's advance was aimed at Washington or Baltimore and to delay it long enough for Federal reinforcements to be sent to the capital. He posted his small force to cover the roads leading to the two cities across the Monocacy River southeast of Frederick and in positions guarding the B&O Railroad bridge and the bridges carrying the Georgetown Pike and the National Road across the river. His forces, supported by a few guns, dug in along the river and manned two blockhouses.

Shortly after dawn on July 9, Early advanced his forces from Frederick. Ricketts's veterans were posted between the railroad bridge and the Georgetown Pike to Washington while the home guard and Ohio 100-day men under Brig. Gen. Erastus B. Tyler protected the National Road to Baltimore. Stephen Ramseur's division approached the Federals via the Georgetown Pike and stiff Northern fire slowed down his forces and compelled him to deploy his troops and unlimber his artillery. Robert Rode's division was stymied by Tyler's forces along the National Road. The Rebels then sought to flank the Federal positions by fording the river at the Worthington-McKinney Ford two miles downstream from the Georgetown Pike bridge, but Wallace shifted forces quickly to counter Early's thrust.

This monument to New Jersey soldiers is on the Monocacy National Battlefield adjacent to the Georgetown Pike, the scene of some heavy skirmishing.

Finally, in mid-afternoon, Maj. Gen. John B. Gordon's division pushed its way across the river and intense fighting broke out in the fields of the Thomas's (Araby) Farm east of the Monocacy. By four-thirty P.M. Wallace feared his small force was in danger of annihilation and he withdrew to the east via the National Road. Early did not pursue Wallace; instead he consolidated his forces on the Georgetown Pike (today's MD355) for a march on Washington. Although he lost more than a third of his force in casualties, Wallace, by delaying Early for twenty-four hours, gained the time needed for three Federal divisions to arrive in Washington, where Early's force would be turned back on July 11 and 12 at Fort Stevens (see **Fort Stevens, The District of Columbia**).

Points of Interest

Many of Frederick's older buildings existed during the Civil War. Of particular Civil War interest are the Hessian Barracks at 24 East Church Street, part of a Federal hospital, the Old City Hall, 124 North Market Street, and the Evangelical Reformed Church at 9–13 West Church Street, where a tired Maj. Gen. Thomas J. Jackson slept through an evening service in September 1862 before marching on Harpers Ferry. The restored Barbara Fritchie House and Museum is at 156 West Patrick Street. Fritchie, an octogenarian resident of Frederick during the brief 1862 Confederate occupation, although she had no contact with Stonewall Jackson except in the legend stemming from John Greenleaf Whittier's patriotic poem, did confront other Confederate troops as they marched west on September 10, 1862.

On his October 1862 visit to the Army of the Potomac after the Battle of Antietam, President Lincoln arrived at and departed from the B&O Railroad station, which is still standing in Frederick on the southwest corner of Market and South streets. Mount Olivet Cemetery, 515 South Market Street, contains the remains of more than 800 Confederate soldiers killed in the Maryland battles, Barbara Fritchie's and Francis Scott Key's graves, and the graves of others. For more information on Frederick sites, including historic bed-and-breakfast inns, contact the Tourism Council of Frederick County, 19 East Church Street, Frederick, MD 21701; 301-663-8687 or 1-800-999-3613.

Also in Frederick is the National Museum of Civil War Medicine, housed in a circa 1830s complex, the former James Whitehill Furniture Factory. The buildings of the factory were used as an embalming center after the Battle of Antietam. The museum, dedicated to the medical history of the Civil War—and featuring such wartime innovations as the universal use of anesthesia and the development of the nursing profession—includes a video program, artifacts, and exhibits depicting a typical camp scene, a field hospital, a hospital ward, and a home-front (civilian) scenario. The museum is open Tuesday through Friday from 10:00 A.M. to 5:00 P.M., opening two hours later on the weekend. Admission is charged. The museum is located at 48 East Patrick Street and the telephone number is 301-695-1864.

The Monocacy National Battlefield, on MD355 southeast of Frederick, has a visitor center, with an electric map, exhibits, and bookstore; monuments and interpretive trails that trace key sites of the July 9, 1864, action on the Worthington Farm and along the Monocacy River. ANTIETAM AND MONOCACY NATIONAL BATTLEFIELDS, P.O. Box 158, Sharpsburg, MD 21782; 301-432-5124 (V/TDD). ❷ 🏃 P

DRIVING TOUR —*Proceed to South Mountain*
READING—*Antietam campaign: Harpers Ferry, West Virginia;*
Early's raid: Fort Stevens, The District of Columbia

SOUTH MOUNTAIN

With the Army of the Potomac in pursuit of units of his invasion force west of South Mountain, Gen. Robert E. Lee fought a delaying action while he waited for Jackson's three converging columns to capture the 13,000 Federals holed up in Harpers Ferry. On September 14, the Union corps advanced on three passes crossing South Mountain. At Fox's Gap and Turner's Gap, they met with heavy Confederate resistance. A late start at Crampton's Gap, farther south, resulted from poor planning and timidity on the part of the Northern commander, Maj. Gen. William B. Franklin. But by four P.M. Franklin's VI Corps stormed Crampton's Gap capturing Confederates, cannons, and stands of colors and inched down into Pleasant Valley on the road to Harpers Ferry. Franklin then inexplicably

Maj. Gen. Jesse L. Reno, USA, led the Federal IX Corps in the Battle of South Mountain after campaigning with Burnside in North Carolina and in Virginia in the summer of 1862. Shortly before his death he met Barbara Fritchie and offered to buy the Stars and Stripes which Fritchie reportedly had waved defiantly days earlier at Stonewall Jackson's troops. Fritchie gave Reno a bunting flag which covered Reno's casket a short time later.

halted his forces. Rebel leaders rallied, called up troops, and blocked the southward march of Franklin's corps toward Harpers Ferry.

After fighting from behind rocks and trees, Southerners under D. H. Hill and James Longstreet withdrew from Turner's and Fox's gaps under cover of darkness. Maj. Gen. Jesse Reno, in command of the Federal IX Corps at Fox's Gap, was shot while reconnoitering at sundown. As he was carried to the rear, he called to Brig. Gen. Samuel S. Sturgis, a classmate in the star-studded West Point Class of 1846, in a calm and cheerful voice, "Hello, Sam . . . I'm dead." Moments later, he was.

Points of Interest

The points of interest for the Battle of South Mountain are in and around two state parks. On US40ALT at the crest of the mountain are historical markers describing the actions at Fox's Gap and Turner's Gap and monuments to Union Maj. Gen. Jesse Reno and Confederate Brig. Gen. Samuel Garland. Just north of Alternate US40 is Washington Monument State Park. It features the first monument built to honor George Washington, erected in 1827. An elevated point on South Mountain, the monument's locale was a Federal signal station. The Turner's Gap fighting occurred east of the park and north and south of the National Road (US40ALT). The park has hiking trails, and picnicking and camping areas. For more information, call 301-432-8065.

Crampton's Gap is located in Gathland State Park on MD17. Here is found one of the few monuments to war correspondents. It was erected in 1896 by Civil War correspondent George A. Townsend, whose nom de plume was "Gath." The park, located on the Appalachian Trail, also features hiking trails, a picnic pavilion, Civil War earthworks, and interpretive markers describing the action at Crampton's Gap. For more information, call 301-293-6860.

DRIVING TOUR and READING—*Proceed to Antietam*

ANTIETAM

The delaying action at South Mountain gained Lee a day, and bolstered by Jackson's capture of Harpers Ferry, he decided to make a stand north of the Potomac rather than return

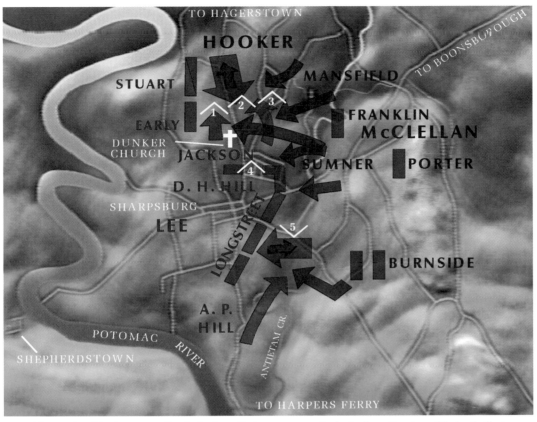

The Battle of Antietam was fought in three distinct sectors and a lack of coordination of Federal efforts prevented General Lee from sustaining a devastating defeat. The battle began at first light in the area of the Dunker Church (cross). Hood's Rebels charged through the West Woods (1) to meet Hooker's I Corps descending on Miller's Cornfield (2). A later attack by Mansfield through the East Woods (3) was also turned back. Sumner's II Corps drove D. H. Hill from Bloody Lane (4). Burnside's delayed advance over the Lower Bridge (5) succeeded in driving the Confederates back on Sharpsburg, until A. P. Hill's force arriving from Harpers Ferry drove the Federals back toward the bridge that now bears Burnside's name.

to Virginia. He selected a good defense position behind Antietam Creek, near the town of Sharpsburg, posting James Longstreet's corps on the right, D. H. Hill's division in the center, and most of Jackson's troops on their arrival from Harpers Ferry on the left. With the Potomac at his back, it was a daring gamble for Lee. But it demonstrated his confidence in his soldiers and his knowledge of General McClellan's strengths and limitations.

The Army of the Potomac began to deploy across the rolling Maryland fields on the afternoon of September 15. This is one of the few battles of the war in which both com-

Confederate soldiers lying along the Hagerstown Pike at Antietam. These men, victims of the battle for Miller's Cornfield, were immortalized by Brady's corps of photographers under Alexander Gardner's direction.

manders chose the field of battle and planned their tactics in advance. But McClellan did not attack on the September 16, except for a probing attack by Maj. Gen. Joseph Hooker's corps on the Rebels' left flank late in the day. By dusk the Yanks pulled back. McClellan thus gave Lee the opportunity to reinforce his position with more troops as they arrived from Harpers Ferry. McClellan also tipped his hand as to where his dawn attack would begin.

At first light on September 17, the soldiers of Maj. Gen. Joseph Hooker's I Corps marched south, toward the Dunker Church landmark, where the Smoketown Road converged with the Hagerstown Pike that stood out against the West Woods green backdrop. Though they pressed hard and into and through Miller's Cornfield one-third mile north of the church, Stonewall Jackson's corps fought just as stubbornly, even after Hooker raked the cornfield with a sheet of cannon fire. Hooker's troops by seven-fifteen A.M. had hammered to within two hundred yards of the church, when "Fighting Joe" was wounded. Brig. Gen. John Bell Hood's division now stormed out of the West Woods, and, in a slashing counterattack, sent the I Corps reeling and regained Miller's Cornfield.

No sooner was Hooker repulsed than Maj. Gen. Joseph Mansfield, leading Nathaniel Banks's former corps, entered the East Woods to challenge the Rebels' hold on Miller's Cornfield. Mansfield was mortally wounded, just before his troops surged forward to regain the cornfield and seize the low ground within several hundred yards of the Dunker Church. Casualties soared as the lead division of Maj. Gen. Edwin "Bull" Sumner's corps charged into the West Woods to be slaughtered by reinforced Confederates, losing 2,260 men in twenty minutes.

Just southeast of Dunker Church, D. H. Hill had positioned his brigades along a sunken farm road. His soldiers threw down rail fences bounding the lane to strengthen their line.

Sumner's other two divisions—first Brig. Gen. William H. French's and then Maj. Gen. Israel B. Richardson's—advanced. Hill's troops beat back French's division, but then "Fighting Dick" Richardson's people took advantage of a mix-up in orders to drive D. H. Hill's reinforced division from the lane since known as Bloody Lane.

When Maj. Gen. William Franklin's VI Corps arrived to steady Sumner's

Federal infantry protect a battery under Capt. Stephen H. Weed performing during the Battle of Antietam. Weed would later rise to brigadier general and become part of the Federal V Corps force sent to save Little Round Top at Gettysburg.

line, he urged Sumner forward. McClellan also sent a staff officer to poll the two generals on resuming the attack. Sumner, who had lost his nerve, replied that his, Hooker's, and Mansfield's corps were cut up and demoralized. Upon receiving the message, McClellan rode to the front and, characteristically, concurred with Sumner not to press the advantage. Yet most of Franklin's corps and Maj. Gen. Fitz John Porter's V Corps, held in reserve, had not been blooded.

Bloody Lane at Antietam National Battlefield was a sunken farm road when the Federals of Maj. Gen. Edwin V. Sumner's corps forced Maj. Gen. D. H. Hill's Confederates from it. Had General McClellan reinforced the breakthrough here, he would have likely broken General Lee's entire line.

Though Longstreet took charge of direct-

Confederate artillerists lying near their shot-riddled caisson in front of the Dunker Church. Alexander Gardner, working for Mathew Brady's Washington, D.C., studios, initiated and supervised the trek of Brady's corps of photographers into the field in the wake of the Union armies.

ing artillery fire at the Federals, who had, after overrunning Bloody Lane, reached the Piper House and orchard, and D. H. Hill personally led a futile counterattack, the battle was over in this sector. McClellan had failed to exploit the weakest part of Lee's line.

Farther south, Maj. Gen. Ambrose Burnside's attack had stalled crossing Antietam Creek. His men didn't find a passable ford until noon. Sharpshooting Georgians under the command of politician Brig. Gen. Robert Toombs held from the bluffs above it the bridge spanning the creek.

At noon Burnside's men successfully charged and crossed the bridge, then, after halting to regroup, by two-thirty P.M. had beat the defenders back into the southeast approaches to Sharpsburg. As Lee's right flank was crumbling, A.P. Hill's soldiers, after a hard-driving seventeen-mile march from Harpers Ferry, struck Burnside's forces in the flank and rear and drove them back to the heights southeast of town.

The Battle of Antietam, or Sharpsburg as the Confederates call it, gave September 17, 1862, the grisly distinction of being the bloodiest day in American history. The total casualties, nearly 23,000, were three times greater than the number of Americans killed and wounded on grim Omaha Beach during the invasion of Normandy on D-Day, June 6, 1944. The number killed at Antietam that day, more than 4,700, exceeded the total of the other three major American conflicts of the nineteenth century combined. During and after this battle Clara Barton tended to the wounded on the Samuel Poffenberger farm. Left for dead on the battlefield, but surviving, was a young captain from Massachusetts who became one of the nation's most respected Supreme Court justices, Oliver Wendell

Holmes, Jr. Holmes, already severely wounded at Ball's Bluff, continued to serve with valor in the Federal army.

McClellan's message to Washington of a great victory achieved was overstated. The Confederates escaped across the Potomac and retreated into the lower Shenandoah Valley meeting little interference from the Army of the Potomac. On the one hand, the victory prompted Lincoln to unveil his preliminary Emancipation Proclamation on September 22, 1862 (see **The White House, The District of Columbia**). On the other, McClellan's failure to follow Lee's retreat and destroy the Army of Northern Virginia ultimately led to his replacement on November 7, 1862, by General Burnside. And the war continued until the resolve shown by the men in the field was fully matched by the resolve of the generals and political leaders.

Points of Interest

Antietam National Battlefield—The battlefield and national cemetery are located along MD65 and MD34 just north and northeast of Sharpsburg. There is a visitor center and extensive roads and trails in the park. The battle's important locations, the East, North, and West Woods; Miller's Cornfield; Bloody Lane; and Burnside Bridge are monumented and interpreted by wayside exhibits. The Dunker Church, destroyed in the 1920s by high wind, was reconstructed during the Civil War centennial; Burnside Bridge has been preserved. ANTIETAM AND MONOCACY NATIONAL BATTLEFIELDS, P. O. Box 158, Sharpsburg, MD 21782; 301-432-5124 (V/TDD).

In Sharpsburg, a historical marker locates the site of Robert E. Lee's headquarters before and after the battle. Historical markers on Branch Avenue and Harpers Ferry Road identify the initial point of contact when A. P. Hill's forces met Burnside's advancing infantry southeast of town. Branch Avenue and the nearby Hawkins's Zouave Monument (off Harpers Ferry Road) are on the Antietam NB tour route, south of Rodman Avenue. Harpers Ferry Road will lead you north to the town of Sharpsburg and the national cemetery, which is just east of the town on Boonsboro Pike.

DRIVING TOUR—*Proceed to Williamsport and Hagerstown*
READING *(chronological)*—*Perryville, Kentucky*

WILLIAMSPORT-HAGERSTOWN

On his retreat, after the Battle of Gettysburg, beginning July 4, 1863, Gen. Robert E. Lee divided his army into three columns. The army wagon train and most of the wounded, guarded by Brig. Gen. John Imboden's cavalry and artillery, proceeded west on the Chambersburg Pike through Cashtown Gap and Greenwood, Pennsylvania, then turned south through the Cumberland Valley. Lee's infantry and artillery marched directly southwest through Fairfield, Pennsylvania, and Monterey Pass while Stuart's cavalry passed through Emmitsburg, Maryland.

Federal mounted forces, headed by the aggressive Brig. Gen. Judson "Kill Cavalry" Kilpatrick, hammered Lee's rear guard. Kilpatrick clashed with Lee's forces on the night of July 4–5 and Stuart's cavalry on July 5. Other Union cavalry skirmished with Imboden's cavalry escorting the trains near Greencastle, Pennsylvania. Union cavalry from Frederick destroyed Lee's Falling Waters pontoon bridge crossing Potomac River. On July 6 and 7 Lee's army arrived at Williamsport and Falling Waters. Heavy rains that began on July 4 caused the Potomac to flood and Lee's troops entrenched on high ground on the Potomac's east bank from Falling Waters north to Williamsport. By July 12, advance elements of the Army of the Potomac arrived in front of Lee's position. Severely buffeted by the Battle of Gettysburg as well, the Federals entrenched opposite their foe.

By the night of July 13, the Potomac water level had begun to drop and the Confederates' new pontoon bridge was positioned, while the Potomac's level had fallen sufficiently to make the Williamsport ford passable. Lee evacuated his entire force to Virginia except for a rear guard of two divisions at Falling Waters. On the morning of July 14, the Federals advanced to Williamsport to find the Rebel trenches empty. Kilpatrick led a mounted charge against the Falling Waters rear guard. Low on ammunition, the Rebels unhorsed many of the Federal cavalry with fence rails and axes. Follow-up attacks by Kilpatrick's and Brig. Gen. John Buford's cavalry failed as Confederate resistance stiffened, although the Rebels suffered heavy casualties, particularly in prisoners, including the mortal wounding of Brig. Gen. James J. Pettigrew. The remaining soldiers of the Confederate rear guard crossed the Potomac and the Federal pursuit ended.

During Lt. Gen. Jubal Early's July 1864 march from the Shenandoah Valley to Washington, one of his brigade commanders stopped long enough in Hagerstown to exact $20,000 from the town to prevent its destruction. City fathers complied on July 8 and Early continued his march toward Frederick.

Points of Interest

In Williamsport (US11), an 1861 Federal earthwork "Battery Doubleday" can be visited in the cemetery overlooking the Potomac. Nearby is a manned Chesapeake & Ohio National Historical Park Visitor Center with exhibits interpreting the canal's history and information about Lee's recrossing of the Potomac and the Battle of Falling Waters. Park rangers can guide you to the cemetery and Battery Doubleday. Historical markers describe the rear-guard action of July 14, 1863, and Lee's retreat across the Potomac. For more information on historical and recreational features of the Chesapeake & Ohio Canal, contact the visitor center in the Great Falls Tavern, 11710 MacArthur Boulevard, Potomac, Maryland 20854; 301-299-3613.

The Washington Confederate Cemetery is located within Rose Hill Cemetery, 600 South Potomac Street in Hagerstown (I-81 at US40) contains the graves of nearly 2,500 Confederate soldiers, many of them killed in the Battles of Antietam and South Mountain. Also located in the cemetery is a handsome memorial to the Confederate dead. The commercial building at 37 East Washington Street is where city fathers paid Early's ransom of $20,000 to spare Hagerstown.

DRIVING TOUR—*Proceed to Harpers Ferry, West Virginia*
READING *(chronological)—Honey Springs, Oklahoma*

MI

WS

MI

Galena

Freeport
Rockford
Fox Lake
Waukegan
Highland Park
Evanston

20
90
94
12

Chicago

Rochelle
De Kalb
Aurora
88
294

30
88
Rock Falls
30

Geneseo
La Salle
Joliet
80
57
Morris

67
Galesburg
39
Kankakee
1

Peoria
El Paso
Watseka
41
24

34
Monmouth
55
Bloomington
65
Logansport

Macomb
24
Danville
74
65

Quincy
51
72
Champaign
31

24
Beardstown
55
Rileysburg
74

Jacksonville
Decatur
57
1
41

36
Springfield
Marshall

55
Terre Haute
70

67
Effingham
70
Bloomington
37
31

Vandalia
Seymour
74

Lawrenceville
65
60

Alton
50
Sandoval
Salem
50
Washington
50
Salem

E. St. Louis
64
Mt. Vernon
Mt. Carmel
Vincennes
65

51
Carmi
41
New Albany
64

45
Evansville
64
Corydon

Carbondale
57

24

Cairo

IL

IN

Valparaiso
South Bend
50
6

30
Columbia City
Fort Wayne
69

Kent-land
Lafayette
Wabash
Decatur
24

Marion
Kokomo
Portland
27

13
Muncie
29

Indianapolis
Richmond

Shelbyville
Columbus
Batesville
Greendale
27

OH

Napoleon
Maumee
Toledo
Sandusky
Lorain
Kingsville
Mentor
Cleveland
90

Defiance
Bowling Green
Fremont
Fostoria
6
Elyria
80
Warren
422

Findlay
199
4
6
71
Akron
Youngstown
75

Lima
24
Mansfield
Bucyrus
30
Wooster
Canton
77

Marysville
68
Marion
23
Columbus
Cambridge
22
70
Morgan's Surrender Monument

Pique
4
68
Zanesville
22
East Liverpool

Springfield
Dayton
71
Circleville
Lancaster
Steubenville

75
Washington Court House
Chillicothe
Athens
74
77

Cincinnati
22
50
Hillsboro
35

Ripley
Portsmouth
52
Ironton
Buffington Is.

The Midwest

The Midwest saw little combat action during the Civil War because of early successes by the Federals in their campaigns to drive the Confederates from Kentucky and the failure of the Rebels to sustain their friends in Missouri to create a buffer between the war-torn South and the nation's breadbasket. The Ohio and upper Mississippi rivers were patrolled by Federal gunboats from the summer of 1861 through the end of the war. Key cities like Cincinnati, alarmed when Edmund Kirby Smith's Army of Kentucky and Braxton Bragg's Army of Mississippi marched into Kentucky in late August and September 1862 but never actually threatened, threw up fortifications, and manned them with militia units.

The Midwest did supply the Federal war effort with thousands of volunteers, with distinguished officers—including Ulysses S. Grant, William T. Sherman, George B. McClellan, and numerous others—and with mountains of material goods. Influential politicians such as Indiana governor Oliver Morton and Illinois congressman Elihu B. Washburne were key supporters of the Lincoln administration war effort. Others, notably Ohio congressman Clement L. Vallandigham, sought to undermine the war effort and negotiate a peace with an independent Confederate States of America. War-weariness and proximity produced strong anti-war sentiments in southern Illinois, Indiana, and Ohio. Exploiting this sentiment as one of his objectives, Confederate cavalry legend Brig. Gen. John Hunt Morgan staged a daring raid into southern Indiana and Ohio in the summer of 1863.

Midwest sites are spread over a large area, so no tour route is designated. They are located on or near major highways as designated on the tour map. You may wish to follow the path of Morgan's Raid, and references are given between points of interest on the raid's route.

Although not in proximity to other Midwest points of interest, the town of Monroe, Michigan, south of Detroit, is worth a visit should you find yourself in that area. Though not a native son, George Armstrong Custer is closely associated with Monroe, the town he later settled in and from where he secured his West Point appointment and met his future wife. Monroe has a number of sites for Custer enthusiasts, including an equestrian statue and a museum.

ILLINOIS

Illinois is the Land of Lincoln, and numerous historical parks and sites, especially New Salem and Springfield, trace his life from Old Salem, where he lived from 1831 to 1837, through his career as circuit lawyer to U.S. Senate candidate to president. Here, the focus is on the sites associated with his life from president-elect until his death, and these are in Springfield, where he maintained a residence and law practice and where he is buried. Other sites include Grant's home in Galena, where he lived and clerked in the leather store managed by his two brothers before the war, and Cairo, one of the North's largest supply and transportation centers and where Grant got his first major command in the war as commander of the Southeast Missouri District.

Although no traces still exist, Camp Douglas, near Chicago, was a Union camp of instruction, holding area for paroled Union soldiers, a large hospital, and prison camp for Confederates.

Cairo

At the confluence of the Ohio and Mississippi rivers, Cairo has spent much of its history combating the rivers' water. This same condition, however, gave nineteenth-century Cairo the distinction of being one of the Mississippi's busiest ports. Never was it more used as such than during the Civil War. Cairo immediately became a huge supply base to support Federal army and navy operations along the Mississippi and beyond. It was also a training camp where large numbers of volunteers gathered to receive their basic training and equipment for Federal service, and then were loaded onto transports for operations to the east, west, and south. Grant arrived at Cairo on September 4, 1861, where he organized an army and, having survived an ill-starred attack on Belmont, Missouri, led the amphibious force that gave the Union victories at Forts Henry and Donelson.

Points of Interest

Cairo is located just south of I-57 exit 1 on US51. Two miles south of the town, at the southern tip of Illinois, is Fort Defiance State Park, site of a fort that was part of the Federal military complex. An observation tower here gives an excellent view of the rivers. In the town of Cairo is the *Tigress* Flagpole monument—the flagstaff was recovered from the packet steamer *Tigress*, which carried Grant to Shiloh, Tennessee, and which was sunk a year later while running the Vicksburg batteries. Also, at 609 Ohio Street is the site of Grant's headquarters in Cairo and the house where his family stayed during his time there. The St. Charles Hotel, of which one wing remains, was used by Federal officers and war reporters. Mound City National Cemetery, 5 miles northeast of Cairo, contains the graves of Union veterans and was the site of the ways where Capt. James B. Eads built three of the seven "city series" ironclad gunboats.

Abraham Lincoln argued the questions of slavery and national unity in a series of debates during his 1858 Illinois campaign for the U.S. Senate. He lost the election to Stephen A. Douglas but gained national attention.

Springfield

Though Lincoln spent his early life in rural Kentucky, Indiana and Illinois, his rise to national prominence began when he moved to Springfield, the Illinois state capital, in 1837, and began his law-practice partnership with John T. Stuart. From their offices in Springfield, Lincoln and Stuart and later Lincoln and Stephen Logan, and finally Lincoln and William Herndon, developed one of Illinois' most successful law firms. Lincoln also honed his political aspirations. This started in 1834 with his election to the first of four terms to the state legislature and matured into a broader base of power. In 1846, he was elected to the House of Representatives for a single term. In 1856 he switched his political allegiance from Whig to the new Republican party and in 1858 ran unsuccessfully for U.S. Senate against powerful Democrat Stephen A. Douglas. Despite losing, he gained national prominence in the race.

It was in Springfield that Lincoln monitored the events of the 1860 Republican National Convention in Chicago and received word of his nomination as presidential candidate. Here too, on the night of November 6, 1860, he learned by telegraph that the electoral vote was carrying him to victory over the other three candidates.

Though he had no opportunity to return to Springfield during the war years, Lincoln's final tragic return to Springfield was in May 1865, when his funeral train pulled into the city and his body was transferred by horse-drawn hearse to its final resting place in Oak Ridge Cemetery.

Points of Interest

Springfield is located at the junction of I-55 and I-72. Most of the sites associated with Lincoln are in a compact area downtown on or near Business Loop 55. The Old State Capitol on City Square is where Lincoln gave his "House Divided" speech. Lincoln departed from the Great Western Station to assume the presidency. The Lincoln-Herndon Law Office was restored in 1968 and is located at Sixth and Adams streets. Lincoln Home National Historic Site, 413 South Eighth Street, 505-425-8025, contains exhibits and Lincoln family possessions. It is the only house Lincoln ever owned and it is where he and his family lived for seventeen years prior to his presidency. Information is locally available for other downtown points of interest related to Lincoln and the Civil War.

North of Springfield, Camp Butler (I-55 exit 100 A-B) was a training camp and a prison for captured Confederate soldiers. Today it is a national cemetery containing the graves of soldiers from both the Union and the Confederacy. Oak Ridge Cemetery is in the northwest part of Springfield, just off IL29. The Lincoln Tomb contains the remains of Abraham and Mary Todd Lincoln and three of their four sons. Eldest son and Civil War officer Robert Todd Lincoln is buried in Arlington National Cemetery.

Galena

Galena was a prosperous city on the Galena River just a few miles from the Mississippi in the mid-nineteenth century. It was located on what was then the richest vein of lead in the country. An explosion in the growth of railroads in the Midwest had lessened the importance of the city of fourteen thousand by 1860. At the J. & S. Grant Leather Goods store, however, business was still booming when Ulysses Grant joined his two brothers that same year in clerking in the store, one of a chain of tannery-related businesses established by their father, Jesse, in several Midwest states. Grant had failed in several businesses in the St. Louis area, but was welcomed without recrimination as an equal partner by his two younger brothers. The Grants settled into a house on High Street.

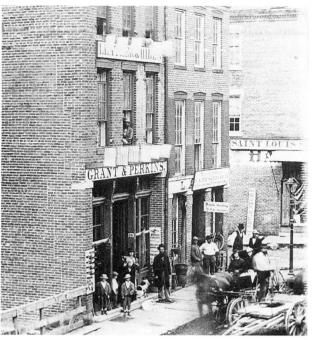

U. S. Grant's father owned this leather goods store in Galena, Illinois, which was operated by Ulysses's two brothers. Ulysses's position as a clerk was short-lived—when the war began, he returned to his first love—the army.

Fortunately for Grant, the Civil War came along and he was able to return to the only profession he knew or cared for—the army. Initially, he organized a militia unit in Galena. Then, in June 1861, with the assistance of Illinois governor Richard Yates and Congressman Elihu B. Washburne, he was appointed colonel of the 21st Illinois, then stationed at Springfield's Sangamon County Fair Grounds. From here, he would go on to Cairo, Illinois, to command large numbers of troops (see **Cairo**). Also in Galena, Grant met his close friend and military adjutant, John A. Rawlins.

Points of Interest

Galena (US20, 75 miles west of Rockford) has an annual tour of historic homes each September. Many of these are associated with U. S. Grant and close associates who were Galena residents. The U. S. GRANT HOME STATE HISTORIC SITE, 307 Decatur,

815-777-0248, is the house Grant and his family occupied in January 1861. A house near-by at 500 Bouthillier was built for the returning hero by admirers and presented to him as a gift on August 19, 1865. The J. & S. Grant Leather Goods store is no longer extant, but the site is marked at 120 South Main, and a replica store is located at 211 South Main. The DeSoto House was Galena's premier hotel during the Civil War. Lincoln spoke here in 1856. The site is marked at Main and Green streets.

Grant used the Illinois Central Railroad depot, at the foot of Bouthillier Street, so often that he remarked to a friend during the war, "I would like to be mayor of Galena, then I might get a sidewalk built from my home to the depot." The home of John A. Rawlins is located at 515 Hill Street, and the Elihu B. Washburne House is at 908 Third Street.

Indiana governor Oliver H.P.T. Morton was one of the most powerful and capable of the Northern war governors. When "Copperhead" sentiments within the state legislature threatened his military support of the Lincoln adminstration, Morton kept the Indiana government running with loans from Washington, the private sector, and profits from the state arsenal until the 1864 elections produced the seating of a Republican majority.

INDIANA

As mentioned earlier, Indiana provided tens of thousands of men and millions of dollars of agricultural and industrial resources to the war effort. It shared a border with Kentucky, where thousands hoped for the South's success. The militia of the North's fifth most populous state was in disarray when war broke out, but thanks to the efforts of Governor Oliver P. Morton, elected in 1860, training camps were organized, a state arsenal was established, war equipment was purchased, and soldiers' health and welfare mechanisms were begun. By war's end, Indiana had supplied Federal forces with 208,300 men.

The Hoosier State was invaded briefly by hostile forces when John Hunt Morgan took his division of Confederate cavalry across the Ohio River at Brandenburg, Kentucky, on July 8–9, 1863, and entered Indiana at Mauckport. Federal forces had been pursuing him since the campaign's beginning on July 2 (see **Kentucky Cavalry Raids and Raiders**). The first significant challenge to his raiders in the North came on July 9 at Corydon, Indiana.

Corydon

On July 9, the day after entering Indiana, John Hunt Morgan's cavalry raiders were opposed by the Harrison County Militia, one of the home guard units called into service by Governor Morton to intercept Morgan. The militia were outnumbered and were easily overwhelmed by Morgan's troopers in a short battle a mile south of town. They surrendered and were held briefly until Morgan's raiders pressed on eastward. In Corydon and elsewhere, the raiders helped themselves to new mounts, supplies, and personal effects of the citizens. The plundering gained the raiders the sobriquet "Morgan's Terrible Men" and dashed Confederate hopes to use the raid to rally the citizens of Indiana's southern counties behind the Peace Democrats campaigning for Southern independence in a negotiated end to the war.

Points of Interest

Corydon, the former capital of Indiana, is located 2 miles south of I-64 exit 105 on IN135. The Battle of Corydon Memorial Park is on Business IN135; take Capitol Avenue south from Corydon to the east side of Old State Road 135. The park has a trail, interpretive markers, and a replica log cabin. It is open every day from 8:00 A.M. until dark and there is no admission. For more information, contact The Harrison County Parks and Recreation Department, 124 South Mulberry Street, Corydon, IN 47112; 812-738-8236.

Efforts have been made to follow Morgan's route through the state and additional markers are located in Harris, Vienna, Lexington, Madison, Salem, Vernon, Versailles, and West Harrison, where Morgan stayed in the American Hotel on July 13, before leaving the state. The site of the hotel is at US52 and State Street.

OHIO

Ohio contributed its extensive manufacturing and mining resources to the Northern war effort, as well as an unusual number of military and political leaders. Although the Republicans controlled state politics throughout the war, some Democrats in the state were vocal opponents of the war. Led by U.S. Congressman Clement L. Vallandigham, who ran unsuccessfully for governor in 1863, the "Copperheads" fostered dissension in Ohio and elsewhere, which sometimes turned ugly. Open resistance to the draft occurred in two Ohio counties in 1863. Maj. Gen. Ambrose E. Burnside, when he assumed command of the Department of the Ohio in 1863, attempted to crack down on the dissidents. He had Vallandigham arrested and tried in a military court. Vallandigham was banished to the South but reentered the state through Canada and continued to exert political influence through the presidential election of 1864.

The majority of Ohioans were solidly behind the Union, however, and it is hard to imagine how the North could have successfully concluded the war without the 319,000 men from the state who served in the Union military. Nearly 25,000 lost their lives in service to the Union.

Cincinnati

A bustling river port and cosmopolitan city, Cincinnati put its defenses on alert and thousands turned out to dig earthworks in September 1862, when first Maj. Gen. Edmund Kirby Smith's Army of Kentucky and then Gen. Braxton Bragg's Army of Mississippi marched northward through Kentucky. Cincinnati was also a command center for Maj. Gen. Ambrose E. Burnside's Department of the Ohio. Ulysses S. Grant and William T. Sherman met here in March 1864 to plan their strategy for the Federal spring campaigns.

Points of Interest

In Cincinnati, Burnside's headquarters is at 24 East Ninth Street. Grant, in March 1864, met Sherman at the Burnet House, Cincinnati's leading hotel during the Civil War. The building is gone but the site is marked at the northwest corner of Third and Vine streets. In the Mount Adams area, off US50 southwest of Hatch Street, remains of the fortifications thrown up to protect the city can be seen on Fort View Place.

Buffington Island

Brig. Gen. John Hunt Morgan's Confederate raiders entered Ohio on July 14 and completed a ninety-mile ride through the suburbs of Cincinnati in thirty-five hours to Pomeroy. By this time, Federal soldiers, including elements of Burnside's 30,000-man Army of the Ohio, were hot on his trail. Union gunboats patrolled the Ohio River, preventing Morgan from returning to Kentucky. On July 19, while attempting to cross the river in Meigs County, Morgan was challenged by Federal soldiers entrenched and on gunboats at Buffington Island. Morgan escaped with 1,200 troopers, but 700 raiders were captured.

Points of Interest

Buffington Island State Memorial on OH124 near Portland features a 4-acre park and a monument to commemorate the battle.

Salineville

Morgan and his remaining force rode northeast, attempting to cross the Ohio River in the vicinity of Wheeling, West Virginia. He was driven farther north into Columbiana County and skirmished at Salineville on July 25. Cornered, Morgan was compelled to surrender with the remainder of his command near West Point (New Lisbon) on July 26. Morgan and some of his officers were incarcerated in the Ohio State Penitentiary in Columbus. On the night of November 27, 1863, Morgan and six officers escaped after tunneling under the stone structure and scaling the outer wall. Morgan arrived safely in Franklin, Tennessee, on December 23.

Points of Interest

On OH518 a few miles west of West Point is Morgan's Surrender Monument. There are picnic facilities at the site. Six miles north in Lisbon, the house at 431 West Lincoln Way is the birthplace of Clement L. Vallandigham. Other Ohio sites not on the tour are William T. Sherman's birthplace and home in Lancaster, southeast of Columbus; the Custer State Monument on OH646 west of Steubenville; and the restored home of the "Fighting McCooks," the family of Federal soldiers that included Maj. Gen. Alexander McCook, Brig. Gen. Edward M. McCook, and Col. Daniel McCook, which is northwest of Steubenville on OH9 at Carrollton.

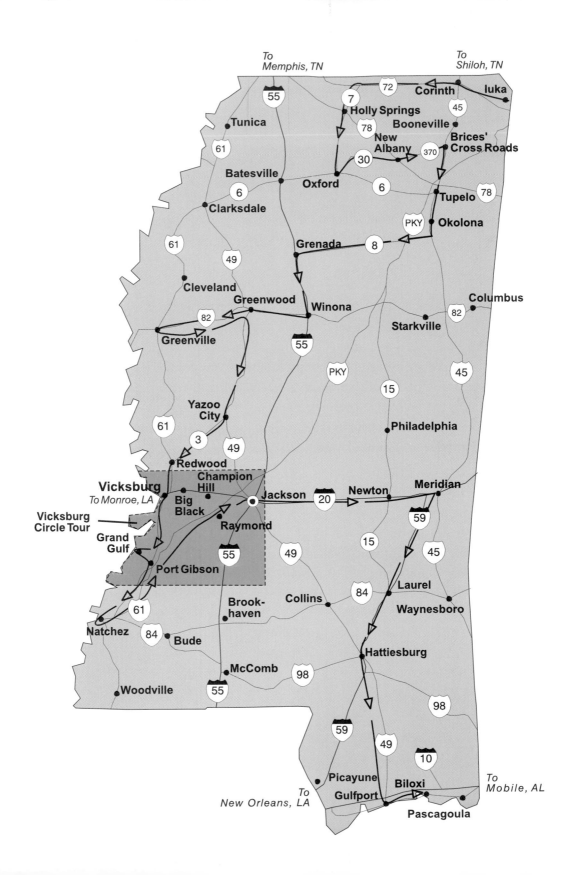

Mississippi

The state that in February 1861 sent Jefferson Davis to Montgomery as provisional Confederate president and on to Richmond as president of the Confederacy, and that sent 80,000 to fight for the South, saw little battle action in the war's first year—only a brief raid on Biloxi by Federal forces who had recently occupied Ship Island off the Gulf coast. But that soon changed. In Mississippi, the second state to secede, both the independent spirit of states' rights and the economic necessity of slavery were supported by most of the population. The Federal objective of controlling the Mississippi River, which for some four hundred miles defines the western border of the state to which the river gave its name, brought war to Mississippi in March 1862.

Coupled with the drive through West Tennessee by forces first under Maj. Gen. Ulysses S. Grant, and then Maj. Gen. Henry W. Halleck, which battled Confederate forces there and drove them to Corinth in northeast Mississippi, U.S. Navy operations on the river in mid-1862 seemed to promise early Federal control of the state. But the Union operations encountered problems of leadership and coordination. The strengths of Mississippi's natural landscape, particularly along the river at Vicksburg, were enhanced as defense positions and the Federal campaigns encountered bitter resistance. Even after the Mississippi River came under Federal control, and the U.S. military established enclaves at Vicksburg, Natchez, Port Hudson, Louisiana, and Memphis, the war continued in the state. Rebel horse soldiers, particularly those led by Nathan Bedford Forrest, pounded the Federals and there was no peace. The Yanks, in turn, waged destructive campaigns designed to destroy the state's economy and break the will to resist, but the spirit remained and Mississippi was one of the last states to be reconstructed and readmitted to the Union after the war.

A tour of Mississippi's battlefield parks and Civil War sites can take from four to seven days—a thorough tour of Vicksburg alone might require two to three days—and be enjoyable. Mississippi has recently added to its already numerous visitor attractions; for example, there are many family entertainment facilities available. A number of bed-and-breakfast accommodations, many in historic plantation homes or town mansions, are available in most of the key Civil War areas. For touring the sites of the campaigns against Vicksburg, the Vicksburg Circle Tour (see **Mississippi Tour Map**) allows you to tour the sites in chronological order.

Mississippi is a good bet any time of the year. It is generally temperate, although during the winter months a chill can often fill the air and the mid-summer months are often hot and humid. And if you need relief from the hot weather, do what Mississippians do—grab a chair on the veranda, prop your feet up, and order a refreshing tall glass of iced sweet tea.

CORINTH-IUKA

Corinth was a vital railroad junction during the Civil War, where the Memphis & Charleston Railroad intersected the Mobile & Ohio, linking important cities, rivers, and coastal areas, and arguably from mid-March to May 29, 1862, strategically the most important place in the Confederacy. The Confederates considered Corinth vital for the concentration of their western armies to lash back at Union armies that, beginning on January 12, 1862, with victories in Kentucky and Tennessee had thrust deep into the Confederate "Heartland."

This painting of the camp of the Confederate 4th Kentucky Regiment at Corinth in May 1862 is by Conrad Chapman, an artist who studied in Europe and who created many fascinating paintings of Southern forces during the war. The relaxed atmosphere portrayed here is in great contrast to the real atmosphere of disease and hardship common for the Rebels during the Siege of Corinth.

Union forces at the same time were massing for a deeper thrust into the South. Forces under Maj. Gen. Ulysses S. Grant gathered at Pittsburg Landing, Tennessee, 22 miles northeast of Corinth, awaiting the arrival of Brig. Gen. Don Carlos Buell's Army of the Ohio from Nashville. Soldiers under Brig. Gen. William T. Sherman in mid-March landing from steamboats sought to reach the Memphis & Charleston Railroad east of Corinth but bad weather hampered their efforts and they withdrew. The impending joining of the two Federal forces caused Confederate general Albert Sidney Johnston to march north from Corinth to attack Grant before Southern forces were fully consolidated, leading to the Battle of Shiloh, April 6–7, 1862, and the subsequent withdrawal of the Rebels to Corinth (see **Shiloh, Tennessee**).

The situation then returned to the way it had been before—the Federals planning a march on Corinth. Maj. Gen. Henry W. Halleck, the Union general with overall command in the west, distrusting Grant, came to the front and assumed command of the combined armies of the Tennessee, the Mississippi, and the Ohio. A cautious leader, Halleck was concerned by rumors that the Rebels outnumbered his large force of 120,000 and 200 guns. The reports were exaggerated and the Confederates, while dug in at Corinth, could have been assaulted rather easily with Halleck's large army, led by aggressive generals such as John Pope and U. S. Grant. Halleck's "army group" marched on April 29 and by May 5 had closed to within five miles of Corinth on the east and north, but then took more than three and a half weeks to dig and inch its way close enough to the railroad crossover to bring it under artillery fire and make Corinth untenable for the Confederates.

Inside the Corinth earthworks, Beauregard's outnumbered troops suffered more from disease and lack of water and rations than from the threat of the opposing army to the north. Employing a campaign of misinformation, staged drama, and careful planning, Beauregard executed a bloodless withdrawal of his army on the night of May 29, pulling back to Tupelo, fifty miles south. While he had successfully saved his army to fight another day, the retreat did not go well with President Jefferson Davis, who was not a Beauregard admirer. Seeing a large section of his home state yielded to the enemy without a fight, Davis replaced Beauregard—when he went on sick leave without clearing it with Richmond—with Maj. Gen. Braxton Bragg, who was promoted to general.

Likewise, Halleck's hollow victory was criticized in Northern newspapers, and the Lincoln administration in mid-July promoted the military scholar and administrator—whose only combat command experience of his army career had been in front of Corinth—to the highest-ranking position in the army, general-in-chief. The position had been previously held by Winfield Scott and then George B. McClellan, who was removed March 11,

1862, when he took the field with the Army of the Potomac. It was well suited to Halleck, who disliked being held responsible for hard decisions. He held that position until March 1864 when U. S. Grant became general-in-chief and Halleck his chief of staff.

With the summer 1862 reshuffling of commands and the reassigning of forces to other areas, Corinth seemed to the Confederates to be ripe for retaking. If the Federals were driven from Corinth, it would open the way for the Confederate forces in northeast Mississippi to reinforce Braxton Bragg's armies that had thrust deep into Kentucky. While much of Grant's army was scattered in posts throughout West Tennessee, Maj. Gen. William S. Rosecrans, with two divisions, held the Corinth enclave.

On September 14, Maj. Gen. Sterling Price, arriving from the Trans-Mississippi in mid-April and under the overall command of Maj. Gen. Earl Van Dorn, attacked a Union outpost at Iuka, driving it from town. Price paused to regroup before crossing the Tennessee River. A combat-seasoned Grant saw an opportunity for a counterattack. He fashioned a pincer attack by sending Rosecrans to converge on Iuka from the southwest, while accompanying Maj. Gen. Edward O. C. Ord's column advancing from Corinth. But Price at the last minute perceived the trap and attacked Rosecrans while Ord's troops waited to hear the sound of the guns. A stiff fight ensued in which the Confederates carried the fight to the Yanks and captured a battery, however Price got away after nightfall.

Maj. Gen. Earl Van Dorn, CSA, was held in high regard by Confederate leadership until his defeats at Corinth and Pea Ridge, Arkansas, proved he lacked the skill to command a large army. This handsome reputed ladies' man did, however, excel later as a cavalry commander until he was killed by a jealous husband on May 7, 1863, in Spring Hill, Tennessee.

A phenomenon called acoustic shadow, a combination of topography and wind, hid the September 19 battle between Price and Rosecrans from Grant and Ord, even though they were only a few miles away. Price then joined his divisions with Van Dorn's, and on October 3, they attacked the Federal position at Corinth with

22,000 soldiers, hoping to seize Corinth, crush Rosecrans's four divisions, and then sweep north into Middle Tennessee. But the screaming assault on Rosecrans's 23,000 man command in ninety-degree heat sapped the troops' energy. Through the rest of the day, the Federals gave ground, withdrawing from one line of entrenchments outside of Corinth to a second and then a third protecting the railroad junction and depot in the town. These interior batteries were held, even as Rosecrans awaited reinforcement from Ord's division en route from Iuka.

Though the sickness of one of his commanders postponed Van Dorn's October 4 daybreak attack until nine A.M., the Confederates moved forward against Battery Powell and Battery Robinett in the face of punishing Union artillery. Savage hand-to-hand combat ensued at Battery Robinett. But once again heat, thirst, and exhaustion, combined with the stubborn resistance of their foe, broke up the Confederate assaults and the Rebels were compelled to withdraw.

Grant, having taken steps to trap the retreating Confederates, implored Rosecrans to help trap them. But "Old Rosey," as his men called him, was slow to join in and Van Dorn escaped after being battered by Ord on the Hatchie River (see **Hatchie Bridge, Tennessee**). Grant, while admiring Rosecrans as a fighter, cooled toward him thereafter for, as Grant believed, allowing the Confederates first at Iuka and then Corinth to escape disaster. But Rosecrans's role in thwarting the Southern offensive in northeastern Mississippi gained Lincoln's attention and the president, in late October, named him to replace Maj. Gen. Don Carlos Buell as commander of the Army of the Ohio (see **Perryville, Kentucky**).

Points of Interest

Corinth is located at the intersection of US45 and MS2. Battery Robinett was a key position during Van Dorn's October 4 on the Federals' final line of fortifications protecting Corinth. Several Confederate attacks against the position were repulsed. At Polk and Linden streets in Confederate Park is a restored portion of the earthwork. There is a monument to Confederate colonel William Rodgers of the 2nd Texas Infantry who was killed in one of the attacks. There are also markers at Battery F and a historic trail is being developed. At MS2 and Seventh Street there is a large Rebel rifle pit, part of Beauregard's second line of defense against the advance of Halleck's forces in the spring of 1862. Homes used as headquarters by Gens. Leonidas Polk, U. S. Grant, and A. S. Johnston are marked. Corinth also has a national cemetery for fallen Union soldiers. For more information, contact the Siege and Battle of Corinth Commission at 601-287-9501.

Iuka, on US72, has a marker for the Battle of Iuka at the entrance of Mineral Springs Park.

DRIVING TOUR—*Proceed to Holly Springs*
READING—*Spring 1862 campaign: New Orleans, Louisiana;*
Fall 1862 campaign: Richmond, Kentucky

GRANT'S FIRST VICKSBURG CAMPAIGN

In November 1862, having successfully beaten back the Confederates' attack on Corinth, Grant was in a position to launch a major offensive on Vicksburg. The experience of the U.S. Navy in the summer of 1862 (see **Vicksburg**) convinced the North that a large army was needed to operate against the Mississippi bastion whose land approaches had been fortified since the Federal warships and gunboats had passed it but had been unable to dislodge the Rebels from it. Grant's plan was to move south along the line of the Mississippi Central Railroad, through Jackson, and march on Vicksburg from the east.

At the same time, and as much to gain the "bulge" on John A. McClernand, a political general who was raising an army on orders from President Lincoln to move on Vicksburg by way of the Mississippi River, Grant ordered Maj. Gen. William T. Sherman to undertake an amphibious expedition down the Mississippi and up the Yazoo River to cooperate with Grant's overland march (see **Chickasaw Bayou**). After getting under way in mid-November from bases at Bolivar and Memphis, Tennessee, and Corinth, Grant's troops, their axis of advance the railroad, occupied Holly Springs, crossed the Tallahatchie, paused at Oxford, and battled and were repulsed by Confederate forces at Coffeeville on December 5. Meanwhile, the Confederates were marshaling forces to interrupt Grant's march.

Holly Springs

A 3,500-man cavalry force under Maj. Gen. Earl Van Dorn, on December 20, attacked Grant's principal supply depot at Holly Springs on the Mississippi Central Railroad, taking 1,500 prisoners, destroying $1.5 million in supplies, and burning several buildings including a new Federal hospital. Though the garrison was warned of the potential of an attack it was surprised when Van Dorn launched his two-pronged charge into the town at daybreak. A key element of an overall plan to disrupt Grant's march, the Holly Springs raid was a resounding success.

Van Dorn's force wended its way back into the Confederate lines, eluding Federal cavalry, which was just returning from pursuit of Nathan Bedford Forrest's cavalry, then raiding Federal bases and destroying Grant's primary supply line—the Mobile & Ohio Railroad—in West Tennessee (see **Jackson, Tennessee**). This was another link in the overall Confederate strategy to frustrate Grant's advance. Grant turned back after the Holly Springs raid but while doing so realized an important thing: The ample supplies gathered in the Mississippi countryside proved his army could live off the land—something he would exploit in his second drive on Vicksburg.

Points of Interest

Holly Springs is on US78. Grant's headquarters there was at 330 Salem Avenue. Other headquarters are marked as well including that of Maj. Gen. Edward O. C. Ord. Several of the churches in the town stood during the war.

Oxford, Mississippi (MS6), was the site of Grant's headquarters immediately before and during the Holly Springs Raid. The town was partly burned by A. J. Smith in August 1864 but the University of Mississippi was spared, possibly due to Grant's friendship with a local doctor. Buildings at the university were used to care for Confederate soldiers wounded in the Battle of Shiloh. The University Museum on Fifth Street have Civil War items on display. The historic homes of several prominent Civil War Mississippians are still standing on the streets of Oxford.

DRIVING TOUR—*Proceed to Brices' Cross Roads*
READING—*Grenada*

BRICES' CROSS ROADS

Early in May 1864, after his Kentucky raid that took him north to Paducah and the "Fort Pillow Massacre," Maj. Gen. Nathan Bedford Forrest and his cavalry corps eluded Federal columns led by Brig. Gen. Samuel Sturgis that chased him out of West Tennessee. He received orders in late May to ride into Middle Tennessee to disrupt William T. Sherman's supply line over the single-track railroad from Nashville to Chattanooga. Confederate Gen. Joseph E. Johnston hoped such a raid would hamstring Sherman's relentless campaign against his Army of Tennessee in northwest Georgia (see **Atlanta Campaign, Georgia**). Forrest, after reaching Russellville, Alabama, and learning that Brig. Gen. Samuel Sturgis had started out from Memphis again in early June, this time with more than 8,100 men to hunt him down, turned back toward Mississippi.

On June 10, at Brices' Cross Roads, in the gently rolling hills of northeast Mississippi, the vanguard Federal cavalry under Brig. Gen. Benjamin Grierson encountered a brigade of Forrest's dismounted cavalry. The troopers held their position until more of Forrest's force arrived on the scene. In slashing attacks Forrest beat Grierson before the Federal infantry arrived. Sturgis's foot soldiers, exhausted from a torridly hot quick-time march, arrived at Brices' Cross Roads, where Forrest—now joined by his fourth brigade—combined frontal and flanking attacks to whip them. The Confederates relentlessly pursued the hapless Yankees for twenty-four hours, keeping them "skeered," capturing more than a thousand of them along with 16 cannons, and more than 100 wagons. Sherman, outraged at the defeat of the numerically superior force by the brilliant Forrest, then directed a new army under Maj. Gen. A. J. Smith to go after Forrest.

Points of Interest

Brices' Cross Roads National Battlefield Site—Located off US45, 6 miles west of Baldwyn, Mississippi, on MS370, at the center of Federal line that was broken by a series of Confederate slashing attacks, is Brices' Cross Roads National Battlefield Site. There is a monument at the site of Brices' House and the surrounding countryside still gives a good idea of how it looked when the clash took place. In the late 1950s the state of Mississippi positioned a number of markers along MS370 locating troop positions. One hundred yards northeast of the monument is a small Confederate cemetery containing the graves of most of the soldiers killed in the battle, with most of them identified. There are no visitor facilities at Brices' Cross Roads beyond an interpretive wayside and a memorial; however, preservation groups, led by APCWS, have acquired more than 750 acres adjacent to the battlefield site and plans are under way to build a visitor center and museum. More information about the battle can be obtained at the Tupelo Visitor Center on the Natchez Trace Parkway, a few miles north of the US45 entrance to the parkway. Information can also be obtained by contacting Superintendent, Natchez Trace Parkway R.R. 1, NT-143, Tupelo, MS 38801; 601-842-1572. ▲ ⅄ 👫 🐎 ⊘ 🏮 ⇌ 👫

DRIVING TOUR and READING—*Proceed to Tupelo*

TUPELO

In early July, Maj. Gen. Andrew J. Smith, with a force of 14,000, started out from Memphis via La Grange, Tennessee, toward the southeast. With Grierson's cavalry again in the lead, Smith's army destroyed a wide swath of northeastern Mississippi, crossing through Ripley and heading south. Lt. Gen. Stephen D. Lee, commanding Confederate forces in the Department of Alabama, Mississippi, and East Louisiana, and General Forrest hoped to trap Smith's column at Okolona, but Smith turned east toward Tupelo. On July 14, with Smith's infantry occupying works at Harrisburg, one mile west of Tupelo, Forrest and Lee launched a series of poorly coordinated attacks on Smith's soldiers. The Federals repulsed all of these with heavy losses to the Rebels.

On July 15, Smith began to withdraw and delivered a stinging repulse at Old Town Creek to Forrest's attack on his rear guard. Forrest was wounded in this action. Although the Confederates held the field, they failed to destroy the Federal force and sustained much higher casualties than they could afford. Smith's columns returned to Memphis while Lee's soldiers hurried south to cope with the threat being mounted against Mobile. The two-day battle proved the ability of the Federals to employ strong columns to keep Forrest tied down in north Mississippi and out of Middle Tennessee where he might, as Sherman feared, cause serious interruption to rail traffic over the Nashville & Chattanooga Railroad at a crucial stage in his Atlanta Campaign.

Points of Interest

Tupelo is located on US45, 2.2 miles east of the Natchez Trace Parkway. The July 14 action occurred at what was then Harrisburg, at the intersection of US45 and MS6, and the July 15 action occurred a few miles north where US45 crosses Old Town Creek. On MS6, 1.2 miles east of the parkway, is the Tupelo National Battlefield Site; this area was behind the Union left flank at the time of the Confederates' July 14 attack. There is a monument and an interpretive wayside exhibit describing the action in the Battle of Tupelo. Further information can be obtained at the Tupelo Visitor Center on the Natchez Trace Parkway, 7 miles north on the parkway. Information can also be obtained by contacting Superintendent, Natchez Trace Parkway R.R. 1, NT-143, Tupelo, MS 38801; 601-842-1572.   **?** **P**

DRIVING TOUR—*Proceed to Okolona*
READING—*Sherman's 1864 Atlanta Campaign: Georgia*

OKOLONA

In February 1864, in conjunction with his march to Meridian, Mississippi, and hopefully beyond to destroy the Southern capacity to produce war goods and wreak havoc on their railroads, Maj. Gen. William T. Sherman ordered a column of cavalry to proceed southeast from Memphis to join him at Meridian. The column commanded by Brig. Gen. William Sooy Smith left Collierville, Tennessee, on February 11, well behind schedule, and rode southeast to rendezvous with Sherman's force, which was marching east from Vicksburg through Jackson.

The advance of Smith's 7,000 troopers and 20 cannons was slow and ponderous. As he proceeded, he was tearing up railroad track and destroying supplies as ordered, and brushing aside Mississippi militia. To the detriment of Smith's progress, his column was picking up more than a thousand ex-slaves seeking protection. During the march Smith learned that Maj. Gen. Nathan B. Forrest was gathering a force to oppose him as he approached the fertile Black Prairie region of Mississippi, south of Okolona.

The reports were true; Forrest, in November of 1863, was detached by President Davis from the Confederate Army of Tennessee and sent to West Tennessee and northern Mississippi with a hodgepodge command including many new recruits enlisted from the area. Forrest was north of Meridian, near West Point, where he had a force of 2,500, many of whom were new recruits who had just undergone brief but rugged training under the tutelage of the "Wizard of the Saddle."

On February 20, Smith's column first skirmished with Forrest north of West Point. Continuing on to West Point, Forrest's detachments accelerated the pressure the next day. By this time Smith felt the Confederates were drawing him into a trap. Concerned for the safety of his force and the ex-slaves following him, he turned his column around on February 21 and started back for Memphis.

On February 22, four miles south of Okolona, Forrest attacked Smith's rear guard. The charge broke the continuity of the Federal column and an eleven-mile running fight ensued which hammered the bluecoats through Okolona and up the Pontotoc Road to Ivey's Hill. Charges continued back and forth all day until the Federals, having already lost a number of men and cannons, broke off the running engagement and retreated to Pontotoc. Forrest's smaller force, low on ammunition, did not pursue them.

Smith's broken command continued its retreat to Memphis, harassed by Mississippi militia. Sherman, not knowing why Smith had been delayed, abandoned plans to go on to Mobile or Selma, evacuated Meridian on February 20, and started back to Vicksburg (**see Meridian**).

Points of Interest

The Battle of Okolona is identified by a historical marker on US45 at the southern edge of the town, in the area where Forrest's "critter cavalry" struck Smith's rear guard on February 22. Nearby is a Confederate cemetery that contains the graves of more than 1,000 soldiers who died in the area.

DRIVING TOUR—*Proceed to Grenada*
READING—*Meridian Campaign*

GRENADA

Lt. Gen. John C. Pemberton, who was a Pennsylvanian by birth and married to a Virginian, assumed command of the Department of Mississippi and East Louisiana, which included Vicksburg, in October 1862. His previous command had been in charge of the department that included the defenses of Charleston, South Carolina, after Robert E. Lee had been recalled to Richmond in March 1862 to become military adviser to President Davis. Serious philosophical problems with the governor of South Carolina had resulted in Pemberton's promotion and reassignment. In December, as Ulysses S. Grant threatened to advance on Jackson, Pemberton established a defense

line behind the Yalobusha River with Grenada at its center. The line was never tested—
Grant turned back after cavalry raids by Nathan Bedford Forrest and Earl Van Dorn
broke up the Mobile & Ohio Railroad, his primary supply line, and destroyed his big
Holly Springs depot (see **Holly Springs**).

Points of Interest

Located on US51, Grenada has two historical markers identifying Pemberton's defense
line as established in December 1862. One is on US51 where it crosses MS8. The other,
on US51 at Grenada Dam on the Yalobusha River, locates the site of a Confederate fort.
There is also a Confederate cemetery in the town and the Bruce Newsome home at 217
Margin Street, which was used as a headquarters by Maj. Gen. Sterling Price.

DRIVING TOUR—*Proceed to Fort Pemberton*
READING—*Chickasaw Bayou*

GRANT'S SECOND VICKSBURG CAMPAIGN

The Confederate surrender of Vicksburg on July 4, 1863, followed a long, hard series of
campaigns by the Federal army and navy against this strategically and symbolically
important southwestern bastion. The emergence of Ulysses S. Grant as "Lincoln's general," as the architect of the ultimate Union victory in the Civil War, was the result of his
successful Vicksburg campaign.

On January 30, 1863, Grant came down the Mississippi from Memphis and reorganized
his army in preparation for another campaign against Vicksburg, his first having failed
following the destruction of his Holly Springs supply depot by Earl Van Dorn's Confederate cavalry, and Maj. Gen. William T. Sherman's repulse at Chickasaw Bayou, both in
December 1862. Concurrent with Grant's new campaign, Maj. Gen. Nathaniel P. Banks
prepared to launch a thrust up the Mississippi from New Orleans, hoping to capture Port
Hudson, the Confederate river stronghold south of Vicksburg that enabled the Confederates to control access to the Red River and the 240 intervening miles of the Mississippi
River (see **Port Hudson, Louisiana**).

The Confederate defenders had little to do with Grant's early difficulties in his Second Vicksburg Campaign. Getting the Federal forces in position to attack the Rebels was the challenge. Grant was determined to access the high and dry ground east of Vicksburg. To do so, he launched a series of amphibious operations from camps occupied by Sherman's and Maj. Gen. John A. McClernand's troops on the Louisiana side of the Mississippi, upstream from Vicksburg. Work was also resumed on a canal project across De Soto Point, Louisiana, and another was begun at Lake Providence (see **Vicksburg Area, Louisiana**).

Yazoo Pass Expedition

The Yazoo Pass Expedition looked toward opening a water route from the Mississippi River near Helena, Arkansas, via Yazoo Pass, Moon Lake, Coldwater, Tallahatchie, and Yazoo rivers to gain a lodgment on the bluffs above Haynes' and Snyder's bluffs. Lt. Col. James H. Wilson, an enterprising young engineer on Grant's staff, surveyed Yazoo Pass and on February 3 exploded mines to breach the levee separating the pass from the Mississippi. By March 2, 1863, gunboats and transports had navigated Yazoo Pass and entered the Coldwater. Confederates got wind of the Yankees' activities and felled trees in the path of the flotilla. Lt. Cmdr. Watson Smith lost his nerve and did not push his gunboats ahead quickly enough to prevent the Rebels from fortifying the narrow neck of land separating the Tallahatchie and Yazoo rivers, near Greenwood. Fort Pemberton, as the work was called, because of high water, was difficult for infantry to assault and Commander Smith was hesitant to attack. When his two ironclads attacked, fire from the fort's big guns held them off. This expedition was soon abandoned.

Points of Interest

Fort Pemberton, at the US49E turnoff near Greenwood, is now identified by a small plot of land and a wayside exhibit. The fort held off Federal gunboats and their supporting infantry divisions for more than three weeks in their failed attempt to open a route to the Yazoo River that would allow Union troops to land above the strong defensive position at Snyder's Bluff.

DRIVING TOUR—*Proceed to Greenville*
READING—*Steele's Bayou Expedition*

Greenville

In April, as first General McClernand's and then Maj. Gen. James B. McPherson's corps marched south from Milliken's Bend through the Louisiana parishes preparatory to crossing the Mississippi, Union forces undertook three diversions to deceive the Confederates as to their intentions. The first of these was the Greenville Expedition. Maj. Gen. Frederick Steele's division sent upriver by boat from Milliken's Bend came ashore at Greenville in early April. Striking inland Steele's soldiers reached Deer Creek and turned south wreaking havoc on the plantations from which the Vicksburg Confederates secured their "hog and hominy." Steele, having drawn the Confederates' attention to his Deer Creek activities, returned to Greenville and then by boat to Milliken's Bend.

Points of Interest

Greenville has several historical markers relating to this Union diversion. North of Greenville on MS1 at Green Groves is a historical marker identifying a plantation once owned by Nathan Bedford Forrest.

DRIVING TOUR—*Proceed to Yazoo City*
READING—*Grierson's Raid*

Yazoo City

Yazoo City, forty-five miles northeast of Vicksburg on the Yazoo River, was the site of a Confederate navy yard. The most famous of Yazoo City's Confederate vessels was the CSS *Arkansas,* an ironclad ram, laid down at Memphis and completed and outfitted at the Yazoo city yard. She was deliberately destroyed by her captain as she developed engine trouble and was threatened by Federal gunboats August 6, 1862, near Baton Rouge, Louisiana (see **Baton Rouge, Louisiana**). The *Arkansas*'s first captain, Isaac Newton Brown, was not present when she was blown up and had advised against her being dispatched to cooperate with the army in the attack on Baton Rouge because of needed repairs to the ironclad's machinery. Brown got a measure of revenge for the loss of his boat. The USS *Cairo,* a Federal ironclad, was destroyed by two of Brown's "infernal machines" (mines) while reconnoitering the Yazoo River on December 12, 1862.

On July 13, 1863, an amphibious force under Brig. Gen. Francis J. Herron advanced to Yazoo City with gunboat support to clear the river of units of Gen. Joseph E. Johnston's army which had ineffectively challenged Grant's forces during the final weeks of the Vicksburg Campaign. Herron occupied the town and the fire-gutted naval facilities. But once again a Federal ironclad, the USS *DeKalb*, fell victim to torpedoes on the Yazoo River and sank.

Points of Interest

There is a historical marker on US49 identifying the naval yard site. The city also has a Civil War museum.

DRIVING TOUR—*Proceed to Steele's Bayou or Chickasaw Bayou*
READING—*CSS* Arkansas: *Baton Rouge, Louisiana;*
(chronological)—Helena, Arkansas

Steele's Bayou Expedition

In mid-March, checkmated before Fort Pemberton, the Federals sought to open another water route that would bring them into the Yazoo River upstream from Haynes' and Snyder's bluffs and downstream from Fort Pemberton. This roundabout route left the Yazoo, ascended Steele's Bayou, passed through Black Bayou, up Deep Creek through Rolling Fork, and then back into the Yazoo via the Big Sunflower River. R. Adm. David D. Porter reconnoitered Steele's Bayou, taking Grant with him. Grant returned to base and approved the Steele's Bayou Expedition.

Supported by General Sherman, Porter, with five ironclads, several tugs, and a mortar scow, left the Mississippi on March 16. Steele's Bayou was navigable through a flooded forest, and Porter's gunboats steamed far ahead of two accompanying troop transports. But as the expedition progressed and the gunboats entered first Black Bayou and then Deer Creek, the channel narrowed. As the gunboats approached Rolling Fork, the last difficult leg of the course before entering the Big Sunflower River, they encountered a tangle of willow trees that they had to force their way through. As the crews attempted to clear these obstacles and to remove trees felled by Confederate scouts, Rebel troops reached Rolling Fork. Porter's gunboats were vulnerable, trapped dead in the water without infantry support. While sailors landed and emplaced a boat howitzer on an Indian mound to keep the butternuts at bay, the ironclads slowly backed down tortuous Deer Creek. Porter frantically sent a message back to the lagging army. "Dear Sherman. Hurry up for heaven's sake. I never knew how helpless an ironclad could be steaming around through the woods without an army to back her."

Sherman's rescue party hastened forward, making a night march. They provided cover for the gunboats as the vessels backed out the way they came. The Steele's Bayou Expedition had failed, as would the Yazoo Pass Expedition which had started six weeks earlier but was aborted one week later.

Points of Interest

One can obtain an idea of the difficulties faced by the Federal gunboats attempting to navigate the twisting bayous and creeks of the delta by traveling on MS16 through Delta National Forest to US61, then south toward Vicksburg. At Rolling Fork is the Indian mound defended by Uncle Sam's "web feet" to buy time for Porter to save his ironclads. The more direct route to Vicksburg is via MS3.

DRIVING TOUR—*Proceed to Chickasaw Bayou*
READING—*Strategy Changes: Grant's Second Vicksburg Campaign*

VICKSBURG AREA

Chickasaw Bayou

A vital element in U. S. Grant's December 1862 converging attack on Confederate Lt. Gen. John C. Pemberton's army behind the Yalobusha in north Mississippi was an amphibious expedition led by Maj. Gen. William T. "Billy" Sherman down the Mississippi River from Memphis.

Sherman departed from Memphis with 22,000 soldiers, picked up another 10,000 at Helena, and entered the Yazoo River. His troop transports were escorted by R. Adm. David D. Porter's Mississippi River Squadron. The failure of Grant to sustain his drive against Pemberton's Yalobusha River line after the destructive Rebel raids on Holly

Springs and the Mobile & Ohio Railroad enabled Pemberton to reinforce the 6,000-man force that, on the approach of Sherman, manned the works centering on Walnut Hills, guarding the northern approaches to Vicksburg. Sherman's forces landed on December 26, skirmished with the Confederates during the next forty-eight hours, and suffered a disastrous repulse on December 29 when they crossed the Chickasaw Bayou and sought to storm the Rebels' Walnut Hills defenses. Having suffered heavy losses, Sherman withdrew from the area on January 2, 1863.

As one of his three April 1863 diversions to cover the southward march of his forces to Hard Times Landing, Grant asked Sherman to make a demonstration against Confederate works on the Yazoo at Snyder's Bluff, four miles upstream from where he had suffered his embarrassing defeat at Chickasaw Bayou the previous December. This diversionary attack, supported by gunboats, on April 29–30, was designed to further confuse Pemberton and to keep the thousands of Rebel troops posted in and around Vicksburg from rushing to Grant's proposed landing site at Grand Gulf, thirty miles south of Vicksburg.

Points of Interest

Located on US61/MS3, 10 miles north of Vicksburg at Redwood, are historical markers for the Chickasaw Bayou battle and Snyder's Bluff. The Confederates from their earthworks and with artillery atop an Indian mound hurled back assaults by Sherman's army in December 1862 and on April 29, 1863, their big guns, from commanding positions on Snyder's and Drumgould's bluffs, dueled with Union gunboats as Sherman undertook his diversion. Less than a month later, on May 19, Federal forces occupied these defenses without firing a shot, the Confederate garrisons having been recalled and redeployed for defense of the Vicksburg perimeter. Depots were then established at Snyder's Bluff and at the mouth of Chickasaw Bayou to supply Grant's forces besieging Vicksburg. The Indian mound, and well-preserved earthworks, at Snyder's and Drumgould's bluffs are extant but are on private property.

DRIVING TOUR—*Proceed to Vicksburg National Military Park*
READING *(1862 chronological)—Stones River, Tennessee;*
1863 Vicksburg campaign: Grand Gulf

Naval Operations at Vicksburg

Farragut's Expedition

In May 1862, after capturing New Orleans (see **New Orleans, Louisiana**) and proceeding upriver with his squadron of saltwater warships, Flag Officer David G. Farragut approached Vicksburg. It was part of his mandate for opening the Mississippi River that the "Hill City" be captured and occupied, thus removing what the North considered to be the last obstacle to control of the river and denying its use to the Confederates. At the same time the city's surrender would reopen the Mississippi River for commerce to the Union states of the "Old Northwest." During a two-week delay to get Farragut's ships ready for continuing the operation upriver, big guns arrived and were mounted at Vicksburg. Upriver, the Federal riverboat squadron had run into difficulties at Fort Pillow, Tennessee, and were dealt a stinging blow by Confederate naval forces at Plum Point Bend (see **Fort Pillow, Tennessee**). When the saltwater Federals demanded the surrender of Vicksburg on May 18, both the military commander and mayor defiantly refused. Farragut reconnoitered the Vicksburg bluffs from the river, and, leaving his gunboats below the city, returned to New Orleans with his deep-draft flagship.

On June 24, Farragut again headed upriver with a larger force, including mortar boats under Cmdr. David D. Porter. On June 25, Porter's bombardment of the city began while a message came to Farragut, anchored below the city, that the Mississippi River Squadron, having been battered along the White River in Arkansas, was now coming downriver to join forces with the oceangoing fleet. Farragut determined to run past the batteries and meet Flag Officer Charles Davis's river gunboats upriver. On June 28, most of his ships successfully challenged the Vicksburg batteries and dropped anchor near the mouth of the Yazoo River, joined there by Davis's Mississippi River Squadron on July 1. The naval guns, even Porter's mortars, had little effect on the cannons mounted to command Vicksburg's hairpin bend and bluffs. Without a sizable army force, the capture of Vicksburg seemed unattainable. The small army force with Farragut began to cut a canal across De Soto Point, Louisiana, but soldiers and sailors alike were suffering from malaria which was prevalent there that summer.

Another problem also developed for the Federal sailors. On July 15, the truth was discovered about the rumored Confederate ironclad being completed upriver on the Yazoo. Three boats sent out in search of the CSS *Arkansas,* including the ironclad *Carondelet,* encountered the Rebel ram on her maiden voyage. The Federal boats were battered by the Confederate ironclad which, though damaged herself, managed to proceed down stream past the combined Federal fleets blasting away at the stationary targets before retiring under the protection of Vicksburg's guns. Farragut's fleet weighed anchor that evening and, in passing Vicksburg, sought in vain to destroy the *Arkansas*. In a week of renewed mortar bombardment and in a July 22 attack by a Federal river ram and the ironclad USS *Essex*, the *Arkansas* suffered casualties but no crippling damage. The *Essex* did witness the death of the *Arkansas*, but that wasn't until several weeks later at Baton Rouge (see **Baton Rouge, Louisiana**).

With the crew's health situation worsening and no progress being made toward a military solution to capturing Vicksburg, Farragut, on July 24, weighed anchor and departed with his entire squadron for Baton Rouge, New Orleans, and the sea. Davis's river fleet headed upriver to a new base at Helena, Arkansas. The first of Vicksburg's successful repulses of Federal efforts to take the "Hill City" was over and the key to the Mississippi, as Lincoln called Vicksburg, was still in the Confederates' pocket.

Porter's Operations

After the January 11, 1863, capture of Fort Hindman at Arkansas Post, R. Adm. David D. Porter had been monitoring the waterways in the vicinity of Vicksburg. With virtually no naval resistance to his activities, Porter sent Lt. Col. Charles Rivers Ellet, who had fought in the Battle of Memphis (see **Memphis, Tennessee**) and was the late Charles Ellet's nineteen-year-old son, to stop Confederate boats bringing supplies from the

The Queen of the West *was one of Charles Ellet's original Federal river rams. She participated in the Battle of Memphis, was damaged while battling the CSS* Arkansas, *pictured here, and ran the Vicksburg batteries on February 2, 1863. She was captured by the Rebels soon afterward, then was retaken and destroyed in a battle with Federal gunboats on Louisiana's Atchafalaya River on April 14, 1863.*

Trans-Mississippi via Louisiana's Red River. Young Ellet, in the *Queen of the West*, ran the Vicksburg batteries on February 2 and went on a twelve-day sortie, attacking six vessels and capturing or disabling them. Ellet finally lost the *Queen of the West*, in a battle with Confederate cottonclad rams and gunboats on the Red River.

The Confederates then refitted the *Queen of the West* and, together with three other vessels, encountered and captured one of Porter's ironclads, the USS *Indianola*, which on February 13 also ran the Vicksburg gauntlet. As the Rebels salvaged their prize, Porter hit upon an idea that would have important implications later in the campaign. At a cost of $8.63, Porter had a coal barge converted into a three-hundred-foot-long dummy gunboat. Porter hoped to use his imposing-looking counterfeit monitor, called the *Black Terror,* to draw attention away from the salvage of the *Indianola.* In this he succeeded. On the night of February 25, Confederate shore batteries at Vicksburg fired away at the *Black Terror* as it drifted downriver. The Rebel salvage crew set the *Indianola* on fire and fled. The advantage of running the formidable Vicksburg batteries at night was an idea whose time soon came.

THE STRATEGY CHANGES IN GRANT'S SECOND VICKSBURG CAMPAIGN

Upon the failure of the Yazoo Pass and Steele's Bayou expeditions and with little hope of success as a result of the De Soto Point and Lake Providence canals, General Grant, under great political pressure from Washington, considered his options. He could not take the entire army back to Memphis and retry the midstate route through Holly Springs (a plan recommended by Grant's two favorite subordinates, McPherson and Sherman); such a move would be considered a retreat and could cost him his job. Lincoln, Grant's staunchest supporter, was under pressure to fire the Illinois general but stood firm as he had earlier when he said, "I can't spare this man, he fights."

Grant's enemies in Washington fanned the fire with accusations that Grant was a drunk. "Tell me the brand of whiskey Grant drinks. I would like to send a barrel of it to my other generals," Lincoln joked. But a serious investigation into Grant's conduct was started by Secretary of War Edwin M. Stanton. In April he sent Assistant Secretary Charles A. Dana to Grant's camp under false pretenses. But Grant and his staff knew the true reason for Dana's mission. Staff members advised the general to be uncooperative, but Grant treated Dana with respect and friendliness and the assistant secretary, writing almost daily, sent favorable impressions of Grant back to Washington. Dana wrote later about U. S. Grant:

"The most modest, the most disinterested and the most honest man I ever knew, with a temper that nothing could disturb . . . not a great man except morally, not an original or brilliant man, but sincere, thoughtful, deep and gifted with courage that never faltered."

Modern historians suspect that Grant was an alcoholic, in the medical sense of the term, a binge drinker. But Grant's belief that drinking was a moral weakness, which reflected the attitudes of the Victorian era, probably made him a stronger person. He fought what he saw to be his weakness. Thanks to his strong character and the support of those close to him, especially his wife and family, there was no evidence his alcoholism affected his leadership as a Civil War general.

The coming of spring offered Grant an option that had not been available during the wet winter months. Just as the flooded waterways of the Mississippi and its tributaries had aided the movement of vessels in the amphibious operations, so the drying of the land and receding of the river helped his new plan. Whether Grant believed that any of the four unsuccessful attempts over the winter to bypass Vicksburg would have worked is debatable, but they did provide direction and purpose to the North's second largest army through the difficult winter. They also had the effect of keeping the bodies of the soldiers strong and their minds sharp. The spring campaign benefited from this fitness.

Grant proposed to march the army overland down the west bank of the Mississippi through the Louisiana parishes to a point south of Vicksburg, and from there to cross the river. The problem was getting the large steamboat and gunboats needed to protect the crossing below the "Fortress City." Grant asked Porter to run the Vicksburg gauntlet.

Porter selected the night of April 16. The run was timed to coincide with a grand ball in Vicksburg

R. Adm. David D. Porter's gunboats running the Vicksburg batteries on the night of April 16, 1863, in this Currier and Ives chromolithograph. In a symbiotic relationship, transports, tugs, and timberclads lashed to the starboard sides of Porter's ironclads provide extra power for the gunboats while the ironclads shield their consorts from the Vicksburg guns.

attended by senior Confederate officers and their staffs. The maneuver was successful. No gunboats were lost, and only one of the transports, loaded with commissary supplies, went down. There were few Federal fatalities during this and a subsequent run of six unarmed steamboats, of which one was destroyed, on April 22. Grant anxiously watched the initial passage of the batteries from his headquarters boat, then rode a horse to New Carthage to greet Porter.

In early May, the tug *George Sturgess* ran the Vicksburg gauntlet but was sunk, causing Porter to note gleefully that she was carrying a group of newspaper reporters with whom Sherman and Porter had been feuding. Most of the crew and scribes were captured.

During the siege of Vicksburg, Federal gunboats continued to prowl the Mississippi River at Vicksburg, supporting land operations with bombardment of the Confederate shore batteries. Though no Confederate vessel appeared to challenge the Federal control of the river after the destruction of the CSS *Arkansas,* the U.S. Navy had to contend with shore batteries and Rebel torpedoes. On May 27, the USS *Cincinnati,* while bombarding water batteries at Wyman's Hill and at the Water Battery below Fort Hill north of Vicksburg, took hits that proved to be fatal. Disabled and not beached properly, the ironclad became a stationary target. Shore batteries pounded the vessel with so much shot she finally sunk near the head of the Mississippi's hairpin bend. Casualties remaining on board turned the sunken gunboat into a watery tomb. Her guns were removed and placed in a battery where Sherman's corps maintained positions on the siege line. After Vicksburg's surrender, the Federals salvaged and repaired the *Cincinnati* and she rejoined the fleet.

The USS Cairo, *one of the original James B. Eads river ironclads, was under the command of Lt. Cmdr. Thomas O. Selfridge when she became the first vessel to be sunk by a torpedo (mine).*

Points of Interest

For the fullest appreciation of Grant's successful twenty-day campaign from the bombardment of Grand

Gulf on April 29 to his arrival before the land approaches to Vicksburg on May 18, take the Vicksburg Circle Tour. The tour includes an initial stop at Vicksburg National Military Park Visitors Center followed by a tour of Fort Hill and the USS *Cairo* Museum to explain the naval operations, then proceeds south of Vicksburg to Grand Gulf and Grant's Mississippi River crossing. From there it continues northeast to Jackson and then west, following the series of battles that the Federals fought with Lt. Gen. John Pemberton's soldiers, forcing them back into the Vicksburg enclave.

Vicksburg National Military Park—Fort Hill and USS *Cairo* Museum—Fort Hill and the USS *Cairo* Museum can be reached by taking exit 4B from I-20 east of Vicksburg to the park's main entrance, then following the park roads north. If you plan to return to the park later on the Circle Tour, a more direct route is to take any I-20 exit into downtown Vicksburg (or continue south on US61 from Redwood) to Fort Hill Avenue, three blocks east of US61, and proceed north to Fort Hill.　🚲 🚌 📷 ♿ 🚶 🏛 P 🚻 $

Fort Hill was one of the key observation points for Confederate guns commanding the Mississippi. It was also the northwest bastion of the Confederate perimeter that guarded the city's land approaches. From Fort Hill there is a commanding view of the Mississippi River and the Yazoo Diversion Canal. The river, however, through natural and man-made efforts, has changed its course drastically since 1863. Gone is the hairpin curve north of Fort Hill that aided in the river's defense. The waterway closest to Fort Hill now is a channeling of the Yazoo River, the Yazoo Diversion Canal, created as part of the effort by the Army Corps of Engineers to facilitate modern Mississippi River commerce. Fort Hill features historical markers that detail its role in the naval operations.

Another water battery, South Fort, is located south of downtown Vicksburg adjacent to the Mississippi River bridges and was built in March 1863 when Grant's canal was under construction to bypass the batteries farther north.

The USS *Cairo* Museum gives a unique look at the role of the navy and its gunboats in the river war. Much of what was the *Cairo* was raised from the Yazoo River in the 1960s and reconstructed in this display, the only full-size exhibit of a Civil War Federal river ironclad. The rediscovery of the USS *Cairo* was made by co-author Edwin C. Bearss and he supervised the recovery and restoration while serving as regional research historian and duty-stationed at Vicksburg National Military Park. The *Cairo* has many of her guns remounted and the adjacent museum building features many recovered artifacts from the ironclad as well as exhibits detailing the river war on western waters.

From Vicksburg, proceed south on US61 to Port Gibson and follow the signs to Grand Gulf. Ten miles south of Vicksburg on US61 is a historical marker for Brierfield, the site of the plantation homes of Jefferson Davis and his brother Joseph. They are located on Davis Island in the Mississippi River and are accessible only by private boat or airplane. Davis's plantation home at Brierfield was destroyed by Federal forces in 1863, except for the plantation's main house. The property was sold while Davis was imprisoned at Fort Monroe, Virginia, from 1865 to 1867, but recovered by Davis in a court of law in 1881. Brierfield was destroyed by fire in 1932.

DRIVING TOUR—*Proceed to Grand Gulf*
READING *(chronological)*—*1862: Little Rock, Arkansas; 1863: Greenville*

Jefferson Davis worked tirelessly as leader of the Confederacy beyond its final days. He was often at odds with other Southern politicians over such issues as central government control, and with some of his generals over his micromanagement of the war. However, Davis was an excellent orator and succeeded in boosting Southern morale in speeches such as those he made during his winter 1862 trip to his home state.

Grand Gulf

Although Grant's movement south had been presaged by the two successful April passages of the Vicksburg batteries by Union gunboats, transports and barges, Pemberton had yet to react. Grant's three diversions had succeeded in masking his intention of landing two infantry corps at Grand Gulf, thirty miles south of Vicksburg. With 10,000 of McClernand's infantry embarked on steamboats and invasion barges at Hard Times, Louisiana, Porter's gunboat squadron assembled to pound Confederate shore batteries at Grand Gulf—Forts Wade and Cobun. On April 29 a five-and-a-half-hour duel took place between Porter's gunboats and the two forts, under the command of Brig. Gen. John S. Bowen. Federal ironclads, fighting the current, knocked out Fort Wade as the Federal troops waited to storm ashore.

But Fort Cobun, on a bluff at the river's edge, seemed to be invincible to the Federal firepower. Porter later called it the strongest position on the river. The gunboats retired and Porter dissuaded Grant from attempting to cross at Grand Gulf.

Porter's gunboats battling the Confederate batteries at Forts Cobun and Wade at Grand Gulf, Mississippi. Porter called Grand Gulf the strongest position on the river.

Points of Interest

Grand Gulf Military Monument—This 400-acre park is a memorial to the river town of Grand Gulf—which struggled through disease and natural disasters in the early 1800s, rendering the community a ghost town by the Civil War—and to the important Civil War battle that occurred there. In the park are Fort Cobun, overlooking the Mississippi's former channel; Fort Wade, several hundred yards inland with its powder magazine visible, and other Confederate earthworks. After Confederate forces evacuated the area on the night of May 2–3, the Federals established a supply base at Grand Gulf. The park also has several restored buildings, an excellent museum of the Civil War, and a coach house with original historic vehicles. Facilities include a picnic area, hiking trails, and RV hookups. GRAND GULF MILITARY MONUMENT Route 2, P.O. Box 389, Port Gibson, MS 39150; 601-437-5911.　🚲 ⛰ 🏠 🖾 ♿ 👫 ❓ 🏛 P ⛱ 🚻 $

DRIVING TOUR and READING—*Proceed to Port Gibson*

Port Gibson

Grant was on the verge of being compelled to push his landing point in Mississippi much farther south, until a black informant confirmed the existence of a good road to the inte-

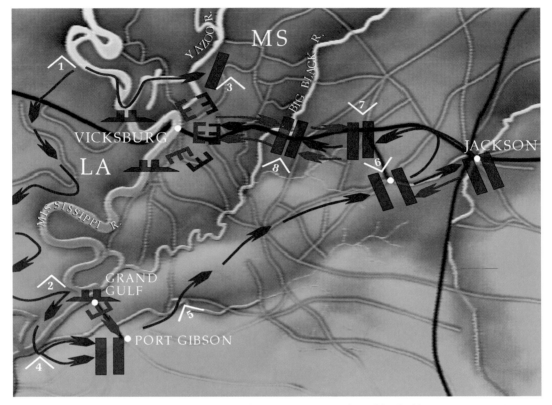

The progression of U. S. Grant's Second Vicksburg Campaign is indicated by the blue arrows. Departing from their bases at Milliken's Bend and Young's Point, Louisiana, (1) the Federal XIII and XVII corps marched to Hard Times, Louisiana, (2) while units of Maj. Gen. William T. Sherman's XV Corps landed near Chickasaw Bayou (3) to create a diversion for the landing downriver. After Confederate batteries held Federal gunboats at bay at Grand Gulf, Grant's forces landed at Bruinsburg (4) and first battled the forces of Maj. Gen. John S. Bowen at Port Gibson. Grant then moved inland, across Bayou Pierre (5) and battled forces organized by Gens. S. John Pemberton and Joseph E. Johnston at Raymond (6) and Jackson. Grant's three corps challenged the Vicksburg garrison of Lt. Gen. John C. Pemberton at Champion Hill (7) and the Big Black River (8) before driving them back into the defenses of Vicksburg.

rior from Bruinsburg, ten miles south of Grand Gulf. On the last day of April, McClernand's corps, along with a division of McPherson's, landed on Mississippi soil and began the last leg of the long road to Vicksburg, one that was on high dry land.

Throughout late afternoon and into the night, the Federals marched toward Port Gibson on the Rodney Road. Pemberton's capable lieutenant, Brig. Gen. John S. Bowen, rushed reinforcements from Grand Gulf to counter McClernand's march inland. But Grant's diversions had so confused senior Southern generals that the response to Bowen's call for reinforcements from Vicksburg was acted upon too late to be effective. Bowen divided his force to cover two converging roads four miles west of Port Gibson.

The A. K. Shaifer House, four miles west of Port Gibson, is where the first shots of the battle were fired shortly after midnight on May 1, 1863. While Mr. Shaifer was serving in the Confederate army at Port Hudson, his wife and sister-in-law remained there, leaving hurriedly when the skirmishing began. Bullet holes still can be seen in the house.

At two A.M. on May 1, Confederate Brig. Gen. Martin E. Green rode forward to check on his pickets along the Rodney Road. He stopped at the A. K. Shaifer House to reassure the frightened women there who were frantically packing their wagon to flee to Port Gibson ahead of the Yankees. Green told them that there was plenty of time, that the Federals did not march at night and would not arrive until the next day. Just then, Confederate pickets and Iowans in the Union vanguard shattered the still air with gunfire and a Federal bullet lodged in the wall of the Shaifer House.

The fighting escalated at daybreak along the Rodney Road as McClernand's lead brigades fought Green near the Magnolia Church. On the other flank, Brig. Gen. Peter Osterhaus sent his diversionary force against Brig. Gen. Edward Tracey's Alabamians on the Bruinsburg Road. The Rebels fought stubbornly and were aided by the terrain—the two roads were on fingerlike ridges separated by vine- and cane-choked ravines. But Grant, arriving in the mid-morning sent brigades of McPherson's corps to back up McClernand's forces. The Confederate right flank finally collapsed under the pressure, and Bowen, concerned about having his force cut off, withdrew to the north of Big Bayou Pierre after the Rebels burned the bridges across Big Bayou Pierre and Little Bayou Pierre northwest and north of Port Gibson. On the morning of May 2 the Federals occupied the town.

With his bridgehead secured, Grant and several aides on May 3 headed for Grand Gulf, which the Confederates had also abandoned. He rendezvoused with Porter's squadron and Grand Gulf was established as a Federal base. Though the supply route from Grand Gulf soon grew long and tenuous, Grant knew that his army could and would live off the land if necessary.

Points of Interest

Claiborne County in Mississippi, which includes Grand Gulf, is a wonderful locale for history buffs, especially of Civil War history. Claiborne County Historical Tours, established by the Mississippi State Parks Commission, provides a brochure with three tours that highlight the Civil War sites. Featured are the A. K. Shaifer House and other sites involved in the Battles of Grand Gulf and Port Gibson; the site of Bruinsburg, the landing point of Grant's forces; and Windsor, the hauntingly beautiful remains of a plantation mansion, burned in the 1890s. Grant's columns, on their march through the loess bluffs, halted near Windsor. Port Gibson—the town that advertises itself by quoting an apocryphal statement by Grant: "The town too beautiful to burn"—retains the unique charm of an old Southern town. Its many churches, all on one street and most predating the war, reflect the diverse cultures of its population. Many of the town's fine large homes, including "The Hill," the boyhood home of Confederate general Earl Van Dorn, were built in the antebellum period. Oak Square is a historically rich bed-and-breakfast inn. There are several other bed-and-breakfast inns in the area. Check with the Claiborne

Corinthian columns are all that remain of Winsdor, one of the most beautiful antebellum mansions in Mississippi. Federal troops marched past the mansion on the road from Bruinsburg to Port Gibson on the night of April 30–May 1, 1863. The plantation home served as a hospital after the Battle of Port Gibson and was undamaged by the war, but burned to the ground in an 1890 fire.

County Historical Tours office on Church Street for brochures and other information.

Enter the Natchez Trace Parkway south of Port Gibson at US61 and proceed either south to Natchez or north to Raymond.

DRIVING TOUR—*Proceed to Raymond (Circle Tour) or Natchez*
READING—*Raymond*

Natchez

Natchez, in 1860, with more than 6,000 people, was Mississippi's largest and most prosperous city, boasting more millionaires than New York City. The Civil War reached Natchez on May 12, 1862, with the arrival of Farragut's gunboats. Fortunately, the war did little to alter the progress of Natchez's legacy. The city promptly surrendered to Cmdr. James S. Palmer. The saltwater navy did not stay, and the only hostile fire directed against Natchez was by the ironclad *Essex* on September 3, 1862. Natchez was not occupied and garrisoned by Federal troops until mid-July 1863, one week after the surrender of Vicksburg. Natchez then was fortified and served the Yankees as an enclave from which Union columns struck out into the hinterland to harass the Confederates and either destroy or carry off cotton. No significant combat occurred in Natchez during the war.

Points of Interest

Natchez, on US61 at the western terminus of the Natchez Trace Parkway, has numerous antebellum mansions within the city and in Adams County. Information about these homes, the historic waterfront, and the annual Natchez Pilgrimage held in February can be obtained at the Canal Street Depot, on the corner of Canal and State streets.

▲ ♿ 👫 🐎 ❷ P ⛱ 🚻

DRIVING TOUR—*Proceed to Raymond*
READING—*Farragut's Expedition*

Raymond

Grant's strategy called for moving his forces—upon the arrival of Sherman's XV Corps from Milliken's Bend by way of Grand Gulf—northeast along the Big Black–Big Bayou Pierre watershed to interpose his army between Vicksburg and Jackson and then execute a ninety-degree turn, and close on Vicksburg from the east. The first heavy fighting in this phase of the campaign occurred on May 12 when McPherson's corps encountered Confederates under Brig. Gen. John Gregg southwest of Raymond. Gregg's brigade, pulled out of Port Hudson, was part of a force being assembled near Jackson, Mississippi.

The Battle of Raymond was McPherson's first major battle as a commander. It was a difficult struggle even though he had three times as many soldiers as Gregg. The Southerners withdrew toward Jackson after six hours, but the engagement had a sobering effect on Grant's plans. This contact with the vanguard of a force Gen. Joseph E. Johnston, Confederate commander in the west, was assembling, and the report that the Mississippi capital was heavily fortified, compelled Grant to change his strategy. Instead of turning toward Vicksburg and leaving a strong Rebel force at his back, he decided to first attack Jackson.

Points of Interest

A turnoff and historical marker just north of Natchez Trace Parkway, milepost 75 alerts you to the Battle of Raymond. Just north of the marker, exit on MS467 and proceed east to Raymond. The beautiful Hind County courthouse was used as a Confederate signal station before and as a hospital after the battle. There is also a Confederate cemetery here. The battle site is 2 miles southwest of Raymond where MS18 crosses Fourteenmile Creek. From Raymond, continue north on MS18, or the Natchez Trace Parkway to Jackson.

DRIVING TOUR and READING—*Proceed to Jackson*

Jackson

Grant defied accepted military principles by dividing his force again in unfamiliar enemy territory. He sent McPherson north to the town of Clinton, while Sherman marched on Jackson by way of Raymond. Most of McClernand's corps bluffed an attack near

Edwards' Station and then occupied Raymond to guard against Pemberton's army, which had crossed the Big Black and had taken post at Edwards.

Joseph E. Johnston had arrived in Jackson from Tennessee on the evening of May 13. He watched Gregg's men stream into town after the Battle of Raymond. Though troops were arriving from Port Hudson, South Carolina, and Tennessee, Johnston—suffering from exhaustion after the long trip west—wired Richmond: "I am too late."

He ordered the evacuation of all troops from Jackson, except a rear guard commanded by John Gregg. Though Sherman had little trouble with the delaying force on the Raymond Road, McPherson, once again, had trouble carrying out his offensive as he advanced east from Clinton and battled outnumbered Confederates in today's Livingston Park. He was hampered by a cloudburst. However, by the late afternoon of May 14, Federal troops raised the United States flag over the Mississippi State House.

Grant spent the night in a Bowman House hotel room vacated earlier in the day by Joseph E. Johnston. Something else belonging to Johnston also came Grant's way: an order to Pemberton, carried by a Southern courier who was a Federal spy. Grant read Johnston's order to Pemberton, who had ventured out of the Vicksburg defenses and had posted three of his five divisions at Edwards' Station. Johnston had outlined a plan for the two Confederate forces to converge and beat Grant's army. The Union commander now ordered McPherson's corps west to link up with McClernand's and drive a wedge in between the Rebel armies.

Grant took action to eliminate Jackson as a manufacturing, supply, administration, and transportation center. While Sherman's men ripped up track and bent heated rails into "Sherman Neckties," making them useless for rebuilding, Grant and "Uncle Billy" visited one of the manufacturing facilities marked for destruction by the invading army. Grant remembered the curious nature of their reception at the mill. "Sherman and I went together into a manufactory which had not ceased work on account of the battle nor for the entrance of the Yankee troops. Our presence did not seem to attract the attention of either the manager or the operatives, most of whom were girls. We looked on for a while to see the tent cloth which they were making roll out of the looms, with "C.S.A." woven in each bolt. There was an immense amount of cotton, in bales, stacked outside. Finally I told Sherman I thought they had done work enough. The operatives were told they could leave and take with them what cloth they could carry. In a few minutes cotton and factory were in a blaze."

A hand-colored woodcut published in Harper's Weekly *showing Federal soldiers tearing up track in the middle of Jackson. Three times Federal troops passed through Jackson and made "Sherman Neckties" from iron rails. Two important rail lines passed through the Mississippi capital during the Civil War.*

Sherman returned to Jackson on July 9, 1863, in pursuit of Johnston's force which had retreated toward the city after the surrender of Vicksburg. With only one serious battle action near Bailey's Hill, south of the city, Johnston's forces were partially invested and on the night of July 16 were forced from the city and retreated to the east. During Sherman's February 1864 campaign to further extend the Federal destruction of the South's ability to support the war effort, Jackson was again visited by the Yankee despoilers. On the march east to Meridian, Mississippi, further destruction of Jackson's commercial enterprises and transportation facilities was targeted. The Federals returned to Jackson briefly in early July 1864 on a raid made by Maj. Gen. Henry Slocum's Vicksburg troops. The destruction wrought by the Yanks on their first three occupations of Jackson resulted in it being called "Chimneyville."

Points of Interest

Despite three Federal torchings of Jackson, several significant buildings survived the war. The old State Capitol now houses the Mississippi State Historical Museum, including its Civil War exhibits. The Governor's Mansion, used as a headquarters by Sherman, and the City Hall escaped the flames. So did several churches; the Oaks House, now a museum, used by Sherman as a headquarters in 1863; and the Manship House, which was on the Confederate line of earthworks. MS18 was the Raymond Road, where Sherman first pushed through the forces defending Jackson. Battlefield Park on Lynch Street south of center city has some remaining Union entrenchments dating to Sherman's July 1863 siege of Jackson.

Information on Jackson's attractions and historic accommodations is available from Metro Jackson Convention and Visitors' Bureau, P.O. Box 1450, Jackson, MS 39215; 800-354-7695. Proceed west on I-20 to exit 27, Bolton and go south across the railroad tracks to Champion Hill Road.

DRIVING TOUR—*Proceed to Champion Hill*
READING—*1863: Vicksburg campaign: Champion Hill;*
(chronological)—1863: After Vicksburg campaign: Hoover's Gap–Liberty Gap,
Tennessee; 1864: Meridian campaign: Okolona

Champion Hill

Near Edwards' Station (now Edwards), General Pemberton—who, but for his battle-impatient subordinates, might have remained posted behind the Big Black ready to counterattack Grant's column should he fail to cross the river—contemplated the order from Johnston. The directive countermanded the personal goal he and Jefferson Davis shared, the unconditional defense of Vicksburg and Port Hudson. He held a council of war, and although some of his subordinates opted to join Johnston, Pemberton decided not to make the rendezvous, and instead adopted the plan advocated by his two senior division commanders. On May 15 the Confederate army marched from Edwards' Station via the Raymond Road. They would then turn south and attack Union reinforcements traveling the Port Gibson Road as they marched east from Grand Gulf. But, on the morning of May 16 when in contact with Grant's troops, a second more urgent order from Johnston caused Pemberton to head northwest, into the gap separating McClernand's and McPherson's corps as they marched west.

The Battle of Champion Hill began. The Alabama Brigade under Brig. Gen. Stephen D. Lee took a defensive stance on Champion Hill as Pemberton's columns reversed direction. Federal Brig. Gen. Alvin Hovey's XIII (McClernand's) Corps division and Maj. Gen. John A. Logan's XVII (McPherson's) Corps division assailed the Rebels and broke the Confederate units on either side of Lee. A slashing counterattack at one-thirty P.M. by Bowen's division drove the Federals from the hill. Particularly hard hitters were soldiers in Col. Francis Cockrell's Missouri Brigade, which would fight with reckless abandon in many western campaigns.

Grant, personally directing the battle, was unshaken by the turnaround. He sent more infantry to the hill and amassed an artillery force to enfilade the Confederates. Pemberton called up Maj. Gen. William W. Loring's force from the southeast, but Loring, facing the bulk of McClernand's corps, delayed his redeployment until it was too late to follow up on Bowen's advance. Pemberton's troops abandoned the fight retreating toward Vicksburg. Only Loring's division, covering the Confederate retreat, rendezvoused with Johnston, several days after it was cut off from Pemberton's army.

Points of Interest

A Guide to the Campaign & Siege of Vicksburg is particularly useful for touring Champion Hill and the Big Black River sites and *Champion Hill: A Battlefield Guide* gives details of that site. Both are available at Vicksburg National Military Park and in local bookstores. Driving west on Champion Hill Road, then taking one of several roads south to Raymond Road leads through the battlefield. The Coker House on Raymond Road (MS467) stood during the battle, and across the highway from and one-third mile west of the house is a monument marking where Confederate Brig. Gen. Lloyd Tilghman was killed in the battle. Travel west on the Raymond Road (MS467) to Edwards and then take US80 or I-20 exit 11 to Big Black River.

⸺⸻⸺

DRIVING TOUR and READING—Proceed to Big Black River

⸺⸻⸺

Big Black River

Grant now headed his three corps toward Vicksburg. What for the Confederates was an embarrassing rear-guard action on May 17 at Big Black Bridge, along the Jackson Road, did little to slow down the Federal advance. On May 18, Grant arrived near the nine-mile perimeter of Rebel fortifications on the hills and hollows east of Vicksburg. The following day he established contact with Union gunboats, which had ascended the Yazoo River. Sherman and Grant sighted the squadron from the Walnut Hills, near the site of Sherman's unsuccessful attack the previous December. Sherman, full of praise for his friend and commander, admitted the error of his doubts in the wisdom of Grant's daring plan to march south, then cross the Mississippi River, and invest Vicksburg from the east.

Points of Interest

The Big Black River battle was fought in the area just east of where what was then the Jackson Road, now called Old Highway 80 (US80), crosses the river. Retreating across an improvised bridge at the present-day railroad bridge, the Confederates burned the steamer *Dot* and the railroad bridge during their retreat. Federal engineers quickly bridged the Big Black and the Federal march toward Vicksburg continued.

DRIVING TOUR—*Proceed to Vicksburg National Military Park*
READING—*Vicksburg Battles*

VICKSBURG BATTLES

May 19 Assault

On the afternoon of May 19, Grant scheduled an assault on the left flank of the Confederate nine-mile defense line. Pemberton, though heavily criticized for his defeats, determined to hold the city. A council of war with his top subordinates bolstered his resolve and the addition of 10,000 troops, who had remained in and around Vicksburg while their comrades had been mauled at Champion Hill and Big Black Bridge, boosted morale in the ranks. It was these troops under Maj. Gens. Martin L. Smith and John H. Forney that now manned the left flank of the defense line. And the sight of these forces in the streets of Vicksburg gave hope to the nervous citizens.

Grant's May 19 offensive centered on Stockade Redan, but only the 13th U.S. Infantry of Col. Giles Smith's brigade gained the ditch fronting the Confederate works. As darkness approached, the action died down. Grant, realizing that Pemberton had a strong defensive position and that proud Vicksburg defenders had regained their will to fight, ordered his army to prepare for an all-out assault. Soldiers established advance gun emplacements and began to dig into a series of ridges just within several hundred yards of the Confederate defenses. Roads were improved to the Yazoo River supply depots. The work continued around the clock. At one point Grant was awakened and watched the house in which he had been sleeping being torn apart to make a bridge.

May 22 Assault

The soldiers of the Army of the Tennessee were confident that a new assault on the works would bring success. Grant's second assault was scheduled for May 22, three days after the May 19 attack. It was to be a synchronized attack along a three-mile front designed to freeze the Confederates in their positions. Early in the morning, Porter's gunboats appeared south of the city and commenced a steady bombardment, augmenting the Federal artillery brought up on the land side. At ten A.M., the guns fell silent and the infantry attack began.

Though individual acts of bravery, such as those of future Medal of Honor recipient Cpl. Thomas H. Higgins of the 99th Illinois, and members of the "Forlorn Hope," were common, the formidable Confederate positions were penetrated only at one point by the Federals. South of the railroad, units of McClernand's corps achieved a breakthrough at the Railroad Redoubt, but a lack of ready reserves made the position tenuous. Grant, eventually encouraged by McClernand's penetration, had the faltering attack in the afternoon renewed on all fronts. Pemberton rushed Waul's Texas Legion, held in reserve, to close the breach pounded in the Rebel line at Railroad Redoubt. Union Brig. Gen. Michael Lawler's brigade in face of the Texans' slashing counterattack was unable to hold on to its gains. No other successes were reported elsewhere along the front and Grant called off the attack.

Vicksburg Siege

The staggering losses of the Federals, with casualties of more than 3,100 and running more than six times those of the Rebels, and the solid defense displayed by the Southerners, prompted Grant on May 25 to begin siege operations. Besides controlling all land access to Vicksburg, Porter's squadron south of the city and his gunboats above Vicksburg sealed the Mississippi River approaches. Federal forces at Milliken's Bend and Young's Point watched the Louisiana side of the river. Thus began one of the longest sieges of a city in our nation's history.

Not content to simply starve out his foe, Grant ordered daily bombardments of Vicksburg. Thirteen saps that approached the Confederate works were dug. Pemberton's force needed to conserve ammunition, so Federal sappers and miners—those responsible for the trenching—worked in relative safety. As the Yanks inched closer to the Confederate lines, the Rebels rolled shells with their fuses lit down into the trenches. Many were thrown back. The Federals also used a weapon rarely before used—a dartlike hand grenade that detonated on impact.

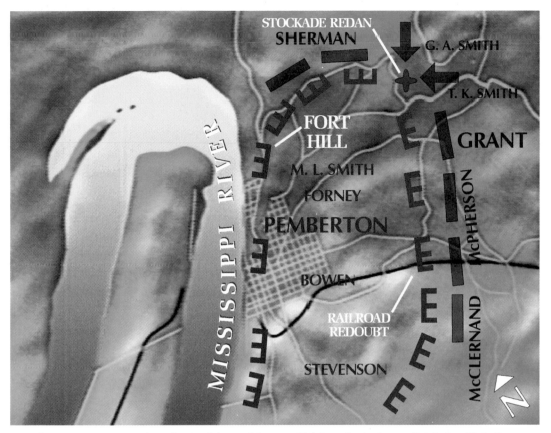

The May 22, 1863, attack on the Confederate defenses at Vicksburg by the forces of Maj. Gen. U. S. Grant focused on a three-and-one-half-mile front centering on strongpoints known as Stockade Redan, 2nd Texas Lunette, and Railroad Redoubt. Maj. Gen. Frank Blair's XV Corps division spearheaded the Stockade Redan attack, supported by other attacks all along the line during the day. No significant gains were made by the Federals and siege operations were soon begun by the North.

On May 25, a truce was called for by Pemberton and eventually agreed to by Grant, thus enabling the Federal dead and few surviving wounded, left on the field since May 22, to be attended to. It also gave troops who were related or knew each other before the war a chance to meet without hostilities. Men from opposing Missouri regiments, and others, exchanged gifts and conversed, usually good-naturedly, during the brief truce. By nightfall the grim work was completed and the time for camaraderie was over. The soldiers returned to their lines to face each other as enemies again.

As the siege continued, Federal troops received visitors from home. On the other side of the lines, there was no such opportunity. Life for the civilians of Vicksburg was grim.

Civilian casualties from the bombardment and fighting were light, but food became increasingly scarce, made worse because there were neither price controls nor rationing and diseases mounted as the siege continued. The twenty-four-hour shellings, interrupted for only three brief periods each day when the artillerists ate, forced many residents to live in caves dug into the Vicksburg bluffs. Despite the privations, many normal activities continued, including the publication of one newspaper.

Outside the works, reporters had surrounded Grant since the beginning of the Vicksburg siege, and while praise was abundant, jealousy and intrigue surfaced. Old animosities divided the senior officers. Senior corps commander McClernand, politically ambitious and feeling slighted, used the press to make public a self-congratulatory address to his XIII Corps, assuming for them much of the credit of the success of the campaign and for their valor in the May 22 Vicksburg assault while casting aspersion on Sherman and McPherson and their corps. Grant was unaware of this address and had not approved its publication as called for by army regulations. Consequently, when this was called to his attention, Grant relieved McClernand on June 18. He was sent back to Illinois and never held a major command again during the war. Maj. Gen. Edward O. C. Ord was named to head the XIII Corps.

The eyes of the Confederacy were now on Gen. Joseph E. Johnston, headquartered in and around Canton, and the army he was amassing from all points in the South east of the Mississippi except Virginia. The morale of the army and civilians in Vicksburg was sustained by the belief that Johnston's army would save them. Grant was concerned that Johnston would attack his force from the rear, either separately or in conjunction with a breakout attempt by Pemberton. Grant called in reinforcements from other theaters to support his army, and on June 22 constituted a seven-division force under Sherman to guard the Big Black River approaches. He refused to send 10,000 reinforcements to Banks, who had commenced his siege of Port Hudson (see **Port Hudson, Louisiana**). Despite urgent telegrams to do something from Secretary of War James Seddon in Richmond, Johnston worried but did not march until it was too late. The only thing he succeeded in destroying was his credibility. A Mobile, Alabama, newspaper suggested Johnston was "fighting Grant daily by giving him a terrible letting alone."

The June 7 attack at Milliken's Bend, Louisiana (see **Vicksburg Area, Louisiana**) and other skirmishes signaled, along with the advent of the "sickly season," the need to force an early conclusion to the Vicksburg siege. Grant made one final attempt to break the stalemate. Soldiers experienced as coal and lead miners were turned to at the head of Logan's approach near the Shirley House. Within two days a forty-five-foot gallery (tunnel) was extending under the 3rd Louisiana Redan. On June 25, more than a ton of gunpowder was exploded in the mine, forming a crater beneath the Rebel position. The Confederates had heard the tunneling and the position was evacuated except for a handful of volunteers working on a counter mine. The 45th Illinois charged into the crater. Taking heavy casualties, the Federals held their ground for a day, then withdrew. Another mine exploded on July 1 and did more damage to the Rebel works, but the Yanks were discouraged by the fate of those involved in the earlier fight, and no assault was attempted. Sharpshooting and artillery shelling did more than these explosions to inflict damage and casualties and further weaken Southern morale.

On July 1, Johnston began a cautious move toward Vicksburg with 30,000 soldiers. Grant also planned a July 6 assault on the city and its defenders, but it was not to be. Seeing an escape attempt as the only realistic chance to save his army, Pemberton polled his four division commanders and learned, to his distress, that privation, disease, and exhaustion would keep a majority of his soldiers from making the effort to break through the Yanks' investing works. Hoping that the Fourth of July spirit would make the Federal commander more benevolent, Pemberton sent his gallant division commander, James S. Bowen, through the lines under a flag of truce on July 3. Bowen, suffering from what proved to be fatal dysentery, volunteered to communicate with Grant, a former St. Louis neighbor. A meeting was arranged between Grant and Pemberton for later in the day. An initial frigid exchange resulted in a retreat from his demand for Pemberton's unconditional surrender.

Grant's decision to parole the 29,500 Confederate prisoners was prudent and practical. His feeling was that many of the defenders, who signed oaths not to fight until exchanged, would desert and not return to the ranks after the arduous ordeal of Vicksburg. The paroles freed Grant of the problems experienced at Fort Donelson in processing the 13,000 Rebels that had been surrendered there unconditionally, and freed more than 75,000 soldiers of his army to conduct further operations against other Confederate commands.

On July 4, 1863, the Confederate defenders marched out of Vicksburg and stacked arms. The Federal army entered. The bluecoats generally maintained an atmosphere of silent respect for their defeated foes. "No word of exultation was uttered to irritate the feelings of the prisoners," wrote Confederate Sgt. Willie Tunnard of the 3rd Louisiana, "on the

In this Harper's Weekly *woodcut, Maj. Gen. Ulysses S. Grant and Lt. Gen. John C. Pemberton converse freely like subordinates discussing sensitive issues related to the surrender of Vicksburg on July 3, 1863. Neither general knew at the time that a great battle was being fought that day at Gettysburg, Pennsylvania.*

contrary, every sentinel who came upon post brought haversacks filled with provisions, which he would give some famished Southerner with the remark, 'Here, Reb, I know you are starved nearly to death.' "

Points of Interest

Vicksburg National Military Park—One of the nation's largest and most monumented national military parks, Vicksburg highlights a number of interesting sites, several of which are described in **Naval Operations at Vicksburg**. At the visitor center, near the park's main entrance at exit 4B from I-20, there is an audiovisual program, a bookstore, and exhibits on the Vicksburg campaigns and siege. Nearby is a section of reconstructed earthworks and an artillery exhibit. A park brochure, detailing the park's 16-mile auto or bicycle tour, is available at the visitor's center. Licensed guided tours are available.

In addition to Fort Hill, South Fort, and the USS *Cairo* Museum, other popular stops along the monument and cannon-studded tour route are Railroad Redoubt; Shirley House, near the place where the two mine explosions occurred; an equestrian statue of Grant at his headquarters site; Stockade Redan; and the Vicksburg surrender site. VICKSBURG NATIONAL MILITARY PARK, Vicksburg, MS 39181; 601-636-0583.

Adjacent to the USS *Cairo* Museum is the Vicksburg National Cemetery. The cemetery was established in 1866 and more than 16,900 Federal soldiers are buried there.

There are numerous other restored and preserved Civil War landmarks in Vicksburg. Many homes were restored or retain their Civil War character. There are bed-and-breakfast accommodations in Vicksburg. The Balfour House, 1002 Crawford Street, was Maj.

Gen. James B. McPherson's headquarters. Earlier, a Christmas Eve 1862 ball under way at the house was interrupted by news that steamboats with Sherman's 32,000-man expedition were passing Lake Providence, Louisiana, en route to attack Vicksburg. Sherman's force ultimately steamed up the Yazoo River to land near Chickasaw Bayou and approach Vicksburg from the north, but were turned back (see **Chickasaw Bayou**). Pemberton's headquarters was down the block at 1018 Crawford Street.

Of particular interest is the Old Warren County Court House, which stood tall on a hill above the city and defied Federal bombardment. The courthouse, on Court Square, sustaining only minor damage, was used as a signal station and hospital. It now houses the Old Court House

The Illinois Memorial is the largest monument at Vicksburg National Military Park and was modeled after the Pantheon in Rome. The memorial temple is inscribed with the names of 36,325 Illinois soldiers who served at Vicksburg.

The Vicksburg courthouse was a visible landmark in the "Hill City" during the Civil War. Miraculously, it escaped serious damage, despite the pounding Vicksburg took from Federal army and navy shelling during the war. The courthouse now is home to the Old Court House Museum.

Museum, which has an outstanding collection of Civil War memorabilia, many focusing on the plight of Vicksburg civilians during the siege. For more information, call OLD COURT HOUSE MUSEUM—Eva W. Davis Memorial at 601-636-0741.

From Vicksburg, head east on I-20 through Jackson to Newton.

DRIVING TOUR—*Proceed to Newton (Newton Station)*
READING *(chronological)—1863: Jackson, Mississippi, or Helena, Arkansas*

GRIERSON'S RAID

In April 1863, while Lt. Gen. John Pemberton contemplated what to do about Steele's column that had landed at Greenville and was now wreaking havoc on the Deer Creek plantations, the second of General Grant's diversions began. This was a daring cavalry raid that turned out to far exceed expectations. Its style was one the likes of which J.E.B. Stuart or James Harrison Wilson would have been proud.

Col. Benjamin Grierson of Illinois was an unlikely hero on horseback. The Pennsylvania-born music teacher, kicked in the face by a horse as a youth, had been coaxed back into the saddle by the war. Starting south from La Grange, Tennessee, Grierson led 1,700 hell-for-leather cavalrymen from Maj. Gen. Stephen Hurlbut's West Tennessee command on a daring expedition to cut Mississippi railroad lines.

Grierson's raid started early on April 17, just hours after Admiral Porter's ironclads ran the Vicksburg batteries. He headed southeast, to Ripley, and down the Pontotoc Ridge, the watershed separating the drainages of the Pearl and Tombigbee rivers, where Confederate general Earl Van Dorn was once based. Unfortunately for the Rebels, Van Dorn and Forrest were far away in Middle Tennessee, and the Confederate leaders whose mission was to cope with Grierson were an unimaginative lot. Grierson foiled their efforts to mount a close pursuit. He sent one third of his force back toward La Grange, covering tracks and drawing off pursuit. A detachment of scouts, risking the consequences of being considered spies if captured, donned gray uniforms and rode east to assess resistance and cut telegraph lines.

On April 24, he reached one of his targets, the Southern Railroad at Newton Station. Grierson, following the destruction of rolling stock, track, and supplies, decided not to return the way he had come. He headed southwest to rendezvous with Grant's army which he expected to cross the Mississippi River. At Union Church he encountered Confederates and changed his route. Grierson then turned his column toward Baton Rouge, a Union enclave. Along the way he made stops to torch rail yards and his weary troopers changed from fire starters to fire fighters as they aided the townspeople in preventing the fires from spreading to homes and businesses. Finally, on May 2, after a bitter fight at Wall's Bridge, Grierson's men tumbled from their saddles for a well-deserved rest, followed by a hero's welcome in Baton Rouge (see **Baton Rouge, Louisiana**). Grierson, with a small number of casualties, had ridden the length of Mississippi, severed two trunk rail lines, and so confused General Pember-

Brig. Gen. Benjamin H. Grierson, USA, enlisted as a private at the beginning of the war and quickly proved his ability as a cavalry commander. After the war he battled hostile Indians in the West and was one of the few nonprofessional soldiers from the Civil War to achieve the rank of brigadier general in the regular army. Grant said Grierson's raid had "taken the heart out of Mississippi."

ton that he gave little thought to Grant's march south and instead scattered his strategic reserve infantry division and exhausted his cavalry in pursuit of Grierson's raiders.

Points of Interest

Newton is on US80, 61 miles west of Jackson at MS15 and just off I-20. This station on the main east-west railroad artery through Mississippi was a major target of Grierson's raid. Movie fans familiar with John Ford's 1958 *The Horse Soldiers*, starring John Wayne, will recall Grierson's Raid and the descent on Newton. The Doolittle CSA Cemetery north of Newton is a family cemetery that also contains the graves of about 100 Confederate soldiers.

DRIVING TOUR—*Proceed to Meridian*
READING—*Snyder's Bluff 1863 assault: Chickasaw Bayou*

MERIDIAN CAMPAIGN

Maj. Gen. William T. Sherman, returning from a Christmas furlough in Ohio, was concerned about increasing Confederate activities in Mississippi, despite the Federal presence there since the surrender of Vicksburg in July 1863 and the follow-up expeditions to Jackson, Yazoo City, and Canton. Sherman requested and received authority to outfit an expedition to destroy Confederate-held railroads in the state and cut a swath of destruction east to Meridian and perhaps beyond. On February 3, Sherman and his 20,000-man force started east over the hard-fought route taken during the victorious drive on Vicksburg. At the same time, a powerful cavalry column prepared to leave Memphis under Brig. Gen. William Sooy Smith, the recently appointed head of Department of the Tennessee horsemen.

Sherman's columns encountered only light resistance as they pushed through Jackson. Confederate forces in the area, under Lt. Gen. Leonidas Polk, retreated to and beyond Meridian in the face of the advance. The Federals arrived in Meridian on February 14. As his men ripped up the railroads, Sherman waited for word of Smith's approach. He had expected the cavalry to arrive there ahead of his two corps.

He waited in vain. Smith was stymied by Nathan Bedford Forrest's cavalry and was en route back to Tennessee by the fourth week in February (see **Okolona**). Sherman, unwilling to venture farther without his cavalry, headed back to Vicksburg by a different route, continuing the destruction to the state's economy that became the hallmark of his subsequent "March to the Sea" and march through South Carolina. The stunned citizens experienced the ugly concept of total warfare that Sherman and other Federal commanders used to destroy the South's logistical base and the Southern people's will to continue the fight. Though the railroads were partially rebuilt as Polk returned to the region, the effects of Sherman's Meridian campaign were lasting. Sherman was also able to reduce the number of troops holding the Mississippi enclaves and redeploy the XVI and XVII corps elsewhere.

Points of Interest

There is a historical marker on US80 east of Meridian describing the campaign. Merrehope, 905 Martin Luther King Jr. Drive, is one of four homes that dates to February 1864 when the Federals raided Meridian.

***

DRIVING TOUR—*Proceed to Biloxi–Ship Island*
READING *(chronological)—Kilpatrick's raid: Richmond Area, Virginia*

***

BILOXI–SHIP ISLAND

The first time in the war that Federal sailors and soldiers stepped on Mississippi soil was on Ship Island, in the Gulf of Mexico. The Confederates resumed work on the Third System fort on the island, but in September 1861 had withdrawn. Capitalizing on the opportunity, the U.S. Navy occupied the island and the army took steps to push construction of the masonry work that was called Fort Massachusetts. The island served as an army and navy base for the Federal operations that in the spring of 1862 led to the capture of New Orleans (see **New Orleans, Louisiana**).

🛏 🚢 🎣 ⊞ ❷ ⊼ ⊪ ⚓ ⚕ **$$$**

Points of Interest

Fort Massachusetts and Ship Island are a unit of Gulf Islands National Seashore. The Ship Island Excursion Ferry provides daily service to the island and fort, which is in excellent condition considering what at times is a hostile environment.

The Biloxi lighthouse, West Beach Boulevard, stood during the Civil War, as did the Church of the Redeemer, where Jefferson Davis worshiped. The lighthouse was painted black following the April 1865 assassination of President Lincoln.

Also near Biloxi on US90 is Beauvoir, a Gulf-front mansion which was the last home of Jefferson Davis. The house and gardens have been restored and the Confederate Museum is in the former Old Veterans' hospital. A nearby Confederate cemetery contains the Tomb of the Unknown Soldier of the Confederate States of America.

DRIVING TOUR—*Proceed to Mobile, Alabama, or New Orleans, Louisiana*
READING—*New Orleans campaign: New Orleans, Louisiana;*
(chronological)—1861: Rich Mountain–Laurel Hill, West Virginia

---

Missouri

Missouri was a battleground from the earliest beginnings of the struggle over slavery. A political football upon its application for admission to the Union, Missouri entered as a slave state but its settlers were diverse groups, not just Southern planters and farmers bringing slaves to reap crops from rich soil of the land. River trading from the earliest settlement of Missouri brought French trappers and traders, a rugged independent breed. Later a large influx of German immigrants following the failure of the 1848 revolution in the "Fatherland" settled in and around St. Louis. These cultures had little use or sympathy for slavery and way of life of the gentleman farmer. The differences led to sectional clashes before the war, and resulted in Missouri having the largest number of incidents of Civil War bushwhacking and guerrilla warfare of any state.

Politically the state remained divided during the war, but it was under Union control. Although Governor Claiborne Fox Jackson at the outbreak of war was sympathetic to the secession movement and Missouri was admitted to the Confederacy as the twelfth state, in the autumn of 1861 on the vote of a rump legislature meeting at Neosho, early Federal strongarm efforts ensured that the state remained in the Union. Action by Capt. Nathaniel Lyon to garrison key cities and subdue secessionist militia further helped tighten the Unionist grip on the most populous sections of the state. Then in July 1861, Lincoln sent Maj. Gen. John C. Frémont, the "Pathfinder," to Missouri to take charge of the politically sensitive area. Frémont, who had explored the Rocky Mountain West, opening it for settlement, and had battled the Mexicans in California, with the result that it was ceded to the United States in 1848, was a military hero with political ambitions. He, in 1856, had lost the bid to become the first Republican president, an honor that Lincoln attained four years later. Although he approached his task with much energy, Frémont's political plans for Union Missouri clashed with good military judgment. His August 30, 1861,

Maj. Gen. John C. Frémont, USA, was a heroic western explorer and loyal Union man. However, in his first command in Missouri he misdirected the Federal effort by fortifying St. Louis while his field armies ranged far from the city ill equipped to battle the Confederates.

unauthorized emancipation proclamation declaring martial law in Missouri and confiscating property of those who took up arms against the United States, and freeing their slaves angered Washington and Lincoln, who rescinded the order and on November 2 removed Frémont from his post. Perhaps Frémont's greatest Civil War accomplishment was in giving Ulysses S. Grant his first significant independent command.

Missouri sent 110,000 men to serve the North and another 40,000 to Southern armies. Many who did not join the organized forces continued to wage a partisan war with or against their neighbors at home. Of the more than 1,160 recorded clashes of arms, a number exceeded only in Virginia and Tennessee, the majority were raids and partisan skirmishes. The Rebels attempted to invade the state and secure it for the Confederacy on several occasions but none of their efforts was successful. Their best opportunity came early in the war, but the Federal victory at Pea Ridge, just below the Arkansas state line, turned back that effort (see **Pea Ridge, Arkansas**). The Federals maintained a large military presence in Missouri throughout the war to guard the waterways and to ensure that the Confederates would not gain control of it through military campaigns or guerrilla warfare.

A tour of Missouri can take from three to four days because there are sites throughout the state. Since so many other significant actions occurred in border areas with states surrounding Missouri, a Missouri-based tour can also include sites of the campaigns touching Kansas, Oklahoma, Arkansas, Kentucky, and Tennessee.

NEW MADRID

When Federal successes in Kentucky and Tennessee compelled the Confederates to abandon the Mississippi River bastion at Columbus, Kentucky, on March 2, 1862, the big guns and many troops formerly posted there were sent to the next stronghold downriver. Island Number 10, in an S-shaped bend in the Mississippi River, was supported by forts and batteries on both sides of the river in Tennessee and Missouri, at Kentucky's southwestern border (see **Island Number 10, Tennessee**). On the Missouri shore, the Confederates occupied earthworks at New Madrid. This was the first objective of Brig. Gen. John Pope's 18,000-man spring expedition, which set out on March 3 from Commerce, Missouri, to Island Number 10 and Tiptonville, Tennessee. During the advance a sortie by horsemen under M. Jeff Thompson, the "Swamp Fox of the Confederacy," was turned back. Pope, after a difficult march through swamps that required the corduroying of roads to bring up cannons and supplies, began a siege of New Madrid.

On March 13, the Confederates hammered with artillery the investing Union lines to screen their plan to give up New Madrid. That night, under cover of a furious thunderstorm they evacuated the town, sending their troops and gunboats to Island Number 10, and Tiptonville. The next day Pope's Federals marched into the vacated earthworks, captured guns and supplies, and planned the next phase of the operation aimed at Island Number 10.

Points of Interest

New Madrid (exit 44 on I-55) has historical markers describing the investment and the siege (March 3–14, 1862). There is an excellent antebellum house in the town, the Hunter-Dawson State Historic Site, with ties to the Civil War action. Call 314-748-5340 for information on hours and admission. The New Madrid Historical Museum, 314-748-5944, has Civil War exhibits. Other downtown buildings also predate the Civil War. A driving tour brochure is available from the New Madrid Chamber of Commerce, 560 Mott Street, New Madrid, MO 63869; 314-748-5300.

DRIVING TOUR—*Proceed to Belmont*
READING—*Island Number 10, Tennessee*

BELMONT

Ulysses S. Grant's first major combat action in the Civil War was at Belmont, Missouri, on November 7, 1861. Grant was under orders to make a demonstration against Columbus, Kentucky, a strategic Confederate position on the Mississippi, to prevent reinforcements being sent to southeast Missouri (see **Columbus, Kentucky**). Grant had 3,500 men on transports steaming south from Cairo, Illinois, on November 6. He was accompanied by two timberclad gunboats. The next day Grant learned of Confederate reinforcements being sent to Missouri and planned an early-morning attack on the Rebel camp at Belmont, across the river from Columbus. Grant landed upriver out of the range of Columbus' guns and, after a minor skirmish, overran the force of about 2,500 under Brig. Gen. Gideon Pillow.

Ulysses S. Grant was appointed brigadier general in the summer of 1861 after successfully organizing and training a number of raw recruits in southern Illinois. In his first field combat assignment at Belmont, Missouri, on November 7, 1861, his forces were cut off, but he did not panic and managed to lead them to safety. The experience taught him lessons which he later used in a series of successful operations.

After the initial Federal success, discipline broke down among the green Federal troops and they began to loot the camp. Grant took steps to bring the force under control again, as Confederate reinforcements from Columbus crossed the river on steamboats and attempted to cut the troops off from their transports. Grant engineered a withdrawal, with the help of fire from the two timberclads; among the last to board was Grant himself. Casualties amounted to about 20 percent of each force, and though it was not really a victory, Grant's coolness and resolve in handling his forces in the eight-hour battle were characteristics, along with the lessons learned from the Battle of Belmont, that stood him in good stead throughout the war.

Points of Interest

The site of the Battle of Belmont, as has often been reported in guidebooks, is not a lost battlefield, but is accessible by secondary roads leading to Belmont Landing, the site of Camp Johnston. There is an interpretive marker at the site of Camp Johnston. There are interpretive markers and exhibits at Columbus-Belmont State Park in Kentucky describing the battle and the role of the Columbus guns and garrison in the fight (see **Columbus, Kentucky**).

DRIVING TOUR—*Proceed to Cape Girardeau*
READING—*Fort Henry, Tennessee*

CAPE GIRARDEAU

The Federals in 1861 commenced construction of four forts at this key Mississippi port town between St. Louis and Cairo, Illinois. On April 26, 1863, Brig. Gen. John S. Marmaduke's division of Confederate horse soldiers on a raid deep into Missouri attacked Cape Girardeau but were repulsed by the Federals manning the forts. Marmaduke withdrew to Jackson, Missouri, after the battle.

Points of Interest

Historical Markers in Cape Girardeau (exit 93 on I-55) indicate the sites of the four Federal forts protecting the city. Fort D, on the northeast corner of Locust and Fort streets, was a key site during the April 26, 1863, attack by Marmaduke's Confederates.

DRIVING TOUR—*Proceed to Fort Davidson (Pilot Knob)*
READING—*Brashear City: Bayou Country, Louisiana*

STERLING PRICE'S 1864 MISSOURI RAID

In the autumn of 1864, Confederate Trans-Mississippi Department commander Gen. Edmund Kirby Smith ordered Maj. Gen. Sterling Price to undertake a large-scale raid deep into Missouri. Similar in size and scope to Lt. Gen. Jubal Early's summer raid on Washington, D.C. (see **Monocacy, Maryland**), though intended to cover more ground, Price's raid had similar objectives—raiding Federal depots to acquire much-needed supplies for the footsore Confederate armies, diverting troops intending to join the Federal commands challenging Hood in Georgia and Lee in Virginia, and reaping whatever

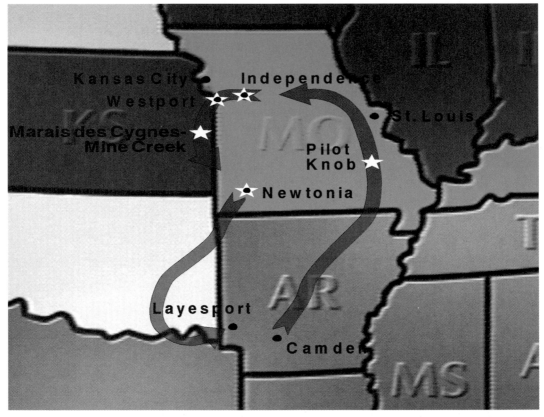

Maj. Gen. Sterling Price's last attempt to reclaim his home state of Missouri for the Confederacy in the autumn of 1864 took his force from Arkansas through three states and the Indian Territory until the demoralized survivors returned to Arkansas in December. Bypassing a strong Federal garrison at St. Louis after failing to capture Fort Davidson (Pilot Knob), Price was dogged by three Union forces which he battled at Independence and Westport, Missouri. During his withdrawal from the state, his rear guard fought off pursuit at Marais des Cygnes and Mine Creek in Kansas and Newtonia in Missouri.

political damage might come to Lincoln's November reelection by threatening such places as, in Price's case, St. Louis and the Missouri capital, Jefferson City.

Price had one more mission Early did not consider: gaining new recruits for the Southern armies. Early clearly had no chance of finding new Confederate recruits in war-torn Virginia and western Maryland; Price had little chance of finding any Southern-leaning recruit who wasn't already in the ranks or content with bushwhacking in his own home area. Some green recruits were picked up along the way, but they were ill equipped and added little to offset an increasing number of Union soldiers being redeployed to oppose and then crush the expedition.

Maj. Gen. Sterling Price, CSA, was a prominent political leader in Missouri when the war broke out. Although he first opposed the state's secession, the seizing of state facilities in St. Louis by Francis P. Blair, Jr., and Nathaniel Lyon outraged him and he offered his services to the Confederacy.

Price started out from Princeton, Arkansas, on August 29 and along the way built up his army by calling upon the cavalry divisions of Maj. Gen. John S. Fagan, Brig. Gen. Joseph O. Shelby, and Brig. Gen. John S. Marmaduke. The combined force of more than 12,000 rode north into Missouri on September 19 and toward their first objective, Fort Davidson near Pilot Knob.

Fort Davidson

Fort Davidson was a stout earthen Federal fort guarding the terminus of the Ironton Railroad, which linked that town and Pilot Knob with St. Louis, eighty miles to the north. Aware that Price was on the move, Missouri Department commander Maj. Gen. William S. Rosecrans received permission from Washington to order a force "The 10,000 Israelites" under Maj. Gen. Andrew J. Smith, then at Cairo, Illinois, en route to reinforce Sherman in Georgia, to disembark at St. Louis to augment Federal garrisons there. At the same time, Brig. Gen. Thomas Ewing, author of General Order No. 11 which made him a wanted man among Missouri Confederates, was en route to Fort Davidson with reinforcements.

The Confederates approached Fort Davidson on the night of September 26. Ewing refused two Rebel demands for surrender. The next day, a six-hour assault on the fort cost the Confederates 1,500 casualties; the Federals lost 184 of their 1,200-man garrison. As the Confederates prepared to assault the fort again that night, the Federals slipped away through a gap in the Confederate ranks. Confederate expectations of capturing the fort's supplies and cannons were frustrated by the Federals, who spiked the guns and lit a slow fuse to the powder magazine which detonated after their escape. Price had paid excessively in lives for Fort Davidson and provided the Federals invaluable time to concentrate forces at St. Louis to frustrate Price's plan to capture the city.

Points of Interest

Fort Davidson State Historic Site—This park is located on MO21 at Pilot Knob. Remains of the Federal earthwork and historical markers can be seen in the park. Camping is available at nearby Taum Sauk and Elephant Rocks state parks. FORT DAVIDSON STATE HISTORIC SITE, P.O. Box 509, Pilot Knob, MO 63663; 573-546-3454.

🏵 ♿ ❓ 🏛 P ⛱ 🚻 $

DRIVING TOUR—*Proceed to St. Louis*
READING—*Centralia Massacre*

St. Louis

Missouri's largest city during the Civil War was a Unionist stronghold. Frémont and subsequent Federal leaders made their headquarters there. Federal forces were posted at Jefferson Barracks and elsewhere in the city; they were summoned to participate in campaigns both in and beyond the state. James B. Eads rebuilt or built his ironclads and mortar boats for the Union army there—the USS *Benton, Carondelet,* and three of her six city series ironclads that were instrumental, in opening up the Mississippi after they were turned over first to the Federal army and subsequently the Union navy.

On May 10, 1861, Nathaniel Lyon, then commanding the U.S. Arsenal in St. Louis, descended on Camp Jackson, a state militia training camp at Lindell's Grove near St. Louis. The pro-secessionist militia was captured and while it was being marched to the arsenal for imprisonment, a riot ensued when fighting broke out between German militia guarding the prisoners and Southern sympathizers. In the ensuing "Battle of St. Louis" more than 28 people lost their lives. Lyon was assisted in his efforts by U.S. congressman and future Federal general Francis P. Blair, Jr. Lyon was promoted to brigadier general of volunteers shortly after the capture of Camp Jackson and the St. Louis riot.

During Maj. Gen. Sterling Price's 1864 Missouri Raid one of his objectives was the capture of St. Louis. The timely arrival of Union Maj. Gen. Andrew J. Smith and his "10,000 Israelites" bolstered the city's defenses and Price wisely decided to bypass St. Louis (see **Sterling Price's 1864 Missouri Raid**).

Points of Interest

A number of extant buildings in St. Louis are Civil War associated. The most important is the U.S. Arsenal, located at the southeast corner of Second and Arsenal. It is currently in use by the U.S. Air Force. The Old Court House at 11 Fourth Street is where the Dred Scott Case was heard, and is a key element of the Jefferson National Expansion Memorial, a unit of the National Park System. The unit's adjacent Museum of Western Expansion has exhibits focusing on the West's role in the sectional crisis and the Civil War. Camp Jackson was located on the present campus of St. Louis University. Historical markers on the campus describe the camp. Jefferson Barracks Historical Park, 10 miles south of downtown at exit 3 on I-255, has a museum in the restored powder magazine, a visitor center, and national cemetery next to the park. On MO30, 8 miles southwest of downtown St. Louis, in the St. Louis suburbs is the U. S. Grant National Historic Site, the home where Grant married Julia Dent and they lived on several occasions before the Civil War and where he planned to return after his presidency. Nearby on land owned by Anheuser-Busch is "Hardscrabble," the log cabin home built by U. S. Grant in the late 1850s. For information on the U. S. GRANT NATIONAL HISTORIC SITE, call 314-842-1867.

DRIVING TOUR—*Proceed to Centralia Massacre*
READING—*Boonville*

CENTRALIA MASSACRE

On September 27, 1864, concurrent with, but not part of Maj. Gen. Sterling Price's Missouri Raid, 30 guerrillas under William "Bloody Bill" Anderson, a former lieutenant of William C. Quantrill (see **Baxter Springs, Kansas,** in **The Northwest**) sacked the town of Centralia. They robbed a stagecoach and held up a passenger train—robbing passengers and killing 24 unarmed soldiers aboard who were going home on furlough. Later in the day, when three companies of Federal cavalry arrived near town, Anderson's men—now reinforced—ambushed them, killing 116. Anderson added revenge for his sister's accidental death a short time before while incarcerated under Order No. 11 to his general hate for Yankees. Among the ruthless gang was seventeen-year-old Jesse James. The Centralia Massacre, the Baxter Springs Massacre, the Sand Creek, Colorado, and Idaho's Bear River massacres, and the Fort Pillow and Poison Spring massacres, in the latter four of which racism was involved, and other similar actions clearly marred what was a war fought with bravery and gallantry on both sides.

Points of Interest

Centralia is located 10 miles north of Columbia on MO124. Historical markers detail the massacre.

———————————

DRIVING TOUR—*Proceed to Boonville*
READING—*Price's raid: Boonville*

———————————

BOONVILLE

On June 17, 1861, Federal troops under Brig. Gen. Nathaniel Lyon routed the Missouri State Guard under Col. John S. Marmaduke four miles east of the town. This resulted in Federal control of key Missouri River counties for vital months before the Confederates gained strength in the state. On September 13 and October 11, 1863, other skirmishes occurred here and following the second Brig. Gen. Jo Shelby's Confederates briefly occupied the town. On October 9, 1864, Maj. Gen. Sterling Price came this way with his cavalry force after bypassing the capital at Jefferson City, which was garrisoned, and skirmished with the Federals on October 9 and 10. With Maj. Gen. Alfred Pleasonton's Union cavalry bearing down on him from the east, Price decided to limit his activities in central Missouri to tearing up railroad track as he headed west up the Missouri River Valley to his next objective, Lexington.

Points of Interest

Boonville, 3 miles north of I-70 exit 101 on MO5, has markers describing the first battle of Boonville and rifle pits remaining from the 1863 skirmishes. Several buildings in the town, including the Vest Home and Thespian Hall, have Civil War association.

DRIVING TOUR—*Proceed to Glasgow*
READING *(chronological)*—*Carthage; Price's raid: Glasgow*

GLASGOW

As an element of Price's 1864 Raid, Brig. Gen. Joseph Shelby took his division to Glasgow on October 15. After shelling the town and the Federal garrison, the Confederates compelled the surrender of the small Union force and burned the city hall and much of the town.

Points of Interest

The city hall in Glasgow on MO87, 25 miles north of Boonville, was used as a Federal stronghold during the battle and was burned. The present city hall was constructed on the site of the 1864 structure. The Methodist church was a Civil War hospital.

DRIVING TOUR—*Proceed to Lexington*
READING—*Price's raid: Lexington*

LEXINGTON

Maj. Gen. Sterling Price, former Missouri governor, who suffered defeat during his 1864 Raid deep into the state and shared credit for the victory at Wilson's Creek on August 10, 1861, with Benjamin McCulloch, on the surge of that success marched north in late August to rid his state of Yankees (see **Wilson's Creek**). His effort focused on Lexington, an important town on the Missouri River forty-two miles east of Kansas City. Price picked up enthusiastic recruits along the way but needed Federal weapons to arm them. The town was held by 3,500 Yankees under Col. James A. Mulligan. On September 12–13, Price's vanguard appeared and drove in Mulligan's outposts. Ordered to hold Lexington at all costs, the Federals barricaded themselves behind earthen ramparts, armed with artillery. Both commanders waited for five days, Price for ammunition, Mulligan for reinforcements (which were driven away by a detachment of Price's force).

On September 18, Price surrounded the Federal position and cut off the Federals' water supply. Artillery bombardment continued the next day—the Confederates shelled the town as well. By September 20, the Federals were being hemmed in by the Confederates, who had tightened their siege lines. Early on September 20, Price's State Guard utilizing mobile-hemp breastworks inched their way to within short range of the Anderson House, a major Yankee stronghold. After several refusals, Mulligan gave in to the wishes of his fellow officers and surrendered at two P.M. Casualties in the long siege were light, but Price's force again dwindled to fewer than 7,000. He was soon compelled to abandon his foothold on the Missouri River and retreat into southwest Missouri as Union columns under Maj. Gen. John C. Frémont numbering more than 38,000 strong converged on Lexington.

On October 20, 1864, Price returned to Lexington with his three-division mounted force. Finally feeling threatened by superior numbers of Federal cavalry and infantry pressing him from the east, Price was hurrying his command west toward Kansas. That afternoon Shelby's division, in the lead, encountered a small Federal force east of Lexington. Though the Yankees were beaten back, the Confederates realized that they then had Union columns to the east and west of them. The Federals encountered at Lexington were United States volunteers and Kansas militia being organized by Department of Kansas commander Maj. Gen. Samuel R. Curtis. The 2,000 bluecoats were led by no-nonsense Army of the Border commander Maj. Gen. James G. Blunt.

Points of Interest

The Battle of Lexington State Historic Site, on MO13A, 10 miles north of I-70 exit 41, has interpretive markers and locates the ramparts used by the Federals. The nearby Anderson House on MO13 was a Federal hospital. BATTLE OF LEXINGTON STATE HISTORIC SITE, P.O. Box 6, Lexington, MO 64067; 816-259-4654.

🛶 ⟜ 🎏 ♿ ❓ 🏛 P 🪑 🚻 $

DRIVING TOUR—*Proceed to Kansas City*
READING *(chronological)—1861: Greenbrier River, West Virginia;*
Price's raid: Independence

INDEPENDENCE

Independence, east of Kansas City, saw a small action in which the Federals were victorious on August 11, 1862. However, the Confederates gained a victory on August 16 when an 800-man Federal contingent of cavalry and infantry under Maj. Emory S. Foster, which had attacked a Confederate camp at Lone Jack the previous day, was bested by a larger force of Rebels. The Federals retreated in good order to Lexington. These were two in a series of small battles in which the Federals drove scattered Confederate forces from the state and reestablished control in much of central and western Missouri. The smoke of gunfire again filled the air on October 22, 1864, as Price's army pressed toward Kansas City. Instead of turning south, Price was leading his columns toward an entrenched force from Kansas under General Blunt.

BYRAM'S FORD

General Blunt's Federal Big Blue River line was attacked by Jo Shelby's Confederate division on October 22. The Rebels probed the line at several fords, until Shelby discovered a weak point in the line at Byram's Ford. Exploiting this point caused the Federals to retreat, but their retrograde did not become a rout. Contesting ground stubbornly, Blunt's people were backed up to the Kansas state line south of Westport, where another line of entrenchments running east-west parallel to Brush Creek was thrown up. By the end of the day, the Confederates occupied the former Federal works on the Big Blue's west bank and Curtis was re-forming his line perpendicular to the Kansas border, setting the stage for the Battle of Westport.

Meantime, Maj. Gen. Alfred Pleasonton's Union force crossed the Little Blue east of Independence, defeated a Rebel brigade in James Fagan's command, and occupied Independence. Marmaduke's division then met Pleasonton about two miles west of Independence, hit the Federals hard, pressed them back, and held them at bay until the morning of October 23. Pleasonton's actions, however, frightened Price and his army, and influenced them, after they had crossed the Big Blue River, to send their wagon trains to Little Santa Fe on the Fort Scott road.

WESTPORT

On the morning of October 23, General Price formed a battle plan to defeat the Federal forces in detail, then take his army into Kansas for the return march south. Encouraged by Shelby to attack and first defeat Curtis, Price left Marmaduke's division to face Pleasonton while he attacked Curtis's force with Shelby's and Fagan's, and they assailed the Federals' Brush Creek line, south of Westport. They drove the militia back, but not for long. The militia, with twice the number of men as the Rebels, held their own and mounted a counterattack.

While this alone was not disastrous for the Confederates, Pleasonton assaulted Marmaduke at Byram's Ford, at eight A.M. Three hours later Marmaduke's men were mauled and they retreated toward Westport. Price was beginning to feel the pinch of the Federal vise. Only savage resistance by Shelby's cavalry in a rear-guard action prevented capture of Price's wagon train and much of his force at Westport, the largest battle in terms of the number engaged to be fought west of the Mississippi River. After narrowly escaping annihilation at Westport, Price began his retreat through Kansas, where pursuing Federals next challenged him at Marais des Cygnes (see **Marais des Cygnes–Mine Creek, Kansas** in **The Northwest**).

Points of Interest

The Battle of Byram's Ford was fought along the Big Blue River and the Battle of Westport was fought in what is now a heavily urbanized section of Kansas City. Critical portions of the Byram's Ford battlefield are preserved and interpreted in parklands administered by

Kansas City Parks and Recreation. There is a series of historical markers along a 32-mile self-guided automobile tour of battle areas from Fifty-first Street and Wornall Road and continuing south to Sixty-third Terrace. The Wornall Home, Sixty-third Terrace and Wornall Road, was used as a hospital by both sides and is operated by the Jackson County Historical Society. Take exit 75-A from I-435 south of downtown Kansas City and drive north to Sixty-third Terrace. Union Cemetery at 227 East Twenty-eighth Street Terrace and Forest Hill Cemetery, a stop on the automobile tour, are worth a visit because of their Civil War graves. A self-guided walking tour and narrative of the Battle of Westport and the Big Blue battlefield pamphlet is available from Monnett Battle of Westport Fund, Inc. of the Civil War Round Table of Kansas City, 1130 Westport Road, Kansas City, MO 64111; 818-931-6620.

Lone Jack, on US50, 21 miles southeast of Kansas City, features the exhibits of the Jackson County Civil War Museum on the site of the battle, and a historic cemetery. For more information, contact the Battle of Lone Jack Museum at 816-566-2272.

DRIVING TOUR—*Proceed to Neosho*
READING—*Price's raid: Marais des Cygnes–Mine Creek, Kansas*

MARMITON

On October 25, after a series of successive defeats at Westport, Missouri, and Marais des Cygnes and Mine Creek in Kansas, Price's column drifted back into Missouri along the Little Osage and Marmiton rivers. Price's wagon trains had difficulty fording the Marmiton, and, as at Mine Creek, the Confederates had to make a stand in this battle also called Charlot's Farm. Here Jo Shelby's cavalry again fought the pursuing Federal force, allowing the rest of Price's column to continue retreating in the direction of Carthage, Missouri.

NEWTONIA

On September 29–30, 1862, a Federal force moved against a Confederate outpost at Newtonia. On September 29, a Union detachment probed the Rebel outposts. The next day, after exchanging artillery fire, the reinforced Federals were confronted by more Confederates, Native Americans, and Texans under Col. Douglas H. Cooper. After several sharp clashes the Federals withdrew. Cooper pursued the Federals but soon came in contact with a larger force under Maj. Gen. John M. Schofield. After several more days of skirmishing, Cooper returned with his brigade and moved into the Indian Territory and the Confederate Missourians pulled back into Arkansas' Boston Mountains. The September 30 Rebel victory at Newtonia was an element in the surge that between September 16 and October 8, 1862, saw armies of the South on the offensive from Maryland in the east to the Indian Territory in the west, and represents the true high tide of the Confederacy.

In the last fight in his long retreat after the Battle of Westport, Maj. Gen. Sterling Price encountered Maj. Gen. James G. Blunt's pursuing force one more time at Newtonia. On October 28, 1864, Blunt surprised Price's force, resting in camps southwest of Newtonia after their rapid flight south from the Marmiton River. Again, Shelby's "Iron Brigade" of cavalry stood in the forefront in first shielding Price's now hapless army and carrying the fight to the foe. But when General Blunt was reinforced, Shelby's rear guard executed an orderly withdrawal. From Newtonia, Price's retreat continued without further serious interruption until his columns crossed Red River and reached Laynesport, Arkansas, in early December.

Points of Interest

The Battle of Marmiton River was fought near US71 in Vernon County.

A marker for the two battles of Newtonia is located on County Road M between Newtonia and Stark City.

DRIVING TOUR—*Proceed to Carthage*
READING *(chronological)*—*1862: Prairie Grove, Arkansas*

CARTHAGE

Carthage was the locale of a number of partisan skirmishes after an initial July 5, 1861, engagement. Col. Franz Sigel led a force of 1,000 Federals into southwest Missouri in search of the pro-secessionist Gov. Claiborne Fox Jackson and his loyal troops. Upon learning that Sigel had encamped at Carthage, on the night of July 4, Jackson took command of the troops with him and formulated a plan to attack the much smaller Union force. Next morning, Jackson closed on Sigel, established a battle line on a ridge ten miles north of Carthage, and induced Sigel to attack him. Opening with artillery fire, Sigel attacked. Seeing a large Confederate force—actually unarmed recruits—moving into the woods on his left, Sigel feared that they would turn his flank and withdrew. The Confederates pursued, but Sigel conducted a successful rear-guard action. By evening, Sigel was inside Carthage and under cover of darkness; he then retreated to Sarcoxie. The battle had little significance, but the pro-Southern elements in Missouri, anxious for any good news, hailed their first victory. This action was a prelude to the Battle of Wilson's Creek.

Points of Interest

There are four historic markers off US71 north of Carthage and in Battle of Carthage State Park on MO96 interpreting the battle. Carter Park, at East Chestnut and River streets, was the site of a rear-guard action.

DRIVING TOUR and READING—*Proceed to Wilson's Creek*

WILSON'S CREEK

The most significant battle west of the Mississippi River in 1861 occurred at Wilson's Creek, near Springfield, on August 10. In July, Brig. Gen. Nathaniel Lyon had swept through Missouri and established a base at Springfield. At the same time, Sterling Price was drilling a force of Missouri State

The Ray House (pictured) and the Ray springhouse are the only structures in the park surviving from the battle. Fighting took place in the cornfield northwest of the house in the Ray cornfield. The house was used as a Confederate field hospital and Nathaniel Lyon's body was brought here after the battle.

The Death of Brig. Gen. Nathaniel Lyon, *a woodcut from a sketch by Frank Leslie's Illustrated Newspaper special artist Henri Lovie, who was at Wilson's Creek. These special artists accompanied the armies into the field and witnessed and recorded many of the war's great events.*

Guards on the Cowskin Prairie in McDonald County. Price was joined at Cassville, Missouri, by Texans, Arkansans, and Louisianans under Brig. Gen. Benjamin McCulloch and the Arkansas State Guard under Brig. Gen. Nicholas B. Pearce. The Confederate force then numbering 12,000 decided to take the offensive against Lyon.

On August 2, Lyon tested the vanguard of the Rebel force—Missouri State Guard—at Dug Springs and, though he bested them, he realized the Confederates outnumbered him and withdrew to Springfield. The Confederates went into camps along Wilson's Creek and planned to attack Lyon, but rain on the evening of August 9 forced a postponement of their offensive.

Despite being outnumbered two to one, Lyon decided to use the element of surprise to attack the Confederates in their camps. On the evening of August 9, he sent a force of 1,200 under Col. Franz Sigel to pass east of the Rebels' camp and attack from the south. Lyon led the rest of the attacking force, about 3,200, and at dawn on August 10 approached the camps from the north. Sigel's flanking attack started well while at the same time Lyon's force surprised the Confederates in their camps along the creek. But the Confederates formed lines of battle and soon the tide reversed. Sigel's Germans were counterattacked by McCulloch's Louisianans and Arkansans, routed and driven from the field.

At the same time, Price's Missourians battled Lyon's soldiers on a scrub oak-clad ridge that has since been known as "Bloody Hill" because of the vicious, sometimes hand-to-hand fighting that occurred there. At nine-thirty A.M. Lyon was killed on Bloody Hill while leading a charge. By eleven A.M. Lyon's successor, Maj. Samuel Sturgis, ordered a withdrawal as the Federals nearly exhausted their ammunition. However, the battle, fought in very hot weather, sapped the Confederates' enthusiasm and they did not pursue the Federals, who retreated first to Springfield and then back to their Rolla railhead. The Battle of Wilson's Creek, or Oak Hills as the Southerners call it, shifted the momentum in Missouri for the next six weeks from the Federals to the pro-secessionist Missourians.

Points of Interest

Wilson's Creek National Battlefield—Much of the battlefield at Wilson's Creek is preserved in a park. The park is located 2 miles south of US60 on MO-ZZ, 10 miles southwest of Springfield. The visitor center has exhibits, bookstore, audiovisual presentations, research library, and a fiber optic battle map. Throughout the year special programs are held and living-history demonstrations are conducted within the park on summer weekends. Brochures are available for a driving or cycling tour through the park.

The highlights on the tour throughout the park include the Ray House, which stood during the battle; Bloody Hill, including a monument where Lyon was killed; and a historic overlook and sites of other battle actions. The park is open every day. WILSON'S CREEK NATIONAL BATTLEFIELD, Route 2, P.O. Box 75, Republic, MO 65738; 417-732-2662.
🚲 ⊠ ♿ 🚶 🐎 ❷ 🏛 P 🚻

Two hundred yards north of the Wilson's Creek National Battlefield visitor center is General Sweeny's Museum featuring artifacts and exhibits interpreting the war in the Trans-Mississippi. General Sweeny's Museum is a must for visitors to the area. Hours are seasonal and admission is charged. For more information, contact General Sweeny's Museum, Route 2, P.O. Box 75B, Republic, MO 65738; 417-732-1224.

DRIVING TOUR—*Proceed to Pea Ridge, Arkansas*
READING—*Lexington*

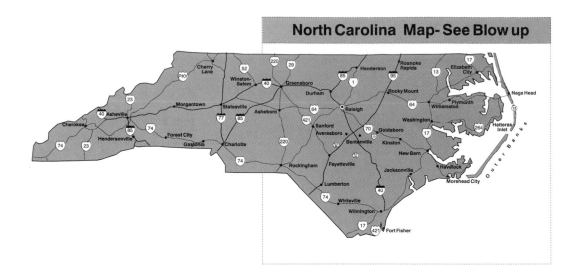

North Carolina Map- See Blow up

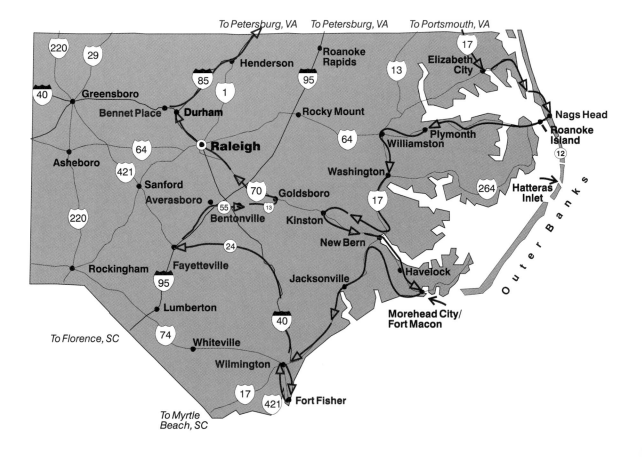

North Carolina

———⊰⋇⊱———

Nnorth Carolina was the last of the eleven states to secede and join the Confederacy. There was strong Unionist sentiment in the western and Piedmont counties of the state and slaveholders in the coastal areas recognized secession as more dangerous to their institution than the status quo. But, when President Lincoln, after the surrender of Fort Sumter, called for 75,000 volunteers to put down the rebellion, Governor John Ellis thundered: "You can get no troops from North Carolina," and on May 20, 1861, a convention meeting in Raleigh adopted a secession ordinance. Ironically, North Carolina sent more of its men to fight for the Confederacy then any other Southern state, and North Carolinians can boast, "First at Big Bethel, farthest at Antietam, Gettysburg, and Chickamauga, and last at Appomattox." One in four Confederate soldiers killed in the war was a North Carolinian.

The first stop on the suggested tour route is Elizabeth City. Hatteras Inlet, located in Cape Hatteras National Seashore, was the site of the first significant war action in North Carolina: the capture of the two Confederate forts. While not on the tour route, Hatteras Inlet can be reached by taking NC12 south from Nags Head, while proceeding from Elizabeth City to Roanoke Island.

HATTERAS INLET

The gateway to Pamlico Sound, Hatteras Inlet was employed by Confederate privateers early in the war to gain access to the Atlantic to raid Yankee shipping. A squadron of warships including the USS *Wabash,* the USS *Cumberland,* the USS *Minnesota,* and others mounting 149 guns, under Flag Officer Silas Stringham, was sent to take the two forts guarding the inlet. Eight hundred and eighty soldiers from Fort Monroe, Virginia, were aboard transports ready to storm ashore. They were commanded by Maj. Gen. Benjamin F. Butler, a Democratic political general from Massachusetts who had gained esteem with President Lincoln for breaking the land blockade of Washington by Maryland secessionists (see **Annapolis Junction, Maryland**), and for his refusal to return fugitive slaves to their owners holding them to be contrabands of war. The two forts that were the objective were Forts Clark and Hatteras on Hatteras Island, and commanding the inlet. On August 28, 1861, the naval attack began. Stringham had his ships cruise in a circle rather than lie at anchor, and the forts' guns were overwhelmed by the naval bombardment.

Only 318 of Butler's men landed because of heavy surf. The Rebels tried to reinforce the forts but were unsuccessful because of the fire of the warships. The Federal landing force finally captured Fort Hatteras when the Rebels evacuated it the next day. At the same time, the navy continued to hammer Fort Clark. Butler demanded and finally received unconditional surrender from the Confederates in the fort and more than 700 prisoners were taken. The Federals garrisoned the forts and relit the Cape Hatteras and Ocracoke lights to facilitate coastal navigation and enable merchant shipping to avoid running afoul of the treacherous Diamond Shoals.

Points of Interest

The Hatteras Island Visitor Center, on NC12 in the Cape Hatteras National Seashore, features a museum of the sea. CAPE HATTERAS NATIONAL SEASHORE, Route 1, P.O. Box 675, Manteo, NC 27954; 919-473-2111. 🚲 ⛺ ⛵ 🏃 ❓ 🏛 P 🚻 🌊 🚻

There are no forts, but the 1823 Ocracoke Lighthouse continues to operate for those navigating Cape Hatteras, known as the "Graveyard of the Atlantic." The foundation of the Cape Hatteras Lighthouse that predated the 1870 tower can be seen. Lighthouse lenses were removed by the Confederates in the early summer of 1861, and the Cape Hatteras light was relighted in 1862 and the Ocracoke light in 1864. A free ferry operates between Hatteras and Ocracoke islands, and there is a toll ferry between Ocracoke and the mainland.

ROANOKE ISLAND

No further incursions into the North Carolina sounds were attempted until mid-January 1862, when a Federal army under Brig. Gen. Ambrose E. Burnside, with naval support, arrived off Hatteras Inlet, its mission to enter Albemarle and Pamlico sounds, and capture Roanoke Island. Armed with an ambitious series of objectives, the most important of which was to capture Goldsboro, a vital railroad junction, Burnside had to raise a force in New England and New York after leading a brigade in the Battle of First Manassas (see

First Manassas, Virginia). Burnside had to compete with other Federal generals who were recruiting for other expeditions, but the force was finally assembled and departed from Fort Monroe, Virginia, in the second week of January 1862.

The Confederates' major stronghold guarding access to the sounds was Roanoke Island. Roanoke Island, bounded on the east by Roanoke Sound and separated from the mainland by Croatan Sound, divided Pamlico and Albemarle sounds. Sand forts and batteries had been built and armed to discourage a naval attack, but there was insufficient manpower to maintain a prolonged defense against an amphibious assault. A small "mosquito fleet" of gunboats was assembled by the Rebels to add some naval muscle to the defense. However, the forts were located toward the north end of the island and the Federal invasion would enter Croatan Sound from the south.

Supported by the firepower of Flag Officer Louis M. Goldsborough's powerful squadron, Burnside's 15,000-man army approached the North Carolina coast in mid-January. Violent storms racked the armada, forcing some heroic rescues as one ship and several small boats foundered. By February 7, under the protection of the warships' 108 guns, the first troops landed at Ashby's Harbor on Roanoke Island.

Under the overall command of former Virginia governor Henry Wise, who was bedridden at the time, the Confederate defenses were in a near-hopeless state of confusion. Goldsborough's squadron had no problem silencing shore batteries near the landing site, and sent the small Southern gunboat squadron scurrying for cover. The next day, February 8, Burnside's three brigades under Brig. Gens. John G. Foster, Jesse L. Reno, and John G. Parke pushed toward the north end of the island. The Confederates held a line of defense covering the island's north-south road protected, they thought, by impassable wetlands on either side. Foster's soldiers hammered the center of the line, and Reno's people maneuvered through the muddy bogs and flanked the Confederate position. The Rebels retreated into a pocket at the island's Northwest Point. While some escaped, more than 2,500 Rebels were captured and the island was secured by the Yankees.

With Roanoke Island in Union hands, other Confederate defenses fronting on the sounds were vulnerable to amphibious attack. On February 10, the Federal gunboats plying Albemarle Sound ascended the Pasquotank River and at Elizabeth City destroyed most of the Rebels' "Mosquito Fleet" vessels. The Federal navy continued up the Chowan River as far as Winton, but turned back after overreaching their army support. The Federal navy lacked the resources to hold Elizabeth City and on April 19 it was occupied by General Reno. When Reno pushed inland he encountered and was bested by Col. Ambrose "Ranse" Wright and his Georgians at South Mills. Evacuating Elizabeth City, the Federals returned to their bases and rejoined the main force. Meanwhile, Burnside had moved against his next objective, New Bern on the Neuse River.

Points of Interest

Elizabeth City—Located on US17 on the Pasquotank River, this town has several buildings that were used by the Federals during their occupation. The Museum of the *Albemarle*, 1116 US Highway South (919-335-1453), is devoted to the history of the CSS *Albemarle* and regional history. At South Mills, 12 miles north of Elizabeth City and just off US17 on NC343, there is a historical marker for the April 19, 1862, battle at South Mills.

Roanoke Island—Between Roanoke Island and the mainland along US64/264 there is an excellent view of Croatan Sound, where Federal warships briefly battled the Confederate "mosquito fleet." Traces of several of Roanoke Island's fortifications are indicated by historical markers. Fort Defiance, just south of US64/264 on NC345, has an interpretive marker and some of the remains are surrounded by a white fence. Markers identify the sites of Forts Bartow, Blanchard, and Huger near Fort Raleigh National Historic Site. The extant remains of the two latter forts are overgrown. Fort Raleigh focuses on Sir Walter Raleigh's 1587 Lost Colony, but at one time the site was a Confederate camp. For more information, contact FORT RALEIGH NATIONAL HISTORIC SITE, c/o Cape Hatteras National Seashore, Route 1, P.O. Box 675, Manteo, NC 27954; 919-473-2111.
♿ ❓ P 🛀 $$

DRIVING TOUR—*Proceed to Plymouth*
READING—*New Bern*

PLYMOUTH

Although Federals ruled the North Carolina sounds and the Union army established and garrisoned enclaves, such as New Bern, Washington, and Plymouth on major rivers discharging into the sounds, the Confederates were not about to concede North Carolina Tidewater to the Yankees. Except for the December 1862 advance to and recoil from Goldsboro by the Union forces intent on severing the Weldon Railroad, and the seventeen day siege of Washington, March 30–April 15, 1863, two years of relative quiet existed in the area. During these months the Confederates were building ironclad rams up the rivers feeding Albemarle and Pamlico sounds, as well as near Wilmington. With whatever materials they managed to scrounge, vessels of a design similar to the CSS *Tennessee* and the CSS *Atlanta* were constructed. The first to see combat action was the CSS *Albemarle*.

In April 1864, Confederates under North Carolina native Brig. Gen. Robert F. Hoke, undertook a campaign to retake Plymouth with the aid of the *Albemarle*. The Rebels attacked on April 17; Federal land forces and gunboats engaged Hoke and the *Albemarle* did not appear. Warned of her approach, the Federal naval commander, Lt. Cmdr. C. W. Flusser, lashed two wooden gunboats, the *Miami* and the *Southfield*, together to use as a ram. The two-gun *Albemarle* came downriver in the early morning hours of April 19. Solid shot and ramming had little to no effect on the Confederate ironclad. The *Albemarle* rammed and sunk the *Southfield* and damaged the *Miami*, killing Flusser. The 2,800-men garrison, without gunboat support, when attacked by Hoke's soldiers and the *Albemarle*, surrendered on April 20.

This is a woodcut of the CSS Albemarle *partially submerged in shallow water in Plymouth, North Carolina, after the October 27, 1864, attack by Lt. William B. Cushing, USN, and his torpedo boat crew. Despite her being protected by an enclosure of floating logs, Cushing managed to explode his torpedo and create a large hole in the* Albemarle's *hull below her waterline. After the Federals captured Plymouth, the* Albemarle *was towed to Norfolk and sold for scrap after the war.*

Federal gunboats attacked the *Albemarle* on May 5 but did her no serious harm. The ironclad broke off the engagement and retired up the Roanoke River. The *Albemarle* did not engage in any further combat action over the summer, but Federal plans for her destruction were under way. After months of planning, a daredevil lieutenant in the Union navy, William B. Cushing, on October 27, 1864, took a steam launch of his own design up Roanoke River to the well-guarded anchorage of the *Albemarle*. Braving a storm of small arms fire, Cushing struck with his launch the log boom protecting the *Albemarle,* smashed through, and exploded a spar torpedo against her hull. The explosion ripped through the hull of the *Albemarle* and she sank in shallow water. Cushing and one of his fifteen-man volunteer crew escaped as their launch was destroyed.

With the threat of the *Albemarle* removed, Federal gunboats returned to Plymouth and pounded the shore batteries. The Rebels evacuated the town on October 31, and the navy occupied it pending the arrival of Yankee soldiers who held the Plymouth enclave until the end of the war.

Points of Interest

Grace Episcopal Church in Plymouth was used as a hospital during the 1864 attack on the town. Ausbon House at the corner of Washington and Third streets has the damage from the 1862 Federal gunboat shelling on its north-facing wall. A museum in Plymouth has artifacts from the 1864 naval actions. On the courthouse lawn is a Battle of Plymouth marker. There is also a marker near the site of *Albemarle*'s sinking.

Farther north on the Roanoke River at Hamilton is Confederate Fort Branch. Efforts have been ongoing for some time to preserve the earthen fortification at Rainbow Bend, which resisted Federal gunboat attempts to proceed up the Roanoke River in 1862 and 1863.

Washington, North Carolina, which was under Federal siege in March and April of 1863, is at the junction of US17 and US264 between Plymouth and New Bern and on the route to either New Bern or Kinston. A self-guided walking tour pamphlet of the town's historic district is available at many downtown businesses in Washington. Included in the tour is the Hollyday House, at 706 West Second Street, which was used as a hospital during the Federal occupation of Washington.

DRIVING TOUR—*Proceed to Kinston*
READING—*Boydton Plank Road–Burgess's Mill, Petersburg, Virginia*

KINSTON

In December 1862, Brig. Gen. John G. Foster undertook an expedition from New Bern to destroy the Wilmington & Weldon Railroad at Goldsboro. The advance was stubbornly contested by hard-drinking Nathan G. "Shanks" Evans's Confederate Brigade near Kinston Bridge on December 14, but the Rebels were outnumbered and withdrew north of the Neuse River in the direction of Goldsboro. Foster continued his movement the next day, taking the River Road, south of the Neuse River. Foster's Union troops reached White Hall on December 16 where Brig. Gen. Beverly Robertson's brigade was holding the north bank of the Neuse River. The Federals demonstrated against the Confederates for much of the day, attempting to pin them in position while the main Union column continued toward the railroad. Foster's people did discover the construction at White Hall of the ironclad that became the CSS *Neuse*, but Robertson's Confederates prevented the Federals from destroying the vessel.

On December 17, Foster's column reached the railroad near Everettsville and began destroying the tracks north toward Goldsboro Bridge. Thomas Clingman's North Carolina brigade delayed the advance but was unable to prevent the destruction of the bridge. His mission accomplished, Foster returned to New Bern where he arrived on December 20.

The CSS *Neuse* was combat-ready in early 1865 to assist in retaking New Bern. By that time, however, the military situation in North Carolina had changed. Confederate forces in eastern North Carolina would soon be called by Gen. Joseph E. Johnston to help oppose the advance of William T. Sherman's "army group." Maj. Gen. John. M. Schofield planned to advance inland from Wilmington in February, at the same time assigning Maj. Gen. Jacob Cox to direct Union forces from New Bern toward Goldsboro. On March 7, Cox's advance was stopped by Robert Hoke's and Johnson Hagood's divisions under Gen. Braxton Bragg's command at Southwest Creek below Kinston. On March 8, the Confederates attempted to seize the initiative by attacking the Union flanks. After initial success in the Battle of Wyse Fork, the Confederate attacks stalled because of faulty communications. On March 9, the Union forces were reinforced and beat back Bragg's renewed attacks the next day after heavy fighting. Bragg withdrew across the Neuse River and was unable to prevent the fall of Kinston on March 14. The CSS *Neuse* participated in the defense of Kinston, but as the Yanks gained the upper hand and closed on the town, the commander of the *Neuse* destroyed his vessel to prevent her capture. Following the capture of Kinston, Schofield's troops converged on Goldsboro where Sherman's "army group" rendezvoused with these forces on March 23, 1865.

Points of Interest

The Richard Caswell Memorial and CSS *Neuse* State Historic Site is located on West Vernon Avenue, just west of Kinston on Business US70. The site features the hull of the CSS *Neuse,* which was salvaged in 1963 along with other artifacts salvaged from the ill-fated ironclad. It is one of only two examples of Confederate ironclad ram construction in existence (see **Columbus, Georgia** for CSS *Jackson*). The site is open daily 9:00 A.M. to 5:00 P.M. with shorter hours on Sunday and in the winter. RICHARD CASWELL MEMORIAL and CSS *NEUSE* STATE HISTORIC SITE, 2612 West Vernon Avenue, P.O. Box 3043, Kinston, NC 28502-3043; 919-522-2091. ♿ ❓ 🏛 P 🚻

On US70 3.5 miles east of Kinston is a wayside exhibit on the Battle of Wyse Fork.

DRIVING TOUR—*Proceed to New Bern*
READING—*Fayetteville–Monroe's Cross Roads*

NEW BERN

After securing Roanoke Island in early February 1862, General Burnside prepared to move against New Bern. The Confederates had thrown up and manned earthworks commanding the Neuse River approaches to the colonial city. Burnside's army sailed from Roanoke Island on March 11 and landed on the west side of the Neuse, eighteen miles downstream from New Bern. On March 14, a foggy and raining morning, Foster's and Reno's brigades, supported by the fire of Federal gunboats, attacked the Confederates, whose left was anchored on the Neuse at Fort Thompson and whose right was ensconced behind Bullen's Creek. Fighting was intense and the North Carolina militia holding the Confederates' center gave way, but a counterattack by the 7th North Carolina momentarily closed the breech. Time soon ran out for the Confederates, as the Federals called up reinforcements and the 7th North Carolina in turn pulled back. Confederate commander Brig. Gen. Lawrence O'Brien Branch called retreat. As soon as the last of the Confederates crossed Trent River, the bridge was torched. Burnside's New Bern victory, besides enhancing his reputation as a "can-do leader," gave Yankees a base on a railroad from which to push their campaign to gain control of the North Carolina sounds.

At the beginning of February 1864, Confederates led by Maj. Gen. George E. Pickett failed to retake New Bern, although they were supported by a dozen small Confederate boats. The strength of the Federal fortifications, counterbattery fire from U.S. gunboats, and the failure of Brig. Gen. Seth Barton, one of Pickett's subordinates, to press an attack caused Pickett to break off the operation on February 2.

Points of Interest
New Bern (spelled New Berne in the 1860s) today is sometimes called Newbern and is a city with a rich historical past. The Craven County Visitor Information Center, 219 Pollock Street, has historical information on New Bern including numerous buildings that existed when Confederate and later Federal forces occupied the city. Tryon Palace, the seat of the royal governor, has been reconstructed and is a state park located at 613 Pollock Street. Among the prominent buildings of Civil War interest is the Charles Slover House, 201 Johnson Street, which was used as a headquarters by Federal generals Burnside and Foster. In 1908 the house was purchased by C. D. Bradham, who developed the beverage on which the Pepsi-Cola formula is based. The Rains House, 411 Johnston Street, was the birthplace of Brig. Gen. Gabriel J. Rains, superintendent of the Confederate Torpedo and Harbor Defense Bureau; and the John Wright Stanley House, New Street, between Middle and Hancock streets, was the birthplace of Brig. Gen. Lewis A. Armistead.

Efforts are under way at the time of this writing to mark and preserve some of the areas in which the 1862 battle was fought.

DRIVING TOUR and READING—*Proceed to Fort Macon*

FORT MACON

The next objective on Burnside's list after New Bern was Morehead City, a port city and the terminus of the railroad running inland to Goldsboro, where it crossed the north-south Weldon RR and the nearby port of Beaufort. Bogue Inlet, giving access to the two ports from the Atlantic Ocean, was guarded by a masonry bastion, Fort Macon. Brig. Gen. John G. Parke's division was sent to take Fort Macon, which had 45 cannons and was located at the east end of Bogue Bay. John G. Parke's division took and garrisoned

Morehead City on March 22, and the next day called on the Confederates defending Fort Macon to surrender. They refused, and General Parke took measures to invest the fort. On March 25 Parke occupied Beaufort.

On March 29, U.S. Navy sailors and marines established a beachhead on Bogue Banks. With gunboat protection, Parke got his forces close enough to establish positions for siege artillery, and on April 26 opened fire on the fort, which soon breached the masonry walls. Within a few hours the fort's scarp began to crumble, and the Confederates ran up a white flag.

Points of Interest

Fort Macon State Park—At the northeast point of Bogue Banks, at the terminus of NC58, is Fort Macon State Park. In it is Fort Macon, a Third System fort, begun in 1826, the linchpin of the Confederate defense of Beaufort harbor until it surrendered to Federal forces on April 26, 1862. The fort's Civil War structural profile is well preserved because it was not modified to serve as part of the Endicott coastal defense system. The site offers a pamphlet featuring a self-guided walking tour. A museum and bookstore are located in the fort; officers' and enlisted men's quarters have been restored. Recreational facilities in the park include picnic areas, hiking trails, and a swimming area. FORT MACON STATE PARK, East Fort Macon Road, P.O. Box 127, Atlantic Beach, NC 28512; 919-726-3775 or 726-8598; FAX: 919-726-2497. ♿ 🚶 ❓ 🏛 P ⛱ 〰

DRIVING TOUR—*Proceed to Wilmington*
READING—*Yorktown, Virginia*

WILMINGTON

Wilmington was destined to become the most important blockade-running port in the Confederacy. Located near the convenient off-shore neutral harbors of the Bahamas and Bermuda, where the trade flourished, it was close to the mouth of the Cape Fear River. The river was entered through New and Old inlets, separated by Smith's Island, while hazardous Frying Pan Shoals made a close inshore blockade by Federal warships difficult. Railroads linked Wilmington with Richmond and other key cities in the South until mid-February 1865. The Confederates realizing this added to the existing Fort Caswell, a Third System masonry fort, and added numerous other fortifications. The most important of these was Fort Fisher, a huge sand fort that protected the base of Confederate Point, separating the Atlantic from the mouth of the Cape Fear River.

Enforcing the blockade of Wilmington became a focal point of U.S. Navy efforts as closure of other Confederate ports and new construction increased the number of vessels available to watch the fifty-mile arc between Old and New Inlets. Blockade-running, while dangerous, was immensely profitable and continued unabated into Wilmington. In the dark early-morning hours of May 6, 1864, the CSS *Raleigh,* a Confederate ironclad, escorted several blockade-runners down the Cape Fear River. Two Federal gunboats engaged the *Raleigh* without serious damage sustained by either side. After daylight, on May 7, four blockaders engaged the *Raleigh* which then grounded near Fort Fisher. Her back was broken and the *Raleigh* was abandoned.

Following the January 15, 1865, capture of Fort Fisher, Wilmington's days were numbered. Confederate Gen. Braxton Bragg divided his command posting Brig. Gen. Johnson Hagood's troops in Fort Anderson, a formidable work on the west bank of the Cape Fear River, seven miles upriver from Fort Fisher, and the rest under Maj. Gen. Robert Hoke to hold the peninsula north of the Sugar Loaf. Federal forces under Maj. Gen. Alfred Terry, reinforced by Union soldiers that arrived by water under Maj. Gen. Jacob D. Cox and supported by warships, began to march upriver. By February 12, they had crossed the river and attacked Fort Anderson. That fort fell on February 19 and additional Federal pressure was applied against new Rebel positions closer to the city. By early morning of February 22, Confederate forces had been withdrawn from Wilmington and the advance of Terry's corps marched in, and Mayor John Dawson surrendered the city to General Terry.

Points of Interest

The Bellamy Mansion, at the northwest corner of Market and Fifth streets, is an antebellum home that was occupied by Federal forces. For information and tours, for which a fee is charged, call 910-251-3700 or FAX a request to 910-763-8154. There are several cemeteries in Wilmington that contain graves of Confederate soldiers, sailors, and civilians including the noted female spy Rose O'Neal Greenhow. There is a national cemetery for Union dead. Across the Cape Fear River from the U.S. Customs House is a historic marker identifying the Confederate navy yard. (For touring Fort Anderson, see points of interest and ferry information under **Fort Fisher**.)

DRIVING TOUR—*Proceed to Fort Fisher*
READING—*Hatcher's Run, Petersburg, Virginia*

FORT FISHER

Fort Fisher, though laid out early in the war, was not the Confederate "Goliath" it became. Wilmington was not threatened and the small Federal blockading force assigned to watch Cape Fear during 1861 was ineffectual. That changed when Col. William Lamb arrived to take command on July 4, 1862. Lamb immediately set to work to build a powerful Confederate earthen fort out of the sand and sod of Confederate Point, the renamed Federal Point separating the Atlantic Ocean and Cape Fear River.

Over the next two years, a one-third-mile series of fifteen traverses, huge mounds of sand linked together, was built across the narrow neck of the point facing north. On the seaward front, the sixty-foot-high Northeast Bastion connected with more sand mounds that ran nearly a mile south along the Atlantic face to connect with the Mound Battery, forming an L-shaped fort. Opposite the Mound Battery, Battery Buchanan protected the entrance to the Cape Fear River. Big seacoast guns were mounted at intervals in the fortifications. A log palisade and ditch protected the north face and beyond that, one of the first electrically triggered land minefields in warfare was created by burying torpedoes under the surface connected by wires to the fort.

The fort was scarcely challenged because of its imposing defenses and Federal priorities elsewhere until late 1864. Then, an amphibious operation by a fleet under recently appointed North Atlantic Blockading Squadron commander, R. Adm. David D. Porter, and Maj. Gen. Benjamin F. Butler was projected to attack and capture Fort Fisher.

Delays compelled the postponement of the expedition until the chilly days of December. One was a plan of Butler's, to which Porter eagerly assented, to run a ship packed with tons of black powder close to the fort's seafront and detonate it to damage or destroy the fort and kill or stun the garrison. The plans proceeded with high hopes and an ex-blockader, the USS *Louisiana,* was selected for the experiment.

On the night of December 23, the *Louisiana* was packed with 235 tons of powder and towed under darkness to the Atlantic side of the fort. Shortly after midnight on Christmas Eve, the fuses were lit by volunteers. The resulting blast destroyed the ship but was hardly noticed in the fort. Troops assumed a boiler had exploded on one of the ships in Porter's squadron which they were aware was off shore. The air had absorbed most of the shock wave from the explosion. At daybreak, Porter sailed his warships, including five iron-

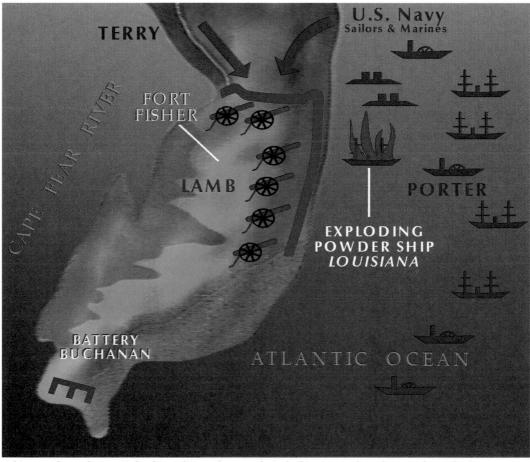

This map shows the two Federal expeditions that were launched against L-shaped Fort Fisher. The first attempt in December 1864 included the failed explosion of the powder boat Louisiana, *bombardment by Federal warships, and a landing by troops under Maj. Gen. Benjamin Butler from the Atlantic northeast of the fort's salient angle. The second combined expedition in January 1865 included the largest fleet of warships ever assembled during the Civil War in one place under R. Adm. David D. Porter and a land attack from the north with two forces: soldiers under Brig. Gen. Alfred H. Terry and a U.S. Navy force of some twenty-two hundred sailors and marines. The second assault resulted in the fort's capture on January 15.*

This photograph taken shortly after the capture of Fort Fisher shows one of the positions where the fort's big guns were mounted en barbette. A 150-pounder Armstrong gun, one of the Fort Fisher's heaviest-caliber weapons, is now on display at the U.S. Military Academy in West Point, New York.

clads, close to the fort and unleashed a day-long bombardment that reached the rate of 115 shells a minute, some huge projectiles from fifteen-inch Dahlgren smoothbores. The bombardment continued at a slower pace on Christmas Day after Butler returned from a fueling stop at Beaufort, North Carolina, where he had gone with his troop transports to ride out a storm.

Butler, on December 25, landed his troops several miles north of the fort. One brigade closed to within several hundred yards of the fort's land front but seeing no appreciable damage to the forts' fighting power, Butler promptly ordered his troops to reembark and prepare to return to Fort Monroe. Because of the angry surf 700 men were stranded on the beach, but were evacuated the next day by navy craft. Although Butler was correct in his assessment that the fort was little damaged, his failure to follow through enabled General-in-Chief U. S. Grant and President Lincoln to sack a general whose political ties were no longer needed and whose military record was frequently an embarrassment. Butler was relieved of duty upon returning to Fort Monroe.

A somewhat humorous footnote to Butler's dismissal was that in mid-January, 1865, as Butler was before a congressional committee in Washington bitterly protesting that he had been unfairly singled out in the failure to take Fort Fisher, word came to the Capitol that Fort Fisher had fallen. Stunned at first, Butler soon led the applause for the conquerors of Fort Fisher.

Porter, after Butler abandoned the expedition, urged Grant to renew the operation and the general agreed. This time Brig. Gen. Alfred H. Terry would lead the army. Rendezvousing at Beaufort, the combined force departed for Fort Fisher on January 12, 1865. The next day the army landed north of the fort, and Porter began another bombardment with forty-four ships that day and continued it on the next. The *New Ironsides* and four monitors continued their fire day and

This is the north face of Fort Fisher from the point of view of the attacking Federal army, navy, and U.S. Marine forces that captured the fort on January 15, 1865. These towering sand mounds were the fort's primary characteristic and some were as high as sixty feet.

night. Instead of the general bombardment like the one carried out in December, Porter ordered the fire directed at specific targets until they were destroyed. (This tactic was a precursor to the methods used for naval gunfire in World War II amphibious landings.) The naval fire on the two days, and part of the third, had the effect of knocking out most of the fort's 75 guns.

On the morning of January 15, 1,800 sailors and 400 marines landed north of the Northeast Bastion. Their afternoon attack was to be coordinated with that of the army. Shortly after three P.M. the navy, hoping to "one-up" the army, attacked first. Uncle Sam's "webfeet" suffered a disastrous repulse. Their effort did divert the defenders' attention away from the army's main attack, which, when it came, was directed against the fort's western flank where it abutted on wetlands. The Federals, after a desperate struggle, seized Shephard's Battery and then fought their way a little at a time through the fort. Gen. Braxton Bragg failed to commit a Confederate division massed north of the fort to prevent Union soldiers from gaining access to it.

The fighting continued along the fort's north front and then south until about nine P.M. Both Colonel Lamb and the general in charge of Wilmington's defense, Maj. Gen. William H. C. Whiting, were wounded. The fort's defenders finally surrendered that night, and 1,900 Confederates were taken prisoner. The capture of Fort Fisher enabled Yankee warships to enter the Cape Fear River. The Confederates destroyed Fort Caswell, but navy Lt. William B. Cushing again was in the center of the action, making a reconnaissance up the river and forcing the surrender of the Rebel batteries at Smithville. The capture of Fort Fisher choked off blockade-running and the port of Wilmington soon fell to Federal forces.

Points of Interest

Fort Fisher State Historic Site—The site, 20 miles south of Wilmington and 3 miles south of US421, is a wonderful park featuring extant remains of the once proud fort. More than half of the land front traverses exist and there is a reconstruction of the palisade that was part of the defense against land attacks. There are also seacoast guns mounted in some of the emplacements and interpretive trails throughout the park. A visitor center and museum enhance the facility. Battery Buchanan rises above the Cape Fear River and a state-run ferry carries cars and passengers to the west bank of the river.

Just a few steps away from the visitor center is the Blockade Runner museum with artifacts from the *Modern Greece* and other blockade-runners that were sunk as they sought to enter or leave the Cape Fear River. The wrecks of the *Modern Greece* and these other vessels are submerged archaeological resources and are listed in the National Register of Historic Places. State headquarters for underwater archaeology is located at Fort Fisher and there are displays on the exploration of the USS *Monitor* at the site. FORT FISHER STATE HISTORIC SITE, 1610 Fort Fisher Boulevard South, P.O. Box 169, Kure Beach, NC 28449; 910-458-5538 or 910-458-0476; FAX 910-458-0477. 🚲 🚢 ♨ ♿ 🚶 ❓ 🏛 P ⛱ 🚻

Other sites on the west side of the Cape Fear River, including the remains of Fort Caswell and Brunswick Town (Fort Anderson) State Historic Site, can be reached by taking the ferry from the end of the peninsula at Fort Fisher, then taking NC211 to NC133 north. At Fort Anderson there are impressive earthen fortifications and a visitor center interpreting the fort's Civil War role and the history of colonial-era Brunswick Town. BRUNSWICK TOWN (FORT ANDERSON) STATE HISTORIC SITE, 8884 St. Philips Road SE, Route 1, P.O. Box 55, Winnabow, NC 28479; 910-371-6613. ♿ 🚶 ❓ 🏛 P ⛱ 🚻

DRIVING TOUR—*Proceed to Fayetteville*
READING— *Wilmington*

FAYETTEVILLE–MONROE'S CROSS ROADS

With the fall of Fort Fisher, the surrender of Wilmington, and the threat to Kinston, the concern of Confederate leaders in North Carolina shifted to the march through South Carolina by Maj. Gen. William T. Sherman's "army group." As Sherman pressed relentlessly ahead, Gen. Joseph E. Johnston was recalled after seven months on the shelf, and living in western North Carolina after Sherman's advance on Columbia, South Carolina (which compelled Johnston and his wife to leave that city). On February 22, Johnston assumed command of the Departments of South Carolina, Georgia, Florida, and Tennessee as ordered by Gen. Robert E. Lee, who three weeks before had been named Confederate general-in-chief. Confederate forces were scarce, but general officers were plentiful, including Braxton Bragg, in command at Kinston; D. H. Hill in eastern North Carolina; Wade Hampton, sent by Lee from the Army of Northern Virginia; Joseph Wheeler's cavalry contingents; Lt. Gen. William Hardee's troops formerly in Savannah and Charleston; and Lt. Gen. Alexander P. Stewart's scattered forces that drifted eastward from the Army of Tennessee.

Sherman entered North Carolina on March 8 en route to Fayetteville, an important Confederate depot on the Cape Fear River. The Federals reached Fayetteville on March 11 as Hardee's soldiers continued to retreat before Sherman's more than 60,000-man army. At Fayetteville, Sherman called for a seventy-two-hour halt and dispatched staffers to Wilmington to procure information about the whereabouts of Maj. Gen. John. M. Schofield's army then advancing from New Bern on Goldsboro by way of Kinston.

Before arriving in Fayetteville, Sherman's cavalry under Brig. Gen. H. Judson Kilpatrick fought a two-day running battle March 9–10 with Hampton's cavalry west of Fayetteville culminating at Monroe's Cross Roads. While stopped at Fayetteville, Sherman received word of his other forces from an army tug, sent up the Cape Fear River from Wilmington by General Terry, recently promoted to major general for his part in the Fort Fisher–Wilmington Campaign. Satisfied that Schofield's force was making progress toward its planned meeting point at Goldsboro, Sherman departed from Fayetteville on March 14 after his soldiers destroyed the U.S. arsenal and other war-related facilities there.

Sherman, aware of Johnston's new command, decided to continue to march his forces in two columns. One, Maj. Gen. Henry Slocum's Army of Georgia, would march north, making a feint toward Raleigh, where Sherman expected Johnston to marshal his scattered forces, while Maj. Gen. Oliver O. Howard's Army of the Tennessee advanced on Goldsboro.

Points of Interest

The North Carolina Arsenal, which Sherman's forces destroyed in March 1865, was located at 822 Arsenal Avenue. The arsenal is now a historical park; directions for a self-guided tour are provided. Several cemeteries in Fayetteville contain graves of Confederate soldiers. There is a marker on US15ALT identifying Confederate earthworks located there. On the Fort Bragg Military Reservation, on the old Yadkin Road, there is a wayside marker describing the Monroe's Cross Roads battle between Kilpatrick's cavalry and the troops under Wade Hampton. Unknown soldiers from this action are buried in the cemetery at nearby Long Street Church.

Another exhibit on the Battle of Monroe's Cross Roads is at the Malcolm Blue Historic Farm, which was occupied by Union officers. The site is located on NC5 south (Blue Street and Bethesda Road) in Aberdeen. For more information on the exhibit or to pre-arrange a tour of the farm, call 910-944-9483, 910-944-7558, or 910-944-1117.

DRIVING TOUR and READING— *Proceed to Averasboro*

AVERASBORO

As Sherman set out from Fayetteville, rains inundated the rural roads of North Carolina, slowing his progress. Johnston was concentrating his forces, but not at Raleigh. Instead, he was at Smithfield, halfway between Raleigh and Goldsboro. Unsure of Sherman's intentions, he ordered Hardee, aided by Wheeler's cavalry, to attack Slocum's column to determine Sherman's intentions. On March 15, skirmishing began as the rain continued to fall. Hardee formed his men into two battle lines south of Averasboro, the most inexperienced of his forces in the front, ready to fall back on veterans when pressed by the Federal advance.

On the morning of March 16, as the rain continued to beat down, the head of Slocum's column came in contact with Hardee's first line of battle at Averasboro. The cavalry and green troops, greatly outnumbered, were forced back to the second line. Slocum's troops also battled and forced back Hardee's second line, but darkness halted the action. During the night, Hardee's men slipped away to join Johnston, satisfied that Slocum's column would remain separated from Howard's for a time.

Points of Interest

The Battle of Averasboro is interpreted at two waysides located on rural roads just west of I-95. Take exit 58 from I-95 and proceed west to US301. The two interpretive pavilions are 6 miles southwest of Dunn on NC82, which intersects with US301 just north of the interstate exit. The first pavilion describes the early action on March 16, the second describes the later fighting. The area retains its rural character and, with the information found on the waysides, conveys a feel for the battle. At the site of the second wayside is a monument and Confederate cemetery.

BENTONVILLE

After the Battle of Averasboro, Slocum's column, which had become badly strung out after the battle, turned east. By this time Joe Johnston, hoping to strike the two corps under Slocum while separated by a day's march from Howard's column, planned a surprise attack at Bentonville, on the Federals' route to Goldsboro. By morning of March 19, Johnston's forces were forming a battle line two miles south of Bentonville. Entrenchments were dug. Hardee's force, marching from Averasboro, did not arrive until the afternoon, bringing the total number of Confederate troops on the field to just over 21,000. The rain finally stopped and the roads, though muddy, were beginning to dry that morning as Slocum's lead division, from Brig. Gen. Jefferson C. Davis's XIV Corps, marched out of the pine forests and into the fields of the Cole plantation. There they were engaged. Earlier in the day, Sherman, who had been accompanying Slocum's Army of Georgia, rode east to join Howard.

When Slocum met the initial resistance at Bentonville, he thought he was faced only by Hampton's cavalry, which had been skirmishing with the advancing Federals on the two previous days, and he sent a message to Sherman stating that aid was not needed. Slocum ordered a general advance, with Brig. Gen. W. P. Carlin's XIV Corps division in the lead. Carlin's advance staggered under the fire of the Confederate line, concealed in trees on the north edge of the Cole plantation. The men fell back and were reinforced by arriving units from Brig. Gen. James D. Morgan's XIV Corps division.

By one-thirty in the afternoon Slocum realized he was in trouble and dispatched a messenger to Sherman. Brigades from Morgan's division formed to the right of Carlin's weak

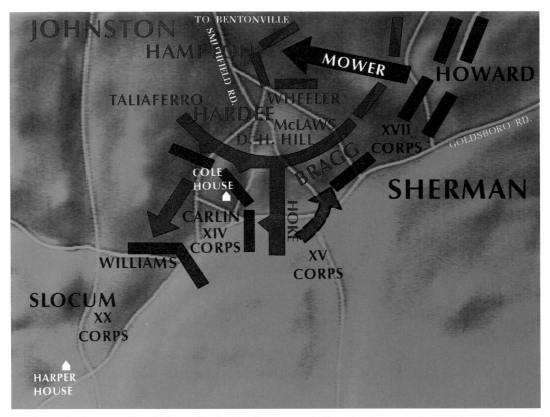

The Battle of Bentonville, which was fought March 19-21, 1865, brought the war to the rural farms of central North Carolina. The Confederate attacks on Maj. Gen. Henry Slocum's XIV and XX corps failed to rout the Federals. At the same time General Sherman ordered Maj. Gen. Oliver O. Howard's army, which had been marching by a separate route to Goldsboro, to rush to Bentonville. By the next afternoon, Sherman's entire "army group" was on the field and the Union soldiers entrenched to conform to a tighter Rebel line of defense drawn by Gen. Joseph E. Johnston. Except for a March 21 attack by two brigades under Maj. Gen. Joseph A. Mower to cut the Confederates' route of retreat, offensive operations were over in the battle. Johnston withdrew his army on the night of March 21.

Federal line. These soldiers threw up log barricades as they dug in. At three P.M. Johnston ordered the Confederates forward and the Federal line was severely challenged. Gen. Braxton Bragg failed to commit his part of the force—Maj. Gen. Robert F. Hoke's division—in a timely manner; however, the Rebels tore into the Federal left, driving it back. Morgan's force was assaulted from front and rear, but held grimly on fighting from behind their log breastworks until reinforcements arrived. And although Confederates continued to assault through the afternoon, their thin ranks were unable to penetrate the Federals, firing from behind their light field-works. The firing sputtered to a halt after dark.

Though Johnston re-formed his line, the opportunity for surprise and isolating Slocum's army was gone as the sun set on the North Carolina landscape on the evening of March 19. He re-formed his troops into a V-shaped line, with his left wing pulled back to

The Harper House at Bentonville Battleground State Historic Site. The Harpers were a family who worked a small farm and owned several slaves. The house was located behind the Federal lines during the battle and was used as a field hospital by Union surgeons. Maj. Gen. Henry Slocum maintained a command post on the property. Today the house, kitchen building, and slave quarters have been restored with period furnishings and the house has three rooms with displays re-creating a Civil War field hospital.

anchor on Mill Creek downstream from the bridge. On March 20, units of Howard's army arrived from Cox's Cross Roads and took position confronting Johnston's left wing, while Slocum's forces re-formed to the south. The only action of the day was heavy skirmishing up and down the line. By nightfall, both of Howard's corps were on the field and the Federal army was again united.

An uneasy stalemate continued on March 21. Johnston hoped that Sherman would launch an attack, but the Ohio general held firm while he prepared to contact Schofield then marching toward Goldsboro. On his own initiative, hard-fighting Maj. Gen. Joseph A. Mower, one of Howard's division commanders, launched a slashing attack with two of his three brigades on the extreme left of the Confederate line. The Rebels were pushed back and the Mill Creek Bridge, their only route of escape, was threatened. A Confederate counterattack, including the 8th Texas Cavalry (Terry's Texas Rangers), stemmed the advance. As Mower was re-forming his lines, orders came from Sherman not to renew the attack. General Hardee's sixteen-year-old son Willie, who had just received his father's permission that day to join the 8th Texas Cavalry, was mortally wounded in the charge against Mower.

That night, the Confederates withdrew over Mill Creek Bridge, an amazing feat considering the number of troops and equipment that had to cross the narrow span. The Rebels marched in the direction of Raleigh, toward, as it was described, "but one end." Not wanting to pursue Johnston until he made contact with Schofield, Sherman marched his united "army group" toward Goldsboro, where he arrived on March 23.

Points of Interest

Bentonville Battleground State Historic Site—Although Bentonville Battleground State Historic Site preserves only a small part of the battlefield, the site of Slocum's March 19 headquarters, a hospital, Union artillery positions, and subsequent Union entrenchments along the line, it is a pristine park. Efforts are constantly under way to expand the acreage of the preserved battlefield. Among the features of the park and area are extant earthworks, interpretive signs, a reconstructed example of a corduroy road, monuments, and a Confederate cemetery. The Harper House served as a hospital during and after the battle and it contains artifacts of and exhibits on Civil War medical care. Several other buildings portray life during the war. The visitor center has an audiovisual presentation and interpretive exhibits. Open every day except Monday in the winter, the site has picnic facilities and trails. BENTONVILLE BATTLEGROUND STATE HISTORIC SITE, 5466 Harper House Road, Four Oaks, NC 27524; P.O. Box 27, Newton Grove, NC 28366; 910-594-0789. ▨ ♿ 👫 ❓ 🏛 P 🍽 👫

Other significant sites in the Battle of Bentonville are identified and interpreted by roadside historical adjacent to the park. From I-95, take US701 south to NC1008 and follow the signs a short distance to Bentonville battleground.

———⊰⊱———

DRIVING TOUR—*Proceed to Bennett Place*
READING—*Fort Stedman, Virginia*

———⊰⊱———

BENNETT PLACE

On April 10, 1865, General Sherman's "army group" left Goldsboro en route to attack Joe Johnston at Smithfield. The Confederates after a brisk skirmish evacuated Smithfield on April 11 and Raleigh, which was occupied by Sherman's vanguard on April 13. Johnston, on April 11, learned of the April 9 surrender of Gen. Robert E. Lee and his army at Appomattox Court House, Virginia, on his army's retreat from Smithfield to Raleigh (see

Appomattox Court House, Virginia). While his troops went into camp in and around Hillsboro, Johnston met at Greensboro on April 12 with President Jefferson Davis.

Johnston, on April 14, sent a note to Sherman, then at Raleigh, based on his knowledge of Lee's surrender. A meeting was set for Monday, April 17, near Durham Station, midway between the two forces. The two generals met in the farmhouse of James Bennett, and returned the following day. Maj. Gen. John C. Breckinridge, now Confederate secretary of war, participated in the April 18 meeting. Remembering Lincoln's desires, when they had met at City Point a few weeks earlier, Sherman worked out terms, subject to the approval of Washington, that Johnston accepted but the U.S. government rejected as too lenient. On April 24, Grant arrived in Raleigh to inform Sherman that the generous terms would have to be modified to conform with his own surrender terms given General Lee.

Thus faced with the possibility of accepting the modified terms or enduring the wrath of an army bent on retribution to Southerners for the assassination of Abraham Lincoln, Johnston on April 26 accepted the terms. Confederate soldiers in Johnston's North Carolina army, after surrendering their arms, were paroled at Greensboro in the first week of May.

Points of Interest

Bennett Place—The reconstructed farmhouse of James Bennett sits at the center of a North Carolina State Historic Site on Neal Road, just off Business US70, west of Durham. Here Joseph E. Johnston and William T. Sherman met on three occasions to work out the terms of surrender and here on April 26, 1865, the surrender documents were signed. The site has a visitor center with interpretive exhibits and a peace memorial. Open every day from April through October, the site is closed Mondays in the winter. BENNETT PLACE STATE HISTORIC SITE, 4409 Bennett Memorial Road, Durham, NC 27705; 919-383-4345; FAX: 919-383-4349. 🎏 ♿ ❓ 🏛 P 🚻

In nearby Raleigh, the State Capitol is the Civil War–era state house. It is a fine example of Greek Revival architecture. For more information on touring the Capitol, which is located at 1 East Edenton Street, call 919-733-4994.

DRIVING TOUR—*Proceed to Petersburg, Virginia*
READING—*surrenders: Citronelle, Alabama*

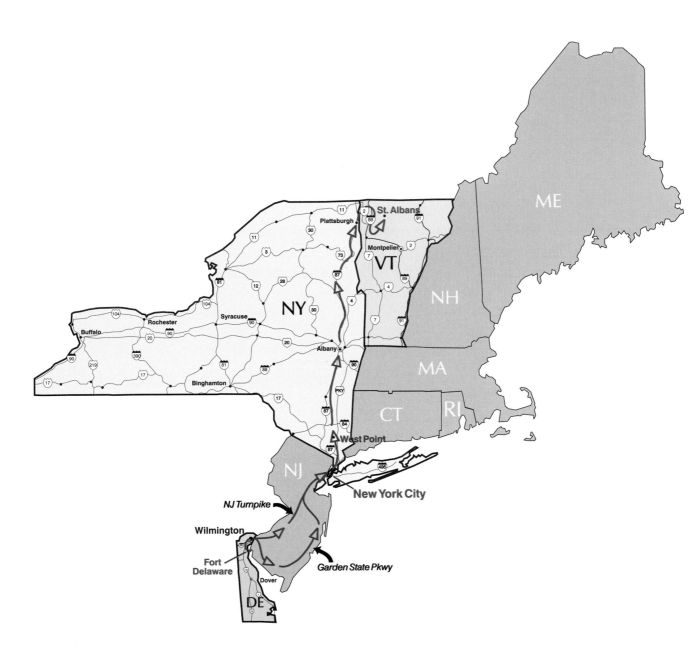

The Northeast

The Mid-Atlantic states, New England, and the Old Northwest (today's Midwest) were the areas of the North that exerted the greatest influence over the actions and policies of the United States government during the Civil War. Manpower, industrial might, and political clout came from these states. With its vast population, its burgeoning industrial capacity, financial, societal, and journalistic powers, the Northeast commanded great influence over the events of the war. Virtually untouched by armed conflict (except in Pennsylvania, a separate chapter) the Northeast has a few sites related to some unusual operations by Confederate operatives. Additional sites of great importance to the period, such as the United States Military Academy, are included.

DELAWARE

A slave state with close ties to the North, Delaware never contemplated seceding. The wartime governors ensured loyalty, though many in the population, including a large number of Quakers, were neutral. Delaware provided eleven organized units to the Federal army and many other volunteers; no Confederate units were organized in the state. Delaware was most valuable for war matériel and consumer goods, particularly the output of the E. I. du Pont powder works in Wilmington. The state also had Fort Delaware, a large Federal prison for Confederate officers and enlisted prisoners of war, as well as a handful of political prisoners.

Fort Delaware

Fort Delaware, a masonry fort located on Pea Patch Island in the Delaware River, was completed in 1859. In August 1863, the prison population was 12,500. Conditions were harsh, especially in the winter. Higher-ranking officers, including several generals and political prisoners, were housed in the fort's buildings. Company officers and enlisted

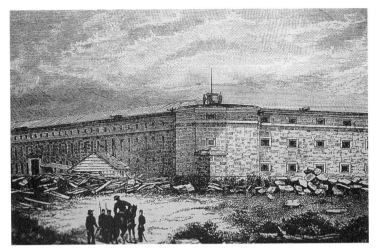

men lived in framed single-story barracks on the island, the grounds of which were flooded during equinoctial storms, leading to comparisons with the notorious Confederate prison Camp Sumter at Andersonville, Georgia (see **Andersonville, Georgia**).

A period illustration of Confederate prisoners at Fort Delaware

Today Fort Delaware is a state park. Access is gained from Delaware City, on DE72, about 20 miles south of Wilmington off US13. Regularly scheduled tour boats leave Delaware City for excursions to the island from April through September.

NEW YORK

No state provided more soldiers—500,000—to the Union army than New York. There were no battles in New York, but in mid-1863 the New York Draft Riots were the nation's most brutal and deadly civil disturbance. It was necessary for Maj. Gen. George G. Meade to send units from the Army of the Potomac to help quell the disturbance. In the autumn of 1864, Confederate agents launched a campaign of terror in Manhattan, but other than making intriguing headlines and panicking a few civilians, the operation had no effect.

Points of Interest

New York City—In the second week of July 1863, the Federal draft law passed by the U.S. Congress the previous March brought turmoil to the nation's largest city when the names of the first draftees were drawn, lottery style. Democratic leaders in the city fomented unrest by convincing many of the immigrant working-class population that they were being drafted to fight to free the slaves in the South who would then come north to compete for available jobs in the city, driving down wages. Consequently, the mob targeted blacks in their wave of hate-induced violence.

There are several sites in Manhattan associated with the New York Draft Riots and identified by historical markers. On Fifth Avenue between Forty-third and Forty-fourth streets is the site of the Negro Orphanage burned by the rioters. On the

The 7th New York Regiment marching down Broadway amid much patriotic fervor on its way to board transports for Washington, D.C., on April 19, 1861. Thomas Nast, the noted Civil War artist, witnessed the scene and sketched it for Harper's Weekly. *Later, he created this oil from his sketch.*

northeast corner of Third Avenue and Forty-sixth Street, a district enrollment office was one of the locations where a lottery wheel was spun to select names of draftees. Crosstown at Forty-sixth and Tenth Avenue, a plaque locates the home of Willy Jones, a laborer whose name was the first drawn in the draft on July 11, 1863.

Among many other buildings and sites in Manhattan with Civil War significance are the Mathew Brady Studio, Broadway at Fulton Street, and Cooper Union, Third Avenue at Seventh Street. Cooper Union—a National Historic Landmark—was one of the premier speaking halls in the nation during the nineteenth century, and many an abolitionist spoke here. Abraham Lincoln's February 27, 1860, speech here was instrumental in his eventually being nominated as the Republican presidential contender. The U.S. Sanitary Commission soldiers' relief organization was also founded here in 1861.

General Grant National Memorial—"Grant's Tomb," as it is often called, is located in Riverside Park at Riverside Drive and 123rd Street on the Upper West Side of Manhattan. Ulysses S. Grant and his wife, Julia, are interred in the sarcophagus. Grant spent his final days in Mount McGregor, New York. He died of throat cancer on July 23, 1885, shortly after completing his Civil War autobiography, *The Personal Memoirs of Ulysses S. Grant.* The site is administered by the National Park Service.

West Point—The United States Military Academy at West Point was established as a military engineering school in 1802 and became the academy for training an officer corps in 1812. More than 1,000 officers who fought for the North and South attended, and most graduated, from West Point. Many would return for tours of duty as instructors. Robert E. Lee was the superintendent from 1852 to 1855. Promising cadets during his tenure were future Union leaders James B. McPherson, John M. Schofield, and Philip H. Sheridan and Confederate generals John B. Hood, James Ewell Brown Stuart, and Stephen D. Lee. The fraternity of the West Point alumni was strong—leading to continued relationships between brother officers and sometimes between officers on different sides of the conflict.

Several of the existing buildings at West Point date to the Civil War era. A complete guide of Civil War sites at the academy is available at the information center at the South Gate. The West Point Museum, near the entrance to the grounds, features extensive Civil War exhibits. Trophy Point, where during the war a battery was manned overlooking the Hudson River, features a display of Civil War artillery and several monuments. Buried in the West Point Cemetery are Civil War notables including George Armstrong Custer.

Across the Hudson River at Cold Spring, the West Point Foundry produced the Union's most widely used rifled gun, the Parrott rifle, designed by a USMA graduate, Robert P. Parrott. The foundry, which turned out 1,700 Parrott rifles during the war, was once visited by President Abraham Lincoln.

West Point is on US9W, 12 miles south of Newburgh, New York.

VERMONT

Like other states of the North, Vermont provided distinguished officers and a surprisingly large number of its young men to the Union war effort. Far removed from the Confederacy, its citizens remained insulated from the direct effects of the war. All that changed in October 1864.

St. Albans

During the summer and fall of 1864, as part of the effort to sway the outcome of Lincoln's reelection, and possibly embroil the United States in a war against Great Britain, Confederate agents based in Canada launched a series of clandestine operations against the Northern states. The largest and most notable was a raid into the border town of St. Albans, Vermont. On October 19, 1864, 22 Confederate soldiers who had drifted down from Montreal and booked rooms in local hotels, appeared on the streets and robbed three St. Albans banks. One civilian was shot, and the raiders carried away $200,000 in cash. Eventually, $70,000 was recovered. The Lincoln administration, as well as Canadian officials, handled the affair diplomatically, and what could have been an explosive international incident was defused.

Points of Interest

The St. Albans Historical Museum on Church Street opposite Taylor Park features, among other exhibits, Civil War artifacts and information about the raid. It is housed in a building that was built in 1861 and used as a school until becoming a museum in the 1970s. Many other buildings in the central area were extant at the time of the raid and before, when St. Albans was a station on the Underground Railroad. The museum is open from 1:00 P.M. to 4:00 P.M. Tuesday through Saturday, June through October. For more information, call 802-527-7933.

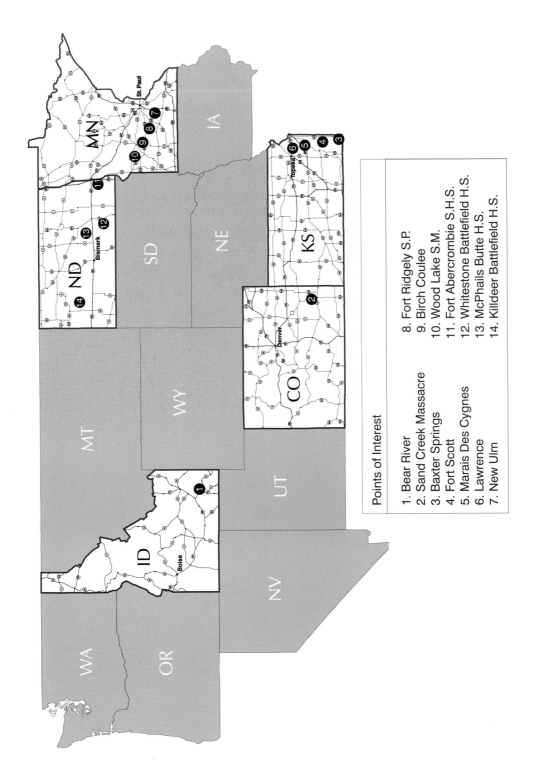

Points of Interest

1. Bear River
2. Sand Creek Massacre
3. Baxter Springs
4. Fort Scott
5. Marais Des Cygnes
6. Lawrence
7. New Ulm
8. Fort Ridgely S.P.
9. Birch Coulee
10. Wood Lake S.M.
11. Fort Abercrombie S.H.S.
12. Whitestone Battlefield H.S.
13. McPhails Butte H.S.
14. Killdeer Battlefield H.S.

The Northwest

The Northwest as defined here includes the states west of the Mississippi River and north of latitude 36°30', except for Missouri, which has its own chapter. Upon the petitioning of Missouri territory to enter the Union as a slave state, latitude 36°30' became the line of demarcation in the Missouri Compromise of 1820 for new territories carved out of the 1803 Louisiana Purchase to enter as slave states (below 36°30') or free (above 36°30'). In February 1861 the Northwest included four states—Oregon, Iowa, Minnesota, and Kansas—and the organized territories of Colorado, Nebraska, Utah, Nevada, Washington, and Dakota. All but Colorado, especially the last two, would see their borders changed by the time they became states.

Most battle action in the Northwest during the Civil War occurred in Kansas, which was granted statehood on January 29, 1861. Though Kansas was above latitude 36°30' and eligible for admission as a free state under the Missouri Compromise of 1820, it became the scene of a sometimes bloody struggle between proslavery and antislavery forces before joining the Union as a state with a constitution prohibiting slavery. That is because U.S. Senator Stephen A. Douglas of Illinois succeeded in amending certain provisions of the Missouri Compromise and replacing them with the Kansas-Nebraska Act of 1854, through which the citizens of a territory would determine whether to petition for statehood as free or slave, the so-called popular sovereignty concept. As freemen and slaveholders rushed to establish residency in the territory, Kansas in the mid-1850s became the crucible for the divisive and violent partisan conflict which would explode into the Civil War. Among the active participants in that pre-war Kansas violence was John Brown—freedom fighter, zealot, abolitionist, madman—depending on a person's perspective.

In other states and territories of the Northwest, the chief problems confronted by the United States government during the Civil War were relations with other peoples, Native Americans who saw their way of life threatened. Indian tribes such as the Sioux,

Shoshones, Cheyennes, and Comanches in the face of the ever-increasing pressure of white settlements and weary of life on reservations sought to drive whites from lands they considered rightfully theirs. The necessity of diverting troops and material from the war effort to cope with these outbreaks, as Indian peoples clashed with white Americans leading to savage warfare—which are documented in *The War of the Rebellion: Official Records of the Union and Confederate Armies*—warrant their inclusion in this guide.

Campaigns and battles between the military and Indians during these years took place in Colorado Territory, Utah Territory, Dakota Territory, and Minnesota. Other states and territories embraced in the "Northwest" were relatively peaceful during 1861–65. Washington Territory and Nevada, which became a state in 1864, were loyal, although pro-Confederate miners could be vocal. U.S. Army detachments and volunteers garrisoned forts, patrolled the western trails, and overawed the Mormons. An important activity in Nebraska Territory was the building of the Union Pacific Railroad, west from Omaha, which would be linked after the war with the Central Pacific at Promontory Point, Utah, in May 1869 to create the nation's first coast-to-coast railway. All of these territories except Utah, as well as the states of Iowa, Minnesota, Oregon, and Kansas, provided soldiers to the war effort, most of them organized into volunteer units. A handful of young men from Utah undoubtedly joined volunteer units from other states or territories or the Regular Army. Some residents of these territories probably fought for the Confederacy.

Points of interest in the Northwest are widely separated in this vast region, and no suggested tour route is offered. Visiting the sites in an area you happen to be in will yield rewards of understanding about the role of the army in the developing western frontier. Kansas sites lie along a north-south line in the eastern part of the state and can be easily accommodated in tours of Missouri, Arkansas, or Oklahoma.

COLORADO

Colorado Territory was becoming an important part of the nation during the Civil War. With new settlers arriving in the territory and "diggings" yielding gold, silver, and other ores, Colorado was growing rapidly. Denver was making the transition from mining camp to territorial capital. Colorado contributed soldiers to the Union war effort—the 1st and 2nd Colorado Volunteer regiments were formed early in the war and contributed to stemming the Confederate campaign to conquer New Mexico and occupy the Denver area (see **Glorieta, New Mexico**, in **The Far West**). After the Confederate invasion was turned back, military attention in the territory was directed toward problems caused by white-Indian difficulties.

Sand Creek Massacre

Efforts to maintain peace with the Plains Indians and other tribes kept violence along the overland trail to a minimum through the winter of 1863–64. By the summer of 1864, white-Indian hostilities in eastern Colorado and western Kansas led the territorial governor to ask Washington for permission to raise a one-hundred-day regiment—the 3rd Colorado Cavalry. Indian attacks, no doubt exaggerated as the news spread, caused panic in Denver. A conference between the governor, and U.S. military commanders on the one side and Arapaho and Cheyenne leaders on the other was held in September 1864, and though it did not end hostilities or result in permanent peace, it seemed to give the tribes security for a time. Black Kettle, a Cheyenne peace chief, and his village were invited to camp near Fort Lyon, on the Arkansas River in eastern Colorado, where they were provided with government rations. Soon Black Kettle moved to a camp forty miles northeast of the fort on Sand Creek. The villagers felt secure that they were complying with the wishes of the government.

On November 29, an expedition of 950 men, including the 3rd Colorado Cavalry, attacked the Sand Creek village at sunrise. Col. John M. Chivington, who had been a hero in the Federal victory at Glorieta Pass more than two years earlier, led the soldiers. The Indians' horses, grazing nearby, were seized to prevent the Indians' escape. A white interpreter in the camp later testified that Black Kettle had raised an American flag over his lodge as the soldiers approached. Despite this, the bluecoats charged the village from three directions, firing indiscriminately on the panicked Indians. Warriors, women, children, and old men were shot. Some of the warriors fought but were no match for the well-armed soldiers. Eventually they were routed and some of the Indians were pursued and shot after the general engagement ended at three P.M. The village was destroyed and the number of dead was more than 150—two thirds of them women and children. Chivington lost 9 killed and 38 wounded.

This attack was condemned in most quarters, though Chivington and others defended the action as necessary as a deterrent to future violence. The opposite resulted. Retaliatory Indian attacks increased, causing a call for more troops, and in early 1865 martial law was declared in the territory. Inquiries were held, opinions were divided, but Chivington and his lieutenants escaped formal censure—though Chivington resigned from the army to avoid a court-martial. One subordinate officer, whose official report indicated the attack was a success, in February 1865 wrote a letter to a Denver newspaper describing the massacre as a disgrace to every officer connected with it. The Sand Creek Massacre continues to be a blight on the reputation of Colonel Chivington and his officers and men.

Points of Interest

At the end of a rural road, 10 miles north of CO96, there is a historical marker describing the Sand Creek Massacre. The marker is on a ridge overlooking the site of Black Kettle's Indian village. Some 40 miles southwest, on US350, is Fort Lyon and the Fort Lyon National Cemetery. A building in the fort, now a museum, was the site of Col. Kit Carson's death. Guide, explorer, and soldier, Carson fought for the Union in the New Mexico battles and in campaigns against Navahos in that state.

IDAHO

Conflicts with Native Americans in what was in 1863 northern Utah Territory, now southern Idaho, increased in late 1862. To replace soldiers of the "Old Army" that in the years since the 1857–58 Mormon Expedition had maintained Federal authority in Utah Territory but had been redeployed to fight Confederates, Col. Patrick Edward Conner with the 3rd California Infantry crossed the high Sierras and entered the Great Basin. Posts were manned along the emigrant route. Conner and most of his command arrived in Salt Lake City on October 20 and established Camp Douglas nearby. Federal officials were concerned that loyalty of the Mormon militia and its ability to guard vital mail and telegraph routes linking the east with California were not adequate. Conner promptly turned his attention to the activities of several Shoshone and Bannock bands that, seeing their way of life being destroyed, had lashed out. There were attacks on miners en route to and from the recently discovered "digging" in today's Montana.

Bear River Massacre

Conner took a column, consisting of California cavalry, infantry, and artillery north from Camp Douglas in late January 1863. The weather was very cold and snow lay two feet deep on the level. On January 29, the cavalry, under Maj. Edward McGarry, dismounted and attacked Bear Hunter's village of Northwestern Shoshones, along Battle Creek, a tributary of Bear River. The frontal attack on the village by the dismounted cavalry failed. But, reinforced by infantry, the village was surrounded, the horse herd stampeded or was captured, and after four hours of desperate fighting, some of it hand-to-hand, the warriors were routed. A few of the more than 300 Indians involved in the battle escaped, but 250 Northwestern Shoshone men, women, and children were dead. Other women and children surrendered and were released. The village was destroyed and the soldiers—having lost 23 killed and 41 wounded in the fight—returned to Camp Douglas. This action, a massacre, broke Indian resistance in the region.

Points of Interest

The site of the Bear River Massacre is in southeastern Idaho off US30, 8 miles northwest of Preston, and a visit to the site, which has changed little in more than 133 years, evokes tragic memories of man's inhumanity to man. A National Historic Landmark, the Bear River Massacre Site is being studied by the National Park Service and recommendations have been forwarded to Congress on how to better protect and interpret the site.

KANSAS

With Kansas torn by prewar bitterness it was logical that the war would bring continued violence. Many partisan incidents occurred, but the state escaped large-scale fights except the two

Three of the Missouri partisans who participated in William C. Quantrill's raids in Kansas and Missouri posing with guns drawn

initiated by organized bands of Missouri Border Ruffians led by William C. Quantrill. Two major battles in Maj. Gen. Sterling Price's September–November 1864 ill-fated raid carried the Confederates deep into Missouri and brought bloodshed to the Jayhawk State. Many Federal units, white, black, and Indian were formed in Kansas and served in campaigns in the Trans-Mississippi, while two cavalry and three infantry regiments participated in battles east of the Mississippi.

Lawrence Massacre

William Clarke Quantrill has been described as the most potent of the Confederate partisan leaders operating from bases in western Missouri. His methods were brutal, his results effective. In the predawn hours of August 21, 1863, he marched his 400 guerrillas—including William "Bloody Bill" Anderson, Cole Younger, George Todd, and Frank James—to the outskirts of Lawrence, Kansas, an abolitionist community before the war and then a stronghold of pro-Union sentiment. After a reconnaissance of the town ascertained that there would be no organized resistance, Quantrill led his force, riding in columns of four, into Lawrence. For four hours they looted, burned, pillaged, and murdered. Though no women or children were harmed, some 150 men and boys, mostly unarmed, were shot and killed. Several prisoners taken in Lawrence were executed on the town's outskirts. Quantrill reportedly had a list of intended victims—on that list was Kansas Senator James Lane, a fiery abolitionist. Lane was in Lawrence but escaped the massacre by fleeing in his nightshirt.

Disappearing as fast as they came, with captured horses and loot, only one

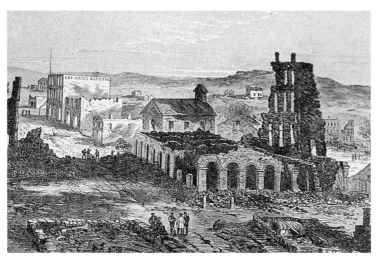

This Harper's Weekly *woodcut shows the severe damage to buildings from the fire set by Missouri partisans during William C. Quantrill's August 1863 raid into Lawrence, Kansas.*

raider was left behind in a drunken stupor to be hanged by the citizenry. Immediately, Federal garrisons in the area were notified, but the raiders made good their escape into Missouri. Lane and others organized a vigilante party to retaliate against the raiders' base in western Missouri, but the group never left Lawrence. As a result of the raid, District of the Border commander Brig. Gen. Thomas Ewing issued General Order No. 11, which compelled all inhabitants of three southwest Missouri counties and part of a fourth to leave the area within fifteen days. This controversial order, against the region held responsible for harboring Quantrill's raiders and other guerrillas, was allowed to stand by the Lincoln administration. Thousands of people were forced from their homes and turned into refugees.

Points of Interest

Little remains of the town Quantrill's raiders sacked and burned on August 21, 1863. The only surviving structure is the First Methodist Church, 724 Vermont Street, used as a morgue. But the city remembers the event. The sites of the Eldridge Hotel, at Massachusetts and Seventh, the Speer House, at 1024 Maryland Street, and the Snyder House, Nineteenth and Haskall streets, all are identified by historical markers describing events that took place that day. At 935 New Hampshire Street is a stone monument to twenty unarmed boys who were shot there. Many of the victims are buried at Oak Hill Cemetery on Thirteenth Street. James Lane, a survivor, is also buried there.

Fort Leavenworth, an important frontier fort northeast of Lawrence (on US73, 15 miles north of I-70 exit 224), was an important Federal army post during the Civil War and is still in use as a U.S. Army facility. There were five Federal camps in the area and the Santa Fe Trail ran through the fort. Fort Sully was built on the post when Jo Shelby's Confederate cavalry was raiding the border area. The fort and the Federal winter quarters are marked with interpretive signs. The Fort Leavenworth post museum has two Parrott rifled cannons and information on locating Fort Sully and the winter camp on the post. For more information, call the post museum at 913-684-3767 between 8:00 A.M. and 4:00 P.M., Monday through Friday.

DRIVING TOUR—*Proceed to Marais des Cygnes and Mine Creek (Mound City)*
READING—*Baxter Springs Massacre*

Sterling Price's 1864 Raid

In the autumn of 1864, Maj. Gen. Sterling Price, who dreamed of recovering Missouri for the Confederacy since the Rebel defeat at Pea Ridge in March 1862 (see **Pea Ridge, Arkansas**), reentered that state with a formidable army, all mounted. Hounded by a series of Federal commands, he was able to slip away from engagements near Kansas City, Missouri, in late October (see **Westport, Missouri**) and began a long and disastrous retreat south into northeast Texas.

Marais des Cygnes–Mine Creek (Mound City)

As Price's forces retreated southward, they were slowed by a cumbersome wagon train, loaded with plunder from happier days of the raid in Missouri. He was pursued by Maj. Gen. Alfred Pleasonton's cavalry division and a separate force under Maj. Gen. James G. Blunt. By the early dawn of October 25, Pleasonton's fast-riding column overtook the rear of Price's force—cavalry and mounted infantry under Maj. Gen. James F. Fagan and Brig. Gen. John S. Marmaduke, first on the Marais des Cygnes River and then on Mine Creek as hundreds of wagons slowly crossed at Mine Creek via a difficult ford. Pleasonton mounted a classic cavalry charge with the head of his column and crashed through the Rebel cavalry, routing them. More than 750 Confederates were captured, including General Marmaduke and Brig. Gen. William "Old Tige" Cabell.

After the initial rout, Price formed the remainder of his force, Brig. Gen. Jo Shelby's cavalry division, to hold the crossing of the Little Osage, three miles southeast of Mine Creek. The delaying action at the Little Osage and later at dusk on Charlot's Farm allowed Price to save his command. The Federals continued pursuit, battling with Price's rear guard until nightfall. Pleasonton then retired his force and marched to Fort Scott. Blunt's column continued to harass Price's force, which had burned most of their wagons after crossing the Marmiton River, and fought them at Newtonia, Missouri (see **Newtonia, Missouri**), then retired. Price's expedition finally ended at Laynesport, Arkansas, on December 2. He returned with less than half the force with which he started the expedition.

Points of Interest

Mound City, on KS52, 6 miles west of US69, has a marker in the national cemetery describing the Battle of Mine Creek. The running battle from Marais des Cygnes to Mine Creek took place along KS7 from Farlinville to Mound City. A new Kansas state park is being developed at Mine Run. The site currently has parking, an information kiosk, and a 2.8-mile interpretive trail which is on two loops through the battlefield. A visitor center is under construction. The park is located 1 mile west of the south intersection of US69 and KS52 in Linn County, 5 miles east of Mound City. On US69 on the way to Baxter Springs is Fort Scott National Historic Site, which served the U.S. Army before the war and was used as a headquarters by the Federal Army of the Frontier.

Maj. Gen. James G. Blunt was born in Maine but moved west early in life. He developed a strong abolitionist stance and was a major champion of using African Americans and Native Americans as soldiers. In many of the battles that he fought he commanded a so-called rainbow coalition of black, white, and Indian soldiers.

Fort Scott National Historic Site—The frontier post of Fort Scott was established in 1842 and served the army as a base of operations for the Mexican War, the exploration of the intermountain west, and the protection of settlers and property in the frontier areas in the mid-nineteenth century. During the Civil War, it was an important base for Federal army operations in Kansas, Missouri, Arkansas, and the Indian Territory. The 1st and 2nd Kansas (Colored) Volunteer Infantry regiments were mustered into the army here. The 1st Kansas had a distinguished record of service beginning with an engagement at Island Mound, Missouri, on October 28, 1862, before they were officially mustered into the U.S. Army on January 13, 1863.

The fort, in the middle of the town of Fort Scott, has been re-created to appear as it did at mid-century, with all important buildings restored or reconstructed. There is a visitor center with a bookstore and a museum, and most of the other buildings contain exhibits. Fort Scott is open every day from 8:00 A.M. to 5:00 P.M. except Thanksgiving, Christmas, and New Year's Day. There are extended hours and some evening programs in the summer. FORT SCOTT NATIONAL HISTORIC SITE, Old Fort Boulevard, Fort Scott, Kansas 66701; 316-223-0310.   🏕 ♿ 🏛 P ⛱ 👫

DRIVING TOUR—*Proceed to Baxter Springs*
READING—*Newtonia, Missouri*

Baxter Springs Massacre

Quantrill and most of his raiders, eluding capture, returned to Kansas in early October. A forced march to northeast Texas, where the guerrillas planned to winter, was interrupted by the October 6, 1863, attack on Fort Blair, a recently built stockade fifty-five miles south of Fort Scott at Baxter Springs. The 95 black and white soldiers manning the fort repulsed the initial assaults of the raiders; however, Quantrill's scouts sighted a small wagon train heading toward the fort. It was the headquarters train of Maj. Gen. James G. Blunt, District of the Frontier commander, and its 100-man escort. Breaking off the attack on the fort, Quantrill formed a line of battle on the edge of the prairie north of the Baxter Springs fort.

The cavalry guarding the train failed to recognize the initial charge as an attack because the raiders were dressed in blue. Before they could get off an effective volley, the raiders were among them. Most of the Kansas horse soldiers were shot down, even those that surrendered. Blunt and a few others managed to escape on horseback, but more than 80 of the Federals including 14 bandsmen, a correspondent for *Frank Leslie's Illustrated*, and other civilians traveling with the train were killed. Quantrill then continued his southward march around the fort and into the Indian Territory. There he was praised by Confederate Maj. Gen. Sterling Price for his efforts, though even among the Rebels, there were those who criticized his methods. Some of the raiders joined organized Confederate units. Others drifted away to form their own marauding gangs. Quantrill and a few followers drifted in and out of Confederate commands in the Indian Territory and Texas until, in early 1865, he decided to carry his personal campaign east, intending to assassinate President Lincoln (see **Kentucky Cavalry Raids and Raiders**).

Points of Interest

Baxter Springs is on US69ALT just north of the Oklahoma state line. A historical marker at the end of East Seventh Street indicates the site of the massacre, and the Baxter Springs museum is a gem with Civil War exhibits and artifacts. The victims of the massacre are buried in Baxter Springs National Cemetery. For more information on Baxter Springs, contact the Baxter Springs Historical Society at 316-856-2385.

MINNESOTA

The tranquillity of Minnesota, seemingly far removed from where Civil War battles raged, was disturbed in the summer of 1862 when the Santee Sioux, embittered by the realization that they had been cheated of their ancestral lands and otherwise by the government and its Indian agents, sought to avenge themselves. In August, led by Chief Little Crow, the Santee Sioux, angered by the Federal government's failure to provide their stipulated annuities and the poor quality of their rations, struck back. They killed some 800 settlers and soldiers, took many prisoners, and caused extensive property damage throughout the upper Minnesota River Valley before they were defeated.

Fort Ridgely

Fort Ridgely, about twelve miles from the Lower Sioux Agency, became the refuge for white civilians. The fort's commander, Capt. John S. Marsh, set out with most of his men for the Lower Sioux Agency. Before reaching the agency, a large number of Santee Sioux surprised the soldiers, killed 25 including Marsh, and pursued the survivors back to the fort. On August 20, about 400 Sioux attacked the fort but were repulsed. Two days later, 800 Sioux attacked again, but the garrison and civilians held the fort.

New Ulm and Birch Coulee

The first attack on New Ulm, a German settlement, came on August 19, when 100 warriors from a position on a bluff fired into the town. The Santee received a hot reception. A late-afternoon cloudburst dampened the Indians' ardor, and with the arrival of the mounted reinforcements for the townspeople, the first fight ended.

The Santee reinforced by 700 Sissetons and Wahpetons returned on August 25 and, after two days of fighting, again withdrew. In the two attacks on New Ulm, the defenders lost 53 dead and 23 wounded. The battle was won by the whites, but much of New Ulm was destroyed. A week later, at dawn on September 2, Sioux warriors surrounded and attacked Minnesota volunteers commanded by Maj. Joseph R. Brown at Birch Coulee, killing 19 soldiers. The next day reinforcements were sent and the Sioux withdrew.

Wood Lake

On September 19, 1862, Col. Henry Hastings Sibley (no relation to Confederate general Henry H. Sibley of New Mexico and Louisiana) set out from Fort Ridgely with 1,500 volunteers to put down the Santee uprising. As they neared Wood Lake on September 23, Sibley's men escaped an ambush by 700 warriors under Chief Little Crow and engaged them in a battle. Sibley's force won the day, inflicting heavy casualties on the Sioux. For this action, Sibley received a promotion to brigadier general. Wood Lake was the first decisive defeat of the Sioux since the uprising began. Most of Little Crow's warriors had seen enough fighting, and they scattered with their chiefs and families, some going to Canada, others joining the Teton Sioux farther west, and many traveling into Devil's Lake country in present-day North Dakota to spend the winter of 1862–63 beyond reach of Sibley's soldiers. Back in Minnesota nearly 2,000 were under guard by late October. The captured warriors deemed responsible for the uprising were brought before a military commission and 307 were sentenced to die. President Lincoln pardoned all but 38 who were publicly hanged at Mankato on December 26, America's largest public execution. The Battle of Wood Lake and its aftermath ended all problems with the Sioux in Minnesota, but they would carry on their war the next spring in Dakota Territory.

Points of Interest

Historic Fort Snelling—In downtown Minneapolis, at the intersection of Hiawatha Avenue and MN5, Historic Fort Snelling is a restored 1820s fort that was the command center for the Federal operations against the Sioux in Minnesota. Some prisoners were also held here. There is an interpretive center and exhibits. For more information, call 612-726-9430. Nearby Fort Snelling State Park, across from the international airport, has day use activities. For more information, call 612-725-2390.

Mankato—Mankato is located at the junction of US169 and US14, 80 miles southwest of Minneapolis–St. Paul. From Mankato, other Minnesota points of interest follow the Minnesota River in a northwest direction. A Sioux Memorial is currently under construction across from the Mankato Public Library to commemorate the executions that took place there. Nearby Minneopa State Park (507-389-5464) has camping and recreational activities. From Mankato, proceed northwest on US14 to New Ulm.

New Ulm—New Ulm has a monument commemorating the two battles fought there, while 8 miles northeast of town on Brown County Road 4 is the Milford Monument commemorating the 52 victims of the Sioux attack which took place there on August 18, 1862. Flandrau State Park has a historic site and recreational activities. FLANDRAU STATE PARK, 1300 Summit Avenue, New Ulm, MN 56073-3664; 507-354-3519.

 ≒ ▲ ➤ ♿ ❷ P ⛴ ≈ ⚥ ⚓ $$$ *

Fort Ridgely State Park—Seventeen of the fort buildings survive as either restorations or as the original foundations. There is an interpretive center at the park and a number of recreational activities are available in the park. The park is located just off MN4 northwest of New Ulm. FORT RIDGELY STATE PARK, Rural Route 1, P.O. Box 65, Fairfax, MN 55332-9601; 507-426-7840.   ▲ ➤ ♿ 🕴 🐎 ❷ ⛴ ⚥ ⚓ $$$ *

At Birch Coulee, just north of the town of Morton, there is a county park at the battle site. Wood Lake State Monument has a wayside exhibit. Follow signs to the site from MN67 southeast of Granite Falls. Also in the area is Upper Sioux Agency State Park,

* annual permit

which has historic exhibits and recreational activities. Call 507-564-4777 for more information. At Joseph R. Brown State Wayside, on County Road 7 south of Sacred Hearth, are the remains of a house destroyed in the 1862 uprising.

NORTH DAKOTA

At the beginning of the Civil War the Dakota Territory, comprising present-day North and South Dakota, much of Montana, and part of Wyoming, had fewer than 2,500 white inhabitants, most of whom had settled in the Red River Valley. Sending a few volunteers to serve in the Federal forces, the territory had only a handful of men to defend the vast region in the event that the Sioux war that had wracked southwestern Minnesota in 1862 spread. The situation became alarming in the summer of 1863 when the Santee Sioux under Chief Little Crow were rumored to be causing trouble. Earlier that year the territory was opened to homesteading. Maj. Gen. John Pope, reassigned from the Eastern Theater after being defeated by Robert E. Lee at the Battle of Second Manassas (see **Second Manassas, Virginia**), launched a two-pronged preemptive campaign into the territory—one column would be led by Brig. Gen. Alfred Sully, an Army of the Potomac veteran, and the other by Gen. Henry Hastings Sibley.

Big Mound

General Sibley led his troops from Fort Ridgely, Minnesota, into the Dakotas, pursuing the Santee Sioux who had joined forces with the Teton Sioux. Having marched all day on July 24, Sibley's scouts at one P.M. reported a large Indian camp a few miles away. Sibley established a camp on a nearby salt lake and set his men to entrenching it for protection. While the troops were making camp, numerous Sioux appeared expressing friendship and began talking with them. Surgeon Josiah S. Weiser, 1st Regiment Minnesota Mounted Rangers, joined the assembly, but soon afterward a Sioux shot and killed him. The scouts attempted to kill the attacker but he escaped. Indians who had hidden behind the surrounding ridges now emerged and attacked. In detachments, the soldiers went out to meet Indians. Sibley, with some men, approached the "Big Mound" on the opposite side of the ravine, and attempted to dislodge those Sioux who were on the upper part of the large ravine firing at the infantry and cavalry with impunity. The Union forces routed these and other well-placed Sioux on the surrounding ridges with accurate artillery fire and forced them into the broken prairie where they fled in confusion. The mounted troops, with some of the infantry and artillery following, set out in pursuit. A running battle ensued for the rest of the day. Before dark, the soldiers broke off the pursuit and returned to camp as ordered.

Dead Buffalo Lake

Following the Big Mound battle, Sibley and his men moved their camp four miles and then rested till the next day. The morning of July 26 they set out and, after marching about fourteen miles, found the Sioux ready for battle. At first, the fighting was long-range, the Indians refraining from closing with the soldiers. The Indians attempted to flank the left side of the camp and stampede the mules. The Mounted Rangers and infantry, though, after heavy fighting, compelled the Sioux to abandon their efforts. Following this setback, the Sioux retreated, ending the battle. Sibley resumed his march the next day, beating them again on July 28 at Stone Lake.

Whitestone Hill

Following General Sibley's victories over the Sioux, he left the area, crossing the James River. The Sioux then recrossed the Missouri River and returned to their old hunting grounds. General Sully decided to find these Sioux and punish them. By September 3, Sully reached a lake where he found remains of recently killed buffalo. A 6th Iowa Cavalry detachment discovered an Indian camp of more than 400 lodges, about three P.M., which they sought to surround until a courier could inform Sully. Word reached Sully around four P.M., and he set out with the rest of the troops, except for the poorly mounted men who remained to protect the animals and supplies. An hour later, Sully and his men arrived at the Sioux camp and observed that the Sioux were attempting to leave. Sully sent in his troops to help the 6th Iowa Cavalry. Although the Sioux counter-attacked, it was to no avail. The Sioux broke under the army's firepower and fled, hotly pursued. Fighting subsided after dark but scattered firing continued. Sully ordered the bugler to sound rally, and the troops stood under arms during the rest of the night. In the morning, Sully established a camp on the battlefield and, during the next two days, sent scouting parties to look for the Indians and ordered the destruction of Native-American foodstuffs and supplies found in the area.

On September 5, a detachment from the 2nd Nebraska and 6th Iowa Cavalry went in search of a surgeon and 8 men missing since the September 3 battle. About fifteen miles northwest of camp, they were attacked by 300 Sioux. The men could not stand up to this number and began a slow retreat while returning fire. As the Indians came closer, the men panicked and stepped up their flight despite entreaties from the officers. They returned to camp and safety, after losing 6 men in the skirmish. Altogether, Sully's men overran a large Sioux camp, destroyed all the Indians' possessions, including four hundred thousand pounds of dried buffalo meat, killed or wounded a large number of men, and captured numerous women and children. This engagement weakened but did not destroy Sioux resistance in the area.

Killdeer Mountain

General Sully wintered on the Missouri River. During the winter, Sully's superior, General Pope, formulated a plan for ending difficulties with the Sioux. He ordered a force of about 2,500 men, commanded by Sully, into the field to find the Sioux and engage them in battle. In addition, he sent infantry behind Sully's force to establish strong posts in the "Indian Country." The two columns rendezvoused on June 30, 1864, and set out against the Sioux. They established Fort Rice on July 7 at the mouth of Cannonball River and moved on. The Sioux, who had been roaming north of Fort Rice, moved across the Missouri River and took a strong position on the Little Missouri River, about two hundred miles from the fort.

On July 26, Sully marched out to engage them in battle and forty-eight hours later he arrived near the Sioux village, which he reported included 5,000–6,000 warriors "strongly posted in wooded country, very much cut up with high, rugged hills, and deep impassable ravines." Sully met with some of the tribal chiefs first, but nothing came of it, so he attacked. Heavy fighting ensued, but eventually the artillery and long-range firearms took effect and the Sioux began losing ground. The retirement turned into flight. The Indians left all their possessions and a running fight of almost nine miles scattered the warriors who were not wounded or killed. Killdeer Mountain broke the back of the Sioux resistance.

Points of Interest

Burman and McPhail's Butte Historic Sites in Kidder County just off I-94 have interpretive waysides, a gravesite, and memorial markers pertaining to the Battle of Big Mound.

Whitestone Battlefield Historic Site (Dickey County, west of US281) and Killdeer Mountain Battlefield Historic Site (Dunn County, west of Killdeer on ND200) have interpretive exhibits on those battles. Other markers in the southeastern part of the state indicate camps of General Sully's command. For more information on North Dakota sites, contact the North Dakota Department of Natural Resources at 701-328-6332.

DRIVING TOUR—*Proceed to Oklahoma, Southwest Missouri, or Northwest Arkansas*
READING—*Kentucky Cavalry Raids and Raiders; Cynthiana, Kentucky*

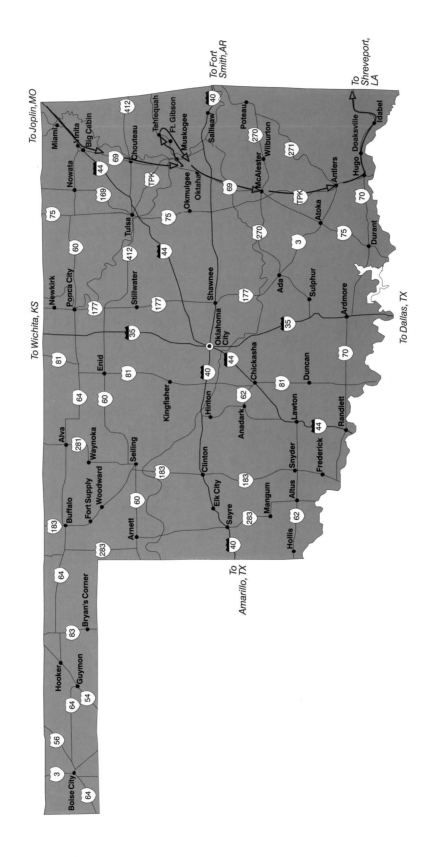

Oklahoma

During the Civil War, Oklahoma was Indian Territory. It included lands that the Federal government ceded to the Five Civilized Native-American Tribes of the Southeast—the Cherokee, Creek, Choctaw, Chickasaw, and Seminole—in exchange for lands they held in the southeastern states in accordance with the government's removal policy. Also living on small reservations were Quapaw and Seneca, while to the west of lands belonging to the "Five Civilized Nations" were Plains Indians. All but the Seminoles had maintained peaceful relations with whites and the Seminoles had been defeated in three wars by the U.S. Army and forcibly removed. Since these tribes had come from the South, some of their leaders and other affluent tribesmen owned slaves, which they brought with them to the Indian Territory. But this in itself was not a valid reason why Native Americans joined the Confederate service and took part in a conflict in which they had nothing to gain and their lives to lose. A stronger reason was the influence that Federal Indian agents Douglas Cooper and Albert Pike, who became Confederate officers, had with leaders; and the humanitarian and generous terms offered by the Confederates in treaties. Pike was made a brigadier general and given the task of negotiating treaties with the Indians west of Arkansas. The terms he offered were equal to or more generous than those in effect with the U.S. government, which was not in full compliance on terms of existing treaties.

On the other hand, those Indians who remained loyal to the Union and even fought in its ranks were expressing loyalty to the Federal government probably because they were satisfied with their treatment. Not all Indians in the Federal army were from the Indian Territory. Delawares Quapaws and Osages living on Kansas reservations joined pro-

Union Cherokees, Creeks, and Seminoles in the three Indian Home Guard Regiments that saw much combat. Most Native Americans in uniform came from and fought in the Trans-Mississippi, primarily in Indian Territory skirmishes and battles. No part of the nation and no peoples suffered as greatly from the hard hand of war. To exacerbate the horrors of war, the Cherokee, Creek, and Seminole nations were plagued by bloody feuds dating to the removal treaties of the 1830s.

Indian Territory military highlights are described in chronological order, while the suggested tour follows a route from north to south. Most action occurred in the eastern part of Oklahoma, although a few skirmishes and raids occurred in the central part of the state and near the Texas border. Because the forts of the territory played an important role in the defense and pacification of the region, those that were occupied by one or both sides during the Civil War are mentioned if they or some of their features are extant.

ROUND MOUNTAIN

Col. Douglas H. Cooper, Confederate commander of the Indian Department, had been unable to reconcile differences with Chief Opothleyahola, who led bands of Unionist Creeks and Seminoles. Cooper set out on November 15, 1861, to "either compel submission . . . or drive him and his party from the country." His force rode up the Deep Fork of the Canadian River toward Chief Opothleyahola's camp, which they found deserted. On November 19, Cooper learned from captured prisoners that part of Chief Opothleyahola's band was at the Red Fork of the Arkansas River. Cooper's men arrived there about four P.M. and the Confederates blundered into Chief Opothleyahola's camp. The red Federals fired into the Rebel cavalry and, in large force, came out to attack them. They chased the Confederates back to Cooper's main force. Darkness prevented Cooper from attacking until Opothleyahola's warriors were within sixty yards. A short fight ensued but Chief Opothleyahola's men broke it off and retreated back to their camp. Cooper set out for Chief Opothleyahola's camp the next morning but found it gone. The Confederates claimed victory because Chief Opothleyahola left the area. This was the first of three encounters between Chief Opothleyahola's Union bands and Confederate troops.

CHUSTO-TALASAH

Following Chief Opothleyahola and his Union force's defeat at Round Mountain, he retreated northeastward, in search of safety. On December 9, 1861, his people were at

Chusto-Talasah, or Caving Banks, on the Horseshoe Bend of Bird Creek when Col. Douglas H. Cooper's 1,300 Confederates—Texans, Creeks, Cherokees, Choctaws, and Chickasaws—attacked Chief Opothleyahola. Chief Opothleyahola knew Cooper was coming and had placed his Creek and Seminole warriors in a strong position at Horseshoe Bend. This was a position similar to that taken up by the "Red Stick" Creeks on March 1814, when they were defeated by Maj. Gen. Andrew Jackson at the Battle of Horseshoe Bend on Alabama's Tallapoosa River. For almost four hours, Cooper attacked and attempted to outflank the Union Indians, finally driving them east across Bird Creek just before dark. Cooper camped there overnight but did not pursue the Federals because he was short of ammunition. Chief Opothleyahola and his bands moved off in search of security elsewhere.

CHUSTENALAH

Although Colonel Cooper and his Confederate Indians and Texans had twice gone out to battle Opothleyahola and his followers, they had failed to crush his bands. More dev-astating for the Rebels, at Chusto-Talasah, on the outskirts of present-day Tulsa, one of the Confederates' Cherokee regiments had switched allegiance. To solve the problem that was rapidly threatening to get out of hand, the Confederates determined to commit an overwhelming force to snuff out the fires of rebellion in the Creek, Seminole, and Cherokee nations.

Col. James McQueen McIntosh and Col. Douglas H. Cooper, commanding the Indian Department, planned a combined attack with each of their columns moving on the camp from different directions. McIntosh left Van Buren, Arkansas, on December 17, with 1,600 Texans and Arkansans. On December 25, he was informed that Cooper's force could not join for a while, but he decided to attack at Chustenalah, near present-day Skiatook, despite being outnumbered. McIntosh attacked the camp at noon on December 26. The Union defenders were secluded in the underbrush along the slope of a rugged hill, but as the Confederate attack came forward, the Native Americans began to fall back, taking cover for a time and then pulling back. The retreat became a rout as the Federals reached their camp. They attempted to make a stand there but were forced away again. The survivors fled and many, though hounded by Colonel Cooper and blizzard conditions, reached Kansas where they found protection. Chief Opothleyahola's bands of Creeks and Seminoles mounted no resistance again, but a number were recruited into Union service and became the core of the 1st Regiment Indian Home Guard.

OLD FORT WAYNE

The first five and one half months of 1862, except in Virginia's Shenandoah Valley, had been a series of Union successes that seemingly doomed the Confederacy. The Indian Territory was no exception. At Locust Grove, in the Cherokee Nation, on July 3, Union forces led by Col. William Weer mauled Col. J. J. Clarkson's Confederates. Before the end of the month, the war turned sour for the Yankees in the Cherokee Nation. Douglas Cooper and his command—Cherokees, Choctaws, Chickasaws, and Texans—swept northeastward into southwest Missouri, as part of the great Confederate August–September advance extending from Tidewater Virginia in the east to the Indian Territory.

Although Cooper more than held his own at First Newtonia on September 30, 1862 (see **Newtonia, Missouri**), the Confederate offensive had crested everywhere. Boldly seizing the initiative, Maj. Gen. John M. Schofield's Army of the Frontier crossed into Arkansas. Brig. Gen. James G. Blunt's Union troops attacked Cooper and his Confederate command on Beatty Prairie near Old Fort Wayne at seven A.M. on October 22. The Confederates put up stiff resistance for a half hour, but overwhelming numbers forced them to retire from the field in haste, leaving artillery and equipage behind.

FIRST CABIN CREEK

In the second week of April 1863, Union forces led by Col. William A. Phillips that included the 1st, 2nd and 3rd Indian Home Guards advanced from camps in northwest Arkansas and occupied Fort Gibson in the Cherokee Nation. Wagon trains traveling south from Fort Scott in Kansas, via the Texas Road, were required to supply the Union toehold on the Arkansas River.

Col. James M. Williams leading the 1st Kansas Colored Infantry escorted a Union supply train from Fort Scott. On July 1, as he approached the crossing of Cabin Creek, he learned that Confederate Col. Stand Watie intended to assault him there. Watie was waiting for reinforcements under the command of Brig. Gen. William L. Cabell to join him before attacking the train. Cabell, however, was detained due to high water on Grand River. Cabin Creek also had high water, preventing a crossing at first, but when it had receded enough, Williams, on July 2, drove the Confederates off with artillery fire and two cavalry charges. The wagon train continued to Fort Gibson and delivered the supplies, making it possible for the Union forces to maintain their presence in Indian Territory.

HONEY SPRINGS

Maj. Gen. James G. Blunt reached Fort Gibson from Fort Scott with reinforcements on July 11, 1863, and assumed command. He learned that Douglas Cooper, now a brigadier general, was camped at Honey Springs Depot with a brigade composed of Native Americans, Texans, and Hispanics. Cooper was said to be bracing for an attack on Fort Gibson, upon arrival of "Old Tige" Cabell and his brigade from Fort Smith, Arkansas. Blunt determined to steal a march on Cooper and attack first.

Blunt began crossing the rain-swollen Arkansas River on July 15, and, by midnight on July 16–17, he had a force of 3,000 men, composed of whites, Indians, and African Americans, marching toward Honey Springs. Blunt skirmished with Rebel troops early on the morning of July 17, and by mid-afternoon, all-out fighting ensued. The Confederates had wet powder, causing misfires, and the problem intensified when rain began. After repulsing one attack, Cooper pulled his forces back to obtain new ammunition. In the meantime, Cooper began to experience command problems, and he learned that Blunt was about to turn his left flank. The Confederate retreat began, and although Cooper fought a rear-guard action, many of his troops counterattacked, failed, and fled. Any possibility of the Confederates retaking Fort Gibson was gone. Following this battle, Union forces controlled Indian Territory north of the Arkansas River.

In the report of the battle, which on both sides involved "Rainbow Coalitions," Blunt commended highly the 1st Kansas Colored Infantry writing, "Their coolness and bravery I have never seen surpassed."

MIDDLE BOGGY DEPOT

In February 1864, Col. William A. Phillips at the head of the Union Indian Home Guard Brigade rode out of Fort Gibson and headed south down the Texas Road carrying the war deep into the Seminole, Creek, Chickasaw, and Choctaw nations. Before returning to Fort Gibson on February 24, he approached to within twenty miles of Fort Washita. The expedition's major engagement occurred at Middle Boggy Depot, on February 13, when Maj. Charles Willett's column surprised a Confederate force. Although poorly armed, the Rebels made a determined stand for a half hour before retiring. The Union forces killed 47 Confederates during the short fight. During Phillips's expedition, he and his men fought with and dispersed numerous Confederate detachments.

SECOND CABIN CREEK

Here, on the prairie west of the ford where the Texas Road crossed Cabin Creek, one of the war's most successful cavalry raids climaxed favorably for the Confederates. A heavily loaded Federal train, numbering 300 wagons and escorted by more than 600 soldiers, had departed Fort Scott, Kansas, en route to Fort Smith, Arkansas, by way of Fort Gibson on September 12. Near the Cabin Creek ford, Confederates were encountered on September 18, and on crossing, the wagons were parked in a quarter circle, preparatory to resisting an attack. It came the next morning. The Confederate attackers belonged to Stand Watie's Indian and Richard Gano's Texas brigades, and they overwhelmed the defenders, panicking the teamsters, and captured more than 250 loaded weapons, valued at $1,500,000.

DOAKSVILLE

The last surrender of Confederate fighting forces was Brig. Gen. Stand Watie's command. Watie and his Cherokee brigade staged daring raids against Federal forces in the Indian Territory, north of the Arkansas, long after other Confederate units in the territory curbed their ardor for combat because of lack of supplies and support by the Confederate government, as well as what seemed to be a hopeless struggle. Watie on June 15, 1864, captured the supply-laden Federal steamer *J. R. Williams* on the Arkansas River. Watie, who was also a Cherokee chief, continued to hold his forces in the field. Finally, Watie on behalf of his Cherokees, as well as his Creeks, Seminoles, and Osages, came to Doaksville, near Fort Towson, and surrendered to Lt. Col. Asa C. Matthews on June 23, 1865.

Points of Interest

The points of interest are listed as you travel north to south along the tour route. Some are off the tour route a short distance, the first being east of I-44 near the Arkansas border. The Battle of Old Fort Wayne was a running fight that moved from northeast to southwest for 2 miles across Beatty Prairie and north of Hog Eye Creek. It is accessible by county roads defining Sections 20, 21, 30, and 31 in Township 4 Range 24 East. The nearest town is Maysville, Arkansas, located at the intersection of AK43 (following the alignment of the historic State Line Road) and AK72. On US59, 17 miles southeast of I-44 exit 301 at Grove, the grave of Cherokee Confederate general Stand Watie is in Polson Cemetery. Watie was the last Confederate general officer to surrender.

The Battles of First and Second Cabin Creek were fought 5 miles east of Big Cabin, south of I-44 exit 282. The sites retain their integrity, there are historical markers, and the trace of the Texas Road and its approach to the ford is apparent. For more information on access to the site, visitors should contact Craig County Historical Society in Vinita. A historical marker indicates the site of Fort Davis, on OK16 just north of Muskogee near the campus of Bacone Indian College. The fort was garrisoned by Confederates in 1862. Four miles south of Tahlequah on US62 is the site of the Park Hill Mission, a religious and educational center for the Cherokee Nation. It was destroyed during the Civil War, though archaeological remains of the Cherokee Female Seminary are extant. The 1845 Murrell home, sacked during the war, has been restored and is a state historic site.

The three-hundred-pound Albert Pike was a New Englander who went west as a young adult; he became a teacher, planter, newspaper publisher, and noted poet. Though his excellent rapport with the Creeks and other tribes in the Indian Territory led to his brigadier generalship in the CSA, his forces performed badly at the Battle of Pea Ridge and he was at odds with Rebel leaders in the Trans-Mississippi thereafter. After the war, he was best known as a national spokesman for Freemasonry.

Fort Gibson, at the confluence of the Arkansas, Grand, and Verdigris rivers, was a strategic point in the Civil War Indian Territory. U.S. troops built the fort in 1824 and occupied it as an active post until 1857 when the troops were redeployed and the buildings and land turned over to the Cherokee Nation. Confederates occupied the post until they were driven from the fort by a Federal advance in April 1863. The Union reactivated the fort in 1863 and during the next eight years most of the structures in the second fort, on the hill overlooking the first fort site, were erected. In 1890 the army again abandoned the fort. The fort is now a state military park, located on OK80 1 mile north of US62, east of Muskogee. The first fort's log stockade, officers' and enlisted men's quarters, blockhouses, guardhouse, and other buildings were reconstructed in the 1930s. A national cemetery that includes graves of Federal Civil War soldiers is located 1 mile east of the fort on US62.

The Battle of Honey Springs was fought north of Oktaha, 14 miles southwest of Muskogee just off US69, and is accessible by the county road leading to Rentiesville. Honey Springs is being developed by the state of Oklahoma as a military park. Land has been acquired and a number of interpretive memorials are positioned at the spring and depot site. There are historical markers at the battle site. In August 1863, Cooper's Confederate forces retreated to Perryville (US69 near McAlester) and established a camp and depot there. Blunt's Federal force pursued the Confederates, but Cooper abandoned the camp before they arrived and retired to Boggy Depot.

Several points of interest are located along US69/75 southwest of McAlester. Boggy Depot, 15 miles southwest of Atoka, has a cemetery with Confederate graves. Fifteen miles farther at Caddo is the site of Fort McCulloch, established by Confederate general Albert Pike and named for Brig. Gen. Benjamin McCulloch, killed at the Battle of Pea Ridge. Douglas Cooper is buried at Fort Washita, OK199/78, 16 miles southwest of Caddo. The Oklahoma Historical Society has reconstructed Cooper's cabin and a barracks at the site of the fort's ruins. At Armstrong, 7 miles southwest of Caddo, are the ruins of the Armstrong Academy. From 1863 to 1883 the academy served the Choctaw Nation as its capital. The Choctaw school was an 1863 Confederate camp.

Doaksville is on US70, 9 miles east of Hugo. The ruins of Fort Towson are located on US70 east of Doaksville. The sutler's building of the 1824 fort has been reconstructed and there is a museum. Some distance from the tour route in southwest Oklahoma at Lawton (I-44) is Fort Sill Military Reservation. The fort was established in 1869 and named by Maj. Gen. Philip H. Sheridan for a West Point classmate, Joshua W. Sill, who was killed fighting as one of Sheridan's brigade commanders at the Battle of Stones River. The post Civil War–era fort is a National Historical Landmark. There is a visitor center with exhibits and an audiovisual program and a museum in the Old Post buildings. Geronimo was imprisoned here and is buried in Apache Cemetery, 2 miles northeast of Fort Sill. Also located at Lawton is the nationally recognized Museum of the Great Plains.

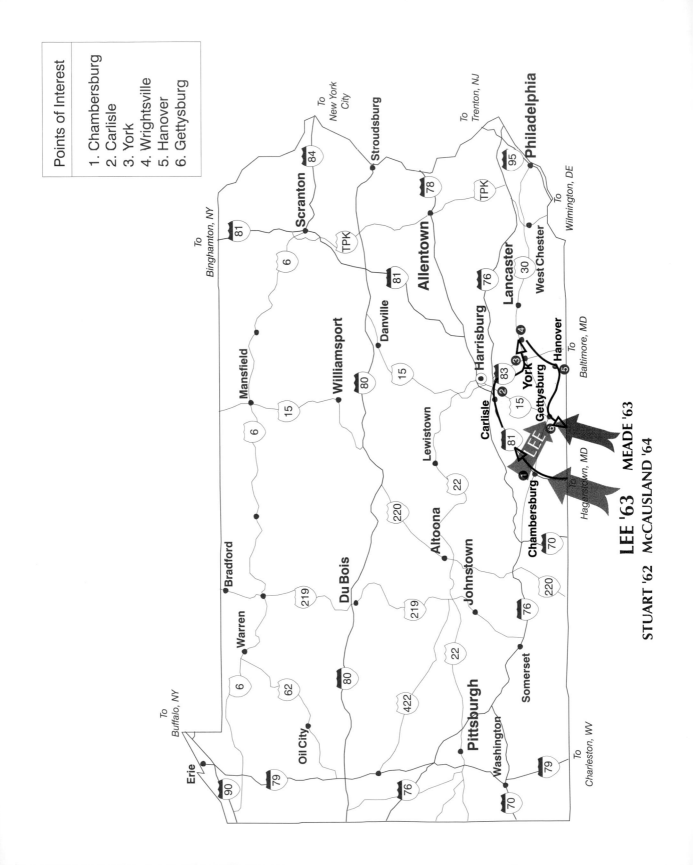

Points of Interest

1. Chambersburg
2. Carlisle
3. York
4. Wrightsville
5. Hanover
6. Gettysburg

LEE '63   MEADE '63

STUART '62   McCAUSLAND '64

Pennsylvania

Pennsylvania, founded by William Penn in 1681, soon became one of the largest and most prosperous of the original thirteen colonies, and is today known as the Keystone State. Pivotal in the formation of the United States, nerve center of the Revolution, and second capital of the nation, Pennsylvania was a focus of commerce, industry, education, and leadership for many decades before the Civil War. During the war, Pennsylvania was in the forefront in providing manpower, money, and industrial production for the Federal war effort. And it was very significant as a battlefield location as well. It was in Pennsylvania that two great armies in blue and gray clashed in what many deem to be the most important battle of the war. The Battle of Gettysburg is often called the "high-water mark of the Confederacy." After Gettysburg most of the South's war effort would be chiefly defensive—pegged to a strategy of obtaining peace and independence by wearing down the North's desire to maintain the Union at any cost.

It was not during the Gettysburg Campaign that the North was invaded by a major force for the first time, but it was in Pennsylvania. Eight and a half months before Gettysburg, in October 1862, a cavalry column under Maj. Gen. J.E.B. Stuart crossed the traditional boundary between North and South, the Mason-Dixon Line, and raided the manufacturing town of Chambersburg. (The concept of the South as "Dixie" is derived from Dixon, the name of one of the two men who surveyed the boundary separating Pennsylvania and Maryland.)

Though the Confederate forays into Pennsylvania were brief, they were well-planned strategic moves by the Southern leadership with many potential benefits, especially if a sustained effort could have been mounted and continued. Unfortunately for the Rebels, "crossing the line" galvanized Northern ire unlike almost anything else. The powerful Union response to Lee's invasion of the North and especially the victory at Gettysburg reversed the sagging fortunes of the North's largest army, the Army of the Potomac, boosting its confidence and eventually, with Lt. Gen. U. S. Grant looking over Maj. Gen. George G. Meade's shoulder, causing the final defeat of Lee's army. Studying the Battle of Gettysburg is indispensable in understanding the Civil War as well as exciting and educational—the "what ifs" will continue to be debated for generations. And visiting the battlefield at Gettysburg, one of the most meticulously maintained and frequently visited, is crucial to that study.

CHAMBERSBURG

The only town in the North to be visited by Confederate forces four times, Chambersburg was an important manufacturing town during the Civil War. One of the South's staunchest enemies, U.S. congressman Thaddeus Stevens, owned several businesses in Chambersburg. The Cumberland Valley Railroad linking Chambersburg with western Maryland was an important supply link in the field for the Army of the Potomac. Finally, Chambersburg was the first sizable community north of the Maryland line in the Cumberland Valley, the northern extension of Virginia's Shenandoah Valley. Primarily for the last reason, but also in part because of the other three, Chambersburg was a convenient target for Rebel raids and for the Confederate march north during Robert E. Lee's 1863 invasion of the North.

In October 1862, shortly after the withdrawal of the Army of Northern Virginia from Maryland after the Battle of Antietam (see **Antietam, Maryland**), Gen. Robert E. Lee asked Maj. Gen. J.E.B. Stuart to conduct a cavalry raid on Chambersburg. Lee was particularly hopeful that the railroad bridge over the Conococheague River be destroyed, interrupting a primary supply route for the Army of the Potomac, then camped along the Potomac in Maryland and Virginia.

Stuart started north at dawn on October 10, crossing the Potomac at McCoy's Ferry above Williamsport, Maryland, and arriving in Chambersburg by nightfall. A small garrison of Federal troops was captured and the town surrendered. That night and part of the next, Stuart's men took supplies or purchased them with Confederate money. They impressed 1,200 strong horses into the service of the Confederacy from nearby farms. Thinking that pursuing Federal cavalry would have learned of his route north, on October 11 Stuart turned his column east to Cashtown, then south through Emmitsburg, Maryland, and back across the Potomac at White's Ford near the mouth of the Monocacy

River. Only 2 Rebels were reported missing and the few injuries sustained by the Confederate troopers were minor.

For a second time Stuart had ridden around Maj. Gen. George B. McClellan's army (see **Peninsula Campaign, Virginia** for the first). Lincoln, already losing his patience with McClellan's constant delays in renewing an offensive against Lee after the Battle of Antietam, responded to a question several days after the Chambersburg raid with an analogy to a children's game: "Three Times Round, and Out. Stuart has been round him twice. If he goes around him once more, gentlemen, McClellan will be out."

In June 1863, Chambersburg was visited twice; the second of these visits was by Lee's army. The first visit was by a cavalry brigade that came on June 15 and returned to Maryland on June 17. Then soldiers of Lee's second corps led by Lt. Gen. Richard S. Ewell arrived in Chambersburg, paused, and on June 26 pushed on to York and Carlisle. The other two corps, six divisions under Gens. A. P. Hill and James Longstreet, camped in and around Chambersburg until Lee ordered his June 29 concentration on Cashtown Gap. Lee maintained his headquarters in Chambersburg until the evening of June 30, when he shifted it ten miles east to Greenwood.

The Rebels made one more uninvited visit to Chambersburg. In late July 1864, recoiling from his raid on Washington, D.C., and defeating a Union force on July 24 at Second Kernstown, Lt. Gen. Jubal Early dispatched a cavalry force led by Brig. Gen. John McCausland to Chambersburg with a written

A number of buildings in Chambersburg were burned on July 30, 1864, by Brig. Gen. John McCausland's Confederate cavalry after the citizens had refused to pay the ransom demanded by Lt. Gen. Jubal A. Early. Most of the town's main area was in flames within ten minutes. This woodcut engraving is from a photograph taken shortly after the fire.

demand for a ransom to spare the town in retaliation for Federal depredations in the Shenandoah Valley earlier in the year. The cavalry brigades of McCausland and Brig. Gen. Bradley T. Johnson, 2,600 strong, arrived in the early-morning hours of July 30 and fired a few cannon shots into Chambersburg. While they waited for a six-hour time limit to expire for the payment of the ransom, the Confederate troopers looted the town. When the citizens refused to pay, the town was torched, businesses and civic buildings first, and soon the fire spread to nearby homes. The Confederates rode out at one P.M., leaving more than four hundred buildings gutted or destroyed by fire.

Points of Interest

Chambersburg, on US30, has a handsome Civil War monument and a historical marker at Messersmith's Woods where Lee headquartered June 26–30. Also marked are a house used by John Brown to collect weapons for his 1859 raid on Harpers Ferry and the Susseratt House, where the fires started by McCausland's raiders were arrested.

LEE'S 1863 INVASION OF THE NORTH (GETTYSBURG CAMPAIGN)

Except for Chambersburg, the other places in Pennsylvania that saw battle action were those affected by Robert E. Lee's 1863 invasion of the north, which climaxed in the Battle of Gettysburg. Confident that he could defeat the Army of the Potomac anywhere after the Battle of Chancellorsville (see **Chancellorsville, Virginia**)—indeed that his army was invincible—General Lee put in motion a plan he had envisioned since his defensive victory over the same Army of the Potomac in December 1862 at Fredericksburg (see **Fredericksburg, Virginia**).

Besides the military benefits that would occur by taking the offensive through striking when the large Federal army was still recovering from a morale-shattering defeat, there was much to be gained both in supplying his army off the enemy's country and in the political-diplomatic area with a successful invasion of the North through Pennsylvania's Great Valley. By doing this, he could transfer the war from beleaguered Virginia, step up the pressure on Washington and Baltimore, and frustrate the Federals' efforts to determine where he would strike next.

These were the arguments Lee gave when he met with President Jefferson Davis and Secretary of War James Seddon in Richmond in mid-May. The president and Postmaster

General John H. Reagan of Texas countered with their concerns—the need to reinforce Vicksburg and/or General Bragg, who confronted Maj. Gen. William S. Rosecrans in Middle Tennessee. In two days of discussions Lee got President Davis to endorse his plan to invade the North.

Lee instructed J.E.B. Stuart to have the cavalry screen the Rebel infantry while tracking the Army of the Potomac. It was a discretionary order that enabled Stuart to employ three of the army's seven cavalry brigades for another of his heretofore successful rides around the Army of the Potomac. But this time the results were less satisfactory.

The Army of the Potomac had remained in the Fredericksburg, Virginia, area when Lee began redeploying his army northwest into Culpeper County. When Hooker received word of this movement he proposed to cross the Rappahannock again and either pitch into Lee's rear or march on Richmond. Lincoln disapproved of both these ideas and instead encouraged Hooker to follow Lee, keeping Washington covered, find a weak part of Lee's column and pitch into the Army of Northern Virginia while it was far from its base.

As his army crossed the Potomac, Hooker informed President Lincoln that he feared Lee, already in Pennsylvania, outnumbered him, and asked that the 10,000 Federals posted in the Maryland Heights area near Harpers Ferry be ordered to reinforce him. Hooker's pleas rang with the familiar "lack of support" theme heard previously from McClellan, and Lincoln, on June 28, sacked Hooker replacing him with Maj. Gen. George Gordon Meade, a tough Pennsylvanian.

Meade, a competent division commander, had been appointed to a corps command before Chancellorsville. Apolitical, hardworking, a perfectionist with a temper, Meade inherited an unenviable task. With the mandate from Lincoln to protect Washington and Baltimore and at the same time take the offensive against Lee's invading army and prevent it from crossing the Susquehanna River, Meade developed his plans. He knew that the Pennsylvania militia had burned the Wrightsville bridge across the Susquehanna River to stop Lee in his advance toward Harrisburg and Philadelphia. Should Lee now turn south to attack Washington, Meade proposed a defense line in Maryland, near the Pennsylvania border, along Big Pipe Creek. At the same time, his army fanned out on a broad front, with its powerful left wing under the capable John Fulton Reynolds, concentrating on Emmitsburg, Maryland, eight miles south of Gettysburg, a Pennsylvania county seat and road hub.

Lee had less knowledge of his opponent's dispositions, but knew, when he learned of the Federal change of command on June 29, that he was facing a different situation with Meade, for whom he had great respect, in command of the army. Lee was determined to concentrate his forces at Cashtown, just east of South Mountain. Lee anticipated battling with Meade. If he won, of which the confident Confederate had little doubt, Cashtown was a good position from which to exploit his success by pushing deep into the Keystone State to wreak political havoc on the North. If he lost, the Cumberland Valley west of South Mountain would screen his route back to Virginia.

Three Federal corps closed on Emmitsburg on June 30. Confederates were marching from Chambersburg, York, and Carlisle to Cashtown while an infantry brigade closed on Gettysburg from the west, but it quickly pulled back after sighting Brig. Gen. John Buford's Federal cavalry division that had come up from Emmitsburg to reconnoiter. Meanwhile, a cavalry battle was being fought at nearby Hanover. The stage was set for one of history's dramatic battles.

Carlisle

When Richard Ewell's II Corps (formerly Stonewall Jackson's corps) marched into Pennsylvania, two of its three divisions were directed toward Harrisburg, the state capital. Ewell arrived at Carlisle, eighteen miles west of Harrisburg, on June 27, where the Pennsylvania militia was evacuating the town without firing a shot. The two divisions encamped in and around Carlisle, while Ewell's third division, under Maj. Gen. Jubal Early, marched to and occupied York.

Confederate cavalry advanced to Camp Hill within two miles of the Susquehanna River, where they saw and shelled Federal entrenchments manned by Pennsylvania militia, under the command of Maj. Gen. Darius N. Couch, former Army of the Potomac corps commander. Ewell decided not to test the defenses and remained in Carlisle until ordered by Lee to Cashtown.

Points of Interest

The Carlisle Barracks on US11 has been a military facility since the mid-eighteenth century. The Hessian Guardhouse, now a museum, built by prisoners during the Revolutionary War, stood during the Civil War. The Army War College at Carlisle Barracks has one of the nation's largest collections of Civil War images and documents. For more

The bridge over the Susquehanna River at Wrightsville, Pennsylvania, was burned by militia units to prevent the Confederates from crossing the river and having a direct march of fewer than one hundred miles to Philadelphia. Confederates scouted the river crossing while Jubal Early's main force was ten miles west at York.

information, contact the U.S. Army Military History Institute, Carlisle Barracks, Carlisle, PA 17013.

The Cumberland County Courthouse in the middle of Carlisle on PA74 has pockmarks from the shelling by J.E.B. Stuart's horse artillery on July 1 during the plumed cavalier's ride to Gettysburg. Several of the nearby churches stood during the occupation. Dickinson College, on West High Street, was used as a campground by Ewell's Confederates occupying the town. For more information on Carlisle sites, contact the Cumberland County Historical Society and the Hamilton Library Association, 211 North Pitt Street, P.O. Box 626, Carlisle, PA 17013; 717-249-7610.

York

Maj. Gen. Jubal Early, in command of a division of Ewell's corps of the Army of Northern Virginia, left the corps in Chambersburg and marched through Gettysburg to York. On June 28 he took the small manufacturing city. He demanded rations and footwear and a $100,000 levy from the town. Under orders to march to Cashtown, and receiving only $28,000, he departed without collecting the rest.

Although under the Confederate's artillery fire, soldiers of the Pennsylvania militia—including African Americans—burned the railroad bridge over the Susquehanna River at Wrightsville, twelve miles northeast of York. This was a major blow to Confederate hopes to cross the river and threaten Philadelphia and other points east. The only other crossing point was at Harrisburg, which was heavily fortified. The problem of crossing the Susquehanna, along with the threat of the Army of the Potomac converging on him under an energetic commander, is the reason Lee changed the strategy of his invasion and ordered his forces to concentrate on Cashtown.

Points of Interest

Historical markers in downtown York on US30 describe the occupation of York by Early's troops on June 28–29, 1863.

Hanover

On June 30, J.E.B. Stuart's cavalry force rode into Pennsylvania, remaining out of touch with the rest of Lee's army. The first real test of his forces since leaving Virginia came when he was challenged by the Federal cavalry division of Brig. Gen. Hugh Judson Kilpatrick sixteen miles east of Gettysburg, at Hanover. Opposing the Confederates were the brigades of Brig. Gen. Elon Farnsworth and Brig. Gen. George Armstrong Custer. Artillery was unlimbered on the heights north of the town and the center square was barricaded. The Confederates charged into the center

The Hanover Center Square and the Central Hotel, which served as Brig. Gen. Judson Kilpatrick's headquarters. Citizens of the town helped Federal cavalrymen barricade the streets as J.E.B. Stuart's cavalry advanced toward Hanover. The Central Hotel building in this 1863 photograph still stands.

of Hanover, briefly scattering the Federal forces, but a mounted counterattack drove them back. Fighting continued on the Carl Forney farm southwest of town. During this phase of the battle, Stuart himself barely escaped capture by jumping his horse across a deep ravine.

Stuart placed his train, including 125 captured Federal wagons, near Mount Olivet Cemetery southeast of Hanover and unlimbered his artillery. During the afternoon, the battle continued with sporadic skirmishing and artillery duels. Stuart finally broke off the engagement when he began to run low on ammunition and rode northeast toward Dover in search of Early's Confederate infantry. This fight further delayed the convergence of the Confederate cavalry with Lee's army converging on Cashtown Gap.

Points of Interest

Hanover has several monuments on the center square, the intersection of PA94 and PA194, relating to the battle, including a handsome equestrian monument honoring the Union Cavalry. A plaque on a building in the southwest corner describes George A. Custer's role in the battle. Many of Hanover's residential buildings were extant during the battle. Mount Olivet Cemetery is 1 mile southeast of the center square on Baltimore Street. On Frederick Street, 1 mile west of the center square, between Forney and Stuart avenues, is where the most intense fighting occurred on the Carl Forney farm. A former school building on Eichelberger Street occupies the site of the Federal artillery position. A few blocks south on Railroad Street is a monument describing Lincoln's short visit to Hanover on November 18, 1863, where he addressed a crowd while en route to Gettysburg.

For more information on these sites and touring historic homes in Hanover, contact the Hanover Area Historical Society, 105 High Street, Hanover, PA 17331; 717-632-3207.

Gettysburg

While Brig. Gen. Judson Kilpatrick was challenging J.E.B. Stuart's cavalry at Hanover, Brig. Gen. John Buford, with two brigades of cavalry, reconnoitered the roads that converged at Gettysburg. The next day, July 1, when Maj. Gen. Henry Heth's infantry marched down the Chambersburg Pike to investigate the Federal forces seen at Gettysburg, Buford's dismounted troopers were waiting on McPherson's Ridge, northeast

Maj. Gen. John F. Reynolds was one of the most promising leaders in the Army of the Potomac before a Confederate killed him on July 1 in McPherson's Woods. Reynolds was born in nearby Lancaster, Pennsylvania.

of the town. These Federal horsemen had been well trained by their commander in dismounted combat and they were armed with breech-loading carbines. On Wednesday, July 1, 1863, one of history's great battles began on ground not selected by the commanders of the two armies, but by the inevitable collision of their advance units.

The skirmish quickly escalated as more and more Rebel infantry units advanced from Cashtown. Buford was in the cupola of the Gettysburg Theological Seminary when Union Maj. Gen. John Reynolds, commander of three corps that had concentrated at Emmitsburg on June 30, rode up. Reynolds, after a brief discussion with Buford, sent a message informing Meade, then at Taneytown, Maryland, of the situation. Reynolds had called up the First Corps at the sound of the opening guns. But for Reynolds, the action at Gettysburg was short-lived. Minutes later, while personally directing the famed Iron Brigade in McPherson's Woods, he was killed, the highest-ranking officer of either army to be slain at Gettysburg. Command of the I Corps passed to the division commander who had been in temporary command while Reynolds scouted ahead, Brig. Gen. Abner Doubleday, who had steadily risen through the ranks since directing artillery at Fort Sumter. Counterattacking blue-coats smashed a Confederate brigade, captured a general, and chased the Rebels back to Herr Ridge. But thousands of Confederates were close at hand and converged on the area.

Following General Heth was another division of A. P. Hill's corps under Brig. Gen. William D. Pender. Vicious fighting took place in McPherson's Woods. Approaching from the north were two divisions of Lt. Gen. Richard Ewell's corps: Maj. Gen. Robert

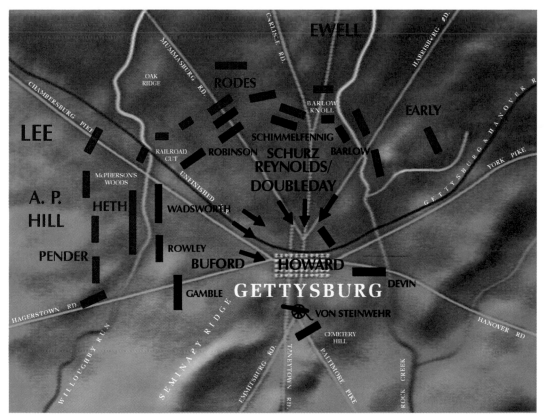

The first day's battle began with the advance of the division of Maj. Gen. Henry Heth southwest along the Chambersburg Pike, which was slowed by Brig. Gen. John Buford's two cavalry brigades under Gamble and Devin. As the Federal cavalry gave way, the Federal I Corps arrived and took up the fight on the McPherson Farm and Oak Ridge. By the afternoon, Maj. Gen. Richard Ewell's corps was arriving from the north and attacked the I Corps brigades of General John Robinson, which fought desperately on Oak Ridge and at the East railroad cut. More Rebels arriving from the north met the XI Corps divisions of Maj. Gen. Carl Schurz. By late afternoon, the Confederates' pressure on the Union line forced the Federals back through the streets of Gettysburg to Cemetery Hill, where artillery chief Henry Hunt had massed cannons to cover the retreat of the Federals. The Union rally at Cemetery Hill prevented a rout as the action died down for the night.

Rodes's division came down the Carlisle Road, and Jubal Early's division marched down the Harrisburg Road.

Maj. Gen. Oliver O. Howard, XI Corps commander, arrived in Gettysburg before noon in time to see the rout of the 147th New York before the Federal rally and defeat of one of Heth's brigades in the middle railroad cut fronting Oak Ridge. He misinterpreted this as a withdrawal of the I Corps under fire and sent a message about it to Meade. With the death of General Reynolds, Howard assumed overall Federal command on the field and, to counter the new threat from the north, ordered Maj. Gen. Carl Schurz's XI Corps division to meet it. But the left flank of Schurz's divisions did not meet the right of the I Corps brigades holding Oak Ridge as Rodes launched his brigades in piecemeal attacks.

By mid-afternoon, pressure from Rodes, Early, and A. P. Hill's two divisions finally drove the Federals back through the streets of Gettysburg. The Rebels pursued them closely and hand-to-hand fighting occurred near Pennsylvania College (now Gettysburg College) which stood in the path of the retreating Yankees. The school was used as a hospital by both sides throughout the battle.

Maj. Gen. George Gordon Meade received command of the Army of the Potomac just three days before the Battle of Gettysburg began. It was an appointment he neither sought nor relished, but accepted as a matter of duty. His aggressive direction of units in all of the Army of the Potomac's previous campaigns brought him to the attention of the Washington leadership.

The Federals retreated through Gettysburg and poured onto the Baltimore Pike, southeast of town, and up onto East Cemetery Hill, a predesignated rallying point. Under cover of artillery and an XI Corps brigade on Cemetery Hill, the Federal rout was stemmed. During the night of July 1, both sides reinforced their positions. The South occupied Oak and Seminary ridges. General Lee made his headquarters near the Widow Thompson House, located between the two ridges. The Federals held Culp's and East Cemetery Hill and Cemetery Ridge running south from Evergreen Cemetery. General Meade arrived during the night and later took over the widow Leister's small farmhouse behind Cemetery Ridge.

A Gettysburg citizen described how the battle had enveloped the town. "It was not safe to be on the street for a moment. The Rebel sharp-shooters were posted in every alley and in many of the houses, picking off our men and horses, while ours were returning the compliment. The cannonade was fierce and incessant, the shell from both sides flew over and into the devoted town."

By the time the sun rose over the eastern edge of Culp's Hill on the morning of July 2, the two great armies were in place, separated by a mile of fields and woods. The next forty-eight hours were to change the tide of the war in the east. The second day's battle could have been decisive if the strategic combination planned by Lee had resulted in routing the Army of the Potomac from its chosen position. But luck and the bravery of individual Union commanders and soldiers made it otherwise.

The farmhouse of Mrs. Lydia A. Leister, a widow, served as Meade's headquarters from the early-morning hours of July 2. The house was heavily damaged in the July 3 bombardment before the Pickett-Pettigrew charge. Mrs. Leister, returning to her farm a few days later, would for years speak of the battle only in regard to the damage it had done to her farm.

Confederate soldiers killed in the fighting on Rose's Farm. These soldiers were photographed by the team led by Alexander Gardner of Washington, D.C., the first photographers to arrive on the field at Gettysburg. The last section of the Gettysburg battlefield to be cleared of bodies was the southern end at Rose's Farm and Devil's Den.

The morning of Thursday, July 2, passed relatively quietly, as battle plans were formulated by the generals. Robert E. Lee, suffering from lack of sleep and an acute illness, met individually with his corps commanders. Giving detailed instructions, he proposed to Longstreet an attack on the Union left, an offensive the Georgian was hesitant to execute, while Ewell was to display a force at the sound of Longstreet's cannons, and if the situa-

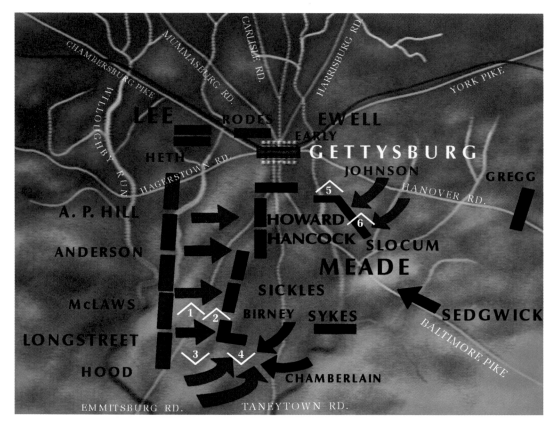

Gen. Robert E. Lee, on July 2, concentrated on the flanks of the Federal fishhook line centering on Cemetery Ridge. But the initial offensive action of the day was begun when the Union III Corps advanced to the Peach Orchard (1). As Maj. Gen. Daniel Sickles exposed the Federal left flank in this position, Lt. Gen. James Longstreet was preparing an echelon advance ordered by Lee, on the same flank. The soldiers of Maj. Gen. John B. Hood's division poured through Devil's Den (3), hitting Sickles's flank and continuing to Little Round Top (4), which was unprotected. However, men from the Union V Corps arrived in time to turn back the Rebels from Little Round Top. Longstreet's advance continued to the north and Maj. Gen. Lafayette McLaws's division met stubborn resistance in the Wheatfield (2). Longstreet's efforts were being checked as Lt. Gen. Richard Ewell launched an assault against the Federal left flank shortly before dusk directed at East Cemetery Hill (5) and Culp's Hill (6). The Confederates were also checked at Cemetery Hill and a fierce night counterattack by the Union XII Corps lasting into July 3 finally dislodged the last threat to the Federal flanks.

tion warranted he could make an all-out attack on the Union right at East Cemetery Hill and Culp's Hill. Sometime after Longstreet left to form the attack, J.E.B. Stuart arrived at Lee's headquarters while his troopers were still making their way to Gettysburg after their foray to places as far afield as Carlisle. Stuart's adjutant Maj. Henry McClellan recounts how Lee, at first very upset, greeted Stuart. "Well, General Stuart, you are here at last." He then turned to Stuart to discuss how the cavalry might be used in the battle at hand.

On the other side of Emmitsburg Road, George Gordon Meade, having had little sleep himself, was described by an aide as "quick, bold, cheerful, and hopeful." The Federal line resembling a fishhook, its barb south of Culp's Hill and its turn on Cemetery Hill, and the tie near the two peaks known as Big and Little Round Top in the south. The southernmost corps was commanded by Maj. Gen. Daniel Sickles, a contro-

Brig. Gen. Joshua L. Chamberlain, USA, was a professor at Bowdoin College when he took a summer sabbatical in 1862. Instead of going to Europe, he joined the Federal army. On July 2 at Little Round Top, as a colonel leading the 20th Maine, he held the extreme left of the Federal line. His heroic leadership by example during this struggle and during his three-year army experience earned him the honor of receiving the Confederate surrender at Appomattox Court House and in later years, the Medal of Honor.

versial political general. (Sickles had created national headlines four years earlier, when he had been acquitted of the murder of his wife's lover through the first American legal use of the plea of temporary insanity.) Without orders, Sickles advanced his III Corps, bands playing, flags flapping in the breeze, to occupy high ground to his front. Meade, surprised to hear of Sickles's maneuver, rode out to meet him, and realizing that the Rebels were massing in the woods to his front after firing a few artillery rounds in that direction, ordered Sickles to hold his tenuous position along Houck's Ridge and the Peach Orchard.

By four P.M., with the arrival of the last Federal units, Maj. Gen. Sedgwick's VI Corps, and Stuart's cavalry, more than 170,000 soldiers were present at Gettysburg. About this time, Longstreet launched his much-delayed offensive. Maj. Gen. John Bell Hood, a hard-driving division commander, was to lead Alabamians, his Texans, Arkansas, and Georgians in an *en echelon* attack of Longstreet's two divisions through the Bushman Farm and Rose's south of the Peach Orchard. But Hood was wounded when Sickles's artillery shelled the woods, so Brig. Gen. Evander M. Law assumed command. Law's objective was Little Round Top, which a scouting party had reported free of Yankees and which was a route to lightly guarded supply wagons. It was also the path to roll up like a rug the vulnerable left flank of the Federal line.

One of the Federal heroes that fateful summer afternoon was an unassuming officer from New York, Brig. Gen. Gouverneur K. Warren, Meade's chief engineer. After accompanying Meade to the Peach Orchard to see Sickles, Warren decided to survey Little Round Top. He was shocked to find the crest of the hill left unguarded by the III Corps redeployment, except for a few signalmen. Through his field glasses, he saw Hood's division coming forward and surmised that an attack on Little Round Top was forming. He also realized the significance of a position which, if occupied by the Rebels, would give

The twilight July 2 attack on Cemetery Hill. The Confederate brigades of Brig. Gen. Harry T. Hays, the "Louisiana Tigers," and Col. I. E. Avery charged the hill and overran the XI Corps infantry and artillery before Maj. Gen. Winfield S. Hancock directed reinforcements to the area who turned back the Confederate advance.

them the opportunity to crush the Union line with a devastating flank attack. Warren had the signalmen wave their flags furiously to create activity, then sent a staffer down to find Federal forces to hold Little Round Top.

First encountered was Col. Strong Vincent's brigade from Maj. Gen. George Sykes's V Corps. Though Vincent had orders to reinforce Sickles, he understood the gravity of the situation and led his brigade to the west face of the hill just before the first Confederates arrived. A fierce battle continued for an hour. Besides Vincent's force, the brigade of Brig. Gen. Stephen Weed battled the Confederates from Hood's division. The 20th Maine, under Col. Joshua Chamberlain, though outnumbered, held off Alabama soldiers attacking the left flank of the Little Round Top enclave, then counterattacked and routed the Rebels. Vincent and two other ranking Federal

The Trostle Farm, where the 9th Massachusetts Battery, ordered to hold the position at any cost, faced the advance of Brig. Gen. William Barksdale's brigade. The photographer Timothy H. O'Sullivan focused on the tragedy of the battle, in this case dead artillery horses, after the directions of Alexander Gardner who supervised the camp photographers. The artillery shell hole in the eaves of the Trostle barn can be seen today.

Union soldiers killed at Gettysburg. Like their Southern counterparts, these unfortunate men were photographed at the southern end of the battlefield according to the research of photo-historian William A. Frassanito, not at the site of Maj. Gen. John F. Reynolds's death on the McPherson Farm, as Alexander Gardner advertised when he first released the photographs.

commanders were killed on Little Round Top. But the timely arrival of reinforcements prevented the area from being taken.

The Confederates' capture of Devil's Den enabled them to use the huge granite boulders as an impregnable fortress. Sharpshooters made life hazardous for Federal soldiers on Little Round Top.

The battle continued to rage in the Peach Orchard and the Wheatfield between Maj. Gen. David Birney's III Corps division, reinforced by eight II and V corps brigades rushing to their assistance, and forces under Brig. Gens. Law and Lafayette McLaws. The soldiers on both sides fought with determination. The Rebels launched six attacks on the Wheatfield and were driven back by six Federal counterattacks before they cleared the area known since as the maelstrom of death.

In one of many touching moments of the American Civil War, eighty-seven-year-old farmer John Wentz emerged from the relative safety of his farmhouse basement in the vicinity of the Peach Orchard late on July 2 to discover his son, whom he had not seen for twenty-four years, manning a Rebel cannon in his front yard.

Sickles's misguided advance was a near disaster for the Union, but Longstreet's slashing attacks were undermined by command failures and irresolution on the part of Lt. Gen. A. P. Hill and Maj. Gen. Richard H. Anderson. General Meade and Maj. Gen. Winfield Scott Hancock showed courage and skill in the redeployment of Federal forces to different parts of the battlefield frustrating Confederate efforts to achieve a decisive breakthrough. The failure of two of Anderson's five brigades to come up *en echelon* and press the Federals as Longstreet's assaults crested and the Yanks counterattacked compelled the Rebels to retire.

As sundown approached, Maj. Gen. Edward Johnson's veteran Confederate infantry soldiers of Ewell's corps advanced and assailed Cemetery and Culp's hills while two of Jubal Early's brigades closed on East Cemetery Hill. In a hard-fought struggle, Federal infantry, with artillery support, held East Cemetery Hill. As he had been doing all day, General Hancock, left wing commander, rushed needed reinforcements to the area to meet the Rebel challenge. Among the Southern forces charging East Cemetery Hill were the famed Brig. Gen. Harry T. Hays's ferocious Louisiana Tigers. With Hays as well were the forces of North Carolinian colonel Isaac Avery. Avery was mortally wounded in the attack and had scribbled a message as he lay dying, "Tell my father I fell with my face to the enemy."

Maj. Gen. George E. Pickett, CSA, was a West Point classmate of Thomas J. Jackson and George B. McClellan. He was in excellent spirits in preparing to lead the charge against the Union center at Gettysburg, believing the position could be carried. Contrary to popular belief, Pickett handled the ill-fated advance with courage and skill.

Twenty-year-old Jenny Wade was killed instantly as a stray Confederate sniper's bullet pierced two doors of her sister's Cemetery Hill house. Nine days later her fiancé, Cpl. Johnston H. Skelly of the 87th Pennsylvania Volunteers, died in Virginia of wounds suffered in the Battle of Second Winchester.

Rebel troops secured a toehold on Culp's Hill that had been virtually abandoned when all but Brig. Gen. George S. Greene's XII Corps brigade left their breastworks earlier in the day to reinforce Union troops battling Longstreet's surge. At four-thirty A.M. on July 3, returning XII Corps soldiers engaged in a furious battle against reinforced Confederates which lasted seven hours. By eleven A.M., the Federal forces turned back the Confederate assault on Culp's Hill, at a tremendous cost, particularly to the butternuts.

During the night of July 2, Meade held a council of war with his top generals. They voted to stand and defend their positions at Gettysburg. As the council broke up, Meade took II Corps commander Brig. Gen. John Gibbon aside. "If Lee attacks tomorrow, it will be on your front," he told the man whose troops held the center of the Union line on Cemetery Ridge.

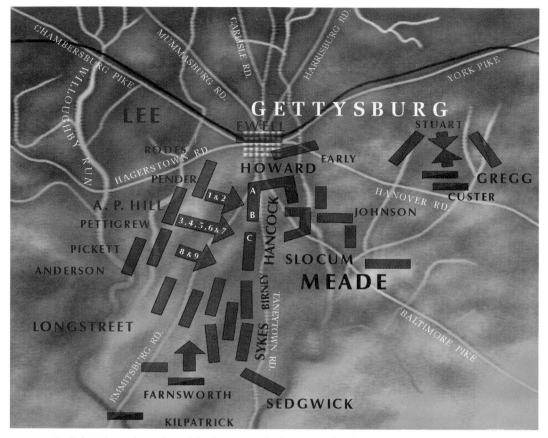

On July 3 the major action of the day occurred when Lee ordered Longstreet to send 12,500 men against the Federal center. Three divisions under Maj. Gens. George E. Pickett and Isaac R. Trimble and Brig. Gen. James J. Pettigrew assaulted the Federal center at three in the afternoon. The brigades of Brocken-brough (1), Davis (2), Lane (3), Marshall (4), Fry (5), Lawrence (6), Armistead (7), Garnett (8), and Kemper (9) led the attack supported by two others. The focus of the attack was a copse of trees at the center of the Federal line held by Gibbon's division (B) of the II Corps. Hays's division (A) also participated in the defense as did elements of Doubleday's division (C), firing into the flank of the two southernmost Rebel brigades as they made a left oblique march to charge the copse of trees. Also in the afternoon, a cavalry battle between Brig. Gen. David Gregg's Federal horsemen and Maj. Gen. J.E.B. Stuart's troopers was fought east of Gettysburg, while Brig. Gen. Judson Kilpatrick ordered Brig. Gen. Elon Farnsworth's cavalry brigade to make a suicide charge against troops of Brig. Gen. Evander Law's division at the base of Big Round Top.

Across town near the Thompson House, Lee was conferring with his lieutenants. Longstreet, as he had earlier, proposed a flanking movement around the Federal left, by Big Round Top. But Lee, curiously encouraged by the setbacks that day, would fulfill Meade's prediction. To lead the charge against the Union center, he selected a division from his native Virginia, led by Maj. Gen. George Pickett. Twelve thousand five hundred

Gen. Robert E. Lee in a photograph taken shortly after the end of the war. At Gettysburg, Lee staged his greatest gamble. After failing to overwhelm the Federal flanks on July 2 he was still optimistic for success and did not view the all-out assault he ordered against the Union center on July 3 as a desperate measure.

A portion of the Gettysburg Cyclorama featuring the Pickett-Pettigrew charge. The cyclorama was first unveiled in Chicago in 1883. It was created in Paris under a team of artists led by Paul Philippoteaux, who traveled to Gettysburg and corresponded with Federal generals Hancock and Doubleday about the battle.

men from Longstreet's and A. P. Hill's corps would cross the open fields in the afternoon of Friday, July 3. Later Longstreet, in bitter opposition to the plan, expressed the feelings he had had at that moment: "My heart was heavy. I could see the desperate and hopeless nature of the charge and the hopeless slaughter it would cause. That day at Gettysburg was one of the saddest of my life."

Except for the culmination of the battle on Culp's Hill, the morning of July 3 was relatively quiet. Rebel sharpshooters continued to harass the Cemetery Hill Yankees. Unlike in modern warfare, civilian deaths in the Civil War were rare and there was only one at Gettysburg. A minié ball from a Rebel musket pierced two doors of the John McClellan home on Cemetery Hill, and killed young Jenny Wade, who had bravely remained there to care for her sister, Mrs. McClellan, and her newborn son.

At one-ten P.M. on a sweltering afternoon, 150 Confederate cannons began the largest artillery barrage ever staged by the South to "soften up" the Federal front. The Union responded with a like number of guns and the ninety-minute duel was heard more than 150 miles away in Pittsburgh. The Rebel guns did little damage to the Federal line; many of the projectiles were misdirected and passed into the rear areas. At three P.M., with courage in their hearts, the 12,000 Confederate infantry began the nearly one-mile advance across open ground between the two ridges. Their focal point was a copse of trees south of Cemetery Hill and north of Little Round Top. A Federal eyewitness described the scene: ". . . an overwhelming relentless tide of an ocean of armed men sweeping upon us! On they move, as with one soul in perfect order . . . over ridge and slope, through orchard and meadow and cornfield, magnificent, grim, irresistible."

Only a few hundred Confederates entered "The Angle" and approached the stone wall fronting Arnold's Rhode Island battery. They were either taken prisoner, killed, wounded, or sought safety in flight. The order

On November 19, 1863, an unknown photographer captured the procession of civilians and soldiers to the dedication of the Soldiers' National Cemetery at Gettysburg as it passed the Wagon Hotel at the junction of the Emmitsburg Road and the Baltimore Pike south of Gettysburg. Lincoln rode to the cemetery with the other marchers.

Abraham Lincoln on the speakers' platform during the November 19 dedication of the Soldiers' National Cemetery at Gettysburg. Lincoln's two-minute address was over before this unknown photographer was ready to capture the historic moment and the president had just again taken his seat to the left of the man standing with the top hat.

was given to retire, and less than 5,000 made it back to Seminary Ridge. General Lee rode out to console the survivors remarking, "All this has been my fault." No more infantry action took place on the battlefield that day. Several miles to the east, at East Cavalry Field, Gen. J.E.B. Stuart's cavalry was being bested by Federal cavalry under Brig. Gen. David Gregg assisted by Brig. Gen. George Armstrong Custer.

The North Carolina Monument on Seminary Ridge at Gettysburg National Military Park. The slogan of North Carolina's Civil War heritage is "First at Big Bethel, farthest at Antietam, Gettysburg, and Chickamauga, last at Appomattox."

South of Devil's Den, Brig. Gen. Judson Kilpatrick ordered Brig. Gen. Elon Farnsworth's horse soldiers to make a suicide charge against the Confederate infantry holding the rugged ground bounding Plum Run. Predictably, the cavalry was routed and Farnsworth killed in the attack. Farther west, north of Fairfield the 6th U.S. Cavalry was soundly whipped by Rebel horsemen under Brig. Gen. William E. "Grumble" Jones.

On July 4, the eighty-seventh anniversary of American independence, rains came to Gettysburg. Both sides anticipated renewed fighting, but none was forthcoming.

That evening, Lee quietly withdrew his army, retracing his steps back to Virginia. Although he would be criticized later, Meade did not pursue. More than 51,000 Union and Confederate casualties, along with the thousands of stragglers, made immediate pursuit difficult.

On November 18, 1863, President Abraham Lincoln took a train from Washington through Hanover Junction and Hanover to Gettysburg. He spent the night in the home of David Willis, a Gettysburg lawyer, on the town square. The next day, November 19, he attended the function for which he had been invited to speak at the last minute. It was the dedication of the Soldiers' National Cemetery at Gettysburg honoring those Union soldiers killed in the battle and whose bodies were then being interred, adjacent to Evergreen Cemetery, on the hill vital to Federal victory. The principal speaker, invited well ahead of Lincoln, was scholar, poet, politician, and orator Edward Everett, whose two-hour speech was well received by the large crowd attending the ceremony. But the world will never forget Lincoln's two-minute address that followed. The Gettysburg Address is one of the masterpieces of the English language, and is the foremost interpretation of the meaning and importance of the Battle of Gettysburg and the American Civil War.

"It is rather for us to be here dedicated to the great task remaining before us—that from these honored dead we take increased devotion to that cause for which they gave the last full measure of devotion; that we here highly resolve that

The East Cavalry Battlefield at Gettysburg, where on July 3, Maj. Gen. J.E.B. Stuart's plan to roam behind the Federal lines was checked by Union cavalry of Brig. Gen. David M. Gregg that included the cavalry brigade of Brig. Gen. George A. Custer. These cannons mark the position of Confederate horse artillery in front of Brig. Gen. Wade Hampton's brigade.

The copse of trees on Cemetery Ridge that was the focal point of the assault of 12,500 Confederates on the afternoon of July 3, 1963. This monument marks the spot as "the high-water mark of the Confederacy."

these dead shall not have died in vain; that this nation, under God, shall have a new birth of freedom; and that government of the people, by the people, for the people, shall not perish from the earth."

Points of Interest

Gettysburg National Military Park—Much of the battlefield is encompassed in Gettysburg National Military Park. Although in certain places, commercial buildings, including the many private Civil War exhibits and attractions, disturb the view, much of the park's landscape reflects the historic scene at the time of the battle. The park contains 3,850 acres with 35 miles of park roads, 1,300 monuments and 400 cannons. Pamphlets, books, and audiotapes are for sale in the park's bookstore describing self-guided auto tours; or knowledgeable licensed guides can lead you through the three days of battles.

The visitor center contains many exhibits and an electric map that gives a narrated account of the battle with lights indicating troop positions and movements. The Gettysburg Cyclorama is housed in another building that overlooks Cemetery Ridge. Among the thousands of monuments and markers on the battlefield is one that identifies the copse of trees near where counterattacking Union soldiers routed the survivors of the Pickett-Pettigrew-Trimble charge who had briefly breached their line. It is a memorial to the Confederacy at the pinnacle of its glory, before the tide of its success slowly ebbed away. It is called the "high-water mark of the Confederacy."

Gettysburg National Cemetery is on Cemetery Hill, adjacent to the park. There are monuments dedicated to the soldiers buried there and a monument commemorating Lincoln's address. The Evergreen Cemetery gatehouse, prominent in battle photographs and paintings, with a compatible addition fronts Baltimore Street.

At Cashtown, 8 miles northwest of Gettysburg on US30, and Fairfield, 8 miles west on PA116, are historical markers describing the events that took place in those communities.

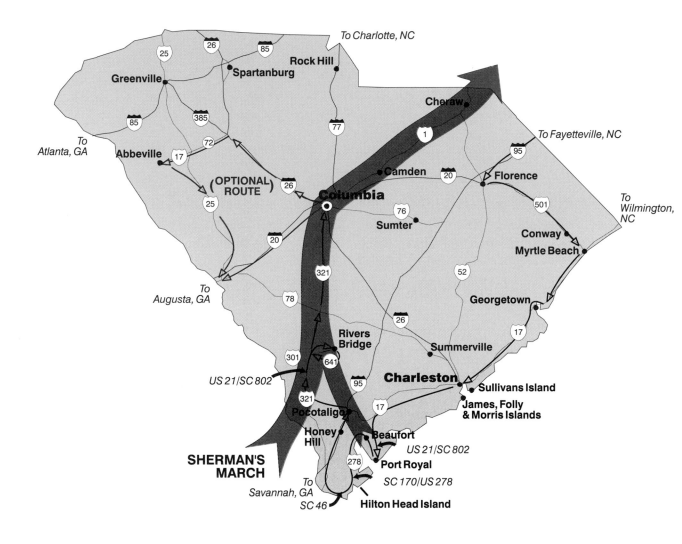

To Charlotte, NC

25 26 85
Rock Hill
Spartanburg
Greenville
Cheraw
1
To Fayetteville, NC
85 385
95
Abbeville 17 72
To
Atlanta, GA
(OPTIONAL ROUTE)
26 Columbia Camden 20 Florence
77
501
To
Wilmington,
NC
25 76
Sumter Conway
20 Myrtle Beach
321
52
78 Georgetown
26 17
Rivers Bridge
301 641 Summerville
US 21/SC 802 95 Charleston Sullivans Island
321 17 James, Folly & Morris Islands
Pocotaligo
Honey Hill Beaufort
US 21/SC 802
SHERMAN'S MARCH
278 Port Royal
SC 170/US 278
To
Savannah, GA
SC 46 Hilton Head Island

South Carolina

In December 1860, South Carolina became the first state to challenge the Federal government's authority to hold the United States together by law or armed force. At the February 1861 Montgomery, Alabama, convention of seceding states, a delegate from South Carolina, Christopher Memminger, headed the committee to draft the constitution of the as yet unformed Confederacy. The Palmetto State saw limited, but savage, conflict within its borders during the war, but for symbolic reasons as much as for strategic advantage, the port city of Charleston was a Union military priority. South Carolina contributed much to sustain the Confederacy, including 63,000 soldiers and a handful of sailors who fought hard and bravely, in places like Stones River, Gettysburg, and Petersburg, to preserve the liberty they believed was being usurped by a domineering Federal government. Nearly a quarter of them did not return.

South Carolina has pleasant weather most of the year, gorgeous scenery, friendly people, and a multitude of sights and activities. Your tour of South Carolina should be a delight. Three to five days is recommended, with Charleston your first stop. Experiencing the city and its history is an excellent introduction to understanding the upper class in the antebellum South. Wending your way through places associated with the Civil War, and learning of the events that happened there, will help you appreciate the many groups who contributed to its history—black and white, Union and Confederate, army and navy.

CHARLESTON AREA

During the Civil War, Charleston, South Carolina, was a bellwether. As the fortunes of the North and South swung back and forth, the military tide in and around Charleston harbor changed, too. The first shots of the war that counted were fired there, on April 12, 1861, both upon and from Fort Sumter. Charleston was the site of the heroic struggle for Morris Island, and its history is replete with the exploits of ironclads, blockade-runners, and a submarine. Though isolated from the sea for much of the war by a naval blockade, in the war years Charleston received supplies from its land accesses and numerous block-ade-runners. The city was never forcibly taken by the North, and from the day the Fed-erals surrendered Fort Sumter, no Union soldier set foot on the island except as a prisoner until February 18, 1865, the day after the Confederate military finally evacuated the city.

You can tour Charleston for one to four days, and visit sites associated with events span-ning the entire war. The tour may include auto, foot, and boat segments.

Fort Sumter

The building of Fort Sumter, a Third System coastal fortification, was begun in 1829, on a man-made island of New England granite. It was still under construction on the night of December 26, 1860, when Maj. Robert Anderson moved his two-company garrison of U.S. Army artillerists there from Fort Moultrie. During the next fifteen weeks the garrison mounted 47 guns: 26 on the barbette (highest) tier and 21 in the case mates of the lower tier. Against these the South Carolinians and Confederates threw up armed, manned batteries on Morris, James, and Sullivans islands, augmenting their guns at Forts Moultrie and Johnson, and at Mount Pleasant. These Confederate guns were commanded by a colorful Louisianian, Brig. Gen. Pierre Gustave Toutant Beaure-gard.

When negotiations failed to convince the U.S. Army to evacuate Fort Sumter, Beauregard, under orders from President Jefferson Davis, demanded surrender. Late on April 11, 1861, South Carolina politician Col. James Chesnut, with others, rowed out to speak directly with Anderson, but by three-thirty A.M. these last-ditch negotiations had reached an impasse. Before leaving, Chesnut informed Anderson that in one hour the fort would be fired upon. At four-thirty A.M. a signal shot rang from Fort Johnson's east mortar battery, and the Confederate batteries unleashed a storm of shot and shell on Sumter.

Short on powder and supplies, and in want of fuses for exploding shells, Anderson elected to fight a defensive battle. After nearly three hours of unanswered Confederate bombard-ment, Capt. Abner Doubleday fired the first Federal shot. The ball passed harmlessly over the Iron Battery on Cummings Point, and the 68 soldiers in Sumter, their 9 officers, 8 bandsmen, and several dozen civilian workers, spent most of the next thirty-three hours fighting fires from Rebel "hot-shot"—cannonballs heated red-hot in furnaces.

Anderson was expecting a relief expedition from the North, commanded by Captain, later Assistant Secretary of the Navy Gustavus Fox. Actually, Fox's supply ships had arrived off the harbor entrance shortly after the firing began, but the powerful warship that accompanied them, the USS *Powhatan,* was directed to reinforce the Fort Picken, Florida, garrison. Over the next day and a half, Fox was unable to devise a plan for the effective supply and reinforcement of the Federal garrison. On the morning of April 13, the flagstaff on Fort Sumter's parade ground was shot away. Though brave soldiers retrieved and again displayed the flag from one of the fort's embrasures, Southern negotiators felt confident enough of their position to return.

Gen. Pierre Gustave Toutant Beauregard, CSA, was an excellent engineer and for four days at Petersburg in June 1864, an outstanding field tactician, and often clashed with President Davis and the Confederate leadership over military issues. He commanded in actions in every major area east of the Mississippi, but was most effective during his first and second tours of duty in Charleston, where he was revered as a hero after he received the surrender of Fort Sumter.

Convinced that his relief was not coming, Anderson accepted the emissaries. The firing stopped at two that afternoon, and by nightfall surrender terms were agreed to, including, at Anderson's insistence, a one-hundred-gun salute to the flag of the United States prior to evacuation. Ironically, the only fatalities in the action occurred during this ceremony, when the accidental explosion of a pile of cartridges killed one U.S. soldier and mortally wounded another. By nightfall the Federals had departed, and the next day they headed north. Fort Sumter was in Confederate hands.

For the Confederates, Fort Sumter was the cornerstone of an impressive array of batteries and forts ringing Charleston harbor. One Yankee officer described the fortifications as "a porcupine's quills turned outside in." In September 1862, when Beauregard returned from duty in the west to command the Department of South Carolina and Georgia, he armed Fort Sumter with powerful rifled guns. The first major test of these new emplacements came on April 7, 1863, when the U.S. Navy attempted to force its

Federal guns inside the casemates of Fort Sumter returned Confederate fire on April 12 and 13, 1861, until the devastated fort was surrendered. This period chromolithograph dramatically portrays the Union artillerists working their guns while garrison commander Maj. Robert Anderson looks on.

way into the harbor (see **Charleston Harbor**).

In August 1863, the Federal army had established guns on Morris Island close enough to Fort Sumter to penetrate its vulnerable southeast-facing gorge wall (see **Morris Island**). More than 45,000 shells were thrown at it by the Union army and navy. Maj. Gen. Quincy A. Gillmore, the Federal army commander, and R. Adm. John A. Dahlgren, in charge of the South Atlantic Blockading Squadron, planned for an amphibious assault together, but that effort went awry.

Beauregard knew that the fort would soon be reduced to rubble, its guns silenced. He removed all but one of its operable heavy guns and replaced his artillerists with 400 infantrymen, led by Maj. Stephen Elliott. On his own, without the Union army, Dahlgren demanded surrender, but Beauregard offered it only if Dahlgren could take and hold the fort. At night, the Confederates placed rows of fraises (sharpened wooden sticks to form an obstruction) around the fort's exterior, removing them during the day to protect them from the bombardment.

In the predawn hours of September 9, 1863, Dahlgren sent a contingent of 500 U.S. Navy and Marine volunteers in small boats to Fort Sumter. But the Confederates were ready for the assault and the landing force was met by the unexpected force of riflemen. The doomed expedition withdrew with 124 casualties, many of whom were taken prisoner. Gillmore had canceled the army assault after the navy landed to avoid confusion.

On November 20, Gillmore sent a small reconnaissance force to test the fort's condition, but the boats were turned back before they reached the island. During the first week of December the bombardment of the fort was increased, until it was abruptly halted on December 6. By this time Fort Sumter was little more than an earthen fortification. On December 11, 1863, a small arms magazine protected by cotton bales in the southwest corner of the fort exploded, starting an intense fire, worsened by exploding shells from Federal warships that left 11 dead and 41 wounded. There was another period of heavy Federal bombardment from July 7 through September 4, 1864, but until the fort's evacuation, in February 1865, the Confederate flag continued to fly.

In a ceremony on April 14, 1865, Maj. Gen. Robert Anderson returned to Fort Sumter with Federal soldiers and Northern dignitaries looking on raised the U.S. flag once again over the fort. It was the same flag that Anderson had taken with him when he surrendered the fort four years earlier.

Fort Moultrie

Fort Moultrie was a Second System masonry coastal fort constructed between 1807 and 1812, and the third fort on this site. The first, a palmetto-log-and-sand structure, turned back His Majesty's British warships on June 28, 1776. The last, a five-sided structure, was completed in 1809 and continued to be modernized until 1947, when it was decommissioned from the nation's coastal defense system.

During the Civil War the fort's masonry walls were reinforced. In late 1860, it was occupied by Maj. Robert Anderson and his garrison while they awaited the completion of Fort Sumter. Pressured by the Charleston secessionists, on the night of December 26 Anderson secretly moved his soldiers from Fort Moultrie to Fort Sumter (see **Fort Sumter**). From that point until February 1865, Fort Moultrie was occupied by Confederate forces. Its guns fired on Fort Sumter on April 12–13, 1861; on the Federal blockading fleet and on R. Adm. Samuel Du Pont's ironclads on their April 7, 1863, attempt to fight their way into Charleston harbor. In this fight the Confederates focused on the *Weehawken* and the *New Ironsides* and saw their flagstaff shot down. By late summer of that year Fort Moultrie had become a sand battery mounting 11 guns and 3 mortars, and in the September 7 engagement with Dahlgren's monitors and the *New Ironsides* a projectile from the *Weehawken* caused an explosion in the fort killing 16 and wounding 12. Fort Moultrie, which gave as good as it took in additional duels with Dahlgren's monitors, was first occupied by Union soldiers from the 3rd Rhode Island Artillery who bested sailors from the monitor *Canonicus* in the race to first hoist their colors over the fort.

Points of Interest

Fort Sumter National Monument—One of Charleston's most important and famous Civil War landmarks is a multifaceted national treasure. Administered by the National Park Service, Forts Sumter and Moultrie are part of the Fort Sumter National Monument. They are open year-round except Christmas Day. For information on getting to Fort Sumter, see the tour boat information below. Fort Moultrie and its visitor center are open 9:00 A.M. to 6:00 P.M. in the summer and 9:00 A.M. to 5:00 P.M. in the winter.

🚌 🛳 🗺 ♿ ❷ 🏛 P 🚻 $$$

Several excursion companies offer tours that pass near Fort Sumter, but only one docks at the fort. Fort Sumter Tours, Inc., provides service from the City Marina in downtown Charleston and from Patriots Point, Mount Pleasant. Boats operate every day except Christmas, generally departing five times beginning at 9:30 A.M. The last boat leaves from City Marina at 2:30 P.M. in the winter and from Patriots Point at 4:00 P.M. in the summer. A fee is charged. Call 803-722-1691 for further information. Free parking and charters are available. Private craft are not allowed to land at Fort Sumter without prior permission. Contact the park superintendent at Drawer R, Sullivans Island, SC 29482.

Fort Sumter Walking Tour—Upon arrival you will be greeted by a park ranger, who will accompany you through the fort's reconstructed sally port. The fort's first reconstruction was begun in the 1870s under the supervision of Maj. Quincy A. Gillmore, the U.S. Army engineer responsible for much of its destruction. Funds were soon exhausted, however, and for more than twenty years no further work was done. The guided tour includes the parade ground and several of the large guns in the casemates. Self-guided tour pamphlets

Guns mounted en barbette at Fort Moultrie such as this ten-inch columbiad exchanged fire with Union warships attempting to enter Charleston harbor.

are available. Be sure to visit the museum located in Battery Huger. This section was built and armed in the late 1890s, when the concerns for national security against sea-based attacks from foreign powers took precedence over Civil War heritage preservation. The museum includes exhibits and artifacts from the Civil War period. Also, climb to the top of the southeast parapet for a bird's-eye view of the entire area. The mountain howitzer represents one seen in several wartime photographs of Fort Sumter.

Fort Moultrie—From Charleston or Mount Pleasant take US17 north to SC703, which crosses to Sullivans Island. At Middle Street, turn right and proceed 1.5 miles to Fort Moultrie. The visitor center is on the right, the fort on the left. Fort Moultrie is well preserved, though as with Fort Sumter, in the late 1890s and early 1900s the army constructed three reinforced-concrete rapid-fire batteries along two of its seafronts. All key parts, including magazines and gun emplacements, are accessible. The fort has an excellent self-guided interpretive exhibit on coastal guns from the War of 1812 through World War II, and examples of many types of Civil War artillery. Tours are also given by park rangers. The Fort Moultrie visitor center has a film, artifacts, and a bookstore. At Fort Moultrie is a monument marking the mass grave of sailors from the *Patapsco,* whose remains were removed from their ship when the wreckage of the monitor was removed from the harbor in the 1870s (see **Charleston Harbor**).

DRIVING TOUR— *1861: proceed to Downtown Charleston;*
1863 Siege of Charleston: proceed to Morris Island

Sullivan's Island

Shortly before the first attack on Fort Sumter, the Confederates built additional batteries on Sullivan's Island (as it was then spelled) to reduce and capture the fort. An ironclad floating battery with four guns was towed to the island's west end. Three batteries were constructed to the west of Fort Moultrie, with five more extending out to the east, including Battery Beauregard. At the eastern tip of the island, Fort Marshall faced the Atlantic Ocean.

The most interesting event associated with Sullivans Island, however, had nothing to do with these batteries, but rather with an incident in the waters off the island's eastern end in early 1864. In their efforts to break the stranglehold of the blockade, the Confederates had been tinkering with secret weapons, especially torpedo launches (see **Charleston Harbor**). But a new, more novel invention showed promise, too. Its chief designer and builder, Horace L. Hunley, had failed in a previous attempt to build a Confederate submarine, but initial tests impressed the Rebel authorities enough to have the manually powered craft brought to Charleston. Two disastrous test runs, however, which together killed thirteen of the vessel's two 9-man crews, caused Beauregard to suspend the CSS *Horace L. Hunley*'s submerged activities. Still, she continued to operate on the surface, well equipped for ramming, with her spar torpedo capable of planting a ninety-pound charge into the bowels of an unsuspecting enemy ship.

Based on Sullivan's Island, the *Hunley* ventured out on several night runs. On the night of February 17, 1864, her inventor in command, the submarine rammed its spar torpedo into the hull of a large wooden warship, the USS *Housatonic,* which sank. But the *Hunley* disappeared, too. For more than 130 years it was not clear whether the submarine's torpedo spar, lodged in the sinking warship, caused the *Hunley* to be dragged to the bottom, or if the sub went down on her own, but divers have recently located its hulk and report she sank while returning to her base. The only land action in the area was at Bull's Bay, about ten miles to the north of Sullivan's Island. On February 13, 1865, gunboats entered Bay Sewee and engaged the Andersonville forts. The Confederates more than held their own against the Union navy as they sought to find a way across the shoals. On February 16 the Federals found the key to success. While several gunboats and part of the army troops from Brig. Gen. E. E. Potter's command continued to threaten Andersonville, two warships and the rest of Potter's troops drove the Rebels from a strong earthwork on Graham's Point. By the next day the Federals held Bull's Bay, which along with the advance of Sherman on Columbia, hastened the Confederate evacuation of Charleston.

Points of Interest

Interpretive signs on Middle Street mark the location of some of Sullivans Island's other Civil War batteries. On US17, 5 miles north of Mount Pleasant, is Boone Hall Plantation. The antebellum estate, established in 1681, has a rebuilt plantation house as well as the original smokehouse and slave quarters. The mansion and historic avenue of oak trees, planted in 1743, have been in many period films and television programs. For information, call 803-884-4371.

Fifty-six miles north of Mount Pleasant on US17 is Georgetown, South Carolina's third-oldest city. If you are on the coastal route heading north to Wilmington, North Carolina, you may want to stop there. The city was the center of a large rice-growing area during the Civil War. Several U.S. Navy sorties were made to the area, though Confederate forces were always sparse and underarmed. The Rice Museum, in the old slave market building downtown, offers a history of the Confederate field soldier's staple food. On the grounds of the private Belle Isle Yacht Club, on Winyah Bay, is Battery White, a Confederate earthwork that mounted two 10-inch columbiads and is largely intact. Check at the yacht club gate for current access.

Charleston Harbor

Charleston has one of the finest harbors on the southeast coast of the United States. It was contested in both the Revolutionary and Civil wars and was prepared for action in all other American conflicts through World War II. Army actions involving the forts and land areas surrounding the harbor are discussed elsewhere—this section is devoted to the naval contests.

In late January 1863, Gen. P.G.T. Beauregard prodded the tiny Confederate navy into action at Charleston. The CSN had two ironclad rams in the harbor, the *Palmetto State* and the *Chicora.* On January 31, they left the Charleston docks to attack the wooden ships of the Federal blockading squadron, including the sloop of war, USS *Housatonic,* 2 gunboats, and 7 converted merchant vessels. Under cover of darkness, the two Confederate vessels approached the *Mercedita* and, at close quarters, the *Palmetto State* fired heavy shot, destroying the *Mercedita*'s steam drum and condenser and forcing her surrender. The *Palmetto State* then joined the *Chicora* in an attack on the *Keystone State.* The Rebel ships were able to avoid a ramming attempt, and the heavily damaged Federal boat got away. The *Housatonic,* at the far end of the line, did not become aware of the attack until daybreak and was only able to fire a few meaningless long-range shots at the withdrawing Confederates.

Though it hardly broke the blockade, as the Confederates claimed, the incident focused the Federals' attention on their need for better protected and armed craft. In fact, they were just then launching and outfitting a group of monitor-class ironclads. The USS *Monitor,* was part of a group sent to South Carolina, but she floundered and sank in a storm off the North Carolina coast on December 30, 1862. R. Adm. Samuel Du Pont, who had captured Port Royal Sound and its forts in November 1861 (see **Port Royal**), was well aware of the importance placed on the capture of Charleston by the Washington leadership and the people of the North. Du Pont in early 1862 employed the North's amphibious capabilities in cooperation with the army to establish coastal enclaves in Florida and compel the Confederates to evacuate the Georgia sea islands and the South Carolina barrier islands. He was convinced that only a combined army-navy effort could be successful. Not everyone agreed.

The Navy Department, particularly Assistant Secretary Gustavus Fox and Secretary Welles, considered the ironclad monitors invincible and the key to a naval attack on the harbor. Additionally, the army commander Maj. Gen. David Hunter, tempered by the Federal defeat at Secessionville (see **Secessionville, James and Folly Islands, and Vicinity**), was reluctant to attack the Charleston fortifications and their large (overestimated by the Federals) supporting force of infantry until the Navy had silenced their principal batteries. Though unconvinced of the monitors' effectiveness, Du Pont planned a trial run. In February and March 1863 he dispatched first one monitor, then several, to attack the earthen fortification guarding Georgia's Ogeechee River, near Savannah (see **Fort McAllister, Georgia**). While the trials provided evidence of the ironclads' resistance to shot and shell, there was debate as to their effectiveness in returning fire. Nevertheless, the Navy Department's support for an attack on Charleston remained unwavering.

At the start of April, Du Pont had seven ironclad monitors at anchorage in Port Royal, as well as the lightly armored, twin tower *Keokuk* and his flagship, an armor-plated ship of the line, the *New Ironsides*. In the early afternoon of April 7, the ships weighed anchor. As they passed Fort Wagner the Confederates held their fire, but once they neared Fort Sumter the Rebel guns commenced firing. Fort Moultrie, the Sullivans Island batteries, and Battery Gregg, at Cummings Point, Morris Island, all joined in. An obstruction, rope netting with mines (torpedoes) attached to it, across the channel between Fort Sumter and Fort Moultrie caused the monitors to slow down, then turn to port ahead of the pivot Du Pont had planned. In the shallow channel the deep-draft *New Ironsides* had difficulty maneuvering.

The ships, stalled and out of line, endured a terrible crossfire. Darkness approached and Du Pont suspended the attack for the day. The ironclads sustained significant damage, especially to their turrets and guns. The *New Ironsides* was relatively unscathed, her draft problems having kept her removed from the center of the action, but to one U.S. Navy officer the *Keokuk* looked "like a colander." The morning of April 8 she flopped on her side in the shallow waters by Morris Island. More important, the Federal guns inflicted little damage and failed to silence any batteries. Du Pont had intended to renew the attack the next day, but when morning came he canceled the order. It's easy to imagine that when Washington that day urgently ordered most of the monitors to New Orleans for operations on the Mississippi, Du Pont felt relief.

A short time afterward, Confederate engineers working at night removed the two heavy Dahlgren guns from the almost fully submerged *Keokuk*. The Dahlgrens were eventually mounted in the Charleston batteries, embarrassing Du Pont and the navy. Despite general agreement that the monitors had made their best effort, the navy's failure and the loss of the *Keokuk* and her guns came to haunt Du Pont. The navy department took the loss hard, and by July Du Pont was relieved of his command. When R. Adm. Andrew H. Foote, the commander designated to replace him, died suddenly, the command of the South Atlantic Blockading Squadron fell to R. Adm. John A. Dahlgren, the former chief of the Bureau of Ordnance.

Dahlgren had no more success in the harbor than Du Pont. His role, primarily, was to enforce the blockade, bombard Confederate shore batteries, and cooperate with the army's offensive to secure Morris Island and bombard Fort Sumter. Once the Rebels evacuated Morris Island, Dahlgren ordered the monitor *Weehawken* to mark the channel between Fort Sumter and Cummings Point, but the ironclad ran aground on September 7, 1863, and, until breaking free in a flood tide the following day, she and other Federal warships dueled with Confederate shore batteries. On October 5, 1863, the Confederate torpedo boat *David* planted an explosive charge on the *New Ironsides*'s hull, which detonated amidships but did little damage. Another monitor, the USS *Patapsco,* was not so lucky. On January 15, 1865, she struck a mine at the harbor entrance, taking 62 of her crew with her to the bottom.

Points of Interest

Charleston harbor is served by a variety of boat tours, which offer the best way to get a feel for the situations of the powerful Federal navy, the Confederate gunboats, and blockade-runners. Excellent views of harbor landmarks, which, in addition to Fort Sumter, include Castle Pinckney, Fort Moultrie, the leeward side of Morris Island, and, in down-

Federal prisoners from the Battle of First Manassas pose in front of a casemate at Castle Pinckney. Introducing a bit of wit into the situation, members of the 11th New York Zouaves placed a sign over their casemate quarters identifying them as "Hotel de Zouave."

town Charleston, the antique spires and Battery Park can be seen from the tour boats. The harbor can also be viewed from Patriot's Point, Battery Park, Fort Moultrie, and other shoreline areas.

Castle Pinckney

Castle Pinckney is a Second System fort constructed in the early nineteenth century. On December 27, 1860, it was commandeered without bloodshed by South Carolina secessionists, one of the first seizures of Federal government property in the rapidly expanding crisis that would lead to war. Though manned early in the war by an elite corps of Charleston militia, it saw limited action because of its distance from the mouth of the harbor. The casemates were converted into barracks and received some of the first Federal prisoners of war from the Battle of First Manassas. It continued as a small prison, with no known escapes. Late in the war it was provided with heavy guns, covered with sand, and made part of the harbor's inner defenses.

Castle Pinckney is located on an ecologically delicate island between downtown Charleston and Patriots Point. Due to the island's fragility and dangerous conditions, the Harbor Authority does not allow visitors on the island. It can easily be seen and photographed from any of the tour boats in the harbor, and from downtown Charleston and Patriots Point.

READING—*prisons: Andersonville, Georgia*

Charleston

Charleston is called the "Cradle of Secession." Led by Robert Barnwell Rhett, Jr., the owner and publisher of the *Charleston Mercury,* and Robert Barnwell Rhett, Sr., the "Father of Secession" who wrote editorials for his son's newspaper, the city's aristocratic class clamored for independence. The tide of secession passed from Charleston harbor and over the state. The two-day secession convention, which was moved to Charleston after an outbreak of smallpox in Columbia, the state's capital, adopted the Ordinance of Secession on December 20, 1861. When the city erupted in noisy demonstrations, some warned that the firecrackers were a portent of war.

Militia units were already a popular draw for the city's young men, and were now joined by companies from around the state. The U.S. Post Office, the Customs House, and the Federal arsenal were seized. On April 12, 1861, Charleston's citizens thronged to the seawalls and quays for a glimpse of the far-off bombardment of Fort Sumter. Once long-range Federal guns were dug in on Morris Island, however, the city itself became a target.

Until the late summer of 1863, the most serious wartime damage to Charleston came from a huge fire, unrelated to any military action, on December 11 and 12, 1861. Hundreds of buildings were burned and gutted, including Secession Hall (Institute Hall), where the signing ceremony for the Ordinance of Secession had been held. On August 21, 1863, however, after Federal army commander Maj. Gen. Quincy A. Gillmore demanded the surrender of Fort Sumter and Fort (Battery) Wagner, an eight-inch Parrott rifle on Morris Island called the "Swamp Angel" fired shells at the city. Beauregard and the

A house along the Battery, which overlooks Charleston harbor. This and many other beautiful buildings in downtown Charleston preserve the city's antebellum heritage.

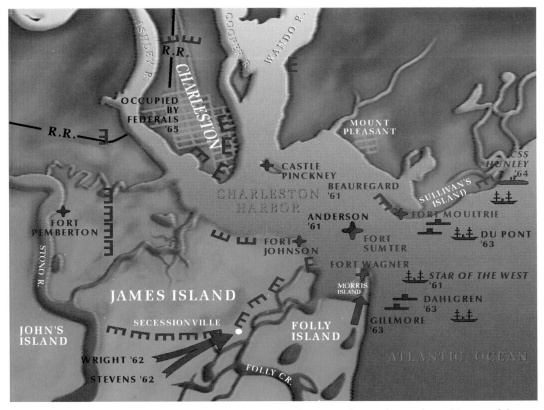

Charleston was under the gun for most of the war. After shots turned away the merchant ship Star of the West *from its resupply mission to Fort Sumter in January 1861 and Fort Sumter fell in April, Federal efforts focused on gaining access to Charleston harbor. Efforts by land and sea through the end of 1864 failed. Charleston was never effectively besieged and Union troops did not march into the city until February 18, 1865, after all Confederate forces evacuated Charleston in the wake of Maj. Gen. William T. Sherman's march through the state.*

Southern leaders protested, complaining that the customary notice had not been given for the evacuation of women and children. Two days later, however, after having fired 36 rounds into the city, the "Swamp Angel" blew up while attempting to fire a thirty-seventh. The Federals dragged more guns into position on Morris Island. Shortly after Christmas night, 1863, they resumed the bombardment and 134 shells were fired into the city. The Confederates retaliated by moving Union prisoners of war to exposed locations near the Battery, but the Federals continued the bombardment on selected days in January 1864. The Federal bombardment continued until other Federal operations took priority. Life in Charleston then regained a degree of normalcy, which lasted until the February 17, 1865, evacuation.

Points of Interest

Charleston is a city of such heritage and beauty that a detailed description of historic sites cannot be given here. An active visitors bureau and the Visitor Reception Center, at 375 Meeting Street, provide information on tour guides, pamphlets, books, a movie, and even surrey rides. The most significant points of interest in Charleston's Civil War history are listed below.

Charleston City Hall on Meeting Street is a landmark that survived the war.

Most of the sites are on or near Meeting Street, the principal north-south street of old Charleston. These include the Civil War–era City Hall; St. Michael's Church, which was used as a Confederate observation post; and the oldest museum in the United States, the Charleston Museum (360 Meeting Street), founded in 1773. On Market Street, east of Meeting, is the Exchange Building, and farther east, on Concord Street, is the U.S. Customs building.

The Embassy Suites hotel, located on Market Street, was the first home—the one seen in period photographs—of the South Carolina State Military Academy, today known most popularly as the Citadel. Another must-see is Battery Park (White Point Gardens), located at the foot of Meeting Street. The park contains several mounted Civil War guns, including one recovered from the USS *Keokuk*. Most of the houses fronting the park date from before the Civil War, and one, at 9 East Battery, still has a piece of a cannon tube from an exploded gun lodged in its roof.

Two museums, one at the Citadel and the Charleston Museum on Market Street, have outstanding Civil War collections. In front of the Charleston Museum is a full-scale reproduction of the *Hunley*.

Secessionville, James and Folly Islands, and Vicinity

James Island is a large sea island and forms most of the southern lip of Charleston harbor. When, in the latter part of 1862, General Beauregard returned to command in Charleston, he decided that the Federals' most feasible land approach would be across James Island. He also believed, based on a Confederate victory on the island in June 1862, they would not attempt to use it. Federal troops, included in the Department of the South under the command of Maj. Gen. David Hunter, landed on James Island on June 2, 1862, near Stono Inlet under the protection of gunboat fire. The Confederates, under the command of Brig. Gen. Nathan G. "Shanks" Evans, constructed a five-mile line of works on the island. In advance of the line, Secessionville, a summer retreat for many well-off Charlestonians, was an unfinished, but formidable fort.

In charge of the Federals' James Island force was Brig. Gen. Henry W. Benham. He was at first content to fire on Secessionville from afar, and succeeded in destroying an unfinished battery, but then having decided that the camp of his subordinate, Brig. Gen. Isaac I. Stevens, was vulnerable, Benham ordered—in the predawn hours of June 16—an advance of his 6,600 soldiers. The Confederates had but 200 soldiers at Secessionville, though reinforcements were en route. Stevens's troops encountered the Rebels posted behind a strong earthwork known as Fort Lamar guarding a narrow neck of land between two marshes. They were beaten back in fierce fighting, and by the time Brig. Gen. Horatio G. Wright's units came up, Rebel reinforcements had arrived. Benham called for naval assistance, but the gunboats were of little help. Some of their shells fell into the Federal ranks. After two and a half hours, Benham called a retreat. With 700 casualties, against 200 for the Confederates, it was a stunning defeat, and Benham was sacked and court-martialed for attacking against orders. There was a small engagement at Simmons Bluff on June 21. On July 9 Major General Hunter ordered all Federals withdrawn, following which the Confederates strengthened the works. However, Federal gunboats continued to patrol the Stone River.

On January 30, 1863, the gunboat *Isaac P. Smith* and another navy vessel *Commodore McDonough* were reconnoitering the Stono near Legaréville. Three masked Confederate batteries opened fire on the *Isaac P. Smith*. She was badly damaged and surrendered before the *Commodore McDonough* could come to her aid.

Then on the morning of December 25, 1863, with twelve guns hastily mounted in masked batteries, on John's Island, the Confederates hoped to catch Federal vessels patrolling Stono Inlet off guard, allowing a supporting infantry force to capture the Federal garrison at Legaréville. The Rebels opened fire on the USS *Marblehead* as she cruised in the inlet. However, the captain of the USS *Pawnee* placed his ship in a position to enfilade the Confederate guns and the fire of the Union warships forced the Rebels to retreat, abandoning two of their eight-inch howitzers.

On February 9, 1864, the Federals landed a larger force onto John's Island, but nothing significant occurred until that summer, when Maj. Gen. John G. Foster, Gillmore's successor in the Department of the South, formulated a five-point plan. Four widely scattered amphibious assaults targeted batteries and railroad lines in the area. On July 2, U.S. gunboats and monitors, having crossed Stono Bar, ascended the river, and the next day opened fire on Battery Pringle on the western side of James Island, commanding the middle reaches of the Stono River. Reinforcements slowed down the Federal advance. This diversion enabled other units to land from small boats and capture a one-gun battery midway between Battery Simkins and Fort Johnson. Caught in the crossfire between Battery Simkins and Fort Johnson, the Federal commander Col. William Gurney failed to commit his reserves and was compelled to surrender himself and 136 officers and men of the 52nd Pennsylvania.

Also on July 2, a force of 1,200 under Brig. Gen. William Birney landed at White Point on Slann's Island and marched toward the Charleston & Savannah Railroad. But they were halted by a Confederate battery on King's Creek and U.S. gunboats on the Dawhoo River shelled the Rebels. Birney, checkmated in his efforts to reach the railroad, received permission to withdraw. Finally, Brig. Gen. John P. Hatch's force landed on John's Island and pushed up the west bank of the Stono and gained a position opposite Battery Pringle, but intense heat caused this assault to also fade when the Rebels brought up the infantry reinforcements. A second July 10 amphibious assault on Fort Johnson was also turned back. Foster abandoned the plan on July 11, although three days earlier, Federal gunboats had pounded Battery Pringle mercilessly.

The final Federal operation against James Island began on February 10, 1965. With Sherman's march toward Branchville and Columbia engrossing the attention of the Confederates in South Carolina, the Federals met slight resistance in their push across the island. A week later the Confederate troops evacuated Charleston and its defenses in the area.

Folly Island, a barrier island on the Atlantic Ocean side of James Island, gave the soldiers of Maj. Gen. Quincy A. Gillmore's command a toehold on the islands south of Charleston harbor. Federal soldiers landed unopposed on Folly Island during the attempt by Du Pont's ironclads to force their way into Charleston harbor on April 7, 1863, and used the island as a base of operations for their subsequent attack on Morris Island.

Points of Interest

To reach James Island, take US17 south from Charleston, across the Ashley River. A little way past the bridge there is a well-marked left turn for Folly Road (SC171). Follow Folly Road south for all sites. For Fort Johnson, turn left on Fort Johnson Drive and follow it until it ends.

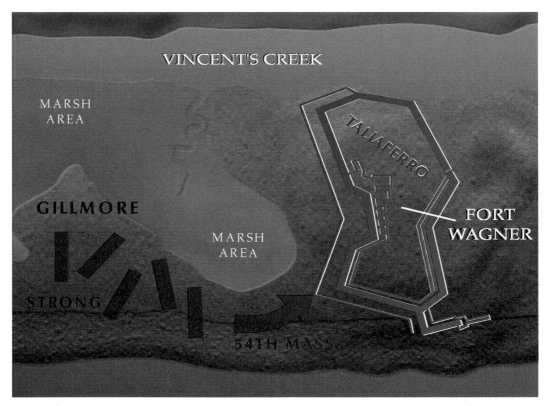

Fort Wagner (Battery Wagner) was well located on Morris Island, forcing the Federals to attack the sand fortress on a narrow front. The second and final assault of the fort at twilight on July 18, 1863, by the division of Brig. Gen. Truman Seymour was spearheaded by a column under Brig. Gen. George C. Strong with the 54th Massachusetts Regiment in the van.

Fort Johnson—Fort Johnson, a pre-Revolutionary War–era fort reactivated on the eve of the attack on Fort Sumter, is currently the home of the South Carolina Wildlife and Marine Resources Center. There are interpretive markers at the site and a small brick powder magazine dating to the eighteenth century. If you look out at Fort Sumter across the bay, you'll get a good idea of how it might have appeared to the Confederate gunners who fired the signal shot that initiated the April 12, 1861, bombardment that triggered the Civil War.

Secessionville—There are historical markers in the Secessionville area that identify Fort Lamar. A reenactment of this battle is held annually, in November, at Boone Hall.

Battery Pringle—Battery Pringle, owned by the Charleston Museum, is located off Folly Road on the east bank of the Stono River. Other earthworks on James Island are held in trust by the South Carolina Battleground Preservation Trust.

Folly Island—Today Folly Island is a popular recreation area and beach. From Folly Island you can get a good view of Morris Island.

Morris Island

One of the southern theater's most significant land campaigns took place on the otherwise desolate barrier island, now slowly eroding away, that guards the southern lip of Charleston harbor. From January through April 13, 1861, Morris Island was a battery position for Southern artillery aimed at Fort Sumter, and by late September 1863 it would serve the North in the same capacity. In between, in the summer of 1863, a vicious struggle to take the island would be waged. Best known for the heroic but ill-prepared charge of the African-American 54th Massachusetts Regiment, the object of this Federal campaign was a

Col. Robert Gould Shaw, USA, was a captain in the 2nd Massachusetts Regiment before being called upon by the state's governor to train and lead a regiment of African-American soldiers. Shaw was more than equal to the task and worked diligently to support his belief that blacks could soldier just as well as whites.

Sgt. William H. Carney, USA, had this to say about his role as color bearer for the 54th Massachusetts Regiment during the July 18, 1863, attack on Fort Wagner: "The old flag never touched the ground, boys."

sand-and-earthen fortification, reinforced with palmetto logs and sandbags, called Fort Wagner, sometimes known as Battery Wagner.

The Confederates had built Fort Wagner on a strategic location at a narrow part of the island, the right anchored on wetland and the left on the choppy waters of the Atlantic Ocean, a location that made the north end of the island all but impossible to overrun. In mid-1863, attempting to gain an advantageous site for their large siege guns, the Federals, under Maj. Gen. Quincy A. Gillmore, launched an attack on Morris Island. In July 1863 P.G.T. Beauregard was in the second of his three tours commanding the Charleston defenses.

Additionally, Brig. Gen. William Taliaferro, a pugnacious veteran of Jackson's Shenandoah Valley Campaign and Second Manassas, rushed from nearby Georgia to take command of Fort Wagner. The Federals had already occupied Folly Island, across Lighthouse Inlet and built a strong base there. On July 10, Brig. Gen. George C. Strong led a Federal force from Folly and overran the rifle pits and batteries on the southern part of Morris, but were then faced with the staggering fire from Fort Wagner. The next day, Gillmore ordered Strong with the 7th Connecticut, and a small supporting force, to storm the fort, but the front between the wetlands and ocean was just 750 yards wide and the units were repulsed.

On July 18, Gillmore, encouraged by division commander Brig. Gen. Truman Seymour, ordered another assault, this time preceded by an eleven-hour bombardment. At twilight, with the 54th Massachusetts Regiment—under the command of Col. Robert Gould Shaw, the son of prominent Boston abolitionists—spearheading the two-brigade attack by Seymour's division, Strong's brigade in the lead advanced to the fort. The soldiers of the 54th fought bravely onto the parapet, but could not long sustain the withering fire. Other units tried to push in behind, but the Confederates raked them with canister and rifle-musket fire. The twenty-five-year-old Gould reached the superior slope of the parapet with sword raised, shouted, "Onward, Fifty-fourth!" and was shot dead. The second brigade of Federals, following behind Strong's units, seized a toehold in Wagner until forced out by the Rebels. In the enveloping darkness, Gillmore finally called off the assault.

The losses were staggering: 1,500 casualties for the Federals, compared with 222 for the Confederates. The 54th lost 281 men. Strong sustained wounds from which he would die; the other Federal brigade commander, Col. Haldimand Putnam, was killed. Seymour and Shaw's second-in-command, Lt. Col. Edward N. Hallowell, were wounded; every other regimental commander was either killed or wounded. Two color-bearers were recipients of Medals of Honor for recovering Federal colors; one of these was Sgt. William H. Carney of the 54th, the first African American to be so honored by the U.S. Army.

Gillmore decided to start lay siege and use his heavy guns on the fort. Over the next several weeks, the Federals pushed parallels—gradually angling trenches—toward it. During bombardments the Confederates retreated to the fort's bombproof, then mounted its parapets to harass Union sappers and miners. By the beginning of September, the four parallels took Union soldiers to the edge of the fort's ditch. On September 6, Beauregard ordered Fort Wagner and Battery Gregg, on Cummings Point, evacuated, and all guns spiked that couldn't be moved. The Federals approached Fort Wagner cautiously and found it abandoned. Fort Wagner, renamed Fort Strong by the Federals, and Battery Gregg were turned into artillery emplacements used to bombard Fort Sumter and other targets.

Points of Interest

Morris Island, under the jurisdiction of the Army Corps of Engineers, is not readily accessible. An experienced guide, with prior permission, can take you to the island in a private craft. Contact the Charleston Visitor Reception Center for more information. Fort Wagner has been lost to the sea by erosion. Battery Gregg and other parts of the island can be explored. The Charleston Lighthouse was a landmark for the island's defenders and attackers. On the seaward side of the island, near Cummings Point, there was a marker which has now disappeared, at the site from which Citadel cadets fired on the *Star of the West,* a merchant ship carrying relief supplies to the Federal garrison at Fort Sumter, on January 9, 1861. The 1990 motion picture *Glory* magnificently, but not accurately, portrayed the events leading up to and including the climactic charge of the 54th Massachusetts on Fort Wagner. In the film the assault was staged, at Jekyll Island, Georgia, as a charge from north of the fort, with the open sea on the Federals' left. The actual assault was from the south.

BEAUFORT AREA

Port Royal

In the fall of 1861, when Washington looked for a success to counter the Confederate victories at First Manassas and Wilson's Creek, it turned to the U.S. Navy, which to that point had little to its credit. The resupply of Fort Sumter had been badly mishandled, and the reinforcement of Pensacola was only slightly more successful. However, in an August expedition to Hatteras Islet, North Carolina, Federal warships had pounded the forts guarding the inlet into submission (see **Hatteras Inlet, North Carolina**).

This period woodcut illustrates the November 7, 1861, attack on Forts Walker and Beauregard in Port Royal Sound by Flag Officer Samuel Du Pont's federal warships. Du Pont's tactic of steaming his ships in an oval formation maximized firepower.

Now, when another victory was needed for the North to gain momentum, the navy was called upon. Secretary of the Navy Welles, a former Connecticut newspaperman, saw valuable public relations in a quick and bold strike, and the benefit of a good coaling station and Federal base near the midpoint of the Confederate Atlantic coast could not be overlooked. For months an assault was planned on

Port Royal, South Carolina, the finest harbor south of New York, which was well protected from the elements, and preparations were made for a secrecy-enshrouded expedition. U.S. Navy Flag Officer Samuel A. Du Pont, a relative of the famous Delaware gunpowder manufacturing family, was selected to command the operation. Much was expected of him. On October 16, warships mounting 148 guns cast off from New York. They were joined by 36 transports carrying 13,000 soldiers, which departed Hampton Roads on October 29, under Brig. Gen. Thomas W. Sherman.

As the expeditionary force made its way south, gales slowed it down and a transport carrying marines and some supply vessels were lost. Diversions intended to confuse the enemy merely wasted time, as the Confederates had already correctly concluded that the attack's aim was Port Royal. At the same time, a Southern officer, Robert E. Lee, assumed command of the region, the newly constituted Department of South Carolina, Georgia, and East Florida.

On November 4, the squadron arrived off Port Royal Sound. Because the Rebels had destroyed or removed the navigational buoys, Du Pont ordered a coastal survey, and while six gunboats took the surveyors in for a closer look, the four-boat Confederate squadron of Josiah Tatnall, mounting eight guns, ventured forth. After a few long-distance exchanges, the "mosquito fleet" retired. The next morning they returned and lured some of the Federal gunboats into range of Fort Walker, on the northern tip of Hilton Head Island, and Fort Beauregard, defending the north shore from Phillips Island. The brief exchange of shots that followed was a preamble. Du Pont had planned on launching his assault that afternoon, but his flagship, the USS *Wabash*, ran aground. By the time she was refloated, night had come.

Gales the next day postponed all offensive operations, but November 7 dawned bright with calm seas. Boilers were stoked, and at nine A.M. the armada steamed toward the channel. The Confederates' position was tenuous. The two forts were short on big guns and their crews were green. A floating battery in the middle of the harbor proposed by Beauregard had not been built. Because of the lack of a good beach and key vessels needed for an army landing, Du Pont first ordered a naval bombardment of Fort Walker. By ten o'clock, one half hour after the first report of Confederate guns, the navy's starboard guns were raking the fort at a rate estimated to be one shell per second. The fort's two rifled guns lacked ammunition and fell from their carriages early on. The inexperienced defenders could do little but show resistance. By the time the Union's lead ships started their second pass, the Rebels were abandoning the fort. Most would later make it to the mainland on steamers or ships from Tatnall's gunboat squadron. By two P.M., Federal navy officers and bluejackets landed and laid claim to the fort.

Over on Phillips Island, the gun crews at Fort Beauregard could do little more than watch the action. All their guns save one, which had burst early on, were outranged by the Federal warships. The garrison heard the cheers of the Federal sailors and, fearing the day was lost, abandoned the fort. By nightfall, the Federal army had landed near Fort Walker, and Du Pont turned Hilton Head Island over to Brig. Gen. Horatio Wright. Despite the iron expended, only 8 sailors and 10 in the fort had been killed. Few on either side were wounded, and because the Federals did not block the escape route, there were few Rebel prisoners.

Seldom in the Civil War was a brother versus brother confrontation more in evidence than at Port Royal. In command of the Confederate defenses at Port Royal was Brig. Gen. Thomas F. Drayton, an aristocratic West Pointer whose expansive plantation was on Hilton Head. The commander of the USS *Pocahontas,* a gunboat in Du Pont's fleet, was Cmdr. Percival Drayton, a Union man of utmost integrity. Later to be Adm. David G. Farragut's right-hand man, Percival Drayton so feared that the late arrival of his vessel off Port Royal Sound because of earlier damage at sea might cause his fellow officers to suspect hesitation, he directed his gunboat to attack the flank of Fort Walker as soon as she rejoined the squadron.

The Federal army had just suffered another devastating setback along the Potomac, northwest of Washington (see **Ball's Bluff, Virginia**), and the victory at Port Royal was an important one. Robert E. Lee quickly assessed the impact of the Port Royal defeat and ordered the undermanned garrisons to evacuate the sea and barrier islands between Charleston and Fernandina, Florida, except for Fort Pulaski, Georgia (see **Savannah, Georgia**). By the following spring, crises in other areas and Lee's belief that the Rebels' coastal defenses were no match for the Federal armada, caused him to form the defense of the region along the railroad that ran inland between Charleston and Savannah. He then stripped the southeast coast of most Confederate infantry units. The Federal army apparently agreed with Lee, and for three years was content to secure Hilton Head Island and other sea islands around Port Royal Sound, and to build forts and support facilities there. They did not venture often or far beyond the guns of the navy's warships.

Hilton Head

After the Federals seized the island of Hilton Head, they turned it into one of the largest Federal supply bases in the South, it served as a staging area for Union operations in South Carolina, Florida, and coastal Georgia. Fort Walker was renamed Fort Welles, after the secretary of the navy, and a town grew up next to the military facilities. Of the dozens of buildings constructed for military purposes, one type of structure had a unique purpose. These buildings were schools for the area's former slaves, the Federal government's first attempt to prepare them for a future of freedom. The first African-American units of the Federal army in the South were organized from former slaves undergoing their initial months of freedom at Hilton Head.

Beaufort

Beaufort, like Hilton Head, was a Federal enclave, with many of the antebellum buildings turned into hospitals, headquarters, and billeting space. Beaufort became a major center for resting and refitting Union troops operating in the region.

At Port Royal on May 16, 1865, Confederate President Jefferson Davis, Vice President Alexander Stephens, Postmaster General John H. Reagan, Maj. Gen. Joseph Wheeler, and President Davis's family were transferred from the tug that had brought them down the Savannah River from Augusta to the oceangoing side-wheel steamer *William P. Clyde*. The president, his family, and Reagan had been captured at Irwinville, Georgia, on May 10 (see **Irwinville, Georgia**). From Port Royal the group was transported north for incarceration (see F**ort Monroe, Virginia**).

Points of Interest

The Port Royal Sound area is an interesting contrast between preservation and development. Beaufort, on the one hand, 24 miles south of I-95 exit 33 on US21, retains much of its antebellum charm and public accessibility, while Hilton Head has become a world-renowned resort area, almost entirely privatized and modernized. From I-95 take exit 21, and follow US278 south for 32 miles to the island. From Savannah take US17ALT north. The new Museum of Hilton Head Island (803-842-9197) intends to recover some of the island's lost heritage; however, remains from Federal forts, including Forts Howell and Sherman, outworks, and Confederate Fort Walker, all on private land, can be toured by contacting the Hilton Head museum. Check with the guard at Hilton Head Plantation, near Skull Creek Marina, for access to Federal Fort Mitchel.

No trace remains of Fort Beauregard, but portions of another Confederate fort still stands, at Sam's Point, on Ladu's Island, near the town of Wilkins, SC802 north of Beaufort. The Nature Conservancy recently purchased Otter Island, which contains remains of a number of Confederate works, but that are not currently accessible. The Parris Island Museum, on the expansive Marine Corps base, SC802 south of Beaufort, contains information and exhibits on Port Royal's Civil War history. Call 803-525-2951 for information.

The past still echoes on the streets of Beaufort, lined with brick homes and commercial buildings from the last century. *A Guide to Historic Beaufort,* published by the Historic Beaufort Foundation, contains much about the city's buildings, many of which were used by the Federals as barracks, hospitals, and headquarters. The book is available at Foundation headquarters, 801 Bay Street, and other locations. The Beaufort County Library at 311 Scott Street also has information on Civil War sites. The Arsenal of Beaufort, established in 1795, and located at 713 Craven Street, features the Beaufort Museum. The present structure dates from 1852; however, portions of it date to the 1790s. For information call 803-525-7471.

Pocotaligo

In October 1862, the Federal army ventured from Port Royal Sound to break up Confederate rail communications between Charleston and Savannah. A force under Brig. Gen. John M. Brannan and Col. William B. Barton was defeated in two battles on October 22–23 at Frampton's Plantation and Caston Plantation by Confederate forces under Brig. Gen. William S. Walker. The Federals lost 32 killed and 180 wounded; the Rebels reported 14 killed and 102 wounded.

Points of Interest

The Pocotaligo battlefield is currently on private lands and is not accessible.

Honey Hill

Supporting Maj. Gen. William T. Sherman's approach on Savannah, Georgia, in late November 1864, Maj. Gen. John G. Foster, commanding the Department of the South,

A view of downtown Columbia, South Carolina, from the location of the Capitol, sketched on February 18, 1865. Federal shelling and blazing cotton bales that burned much of the city during the brief Federal occupation caused chaos in Columbia and delayed the completion of the new state capitol building.

moved to cut off the Savannah defenders' escape route and block Confederate reinforcements from reaching the city by rail from Charleston. Foster brought together 5,500 soldiers and sailors at Hilton Head on transports and steamed up Broad River, his objective the Charleston & Savannah Railroad depot at Gopher Hill, today's Ridgeland, near Grahamville. The Confederates, informed of the operation, rushed troops to the area. The only available units were 2,000 Georgia militia and reserves under Maj. Gen. G. W. Smith, and a handful of artillery and cavalry. Although the militia were bound by Governor Joseph Brown of Georgia to serve within the state, Lt. Gen. William Hardee convinced Smith to rush them across the Savannah River and to Grahamville by rail.

Their presence proved decisive. Under the command of Brig. Gen. John P. Hatch, the Federals disembarked at Boyd's Neck for the cross-country march to Gopher Hill. Hatch forged ahead with one brigade, sailors and marines, and eight boat howitzers, but the expedition became disoriented and did not reach Bolen Church, five miles from the railroad, until nine A.M. on November 30. By this time Smith's force had manned earthworks built for the purpose of protecting the railroad three miles south of Grahamville at Honey Hill. After driving Rebel pickets back to this ridge fronted by Euhaw Creek, Hatch was faced with assailing the Confederate defenses head-on because of the difficult terrain.

Hatch launched three frontal attacks which withered under the fire of the Rebel artillery and rifle-muskets. With ammunition running low and news of Confederate reinforcement, Hatch abandoned the attack and withdrew from the area, and the railroad linking Charleston to Savannah remained open to facilitate Confederate troop movements.

Federal casualties were 746 compared with more than 150 for the Confederates. The Federal campaign continued with strikes at the railroad near the Coosawhatchie River on December 6–9.

⸻ ✦ ⸻

DRIVING TOUR— *To Rivers Bridge*
READING— *The March to the Sea, Georgia*

⸻ ✦ ⸻

Points of Interest

Units of the 54th Massachusetts and 55th Massachusetts regiments were involved in this action. Bolen Church was a battlefield landmark located on Grahamville Road (SC462) at US278. Take US278 east to SC462. US278 bisects the battlefield, and Honey Hill is 2.5 miles west of the intersection. There is a historical marker at the battle site, which possesses great integrity, and remains of the Confederate earthworks on Honey Hill.

SHERMAN'S MARCH THROUGH SOUTH CAROLINA

In late January 1865, Maj. Gen. William T. Sherman marched northward from Savannah, Georgia, pushing the Confederates before him. All eyes turned to Charleston. The Federals finally had a major "army group" that could move on the city from the landward side, while its navy and other army units controlled the barrier islands of the southeast coast. But Sherman had other plans. He froze Lt. Gen. William J. Hardee's force guarding the railroad and Charleston by sending Maj. Gen. O. O. Howard's right wing to Beaufort, perplexing Gen. P.G.T. Beauregard, who had returned to command the region for the third time. With Sherman in position to march toward either Charleston, or Augusta, Georgia, Beauregard tried to ready his army to respond to a threat in either direction. On February 1, Sherman's left wing—two corps under Maj. Gen. Henry Slocum and cavalry under Brig. Gen. Judson Kilpatrick—crossed into South Carolina thirty miles north of Savannah at Sister's Ferry.

Sherman's objective was Columbia, South Carolina's capital, where good roads led to North Carolina. The only more devastating blow, Sherman knew, would be the capture of Charleston. In the end, the Union would net both cities. To prepare for the march he organized a special unit, consisting of Michigan lumbermen and rail-splitters from

Indiana and Illinois, as well as former slaves, that bridged rivers and swamps and built corduroy roads at the rate of twelve miles a day for the nearly 3,000 wagons and 68 artillery pieces accompanying the 62,000-man force. Sherman's fast-stepping and high-spirited western infantry prompted Confederate general Joseph E. Johnston to remark, "I made up my mind that there had been no such army in existence since the days of Julius Caesar."

The Federal troops and their commander were confident their march would devastate Southern morale. It was felt that South Carolina, the birthplace of secession, needed to be taught a lesson, and the torch was the instrument of instruction. "I want to see the long deferred chastisement begin," one officer wrote. "If we don't purify South Carolina it will be because *we can't get a light.*" And Sherman's soldiers sang, "Hail Columbia, happy land! If I don't burn you, I'll be damned," as they drew nearer.

Sherman's two wings, by February 9, were camped along the South Carolina Railroad from its crossing of the Edisto River east of Midway to Blacksville. Howard, advancing inland from his landing point at Beaufort, quickly reached Pocotaligo. After breaking the Charleston & Savannah Railroad, Howard's troops forged ahead, striking the Charleston & Augusta Railroad east of Branchville, and destroyed more than fifteen miles of track while awaiting Slocum's column, traveling the more difficult inland route. Kilpatrick's cavalry swung farther to the west to Aiken, and besides threatening Augusta, guarded Slocum's left flank against Maj. Gen. Joseph Wheeler's cavalry, which had little impact on the Federal progress. The only serious fighting to that point was at Rivers Bridge.

Rivers Bridge

On February 2, Howard's wing encountered a formidable obstacle at Rivers Bridge. The Salkehatchie was at flood stage, a dank mile-and-a-half-wide swamp. The approach to the bridge was over a narrow causeway commanded for much of the way by Confederate artillery.

Maj. Gen. Joseph Mower, a bold, hard fighter, ignored the strength of the Rebels' position and called up the 63rd Ohio Infantry. With mighty oaths he told the Ohioans to get across the causeway and not halt until the north side of the river was gained. The foolhardy charge was repulsed with ease by Confederate cannons, which scattered the 63rd soldiers. Many of the wounded Yanks had to spend a miserable night in the swamp, clinging to trees to avoid drowning.

Mower was undaunted. On the morning of February 3, he turned his troops to cutting two roads through the swamp with expectations of outflanking the Confederates. At the same time his troops continued to occupy the Confederates' attention by probing their front. Throughout the day Mower's people toiled in mud and water up to their waists and by dark they met with success. Outflanked, the Southerners withdrew in a hurry, and the road north to the Charleston & Augusta Railroad was open.

Taking a two-day break alongside the South Carolina Railroad, Sherman's army wreaked havoc on the right-of-way. Then the forward march was resumed on February 12, and the army's two wings now crossed the North Fork of the Edisto on a broad thirty-mile front. As the two wings approached Columbia they converged. Beauregard was in the process of consolidating his scattered forces, including those of the Army of Tennessee, beginning to arrive at Chester, South Carolina, fifty miles north of Columbia after a long journey from Tupelo, Mississippi. But the Confederate transportation problems, Hardee's indecision when faced with conflicting orders from Beauregard and Richmond about when to evacuate Charleston, and Sherman's feints and fast-marching troops doomed Columbia without a fight.

Points of Interest

Rivers Bridge State Park is located on SC641 between US321 and US601. The park features interpretive markers about the battle and recreational facilities. For more information, call 803-267-3675.

Columbia

By February 16, Sherman's vanguard had crossed the Saluda River and was on the outskirts of Columbia. That night, with Beauregard transferring his headquarters to Chester, leaving Maj. Gen. Wade Hampton, a Columbia native, in charge of rear-guard cavalry, Union artillery shelled the city. Fleeing civilians, many of whom had come to the capital as refugees, crowded trains and wagon roads, but not all who wanted to leave could be accommodated. Authorities ordered bales of cotton, removed from city warehouses, piled in the streets for transportation to and burning in the fields outside the city. But Sherman's army came on too quickly for this to be accomplished.

The morning of February 17, under orders from Hampton, the mayor and other city officials surrendered the city. Sherman and his staff rode into Columbia, accompanied by a brigade of the XV Corps. Some of the cotton bales were smoldering, and a swirling wind blew blazing tufts of loose cotton through the streets. By dark, the Federal troops were fueled by alcohol, and a night of terror had begun. Sherman, who expressed no surprise or regret at the ensuing conflagration, nevertheless called in other Federal units camped outside the city to extinguish the firestorm and restore order and control. Eighty-four of Columbia's 124 blocks had caught fire, and public buildings, stores, homes, and churches went up in smoke. It was an excessive yet effective demonstration of the North's power, and tremendously demoralized the South.

By February 20, Sherman's army was on the march again. While Kilpatrick's cavalry feinted toward Chester, on the road to Charlotte, North Carolina, Sherman swung the army northeast, toward Cheraw. His destination was Goldsboro, North Carolina, via Fayetteville, where he expected to link with the forces under Maj. Gen. John M. Schofield. On February 22, Schofield's troops had occupied Wilmington (see **Wilmington, North Carolina**). Along the way, another sizable town, Camden, was visited by the Federal troops, before the "army group," delayed for some days by heavy rains, took advantage of improved weather to quicken their pace toward the North Carolina border. On March 3 there was a sharp skirmish at Cheraw between Mower's vanguard and Confederate cavalry guarding the bridge across the Great Pee Dee. By the afternoon of March 6 Sherman's right wing was across the Great Pee Dee and Slocum's left wing had crossed into North Carolina.

Points of Interest

Columbia—South Carolina's capital recovered from the devastating blow it suffered in February 1865 and by the 1960s urban renewal had destroyed more antebellum homes than Sherman's soldiers did. Today it remains a charming city of the Old South. Some of the Civil War–era landmarks survive, rebuilt to their antebellum splendor. US321, the highway that traces the march of Sherman's columns from Savannah, Georgia, enters the city from the west, joining US21 and US176 to become Knox Abbot Drive and changing to Blossom Street after the road crosses the Congaree River. From the west bank of the Congaree, Sherman's artillery fired at the old State House and new Capitol, then under construction at Assembly and Gervais streets.

The granite state house was begun in 1855, and in 1863, when war forced a cessation of construction, the exterior was nearly complete. It was still unfinished when Federal troops entered the city. Scars from the war are still visible on the building's exterior: bronze stars mark the locations of pockmarks and indentations caused by Federal artillery shells. The wooden state house was burned on the night of February 17. A plaque in the capitol park marks its location. Other points of interest in the capitol park are the Confederate memorial and a large bronze statue of native son Lt. Gen. Wade Hampton astride a horse. For interior tours of the state house, contact the tour desk at 803-734-2430. Tours are given Monday through Friday. The State Museum features Civil War artifacts.

Directly across from the capitol on Assembly Street is a visitor center, which has information on Columbia's antebellum buildings and other attractions, including a museum that contains a large number of Confederate artifacts. Three major churches downtown survived the 1865 fire, and another is built on the site of one that had burned. The Federals mistakenly torched the Methodist Church after being told by the black sextant of the First Baptist Church—which was site of the first Secession Convention in December 1860—that the Methodist Church was the First Baptist Church. The First Baptist Church still stands at 1306 Hampton Street.

Other antebellum buildings with Civil War ties include the beautiful Hampton-Preston Mansion, 1615 Blanding Street, which was ordered by Sherman to house orphans and was thus spared the torch; the Chesnut Cottage, the home of South Carolina politician James Chesnut and his wife, diarist Mary Chesnut, 1718 Hampton Street; the Maxcy Gregg House, home of the Confederate general, at 1518 Richland Street; and The Palmetto Armory, 1802 Lincoln Street, which supplied Confederate arms.

The Governor's Green is a 9-acre complex consisting of three antebellum structures, including the Governor's Mansion. There is a gift shop on the grounds. Tours of the mansion and its grounds are by advance reservation only. Governor's Green, 800 Richland Street, Columbia, SC 29201; 803-737-1710.

Located to the southeast of downtown is the Millwood Ruins, the mansion house on the then 13,000-acre estate of General Wade Hampton, CSA, who was in 1860 considered one of the wealthiest men in the South. The mansion and outbuildings were burned by Sherman's forces. Graceful columns of the once palatial house remain and the grounds are splendid. Tours can be arranged by calling 803-252-7742 in advance.

***

DRIVING TOUR— *To Abbeville (optional) or Augusta, Georgia*
READING— *Fayetteville–Monroe's Cross Roads, North Carolina*

Abbeville—For those interested in the flight of Jefferson Davis, a side trip to Abbeville provides an enlightening stop along his route. The Burt-Stark House was where Davis's wife Varina and their four children took refuge after the fall of Petersburg. On May 2, Davis traveled to Abbeville from Charlotte, North Carolina, although Varina and the family had already gone on to Washington, Georgia. It was at the Burt-Stark House, in a conference with his remaining cabinet members—including Secretary of War John C. Breckinridge, Gen. Braxton Bragg, and three brigadier generals—that Davis recognized that there was no longer any support east of the Mississippi for resisting the Federals. The Burt-Stark House, a National Historic Landmark, is located on US17 in Abbeville, South Carolina. For tour information, call 864-459-4600. From Columbia, take I-26 north to exit 54, Clinton. Take SC72 west from Clinton 41 miles to Abbeville. From Abbeville you can take US25 south to connect with I-20 and proceed either to Columbia, South Carolina, or Augusta, Georgia.

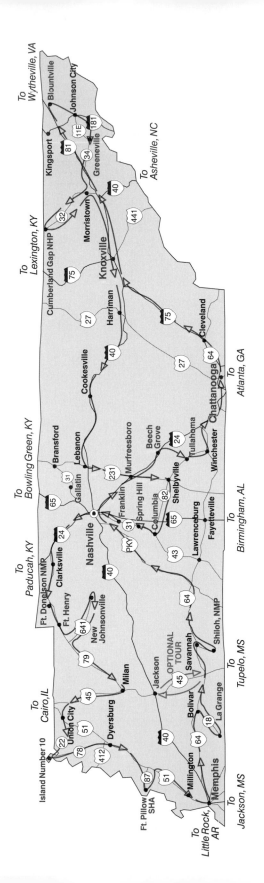

Tennessee

Tennessee was involved in many campaigns crucial to the Federal forces' winning the war and preserving the Union. The battles in the eastern theater of the war, primarily in Virginia, were necessary to Northern success in essence because they prevented sustained drives by Gen. Robert E. Lee and his Army of Northern Virginia which could have led the South to victory, a negotiated peace, or foreign intervention favorable to the Confederacy. The maneuverings and campaigning of the large armies in Virginia and north of the Potomac, with the Confederate Army of Northern Virginia and the Union Army of the Potomac on center stage, played out a mammoth chess game, with moves and countermoves leading to a virtual stalemate for most of the four years of war. On the other hand, Union victories in the West enabled U. S. Grant, William T. Sherman, William S. Rosecrans, and other Federal leaders to control or invade and devastate large sections of the Southern heartland, reduce the ability of the Confederacy to transport and supply its forces, and tie up Rebel manpower while an increasing number of Federal soldiers were committed to Virginia. Tennessee became a part of most of these important campaigns.

More battles, engagements, and skirmishes were fought in Tennessee than in any other state except Virginia. In the initial efforts by Grant and other generals to control the western rivers, battles such as Fort Donelson, Shiloh, and Island Number 10 were fought in Tennessee. The invasion of the North through Kentucky by Confederate forces under Gens. Braxton Bragg and Edmund Kirby Smith was slowed because Federal occupation of key areas of Tennessee allowed troops to be redeployed to enable Maj. Gen. Don Carlos Buell to recover the initiative and defeat Bragg's army at Perryville, Kentucky, while the Union armies of the Tennessee and the Mississippi thwarted the Confederates in northeast Mississippi (see **Perryville, Kentucky,** and **Corinth-Iuka, Mississippi**). The slow, steady pressure of Union forces on the Rebel Army of Tennessee at Stones River, Tulla-homa, and Chattanooga opened the road to Georgia for Sherman's capture of Atlanta and March to the Sea. Union armies operating in eastern Tennessee allowed the politically sensitive area to come under Federal control. And the last fitful Confederate attempt to rampage in the west was stopped by Northern soldiers at Franklin and Nashville.

More than just a battleground, however, Tennessee was strategic for its transportation, food production, and manufacturing capabilities. As these neccessary resources were lost by the South and gained by the North, the already unequal balance between the two sides in the ability to make war increased. Important as well was the political climate in the last state to join the Confederacy, and Washington put increasing effort into weaning the populace away from the Southern union as more and more of the state came under Federal control. Finally, Tennessee was a huge source of manpower—186,652 men and a number of talented officers joined the ranks of the Confederacy. The North enrolled 31,092 troops from Tennessee—many of whom were ex-slaves formed into regiments of United States Colored Troops.

Surrounded by states with important Civil War sites, Tennessee boasts enough important and interesting battlefields to warrant a five-to-six-day itinerary. The suggested tour (see the **tour map**) is an oval-shaped route following the state's geography, beginning and ending in Nashville. There are interstate and major highway junctions allowing side trips to nearby sites in adjoining states. Tennessee contains several expansive and well-preserved battlefields in rural areas such as Shiloh, Fort Donelson, and Stones River, now in a growing metropolitan area. The important battles and campaigns in the urban areas of Nashville, Memphis, Knoxville, and Chattanooga should not be overlooked. Details are given on how to obtain a perspective of the battles by visiting sites in these areas as well. The first stop heading northwest from Nashville is Fort Donelson, with an optional stop in Clarksville (see **Fort Donelson Points of Interest**). Since the Forts Henry and Donelson campaigns are discussed in chronological order, Fort Henry is the first entry.

FORT HENRY

On January 30, 1862, Department of the Missouri commander Maj. Gen. Henry W. Halleck, whose region extended east to the Cumberland River in Kentucky, after much delay approved an expedition urged by Brig. Gen. U. S. Grant and Flag Officer Andrew H. Foote up the two important rivers leading through Kentucky to Tennessee, the Cumber-

land and the Ten-
nessee. Grant's plan
which he executed
along with Flag Of-
ficer Foote, whose
gunboats were at that
time assigned to the
army, was to first
capture Fort Henry
guarding the Ten-
nessee River just
inside the Tennessee
border with a com-
bined land and water
assault.

Federal city-class gunboats and the Essex, *supported by three timberclads, fire on Fort Henry on February 6, 1862, reducing it and forcing its surrender. The fort was poorly located on low land subject to flooding. Through an unusual arrangement that existed early in the western war, the Federal gunboats were under the overall command of the army, but the individual squadrons and vessels were commanded by U.S. Navy officers. U. S. Grant and Flag Officer Andrew H. Foote used this cooperation to maximum effect.*

Fort Henry and Fort
Donelson, on the
Cumberland River, were the southernmost points in the Confederate line and formed
a concave arc anchored in the east on Cumberland Gap, in the center on Bowling
Green, and in the west on Columbus, Kentucky. The forts were constructed in mid- to
late-1861 at an ill-advised location where the two rivers closed to within ten miles of
each other and then flowed north in parallel courses into the Ohio River. Brig. Gen.
Lloyd Tilghman, given command of the forts in November 1861, immediately recognized their weaknesses—particularly those of Fort Henry, located on low ground subject to flooding and commanded by high ground to the east. Tilghman set about to
construct a new fort—Fort Heiman—on the Tennessee across from Fort Henry, but
before it could be completed, Federal forces were on his doorstep.

On February 4, the expedition arrived from Paducah below Fort Henry. The infantry
under Brig. Gen. John A. McClernand and Brig. Gen. Charles F. Smith were put ashore
on both sides of the Tennessee. On February 6, Foote's squadron, 4 river ironclads and 3
wooden gunboats, proceeded upriver to bombard the fort. Tilghman sent his infantry
force overland to Fort Donelson. Only the heavy artillerists remained. With the 4 ironclads presenting an ominous front line to the fort, Foote opened fire at twelve-thirty P.M.
The action lasted less than two hours. Although many shots from the fort hit the iron-

clads, only the USS *Essex* was disabled. Tilghman surrendered the fort to Foote and Grant's force, after struggling through the muddy approaches, arrived to take control of Fort Henry.

Points of Interest

Fort Henry is now beneath Kentucky Lake; however, some of the fort's outer works are extant. From US79, turn north 1 mile east of Kentucky Lake on Fort Henry Road. Travel 2 miles north to a sign for Boswell Landing and turn left. When the paved road bears right at 0.5 mile, take the dirt road straight for 0.1 mile. At the end of the road, there is a parking area and a trailhead wayside exhibit; the earthworks are on both sides of the road. Fort Heiman is now a housing development, but its site can be reached by traveling west on US79 across Kentucky Lake to TN119, which becomes KY121. Just across the Kentucky border at New Mount Carmel Church, a road leads to the west. Take this road which bears to the right after 0.5 mile for another 1.5 miles and enter the Fort Heiman housing development by turning right off the main road. In 0.25 mile are the earthworks of the fort.

DRIVING TOUR—*Proceed to Johnsonville*
READING—*Fort Donelson*

FORT DONELSON

Elated with the ease at which Fort Henry was taken, Grant and Flag Officer Foote straightaway made plans to capture Fort Donelson on the Cumberland River. Immediately after the surrender of Fort Henry, Foote sent his 3 wooden gunboats up the Tennessee. They destroyed a railroad bridge and chased and captured several Confederate vessels until they were stopped by Muscle Shoals at Florence, Alabama. Foote meanwhile had returned with all but one ironclad to Cairo, Illinois, for repairs. Grant was anxious to invest the fort as quickly as possible, but it was February 12 before the USS *Carondelet* returned down the Tennessee, entered the Cumberland, and steamed upriver to Fort Donelson.

Fort Donelson was an extensive earthen fort with outlying rifle pits and two tiers of water batteries. Flooded creeks emptied into the Cumberland upstream and downstream from the fort. In command at Donelson was Brig. Gen. Gideon J. Pillow. Department commander Gen. Albert Sidney Johnston, from his headquarters in Bowling Green, Kentucky, dispatched reinforcements to the fort, but erred in not going to Fort Donelson himself to take command. As a result, leadership was the greatest Confederate weakness at the fort. In addition to Pillow, Brig. Gen. John B. Floyd arrived with his command as did Brig. Gen. Simon B. Buckner's forces. Buckner, the only professional soldier among the three, was outranked by two of the less-qualified political generals in the Confederate army.

On February 12, Grant arrived in front of the Fort Donelson perimeter after an overland march from Fort Henry. The next day he spread his forces in a thin line on the land approaches to the rifle pits and his probes found the defenses too strong for an immediate assault. He then awaited reinforcements and Foote, who was en route from Cairo with three city-class ironclads, two of which had just been outfitted and manned. Two wooden gunboats were recalled from the Tennessee River. The *Carondelet* engaged the water batteries twice on February 13, but her fire was ineffective. That night Foote arrived with his squadron and fresh troops, which, along with the arrival of Brig. Gen. Lew Wallace's command from Fort Henry, swelled Grant's army to 27,000—10,000 more than the combined commands of the three Rebel generals.

Shelling by Foote's gunboats on the afternoon of February 14 was ineffective. Two of the ironclads received damage to their steering, a third received a waterline hit, and Foote was wounded in the action. Perhaps encouraged by the work of the gunners and concerned about the increased strength of Grant's investing army, Pillow the next morning launched a savage attack on the Union right, while Grant was aboard Foote's flagship consulting with the wounded navy commander. The Confederates achieved sweeping initial successes against the position on the right, held by soldiers of Brig. Gen. John A. McClernand's reinforced division, but the Confederates, although they had first hammered and then rolled back four Union brigades, were stymied by a paralysis in their high command. By that time Grant returned and, deducing the Rebels were trying to break out of the fort, ordered a counterattack along the line. By the end of the day the armies on the Confederate left and center had returned to near their original positions. But on the Rebel right, C. F. Smith had stormed and occupied part of the works commanding the Confederates' water batteries.

The night of February 15, fearing defeat, Floyd and Pillow planned an escape. They yielded command, placing Buckner in charge of the fort. Floyd, wanted in Washington for unscrupulous acts committed while he was secretary of war, fled to Nashville on a steamboat with about 2,000 Virginia soldiers. Pillow escaped separately. A rising cavalry commander, Lt. Col. Nathan Bedford Forrest, led his troopers and some foot soldiers out of the area on a flooded road leading toward Nashville.

The next morning when Buckner sent word to Grant for the appointment of commissioners to negotiate surrender terms, Grant replied, "No terms except an unconditional and immediate surrender can be accepted." While Buckner considered the reply "ungenerous and unchivalrous," he surrendered. Later that day he and his friend and West Point classmate, Ulysses S. Grant, sat down at the Dover Hotel and visited. The dandified Buckner was treated with the respect he was accustomed to by his Federal captors. Grant even settled an old debt with Buckner. The friendship endured. Buckner, who lived into the twentieth century, was one of the last Civil War personalities to visit Grant when he was terminally ill and living at Mount McGregor in upstate New York. Buckner also acted as a pallbearer at Grant's funeral.

Points of Interest

Fort Donelson National Battlefield—Fort Donelson is located on US79, 37 miles west of I-24. The park includes the fifteen-acre fort, the two water batteries, miles of Confederate outer works, and the historic Dover Hotel, where the generals met. Enter the park on Battlefield Memorial Highway. The park has a visitor center with exhibits and a film. Reconstructed log huts, the type that were occupied by the Confederate soldiers in the winter of 1861–62, are exhibited in the park and used during living history interpretations. A driving tour of the park leads through the earthworks and to the lower water battery, where a thirty-two-pounder mounted en barbette, a reconstructed powder magazine, and an unsurpassed view of the Cumberland River (now Lake Barkley) can be seen. The park also contains a national cemetery and a UDC monument. FORT DONELSON NATIONAL BATTLEFIELD, P.O. Box 434, Dover, TN 37058; 615-232-5348. ♿ 🚶 ❓ 🏛 P 🪑 🚻

In Clarksville, which is 6 miles west of I-24, numerous small skirmishes were fought. The ironworks here was an important source of construction matériel for the South in the war's first months. The city has several museums with Civil War exhibits, two cemeteries where Confederate soldiers are buried, and a Confederate earthwork on high ground commanding the confluence of the Red and Cumberland rivers.

<hr />

DRIVING TOUR—*Proceed to Fort Henry*
READING *(chronological)*—*Roanoke Island, North Carolina*

<hr />

JOHNSONVILLE

In the autumn of 1864 Atlanta was in Federal hands. The South began searching for a way to hurt Maj. Gen. William T. Sherman's "army group" as it occupied the strategic city, perhaps even compelling the Union armies to withdraw from northwest Georgia. A battlefield victory was unlikely, but attacks on Sherman's source of supplies, a chain of rail and river depots and connections leading more than four hundred miles north to the Ohio River, was a plausible means to check and turn back the huge Federal force. Maj. Gen. Joseph Wheeler had made a raid into northwest Georgia and East and Middle Tennessee in mid-August and early September that had been a strategic disaster when Sherman's maneuvers south of Atlanta had been made without the Rebels having much cavalry at hand (see **Battle of Jonesboro, Georgia**). Union garrisons and repair crews prevented Wheeler from scoring any effective and lasting damage to Sherman's communications. One month after Gen. John Bell Hood unfolded his plan to President Davis to employ the Army of Tennessee as a large raiding force for the same purpose (see **Palmetto, Georgia**), Lt. Gen. Richard Taylor was tapping a famed commander in his department to employ his cavalry corps in a manner in which that commander, Nathan Bedford Forrest, had previously enjoyed great success.

Under discretionary instructions from Taylor, who was wise enough to leave the details to Forrest, to attack Federal installations in West Tennessee, the "Wizard of the Saddle" led 3,000 men, not all of whom had horses, from his Jackson, Tennessee, headquarters in late October. His target was Johnsonville, a Tennessee River depot at the head of seasonal navigation on the river. Because of drought-caused low water, navigation on the Cumberland River to Nashville was uncertain, so Johnsonville and its seventy-eight-mile rail link east to Nashville took on added importance.

Forrest first headed north of Johnsonville to Fort Heiman, an abandoned earthwork near the Kentucky border that was to replace Fort Henry if Grant had been patient enough to allow the Confederates to complete it. With cannons unlimbered at and downstream from Fort Heiman and upstream five miles at Paris Landing, Forrest's advance under Brig. Gen. Abraham Buford captured three supply-laden steamers and a tinclad (lightly armored) gunboat, the USS *Undine,* on October 29–30. Forrest himself arrived on October 29 and pressed some of his cavalrymen into service to man the *Undine* and the captured transport *Venus* for his own navy of "horse marines." By the time Forrest's boats and ground forces started for Johnsonville on November 1, word of Forrest's presence had reached the Federal army and navy commanders at Paducah, Kentucky. Six gunboats started upstream for Johnsonville, but two gunboats already at Johnsonville intercepted Forrest's navy on November 2 and destroyed the *Venus.*

Forrest's main concern was the placement of his artillery on the west bank of the Tennessee River, above and below Johnsonville. The town and depot, on the river's east bank, contained two wharves, rail sidings, warehouses, and a fort, Fort Johnson. Besides the 2 gunboats engaged on November 3, a third was docked at Johnsonville along with 11 transport steamers and 18 barges. The 1st Kansas Battery, the 43rd Wisconsin, portions of three regiments of USCTs, and armed quartermaster employees and 20 troopers from the 11th Tennessee Cavalry made up the approximately 2,000-man garrison. Though the 6 gunboats that had steamed upriver arrived below Johnsonville by the morning of November 4, the Confederate guns held them to long-distance firing. In the meantime, the *Undine* inadvertently created a diversion for the repositioning of some of the Rebel guns by again challenging the *Key West* and the *Tawah,* reinforced by a third tinclad, the USS *Elfin.* But the Confederate "horse marines," overwhelmed by Union firepower afloat, ran the *Undine* aground and set her afire.

At two P.M. on November 4, Forrest's well-placed artillery commenced firing on the Federal vessels, Fort Johnson, and the dock facilities. The Federal garrison returned fire as did the gunboats, but the Rebel guns were sited too high for the gunboats' cannons and were too well hidden to receive much fire from the fort. The three tinclads received damaging hits and the Federal navy commander scuttled his boats, for which he was later criticized. By nightfall, with Fort Johnson silenced, the docks, boats, and barges ablaze, and the garrison and government employees panic-stricken, Forrest left Johnsonville, marched his command six miles before dawn, and reported to General Hood on November 14 at Florence, Alabama. At a cost of 2 killed and 9 wounded, he had destroyed 33 vessels including barges and more than $6 million of Federal property and taken 150 prisoners. As successful as the raid was, Forrest did not slow down Sherman, whose command in mid-November cut its supply line and departed for the Atlantic coast, supplying itself from the countryside (see **The March to the Sea, Georgia**).

Points of Interest

Two Tennessee State Historic Areas commemorate the Johnsonville raid. Nathan Bedford Forrest SHA is on the Tennessee River's west bank, near where Forrest sited his artillery, and New Johnsonville SHA is on the location of the Johnsonville depot. They can be reached by traveling on US79 west to Paris, then taking US641 south for 22 miles. Nathan Bedford Forrest SHA, which has a visitor center, programs, and demonstrations, is east of US641 at the end of TN191; New Johnsonville SHA is across the river and north of US70 at New Johnsonville. For more information, contact NATHAN BEDFORD FORREST STATE HISTORIC AREA, Eva, TN 38333; 901-584-6356.

△ ⊷ ♿ ⅋ ❷ P ⊓ ⍕

DRIVING TOUR—*Proceed to Tiptonville*
READING—*The March to the Sea, Georgia*

ISLAND NUMBER 10

Though victories at Forts Henry and Donelson, victories that earned U. S. Grant a promotion to major general of volunteers, broke the center of the Confederate line in Kentucky and Tennessee, the opening of the Mississippi River was still a top Federal priority. The Confederates on March 2, 1862, evacuated their stronghold of Columbus, Kentucky, on the Mississippi after losing the two forts, and its guns were moved downriver to the next stronghold at Island Number 10, Tennessee (see **Columbus, Kentucky**). This island, the tenth island in the Mississippi south of its confluence with the Ohio River, was on a double-hairpin bend in the Mississippi. More than 50 Rebel guns covered the river in this position of natural defense just south of the Kentucky border.

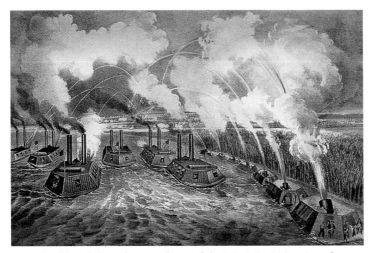

Federal ironclads and mortar boats of the Mississippi River Squadron blasting away at Island Number 10 in March 1862. The shelling did not break Confederate resistance there and it was necessary for the Union navy to pass the fort with ironclads and assist with the landing of army troops south of Island Number 10 before the stronghold fell.

Brig. Gen. John Pope, in command of the Federal Army of the Mississippi, marched down through Missouri and, after a ten-day siege, occupied New Madrid, which guarded the upper bend of the downriver hairpin, after the Confederates evacuated the town on March 13, 1862 (see **New Madrid, Missouri**). From there he established batteries opposite Tiptonville, Tennessee, and upriver from there. Crossing the Mississippi would gain the Federal army a position from which Island Number 10 could be isolated, but Pope needed the navy's help—transports would be required and gunboat protection from Rebel gunboats patrolling the river.

Flag Officer Andrew Foote was then at Cairo, Illinois, repairing and adding to the Federal river squadron after the navy's role in the capture of Fort Donelson. On March 14, Foote left Cairo with 5 city-class ironclad gunboats and his mighty flagship, the *Benton,* also an ironclad, and 10 mortar boats. Arriving in front of the Island Number 10 defenses during bad weather the next day, he began a mortar bombardment of the Confederate batteries before dawn on March 16 and on March 17 the gunboats joined the day-long shelling. After a second day of intense shelling, Foote, made cautious by his experience at Fort Donelson, continued a limited harassing fire on the defenses. He repeatedly turned down as too dangerous appeals by Pope to have an ironclad run the gauntlet. Federal army engineers did in the meantime establish a route to get shallow-draft transports downriver to Pope by clearing trees from St. Johns Bayou through flooded Missouri wetlands that bypassed Island Number 10 discharging into the Mississippi upstream from New Madrid.

On April 4, Cmdr. Henry Walke of the USS *Carondelet*, who had previously volunteered to run the Island Number 10 batteries when others including Foote considered it too dangerous, received the naval commander's permission to make an attempt. Special preparations were made, including lashing a coal barge to the ironclad's port side, which would receive the most fire, to protect her port magazine. The night of April 4 was selected because stormy weather would mask the run. Getting under way shortly after ten P.M., the *Carondelet* silently passed two batteries before she was discovered by the Confederate gunners. Then, suddenly, she felt the heat of the guns but continued downriver at full speed and unharmed, finally passing the floating battery, which previous Federal shelling had beached. Two nights later, the USS *Pittsburg* also ran the batteries successfully.

The two ironclads shelled the batteries below Island Number 10 on April 7 and guarded the army's river crossing. Tiptonville was quickly in Federal hands and by the afternoon, Pope's presence compelled the Confederate commander to initiate action for surrender of Island Number 10. The army did not lose a man in this operation. The total loss of the combined Union force was 17 killed and 34 wounded (Rebel casualties in the action were light as well). The Federals captured 7,000 Confederates, 158 cannons of which 123 were big guns, and Island Number 10.

Points of Interest

Island Number 10 of the 1860s has been completely lost to the Mississippi's currents—it ceased to exist less than three decades after the Civil War. In Tiptonville (TN21), where Pope's forces first landed on April 7, a historical marker on the courthouse lawn details the action. Other historical markers for the battle are on TN22 and TN78 north of Tiptonville, and from the levee a good view can be had of the place in the river where Island Number 10 was formerly located. The best sites related to the action are in New Madrid, Missouri, including the New Madrid Historical Museum, which features artifacts from Island Number 10 and the fighting at New Madrid and elsewhere in the campaign (see **New Madrid, Missouri**).

DRIVING TOUR and READING—
Proceed to Fort Pillow–Plum Point Bend

FORT PILLOW–PLUM POINT BEND

The next target in the Federals' Mississippi River Campaign was the next downriver stronghold, Fort Pillow. Flag Officer Foote prepared to steam his squadron downriver to attack the fort, which mounted 40 guns both in water batteries just above the flood plain and on high bluffs guarding another of the Mississippi's numerous hairpin turns, departing from New Madrid on April 11. On April 12, Foote's ironclads were overtaken by General Pope's transports fifty river miles below New Madrid and the combined force steamed downriver to a point just out of range of the fort's guns. While en route, 5 Confederate gunboats came upriver and at long range engaged the Yankees, but fire from the Federal ironclads forced them back downriver below the fort.

On April 14 Foote positioned mortar boats in the lee of Craighead Point on the Arkansas shore of the river and lobbed thirteen-inch shells at Fort Pillow, awaiting the landing of Pope's infantry on the Tennessee shore north of the fort. But that afternoon, Pope reported that after putting ashore several regiments, they had encountered a swamp and were unable to gain the fort's rear. The two Federal leaders discussed cutting a canal on the Arkansas side of the Mississippi to allow transports and some ironclads to bypass Fort Pillow and attack from the south. Two days later, on April 16, Pope and most of his force were ordered by department commander Maj. Gen. Henry W. Halleck to join the forces of Grant and Buell on the Tennessee River, near Pittsburg Landing, to participate in the advance on Corinth, Mississippi, so the combined army-navy attack on Fort Pillow was shelved (see **Corinth, Mississippi**).

Over the next three weeks, Foote maintained a harassing fire on the fort with his mortar boats, but with his ankle wound sustained at Fort Donelson failing to heal, the navy commander asked to be relieved to take a rest in the north. On May 9, amid the cheers of his admiring sailors, Foote departed, and was replaced by Capt. Charles H. Davis, who had been second-in-command to Flag Officer Samuel Du Pont in the South Atlantic Blockading Squadron during and in the three months following the successful Port Royal Expedition (November 1861). The next day, as the designated mortar boat—No. 16—moored downriver from the squadron to begin the daily bombardment of the fort, accompanied by the ironclad *Cincinnati*, smoke was spotted around Plum Point Bend. Shortly after seven A.M., 8 Confederate rams, recently arrived from New Orleans under the command of Capt. James E. Montgomery, rounded the bend, intent on engaging and either sinking or capturing the *Cincinnati*. The iron prowls, or rams, on these vessels, which, combined with their rapid speed were their chief means of offense, took naval warfare back to the days of the ancient galleons, before the introduction of gunpowder. They carried few big guns and their sharpshooters, provided by the colorful partisan fighter M. Jeff Thompson, served as marines to pick off Yankee skippers and gunners. The engines were protected with cotton bale and pine bulwarks.

The *Cincinnati*, warned by the approaching smoke, got under way and, along with the fire of the *Mortar Boat No. 16*, challenged the Rebel fleet. Another ironclad, the USS *Mound City*, was signaled and joined the Battle of Plum Point Bend, but the action lasted only one hour. In that time, however, the Confederate vessels the *General Bragg*, *General Sterling Price*, and *General Sumter* rammed the *Cincinnati*, while the *General Earl Van Dorn* rammed the *Mound City*. Both Federal ironclads were run close into shore, where they sank with their upperworks above water. Subsequently, they were refloated, taken upriver, and repaired. Captain Montgomery then ordered his boats back to Fort Pillow before any serious damage was dealt to them. Casualties on both sides were light, although a Confederate sharpshooter wounded the *Cincinnati*'s captain, Cmdr. Roger N. Stembel.

After Gen. P.G.T. Beauregard evacuated Corinth on the night of May 29–30, Fort Pillow was outflanked. On June 3, with the Rebel ram fleet steaming downriver to Memphis, the fort was evacuated. The next day Federal soldiers attached

This woodcut dramatically illustrates the massacre of African-American soldiers at Fort Pillow on April 12, 1864. Maj. Gen. Nathan Bedford Forrest denied official responsibility for the massacre after his cavalry overran the fort. Other accounts give various explanations why only 62 of the 262 blacks at the fort were taken prisoner and a total of 231 Federals were killed. The controversy, which aroused passions against Forrest's command at the time, exists today and the facts of what really happened at Fort Pillow have not been fully explained.

to Davis's squadron occupied Fort Pillow. The Federal navy, learning from the Plum Point Bend embarrassment, improved the defensive characteristics of the ironclads, and reinforced by Col. Charles Ellet, Jr.'s 3 rams which in combat proved far superior in construction to Montgomery's rams, prepared to battle the Rebel boats for Memphis.

Fort Pillow was garrisoned by Federal troops for much of the time without incident until the spring of 1864. Maj. Gen. Nathan B. Forrest had continued to operate with his new cavalry corps in northern Mississippi, West Tennessee, and Kentucky's Jackson Purchase, after his successful pursuit of Brig. Gen. W. S. Smith's cavalry in February (see **Okolona, Mississippi**) and his March 25 attack on and repulse at Paducah, Kentucky. The most noteworthy event of his campaign against Federal garrisons came on April 12, 1864, when Forrest attacked Fort Pillow. In that month the Union garrison at Fort Pillow, a Confederate-built earthen fortification and a Union-built inner redoubt overlooking the Mississippi River, comprised 295 white Tennessee troops and 262 U.S. Colored Troops under the command of Maj. Lionel F. Booth. Forrest attacked the fort on April 12 with a cavalry division of approximately 2,500 men and seized the older intermediate works, with high knolls commanding the Union position, to surround Booth's force. Rugged terrain prevented the gunboat *New Era* from providing effective fire support for the Federals. The garrison was unable to depress its artillery enough to cover the approaches to the fort. Rebel sharpshooters on the surrounding knolls began firing into the fort, killing Booth. Maj. William F. Bradford then took over command of the garrison. The Confederates launched a determined attack at eleven A.M., occupying more strategic locations close to the fort, and Forrest demanded unconditional surrender. Bradford asked for an hour of consultation, and Forrest granted twenty minutes. Bradford refused surrender and the Confederates renewed the attack, overran the fort, and drove the Federals down the river's bluff into a deadly crossfire. Casualties were high and only sixty-two of the U.S. Colored Troops survived the fight. Many accused the Confederates of perpetrating a massacre of the black troops, and that controversy continues today. The Confederates evacuated Fort Pillow that evening so they gained little from the attack except a temporary disruption of Union operations and much war matériel which they carried off. The "Fort Pillow Massacre" became a Union rallying cry and cemented resolve to see the war through to its conclusion.

Points of Interest

Fort Pillow State Historic Area—Although the Mississippi River has changed course and is now several miles south of Fort Pillow, there is much to see and do at this park, located 1 mile north of TN87 on TN207. There is a visitor center and bookstore near the entrance. A separate interpretive center near the fort has displays and an audiovisual program. Confederate earthworks, on a 5-mile trail, include the outerworks and the intermediate works. Across a suspension footbridge is the reconstructed Federal fort that Forrest attacked, with canvas tents and artillery added to reset the scene. From the bluff, the former channel of the Mississippi, now Cold Creek and Cold Creek Chute, can be seen. The park, open year-round, provides a variety of recreational opportunities, including tent camping with facilities, hiking, and fishing. FORT PILLOW STATE HISTORIC SITE, Route 2, P.O. Box 108 B-1, Henning, TN 38041; 901-738-5581.

🚴 🎣 ⛺ ♿ 🚶 ❓ 🏛 P 🪑 🚻

DRIVING TOUR—*Proceed to Memphis*
READING—*1862: Memphis; Forrest's 1864 raid: Paducah, Kentucky*

Memphis

After the Confederates evacuated Fort Pillow, Captain Davis steamed his squadron downriver on June 5 to Island Number 45, a few miles north of Memphis. Now accompanying the five ironclads was Col. Charles Ellet's "Ram Fleet." A civil engineer hailing from western Pennsylvania, Ellet proposed the design of his streamlined, unarmed riverboat ram to the U.S. Navy Department in 1861 when word came north that the Confederates were building ironclads. The navy rejected Ellet's proposal, but shortly after the USS *Monitor*–CSS *Virginia* battle at Hampton Roads, Ellet received an audience with Secretary of War Edwin Stanton, who commissioned Ellet a colonel and gave him the green light to build his ram fleet at Pittsburgh.

Ellet purchased 9 fast steamers and strengthened their bows, while running heavy shock-absorbing timbers from stem to stern. Ellet arrived with the first of his rams above Fort

Pillow on May 25, and though he was under no obligation to take orders from Davis, cooperated with the naval leader. At four A.M. on June 6 the ironclads and rams, the former leading, got under way, dropping downriver. Meanwhile, shortly after daylight, 8 Confederate rams got under way from the city's landing and, after a short run downstream to organize, turned to face the Union attack fleet, led by the 5 ironclads: the flagship USS *Benton, Louisville, Carondelet, Cairo,* and *St. Louis.*

The Confederate gunboats fired opening shots at five-forty A.M. and the battle began. After the opening rounds—the boats avoided directing fire into the city as ten thousand Memphis citizens crowded the bluffs to watch the action—Davis's 5 ironclads rounded to and headed upriver. Two of Ellet's rams then darted out from behind and passed through the ironclads. Charles Ellet commanded one, the *Queen of the West,* while his brother Alfred conned the *Monarch.* In the ninety-minute engagement the *Queen of the West* rammed and sunk the Confederate gunboat *General Lovell,* but in the collision, the Federal ram was damaged and Charles Ellet was wounded—he died several weeks later. The Union ironclads disabled two Rebel boats and the *Monarch* rammed one, the *General Beauregard,* which sunk after the *Monarch* took her in tow. The Federals maintained a running fight for ten miles with the Confederate gunboats. By the time the day ended, 7 of the 8 Rebel rams were sunk, damaged or captured. Only the swiftest, the *General Earl Van Dorn,* escaped.

With the destruction of the fleet, amid the

This painting of the Battle of Memphis is by Alexander Simplot. The Federal river rams under the command of Col. Charles Ellet battle Confederate gunboats as U.S. Navy ironclads approach the battle from the north. The action was fought in the Mississippi River directly in front of the city and Memphis residents flocked to the bluffs to see it.

moans of the onlookers, the Confederate garrison, commanded by Brig. Gen. M. Jeff Thompson of the Missouri State Guard, evacuated the city. Davis sent a formal demand for surrender to the mayor, who yielded the defenseless city. By the evening of June 6, Federal soldiers were occupying it.

With its significant railhead, docks, and shipyards, Memphis became a vital Federal base depot and command center. First Maj. Gen. William T. Sherman and then Maj. Gen. U. S. Grant (the latter briefly) headquartered there for a time preparing for their campaigns against Vicksburg, and thereafter Maj. Gen. Stephen Hurlbut commanded the Memphis area until the spring of 1864. But then all hell broke loose. At four A.M. on August 21, 1864, Maj. Gen. Nathan Bedford Forrest made a daring raid on Memphis, which was occupied by 6,000 Federal troops. The raid was not an attempt to capture the city; it had three objectives: to capture three Union generals posted there; to release Southern prisoners from Irving Block Prison; and to cause the recall of Union forces from northern Mississippi. While striking northwestward for Memphis with 2,000 cavalry, Forrest lost about a quarter of his strength because of exhausted horses. Forrest knew that surprise was essential. So taking advantage of a dawn fog and claiming to be a Union patrol returning with prisoners, the Confederates captured the sentries manning the Hernando Road checkpoint. Galloping through the streets and exchanging shots with Union troops, the raiders split to pursue separate missions. One Union general was not in his quarters and Maj. Gen. C. C. Washburn, who had replaced Hurlbut, escaped to Fort Pickering dressed in his nightshirt. The attack on Irving Block Prison also failed when Union troops stalled the main body at the State Female College. After two hours, Forrest withdrew, cutting telegraph wires and taking 500 prisoners and large quantities of supplies, including many horses. Although Forrest failed in Memphis, his raid caused the recall of formidable Union forces from northern Mississippi.

Points of Interest

From the bluffs of Memphis, on Arkansas Riverside Drive, between I-55 and I-40, one can get a feel for the view of the Mississippi River as Memphis citizens saw it during the June 6, 1862, battle. Mud Island breaks into the river on the Memphis shore and is reached by monorail. The modern Mississippi River Museum there contains exhibits about the battle, ship models, and a walk-through replica of a portion of a Federal city-class ironclad. Admission is charged, which includes the monorail fare, as there is no parking on the island. For more information, call 901-576-7241.

There are many historical markers in Memphis on buildings and at sites with Civil War ties. Among the most notable is the one for the Gayoso Hotel, no longer extant on Front Street between Gayoso and McCall, where Capt. William H. Forrest rode into the lobby in search of General Hurlbut during the August raid of the city. Another marker at 1327 Mississippi Boulevard locates a Rebel battery position during the raid. Nathan Bedford Forrest had several homes in Memphis. The site of one is designated, an early home on Adams Avenue between Second and Third, as is the house of his brother, 693 Union Avenue, where Forrest died in 1877. He and his wife are buried in Forrest Park under a handsome equestrian monument of the general.

Elmwood Cemetery at Walker Avenue and Neptune Street contains Confederate graves; there is a national cemetery on Raleigh Road which features a monument to Illinois soldiers. Court Square on North Main Street between Jefferson and Court Avenue was the location of a Federal prison during the Civil War. At Second Street and Madison Avenue, the Confederates maintained the state capitol between the fall of Nashville and the fall of Memphis.

Fifty miles east of Memphis on TN57 is the village of LaGrange, which was a major Federal base for much of the war. From here, Col. Benjamin H. Grierson began his raid into Mississippi in conjunction with U. S. Grant's Second Vicksburg Campaign (see **Newton Station, Mississippi**). A historical marker on TN57 describes the raid. The town has many antebellum homes and was used as a location for the 1958 film *Horse Soldiers* about Grierson's Raid. You may wish to continue east on TN57 to Hatchie Bridge, or take TN18 north to Bolivar and continue the tour to Shiloh.

DRIVING TOUR—*Proceed to Hatchie Bridge*
READING—*Farragut's Expedition, Mississippi*

HATCHIE BRIDGE

After the repulse of Maj. Gen. Earl Van Dorn's Confederate army at Corinth (see **Corinth, Mississippi**) on October 3–4, 1862, Van Dorn retreated to the northwest and crossed the state line into Tennessee, camping for the night near Pocahontas. The next morning, Van Dorn's vanguard crossed the Hatchie at Davis's Bridge, and encountered Union troops under Maj. Gen. Stephen A. Hurlbut that had marched first south from Bolivar, Tennessee, and then west to Middleton. The Federals, in savage fighting, during which Maj. Gen. E.O.C. Ord arrived and assumed command and then was wounded, pushed the Confederates back across Davis's Bridge. If Maj. Gen. William S. Rosecrans had driven his pursuing columns harder following Van Dorn's defeat at Corinth, it could have been disastrous for the Confederates. But Van Dorn escaped back into Mississippi over a road crossing the Hatchie at Crum's Mill. Van Dorn then retreated to Holly Springs, via Ripley. Casualties in the battle exceeded 600 on each side.

Points of Interest

On TN57, where it crosses the Hatchie River near the town of Pocahontas, there is a historical marker describing the action. Davis's Bridge and the adjacent battlefield are part of the Siege and Battle of Corinth National Historic Landmark. Continue east on TN57 to TN22, then turn north to get to Shiloh National Military Park.

Gen. Albert Sidney Johnston was looked on to be one of the heroes of the Confederacy by Southern leaders and the people early in the war. Trouble plagued his command in Kentucky and Tennessee during late 1861 and early 1862, when Brig. Gen. U. S. Grant's forces captured key positions in the center of the long Confederate front in the region. Johnston designed the offensive at Shiloh to drive the Federals from the upper reaches of the Tennessee River, but he was killed before seeing the battle through to its conclusion.

DRIVING TOUR—*Proceed to Shiloh*
READING—*Perryville, Kentucky*

SHILOH

While the Federal navy and Army of the Mississippi were operating against New Madrid and Island Number 10, Maj. Gen.

Ulysses S. Grant's Army of the Tennessee had ascended the Tennessee River and had gone into camp at Pittsburg Landing, the closest all-weather landing to the Confederate stronghold and strategic railroad town of Corinth, Mississippi, and Crump's Landing upriver from Savannah, where Grant established his headquarters. Grant awaited the arrival of the Army of the Ohio under Maj. Gen. Don Carlos Buell, marching overland from Nashville. The combined armies would then, under the overall direction of department commander Maj. Gen. Henry W. Halleck, march on Corinth.

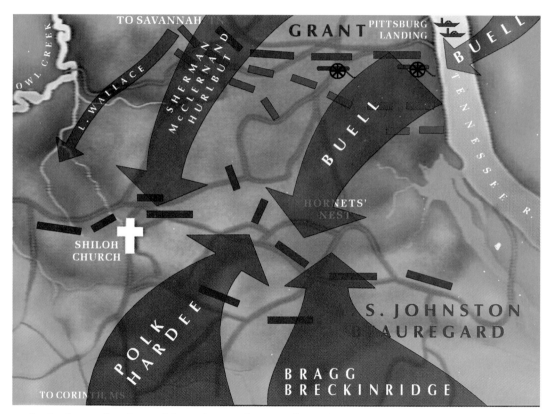

On Sunday, April 6, the Confederate forces under Gen. Albert Sidney Johnston (red arrows) surprised Maj. Gen. U. S. Grant's forces and overran their camps in the vicinity of Shiloh Church (blue blocks). After a day of heavy fighting, Grant was able to fashion a steady line on bluffs opposite Pittsburg Landing (blue blocks at top) with the help of artillery and gunboats on the Tennessee River. The last pocket of Union resistance at the Hornets' Nest helped slow the Rebel advance and the Confederates halted for the night in front of the Federal line (red blocks). That night, the arrival of Maj. Gen. Don Carlos Buell's Army of the Ohio helped Grant's forces on the morning of April 7 to retake the same ground taken from them the day before. The Confederates, led by Gen. P.G.T. Beauregard, who took command when Johnston was killed on April 6, retraced their footsteps toward Corinth, Mississippi.

But the Confederate leadership hoped to attack and crush the Army of the Tennessee's five divisions camped at Pittsburg Landing before Buell arrived. In the weeks following the loss of Fort Donelson and the evacuation of Nashville, Gen. Albert Sidney Johnston used the railroads to rush troops from the Gulf Coast to reinforce his newly constituted Army of the Mississippi, numbering 44,000, gathered in and around Corinth. News of the rapid approach of Buell's troops caused the Confederates to plan their strike before the arrival at Corinth of Maj. Gen. Earl Van Dorn's Army of the West, then en route from northwest Arkansas. With Gen. P.G.T Beauregard as second-in-command, and corps led by Maj. Gens. Braxton Bragg, William Hardee, Leonidas Polk, and Brig. Gen. John C. Breckinridge, Johnston planned a surprise attack on the Federal camps.

On Sunday morning, April 6, while Grant was at his Savannah headquarters where he was coordinating the deployment of Buell's army, one division of which had reached Savannah on the evening of April 5, the Confederates assailed and surprised the soldiers of Brig. Gen. Benjamin Prentiss's division camped southeast of Rhea's Field and Brig. Gen. William T. Sherman's in their camps around Shiloh Meeting House. Because Grant had expected the Rebels to remain in Corinth, key subordinates had ignored reports from pickets that the Southerners had taken position the previous afternoon within one mile of the Federal encampments. Despite being taken by surprise, most of the Yankee soldiers, including many new recruits in Sherman's and Prentiss's divisions, did not panic and run. Instead, ground was given stubbornly in the face of slashing attacks, first as Hardee's, then Bragg's and Polk's battle lines were committed in human waves.

As the Federal lines were pushed back, Union troops rallied along a farmer's trace connecting the Corinth and Hamburg roads that was to become the Hornets' Nest. Brigades from Prentiss's command and that of Brig. Gen. W.H.L. Wallace—6,000 men in all—held the Hornets' Nest for more than seven hours against numerous piecemeal attacks launched by Bragg. Meanwhile, on the Federal left, Albert Sidney Johnston, while directing Confederate attacks near Sarah Bell's Peach Orchard, was mortally wounded at two-thirty in the afternoon. Beauregard assumed command, but the Rebel advance was slowing. It was not until five-thirty P.M. that the Confederates, having forced back the Union left and right, massed 62 artillery pieces and hammered the defenders of the Hornets' Nest. Assailed from the front and with Confederates closing in on their flanks, the Union center at the Hornets' Nest gave way.

Though Confederates captured more than 2,000 prisoners there, the Hornets' Nest stand by Prentiss's and W.H.L. Wallace's people gave Grant time to form a new line, backed by

53 cannons, on the high ground behind Tilghman and Dill branches. The Union left was anchored on the Tennessee River and the right on the Snake Creek bottom. By this time, Grant received reinforcements: Brig. Gen. Lew Wallace's division on the right and the first of Buell's army, Brig. Gen. William Nelson's division, on the left. Two timberclad Union gunboats—the USS *Tyler* and the USS *Lexington*—added their fire to the army's and the Confederates could not sustain a drive against the final Federal line as darkness fell.

Buell's men throughout the night continued to disembark from steamboats at Pittsburg Landing. By the morning of April 7, Grant's effective force numbered more than 39,000. At six A.M. Beauregard, unaware of the number of Federal reinforcements, prepared to resume the Southern attack. But he was too late, as Buell's Army of the Ohio troops on Grant's left had already seized the initiative. Lew Wallace's division on the Yankee right soon moved out. Grant's troops advanced in a broad front, rolling up the Confederates who had spent the night in the camps of four of his five divisions. After one last attempted thrust in mid-afternoon at Water Oaks Pond, Beauregard ordered a Confederate withdrawal, which by April 8 carried his army back to Corinth. A pursuit force, Sherman's badly mauled division, sent south by Grant on April 8, was met by the Rebel rear guard under Lt. Col. N. B. Forrest at Fallen Timbers. Sherman then broke off the pursuit.

Casualties at the Battle of Shiloh, or Pittsburg Landing as the North called it, were the largest in the war up to that time—nearly 24,000 casualties or about 25 percent of the number engaged. This figure was greater than in all the battles fought in the Revolutionary War which lasted more than eight years. After Shiloh, it is said, the South did not smile again. Though he was criticized for being caught off guard, Grant's cool handling of the battle and his timely reinforcements blunted the Confederate attempt to regain the initiative, drive the Union forces from West and Middle Tennessee, and carry the war deep into Kentucky. It also continued the Union campaign to carry the war into Mississippi and sever the Confederacy along the "Father of Waters." The bloody battle was a harbinger of how the war was to be fought in the three years following the Battle of Shiloh.

Points of Interest

Shiloh National Military Park—Most of the battlefield is encompassed in this beautiful military park, 22 miles northeast of Corinth, Mississippi, on TN22. The park visitor center, Grant Road east of TN22, has uniformed interpreters, exhibits, and a 25-minute film program. A driving tour begins at the visitor center which is located near the eastern anchor of Grant's final line of April 6. Nearby is the Shiloh National Cemetery.

The major sites of the battle are all marked with interpretive waysides and monuments. Artillery pieces—primarily original tubes on replica carriages—can be seen from the tour route as well. Shiloh Methodist Church has been reconstructed on the site of the meeting house. Short walks on trails leading from the park roads take you to Rhea Spring, a peaceful area adjacent to the camps of Sherman's division that were overrun on that Sunday morning; the Manse George Cabin located in the Peach Orchard, and the site of Albert Sidney Johnston's death. There are also Indian mounds along the Riverside Drive park road, and a river overlook at the Left Flank tour stop. The park is open every day; the visitor center is open every day except December 25. SHILOH NATIONAL MILITARY PARK, Shiloh, TN 38376; 901-689-5275.

🚲 🗺 ♿ 🚶 ❓ 🏛 P 🍽 🚻 $

DRIVING TOUR—*Proceed to Jackson or Murfreesboro*
READING—*Island Number 10*

JACKSON–PARKER'S CROSS ROADS

There are several sites not on the tour route in the vicinity of Jackson, Tennessee, that you may want to tour prior to entering the Natchez Trace Parkway for a scenic drive to Murfreesboro. Two of the actions in the Jackson area were part of Brig. Gen. Nathan Bedford Forrest's Christmas 1862 raid. The other was a September 1, 1862, engagement between Confederate cavalry led by Brig. Gen. Frank C. Armstrong and detachments from two Illinois infantry regiments, a company of Ohio cavalry, and a company of Illinois artillery. The Federals bested the Rebel horsemen in this Battle of Britton's Lane.

In mid-December 1862, Brig. Gen. Nathan Bedford Forrest began a raid into West Tennessee designed to destroy Maj. Gen. U. S. Grant's railroad supply lines during his first

Vicksburg campaign (see **Holly Springs, Mississippi**). Starting out from Columbia, in Middle Tennessee, on December 11, Forrest's brigade of 2,100 cavalrymen crossed the Tennessee River near Clifton and headed toward Jackson on the Mobile & Ohio Railroad. Along the way, on December 18, he fought a running battle, beginning east of Lexington, with cavalry under Col. Robert G. Ingersoll. The Federal horse soldiers were routed and the following day Forrest demonstrated in front of Jackson while his people tore up the Mobile & Ohio. Forrest continued north, fighting skirmishes and tearing up track. He spent Christmas in Union City, Tennessee, and crossed into Kentucky, destroying trestles near Moscow.

As Forrest's brigade was riding back toward Middle Tennessee, the first serious challenge to his raid came from two Federal brigades of infantry—Cyrus Dunham's and John W. Fuller's—sent out after him by the commander of the Jackson garrison. The Battle of Parker's Cross Roads was fought near Red Mound, northeast of Jackson, on December 31. Dunham's and Forrest's march routes brought them into contact at Parker's Cross Roads. Skirmishing began about nine A.M., with Forrest taking an initial position along a wooded ridge northwest of Dunham at the intersection. Confederate artillery gained an early advantage. Dunham pulled his brigade back a half mile and redeployed, facing north. His Federals repelled frontal feints until attacked on both flanks and rear by Forrest's mounted and dismounted troops. During a lull, Forrest sent Dunham a demand for an unconditional surrender. Dunham refused and was preparing for Forrest's next onset when Fuller's Union brigade arrived from the north and surprised the Confederates with an attack on their rear; Confederate security detachments had failed to warn of Fuller's approach. "Charge 'em both ways," ordered Forrest. The Confederates briefly reversed front, repelled Fuller, then rushed past Dunham's demoralized force and withdrew south to Lexington.

After the Battle of Parker's Cross Roads, Forrest's men recrossed the Tennessee River as before at Clifton on January 1, 1863, and made their way back into Middle Tennessee. The Federals probed and pursued Forrest cautiously through New Year's Day but never seriously engaged his forces.

Points of Interest

A monument to the unknown soldiers who fell at Britton's Lane and a historical marker are located at TN18 and Collins Road in Medon, between Bolivar and Jackson.

In Jackson, located on I-40, there are markers identifying Confederate Camp Beauregard (US70 and TN20), an early Rebel training camp, a Confederate monument at the courthouse, and graves of Southern soldiers in Riverside Cemetery. A historical marker at 512 East Main Street marks a home used as a command post by U. S. Grant before and after the Battle of Corinth, October 3–4, 1863.

A historical marker on TN22 at Parkers Crossroads, just north of I-40, describes the Battle of Parker's Cross Roads. Other historical markers for Forrest's Christmas raid are at Chesterfield (TN20) where Forrest battled Ingersoll along the Beech River on December 18; at Clifton (TN 114 near US64) where the Rebel troopers crossed and recrossed the Tennessee River; and northwest of Jackson at Humboldt (US45W), Trenton (US45W and TN54), Kenton (US45W), and Union City (US45W). The latter four markers describe engagements and actions by Forrest and his command on their December raid that shut down traffic on the Mobile & Ohio Railroad through the first week of March 1863.

A driving tour has been established of the Parker's Cross Roads battlefield. For information and literature on the tour, stop at the Cotton Patch Restaurant in Wildersville on TN22 south of the I-40 interchange or telephone them at 901-968-3533.

DRIVING TOUR— *Proceed to Murfreesboro*
READING— *Chickasaw Bayou, Mississippi*

MURFREESBORO

In June 1862, after performing admirably at the Battle of Shiloh, Nathan Bedford Forrest was promoted to brigadier general and sent to Chat-

A Civil War photograph of Murfreesboro Courthouse, a landmark in this town south of Nashville, an important Federal base. The Confederates captured Murfreesboro and its garrison in the summer of 1862 and the Federals regained it the following winter. The town was again garrisoned, and as late as December 7, 1864, again came under attack by the Rebels.

tanooga to organize a cavalry brigade. Under orders from Maj. Gen. E. Kirby Smith, Forrest left Chattanooga on July 9 with two cavalry regiments and joined other units on the way, bringing the total force to 1,400. His major objective was to strike Murfreesboro, an important Union supply center on the Nashville & Chattanooga Railroad, at dawn on July 13. The Murfreesboro garrison was camped in three locations and included detachments from four units made up of infantry, cavalry, and artillery, under the command of Brig. Gen. Thomas L. Crittenden who had arrived on July 12. Between four-fifteen and four-thirty A.M. Forrest's cavalry surprised the Union pickets on the Woodbury Pike, east of Murfreesboro, and quickly overran a Federal hospital and the camp of the detachment 9th Pennsylvania Cavalry Regiment. Additional Rebel troops attacked the camps of the other Union commands and the jail and courthouse. By late afternoon all of the Union units numbering more than 1,000 had surrendered to Forrest's force. The Confederates destroyed much of the Union supplies and tore up railroad track in the area, but the principal result of the raid was the diversion of Union forces from a drive on Chattanooga. This raid, along with Morgan's raid into Kentucky, made possible Bragg's concentration of forces at Chattanooga and his early September invasion of Kentucky. Forrest returned to McMinnville with his captives and on July 18 began a nine-day raid to occupy the attention of Brig. Gen. William Nelson's division diverted to Middle Tennessee from north Alabama in the vicinity of Nashville, though he avoided Murfreesboro as he traveled northwest to the outskirts on Nashville and on his return.

Murfreesboro was evacuated by the Federals on September 6, when the Confederates, having stolen several marches on Buell's army, invaded Kentucky, compelling the Federal forces to enter into a race for Munfordville. After retreating from Kentucky, following the Battle of Perryville (see **Perryville, Kentucky**), Confederate Gen. Braxton Bragg took position in and around Murfreesboro with his Army of Tennessee. Here he remained until challenged by the Federals in the Battle of Stones River.

STONES RIVER

If there was one glimmer of hope in the winter of 1862–63, the season of Fredericksburg, Holly Springs, and Chickasaw Bayou, described by one Northern officer as "our Valley Forge," it was in Middle Tennessee. On December 26, the 42,000-man Army of the Cumberland marched southeast from Nashville. Their commander since October 30, Maj. Gen. William S. Rosecrans, commended by Lincoln for his leadership in the Battle of Corinth, nevertheless was slow to heed the president's well-known desire to take the war to the enemy. But when Rosecrans moved, it was with a carefully considered plan evincing a keen appreciation of strategy and tactics.

Although Confederate Gen. Braxton Bragg was controversial, he still commanded more than 35,000 soldiers in the Murfreesboro area. Only days earlier, Jefferson Davis had ordered Bragg to send 10,000 men to Lt. Gen. John C. Pemberton in Vicksburg, reducing his strength. But, cavalry was still a key element of the Army of Tennessee. Besides the strategic raiding provided by Nathan Bedford Forrest and John Hunt Morgan, Bragg had a cavalry corps under twenty-six-year-old Brig. Gen. Joseph Wheeler for nearby tactical operations. In the last few days of December, Wheeler duplicated J.E.B. Stuart's earlier feats with a ride around the enemy.

While Wheeler succeeded in destroying and capturing ammunition and supplies, the Federal advance continued south. On December 29, Rosecrans's vanguard arrived two miles northwest of Murfreesboro to challenge the Rebels' positions astride Stones River. When the troops made camp on the evening of December 30, neither the officers nor men were aware that the enemy generals had devised the same battle plan as their own leaders: to turn the opposing army's right flank and cut it off from its base. As the soldiers of both sides prepared to bed down for the night, a battle of the bands developed, each challenging the other with their own patriotic songs. Then someone started a rendition of "Home Sweet Home" which was picked up by bands in both armies. Soon soldiers North and South were filling the cold night air with that nostalgic song.

At daybreak on December 31, 13,000 Rebels tore into the Union right flank. In several hours of savage fighting, the Northern line was

The assault on the Federal lines of the Army of the Cumberland on December 31 by the Confederate Army of Tennessee was immortalized later by an Ohio soldier, Pvt. E. Matthews, in a series of drawings.

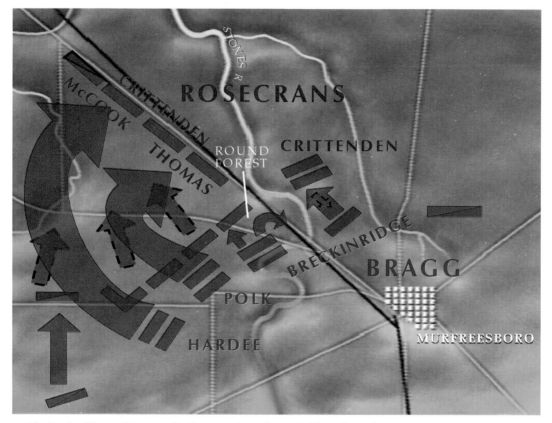

The Battle of Stones River was fought over a three-day period from December 31, 1862, to January 2, 1863. On the evening of December 30, both Federal commander Rosecrans and Confederate commander Bragg discussed similar battle plans with their subordinates—to turn the opposing army's right flank and cut it off from its source of supplies. If successful, the Federal plan would have forced the Rebels away from their base at Murfreesboro. The Southerners planned to drive the Federals beyond the railroad and turnpike connection that ran northwest to Nashville. The Confederate offensive started first and, though it jackknifed the Union line, Rosecrans formed a new line defending the railroad and pike. After only light skirmishing between the two forces on January 1, Bragg ordered Breckinridge's division to attack a position that had been recently occupied by the Federals east of Stones River. The disastrous assault failed, and the Northerners counterattacked, driving the Rebels back and taking prisoners. The spirit of the Rebel offensive broken, Bragg withdrew to the south the next night.

hurled back three miles, folded almost on itself in the area of the Nashville Pike and the railroad. Total disaster was avoided for the North thanks to the foresight of Brig. Gen. Philip Sheridan, who had his division up before dawn and awaiting the Southern attack. At terrible cost to his force, Sheridan was able to blunt the onslaught and fight a skillful delaying action before his bloodied command was forced to retreat.

Though Rosecrans had begun his own offensive in the morning, he soon abandoned the attack. Instead, he rode along his line, determinedly holding it together. By noon, the hinge of the jackknifed Union front was near a bend in Stones River known as Round Forest or Hell's Half Acre. Bragg was intent on breaking this position against which he had already sent two brigades. He ordered the division of former U.S. vice president John C. Breckinridge against it. The Rebels attacked piecemeal with four brigades and suffered heavy casualties; the Yanks grimly held their ground. Bragg, however, believed the Federals to be withdrawing and telegraphed news of a great victory to Richmond. Braxton Bragg's victory celebration was premature; Rosecrans and his commanders decided to hold their ground.

The Army of the Cumberland celebrated New Year's Day, 1863, by redefining and strengthening its defensive position. As Lincoln was signing the Emancipation Proclamation into law, Rosecrans sent Col. Samuel Beatty's division to occupy commanding ground east of Stones River, near McFadden's Ford.

On January 2, Bragg ordered Breckinridge to take this ground. The Kentucky general protested, pointing out that the Federal artillery west of the river would enfilade his attacking line. Bragg insisted and Breckinridge's prediction came true; his men were raked by 57 cannons. The brave but futile late-afternoon assault lasted only an hour and added 1,600 to the more than 10,000 Southern casualties at Stones River. The Federals counterattacked and drove back the survivors of Breckinridge's division.

Unable to find a way to repulse the quickly rein-

This view of Stones River National Battlefield shows a portion of the Federal line held on the morning of December 31, 1862, by the division of Brig. Gen. Philip H. Sheridan. The rocky cedar woods were stoutly defended for a time by Sheridan's soldiers, who were up early in anticipation of launching an attack. Instead, the Rebels launched a powerful assault that eventually drove back Sheridan's men and the rest of the Union line.

forced units of the Army of the Cumberland, Bragg was forced to withdraw on the night of January 3–4 to the vicinity of Tullahoma, forty miles to the south. And though the criticism of Bragg by his subordinates reached a new level of discontent, replacing him was a difficult challenge for Jefferson Davis. Gen. Joseph E. Johnston found the spirits of Bragg's enlisted men high, and stated so to Davis as he also refused to take Bragg's job himself. So the controversial and moody commander stayed on.

Added together the total casualties of both sides at Stones River, called Murfreesboro by the South, created the highest percentage of killed and wounded to number engaged of any major Civil War battle. The Battle of Stones River, which cost the Union 12,900 casualties, was little better than a stalemate, but for President Lincoln it was the only good news of a hard winter. "God bless you, and all with you," he wired to Rosecrans. The president wrote to "Old Rosy" later: "I can never forget . . . you gave us a hard earned victory which, had there been a defeat instead, the nation could hardly have lived over."

Points of Interest

Stones River National Battlefield—The park is located northeast of I-24 exit 78 and includes areas of the battlefield where Union soldiers of General Rosecrans's army battled the forces of Confederate generals Leonidas Polk and Breckinridge and several satellite areas, including Fortress Rosecrans and Brannan Redoubt. The park visitor center has a museum and audiovisual presentation. Uniformed park rangers can orient you to the battlefield and provide a brochure for a driving tour of the park. An audiotape tour is also available for rent or purchase. Throughout the summer, talks and living history programs are given. The battlefield includes Round Forest, a portion of the January 2 Federal artillery position overlooking Stones River which enfiladed Breckinridge's attack, and Sheridan's portion of the line which slowed the initial Confederate drive. A national cemetery is located in the park and historical markers identify sites outside the park. The park is open every day except December 25. STONES RIVER NATIONAL BATTLEFIELD, 3501 Old Nashville Highway, Murfreesboro, TN 37129; 615-893-9501 (TDD). 🚲 🏕 ♿ 🚶 ❓ 🏛 P 🪑 🚻

In Murfreesboro there are several points of interest. A historic marker on East Main Street at Jordan locates the home where on December 14, 1862, John Hunt Morgan married Martha "Mattie" Ready. The wedding was performed by Leonidas Polk and most of the general officers of the Army of Tennessee were in the wedding party. Oaklands, North Maney Avenue, is an antebellum mansion that was the headquarters for the Federal garrison that surrendered to Gen. Nathan Bedford Forrest on July 13, 1862. Many Southern notables were entertained by the mansion's owner, Dr. James Maney. Evergreen Cemetery has Confederate graves and a monument; there is another Confederate monument on the courthouse square. The buildings of Union University, now occupied by Central High School, were used as a hospital by both sides.

DRIVING TOUR and READING—*Proceed to Hoover's Gap*

HOOVER'S GAP–LIBERTY GAP

In the spring of 1863, the Lincoln administration endeavored to have the commanders of its three major armies launch coordinated attacks on the Virginia, Tennessee, and Mississippi fronts. While Maj. Gen. Joseph Hooker prepared to outflank Gen. Robert E. Lee's entrenched Rebels at Fredericksburg, and Ulysses S. Grant landed his Army of the Tennessee at Bruinsburg, south of Vicksburg, Maj. Gen. William S. Rosecrans passed the time refitting and resting his army at Murfreesboro, gained four

The heaviest fighting in the Federal Army of the Cumberland's drive from Murfreesboro to Chattanooga in June 1863 occurred here at Beech Grove, where Col. John T. Wilder's "Lightning" Brigade was attacked by a superior number of Confederates and held the position until reinforced. Today the area is commemorated by a small state park and Confederate cemetery.

months earlier after the Battle of Stones River. While General Lee began his invasion of the North and Grant besieged Vicksburg, Rosecrans dismissed urgent warnings and telegrams from Secretary of War Edwin M. Stanton and General-in-Chief Henry W. Halleck—he was not ready.

When Rosecrans finally did move his army on June 23, 1863, the march was characteristically swift and decisive. Through careful preparation and swift execution, Rosecrans strategically maneuvered his four infantry and one cavalry corps through three mountain gaps, ending up on both flanks of his opponent, Gen. Braxton Bragg. The Federal advance on Hoover's Gap was led by a brigade of mounted infantry under Col. John T. Wilder, brandishing Spencer seven-shot rifles. On June 24, Wilder's brigade cleared Hoover's Gap and Beech Grove of Rebel pickets and then repulsed a counterattack by Brig. Gen. William Bate's Confederate infantry. Other Federal units feinted east and west of the main column of Maj. Gen. George Thomas's corps, which followed Wilder. Maj. Gen. Thomas L. Crittenden's corps marched on McMinnville while Maj. Gen. Alexander McCook's corps clashed with Confederate forces at Liberty Gap on June 24–25 and then marched through Bell Buckle.

Points of Interest

Beech Grove Memorial State Park—The park is located on a hill just east of I-24 and north of TN64, and features a Confederate cemetery with a monument to unknown Confederate soldiers. At Christiana (TN269) a historical marker describes the action at Liberty Gap, 6 miles south, where a division of Maj. Gen. Alexander McCook's corps battled elements of Maj. Gen. Patrick Cleburne's division. At Shelbyville, on US41A and US241, there are markers describing the Army of the Cumberland march and a Confederate monument at the courthouse. Another historical marker identifies the meeting point of Andrews' Raiders before traveling to Georgia. Tullahoma (TN55) has a Confederate cemetery and a historical marker locating Bragg's headquarters.

DRIVING TOUR and READING—*Proceed to Chattanooga*

CHATTANOOGA AREA

Chattanooga

In Chattanooga, Gen. Braxton Bragg positioned his two corps to defend the city. He was given sufficient time to improve the defenses of the city; General Rosecrans, after the rapid southeastward march through Middle Tennessee, paused in the Tullahoma area for six weeks to rest his army, rebuild his railroad supply line, and wait for the corn and wheat to ripen. In the meantime, Bragg appealed to Richmond for reinforcements while at the same time corps commander William J. Hardee was transferred to Mississippi. But by mid-August, Rosecrans was ready to move again. After much delay, Maj. Gen. Ambrose E. Burnside was marching his Army of the Ohio southeast through Kentucky toward Knoxville (see **Knoxville**). Bragg assumed Rosecrans would approach Chattanooga from the north, with Burnside in supporting distance to the northeast.

That is what Rosecrans hoped Bragg would believe, but his intentions were again different. Rosecrans supported his ruse by sending three infantry brigades and cavalry—including Wilder's mounted infantry, who had earned their comrades' admiration and the nickname the "Lightning Brigade"—under Brig. Gen. William B. Hazen, on a long march through the mountains north of Chattanooga. On August 21, a Confederate "day of prayer and fasting" in Chattanooga was interrupted by Federal artillery fire from Stringers Ridge on the far bank of the Tennessee River.

Rosecrans concentrated two of the Army of the Cumberland's three infantry corps near Stevenson, Alabama, where the railroad from Nashville joined the east-west Memphis & Charleston running to Chattanooga (see **Stevenson, Alabama**). Hazen's force, as well as Thomas Crittenden's corps, remained northeast of Chattanooga. By the time Bragg's intelligence revealed the location of Rosecrans's army, the Union force was already crossing the Tennessee River near Stevenson. Bragg vacillated, even as he received reinforcements; Maj. Gen. Simon Buckner and the rest of his force were ordered south from Knoxville, and other reinforcements from Mississippi under Maj. Gen. William H. T. Walker came. Finally, admitting that he had again been outmaneuvered, Bragg withdrew from the "Gateway City" without firing a shot on September 7.

Rosecrans was ecstatic. Sending Crittenden's corps into Chattanooga to follow up Bragg's retreat, he dispatched his other two corps on separate routes through northwest Georgia to get onto Bragg's flank and into his rear. Although corps commander George Thomas suggested to Rosecrans that he first consolidate the Army of the Cumberland in Chattanooga and fortify the city, "Old Rosy" was convinced that the Army of Tennessee was in panic-stricken retreat and that Bragg would not turn to fight north of Atlanta. Events proved him wrong and Rosecrans would come to grief at the Battle of Chickamauga (see **Chickamauga, Georgia**).

After defeat at Chickamauga, the Federal Army of the Cumberland retreated into the protection afforded by Chattanooga, and by September 22 all units had reached the fortified town. Defenses were quickly improved. They were cautiously followed by the Army of Tennessee, and General Bragg, appalled by the casualties suffered by his army, did not land a knockout blow on his opponent. Instead, he was content to besiege Rosecrans while he sorted out internal dissension in his army.

The Rebels soon established an investment line anchored on the left on Lookout Mountain (after Rosecrans unwisely withdrew a brigade from the strategic position), the center in Chattanooga Valley and the right on Missionary Ridge, with Rebel cavalry ranging west and northeast of Chattanooga, effectively sealing off the Union Army except for a tenuous wagon road to the northwest across Walden's Ridge. The Army of the Cumberland became the first major Federal force to be besieged. To add to the Federals' discomfort, Bragg sent Maj. Gen. Joseph Wheeler on a cavalry raid. On September 29–30, Wheeler crossed the Tennessee River some forty miles upriver from Chattanooga and the next day in the Sequatchie Valley came upon a large train at Anderson's Cross Roads. As Wheeler's force was plundering the train, Col. Edward M. McCook's Federal cavalry attacked the Rebel horsemen, nearly capturing Wheeler. Wheeler's cavalry then raced ahead to McMinnville, where they captured the garrison, but close pursuit by Federal horse soldiers, particularly those led by Brig. Gen. George Crook, limited damage to the Nashville & Chattanooga Railroad south of Murfreesboro. At Farmington, on October 7, Crook's people overtook and mauled one of Wheeler's divisions. On October 9 Wheeler's exhausted corps, having failed to significantly damage the railroad, recrossed the Tennessee River at Muscle Shoals. But the destruction of wagons and loss of mules at Anderson's Cross Roads was devastating to the Federals.

Fretful over the sudden reversal of fortune in Tennessee, Lincoln searched for a solution to his leadership problems there. He saw it in U. S. Grant. The Army of the Tennessee commander was recovering from an injury caused by a fall from an unfamiliar horse while he was visiting Maj. Gen. Nathaniel Banks in New Orleans in mid-September. It was rumored that drunkenness caused the mishap. (The criticism of Grant's drinking continued to melt away with his successes, prompting Southern diarist Mary Chesnut to observe wryly, "Since Vicksburg they have not a word to say against Grant's habits. He has the disagreeable habit of not retreating before irresistible veterans.")

Lincoln named Grant to command the newly constituted Division of the Mississippi. The division included the Departments of the Ohio, Cumberland, and Tennessee. Grant's headquarters were to be in the field, which, with the armies in Mississippi idle, was Chattanooga. Maj. Gen. W. T. Sherman with four divisions of the Army of the Tennessee had been boated from Vicksburg to Memphis and were en route to Corinth and rebuilding the Memphis & Charleston Railroad. Two corps from the then idle Army of the Potomac in northeast Virginia were also ordered to relieve the Army of the Cumberland. Lincoln placed Maj. Gen. Joseph Hooker in charge of this force and gave Grant the option to relieve General Rosecrans. Grant was not a Rosecrans fan, and on October 18 he ordered Rosecrans to turn over his army to Maj. Gen. George H. Thomas.

While the besieged Federals awaited relief from Bragg's infantry and artillery investing Chattanooga, key subordinates of the Rebel chief awaited relief from him. Though shortly after Chickamauga, Bragg rid himself of General Polk and a troublesome division commander, a number of the army's generals petitioned President Davis to replace Bragg as army commander. Jefferson Davis saw the need for his personal intervention and arrived at Bragg's headquarters on October 9 to resolve the controversy. James Longstreet and the other three corps commanders present gave Bragg a lack of confidence vote in front of their leader and the Confederate president.

Though Davis had already decided to keep Bragg as commander of the Army of Tennessee before the meeting, he hoped to ease the situation surrounding the stormy commander. Several generals were transferred or shunted aside and Davis subsequently endorsed a special mission for Longstreet—to march northeast with his corps and Wheeler's cavalry and crush Burnside's army and retake Knoxville. Back in Richmond, Davis offered Bragg some tactical advice to continue the success of the siege. "It is reported here that the enemy are crossing at Bridgeport [Alabama]. If so, it may give you the opportunity to beat the detachment moving up to reinforce Rosecrans as was contemplated. You will be able to anticipate him, and fight with the advantage of fighting him in detail."

Meanwhile, Bedford Forrest, most of his horse soldiers reassigned to Wheeler and participants in his ill-fated raid, had had a stormy confrontation with General Bragg in which he had declared he would not again serve under Bragg. Forrest was, with the approval of President Davis, sent to northeast Mississippi with a small detachment and ordered to assume command of Confederate forces there.

Brown's Ferry and Wauhatchie

When Grant arrived in Chattanooga on October 23, things began to quicken for the Federals. Bragg did not defeat the XI and XII corps of the Army of the Potomac in detail as suggested by Davis. Instead, the expeditionary force, the lead elements of which arrived at Bridgeport on October 1, only six days after being ordered west, seized the initiative. In a plan perfected by the new chief engineer in Chattanooga, Maj. Gen. William F. "Baldy" Smith, and approved by Rosecrans before his departure, Federal forces in Chattanooga prepared to take Brown's Ferry from the Confederates and establish a bridgehead on a portion of the Tennessee River out of range of the Rebel guns. In the predawn hours of October 27, soldiers from William Hazen's brigade floated silently downriver in pontoon boats while a larger infantry force led by Brig. Gen. John Turchin marched overland to Brown's Ferry. At the same time Hooker, with three divisions, marched northeast through Lookout Valley in support.

Hazen's men rowed their boats ashore and surprised Confederate pickets. As fighting broke out, Turchin's overland force used the boats to cross the river, and the Rebels withdrew, unable to hold out as Federal reinforcements arrived continuously. By midafternoon, the pontoons were being planked over and a bridge was in place creating a supply line, which soon was fed by boats steaming up the Tennessee River to Kelley's Ferry, and was dubbed the "Cracker Line" by the grateful Army of the Cumberland soldiers, in honor of receiving shipments of the usually despised army hardtack or "crackers."

The Confederates, slow to react to the presence of Hooker's expeditionary force, behaved even more strangely when the advance from Bridgeport was confirmed. Longstreet, in command of that sector, sent John Bell Hood's division, commanded by Brig. Gen. Micah Jenkins after Hood was wounded at Chickamauga, to make a night attack on the southernmost division of Hooker's force. That was the division of Brig. Gen. John W. Geary, one of the more interesting of the politician-generals in the Federal army, camping in Lookout Valley near Wauhatchie railroad station. Sending the brigade of Brig. Gen. Evander M. Law to the north to isolate Geary from the rest of Hooker's force, camped south of Brown's Ferry, Jenkins launched a determined night attack against Geary.

The November 24, 1863, Federal advance on Lookout Mountain is commemorated in this painting by James G. Walker who was present with Federal forces at Chattanooga during the campaign. Maj. Gen. Joseph Hooker, on the white horse in the center, prepares orders for his staff as his soldiers form at the base of the mountain.

Confusion reigned in the moonlit battle. Geary's men held a good defensive position against the unseen enemy, but Jenkins's men pressed Geary's flanks and Geary's son was killed while directing an artillery battery. Farther north, two XI Corps divisions ordered by Hooker to reinforce Geary failed to reach Wauhatchie, though a bayonet charge was mounted which drove Law from his hilltop position. The XI Corps soldiers, much maligned for their poor performance at Chancellorsville and Gettysburg, fought bravely and gained respect in this attack. As Geary desperately held on, the Confederates mysteriously withdrew about three-thirty A.M. on October 29 and the "Cracker Line" was secure.

A legend that sprang from the Battle of Wauhatchie was that some stampeding mules were mistaken in the darkness as a cavalry charge by the Rebels. Grant was amused when his quartermaster petitioned for the mules to receive brevet (honorary) promotions to horses for their part in the Battle of Wauhatchie.

Orchard Knob–Lookout Mountain

In mid-November, Sherman arrived in the Chattanooga area with his 17,000 Army of the Tennessee veterans, bringing the total number of Federals to more than 70,000. Grant then devised a plan to break the siege of Chattanooga, one that was also taking its toll on the Confederate soldiers, who were suffering themselves from lack of supplies and cold and wet conditions. Grant sent Sherman to the north side of the Tennessee River with instructions to recross the river and attack the right flank of Bragg's line on Missionary Ridge. To the west, Hooker was to seize Lookout Mountain, cross Chattanooga

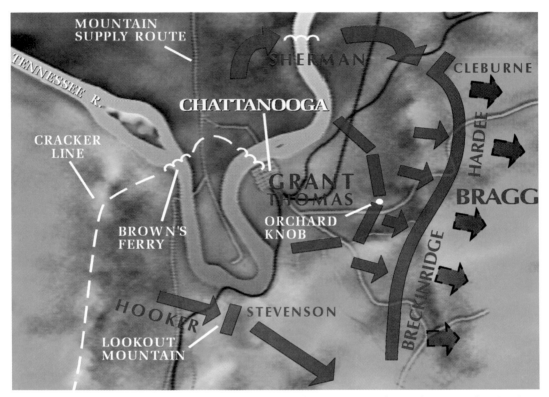

The Federal campaign to break the siege at Chattanooga in late 1863 spanned more than a month. First, in late October, the actions at Brown's Ferry and Wauhatchie opened the "Cracker Line" for Federal supply. Then, in late November, Grant launched a series of breakout assaults; on November 23, the Army of the Cumberland moved forward and captured Orchard Knob. On November 24 and 25, Grant ordered flanking operations; by Maj. Gen. Joseph Hooker's force, which captured Lookout Mountain and marched forward to Chattanooga Valley on the Rebel southern flank, and by Maj. Gen. William T. Sherman's attack on the northern flank along Missionary Ridge. The Confederate Army of Tennessee was routed on November 25 by the unplanned assault of Missionary Ridge by the Army of the Cumberland.

Valley, and approach Missionary Ridge extending northeast-southwest for many miles via Rossville Gap.

To the Army of the Cumberland, Grant gave an assignment that was to be a demonstration. The Confederates held a prominent hill, Orchard Knob, midway between the Federal position in Chattanooga and the Rebel rifle pits at the base of Missionary Ridge. Two divisions of Maj. Gen. Gordon Granger's reconstituted IV Corps, under Brig. Gens. Philip H. Sheridan and Thomas J. Wood, appeared in the afternoon to be drilling outside the Federal fortifications. Even the Confederates came out to watch. Then suddenly at one-thirty P.M., a signal cannon was fired and the two divisions rushed Orchard Knob.

Within one hour the Rebels were pushed back to their rifle pits at the base of Missionary Ridge. The demonstration exceeded expectations—Thomas brought up units to support the forward line and Grant moved his headquarters to Orchard Knob.

The success encouraged Grant to order General Hooker to proceed beyond Lookout Mountain through Rossville Gap after the attack on the mountain planned for the following day.

On November 24, the fighting started when Hooker's three divisions scaled the precipitous western face of Lookout Mountain about eight A.M. and gained the bench at the Cravens House. The fog and mist that lingered throughout the day later gave this action the name the "Battle Above the Clouds." The action culminated when the Union soldiers captured key positions around the Cravens House two thirds the way up the mountain. That night, Bragg withdrew all Confederate forces from Lookout Mountain. The success of Hooker's troops in driving the Rebels from the mountain fortified the resolve of the Federals. On the same day Sherman moved forward from a hidden camp north of the Tennessee River, crossed on pontoons, and gained a foothold in the northern extension of Missionary Ridge, known locally as Billy Goat Hill.

Missionary Ridge

The next day, November 25, as the Stars and Stripes flew from the top of Lookout Mountain and Hooker's advance elements were crossing Chattanooga Valley on their way to challenge Maj. Gen. John C. Breckinridge's Confederates at Rossville Gap, Sherman's force was advancing against Tunnel Hill, where the East Tennessee & Georgia Railroad ran underground for a short distance before entering Chattanooga. The position was held by Maj. Gen. Patrick Cleburne's division. Nearby was Maj. Gen. Carter L. Stevenson's division, which had arrived overnight from Lookout Mountain. Sherman was reinforced by part of Maj. Gen. Oliver O. Howard's XI Corps, which marched north on the near side of the river after the Rebels were cleared from Orchard Knob.

The reinforcements did not help Sherman. At day's start, his troops found themselves confronted by the well-defended Tunnel Hill, the route to unhinge and roll up the Confederate line on Missionary Ridge from the north. Cleburne's soldiers, inspired by their leader, turned back repeated assaults across the rugged terrain by the Union forces.

Despite their success against Orchard Knob, Grant did not have confidence in Thomas's Army of the Cumberland soldiers with the cloud of the Chickamauga defeat hanging over them. Grant's plan did not call for their use if the flank assaults succeeded. As reports of Sherman's plight became known, however, Grant asked Thomas to demonstrate against the center to divert reinforcements from adding to the difficulties Sherman was having with Cleburne. Thomas's objective was to be at the rifle pits at the base of the ridge but poor command and engineering work by the Confederate leadership left the center curiously vulnerable.

After some delay and with darkness not far away, the Army of the Cumberland troops began a parade ground–like advance across a gradual slope to the first Confederate line of defense at the base of Missionary Ridge. The momentum they felt after rushing and gaining the rifle pits was contagious. In a dramatic parallel charge up the steep ridge slopes, not unlike the sweep of Pickett's, Pettigrew's, and Trimble's troops across the fields of Gettysburg, except that the terrain was far more treacherous, regiment after regiment raced to the top shouting "Chickamauga, Chickamauga" as they went. Hindered by confusing orders, the Rebels fled in a manner not unlike the Yankee retreat from the "River of Death." The poorly located Rebel artillery could not fire on the advancing Federals without hitting their own forces. As Grant and Thomas watched in amazement, the inspired men of the Army of the Cumberland climbed and took the ridge.

The rout began immediately as Confederate soldiers streamed down the back of the ridge toward Georgia. Hooker, who had already been successful in driving the Rebels from the Rossville Gap area and Sherman, with Cleburne desperately fighting a rear-guard action, joined forces with Thomas by nightfall. The next day the combined Federal forces pushed Bragg's army beyond Rossville and into Georgia. The disgraceful defeat at Missionary Ridge toppled Bragg from command of the Army of Tennessee.

Points of Interest

Chickamauga and Chattanooga National Military Park—The national military park, which is the nation's largest, commemorates the Battle of Chickamauga (see **Chickamauga, Georgia**) and the battles in and around Chattanooga in the autumn of 1863. In Chattanooga there are several reservations which make up the battlefield park. The best place to start is Lookout Mountain. From I-24, take Broad Street (US64/72 and US11/41) a short distance to Scenic Highway, which winds up the mountain to East Brow Road and Point Park. You can also take public transportation to the lower station of the Lookout Mountain Incline Railway, which climbs to the Cloud High Station, a short distance from Point Park. Across from Point Park is the visitor center for the Chattanooga unit. Uniformed park rangers are available to answer questions, and there are exhibits and an audiovisual presentation. Although no fighting in the Battle of Lookout Mountain was fought on the mountaintop, the Confederates emplaced artillery on the crest and several battery positions are indicated with markers and cannons. The New York Peace Memorial is also in the park.

A short trail down from the northern crest leads to the Adolph S. Ochs Museum and Overlook. From here and from the crest are excellent views of the Tennessee River, Moccasin Bend, Signal and Raccoon mountains, Missionary Ridge, Orchard Knob, and the city of Chattanooga. The museum has exhibits on the battle and weapons; there are landmark locators on the observation deck. Lookout Mountain was a popular site for Federal soldiers to be photographed and rock outcroppings near the crest of the mountain can be seen in a number of Civil War–era photographs.

When you return down the mountain via Scenic Highway, note the turnoff that leads to the Cravens House, the scene of decisive action on the mountain. The house, the only structure in the Chattanooga Unit that existed during the battle, has been restored and markers and monuments describe the action that took place around it. For more information on CHICKAMAUGA AND CHATTANOOGA NATIONAL MILITARY PARK, call the Chickamauga Visitor Center at 706-866-9241.

From Scenic Highway, return to US64/72 and US41/11 and drive west to the Y intersection, then follow US11 south. In a few miles you begin to see state historical markers along the highway descriptive of the Battle of Wauhatchie. A turnoff to Brown's Ferry Road will lead to four NPS sites associated with the Wauhatchie battle. Consult the NPS map and visitor center ranger for more specific locations. The present-day railroad follows the right-of-way of the Nashville & Chattanooga. Return to US11 and I-24 and cross the river to Moccasin Bend, following the US27 limited-access highway north through Chattanooga. At the Mountain Boulevard (US127) exit there is a historical marker for the Battle of Brown's Ferry which was fought to the west along the river south of Williams Island. On TN27ALT at the junction with the road to Baylor School is a historical marker describing the capture there of James J. Andrews after he escaped from a Chattanooga jail while being held following his raid into Georgia. The Signal Mountain reservation of the national park can be reached from US127, 9 miles north of Chattanooga. There was no fighting at that location but the highway follows

A portion of the Confederate line on Missionary Ridge is commemorated by a monument and cannons along Crest Road. Here on November 25, 1863, Army of the Cumberland soldiers charged up the steep slopes of Missionary Ridge and overwhelmed the corps of Lt. Gen. William Hardee and Maj. Gen. John C. Breckinridge, who were manning these poorly sited positions.

the mountain supply road the Federals were forced to use for more than a month of the siege and Signal Mountain was used by Federal signalers.

Return to the city of Chattanooga via TN27 or proceed north on US27 to TN153, then south on TN153 to the Hixson Pike exit. Turn right and proceed to Ozark Road. From this concealed camp, Sherman and four divisions crossed the river on a pontoon bridge on November 24. Return to Chattanooga via the Market Street Bridge. On TN58, Amnicola Highway, are historical markers describing Sherman's position on South Chickamauga Creek, before launching his attack on Tunnel Hill. Historical markers track Sherman's advance through the area and the NPS Sherman Reservation and 73rd Pennsylvania Reservations are on Wilder Avenue east of TN58. Parking at these two sites, and on Missionary Ridge, is limited.

Visitors can ride the rails in cars pulled by vintage steam locomotives through historic Tunnel Hill, the key sector that Patrick Cleburne successfully defended against Sherman's advance. Two depots of the Tennessee Valley Railroad, one at 2200 North Chamberlain Avenue and the other at 4119 Cromwell Road, are on either side of the mountain tunnel. For more information on the railroad, call 615-894-8028.

🚌 ❄ ♿ P ⛱ 🚻 $$

From Sherman Reservation, proceed south on North Crest Road, which runs along the top of Missionary Ridge. There are six NPS reservations along Missionary Ridge and historical markers and cannons along Crest Road. Convenient parking is available only at the Bragg Reservation (Bragg's headquarters), but the drive is scenic and informative. From North Crest Road, continue south to the Iowa Reservation and return to Chattanooga by taking Rossville Boulevard (US27) north. A shorter route is to take Shallowford Road west from North Crest Road and return to Chattanooga via McCallie Avenue.

The most important sites in Chattanooga are the NPS reservation at Orchard Knob, north of McCallie Avenue on Orchard Knob Avenue and the national cemetery on Holtzclaw Avenue. Besides containing the graves of Union soldiers killed in the battles of Chickamauga and Chattanooga, and those who died in hospitals in the area, the cemetery contains the graves of James J. Andrews and other Andrews' Raiders who were executed. A memorial featuring a small replica of the General locomotive is in the center of the plot. There are excellent views of Lookout Mountain and Missionary Ridge at the cemetery.

Historic buildings and structures in Chattanooga with Civil War ties include Bragg's headquarters, 407 East Fifth Street; the Breckinridge headquarters, 415 Poplar Street; College Hospital at West Eleventh and Cedar streets; Fort Sheridan at 1219 East Terrace; Thomas J. Woods's headquarters at 504 Vine Street; and Joseph Wheeler's headquarters at 515 Douglas Street. The Grant House at 110 East First Street was used as a headquarters by Grant and Sherman; Federal generals James A. Garfield and Joseph J. Reynolds occupied the house at Fourth and Walnut streets. The 10th Ohio Volunteer Infantry Camp is marked at 654 Houston Street. Reportedly, the first Confederate shells fired from Lookout Mountain during the siege fell here. A monument on the lawn of the county courthouse honors Confederate general Alexander P. Stewart and there is a Confederate cemetery bounded by Lansing, Palmetto, East Third, and East Fifth streets.

DRIVING TOUR and READING—*Proceed to Knoxville*

KNOXVILLE AREA

Campbell's Station

In the chess game that was played out in Tennessee in November 1863 between the Confederate Army of Tennessee, then posted on the mountains and ridges commanding most of the approaches to Chattanooga, and the combined Federal forces in and around Chattanooga and Knoxville, under the overall command of Maj. Gen. Ulysses S. Grant, the first pieces moved were the 10,000 soldiers of the Army of Northern Virginia under Lt. Gen. James Longstreet and 5,000 cavalry led by the "Mighty Bantam," Maj. Gen. Joseph Wheeler. Following an earlier suggestion of President Davis, Gen. Braxton Bragg ordered Longstreet northeast on November 4, as much to rid himself of a general who no longer had respect for his leadership as to beat Maj. Gen. Ambrose E. Burnside's Army of the Ohio and drive the Federals from Knoxville. Longstreet had little enthusiasm for the project and warned of the danger of splitting the already vulnerable force at Chattanooga. "We thus expose both to failure, and really take no chance to ourselves of great results," he wrote.

After weeks of resisting efforts to loosen his grip on Knoxville and much of East Tennessee by reinforcing the Federals holed up in Chattanooga, General Burnside suggested to Grant that by marching southwest to oppose Longstreet's approach well beyond Knoxville's fortifications and then pulling slowly back into the city, he might draw off the Georgian and thus contribute to the success of the campaign Grant planned to beat Bragg's army and lift the siege of Chattanooga (see **Chattanooga**). Grant liked the idea and in the second week of November, Burnside took the field with 5,000 soldiers. Burnside was unaware that supply and transportation difficulties were hampering Longstreet's progress, though the fighting spirit of his men soared as the campaign unfolded.

The first clash of the two forces came on November 14, when Wheeler's cavalry, accompanying Longstreet's column, rode ahead to test the Knoxville defenses, via Maryville. Their advance was resisted by Burnside's cavalry under energetic Brig. Gen. William P. Sanders. Though outnumbered by the Confederate horsemen, Sanders's command fought a delaying action for two days and Wheeler could only study the strength of the Knoxville defenses from commanding ground south of the Tennessee River. Wheeler, because of difficulty in recrossing the Tennessee, did not rejoin

Longstreet's columns until midafternoon on November 17, the day after the Campbell's Station fight.

At the same time Burnside, confronted by Longstreet's army, was withdrawing to Knoxville, picking up the Federal garrison at Loudoun en route. Feeling he could do no more to slow down the larger Rebel force and fearing he would be cut off from Knoxville, Burnside began his retrograde movement along the railroad. Following parallel routes, Longstreet and Burnside raced for Campbell's Station, a hamlet where the Concord Road, from the south, intersected the Kingston Road to Knoxville. Burnside hoped to reach the crossroads first and continue on to safety in Knoxville; Longstreet planned to reach the crossroads and hold it, which would prevent Burnside from gaining Knoxville and force him to fight outside his earthworks. By forced-marching on a rainy November 16, Burnside's advance reached the vital intersection and deployed first. The main column arrived at noon with the baggage train close behind. Scarcely fifteen minutes later, Longstreet's Confederates approached. Longstreet attempted a double envelopment: attacks timed to strike both Union flanks simultaneously. Maj. Gen. Lafayette McLaws's Confederate division struck with such force that the Union right had to redeploy, but held. Brig. Gen. Micah Jenkins's Confederate division maneuvered ineffectively as it advanced and was unable to turn the Union left. Burnside ordered his two divisions astride the Kingston Road to withdraw three quarters of a mile to a ridge in their rear. This was accomplished without confusion, and Longstreet, miffed at the misfire, called off any further attacks. Sanders's cavalry arrived to become Burnside's rear guard and the Federals got back to the Knoxville defenses with all but a handful of abandoned wagons, though Sanders was killed in a clash of cavalry on November 18.

Points of Interest

In Farragut, Knox County, southwest of Knoxville, near Farragut High School on US11/70 is a Tennessee State Historical Marker describing the Battle of Campbell's Station.

Knoxville

A hundred miles northeast of Chattanooga, Knoxville was the major city in an area of Tennessee that had never wholeheartedly embraced the state's decision to join the Confederacy. Unionists, mostly small farmers, in East Tennessee endured persecution from Confederate authorities and citizens in the region. Abraham Lincoln had longed for a military effort to relieve the Tennessee Unionists, but it was not until the summer of 1863 that a sustained campaign was mounted in the region by General Burnside, eager to redeem a reputation tarnished by defeat while he was commanding the Army of the Potomac at Fredericksburg (see **Fredericksburg, Virginia**).

Though Burnside lost precious months after the formation of a reconstituted Army of the Ohio with headquarters at Cincinnati, because of the need to rush two divisions to Mississippi during the Vicksburg siege, like his comrade to the south, William S. Rosecrans, when he marched, it was with alacrity. In mid-August, he marched south through Kentucky, just as Rosecrans was beginning the campaign that led to his September 9 occupation of Chattanooga. Concern for the latter prompted Gen. Braxton Bragg to order Maj. Gen. Simon B. Buckner and most of his small army to evacuate Knoxville and join him in northwest Georgia.

Despite the obstacles in traversing rugged terrain, Burnside's columns covered as much as thirty miles a day. With minimal resistance from the enemy, Burnside's cavalry entered Knoxville on September 2, with the general and his main force arriving to a hero's welcome the next day. Intent on holding the city, Burnside commenced the building of fortifications, while he released some cavalry requested by General Rosecrans and planned a campaign against the Confederate saltworks and leadworks in southwestern Virginia. After the defeat of the Army of the Cumberland at Chickamauga (see **Chickamauga, Georgia**), Washington became increasingly insistent that Burnside march southwest to Chattanooga to aid Rosecrans in beating back Bragg's investing army. Burnside resisted these pleas from the War Department and Lincoln, who were seemingly insensitive to the fact that Confederate forces were marching into Tennessee from southwest Virginia to wrest from Burnside the gains he had made thus far (see **Blountville** and **Blue Springs**).

Washington reversed its position, however, once Grant stabilized the situation in Chattanooga, and Knoxville was endangered by the northeastward march of Lt. Gen. James Longstreet's Rebel force. Burnside was unconcerned, however, despite his own tenuous supply situation and the Confederate threat, and even attempted to cooperate strategically with Grant in the region by disrupting Longstreet's march (see **Campbell's Station**).

Fort Sanders

By November 17, Longstreet had pushed Burnside's forces back into the defenses of Knoxville and the Federal Army of the Ohio found itself besieged. Burnside was optimistic. Formidable fortifications formed three sides of a rectangle around the city and the Tennessee River constituted the fourth side to the south. Cleared ground outside the works gave good fields of fire, while Federal cavalry held the southern heights, keeping pontoon bridges open across the Tennessee. The Yankees had provisions and ammunition that would sustain them for several weeks and the Confederates logistic problems were difficult and would be compounded if Grant's "army group" beat Bragg's Army of Tennessee in the anticipated battle of Chattanooga.

Realizing time was not on his side, Longstreet planned an attack against a strong earthen redoubt that anchored the northwest angle of the Union defense line, Fort Sanders, renamed for Burnside's slain cavalry chief. A wide creek bed not far from the fort created an opportunity for attackers to form out of the sight of the fort's garrison. Longstreet planned the attack for November 24, but there were delays, first awaiting reinforcements from Chattanooga, then because of rain. With rumors in the air of a decisive Federal victory at Missionary Ridge, Longstreet ordered the attack for dawn on November 29.

At eleven P.M. Rebel sharpshooters advanced to take the outlying rifle pits. After a brief artillery bombardment three brigades of Maj. Gen. Lafayette McLaws's division charged, supported by one of Micah Jenkins's. But as the Confederates raced across the open snow-covered fields from the creek bed in which they had formed—one hundred twenty yards from the fort—at dawn they encountered several unpleasant developments. First, the Yankees had strung telegraph wire between the stumps of the trees cleared in front of the fort, tripping the first wave of Rebels as they ran full speed for the fort's ditch. Second, the moat in front of the fort was deeper than the Confederate officers had thought, and the water in it was ice-cold. Icy also were the fort's parapets, and without scaling ladders the Rebels had a difficult time climbing them. Those few who made it were taken prisoner by the 79th New York, who took the brunt of the attack, and the other defenders, all of whom had been alerted to the danger by the night's skirmishing. The attack was over in twenty minutes.

The attack on Fort Sanders demonstrated the strength of Knoxville's defenses and the assault, although on a much smaller scale, was a slaughter akin to the previous December's assaults on Marye's and Willis Heights at Fredericksburg when the two generals' roles were reversed (see **Fredericksburg, Virginia**). Without the aid of the relief column under Maj. Gen. William T. Sherman, which General Grant had dispatched to Knoxville immediately after the Union victory at Chattanooga, Burnside and his men turned away the ill-advised Confederate onslaught. Longstreet lifted the siege on the night of December 4, forty-eight hours before Sherman arrived, and withdrew northeast toward Virginia, halting at Rogersville on December 9, where he was cut off from rejoining the Army of Tennessee in northwest Georgia and instead returned the following spring to Virginia.

Points of Interest

Knoxville, like many other Civil War battle sites that have become large metropolitan areas, has scattered sites, most of them identified by historical markers. Knoxville can be reached from I-75/40. Exit onto US11/70, Kingston Pike, and drive east toward the downtown area. Confederate Memorial Hall, 3148 Kingston Pike, was called Bleak House during the war and was headquarters for Generals Longstreet and McLaws. A sharpshooter stationed in the house killed Union Brig. Gen. William P. Sanders during the November 18, 1863, skirmish. The house is open for tours and contains period furnishings and historical displays. North of Kingston Pike on the lawn of the Second Presbyterian Church is a historical marker indicating the site of Sanders's death.

The west flank of the Union fortifications began at Second Creek, which you cross as Kingston Pike becomes Cumberland Avenue. A historical marker at Neyland Drive along the Tennessee River at Second Creek indicates the west anchor of the Union fortifications on the river. Another marks the Confederate batteries on Cherokee Heights, south of the river. Poor-quality powder prevented Rebel cannons from firing effectively from the heights during the attack on Fort Sanders, more than 1 mile north. These markers are on the University of Tennessee campus, as is one locating Federal fort Byington at the main entrance on Cumberland Avenue. Two blocks north of the university's Sophronia Strong Hall, where there is a historical marker, is the site of Fort Sanders, at Sixteenth Street and Clinch Avenue. A monument to the 79th New York is at the intersection. Two blocks away, at Seventeenth Street and Laurel Avenue is the UDC Confederate Monument. The Confederates camped during the siege at what is today's Knoxville College, 1400 College Street.

Farther east on Cumberland Avenue in the central city area are markers for the site of the J. H. Crozier home, Burnside's headquarters, at the First Tennessee Bank building, City

Hall, at Broadway and Henley, which was used as a hospital and barracks; the site of Battery Wiltsie, on Vine Avenue near Market, the site of Fort Huntington Smith, at Green Elementary School on Summit Hill Drive; and the site of the Union pontoon bridge that connected with the fortifications south of the river, at Central Avenue in Centennial Park. The eastern flank of the Union defenses is indicated by a marker on Riverside Drive, a short distance east of the park.

There are two Civil War cemeteries in Knoxville. The Confederate cemetery is on Bethel Avenue, approximately 1 mile east of center city off Vine Avenue. National and Old Gray cemeteries contain the graves of Federal soldiers killed in the area. They are located together, north of center city just west of Broadway between Tyson and Cooper streets. W. G. "Parson" Brounlow is buried in Old Gray.

Two Federal forts south of the Tennessee River are Fort Dickerson, located in Fort Dickerson Park on Fort Dickerson Road just west of Chapman Avenue (US441/TN71). A few hundred yards to the southeast, Fort Stanley is indicated by a historical marker on Chapman Highway and Woodlawn Pike.

<hr />

DRIVING TOUR—*Proceed to Dandridge*
READING—*Bean's Station*

<hr />

MOSSY CREEK

Brig. Gen. Samuel D. Sturgis received a report on the night of December 28, 1863, that a brigade of enemy cavalry was in the neighborhood of Dandridge. Surmising that the Rebel cavalry force was divided, Sturgis decided to defeat it in detail and ordered most of his troopers out toward Dandridge on two roads. After these horse soldiers marched, Maj. Gen. William T. Martin, commander of Longstreet's Confederate cavalry, now reunited, attacked the remainder of Sturgis's force at Mossy Creek, commanded by Col. Samuel R. Mott, at nine A.M. on December 29. Sturgis then sent messages to his subordinates on the way to Dandridge to return promptly if they found no enemy there. The Confederates advanced, pushing the Federals before them. Some of the Union troopers who had set out for Dandridge returned. Around three P.M., fortunes changed as the Federals began driving the Confederates. By dark, the Rebels were back where they had begun the battle. Union pursuit was not mounted that night, and Martin retreated from the area.

DANDRIDGE

On January 14, 1864, Union forces under Maj. Gen. John G. Parke advanced on Dandridge, south of the East Tennessee & Virginia Railroad, forcing Lt. Gen. James Longstreet's Confederate troops to fall back. Longstreet rushed up reinforcements on January 15 to meet the enemy and threatened the Union base at New Market. On January 16, Brig. Gen. Samuel D. Sturgis, commanding the Cavalry Corps, Army of the Ohio, rode forward to occupy Kimbrough's Cross Roads. Within three or four miles of his goal, Sturgis's cavalry met Rebel troops, forcing them back toward the crossroads. As the Union cavalry neared the crossroads, they discovered an enemy infantry division with artillery that had arrived the day before. The Union cavalry, unable to dislodge these Rebels, was compelled to retire to Dandridge. About noon the next day, Sturgis received information that the Confederates were preparing for an attack and formed his men into battle line. About four P.M., the Confederates advanced and the fighting escalated. Combat continued until after dark with the Federals occupying the same battle line as when the fighting started. The Union retreated to New Market and Strawberry Plains during the night, but the Rebels were unable to pursue because of the lack of cannon, ammunition, and shoes.

FAIR GARDEN

Following the Battle of Dandridge, the Union cavalry moved to the south side of the French Broad River and disrupted Confederate foraging and captured numerous wagons in that area. On January 25, 1864, General Longstreet instructed his subordinates to do something to curtail Union operations south of the French Broad. On January 26, General Sturgis, having had various brushes with Confederate cavalry, deployed his troopers to watch the area fords. Two Confederate cavalry brigades advanced from Fair Garden that afternoon but were checked about four miles from Sevierville. Other Confederates attacked a Union cavalry brigade, though, at Fowler's on Flat Creek, and gained two miles. No further fighting occurred that day. Union scouts observed that the Confederates had concentrated on the Fair Garden Road, so Sturgis ordered an attack there in the morning. The cavalry division led by Col. Edward M. McCook—one of Ohio's famed fourteen "Fighting McCooks"—in pea soup like fog assailed and drove back Maj. Gen. William T. Martin's Confederates. About four P.M., McCook's men charged with sabers and routed the Rebels. Sturgis set out in pursuit on January 28, and captured and killed more of the Rebels.

The Union forces, however, observed three of Longstreet's infantry brigades crossing the French Broad River. Cognizant of his people's weariness from fighting, lack of supplies, ammunition, and weapons and the overwhelming strength of the enemy, Sturgis resolved to evacuate the area. But, before leaving, Sturgis determined to attack Brig. Gen. Frank C. Armstrong's Confederate cavalry division three or four miles away, on the river. Unbeknownst to the Federals, Armstrong had strongly fortified his position and three infantry regiments had arrived to reinforce him and the Union troops suffered severe casualties in the attack. The battle continued until dark, when the Federals retired from the area.

Points of Interest

In Dandridge (TN92 just south of I-40 at US25/70), there is a historical marker on the courthouse lawn for the December 24, 1863, skirmish near Dandridge and the December 27, 1863, engagement at Mossy Creek. Several engagements were fought near here January 16–17, 1864. The cavalry fights on January 26–28 culminating in the January 27 engagement at Fair Garden took place south of the French Broad River and on US411 between Newport and Sevierville.

DRIVING TOUR—*Proceed to Bull's Gap (Blue Springs)*
READING *(chronological)—sinking of the USS* Housatonic:
Charleston Harbor, South Carolina

BLUE SPRINGS

Maj. Gen. Ambrose E. Burnside, commander of the Department of the Ohio, undertook an expedition into East Tennessee to clear the roads and passes to Virginia, and, if possible, secure the lead and saltworks beyond Abingdon. In late September 1863, Confederate Brig. Gen. John S. "Cerro Gordo" Williams, with his 1,500-man cavalry force, set out to disrupt Union communications. He wished to take Bull's Gap on the East Tennessee & Virginia Railroad. Williams first drove Federal cavalry from Jonesboro, Tennessee, on September 29, then met Brig. Gen. Samuel P. Carter's Union horse soldiers at Blue Springs, midway between Bull's Gap and Greeneville on October 3.

Carter, not knowing how many of the enemy he faced, withdrew. Carter and Williams skirmished for the next few days. On October 10, Carter approached Blue Springs in force. Williams had received some reinforcements. The battle began about ten A.M. with Union cavalry engaging the Confederates until afternoon while another mounted force attempted to place itself in a position to cut off a Rebel retreat. Capt. Orlando M. Poe, the chief engineer, performed a reconnaissance to identify the best location for making an infantry attack. At three-thirty P.M., Brig. Gen. Edward Ferrero's 1st Division, IX Army Corps, moved up to attack, which he did at five P.M. Ferrero's men broke the Confederate line, causing heavy casualties, and advanced almost to the enemy's rear before being checked by a battery of 4 cannons and 4 Williams Rapid-Fire Guns (a carriage-mounted breech-loading artillery piece capable of firing 20 one-pounder shells per minute when working properly; invented by Kentuckian R. S. Williams, no relation to the Confederate commander). After dark, the Confederates withdrew and the Federals took up the pursuit in the morning. Within days, Williams and his men had retired to Virginia.

BULL'S GAP

Some thirteen months later, in November 1864, Confederate Maj. Gen. John C. Breckinridge undertook an expedition into East Tennessee, anticipating that Southern sympathizers would bolster his force and help drive the Yankees from the area. The Federals initially retired in the face of this advance and, on November 10, were at Bull's Gap on the East Tennessee & Virginia Railroad. The Confederates attacked them on the morning of November 11 but were repulsed. Artillery fire continued throughout the day. The next morning, both sides attacked; the Confederates sought to strike the Union forces in the flanks but made little headway. The next day firing occurred throughout the day, but the Confederates did not assault the Union lines because they were redeploying to flank them on the right. Before making the flank attack, the Union forces, short on everything from ammunition to rations, withdrew from Bull's Gap during the night. Breckinridge pursued, but the Federals received reinforcements and foul weather played havoc with the roads and streams. Breckinridge, with most of his force, then abandoned the expedition and returned to southwest Virginia.

Points of Interest

Bulls (Bull's) Gap is located on US11E/TN34, 3 miles north of I-81 exit 23. Historical markers between Bulls Gap and Greeneville describe the Blue Springs skirmishes and battle and identify traces of earthworks. At Russellville, 8 miles west of Bulls Gap, a historical marker in front of a house across the street from the post office calls attention that the dwelling served as Longstreet's headquarters as his corps camped in the area during the winter of 1863–64.

DRIVING TOUR—*Proceed to Greeneville*
READING—*Wauhatchie and Brown's Ferry*

GREENEVILLE

Greeneville, Tennessee, was the home of Andrew Johnson, the former tailor and East Tennessee politician who was appointed military governor of Tennessee in 1862, after Federal victories placed much of the state in Union control. It was also the location of the death of Confederate Brig. Gen. John Hunt Morgan, the dashing and daring cavalry leader whose raids through the region vexed Yankee commanders for more than three years.

On September 3, 1864, a Federal cavalry force under Brig. Gen. Alvan C. Gillem, who had had several run-ins with Morgan before, tracked Morgan's raiders to Greeneville. Morgan had been battling Federal forces raiding the saltworks in southwest Virginia. Morgan was sleeping in the upstairs bedroom of Mrs. Catherine Williams, a wealthy widow, when the Union cavalry, tipped off by local Unionists, entered Greeneville in the early-morning hours of September 4 in search of the Rebel cavalry chief. Alerted, Morgan leapt out an upstairs window and was gunned down by Federal trooper Andrew G. Campbell of the 13th Tennessee Cavalry, who discovered him in a grape arbor behind the hotel. The Federals allowed local citizens to recover and dress Morgan's body, which was soon returned to his widow in Shelbyville, Tennessee, and later his remains were taken to Lexington, Kentucky, for reinterment.

Points of Interest

The Andrew Johnson National Historic Site in Greeneville includes Johnson's restored home and tailor shop and a national cemetery, where Johnson is buried. The visitor center for the site is at the corner of Depot and College streets, one block east of Main Street. The other sites are within walking distance of the visitor center. Call 615-638-3551 for more information. Also in Greeneville on the courthouse lawn are a Grand Army of the Republic Union Monument and the Morgan Monument. The restored Dickson-Williams Home in the center of Greeneville is where Morgan's body was taken after he was shot and killed nearby.

⸺⸻✠⸻⸺

DRIVING TOUR—*Proceed to Blountville*
READING *(chronological)*—*Second Cabin Creek, Oklahoma*

⸺⸻✠⸻⸺

BLOUNTVILLE

In September 1863, Confederate forces under Department of East Tennessee commander Maj. Gen. Samuel Jones attempted to counter the Federal occupation of East Tennessee by Maj. Gen. Ambrose E. Burnside. The Confederates wanted to retain the East Tennessee & Virginia Railroad, a priority of Burnside, and the two sides skirmished at Blountville and Carter's Depot on the railroad for several days. On September 22, the Confederates invited attack at Blountville as a Federal cavalry brigade under Col. John W. Foster crossed the Watauga River. Despite being lured into attacking a prepared Confederate position defended by Col. James E. Carter, the Union force drove them from the town. An artillery duel during the four-hour fight fired several Blountville homes. Too weak to oppose

Burnside's force in the area, the Rebels withdrew to Zollicoffer and the Federals tightened, for the time, their hold on the railroad.

Federal cavalry again skirmished with the Rebels at Blountville on October 13, 1863, as the Confederates of Jones's command completed their withdrawal into Virginia after again unsuccessfully challenging Burnside's efforts to occupy the region.

Points of Interest

Blountville is located on TN37, just south of US81 exit 69. The only points of interest in the town are a monument on the courthouse lawn to Sullivan County soldiers and a historical marker describing the September 22, 1863, battle. Unless you are proceeding northeast on I-81 to southwest Virginia, Blountville is far removed from other Tennessee sites. If you go to Blountville, continue the tour by taking US11W west to Bean Station. On the way at Rogersville, which was Longstreet's camp immediately after his abandonment of the Knoxville siege, there is the Hale Street Inn, established in 1824, which is still a hotel. It was a Union headquarters during the war and the building across the street from it was occupied by the Confederates when they held the town. Historical markers in Rogersville also describe a November 6, 1863, engagement at Big Creek, 2 miles east where the Confederates bested the Yankees; and, in front of Lyons Hospital, the birthplace of Confederate general Alexander P. Stewart.

DRIVING TOUR—*Proceed to Bean Station (Bean's Station)*
READING—*Blue Springs*

BEAN'S STATION

Lt. Gen. James Longstreet abandoned the Siege of Knoxville, on December 4, 1863, and retreated northeast toward Rogersville. Union Maj. Gen. John G. Parke pursued the Confederates but not too closely. Longstreet continued to Rutledge on December 6 and Rogersville on December 9. Parke sent Brig. Gen. J. M. Shackelford ahead with 4,000 cavalry and infantry to search for Longstreet.

On December 13, Shackelford was near Bean's Station on the Holston River. Longstreet decided to countermarch and hammer his pursuers. Three Confederate columns and artillery approached Bean's Station to catch the Yankees in a vise. By two A.M. on December 14, one column was skirmishing with Union pickets. The pickets held out as best they could and warned Shackelford of the Confederate presence. He deployed his force for an assault. Soon, the battle started and continued throughout the day. Rebel flanking attacks occurred, but the Federals held until Rebel reinforcements tipped the scales. By nightfall, the Federals retreated from Bean's Station through Bean's Gap and on the Blain's Cross Roads. Longstreet set out to attack the Yankees again the next morning, but as he approached them at Blain's Cross Roads, he found them well entrenched. Longstreet withdrew and the Federals soon left the area. The Knoxville Campaign ended following the Battle of Bean's Station. Longstreet soon went into winter quarters at Russellville. Except for some minor skirmishes at the end of the month and in early January, Longstreet's corps remained secure in its camps until ordered back to Virginia in mid-April 1864. The Federals maintained control of Knoxville until the end of hostilities.

Points of Interest

Bean's Station, now Bean Station, is located on US11W at TN32. The retreat of Longstreet's forces and the Federal pursuit followed a route that US11 now approximates, from Knoxville through Rutledge and north to Rogersville. Three miles west of Bean Station US11W intersects with US25E, which continues north to Cumberland Gap.

DRIVING TOUR—*Proceed to Cumberland Gap*
READING—*Mossy Creek–Dandridge*

CUMBERLAND GAP

Cumberland Gap was the natural gateway to Kentucky used by Indians and settlers—especially after Daniel Boone and his companions laid out the Wilderness Trail in the 1770s—for generations. In the Civil War, Cumberland Gap was contested, but its importance was not as significant as first thought because other gaps to the west enabled troops to bypass its garrison. The Confederates seized the gap after Kentucky's neutrality was violated in September 1861. They held and fortified it until June 18, 1862, when Federals under Brig. Gen. George W. Morgan, passing through Rogers and Big Creek gaps, threatened to envelop the garrison, compelling the Confederates to evacuate the flawed stronghold. The Federal occupation lasted only three months. Maj. Gen. Edmund Kirby Smith's mid-August 1862 invasion of Kentucky took him

A cannon at Fort Lyon in the Cumberland Gap National Historical Park. The gap was long a pioneer route into the rich lands of Kentucky. Before that, Native Americans crossed the natural portal. Considered a key passage for Civil War armies, it was stoutly defended at times by both Yanks and Rebels. The major campaigns in Kentucky and East Tennessee, however, bypassed Cumberland Gap.

west of Cumberland Gap through Big Creek Gap, on to victory in the Battle of Richmond, and deep into the bluegrass country. Confronted by Confederates to his front and with Smith's army deep in his rear, General Morgan and his 10,000 men evacuated Cumberland Gap on September 17. Badgered by pursuing Confederates, Morgan's command in sixteen days retreated 219 miles across the rugged Cumberland Mountains of eastern Kentucky, crossing the Ohio at Greenup on October 3.

Maj. Gen. Ambrose E. Burnside's Army of the Ohio in mid-1863 began its advance south from Camp Nelson through Kentucky with the objective of capturing Knoxville. Burnside sent a division under Col. John F. DeCourcy by way of the "Wilderness Road" to occupy the attention of the Confederates holding Cumberland Gap while he marched the rest of his army in three columns to the west, bypassing the gap. DeCourcy failed to initiate an attack against the Rebel brigade under Brig. Gen. John W. Frazer holding Cumberland Gap. Burnside then ordered Brig. Gen. James M. Shackelford's cavalry to approach the gap from the south via Powell River. Shackelford arrived on September 7, invested the gap on the Tennessee side, and demanded surrender. Frazer, ensconced behind strong defenses, having received orders to hold out at all costs despite the Rebel evacuation of Knoxville, refused.

For forty-eight hours the Confederates held out against the Federal forces pressing them from both sides of the gap. Burnside, impatient for a closure, accompanied a fast-marching brigade of infantry from Knoxville to Cumberland Gap, and in the presence of overwhelming odds Frazer, on September 9, surrendered unconditionally his garrison numbering 2,500 officers and men and 12 cannons. The Federals held the gap for the remainder of the war.

Points of Interest

Cumberland Gap National Historical Park—Located on US25E, Cumberland Gap marks where three states, Kentucky, Virginia, and Tennessee, share a border. The national park includes more than 20,000 acres of these three states. Most of the park's interpretive features focus on cultural history highlighting the role of the gap in the Wilderness Road and the migrations of Native Americans and white settlers through the area. There, however, are pristine examples of the defensive works thrown up by both Northern and Southern soldiers. Among these are Fort McCook and Fort Lyon, which can be accessed on a driving tour of the park. Other earthworks are on short hiking trails and the Pinnacle Overlook gives a magnificent view of the area.

A wonderful view of the gap is available from US25E just before entering it. The visitor center, open daily except December 25, is on the Kentucky side of the park and features exhibits and information on interpretive programs. The park offers a variety of recreational facilities. CUMBERLAND GAP NATIONAL HISTORICAL PARK, P.O. Box 1848, Middlesboro, KY 40965; 606-248-2817. ⚅ ▲ ◂ ▦ ♿ 🚶 ❓ P ⛱ 🚻

Just south of Cumberland Gap NHP in Harrogate, Tennessee, is the Lincoln Memorial University and The Abraham Lincoln Museum. For more information on the museum, call 615-869-6354; FAX 615-869-6350.

***

DRIVING TOUR—*Proceed to Columbia*
READING—*Blountville*

COLUMBIA

When Gen. John Bell Hood and the Army of Tennessee departed Florence, Alabama, on November 21, 1864, the underfed, ill-supplied force of 38,000 was full of hope. For Hood, the vision of a decisive offensive to defeat the still scattered Federal forces in Tennessee, push on to Nashville and perhaps beyond, and compel Maj. Gen. William T. Sherman to abandon his march through Georgia to come after the Rebels was in keeping with his desire to emulate the daring campaigns of his idol, the late Stonewall Jackson. For the men, with many Tennesseans among them, it was a chance to go home and to avenge the series of bitter defeats the army had suffered.

Hood's army crossed into the state in three columns, each consisting of a corps that, from west to east, was under the command of Maj. Gen. Benjamin F. Cheatham, Lt. Gen. Stephen D. Lee, and Lt. Gen. Alexander P. Stewart. Maj. Gen. Nathan B. Forrest's cavalry, whose return from the raid on Johnsonville caused a delay in Hood's departure (see **Johnsonville**), reinforced by William H. "Red" Jackson's division, rode in front of the infantry. At this time, Maj. Gen. John Schofield commanded two Federal corps, the IV and the XXIII, more than 22,000 strong, at Pulaski in south central Middle Tennessee. The reorganized Union cavalry, under Brig. Gen. James H. "Harry" Wilson, who had served under U. S. Grant at Vicksburg and in the Virginia "Overland Campaign," and under Philip Sheridan in the Shenandoah Valley, discovered the Confederate march when they began skirmishing with Forrest's horsemen on November 22 at Lawrenceburg, Tennessee.

At stake was the important crossroads at Columbia, where the railroad and turnpike to Nashville crossed Duck River. Hood's three corps were converging to march on Columbia from the southwest while, on November 22, Schofield began marching his five divisions, artillery, and wagons due north to Columbia. Schofield arrived at Columbia on November 24, just ahead of Forrest's cavalry. The Federal vanguard dug entrenchments south of Duck River while skirmishing with Forrest's horse soldiers, on November 24 and 25. Hood's infantry closed in on November 26 but did not assault. On the night of November 27–28, Schofield's army withdrew to the north bank of the river. Having been bested in the race for Columbia by the Northerners, Hood pinned Schofield's force in position by skirmishing and firing artillery shells across the river while Forrest's Confederate cavalry rode east to search for upstream crossings.

A location was found for laying the Rebel pontoon bridge at Davis's Ford, three miles east of Columbia, and Hood ordered most of his army north, hoping to get behind Schofield at Spring Hill and cut him off from his escape route to Nashville. Two divisions of Lee's corps with most of the artillery remained in Columbia south of Duck River to occupy Schofield's attention. Without confirmed knowledge of Hood's plan but aware that Rebels were crossing the river, Schofield dispatched an infantry force, his reserve artillery, and a wagon train ahead to Spring Hill. Hood's flanking march, which was undertaken on a poor road, was confirmed by the morning of November 29 and by midday the remainder of Schofield's two corps—less the rear guard—were on the Franklin Pike en route to Spring Hill.

Points of Interest

Columbia, home of U.S. President James K. Polk, is located 49 miles southwest of Nashville at the intersection of US31, US43, and US412 and is 9 miles west of I-65. At Ashwood, on US43, 7 miles southwest of Columbia, there is a historical marker for the November 24, 1864, fight between Forrest's cavalry and the Federal horsemen of Col. Horace Capron. Forrest drove Capron back to Columbia while screening the advance of Stewart's infantry corps. At Columbia's city limits on US31, a historical marker describes the three-day standoff in the city. At the northeast corner of 7th and Garden streets is the site of the Masonic Lodge where on June 13, 1863, Lt. Wills Gould shot Brig. Gen. N. B. Forrest. Just off the northeast corner of the square on North Main, across from the police station, is the Nelson House where Gould died after being knifed by Forrest. The Athenaeum at 808 Athenaeum Street is an antebellum structure that served as headquarters of Brig. Gen. John S. Negley and Maj. Gen. John M. Schofield. Several antebellum homes, including one with the unusual name Rattle and Snap, have been restored and are open for touring. At Ashwood, St. John's Episcopal Church, built in 1842, is reportedly Tennessee's last remaining plantation church and the initial burial place for Maj. Gen. Patrick R. Cleburne. Civil War soldiers are buried in Columbia's Rose Hill Cemetery and the churchyard of Zion Presbyterian Church.

DRIVING TOUR and READING—*Proceed to Spring Hill*

SPRING HILL

One of the greatest leadership blunders to befall the ill-fated Confederate Army of Tennessee, which saw more than its share of mismanagement, was the escape of Maj. Gen. John M. Schofield's two-corps army at Spring Hill, Tennessee, on November 29, 1864. Gen. John B. Hood had sent the division of Maj. Gen. Patrick Cleburne ahead to Spring Hill in the van of his flanking march around Schofield's position north of Duck River. Cleburne's attack, and a previous mounted attack from the east along the Mount Carmel Road by Forrest's cavalry, were checked by a defensive line thrown up covering the approaches to the village by Federal Maj. Gen. David S. Stanley. Stanley was rushed ahead to Spring Hill to augment the small garrison there, and his lead brigade under Col. Emerson Opdycke arrived in time to repulse Forrest, who, having bested and then outfoxed Harry Wilson, had headed west on Mount Carmel Road. Stanley then positioned his troops northeast and southeast of Spring Hill, protecting the wagon train, reserve artillery, and railroad west of the village. Another Union force guarded the Rutherford Creek crossing of the Columbia–Spring Hill Road.

Hood was on hand for the advance of Cleburne's division, which upon encountering resistance altered the axis of its advance, but soon retired from the field to set up headquarters at the Absalom Thompson Home south of Spring Hill. As the rest of Maj. Gen. Benjamin F. Cheatham's Confederates arrived near Spring Hill, they were formed into a line of battle on Cleburne's right and left but an assault was never launched against the smaller Yankee infantry force and vulnerable artillery and trains parked nearby. Confusing orders and countermanded orders emanated from Hood's headquarters, while Cheatham focused his attention on the assault that never came. Stewart's corps arrived well after Hood had expected them on the field, then got lost while deploying.

By the time Schofield's remaining divisions were approaching Spring Hill, the Confederates of Cheatham's and Stewart's corps were preparing rations and preparing to bed down for the night. Stephen D. Lee's corps, having crossed Duck River, was still on the march from Columbia. In Hood's defense, a fall from his horse added to the chronic pain he felt from his previous battle wounds that had withered his left arm and cost him his right leg at the hip, and exhaustion and painkillers clouded his judgment. Inaction and obstinacy among subordinates enhanced the chances for missing the opportunity to cut off and maul or destroy Schofield. Even the usually reliable Forrest failed to sustain his Franklin Pike roadblock north of Spring Hill as Hood believed he was doing.

Frustration was felt by some Confederate pickets who detected the sound of Schofield's column passing north through Spring Hill on the moonless night of November 29. Some Federals accidentally stumbled into Confederate camps and were captured or allowed to leave again. No attack orders were issued to the Rebels, although an order to investigate reports of the Yankee march which Hood supposedly issued to Cheatham may or may not have reached the veteran commander. As a result, Hood and the rest of the Army of Tennessee awoke the next morning to discover the Yankees were well on their way to Franklin.

Points of Interest

Spring Hill is located on US31, 8 miles south of Franklin and 15 miles north of Columbia. A number of private residences in the town are extant which were landmarks during the Civil War. Most of these are located along or near US31, including Rippavilla, the home of Confederate Maj. Nathaniel Cheairs, a short distance south of the town on US31, which is now being restored by the Maury County Historical Society. An angry and disappointed John Bell Hood and his senior officers breakfasted there before riding to Franklin on the morning of November 30. On Main Street in Spring Hill are the Martin Cheairs House and the McKissack House. The former was a headquarters of Confederate general Earl Van Dorn in May 1863, as was "White Hall," the home of Dr. Aaron White on Duplex Road. The Martin Cheairs House is now part of the Tennessee Orphans Home. Van Dorn was killed in the Martin Cheairs House May 7, 1863, by Dr. George Bodley Peters for having amorous relations with the doctor's wife, Jessie McKissack Peters. General Schofield stopped briefly at the McKissack House while traveling through Spring Hill during the Federals' silent march on the night of November 29.

Tennessee State Historical Markers call attention to the Absalom Thompson House, (Hood's headquarters) and the Ewell Farm, the last home of Confederate Lt. Gen. Richard S. Ewell. The APCWS has taken the lead in purchasing several hundred acres of land east of US31, south of Spring Hill, across which Cleburne's division engaged Brig. Gen. Luther Bradley's bluecoats.

DRIVING TOUR and READING—*Proceed to Franklin*

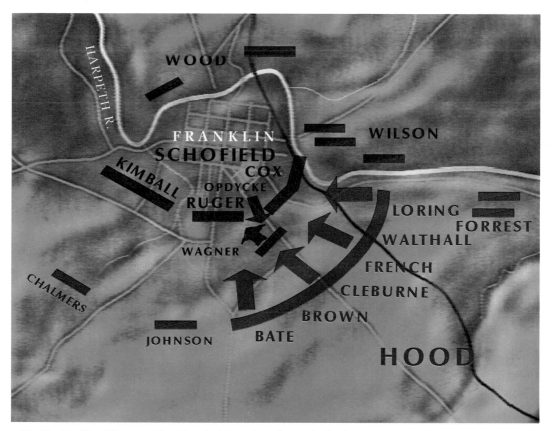

The Battle of Franklin was a short but decisive action, the result of a desperate attempt by Confederate general John Bell Hood to redeem his missed opportunity when he allowed Maj. Gen. John M. Schofield's two-corps Union force to escape at Spring Hill, Tennessee. As a result, Hood did what he promised his men at the beginning of the campaign that he would not do; he ordered a frontal assault against the hastily built but well-defended Federal entrenchments at Franklin. The result was a futile attack that consumed more Southern casualties than any other single Confederate charge in the war.

FRANKLIN

On the morning of November 30, 1864, Maj. Gen. John M. Schofield determined to make a defensive stand at Franklin, twenty miles south of Nashville. The problems of getting his trains and artillery across Big Harpeth River on Franklin's northern edge compelled him to turn and fight the Confederates whom his army had slipped past at Spring Hill during the previous night. Upon arriving at Franklin in the early daylight, Schofield determined to utilize the works thrown up by Union forces in the spring of 1863 when Maj. Gen. W. S. Rosecrans determined to position his left flank at Franklin. These fortifications, covering the approaches to the town from the south, were anchored on the Big Harpeth up and downstream from Franklin. General Hood, disgusted with the Confederate failure to trap and destroy Schofield's army at Spring Hill, which he blamed on subordinate commanders and the defensive-minded timidity instilled in the rank and file by Gen. Joseph E. Johnston, decided to launch a frontal attack against Schofield's Franklin fortified position.

Although most of his artillery and one of his three infantry corps were not yet on the field, Hood ordered the assault by 23,000 soldiers at four P.M., in the waning hours of an Indian summer's day. Schofield had two brigades under Brig. Gen. George D. Wagner in an advanced position along the Columbia Pike. Waves of Confederate soldiers streamed down from the knobs south of Franklin and routed Wagner's people. Raising the cry "Into the works with them!" the Rebels surged ahead hard on the heels of Wagner's men keeping the rest of the 20,000 entrenched Federals from firing until the Confederates were on top of them. The fire of the two-corps Federal line was deadly; still many Rebels crossed the line of entrenchments. A savage counterattack by Col. Emerson Opdycke's "Tigers," stationed in reserve north of the Carter House prevented a breakthrough. Opdycke plugged a gap in the Federal line and with soldiers of Ruger's and Reilly's divisions to the right and left held off portions of four attacking Rebel divisions.

Forrest, with one of his three cavalry divisions that had forded the river upstream, clashed with Wilson's cavalry inconclusively. The flanks of the Federal line were never seriously threatened and the principal fighting ranged in front of the Union defenses anchored on the left by the Big Harpeth and on the right at the locust grove 250 yards west of the Carter House.

The battle lasted well into the night and when it was over, the Rebels in the Army of Tennessee proved their mettle—Schofield withdrew north. But the price was high. The Confederates suffered more casualties than had Ulysses S. Grant at Cold Harbor on June 3, 1864, or the Army of Northern Virginia during the Pickett-Pettigrew charge at Gettysburg. Five Southern generals were killed, including the talented Patrick Cleburne, and one other died later; five were wounded and one was captured. The total Confederate casualties were more than 7,000; the Union lost 2,326.

Points of Interest

Although Franklin is a small city, its growth, particularly during the last forty years, has impacted much of the battlefield, though several historical markers describe the battle and some landmarks remain. Chief among these are the Carter House and Carnton Plantation. The Carter House was at the center of the Federal line, where Col. Emerson

The Carnton Plantation in Franklin is located southeast of the community in the area from which the Confederate attack began; after the battle it was used as a hospital. The bodies of four slain Confederate generals were laid out on the rear veranda of the house where survivors of the charge came to mourn their fallen leaders.

Opdycke's brigade counterattacked and with reinforcements held off human waves of Confederate assaults. The Carter House and the grounds around it are currently part of a Tennessee state historic site and National Historic Landmark, which features a video tour, Battlerama, artifacts, and tours of the house and grounds. Nearby on Columbia Avenue, historical markers identify key locations of the attack. A fee is charged. THE CARTER HOUSE, 1140 Columbia Avenue, Franklin, TN 37064; 615-791-1861.
✽ ♿ ❓ 🏛 💲

Carnton Plantation was built in 1826 by Randal McGavock. On the porch of the restored mansion, the bodies of four of the five Confederate generals killed in the Battle of Franklin—Patrick Cleburne, Hiram Granbury, O. F. Stahl, and John Adams—were laid out after the fighting stopped. Col. John McGavock, Randal's son, returned after the war and established a Confederate cemetery on the property. The cemetery contains the remains of 1,500 Confederates killed in the battle. The house and property are open for tours. There is a fee and a visitor facility. HISTORIC CARNTON PLANTATION, 1345 Carnton Lane, Franklin, TN 37064; 615-794-0903. ♿ ❓ 💲

Across Columbia Pike from the Carter House, the Lotz House was also in the midst of the fighting. Opdycke's men charged through the yard of the two-story home on their way to stem the Confederate advance. After the battle, wounded soldiers in blue and gray received care in the mansion. It has been restored and houses a museum of Civil War and Old West artifacts. THE LOTZ HOUSE MUSEUM, 1111 Columbia Avenue, Franklin, Tennessee 37064; 615-791-6533.

Other Civil War points of interest in Franklin include the Harrison House on US31, 3.5 miles south, in which Hood held his final staff meeting before the battle and where mortally wounded Confederate Brig. Gen. John H. Kelly was brought on September 2, 1864, and probably died on September 4 from wounds received on Maj. Gen. Joseph Wheeler's August–September 1864 raid; a marker indicating the site of the home of Confederate naval commander Matthew Fontaine Maury, US431 north of Franklin; St. Paul's Episcopal Church, which was used as a barracks and hospital; Fort Granger, the largest Union earthwork, at Franklin constructed in 1863, site of General Schofield's command post during the Battle of Franklin and the hanging of Lt. Col. W. Orton Williams and Lt. W. G. Peter, kin of Gen. Robert E. Lee, by Union forces on June 9, 1863; and Winstead's Hill, 2 miles south on US31, from which Hood and his staff observed the November 30 attack. Fort Granger has been restored and is open to the public. The Sons of Veterans' Winstead's Hill wayside provides an excellent overview of the battlefield and features a memorial honoring General Cleburne.

DRIVING TOUR and READING—*Proceed to Nashville*

NASHVILLE

Despite staggering losses at Franklin, which reduced his effective force to a little more than 23,000, Gen. John Bell Hood marched the Army of Tennessee to the doorstep to Nashville. Even the aggressive Hood realized that a frontal assault on the Federals was futile. Union forces had occupied Nashville for thirty-three months, since shortly after the surrender of Fort Donelson, and it was one of the most fortified cities in the nation. Union engineer, Brig. Gen. James St. Clair Morton, had overseen construction of sophisticated earthworks at Nashville in 1862–63, strengthened by others, into which Union troops deployed. With Schofield's force joining his own after retreating from Franklin, Maj. Gen. George H. Thomas had more than 50,000 defenders in Nashville and had had ample time to perfect the city's defenses. Hood hoped to lure Thomas into attacking him and, after repelling that assault, to counterattack. Hood hoped for reinforcements from the Trans-Mississippi, but this was a bad dream because they could not pass Federal gunboats, which patrolled the Mississippi River. Hood took up a defensive position on the knobs two miles south of Nashville: a five-mile line extending from the Nashville & Chattanooga Railroad in the east to the Hillsboro Pike in the west. An understrength infantry brigade and Brig. Gen. James R. Chalmers's cavalry division watched the four-mile gap between the Hillsboro Pike and the Cumberland River.

During the first eight days of December, the Confederates held their positions, but Thomas was in no hurry to attack. His well-known ponderous style unnerved the Washington leadership, who viewed Hood's threat as they had Jubal Early's early July advance to the gates of the nation's capital. At City Point, Virginia, Lt. Gen. U. S. Grant was also concerned. Uncharacteristically, he became unnerved after a series of telegrams to "Old Slow Trot" failed to move the Nashville commander. Grant, not fully understanding the desperate condition of Hood's army, feared the Confederates would bypass Nashville and invade Kentucky wreaking havoc, just as the Northern public was beginning to see the war was finally coming to a successful conclusion.

Just as Thomas was ready to attack on December 8, a severe winter sleet and snow storm paralyzed troop movements, and he postponed his battle plan. By the evening of December 14 when the weather had moderated and the ice had melted and Thomas telegraphed the War Department that he would attack the next day, Grant had lost his nerve and had left City Point and was en route to Washington. From there he would travel west to relieve Thomas, replacing him with Maj. Gen. John A. Logan.

Thomas saw flaws in the Confederate plan. The Rebels held the four primary roads approaching Nashville from the south, but their lines were too extended. Hood ordered the construction of five detached redoubts on his left flank covering approaches to the Hillsboro Pike, held by A. P. Stewart's corps, but they were not connected by rifle pits and were vulnerable themselves. Hoping to lure Thomas into leaving his fortifications, Hood ordered Forrest's cavalry to capture blockhouses guarding the Nashville & Chattanooga Railroad and to attack the Federal garrison at Murfreesboro ensconced in Fortress Rosecrans. Thomas did not take the bait, feeling the Fortress Rosecrans garrison could handle the situation. The most severe consequence of this order was for the Confederates, who were without Forrest and most of the Southern troopers needed to guard the flanks of their Nashville investment line. A few remaining Rebel horsemen did spar with Union gunboats on the Cumberland River downstream from Nashville, which had a low water level at the time. The Yankee gunboats could not effectively return the fire of two ten-pounder Parrott rifles Lt. Col. David C. Kelley's men manned on shore. The Confederates blockaded the river and captured two Federal transports which the Yankees subsequently recaptured.

On December 15, as Grant was in Washington preparing to leave for Tennessee, Thomas attacked with the speed of lightning and the force of thunder, though the offensive, at first had a different character. A heavy fog delayed the start, then the mostly African-American units of Maj. Gen. James B. Steedman's Chattanooga garrison, assigned to a diversionary attack on the Rebel right, met with stout resistance from hard-drinking, hard-fighting Maj. Gen. B. Frank Cheatham's Confederates. West of Nashville, Wilson's cavalry and Maj. Gen. A. J. Smith's "10,000 Israelites," advancing via the Hardin Pike, brushed aside small numbers of Confederates, and, executing a left wheel, closed on the Confederates posted in the five redoubts anchoring Hood's left on the Hillsboro Pike. Brig. Gen. Thomas J. Wood's IV Corps at noon, with Smith's "Israelites" approaching the Hillsboro redoubts, in the center advanced and seized Montgomery Hill now lightly defended following Hood's decision to concentrate his forces on defense of a line of works farther south thrown up on December 10.

By the afternoon, the situation began to change. Spurred on by competition from Maj. Gen. A. J. "Whiskey" Smith's "Israelites," recently arrived from Missouri, Brig. Gen. Edward Hatch's dismounted cavalry charged the westernmost redoubt, No. 5. The Yankee troopers and Smith's infantry charged the hilltop redoubt in parallel lines and the few defenders were routed. The capture of Redoubt No. 5 led to the other redoubts falling like dominos, as other Federal brigades of Smith's command and Wood's divisions joined in the attack. Hood was unable to redeploy soldiers of Lee's corps from his center in time to prevent the collapse of Stewart's front. Maj. Gen. Edward C. Walthall's hard-fighting division tried to hold their ground, but the numbers in their front were overwhelming. By dusk, the Confederate left had given way.

Several senior Federal officers that night expected the rout of Hood's left to signal a Confederate retreat. General Schofield, however, correctly predicted that his former West

Point classmate had not abandoned the field. Dawn proved him right. Hood had formed a shorter line, his left anchored on a steep unnamed knob and his right on Overton Hill about a mile and a half south of his December 15 line. Thomas wasted no time in ordering a follow-up to the previous day's success. Again, the focus was on the Confederate left. On the Federal left, another diversionary attack went forward against Overton Hill, defended by S. D. Lee's corps. In this action the 13th U.S. Colored Troops displayed extraordinary valor in battling abatis and other obstacles to gain a toehold near the Southern line, but the Confederates in this sector stood tall and repulsed the charges of Steedman's division and Abel Streight's and P. Sidney Post's brigades.

On the Federal right, subordinates dawdled and it fell upon the commander of A. J. Smith's first division, Brig. Gen. John McArthur to take the initiative as the day wore on and a light rain set in. McArthur was a distinguished fighter in western Federal campaigns since Shiloh but his independent style, like that of his superior, "Whiskey" Smith, prevented him from gaining a higher command. At four P.M. on December 16, McArthur ordered his men to storm the knob anchoring the western flank of the Rebel line. Shy's Hill, as it became known after the battle (for Confederate Col. William Shy, killed in its defense), proved to be less of an obstacle than the other Federal commanders expected. Observing the charge of McArthur's men, Thomas ordered his right wing to advance. The result was a rout. Though many of the Rebels fought gamely, they could not sustain the pressure, and the badly defeated army headed south down the Franklin Road, the one escape route through the Brentwood Hills still open.

The disintegration of the Army of Tennessee came on that rainy afternoon of December 16. Many Rebels surrendered, others dropped their arms and fled. The shattered remains of Hood's army with losses in the campaign reducing their number to one third of that which started north from Florence, Alabama, were pursued by Wilson's Federal cavalry and Wood's IV Corps. Bedford Forrest, aided by a picked infantry force led by General Walthall, fought several successful rear-guard actions as the Confederate force bowed out of Tennessee, reentered Alabama, crossed the Tennessee River at Bainbridge, Alabama, on December 26–28, and ended their flight in Tupelo, Mississippi, in early January 1865.

Grant, learning on the evening of December 15, of the victory at Nashville, returned to Virginia and sent a congratulatory telegram to Thomas: "The armies operating in the vicinity of Petersburg have fired two hundred guns in honor of your great victory."

Points of Interest

A number of historical markers for the Battle of Nashville are scattered throughout the metropolitan area. The best guide to the sites is a self-guided driving tour published jointly by the Tennessee Historical Society and Metropolitan Historical Commission. It can be obtained from the Metropolitan Historical Commission, 400 South Broadway, Suite 200, Nashville, TN 37203, 615-862-7970, or from the Tennessee State Museum, across from the Civil War–era State Capitol, also worth a visit. The state museum has a large Civil War collection. Nearby at Fifth Avenue and Church Street is the Downtown Presbyterian Church, which was used as a Federal hospital. Its spires can been seen in Civil War–era photographs. St. Mary's Catholic Church, built in 1844, at Charlotte Street and Fifth Avenue, also served as a hospital, while the Federals used the Church of the Holy Trinity, Sixth Avenue at Lafayette Street, as a Federal powder magazine and butcher shop. This church received postwar reparations from the U.S. government.

Fort Negley at Chestnut Street and Ridley Boulevard is the largest of the Nashville forts. Reconstructed under the Emergency Conservation Program in the 1930s, the massive earth and stone structure is being restored as a city park and interpretive center. Fort Negley was manned by the 13th USCT before and during the battle. On Franklin Pike near the I-440 overcrossing is the beautiful Battle of Nashville Peace Monument. Pull into the parking lot of the apartment complex west of the pike for a better view. Redoubt No. 4, the Shy's Hill earthworks, Overton (Peach Orchard) Hill, and a stone wall used by soldiers of Stewart's corps as they desperately tried to hold off the Federal assault on December 16 can be located by following the driving tour given in the pamphlet referenced above, or one appearing in a *Blue & Gray Magazine* issue on the Battle of Nashville (see **Bibliography**). Shy's Hill is on public property and can be accessed by a trailhead located on Benton Smith Road.

Civil War cemeteries in Nashville include the national cemetery with its Minnesota memorial on US31E and Mount Olivet Cemetery on US70N southeast of Nashville. Buried in Old City Cemetery on Fourth Street near Fort Negley are Confederate generals Richard Ewell, Bushrod Johnson, and Felix Zollicoffer.

Sunnyside is a building located in Sevier Park (Twelfth and Kirkwood avenues). The antebellum mansion was in the middle of the first day's fighting and still shows battle scars. Woodlawn, on Woodmont Avenue near Harding Road, served as Brig. Gen. James H. Wilson's headquarters for a time. Belle Meade, on US70S (West End Avenue) was headquarters for Forrest's subordinate, Brig. Gen. James R. Chalmers. Tours of this house can be arranged; admission is charged. Traveler's Rest, 6.5 miles south of the center of Nashville just off US31 (Franklin Pike), was Hood's headquarters during the battle. Part of the Battle for Overton Hill, located just to the north, was fought on the grounds of this estate. At Brentwood, 9 miles south of Nashville on the Franklin Road (US31), a historical marker identifies a beautiful mansion which served as Hood's headquarters during the northward Confederate march to Nashville.

North of Nashville at Gallatin, US31E/TN25, Col. John Hunt Morgan captured a 200-man Federal garrison on August 12, 1862, and then destroyed the railroad bridge south of town and a tunnel 6 miles north of Gallatin. Morgan had previously raided Gallatin on March 16 and captured a garrison and supply train. There is a historical marker on US31E and a Confederate monument at the Trousdale Mansion.

DRIVING TOUR—*Proceed to Kentucky*
READING—*Petersburg Assault, Virginia*

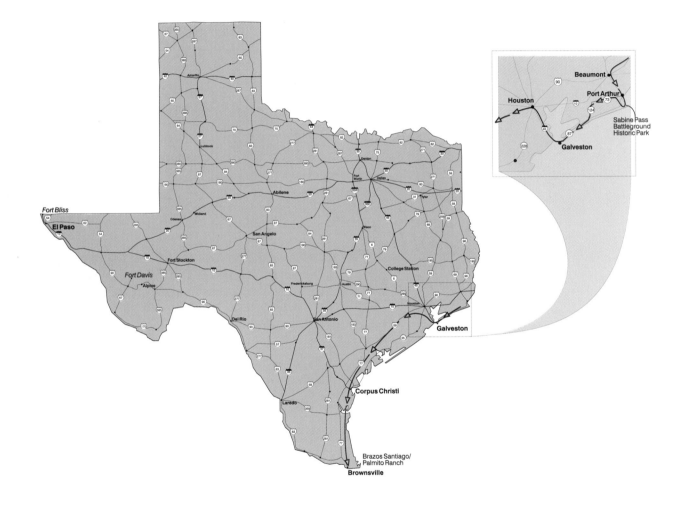

Texas

Texas, the largest state geographically in the Confederacy, had more impact on the Southern war effort as a source of manpower and matériel than as a battle zone. Yet from the 1861 staging area for the Confederate invasion of New Mexico from El Paso, then called Franklin, to the last recorded land action of the war, the Lone Star State was the scene of some interesting and unique small-scale battles in the years 1862, 1863, and 1865. The Federals held only small coastal enclaves of the state and generally for only brief periods. The most ambitious campaign for the invasion of Texas by the North, the Red River Campaign in 1864, never quite reached the state (see **Red River Campaign, Louisiana**).

In addition to the actions described below in which blood was shed, two other Federal campaigns into Texas were mounted. Like Sabine Pass, Galveston, and Corpus Christi, Union occupation in these exercises was brief. The first occurred in August 1862, when the California Column under Brig. Gen. James H. Carleton entered the extreme western part of Texas from New Mexico. Carleton's three companies of the 1st California Cavalry occupied El Paso and captured, then paroled, a few wounded Confederate soldiers and surgeons at Fort Bliss. Detachments from the main force then rode east and, on August 22, occupied abandoned Fort Quitman and reconnoitered as far east as Fort Davis. By the end of the month, feeling as the Confederates had that the dusty, arid plains and mountains of West Texas were not worth being held in the face of hostile Indians, the Californians in September withdrew to New Mexico. Although Texans talked about raising new expeditions to ride through West Texas and descend on New Mexico again, none was ever mounted.

The other virtually bloodless Federal incursion into Texas occurred in the fall of 1863. Concerned with the mid-summer occupation of Mexico City by French troops and rumors of intrigues, the Lincoln administration was anxious to reestablish Federal control along the lower Rio Grande. Not only did this policy lead to the cancellation by the

War Department of Grant's second request for an advance to capture Mobile, Alabama, in favor of a Federal approach to Sabine Pass, but it also led to an amphibious landing on Texas's southern coast. On November 2, 1863, a 3,500-man division led by Maj. Gen. Napoleon Jackson Tecumseh Dana and accompanied by Department of the Gulf commander Maj. Gen. Nathaniel P. Banks (for history of Banks's Gulf Department leadership see **Galveston**) landed at Brazos Santiago, at the mouth of the Rio Grande. Four days later Brownsville was occupied, closing the lower Rio Grande to international trade.

The Federals proceeded north by water from camps on Brazos Island to Mustang Island, near Corpus Christi. On November 17, aided by fire from the USS *Monongahela,* they captured the Confederate battery guarding the entrance to Aransas Pass. Their next target was Fort Esperanza protecting Pass Cavallo and the entrance to Matagorda Bay, which they laid siege to and overwhelmed on November 29. In December the Federals landed on the Matagorda Peninsula and occupied Indianola. But Banks, after determining that the Confederates had marshaled a formidable force at Velasco guarding the Brazos River approach to Galveston, was satisfied in having secured the coastal enclaves established to that point and returned to New Orleans. In June 1864 the Union withdrew its troops from the Matagorda Peninsula and in July further reduced its manpower on the Texas Gulf Coast by evacuating Brownsville.

The Lone Star State continued to resist Federal inroads and defy the blockade until June 2, 1865, when Gen. Edmund Kirby Smith accepted the terms of a May 26 agreement drawn up in New Orleans. The agreement called for the surrender of Confederate forces in Kirby Smith's Trans-Mississippi Department at Galveston.

SABINE PASS

The strategic inlet of Sabine Pass was of interest to Federal leaders searching for a gateway to the interior of Texas. The Sabine River, which discharges into the Gulf of Mexico, was a direct route to the rich cotton fields of northeast Texas. Three times Federal attacks on the pass yielded little, and twice the incursions came to grief.

On September 24–25, 1862, three Federal vessels of the West Gulf Blockading Squadron commanded by Acting Master Frederick Crocker bombarded the Confederate fort protecting the entrance to Sabine Pass, called Fort Sabine. The Rebel gunners spiked their guns, then buried them in the sand and fled inland. A landing party from the Union warships captured Sabine City, burned Wingate's Sawmill, and destroyed the railroad bridge to Beaumont over Taylor's Bayou. Without a supporting army force, however, the Federal sailors, fearing the presence of yellow fever, returned to their vessels on September 29, though they continued to blockade the entrance to the pass.

The area was quiet until January 1863, when daring Confederate naval attacks down the coast inspired the officers and men of 2 cottonclad gunboats, the CSS *Josiah Bell* and the CSS *Uncle Ben,* to engage and capture 2 blockading gunboats, the USS *Morning Light* and the USS *Velocity,* in a surprise attack on January 21. This action briefly lifted the blockade of Sabine Pass. The Confederates then began to strengthen defenses in the area and build a new fort upriver from Fort Sabine, designated Fort Griffin, after the commander of the forces in the area. In April 1863, Federal navy personnel in the area, led by Cmdr. Abner Read, used the abandoned Sabine Lighthouse, on the Louisiana side of the river, to observe the Confederate buildup. Read planned to attack the Rebel force, but these plans were dashed when the Southerners became aware of what was planned. On April 18, the Texans surprised Read's landing party, wounding Read and capturing and killing 8.

In August 1863, General-in-Chief Henry W. Halleck again pushed for Federal action in the area. A joint army-navy expedition was planned—four gunboats and twenty transports led by recently promoted Lt. Frederick Crocker, who had commanded the September 1862 incursion into Sabine Pass and had captured Sabine City; and 5,000 troops under the command of Maj. Gen. William B. Franklin. The gunboats crossed the bar into the river on September 8. The Confeder-

A monument to the defenders of Fort Griffin at Sabine Pass Battleground State Historic Park features a bare-chested Dick Dowling holding a spyglass in one hand and a torch to ignite artillery fuses in the other.

ates were aware of the impending attack, and Maj. Gen. John B. Magruder, the overall commander in Texas, ordered the fort abandoned.

No senior Confederate officer was at Fort Griffin on September 8, but Jr. Lt. Richard Dowling and the 46 Irish dockworkers in his command, the Davis Guard, were spoiling for a fight. They waited at their guns while the Federal gunboats pounded the rail-iron-reinforced earthworks. Then, when the closest U.S. Navy ships were within 1,200 yards, Dowling unleashed an artillery barrage that crippled 2 gunboats, the USS *Sachem* and the USS *Clifton.* The disabled *Sachem* was snared by the CSS *Uncle Ben* and USS *Clifton,* badly pummeled and with Crocker aboard, surrendered to Dick Dowling and his men. The USS *Arizona* picked up survivors and backed down the channel. A hysterical junior officer in command of the fourth gunboat, the USS *Granite City,* convinced Franklin that Rebel reinforcements were arriving, and Franklin canceled the troop landing.

Jefferson Davis called the battle at Fort Griffin the "Thermopylae of the Civil War." Without losing a man, Dowling's command caused 100 Federal casualties, captured 2 ships, and took 350 prisoners. The Confederate Congress thanked Dowling's force and ordered a special medal to be struck for the garrison, the only one given to Southern soldiers in the war. The action, along with the Confederate victory at Chickamauga (see **Chickamauga, Georgia**) dampened expectations in the North and abroad that the war would be over by New Year's Day, 1864.

Points of Interest
A 56-acre state park commemorates the location of Fort Griffin and the battle that took place there. From I-10 proceed south through Port Arthur via TX87 to the city of Sabine Pass. At the intersection of TX87 and Texas Farm Road (FM) 3322 stands a monument to Dick Dowling. Take FM3322 south for 1.5 miles to the entrance to Sabine Pass Battleground State Historical Park. A monument, topped by a handsome sculpture of Dick Dowling, commemorates the battle. On a clear day, across the channel on the Louisiana shore, you can see Sabine Lighthouse, built in 1856 and used by the U.S. Navy's Abner Read and his scouting party.

The park is open for daylight use only. Popular activities include fishing and picnicking; the park also has a boat ramp. Nearby Sea Rim State Park has campsites. For more information, contact Park Superintendent, SABINE PASS BATTLEGROUND/SEA RIM STATE PARK, P.O. Box 1066, Sabine Pass, TX 77655; 409 971 2451.

🛶 🐟 ❷ P ⛱

DRIVING TOUR—*Proceed to Galveston*
READING *(chronological)*—*1862 battle: Newtonia, Missouri;*
1863 battle: Chickamauga, Georgia

GALVESTON

One of the objectives of the new Department of the Gulf commander, Maj. Gen. Nathaniel Banks, in the autumn of 1862 was an incursion into Texas. While not a primary objective in the overall scheme that President Lincoln's War Department had planned for Banks, the Massachusetts political general delayed his departure up the Mississippi to reoccupy Baton Rouge while awaiting reinforcements and heavier artillery. So Texas took center stage in late December for political and economic interests. Prodding Banks to action were two factions: Texas Unionists led by Brig. Gen. Andrew Jackson Hamilton, designated to be military governor of the state by the U.S. government, and New Englanders interested in curing the current cotton shortage in the Northeast by colonizing and revitalizing Texas's vast cotton-growing lands.

The Federal navy had seized the harbor on October 5. On November 29, Maj. Gen. John B. Magruder had arrived in Houston from Virginia and assumed command of the Confederate District of Texas, New Mexico, and Arizona. By the time Banks dispatched troops to occupy the important port of Galveston on December 22, 1862, Confederate countermeasures had been planned. Magruder had created a 2-boat fleet of cottonclad gunboats and organized a force of 500 grim fighting men, including Col. Tom Green's survivors from Sibley's ill-fated New Mexico expedition (see **New Mexico**).

Banks's vanguard—three companies of the 42nd Massachusetts Volunteers—landed at Galveston on December 24 and barricaded the wharf area. The U.S. Navy presence in the harbor consisted of 5 gunboats from the West Gulf Blockading Squadron. Early on January 1, 1863, Magruder's land force crossed an unguarded bridge from the mainland but was stymied by the Federal defenses. Then the 2 Confederate cottonclads went into action. After a rough start, in which the Rebel cottonclad *Neptune* sank in six feet of water, Rebel marines from the *Bayou City* boarded and captured the *Harriet Lane*, while USS *Westfield* ran aground and was destroyed by her captain. The other three Federal gunboats first surrendered, then fled. With no naval support, the small Union garrison surrendered. The Union loss in casualties and prisoners was more than 300 soldiers and sailors, 15 cannons, *Harriet Lane*, and the *Westfield*, as well as the support vessels. The Southerners lost just 27 killed and 177 wounded in recapturing Galveston and 3 regaining possession of the bay.

Magruder's bold strike caused R. Adm. David G. Farragut to send six gunboats and the USS *Brooklyn*, a formidable screw steamer, from Mobile to Galveston. It also killed the colonization plan for Texas for a time. The Rebels, however, were not finished punishing the Federal navy. On January 11, the *Brooklyn* and her consorts spotted a Rebel merchantman approaching Galveston harbor. The USS *Hatteras* was sent to investigate the suspicious ship, which failed to make a run for the open sea. No mere merchantman, this was CSS *Alabama*, under the command of Capt. Raphael Semmes. Semmes had approached the bay, unaware of the Confederate recapture of Galveston, in anticipation of attacking and dispersing Banks's fleet of transports, which a captured Boston newspaper had told him were heading for Texas. Upon being sighted by the Union ships, Semmes headed back out to sea. His tactic was to decoy the Yankees into close range before identifying his ship. His parting shot was the sinking of the *Hatteras* with a shocking broadside, even though the *Alabama* was outgunned by her victim 10 guns to 8. After plucking 118 survivors out of the water, Semmes swiftly departed, en route to Jamaica, before the *Brooklyn* and the other gunboats reached the area. (See **Confederate Cruisers** in **International**.)

The *Harriet Lane* was converted to a blockade-runner. She escaped Galveston, ending up in Habana, while other runners continued to use the port of Galveston throughout the war, despite the tightening blockade. The last ship sunk by the Federal blockading force was a notoriously fast British vessel, the *Denbigh*. She was destroyed on May 24, 1865.

Points of Interest

A free ferry operated by the state of Texas connects Galveston with Port Bolivar across the bay (TX87). The land action centered around the wharf area of Galveston. The most notable part of the city is the restored nineteenth-century wharf area called The Strand. Hendley Row, a large brick warehouse here, had a cupola, not extant, which was used as an observation post by Union and Confederate observers at various times.

Across a small inlet is Pelican Island, where the *Westfield* ran aground and was blown up. Seawolf Park is located on the island.

DRIVING TOUR—*Proceed to Corpus Christi*
READING *(chronological)—Stones River, Tennessee*

CORPUS CHRISTI

In early 1862, shortly after the Federal blockade had tightened along the Texas coast, an ambitious Yankee sailor, Acting Lt. John W. Kittredge, captain of a blockader, the USS *Arthur,* was patrolling along the central coast of Texas, north of Corpus Christi. Not content with the long odds of capturing blockade-runners in the open sea, he wanted to get into the harbors and confront them there. He initiated a series of landings along the coast, starting with a landing on St. Joseph Island on April 22, 1862.

By August 1862, Kittredge had increased the size of his force to 5 vessels and was determined to attack Corpus Christi. Maj. A. M. Hobby, leader of the small Confederate force there, prepared for attack by readying some Mexican War artillery and a handful of infantry. On August 13, Kittredge employed the gunboat USS *Sachem* to remove obstacles placed in the channel; he then entered Corpus Christi Bay. He captured 1 vessel—the CSS *Breaker*—then, landing under a flag of truce, demanded the surrender of the town within twenty-four hours.

By August 16, after delaying his ultimatum but receiving no surrender, Kittredge was surprised when artillery—6 Rebel guns dug into the beach—fired on his ships. The Federal ships moved out of range without sustaining any serious damage; however, their fire proved fruitless against the Confederate sand batteries. After a day of relative quiet, Kittredge early on the morning of August 18 ordered a party of 30 U.S. sailors, armed with a twelve-pounder rifled boat howitzer, to land on the beach and attack the Confederate flank. Despite being supported by naval gunfire, the party was beaten back in a Rebel counterattack that included cavalry. Kittredge then withdrew his force from the bay. A month later, on September 14, Kittredge was captured while landing down the bay in a raid on a place called Flour Bluff. After a month in a San Antonio prison, he was paroled. He would not attempt to capture Corpus Christi again.

In an unrelated action, German settlers in the hill country near San Antonio opposed Confederate conscription and sought to escape across the Rio Grande. On August 13, 1862, they were attacked by Rebel soldiers as they were fording the Neuces River near Fort Clark.

Points of Interest

In Corpus Christi, the Centennial House, built in 1849, served as a Confederate Hospital. It is located at 411 North Broadway. Across the street, at 401 North Broadway, is a historical marker indicating the location of the Kinney Stockade, where the Confederate guns defending the city were situated before being moved to the beach. In the downtown area are a Confederate Memorial and Memorial Fountain. Nearby, the Merriman House, open for tours, is a Greek Revival house used as a hospital during the Civil War. Old Bayview and Banquete cemeteries contain the graves of Confederate soldiers.

Take TX361 north to Mustang Island State Park, the area where General Banks's November 1863 expedition captured a Rebel fort, and continue to Port Aransas, where Kittredge made landings before his attack on Corpus Christi. Historical markers tell of the importance of Aransas Pass in blockade-running and point out the restored, privately owned Aransas Pass Light Station, built in 1855 and sabotaged by the Union sailors who landed there. They stole the lens and buried it in the sand nearby to shut down the lighthouse and disrupt blockade-running traffic.

At Comfort, US87 and I-10, 52 miles northwest of San Antonio, a monument near the high school commemorates the August 13, 1862, Rebel attack on German settlers.

DRIVING TOUR—*Proceed to Palmito Ranch*
READING—*Sabine Pass*

PALMITO RANCH

The last land engagement of the Civil War occurred in the Texas-Mexico border area within sight of the Rio Grande, near Brownsville. Confederates under the command of Col. John S. Ford routed a Federal force after a two-day running battle, May 12–13, 1865. The Rebels, although victorious in the battle, were among those troops surrendered by the military convention in New Orleans. They consequently surrendered to their captives after this battle, which is also known as the Battle of Palmito Hill.

Points of Interest

A historical marker 12 miles east of Brownsville on TX4 denotes the action. Also, north of Brownsville is the newly created Palo Alto Battlefield National Historic Site—where the first major battle in the Mexican War occurred, on May 8, 1846. Many a Civil War general got his first combat experience in the Mexican War, including the campaign which began here. For more information on this developing park, which is open daily, contact the superintendent from 8:00 A.M. to 4:30 P.M. Monday through Friday. PALO ALTO BATTLEFIELD NATIONAL HISTORIC SITE, 1623 Central Boulevard, Suite 213, Brownsville, TX 78520; 210-541-2785.

The Port Isabel Lighthouse, begun in 1851, at Port Isabel State Historic Park, was used as an observation post by both Confederate and Federal forces. The park is located 24 miles north of Brownsville on TX48.

DRIVING TOUR—*Proceed to West Texas and New Mexico*
READING—*surrenders: Doaksville, Oklahoma*

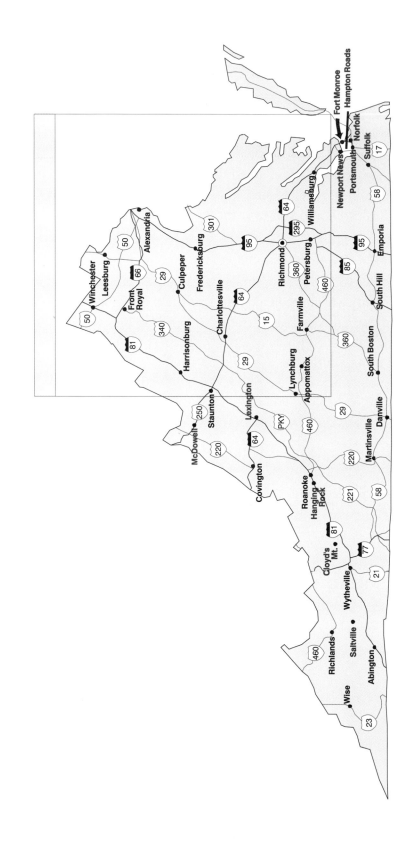

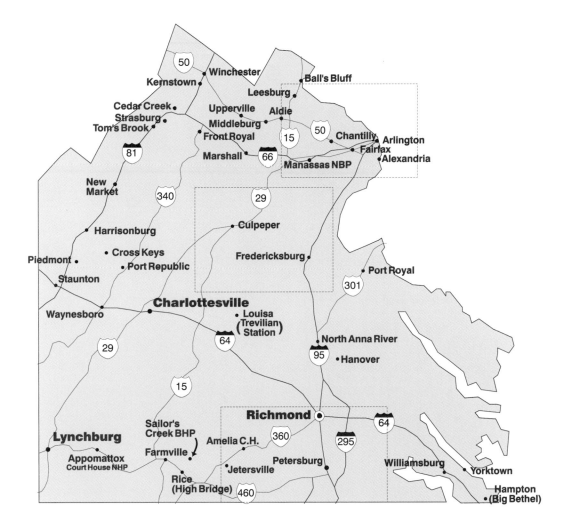

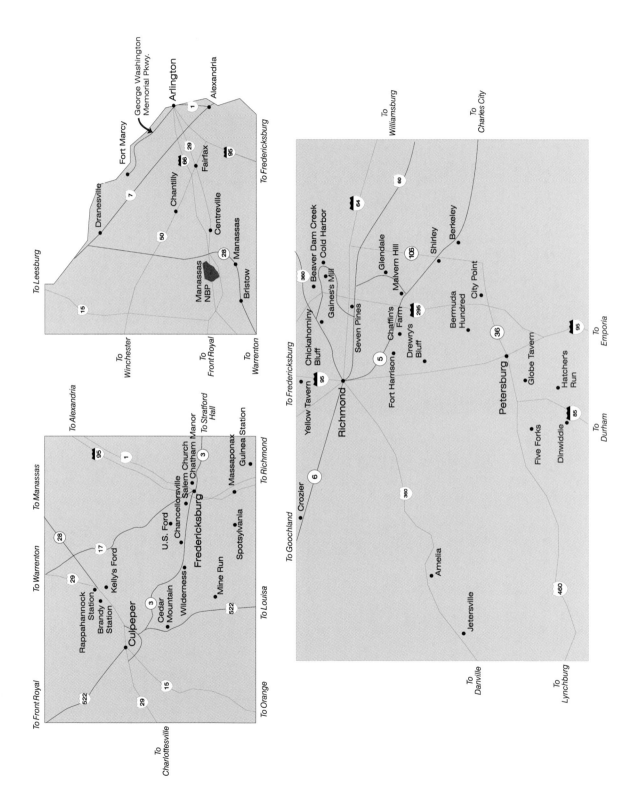

Virginia

I f there is a town or battle that immediately comes to mind, in even the most casual student of the Civil War, it is probably Gettysburg. If there is a state, it is definitely Virginia. More battles, skirmishes, raids, and actions occurred in the Old Dominion State than in any other. Virginia sent sixty-three infantry regiments, twenty-three cavalry regiments, and a number of artillerists, sailors, and marines to fight for the Southern cause. Richmond served as the Confederate capital from May 29, 1861, to April 3, 1865. Virginia also contributed the most general officers to the Confederate army.

The constant presence of the armies of Gens. P.G.T. Beauregard, Joseph E. Johnston, and finally, from June 1, 1862, until the end at Appomattox Court House, Robert E. Lee, kept the Federal leadership in Washington on edge, and the large armies of the eastern theater occupied. It is hard to imagine how the Confederacy would have lasted for more than a few months without Virginia's manpower, materials, and military leadership, as well as her political and geographic presence. She didn't do this immediately though—it was not until after the firing on Fort Sumter that the Virginia Convention seriously debated secession. As late as April 18, 1861, Francis Blair, Sr., confidant of presidents beginning with Andrew Jackson, was meeting with Robert E. Lee in the Blair House in Washington to offer him command of the Federal forces assembled in and around the District of Columbia.

A tour of Virginia can take a week or more. You might divide the exploration of Virginia's battlefields and historic sites into several trips, perhaps seasonal journeys to, say, the Shenandoah Valley and western Virginia in the autumn, the peninsula and Richmond-Petersburg in the spring, and the Washington, D.C., and central areas in the summer. Sections of Virginia can also be covered in tours of neighboring states.

Suggested stops are the Washington, D.C., area, particularly historic Alexandria; Fredericksburg; the Culpeper area; the lower Shenandoah Valley from Winchester to New Market; the Lexington or Lynchburg area; the Richmond-Petersburg area; and the

Williamsburg-Yorktown-Norfolk area. All of these places have historic accommodations, many bed-and-breakfast inns that have Civil War interest, fine dining, camping opportunities, and a number of family recreational activities. Virginia also has more than a few antique and artifact shops and flea markets which have authentic and reproduction items of Civil War vintage.

WASHINGTON, D.C., AREA

Arlington

Though nothing beyond minor skirmishes occurred on the hills directly across the Potomac from Washington—the Federal army occupied the area in May 1861—Arlington served as a camp and training ground for the Union army during the Civil War. The county took its name from Arlington House, the Custis-Lee mansion that stands at the top of a hill overlooking the Potomac. It was Robert E. Lee's pre-war home, built by the father of Lee's wife, and was taken over by the Federal army and used as a headquarters building shortly after Lee vacated it upon resigning his U.S. Army commission and following his state into the Confederacy.

Fort Ward was one of the forts constructed in Federal-occupied Virginia for the defense of Washington. The heavy artillery pieces that the reconstructed fort features are typical of those these forts mounted.

Points of Interest

Arlington National Cemetery—Established in 1864, the nation's largest military cemetery contains the graves of many Civil War soldiers, sailors, and marines, including noted officers David Dixon Porter, George Crook, Philip H. Sheridan, and Philip Kearny. Arlington House, in the cemetery, is the nation's Robert E. Lee Memorial, containing many Lee artifacts and exhibits.

Fort Marcy on the George Washington Memorial Parkway and Fort C.

F. Smith in Rosslyn are two of the better-preserved earthen forts from the Washington defense line. Fort Myer, also in the system, is the only one currently in use as a US Army facility. It was formed from several forts and batteries on the west side of Arlington Hill.

***

DRIVING TOUR— *Proceed to Alexandria*
READING— *Washington fortifications: The Defense of Washington, The District of Columbia*

***

Alexandria

The largest city in northeast Virginia when the Civil War broke out was Alexandria. It was an important port on the Potomac River and has much tradition beginning in its colonial period. The first celebrated death of the Civil War occurred in Alexandria when Col. Elmer Ellsworth, a friend of Abraham Lincoln's and leader of a Zouave Militia unit—the 11th New York—made up primarily of New York City firemen, took his unit to occupy Alexandria. Seeing a secession flag atop the Marshall House hotel he personally went to the garret and tore it down. On the way downstairs, he was shot by the hotel's proprietor who was in turn killed by one of Ellsworth's men.

From May 24, 1861, Alexandria served as a major supply and transportation center for the Federal army. From Alexandria, the only railroads into northern Virginia linked with the Potomac wharves and the railroad to Washington.

Points of Interest

Alexandria has numerous points of historical interest including those associated with Robert E. Lee, who lived in Alexandria as a youth. Several of the Washington defense forts are marked with historical markers and there is a national cemetery in Alexandria. The Marshall House was located at 480 King Street. The site is now occupied by a modern Holiday Inn hotel which has a plaque on the west wall pertaining to the Marshall House.

Fort Ward Museum and Historic Site—This city of Alexandria park features one of the larger forts in the Washington defenses, partly original and partly reconstructed, with heavy artillery pieces in place. The museum has a number of exhibits including one on the Washington Defense System. There is no admission charge and picnicking is permitted in the park. FORT WARD MUSEUM AND HISTORIC SITE, 4301 W. Braddock Road, Alexandria, VA 22304; 703-838-4848.   ♿ ❷ 🏛 P 🚻

DRIVING TOUR—*Proceed to Dranesville and Fairfax*
READING *(chronological)*—*Philippi, West Virginia*

Dranesville

On December 20, 1861, an engagement in Dranesville resulted from contact between a Confederate foraging party guarded by a task force led by flamboyant Brig. Gen. J.E.B. Stuart and a Union column headed by Brig. Gen. Edward O. C. Ord. Stuart attacked the Union force to protect his foragers but was repulsed. Reinforced, he returned the next day to pick up his dead and wounded.

Fairfax

One of the earliest land actions of the war, more an exchange of shots than a battle, occurred at the courthouse here on June 1, 1861. Fairfax Court House, now Fairfax, was a stop on the route of Brig. Gen. Irvin McDowell's forces on their July 1861 southwest march to attack the Confederates at Manassas. After the rout of the Federals at First Manassas, Col. J.E.B. Stuart led his 1st Virginia Cavalry to Fairfax and made camp on Munson's Hill. Stuart monitored Federal movements and created a defense line of "Quaker Guns"—tree trunks disguised to look like cannons, to overawe Union observers. Stuart evacuated the position on September 28, 1861.

Lt. Col. John S. Mosby, in command of an independent group of Virginia partisan rangers, began to build a fearsome reputation among Union officers and men when he captured Brig. Gen. Edwin H. Stoughton from his bed in Fairfax Court House on March 8, 1863.

Points of Interest

On VA7 at Dranesville there is a historical marker for the Battle of Dranesville. On the lawn of the Fairfax courthouse are several monuments and the part of the building facing VA236 is the original courthouse which was used as a headquarters. Just south of the courthouse a historical marker on VA123 identifies the William Presley Gunnell House, now the vestry house for Truro Parish Episcopal Rectory, where Mosby captured General Stoughton.

Southeast of Fairfax at the intersection of Burke Lake Road (VA645) and Burke Road (VA652), a historical marker indicates the site of Burke's Station. During his Christmas 1862 cavalry raid, J.E.B. Stuart used the Union military telegraph here to complain about the poor quality of Federal mules that Stuart was appropriating from the Northern army on his raid. This is one of the best-known humorous incidents of the war and a testament to Stuart's dash and daring. Also at Burke Station is St. Mary's Catholic Church, used as a Union hospital during the Second Manassas Campaign and the place where Clara Barton first nursed and comforted wounded soldiers.

DRIVING TOUR—*Proceed to Chantilly*
READING *(chronological)—First Manassas*

Chantilly

Moving quickly to capitalize on his Second Manassas victory, Gen. Robert E. Lee sent Stonewall Jackson and his force north on August 31. Maj. Gen. John Pope had organized an effective rear guard on September 1, 1862, at Ox Hill, near Chantilly, approximately halfway between the Manassas battlefield and Washington, and in a severe thunderstorm the Federals stood firm in this fiercely contested battle. Two Union generals, Maj. Gen. Philip Kearny and Brig. Gen. Isaac Stevens, were killed in the action. Pope's army took advantage of the check given the Confederates in this brief but bloody stand-up fight, and reached the safety of Washington's defenses.

Nevertheless, General Lee's accomplishments in his first three months of command were tremendous. He had carried the war from five miles outside of Richmond to twenty miles from the Union capital. All this occurred in nine action-filled weeks. And his force of stolid veterans, to be known from the summer of 1862 forward as the Army of Northern Virginia, established a fighting reputation second to none.

Points of Interest

A small Fairfax County park on Ox Hill Road just south of US50 commemorates the Battle of Chantilly. There are monuments to Generals Kearny and Stevens. The rest of the hilly battlefield has been developed with housing tracts and office complexes. The park helps to capture the spirit of the fierce fight that took place there that thunderstorm-punctured September afternoon.

DRIVING TOUR—*Proceed to Centreville-Manassas*
READING—*Frederick, Maryland*

FIRST MANASSAS

In July 1861, the first major offensive operation of the Civil War got under way. The Washington area secured by the influx of volunteers, and most of them two thirds or more of the way through their service commitment, the Federal leadership saw the need to begin a campaign to conclude the "ninety-day" war. Richmond, the Confederate capital one hundred miles to the south, was the objective as was the Confederate force under the command of Brig. Gen. P.G.T. Beauregard, standing in the way. Beauregard formed his force of 22,000 inexperienced and ill-equipped soldiers into a six-mile line along Bull Run, protecting the important railroad junction at Manassas.

Leading the Federal army was Brig. Gen. Irvin McDowell, a protégé of the aging Maj. Gen. Winfield Scott, general-in-chief of the army, who was too infirm to take the field, and powerful Secretary of the Treasury Salmon P. Chase. McDowell had 35,000 men divided into five divisions under five older officers, but none had led the number of troops into battle before that they now controlled. In fact, there had never been an army this large operating in North America. Political pressure compelled McDowell to begin his march south before he felt prepared to move his ninety-day soldiers. The Federals advanced from camps around Washington on July 16 and reached Fairfax Court House midday on July 17.

A key necessity of the campaign was for the Federal commander who had crossed the Potomac and seized Harpers Ferry in early July (see **Harpers Ferry, West Virginia**), Maj. Gen. Robert Patterson, to keep the Rebel forces in the lower Shenandoah Valley occupied to prevent their commander, Brig. Gen. Joseph E. Johnston, from sending units to rein-

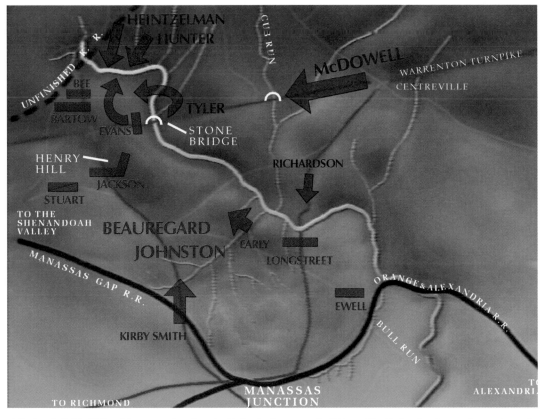

The battlefield of First Manassas showing the Federal advance to Bull Run. The Federals advanced west through Centreville and paused briefly. Brig. Gen. Irvin McDowell sent a force ahead under Brig. Gen. Daniel Tyler, a brigade of which under Col. Israel B. Richardson engaged the Confederates under Brig. Gen. James Longstreet in an unproductive fight on July 18 at Blackburn's Ford. Early on the morning of July 21, McDowell sent most of his force on a flanking march to the north to cross Bull Run at Sudley Springs. Tyler demonstrated at the Stone Bridge, but unconvincingly, leading Col. Nathan Evans to shift his force soon reinforced by the brigades of Brig. Gen. Bernard E. Bee and Col. Francis S. Bartow to meet the Federal advance from the north. The Federal advance slowed when it reached Henry Hill and the Confederate line held by Stonewall Jackson's Virginians, allowing Beauregard and Johnston to reinforce their army with units arriving from several directions. The rout began in mid-afternoon, and the Union soldiers began a hasty retreat over the Stone Bridge and other crossings to Centreville and then back to Washington.

force Beauregard. In this Patterson failed. Johnston left a cavalry screen at Winchester which fooled Patterson badly and on July 18 marched his force to Piedmont (now Delaplane) to shuttle them via the Manassas Gap Railroad to reinforce Beauregard. Although inadequate rail rolling stock and a derailment delayed the rail movement, the arrival of Johnston's soldiers from the Valley command raised Confederate strength at Manassas to nearly that of the Federals.

Meanwhile, the Federal vanguard pushed ahead to Centreville, which the Confederates had evacuated, and McDowell ordered their commander, Brig. Gen. Daniel Tyler, to probe the area for Confederate positions. Tyler's advance on July 18 met with resistance at Blackburn's Ford. Though he had been ordered by McDowell not to engage the enemy, Tyler ordered his artillery unlimbered and Confederate artillery from across Bull Run replied. Concealed Rebel troops under the command of Brig. Gen. James Longstreet gave a few Union regiments their first taste of combat as they approached the stream. McDowell arrived and ordered Tyler to disengage. During the artillery duel a Federal shell crashed harmlessly into the chimney of a house where McDowell's West Point class-mate P.G.T. Beauregard was having dinner.

McDowell then spent two more days reconnoitering and formulating a battle plan. During this time, Johnston's troops began arriving at Manassas Junction. McDowell decided to launch a demonstration against the Stone Bridge, which carried the Warrenton Turn-pike over Bull Run, and employ two divisions to flank the Confederate line to the north, crossing at Sudley Springs. Before dawn on Sunday, July 21, on what would prove to be a hot and dusty day, the Federal force started out. The advance moved along slowly as artillery accompanied the march.

The feint at the Stone Bridge by Tyler was not convincing to South Carolinian Col. Nathan G. "Shanks" Evans. He left a small force there and marched the rest of his brigade to oppose the reported Federal advance from Sudley Springs. His 1,000 men were opposed by 6,000 Federals from Col. David "Black Dave" Hunter's division at Matthews Hill. Other Rebel units arrived to reinforce Evans, but McDowell pushed more units for-ward across Sudley Ford, and Tyler's troops, having discovered a farm ford, crossed Bull River upstream from the Stone Bridge. The telling weight of the Federal advance pushed the Confederates south, and they fell back to the cover of Henry Hill, where there was a house occupied by an invalid widow, Judith Henry, who refused to leave it. On the far crest of the hill, a brigade from Johnston's force commanded by Brig. Gen. Thomas J. Jackson with supporting artillery held a firm line. Seeing Jackson and his force, Brig. Gen. Barnard Bee shouted a command to his retreating brigade, "Look! There is Jackson standing like a stone wall! Rally behind the Virginians!"

Though Bee was mortally wounded shortly after uttering his legend-making exclamation, his troops and the rest of the forces retreating from Matthews Hill formed behind and alongside Jackson's unwavering line. Johnston, directing reinforcements, and Beauregard, controlling the battle line, managed to bring up enough reinforcements to maintain their

Henry Hill position. McDowell unleashed a rain of artillery fire but the Federal guns were overwhelmed by a Confederate counterattack, and before the fighting on the hill ended were recaptured and captured four more times. One of the unique elements of this battle—called First Bull Run by the North, First Manassas by the South—was the variety of styles and colors of uniforms worn by the units of both sides; many were attired in their state militia garb. Two Henry Hill Federal cannons on occasion were taken by bluecoated Southerners, mistakenly identified by the artillery commander as infantry reinforcements.

Brig. Gen. Thomas J. Jackson in command of Virginia forces that arrived at Manassas from the Shenandoah Valley and formed a defense line on Henry Hill. Jackson's stand became the rallying point for Confederate soldiers as they fell back before the early Federal advances and was the focus of the battle for much of the day. Jackson's command of this line that stabilized the Rebel position and allowed them to later gain victory on the field earned him the endearing nom de guerre "Stonewall."

About four P.M., the Federal right flank began to crumble and Beauregard ordered an attack that swept the field. As the Northern soldiers were forced off Henry Hill, most recrossed at Sudley Ford and a bridge on the next stream east, Cub Run. Soldiers, wagons, limbers, and horses tangled in a cacophony of confusion. An artillery shell into the Cub Run bridge turned the retreat into a rout and officers lost all control of their rookie soldiers. When word of the impending battle had reached Washington, politicians, reporters, and spectators had ridden out for a look. They too became part of the fleeing mass as the Union soldiers backtracked to Centreville and beyond. Some Confederate units pursued the Yanks as far as Centreville, but most of the Federal force drifted back to Washington through the night.

Jefferson Davis had traveled to the field that day from Richmond and observed the final phase of the battle. When he questioned his senior commanders why a more vigorous pursuit hadn't been made, Johnston offered the president a reply which he explained later, "Our army was more disorganized in victory than the Federal army was in defeat." Casualties were light compared to later conflicts: 4,878 total casualties for both sides for nearly 71,000 engaged. Not included in this statistic was Judith Henry, mortally wounded as the battle raged around her house. Two products of the battle were a Confederate battleflag, which became more popular on the field than the Stars and Bars, which was similar to the Stars and Stripes of the Federal army. And the soon-to-be-famous "Rebel Yell" first rang out during that afternoon's counterattack.

SECOND MANASSAS

On August 28, 1862, great land forces in blue and gray were once again poised to clash on the farmland and wood lots west of Bull Run. Rather than a one-day battle, Second Manassas was a series of developing maneuvers fought by experienced veterans. The battle was brought on by Gen. Robert E. Lee, who split his force to challenge the new Federal Army of Virginia under Maj. Gen. John Pope (see **Cedar Mountain**). Lee sent Jackson and his fast-marching force to Manassas Junction to destroy Pope's main supply base and link to Washington while he advanced north separately with the slower-moving corps of James Longstreet. Having driven Maj. Gen. George B. McClellan's proud army from Richmond's gates and eventually from the Virginia peninsula, in the Seven Days' Battles and during the ensuing weeks, Lee was anxious to confront Pope before his force and McClellan's could combine.

Jackson's destruction of the Manassas Junction supply depot on August 27 brought Pope forward to "bag" Jackson as he boasted, but Jackson marched north and placed his men along an unfinished railroad grade running southwest from Sudley Springs. Pope's forces marched and countermarched in a fruitless search for Jackson on August 28 until six P.M. when the "Black Hat" brigade of Indiana and Wisconsin soldiers under Brig. Gen. John Gibbon marched northeast along the Warrenton Turnpike in front of Jackson's right flank at Brawner's Farm. Jackson attacked and the "Black Hat" brigade as reinforced put up a spirited defense. Both sides fought savagely for two hours until dark in the Battle of Brawner's Farm (also called Groveton).

The next morning Pope formed a line with his army and the first units arriving from McClellan's command. But a day spent in savage, unsupported thrusts at Jackson's position was unproductive. Maj. Gen. Joseph Hooker's division scored a momentary breakthrough that was erased by a Rebel counterattack. Late in the day, Maj. Gen. Philip Kearny's division broke through Jackson's left and drove the Confederates back to Stony Ridge, but the Southerners rallied and Pope did not exploit the advantage. The mid-afternoon arrival of the 31,000 men in Longstreet's corps extended the Confederate line one mile farther south. Maj. Gen. Fitz John Porter detected the reinforcement of Jackson's right flank but refused to attack as ordered by Pope. Pope disregarded the presence of Longstreet and directed Porter to attack again the next day.

When Pope resumed his probes on August 30, he was convinced he could finish off Jackson. Jackson's response to Porter's advance in mid-afternoon taxed his forces and he had to call on Longstreet for reinforcements. At one point part of Jackson's command, their ammunition exhausted, threw rocks at the Federal soldiers twenty yards away.

Pope sent his bluecoats into the gaping pincers of a giant claw. On the Union left, north and south of the Warrenton Turnpike, two brigades were engulfed when Longstreet launched his counterattack. Longstreet's people closed on Chinn Ridge. Pope rushed his reserves to Chinn Ridge. The Federals fought stubbornly but slowly gave ground when hammered again and again by Longstreet's repeated assaults. They did gain time enough for Pope to form another line on Henry Hill, anchored by Brig. Gen. John F. Reynolds's Pennsylvanians and Lt. Col. William Chapman's "Regulars." The Federal stand on Henry Hill, echoing Jackson's heroics more than a year earlier, bought time and as the sun set, the Federals began an orderly retreat across Bull Run's Stone Bridge.

The casualty figures for Second Manassas (Second Bull Run) were staggering when compared to the first—nearly 24,000 killed, wounded, captured, and missing. The Confederate pursuit of the Union forces marching back to Alexandria, even as more units from McClellan's Army of the Potomac arrived at Centreville to reinforce Pope, was checked on September 1 at Chantilly (see **Chantilly**). The victory gave Confederate morale a tremendous boost. On the Federal side, the battle altered the military careers of three Federal officers: Pope was sent to Minnesota to fight the Sioux; McDowell was shelved until reassigned to a desk job in California; and Porter was cashiered—he spent nearly sixteen years clearing his name.

McClellan did not escape the ire of Lincoln and others in Washington for his role in the disaster. Word circulated that "Little Mac" had mismanaged the sending of reinforcements, secretly hoping that Pope would fail at Second Manassas, paving the way for a triumphant George McClellan to step into the breach and save the day. McClellan did lead the Army of Potomac, including the forces of Pope's short-lived Army of Virginia, into battle again, but only because at that time he was, in Lincoln's opinion, the only Federal officer capable of reorganizing the dispirited soldiers, and getting them battle-ready.

Points of Interest

Manassas National Battlefield Park—The 5,000-acre park includes most of the sites associated with the two battles. The park is located on VA234 just off I-66. The visitor center, located on Henry Hill, features exhibits, a slide program, and a battle map that shows troop movements on a 3-D scale model of the battlefield. There is a walking trail of Henry Hill on which is a reconstructed Henry House, Judith Henry's grave, and an equestrian statue of Stonewall Jackson.

Audiotapes are available for driving tours of the battlefield. First Manassas landmarks include the Stone Bridge, the Stone House, the chimney and foundations of the James Robinson House (rebuilt), and Matthews Hill. Second Manassas landmarks include Brawner's Farm, the Groveton Confederate Cemetery, the Deep Cut along the Unfinished Railroad, Sudley Church, and Chinn Ridge. Two of the oldest Civil War monuments, the Groveton monument on the Deep Cut walking trail and the First Manassas monument on the Henry Hill trail, both erected in 1865, are in the park. MANASSAS NATIONAL BATTLEFIELD PARK; 703-361-1334.   🚲 🗺 ♿ 🥾 🏛 P 🪑 🚻

On US29 in Centreville, several historical markers describe Confederate fortifications erected in 1861 and early 1862, and the Federal advance to Manassas beginning on July 16, 1861.

DRIVING TOUR—*Proceed to Bristoe Station or Ball's Bluff*
READING *(chronological)*—*Carnifax Ferry, West Virginia*

BRISTOE STATION

After advancing into the Piedmont in the months after the Battle of Gettysburg, Maj. Gen. George Gordon Meade tested Robert E. Lee's line along the Rapidan River, looking for an opportunity to turn his flank. In mid-October 1863, the Federals received a scare when Lee, satisfied that Meade's Army of the Potomac had been weakened by the transfer of Maj. Gens. Oliver O. Howard's and Henry Slocum's corps to Middle Tennessee, advanced. Lee moved to place two corps between the Army of the Potomac and Washington. Though outnumbering the Confederates, the Union force backpedaled toward Washington, skirmishing heavily with the corps of Lt. Gens. Richard Ewell and A. P. Hill. But on October 14, the impetuous Hill failed to gather proper intelligence and sent two brigades into a crossfire at Bristoe Station. Hill's repulse allowed the Federals the opportunity to establish a strong position east of Bull Run near the Manassas battlefield. By October 17, Meade had reversed the flow of action. The Southerners pulled back west of the Rappahannock River as J.E.B. Stuart's cavalry covered the withdrawal (see **Buckland**).

Points of Interest

Bristoe Station (now spelled Bristow) is on VA619, 5 miles southwest of the city of Manassas. There are currently historical markers on VA28 to indicate the action that occurred parallel to the present railroad right-of-way. Six miles west of Warrenton on VA613 is a historical marker identifying the starting point of the raid on Maj. Gen. John Pope's Catlett's Station headquarters by Stuart's cavalry on August 22, 1862, in the Second Manassas Campaign.

DRIVING TOUR—*Proceed to Ball's Bluff*
READING—*Buckland*

LOUDOUN AND FAUQUIER COUNTIES

Ball's Bluff

After Maj. Gen. George B. McClellan was called to Washington in July 1861as general-in-chief of the Federal army, he concentrated on creating the Army of the Potomac. He retooled the mechanisms of administration, training, and supply and instilled a spirit of dedication and teamwork among the soldiers. While McClellan staged reviews, Washington wanted battles—and victories. So in October, McClellan, in an attempt to clear the Confederates from Leesburg and the Potomac River northwest of Washington, asked Brig. Gen. Charles P. Stone to make a demonstration across the river.

Stone assigned the brigade of Lincoln's friend and U.S. senator from Oregon, Col. Edward Baker, to the task. Perhaps unwisely, Stone gave Baker, with little military experience, too much discretion in deciding on a battle plan. Baker, in search of a victory to enhance his personal fame, crossed the Potomac on October 21 beneath sixty-foot cliffs at Ball's Bluff, near Leesburg. He lacked sufficient small craft to get his command over the river as a unit, and when the soldiers struggled up the bluffs into a small field above, the Confederates under hard-drinking Brig. Gen. Nathan G. "Shanks" Evans were waiting for them. Baker was killed and his command routed. Some of the Federals were shot while fleeing across the river, a number were drowned, and hundreds captured.

As Lincoln and official Washington grieved the death of Baker, the new joint Congressional Committee on the Conduct of the War, dominated by Radical Republicans searching for military commanders who were "soft" on slavery, fingered Stone in this second stunning Federal defeat in Virginia. Stone was given little opportunity to mount a defense and McClellan avoided involvement. The result was that Stone was imprisoned without cause for more than six months and his military career was ruined.

Points of Interest

Ball's Bluff is located on the Potomac River east of Leesburg and is accessed from US15. The battleground is a gem and is included in a 60-acre park administered by the Northern Virginia Parks Authority. There is parking, trails, interpretive markers, and a wayside exhibit. The bluffs and river area look very much as they did during the battle. On the trail is the nation's smallest (in size) national cemetery. On US15 north of Leesburg are several historical markers identifying Potomac crossings of the Armies of the Potomac and Northern Virginia.

DRIVING TOUR—*Proceed to Aldie, Loudoun Valley*
READING *(chronological)—Belmont, Missouri*

Loudoun Valley

When Robert E. Lee began his invasion of the North in June 1863, the reorganized Federal cavalry of the Army of the Potomac was enjoying its first successes in challenging Maj. Gen. J.E.B. Stuart's elite cavalry corps. Operating independently to screen (mask) the march north of Lee's infantry force, Stuart was surprised by Union horsemen at Brandy Station on June 9, and though the Federals broke off the day-long engagement, a clear message was sent to Stuart that he would no longer be able to dominate the equestrian war (see **Brandy Station**). Eight days after that great cavalry battle, in the beautiful Loudoun Valley, Maj. Gen. Alfred Pleasonton's cavalry again engaged Stuart's troopers as the horsemen in blue passed through gaps in the Bull Run Mountains and sought to gain the Blue Ridge gaps to determine the Army of Northern Virginia's intentions.

At Aldie, on June 17, Brig. Gen. H. Judson Kilpatrick's horsemen, with the 1st Massachusetts Cavalry bearing the brunt of the fight, engaged Stuart's forces. Five miles farther west at Middleburg, Col. Alfred Duffié's Federal cavalry was trapped by a portion of Stuart's command, but fought his way out with heavy losses. Stuart fell back to the west and Brig. Gen. David Gregg's horse soldiers assaulted Stuart's new position two miles west of Middleburg on June 19, forcing him to fall back on Goose Creek. On June 21, Pleasonton forced Stuart from behind Goose Creek and beyond Upperville, with cavalry under Gregg, Brig. Gen. John Buford, and infantry support. Stuart withdrew through Ashby's Gap on June 22. Though he had successfully masked the movement of Lee's force, Stuart, in an effort to reclaim his reputation which had suffered at the hands of the hard-fighting Federal troopers at Brandy Station though had been redressed in the Loudoun Valley clashes, started out on another ride around the Army of the Potomac on June 25. The Rebels soon crossed the Potomac into Maryland.

Though he had successfully ridden around the Union army twice in 1862, this ride did not achieve Stuart's ambitious expectations. The ride was challenged and it denied Lee his "eyes," as he called Stuart's cavalry, when he needed them more than ever (see **Federal 1862 Campaign Against Richmond (Peninsula Campaign), Virginia; Rockville** and **Westminster, Maryland; Chambersburg** and **Hanover, Pennsylvania**).

Points of Interest

At Aldie, 0.5 mile north of US50 on VA734 is a monument to the 1st Massachusetts Cavalry that was involved in the battle there. On US50 at Middleburg and Upperville are historical markers that describe actions that took place there. An even better illustration is found in the countryside with its roads, rock walls, old stone bridges, towns, and villages that retain a mid-nineteenth century character.

DRIVING TOUR—*Proceed to Buckland, Thoroughfare Gap, and Marshall*
READING *(chronological)—Second Winchester;*
Stuart's Cavalry: Rockville, Maryland

Thoroughfare Gap

On August 28, 1862, Maj. Gen. James Longstreet was opposed by Federal forces at Thoroughfare Gap as he marched to meet Stonewall Jackson's corps on the plains of Manassas. After a short fight, the Federals at dusk abandoned their position commanding the eastern exit from the gap, and on the morning of June 29, Longstreet's corps pushed ahead to rendezvous with Jackson's troops. The previous day, a short distance to the west of Salem (now Marshall), Gen. Robert E. Lee narrowly escaped capture after his staff opposed a dash by the 9th New York Cavalry.

Buckland

After the defeat of A. P. Hill's corps at Bristoe Station on October 14, 1863, Robert E. Lee was unable to continue his advance toward Washington, D. C. (see **Bristoe Station**). Maj. Gen. J.E.B. Stuart's troopers were asked to cover the retrograde of Lee's army as it marched southwest through Fauquier County. Stuart's defeat of one of Brig. Gen. Judson Kilpatrick's cavalry brigades near Buckland Mills on October 19, called the "Buckland Races" because of the inglorious flight of the Federal troopers east along the Warrenton Turnpike, was the final battle in this last offensive campaign of the Army of Northern Virginia.

Points of Interest

On VA55 near Marshall are several historical markers. One describes events at Rectortown, 4 miles north on VA713, where Maj. Gen. George B. McClellan was relieved of command on November 7, 1862, and replaced by Maj. Gen. Ambrose Burnside (see **Fredericksburg**). On VA211, 3 miles west of Buckland, there is a historical marker identifying the site where McClellan issued his farewell address to his army that same day. Other historical markers on VA55 between Marshall and Gainesville describe the engagement at Thoroughfare Gap, Lee's near capture, and the "Buckland Races." The Warrenton Turnpike, along which the Federal troopers fled east, is now US29. In Thoroughfare Gap at the cul-de-sac at the end of VA617 is Chapman's Mill, cockpit of Longstreet's August 28, 1862, scrap.

DRIVING TOUR—*Proceed to Kernstown*
READING *(chronological)—1862: Second Manassas; 1863: Rappahannock Station*

LOWER SHENANDOAH VALLEY AREA

Virginia's Shenandoah Valley, an expansive and fertile region drained by the Shenandoah River and its tributaries, bounded on the east by the Blue Ridge and on the west by the Allegheny Mountains, served the Confederacy in two ways. First, it was a protected and convenient corridor for the movement of armed forces, against the soft underbelly of the North through Maryland and Pennsylvania's Cumberland Valley. With its several railroads and macadamized Valley Turnpike, the Shenandoah Valley linked the Old Dominion State with southwest Virginia. Second, the Valley, with no plantations and few slaves, and with an economy based on the production of staples, was a strategic area for the Confederacy, because, like all armies, the soldiers of the South marched on their stomachs.

The Valley was hardly disturbed in the first year of the war, merely inconvenienced by the Federal occupation of Harpers Ferry and the subsequent maneuvers of Union troops, and by the presence of Brig. Gen. Joseph E. Johnston's Valley soldiers before they left to board railroad cars en route to Manassas Junction (see **First Manassas**). But, beginning in March 1862, the Valley saw much death and devastation, beginning with Stonewall Jackson's Valley Campaign, continuing with Lee's second invasion of the North in 1863, the spring 1864 Federal offensive, Jubal Early's Washington Raid in the summer of 1864, and finally Maj. Gen. Philip H. Sheridan's Valley Campaign beginning on August 7, 1864, that by October 20 crushed Confederate resistance in the Valley and concurrently undertook a campaign of destruction that had a ruinous effect on the Valley and from which it took several generations to recover.

First Kernstown

In March 1862, as Maj. Gen. George B. McClellan prepared for his major campaign against Confederate forces in Virginia by marching up the Peninsula between the James and York rivers southeast of Richmond, a battle occurred that gave credence to the Lincoln administration's fears for Washington's security. Gen. Joseph E. Johnston had given a vital mission to a hero of First Manassas, Maj. Gen. Thomas J. Jackson, who, the previous November, had crossed the Blue Ridge Mountains and assumed command of the Confederate Valley District. Stonewall Jackson, in command of a small army, had the task of defending the Lower Shenandoah Valley against Maj. Gen. Nathaniel Banks's 30,000-man army. On March 12, Banks, having crossed the Potomac River, occupied Winchester in the Shenandoah Valley. By March 20, Banks and two of his three divisions were leaving the Valley en route to Manassas. McClellan wanted to redeploy Banks's soldiers in the defense of Washington, freeing other units to participate in his Peninsula Campaign.

On March 23, Jackson marched against the division of Banks's army still in Winchester. At Kernstown, just south of Winchester, Jackson attacked what he thought was a four-regiment rear guard, but clashed with an entire 9,000-man division. The Rebels were mauled and compelled to retreat. This tactical defeat, however, turned into a strategic victory for the South. The threat of Jackson's force sent a shock wave through Washington. Not only was the transfer of Banks's two divisions headed for Washington canceled, but Maj. Gen. Irvin McDowell's 35,000 men were detached from McClellan's command. McDowell was kept in front of Washington while Banks returned to the Valley. The strength of McClellan's Peninsula Campaign force was slashed in favor of the defense of Washington. From this inauspicious beginning, Jackson fashioned one of the most brilliant and most studied campaigns of the Civil War.

Second Kernstown

After being turned back from the gates of Washington, Lt. Gen. Jubal Early withdrew his Army of the Valley in July 1864 across the Potomac River near Leesburg to Berryville, east of Winchester. The Federal forces that had arrived to defend Washington, the VI and XIX corps, were led in pursuit of Early by Maj. Gen. Horatio Wright, the VI Corps's commander. Joining him were the forces from West Virginia under Maj. Gen. David Hunter that in mid-June had threatened Lynchburg (see **Lynchburg**). Hunter's infantry, redesigned the VII Corps and led by Brig. Gen. George Crook, spearheaded Wright's army. Wright pushed Crook ahead toward Early's position. At Cool Spring on July 18, Early defeated a portion of Crook's command. Two days later, on July 20, one of Early's divisions was soundly defeated at Rutherford's Farm, north of Winchester, by Union cavalry led by Brig. Gen. William W. Averell. Early withdrew to Fisher's Hill to regroup.

Assuming Early was departing the Valley, Wright ordered the two corps sent from Petersburg and Hampton Roads to return to Washington to board steamers to be redeployed to the Petersburg front. Crook's command, numbering 9,500, was left to guard the Valley. Early saw the opportunity to use his larger force to drive Crook from the Valley. On July 24, Early marched north. Crook took position at Kernstown. The Rebels pressed Crook's center at noon, with Maj. Gen. John B. Gordon's division in the lead. The Federals resisted stubbornly. The division of Brig. Gen. James A. Mulligan and the brigade led by Col. Rutherford B. Hayes, future U.S. president, fought valiantly from behind stone walls around Opequon Church. But Early's veterans, some of whom had fought here with Stonewall Jackson, pressed forward. Mulligan, a fighting Irishman, was mortally wounded, and the outnumbered Federals retreated through Winchester, losing a number of men, many of whom were captured. Crook withdrew his force across the Potomac before returning to Harpers Ferry. Early's continued presence in the Shenandoah Valley prompted Grant to return the VI and XIX corps there under a new overall commander for the region.

Points of Interest

Both the battles at Kernstown took place around Opequon Presbyterian Church, which is just west of the Valley Pike, US11, 3 miles south of Winchester. The present church, rebuilt on the site of the church that stood during the battles, has some artifacts and a painting of the First Kernstown battle. The cemetery was part of the battlefield as was the stone wall west of the church. An interpretive wayside on US11 and another in front of the church describe the Kernstown battles. For information on the church, call 703-662-1843.

Lt. Gen. Thomas Jonathan "Stonewall" Jackson, CSA, was of humble beginnings, but he applied himself to his studies and graduated seventeenth in his West Point class. He served in the peacetime army and as a professor at the Virginia Military Institute. His aggressive style motivated his soldiers and they became reliable and steady veterans under him. As an independent commander and teaming with Robert E. Lee, he distinguished himself in engineering a number of key Confederate victories in Virginia.

DRIVING TOUR—*Proceed to Front Royal and Winchester*
READING— *1862: Jackson's Valley Campaign; Early's 1864 campaign: Chambersburg, Pennsylvania*

Jackson's Valley Campaign

It was Robert E. Lee, who, having returned to Richmond in early March from his assignment to perfect coastal defenses in South Carolina, Georgia and Florida, to advise Jefferson Davis, shaped the strategy that made Jackson's force an instrument that wrecked McClellan's Peninsula Campaign, which was designed to capture Richmond and end the war. Jackson's credo of mystifying the enemy worked well in Lee's plan to play on the fears of concerned Washington leadership, diverting Federal attention from Richmond. From April 30 to June 10, 1862, Jackson's "foot cavalry," as they came to be known, logged 431 miles by shoe leather, if they had shoes, and by occasional rail transportation. The key to the rapid and skilled movement of Jackson's force was his thorough knowledge of the Shenandoah Valley's geography, from the lower Valley to the southern end, near Jackson's home in Lexington.

Responsible for this geographic information was Jackson's topographic engineer, Jedediah Hotchkiss, a thirty-three-year-old former teacher and school master. Though Hotchkiss's commission while serving under Jackson was never approved by the Confederate Congress, he was called a captain. He was the Civil War's most prolific mapmaker.

Battles of Front Royal and First Winchester

After his stunning victory at McDowell, Stonewall Jackson reentered the Shenandoah Valley with his fast-moving infantry column. He made another dogleg move, which turned into a brilliant piece of strategy. He took the Stonewall Division down the west side of the Valley toward Strasburg, then, at New Market, veered off toward Luray, crossing Massanutten Mountain through New Market Gap. He left his cavalry under Col. Turner Ashby in the western Valley to keep Maj. Gen. Nathaniel Banks thinking the main force was headed for Strasburg. At Luray, on May 21, he was reinforced by Maj. Gen. Richard S. Ewell's division that had come down the Page Valley from Conrad's Store (present-day Elkton). On May 22, with Ewell's force bringing his strength to 17,000 men, Jackson marched down the Page (Luray) Valley and on May 23 attacked the Federal outpost at Front Royal. The short engagement, which included fighting between the 1st Maryland Regiment, CSA, and the 1st Maryland Regiment USA, netted Jackson 904 prisoners, 2 cannons, and a cache of arms. The surprise attack sent Banks heading northwest to Winchester. The Federal commander divided his army the following day after the Rebels struck his attenuated column at Middletown. Banks formed battle lines south of Winchester, but the troops were overwhelmed by Jackson's men on May 25. Jackson pursued Banks through the town.

The defeat at Winchester caused Banks's tattered division to flee across the Potomac. Jackson pursued his foe to Harpers Ferry, feigned a crossing of the Potomac, then turned his weary troops south again.

This woodcut dramatically depicts the First Battle of Winchester, which was fought on May 25, 1862. Stonewall Jackson's larger force defeated the Federal force of Maj. Gen. Nathaniel Banks after Brig. Gen. Richard Taylor's Louisiana Brigade led a charge that broke the Union line.

It was as if "Old Jack," as his troops called him, had peered inside Lincoln's head.

Second Winchester

Winchester was one of the most contested locations in the Civil War, changing hands seventy-two times. In mid-June 1863, during Robert E. Lee's second invasion of the North, the Army of the Potomac under Joseph Hooker lagged well behind the Confederate advance. The only force that stood in the way of Lee's northbound columns was a Federal division in Winchester under Maj. Gen. Robert H. Milroy. Milroy had prepared earthworks on the commanding ridges west and north of the town, but the number of Confederates opposing him made resistance virtually impossible. From June 13 to 15, Lt. Gen. Richard Ewell's corps, led by the advance of Jubal Early's division to the west against Milroy's fortifications, pushed unrelentingly from three directions. Milroy's wagon train and much of his command were captured north of Winchester at Stephenson's Depot by Maj. Gen. Edward Johnson's division in the early-morning hours of June 15.

SHERIDAN'S 1864–65 SHENANDOAH VALLEY CAMPAIGN

After the frustrating efforts by Generals Wright and Cook to drive Jubal Early from the Shenandoah Valley failed, Grant discussed privately with Lincoln the idea that he saw as the solution—appointment of a tough, no-nonsense soldier who would cut through the administrative logjam now paralyzing action in the Valley. By superseding ineffective generals and going after Early with a unified command, an army could then concentrate on cutting Lee's supply line, destroying the Valley harvests and chasing down John S. Mosby's and Hanse McNeill's partisan rangers.

Grant's selection, after careful consideration, was Philip Sheridan. Lincoln concurred, though the rest of official Washington had misgivings about giving the command of an army of three infantry corps and three cavalry divisions to the thirty-three-year-old Westerner. But Grant knew that Sheridan would be aggressive in achieving the desired objectives, and gave him instructions to lay waste to the Valley: ". . . it is desirable that nothing be left to invite the enemy to return. Take all provisions, forage, and stock wanted for use of your command. Such as cannot be consumed, destroy."

Sheridan's first drive up the Valley Turnpike commencing on August 10 belied the character of future events. After learning of Early's reinforcement by Maj. Gen. Fitzhugh Lee's cavalry and Joe Kershaw's infantry from Petersburg, Sheridan backed away from a confrontation at Cedar Creek. Early delighted in the timidity of the new commander, stalking the Federals' return march to strongly fortified Harpers Ferry and Halltown. But a month later, when

(left to right) Gens. Wesley Merritt, Philip Sheridan, and George Crook, Col. James Forsyth, and George A. Custer. Maj. Gen. Philip H. Sheridan meets with his commanders Brig. Gens. Alfred Torbert, George A. Custer, and Wesley Merritt during the Shenandoah Valley campaign of 1864–65. Cavalry was a critical element of the operation that had the dual purpose of shutting down the activities of Lt. Gen. Jubal Early's Confederate force and partisan rangers operating in the Valley and of destroying the crops which, if harvested, would be used to feed the Rebels on the lines at Petersburg and Richmond.

Grant visited Charles Town to press his own plan for a new advance, Sheridan told him that a young woman spy had sent him important information. Early's infantry and artillery reinforcements were returning to Petersburg and the time was right to go on the offensive.

Third Winchester (Opequon)

By the time Grant landed back at City Point on September 19, Sheridan had already moved his army southwest and struck a blow against Early's main force. The battle, called Third Winchester or Opequon Creek, was not an overwhelming victory for the North. As the Federals approached Winchester from the east, the large column bogged down. Attacks were uncoordinated and Early recalled his scattered units. Sustained pressure finally crushed the Rebel cavalry on the left and Early's army was sent "whirling through Winchester." The Federals sustained higher casualties, but the Confederates lost veteran Maj. Gen. Robert Rodes, who was killed while sending his division into a counterattack. Early's army escaped to a strong position at Fisher's Hill south of Strasburg.

Points of Interest

The Battle of Front Royal is commemorated by a monument on US340/522 just north of Front Royal's downtown area. A few blocks south of the monument at 101 Chester Street is the Belle Boyd Cottage, where the Confederate spy Belle Boyd lived for a time with her aunt and uncle. It was then that she eavesdropped on Federal General Banks at her uncle's hotel, then relayed Federal troop movements to Stonewall Jackson. The cottage, with period furnishings, is on the property of the Warren Heritage Society, which also has a library and museum. The cottage has period furnishings. Next door is a Civil War Cavalry Museum. WARREN HERITAGE SOCIETY, 703-636-1446.

The Frederick County Courthouse in Winchester was used as a hospital beginning with First Kernstown. The house used by Stonewall Jackson as a headquarters before and after the Romney Expedition (January 1–16, 1862) is a historic house museum featuring Jackson artifacts. It is located at 415 North Braddock Street. At Braddock and Piccadilly streets is a large mansion that was used as a headquarters by Nathaniel Banks in 1862. Maj. Gen. Philip Sheridan left this house on the morning of October 19, 1864, and later began his famous ride to Cedar Creek that snatched victory from the jaws of defeat.

Col. John Singleton Mosby was a pre-war lawyer who organized the most effective band of partisan cavalry rangers in northern Virginia after serving under J.E.B. Stuart during the war's first months. His strict discipline and effective tactics were often praised by Confederate leaders; his guerrilla raids tied up a great number of Federal soldiers. U. S. Grant, in 1864, ordered Mosby and his raiders to be captured and hanged without a trial; however, the two men became friends after the war.

Winchester has the large Confederate Stonewall Cemetery and a national cemetery next to each other on the east end. To the east along VA7 are historical markers for Third Winchester. The Federals advanced from Berryville along this road. South of Winchester on US11 are interpretive way stations describing First Winchester and historical markers relating to the second and third battles. The Star Fort is located just east of US522 north of town. It was captured by the Federals during the battle of Third Winchester after Early's forces occupied it earlier in the summer. Other 1863 earthworks are off US522 west of Winchester, but they are all currently on private property. The Kurtz Cultural Center in downtown Winchester has information and exhibits on the city and Frederick County in the Civil War.

DRIVING TOUR—*Proceed to Fisher's Hill*
READING—*1862: Harrisonburg; 1863: Chambersburg, Pennsylvania; 1864: Fisher's Hill*

Fisher's Hill

Not wanting to rest on his Battle of Winchester laurels, even though congratulatory messages were arriving from Washington and elsewhere, Sheridan advanced on September 20 to a position on Cedar Creek. He studied Early's formidable Fisher's Hill defenses. He moved to turn Early's left flank with Crook's two divisions while Emory and Wright demonstrated against the Rebels' front. Sheridan, on September 22, dealt Early a second major defeat. But the planned interception of Early's retreat at New Market was bungled by Sheridan's cavalry leader, Brig. Gen. Alfred Torbert, and Early withdrew to Rockfish Gap. Instead of pursuing Early farther, Sheridan suggested to Grant that he retrace his steps down the Valley, implementing the planned campaign of destruction. "I think the best policy would be to let the burning of the crops in the Valley be the end of the campaign," Sheridan wrote, "and let some of the army go somewhere else."

The idea was well received by Grant, anticipating the return of the veteran VI Corps to the Petersburg front. Sheridan, in carrying out "The Burning," laid waste to the Shenandoah Valley. The unfortunate residents, even pro-Union families, were compelled to abandon the area in the wake of the scorched earth campaign. Early cautiously followed Sheridan north—the cavalry at the head of the Confederate columns skirmished with Union horse soldiers screening the retrograde. But the most fearsome aspect of "The Burning," as Valley residents called the campaign, was the vicious war of terror and revenge waged first by Brig. Gen. George A. Custer and responded to by Lt. Col. John S. Mosby and other Rebel partisans. Ambushes, executions of prisoners, and other criminal acts occurred, countered with fires of retribution set by the Federals. Mosby eventually offered a truce to curtail the escalation of atrocities, but continued to harass Federal installations and sympathetic civilians.

Points of Interest

The Association for the Preservation of Civil War Sites (APCWS) is a nonprofit organization that is acquiring or adding to important Civil War battlefields by purchasing the properties from private owners. A portion of the Fisher's Hill battlefield is one of those acquisitions. It is on VA601, 1 mile west of US11 just south of Strasburg. The site has interpretive markers and trails. For more information, contact ASSOCIATION FOR THE PRESERVATION OF CIVIL WAR SITES, 11 Public Square, Suite 200, Hagerstown, MD 21740.

Hupp Hill (0.8 mile north of Strasburg on US11) has earthworks constructed by the Federals in late October 1864 and a Civil War museum. In Strasburg at the water tower is a fort constructed by Nathaniel Banks's forces in 1862.

DRIVING TOUR—*Proceed to Tom's Brook, Cedar Creek (Middletown)*
READING—*Cedar Creek*

Cedar Creek

By October 8, 1864, Sheridan was back at Cedar Creek. On October 9, a cavalry action involving Brig. Gen. George A. Custer, his Rebel classmate, Thomas Rosser, and others announced the presence of the Confederates. The fight is known by most people as the Battle of Tom's Brook, but in the bitter days following "The Burning," Valley residents called it the "Woodstock Races," because the Rebel horsemen were driven from the field and south to Columbia Furnace, and it was reminiscent of the Federal flight to Buckland. Early, thinking the VI Corps had departed from the Union force en route back to the Army of the Potomac, planned an attack. But Sheridan, following an October 13 fight at Hupp Hill, recalled the veterans before they passed Ashby's Gap.

Satisfied with the defensive arrangements at the Northern camps on Cedar Creek, Sheridan left for a Washington meeting on the future plans for his army on October 15, promising to be back in several days. Meanwhile, Early approved the attack plan proposed by division commander Maj. Gen. John B. Gordon to turn the Yankees' flank left at Cedar Creek and roll it up. Despite odds of two to one against him, Early, at

The Belle Grove Mansion was a landmark on the battlefield of Cedar Creek. It was the command post for the Federal VI Corps and Maj. Gen. Philip H. Sheridan's Shenandoah Valley army. The home was in the middle of the XIX Corps camps and the battle was waged all around it. Today the mansion is owned by the National Trust for Historic Preservation.

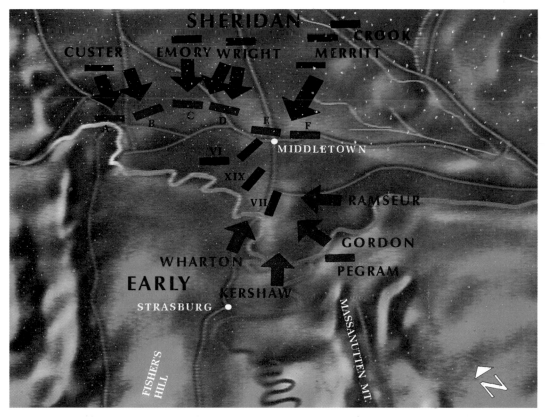

The Battle of Cedar Creek began in the early-morning hours as Lt. Gen. Jubal Early's three-column attack drove three Federal corps from their camps on Cedar Creek. The second division of the Union VI Corps stubbornly held out just north of Middletown after other Yankee resistance had broken down. Despite the urging of wing commander Maj. Gen. John B. Gordon to continue the attack, Early had his troops form a defensive line in the afternoon. By that time, Maj. Gen. Philip H. Sheridan had rallied his forces and orchestrated a stinging Federal counterattack spearheaded by his cavalry corps. The Rebels were forced back beyond Strasburg, losing many of their wagons and much of the Federal gear they captured during the rout. The Battle of Cedar Creek broke the back of Early's army and gave the Federals control of the Shenandoah Valley for the rest of the war.

dawn October 19, struck. He first routed Crook's VIII Corps from their camps, and continued to advance through the camps of Emory's XIX Corps. A brief rally by units of these two corps east of the Valley Pike enabled Maj. Gen. Horatio Wright to form his VI Corps into a line west of Meadow Brook. The Federals again gave way and were pushed back and finally broke and retreated. Only Brig. Gen. George W. Getty's division of the VI Corps remained in contact, stubbornly resisting Confederate pressure for more than an hour in the cemetery northwest of Middletown.

During the opening phase of the battle, Sheridan was riding back to Cedar Creek from Winchester at a leisurely pace after his meeting in Washington. The distant gunfire concerned him and he learned from frightened fugitives of the attack and routs of two of his three corps. Spurring his horse forward into a gallop, he rallied the increasing number of Union stragglers walking away from the battle. Enlisting the help of a young VIII Corps staffer, Capt. William McKinley, the future U.S. president, he formed the stragglers into a line of battle.

Inspired by "Sheridan's Ride," the Federals who still held the field and those encouraged by Sheridan to return to the front made a determined counterattack at four P.M., led by a massed cavalry assault by the troopers of Brig. Gen. George A. Custer on the Rebel left. Maj. Gen. John Gordon, who had pleaded with a hesitant Early to continue to push forward after the initial gains, was hit with the full force of the Union counterattack. First Gordon's division and then the rest of the Confederates were pushed back and retired from the field. At a bridge south of Strasburg the retreat became a rout. Early withdrew to Rude's Hill near New Market. After the Battle of Cedar Creek, no serious Confederate threat was mounted to challenge Federal control of the Lower Shenandoah Valley.

Points of Interest

A 25-acre tract constituting part of the Tom's Brook battlefield has been acquired by APCWS and gives an excellent overview of the rolling pastures where the cavalry clashed on October 9. It is located on VA652 off I-81 exit 291.

An important part of the Cedar Creek battlefield has been preserved by the Cedar Creek Battlefield Foundation. This is the portion of the battlefield where the camps of the

On the morning of October 19, 1864, Maj. Gen. Philip H. Sheridan was returning to his headquarters at the Federal camp on Cedar Creek from Winchester when he encountered demoralized Federal soldiers retreating north. His efforts to rally the soldiers as he rode among them led to a counterattack and victory for the Union in the Battle of Cedar Creek and was thereafter immortalized as "Sheridan's Ride."

Federal XIX and VI corps were located. The park is on US11 just south of Middletown. An annual reenactment of the battle is held in October. Nearby is Belle Grove Plantation. The mansion, which served as a Federal headquarters, is open for touring and special events. CEDAR CREEK BATTLEFIELD FOUNDATION, INC., P.O. Box 229, Middletown, VA 22645; 703-869-2064. 🖾 ♿ ❷ 🏛 P ♟ $$

On US11 north of Middletown is a historical marker locating the "end" of Sheridan's ride and the left flank of the line from which his rallied and reorganized army counterattacked and drove the Confederates to and beyond Cedar Creek.

DRIVING TOUR—*Proceed to New Market*
READING (*chronological*)—*1864: Sterling Price's 1864 Missouri Raid, Missouri*

NEW MARKET

Nathaniel Banks's Red River Campaign in Louisiana (see **Red River, Louisiana**) was winding down as one of the South's most fascinating victories was scored over another controversial general in the Shenandoah Valley. Maj. Gen. Franz Sigel, the German-born inspirational leader of the 200,000 German-American troops in the Federal armies, had begun a march up the Shenandoah Valley from Martinsburg, West Virginia. His slow advance was appreciated by the controversial, though able, general commanding Confederate forces in southwest Virginia, John C. Breckinridge. After chafing under the command of Gen. Braxton Bragg, with whom he shared no affection, for thirteen months in the west, the former U.S. senator, vice president, and presidential candidate finally got a regional command of his own, albeit a most difficult one. With only a handful of troops to work with, Breckinridge reluctantly pressed the cadets of the Virginia Military Institute in Lexington into service. Though Lee and the political leaders of Virginia had sanctioned their use, it was with hesitation that the Confederate leadership risked placing the South's future military leaders in harm's way. But on May 13 the 264 VMI cadets, excited to get in on the action, joined the northward march of the Rebels at Staunton.

While Breckinridge's infantry trudged north, several events hastened his resolve to stop General Sigel. Brig. Gen. John D. Imboden had been hitting Sigel's winding column, pri-

Cadet Thomas Garland Jefferson fought with 263 of his Virginia Military Institute classmates in the Battle of New Market on May 15, 1864. Jefferson, a descendant of President Thomas Jefferson, was one of ten VMI cadets killed in the battle.

marily with lightning cavalry raids. This caused Sigel to slow his advance even more. And Maj. Gen. George Crook's victory at Cloyd's Mountain just days before threatened the Valley from the opposite end (see **Cloyd's Mountain**). Breckinridge decided to defeat Sigel, then turn his attention to Crook.

On May 13, Imboden's cavalry skirmished with Sigel's vanguard south of Mount Jackson. By the next evening, Imboden broke contact and rendezvoused with the rest of his small force. Imboden decided to make a stand at New Market. Like many small towns in the Shenandoah Valley, New Market bounded the Valley Pike and served the people whose farms dotted the countryside. One of the prominent wheat farms in the area belonged to the Jacob Bushong family.

Late on May 14, the Federals began to arrive at New Market. Breckinridge turned out his little army long before daybreak on May 15, after Imboden communicated his intention to make a stand south of the village. By six A.M. Breckinridge had drawn a line south of New Market, his left flank anchored on Shirley's Hill and his right on Smith Creek. Sigel's commander on the ground committed one brigade to occupy the town, but the rest of Sigel's nearly 9,000 men were strung out down the turnpike as far north as Woodstock.

Sigel, who arrived at noon, directed the brigade in New Market to pull back and join his forces now arriving north of town. Sigel consolidated his line resting his right on Bushong's Hill and placed skirmishers in Bushong's orchard. When the Federals did not advance, Breckinridge felt compelled to attack. Though weakened by the assault, the Northern line held and checked the Rebel advance. By mid-afternoon, a serious gap appeared in the Southern line, the 30th and 51st Virginia pulled back. The VMI cadets were committed. To avoid having this gap exploited by the Federals, General Breckinridge called up the VMI battalion. The cadets pressed forward in a determined attack, their uniforms spattered with mud and blood. Their attack galvanized the Rebels into action as the units passed to the east and west of the Bushong House, to the cadets' right and left, and the Federals gave way.

There were VMI cadets among the casualties treated at the Bushong farmhouse that day, while ten of their school comrades were killed or mortally wounded in the action. A rout was avoided and pursuit was discouraged by the quick thinking of artillery Captain Henry Du Pont. A scion of the famous Delaware family, Du Pont staggered his cannons in sections on the slope west of and paralleling the Yankees' withdrawal down the Valley Turnpike.

The Battle of New Market zeroed out for the time the strategic hammer blow Grant had been hoping for in the Shenandoah Valley. Sigel within a week was replaced by aging war-horse Maj. Gen. David Hunter, whose way of war earned him the nom de guerre "Black Dave." Lee called the hard-fighting Breckinridge and his division east of the Blue Ridge Mountains in the third week of May to help fill the ranks of men lost in the bitter Wilderness and Spotsylvania fighting. The Valley command fell to Brig. Gen. William "Grumble" Jones, who was killed when Hunter crushed and routed his army at Piedmont on June 5 (see **Piedmont**). Despite these misfortunes, the Confederates in the Shenandoah Valley would see Hunter fumble in front of Lynchburg in mid-June and then blunder as he retreated into the West Virginia mountains, opening the Shenandoah Valley for Jubal Early's march to the gates of Washington. And the battle in which the young VMI cadets won their battle honors and suffered marked the start of a terrible six-month struggle for the Shenandoah Valley.

Points of Interest

New Market Battlefield and the Hall of Valor—This park, administered by the Virginia Military Institute, is located just west of I-81 at New Market. The property contains the battlefield on the Bushong Farm, including the Bushong House. The farmlands and buildings look much as they did when the VMI cadets and other soldiers tramped across the "Field of Lost Shoes" during that rainy muddy day of May 15, 1864. The Hall of Valor has exhibits, artifacts, and a film program about the Battle of

New Market and Shenandoah Valley campaigns. There are wayside exhibits, trails, and monuments. NEW MARKET BATTLEFIELD PARK, P.O. Box 1864, New Market, VA 22844; 703-740-3102. 🚲 🏕 ♿ 🚶‍♂️ ❷ 🏛 P ⛱ 🚻 $$

DRIVING TOUR—*Proceed to Harrisonburg*
READING *(chronological)*—*1864: Bermuda Hundred, Virginia*

HARRISONBURG

Following the May 25, 1862, rout of Maj. Gen. Nathaniel P. Banks's army at Winchester, President Lincoln, Secretary of War Stanton, and the Washington-based army staff viewed the Shenandoah Valley situation with alarm. Lincoln decided to eliminate the cause of the problem, Stonewall Jackson. He ordered Maj. Gen. John C. Frémont to enter the upper Valley in pursuit of the Rebels. He also ordered the forces of Irvin McDowell, then pushing south from Fredericksburg for a proposed linkup with McClellan's army, to countermarch and head for the Valley by way of Manassas Gap. McDowell, as well as McClellan, protested this decision.

Lincoln hoped to trap Jackson between the two Federal forces. But Frémont entered the Valley by way of Wardensville and Strasburg and McDowell's lead division under Brig. Gen. James Shields, whose troops had defeated Jackson at Kernstown, turned south at Fort Royal and made his way slowly up the Page Valley via a muddy road. Jackson slipped between the Federal columns, arriving in Port Republic on June 6.

Turner Ashby and the Confederate cavalry clashed repeatedly with the blue horsemen spearheading Frémont's column, and on June 6, Federal cavalry and infantry battled the Rebels on the Port Republic road southeast of Harrisonburg. The daring Ashby, recently promoted to brigadier general, was killed. Frémont then halted at Harrisonburg and closed in on Ewell's force, camped a few miles to the southeast at Cross Keys.

Points of Interest

One and one half miles southeast of Harrisonburg on US33 is a turnoff to a small park, which is the area where the June 6, 1862, battle was fought. The park has a monument identifying the site of Ashby's death and an interpretive wayside.

DRIVING TOUR and READING—*Proceed to Cross Keys and Port Republic*

CROSS KEYS

Maj. Gen. Richard Ewell's Confederates were bivouacked in and around Cross Keys. On June 8, Frémont made an uncoordinated attack on Ewell and was beaten back. Shields's vanguard under Col. Samuel S. Carroll having reached Conrad's Store (present-day Elkton) was near Port Republic, where Jackson controlled the only bridge over North River just above the head of the South Fork of the Shenandoah River. All rivers were swollen from spring rains. Carroll's cavalry nearly captured Jackson in a June 8 raid through Port Republic, but Jackson repulsed them with artillery and then drove them off with an infantry regiment.

PORT REPUBLIC

On June 9, Jackson attacked Brig. Gen. Erastus Tyler who had reinforced Carroll northeast of Port Republic. The Confederates were spearheaded by the famous "Stonewall Brigade," Jackson's staunch defenders from First Manassas. In the beginning, the battle took a turn in favor of the North as Tyler's men fought gallantly, carrying the fight to the Rebels. By noon, however, Jackson prevailed when Ewell's force arrived on the field. Ewell attacked Tyler's flank while Brig. Gen. Richard Taylor and his Louisianians, after a desperate hand-to-hand struggle, captured the 6-gun Federal battery located at the Coaling. Frémont's troops, stranded on the opposite side of the swollen South Fork by the destruction of the North River bridge, were prevented from coming to Tyler's aid.

Still, Jackson realized the peril of being cut off by a growing Federal force. He withdrew in a timely manner. The two Union columns abandoned their efforts to defeat Jackson and pulled back, Frémont to Harrisonburg west of the Massanutten and Shields to Luray. In five weeks, Jackson scored five victories, occupying the attention of three Union armies numbering more than 50,000 soldiers and wrecking McClellan's campaign plans that called for concentration of an overwhelming force on the approaches to Richmond and then fighting a decisive battle that the North could not lose.

The Confederate leadership in Richmond was enthusiastic. General Thomas J. "Stonewall" Jackson's Shenandoah Valley Campaign was a resounding success. Richmond was spared in the spring of 1862, in large part due to Jackson's efforts, marking him as a "great captain."

Points of Interest

On VA276, Keezletown Road, there is an interpretive wayside describing the Battle of Cross Keys. On US340 there are Battle of Port Republic interpretive markers. The Frank Kemper Home in Port Republic on VA659 served as a hospital and morgue. Turner Ashby's body was brought there after he was killed at Harrisonburg and there Jackson paid his respects to his fallen subordinate. The Port Republic Historical Society has opened an excellent museum in the Frank Kemper House. The museum is open on Sunday afternoon and by appointment for groups.

The APCWS has acquired The Coaling, the site of a key phase of the battle where Richard Taylor's command captured a Federal artillery position in hand-to-hand fighting. A vista has been opened, a trail opened, and wayside markers sited. It is located at the intersection of US340 and VA708. Grace Episcopal Church, which stood during the battle, is at the base of The Coaling. For more information, contact ASSOCIATION FOR THE PRESERVATION OF CIVIL WAR SITES, 11 Public Square, Suite 200, Hagerstown, MD 21740.

<hr />

DRIVING TOUR—*Proceed to Piedmont*
READING *(chronological)—1862: The Seven Days' Battles*

<hr />

PIEDMONT

After the Battle of New Market, the focus of Virginia operations momentarily shifted away from the Shenandoah Valley. Most of Breckinridge's force that had opposed Sigel joined Lee's army east of the Blue Ridge Mountains and participated in the Battles of North Anna and Cold Harbor. The VMI cadets returned to Lexington, and the only Confederate force in the Valley was Imboden's cavalry. Sigel, returning to Cedar Creek with his demoralized force, was relieved of his command at Belle Grove by Maj. Gen. David Hunter.

Hunter reorganized Sigel's divisions and on May 26 commenced a new march up the Shenandoah Valley. His aim was to destroy the South's ability to wage war, by destroying the region's agricultural economy. This had been practiced in the west by Maj. Gen. William T. Sherman in his February 1864 Meridian Expedition. Persons aiding partisans had their homes destroyed as Hunter advocated a hard war. After bypassing a prepared Confederate position at Mount Crawford and encountering delays in crossing the North River at Port Republic, Hunter approached the village of Piedmont, where Brig. Gen. William E. "Grumble" Jones, who had arrived from southwest Virginia with reinforcements, made another attempt to block his advance.

After skirmishing with Imboden's cavalry and driving them back on the morning of June 5, 1864, Hunter, at Piedmont, met Jones's infantry and cavalry. Jones was killed as the Federals advanced through a gap between the Confederate line of infantry and cavalry. The Rebels, routed, retreated to Waynesboro and Hunter on June 6 occupied Staunton. Here he was joined on June 8 by George Crook's infantry and Averell's cavalry which had marched east from Meadow Bluff, West Virginia. Hunter on June 11 continued his march south to Lexington.

Points of Interest

The village of Piedmont is on VA608, 13 miles northeast of Staunton. A historical marker on the road details the battle.

———————

DRIVING TOUR—*Proceed to McDowell*
READING—*Hunter's campaign: Lexington*

———————

McDowell

Jackson's first target in his Shenandoah Valley Campaign in the spring of 1862 was the western Virginia–based army of Maj. Gen. John C. Frémont. Frémont planned to mount an offensive into East Tennessee, toward Knoxville, which was a favored goal of President Lincoln. Jackson's presence kept Frémont's attention focused east. On April 30, Jackson marched his troops out of the Valley, leaving a 7,000-man division under Maj. Gen. Richard Ewell, which had just entered at Conrad's Store. Then, east of the Blue Ridge, Jackson at Mecham's Station entrained his people onto cars of the Virginia Central Railroad and on May 4–5 shuttled them back to Staunton, in the upper Valley. From there, he marched west, linking up with Brig. Gen. "Allegheny Ed" Johnson's 2,800 men, who in the face of a relentless advance by Brig. Gen. Robert Milroy's Union brigade, had fallen back in successive stages from Camp Allegheny to West View six miles west of Staunton. The combined force of 9,000 men clashed with Milroy's and Brig. Gen. Robert Schenck's troops of Frémont's advance guard, near the village of McDowell on May 8. The battle forced a Federal retreat and Jackson was elated. Having made his point to Frémont, Jackson headed east to call on Banks again, with his force numbering 10,000. Banks's intelligence reported that Jackson outnumbered him. He withdrew north from Harrisonburg to Strasburg.

Points of Interest

APCWS purchased a portion of the McDowell battlefield, Sitlington Hill, where some of the heaviest fighting occurred, in 1990 and it is open to the public. This is adjacent to land previously acquired by the Lee-Jackson Foundation. The site is off US250, 30 miles west of I-81, and there is a small parking area. Getting to the site requires a short but steep hike. There is a UDC monument near the parking lot along US250. For more information, contact ASSOCIATION FOR THE PRESERVATION OF CIVIL WAR SITES, 11 Public Square, Suite 200, Hagerstown, MD 21740.

DRIVING TOUR—*Proceed to Waynesboro*
READING—*Battles of Front Royal and First Winchester*

WAYNESBORO

On March 2, 1865, the last battle was fought in the Shenandoah Valley, on its extreme eastern flank, after nearly four years of hostile conflict and suffering in Virginia's most beautiful and agriculturally productive region. Maj. Gen. Philip H. Sheridan, with two cavalry divisions, rode south from Winchester on February 27. By this time, Lt. Gen. Jubal Early's force in the Valley numbered fewer than 2,000 and he could do nothing other than fall back from a Federal force five times as large. The Federals overtook Early's force at Waynesboro, and the attack on Early's infantry, brilliantly staged by Brig. Gen. George A. Custer with dismounted troops, captured 1,600 Rebels, their wagons, cannons, and flags. Sheridan's force then launched a destructive campaign through the Piedmont en route to join Grant's forces in the Richmond-Petersburg area.

Points of Interest

A cemetery in Waynesboro contains historical markers about the battle and graves of some of the Confederates killed in the battle. There is a Confederate monument in the cemetery.

DRIVING TOUR—*Proceed to Cedar Mountain*
READING—*Virginia, 1865: Fort Stedman and Petersburg*

CULPEPER AND ORANGE COUNTIES

Cedar Mountain

General Lee capitalized on momentum gained by his victory over McClellan's Army of the Potomac in the Seven Days to send Maj. Gen. Stonewall Jackson and his wing by rail to Gordonsville, eighty miles southwest of Washington. President Lincoln and Secretary of State Stanton had brought in a new commander from the West, Maj. Gen. John Pope, to consolidate the troubled corps of Frémont, Banks, and McDowell. They had high hopes for Pope, the bombastic hero of Island Number 10, and his newly formed Army of Virginia.

Jackson encountered Banks, in command of a portion of Pope's army, at Cedar Mountain on August 9. Both sides suffered heavy casualties. The Rebels prevailed in the fight, but Banks slowed the Rebel

A wartime view of Cedar Mountain, south of Culpeper, Virginia. Even though Maj. Gen. John Pope had just taken control of the new Federal Army of Virginia, in his first defeat on August 9, 1862, at Cedar Mountain the Union soldiers on the field were commanded by Maj. Gen. Nathaniel Banks, who had already been defeated by the Confederate commander Gen. Stonewall Jackson several times. Most of the fighting took place in the fields in front of the mountain.

advance. Lee, satisfied that McClellan was withdrawing from the peninsula, acted quickly to join Jackson and kept the armies of Pope and McClellan from combining along the Rapidan River in northern Virginia.

Points of Interest

There is a historical marker locating the Battle of Cedar Mountain on US15 south of Culpeper, and several nearby monuments. Cedar Mountain itself is visible for miles in any direction. Views of the northwest, where most of the fighting took place in fields west and northwest of the mountain, are those seen in period photographs. The scene and road network, except for some changes in the alignment of US15, are little changed.

DRIVING TOUR— *Proceed to Kelly's Ford*
READING *(chronological)—1862: Thoroughfare Gap and Second Manassas*

Kelly's Ford

In response to a February 24–26, 1863, Confederate cavalry raid to Hartwood Church on

part of the reorganized Army of the Potomac Cavalry Corps, Brig. Gen. William W. Averell received permission to attack the cavalry of Confederate Brig. Gen. Fitzhugh Lee, camped east of Culpeper Court House. Lee and Averell were close friends before the war and it was Lee who was responsible for the February 25 raid that penetrated

Federal soldiers crossing the Rappahannock River at Kelly's Ford. The March 17, 1863, action, which began as a Yankee raid, developed into a dismounted and mounted cavalry battle. It was a signal to the Confederates that the reorganized Union cavalry was going to challenge the dominance the Southerners had previously enjoyed.

to Hartwood Church in which 150 Federal horsemen were captured. Lee left Averell a note jokingly asking for a return visit and a gift of a sack of coffee.

The March 17 return visit started well for the Yanks as Averell's Federals forced their way across the Rappahannock River at Kelly's Ford and mounted a succession of charges which the Rebels countered. The action combined classic saber charges, dismounted musket and carbine fire, and artillery, with the Federals dominating the artillery. Averell withdrew after about seven hours, leaving a sack of coffee and a note for Lee. His light-heartedness was tempered, however, by the killing and wounding of men, of whom the Confederates suffered the most, including the death of the "Gallant" Maj. John Pelham, who was at the battle only as an observer. The better performance of the previously dominated Federal cavalry in this battle was a prelude to the next major action for the Army of the Potomac horsemen, fought nearby at Brandy Station.

Brandy Station

In his second invasion of the North beginning in June 1863, Gen. Robert E. Lee relied on his trusted cavalry chief, Maj. Gen. J.E.B. Stuart, to form a barrier or screen to mask the redeployment of Lee's infantry, their crossing of the Blue Ridge, and their march north through the Shenandoah Valley. Initially, Stuart did a credible job of screening Lee's movements. The Federals received erroneous scouting reports that a Confederate raid toward Washington was imminent. The Federal cavalry was sent to investigate Lee's movements.

Brig. Gen. John Buford, one of the best of the rising new Northern cavalry leaders, reported to Army of the Potomac commander Maj. Gen. Joseph Hooker on June 5, 1863, information "which I consider reliable, that all of the available cavalry of the Confederacy is in Culpeper County. Stuart . . . is going to make a raid." Hooker ordered the recently appointed head of the Federal Cavalry Corps, Maj. Gen. Alfred Pleasonton, to seek out and destroy Stuart's force.

Pleasonton, prone to exaggeration and disliked by some of his officers, was nevertheless a capable fighter and excellent administrator. He moved his 11,000-man combined cavalry-infantry force into Fauquier County, across the Rappahannock River from a whistle stop on the Orange & Alexandria Railroad called Brandy Station.

On June 8, as the infantry from Ewell's and Longstreet's corps settled into temporary camps near Culpeper Court House, Robert E. Lee rode east to witness an event planned for him by Stuart. It was a grand review of the cavalry, 10,000 strong. The seemingly

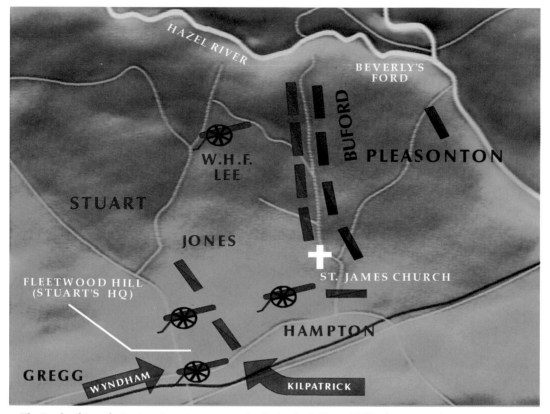

The Battle of Brandy Station, June 9, 1863, was fought in the fields and hills of eastern Culpeper County. After crossing the Rappahannock River at Beverly's Ford, the Federal division of Brig. Gen. John Buford became locked in combat with Brig. Gens. William E. "Grumble" Jones's and "Rooney" Lee's cavalry at St. James Church and the Cunningham Farm. To the south, Brig. Gen. David M. Gregg's horsemen crossed at Kelly's Ford and approached Fleetwood Hill from the south. Buford drove Lee back, while J.E.B. Stuart's troopers turned back mounted attacks near his headquarters on Fleetwood Hill. Despite holding the hill, the Rebels were shaken by the powerful and determined attacks by Maj. Gen. Alfred Pleasonton's Union cavalry command.

invincible horsemen paraded in columns and lines that extended three miles across the lush green pastures of Auburn Plantation. Among the troopers were those under Brig. Gen. "Rooney" Lee, who proudly rode for the father of their commander. The elder Lee later called this pageant "a splendid sight." This was the second of two grand reviews, an earlier and more splendid one having taken place on June 5.

As the Rebel troops bedded down for the night on June 8, they were unaware of activities just to the east. Pleasonton divided his force into three columns; one under Buford headed north to cross the Rappahannock at Beverly's Ford, the other two, commanded by Brig. Gen. David M. Gregg and Col. Alfred Duffié, crossed the river at Kelly's Ford. Horse artillery and two brigades of infantry accompanied the troopers. Pleasonton's plan called for the columns to converge on Brandy Station, then attack Stuart's cavalry in their encampment between Brandy Station and Culpeper. Pleasonton rode along with Buford's column. On his staff was an impetuous young cavalry captain, George Armstrong Custer.

At six-thirty A.M. on the foggy morning of June 9, the 8th New York Cavalry ran headlong into pickets of Brig. Gen. William "Grumble" Jones's brigade at Beverly's Ford and overwhelmed the surprised Southerners. This action, in which the able Union colonel Benjamin Grimes Davis lost his life, began the Battle of Brandy Station.

The Federal cavalry approached St. James Church, where Rebel horse artillery was dangerously exposed. But the Confederates held the charging cavalry off while Jones's brigade was supported on the right by Brig. Gen. Wade Hampton's troopers and on the left by Rooney Lee's brigade, who posted themselves behind a stone wall on the Cunningham property.

At eight A.M. Buford was in front of the Rebel line at St. James Church. He sent the 6th Pennsylvania Cavalry, Rush's Lancers, in a dramatic charge against the middle of the line. They were supported by the regulars of the 6th U.S. Cavalry. Rather than being "tailors and shoe clerks," a disparaging Southern term for Federal cavalrymen, these horsemen were the elite of Philadelphia society. They proved themselves able in this opening melee, as did many Northern "tailors and shoe clerks," before this day was over. The 6th Pennsylvania no longer armed with lances, did not penetrate the Rebel position. Their retreat was orderly, but with heavy casualties. Leaving part of his force in front of the church under Col. Thomas Devin, Buford took the rest of his men and headed north to engage Rooney Lee's troopers who threatened the Union line of retreat across Beverly's Ford.

Buford threw his cavalry at the daunting position of Lee's dismounted units at the Cunningham place. Rooney Lee, a Harvard graduate, had picked ideal terrain for his defense. It was amazing to Buford's men, therefore, that at mid-morning Lee's troopers began to withdraw from this strong position. It was equally surprising to Devin that the Rebels fell back from St. James Church. The reason—Gregg's forces finally exploded onto the scene, threatening Stuart's former headquarters on Fleetwood Hill's commanding heights.

Gregg had crossed the river at Kelly's Ford much earlier, but had to wait for Duffié who became lost in the woods. When the battle first began, Stuart had dispatched Brig. Gen.

Beverly Robertson's cavalry to defend the Kelly's Ford road. Gregg outwitted this move by using his infantry to occupy Robertson's attention and, hearing the battle to the north, headed in that direction on a road farther west.

Duffié continued east to his assigned pivot point. He met resistance from the 2nd South Carolina at Stevensburg and later other Rebel cavalry at Jones Run. He finally aborted his mission and rendezvoused with Gregg too late to be of assistance in the fight for Fleetwood Hill and worse, missing an opportunity to discover Longstreet's corps camped near Culpeper.

Much of the ten-hour battle revolved around the long north-to-south ridge, Fleetwood Hill. While Buford encountered stubborn resistance from Rooney Lee at the northern end of the ridge, two of Gregg's brigade assailed the southern end. The English gentleman and soldier of fortune Sir Percy Wyndham led cavalry units from New York, Pennsylvania, and Maryland to the west face of the hill, where a single cannon defended the approach to Stuart's former headquarters. They collided with the 12th Virginia, racing to defend the hill. The Federals cut up the 12th, but two other Virginia units followed up and pushed Wyndham back.

The fighting here was vicious, personal, boot to boot, and saber to saber. Arriving after Wyndham, hard-driving Col. Judson Kilpatrick sent his troops up the southeastern slope of the ridge. All but the 1st Maine, nicknamed the "Puritans," were repulsed by Cobb's Georgia legion and others. The Maine

The battlefield at Brandy Station has been at the center of preservation efforts for some time. Besides its historical significance, Brandy Station has put the question of land use in this largely rural area to public debate. In the meantime, much of the battlefield area, though privately held, can be viewed from the country roads in the area. A few historical markers exist on the field.

horsemen rode over the hill and beyond supporting forces. They found an escape route back to the Union line.

Much to Stuart's chagrin, the Federals remained on the field of battle until late afternoon although the Rebels now controlled Fleetwood Hill with a line more than two miles long. Rebel cavalry arrived from the north and joined the foray and Buford, already under orders from Pleasonton to withdraw, rode back over the Rappahannock by the way he came.

Robert E. Lee arrived to witness the closing moments of the battle and "expressed great admiration of the grit and courage manifested by soldiers on both sides," an aide reported. While the skillful use of resources enabled Stuart to hold his position while sustaining lower casualties, he was clearly embarrassed at having been surprised by Pleasonton. The Federal cavalry displayed skill and valor that boded well for future battles in the Gettysburg Campaign and beyond. And this, the largest cavalry battle to be fought in the Western Hemisphere, became one of the memorable events of the war.

Rappahannock Station

Maj. Gen. George G. Meade had requested permission from Washington to shift his army east to Fredericksburg to flank the Confederate forces in northern Virginia, but after the scare caused by General Lee's mid-October march toward Washington (see **Bristoe Station**), the request was denied. To capitalize on the success achieved in forcing the Army of Northern Virginia to abandon its advance on reaching Bull Run and retire behind the Rappahannock, Meade on November 7, 1863, launched an attack on Lee's fortifications guarding the Rappahannock River at Kelly's Ford and Rappahannock Station. More than 1,600 Confederates from Jubal Early's division holding the bridgehead were isolated and captured north of the river at Rappahannock Station while the Northerners crossed with minor losses at Kelly's Ford capturing a number of North Carolinians from Robert Rodes's division. Federal control of the Rappahannock crossings compelled Lee to retreat south of the Rapidan River.

Points of Interest

Kelly's Ford, Brandy Station, and Rappahannock Station are on US29 in Culpeper County. There are a few historical markers along the highway. Just south of the Rappahannock River on US29 at Elkwood is a monument and historical marker describing Maj. John Pelham's death. There is a second memorial at the site where he received his mortal wound. This is accessed by a trail leading from a parking area on VA674. On

VA676 a mile north of US29 is the location of the former St. James Church. On Fleetwood Hill, VA688, a mile southwest of where VA676 and US29 intersect, but north of and parallel to US29, is a monument on the ridge that sustained the most protracted fighting of the Brandy Station battle. That area also served as a winter quarters for the Army of the Potomac in the winter of 1863–64. Much of the battlefield is being acquired for preservation and interpretation by APCWS. For information, contact 11 Public Square, Suite 200, Hagerstown, MD 21740.

The charming colonial town of Culpeper is a few miles southwest of Brandy Station on US29. The town was occupied alternately by both armies. There are antebellum homes and buildings and the Culpeper Tourist Council has provided a walking tour pamphlet of the sites. One is the Culpeper Cavalry Museum, 133 West Davis Street, which features artifacts from Brandy Station.

———————

DRIVING TOUR—*Proceed to Mine Run*
READING *(chronological)—After Kelly's Ford: Stoneman's Raid; after Brandy Station: Loudoun Valley; after Rappahannock Station: Mine Run*

———————

Mine Run

Except for a continuing rash of cavalry engagements, only one major action took place in the rolling hills of the Piedmont in the last weeks of 1863 and the first five weeks of 1864. Perceiving Lee's right flank to be weakened, Meade sent his army in the last week of November across the Rapidan. But the slow Federal advance by Maj. Gen. William French, in command of the III Corps, and George Sykes, commanding the V Corps, enabled the Rebels to take up a strong defensive stance behind Mine Run. Meade wisely canceled the all-out attack scheduled for the morning of November 30 on the Rebel works to avoid needless bloodshed and in frightful weather pulled back and recrossed the Rapidan. The two armies then settled into their winter camps.

Points of Interest

Six and one half miles east of Unionville (VA20) is Lee's Mine Run line. Here the two armies skirmished in late November 1863. Lee's defensive line blocked Meade's ability to establish a position south of the Rapidan River and the Army of the Potomac withdrew to camps north of the Rapidan and Rappahannock rivers. There are historical markers and earthworks on private lands here and at Locust Grove (VA20), where Meade assembled his forces.

DRIVING TOUR—*Proceed to Fredericksburg*
READING *(chronological)*—*Chattanooga, Tennessee*

Stoneman's Raid

As part of Maj. Gen. Joseph Hooker's spring 1863 offensive, Maj. Gen. George Stoneman took the reorganized Federal cavalry, 10,000 strong, on a raid to disrupt Confederate lines of communication. The raid was supposed to begin in mid-April, but flooded rivers forced a postponement until April 29, when the cavalry crossed the Rappahannock River at Kelly's Ford with three of Hooker's seven infantry corps. On April 30, most of Stoneman's raiders crossed the Rapidan turning the left flank of the Army of Northern Virginia northwest of Fredericksburg.

Stoneman then separated his force into three columns. Brig. Gen. William W. Averell's column failed to cross the Rapidan and inflict any damage on the Orange & Alexandria Railroad in Orange County. Stoneman rode with the other columns—the divisions of Brig. Gen. John Buford and Brig. Gen. David Gregg. That force got between Lee and Richmond, but inflicted little destruction on the railroad or Lee's supply line south of Fredericksburg. The greatest impact of the raid was felt by Hooker's army, which lacked cavalry reconnaissance and support during the Battle of Chancellorsville (see **Chancellorsville**).

Points of Interest

There are historical markers for the crossing point at Kelly's Ford on the Rappahannock River where Stoneman's cavalry force crossed on April 29, 1863. Another historical marker in Ashland describes the raid launched against the railroad there (see **Louisa**).

DRIVING TOUR—*Proceed to Fredericksburg*
READING—*Chancellorsville*

FREDERICKSBURG AREA

Fredericksburg

Fifty miles north of Richmond, Fredericksburg was the principal city between Washington and the Confederate capital. The Rappahannock River, which flowed on the northern side of this charming colonial city, had long been a Rubicon for the Army of the Potomac. But Maj. Gen. Ambrose E. Burnside chose to avoid relying on the rail line through Manassas; instead he marched the army quickly to Falmouth, across the river from Fredericksburg. By November 17, 1862, Maj. Gen. Edwin V. Sumner's right grand division was at Falmouth. This redeployment impressed Lincoln and opened a railroad supply line from Aquia Landing on the Potomac north of Fredericksburg. The move concerned Lee, who had only a few troops in the area. But a Northern snafu in supporting Burnside's campaign soon dissipated any fears Lee had about being undermanned.

Because the Rebels had destroyed all the bridges over the Rappahannock, Burnside had to rely on pontoon bridges—small boats supporting a timber roadway—to effect a crossing. Due to poor staff work by General-in-Chief Henry W. Halleck in Washington and obstacles in getting the pontoons from Berlin on the Potomac below Harpers Ferry to Fredericksburg, the pontoon train did not arrive until late November. By that time Lee had transferred most of his 75,000 veterans to Fredericksburg.

Burnside had never wanted a battle at Fredericksburg; he simply wanted to bridge the river and engage the enemy on more favorable terrain for the Federals farther south. But now,

Federal engineers brave sniper fire as they bridge the Rappahannock River at Fredericksburg on December 11, 1862. Maj. Gen. Ambrose Burnside sent infantry across the river in pontoon boats to drive off the sharpshooters after a cannonade by massed Federal artillery on Stafford Heights failed to dislodge them.

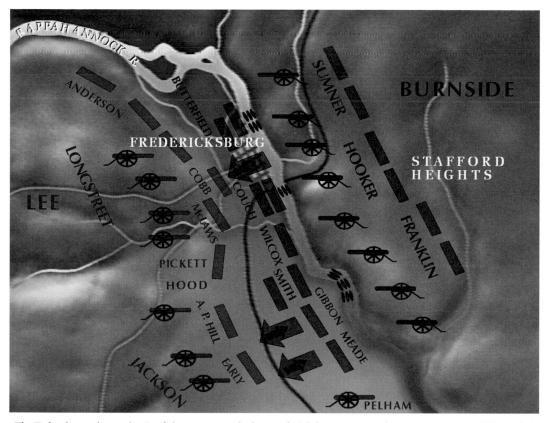

The Federal assaults on the Confederates entrenched at Fredericksburg on December 13, 1862, was a difficult challenge under ideal circumstances. The best chance of success was in front of Franklin's grand division south of the town. Although Maj. John Pelham's horse artillery enfiladed the Union left for a time, the divisions of Brig. Gens. George G. Meade and John Gibbon forged ahead against Jackson's front. Had Franklin supported the advance, a breakthrough was possible. Unaided, the soldiers of Meade and Gibbon were driven back. In town, the charge of Sumner's grand division, supported by part of Hooker's force, against the massed infantry and artillery of Longstreet's corps, was destined for failure despite the determination and bravery of the soldiers.

with the Army of Northern Virginia at his front, and political pressure for an offensive at his back, Burnside planned his strategy.

Burnside had reorganized the Army of the Potomac into three grand divisions; the right grand division under Maj. Gen. Edwin V. Sumner had arrived first on the Rappahannock. Had it not been for the commencement of heavy rains, and unwarranted concerns on Sumner's part, his troops might have crossed the river upstream at Scott's or Banks's fords prior to the arrival of the main Confederate force. The left grand division was under the command of Maj. Gen. William B. Franklin—number one in U.S. Grant's 1843 class at West Point—and the center under Maj. Gen. Joseph Hooker. "Fighting Joe" Hooker, an opportunistic officer, well liked by some of his colleagues and mistrusted by others, was openly critical of Burnside's plans. He had lobbied for Burnside's position and Burnside had agreed to take command of the army partly to keep it from Hooker.

Burnside spent another two weeks after the arrival of the pontoons deciding what to do. Lincoln and Halleck visited the army and Halleck suggested a crossing twenty miles downstream, at Skinker's Neck near Port Royal. Burnside abandoned this idea when the Rebels redeployed two divisions to meet that crossing.

Thinking that he would surprise the enemy by hitting them head-on, Burnside elected to cross the river at Fredericksburg. The only surprise to Lee was the folly of this choice. The Rebels had several weeks to strengthen their defensive position. Even among the Federals, there was disbelief in that approach. A New Jersey colonel wrote to his wife, "I can't think that we will move across here. The loss of life would be terrible."

On December 11, the Federal engineers began the difficult task of laying the six bridges. At Franklin's crossing site downstream of Fredericksburg, the operation was completed without incident. But in town, a reinforced brigade of Mississippi and Florida sharpshooters fired on the engineers with deadly accuracy. One hundred and forty-six Union artillery pieces, spaced along Stafford Heights with careful planning, shelled the town with a two-hour cannonade but failed to dislodge the persistent snipers.

Finally, Burnside sent infantry across the river in pontoon boats and they drove the Southerners from town. Three more pontoon spans were completed and late on December 11 Federal troops crossed the bridges and occupied the city. In angry reaction to the effectiveness of the Rebel sharpshooters, the Federal troops engaged in looting and destruction of the city from which many of the citizens had fled weeks earlier. This rampage was one of the ugliest incidents of its kind in the war up to that time.

The crossing and massing of Federal troops continued throughout December 12. The Confederates saw the men of Franklin's grand division mass near Hamilton's Crossing, opposite Jackson's corps. On the high ground west and upstream from town, Longstreet's corps had extended a line that centered on Marye's and Willis heights. At the foot of this gradual rise, he placed the reinforced brigade of Brig. Gen. T.R.R. Cobb behind a stone wall. This position flanked by sunken Telegraph Road offered much protection for the defenders. Broad fields separated the Rebels from the Federals, who were forming in town out of sight of the Confederates.

December 13, 1862, dawned cold and damp. A heavy mist obscured all movement, but the sounds of marshaling soldiers indicated an impending attack. About ten A.M. the fog suddenly lifted like a curtain, and south of Fredericksburg, Franklin's grand division, supported by part of Hooker's, advanced on the Rebel right. They first encountered 2 guns of John Pelham's horse artillery of Stuart's cavalry on open ground far in advance of the Confederate position. "It is glorious to see such courage in one so young," Lee said of the twenty-four-year-old Alabama major, whose reckless heroics slowed down the Union offensive. Pelham's cannons were neutralized, but soon the woods and fields in front of the Union infantry were swept by the fire of Jackson's artillery on Prospect Hill. Still, the Federals pressed forward. A division of Pennsylvanians under Brig. Gen. George Gordon Meade found a seam in Jackson's line and stormed ahead. Here, Burnside's unclear instructions to Franklin endangered the best opportunity for a breakthrough. Franklin understood his advance to be only a probing attack. Despite the urging of subordinates, Franklin refused to follow up the breakthrough without specific orders. The Rebels closed the gap and first hurled back Meade's advance and then turned on and mauled Brig. Gen. John Gibbon's division, which had pressed forward on Meade's right. Counterattacking Confederates were turned back as they sought to pursue the fleeing Yanks.

In Fredericksburg, the Federals were faring less well. Sumner's right grand division was hammered by Cobb's brigade, artillery, and other infantry. Sumner himself had been restrained from crossing the river to lead his troops into battle; he was considered too impetuous by the high command. But his gallantry had rubbed off on his soldiers. Joined by several of Hooker's divisions, the soldiers advanced across the upward sloping fields, slowed by fences, orchards, houses, and a drainage canal; charging, but never reaching the Georgians and North Carolinians who fired their rifle-muskets so rapidly as to achieve a machine gun–like effect.

The bravery of these men awed those on both sides of the line. Longstreet wrote later, "Before the well-directed fire of Cobb's Brigade, the Federals had fallen like the steady dripping of rains from the eaves of a house. Our musketry alone killed and wounded at least 5000; and these, with the slaughter by the artillery, left over 7000 killed and wounded before the foot of Marye's Hill. The dead were piled sometimes three deep, and when morning broke, the spectacle that we saw upon the battlefield was one of the most distressing I ever witnessed. The charges had been desperate and bloody, but utterly hopeless. I thought, as I saw the Federals come again and again to their death, that they deserved success if courage and daring could entitle soldiers to victory."

As the afternoon passed, more Confederates—South Carolinians led by dashing Brig. Gen. Joseph Kershaw—reinforced their comrades behind the stone wall. The short December day finally drew a curtain of twilight over the carnage after six charges. A newspaper reporter observed: "It can hardly be in human nature for men to show more valor, or generals to manifest less judgment."

In mental agony, Burnside assumed full responsibility. "Oh, those men, those men over there! I cannot get them out of my mind!" But he expressed displeasure with Hooker and Franklin for deliberately misunderstanding his orders. To assuage his grief, Burnside planned a desperation assault the next day, intending to lead his former command, the IX Corps, personally, but subordinates convinced him to abandon the idea. After only light skirmishing the next two days, the Federals quietly withdrew back across the river on the night of December 15–16.

Five weeks after withdrawing from Fredericksburg, the Federals embarked on a new offensive. Unusually cold dry weather in January prompted Burnside to plan to ford the Rappahannock above Fredericksburg. This would place the Union forces on Lee's left flank and force the Rebels away from their previously prepared defensive positions. Many of Burnside's subordinates were critical of the plan, especially Generals Hooker and Franklin, who affected the already low morale of the troops by openly disagreeing with Burnside.

Misfortune visited Burnside again. Heavy rains, then sleet and snow, inundated the expedition. The Virginia roads turned into ribbons of mud and bogged down the operation. The "Mud March" was abandoned on January 22.

The Confederate defenses on the heights behind Fredericksburg would be tested again in May 1863 as part of the next Federal offensive that resulted in the Battle of Chancellorsville.

Points of Interest

Fredericksburg and Spotsylvania County Battlefields Memorial National Military Park—The park includes seven major units, devoted to preserving and interpreting the Battles of Fredericksburg, Chancellorsville, the Wilderness, and Spotsylvania and related events. The Fredericksburg Unit includes many sites associated with the December 1862 battle. Fredericksburg is located just east of I-95 on US1 at VA3. The Fredericksburg Battlefield Visitor Center on BUS1 has exhibits and information on the park's points of interest. Behind the visitor center is the Sunken Road, and Marye's and Willis heights. Interpretive signs and markers locate the positions of Cobb's brigade and other Confederate units that opposed the six Federal charges on December 13, 1862. On May 2, 1863, the division of Maj. Gen. John Gibbon, on its way to rendezvous with Hooker's forces at Chancellorsville, overran the Confederates of William Barksdale's Mississippi Brigade posted here under Jubal Early. The mansion on Marye's Heights, now part of Mary Washington College, stood during the battle. The heights are the location of the Fredericksburg National Cemetery.

A driving tour along a park road, Lee Drive, will lead you to the heights where Longstreet's and Jackson's artillery was located. Also on Lee Drive is the Federal breakthrough, where Meade's division charged the woods and found a seam in Jackson's line. At the intersection of VA2 and VA608 there is a monument identifying the site where John Pelham committed his horse artillery to oppose the Federal advance.

As you approach Fredericksburg from the south on VA2, the Rappahannock River is on your right. The streets nearest to the river are where the Rebel sharp-shooters held off the

Marye's Heights at Fredericksburg. The stone wall at the foot of this rise was the scene of the bloodiest fighting at the Battle of Fredericksburg. Artillery on the crest of the hill added to the intense fire of Cobb's infantry as the Federals advanced against the position. The house on Marye's Heights, now part of Mary Washington College, survived the two battles at Fredericksburg.

Federals laying the pontoon bridges. Despite the heavy shelling of Fredericksburg, many of the buildings on Caroline, Sophia, and adjoining streets survive. A small unit of the park just off BUS17 north of William Street was one of the Federal crossing sites in Fredericksburg.

On the east bank of the Rappahannock River is Chatham

Manor, known during the Civil War as the Lacy House. This riverfront home was used as a Federal headquarters and hospital. The building has exhibits on medical care during the Civil War. Among those who cared for wounded soldiers here were Clara Barton and the poet Walt Whitman. From Chatham Manor's front lawn there is an excellent view of Fredericksburg across the river where two pontoon bridges were laid. 🚲 ♿ 🚶 ❓ 🏛 P 🧺 🚻

Two sites east of Fredericksburg near Port Royal relate to John Wilkes Booth's flight from Washington, D.C., after he assassinated Abraham Lincoln. Cleydael, VA206 a mile and a third west of VA218, is a summer home circa 1859, which in 1865 belonged to Dr. Richard Stuart, a kinsman of Robert E. Lee's family. On Sunday evening, April 23, a suspicious Dr. Stuart, aware of the assassination and Booth's flight, refused to aid Booth, who with David Herold came to his door seeking assistance.

On US301, 2 miles south of Port Royal on the Fort A. P. Hill Military Reservation, is a historical marker indicating the site of the Richard Garrett Place. Here on April 26, 1865, Booth and Herold were cornered in a tobacco shed by New York cavalry. Herold surrendered but Booth remained armed inside the shed, even after the structure was torched. Sgt. Boston Corbitt, a New York cavalryman, shot Booth through an opening in the burning building. Booth was dragged from the barn alive, but paralyzed by the wound in his spinal column. The twenty-six-year-old Booth was laid on the porch of the farmhouse where he died the next morning.

Twenty-one miles east of the intersection of US301 and VA3 on VA3 is Stafford Hall, the birthplace of Robert E. Lee. A few miles west of Stafford Hall is the George Washington Birthplace National Monument.

DRIVING TOUR—*Proceed to Chancellorsville*
READING *(chronological)*—*Grant's First Vicksburg Campaign, Mississippi*

Chancellorsville

Spring of 1863 brought the Army of the Potomac another new commander. Shortly after the "Mud March," Lincoln replaced Burnside with Maj. Gen. Joseph Hooker. Lincoln's appointment was made with some reservations because Hooker's reputation for intrigue and rowdiness was well known. As he had with past commanders, Lincoln expressed his views in his straightforward, fatherly advice. He let Hooker know his feelings on the general's earlier undermining of Burnside: "You have taken counsel of your ambition . . . in which you did a great wrong to the country, and to a most meritorious and honorable brother officer. I have heard, in such way as to believe it, of your recently saying that both the Army and the Government needed a dictator. Of course it was not for this, but in spite of it, that I have given you the command. Only those generals who gain successes can set up dictators. What I now ask of you is military success, and I will risk the dictatorship."

Hooker was a popular choice with the men of the Army of the Potomac. He improved conditions in the camps and hospitals—cashiering corrupt quartermasters, bettering the quality of the rations, and improving morale by creating distinctive badges for each corps. He took the important step of organizing the cavalry into a separate corps, based on the successful Confederate model. Amnesty was granted to AWOL soldiers. The reforms worked. Sickness and desertion declined, AWOLs returned and morale improved throughout the army. A soldier in the ranks wrote, "Under Hooker, we began to live."

Lincoln was pleased with the condition of the army when he visited Hooker along the Rappahannock in early April. But he raised an eyebrow at Hooker's self-congratulatory attitude and reminded him of the job at hand. "The hen is the wisest of all the animals in all creation," the president told him, "because she never cackles until the egg is laid."

The increasing strength of the Army of the Potomac was of concern to Lee, who had recently cut his own force to 60,000 men. In late February, Lee sent Longstreet south with two divisions to confront continuing Union threats in Tidewater Virginia and North Carolina (see **Suffolk**). Lee's cavalry was also scattered in search of better forage as well as the reporting of Federal troop movements.

Still, Lee's men remained in command of the heights behind Fredericksburg and had a ten-mile network of trenches commanding the Rappahannock. Rations were being sent from Longstreet's expedition near Suffolk, Virginia, to feed the hungry soldiers and morale was high among these proud fighters. These opportunities for Lee's army to rest and refit between campaigns were a result of the failure of the Army of the Potomac commanders to keep constant pressure on the Army of Northern Virginia. This situation continued until Grant came east in March 1864.

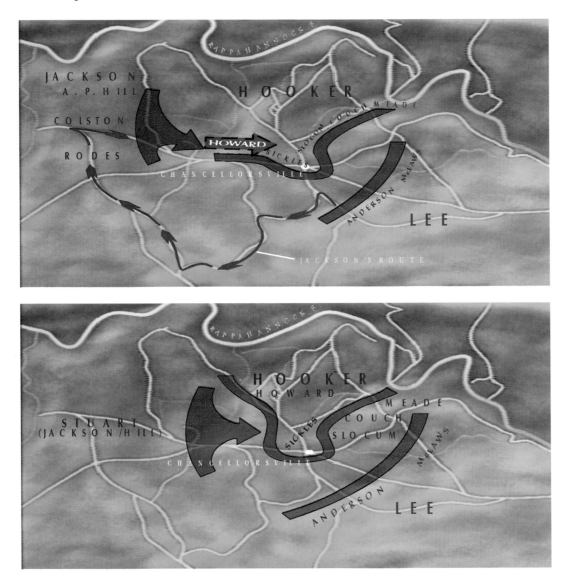

The Battle of Chancellorsville was fought on three fronts—at Chancellorsville, at Fredericksburg, and at Salem Church, several miles away. On May 2, Stonewall Jackson marched his force around the flank of the Federal army, leaving Lee with just two divisions to face three corps of the Army of the Potomac. Jackson's evening attack on May 2 routed the weakest corps in the Army of the Potomac, Maj. Gen. Oliver O. Howard's XI Corps. As a result Hooker, who had already drawn in his line, fell back to an even shorter line centering on the Chancellorsville intersection. When J.E.B. Stuart temporarily commanded the wounded Jackson's corps on May 3 and 4, the Federals at Chancellorsville were battling Rebels on two fronts. Maj. Gen. John Sedgwick's Federal VI Corps was prevented from coming to Hooker's aid when Rebels at Salem Church put up a spirited fight. On the night of May 5, Hooker recrossed the Rappahannock River over the fords north of his position.

With the exclamation, "May God have mercy on General Lee, for I will have none," Hooker launched his offensive to bring the Rebels out of their trenches for a fight on ground of his choosing. The reorganized cavalry, 10,000 strong, crossed the Rappahannock at Kelly's Ford on April 29 and headed south to cut the supply lines to Lee's army and further distract the Rebel cavalry (see **Stoneman's Raid**). Hooker left Maj. Gen. John Sedgwick's reinforced VI Corps at Fredericksburg to feign an attack and keep Lee's force there. Hooker took three infantry corps, 42,000 men, on a swift twenty-seven-mile march around Lee's left flank. By the evening of April 30, most of this force was concentrated around a mansion inn at a crossroads called Chancellorsville. Much of the area surrounding this hamlet was a dense forest with heavy underbrush known locally as The Wilderness.

Hooker's converging attack placed Lee in a virtual checkmate. But like those who had preceded him, Hooker seemed unaware of the nerve and instinct of gambling "Bobby" Lee and the resolve of those whom he commanded. Lee assumed correctly that the chief Federal threat was at Chancellorsville. He left only 10,000 men entrenched at Fredericksburg under Maj. Gen. Jubal Early and marched the rest of his infantry and artillery toward Chancellorsville. On May 1, they clashed with the advance division of Hooker's force near Zoan Church, on open ground favorable to the Yanks east of Chancellorsville.

Rather than pressing this attack in which the North had advantage in numbers and cannons, Hooker ordered the troops back into a defensive position at Chancellorsville, where the thickets reduced their firepower and numerical advantage. Hooker's corps commanders feared their leader had lost his nerve even before Lee displayed the extent of his.

Lee and Stonewall Jackson conferred on the night of May 1–2. As the two commanders assessed the strength of Hooker's well-defended line and how to attack it, J.E.B. Stuart brought scouting reports indicating that Hooker's right flank was "in the air," that is, vulnerable to attack, three miles west of Chancellorsville. This was the opportunity Lee had hoped for and Jackson's combat-tested veterans were the soldiers to take advantage of the situation.

Guided by a local resident and screened by Stuart's cavalry, Jackson took 29,000 infantry and artillery on a roundabout twelve-mile march through The Wilderness early on May 2. Lee was left with only 13,000 men facing Hooker's front, while Early still faced almost three-to-one odds at Fredericksburg. This chance to overwhelm Lee was missed by the Federals. The only Federal attack on May 2 occurred when Maj. Gen. Daniel Sickles's III

Corps discovered Jackson's column and reported the discovery to Hooker. But the Army of the Potomac commander chose to see this as a retreat of Lee's army to the southwest. Sickles, with most of his corps and one brigade of the XI Corps, started out in pursuit of Jackson. Unable to penetrate Stuart's cavalry screen the Yanks were unable to ascertain the Confederates' intentions.

Thus, at five-fifteen P.M. on May 2, 1863, the soldiers of Maj.

These dead soldiers at the foot of Marye's Heights are Confederates photographed a few days after the Federal VI Corps overran the stone wall on May 3, 1863, as part of the Chancellorsville battle. The Rebels had held off furious Federal attacks on this sunken road the previous December. However, when Lee marched the majority of the Confederate force to oppose Hooker at Chancellorsville, Maj. Gen. Jubal Early had only a handful of Southern soldiers remaining in Fredericksburg to counter the powerful Union attack.

Gen. O. O. Howard's XI Corps were ill prepared for the gray-clad thunderbolt approaching from the west, and after a brief stand near Wilderness Church, Howard's corps collapsed. As Union troops were redeployed to check Jackson's surge, this fight turned into a rare Civil War night-combat action that was especially costly for both sides. Reconnoitering in The Wilderness after dark, Stonewall Jackson was shot and wounded by his own men while returning to his lines.

When Jackson went down, A. P. Hill assumed command but was also soon wounded. J.E.B. Stuart stepped in to take their place for the ensuing action. Jackson's left arm was amputated near Wilderness Tavern, five miles west of the Chancellorsville crossroads. He was moved to the Chandler's office at Guinea Station on the rail line to Richmond, behind the lines south of Fredericksburg. Here he developed pneumonia before being moved to a hospital in the Confederate capital. On Sunday, May 10, eight days after being wounded, he uttered the words, "Let us cross over the river, and rest under the shade of the trees," and died.

Severely disheartened by Jackson's loss, the Rebels nevertheless engaged in some of the hardest fighting of the war on May 3. On the previous day, Hooker had ordered Sedgwick to take the heights behind Fredericksburg and push toward Lee's rear at Chancellorsville. Sedgwick's force the next morning overran the previously impregnable Sunken Road and Marye's and Willis heights behind Fredericksburg. But on May 3, his forces were stopped in bitter fighting by the brigade of Brig. Gen. Cadmus M. Wilcox, fighting from within and around Salem Church. The Confederates at Chancellorsville seized the high ground of Hazel Grove, drove the bluecoats, with often bitter fighting from Fairview, and pressed closer to Hooker's Chancellorsville headquarters. Hooker was stunned by an artillery shell striking one of the mansion's columns. He subsequently ordered his forces into a tight defensive arc with the left entrenched behind Mineral Spring Run and the right on the Rapidan.

The next day passed without any major change in the lines along Hooker's front. At Salem Church an all-out attack on Sedgwick's reinforced VI Corps by three of Lee's divisions misfired. On the night of May 4, the Army of the Potomac corps commanders held a council of war. The majority of commanders voted to remain south of the Rappahannock and continue the battle, but Hooker disregarded the vote and ordered a withdrawal. Fighting Joe had had the fight knocked out of him.

Lee's only regret was that Sedgwick's withdrawal across the Rappahannock at Scott's Ford on the night of May 4 and Hooker's on the night of May 5 at U.S. Ford enabled the Federals to escape without further embarrassment. The Confederate victory, for a time, took the war away from this part of Virginia. More important, Lee acted on the invincibility he perceived in his army. With his depleted force, made weaker by nearly 13,000 casualties at Chancellorsville, Lee could not afford to sit and wait for a refitted Army of the Potomac to strike again, with better leadership and new resolve. He determined to again take the war to the North.

Points of Interest

Fredericksburg and Spotsylvania County Battlefields Memorial National Military Park—The Chancellorsville Battlefield Unit of the park has a visitor center, located just north of VA3 on Bullock Road, and numerous wayside exhibits. If you are traveling west on VA3 from Fredericksburg, you first arrive at Old Salem Church. The brick church stands where fierce fighting took place on May 3–4, 1863. There is a parking lot behind the church, and pamphlets are available at the site for a short walking tour. The Chancellorsville driving tour is circular. The visitor center is located where units from the Federal III and XII corps were posted on the evening of May 2 and morning of May 3. The center has exhibits, a bookstore, and an audiovisual program.

On the drive northeast from the visitor center along Bullock Road, there is a marker at the intersection of Ely's Ford Road, VA610, that marks the apex of Hooker's final line. After a right turn on VA610, at the intersection of VA3, are the ruins of Chancellorsville, where Hooker maintained his headquarters. This was a focus of action on May 3. Continue east on VA3, 1.5 miles to McLaws Drive, turn right onto McLaws Drive and you come to the intersection of McLaws Drive and the Orange Plank Road (VA610), where Lee and Jackson met on the night of May 1–2 to plan their bold strategy. By continuing to make right turns on Furnace Road, Jackson Trail East, and VA613, you can follow Jackson's flanking march and reenter VA3 where his force emerged from The Wilderness to deploy and begin the May 2 attack. 🚲 ♿ 🚶 ❓ P ⛱ 🚻

Returning east on VA3 toward Bullock Road, you pass Wilderness Church as well as a monument indicating the point at which Jackson was mortally wounded by soldiers of the 18th North Carolina Infantry, and Hazel Grove, just south of VA3 on a park road.

At Guinea Station, 15 miles south of Fredericksburg on VA606 east of I-95, is the Stonewall Jackson Shrine. Stonewall Jackson, having had his left arm amputated near Wilderness Tavern, arrived here, at the Fairfield Plantation of T. C. Chandler, on May 4 in an ambulance to await transportation to a Richmond hospital on the railroad. Pneumonia complicated his wound and he died in the clapboard office building on May 10, 1863.

DRIVING TOUR—*Proceed to the Wilderness*
READING—*Brandy Station*

GRANT'S SPRING 1864 VIRGINIA CAMPAIGN

On March 9, 1864, having been called on short notice to Washington, Ulysses S. Grant was commissioned lieutenant general and made general-in-chief. The three-star-general status, the first since George Washington, had been authorized by Congress with Grant in mind. Lincoln was confident that Grant would use the rank and position to end the war, rather than advance any political ambitions he might have. The president's supposition was correct. With Halleck remaining in Washington in the lesser post of chief of staff but continuing his capable administrative functions, Grant, who refused to run the Federal armies from Washington, returned to the field with a plan that would receive Lincoln's endorsement.

Grant's proposal was simple and direct—a coordinated attack by all armies of the Union, now that they were all under his control. Sherman, elevated by Grant to commander of the Military Division of Mississippi, would go after Joseph E. Johnston's Army of Tennessee. Grant would accompany the Army of the Potomac in Virginia and campaign against Lee. Meade offered to resign, suggesting that Grant may want to bring in his own commander from the west, but Grant declined the offer. Even though he brought in tough Maj. Gen. Philip Sheridan to take charge of the cavalry and his own presence with the army reduced Meade's role significantly, the two generals successfully maintained an efficient working relationship through the end of the war. Grant then issued an order to Meade that characterized strategy of the campaign: "Wherever Lee goes, there you will go also."

Lt. Gen. Ulysses S. Grant was confident that the success of a coordinated and concerted effort by all Federal armies in the field would succeed. In the case of the two principal armies he was correct: slow steady pressure by the Army of the Potomac in Virginia bottled up Gen. Robert E. Lee's Army of Northern Virginia and within six weeks placed the Confederate capital under siege, while the drive through northwest Georgia by Maj. Gen. William T. Sherman's "army group" threatened the strategic city of Atlanta. However, lesser tasks given to smaller commands under political generals led to Northern defeats and waste of resources.

The Wilderness

On the east side of the Blue Ridge, the key campaign, the one that brought the new Federal lieutenant general to Virginia, began. On the night of May 3, 1864, Grant and Meade began their advance. The Army of the Potomac was now divided into three infantry corps: the II under Maj. Gen. Winfield S. Hancock, who had recovered from his Gettysburg wound; the V led by Maj. Gen. Gouverneur K. Warren, who had replaced George Sykes; and the VI Corps whose leader continued to be Maj. Gen. John Sedgwick. Ambrose E. Burnside and his IX Corps, returning from East Tennessee, joined the force but until the fourth week of May reported to Grant. With many in this army approaching the end of their three-year enlistments, Grant hoped his campaign would be swift and decisive. The army crossed the Rapidan River and entered The Wilderness, which Grant wanted to traverse as quickly as possible. But Lee was not going to let this dense scrub forest, his ally in two previous Federal offensives, be passed without a fight. He pressed two corps west from their encampments near Orange Court House. Longstreet's corps, having returned from winter quarters in East Tennessee, marched from camps near Gordonsville.

On the morning of May 5, the Federal march through The Wilderness was interrupted. Major General Warren's V Corps's skirmishers clashed with Ewell's II Corps on the Orange Turnpike. The fight between Warren's and Ewell's lead divisions raged across a clearing on the Saunders Farm. Waves of blue and gray ebbed and flowed across the cleared ground and into the woods beyond.

Union horse soldiers were the first to meet Lt. Gen. A. P. Hill's corps as it advanced east on the Orange Plank Road. The plank road cut the barest sliver of daylight through the dark, smoke-filled woods. Thanks to the delaying action of the cavalry, Brig. Gen. George W. Getty's division of the Federal VI Corps reached there first and held the vital intersection of the Orange Plank and Brock roads. A follow-up attack on Hill by Hancock's II Corps was poorly coordinated and finally halted by Rebel reserves, but Hill's corps was hard hit. Despite Sedgwick's aid to Warren, the Federals failed to dislodge Ewell from the woods west of and north and south of Saunders's field. Spades were now trump and the soldiers in blue and butternut entrenched whenever there was a respite from the savage combat.

Lee still saw The Wilderness situation in a positive light that night, even though Hill's command was cut up and scattered. He was confident that Longstreet would arrive in time from Gordonsville to back up Hill's position on the right. Grant pushed for a dawn

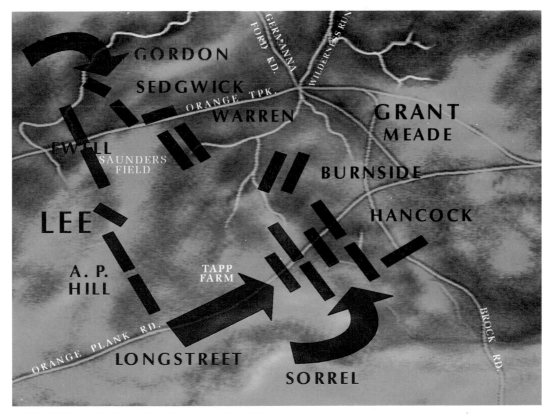

The Wilderness battle was fought over two days in May as Gen. Robert E. Lee sought to challenge the march of the Federal Army of the Potomac across the Rapidan River and southeast toward Richmond. While two Union corps challenged Lt. Gen. Richard Ewell's corps on and around the Saunders Farm, Maj. Gen. Winfield S. Hancock's II Corps hammered Lt. Gen. A. P. Hill's Rebels along the Brock Road. Only the timely arrival of Lt. Gen. James Longstreet's corps on May 6 averted a Confederate rout. Longstreet's two-pronged counterattack drove the Federals back to a defensive position along Brock Road and Brig. Gen. John B. Gordon's flanking attack on the Federal right late on May 6 hammered, but did not break, the Union line. Lt. Gen. Ulysses S. Grant then ordered the Federal force to march southeast around the Confederate position to the Spotsylvania Court House.

attack the morning of May 6. The Union right gained no ground on the Orange Turnpike, but Hancock's sledgehammer blows broke up Hill's weakened corps on the Orange Plank Road. With Longstreet still not on the field, Lee sensed disaster in this area and attempted to rally units for a do-or-die stand across the Widow Tapp Farm. At this critical moment, Longstreet's vanguard arrived. Concerned for Lee's safety, soldiers from the Texas-Arkansas brigade sent Lee to the rear. Longstreet's men first stalled the Union advance, then surprised the Federals with a thunderous two-pronged counterattack that first rolled up the Union left like a wet carpet.

As Longstreet and other officers rode forward during this offensive in the confusing and tangled woodland, they were accidentally fired upon by Virginians in the flanking force. Longstreet was seriously wounded. The Confederates, however, forced Hancock's men back to breastworks covering the Brock Road. Gunfire exchanges sparked raging blazes in the dry timber, trapping many wounded soldiers not evacuated in time.

In this illustration, from a sketch by an illustrated newspaper's special artist, Federal soldiers carry a wounded man from The Wilderness battlefield on a makeshift stretcher. The Wilderness underbrush was so dense, artillery and small arms fire easily ignited spot incendiaries in many of the wooded areas on the battlefield.

About four P.M. Longstreet's men launched an attack on these works, but the Confederates were beaten back. At dusk Brig. Gen. John B. Gordon of Ewell's corps hit Sedgwick on the other flank. Gordon achieved local success but darkness and stiffening resistance first checked then blunted the Rebel surge. Both sides were left to assess their staggering casualties.

Among the Federal casualties captured and being treated behind the lines was an older general who had commanded the I Corps's elite first division, Maj. Gen. James Wadsworth. The political general, whose wealth had given him multimillionaire status in a time when that was a rare feat for any individual, died a lonely death in a Confederate hospital, treated by his foe with the respect due to him.

Grant rose early on the morning of May 7. By this time Assistant Secretary of War Charles A. Dana, dispatched by Lincoln and Stanton for news from the front, had arrived at Grant's headquarters. Expecting to report the withdrawal of the Army of the Potomac after apparent defeat in The Wilderness, Dana and others were surprised when Grant issued orders for Meade to march to Spotsylvania Court House, skirting Lee's right flank. Cheers went up as the news reached the ranks; the soldiers also expected a retreat to reorganize, an action that had followed, as night follows day, whenever they had advanced to break Lee's defenses in the Piedmont. In Grant, Lincoln had found a military leader who shared his vision of how victory could be achieved. A race to the southeast began as both armies raced to get to the strategic crossroads first. After his troopers first screened the infantry move to Spotsylvania, Maj. Gen. Philip Sheridan received permission from Grant to embark on his first independent mission as cavalry commander. He established a lasting reputation for guts and initiative (see **Yellow Tavern**).

Points of Interest

Fredericksburg and Spotsylvania County Battlefields Memorial National Military Park—Just a few miles west of the Chancellorsville battlefield visitor center is the eastern edge of The Wilderness battlefield. The Wilderness Unit has no visitor center, but there are several interpretive stops. East of the intersection of VA3 and VA20 is a remaining portion of the chimney of The Wilderness Tavern, a landmark during the battle and close to the site of Grant's headquarters. Turning west on VA20, you enter the area of Saunders's field, where the Federal V Corps and later the VI Corps battled Lt. Gen. Richard Ewell's II Corps for two days. Elwood (the Lacy House) was Warren's headquarters; in its garden is buried Stonewall Jackson's amputated left arm. Elwood is on NPS land and accessible with NPS permis-

The Wilderness was fought on May 5 and 6, 1864, in a heavily wooded area south of the Rapidan River in Piedmont Virginia. Several farms dotted the area, among them the Saunders Farm. This field was at the center of the battle between Ewell's Confederates and Warren's Federals. It is now part of the Fredericksburg and Spotsylvania County Battlefields Memorial National Military Park.

sion through the Chancellorsville Visitor Center. There is an exhibit shelter and walking trails to important sites on this, the northern sector of the battlefield.

Taking Hill-Ewell Drive south from VA20, you travel through the dense portion of The Wilderness through which Federal cavalry rode to gain the Orange Plank Road at Parker's Store. VA621 at this point is the Orange Plank Road. Just west of the intersection with Hill-Ewell Drive is the Widow Tapp Farm, where Robert E. Lee stood tall until the first of Longstreet's units arrived. Return east on VA621 to the Orange Plank Road's intersection with Brock Road. Here are remains of entrenchments dug with haste by the Federal II and VI corps. South of VA621 is the unfinished railroad grade upon which a portion of Longstreet's corps was deployed by the Georgian's chief of staff, Col. G. Moxley Sorrel, to flank the Union II Corps's position.　🏃 ❷ P 🪑 🚻

DRIVING TOUR—*Proceed to Spotsylvania*
READING—*Yellow Tavern*

Spotsylvania

General Lee had little time to mourn the May 12 death of J.E.B. Stuart, mortally wounded at Yellow Tavern. Though he successfully shifted his lead divisions under Lt. Gen. R. H. Anderson, now commanding the I Corps in place of the wounded Longstreet, to a strategic position west of Spotsylvania Court House, the swift-moving Army of the Potomac, rejuvenated by Grant's determination, marched on roads parallel to the Rebels and momentarily had a head start on Anderson's veterans. This move was anticipated by Lee, who also had respect for Grant and his determination to press forward.

The action at Spotsylvania started almost immediately on May 8. Fitzhugh Lee's cavalry delayed General Warren's V Corps, screened by Wesley Merritt's horse soldiers, advancing down the Brock Road until Anderson arrived on the double at Laurel Hill just minutes ahead of the Yankee infantry. Warren's assaults were repulsed. The Rebels expanded the initial defense line into an elaborate system of earthworks and the Federals matched these with spadework of their own. Maj. Gen. "Uncle John" Sedgwick was killed by a sniper's bullet on May 9 after assuring a frightened soldier that no sniper could shoot an elephant from the distant position the Confederates held. One of the North's most beloved commanders joined the lengthening list of Federal casualties in Grant's

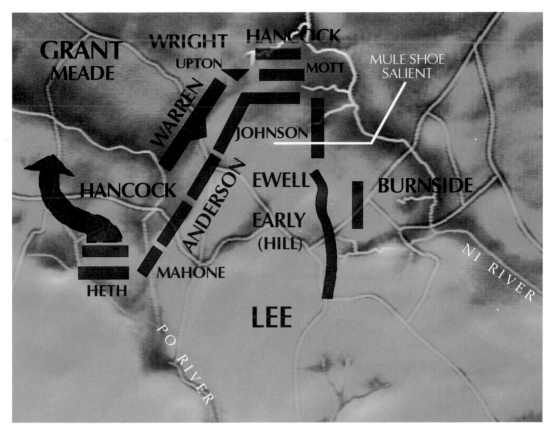

The struggle for control of the important intersection at Spotsylvania Court House began almost immediately after the two armies broke contact in The Wilderness and marched on parallel routes to positions west of the village. Preceded by cavalry, which battled on the road to Spotsylvania at Todd's Tavern, the two armies squared off on May 8, when Maj. Gen. Gouverneur Warren's V Corps met Lt. Gen. Richard H. Anderson, in command of the wounded Longstreet's corps, on May 8. The next day, the two armies entrenched. An offensive by Hancock south of the Po River, on the Confederate left, was stalled and Hancock's soldiers were shifted to the center of the long line that quickly developed. On the evening of May 10, Col. Emory Upton attacked the Mule Shoe portion of the Confederate line and early on the morning of May 12, Grant ordered Hancock's entire corps to attack the Mule Shoe. In twenty hours of bitter fighting in a driving rainstorm the Federals captured a Rebel division, but Lee formed a new line. The failure of either side to make additional progress against their entrenched foe caused Grant to pull up stakes and continue to march toward Richmond around Lee's right flank.

campaign, not yet a week old. That same day, Grant sent Hancock's corps to turn the Confederate left, but the effort unraveled as the woods and the Po River slowed the advance enough for Lee to shift his troops. On May 10, Federal attacks by the II and V corps against Anderson's butternuts posted in the Laurel Hill earthworks were repulsed with heavy Union losses. At six P.M. VI Corps soldiers prepared to assail the sector on the west face of the Mule Shoe Salient held by Brig. Gen. George Dole's Georgians. Col. Emory Upton emerged as a Union hero, leading twelve regiments over the imposing breastworks. But Brig. Gen. Greshom R. Mott lacked the resolve to bring up his support division as planned. Savage Rebel counterattacks drove Upton's force back as darkness set in.

Grant saw the value in this attack formation and ordered a similar assault targeted on the apex of the Mule Shoe in the pre-dawn hours of May 12. Hancock's II Corps started the attack at four-forty A.M. and they overwhelmed Edward Johnson's division, taking several thousand prisoners including "Allegheny Ed."

Once again, the determined Southerners rose to the occasion and resisted the breakthrough. The fighting lasted all day and into the night and by two A.M. on May 13 Lee established a new defensive line across the base of the Mule Shoe Salient. Despite five more days of skirmishing and a May 18 Union attack on Southern fortifications thrown up during the Mule Shoe struggle, the Rebel line held. Then, on May 19, in a hard-fought struggle at the Harris Farm, east of the Ni River, the Federals hammered Ewell's II Corps Confederates as they made a forced reconnaissance.

Grant learned of Sigel's defeat in the Shenandoah Valley, which kept Lee's left flank out of danger. That failure and the futility of further action against this strong position caused Grant to order another march around Lee's right flank. On the night of May 20–21, the Army of the Potomac broke camp and headed southeast for the North Anna River.

Points of Interest

Fredericksburg and Spotsylvania County Battlefields Memorial National Military Park—When you proceed from The Wilderness to Spotsylvania via VA613, Brock Road, you are following the route which Warren's V and Hancock's II corps used on the march to Spotsylvania Court House. Midway on the route is the site of Todd's Tavern (at VA612). Here on May 7, Federal cavalry massed to hold the intersection against a thrust by J.E.B. Stuart's horsemen and keep the road open for a planned night march known only to top Federal commanders.

Your tour of Spotsylvania begins when you enter the park unit at Grant Drive and turn left. At the intersection is a monument marking the site where Maj. Gen. John Sedgwick fell to a sniper's bullet. Here also is the Spotsylvania Exhibit Shelter, which will orient your tour. Before continuing northeast on Grant Drive, take the walking tour west along Hancock Road and south to the crest of Laurel Hill following in the steps of Union soldiers in the May 8 and May 10 assaults. Federal earthworks are viewed here. As you continue the tour east on Grant Road and the connecting park roads you come to the Mule Shoe. A short walking tour takes you along the earthworks that remain from this bitter struggle. Interpretive markers along the park roads indicate the position of Lee's reformed line and Burnside's position on the Federal left flank.   🚲 🚶 ❷ P ⛵ 🚻

Northeast of the national park property is a parcel acquired by APCWS that contains a monument to the 1st Massachusetts Heavy Artillery Regiment. This is the location of the May 19 attack by Ewell's corps on its forced reconnaissance after General Meade shifted his forces east of the former Federal works centering on the Mule Shoe. The "heavies," as they were called, were former artillerymen from the Washington, D.C., defenses pressed into service as infantrymen by Grant's continuing need for replacements. Although they were expected to perform poorly, they showed courage and resolve in resisting the attack of Ewell's 6,000-man force. The monument and the Harris House which served as a hospital are on the site, which is surrounded by a working farm. Check with park service personnel at either the Fredericksburg or Chancellorsville visitor centers for current access.

This photograph is one in a series of unique candid pictures in which photographer Timothy O'Sullivan captured Grant, his staff, and Army of the Potomac commanders meeting in the yard of Massaponax Baptist Church on May 21, 1864, as the Federal armies were marching from Spotsylvania Court House to the North Anna River.

At Spotsylvania Court House (intersection of VA608 and VA208) is the Spotsylvania County Museum, in the Old Berea Christian Church. This example of antebellum Gothic Revival was used as a hospital during the war, and now it houses a collection of local artifacts. For more information on the museum, call 703-582-7167. Nearby Christ Episcopal Church was built in 1841 and shows evidence of the shelling that scarred the area in May 1864. The existing Spotsylvania courthouse at the intersection of VA608 and VA208 utilizes the front columns from the Civil War–era courthouse. The Spotsylvania Confederate Cemetery is off VA208 northeast of the intersection. For general information on sites and attractions in Spotsylvania County, contact the Spotsylvania Visitors' Center, 4707 Southpoint Parkway, Fredericksburg, VA 22407; 703-891-TOUR or 1-800-654-4118.

From Spotsylvania Court House, proceed east on VA608 to the intersection of US1. At this intersection is Massaponax Baptist Church. Here, after the armies began marching from Spotsylvania, Grant held a meeting with his staff and generals. Pews were removed from the church and placed under a large shade tree. Photographer Timothy O'Sullivan, who had been following the Federal armies in Virginia for almost two years in the employ of Alexander Gardner of Washington, hauled his large stereo camera to the second story of the church and from the front window recorded a unique series of candid images of Grant, Meade, and other officers of the Army of the Potomac.

DRIVING TOUR—*Proceed to North Anna River*
READING—*New Market*

North Anna River

While Maj. Gen. George G. Meade marched the Army of the Potomac ever closer to Richmond, maintaining a supply line open to tidewater rivers to the east, Lee kept his army moving as well. Much to Lee's dismay, the days of Union commanders who had allowed their army to rest and refit were gone. While the battles of The Wilderness and Spotsylvania took a terrible toll on the Federal forces, Grant knew that Lee's army was suffering heavy losses too, so he continued to press forward, certain that the North could win a war of attrition. Lee's position south of the North Anna River, long considered one of the last strong defensive lines north of Richmond, was immediately challenged by Grant. Warren's V Corps crossed the river at Jericho Mill on May 23 so swiftly that Lee was caught unprepared and A. P. Hill botched the counterattack. By the time Hancock's corps crossed at Chesterfield Bridge the next day, Lee had prepared a defensive position that broke Grant's force into three parts. Lee would be able to shift forces as different parts of his inverted-V-shaped line were tested. By May 26 the three-day battle was over, and Grant pulled all his forces back north of the river. But with Longstreet seriously wounded and out of action, and with Ewell, A. P. Hill, and Lee himself ill and exhausted, the Confederate army was unable to deliver a decisive counterblow to send the Army of the Potomac reeling. So Grant resumed his jug handled movements around the Rebel right flank to test the Southern army at another point, somewhere south of the Pamunkey River.

Points of Interest

US1 crosses the North Anna River 23 miles south of Massaponax Church (VA608). This is close to where the old Telegraph Road crossed the North Anna River. Winfield S. Hancock's Federals captured the bridge in a dramatic May 23 charge. But Ewell's troops, holding the right of Lee's inverted-V-shaped line, on May 24 stalled Hancock's corps. There are few markers describing this action but by parking south of the river along the road, you can get a good view of the largely undisturbed landscape. Do not attempt to cross the river by foot; the US1 bridge is narrow and traffic moves fast.

Mount Carmel Church, which is identified by a historical marker on US1 north of the North Anna was Grant's headquarters on May 24. East of US1 on VA684 is Doswell, formerly Hanover Junction. This crossover of the Virginia Central Railroad and the Richmond, Fredericksburg & Potomac was a key strategic position that Lee's North Anna line sought to protect.

A little more than a mile south of the river, VA684 intersects US1. Turn left and proceed 2.8 miles. Here land administered by Hanover County has been set aside to commemorate the May 24 attack by Brig. Gen. James Ledlie's IX Corps brigade. Ledlie was drunk when he sent his Yanks in a futile charge against Rebel works defended by Brig. Gen. Billy Mahone's division. Ledlie's soldiers were repulsed with heavy casualties. For more information on the park, which features some of the best and most pristine Virginia earthworks, call Hanover County Parks at 804-798-8062.

From this point you can continue northwest on VA684, via VA601 and VA618, to Louisa (Jericho Mill, several miles northwest on the river, where Warren's V Corps crossed the North Anna on May 23 and fought A. P. Hill's Confederates, is not accessible). Or you can return to US1 and drive south to one of several more direct routes to Louisa, which is 37 miles northwest of US1 via Ashland.

DRIVING TOUR— *Proceed to Trevilian Station (Louisa)*
READING— *Totopotomy Creek–Cold Harbor*

Trevilian Station

On May 31 and June 1, 1864, having secured the crossroads at Cold Harbor pending the arrival of Federal infantry, two divisions of Maj. Gen. Philip H. Sheridan's cavalry corps prepared for a new mission—the destruction of the railroad linking Richmond and Charlottesville. They would then link up with David Hunter's Shenandoah Valley army at Charlottesville. Most of General Lee's cavalry, under new leader Maj. Gen. Wade Hampton, was sent in pursuit of Sheridan. On June 11, Sheridan attacked one of Hampton's divisions at Trevilian Station. Sheridan drove a wedge between the Confederate brigades, throwing them into confusion. On June 12, fortunes were reversed. Hampton dismounted his troops and drew a defensive line across the railroad and the road to Gordonsville. From this advantageous position, he beat back several determined dismounted assaults. Sheridan withdrew after destroying about six miles of the Virginia Central Railroad. Confederate victory at Trevilian prevented Sheridan from reaching Charlottesville and cooperating with Hunter's army in the Valley. This was one of the bloodiest cavalry battles of the war.

Points of Interest

The battlefield of Trevilian Station (now Trevilians) is 4.5 miles west of Louisa, on US33. Historical markers indicate the point where Hampton's line crossed the road and describe Custer's June 11 attack and repulse. On June 11, Brig. Gen. George Custer and his brigade, approaching via an unguarded road, charged into Trevilian Station, and captured a large number of horses belonging to dismounted Rebel cavalry who were battling Alfred Torbert's other Union brigades. But a slashing counterattack by Brig. Gen. Tom Rosser's Laurel Brigade scattered Custer's people and enabled the Confederates to pull back and regroup.

Louisa was raided by the Army of the Potomac cavalry under Maj. Gen. George Stoneman on May 2, 1863. Proceed south from Louisa on US33 to Ashland.

Ashland, 11 miles east of the intersection of US33 and VA54 at US1, was raided by Federal cavalry on several occasions. On May 3, 1863, Maj. Gen. George Stoneman came through Ashland as he struck at and disrupted the Army of Northern Virginia's communication lines in conjunction with Maj. Gen. Joseph Hooker's campaign that resulted in the Battle of Chancellorsville. On March 1, 1864, Brig. Gen. H. Judson Kilpatrick's cavalry stopped at Ashland en route to the northern approaches to Richmond. Early on May

11, 1864, some of Maj. Gen. Philip H. Sheridan's people raided Ashland only hours before Sheridan's main column encountered J.E.B. Stuart and his hard-riding horsemen at Yellow Tavern.

DRIVING TOUR—*Proceed to Yellow Tavern*
READING—*Lynchburg*

RICHMOND AREA

Yellow Tavern

On May 9, 1864, Maj. Gen. Philip H. Sheridan struck out on his own to draw J.E.B. Stuart away from the Spotsylvania action and into a fight to the death with the Union horsemen. He took 10,000 troopers on a ride around the Confederate right flank anchored at Spotsylvania Court House and then headed south toward Richmond. A deliberate pace and stops to tear up track and destroy supplies were intended to draw out and invite attack by J.E.B. Stuart's Southern horsemen. Such guile would have, two years earlier, been flirting with disaster for Yankee troopers. But with superior numbers and leadership and repeating carbines, the Federal rear guard held off pursuing Rebel horsemen while the vanguard closed on Richmond. Finally, on May 11 at Yellow Tavern, the hard-driving Stuart forced a showdown and his troopers were defeated. Most seriously, Stuart, never afraid of battle himself, was mortally wounded. The dashing and daring young cavalry chief, not yet thirty-one years old, would ride no more. The sadness of losing this intelligent, handsome, witty, and charming man, who epitomized so many of the characteristics that were part of the pre-war Southern culture, was felt from the newest recruits to General Lee, who had fully appreciated Stuart's unique ability. His death on May 12 was a bitter pill for the Confederacy.

Points of Interest

At Yellow Tavern there is a handsome monument marking the site where J.E.B. Stuart was mortally wounded. The monument, which can be difficult to locate because it is on a hill above the level of the road, is on Old Telegraph Road 0.5 mile east of US1 at VA677. The monument was erected in 1888 by veterans of Stuart's cavalry.

DRIVING TOUR—*Proceed to Northern Richmond*
READING—*Spotsylvania*

Kilpatrick's Raid

In early 1864, an opportunistic cavalry officer used Lincoln's desire to advance his Amnesty and Reconstruction program, announced the previous December, to further his own quest for glory. Brig. Gen. Judson Kilpatrick, whose exploits at Hanover, Gettysburg, Buckland, and elsewhere had earned him the nom de guerre "Kill Cavalry," bypassed Army of the Potomac commander Maj. Gen. George G. Meade and other army brass to secure President Lincoln's interest in his proposal for a major cavalry raid on Richmond. Kilpatrick assured the president that—besides battling the weak forces guarding the Confederate capital, freeing Union prisoners in the city's principal POW compounds and putting a scare into General Lee—his troopers would distribute leaflets along the way announcing the president's amnesty offer. Kilpatrick was given more than 3,600 horse soldiers and a well-known Washington personality as his chief subordinate. Col. Ulric Dahlgren, twenty-one-year-old adventure-seeking son of the Federal admiral, who had already given a leg in defense of the Union, led a column of the cavalry force. On February 28, the cavalry slipped across the Rapidan River at Ely's Ford and pushed toward the Rebel capital without pursuit. Kilpatrick's raid was initially screened by a successful dash toward Charlottesville by another daring trooper, Brig. Gen. George A. Custer, and maneuvers by infantry of the VI Corps.

South of Spotsylvania Court House, Kilpatrick detached Dahlgren's column to swing to the west, cross the James River, and approach Richmond from the west while his own force charged in from the north. He hoped his troopers could hold the attention of the city's garrison while Dahlgren liberated Federal captives at Belle Isle and Libby prisons. But when Kilpatrick tested the Richmond defenses on March 1, he ran into resistance from home guards stiffened by army units. He failed to get any response to his signal rockets from Dahlgren. After an afternoon's five-hour fight, Kilpatrick withdrew to the east, as his rear guard was hammered by a pursuit force bearing down on him from the north led by Maj. Gen. Wade Hampton. Some twenty-four hours later, part of Dahlgren's force overtook and linked up with Kilpatrick. They had failed to get across the flooding James River and, turning east, skirmished west of Richmond. On March 2, Dahlgren was killed in an ambush at a site since known as Dahlgren's Corner, near Walkerton in King and Queen County. Papers taken from Dahlgren's body disclosed that he planned to assassinate Davis and other Rebel leaders and set fire to downtown Richmond, a charge heatedly denied by the Lincoln administration. The failed raid became a propaganda tool for the Confederates.

Points of Interest

In addition to Ashland, previously mentioned, Kilpatrick's ride took him south to Richmond's intermediate defense line, where he was turned back on March 1. A historical marker at Laburnum and Chamberlayne avenues, on US301/VA2, 2 miles south of I-95 exit 82, marks the site of the skirmish. Kilpatrick next contemplated a night attack down the Mechanicsburg Pike (US360), but Hampton's pursuing cavalry caught up to him and assailed his rear guard. After fighting off the cavalry and having failed to receive word from Dahlgren, Kilpatrick took his force east to the protection of friendly forces that had marched up the Virginia peninsula to New Kent Court House.

Dahlgren's force was frustrated in attempting to cross the James River in Goochland County near Crozier. Take Laburnum Avenue west and follow signs for I-64 west. Take the interstate to exit 167 then south 5 miles on VA670 to Crozier. At this point you will follow Dahlgren's route east on VA6 along the James River. Dahlgren visited the home of Confederate Secretary of War James A. Seddon at Sabot Hill while his men plundered the estate. A historical marker 2.6 miles east of Crozier marks the 1855 house. Then go on to Tuckahoe (VA650), a National Historic Landmark that includes the schoolhouse where Thomas Jefferson began his studies. Farther east on VA650 is a historical marker indicating the site where Dahlgren hanged his African-American guide beside the road on March 1. The guide brought Dahlgren's force to a James River ford near Dover Mills, but when the water was found to be too deep for crossing, Dahlgren thought the man had deceived him.

Continue east on VA650. Just across the Henrico County line, Dahlgren and his force in the early evening of March 1 clashed with Rebels who blocked the road. Dahlgren then turned first northwest and then northeast crossing the Mattaponi and was killed the next night at Walkerton, near King and Queen Court House, 32 miles northeast of Richmond.

Follow VA650 east to Parham Road (VA150). Take Parham Road north to US33, then north a mile to Hungary Road. Dahlgren was secretly buried at the intersection of Hungary Road and Hungary Springs Road. In October 1865 his body was removed to the North and on November 1 reinterred in Philadelphia's Laurel Hill Cemetery. A historical marker on VA631, 2.5 miles northwest of King and Queen Court House, identifies the site of Dahlgren's death.

Also related to the Kilpatrick raid was the strike by Brig. Gen. George A. Custer on Rio Hill, near Charlottesville. This is as close as the famed University of Virginia city came to a Federal threat during the war until March 3, 1865, when Maj. Gen. Philip H. Sheridan's cavalry en route from the Shenandoah Valley to join Grant's "army group" at City Point passed through. You may wish to visit Charlottesville and Rio Hill while traveling between the Shenandoah Valley and Orange County. A historical marker on US29, 5.75 miles north of Charlottesville, describes the Battle of Rio Hill, February 29, 1864. After Custer beat back weak opposition he burned the covered bridge across the Rivanna River and three gristmills. A few homes were also plundered, prompting one Northern officer to describe the Yanks to a young woman pleading that her home be spared: "Madam, we are agents of unrelenting destiny." The description characterizes the role of the Federal soldiers late in the conflict as destroyers of the South's means to wage war as well as of its armies. The gristmills were quickly rebuilt and continued to turn out flour for the Confederacy.

DRIVING TOUR—*Proceed to Hanover (Hanover Court House—
Stuart's 1862 Ride Around McClellan)*
READING *(chronological)*—*Red River Campaign, Louisiana*

FEDERAL 1862 CAMPAIGN AGAINST RICHMOND (PENINSULA CAMPAIGN)

As spring of 1862 approached, Maj. Gen. George B. McClellan remained at odds with President Lincoln over the conduct of the war in the eastern theater. Joseph Johnston's Confederate army was still centered near Manassas Junction, watching and waiting. Maj. Gen. Ambrose Burnside's capture and occupation of key points on North Carolina sounds caused concern in Richmond that the Federals would strike northward toward

Norfolk (see **Roanoke Island, North Carolina**). Unwilling to challenge Johnston head-on, McClellan proposed a landing at Urbanna on the peninsula between the Rappahannock and York rivers. This move would place his army closer to Richmond than Johnston's. But Johnston in early March withdrew to a position behind the Rappahannock and McClellan was compelled to rethink his strategy.

The idea of transporting the Army of the Potomac by water to a strategic position deep within the Confederacy appealed to McClellan. He now eyed the peninsula between the James and York rivers in Tidewater Virginia. Reluctantly, Lincoln approved the plan. But the political aspect of running the war and the Lincoln administration's concerns for the security of Washington affected this campaign, and relations between the president and McClellan, who was a Democrat with political aspirations. It did not help McClellan that Johnston's withdrawal from Centreville and Manassas Junction revealed defenses not nearly as strong as imagined by McClellan in his reluctance to take the offensive. "Quaker Guns" were fodder for "Little Mac's" enemies. Lincoln, eager for a military success, urged McClellan to act quickly, ignoring the general's cautious attitude. McClellan became increasingly resentful of interference

Maj. Gen. George Brinton McClellan, USA, was a brilliant organizer and administrator who entered the Civil War with outstanding military credentials. Early successes in western Virginia led to his appointment as general-in-chief in 1861. He created the Army of the Potomac from the demoralized survivors of First Manassas, but disagreed with the Lincoln administration which was anxious for offensive operations. Always cautious and willing to overestimate the obstacles against him, McClellan missed opportunities in his drive up the Virginia peninsula and allowed Gen. Robert E. Lee to maneuver the Federal army into eventual withdrawal.

by Lincoln and Secretary of War Edwin M. Stanton, whom he considered amateurs in handling the army.

Lincoln and Stanton were understandably concerned about the security of Washington. It was of paramount political importance that the capital, so exposed to Confederate forces in northern Virginia, be secured. The forts surrounding the city were strengthened. A 20,000-man garrison under influential Republican Brig. Gen. James S. Wadsworth manned the Washington defenses.

In another move with political implications, Maj. Gen. John C. Frémont was named to head the new Mountain Department in western Virginia. As ships and boats were being readied to transport his army to the peninsula, McClellan's military authority was reduced by Lincoln to commander of the Army of the Potomac. Lincoln reasoned that while McClellan was with the army in Tidewater Virginia he could not exercise effective control as general-in-chief over other forces, especially those left to defend the capital. McClellan, however, saw the move as a deliberate slight and was offended. Lincoln's and Stanton's efforts to collectively perform McClellan's duties as general-in-chief were unsatisfactory and in a step of lasting importance Maj. Gen. Henry W. Halleck was appointed to the post in mid-July.

The confidence President Jefferson Davis had in Gen. Joseph Johnston further eroded following Johnston's decision to pull back from Centreville to a position behind the Rappahannock River. While ultimately a good decision in light of Federal strategy, the hasty withdrawal left behind invaluable supplies and increased existing mistrust between Johnston and the Confederate president. The appearance of the Army of the Potomac in front of the Yorktown-Warwick line on the lower peninsula compelled Johnston to uproot his army again. The Federal campaign for Richmond in 1862, just as the first colonization of Virginia, began in the Tidewater region where rivers, streams, and the topography plagued both armies.

READING— *Yorktown*

Stuart's June 1862 Ride Around McClellan

On June 1, 1862, after Robert E. Lee assumed command of the Confederate forces around Richmond, he put the soldiers to work building fortifications confronting McClellan's large Federal army then threatening the capital. This action gave the critics of Lee, who had yet to be tested in significant combat, more ammunition for derisive commentary. They called him the "King of Spades." But Lee was already planning a campaign to drive the Federals back down the peninsula. First he ordered a reconnaissance by his October 1859 subordinate in the capture of John Brown at Harpers Ferry.

Lee asked Brig. Gen. James Ewell Brown Stuart, well known for his resplendent dress and horsemanship, to lead 1,200 troopers on an information-gathering raid. On June 12, Stuart started on the ride that established his cavalry corps as an indispensable part of Lee's army. Riding north from Richmond, Stuart first confirmed Lee's suspicion that Brig. Gen. Fitz John Porter's V Corps had not refused (bent back for a stronger defensive position) and fortified its right flank north of Totopotomy Creek. Stuart continued east, turning away the only opposition to his ride, Federal cavalry from the command of Brig. Gen. Philip St. George Cooke, Stuart's father-in-law. Stuart's column then continued its one-hundred-mile ride south, and finally west around the Army of the Potomac. The Confederate horsemen arrived back in Richmond on June 15 bolstering Southern morale with their daring.

While the Federal army east of Richmond in 1862 lacked a cavalry leader the caliber of J.E.B. Stuart, it had another form of reconnaissance that McClellan used frequently. Thaddeus S. C. Lowe brought his gas-filled balloons to the peninsula after successfully demonstrating his technology to Lincoln and other Washington leaders (see **The District of Columbia**). Lowe and others aloft in the balloons telegraphed information concerning Confederate troop movements to Federal commanders on the ground. One balloon was launched from a river tender, in effect making the world's first aircraft carrier. Before the Peninsula Campaign ended, the Confederates put a balloon aloft. Made from ladies' dresses, the balloon was patched together from various styles of silk bolt cloth.

Spies were also an important form of reconnaissance for both sides. General McClellan relied heavily on the troop estimates given to him by Alan Pinkerton and his band of civilian operatives. The dramatically exaggerated estimates of enemy forces made by Pinkerton reinforced McClellan's existent caution. Another of McClellan's operatives was a Canadian woman, Sarah Emma Edmonds. Edmonds had emigrated on her own to Michigan as a

Maj. Gen. James Ewell Brown Stuart, CSA, was a skilled cavalry leader who possessed a flamboyant and gregarious style. Always impeccably dressed, a lover of music and finery, and having a sense of humor that touched his troops and often his enemies, Stuart was also a great leader of men who utilized cunning and intelligence in battle. Never afraid to be in the middle of the action when his cavalry troopers were in battle, Stuart lost his life while fighting the enemy at Yellow Tavern, Virginia, in 1864.

teenager in search of adventure. When Lincoln put out the call for volunteers, she had joined a Michigan regiment, disguised as a man. Because of her slight build, Sarah, as a man, had served as a nurse beginning at First Manassas. By the time she joined the Army of the Potomac in the Peninsula Campaign, her dream of adventure reached new heights. After volunteering for a reconnaissance operation, Sarah quickly became one of McClellan's most reliable agents, frequently crossing enemy lines returning with information valuable to the North.

Among the dozens of operatives providing intelligence to the South was nineteen-year-old Belle Boyd. From her homes in Front Royal and Martinsburg, Boyd eavesdropped on and charmed information from Federal officers (see **Front Royal**). Her reports were forwarded to Stonewall Jackson, who personally thanked her for her help in his 1862 Shenandoah Valley Campaign.

Points of Interest

Stuart's column skirted the South Anna River and, on June 13, passed through Hanover Court House (Hanover—US301/VA2, 3 miles east of I-95 exit 92). The Rebel horsemen rode by Enon Church and beyond Haw's Shop (now Studley) and crossed the Totopotomy. Between the Totopotomy and US360, Stuart's horse soldiers clashed with Federal cavalry. Confederate Capt. William Latané was killed in that action, the only fatal casualty Stuart's expedition suffered. From Old Church, Stuart continued southeast toward Tunstall's Station. A historical marker at Talleysville (VA33) indicates the place where his command stopped to rest before turning south and crossing the Chickahominy River at Forge Bridge. Stuart then led his command on to Charles City Court House, and returned to Richmond via the Charles City Road (present-day VA5) on June 15.

**DRIVING TOUR—*Proceed to Chickahominy Bluff–Beaver Dam Creek–Gaines's Mill*
READING— *The Seven Days' Battles***

THE SEVEN DAYS' BATTLES

Armed with Stuart's information Robert E. Lee awaited only the arrival of Stonewall Jackson's troops from the Shenandoah Valley. Lee then formed his army into seven "corps" under Jackson, and Maj. Gens. Ambrose Powell Hill, Daniel Harvey Hill, James Longstreet, John B. Magruder, Benjamin Huger, and T. H. Holmes.

Oak Grove

Lee's plan called for A. P. Hill's, D. H. Hill's, and J. Longstreet's divisions to cross the Chickahominy and assail Fitz John Porter's Union corps, as Jackson's divisions crossed Totopotomy Creek and outflanked Union troops posted behind Beaver Dam Creek, and cut the Federal supply line from the White House Landing on the Pamunkey River to Fair Oaks Station. But the Seven Days' Battles began by a Federal advance against Confederates posted at Oak Grove, near Fair Oaks, on June 25. McClellan advanced his skirmish lines north and south of

Gen. Robert Edward Lee, CSA, brought intelligence, compassion, and bravery to his role as Confederate army commander. Perhaps his best attribute was his ability to assess the risks of daring gambles, and act on them.

the Williamsburg Road with the objective of bringing Richmond within range of his siege guns. Union forces attacked over swampy ground with inconclusive results, and darkness halted the fighting. McClellan's attack was not strong enough to derail the Confederate offensive that already had been set in motion. The next day, Lee seized the initiative by attacking at Beaver Dam Creek north of the Chickahominy.

Beaver Dam Creek

Lee's offensive took shape on the morning of June 26, the day Jackson had promised to have his troops strike Porter's exposed flank. But Jackson failed to appear by midafternoon and the impulsive A. P. Hill started the attack himself, under less than ideal conditions. The Federals were entrenched behind Beaver Dam Creek, near Mechanicsville. They fought stubbornly and the Rebels sustained heavy casualties. But McClellan who believed he was outnumbered two to one solved Lee's dilemma by directing Porter to fall back during the night to a position near Gaines's Mill.

Gaines's Mill

The only tactical victory of the Seven Days' Battles for the Confederates came on June 27 at Gaines's Mill. The Federals of Porter's large reinforced corps, more than 36,000 strong, were still isolated from the rest of the Army of the Potomac by the Chickahominy. But the Yanks maintained a stout defensive position on high ground overlooking Boatswain Creek. Only after five hours of vicious fighting and failed Confederate charges did the stalemate break. At seven P.M., the Rebels, spearheaded by the brigades of Brig. Gen. John Bell Hood and Col. Evander M. Law of Jackson's corps and supported by Brig. Gen. George E. Pickett's brigade of Longstreet's division, pierced the left of the Federal line, resulting in a dusk coordinated assault that sent Porter's troops reeling back toward the Chickahominy. The Federals, under the cover of darkness, retreated across the river.

Once again, the Southern casualties were higher than those of the North. But the breakthrough and subsequent withdrawal led McClellan to begin the next day to change his base from White House on the Pamunkey River to Harrison's Landing on the James. No matter what McClellan called it, this was a retreat.

Points of Interest

Richmond National Battlefield Park—The main visitor center for Richmond NBP is located at 3215 East Broad Street, Richmond, on the site of the Chimborazo Hospital, the Confederacy's largest military hospital. The visitor center and the hospital site are discussed later under Richmond points of interest. If you are not familiar with the ten-unit Richmond NBP, which includes sites scattered over a wide area, you will want to stop at the visitor center first. A brochure describing a driving tour of all units within the park's jurisdiction and other important sites is available and park rangers are on duty to answer questions. This tour of the 1862 battle site begins with the Chickahominy Bluff Unit of the park located on US360 north of Laburnum Avenue and 2 miles south of I-295 exit 37.

Chickahominy Bluff was part of an intermediate defense line protecting Richmond. The works here were constructed subsequent to the Seven Days' Battles and were manned by Confederate forces defending Richmond whenever the city was threatened beginning in June 1863 until the April 2–3 evacuation. Traces of the earthworks are visible. From a bluff here, Lee observed the opening of the June 26 attack at Beaver Dam Creek. From Chickahominy Bluff, drive north on US360 to VA156 (formerly the Mechanicsville Road, now Battlefield Park Route), turn right, and proceed to the Beaver Dam Creek Unit. You will be following the route taken by the Confederate forces in the June 26 attack.

After driving the Union outposts from Mechanicsville in mid-afternoon on June 26, the Rebels faced the formidable defense line that the Federals had previously established behind Beaver Dam Creek, north and south of Ellerson's Mill. Today, the small Richmond NBP Unit here shows the extent of the natural obstacles faced by the Confederate soldiers. The stream and millpond and a brush-choked slope awaited those Rebels who managed to clear the abatis and withering artillery and rifle-musket fire from across the creek. The Federals had dug earthworks on the opposite bank, which are not visible today through the underbrush. It is easy to see why the Southern offensive, uncoordinated as it was, failed against this strong position.

Proceed east on the Battlefield Park Route to the turnoff (VA718) for the Watt House–Gaines's Mill Unit. Along the road are numerous historical markers indicating troop positions and movements prior to the Battle of Gaines's Mill. At 1.5 mile there is a marker at Walnut Grove Church for the point where Jackson and Lee met on the morning of June 27. Just before the turnoff to the Watt House there is a marker indicating the site of Gaines's Mill, where South Carolinians of A. P. Hill's advance guard attacked

Porter's rear guard. The Federals here quickly retreated to the protection of the defenses behind Boatswain Creek. Maj. Gen. Philip H. Sheridan's cavalry burned the mill during their 1864 raids into the area.

The Watt House is the restored 1835 farmhouse used by Fitz John Porter as his headquarters during the fighting on June 27. The interior of the house is not open to the public. A history trail leads down the west slope of the plateau to the Breakthrough Point, where the seven P.M. attack by Hood's brigade and the others broke the Federal line. Traces of the shallow Federal works here remain. From the Watt House, return to the Battlefield Park Route and continue east to the Cold Harbor Unit. More historical markers are along the road south of the Cold Harbor intersection indicating sites of Jackson's and D. H. Hill's June 27 attacks on the right flank of the Federal line.   🚲 ♿ 🚶 ❓ 🏛 P 🚏 🚻

DRIVING TOUR—*Proceed to Totopotomy Creek–Cold Harbor*
READING—*Savage's Station–White Oak Swamp–Glendale*

Totopotomy Creek–Cold Harbor

With no hope of Maj. Gen. Benjamin F. Butler's Army of James, then "corked as if in a bottle" on Bermuda Hundred, being able to seriously threaten Richmond from the south, U. S. Grant was even more determined to prevent Lee from taking a position behind the Richmond defenses. Grant pulled the Army of the Potomac back across the North Anna and had General Meade turn his columns southeast and pass around General Lee's right flank. On May 27–28, 1864, the Army of the Potomac crossed the Pamunkey River at two places, still hoping to confront Lee's army in a vulnerable position northeast of the Confederate capital. Lee, still infirm and unsure of Grant's plans, sent the Rebel cavalry under his nephew, Fitzhugh Lee, and Wade Hampton to determine if reports of Federals across the Pamunkey were correct. A raging cavalry battle, the largest since Brandy Station, took place at Haw's Shop on May 28, and confirmed the reports of Grant's crossing of the Pamunkey.

By the time Grant had turned the Federal force to the southwest, toward Richmond, Lee had taken up a defensive position behind Totopotomy Creek. Realizing Grant would continue to go around this strong defensive position, Lee ordered an offensive. The May 30 attack on Warren's V Corps by Jubal Early, in command of Ewell's II Corps since May

27 when Ewell had gone on prolonged sick leave, was disjointed and it failed. Then Lee received more bad news. He learned that Maj. Gen. William F. "Baldy" Smith's corps had been detached from Butler's command at Bermuda Hundred and was arriving on transports at White House Landing to reinforce Grant's force.

Both commanders then had the same objective, the strategic crossroads at Old Cold Harbor, near the site of Lee's Gaines's Mill victory against the Army of the Potomac nearly two years earlier. Grant sent Sheridan with his cavalry to take and hold the crossroads at Cold Harbor, but Fitzhugh Lee was there to meet them. Still, Sheridan took the crossroads on May 31 and held it under orders from Meade even though Lee sent two infantry divisions to recover the crossroads on the morning of June 1. The Yankee cavalry, many armed with Spencer 7-shot repeating carbines, held Cold Harbor until relieved. Sheridan's rapid-firing troopers were relieved by units from Wright's VI and Smith's XVIII corps on June 1, and Lee's repulsed infantry dug in west of the crossroads. Eventually, the Rebel line extended seven miles from northwest to southeast, anchored by the Totopotomy Creek on the north, and the foreboding Chickahominy River on the south.

Meade ordered an attack in the late afternoon of June 1, and the two corps succeeded in a breakthrough north and south of the Mechanicsville Road. R. H. Anderson's counterattack stabilized the situation for the Rebels. The Federals, however, took more than 800 prisoners and inched closer to the earthworks on the Confederate right.

Meade's forces were strung out and the decision to attack, made by Grant the evening of June 1, could not be executed until the morning of June 3. Grant and his officers made the decision to go ahead even as Lee strengthened his lines and his soldiers dug in. In thirty minutes just after dawn on June 3, 1864, the needless slaughter of a great number of the 45,000 attacking Federal troops occurred. Many, who had foreseen their destiny the night before and pinned slips of paper with their names to their uniforms, did not return from the charge toward the two miles of Rebel trenches assailed in the morning's human wave assaults. Grant at last saw the impossibility of a frontal assault on strong entrenchments. He took full responsibility, saying, "I regret this assault more than any one I have ordered."

The Federal casualties at Cold Harbor that day numbered more than 7,000; the Confederates 1,500. After a brief truce on June 7 to clear the field, Grant was on the move again. But the war of attrition, which critics wrongly accused Grant of waging with no regard for his soldiers, was beginning to turn the spring 1864 overland campaign into a morale booster for the Confederacy. Grant began to appear as a political liability for Lincoln's reelection hopes. The war of attrition was Lee's strategy for protecting his decreasing military assets and fostering war weariness in the North.

Points of Interest

The May 28 cavalry battle at Haw's Shop (Enon Church) and the May 30 Confederate attack near Bethesda Church are identified by historical markers, and can be reached by state highways. Enon Church (Haw's Shop) is north of Totopotomy Creek, east of the intersection of VA606 and VA643. Bethesda Church, which was also the northern flank of the Federal line during the Cold Harbor battle and held by Burnside's corps, is about 4 miles northeast of Mechanicsville on US360 at the intersection with Pole Green Road (VA627). On the north side of VA627 several hundred yards east of the intersection with VA643 is a monument to the 36th Wisconsin Infantry.

The Cold Harbor Unit of Richmond NBP is 1 mile east of Gaines's Mill. This unit features a short driving tour starting at a manned interpretive shelter that features an electric map of Grant's overland campaign and the June 3 battle. There is a small picnic area behind the exhibit shelter. The park road travels north along the Confederate line held by Hoke's and Kershaw's divisions, with a stop behind the Confederate works. The earthworks are well preserved and the pine woods that separate them from the Federal works to the east give the same picture of the terrain as it was seen in the desperate early-morning charge of the three Federal corps on June 3. Attacking in this area were elements of the VI and XVIII corps. The Federal line at the next stop was the line that began with the shallow trenches dug by each survivor of the charge. Later expanded, the trenches served as protection for the Union troops until they withdrew on the night of June 12–13 for their march to and crossing of the James River.

The auto tour ends on VA156. A quarter mile to the east is a national cemetery and the Garthright House. Although it is not open for tours, the Garthright House, part of which was built in the early 1700s, was used as a Federal hospital after the Battle of Cold Harbor and later as a Confederate hospital. A short distance to the east, where VA156 intersects with VA632 and VA619, is the Cold Harbor crossroads, the site of the Civil War–era tavern that gave the area and the battle its name. Continue south on VA156 to the Chickahominy River.

The only Federal breakthrough during the June 3 attack was short-lived. Brig. Gen. Francis Barlow's division of Hancock's corps overran the salient held by Maj. Gen. John C. Breckinridge west of VA156 south of Cold Harbor. A furious counterattack led by Brig. Gen. Joseph Finegan turned back the Yankees and sealed the breach in the Confederate line. Finegan displayed the ferocity he had shown in the Battle of Olustee a few months earlier (see **Olustee, Florida**). He had been placed in command of brigade after being ordered north with several battalions of Florida soldiers to reinforce Lee.

DRIVING TOUR—*Proceed to Seven Pines*
READING—*Trevilian Station*

Seven Pines

On May 31, 1862, Gen. Joseph E. Johnston, with his back against Richmond, readied a complex plan of attack to assail the two corps of General McClellan's Army of the Potomac, then south of the Chickahominy. These troops were isolated from the larger force to the north to whom they were linked by several bridges spanning the rain-swollen river. Things went wrong almost immediately in this battle called Fair Oaks by the North and Seven Pines by the South. The Rebel advance started late and was uncoordinated. Stout resistance by the Federal IV Corps, subsequently reinforced by Brig. Gen. Philip Kearny's III Corps division, slowed the advance. The II Corps, commanded by veteran Maj. Gen. Edwin V. "Bull" Sumner, crossed the Chickahominy at Grapevine Bridge and at dusk checked the Confederate surge.

The 5th Cavalry was one of a handful of regular army units that kept their original designations in the Union army. Here they are mounting a charge to cover the withdrawal of Federal artillery at Gaines's Mill.

At twilight on May 31, Johnston was severely wounded. He was replaced temporarily by Maj. Gen. G. W. Smith, who ordered the attack renewed at dawn. The June 1 Confederate assault fared no better when Maj. Gen. James Longstreet, sensing a failure in the making, did not respond and asked for reinforcements to stay a Union counterattack that was battering Pickett's and Armistead's brigades. Gen. Robert E. Lee, who rode out from Richmond and assumed command of Johnston's army, recalled the troops and ordered the Rebels back to their original positions.

Though the Confederates sustained higher casualties, the battle had a sobering effect on McClellan, who redoubled his natural caution. Still confident that Maj. Gen. Irvin McDowell's corps would be arriving overland from Fredericksburg to support his right, McClellan did not contemplate an immediate offensive against the Confederate force which he was convinced not only outnumbered him but also was receiving reinforcements from the south. He planned to establish a strong defensive line and then bring up heavy siege artillery to invest and reduce the Richmond defenses. But the rain and muddy conditions slowed progress to a crawl and eventually General Lee boldly seized the initiative that would determine the outcome of the 1862 Richmond campaign.

Points of Interest

VA156 crosses the Chickahominy River at Grapevine Bridge. Seeing the murky swamplike river makes it understandable why it was a deterrent to military operations. Over a bridge here Sumner's Federal corps crossed to participate in the Battle of Seven Pines. After the Battle of Gaines's Mill part of Porter's corps withdrew across the bridge and then destroyed it. Jackson's Confederates, delayed in having to rebuild the bridge on June 29, did not get into the rear of the Federal army as planned during the June 29 action at Savage's Station. A short distance farther south a historical marker describes the June 27 action at Golding's Farm, in which Rebels south of the Chickahominy attacked Hancock's brigade, holding a position south of the river. Then darkness ended the inconclusive fighting.

Continue south on VA156, Battlefield Park Route, to US60, Williamsburg Road. As you travel east on US60 from Richmond International Airport you are following the route of Longstreet's and D. H. Hill's forces as they marched toward the Battle of Seven Pines. There are many historical markers related to the action on US60. One at Sandston indicates the first Federal line, the farthest west, which was broken by Hill's grim fighters. The Confederates reinforced by Micah Jenkins's South Carolinians then attacked a second, stronger line McClellan's forces formed at Seven Pines. The Seven Pines

National Cemetery, on Williamsburg Road, was part of this battlefield. This line was broken also, but the reinforced Federals withstood the continuing attacks on May 31. The battle resumed the next day and soldiers of Sumner's corps prevented the Confederates from breaking the third Federal line, identified by a marker 1.3 miles east of Seven Pines. One mile northwest of Seven Pines, on VA33 at the railroad crossing, is Fair Oaks. The Confederates had less success attacking the right wing of McClellan's force at Fair Oaks during the two-day battle. There are no historical markers in the area—where General Johnston was wounded—but the action took place in the vicinity of the VA33 crossing over the railroad.

DRIVING TOUR—*Proceed to Savage's Station–White Oak Swamp–Glendale*
READING—*Stuart's June 1862 Ride Around McClellan*

Savage's Station–White Oak Swamp–Glendale

At Savage's Station on the Richmond & York River Railroad on June 29 and at White Oak Swamp and Glendale on June 30, the Confederate assaults were uncoordinated; confusing roads led to the late arrival of units and the soldiers of both sides became disorganized in the swampy morass. The Federals fought as valiantly as their foes, but McClellan continued his retreat south to Harrison's Landing.

Points of Interest

A half mile north of Seven Pines, the morning of June 29 opened with a skirmish at Allen's Farm. The Federals then fell back to Savage's Station, 3.6 miles east of Seven Pines. The Federal line extended north-south from the railroad across the Williamsburg Road. Historical markers on Meadow Road (VA156) describe the action. On US60, 4.9 miles east of Bottoms Bridge, is a historical marker locating Long Bridge, one of the points at which the Army of the Potomac crossed the Chickahominy River on its way to the James River and Petersburg.

Continue a short distance east of the Savage's Station historical markers, then south on VA156, the Battlefield Park Route. About 3 miles southeast of the intersection of US60 and VA156 is a historical marker for the action at White Oak Swamp. On June 30, while the battle at Glendale raged 4 miles to the southwest, Jackson was stymied on the north side of White Oak Swamp by artillery of Brig. Gen. William Franklin's reinforced VI Corps. The Federals beginning on June 28 and continuing for forty-eight hours had been crossing White Oak Swamp here and had destroyed the bridge. Jackson was unable to cross the swamp until July 1.

Continue south on VA156 to the Darbytown Road. Here historical markers describe the June 30 Battle of Glendale (Frayser's Farm). First Longstreet's and then A. P. Hill's troops attacked four Union divisions positioned here west of the Quaker Road, as VA156 was then called, and stood between the Confederates and McClellan's wagon trains with the best opportunity General Lee would ever have to drive a wedge into the Army of the Potomac and defeat it in detail. The center and left of the Union line extended from this intersection south to the Glendale National Cemetery and Willis Church. Farther south on the New Market Road (VA5), west of Malvern Hill, Federal general George Sykes's V Corps division held off Confederate general T. H. Holmes's division attempting to get between McClellan's army and the river. North of Glendale on the Charles City Road the Federals felled trees across the road which Huger's Confederates took time to clear, delaying their advance in what was called the "battle of the axes." Continue south on VA156 to the Malvern Hill unit of Richmond NBP.

<hr />

DRIVING TOUR—*Proceed to Malvern Hill*
READING—*Malvern Hill*

<hr />

Malvern Hill

At Malvern Hill on July 1, Fitz John Porter established a strong defensive position with his artillery on commanding ground zeroed in on the hill's gentle northern approach. Confederate attempts to position and sight artillery to converge their fire on the Union cannons misfired. Confusing and misinterpreted orders caused uncoordinated Rebel attacks to be launched against the Federals' all but impregnable position which resulted in frightful Confederate losses. This action ended the Seven Days' Battles. With the Army of the Potomac under the protection of U.S. Navy gunboats at Harrison's Landing, on July 2, Lee launched no new attacks. Lee's gamble in the Seven Days' Battles resulted in more than 20,000 Confederate casualties. Yet McClellan insisted on changing his base and withdrawing his army to Harrison's Landing though throughout the campaign many of his generals—particularly trigger-tempered division leaders Hooker and Kearny and the grizzled veteran Sumner—were ready to turn on Lee and continue to Richmond.

The Seven Days' Battles established Lee as a premiere Confederate general, though he was convinced that a greater victory, the destruction of McClellan's army, was possible. Learning from the experience, Lee set about to rid his army of ineffective generals. He organized two wings under Jackson and Longstreet, establishing a pair of cohesive fighting units. He never publicly reprimanded Jackson for the lapses that were so costly in lost lives to other commanders.

Thanks to careful staff work by War Department staff officers, McClellan's irrational rage toward President Lincoln and Secretary Stanton, whom he blamed for lack of support in the campaign, was muted. "Little Mac" managed to keep his job for a time. But a new personality soon came forward to take center stage for the Union in the East.

Points of Interest

The last of the Seven Days' Battles, fought on July 1, 1862, centered on Malvern Hill's commanding ground. The Federals did not entrench—the massed artillery and infantry units on the hill, supported by gunboat fire from Union warships on the James River, turned back the piecemeal Confederate assaults. Recent acquisitions have expanded this important battlefield, which features an interpretive shelter and walking trail. By law, no Federal funds are to be used to buy additional property for the Richmond National Battlefield Park, and additional acquisition must come through private efforts, such as that of the APCWS to buy additional land at Malvern Hill and Glendale. In this APCWS has been extraordinarily successful. Its land acquisitions at Malvern Hill and Glendale total more than 750 acres and when this land is conveyed by APCWS to the American people it will double the acreage of Richmond National Battlefield Park.

The Federal change of base to the James River brought the Federals to Harrison's Landing. Berkeley Plantation on VA5, 9 miles southeast of Malvern Hill, was the birthplace of President William Henry Harrison and served as McClellan's headquarters after the change of base. The plantation is open for tours; call 804-829-6018 for information. Shirley Plantation, on VA608 just west of VA5, about 6 miles southeast of Malvern Hill, was the birthplace of Robert E. Lee's mother, Anne Hill Carter. Call 800-232-1613 or 804-

829-5121 for information. Charles City, also on VA5, features historical markers describing the sites where Grant's army crossed the James River, Hancock's corps of steamboats at Wilcox's Landing, and the other three corps crossed on a half-mile pontoon bridge at Windmill Point. At Wilcox's Landing (present day Wilcox's Wharf) at the dead end of VA618, 2 miles west of Charles City, is a country park from which there are excellent views of the James River both upstream and downstream.

DRIVING TOUR—*Proceed to New Market Heights–Fort Harrison*
READING—*Cedar Mountain*

Chaffin's Farm–New Market Heights

As part of General Grant's strategy for tightening the investment of Petersburg and cutting off supplies to Lee's army defending Richmond and Petersburg in late September 1864, an attack was launched on the Confederate line at Chaffin's Farm southeast of Richmond. An attack there had the added advantage of keeping Lee's forces spread thin and affecting any further reinforcements to Lt. Gen. Jubal Early's command in the Shenandoah Valley from Lee's strapped manpower pool. While Meade's army on the left flank of the Federal line at Petersburg made another lunge for the Southside Railroad, Grant ordered the Army of the James to attack north of the James toward Confederate Forts Harrison and Gilmer.

Maj. Gen. David B. Birney's X Corps and Maj. Gen. Edward O. C. Ord's XVIII Corps crossed the James River on the night of September 28–29 and advanced north in an early-morning fog. The X Corps, with fourteen regiments of black soldiers, primarily United States Colored Troops, assailed the advanced line of defense covering New Market Heights. Though they were greatly outnumbered, the Confederates under Brig. Gen. John Gregg had an advantageous natural defensive position, with rifle pits, artillery emplacements, and abatis obstructing the approach. The determined Federals pushed through the abatis and finally charged the heights and took them. Thirteen black soldiers and two white officers were recipients of Medals of Honor for heroics in this action.

Three miles to the west, Ord's two divisions stormed Fort Harrison. The Federal charge surprised the defenders and by eight A.M. Fort Harrison was in Federal hands. But Fort Gilmer to the north was defended by a greater number of troops and the X Corps division assigned to take it met with a withering fire. A follow-up attack by Brig. Gen. William Birney's black brigade gained the ditch fronting Fort Gilmer but was then beaten back in a savage no-quarter struggle.

The loss of Fort Harrison was a serious blow to Lee, who rushed two divisions north from Petersburg and went himself to direct an attack to retake the fort the next day. The Federals anticipated the attack and overnight reoriented the fort to confront the Confederates. A number of Federal soldiers were armed with repeating rifles, increasing their advantage against the furious Southern assaults. The Confederate casualties on September 30 were high. The Federals lost more in the two-day battle: 3,300 to 2,000. The Rebels constructed new outer works between the Fort Harrison line and Richmond. The Federals renamed Fort Harrison Fort Burnham after a general killed in the battle, built a new work—Fort Brady—to the south on a bluff overlooking the James River, and connected Forts Harrison and Brady with trenches.

Points of Interest

Interpretation of the Union September 29–30 offensive north of the James River is centered at Fort Harrison. From the intersection of VA156 and VA5 south of Malvern Hill, take VA5 north toward Richmond. The first battlefield you come to is New Market Heights. Starting at the intersection of Kingsland Road and running north along VA5 (New Market Road) for about 1 mile is the Confederate position. Between Turner Road and Fourmile Creek is a pull-off and a historical marker describing the September 29, 1864, attack on New Market Heights by a division of African Americans. Return to Kingsland Road, which turns into VA5, and turn south. The Federals formed for the attack along Kingsland Road in the vicinity of Deep Bottom Road. Take Deep Bottom Road south until it dead-ends into a park. There is a lovely view of the James River here. The Federal X Corps crossed the James on pontoon bridges at Deep Bottom preparatory to attacking New Market Heights and assaulting Fort Gilmer. There was also fighting at Deep Bottom and beyond on July 27–30 and August 13–20, 1864. Today there is a picnic area and boat launch at the county park.

Return to Kingsland Road and turn left. In a short distance you enter the Fort Harrison unit of Richmond NBP. Turn left on Hoke-Brady Road; the road dead-ends at Fort Brady. This fort was established by the Federals after the capture of Fort Harrison to command the James River and prevent a sortie by the Confederate James River Squadron. Fort Brady offers an excellent view of the James. Return north on Brady-Hoke

Road to Fort Hoke at the intersection of Battlefield Park Road. This fort was a small work erected by the Confederates along the line connecting Fort Harrison with the Chaffin's Bluff defenses. Continuing north on Battlefield Park Road, you come to Fort Harrison. The visitor center here is open during the three summer months.

Fort Harrison has a self-guided walking tour, a picnic area, and rest rooms. Fort Harrison features the works constructed by the Confederates and the additions made by the Federals beginning immediately after its capture. The national cemetery at Fort Harrison is on a park road just northeast of the fort. Continue north on Battlefield Park Road past the remains of Confederate Forts Johnson, Gregg, and Gilmer and you reach New Market Road (VA5) again. You will want to stop at the Fort Gilmer wayside which interprets the September 29, 1864, attack on the fort by Union troops, both white and black. Turn right and follow to I-295. Take the interstate south across the river to exit 15 which is VA10. You then enter the area known as Bermuda Hundred.

DRIVING TOUR—*Proceed to Bermuda Hundred*
READING—*Boydton Plank Road–Burgess's Mill, Petersburg Area*

Bermuda Hundred

As the Army of the Potomac slugged southward through the Piedmont, Lt. Gen. U. S. Grant hoped that Maj. Gen. Benjamin F. Butler's Army of the James had ascended the James River as ordered, occupied Bermuda Hundred, and advancing northwestward would rendezvous with the Army of the Potomac on the James upstream from Richmond. But long before Grant reached the North Anna River, Butler had put his army in a hopeless defensive position. After landing at Bermuda Hundred, a tongue of land west of the confluence of the James and Appomattox rivers, Butler first entrenched his army, rather than boldly striking out with a swift and powerful blow against the hastily fortified and understrength forces then commanded by Maj. Gen. George E. Pickett. A skirmish with Pickett's command at Port Walthall on May 7 on the railroad west of Bermuda Hundred convinced Butler to return to the fortifications to rethink his strategy. Though Butler's cavalry, sweeping west from Suffolk under Brig. Gen. August V. Kautz, was successful in tearing up the rail lines south and west of Petersburg, the U.S. Navy lost two ships to torpedoes and shore batteries on the James River, giving Butler pause. A mutual dislike between Butler and his two corps commanders, Maj. Gen. Quincy A. Gillmore and Maj. Gen. William F. "Baldy" Smith, added to the problems of the Army of the James.

The delay in offensive action allowed Confederate reinforcements to arrive from the south, despite the damaged railroads. Gen. P.G.T. Beauregard, recently given command of Confederate forces in southside Virginia, arrived to take charge of the defense. On May 13, after deciding not to venture south toward Petersburg, Butler put his army in motion and attacked and carried the outworks of the Confederate defenses anchored on Wooldridge Hill, compelling the Confederates to retire to their inner works. By that time the Creole general had built up his army to two thirds the size of Butler's fighting force and, on May 16, assailed the Federals awaiting Butler's next order. The result was that the Army of the James was forced back into Bermuda Hundred behind their entrenchments. Grant described Butler's position as if he were "in a bottle, tightly corked." Beauregard kept an eye on Butler's troops while detaching General Pickett with 4,000 soldiers to reinforce Lee on the North Anna River (see **North Anna River**).

Points of Interest

There are several historical markers on Bermuda Hundred detailing the operations of the Army of the James during its occupation of the area from May 1864 through April 2–3, 1865. Proceed west on VA10 to the Ware Bottom Spring Road (VA898) which veers to the left. At Ramblewood Road (VA617), turn left. This is the Parker's Battery unit of Richmond NBP. The battery served the Confederates during the time when Butler's Army of the James was bottled up on Bermuda Hundred. Parker's Battery became part of the Howlett Line, which was part of the Richmond to Petersburg defense line. The Federal works which Butler ordered constructed after his repulse in the May 16, 1864, Battle of Drewry's Bluff were 1 mile east of this line.

Nearby, also accessible by boat, is the Henricus Historical Park, where the town of Henrico was established in 1611. The park is located near Dutch Gap, a neck of land on a large curve in the James River. Here in August 1864 Benjamin Butler ordered the construction of a canal across the 174-yard neck to allow Federal warships to bypass Confederate guns at Trent's Reach and obstructions placed in the 5-mile bend in the river by the Confederates. The project kept Butler's troops, many of them blacks, busy digging under sniper fire and occasional artillery shelling until January 1, 1865, when Butler, dissatisfied with the progress of the canal, ordered a large charge exploded. The explosion caved in part of the canal which had previously been dug by hand. Grant allowed the project to continue to keep soldiers of the Army of the James occupied. The canal project continued after Grant removed Butler from command in January 1865, replacing him with Maj. Gen. Edward O. C. Ord. After the war the U.S. Congress appropriated moneys and the canal was completed. The present channel of the James River follows the alignment of the Dutch Gap Canal.

From Parker's Battery, return to VA89 and continue west until its intersection with US1. Turn right (north) on US1. On the way to Drewry's Bluff there are several Virginia historical markers describing the Howlett Line, and battles between the Rebels and the Army of the James in May 1864, including the fight at Proctor's Creek on May 13–14, 1864. Chesterfield County maintains and interprets the Battle of Drewry's Bluff in a small park at Fort Stevens. A brochure on the Bermuda Hundred Campaign includes site directions and is available for a small fee from Chesterfield Historical Society, P.O. Box 40, Chesterfield, VA 23832; 804-748-1026.

DRIVING TOUR—*Proceed to Drewry's Bluff*
READING—*Spotsylvania*

"Fort Darling" at Drewry's Bluff was a formidable obstacle for the Federal navy in ascending the James River to Richmond. This battery was looking downriver and its fire met the Union warships as they rounded a bend in the river. The fort is now part of the Drewry's Bluff Unit of Richmond National Battlefield Park.

Drewry's Bluff

In April and May 1862 rains turned the peninsula roads into ribbons of mud. Water, mud, and disease in the swampy area became the most formidable foes for McClellan's army for much of the campaign. As a result, Federal army operations all but bogged down and the Union navy took up the torch. The ironclad *Virginia* (*Merrimack*) having been destroyed by her crew on

May 11, following the Confederate withdrawal from Norfolk, five Federal gunboats—including the ironclads *Galena, Monitor,* and *Stevens Battery*—steamed up the James River toward Richmond. On May 15 they engaged Rebel shore batteries at Drewry's Bluff. The USS *Monitor* could not elevate her guns high enough to hit Southern artillery on the ninety-foot-high Drewry's Bluff, and the Federal navy was repulsed. If McClellan had supplied troops to assist in the operation, the results might have been different, but he reported to Secretary of War Stanton in Washington that he was not ready to cooperate with this naval operation. After four hours the gunboats disengaged, forcing the army to take the next initiative in the Peninsula Campaign.

Points of Interest

The Drewry's Bluff Unit of Richmond NBP is located on Fort Darling Road (VA1435). Turn right from US1 just north of I-95 exit 64 onto Bellwood Road (VA656), then left on Fort Darling Road just after passing under the interstate. Fort Darling is the name the Federals gave to the imposing earthen fort on the bluff here.

A short trail leads you to the earthen fort which is intact. A large 8-inch columbiad stands guard over the James River. Interpretive signs describe the 1862 naval action and the subsequent use of the fort as a training area for Confederate sailors and marines. 🚶 ❷ P

From Drewry's Bluff, follow US1 south. Historical markers identify the area where the Confederates battled the Army of the James. The Federals captured the outworks on May 14, 1864, but a Confederate counterattack on May 16 retook the works and drove the Federals back into the Bermuda Hundred peninsula. Continue south on US1 to Petersburg or to exit 64 of I-95 and proceed south to Petersburg. The entrance to Petersburg National Battlefield is on East Washington Street (VA36), which can be reached from US1 or I-95 exit 52.

DRIVING TOUR—*Proceed to Petersburg Area*
READING—*Seven Pines*

PETERSBURG AREA

Petersburg

By summer of 1864 the most important city in Virginia after Richmond was Petersburg, twenty-three miles south of the Confederate capital. All but one railroad bringing supplies to Richmond and the Army of Northern Virginia from the South passed through Petersburg; five lines in all, radiating in all directions, including the Richmond & Petersburg Railroad linking the two cities. The city on the Appomattox River was a transportation hub not only because of the railroads, but also because a similar array of roads entered from all directions, including two plank roads.

The Confederate leadership recognized the strategic importance of Petersburg while McClellan's Army of the Potomac threatened Richmond from the east. Work began on a perimeter of fortifications even as McClellan's army hunkered down in its Harrison's Landing encampment in July 1862. The line guarding approaches to the city had a ten-mile perimeter, anchored east and west on the Appomattox, known as the "Dimmock line," after Capt. Charles H. Dimmock, the engineer in charge of the year-long construction. The Dimmock line included 55 artillery batteries but an insufficient number of men to defend it, even after Gen. P.G.T. Beauregard assumed command of the defense of southside Virginia and Petersburg in May 1864.

The initial Federal assault on Petersburg did not come from Lt. Gen. U. S. Grant and the Army of the Potomac, then battling Robert E. Lee's Army of Northern Virginia northeast of Richmond, but from the Army of the James under Maj. Gen. Benjamin Butler. Despite Beauregard successfully outfoxing Butler, which resulted in the Army of the James being bottled up on the Bermuda Hundred peninsula, raids on the railroads north and south of Petersburg were launched, tying up Southern forces in guarding and repairing the lines. On June 9, Butler's forces advancing in two columns attacked the Dimmock line east of Petersburg. The infantry demonstrated while Brig. Gen. August V. Kautz's cavalry stormed Battery 29 guarding the Jerusalem Plank Road and thundered ahead until checked and turned back by home guards in the fight called the "battle of old men and young boys" by Petersburgers. The attack revealed the weaknesses of the Petersburg defenses and helped Grant formulate his next move.

As Grant began to march southward again after the Battle of Cold Harbor, he succeeded in confusing Lee as to his plans. Much of Lee's cavalry force was pursuing Maj. Gen.

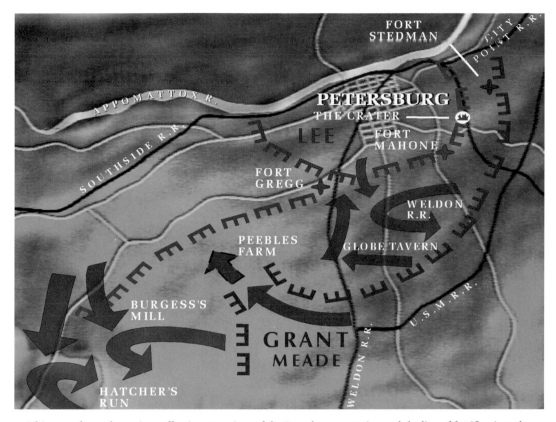

This map shows the various offensive operations of the Petersburg campaign and the line of fortifications that began east and south of the city and extended to the west over the months of the siege. The initial Federal assault in June 1864 was fought over the fortifications east of the city. After establishing a line of defense, Grant ordered attacks against the railroads and roads leading into Petersburg to turn the Confederate right and stop the flow of supplies to the Confederates behind the Petersburg fortifications. These assaults included battles at Globe Tavern August 18–21, Reams Station August 25, Peebles Farm September 29, and Boydton Plank Road–Burgess's Mill October 27, 1864. In early 1865 Grant renewed the effort to turn the Confederate right with the Battle of Hatcher's Run on February 5. In addition, the Battle of the Crater, fought on July 30, 1864, was not part of Grant's strategy for defeating the Confederates at Petersburg and in fact was a Federal disaster. After the initial Federal assault on Petersburg in June 1864, Lee launched only one offensive operation on the front, the attack on Fort Stedman on March 25, 1865. Petersburg fell after the Union assault on April 2, 1865.

Philip H. Sheridan's cavalry corps northwest of Richmond (see **Trevilian Station**) and Grant on June 13 undertook a diversion by the V Corps spearheaded by Brig. Gen. James H. Wilson's cavalry at Glendale, south of the Chickahominy, to mask his movement across the James River. This commotion allowed Grant to slip around Lee's army, holding closely to forts and fortifications around Richmond, and drive on his new objective,

Petersburg. Grant first sent the XVIII Corps, under Maj. Gen. William F. "Baldy" Smith, across the Appomattox River on a pontoon bridge at Broadway Landing on June 15. At the same time, the Army of the Potomac was crossing the James River farther east.

The attack on the Dimmock line began about seven P.M. on June 15. Smith's men captured Batteries 5 through 11 from Beauregard's 4,000 defenders, but Smith then hesitated. By the time Hancock's Union II Corps arrived to back him up, Rebel infantry were streaming south from Drewry's Bluff to stiffen the defense. Batteries 4 and 12 through 14 were captured in attacks on June 16 and 17 but new Rebel trenches closer to the city were sited and dug in the early-morning hours of June 18 as Lee arrived with most of his force. With 90,000 men across the James, Grant launched a massive assault on the Confederates on June 18. The Rebels pulled back to the new line of fortifications and held off the assaults until darkness halted the action.

Grant's force had cut two railroads in to Petersburg and gained control of several important roads, but the four-day assault was costly—more than 10,000 Federal casualties were tallied. Grant was left with no choice but to commence siege operations at Petersburg, though officially siege operations were not ordered until July 9. At the same time Grant continued to look for ways to break the Rebels' contact with their sources of supply. The Federals began to strengthen and fortify the positions captured in the initial assaults. At the same time, thrusts were made to the southwest to continue to cut railroads and roads into Petersburg. The Union probe toward the Petersburg & Weldon Railroad, known in reports in its abbreviated form, the Weldon Railroad, on June 22–23 was halted by two Confederate divisions, but the Jerusalem Plank Road fell to the Northerners and raiding Yankee cavalry pulled up and twisted track on the railroad. The Weldon Railroad would continue to be the focus of Federal attempts to encircle Petersburg and cut off supplies to the Southerners.

Points of Interest

The first stop in Petersburg National Battlefield is the visitor center. Exhibits and an automated sound-and-light map show orient you to the treasures found in this expansive and interesting park. Park rangers are on duty during the visitor center's open hours of 8:00 A.M. to 7:00 P.M. (shorter hours in the winter months) to answer questions. A short walking tour from the visitor center leads you to Confederate Battery 5. This was one of the first positions taken in the June 15 Federal attack. Guided tours are given of this position, which became Federal Battery 4 after its capture. A farther walk down a hill from Battery 5 leads you to a 13-inch mortar in its approximate siege position representing "the Dictator." Park rangers give scheduled talks on the siege at this location. 🚲 🅿️ ♿ 🏃 🏛 P 🍽 🚻 $

Continue your driving tour southbound on the one-way park road to Confederate Battery 8, also captured on June 15. This position was part of the Federal line from which artillery fire helped to turn back the Rebel attack on Fort Stedman. Tour stop three features a reconstructed Union camp including huts, earthworks, lateral trenches, fraises, gabions (dirt-filled wicker baskets), and bombproofs. A sutler store has also been built to reflect the importance of the sutlers—licensed merchants in the camps of both armies who sold items not supplied by the respective war departments to the soldiers. In the summer season demonstrations at this location include rifle-musket drill and firing as well as medical procedures. East of tour stop three was Meade's Station, a major depot on the U.S. Military Railroad built by the Federals.

On the way to the next tour stop is a picnic area. Tour stops four and five (Fort Stedman) are described later in that section.

The Crater

The developing stalemate of the siege of Petersburg was broken once during the month of July 1864. The 48th Pennsylvania Infantry Regiment of Burnside's IX Corps, former coal miners, began to drift a gallery under the Rebel works. The design was conceived by their commander, Lt. Col. Henry Pleasants, a brilliant engineer. He developed a unique ventilating system that allowed the gallery to extend more than 500 feet and form a T-shape directly under the Confederate works at Elliott's (Pegram's) Salient. Four tons of black powder were placed in barrels at the end of the mine. After the explosion, Burnside's infantry was to rush toward the crater formed by the blast and fan out on either side, rolling back the Confederates holding the works north and south of the crater, and then lunge west and seize the high ground overlooking Petersburg. The attack was preceded by a demonstration at Deep Bottom, north of the James, by General Hancock, to draw more Rebel troops from Petersburg, and a furious cannonade along the line. The Confederates were suspicious that a gallery was being dug, but believing one could not be extended more than 400 feet, were digging in the wrong places to uncover it.

A critical flaw arose in the plan when Meade and Grant discovered that the troops Burnside was drilling to lead the assault were the black soldiers of Brig. Gen. Edward

Ferrero's division. Fearing the political turmoil that would be caused by appearing to sacrifice African-American soldiers if the plan failed, Meade and Grant ordered Burnside to have one of his three white divisions spearhead the attack. After the division commanders drew straws, the lead fell to the division of Brig. Gen. James H. Ledlie, an officer with political connections whose most noteworthy trait was taking to the bottle in pressure situations.

The assault was planned for the predawn hours of July 30. The long fuse was lit, but nothing happened. Two 48th Pennsylvania Volunteers crawled into the gallery, respliced the fuse, and at four-forty in the morning, the earth shook. The blast sent a shock wave across the trenches at Petersburg; dirt clogs as large as houses were thrown into the air; 286 Confederates were immediately killed or wounded. But confusion reigned among Ledlie's men as they charged the crater while their division commander remained behind, allegedly drinking. They gawked at the destruction in the crater rather than fanning out as Ferrero's division had been trained to do. As the other three divisions pressed forward, the Confederates regained their composure and began firing mortar shells into the mob stalled in the crater. Rebel general, Petersburg resident William "Billy" Mahone, although small in stature, was a giant on this day as he masterminded a series of slashing counterattacks that spelled disaster for the Federals.

Despite heroics by Ferrero's division (Ferrero himself remained behind in the bombproof with Ledlie), the Battle of the Crater turned into a tragic reverse for the Army of the Potomac. As a result, Burnside was relieved of command, Ledlie was forced to resign from the army, and Ferrero, through an oversight, was merely assigned to an unimportant command. Grant never again used a mine as a tactical weapon.

Points of Interest

Two tour stops are important to the Battle of the Crater. Tour stop seven is the Federal Fort Morton, Burnside's headquarters. The chimney of Spring Garden's kitchen which survived the war is here. Park at tour stop eight. The footpath leads you to the entrance to the gallery and the crater. Interpretive signs and monuments are features here. Behind the crater is the area where counterattacking Confederates of Mahone's division surged across open fields. A monument to Mahone marks the Confederates' approach to the crater.

Globe Tavern

While Hancock's command demonstrated north of the James River at Deep Bottom, the Union V Corps and elements of the IX and II corps under command of Maj. Gen. G. K. Warren were withdrawn from the Petersburg entrenchments to operate against the Weldon Railroad. At dawn on August 18, Warren advanced, driving back Confederate pickets until reaching the railroad at Globe Tavern. In the afternoon, Brig. Gen. Henry Heth's division attacked, driving one of Warren's divisions back to the tavern. Both sides entrenched during the night. On August 19, Maj. Gen. William Mahone, whose division had been hastily returned from north of the James River, attacked with five infantry brigades, rolling up the right flank of Brig. Gen. Samuel W. Crawford's division. Heavily reinforced, Warren counterattacked and by nightfall had retaken most of the ground lost during the afternoon's fighting. On August 20, the Federals laid out and entrenched a strong defensive line covering the Blick House and Globe Tavern and extending east to connect with the main Federal lines at Jerusalem Plank Road. On August 21, A. P. Hill probed the new Federal line for weakness but could not penetrate the Union defenses. With the fighting at Globe Tavern, Grant succeeded in extending his siege lines to the west and cutting Petersburg's primary rail connection with Wilmington, North Carolina.

Ream's Station

While the Confederates lost use of the Weldon Railroad into Petersburg, the line still brought supplies up from North Carolina to Stony Creek Station, thirty miles to the south, where they were redistributed into wagons for transport to Petersburg. As a result, Grant ordered destruction of the railroad track south of Globe Tavern. The task was handed to Maj. Gen. Winfield Scott Hancock's II Corps and Brig. Gen. David M. Gregg's cavalry. The once proud corps had been wracked by casualties in the spring and summer campaigns and by August numbered many inexperienced conscripts. On August 25, the Confederates led by Maj. Gen. Henry Heth surprised Hancock's people and captured more than 2,000 at Ream's Station, five miles south of Globe Tavern.

Peeble's Farm

Three weeks after the Battle of Ream's Station, the Army of Northern Virginia cavalry under Maj. Gen. Wade Hampton helped relieve the Confederates' supply problems by staging a raid deep behind the Federal lines at Coggins' Point. On September 16 the Rebel horsemen surprised cavalry guarding a herd of cattle, capturing more than 300 troopers and almost 2,400 beeves, which they drove back into the Confederate lines. The impact of this spectacular raid and the Ream's Station victory were short-lived for the beleaguered Southerners. Grant ordered the westward extension of the Petersburg investment lines in late September.

On September 29, the Federals launched the third of what had become a familiar pattern of one-two punches against the Confederate lines guarding Petersburg and Richmond. In conjunction with the attack on Fort Harrison southeast of Richmond (see **Chaffin's Farm–New Market Heights**), the Army of the Potomac advanced on the Rebel works at Peeble's Farm west of the Globe Tavern. In three days of fighting the Federals forced the Confederates from their works along Squirrel Level Road. The Southerners successfully resisted any further gains toward the Southside Railroad, the last Confederate-controlled railroad from southside Virginia into Petersburg, but they were compelled to extend their lines three miles farther to the west to match an equal extension of Federal works. The Union soldiers constructed the largest fort at Petersburg, Fort Fisher, along this section of the line that was refused westward of the Squirrel Level Road.

Boydton Plank Road–Burgess's Mill

On October 27, the Federals again sought to reach the Southside Railroad. Standing in their way were Confederate defenses covering the Boydton Plank Road, north of Hatcher's Run. This thrust was made in conjunction with a demonstration against the defenses of Richmond north and south of Fair Oaks by Butler's Army of the James. Meade's Federals moved forward in two columns drawn from the II and V corps, preceded by Gregg's horsemen. At Burgess's Mill, where Boydton Plank Road crossed Hatcher's Run, Hancock's II Corps divisions were stopped by fierce Confederate resistance along the plank road and a charge by Wade Hampton's Confederate cavalry. Adding to the Northern problems was a lack of coordination between the two Federal corps commanders, Warren and Hancock, and the II Corps finding itself isolated retreated. Hancock, never having recovered from his Gettysburg wound and feeling discouraged by his inability to gain the kind of acclaim with his inexperienced soldiers that he achieved with previous commands, took sick leave, left the Army of the Potomac, and when he returned to duty, headed the Invalid Corps that helped defend Washington.

After the Battle of Burgess's Mill, there were no serious actions over the winter months. The siege settled into a pattern of picketing and sniping, with small skirmishes erupting from time to time along the nearly thirty-five miles of Confederate earthworks extending from east of Richmond to southwest of Petersburg. The Federals employed large-caliber siege guns and mortars, including the huge thirteen-inch mortar "the Dictator," to throw shells into Petersburg two miles away. The bombardment did little damage and the Confederate soldiers and citizens of Petersburg quickly adapted to living with the nuisance, much as those at Vicksburg had done eighteen months earlier.

The greatest problems for Lee's army in the winter of 1864–65 were sickness and disease, as well as lack of food and proper shelter for the cold winter months. Morale faltered as hunger pangs took on greater importance and desertion greatly increased, particularly among units from Georgia and South Carolina concerned about suffering caused by Sherman's "March to the Sea" and then into the heart of South Carolina. The Federals did not suffer nearly as much as their foes: Supplies arrived daily; many cabins, some elaborate, were built by the soldiers behind their line; and entertainment was occasionally imported or invented. One unit formed its own theater troupe. A U.S. Military Railroad line was built from City Point to speed the movement of supplies along the extensive line of Federal trenches.

Points of Interest

South of the Crater, the park road ends at Crater Road (US301), formerly Jerusalem Plank Road. Turn left (south) on Crater Road to Flank Road, where the park continues. The June 22–23 Federal attack toward the Weldon Railroad began at this intersection. Continue west on Flank Road to the intersection of Halifax Road (VA604). In 1864 present-day Halifax Road occupied the right-of-way of the present-day Southern Railroad while the Weldon Railroad was located on today's Halifax Road. The Battle of Globe Tavern was fought here. The tavern was 0.5 mile southeast of this intersection. Ream's Station was near where VA604 crosses the present-day railroad tracks 6 miles south of Flank Road. Besides the action here on August 25, Brig. Gen. August Kautz's Federal cavalry raided the station on June 22 during Brig. Gen. James H. Wilson's cavalry raid. Wilson's and Kautz's cavalry ranged as far west as Burke's Station and the Stanton River Bridge, where they battled Rebel cavalry and home guards on June 23–25. On June 29 Confederates led by Billy Mahone and "Rooney" Lee thrashed Wilson's and Kautz's cavalry at Ream's Station as they were returning from their raid on the railroads west of Petersburg.

Continue west on Flank Road to VA675, formerly Vaughan Road. Just south of Flank Road is Poplar Grove National Cemetery with graves of 4,000 unknown Union soldiers and more than 2,000 marked graves, most of which are Civil War veterans. This area was seized by the Federals during the Battle of Globe Tavern and was the camp of the 50th New York Engineers. Their famous log church was constructed here during the winter months.

From Poplar Grove, return north on VA675 and continue west on Flank Road to VA613, Squirrel Level Road. On September 29–October 2, 1864, soldiers of General Meade's Army of the Potomac, after a 2-mile advance, were stalled here short of Boydton Plank Road in the Peeble's Farm battle. Continue west on Church Road (VA672) to US1 and turn left. Three miles south a wayside marker indicates the site of Burgess's Mill and the Confederate trenches here.

Hatcher's Run

By February 1865, Grant was on the move again, looking to advance to and beyond the Boydton Plank Road. The advance began on February 5 and fighting again took place along Hatcher's Run. Brig. Gen. David M. Gregg's Union cavalry reached but could not maintain their toehold on Boydton Plank Road. After three days of battling in the bitter cold, soldiers of Warren's V Union Corps who had crossed Hatcher's Run were recalled. The Confederate major general John Pegram—who on January 19, 1865, had married the vivacious belle of Richmond society, Hetty Cary—was killed in the action. General Lee was compelled at the same time to extend his increasingly dwindling force another two miles to prevent the Union forces from perfecting their investment of Petersburg.

Points of Interest

A mile south of the Burgess's Mill marker is Dabney Mill Road (VA613). Turn left and continue east for 2.5 miles. A historical marker locates the site of the Battle of Hatcher's Run, a portion of which is preserved in a wooded parcel acquired with APCWS funds. Though there are currently no trails here, a short walk through the woods south of the road will bring you to a granite monument to Confederate general John Pegram, killed nearby.

Fort Stedman

By March the situation had turned from bad to worse for the Confederacy. Not only was Maj. Gen. William T. Sherman advancing through North Carolina to coordinate his "army group" with Grant's, the last great Confederate port on the Atlantic, Wilmington, had been occupied on February 22, five weeks after the fall of Fort Fisher (see **Fort Fisher, North Carolina**). At the same time, Maj. Gen. Philip H. Sheridan was sweeping through the Piedmont with his cavalry after crushing the last of Lt. Gen. Jubal Early's Shenandoah Valley force at Waynesboro on March 2. Rebel hopes for a negotiated end to the war were dissolved after a February 3, 1865, meeting of senior Confederate officials with President Lincoln at Hampton Roads, Virginia (see **Hampton Roads**). Lee, after conferring with President Davis in Richmond, ordered an attack at Petersburg to cover his evacuation of Petersburg and rapid march to North Carolina to join with the forces of Gen. Joseph E. Johnston and then give battle to Sherman's "army group."

To lead the attack, Lee selected Maj. Gen. John B. Gordon, a former Georgia lawyer who had established himself as one of the

Maj. Gen. John B. Gordon, CSA, was a pre-war Georgia lawyer with no professional military experience. He raised a company of soldiers, was elected its captain, and served in Robert Rodes's Alabama brigade in Bloody Lane at Antietam. A capable organizer and aggressive fighter, Gordon became one of Robert E. Lee's most trusted subordinates. Lee's confidence in Gordon led to his decision to have the Georgian lead the Confederate offensive launched against Fort Stedman at Petersburg.

South's most capable fighting generals. Gordon reconnoitered the Federal lines and determined the best place for an attack was at Fort Stedman, near the Military Railroad, the Federal army's main supply route. If Grant contracted his lines to protect the railroad, Lee could send several divisions to aid Johnston; if the attack failed, the resulting uproar would buy the Army of Northern Virginia time to evacuate Petersburg and Richmond in an orderly fashion.

Gordon worked out the details of the March 25 attack. Teams of pioneers would cut their way through the obstacles fronting the fort while three companies of volunteers posing as deserters would subdue the pickets and surprise the fort's defenders. The assault got under way at four A.M. and was initially successful. Fort Stedman and nearby batteries were captured with many of the defenders roused from their sleep only to find themselves taken prisoner. The three companies spearheading the attack rushed ahead to cut telegraph wires and disrupt the military railroad. But as the Rebel infantry divisions filed through and began fanning out to capture batteries along the Federal line, resistance stiffened. Union defenders of Fort Haskell, south of Battery XII and north of Battery XIII, stood tall and hurled the Rebels back. Those Confederates who pushed behind the lines had difficulty finding their objectives and were met by artillery fire and rallying infantry near the old Dimmock line in the Federal rear.

The Rebels were rolled back to the area of Fort Stedman, where at seven-thirty A.M. they were attacked by a fresh division under Brig. Gen. John F. Hartranft. The Confederates resisted the attack but by then Lee had sent an order for Gordon to withdrawal. Many Confederates surrendered when the ground between the lines was raked by Federal artillery fire, blocking their escape. The attack on Fort Stedman was a disaster for the Rebels as counterattacking the Federals restored their line and inflicted prohibitive heavy casualties on Lee's veterans. Worse, VI Corps soldiers in the Fort Fisher sector advanced and seized the Confederate picket line, giving them a springboard from which they scored a massive breakthrough on April 2. Lee began to make plans for evacuating Petersburg.

Points of Interest

Fort Stedman is tour stop five in the core area of Petersburg National Battlefield. If you are returning to the park, it is necessary to return to the main entrance and drive along the one-way park road tour to Fort Stedman. Just before Fort Stedman at tour stop four is Harrison's Creek. This ravine was the site of the farthest advance of Gordon's force before Federal artillery on a ridge to the east turned back the Rebels. Park at Fort Stedman and take the short walking tour of the fort, which is well preserved, and the ground across which Gordon attacked on March 25, 1865, and over which soldiers of the Union II Corps advanced on June 18, 1864, to meet a terrible fate. In the latter attack, the 1st Maine Heavy Artillery suffered the largest number of casualties of any Civil War unit in one day. Interpretive signs, battlefield art, and monuments—including the 1st Maine Heavy Artillery's—detail the June 18, 1864, and March 25, 1865, attacks. During the summer there are reenactments of Louisiana's Washington Artillery's advancing of a six-horse artillery unit and unlimbering and firing a 12-pounder Napoleon smoothbore cannon, as well as firing of a Coehorn mortar.

Five Forks

Even as Lee was making preparations to evacuate Petersburg and Richmond, Grant was making plans to complete the investment of the Confederate army. The day before the attack on Fort Stedman, Grant ordered the Army of the Potomac II and V corps to concentrate along Hatcher's Run. Maj. Gen. Edward O. C. Ord with three Army of the James infantry divisions was to cross the James and occupy the earthworks on the left of Wright's VI Corps from which the II and V corps were withdrawn. Grant's intent was to turn Lee's right flank beyond where his entrenchments terminated northeast of Dinwiddie Court House and eastof Five Forks' strategic crossroads. On March 26, Sheridan arrived at Petersburg with his victorious cavalry force of 10,000 after the completion of their destructive march from the Shenandoah Valley. He joined his cavalry with the other commands assigned to the expedition. Grant placed Sheridan in charge of the four-division mounted force.

The "win-the-war" offensive began on March 29 with the II and V corps, Army of the Potomac, moving out along with Sheridan's cavalry. Sheridan's vanguard reached Dinwiddie Court House by dark, but heavy rains bogged down the troopers, as well as the infantry. Robert E. Lee meanwhile rushed Maj. Gen. Fitzhugh Lee and three mounted divisions and Maj. Gen. George Pickett's reinforced infantry division to Five Forks to protect the crossroads that led to the Southside Railroad and Lee's line of retreat. On March 31, Pickett attacked Sheridan's horsemen in the Battle of Dinwiddie Court House, and, though the Rebels gained ground, Sheridan called up Custer's division and at dark still clung to the village. Maj. Gen. Gouverneur K. Warren's V Corps, after a day-long fight with Confederate infantry at White Oak Road, was ordered to report to Sheridan. Pickett pulled back to Five Forks and had his men throw up breastworks. Lee, disappointed to hear that Pickett did not hold his advanced position near Dinwiddie Court House, ordered Five Forks held at all costs.

The Confederates' defensive position fronted White Oak Road, covered the intersection, and anchored its left at the "return," a 200-yard breastwork forming a right angle to their main line of resistance. The rain stopped on April 1. Toward afternoon, Pickett, convinced that the Federals would not attack that day, accepted an invitation of cavalry general Thomas Rosser to a shad bake north of Hatcher's Run which Fitzhugh Lee also attended. At four P.M. Sheridan attacked, his dismounted cavalry occupying the attention of the Confederates positioned behind breastworks fronting White Oak Road east and west of Five Forks, while Warren's three infantry divisions advanced on and overwhelmed the Rebel brigade holding the "return." As Pickett raced back to the front line, Col. Willie Pegram, the younger brother of John Pegram, killed at Hatcher's Run, protected the center of the line with his artillery. Pegram was killed and by the time Pickett returned, his command was disintegrating—the Federal infantry swept across Ford Road and captured more than 3,200 prisoners before the battle ended at dusk. Total Federal casualties were less than 1,000.

The Battle of Five Forks is considered the Waterloo of the Confederacy. It broke the back of the Army of Northern Virginia and hastened the evacuation of Petersburg and the fall of Richmond. The battle convinced Grant to abandon completing an investment of the city in favor of an all-out attack on the Petersburg works set for four-forty A.M., April 2.

Points of Interest

Several sites were involved in the action leading up to the Battle of Five Forks on April 1. At the intersection of White Oak and Claiborne roads, APCWS has purchased 30 acres which are being developed with Dinwiddie County and include the site of the March 31, 1865, Battle of White Oak Road and formidable Confederate earthworks anchoring the right of the Southern line. From Petersburg NB, or the Hatcher's Run site, travel to the intersection of US1 and VA613 (White Oak Road). Take VA613 west for 2.75 miles to Claiborne Road (VA631) and park in the grassy area near the corner. Earthworks and battery positions of the Confederate line are located on both sides of the busy road; use caution when crossing the highway. On March 31, Maj. Gen. Bushrod Johnson's under-strength division, with General Lee looking on, attacked Warren's corps as it crossed White Oak Road. The Confederates were initially successful routing one of Warren's divisions and driving back a second. The tide then turned. Warren's forces counterattacked, the Confederates' gains were erased, and they retreated into their earthworks. The fight here kept these troops of R. H. Anderson's corps pinned in their entrenchments on April 1 while the action raged at Five Forks, 5 miles to the west.

At Dinwiddie Court House (US1), a historical marker identifies Sheridan's March 29 advance north from here. General-in-Chief Winfield Scott, a native of the town, had a law office here which is extant. A Confederate monument stands at the courthouse. At Chamberlain's Bed, a stream 1.1 miles northwest of the town, Maj. Gen. George E. Pickett and Maj. Gen. Fitzhugh Lee on March 31 challenged Maj. Gen. Philip Sheridan's advancing troopers and drove them back to Dinwiddie Court House. Pickett then withdrew to Five Forks.

The Five Forks unit of Petersburg National Battlefield is a new addition to the park and not yet fully developed. There is a small visitor facility at the unit, a monument, and interpretive signs. Five Forks is at the intersection of VA627 and VA613, 5 miles north of Dinwiddie Court House and 13 miles southwest of Petersburg. ❷ P 👫

The April 2, 1865, Federal attack on the Petersburg defenses, dramatically portrayed in this lithograph, overwhelmed the Confederates holding the city after Maj. Gen. Philip H. Sheridan's victory at Five Forks. After stubborn resistance at several points along the line, the Rebels withdrew to a tighter ring of defense at Petersburg, enabling Lee to successfully evacuate most of his army that night.

Petersburg Assault

The general assault on Petersburg was ordered for dawn the next day, Sunday, April 2. A signal gun began the attack at four-forty A.M., but heavy fog kept fighting localized until seven A.M. By that time the Federals had made major gains. Maj. Gen. Horatio Wright's VI Corps, forming on the ground seized on March 25, advanced and scored a massive breakthrough along the front a mile north of Fort Fisher and swept across Boydton Plank Road. Confederate Lt. Gen. A. P. Hill was killed while rallying his forces in vain. Only stubborn resistance of Rebels at Forts Gregg and Baldwin (Whitworth) prevented Federal troops of Maj. Gen. John

A photograph of a Confederate soldier killed in the April 2 Federal assault on Petersburg, taken at Confederate Fort Mahone the next day by a photographer following the Union forces into the city.

Gibbon's corps from spilling into the streets of Petersburg from the west. Farther east, the defenders of Fort Mahone prevented a breakthrough southeast of Petersburg. The death stand of the defenders of Fort Gregg allowed Lee to form a last-ditch defense along parts of the inner defense line behind Rohoic Creek west of the city. As he organized the withdrawal of his forces to the north, he sent word to President Davis in Richmond that the capital must be evacuated (see **The Fall of Richmond**).

The Confederates, of whom about 28,000 remained in Petersburg on the evening of April 2, successfully withdrew across the Appomattox River and marched west on roads to Amelia Court House. Grant was prepared to renew the assault the next morning, but by three A.M., the Federals learned that the city had been evacuated by Rebel troops and an hour later Petersburg fell. By eight A.M. Richmond had surrendered also. Leaving occupation forces in Petersburg and Richmond, Grant and the rest of the Federal army headed west to intercept the Army of Northern Virginia in its flight toward North Carolina.

Points of Interest

Points of interest relating to the April 2 attack on Petersburg and its capitulation are clustered in three areas southeast and southwest of downtown Petersburg. Returning to Petersburg from Five Forks via VA613 and US1, you find a historical marker on US1 near that intersection (2.8 miles southwest of Petersburg) describing the death of A. P. Hill. A monument locating the site of Hill's death is in a subdivision 0.5 mile to the west. From there, travel northeast on US1 to VA142. East of US1 is Fort Gregg, one of the last Confederate positions to fall on April 2. South on Church Road is Federal Fort Fisher, the largest earthen fort in Petersburg and the location from which the signal shot was fired to start the April 2 assault. As you travel east on VA142 you pass the Confederate forts and trenches in Petersburg NB that were assaulted. After you pass Wilcox Lake and leave the national battlefield there are two more forts: Fort Walker and Fort Mahone, near the intersection of Sycamore Street and Crater Road. Fort Mahone was the scene of bitter fighting that day. A large monument to Pennsylvania soldiers is nearby. Pamplin Park, a new park that features a walking trail, visitor center, and excellent earthworks, is on the site of the VI Corps breakthrough. To contact Pamplin Park, call 807-861-2408.

Often linked to Fort Mahone in accounts of the Petersburg siege is Fort Sedgwick on Crater Road. The two forts were relatively close together. Fort Sedgwick was nicknamed "Fort Hell" because it received so much Rebel artillery fire. Fort Sedgwick has long disappeared and there is now a shopping center on the site. Between the two forts at the intersection of Sycamore Street and Crater Road is a monument to Col. George W. Gowen, who was killed while leading the 48th Pennsylvania in the assault on Fort Mahone. Gowen's monument stands in the midst of a concentrated commercial area that gives little indication of the desperate struggle that occurred on this site.

North of the Gowen Monument at 319 South Crater Road is Old Blandford Church and Interpretive Center. The church, built in 1735, has fifteen Tiffany stained-glass windows, most of which commemorate forces contributed by different states of the Confederacy. The church cemetery contains the graves of more than 30,000 Confederate soldiers. It was located just behind the Rebel line but miraculously escaped significant damage during the siege.

Several sites in downtown Petersburg are of interest. The city has a number of antebellum homes and commercial buildings. The Petersburg Visitor Center in the 1815 McIlwaine House at the east end of Old Towne has information on historic sites, museums, shops, bed-and-breakfast inns, and other visitor attractions and services in the area. For more information, call 804-733-2400 or 800-368-3595. Farmers Bank, 19 Bollingbrook, is one of the oldest extant bank buildings in the United States and can be toured. The siege museum in the 1839 Exchange Building features exhibits on the effect of the war and the siege of Petersburg on the civilian population. City Hall on North Sycamore Street was formerly the U.S. Customs House and Post Office. It was occupied by the Confederates. The courthouse, also on North Sycamore, was a landmark during the siege. Its tower clock could be seen in the Yankee trenches. North Carolina Hospital at Perry and Brown streets was one of several Confederate tobacco warehouse hospitals in Petersburg. Niblo's Tavern at Bollingbrook and Second Street was a favorite gathering point for Confederate officers.

The 1823 Centre Hill Mansion on Centre Hill Court near Adams and Tabb streets is one of Petersburg's finest homes. Lincoln visited here after the city fell. The restored mansion can be toured. Other houses in Petersburg with Civil War significance are Maj. Gen. George Pickett's headquarters when he was commander of the Confederate Department of Southern Virginia before Beauregard assumed command of the region. It is located at Washington and Perry streets. The Mahone House on South Sycamore Street was the home of Confederate general William Mahone. The Wallace House at the intersection of South Market and Brown streets was the site of an April 3, 1865, meeting between Lincoln and Grant just hours after the city fell. It was the last time Lincoln and Grant met before Grant rode off in pursuit of Lee while Lincoln, after visiting Richmond and staying a few more days at City Point, returned to Washington.

Other sites in Petersburg associated with Robert E. Lee are St. Paul's Church on North Union Street—Lee's pew is marked and the building displays shell damage—and Lee's headquarters at the Beasley-Williamson House at 558 High Street. This building was his headquarters only during November 1864. Other sites include the Clay House on US1, 7.5 miles north of Petersburg, Lee's headquarters when he first arrived in the area on June 17, 1864, and two other buildings no longer extant. Lee had to change the location of his headquarters at least once to escape Federal artillery fire after the Yankees discovered the position. Lee Memorial Park is on Johnson Road near Confederate Fort Walker. The city park contains earthworks.

City Point

From the time Benjamin Butler's Army of the James landed at City Point, at the confluence of the James and Appomattox rivers, the small port town took on enormous significance to the Federal army. On June 15, 1864, Lt. Gen. U. S. Grant established his headquarters here to direct the campaign against Petersburg. A tent city sprung up on the lawn of the Epps Mansion, on a bluff overlooking the rivers' confluence, that became the nerve center of the campaign and of Grant's direction of the war efforts elsewhere as general-in-chief. Over the winter, cabins replaced the tents and a telegraph line was laid to Fort Monroe at Hampton Roads.

The sheds of the special U.S. Military Railroad depot which was established at City Point to carry supplies to the Federal forces besieging Petersburg. The U.S. Military Railroad branched from the City Point Railroad near the Appomattox River and ran behind the Federal lines. Besides the railroad facilities, the City Point base included wharves, hospitals, prison pens, a bakery, and the headquarters cabins of Grant and his staff.

Not only was City Point the headquarters for the

armies besieging Petersburg and Richmond, it was their chief supply and operations center. A new wharf was built to accommodate the mountain of supplies and thousands of soldiers arriving (and sometimes departing) from vessels coming up the James River from Fort Monroe. The City Point Railroad was repaired and a new U.S. Military Railroad extended south and then west from the City Point Railroad to continue the supply line behind the Federal works fronting Petersburg. In addition, warehouses, shops, and depots were constructed to supply the Federal forces. Hospitals were built, as were prison stockades to accommodate the prisoners from the Petersburg actions. City Point was shielded by earthworks extending from the Appomattox River on the north to the James River on the east.

Aware of the importance of City Point, the Confederates planned to do something destructive. Only once did an opportunity lead to action. On August 9, 1864, two Confederate agents got a timed explosive device aboard an ammunition barge. The device detonated about noon, killing 43 and injuring 126, including members of Grant's staff. The general-in-chief, having just returned from a meeting with General Sheridan in Monocacy Junction, Maryland, narrowly escaped injury himself as he sat in the yard of the Epps Mansion. The immense damage done, however, was repaired and supplies were replaced   this successful sabotage failed to slow down the Federal war machine intent on victory at Petersburg.

On two occasions President Lincoln visited Grant's headquarters here. In March 1865, he stayed for several weeks as the ten months' operations around Petersburg were climaxing. Grant and Lincoln met with R. Adm. David D. Porter and Maj. Gen. William T. Sherman on March 28 aboard the presidential yacht *River Queen,* at which time Lincoln discussed with the three officers his desire to be lenient with the former Confederates once the Rebels laid down their arms. That was not to be after a shot rang out in Ford's Theatre on April 14, 1865. But all three officers were impressed by the compassion that Lincoln displayed in regard to the Southerners and it added to their existing impression of the greatness and goodness of the man.

Points of Interest

The City Point Unit of Petersburg National Battlefield at Hopewell is located on VA36, 12 miles northeast of Petersburg. Besides possessing a commanding view of the Appomattox and James rivers where a huge Federal supply depot, wharves, shops, and railroad facilities once stood, the property highlights the restored Epps Mansion and the restored and refurnished cabin that General Grant used as his headquarters in the winter of 1864–65.   ♿ ❷ P ⛱ ⚥

DRIVING TOUR—*Proceed to Richmond*
READING—*The Fall of Richmond*

RICHMOND

Richmond was the most important city in the Confederacy during the war. Like Washington, it served as the nerve center of the war effort. While the Confederate states' capitol, which was the Virginia State House, served as a meeting place for the Confederate Congress to debate, enact legislation, and hear addresses by public officials such as the president, the role of the Southern legislature was even more limited than that of its Northern counterpart. The Confederacy disdained central governmental control and many of the political decisions in the South were still made at the state level. The primary political power of the Confederacy lay with President Jefferson Davis. For that reason, most of the important decisions of the Confederacy, especially the conduct of the war, were made in Davis's office in a house on Clay Street, the "White House of the

The Virginia State House served as the capitol of the Confederacy for nearly four years. Shortly after the fall of Richmond, the city started to rebuild. Except for some broken windows, the State House escaped damage during the war and soon returned to its former role as a meeting place for the Virginia legislature. Among the men on the portico in this 1865 photograph is photographer Mathew Brady.

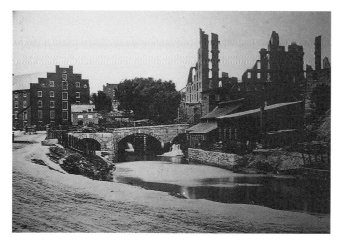

The ruins of the Gallego Flour Mills, which were totally destroyed by the fire that ravaged the Shockoe District of Richmond on the night of April 2–3, 1865. The Gallego Flour Mills provided processed flour which supplied bread to the Confederate army for four years of war.

Confederacy," and in the other offices of the executive branch.

Throughout the war Richmond was an important center for the manufacture and distribution of war materials. The huge Tredegar Iron Works on the James River turned out iron for all types of armament. The state arsenal manufactured rifle-muskets and ammunition. Many other factories in Richmond and Manchester, across the James, turned out war goods and other necessities for the armed forces and civilian populations. As is the case today, Richmond was an important center for processing Virginia's primary cash crop, tobacco.

A seemingly endless number of wounded soldiers made their way to the capital during the war. Richmond had the South's largest military hospital, Chimborazo, composed of a large number of one-story buildings on the bluffs east of downtown, which contained seven thousand beds. Among Richmond's care givers was Sally L. Tomkins, who used her widow's inheritance to run a private hospital for soldiers with a high rate of success. She was the only woman to receive a Confederate army officer's commission.

Richmond also had a number of facilities for Federal prisoners of war. The best known are Libby Prison, an old warehouse in downtown Richmond, which was used to house officers, and Belle Isle, an open-air prison on an island in the James River. Belle Isle was quickly filled to capacity, forcing the Confederates to build more prisons farther south. The prisoners lived in tents or in the open and the harsh conditions were similar to the North's Point Lookout. Libby Prison's conditions were little better. The close quarters and meager food fostered disease among its officer inmates. Numerous escapes were attempted. The most famous was via a tunnel constructed through the efforts of Col.

Thomas E. Rose. On the night of February 9, 1864, 109 officers escaped through the tunnel. Forty-eight, including Rose, were recaptured.

While Richmond managed to remain calm through the several Federal threats to the city prior to April 1865, one period of unrest affected the city in the spring of 1863. A shortage of food products entering the city sent prices skyrocketing and on April 2, 1863, what started as an orderly march of primarily women to the city's business district turned into an unruly rampage of looting. The riot was not brought under control until Jefferson Davis came out into the streets and addressed the mob. After his appeals of reason failed to stop the looting, Davis ordered the crowd to stop within five minutes or be fired upon. The mob scattered

This photograph of Richmond was taken when the Confederate capital was a busy supplier of war materials to the Rebel armies. In the distance across the James River are the mills of Richmond's companion city, Manchester. In the foreground is the waterside industrial area of Shockoe.

and some participants were rounded up later. Several ringleaders of the "Bread Riot" were convicted and sentenced to prison.

THE FALL OF RICHMOND

After the Federal attack and breakthrough of April 2, 1865, at Petersburg, Lee sent an urgent message to Jefferson Davis in Richmond advising him of the need to evacuate the capital. Davis was reached in St. Paul's Church, near the capitol, where he was attending Sunday service. Before day's end, Richmond was a city in panic. Government officials hurriedly packed documents and the contents of the treasury. Davis and the remaining Confederate cabinet boarded a train for Danville, Virginia, to reestablish the seat of government there. Many of the city's residents also clamored for passage on the southbound trains, which ran as frequently as the limited rolling stock allowed.

That night the city was in flames. At three A.M. fires started to destroy military stores raged out of control in the Shockoe area near the river and spread north into the business district. The state arsenal went up in flames, the bridges across the James River were torched, and the Confederate river fleet at Drewry's Bluff and the Rocketts, their magazines set to explode, was scuttled. Roving mobs looted stores and added to the destruction suffered by the city. The next morning, April 3, Federal troops entered the city, among them African-American soldiers of the XXV Corps, and restored order. The streets were filled with Richmond's slave population, who greeted their liberators with boisterous celebrations. President Abraham Lincoln and his son Tad arrived in Richmond on April 4, accompanied on a brief tour of the city by R. Adm. David D. Porter.

Points of Interest

A tour of Richmond begins at the Richmond National Battlefield Park Chimborazo Visitor Center at 3215 East Broad Street. The visitor center is on the site of the old Chimborazo Hospital, though none of the hospital's buildings remains. A brochure available at the visitor center diagrams the hospital's many buildings and orients them to existing streets and the visitor center. The center also has an audiovisual program on the Civil War defenses of Richmond, exhibits on the defense system, Civil War medicine, especially relating to the work of the Confederate Medical Corps, and exhibits and artifacts pertaining to the use of reconnaissance balloons and their employment during the Peninsula Campaign.

A short distance from the visitor center is Libby Hill Park, 27–29 East Franklin Street, which features a large monument dedicated to Confederate soldiers and sailors. At the foot of the bluff on the James River side of Libby Hill Park is the site of the Rocketts, the Confederate Navy Yard. Also in East Richmond is St. John's Episcopal Church at 24th and Broad streets, the eighteenth-century landmark where Patrick Henry gave his famous "liberty or death" speech. The Van Lew House, replaced by Belle Vue School, was on Grace Street between 23rd and 24th streets. It was the home of Elizabeth Van Lew. She helped Federal prisoners in Richmond escape. Libby Prison for officers was located at 20th and Cary streets; a historical marker is at the site. At 1701 Williamsburg Road is the Richmond National Cemetery. Of the 6,000 graves of Union soldiers, less than 10 percent are identified.

As you return to the center of Richmond on Williamsburg Road, the most striking building is visible is the Virginia State Capitol in Capitol Square between 9th Street and Governor's Street. The building's exterior, except for the wings, is largely unchanged from the time when the Virginia convention passed the state's ordinance of secession and when the Confederate Congress met. In the capitol and on Capitol Square are monuments to Confederate leaders. When Lincoln visited the capital on April 4, 1865, he admired the statue of George Washington in the northwest corner of Capitol Square. Washington's outstretched arm is pointing toward the southwest, the general direction of Danville. "Washington is looking at me and pointing at Jefferson Davis," the president remarked.

Across 9th Street from Capitol Square on Grace Street is St. Paul's Church. Jefferson Davis was attending Sunday service here when he received word on April 2, 1865, of the Federal assault on and breakthrough at Petersburg. Lee recommended the evacuation of the capital. Just north of Capitol Square on 11th Street is the Old City Hall, in use until 1870. Three blocks north of Capitol Square at 12th and Clay streets is the White House of the Confederacy, the home that Jefferson Davis and his family occupied for four years and where Davis maintained an office in which he conducted many of his duties. The White House of the Confederacy is faithfully restored and contains much of its original furnishings and other artifacts. Next to the mansion is the Museum of the Confederacy, which houses one of the nation's outstanding collections of Civil War artifacts, certainly as it applies to Confederate memorabilia, and an archive and research library. Admission is charged to the museum and mansion. For more information, call the Museum of the Confederacy at 804-649-1861.

Other points of interest in central Richmond are the Valentine Museum, located in an antebellum home at 1015 East Clay Street, which has Civil War exhibits and a research library. The Lee House, 707 East Franklin Street, was the Lee family's wartime residence. The Tredegar Iron Works are located at the south end of 6th Street between the Kanawha Canal and the James River. A number of the buildings and facilities have been restored, and hopefully will again be open to the public in the near future. Gamble's Hill Park at the south end of 3rd and 4th streets gives an excellent bird's-eye view of the area. The Shockoe section of the city between the river and Main Street was the area most affected by the fire on the night of April 2–3, 1865. At 8th and Byrd streets the Kanawha Canal Locks give an indication of the old waterway that brought boat traffic from Buchanan and Lynchburg parallel to the largely unnavigable section of the James River.

In the western part of the city are several other points of interest. Hollywood Cemetery at Cherry Street and Idlewood Avenue west of downtown contains the graves of Jefferson Davis, J.E.B. Stuart, George Pickett, Fitzhugh Lee, and many other Confederate officers and thousands of enlisted men. The northwest continuation of Franklin Street is called Monument Avenue, named for its series of monuments to Confederate leaders—J.E.B. Stuart, Robert E. Lee, Jefferson Davis, Stonewall Jackson, and Cmdr. Matthew Maury. All but Davis were native Virginians. The Virginia Historical Society is located in Battle Abbey at 428 North Boulevard Avenue. The postwar building houses, among its vast historical society collection of documents, pictures and artifacts, four two-story murals interpreting the four seasons of the Confederacy. For more information on the Virginia Historical Society, call 804-342-9658.

DRIVING TOUR—*Proceed to Amelia Court House*
READING—*The Road to Appomattox*

THE ROAD TO APPOMATTOX

Amelia Court House

Lee's next objective after evacuating Petersburg on the night of April 2–3 was to join his soldiers with the Confederate forces from Richmond and Bermuda Hundred at Amelia Court House, on the Richmond & Danville Railroad west of Richmond. The survivors of Five Forks were also marching to the concentration point separately. Here his army was to receive provisions, but when the hungry soldiers arrived on the evening of April 4, only an ordnance train was waiting at the station. A breakdown in communication had resulted in a failure to send from Danville by rail the expected rations and forage. Food was scarce at the local farms, having been collected earlier for the army's use at Petersburg, and invaluable time was lost as foraging parties scrounged the neighborhood for food and provender. So the new supply of ammunition, as well as part of Lee's artillery and wagon train, were left behind as the Richmond forces under Lt. Gen. Richard Ewell arrived and joined the march.

Federal cavalry pursuing Gen. Robert E. Lee's retreating forces near Jetersville. The ability of the large Union cavalry force to ride ahead, block the route of retreat, and destroy supplies enabled the Federal infantry to quickly close up on the Rebel soldiers marching west from Richmond and Petersburg. The depleted Confederate cavalry corps was unable to successfully challenge the Federal horsemen, who were well led, larger in number, and well supplied.

Jetersville

By the time Lee's columns were re-formed and marching again on April 5, their twenty-four-hour head start over the Federal army was lost. Sheridan's cavalry had followed the direct route west from Petersburg, shadowing and then outdistancing Lt. Gen. Richard H. Anderson's columns slogging along the south bank of the Appomattox River. Brig. Gen. George A. Custer's horsemen hammered Rooney Lee's cavalry at Namozine Church on April 3. Federal infantry was not far behind. Sheridan's troopers arrived at Jetersville on April 4 and formed a line behind light entrenchments, blocking the road to Burkeville (Burke's Station) where the two railroads, the Southside and the Richmond & Danville, crossed and where Lee hoped to receive supplies from the south.

When a forced Confederate reconnaissance on April 5 determined that three corps of Union infantry, under General Meade, were backing up the Yankee horsemen while other Federal infantry units were fast approaching, Lee was compelled to march his army to the west. His new objective was Farmville, where supplies from Lynchburg were due to arrive to ease the growing hunger of the Rebels. Another difficult night march, on increasingly poor roads, was ordered.

Points of Interest

From Richmond, take US360 southwest. At the bridge over the Appomattox River, 8 miles east of Amelia Court House, then called Goode's Bridge, a historical marker calls attention to the crossing of the Confederates from Petersburg. The courthouse square in Amelia Court House (US360 Business) has a Confederate memorial and a Coehorn mortar used by the Confederates at Petersburg. The present-day rail line runs along the same route as that of the Richmond & Danville from which Lee's men had hoped to draw supplies here. Several other markers along US360 southwest of the town describe the march of the Federal pursuit forces.

At Jetersville (US360, 9 miles southwest of Amelia Court House) there are historical markers indicating Lee's change of route to the west via Amelia Springs, formerly a summer resort. At 0.7 mile southwest of Jetersville a historical marker pinpoints Sheridan's position blocking the road to Burkeville.

DRIVING TOUR and READING—*Proceed to Sailor's Creek*

Sailor's Creek

On the night march of April 5 which carried through the next morning, the three parts of Lee's army, increasingly losing stragglers along the way, lost touch with one another. Longstreet's corps, in the van, arrived at Rice's Station by noon to protect the Southside Railroad—on which supplies would be arriving from Lynchburg—from Maj. Gen. Edward O. C. Ord's Army of the James then making a forced march alongside the railroad from Burkeville to intercept the Rebels. But the three small corps following

Longstreet became separated behind Longstreet's trains. On the afternoon of April 6, Lee, accompanied by the III Corps division of Maj. Gen. William Mahone, left Rice's and backtracked to high ground west of Big Sayler's Creek, a confluent of a two-branch stream that flows north into the Appomattox River twelve miles east of Farmville.

Riding east from the crest toward dusk, Lee observed the disorganized flight of hundreds of Confederate soldiers scrambling up the slope toward him, prompting him to utter an uncharacteristically alarmed exclamation, "My God! Has the army been dissolved?" What Lee saw were the survivors of the corps of R. H. Anderson, routed in one of three actions which made up the Battle of Sailor's Creek. Earlier in the day Anderson's force had been delayed by fighting the Federal cavalry on their southern flank. Anderson failed to get word to Longstreet that he had halted. As a result, a gap opened between Longstreet's wagon train and Anderson's corps, and Maj. Gen. George Crook alertly thrust his cavalry division into it. Crook was then joined by two other cavalry divisions under Brig. Gen. Thomas Devin and Brig. Gen. George A. Custer in fighting Anderson's two divisions, led by George Pickett and Maj. Gen. Bushrod Johnson, at a crossroads near the Marshall Farm. Sustaining only 172 casualties, the Federals routed the Rebels and inflicted a loss of 2,600, most of which were prisoners, including the capture of two general officers.

Just to the north of the intersection, Lt. Gen. Richard Ewell formed a battle line from Joseph Kershaw's veterans and his force of reservists, heavy artillerymen, and naval and marine corps personnel from the Richmond defenses under Maj. Gen. G. W. "Custis" Lee. He had already diverted the latter part of the wagon train to a road farther north, but failed to report the change to Maj. Gen. John B. Gordon, battling Maj. Gen. Andrew A. Humphreys's Federal II Corps which had marched in pursuit of the Rebel army from Jetersville. Ewell then was confronted by the 10,000-man VI Corps of Maj. Gen. Horatio Wright on the Hillsman Farm. Wright unlimbered 20 cannons about five P.M. and fired shells at the 3,600-man Confederate force on a parallel ridge across Little Sayler's Creek. The Federals then assaulted the ridge but were beaten back. After a Rebel counterattack was also turned back, the VI Corps re-formed and their second charge shattered the Confederate line. Ewell, his staff, 7 other generals, and more than 3,400 Confederates were captured in the fight west of the Hillsman Farm.

A few miles to the north, John B. Gordon was being steadily pressed by Humphreys's column. What he did not know was that his corps was isolated and that the deep valley

The Hillsman House at Sailor's Creek Battlefield Historical State Park was used as a Federal field hospital after the battle. The handmade colonial structure features brick nogging daubed in clay, beaded weatherboarding, and gutters fashioned from heart pine.

road his force was slowly withdrawing along was clogged by the supply train, having difficulty negotiating the double bridge over the confluence of the two branches of Sayler's Creek. After fighting from among the wagons, Gordon broke off the engagement after dark, losing a number of the wagons and enough soldiers to bring the total Confederate prisoner count for the day to more than 8,000.

The Battle of Sailor's Creek gave April 6, 1865, the distinction of being "Black Tuesday" in Confederate minds. The only factors that allowed the Army of Northern Virginia to escape annihilation that day were the safe passage of Longstreet's corps and Fitzhugh Lee's cavalry to Rice and High Bridge, and the rear guard that Mahone formed to allow a few of those engaged in the battle, chiefly from Gordon's corps, to escape to the west and re-form.

Points of Interest

Sailor's Creek Battlefield Historical State Park—Most of the battlefield of Sailor's Creek (the spelling of the battle and the state park were changed by the state of Virginia although the body of water is still called Sayler's Creek) is preserved in or nearby this state facility. From Jetersville, take US360 for 2 miles southwest to VA307; travel west for 5 miles to VA616 then 4 miles north to VA617, then west to the park entrance. A driving tour along VA617 takes you to the key sites of the battle. The Hillsman House, dating from the eighteenth century, has many fine hand-crafted features. Bloodstains extant on the floors attest to its use as a Federal field hospital treating casualties of both sides after the battle.

A short walking tour from the Hillsman House parking lot takes you to the position of the Federal VI Corps overlooking the valley of Sayler's Creek to the southwest. Interpretive signs, a painting, and reproduction cannon set the scene for the battle between Wright's forces here and Ewell's forces across the valley. Continue your tour by continuing on VA617 across Little Sayler's Creek and up the hill to the overlook alongside the road where the battle is interpreted from the Confederates' perspective. Here there is a trail and a Confederate memorial. Turn around and return on VA617 to Hott's Corner and the intersection with VA618; turn left at the intersection. The Lockett Farm is at the top of the next hill. From this position, Maj. Gen. Andrew Humphreys's II Corps drove John B. Gordon's rear guard into the valley formed by the confluence of the two branches of Sayler's Creek. There is a monument in front of the extant Lockett House. Continue down the hill to the creek bed—parking is difficult here but the creek is visible in this heavily wooded section where Gordon's troops battled from amid the stalled wagon train.

Continue south on VA618 to VA619. A short distance to the south, VA619 meets VA617. Turn left (east) on VA617. Shortly you reenter the state park. Interpretive markers describe Sheridan's cavalry attack on Maj. Gen. R. H. Anderson's corps. Continue on VA617 to its intersection with VA307 and travel west to Rice. For more information on Sailor's Creek Battlefield Historical State Park, contact Twin Lakes State Park, Green Bay, VA 23942; 804-392-3435. Twin Lakes State Park is nearby and has recreational facilities. 🚲 ♿ 🚶 ❷ P 🪑 🚻

DRIVING TOUR and READING— *Proceed to High Bridge–Farmville*

High Bridge–Farmville

As the Confederates marched on April 6 toward Farmville, the cavalry of Maj. Gen. Fitzhugh Lee rushed to intercept a flying Federal column from Maj. Gen. Edward Ord's army intent on destroying the bridges on the Southside Railroad. Their major target was High Bridge, iron and wood spans built on twenty-one brick piers standing 126 feet above the valley, which carried the railroad over the Appomattox River east of Farmville. Lee's cavalry led by Fitzhugh Lee and Tom Rosser in a savage fight killed, wounded, or captured the entire Federal contingent of 900.

The morning of April 7 Robert E. Lee anxiously awaited word of the safe crossing of the Sailor's Creek survivors at High Bridge even as Longstreet's veterans who had marched from Rice's Station to Farmville were beginning to draw rations from the boxcars that had arrived from Lynchburg. A new crisis soon developed, however. Mahone, after covering the river crossing of the Sailor's Creek survivors, left the area without overseeing destruction of the railroad and wagon bridges. By the time the engineers secured his permission to torch the vital bridges, Humphreys's II Corps appeared on the river's south bank. The railroad bridge was soon engulfed in flames and four of the twenty-one spans destroyed, but the adjacent wagon bridge, made of hardwood, caught fire slowly and the Federals, in an operation similar to that at Remagen in March 1945, put out the fire and crossed the bridge. Despite Mahone's efforts to return and counterattack with his division, the Federals had a foothold on the west side of the river and a clear approach to Farmville, disrupting Lee's plans to allow his tired and hungry soldiers to rest and ration themselves there.

The Confederates next formed a line of battle at Cumberland Church, north of the Appomattox after crossing and destroying the Farmville bridges. At Cumberland Church, Mahone held back Humphreys's advance, while George Crook's cavalry, who had forded the Appomattox upriver from Farmville, was turned back by Fitzhugh Lee's cavalry south of Cumberland Church. Though Lee avoided having his army cut off at Farmville, the results of the mistakes early in the day were grim. Few of the rations delivered to Farmville got in the hands of the Army of Northern Virginia soldiers. And they would have to make another night march in order to stay ahead of the Federals and reach the next place where rations could be had at Appomattox Station, thirty miles west.

U. S. Grant was in Farmville by the evening of April 7, watching some of his 80,000-man force hold a torchlight parade, as they marched through the town in pursuit of the fleeing Rebels. His plan was in place. The infantry corps of Humphreys and Wright would tail the Confederate column north of the Appomattox, while Sheridan's cavalry, followed closely by the infantry of Ord and Charles Griffin, raced ahead along the railroad and captured Appomattox Station. The Federals would then block the route of Lee's army south, toward Gen. Joseph E. Johnston in North Carolina, or west toward Lynchburg. It was at Farmville that Grant composed and sent between the lines his first request for the surrender of the Army of Northern Virginia.

Points of Interest

A historical marker 2.25 miles north of US460 at the intersection of VA619 and VA688 is the closest to High Bridge. The 21-span structure, extant and in use by the railroad, is located 1 mile north of this site. Continue west on US460 and enter Farmville on

US460 Business. The site of the Prince Edward Hotel, occupied by Lee on the night of April 6 and Grant on the night of April 7, is identified by plaques. The innkeeper told Grant he was staying in the same room Lee had occupied the night before, but put him up in a different and—undoubtedly because he was a typical Virginian who revered Lee—less elegant chamber.

From Farmville, take US15 north across the Appomattox River and past the site of the engagement at Cumberland Church, which is extant. At Sheppards, turn left (west) onto VA636. Part of Lee's army traveled this route on April 8, pursued by Humphreys's II Corps. On VA636 a historical marker identifies Clifton, the house where Grant spent the night of April 8. Here he corresponded with Lee. Grant left the house early on April 9 to travel to the Federal front at Appomattox Court House. The house is a private residence but can be seen from the road. Continue west on VA636 through the Buckingham Appomattox State Forest to VA24, then southwest to Appomattox Court House. Holliday Lake State Park in the state forest has recreational facilities. For information, call 804-248-6308.

DRIVING TOUR and READING—*Proceed to Appomattox*

Appomattox Court House

The evening of April 7 Grant's first surrender message reached Lee at Cumberland Church under a flag of truce. Lee composed and sent a message to Grant asking under what terms a discussion might occur. The next day the Rebels continued to slog toward Lynchburg, though their march was relatively quiet. Increased straggling and exhaustion of the soldiers decreased the ranks faster than the skirmishing around Farmville had the previous day. Though relatively close to the gray cavalry trailing the corps of Maj. Gen. John B. Gordon, in the lead, and Lt. Gen. James Longstreet, the Federals did not attack the column on April 8. Instead, they advanced on both sides of the Appomattox River toward the same goal as the Confederates, Appomattox Station.

Though Grant's reply to Lee's April 7 letter offered terms much more liberal than one would assume were in line with his "unconditional surrender" reputation, Lee's letter rejected the notion of surrender. Grant was unwilling to accept Lee's terms for a "restoration of peace" and negotiations broke down for the moment. The Southern leader was holding open the possibility of beating the Federals to the depot or breaking through their lines if he didn't.

As evening set in, Lee and the lead elements of Gordon's corps approached Appomattox Court House from the northeast. Appomattox Station was another three miles to the southwest. As the sun began to set, the first option Lee had considered no longer existed—Union campfires southwest of Appomattox Court House showed the Federals had won the race. Maj. Gen. Philip H. Sheridan's cavalry had captured four Confederate supply trains at Appomattox Station earlier in the day. In a meeting with his top lieutenants Lee determined the only alternative to surrender would be a breakout attempt by the smaller Confederate force.

On Palm Sunday morning, April 9, the exhausted soldiers of Gordon's Corps and Maj. Gen. Fitzhugh Lee's cavalry attempted to break through Sheridan's troopers blocking the road west of Appomattox Court House. But the shrill Rebel yells that marked this charge would be the last for the Army of Northern Virginia soldiers. Sheridan's cavalry initially gave way, but only to allow the infantry corps of Maj. Gen. John Gibbon, reinforced by two brigades of Brig. Gen. William Birney's division of the African-American XXV Corps, to enter the fight. Longstreet, pressed by Maj. Gen. Andrew A. Humphreys's II Corps coming from the northeast, could offer no assistance. Federal cavalry flanked the infantry, preventing all but the Rebel cavalry from breaking out and making its way west to Lynchburg. All but surrounded by Union troops, Lee rejected the idea put forth by some of his officers that the army take to the hills to fight as guerrillas. He sent a message to Grant to request a meeting for the purpose of surrendering his army. Flags of truce gradually brought the fighting to a halt.

That same afternoon, April 9, 1865, Lee and Grant met in the parlor of Wilmer McLean's brick home in Appomattox Court House. McLean had brought his family to Appomattox County after the armies of blue and gray had overrun, for the second time, his farm west of McLean's Ford crossing Bull Run following the Second Battle of Manassas. Lee and a staff officer arrived first. Grant, who had received Lee's request for the meeting while on his roundabout ride to the front, arrived thirty minutes later accompanied by staff and several general officers. After introductions and Grant remarking about an encounter with Lee in the Mexican War, the two great generals sat down to work out the terms of surrender. The terms Grant was offering were substantially the same as those he previously offered in his messages to Lee.

Army of Northern Virginia soldiers furl a battle flag in this stirring Richard Brooke painting of the surrender ceremony at Appomattox Court House. In their handling of the troops' surrender, the conquering Federal forces allowed the Confederates to maintain dignity in defeat. Brig. Gen. Joshua L. Chamberlain was given the honor of supervising the surrender for the combined Union forces at Appomattox Court House. For the Confederate Army of Northern Virginia, Robert E. Lee's trusted subordinate, Maj. Gen. John B. Gordon, handled the details of surrender. The ceremony took place on April 12, 1865.

As the Army of Northern Virginia commander read the document, Grant looked for a reaction from Lee. He wrote later, "What General Lee's feelings were I do not know, as he was a man of much dignity, with an impassable face . . . it was impossible to say whether he felt inwardly glad that the end had finally come, or felt sad over the result and was too manly to show it. Whatever his feelings they were entirely concealed from my observation; but my own feelings, which had been quite jubilant on the receipt of his letter, were sad and depressed. I felt like anything rather than rejoicing at the downfall of a foe who had fought so long and valiantly, and had suffered so much for a cause, though the cause was, I believe, one of the worst for which a people ever fought."

After some minor changes, particularly one in which Grant allowed those in the army who owned horses or mules to be allowed to leave with them, Col. Ely Parker—a Seneca chief and member of Grant's staff—drafted a final agreement that was signed by Grant and Lee. Grant then ordered 25,000 rations for the Confederates—for this and the concession on the horses and mules Lee expressed his appreciation. The two men then shook hands and departed separately. Souvenir hunters snapped up most of McLean's furnishings as Lee rode back to his headquarters camp, surrounded by Southern soldiers who showed only their love for him for the difficult decision he had had to make.

The details of signing paroles for the more than 28,000 Confederates and the surrendering of arms were arranged by three senior officers from each army. Brig. Gen. Joshua L. Chamberlain was given the honor of formally receiving the surrender of the Army of Northern Virginia's infantry. Grant did not wait at Appomattox Court House for the formal surrender; after a short meeting with Lee on Monday—April 10—he left for City Point en route to Washington to begin the process of winding down the war effort on behalf of the Union armies then costing the U.S. government $4 million each day. After delivering a stirring farewell address to his men, Lee remained in his headquarters tent through Wednesday April 12, but did not attend the day's formal surrendering of arms ceremony. That day he departed for Richmond.

On April 12, the Federal army marched into the "surrender triangle" at Appomattox Court House and formed ranks facing each other alongside the Lynchburg Stage Road. Shortly, the tattered but proud gray soldiers passed between the solemn lines of blue soldiers, stacked their arms and furled their flags. The respect given by the Federal officers and soldiers to their defeated foes was appreciated by the Southerners. Brig. Gen. E. Porter Alexander, artillery commander for the Army of Northern Virginia's I Corps, wrote later, "Grant's policy of conciliation was followed by everyone in his army, even to the teamsters along the roads . . . [after the surrender], in riding forty miles through the troops and trains of the Federal army, I met with not a single word or look which did not seem inspired with kind feeling and a disposition to spare us all the mortification possible. I think no one who was not at that surrender can fully appreciate the calamity wrought to the South by the assassination of President Lincoln. For Wilkes Booth slew also the kindly and generous sentiment which already inspired the army, and which would doubtless soon have pervaded the whole country."

Points of Interest

Appomattox Court House National Historical Park—This 1,325-acre historical park commemorates the last battle action of the Army of Northern Virginia and its subsequent surrender. The village saw a decline shortly after the war as the commercial center in the region moved to Appomattox Station on the railroad. The McLean House was dismantled with plans to move it to Washington but the project failed. The courthouse burned in 1892. The decline of the village was a blessing for posterity. By the 1930s efforts were under way by the National Park Service that led to the preservation of the village itself as a historical tribute. Today the carefully restored village is one of the most beautiful of Civil War sites.

From the site of Lee's headquarters east of the village to the site of Grant's headquarters southwest of the Appomattox Court House, the park contains all the important battle- and surrender-associated sites. The reconstructed courthouse contains the visitor center featuring pamphlets on walking tours of the village, park rangers to answer questions, and rest rooms. There is a museum on the building's second floor with exhibits, an electric map, and an auditorium where interpretive audiovisual shows are presented. All the other buildings in the park are either historic structures or have been reconstructed to give the village its 1865 appearance except for the Appomattox County Jail, completed in 1870. Exhibits and living history interpreters in the houses and commercial buildings of the village explain life in this rural village as it existed for its inhabitants in the 1860s. Before the Civil War, Joel W. Sweeney, musician, minstrel, and inventor of the five-string banjo, lived here. His grave is in the park. Sweeney's brother Sam was also an entertainer who served with J.E.B. Stuart's cavalry.

The McLean House is fully restored and the parlor has been refurbished to look as it did to those who witnessed the epic event that took place there on the afternoon of April 9, 1865. On the opposite side of the courthouse from the McLean House and a few hundred yards up the Old Richmond–Lynchburg Stage Road is Surrender Triangle, where the April 12 surrender ceremony took place. Among other features of the park are the North Carolina Monument, which locates the farthest advance of Gordon's April 9 morning attack and a Confederate cemetery, which contains the graves of 18 Southern soldiers and 1 unknown Union soldier killed in battle that day.

From Appomattox Court House continue south on VA24 to the town of Appomattox (formerly Appomattox Station) and US460 to Lynchburg. At the park visitor center, as well as the Petersburg NB visitor center, you can secure information and literature about the acclaimed twenty-stop radio tour that follows and interprets "Lee's Retreat" from the outskirts of Petersburg to Appomattox. APPOMATTOX COURT HOUSE NATIONAL HISTORICAL PARK, P.O. Box 218, Appomattox, VA 24522; 804-352-8987.
♿ 🚶 ❓ 🏛 P 🚻 👫 💲

DRIVING TOUR—*Proceed to Lynchburg and Western Virginia*
READING—*surrenders: Bennett Place, North Carolina*

SOUTHEASTERN VIRGINIA

Naval Action at Hampton Roads

In March 1862, the long-awaited appearance of the Confederate ironclad CSS *Virginia* launched a new era in naval warfare. The Federal government had known about the existence of the ironclad for nearly a year, since plans for her construction had been communicated to the U.S. Navy Department shortly after rebuilding the vessel began. The *Virginia* was built from the hulk of the Union warship *Merrimack*, scuttled during the evacuation of the U.S. Navy base at Norfolk in April 1861. Confederate forces arrived in time to salvage the burning *Merrimack* and from her hull, naval engineers began the process of rebuilding a 10-gun armor-plated warship under the guidance of Confederate navy secretary Stephen Mallory.

On her maiden voyage the CSS *Virginia* targeted Federal vessels lying at anchor in Hampton Roads. The U.S. Navy was then based at Newport News, after the evacuation of Norfolk and the Gosport Navy Yard at Portsmouth, where the *Virginia* was built. Hampton Roads is the large body of water formed by the confluence of the James and two other rivers before they flow into the Chesapeake Bay. To the north, Fort Monroe guarded the mouth of the roads, and control of Hampton and Newport News enabled the Federals to maintain protected anchorages and support facilities in what was otherwise the Confederate-held Tidewater region of Virginia. On March 8, 1862, at eleven A.M. the CSS *Virginia* steamed down the Elizabeth

The sinking of the USS Cumberland *on March 8, 1862, by the CSS* Virginia. *The havoc wrought by the Confederate ironclad at Hampton Roads led to the first duel of ironclad ships the next day as the USS* Monitor *arrived to challenge the* Virginia. *The wooden hulls of the* Cumberland *and her sister ship the USS* Congress *were heavily damaged by shot from the* Virginia *as the ironclad closed range on the Federal warships. Though the* Cumberland *and the* Congress *returned fire, their solid shot merely bounced off the superstructure of the* Virginia, *which consisted of heavy timbers reinforced with iron plates and rails.*

River and into Hampton Roads at five knots under the command of Flag Officer Franklin Buchanan. Rumors of the ironclad's imminent appearance had died down over the months while her construction suffered delays and Federal sailors were somewhat surprised when a Union gunboat lookout shouted, "That thing is coming down!"

At that time five powerful warships were on blockade duty in Hampton Roads, including the steam frigates USS *Minnesota* and USS *Roanoke,* as well as three sailing vessels, the USS *St. Lawrence,* the USS *Congress,* and the USS *Cumberland.* The latter two, guarding the mouth of the James River, were stationed nearest to the *Virginia.* Buchanan was determined to attack the *Cumberland* and the *Congress* first, then head east to attack the other Federal warships. The *Virginia* was sluggish and hard to steer and Buchanan navigated carefully to avoid running aground. After ninety minutes, the *Virginia* closed to within one mile of the anchored *Cumberland* and fired one shot from her bow pivot gun, which tore into the *Cumberland's* gundeck. The guns of the two Federal warships, nearby gunboats, and the shore batteries at Newport News fired on the *Virginia,* but the shots glanced off the iron superstructure.

The *Virginia,* using a mile of water to gain momentum, rammed the *Cumberland* with an iron prow designed for doing that. A huge hole opened at the waterline, and as the *Cumberland* began to list, the *Virginia* was dragged down as well, her ramming prow stuck in the side of the crippled ship. Finally the *Virginia* wrenched free but wrested off and lost her iron prow. Maneuvering through deeper water and accompanied by Confederate gunboats, the *Virginia* returned to engage the USS *Congress* even as the *Cumberland* was slipping beneath the waves. The *Congress* was towed to shallow water but could not aim more than two guns at the *Virginia* and her gunboat consorts. Several well-placed shells damaged the *Congress* and killed her skipper. The Federal ship hoisted a white flag but Northern shore batteries continued to fire on the *Virginia,* so Buchanan ordered hot-shot fired at the *Congress.* Buchanan came out onto the deck of the *Virginia* and was wounded by a sharpshooter. Lt. Catesby ap Jones assumed command of the *Virginia* as the *Congress* raged into an inferno from the hot-shot shells fired from the *Virginia.*

Jones wanted to turn next to the USS *Minnesota,* which had come from her station near Fort Monroe to aid the two sailing ships, but the day when ships were wood and the men iron had passed. En route, the *Minnesota* ran aground and presented an easy target for the *Virginia.* However, the Confederate ironclad's pilots feared the lowering tide and convinced Jones to abandon the fight for the day. By dusk, the *Virginia* was settling into anchorage near Sewell's Point at the mouth of the Elizabeth River. Plans were formulated to continue the destruction of the Federal blockading squadron at dawn.

During the night of March 8, the closest thing to a miracle occurred for the U.S. Navy. The *Monitor* arrived in Hampton Roads. The novel first Federal ironclad had had a rough course from cardboard model to maiden voyage. Angered by previous contacts with the U.S. Navy, *Monitor* designer John Ericsson, a brilliant Swedish-born naval architect and builder, did not aggressively pursue the invitation of the navy for ironclad designs until a competitor, Cornelius Bushnell, realized the superiority in design of the Ericsson *Monitor* and presented it to the navy's Ironclad Board. With Lincoln's endorsement, the skeptical board awarded contracts to both Bushnell and Ericsson, but Ericsson's design was the first to be built and would have the greatest influence on U.S. Navy ship design in the Civil War and afterward. Ericsson's contract called for a one-hundred-day construction schedule and though the building was completed efficiently and in half the time it took the Southerners to convert the *Merrimack,* the *Monitor* was undergoing last-minute outfitting when she left Brooklyn, New York, under tow for the trip down the Atlantic to Hampton Roads.

At nine P.M., March 8, the *Monitor* arrived in Hampton Roads under the command of Lt. John Worden and reported to the acting commander of the North Atlantic Blockading Squadron, Capt. John Marston. The *Monitor* was ordered to go to the aid of the *Minnesota,* still grounded. Worden had no trouble locating the *Minnesota* as the night sky was illuminated by the burning *Congress.*

At dawn the CSS *Virginia* weighed anchor and steamed toward the *Minnesota.* Crowds were already gathering in boats and on the Confederate shoreline to witness the *Virginia* at work. But as the Rebel ironclad approached the *Minnesota,* the *Monitor* appeared from behind the warship. The crew of the *Virginia* recognized immediately the distinctive design—the single iron turret mounted amidships on the low flat iron hull, the "cheese box on a raft" or "tin can on a shingle" as the widely publicized Ericsson craft was derisively called. Whether or not she would prove to be a formidable opponent for the Southern ironclad would be shortly discovered when the *Virginia* opened fire at 8:06 A.M. on March 9, 1862.

The first shot passed over the *Monitor* and struck the side of the *Minnesota.* The frigate responded with a broadside and the *Virginia* also launched a full broadside at the *Monitor,* but the shots glanced off the Federal ironclad. From that moment on the two ships fought with intensity, often at close range. The *Monitor* had superior maneuverability and speed but the *Virginia* commanded greater firepower and could deliver it faster than the two big shell guns in the slow-moving turret of the *Monitor* could be fired. After two hours, Jones and his crew, seeing no appreciable damage to the *Monitor* occurring from gunfire alone, decided to ram the ironclad, but after taking an hour to maneuver into position, the *Virginia* only managed a glancing blow as the *Monitor* sheared away from the impact. The *Monitor* delivered some point-blank shots at the *Virginia*'s aftergun casemate that knocked down and stunned a number of the soldiers inside the casemate manning the cannon.

About noon the *Virginia* fired a shot that exploded at the eyeslit in *Monitor*'s raised pilot-house. The impact blinded Worden permanently in one eye. In the confusion that followed, the command was assumed by the gunnery officer, Lt. S. Dana Greene, who received orders from Worden to continue the fight if possible. But in the moments just after Worden's injury, the *Monitor* sheered into shallow water away from the *Virginia*. Jones assumed the Federal ironclad was breaking off the contest and turned his attention to the *Minnesota*. His pilots, however, again warned of the dangers of the lowering tide and so with leaking caused by damage and ammunition running low, the *Virginia* headed for the Elizabeth River. The Federals fired a few more parting shots, then, satisfied that the *Minnesota* was out of danger, did not pursue the contest. After four hours of almost continuous contact the crews welcomed the relief from further action.

While the contest was tactically a draw, the *Monitor* successfully protected the grounded *Minnesota* and though the *Virginia* reappeared in Hampton Roads a month later after undergoing repairs, the presence of the *Monitor* prevented any further destruction of the Federal blockading fleet by the Confederate ironclad. The successful duel of the two ironclads, the first in history, caused both sides to accelerate construction of more ironclad vessels; the South produced several more of the *Virginia* design, the U.S. Navy ordered fifty-six monitors. The battle launched a bold new era in naval ship design and combat.

Neither of these historic ships lasted the year, however. When Confederates evacuated Norfolk on May 10, 1862, following the landing of Federal troops across the Ocean View beaches east of Sewell's Point as President Lincoln looked on, the CSS *Virginia* was set afire by her crew and scuttled off Craney Island on May 11 to prevent her capture. The USS *Monitor* was lost in a gale off Cape Hatteras, North Carolina, on December 30, 1862, while being towed to Port Royal, South Carolina, to participate in naval operations against Charleston. Sixteen crewmen were lost in the nighttime sinking.

Fort Monroe

The Tidewater area continued to play a major role in Federal operations in Virginia. In the spring of 1862 more than 100,000 Federal troops arrived in the area for the Peninsula Campaign. Fort Monroe (sometimes called Fortress Monroe) on Old Point Comfort, held continuously by the Federals throughout the war, served as a command center while hospitals and other support facilities sprang up in the area. Maj. Gen. Benjamin Butler used the fort as a command post on several occasions, including during the period in 1864 when he gathered forces for his Army of the James to launch an offensive against Richmond by boating his Army of the James up James River and occupying City Point and Bermuda Hundred. A direct telegraph line linked the fort with the War Department in Washington and another, established between Fort Monroe and City Point, enabled U. S. Grant to have immediate communication with Washington as he directed Federal operations at Petersburg.

The Hampton Roads peace conference was held on February 3, 1865, aboard the presidential yacht *River Queen,* anchored just off Fort Monroe. The meeting between President Lincoln, Secretary of State William Seward, and three Southern emissaries including Vice President Alexander Stephens did not bring peace, but the emissaries left with the clear message that the resolve of the Federal government would keep the nation at war until the Union was reunited. Four months later on May 22, 1865, Jefferson Davis arrived at Fort Monroe, involuntarily. He was imprisoned in one of the casemates there until October 1865, and then lodged in Carroll Hall, a two-story brick building, no longer extant (see **Irwinville, Georgia**). His wife joined him there in May 1866, staying in nearby quarters through May 13, 1867, when Davis was released on a bond of $100,000 with no charge being made against him for his role in the dissolution of the Union.

Points of Interest

In the Norfolk-Portsmouth area are several sites associated with army and especially naval events and personalities in the brief period in 1861–62 when the area was contested. Beginning at Portsmouth's west end, which can be reached from Suffolk via US17 or Newport News via I-664 and the Monitor Merrimac Memorial Bridge Tunnel, you can travel east to I-64 and cross to Fort Monroe and the Virginia peninsula. The Tidewater tour is a circle route and depending at what point of the compass you enter the circle you can follow the tour in any combination and leave near your entrance point. For example, if you enter the area from western Virginia via US58, you can follow the route suggested and depart the area on US17 heading south to Elizabeth City, North Carolina. If you are traveling southeast from Richmond, you can still follow the same order, or visit Suffolk first and return to Richmond via Williamsburg.

Fort Nelson was a Revolutionary War–era fort that was refortified by the Confederates in 1861. It was located near the Chesapeake-Portsmouth city limits; a historical marker on VA337 describes the fort. Another historical marker on VA337 locates Craney Island, which is 4 miles north of VA337 at the mouth of the Elizabeth River. Here on May 11, 1862, the Confederates destroyed the CSS *Virginia.* The island is currently restricted U.S. Navy property, but is visible from harbor cruises and waterfront locations in the northern portions of Portsmouth and Norfolk. The *Virginia* was built at the Norfolk (Gosport) Navy Yard, at the south end of First to Fourth streets in Portsmouth. Most of the existing artifacts from the *Virginia*, as well as exhibits about the vessels, are found in the museums of the Tidewater area, especially the Portsmouth Naval Shipyard Museum (at the foot of High Street in Portsmouth) and the Hampton Roads Naval Museum, at The Waterside, 333 Waterside Drive in Norfolk (804-444-8971). *Monitor* artifacts have been curated and are on exhibit at Newport News's Mariners Museum.

Other sites in Portsmouth include the Butt House, 327 Crawford Street, which was used as a Federal commissary headquarters; the Porter House, 23 Court Street, the home of naval architect John L. Porter, who played a major role in building the CSS *Virginia* and was a relative of Fitz John and David D. Porter; and the U.S. Naval Hospital which contains on its grounds graves of Confederate and Union sailors and a stone cairn, a memorial to the men lost on the USS *Congress* and the USS *Cumberland* on March 8, 1862.

Norfolk has historical markers locating Camp Talbot, at Oak Grove Road and Granby Street, a Confederate camp during the Rebel occupation of the city; the site of the U.S. Customs House at Main and Granby streets, used as a Federal prison during the war; Fort Norfolk, at the west end of Front Street, which was occupied by troops of both sides; and Ocean View, indicating the site where Federal general John E. Wool landed with 6,000 men to reoccupy Norfolk on May 10, 1862. Several companies offer harbor cruises that cruise the waters of Hampton Roads where the CSS *Virginia* and the USS *Monitor* battled and which were traversed by numerous other vessels involved in the war effort. For information on harbor cruises, contact the Norfolk Convention and Visitors Bureau at 804-441-1852 or 800-368-3097.

Cross the I-64 Hampton Roads Bridge Tunnel and take the first exit in Hampton, traveling on VA143 south to Fort Monroe on Old Point Comfort. Fort Monroe is a U.S. Army facility, the only Third System fort still part of an active military base. There are many sites in the fort, a National Historic Landmark, that relate to its Civil War–era period and a brochure is available to tour the site. The house that Lincoln stayed in during a visit to the fort, Quarters Number One, is marked as is one occupied before the war by Robert E. Lee, then a lieutenant in the U.S. Army Corps of

Engineers. The fort itself is in excellent condition and the bastions and casemates of the fort contain markers and artillery pieces. A water-filled moat surrounds the fort. Hampton Roads and Fort Wool, a Third System fort built on the "Rip Raps" in the roads, are visible from the barbette tier.

Within the fort is the Casemate Museum which has numerous exhibits and a treasured archive. Among the exhibits are those on the role of coastal artillery in the Civil War and other wars, restored living quarters, and the casemate prison cell of Confederate president Jefferson Davis. The museum is open daily from 10:30 A.M. to 4:30 P.M. except Thanksgiving, Christmas, and New Year's Day. THE CASEMATE MUSEUM, P.O. Box 341, Fort Monroe, VA 23651; 804-727-3391 or 727-3973.

From Fort Monroe, return north on VA143 which becomes US60. Newport News is the nearest of the Tidewater cities to the area of Hampton Roads where the USS *Virginia* attacked the Federal blockading squadron and where the first battle of ironclads occurred the next day. A historical marker just off US60, on Chesapeake Avenue between La Salle Avenue (VA167) and East Avenue, describes the action.

Newport News has three museums that feature Civil War exhibits. The War Memorial Museum of Virginia is located at 9285 Warwick Road (US60) in Huntington Park. Mariners Museum is on Museum Drive just west of Warwick Road at VA312. The Mariners Museum, with USS *Monitor* artifacts, is a must for naval enthusiasts. For information, call 804-596-2222. At the north end of Newport News on US60 at VA105 (Fort Eustis Boulevard) is Fort Eustis. The active military base has a Civil War–era earthen fort and the U.S. Army Transportation Museum and Research Library, which includes exhibits on Civil War military vehicles. For information, call 804-878-1182 or 878-1183.

DRIVING TOUR—*Proceed to Big Bethel*
READING—*Jackson's Valley Campaign*

Battle of Big Bethel

On June 10, 1861, one of the first actions of the Civil War occurred just north of Fort Monroe on the Virginia peninsula. To reconnoiter the strength of Confederate-held positions in Virginia, Federal forces launched probes in northern Virginia at Fairfax Court House, at Aquia Landing on the Potomac near Fredericksburg, and on the Virginia peninsula north of Fort Monroe. The Federals advanced to Back Creek where they confronted Virginia and North Carolina soldiers stationed behind earthworks and under the command of Col. John B. Magruder. Magruder's headquarters was near Bethel Church, on the north bank of the creek, from which the battle derived its name.

U.S. regulars and volunteer soldiers from New York, Massachusetts, and Vermont attacked in a confused and piecemeal fashion and a Federal unit dressed in gray received friendly fire. Though outnumbering the Confederates more than four to one, the Union forces saw their offensive fail disastrously, losing 18 killed, including a volunteer officer who was also a talented author, Maj. Theodore Winthrop. The Confederates had only 1 man killed in the battle.

Points of Interest

Several monuments commemorating the Battle of Big Bethel are located on a portion of the battlefield in Bethel Park, located on Big Bethel Road at the corner of Sanders Road. Big Bethel Road can be reached by taking VA134 north from I-64. The park is open Saturday and Sunday from 6:00 A.M. to 8:00 P.M. and Monday and Friday from 11:00 A.M. to 8:00 P.M. For more information, call Bethel Park at 804-766-3017.

DRIVING TOUR—*Proceed to Yorktown*
READING—*Rich Mountain–Laurel Hill, West Virginia*

Yorktown

When Maj. Gen. George B. McClellan landed his Army of the Potomac at Fort Monroe and Newport News to begin his drive up the Virginia peninsula, his first objective was a Confederate line drawn across the peninsula between the York and Warwick rivers. The Rebels were led by Maj. Gen. John B. Magruder. "Prince John" had established a reputation early on—being able to accomplish much with few resources—at the Battle of Big Bethel, fought nearby prior to First Manassas. On

April 5, 1862, 55,000 of McClellan's soldiers advanced and came up against the York-town-Warwick line. A master of theatrics, Magruder moved his troops around nois-ily, giving the impression of having a larger force than he had. McClellan bought into the deception. Union soldiers turned to with shovels and axes opening roads, throw-ing up earthworks, establishing batteries to batter the Rebel works, and probing for soft points in the Confederate line. On April 16, at Dam Number 1 (Burnt Chim-neys), there was a hard-fought local engagement as soldiers of the Vermont Brigade crossed the Warwick and momentarily gained a toehold inside the Rebel works. A Confederate counterattack sent the Vermonters back across the Warwick. Union artillery blasted away at Yorktown for several weeks. Gen. Joseph E. Johnston hastily marched his army from the Rappahannock to the peninsula, and appreciated the time McClellan afforded him. By May 3, McClellan, his powerful breaching batteries in position, was ready to begin a bombardment that would hopefully obliterate the Yorktown defenses. Johnston, knowing this and having bought four weeks, withdrew from the Yorktown-Warwick line on the night of May 3–4.

Points of Interest

Colonial National Historical Park—Several sites that relate to the siege of Yorktown are included in the Colonial NHP, although the park and the restored village of York-town are primarily devoted to the spectacular victory of the American and French allies over Lord Charles Cornwallis's British army in October 1781. The Confeder-ates modified and strengthened the British fortifications at Yorktown, and the British works at the park's visitor center are the Confederate earthworks. Federal siege artillery was positioned west of Wormley Creek and Pond. The national cemetery at Yorktown contains 2,200 Union soldiers' graves. There is also a small Confederate section next to the national cemetery.

Many of the restored original buildings in Yorktown witnessed the 1781 surrender of Cornwallis's British army to the French and American allies. Somerwell House at the corner of Main and Church streets was a hotel during the Civil War. From York-town, drive west on Colonial Parkway to Williamsburg. Along the way, a historical marker west of Jones Mill Pond indicates the area where Capt. George A. Custer located a ford that enabled Brig. Gen. Winfield S. Hancock's brigade to cross the pond.

At the south end of the Warwick River line Newport News Park commemorates the Bat-tle of Dam Number 1. Ten miles of original fortifications can be viewed from wooded nature trails and there is an interpretive center. For more information, contact Newport News Park, 13560 Jefferson Avenue, Newport News, VA 23603; 804-886-7912.

🚲 🎪 ♿ 🚶‍♂️ ❓ 🏛 P 🍽 🚻

DRIVING TOUR and READING—*Proceed to Williamsburg*

Williamsburg

Gen. Joseph E. Johnston, though his decision was not welcomed by President Davis, decided to evacuate the Yorktown-Warwick line and withdraw up the peninsula. He began his evacuation on the night of May 3. The next day rain poured down, and the Union cavalry came on so rapidly that the Confederate rear guard at Williamsburg, under big, burly Maj. Gen. James Longstreet, formed a defensive line centered on Fort Magruder. On May 5 occurred a bitterly fought delaying action. Longstreet's people resisted attacks by the commands of Brig. Gens. Joseph Hooker, Philip Kearny, and William F. "Baldy" Smith. Johnston recalled other forces to help Longstreet, but a hastily organized counterattack by Jubal Early's Virginia–North Carolina Brigade on Brig. Gen. Winfield S. Hancock misfired and led to heavy Confederate losses. Still, the Williamsburg fight allowed Confederate wagon trains and artillery time to escape. Though sustaining more than 1,700 casualties in the battle, Longstreet evacuated his force, joining the rest of the Rebel infantry marching up the peninsula.

Points of Interest

Besides the restored colonial town of Williamsburg, the city has several sites of interest in its Civil War history. Two markers on US60 indicate the site of Fort Magruder and describe the battle. The battlefield, except for Fort Magruder, Redoubts Nos. 12 and 13, and land embraced in Colonial National Historical Park, has been lost to development. Parts of Fort Magruder, located on VA143, have been preserved by the UDC. Whitaker's House, on US60 1.5 miles southeast of Williamsburg, was the headquarters of Federal general William F. "Baldy" Smith during the battle. In the city the lawn of the Coke-Garrett House on the east end of Nicholson Street was used to care for the wounded during the battle, as were the Baptist Church and the courthouse. The Palmer House was the headquarters of Joseph E. Johnston and later George B. McClellan.

William and Mary College had 90 percent of its students join the Confederate forces and the school closed down for the war's duration in May 1861. College buildings were used to care for the wounded during and after the Battle of Williamsburg and a September 9, 1862, Confederate raid netted the South 33 Federal prisoners bivouacked on the campus.

DRIVING TOUR—*Proceed to Suffolk*
READING—*Drewry's Bluff*

Suffolk

Lt. Gen. James Longstreet returned to Tidewater Virginia and North Carolina with two divisions of his corps in the winter of 1862–63. A threat was developing here from Federal troops based in Suffolk and from Maj. Gen. John Foster's force in North Carolina (see **New Bern, North Carolina**). The most positive aspect of this operation for the Army of Northern Virginia was the wealth of hog and hominy that Longstreet's men found in this unscarred region. The supplies were forwarded to Lee's army, in its camps south of the Rappahannock River.

In April, Longstreet closed on the Federal fortifications guarding Suffolk. On April 13, Confederate troops pushed their left flank to the Nansemond River and constructed a battery on Hill's Point, which closed off the garrison to Union shipping. Union gunboats, on April 14, attempted to run the batteries at the Norfleet House slightly upstream, but the *Mount Washington* was crippled. The Federals, at the same time, constructed batteries to command the Confederate works at Norfleet House. On April 15, these batteries were unmasked and opened fire, driving the Confederates out of this important position. Four days later, on April 19, a Union infantry force on Hill's Point at the confluence of the forks of the Nansemond River, assaulted Fort Huger from the rear, quickly capturing its garrison, thus reopening the river to Union shipping. On April 24, Brig. Gen. Michael Corcoran's Union division had mounted a reconnaissance-in-force from Fort Dix against Maj. Gen. George E. Pickett's extreme right flank. The Federals approached cautiously and were repulsed. On April 29, Gen. Robert. E. Lee, his army threatened by the crossing of the upper Rappahannock by three corps of the Army of the Potomac, directed Longstreet to disengage from Suffolk and rejoin the Army of Northern Virginia at Fredericksburg.

Points of Interest

A historical marker 1.5 miles north of Suffolk on VA10 locates Longstreet's main line of works during the siege. Another marker on US460 near the downtown area describes the Federal occupation and Confederate siege of Suffolk.

DRIVING TOUR—*Proceed to Southwestern Virginia or Tennessee*
READING *(chronological)—Fort McAllister, Georgia*

WESTERN AND SOUTHWESTERN VIRGINIA

Lynchburg

On June 12, 1864, Gen. Robert E. Lee dispatched Lt. Gen. Jubal Early's II Corps to Lynchburg to meet the threat posed by Maj. Gen. David Hunter's march down the Shenandoah Valley and his crossing of the Blue Ridge. Lynchburg was an important railroad, hospital, and supply center for Lee's army and was defended by two brigades of cavalry, an infantry division, and home guards prior to the timely arrival by rail from Charlottesville of Early's vanguard on June 17. The Federals meanwhile had deployed and, driving back Rebel cavalry, closed on the city from the southwest. Although the last of Early's troops did not detrain from the overtaxed railroad until the morning of June 18, they were in time to checkmate Hunter's probing attacks. Awed by what he mistakenly believed to be overwhelming numbers of Rebels, Hunter lost his nerve and disengaged that night and began a roundabout withdrawal into West Virginia.

Points of Interest

Lynchburg is on US460, 24 miles west of Appomattox. Lynchburg has a number of historical markers relating to the defenses of the city. Downtown at Ninth and Church streets is a marker describing the June 17–18, 1864, Battle of Lynchburg.

Nearby is a Confederate monument and a few blocks away there is a commanding view of the James River. Other historical markers call attention to portions of the city's defense line, particularly along Polk and Floyd streets. The Confederate section of the Old City Cemetery near the intersection of Fifth and Taylor streets is the final resting place of 2,701 Confederate soldiers from fourteen states who died in Lynchburg hospitals. Adjacent to the Confederate cemetery is the Pest House Medical Museum.

From the downtown area, travel southwest on Twelfth Street which becomes Fort Avenue. Fort Early, at Fort Avenue and Vermont Street, was part of the defenses built in 1864 and has been restored. It is now a park and museum interpreting the Battle of Lynchburg. Admission is charged and it is well worth a stop. Named for Lt. Gen. Jubal Early, the park has a monument to the Confederate general. Early is buried along with Brig. Gen. James Dearing, Col. Thomas Munford, and other Confederates in Spring Hill Cemetery, nearby on Fort Avenue and Oakley Street. Just south of Fort Street on US29, Sandusky is a house that was used as a headquarters by Federal general David Hunter. Capt. William McKinley (the twenty-fifth president) roomed here while serving as a staff officer under Hunter.

The South River Meeting House (5810 Fort Avenue), built in 1757 and remodeled in 1765, was a centerpiece in the June 17, 1864, skirmishing where Union soldiers pushed back the Confederate horse soldiers as they bought time to facilitate Early's successful defense of Lynchburg. Tours are available with three days' advance notice. To arrange for a tour, call 804-239-2548. Old Courthouse Museum (Ninth and Court streets) has collections highlighting Civil War objects and Lynchburg's role in the Civil War. There is an admission charge.

Traces of Fort McCausland, another Confederate fort protecting Lynchburg's western approaches, can be seen at Langhorne Road near Clifton Street. Cavalry skirmished near here on June 18. Across the James River in Madison Heights other Confederate defensive works are visible off VA210, 0.5 mile south of US29. There are also earthworks on a hilltop 200 yards east of a historical marker on US501 just east of Lynchburg.

Lexington can be reached by taking US501 north from Lynchburg following the James River gorge through the Blue Ridge Mountains, a 49-mile scenic drive that crosses the Blue Ridge Parkway.

A city that is identified with the last days of the Confederacy in Virginia is Danville, at the junction of US29 and US58, 67 miles south of Lynchburg. Here President Jefferson Davis and officials of the Confederate government established a temporary capital that remained from their arrival on April 3 to the post-Appomattox flight on April 10. Davis stayed at the home of Maj. W. T. Sutherlin (975 Main Street) and conducted the business of government there including the last official cabinet meeting of the Confederate government. The home is now the Danville Museum of Fine Arts and History. Danville also has a Confederate Memorial at Sutherlin Avenue and Main Street. There are also traces of Confederate earthworks, ordered dug as Davis arrived and under the command of rear admiral, now "Brigadier General," Raphael Semmes and his force of former Confederate marines, sailors, and artillerymen who, like Davis, traveled to Danville after the fall of Richmond and Petersburg. Also in Danville is a national cemetery at 721 Lee Street, where remains of Union prisoners kept in the six Danville prisons are buried. One of the prison buildings—Prison No. 6—at 300 Lynn Street is extant.

DRIVING TOUR—*Proceed to Lexington or Danville*
READING—*Hanging Rock*

Lexington

On June 11, 1864, Federal general David Hunter's army entered Lexington, following a brisk skirmish with Brig. Gen. John McCausland's cavalry. During the engagement some of McCausland's sharpshooters fired on Hunter's soldiers from Virginia Military Institute's grounds. The Yankees burned the Virginia Military Institute barracks, classrooms, and other buildings because of the involvement of the corps of cadets in the Battle of New Market (see **New Market**) and ex-Governor John Letcher's home. Hunter's forces on June 14 headed south to Buchanan and then crossed the Blue Ridge en route to Lynchburg.

Points of Interest

Lexington is located on US11 easily accessible from I-81. Home to Stonewall Jackson before the Civil War and Robert E. Lee after the war, Lexington retains much of its nineteenth-century character. The Lexington Visitor Center, 106 E. Washington Street, is centrally located and a good place to begin. It is open daily. For more information, call 540-463-8768.

Lee Chapel (on the Washington and Lee campus) is the site where Robert E. Lee and his family are buried. Lee served as president of this institution after the war. Lee's office was in one of the rooms here. It's preserved in much the way he left it. He died at his home at the university in 1870. His horse, Traveller, is buried just outside. Open 9:00 A.M. to 5:00 P.M. Monday through Saturday and 2:00 P.M. to 5:00 P.M. on Sundays. Admission is free. For more information, call 540-463-8768.

"Stonewall" Jackson House (8 E. Washington Street), a modest structure built in 1801, was home to Virginia Military Institute professor Thomas Jonathan Jackson for two years before the Civil War. Restored, it now contains many of his possessions and period pieces. Guided tours are given on the hour and half hour. For more information, call 540-463-2552.

"Stonewall" Jackson Memorial Cemetery (South Main Street) is the eighteenth-century cemetery where Jackson lies among hundreds of his fellow Confederates, two Virginia governors, and Revolutionary War soldiers. The statue of Jackson above his grave was dedicated in 1891. The cemetery is open from dawn to dusk.

Virginia Military Institute Museum—The cadet barracks were rebuilt on the footprint of the barracks torched at Hunter's orders. In the years since the barracks have been enlarged and constitute a quadrangle. The superintendent's quarters is the only extant building that survived Hunter's June 1864 visit to Lexington. Located in the basement of Jackson Memorial Hall (built in 1915) is the VMI Museum. The museum has an outstanding collection of Civil War artifacts including the bullet-torn raincoat Jackson wore at Chancellorsville on the evening of May 2, 1863. Little Sorrel, Jackson's favorite horse, has been mounted and is on display. The museum is open 8:00 A.M. to 5:00 P.M. Monday through Saturday and 2:00 P.M. to 5:00 P.M. on Sundays. Admission is free. For more information, call 540-464-7232. ❷ 🏛 P 🚻 $

DRIVING TOUR—*Proceed to Roanoke (Hanging Rock)*
READING—*Lynchburg*

Hanging Rock

On June 21, 1864, after being repulsed at Lynchburg by the forces of Lt. Gen. Jubal Early, Maj. Gen. David Hunter's rear guard fought a skirmish here against Brig. Gen. John McCausland's cavalry. After this battle near Salem, in which he spiked and lost 8 cannons, Hunter retreated northwest through New Castle and on to Lewisburg, West Virginia.

Points of Interest

On VA311, 0.4 mile northwest of I-81 exit 141, is a historical marker for the Battle of Hanging Rock. Hanging Rock is directly across the road. The route number at the exit is VA419 which merges into VA311 within 0.4 mile of the exit.

DRIVING TOUR—*Proceed to Cloyd's Mountain*
READING—*Early's campaign: Monocacy, Maryland*

Cloyd's Mountain

In late April and early May 1864, Lt. Gen. U. S. Grant launched a multipart offensive aimed at destroying Gen. Robert E. Lee's Army of Northern Virginia. Armies led by Maj. Gens. George G. Meade and Benjamin F. Butler would converge from different directions on Richmond; Maj. Gen. Franz Sigel's column would occupy the Rebels' attention in the lower Shenandoah Valley; Brig. Gen. George Crook's force marching from Gauley Bridge, West Virginia, was to pass through New River Narrows and destroy the vital bridge carrying the Virginia & East Tennessee Railroad across the New at Dublin Station; and Brig. Gen. William Averell and his cavalry riding south from Logan, West Virginia, were to cross the mountains into the Great Valley and destroy the Saltville saltworks.

On May 9, Crook's three brigades, having crossed Cloyd's Mountain on the south side of Back Creek engaged a patchwork Confederate force under Brig. Gen. Albert Jenkins. Fighting was furious and hand to hand. Casualties were heavy for the size of the forces engaged: for the Union, 10 percent; for the Confederates, 23 percent. Jenkins was mortally wounded. Crook then advanced to Dublin and burned the New River railroad bridge. He then rendezvoused with Averell's cavalry, and the united column withdrew to Meadow Bluff, West Virginia.

Points of Interest

The battlefield, privately owned, is a beautiful pastoral landscape and can be viewed from VA100, which follows the historic alignment of the Dublin-Pearisburg Turnpike. There are two historical markers describing the battle—one on VA100, 5 miles north of Dublin, and a second at VA100 in Dublin. Midway between Dublin and the battlefield on VA100 is a pull-out at the gravesite of Lt. Christopher Cleburne, CSA, the younger brother of Confederate general Pat Cleburne, killed in a skirmish on May 10, the day after the Cloyd's Mountain battle.

DRIVING TOUR—*Proceed to Saltville*
READING *(chronological)—Spotsylvania; Sheridan's 1864–65*
Shenandoah Valley campaign: New Market

Saltville-Marion

Union cavalry and infantry raiders led by Brig. Gen. Stephen Burbridge, departing from Mount Sterling, Kentucky, on September 20, 1864, attempted to destroy the saltworks near Saltville. Burbridge was delayed at Clinch Mountain and Laurel Gap by a makeshift Confederate force, enabling Brig. Gen. Alfred E. Jackson to concentrate troops near Saltville to meet him. On the morning of October 1, the Federals attacked but made little headway. Confederate reinforcements continued to arrive during the day. After day-long fighting, Burbridge retired without accomplishing his objective. Afterward, Confederate soldiers were said to have murdered, captured, and wounded black soldiers.

Departing from Knoxville, Tennessee, on December 10, 1864, and riding through Cumberland Gap, Maj. Gen. George Stoneman's mounted expedition advanced on the important lead mines and salt ponds around Marion and Saltville. At Marion on December 17–18, Stoneman defeated a makeshift force of Confederate defenders led by Maj. Gen. John C. Breckinridge. On December 18, the Federals destroyed the leadworks and mines. After determined skirmishing on the part of the outnumbered Confederate defenders, the Federals captured and destroyed the Saltville saltworks on December 20, accomplishing the objective of their raid.

Points of Interest

There are two historical markers referencing the Battle of Marion. The first is on US11 at Marion and the second is on US11 east of the corporate limits. The Marion battlefield embraced both sides of the Middle Fork of the Holston River upstream and downstream from the US11 bridge, including the ridge on the right side of the road, which was defended by the Confederates. The wooden covered bridge, the focal point of the fight, stood just downstream from the present-day bridge. Its abutments are evident today.

There are two historical markers interpreting the Saltville battles—the first is on US11, 4.1 miles west of Chilhowie, and the second on VA91 at Saltville. In the town, which exhibits a handsome landscape, is a park featuring a reconstructed saltworks that made the town the "Salt Capital of the Confederacy." Remains of Confederate forts are currently on private property. Among Saltville's surviving historic structures is the log house owned by J.E.B. Stuart's brother, where Flora Stuart and her two children lived for several years after her husband's death at Yellow Tavern.

———⊷∙◆∙⊷———

DRIVING TOUR—*Proceed to Elizabeth City, North Carolina*
READING—*Virginia campaigns: Stoneman's Raid to Chancellorsville*

———⊷∙◆∙⊷———

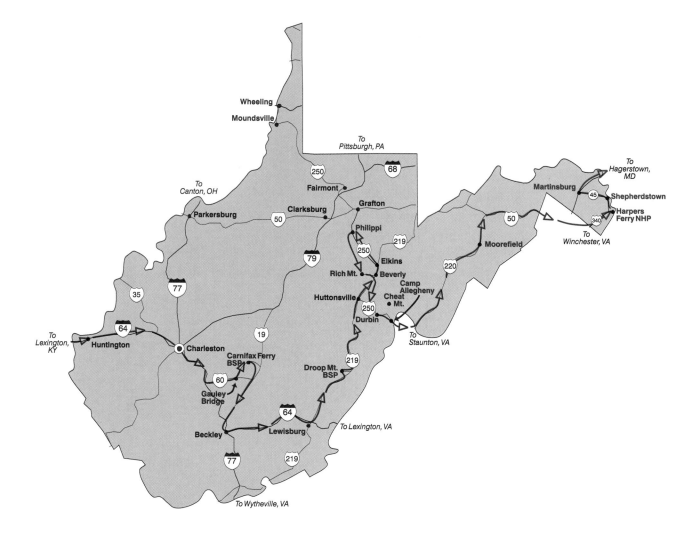

Wheeling

Moundsville

To
Pittsburgh, PA

250

68

To Canton, OH

Fairmont

Parkersburg

Clarksburg

Grafton

50

Philippi

219

250

Elkins

79

Rich Mt.

Beverly

Camp Allegheny

Huttonsville

Cheat Mt.

250

Durbin

35

77

19

To Hagerstown, MD

Martinsburg

Shepherdstown

45

Harpers Ferry NHP

50

340

To Winchester, VA

Moorefield

220

To Staunton, VA

To Lexington, KY

Huntington

64

Charleston

Carnifax Ferry BSP

60

Gauley Bridge

Droop Mt. BSP

219

64

Beckley

Lewisburg

To Lexington, VA

77

219

To Wytheville, VA

West Virginia

T here was no West Virginia when the Civil War began. But residents of the thirty-four counties in and west of the Allegheny Mountains shared more cultural, social, economic, and transportation ties with the Northern states of Ohio and Pennsylvania than with the planters, farmers, and politicians of Piedmont and Tidewater, Virginia. After the Richmond Convention passed the secession ordinance, Western delegates returned home, mass meetings were held, and at the first Wheeling Convention on May 13, 1861, the foundation for statehood was laid. This led to the second Wheeling Convention which convened on June 11, 1861. A "Restored Government of Virginia" was established and Frances H. Pierpont chosen as governor. Congressmen from the "restored state" were seated in the U.S. Congress. This secession from Virginia without that state's permission is without precedence in the nation's history and has been questioned as to its constitutional legality.

The "Restored Government of Virginia" supported the formation of a new state and the first constitution was drafted in February 1862, and on April 3, 1862, the constitution was ratified by an overwhelming vote. On December 31, 1862, President Abraham Lincoln signed legislation authorizing the admission of the new state of West Virginia.

Lincoln had reservations after Congress passed the bill, based on constitutional questions and the need to include a gradual abolition of slavery in the new state. But he signed it into law on April 20, 1863, and two months later—on June 20—West Virginia was admitted into the Union, as the thirty-fifth state. Thus the Civil War, which exacerbated long-standing intrastate social, economic, and political grievances, provided the only instance in American history where a new state was formed from an existing one.

Militarily, West Virginia garnered early attention because the crucial east-west railroad link, the Baltimore & Ohio, ran through the state; the Chesapeake & Ohio Canal paralleled the Potomac River from Harpers Ferry to Cumberland; the Ohio River along its northwestern border would provide the Confederacy with a defensible frontier; and three transmountain turnpikes offered Union columns what on paper looked like inviting routes for carrying war into the Shenandoah Valley. The state witnessed smaller actions and cavalry raids throughout most of the war, and guerrilla warfare and bushwhacking plagued the citizenry as not all of the area's residents were in favor of the breakaway state. Harpers Ferry, on the extreme end of the Mountaineer State's eastern panhandle, was the location of a Federal armory and arsenal and at the confluence of important waterways. It changed hands several times during the war. West Virginia sent 32,000 of its sons into the Federal ranks, while 10,000 men joined the armies of the South.

Civil War touring sites in West Virginia can be divided into three regions—east, central, and west. Autumn—the color season—is a wonderful time to visit the state, and an informative and relaxing vacation can be planned around visiting the sites in West Virginia and in some of its neighbors. With an abundant wilderness and bucolic landscapes and friendly people, West Virginia provides a wide variety of recreational facilities and activities for visitors as well.

CARNIFAX FERRY

The Kanawha Valley was one of the important areas of West Virginia occupied by a Federal column after a clash at Seary Creek on July 16, 1861. Determined to rid the area of the Federal menace, two former governors of Virginia, Brig. Gens. Henry A. Wise and John B. Floyd, raised separate commands and marched into the area. Besides a lack of experience and good military judgment, the two disliked each other. Jefferson Davis had sent Gen. Robert E. Lee to the western part of Virginia in his first field command to advise the local commanders. But Lee was trying to sort out the problems farther east near Beverly when Floyd marched northwest to Carnifax Ferry, crossed the Gauley, and established a fortified camp with the river at his back. On August 26, a skirmish occurred several miles north of Carnifax Ferry involving Floyd's Virginians and the 7th Ohio at Cross Lanes, also called Kessler's Cross Roads, that resulted in the Ohioans' rout.

Brig. Gen. William S. Rosecrans, who had succeeded to command when Maj. Gen. George B. McClellan was called to Washington, took the field marching south from

Clarksburg. On September 10, Rosecrans's larger force pushed in the pickets and Floyd's troops took refuge in their fortified camp. Wise, who had previously warned Floyd against maneuvering in front of Rosecrans's force, was a few miles away, and had refused to send reinforcements. Floyd held his ground until dark in bitter fighting and then escaped across the Gauley. Rosecrans did not either harass or pursue him because of the fatigue of his men. Floyd's withdrawal added to the problems being experienced by the Rebel commands in West Virginia.

Points of Interest

Ten miles southwest of Summersville on US19 is Carnifax Ferry Battlefield State Park. Here there are historic Confederate earthworks, markers, and a museum interpreting the battle. To the northwest of Carnifax Ferry on WV39 is a marker, for the Battle of Cross Lanes. Miller Tavern at Gauley Bridge on US60 was a headquarters for Federal officers, including future U.S. Presidents Rutherford B. Hayes and William McKinley, operating in West Virginia. Piers from the Old Gauley Bridge burned by the Confederates are extant and can be seen upstream from the US60 bridge. For more information on the state park, call 304-558-2766 or 800-CALLWVA.

DRIVING TOUR—*Proceed to Lewisburg*
READING—*Cheat Mountain*

PRINCETON-LEWISBURG

By early May 1862 Union forces in today's West Virginia were positioned to breach the Alleghenies and debauch into Virginia's Great Valley at two points more than one hundred miles apart. Brig. Gen. Robert H. Milroy's column, its axis of march the Staunton-Parkersburg Turnpike, advanced from Cheat Mountain and occupied, in succession, Camp Allegheny (now West Virginia) and Monterey, McDowell, and Shenandoah Mountain, Virginia. Retreating before the oncoming Federals, Confederate general Edward Johnson pulled back to West View, six miles west of Staunton, Virginia, where he soon linked up with Stonewall Jackson to defeat Milroy at the Battle of McDowell (see **McDowell, Virginia**).

Union soldiers of Brig. Gen. Jacob D. Cox's District of Kanawha threatened the East Tennessee & Virginia Railroad. The Federals, by mid-May, although ousted from Pearisburg, Virginia, held Mercer County (now West Virginia) and braced for a lunge at the railroad. Confederate Brig. Gen. Humphery Marshall arrived from Abingdon, Virginia, with the Army of East Kentucky. Boldly seizing the initiative, Marshall bested Cox's two brigades during three days of fighting, May 15–17, centering on Princeton Court House in Mercer County. Breaking contact with the Confederates on the night of May 17–18, Cox withdrew twenty miles to Camp Flat Top.

Also responding to the threat to the railroad and the western part of Virginia, Confederate forces led by Brig. Gen. Henry Heth, after a long, hard march from Pearisburg, Virginia, by way of the New River Narrows, at five A.M., May 23, 1862, attacked Col. George Crook's brigade encamped on high ground at the western edge of Lewisburg. (The Union camp is now the location of the Confederate cemetery.) Crook's reaction was prompt and vigorous. The Federals formed a battle line and advanced through the town, driving the Confederates from the ridge east of town where the General Lewis Inn now stands. Upon learning that Maj. Gen. Thomas J. "Stonewall" Jackson's army had routed Maj. Gen. N. P. Banks's division at Winchester on May 25 and driven it across the Potomac, Crook evacuated Lewisburg and pulled back to Meadow Bluff.

In the fight ninety-five Confederates were killed and buried by the victorious Yanks without ceremony in a trench in the yard of the Old Stone Church. After the war, the soldiers' remains were removed from the churchyard and interred in a cross-shaped mass grave in the present Confederate cemetery.

Points of Interest

Princeton—Though not on the tour route, Princeton Court House, now Princeton, is on US19 just off I-64/77, 27 miles south of Beckley, near the Virginia border. Historical markers on US19 describe the three-day battle.

Lewisburg—Several sites associated with the Battle of Lewisburg can be toured, including the ridge on the east end of town, where the General Lewis Inn stands. Part of the inn dates from 1834. For information on the historic inn and restaurant, call 304-645-2600 or 800-628-4454. The 1796 Old Stone Church, the John Wesley Methodist Church, the Greenbrier Public Library, where soldiers made etchings on the walls, and the Confederate cemetery are all part of a downtown walking tour. A walking tour pamphlet and other information about the historic sites in Lewisburg are available from the Lewisburg Visitors Center, 105 Church Street, Lewisburg, WV 24901. The center's hours are 9:00 A.M. to 5:00 P.M. Monday through Saturday and 1:00 P.M. to 5:00 P.M. Sunday. More information can be obtained by calling the visitor center during these hours at 304-645-1000 or 800-833-2068. Lewisburg holds a biannual reenactment of the battle in June and nearby White Sulphur Springs (US60) holds an annual reenactment in August at the Greenbrier State Forest to commemorate an action fought there.

DRIVING TOUR—*Proceed to Droop Mountain*
READING—*Battles of Front Royal and First Winchester, Virginia*

DROOP MOUNTAIN

In November 1863, Brig. Gen. William W. Averell, Federal cavalry leader, left Beverly to raid and wreak havoc on the East Tennessee & Virginia Railroad. At Lewisburg, he was to rendezvous with a column marching east led by Brig. Gen. Alfred N. Duffié that was to start from Charleston. Averell's column pushed back a contingent under Col. William L. Jackson through several positions until the Rebels dug in on Droop Mountain, a formidable barrier, where they were reinforced. On November 6, with the combination of a flanking attack and an advance up the steep face of the mountain, Averell's force defeated the Confederates on Droop Mountain. Averell rendezvoused with Duffié the next day at Lewisburg, but the two decided to abandon the campaign because of poor road conditions and troop fatigue without proceeding with their mission of breaking up the railroad.

Points of Interest

Droop Mountain Battlefield Park, a West Virginia state park 25 miles north of I-64 exit 169 on US219, has a visitor center, monuments, breastworks, and interpretive trails. For more information, call 304-653-4254.

———————

DRIVING TOUR—*Proceed to Philippi*
READING—*Mine Run, Virginia*

———————

PHILIPPI

One of the first actions in the war and the "first battle" occurred in central West Virginia. Maj. Gen. George B. McClellan, himself a former railroad executive, seized one of the first Federal advantages in the war by rushing volunteer troops on the Baltimore & Ohio Railroad from Ohio and Indiana into what was then western Virginia. Arriving at Grafton, the troops disembarked and reinforced loyal-to-the-Union Virginia troops under Col. Benjamin F. Kelley sent south from Wheeling. In two columns the Federals marched south thirty miles to attack the camp of green Virginia Confederate volunteers at Philippi. On the rainy morning of June 3, 1861, the Federals surprised the Rebels. Lacking proper equipment, the Confederates fled, giving rise to the name given to the battle, the "Philippi Races." The victory gave McClellan confidence and he arrived in person to direct a campaign aimed at securing the vital Tygart Valley and much of the Staunton-Parkersburg Turnpike for the Union.

Points of Interest

The Tygart River covered bridge on US250 is extant. Adjacent to the bridge is the former railroad depot, an outstanding museum maintained by the Barbour County Historical Society. On the opposite side of the river is an interpretive wayside highlighting the war's "first battle." For more information, call the Barbour County Historical Museum at 304-457-4846.

DRIVING TOUR—*Proceed to Rich Mountain–Laurel Hill*
READING—*Big Bethel, Virginia*

RICH MOUNTAIN–LAUREL HILL

When Maj. Gen. George B. McClellan arrived in western Virginia on June 23, 1861, as commander of the Department of the Ohio, his force had swelled to 20,000. He advanced south up the Tygart Valley. There, a Confederate command from Virginia under Brig. Gen. Robert S. Garnett had entrenched to protect the Staunton-Parkersburg Turnpike that led through Beverly to the Shenandoah Valley. With poor transportation to haul supplies into the area, the Confederates had been subsisting mostly on rations and by raiding the farms and homes of Union residents.

McClellan started his advance on July 6. Rich Mountain to the west bounded Tygart Valley; Laurel Hill flanked the Tygart River Valley on the east; one branch of the turnpike which forked at Beverly passed over Rich Mountain and the other by Laurel Hill en route to Philippi, Grafton, and beyond. On July 7, the Federals began a four-day skirmish with Garnett's Confederates entrenched on Laurel Hill. McClellan had divided his force and with three brigades he moved against the formidable Rich Mountain position held by less than a third of Garnett's force. On July 11, Federals led by Brig. Gen. William S. Rosecrans charged and, after a bitter fight, sized up the gap through which the turnpike crossed Rich Mountain. Most of the Rich Mountain defenders surrendered on July 12 near Beverly, and Garnett, flanked out of his Laurel Hill position, withdrew toward St. George. During a rear-guard action at Corrick's Ford on July 13, Garnett was killed, the first general to be killed in the war. The Battle of Rich Mountain, the Laurel Hill skirmishes, and the Corrick's Ford engagement brought McClellan acclaim in Washington and the press and shaped his future and that of the Union Army.

On January 11, 1865, Union and Confederate forces again clashed in the vicinity of Rich Mountain during the cavalry battle at Beverly in which Federal horsemen were routed and 580 were captured.

Points of Interest

The Battle of Rich Mountain is preserved and interpreted by a coalition of organizations interested in preservation. Take US219/250 south to Beverly and go west on Rich Mountain Road. Protected areas of the battle site include Camp Garnett and its Confederate entrenchments, the crest of the mountain at the site of the Hart Farm, and the old Staunton-Parkersburg Turnpike. The Hart House was used as a hospital after the battle. There is parking, foot trails and interpretive markers at the site. Beverly is a time capsule with the Randolph County Museum and many National Register homes. The See/Ward House on US219/250 near Mill Creek was the location of a Federal camp during McClellan's campaign and was used as a hospital. The Mount Iser cemetery in Beverly has a Confederate monument; 18 miles north of Beverly, 8 miles north of Elkins, at Belington (US250/WV92) are roadside markers and earthworks associated with the Laurel Hill action. A mile south of Parsons is a marker identifying Corrick's Ford, the site of General Garnett's death.

DRIVING TOUR—*Proceed to Cheat Mountain*
READING—*Carnifax Ferry*

CHEAT MOUNTAIN

At the same time Brig. Gen. John B. Floyd was being defeated by Brig. Gen. William S. Rosecrans at Carnifax Ferry on the Gauley, Robert E. Lee was attempting to drive Federals from the Tygart Valley and their Cheat Mountain bastion astride the Staunton-Parkersburg Turnpike they had secured as a result of their July 1861 victories. With 15,000 men, Lee outnumbered the Federal forces guarding Cheat Mountain and holding the Tygart Valley. He planned to maneuver five converging columns through rugged terrain to trap Brig. Gen. Joseph J. Reynolds's Union command, which was divided into two wings separated by seven mountainous miles.

The heavy rains that had drenched the region since mid-August were still falling as the Confederates advanced on September 10. Confederate attacks were uncoordinated, and the Federal defense was so stubborn that Col. Albert Rust (leading the attacks) was convinced that he confronted an overwhelming force. He actually faced only about 300 determined Federals. Lee called off the attack and, after maneuvering in the vicinity, withdrew to Valley Head on September 17. The Battle of Cheat Mountain began a wave of criticism, which Lee endured, for the poor showing in the mountains of western Virginia.

GREENBRIER RIVER

The Federals who had repulsed the Rebel attack on Cheat Mountain determined to go on the offensive. During the night of October 2–3, Brig. Gen. Joseph Reynolds with two brigades advanced from Cheat Mountain to reconnoiter the Confederate position at Camp Bartow on the Greenbrier River. Reynolds drove in the Confederate pickets and opened fire with his artillery. After sporadic fighting and an abortive attempt to turn the Confederates' right flank, Reynolds withdrew to Cheat Mountain.

Points of Interest

At Bartow on the Greenbrier River a few miles east of Cheat Mountain is a marker identifying Camp Bartow. On the south side of the river behind Traveler's Repose at the junction of US250 and SR28 are some well-preserved Confederate trenches. Cheat Summit Fort is interpreted by U.S. Forest Service facilities. For more information, call 304-636-1800 or 800-333-SAVE.

DRIVING TOUR—*Proceed to Camp Allegheny*
READING—*Ball's Bluff, Virginia*

CAMP ALLEGHENY

In December 1861, Confederate forces under Col. Edward Johnson occupied the summit of Allegheny Mountain to defend the Staunton-Parkersburg Turnpike. A Union force under Brig. Gen. Robert Milroy attacked Johnson on December 13. Fighting continued for much of the morning as each side maneuvered to gain the advantage as the bluecoats scrambled up the mountain's steep slope to get at the Rebels posted behind earthworks. Finally, Milroy's troops were repulsed, and he retreated to his Cheat Mountain camps. At the year's end, Edward Johnson remained at Camp Allegheny with five regiments, and Henry Heth was at Lewisburg with two regiments.

Points of Interest

Allegheny has been developed by the U.S. Forest Service. Contact the ranger office in Bartow at 304-456-3335 or 800-333-SAVE.

DRIVING TOUR—*Proceed to Moorefield*
READING—*Mill Springs, Kentucky*

MOOREFIELD

Early in August 1864, a savage cavalry action occurred in the beautiful valley of the South Branch of the Potomac in eastern West Virginia. Brig. Gen. John McCausland led his brigade and that of Brig. Gen. Bradley T. Johnson on a raid that struck and burned downtown Chambersburg, Pennsylvania (see **Chambersburg, Pennsylvania**) in conjunction with Lt. Gen. Jubal Early's advance to the Potomac following his July 24 victory at Second Kernstown. Ordered to pursue McCausland's raiders, who had returned to West Virginia, Brig. Gen. William Averell's Union cavalry followed the Rebels across the Potomac.

In the predawn hours of August 7, Averell's cavalry overran the camps of first Johnson's then McCausland's cavalry near the South Branch of the Potomac River. Averell captured more than 400 prisoners and sapped the morale and effectiveness of the Confederate cavalry, which thereafter performed poorly in the remainder of the 1864 Valley Campaign.

Points of Interest

There are battle markers on US220 for the Moorefield battle, and just off the highway is the 1818 McNeill Mansion. Several of the McNeill men led a group of Confederate rangers who attacked Federal facilities and supply trains.

DRIVING TOUR—*Proceed to Harpers Ferry*
READING—*Sheridan's 1864–65 Shenandoah Valley Campaign, Virginia*

HARPERS FERRY

The most significant town in what was to become West Virginia was Harpers Ferry. Strategically located at the confluence of the Potomac and Shenandoah rivers, it was an important transportation hub on both the Baltimore & Ohio Railroad and the Chesapeake & Ohio Canal. Harpers Ferry was also home to a Union arsenal

The piers of the Baltimore & Ohio Railroad bridge over the Potomac River at Harpers Ferry after the bridge was burned in 1861. The bridge was rebuilt by Federal forces.

and armory, the latter one of two locations in the United States where rifle-muskets were manufactured by the government in the pre-war years (the other was Springfield, Massachusetts).

Harpers Ferry became one of the place names associated with the events that shaped the Civil War in mid-October 1859, when John Brown's abolitionist "Army of Liberation," many of whom had been involved in the border wars in Kansas, came east with the intention of starting a slave uprising in the South. Although Brown had planned the campaign for more than two years, he failed to map out tactical considerations when his army of twenty-two struck. Brown and eighteen of his men on the night of October 16 left Maryland's Kennedy Farm and slipped across the Potomac and seized the armory and arsenal. He failed to pass the word along to potential slave recruits in the area and the only crowd he drew was of armed citizens and the Virginia and Maryland militia, who battled Brown and his followers.

After Brown and the remaining members of his expedition barricaded themselves in the armory's firehouse, they were overwhelmed by a contingent of U.S. marines led by Lt. Israel Green under the overall command of Lt. Col. Robert E. Lee. Brown and six co-conspirators were tried in nearby Charles Town. Brown was convicted and hanged in Charles Town, on December 2, 1859. The other six went to the gallows at later dates. The Harpers

Ferry Raid led to charges and countercharges in the national turmoil over slavery and Brown was deemed to be a martyr by those who opposed slavery and later his name became a rallying cry for the Northern righteous.

Immediately upon Virginia's April 17, 1861, secession from the Union, the armory and arsenal again became a focal point in the struggle. Virginians seized it, but U.S. Army soldiers had already torched the arsenal. Still, the Confederates were able to salvage the armory's musket-making machinery and tools and move them first to Richmond and then to Fayetteville, North Carolina. In early July the Federals reoccupied Harpers Ferry. The town changed hands several more times before the late winter of 1862, and would then be threatened by Confederate forces operating in Virginia's nearby Shenandoah Valley, and, during Robert E. Lee's first invasion of the North, would become the objective of converging Confederate columns.

More than 13,000 Federals would find themselves in the eye of a hurricane in mid-September 1862 in the days before General Lee's first invasion of the North climaxed at Antietam (see **Antietam, Maryland**). A key to Lee's plan was the capture of Harpers Ferry and its defenders. Lee sent three columns, the largest led by Maj. Gen. Thomas J. Jackson, that closed in on the Federals from three directions. Artillery was placed on heights commanding the town. As the Rebels hemmed in the Union force, they failed to close the escape route used by Col. Benjamin F. "Grimes" Davis and 1,300 cavalrymen. On the morning of September 15, Confederate cannons again roared. Federal garrison commander Col. Dixon Miles was mortally wounded by an exploding shell before all the Confederate guns ceased fire and the Northern troops raised the white flag. The surrender of the more than 12,000 Federals at Bolivar Heights was the largest surrender of U.S. troops until that grim day in mid-April 1942 when U.S. Army and Philippine soldiers laid down their arms on Bataan.

The Federals again garrisoned Harpers Ferry after Lee's forces recrossed into Virginia following their September 17, 1862, defeat at Antietam. The Confederates bypassed Harpers Ferry during Lee's June 1863 march into Pennsylvania. During Lt. Gen. Jubal Early's July 1864 raid into Maryland and to the gates of Washington, D.C., Harpers Ferry was evacuated by its Union garrison, who took position in the formidable Maryland Heights fortifications. Harpers Ferry served first as Maj. Gen. Philip H. Sheridan's headquarters and then as his base for his 1864 victorious Shenandoah Valley Campaign (see **Winchester, Virginia**).

Points of Interest

Harpers Ferry National Historical Park—This national historical park encompasses much of the old town, including the site of the arsenal and part of that of the armory at the point of land where the Potomac and the Shenandoah rivers meet. Many of the buildings have been restored; the visitor center and book-

The piers of this Civil War–era bridge still stand in the Potomac River next to the modern railroad bridge.

store are in the Stage Coach Inn on Shenandoah Street. The rich history of the town is detailed in the exhibits and restored buildings. Also part of the park are museums on Harpers Ferry Civil War history, black history, and the John Brown Raid. Shuttle buses are available at the entrance to the park off US340; parking on the narrow streets is restricted. The park is open every day but Christmas. During most of the year park rangers give interpretive talks and demonstrations. There are many special events throughout the year. 🏞 ♿ 🧑‍🤝‍🧑 ❓ 🏛 P* 🚏 🚻 $$

Among the sites of interest in Harpers Ferry Civil War history are the armory Fire House, which has been relocated several times and now occupies a site some 40 yards east of its original position; the archaeological remains of several arsenal buildings; the site of Hall's Rifle Works and other Virginias Island industrial facilities; and the ruins of the Episcopal church. In the rivers are piers from the Civil War–era railroad bridge.

Bolivar Heights is also part of the national historical park. It is located across from the park entrance just off US340. There are earthworks and interpretive signs. This is the site of the surrender of the more than 12,000 Federal troops to Stonewall Jackson's force. Maryland Heights, across the Potomac and Loudon Heights east of Shenandoah, is where Confederate artillery was emplaced during the September 1862 investment. There

*Parking at entrance; shuttle buses to historic town

are hiking trails with a high level of difficulty. Access to the trails and to the C&O Canal NHP can be reached by using the pedestrian crossing adjacent to the modern railroad bridge. Check with park personnel for further information on hiking trails. The park is open every day but Christmas.

Also in the area but outside the national park are the Harpers Ferry Cemetery and three buildings on Washington Street—Thomas J. Jackson's headquarters, now a private residence, and the Bolivar Methodist Church and St. John's Lutheran Church, which were used as hospitals.

SHEPHERDSTOWN

On the night of September 18, 1862, Gen. Robert E. Lee withdrew from Antietam battlefield and recrossed the Potomac at Boteler's Ford (Pack Horse Ford). The next day a detachment of Brig. Gen. Fitz John Porter's V Corps, the Army of the Potomac, crossed the river at the ford, attacked the Confederate rear guard commanded by Brig. Gen. William Pendleton, and captured 4 guns. Early on September 20, Porter pushed elements of two divisions across the Potomac to establish a bridgehead. Hill's division counterattacked while many of the Federals were crossing and nearly annihilated the 118th Pennsylvania (the "Corn Exchange" Regiment), inflicting 269 casualties. This rear-guard action discouraged Federal pursuit.

Points of Interest

Shepherdstown, 10 miles north of Harpers Ferry on WV230, has roadside markers describing the September 19–20 battle 1 mile east of town on Secondary Route 17. Elmwood Cemetery has a monument to the 577 Confederate soldiers buried there, including a number from the Battle of Antietam. Among the Confederates buried in Elmwood are Col. Henry Kyd Douglas, author of *I Rode with Stonewall,* and Brig. Gen. William W. Kirkland.

Martinsburg, on US11, 7 miles west of Shepherdstown, was an important railroad center during the war; repair shops for the B&O Railroad were here. It was also used as a Federal headquarters. There are several buildings in the town that were used by the military during the war. These include the Flick House, Boydville, the B&O Railroad Station, Benjamin Reed Boyd House, Berkeley County Courthouse, Newborn Hall, and Greenhill

Cemetery. On June 14, 1863, concurrent with the Second Battle of Winchester, there was a battle at Martinsburg between Maj. Gen. Robert E. Rodes's division of Ewell's corps spearheading Lee's second invasion of the North and Union troops led by Brig. Gen. Daniel Tyler. Historical markers describe the action.

DRIVING TOUR—*Proceed to Maryland*
READING—*Lee's 1862 Invasion of the North: Antietam, Maryland*

APPENDIX A

Washington, D.C., area forts as listed by number on the map on page 62 — District of Columbia

1. Fort Franklin, Fort Ripley, Fort Alexander
2. Fort Massachusetts (Stevens)
3. Fort Slocum
4. Fort Totten
5. Fort Bunker Hill
6. Fort Saratoga
7. Fort Thayer
8. Fort Lincoln
9. Fort Gaines
10. Fort Pennsylvania (Reno)
11. Fort De Russy

12. Fort Mahan
13. Fort Marcy
14. Fort Du Pont
15. Fort Davis
16. Fort Corcoran
17. Fort De Kalb
18. Fort Cass
19. Fort Albany
20. Fort Runyon
21. Fort Baker
22. Fort Ricketts

23. Fort Stanton
24. Fort Snyder
25. Fort Carroll
26. Fort Ramsay
27. Fort Barnard
28. Fort Blenker
29. Fort Ward
30. Fort Greble
31. Fort Worth

APPENDIX B

Locations for a selection of motion pictures and television programs featuring Civil War battles and incidents.

Name	Date Released	Director
1. *The Birth of a Nation*	1915	D. W. Griffith

Location Comments: Griffith's Fine Arts Studio (Sunset Boulevard and Vermont Avenue, Hollywood) was used for sets including Ford's Theatre; battle scenes, including Petersburg trenches, were filmed in the east San Fernando Valley (Los Angeles and Burbank).

Name	Date Released	Director
2. *The General*	1927	Buster Keaton

Location Comments: The entire film was shot in Oregon, near the town of Cottage Grove (part of a trestle built over the Row River remained for some time afterward).

Name	Date Released	Director
3. *Gone With the Wind*	1939	Victor Fleming

Location Comments: The first scene shot, the evacuation and burning of Atlanta, was shot on December 11, 1938, on the MGM back lot, Culver City, California; interiors were shot at Selznick Studios, now Culver Studios, 9336 Washington Boulevard, Culver City.

Name	Date Released	Director

4. *They Died With Their Boots On* 1941 Raoul Walsh
   Location Comments: Shot at Warner Brothers Studios and the Warner Ranch and environs, Burbank, California.

5. *The Red Badge of Courage* 1951 John Huston
   Location Comments: Many scenes shot on John Huston's ranch, San Fernando Valley, California.

6. *The Raid* 1954 Hugo Fregonese
   Location Comments: Shot at Twentieth Century–Fox Studios and the Fox back lot, Century City, Los Angeles, California.

7. *The Great Locomotive Chase (Andrews' Raiders)* 1956 Francis D. Lyon
   Location Comments: Shot on location in northwest Georgia, including the Tallulah Falls Railway.

8. *Raintree County* 1957 Edward Dmytryk
   Location Comments: Shot in Hollywood and on location in Kentucky, Tennessee, and Mississippi.

9. *The Horse Soldiers* 1958 John Ford
   Location Comments: Exteriors shot on location in Clarence and Natchitoches, Louisiana, Natchez, Mississippi, and La Grange, Tennessee. Interiors were shot at Samuel Goldwyn Studios and MGM Studios.

10. *The Good, the Bad, and the Ugly* 1967 Sergio Leone
    Location Comments: Shot in Burgos, Spain, and on location in central and southern Spain.

11. *The Beguiled* 1971 Don Siegel
    Location Comments: The exterior of the girls' school was a home in Baton Rouge, Louisiana; the rest of the film was shot at Universal Studios, Universal City, Los Angeles, California.

12. *The Red Badge of Courage* (television movie) 1974 Lee Philips
    Location Comments: Shot on location in Nogales, Arizona.

13. *The Blue and the Gray*   1982   Andrew V. McLaglen
    Location Comments.   Shot on location in Fort Smith, Van Buren, and Fayetteville,
    Arkansas; the Battle of First Manassas was shot at Prairie
    Grove Battlefield State Park.

14. *Glory*   1989   Edward Zwick
    Location Comments: Shot on location in Jekyll Island, Georgia; Savannah, Georgia,
    was used for Boston, Massachusetts.

15. *Gettysburg*   1993   Ronald F. Maxwell
    Location Comments: Shot in Gettysburg, Pennsylvania, and environs; some scenes shot
    at Gettysburg National Military Park.

BIBLIOGRAPHY

Alexander, E. Porter. "With Lee at Appomattox." *American History Illustrated* 22 (September 1987): 40.

Alexander, Ted. "The General's Tour—Gettysburg Cavalry Operations, June 27–July 3, 1863." *Blue & Gray Magazine* 6 (October 1988): 8.

American Heritage. *The American Heritage Picture History of the Civil War.* Edited by Richard M. Ketchum. New York: American Heritage Publishing Co., Inc, 1960.

Anderson, Bern. *By Sea and by River: The Naval History of the Civil War.* New York: Da Capo Press, Inc., 1989.

Black, Robert C. III. *The Railroads of the Confederacy.* Chapel Hill: University of North Carolina Press, 1952.

Bradford, Ned, ed. *Battles and Leaders of the Civil War.* Vol. 1, *The Opening Battles.* 1883. Reprint. Edison, N. J.: Castle, 1985.

———*Battles and Leaders of the Civil War,* Vol. 2, *The Struggle Intensifies.* 1883. Reprint. Edison, N. J.: Castle, 1985.

———*Battles and Leaders of the Civil War,* Vol. 3, *The Tide Shifts.* 1883. Reprint. Edison, N. J.: Castle, 1985.

———*Battles and Leaders of the Civil War,* Vol. 4, *Retreat with Honor.* 1883. Reprint. Edison, N. J.: Castle, 1985.

Cassidy, John M. *Civil War Cinema* (a pictoral history of Hollywood and the war between the states). Missoula, Mont. Pictoral Histories Publishing Co., 1986.

Colton, Ray Charles. *The Civil War in the Western Territories: Arizona, Colorado, New Mexico, and Utah.* Norman: University of Oklahoma Press, 1959.

Cromie, Alice. *A Tour Guide to the Civil War.* 3rd rev. ed. Nashville, Tenn.: Rutledge Hill Press, 1990.

Cullen, Joseph P. *Richmond National Battlefield Park, Virginia.* Washington, D.C.: National Park Service, 1961.

Davis, George B. et al. *The Official Military Atlas of the Civil War.* New York: The Fairfax Press, 1983.

Denny, Norman R. "The Devil's Navy." *Civil War Times Illustrated* 35 (August 1996): 24.

Faust, Patricia L., ed. *Historical Times Illustrated Encyclopedia of the Civil War.* New York: Harper Perennial, 1986.

Foote, Shelby. *The Civil War: A Narrative,* Vol. 1, *Fort Sumter to Perryville.* New York: Random House, 1974.

———*The Civil War: A Narrative,* Vol. 2, *Fredericksburg to Meridian.* New York: Random House, 1974.

————*The Civil War: A Narrative*, Vol. 3, *Red River to Appomattox*. New York: Random House, 1974

Frassanito, William A. *Gettysburg: A Journey in Time*. New York: Charles Scribner's Sons, 1975.

Futch, Ovid L. *History of Andersonville Prison*. 9th ed. Gainesville: University Press of Florida 1988.

Georgia Civil War Historical Markers. 2nd ed. Atlanta: Georgia Department of Natural Resources State Parks, Recreation & Historic Sites Division, 1982.

Glatthaar, Joseph T. *Forged in Battle: The Civil War Alliance of Black Soldiers and White Officers*. New York: Free Press, 1990.

Gragg, Rod. *Confederate Goliath: The Battle of Fort Fisher*. New York: HarperCollins, 1991.

Harper Brothers. *Harper's Pictorial History of the Civil War*. New York: The Fairfax Press, 1866.

Holzer, Harold, and Mark E. Neely, Jr. "Cycloramas." *Civil War Times Illustrated* 35 (August 1996): 32.

Jacobs, Charles T. *Civil War Guide to Montgomery County, MD*. Rockville, Md. The Montgomery County Historical Society and the Montgomery County Civil War Round Table, 1983.

Kennedy, Frances H., ed. *The Civil War Battlefield Guide, The Conservation Fund*. Boston: Houghton Mifflin Company, 1990.

Kerby, Robert L. *Kirby Smith's Confederacy: The Trans-Mississippi South, 1863–1865*. New York: Columbia University Press, 1972.

Leech, Margaret. *Reveille in Washington 1860–1865*, special ed. New York: Time Inc. 1962.

Lykes, Richard Wayne. *Petersburg National Military Park, Virginia*. 1951. Reprint. National Park Service, 1961. Washington, D.C.

McPherson, James M. *Battle Cry of Freedom: The Civil War Era*. New York: Oxford University Press, 1988.

Martin, Jane A. *The Civil War Spies, Scouts and Raiders: Irregular Operating*. New York: Time-Life Books, Inc., 1985.

Miles, Jim. *Fields of Glory: A History and Tour Guide of the Atlanta Campaign*. Nashville, Tenn.: Rutledge Hill Press, 1989.

Nevin, David. *The Civil War: Sherman's March, Atlanta to the Sea*. Alexandria, Va.: Time-Life Books, 1986.

Page, Dave. *Ships Versus Shore*. Nashville, Tenn.: Rutledge Hill Press, 1994.

Perry, Milton F. *Infernal Machines: The Story of Confederate Submarine and Mine Warfare*. Baton Rouge: Louisiana State University Press, 1965.

Porter, General Horace. *Campaigning with Grant*. Bloomington: University of Indiana Press, 1961.

Roth, David E. "The General's Tour—The Mysteries of Spring Hill, Tennessee" (historical background text). *Blue & Gray Magazine* 2 (1964): 12.

Salmon, John S. *A Guidebook to Virginia's Historical Markers.* rev. ed. Charlottesville: University Press of Virginia, 1994.

Sauers, Richard A. "The General's Tour—Laurels for Burnside: The Invasion of North Carolina, January–July 1862." *Blue & Gray Magazine* 5 (May 1988): 5.

Scaife, William R. *Allatoona Pass: A Needless Effusion of Blood.* Atlanta: Etowah Valley Historical Society, 1995.

———*The Campaign for Atlanta.* Saline, Mich.: McNaughton & Gunn, Inc., 1993.

———*The March to the Sea.* 2nd ed. Saline, Mich.: McNaughton & Gunn, Inc., 1993.

Simons, Gerald. *The Civil War: The Blockade, Runners and Raiders*, Alexandria, Va.: Time-Life Books, 1983.

Stackpole, General Edward J., and Wilbur S. Nye. *The Battle of Gettysburg: A Guided Tour.* Harrisburg, Pa: Stackpole Books, 1960, 1963.

Sword, Wiley. "The General's Tour—The Battle of Nashville." *Blue & Gray Magazine* 11 (December 1993): 12.

Symonds, Craig L. *A Battlefield Atlas of the Civil War.* 5th ed. Baltimore, Md.: The Nautical and Aviator Publishing Company of America, 1988.

Talley, Mike, ed. *Texas State Travel Guide.* Austin, Tex.: R. R. Donnelley & Sons, 1994.

Walsh, Raoul. *Each Man in His Time.* New York: Farrar, Straus & Giroux, 1974.

Young, Bennett H. *Confederate Wizards of the Saddle: Being Reminiscences and Observations of One Who Rode with Morgan.* 1914 Reprint. Kennesaw, Ga.: Continental Book Company, 1958.

PICTURE CREDITS

The following is a list of photographs, paintings, and illustrations used in the book. The credited sources of all period works are to the original collections where paintings reside and where they were photographed. In the case of photographs, newspaper engravings, and illustrations, these collections are cited where the period prints or duplicates reside and where they were copied. The key to photographers who recopied these works is as follows: SG—Susan Gristina; MAP—Mary Ann Prall; AW—Andrew Wertz; JW—Jay Wertz. All present-day battlefield scenes, unless otherwise indicated, were photographed by Jay Wertz. (MASS-MOLLUS/USAMHI)—Massachusetts Commandery, Military Order of the Loyal Legion of the United States and the U.S. Army Military History Institute, Carlisle Barracks, Pennsylvania.

Alabama-6: Prints and Photographs Division, Library of Congress, Washington, D.C.–JW; Alabama-11: Prints and Photographs Division, Library of Congress, Washington, D.C.–JW; Alabama-17: U.S. Naval Academy/Beverly R. Robinson Collection; Alabama-18: National Archives, Washington, D.C.–JW; Alabama-19: Prints and Photographs Division, Library of Congress, Washington, D.C.-JW; Alabama-21: MASS-MOLLUS/USAMHI–AW; Alabama-25: Historic Blakeley State Park.

Arkansas-31: Pea Ridge National Military Park photographed by Marv Lewis; Arkansas-38: Prairie Grove Battlefield State Park photographed by Marv Lewis; Arkansas-40: U.S. Naval Academy/Beverly R. Robinson Collection; Arkansas-44: Prints and Photographs Division, Library of Congress, Washington, D.C.–MAP.

District of Columbia-53: West Point Museum Collection, United States Military Academy, West Point, New York; District of Columbia-54: Brady-Handy Collection, National Archives, Washington, D.C.–JW; District of Columbia-55: Courtesy of The Architect of the U. S. Capitol; District of Columbia-58: National Archives, Washington, D.C.–JW; District of Columbia-68: Fort Stevens, Rock Creek Park.

The Far West-86: MASS-MOLLUS/USAMHI–AW.

Florida-106: Fort Pickens, Gulf Islands National Seashore photographed by Michael Myles; Florida-110: Natural Bridge State Historic Site photographed by Michael Myles; Florida-117: Castillo de San Marcos National Monument; Florida-125: Olustee Battlefield State Historic Site photographed by Michael Myles.

Georgia-132: Courtesy of the Atlanta History Center; Georgia-134: Brady-Handy Collection, National Archives, Washington, D.C.–MAP; Georgia-135: Valentine Museum, Richmond, Virginia–JW; Georgia-139: Prints and Photographs Division, Library of Congress, Washington, D.C.–MAP; Georgia-140: Chickamauga and Chattanooga national Military Park; Georgia-141: MASS-MOLLUS/USAMHI–JW; Georgia-143: Prints and Photographs Division, Library of Congress, Washington, D.C.–MAP; Georgia-146: Brady-Handy Collection, National Archives, Washington, D.C.–MAP; Georgia-151: Prints and Photographs Division, Library of Congress, Washington, D.C.–SG; Georgia-153: Prints and Photographs Division, Library of Congress, Washington, D.C.–SG; Georgia-162: Brady-Handy Collection, National Archives, Washington, D.C.–JW; Georgia-164: Brady-Handy Collection, National Archives, Washington, D.C.–MAP; Georgia-167: New Hope Church wayside; Georgia-168: Pickett's Mill State Historic Site; Georgia-174: Kennesaw Mountain National Battlefield Park; Georgia-176: Kennesaw House, Marietta; Georgia-181: Courtesy of the Virginia Historical Society–JW; Georgia-193: Prints and Photographs Division, Library of Congress, Washington, D.C.–MAP; Georgia-191: Brady-Handy Collection, National Archives, Washington, D.C.–SG; Georgia-192: Courtesy of the Atlanta Cyclorama–JW; Georgia-193: Brady-Handy Collection, National Archives, Washington, D.C.–JW; Georgia-194: Courtesy of the Atlanta Cyclorama–JW; Georgia-196: McPherson Monument, Atlanta; Georgia-197: Oakland Cemetery, Atlanta; Georgia-198: Sweetwater Creek State Park; Georgia-208: Prints and Photographs Division, Library of Congress, Washington, D.C.–SG; Georgia-207: Prints and

Photographs Division, Library of Congress, Washington, D.C.–SG; Georgia-209: Warren House, Jonesboro; Georgia-223: MASS-MOLLUS/USAMHI–AW; Georgia-231: MASS-MOLLUS/USAMHI–JW; Georgia-235: MASS-MOLLUS/USAMHI– JW; Georgia-238: Fort McAllister Historic Park.

International-247: Prints and Photographs Division, Library of Congress, Washington, D.C.–SG; International-249: West Point Museum Collection, United States Military Academy, West Point, New York; International-250: Prints and Photographs Division, Library of Congress, Washington, D.C.–MAP; International-254: U.S. Naval Academy/Beverly R. Robinson Collection.

Kentucky-269: Prints and Photographs Division, Library of Congress, Washington, D.C.–SG; Kentucky-272: MASS-MOLLUS/USAMHI–JW; Kentucky-280: Prints and Photographs Division, Library of Congress, Washington, D.C.–MAP.

Louisiana-286: U.S. Naval Academy/Beverly R. Robinson Collection; Louisiana-289: Prints and Photographs Division, Library of Congress, Washington, D.C.–MAP; Louisiana-291: MASS-MOLLUS/USAMHI–JW; Louisiana-295: Prints and Photographs Division, Library of Congress, Washington, D.C.–JW; Louisiana-297: Brady-Handy Collection, National Archives, Washington, D.C.–MAP; Louisiana-300: U.S. Naval Academy/Beverly R. Robinson Collection; Louisiana-302: MASS-MOLLUS/USAMHI–AW; Louisiana-303: Port Hudson State Commemorative Area; Louisiana-305: Courtesy of the Navy Memorial Museum, Washington, D.C.; Louisiana-310: Mansfield State Commemorative Area; Dog Trot House, Pleasant Hill.

Maryland-320: MASS-MOLLUS/USAMHI–JW; Maryland-322: Prints and Photographs Division, Library of Congress, Washington, D.C.–JW; Maryland-324: MASS-MOLLUS/USAMHI–JW; Maryland-330: Prints and Photographs Division, Library of Congress, Washington, D.C.–JW; Maryland-331: Monocacy National Battlefield photographed by Andrew Wertz; Maryland-333: MASS-MOLLUS/USAMHI–JW; Maryland-336: Prints and Photographs Division, Library of Congress, Washington, D.C.–MAP; Maryland-337: West Point Museum Collection, United States Military Academy, West Point, New York; Antietam National Battlefield; Maryland-338: Brady-Handy Collection, National Archives, Washington, D.C.–SG.

The Midwest-345: Prints and Photographs Division, Library of Congress, Washington, D.C.–JW; The Midwest-347: Chicago Historical Society; The Midwest-348: Brady-Handy Collection, National Archives, Washington, D.C.–MAP.

Mississippi-354: Valentine Museum, Richmond, Virginia–JW; Mississippi-356: Prints and Photographs Division, Library of Congress, Washington, D.C.–MAP; Mississippi-371: U.S. Naval Academy/Beverly R. Robinson Collection; Mississippi-373: U.S. Naval Academy/Beverly R. Robinson Collection; Mississippi-374: MASS-MOLLUS/USAMHI–JW; Mississippi-376: Brady-Handy Collection, National Archives, Washington, D.C.–MAP; Mississippi-377: U.S. Naval Academy/Beverly R. Robinson Collection; Mississippi-379: Grand Gulf Military Monument; Mississippi-380: Windsor Mansion, Port Gibson, Mississippi; Mississippi-384: Courtesy of the Mississippi Department of Archives and History, Jackson, Mississippi; Mississippi-392: Collection of Jay Wertz; Mississippi-393: Vicksburg National Military Park; Old Courthouse Museum, Vicksburg; Mississippi-395: MASS-MOLLUS/USAMHI–AW.

Missouri-400: MASS-MOLLUS/USAMHI–JW; Missouri-402: Prints and Photographs Division, Library of Congress, Washington, D.C.–JW; Missouri-405: Prints and Photographs Division, Library of Congress, Washington, D.C.–MAP; Missouri-415; Wilson's Creek National Battlefield photographed by Marv Lewis; Missouri-416: Prints and Photographs Division, Library of Congress, Washington, D.C.–JW.

North Carolina-423: National Archives, Washington, D.C.–JW; North Carolina-432: MASS-MOLLUS/USAMHI–AW; North Carolina-433: Fort Fisher State Historic Site; North Carolina-439: Bentonville Battleground State Historic Site.

The Northeast-444: MASS-MOLLUS/USAMHI–AW; The Northeast-447: Courtesy of the Seventh Regiment Fund, Inc.

The Northwest-453: Prints and Photographs Division, Library of Congress, Washington, D.C.–SG; The Northwest-454. Prints and Photographs Division, Library of Congress, Washington, D.C.–MAP; The Northwest-457: Prints and Photographs Division, Library of Congress, Washington, D.C.–SG.

Oklahoma-473: Prints and Photographs Division, Library of Congress, Washington, D.C.–SG.

Pennsylvania-479: Prints and Photographs Division, Library of Congress, Washington, D.C.–MAP; Pennsylvania-483: Prints and Photographs Division, Library of Congress, Washington, D.C.–MAP; Pennsylvania-484: Courtesy of Hanover Area Historical Society; Pennsylvania-486: Brady-Handy Collection, National Archives, Washington, D.C.–MAP; Pennsylvania-488: Prints and Photographs Division, Library of Congress, Washington, D.C.–JW; Brady-Handy Collection, National Archives, Washington, D.C.–MAP; Pennsylvania-489: MASS-MOLLUS/USAMHI–AW; Pennsylvania-491: Prints and Photographs Division, Library of Congress, Washington, D.C.–MAP; Pennsylvania-492: Brady-Handy Collection, National Archives, Washington, D.C.–SG; Prints and Photographs Division, Library of Congress, Washington, D.C.–MAP; Pennsylvania-493: Prints and Photographs Division, Library of Congress, Washington, D.C.–MAP; MASS-MOLLUS/USAMHI–AW; Pennsylvania-495: Gettysburg National Military Park–JW; Prints and Photographs Division, Library of Congress, Washington, D.C.–MAP; Pennsylvania-497: MASS-MOLLUS/USAMHI–JW; Brady-Handy Collection, National Archives, Washington, D.C.–JW; Pennsylvania-498: Gettysburg National Military Park; Pennsylvania-499: Gettysburg National Military Park; Pennsylvania-500: Gettysburg National Military Park photographed by Andrew Wertz.

South Carolina-505: Prints and Photographs Division, Library of Congress, Washington, D.C.–JW; South Carolina-506: U.S. Naval Academy/Beverly R. Robinson Collection; South Carolina-508: Fort Sumter National Monument; South Carolina-514: Prints and Photographs Division, Library of Congress, Washington, D.C.–MAP; South Carolina-515: White Point Gardens, Charleston; South Carolina-517: Prints and Photographs Division, Library of Congress, Washington, D.C.–JW; South Carolina-521: MASS-MOLLUS/USAMHI–AW; South Carolina-522: National Archives, Washington, D.C.–JW; South Carolina-524: U.S. Naval Academy/Beverly R. Robinson Collection; South Carolina-529: Prints and Photographs Division, Library of Congress, Washington, D.C.–SG.

Tennessee-539: U.S. Naval Academy/Beverly R. Robinson Collection; Tennessee-546: U.S. Naval Academy/Beverly R. Robinson Collection; Tennessee-549: Prints and Photographs Division, Library of Congress, Washington, D.C.–MAP; Tennessee-552: Chicago Historical Society; Tennessee-555: Prints and Photographs Division, Library of Congress, Washington, D.C.–JW; Tennessee-561: MASS-MOLLUS/USAMHI–JW; Tennessee-563: Prints and Photographs Division, Library of Congress, Washington, D.C.–JW; Tennessee-565: Stones River National Battlefield; Tennessee-567: Beech Grove Memorial State Park; Tennessee-573: Courtesy of Chickamauga and Chattanooga National Military Park; Tennessee-578: Chickamauga and Chattanooga National Military Park; Tennessee-593: Cumberland Gap National Historical Park; Tennessee-601: Historic Carnton Plantation, Franklin.

Texas-611: Sabine Pass Battleground State Park.

Virginia-622: Fort Ward Museum and Historic Site, Alexandria; Virginia-629: Prints and Photographs Division, Library of Congress, Washington, D.C.–JW; Virginia-639: MASS-MOLLUS/USAMHI–JW; Virginia-641: Prints and Photographs Division, Library of Congress, Washington, D.C.–MAP; Virginia-642: Brady-Handy Collection, National Archives, Washington, D.C.–SG; Virginia-644: Prints and Photographs Division, Library of Congress, Washington, D.C.–MAP; Virginia-646: MASS-MOLLUS/USAMHI–JW; Virginia-648: Prints and Photographs Division, Library of Congress, Washington, D.C.–MAP; Virginia-650: Courtesy of the Virginia Military Institute; Virginia-657: MASS-MOLLUS/USAMHI–JW; Virginia-658: MASS-MOLLUS/USAMHI–JW; Virginia-662: Brandy Station, Culpeper County; Virginia-666: Prints and Photographs Division, Library of Congress, Washington, D.C.–MAP; Virginia-671: Fredericksburg and Spotsylvania County Battlefields Memorial National Military Park; Virginia-676: Brady-Handy Collection, National Archives, Washington, D.C.–SG; Virginia-679: Prints and Photographs Division, Library of Congress, Washington, D.C.–MAP; Virginia-682: Prints and Photographs Division, Library of Congress, Washington, D.C.–SG; Virginia-683: Fredericksburg and Spotsylvania County Battlefields Memorial National Military Park; Virginia-687: Brady-Handy Collection, National Archives, Washington, D.C.–JW; Virginia-695: Brady-Handy Collection, National Archives, Washington, D.C.–MAP; Virginia-698: Prints and Photographs Division, Library of Congress, Washington, D.C.–MAP; Virginia-699: National Portrait Gallery,

Index

Page numbers in *italics* refer to maps and illustrations.

Abbeville, S.C., 535
Abraham Lincoln Museum, Harrogate, Tenn., 594
Abraham Lincoln National Historic Site, Hodgenville, Ky., 277
Absalom Thompson House, Spring Hill, Tenn., 597, 598
Adams, Charles Francis, 248, 249
Adams, Dan, 271
Adams, John, 601
Adams, Silas, 198
Adela, USS, 108
Adolph S. Ochs Museum and Overlook, Lookout Mountain, Chattanooga, Tenn., 577
Agnes Scott College, Decatur, Ga., 196
Aiken, S.C., 231
A. K. Shaifer House, Port Gibson, Miss., 379, 380
Alabama, xxxii, 1–27
Alabama, CSS, 63, 214, 243, 248, 251, *252*, 253–255, *254*, 257
    USS *Brooklyn* sunk by, 614
Alabama, USS, 14
Alabama Department of Archives and History, 12
Alabama Historical Commission, 23
Alaska, 277
Albatross, USS, 301–302
Albemarle, CSS, 422, 423–424, *423*
Albuquerque, N.Mex., 75, 89, 90, 95, 97
Alcatraz, San Francisco, Calif., 82–83
Alexander, E. Porter, 230, 749
Alexander Eaton house, Smyrna area, Ga., 180
Alexander H. Stephens Historic Site, Crawfordville, Ga., 229
Alexandria, La., 304–307, 312
Alexandria, Va., 623–624
Alexandria-Pineville Convention and Tourist Bureau, Alexandria, La., 306
Allatoona Pass, Battle of, 161–163, *162*
Allen, Henry W., 294
Allen's Farm, Seven Pines, Va., 707
Amelia Court House, Va., 739, 741
Amelia Island Lighthouse, Fernandina Beach, Fla., 118
American Hotel, West Harrison, Ind., 349
Anderson, George W., 238
Anderson, Richard H., 103–104, 494, 684–685, *685*, 703, 728, 740, 742, 744

Anderson, Robert, 260, 504–505, *506*, 507
Anderson, William "Bloody Bill," 408, 454
Anderson Cottage, Washington, D.C., 68
Anderson House, Lexington, Mo., 410, 411
Anderson's Cross Roads, Tenn., 570
Andersonville, Ga., 61
Andersonville National Historic Site, Andersonville, Ga., 219
Andersonville Prison, Ga., 200, 215–219, 222, 326, 444
Andrew Johnson National Historic Site, Greeneville, Tenn., 590
Andrews, James J., 131–132, 161, 176, 198, 577, 579
Annapolis, Md., *324–325, 324*
Annapolis Junction, Md., 323–324
Antietam, Battle of, 267, 271, 332, 334–339, *335, 336, 337, 376*, 478, 479, 782, 784
Antietam and Monocacy National Battlefields, Sharpsburg, Md., 333, 339
Apache Canyon, Battle of, *91*, 92, 93, 95
Apache Cemetery, Lawton, Okla., 475
Apache Pass, Battle of, 78–80
Apalachicola, Fla., 101, 107–108
Appomattox Campaign, 739–749
    Lee's surrender in, 70, 212, 440–441, 746–749
    Sailor's Creek battle in, 741–743
Appomattox Court House, Va., 13, 25, 746–749
Appomattox Court House National Historic Park, Appomattox, Va., 750–751
Aransas Pass Light Station, Port Aransas, Tex., 616
Archer, James J., *496*
Archibald Howell House, Marietta, Ga., 177
Arizona, *74*, 75, 76–80
Arizona, USS, 612
Arkansas, *28*, 29–49
Arkansas, CSS, 294, 300, 366, 370–371, *371*, 374
Arkansas Post, Ark., 29, 38–40
Arkansas Post National Memorial, Gillett, Ark., 40
Arlington, Va., 621–623
Arlington House, Arlington, Va., 621
Arlington National Cemetery, Arlington, Va., 621
Armistead, Lewis A., 80–81, 82, *496*
    birthplace of, 427

Armstrong, Frank C., 166, 559, 587
Armstrong, James, 102–103
Armstrong Academy, Armstrong, Okla., 474
Army of East Kentucky (Confederate), 774
Army of Georgia (Union), 435, 437
Army of Kentucky (Confederate), 260, 343, 350
Army of Mississippi (Confederate), 153, 157, 278
Army of Northern Virginia (Confederate), 25, 136, *136*, 144, 146, 151, 212, 320, 329, 339, 435, 481, 537, 580, 600, 625, 636, 665, 667, 673, 716, 721, 725, 743, *748*, 749, 762, 767
Army of Tennessee (Confederate), 132, 133, *141*, 142, 145–146, *145*, 147, 150, 152, 176, 179, 185, 204, 205, 210, 211, 212, 278, 360, 362, 435, 532, 538, 562, 563, 567, 570, 571, *574*, 576, 580, 583, 584, 595, 597–598, 600, 602, 605, 679
Army of the Cumberland (Union), 5, 133, 134, *145*, 147, 158, 165, 167, 169, 171, 172, 173–174, *173*, 176, 181, 184–185, *187*, 188–189, 190, *190*, 203, 281, 562, 565–566, *567*, 569–570, 571, 572, 574, *574*, 582
    at Missionary Ridge, 575–576
Army of the Frontier (Union), 35, 45, 470
Army of the James (Union), 702, 710, 712–714, 715, 716, 722, 727, 732, 741, 755
Army of the Mississippi (Confederate), 2, 260, 274, 278, 343, 350, 557
Army of the Mississippi (Union), 39, 546, 555
Army of the Ohio (Union), 1, 4, 135, *145*, 147, 154, 190, 201, 203, 265, 276, 278, 350, 355, 357, 556, *556*, 558, 569, 580, 582, 583, 586, 593
Army of the Potomac (Union), 67, 199, 266, 328, 332, 335, 339, 340, 356, 444, 478, 480–481, 484, *488*, 489, 537, 571, 572, 582, 631, 634, 635, 641, 646, 657, 658, 659, 664, 665, 666–667, 673, *674*, 677, 679, 680, 682–683, 688–689, *695*, 702, 716, 718, 727, 759
    McClellan and, 633, 695, 696

Army of the Potomac (Union)
    (*continued*)
  Meade named commander of,
    329–330
  Stuart's ride around, 697–698
Army of the Southwest (Union), 30
Army of the Tennessee (Union), 4, *145*,
    152, 153, 156, 159, 161, 171,
    173, 178, 190–191, *190*, 194,
    195, 196, 200, 203, 208, 436,
    537, 556, 557, 567, 570–571
Army of the Valley (Confederate), 638
Army of the West (Confederate), 557
Army of Virginia (Union), 266, 632, 657
Army War College, Carlisle Barracks,
    Carlisle, Pa., 482–483
Arnold (battery commander), 498
Arnold, L. G., 114
Arnold, Samuel, 72
Arsenal of Beaufort, Beaufort, S.C., 528
Arthur, USS, 615
Asboth, Alexander, 107
Ashby, Henry, 211–212
Ashby, Turner, 640, 652, 653, 654
Ashland, Va., 665, 690–691, 693
Ashley Oaks Mansion, Jonesboro, Ga.,
    209
Ashwood, Tenn., 596
Association for the Preservation of
    Civil War Sites (APCWS),
    Fredericksburg, Va., 645
Athenaeum, Columbia, Tenn., 596
Athens, Ala., 2–4
Atlanta, Battle of, 190–195, *190*
  painting of, 195
Atlanta, CSS, 240, 423
Atlanta, Ga., vii, 129, *130*, 538, 543
  Federal occupation of, 205–226, *206*
  Hood's evacuation of, 204–205
  siege of, 202
  Underground in, 206–207
Atlanta, USS, 240
Atlanta Campaign, 129, 133, 143,
    144–184, *145*, *173*
  Allatoona Pass battle in, 161–163
  Caswell engagement in, 158–159
  Chattahoochee River engagement in,
    183–184
  Dallas engagement in, 166–167
  Dalton engagement in, 150
  Dug Gap engagement in, 151–152
  Ezra Church battle in, 199–202
  Johnston's delaying tactics in, 156
  Johnston's River Line in, 178–180,
    181
  Kennesaw Mountain battle in,
    170–174
  Kolb Farm battle in, 170–171, 174
  Lost-Pine-Brushy Mountain Line in,
    169–170
  New Hope Church battle in,
    164–165

New Manchester engagement in,
    198–199
  Pickett's Mill battle in, 165–166
  Resaca Battle in, 152–156
  Rocky Face Ridge engagement in,
    148–149
  Rome Cross Roads engagement in,
    156–157
  Roswell engagement in, 180,
    182–183
  Ruff's Mill battle in, 178, 180
  Smyrna Line in, 177–178
  strategy for, 147
  Tunnel Hill engagement in, 147–148
  Utoy Creek battle in, 201
Atlanta Cyclorama, *192*, *194*, 195, 197
Atlanta History Center, Atlanta, Ga.,
    189
Atlantic, USS, 103
Atzerodt, George, 72
Augur, Christopher C., 67
Augusta, Ga., 230–232
Augusta Arsenal, Augusta, Ga., 231
Augusta Powder Works, Augusta, Ga.,
    230–231, *231*
Augustus Hurt House, Atlanta, Ga.,
    197
Ausbon House, Plymouth, N.C., 424
Austin, Tex., 101
Averasboro, Battle of, 436–437
Averell, William W., 638, 655, 658, 665,
    767–768, 775–776, 778
Avery, Isaac E., *492*, 494

Bahamas, 256
Bahía, Brazil, 256
Bailey, Joseph, 306
Bailey, Theodorus, 109, 290
"Bailey's dams," *305*, 306, 312
Baird, Absalom, 134, 170, 179, 232, 233
Baker, Edward, 633–634
Baldwin County Convention and
    Visitors Bureau, Milledgeville,
    Ga., 228
Balfour House, Vicksburg, Miss.,
    392–393
Ball's Bluff, Battle of, 633–634
Baltimore, Md., 319, 321–323, *322*
Banks, Nathaniel P., 15, 45, 46, 285,
    290, 294, 296, *297*, 298, 336,
    364, 390, 570, 610, 613, 616,
    657
  Alexandria operations and, 304–306
  at Cedar Mountain, 657–658
  at First Winchester, 640–641, 652,
    774
  at Port Hudson, 300–302
  in Red River Campaign, 307–309,
    311–312, 314
  in Valley Campaign of 1862,
    637–638, 640–641, 643, 646,
    652, 656

Banquete cemetery, Corpus Christi,
    Tex., 616
Barbara Fritchie House and Museum,
    Frederick, Md., 332
Barbour County Historical Society,
    W.Va., 776–777
Barksdale, William, *493*, 671
Barlow, Francis, 704
Barnard, John G., 64
Barnes, Joseph K., 61
Barnsley Gardens, Ga., 158, 159
Barrett, James, 77, 78
Barton, Clara, 53, 219, 338, 625, 672
Barton, Colonel, 528
Barton, Seth, 427
Barton Academy, Mobile, Ala., 13
Bartow, Francis S., *627*
Bate, William, 166, 168, 188, 189, 193,
    568
Bates, Edward, *55*
Baton Rouge, La., 293–295
Battery Beauregard, Sullivan's Island,
    S.C., 509
Battery Buchanan, Fort Fisher, N.C.,
    430, 434
Battery Doubleday, Williamsport, Md.,
    341
Battery Gladden, Mobile, Ala., 14
Battery Gregg, Morris Island, S.C., 512,
    523
Battery Huger, Fort Sumter,
    Charleston, S.C., 509
Battery Jamison, Washington, D.C., 66
Battery Kemble, Washington, D.C., 65
Battery Park, Charleston, S.C., 514, 517
Battery Pringle, James Island, S.C., 519,
    521
Battery Robinett, Corinth, Miss., 357
Battery Rodgers, Va., 326
Battery Simkins, S.C., 519
Battery White, Georgetown, S.C., 511
Battery Wiltsie, Knoxville, Tenn., 585
"Battle Above the Clouds," 575
Battlefield Park, Jackson, Miss., 384
Battleground National Cemetery,
    Washington, D.C., 68
Battle Grove Cemetery, Cynthiana, Ky.,
    274
Battle of Baton Rouge State
    Monument, Baton Rouge, La.,
    294
Battle of Carthage State Park,
    Carthage, Mo., 415
Battle of Corydon Memorial Park,
    Corydon, Ind., 349
Battle of Lexington State Historic Site,
    Lexington, Mo., 411
Battle of Lone Jack Museum, Westport,
    Mo., 413
Battle of Nashville Peace Monument,
    Nashville, Tenn., 606
"battle of the axes," 708

Baxter Springs, Kans., 459
Baxter Springs Massacre, 408, 458–459
Baylor, John R., 76, 83–84, 85, 86, 98
Bayou City, CSS, 614
Bayou Fourche, Ark., 43–44
Bayport, Fla., 112
Bean's Station, Battle of, 591–592
Bear Hunter, 453
Bear River Massacre, 408, 452–453
Bearss, Edwin C., 375
Beasley-Williamson House, Petersburg,
    Va., 732
Beatty, Samuel, 565
Beaufort, S.C., 527–528
Beaufort County Library, Beaufort,
    S.C., 528
Beaufort Museum, Beaufort, S.C., 528
Beauregard, P.G.T., 12, 210, 231, 239,
    261, 291, 292, 355, 357, *505,*
    530, 532, 549, *556,* 557, 558,
    619, 627, 713, 716, 718, 731
  Charleston defense and, 510, 511,
    515–516, 518, 522, 523, 525
  at First Manassas, 626–629
  at Fort Sumter, 504, 505–506
Beauregard, René, 291
Beauregard House, Chalmette, La., 291
Beauvoir Mansion, Biloxi, Miss., 397
Beaver Dam Creek, Battle of, 700, 701
Bee, Barnard E., *627,* 628
Beecher, Henry Ward, 58
Beech Grove Memorial State Park,
    Tenn., *567,* 568
Belington, W.Va., 778
Bellamy Mansion, Wilmington, N.C.,
    429
Belle Boyd Cottage, Front Royal, Va.,
    643
Belle Grove Mansion, Middletown, Va.,
    646, 649
Belle Isle Prison, Richmond, Va., 692,
    735–736
Belle Meade, Nashville, Tenn., 606–607
Bellevue Plantation, Perkins, Ga., 233
Belmont, Battle of, 261, 344, 402
Ben Hur (Wallace), 330
Benjamin, Judah P., 113, 292
Benjamin Reed Boyd House,
    Martinsburg, W.Va., 784
Bennett, James, 441
Bennett Place State Historic Site,
    Durham, N.C., 441
Benton, USS, 406, 546, 552
Bentonville, Battle of, 437–440, *438, 439*
Bentonville Battleground State Historic
    Site, Newton Grove, N.C., 440
Berkeley County Courthouse,
    Martinsburg, W.Va., 784
Berkeley Plantation, Va., 709
Bermuda, 256
Bermuda Hundred, Va., 702, 703,
    712–713, 715, 716

Bernard, Simon, 22
Bethesda Church, Va., 704
Beverly, W.Va., 778
Big Bethel, Battle of, 758–759
Big Black River, Battle of, 386–387
Big Creek, Battle of, 591
Big Mound, Battle of, 462–463, 464
Big Shanty, Ga., 131, 132, 133, 161
Biloxi, Miss., 397
Birch Coulee, Minn., 460, 461
Birney, David, 494, 710
Birney, William, 519, 711, 747
"Bivouac of the Dead, The" (O'Hara),
    275
Blackbird Marsh Nature Trail, Fort
    Pickens, Fla., 106
Black Kettle, 451
Black Terror, USS, 372
Blair, Francis, Jr., 178, 179, 192,
    193–194, 196, 204, *223, 389,*
    407
Blair, Francis, Sr., 619
Blair, Montgomery, *55,* 61
Bliss, Phillip P., 161
blockade-runners, 250–251
Blount's Plantation, Ala., 6
Blountsville, Ala., 6
Blountville, Battle of, 590–591
Blue & Gray Magazine, 606
Blue Springs, Battle of, 587–588
Blunt, James G., 35–36, 37, 43, 410,
    411, 414, 456, *457,* 458, 470,
    471, 474
Blunt House, Dalton, Ga., 151
Boggy Depot, Okla., 474
Bolen Church, Honey Hill, S.C., 530
Bolivar Heights, Harpers Ferry, W.Va.,
    783
Bolivar Methodist Church, Harpers
    Ferry, W.Va., 784
Boone, Daniel, 592
Boone Hall Plantation, Mount
    Pleasant, S.C., 510
Boonville, Mo., 408–409
Booth, John Wilkes, 54, *54,* 70–72, 73,
    115, 283, 319, 327–328
  death of, 672
  grave of, 323
Booth, Lionel F., 550
Borden House, Prairie Grove, Ark., 37,
    38
Bostwick-Fraser House, Marietta, Ga.,
    177
Bowen, John S., 376, 378–379, *378,*
    385, 386, 391
Bowling Green, Ky., 279
Boyd, Belle, 643, 698
Boydton Plank Road, Battle of, *717,*
    722–723
Boynton, H. V., 139
Bradford, William F., 550
Bradham, C. D., 427

Bradley, Luther, 598
Brady, Mathew, 61, *336, 338, 734*
Bragg, Braxton, 1–2, 4, 5, 6, 80–81,
    103, *135,* 144, 185, 260, 278,
    280, 281, 292, 343, 350, 355,
    425, 429, 433, 435, 438, 537,
    557, 562, 568, 573, 575, 579,
    580, 582, 583, 649
  at Chattanooga, 569–571
  at Chickamauga, 133–137, 139, *141,*
    142
  Forrest's confrontation with,
    571–572
  Frankfort occupation and, 274–276
  gravesite of, 13
  at Perryville, 268, 269, 271–272
  at Stones River, 563, *564,* 565–566
Bragg Reservation, Chattanooga,
    Tenn., 579
Branch, Lawrence O'Brien, 426
Brandy Station, Battle of, 634–635,
    659–663, *660, 662,* 702
Brannan, General, 528
Brannan, John, 113–114, 120–121
Brawner's Farm, Battle of, 630
Brazil, 253
Breaker, CSS, 615
Breakthrough Point, Richmond, Va.,
    702
Breckinridge, John C., 78, *138,* 273,
    293–294, 300, 441, 535, 557,
    564, 565, 566, 575, 579,
    588–589, 649–650, 651, 654,
    704, 768
Breckinridge, William C. P., 222
Brentwood, Tenn., 607
Brices' Cross Roads, Battle of, 359–360
Brices' Cross Roads National
    Battlefield Site, Baldwyn, Miss.,
    360–361
Bridgeport, Ala., 1–2, 4
Bristoe Station, Va., 632–633, 636
Britton's Lane, Battle of, 559, 560
Brockenbrough, John M., *496*
Brooklyn, USS, 18, 19, 103, 287, 289,
    614
Brownlow, W. G., 585
Brown, Isaac Newton, 366
Brown, John, 449, 480, 781–782
Brown, Joseph E., 178, 225, 230, 529
Brown, Joseph R., 460
Brownlow, James, 183, 184
Brown's Ferry, Tenn., 572, 577
Brown's Mill, Battle of, 211
Brownsville, Tex., 610, 617
Brunswick Town-Fort Anderson State
    Historic Site, Winnabow, N.C.,
    434
Buchanan, Franklin, 16, 18, 19, 20, 21,
    63, 320, 752–753
Buchanan, James, 52, 53, 83

Buchanan, Robert C., 320
Buckland, Battle of, 636
Buckner, Louisa, 61
Buckner, Simon B., 135, 137, 278, 280,
    313, 541, 542, 569, 582
Buell, Don Carlos, 1, 4, 131, 263,
    275–276, 277, 278, 281, 355,
    357, 537, 548, 556, *556,*
    557–558, 562
  at Perryville, 268–272, *269*
Buffington Island, Ohio, 350–351
Buffington Island State Memorial,
    Portland, Ohio, 351
Buford, Abraham, 263, 544
Buford, John, 340, 482, 485–486, *487,*
    635, 659–663, *660,* 665
Bulloch, James, 183, 248, 251, 253,
    255
Bulloch Hall, Roswell, Ga., 183
Bull Run, Battles of, *see* Manassas,
    Battles of
Bull's Gap, Battle of, 588–589
Burbridge, Stephen Gano, 274, 275,
    282, 298, 768
Bureau of Engraving, Washington,
    D.C., 58
Burgess's Mill, Battle of, *717,* 722–723,
    724
Burke's Station, Va., 625, 723
Burman Historic Site, Kidder County,
    N.Dak., 464
Burnet House, Cincinnati, Ohio, 350
Burnside, Ambrose E., 135, 143, 298,
    324, 338, 339, 350, 587–588,
    593–594, 680, 687, 694, 704
  at Blountville, 590–591
  Crater Battle and, 719–720
  at Fredericksburg, 666–670
  Hooker's replacement of, 672–673
  Knoxville Campaign and, 569, 571,
    580–584
  McClellan replaced by, 636
  Mud March and, 670
  at New Bern, 426
  Roanoke Island Expedition and,
    420–422
Burnt Chimneys (Dam Number 1),
    Battle of, 760
Burt-Stark House, Abbeville, S.C., 535
Bushnell, Cornelius, 753
Bushong, Jacob, 650
Bushong House, New Market, Va., 651
Butler, Benjamin F., 286, 287–288, 290,
    292, 293, 294, 296, 322, 323,
    324–325, 419–420, 430, *431,*
    702, 703, 716, 722, 732, 755,
    767
  at Bermuda Hundred, 712–714
  Grant's dismissal of, 432, 714
Butterfield, Daniel, 160
Butt House, Portsmouth, Va., 757
Byram's Ford, Battle of, 411–413

Cabell, William L., 46, 456, 470–471
Cabin Creek, First Battle of, 470–471,
    473
Cabin Creek, Second Battle of, 472,
    473
Cairo, Ill., 344–345
Cairo, USS, 63, 214, 366, *374,* 375, 552
Calhoun, James M., 205, 206
California, *74,* 75, 80–83
California Column, 77, 78, 79, 84, 98
  organization of, 81
Calloway, William, 77–78
Camden, Ark., 29, 46, 48–49
Camden Campaign, 45–49
Camp Allegheny, W.Va., 779–780
Camp Bartow, Bartow, W.Va., 779
Camp Beauregard, Jackson, Tenn., 561
Campbell, Andrew G., 590
Campbell's Station, Battle of, 581
Camp Bisland, Morgan City, La., 297
Camp Butler, Springfield, Ill., 346
Camp Douglas, Ill., 344
Camp Douglas, Utah, 452, 453
Camp Garnett, Beverly, W.Va., 778
Camp Jackson, St. Louis, Mo., 407
Camp Oglethorpe, Macon, Ga., 200,
    222
Camp Parole, Annapolis, Md., 325
Camp Talbot, Norfolk, Va., 757
Camp Wildcat Battle Monument,
    Livingston, Ky., 266
Canada, 446
  Fenian raid on, 247
  St. Alcans raid and, 446–447
Canby, Edward R. S., 8, 17, 23, 24, 78,
    79, 83, 84, 85, *86,* 90, 313
  Confederate surrender and, 26–27
  Peralta Battle and, 97–98
  Valverde Battle and, 86–87, 88
Cane-Bennett Bluff, Shreveport, La.,
    314
Canehill, Ark., 36, 37
Canonicus, USS, 507
Cantey, James, 153
Cape Girardeau, Mo., 49, 403
Cape Hatteras National Seashore,
    Manteo, N.C., 420
Capron, Horace, 222, 596
Carleton, James H., 77, 78–79, 80, 81,
    84, 609
Carlin, William P., 271, 437
Carlisle, Pa., 482–483
Carlisle Barracks, Carlisle, Pa., 482
Carney, William H., *522,* 523
Carnifax Ferry, Battle of, 772–773
Carnifax Ferry Battlefield State Park,
    W.Va., 773
Carnton Plantation, Franklin, Tenn.,
    601, *601*
Carondelet, USS, 370, 406, 540–541,
    547, 552
Carpenter, Francis B., *55*

Carr, Eugene A., 31, 32, 33
Carroll, Samuel S., 320, 653
Carroll Hall, Fort Monroe, Va., 756
Carson, Christopher "Kit," 88, 97, 452
Carter, Anne Hill, 709
Carter, James E., 590
Carter, Samuel P., 588
Carter House, Franklin, Tenn., 600
Carter Park, Carthage, Mo., 415
Carthage, Mo., 414–415
Cary, Hetty, 724
Cascade Springs Nature Preserve,
    Atlanta, Ga., 202
Casement Museum, Fort Monroe, Va.,
    758
Cashtown, Pa., 501
Cassville, Ga., 158–159, 160
Castillo de San Marcos, St. Augustine,
    Fla., *117,* 118, 119
Castle Pinckney, Charleston, S.C., 513,
    514, *514*
Caston Plantation, Battle of, 528
Catherine State Park, Hot Springs,
    Ark., 49
Catoosa Springs, Ga., 144
Cedar Creek, Battle of, 646–648, *647*
Cedar Creek Battlefield Foundation,
    Middletown, Va., 648–649
Cedar Key, Fla., 101, 111, 116
Cedar Mountain, Battle of, 657–658,
    657
Centennial House, Corpus Christi,
    Tex., 616
Central Hotel, Hanover, Pa., *484*
Centralia, Mo., 408
Central Louisiana State Hospital,
    Alexandria, La., 306
Centre Hill Mansion, Petersburg, Va.,
    731
Centreville, Va., 632
Chaffin's Farm, Battle of, 710
Chalk Bluff, Ark., 49
Chalk Bluff Park, St. Francis, Ark., 49
Chalmers, James R., 278, 603, 607
Chalmette, La., 291
Chamberlain, Joshua L., *491,* 493, *748,*
    749
Chamberlain's Bed, Dinwiddie Court
    House, Va., 728
Chambersburg, Pa., 477, 478–480, *479,*
    780
Champion Hill, Battle of, 263,
    385–386, 387
Chancellorsville, Battle of, 192, 199,
    480, 665, 670, 672–677, *674,*
    690
Chandler, T. C., 678
Chantilly, Battle of, 625–626, 631
Chapman, Conrad, *354*
Chapman, William, 631
Chapman's Mill, Thoroughfare Gap,
    Va., 636

Charles City, Va., 710

Charles Slover House, New Bern, N.C., 427

Charleston, S.C., 13, 15, 503–504, 513–517, *515, 516, 517*

Charleston Harbor, 506, 507, 511–514

Charleston Lighthouse, 523

Charleston Mercury, 515

Charleston Museum, Charleston, S.C., 517

Charleston Visitor Reception Center, Charleston, S.C., 517, 523

Charlot's Farm, Battle of, 413

Charlottesville, Va., 694

Chase, Salmon P., 53, *55,* 56, 626

Chatham Manor, Fredericksburg, Va., 671–672

Chattahoochee, CSS, 108, 213–214

Chattahoochee River National Recreation Area, Dunwoody, Ga., 184

Chattanooga, Tenn., 1, 2, 4, 131, 133, 134, 143, 538
    siege of, 570–574, *574*

Cheairs, Nathaniel, 598

Cheatham, Benjamin F., 171, 172, 186, 187, 188, *190,* 191, 193, 194, 195, 199, 271, 595, 597–598, 604

Cheat Mountain, Battle of, 778–779

Cheat Summit Fort, W.Va., 779

Cherbourg, France, 256

Chesapeake and Ohio Canal, Washington, D.C., 69

Chesapeake & Ohio National Historical Park, Williamsport, Md., 341

Chesnut, James, 135, 504, 534

Chesnut, Mary Boykin, 135–136, 534, 571

Chesnut Cottage, Columbia, S.C., 534

Chesterfield Historical Society, Chesterfield, Va., 714

Chickahominy Bluff, Richmond, Va., 701

Chickamauga, Battle of, 129, 133–139, *136, 138, 141,* 148, 277, 570, 575–576, 582, 612

Chickamauga and Chattanooga National Park, Fort Oglethorpe, Ga., 139–141, *140,* 576–577

Chickasaw, USS, 17, *18,* 21

Chickasaw Bayou, Miss., 38–39, 364, 368–369, *378,* 393

Chicora, CSS, 511

Chimborazo Hospital, Richmond, Va., 735, 737

Chinn Ridge, Manassas Battlefield, Va., 632

Chivington, John M., 79, 90, 92, 94, 97, 98, 99, 451–452

Choctaw, USS, 316

Christ Episcopal Church, Mobile, Ala., 13

Christ Episcopal Church, Spotsylvania, Va., 687

Churchill, Thomas J., 39, 267, 311

Church of the Holy Trinity, Nashville, Tenn., 606

Chustenalah, Battle of, 469–470

Chusto-Talasah, Battle of, 468–469

Cincinnati, Ohio, 350

Cincinnati, USS, 374, 548–549

Citronelle, Ala., 26–27

City Hall, Charleston, S.C., 517

City Hall, Knoxville, Tenn., 584–585

City Hall, Macon, Ga., 225

City Hall, Mobile, Ala., 13

City Hall, Petersburg, Va., 731

City Point, Va., 732–733, *732,* 755–756

Civil War Cavalry Museum, Front Royal, Va., 643

Civil War Tours, Atlanta, Ga., 181

Claiborne County Historical Tours, Port Gibson, Miss., 380–381

Clarkson, J. J., 470

Clarksville, Tenn., 542–543

Clay, Cassius M., 268

Clay House, Petersburg, Va., 732

Clayton-Mooney House, Allatoona Pass, Ga., 163–164

Cleburne, Christopher, 768

Cleburne, Patrick, 42, 137, 150, 171, 172, 178, 179, 180, *187,* 188, 192, 193, 194, 203, 209, 267, 568, 575–576, 578, 596, 597, 598, 601, 602, 768
    at Chickamauga, 134, 137
    death of, 600
    at Pickett's Mill, 165–166
    at Ringgold Gap, 142–144, *143*

Cleydael, Va., 672

Clifton, USS, 612

Clifton House, Va., 746

Clingman, Thomas, 425

Clisby Austin House, Tunnel Hill, Ga., 148

Cloud, William F., 43, 44

Cloyd's Mountain, Battle of, 650, 767–768

Coaling, The, Port Republic, Va., 653, 654

Cobb, Howell, 129, 221–222

Cobb, T.R.R., 668, 669, 671

Cochise, 79

Cockrell, Francis M., 24, 175, 385

Coke-Garrett House, Williamsburg, Va., 761–762

Coker House, Miss., 386

Cold Harbor, Battle of, 600, 654, 703

College Hospital, Chattanooga, Tenn., 579

Collins, Napoleon, 253

Colonel Lovell, CSS, 552

Colonial National Historical Park, Yorktown, Va., 760, 761

Colorado, *448, 449, 450–452*

Colquitt, Alfred, 126

Columbia, S.C., *529,* 530, 532–534

Columbia, Tenn., 595–596

Columbus, Ga., 213–215

Columbus, Ky., 260–261, 402, 545

Columbus-Belmont Battlefield State Park, Columbus, Ky., 261–262, 403

Comfort, Tex., 616

Commodore McDonough, USS, 519

Compromise of 1850, 75

Concord Covered Bridge Historic District, Smyrna area, Ga., 180

Confederacy, 503
    battleflag of, 630
    blockade of, 245
    foreign intervention sought by, 245–247
    "high-water mark" of, *500,* 501
    King Cotton diplomacy of, 246
    ocean raiders used by, 251–253
    political power in, 734–735

Confederate Battery 5, Petersburg, Va., 718–719

Confederate Battery 8, Petersburg, Va., 719

Confederate cemetery, Knoxville, Tenn., 585

Confederate Memorial, Corpus Christi, Tex., 616

Confederate Memorial, Danville, Va., 765

Confederate Memorial Hall, Knoxville, Tenn., 584

Confederate Museum, Biloxi, Miss., 397

Confederate Museum, Hamilton, Bermuda, 256

Confederate Museum, New Orleans, La., 292

Confederate Naval Foundry, Selma, Ala., 10

Confederate Naval Museum, Columbus, Ga., 214

Confederate Stonewall Cemetery, Winchester, Va., 644

Confederate War Memorial, St. Augustine, Fla., 119–120

Congress, Confederate, 312, 612, 734, 738

Congress, U.S., 444, 679, 714, 771

Congress, USS, 752–753, *752,* 754, 757

Congressional Cemetery, Washington, D.C., 61

Congressional Committee on the Conduct of the War, 634

Congressional Medal of Honor, 132, 388, *491,* 523, 710

Connelly, Henry, 89, 97

Constellation, USS, 323
Constitution, U.S., 60
Constitution, USS, 324
Cook, Ferdinand, 226
Cooke, Philip St. George, 697
Cool Springs, Battle of, 638
Cooper, Douglas H., 413–414, 467–469, 470, 471, 474
Cooper's Furnace Historic Site, Allatoona Pass, Ga., 163
Cooper Union, New York, N.Y., 445
"Copperheads," 350
Corbit, Charles, 321
Corbitt, Boston, 672
Corcoran, Michael, 762
Corinth, Miss., 354–358, *354*
Cornwallis, Charles, 760
Corpus Christi, Tex., 609, 615–616
Corrick's Ford, W.Va., 777, 778
Corse, John M., 161–162, 203
Corydon, Ind., 349
Cotton, 296
Cotton Patch Restaurant, Wildersville, Tenn., 561
Couch, Darius N., 482
Courtland, Ala., 4
Court Square, Memphis, Tenn., 554
Cox, Jacob D., 183, 202, 425, 429, 774
Craig County Historical Society, Vinita, Okla., 473
Craney Island, Va., 756–757
Crater, Battle of the, *717,* 719–720
Craven, Thomas A., 113
Craven, Tunis A. M., 18–19
Craven County Visitor Information Center, New Bern, N.C., 427
Cravens House, Lookout Mountain, Tenn., 575, 577
Crawford, Samuel W., 721
Crawford House, Perryville, Ky., 272–273
Crawford-Talmadge Plantation, Lovejoy's Station, Ga., 210
Crawfordville, Ga., 229
Creole, 104
Crittenden, George B., 83, 259, 265–266
Crittenden, John J., 259, 275
Crittenden, Thomas L., 133–134, 135, 137, *138,* 139, 141, *141,* 259, 268, 270, 271, 275, 562, 568, 569
Crocker, Frederick, 610–611, 612
Crook, George, 570, 621, 638, 641, *642,* 645, 647, 650, 655, 742, 745, 767–768, 774
Crosman, Alexander, 109
Cross Keys, Battle of, 653, 654
Crossland, Edward, 9
Cross Lanes, Battle of, 772, 773
Crozier, J. H., 584
Crozier, Va., 693

CSS *Alabama* Commission, Paris, France, 257
CSS *Neuse* State Historic Site, Kinston, N.C., 426
Culpeper Cavalry Museum, Culpeper, Va., 664
Culpeper Tourist Council, Culpeper, Va., 664
Cumberland, USS, 419, 752–753, *752,* 757
Cumberland Church, Farmville, Va., 745, 746
Cumberland County Courthouse, Carlisle, Pa., 483
Cumberland County Historical Society, Carlisle, Pa., 483
Cumberland Gap, Battle of, 592–594
Cumberland Gap National Historic Park, Middlesboro, Ky., *593,* 594
Curtis, Samuel R., 30–32, 33, 35, 41, 410, 412
Cushing, William B., *423,* 424, 434
Custer, George Armstrong, 294, 343–344, 446, 484, 485, 499, *500,* 642, *642,* 645–646, 648, 656–657, 661, 690, 692, 694, 740, 742, 760
Custer State Monument, Steubenville, Ohio, 351
Cynthiana, Ky., 273–274, 282

Dahlgren, John A., 63, 64, 238, 506, 507, 513
Dahlgren, Ulric, 692–694
Dakota Territory, 449, 450
Dallas, Battle of, 166–167
Dallas, Ga., 168–169
Dalton, Ga., 150–151
Dam Number 1 (Burnt Chimneys), Battle of, 760
Dana, Charles A., 372–373, 682–683
Dana, Napoleon Jackson Tecumseh, 610
Dandelion, 238
Dandridge, Battle of, 586
Danville, Va., 765
Danville Museum of Fine Arts and History, Danville, Va., 765
Darien, Ga., 242–243
Dauphin Island Park and Beach Board, Mobile, Ala., 22
David, CSS, 513
Davidson, John W., 43
Davis, Benjamin F. "Grimes," 661, 782
Davis, Charles F., 370
Davis, Charles H., 548, 549–553
Davis, Jefferson C., 31, 33, *136,* 149, 157, 158, 172, 175, 204, *223,* 234, 437, 441
    Nelson affair and, 276–277

Davis, Jefferson F., 11, 30, 85, 113, 149, 199, 207, 210, 218, 231, 253, 275, 292, 294, 295, 353, 355, 363, *376,* 385, 535, 563, 566, 571, 572, 580, 612, 640, 693, 696, 730, 765, 772
    Bread Riot and, 736
    fall of Richmond and, 736–737, 738
    Federals' capture of, 220–221, 527
    Gettysburg Campaign approved by, 480–481
    gravesite of, 739
    imprisonment of, 756, 758
    inaugural address of, *11,* 12
    Johnston relieved by, 185–186, *189*
    last home of, 397
    plantation home of, 376
    political power of, 734–735
    Richmond home of, 734–735, 738
    Toombs and, 230
Davis, Joseph, 376
Davis, Joseph R., *496*
Davis, Varina, 220, 535
Davis's Cross Roads, Chickamauga, Ga., 134, 142
Dawson, John, 429
Day's Gap, Ala., 5–8
Dead Buffalo Lake, Battle of, 463
Dearing, James, 764
Decatur, Ala., 4–5
Decatur, Ga., 185, 191, 195
Declaration of Independence, 60
DeCourcy, John F., 593
Deep Bottom, Va., 711, 719, 721
Deerhound, 255
De Gress, Francis, 192, 194–195, 237–238
DeKalb, USS, 367
Delaware, *442,* 443–444
Denbigh, 614
DeSoto Hill, Rome, Ga., 158
De Soto House, Galena, Ill., 348
Devin, Thomas, *487,* 661, 742
Dexter Niles House, Atlanta, Ga., 189
Dickinson College, Carlisle, Pa., 483
Dickison, John, 111
Dickson-Williams Home, Greeneville, Tenn., 590
Dimmock, Charles H., 716
Dinwiddie Court House, Battle of, 727
Dinwiddie Court House, Va., 728
District of Columbia, *50,* 51–73, *53, 62,* 619
    bridges of, 69
    cemeteries of, 61
    Early's raid on, 66–68, *68,* 139, 326, 330–332, 340, 637
    equestrian statues in, 60
    forts system of, 64–69
    Maryland sites near, 326–328
    Virginia sites near, 621–626
Dix, Dorothea, 61

Dix-Hill cartel, 325
Doaksville, Okla., 472, 474
Dodd, Theodore H., 85, 86–87, 88
Dodge, Grenville M., 4, 6, 178, 179, 193, 194, 195
Dole, George, 686
Doolittle C.S.A. Cemetery, Newton, Miss., 395
Doswell (Hanover Junction), Va., 689
Dot, 387
Doubleday, Abner, 486, *496, 497,* 504
Douglas, Henry Kyd, 784
Douglas, Stephen A., 346, 449
Douglass, Frederick, 61
Dover Hotel, Dover, Tenn., 542
Dowling, Richard, *611,* 612
Downtown Presbyterian Church, Nashville, Tenn., 606
Dranesville, Battle of, 624
Drayton, Percival, *17, 20,* 116, 526
Drayton, Thomas F., 526
Drewry's Bluff, Battle of, 713, 714–715, *714*
Droop Mountain, Battle of, 775–776
Droop Mountain Battlefield Park, W.Va., 776
Dr. Samuel A. Mudd House, Md., 328
Drum Barracks, Wilmington, Calif., 82
Dry Tortugas, Fla., 113
Duffie, Alfred, 635, 661, 775–776
Dug Gap, Ga., 150, 151–152, *151*
Dug Gap Battlefield Park, Dug Gap, Ga., 152
Dug Springs, Mo., 416
Dunham, Cyrus, 560
Du Pont, Henry, 651
Du Pont, Samuel A., 116–117, 118, 120, 237, 240, 507, 511–513, 520, *524,* 525–526, 548

Eads, James B., 345, *374,* 406
Earle, R. G., 159
Early, Jubal A., *62,* 319, 341, 404–405, 479, 482, 483, 487, 488, 494, 603, 651, 671, 675, *676,* 702, 710, 725, 761, 767, 780, 782
  at Cedar Creek, 646–648
  gravesite of, 764
  at Second Kernstown, 638–639
  Shenandoah Valley Campaign and, 641–648
  Washington raid of, 66–68, 139, 326, 330–332, 340, 637
  at Waynesboro, 656–657
East Cavalry Battlefield, Gettysburg, Pa., *500*
East Martello Museum, Key West, Fla., 115
East Point, Ga., 207–208
Eastport, USS, 311–312
Ebenezer Church, Battle of, 9

Ebenezer Creek, Springfield, Ga., 233–234
Edmonds, Sarah Emma, 697–698
VIII Corps, U.S., 647–648
XVIII Corps, U.S., 703, 704, 710
1842 Inn, Macon, Ga., 225
Eisenhower, Dwight D., 33
Eldridge Hotel, Lawrence, Kans., 455
election of 1864, 122, 205, 307, *348, 350,* 703–704
XI Corps, U.S., *487,* 488, *492,* 572, 573, 575, *674,* 676
Elfin, USS, 544
Elizabeth City, N.C., 422
Elizabethtown, Ky., 277
Elkhorn Tavern, Battle of, *see* Pea Ridge
Elkin's Ferry, Ark., 46, 48
Elkwood, Va., 663–664
Ellen, USS, 120
Ellet, Alfred, 552
Ellet, Charles, Jr., 550, 551–552
Ellet, Charles Rivers, 371–372
Elliot, Jonas D., 3
Elliot, Stephen, 506
Ellis, John, 419
Ellsworth, Elmer, 623
Ellsworth, George, 281
Elmwood Cemetery, Memphis, Tenn., 554
Elmwood Cemetery, Shepherdstown, W.Va., 784
Elmwood Inn, Perryville, Ky., 273
Elwood (Lacy House) Wilderness Battlefield, Va., 683–684
Elzey, Arnold, 323
Emancipation Proclamation, 54, *55,* 56, 246, 307, 339, 565
Emory, William H., 310–311, 320, 645, 647
Enon Church (Haw's Shop), Mechanicsville, Va., 704
Epps Mansion, City Point, Va., 732–733
Ericsson, John, 753–754
Essex, USS, 294, 300, 371, 381, *539,* 540
Estevan Hall, Helena, Ark., 42
Etowah Valley Historical Society, Cartersville, Ga., 163
Evangelical Reformed Church, Frederick, Mo., 332
Evans, Beverly D., 226
Evans, Nathan G. "Shanks," 425, 518, 627, 628
Everett, Edward, 500
Evergreen Cemetery, Murfreesboro, Tenn., 567
Ewell, Richard S., 83, 479, 482, 483, 486, *487,* 490, *490,* 494, 598, 606, 633, 640, 641, 652, 653, 656, 659, 680, *681,* 682, 683, 686, 688, 689, 702, 739, 742, 744, 785

Ewell Farm, Spring Hill, Tenn., 598
Ewing, Thomas, 406, 455
Exchange Building, Petersburg, Va., 731
Eyre, Edward E., 79
Ezra Church, Battle of, 199–201

Fagan, James F., 46, 47, 412, 456
Fagan, John S., 405
Fairfax, Va., 624–625
Fairfield, Pa., 501
Fairfield Plantation, Guinea Station, Va., 678
Fair Garden, Battle of, 586–587
Fair Oaks, Marietta, Ga., 177
Fair Oaks National Cemetery, Fair Oaks, Va., 706–707
Fair Oaks (Seven Pines), Battle of, 178, 705–706
Fallen Timbers, Battle of, 558
Falling Waters, Battle of, 340, 341
Farmers Bank, Petersburg, Va., 731
Farmville, Va., 744–747
Farnsworth, Elon, 484, *496,* 499
Farragut, David G., 24, 104, 254, *289, 293*–294, 315, 381, 526, 614
  at Mobile Bay, 13, 14–17, *17,* 19, 20–21
  at New Orleans, 287–290, 292
  Vicksburg Expedition of, 370–371
Far West, *74,* 75–99
Fayetteville, Ark., 29
Fayetteville, N.C., 435–436
Featherston, Winfield, 188
Federal Battery 4, Petersburg, Va., 718
Federal Hill, Baltimore, Md., 322
"Federal Triangle," 60
Fernandina, Fla., 116–118
Fernandina, USS, 237
Ferrero, Edward, 588, 719–720
V Corps, U.S., 272, 337, *490,* 493, 665, 680, 683, 684, 685, *685,* 686, 688, 689, 692, 697, 702–703, 708, 717, 721, 724, 727, 784
XV Corps, 154, 166, 169, 171, 172, *190,* 192, 195, 196, 200–201, 203, 237–238, 314, *378,* 382, 532
54th Massachusetts Colored Infantry, 61, 126, 242, *520,* 521, 522–523, 524, 530
"Fighting McCooks" home, Steubenville, Ohio, 351
Finegan, Joseph, 120, 121, 126, 705
Fingal, 240
Fire House, Harpers Ferry, W.Va., 783
I Corps, U.S., 336, 486, *487,* 488, 682
First Baptist Church, Columbia, S.C., 534
First Methodist Church, Lawrence, Kans., 455
First Presbyterian Church, Fernandina Beach, Fla., 118

First Presbyterian Church, Marietta, Ga., 177
Fisher's Hill, Battle of, 645
Five Forks, Battle of, 727–728, 729
Flandrau State Park, New Ulm, Minn., 461
Flanigan, Harris, 43
Fleetwood Hill, Brandy Station, Va., 661–662, 664
Flick House, Martinsburg, W.Va., 784
Florida, *100*, 101–127
Florida, CSS, 13, 64, 214, 248, 251–253, 256
Floyd, John B., 83, 541, 772–773, 778
Flusser, C. W., 423
Folly Island, S.C., 520, 521, 522
Foote, Andrew H., 513, 538–540, 546–547, 548
Ford, Henry Clay, 73
Ford, James H., 85, 90
Ford, John S., 617
Ford, John T., 71, 73
Ford's Theatre, Washington, D.C., 60, 70–72
Ford's Theatre National Historic Site, Washington, D.C., 73
"Forlorn Hope," 388
Forney, John H., 387
Forrest, Jesse, 3
Forrest, Nathan Bedford, 6, 7, 9, 38–39, 223, 353, 361, 366, 394, 396, 563, 567, 595, 597, 600
    Bragg's confrontation with, 571–572
    at Brices' Cross Roads, 359–360
    at Chickamauga, *136*, 137
    1862 Tennessee raid and, 559–562
    at Fallen Timbers, 558
    Florence raid and, 2–3
    at Fort Donelson, 282, 542
    Fort Pillow Massacre and, 549, 550
    gravesite of, 554
    Johnsonville raid and, 543–545
    Kentucky raids of, 282
    Memphis home of, 554
    Memphis raid and, 553
    at Nashville, 603–605
    at Okolona, 362–363, 364
    Paducah raid of, 262
    at Perryville, 268–269, 271
    Streight's raid and, 5–7, 157, 158
    surrender of, 27
Forrest, William H., 554
Fort Anderson, Paducah, Ky., 262–263
Fort Anderson, Wilmington, N.C., 429, 434
Fort Anderson State Historic Site and Brunswick Town, Winnabow, N.C., 434
Fort A. P. Hill Military Reservation, Port Royal, Va., 672
Fort Baldwin, Va., 729–730

Fort Barrancas, Fla., 102, 103, 104–105
Fort Bartow, Roanoke Island, N.C., 422
Fort Bayard, Washington, D.C., 65
Fort Beauregard, La., 305
Fort Beauregard, St. Phillips Island, S.C., *524*, 525–526, 528
Fort Blakely, Mobile, Ala., 13, 23, 24–25, *25*, 26
Fort Blanchard, Roanoke Island, N.C., 422
Fort Bliss, Tex., 609
Fort Boggs, Savannah, Ga., 241
Fort Bowie National Historic Site, Willcox, Ariz., 80
Fort Brady, Va., 711
Fort Bragg Military Reservation, Fayetteville, N.C., 436
Fort Branch, Hamilton, N.C., 424
Fort Brooke, Tampa, Fla., 112
Fort Bunker Hill, Washington, D.C., 66
Fort Burnham, Va., 711
Fort Butler, Donaldsonville, La., 299
Fort Carroll, Washington, D.C., 65
Fort Caswell, Wilmington, N.C., 429, 434
Fort C. F. Smith, Rosslyn, Va., 621–623
Fort Chaplin, Washington, D.C., 64
Fort Clark, Hatteras Inlet, N.C., 420
Fort Clark, Tex., 616
Fort Clinch, Fernandina, Fla., 116–117
Fort Clinch State Park, Fernandina Beach, Fla., 117–118
Fort Cobun, Grand Gulf, Miss., 376–377, *377*
Fort Craig, Munfordville, Ky., 278, 279
Fort Craig, N.Mex., 85–87, 88
Fort Curtis, Helena, Ark., 41
Fort D, Cape Girardeau, Mo., 403
Fort Darling, Drewry's Bluff, Va., *714*, 715
Fort Davidson, Mo., 405–406
Fort Davidson State Historic Site, Pilot Knob, Mo., 406
Fort Davis, Tex., 81, 609
Fort Davis, Washington, D.C., 65
Fort Defiance, Roanoke Island, N.C., 422
Fort Defiance State Park, Cairo, Ill., 345
Fort Delaware, Delaware City, Del., 443–444, *444*
Fort De Russy, La., 305, 306
Fort De Russy, Washington, D.C., *62*, 65, 66
Fort De Soto Park, Tampa, Fla., 112–113
Fort Dickerson, Knoxville, Tenn., 585
Fort Dix, Va., 762
Fort Donelson, Tenn., 104, 259, 261, 278, 344, 537, 538, 539, 540–542, 546
Fort Donelson National Battlefield, Dover, Tenn., 542

Fort DuPont, Washington, D.C., 65
Fort Early, Lynchburg, Va., 764
Fort Esperanza, Tex., 610
Fort Eustis, Newport News, Va., 758
Fort Fillmore, N.Mex., 84–85
Fort Fisher, Petersburg, Va., 722, 725, 730
Fort Fisher, Wilmington, N.C., 429, 430–434, *431, 432, 433*, 725
Fort Fisher State Historic Site, Kure Beach, N.C., 434
Fort Foote, Md., 326–327
Fort Gadsden State Historic Site, Sumatra, Fla., 108
Fort Gaines, Mobile, Ala., *15*, 16, 17, 21, 22
Fort Gaines Historic Site, Dauphin Island, Ala., 22
Fort Gibson, Okla., 473–474
Fort Gilmer, Phenix City, Ala., 215
Fort Gilmer, Va., 710–711, 712
Fort Granger, Franklin, Tenn., 602
Fort Grebel, Washington, D.C., 65
Fort Gregg, Va., 712, 729–730
Fort Gregg, Washington, D.C., 65
Fort Griffin, Sabine Pass, Tex., 611–612, *611*
Fort Harrison, Va., 710–711, 712, 721
Fort Haskell, Petersburg, Va., 726
Fort Hatteras, Hatteras Inlet, N.C., 420
Fort Heiman, Tenn., 540, 544
Fort Henry, Tenn., 104, 259, 261, 344, 538–540, 544
Fort Higginson, Jacksonville, Fla., 123
Fort Hill, Dalton, Ga., 151
Fort Hill, Vicksburg, Miss., 375, 392
Fort Hindman, Ark., 39, 40, *40*
Fort Hoke, Va., 712
Fort Howell, Beaufort, S.C., 527
Fort Huger, Roanoke Island, N.C., 422
Fort Huger, Va., 762
Fort Humbug Memorial Park, Shreveport, La., 314
Fort Huntington Smith, Knoxville, Tenn., 585
Fort Jackson, Port Sulphur, La., 286, *286*, 288, 290, 291
Fort Jackson, Rome, Ga., 157
Fort Jackson, Savannah, Ga., 241–242
Fort Jefferson, Dry Tortugas, Fla., 113, 114, 115, 328
Fort Johnson, Johnsonville, Tenn., 544
Fort Johnson, S.C., 504, 519, 520, 521
Fort Johnson, Va., 712
Fort Lamar, James Island, S.C., 518, 521
Fort Leavenworth, Kans., 455
Fort Lincoln Park, Washington, D.C., 66
Fort Lookout, Camden, Ark., 48
Fort Lyon, Colo., 452
Fort McAllister, Ga., 237–238, *238*

Fort McAllister Historic Park, Richmond Hill, Ga., 238–239
Fort McCausland, Lynchburg, Va., 764
Fort McCulloch, Caddo, Okla., 474
Fort McDermott, Ala., 25
Fort McHenry National Monument and Historic Shrine, Baltimore, Md., 323
Fort McIntosh, Mobile, Ala., 14
Fort McNair, Washington, D.C., 62
Fort Macon, Morehead City, N.C., 427–428
Fort Macon State Park, Atlantic Beach, N.C., 428
Fort McPherson, Ga., 208
Fort McRee, Fla., 102, 103
Fort Magruder, Williamsburg, Va., 761
Fort Mahan, Washington, D.C., 64
Fort Mahone, Petersburg, Va., *729,* 730, 731
Fort Marcy, Arlington, Va., 621
Fort Marion, St. Augustine, Fla., 118
Fort Marshall, Sullivan's Island, S.C., 509
Fort Mason, San Francisco, Calif., 82–83
Fort Massachusetts, Ship Island, Miss., 397
Fort Mitchel, S.C., 528
Fort Monroe, Old Point Comfort, Va., 751, 755–758
Fort Morgan, Mobile, Ala., *15,* 16, 18, 19, 20, *20,* 23
Fort Morton, Va., 720
Fort Moultrie, Charleston, S.C., 504, 507, 508, *508,* 509, 512, 513
Fort Negley, Nashville, Tenn., 606
Fort Nelson, Portsmouth, Va., 756
Fort Norfolk, Norfolk, Va., 757
Fort Pemberton, Greenwood, Miss., 365, 367
Fort Pickens, Fla., 101, 102, 103, 104–106, *106*
Fort Pike State Commemorative Area, La., 292–293
Fort Pillow, Tenn., 293, 370, 548–552
massacre at, 408, *549,* 550
Fort Pillow State Historic Site, Henning, Tenn., 551
Fort Point National Historic Site, San Francisco, Calif., 83
Fort Powell, Mobile, Ala., 16, 17, 21
Fort Pulaski, Cockspur Island, Ga., 234–236, *235,* 239
Fort Pulaski National Monument, Cockspur Island, Ga., 236
Fort Quitman, Tex., 609
Fort Raleigh National Historic Site, Manteo, N.C., 422
Fort Reno, Washington, D.C., 65, 66
Fortress Rosecrans, Murfreesboro, Tenn., 603–604

Fort Rice, N.Dak., 464
Fort Ricketts, Washington, D.C., 65
Fort Ridgely, Minn., 459
Fort Ridgely State Park, Fairfax, Minn., 461
Fort St. Catherine, St. George, Bermuda, 256
Fort St. Philip, La., 286, *286,* 288
Fort Sanders, Knoxville, Tenn., 583–584
Fort Scott National Historic Site, Fort Scott, Kans., 457–458
Fort Sedgwick, Petersburg, Va., 730–731
Fort Sherman, Beaufort, S.C., 527
Fort Sill Military Reservation, Lawton, Okla., 474–475
Fort Slocum, Washington, D.C., *62,* 66
Fort Slocum Park, Washington, D.C., 68
Fort Smith, Ark., 29, 38, 43, 44, 45
Fort Smith National Historic Site, Fort Smith, Ark., 37–38
Fort Snelling, Minneapolis, Minn., 461
Fort Southerland, Camden, Ark., 48
Fort Stanley, Knoxville, Tenn., 585
Fort Stanton, Washington, D.C., 65
Fort Star, Morgan City, La., 297
Fort Stedman, Petersburg, Va., *717,* 724–726
Fort Stevens, Va., 714
Fort Stevens, Battle of, 52, *62,* 66–69, *68*
Lincoln's visit to, 67–69
Fort Stevens, Washington, D.C., *62,* 66
Fort Stovall, Rome, Ga., 157, 158
Fort Sully, Kans., 455
Fort Sumter, S.C., 29, 57, 103, 419, 503, 504–507, *506,* 512, 515, *516,* 521, 524, 619
walking tour of, 508–509
Fort Sumter National Monument, Charleston, S.C., 508
Fort Sumter Tours, Inc., Charleston, S.C., 508
Fort Tejon State Historic Park, Calif., 82
Fort Totten, Washington, D.C., *62,* 66
Fort Towson, Okla., 474
Fort Tyler, West Point, Ga., 212–213
Fort Union National Monument, Watrous, N.Mex., 96
Fort Wade, Grand Gulf, Miss., 376, 377, *377*
Fort Wagner, Morris Island, S.C., 515, *520,* 522–523
Fort Walker, Atlanta, Ga., 197
Fort Walker, Hilton Head Island, S.C., *524,* 525–526, 527
Fort Walker, Petersburg, Va., 730, 732
Fort Ward, Alexandria, Va., *621,* 622
Fort Ward Museum and Historic Site, Alexandria, Va., 623–624
Fort Washington, Md., 327

Fort Welles, Hilton Head Island, S.C., 527
Fort William, St. Marks, Fla., 108, 109
Fort Wool, Va., 758
Fort Zachary Taylor, Key West, Fla., 113–114
Fort Zachary Taylor State Historic Site, Key West, Fla., 114
Foster, Emory S., 411
Foster, John C., 238, 240
Foster, John G., 421, 425, 519, 528–529
Foster, John W., 590
IV Corps, 154, 156, 184, 199, 208, 588, 595, 596, 705
XIV Corps, U.S., 133, 134, 147, 156, 170, 203, 204, 232, 233–234, 437
Fox, Gustavus, 287, 505, 512
Frampton's Plantation, Battle of, 528
France, 266
Mexico and, 247–248, 298, 308, 609
U.S. Civil War and, 245–246
Frankfort, Ky., 274–275
Frankfort Cemetery, Frankfort, Ky., 275
Frankfort State Arsenal, Frankfort, Ky., 275
Frank Kemper Home, Port Republic, Va., 654
Franklin, Battle of, 538, 599–600, *599, 601,* 612
Franklin, William B., 298–299, 305, 309, 333–334, 337, 611, 667–670, *667,* 708
Frassanito, William A., *493*
Frayser's Farm (Glendale), Battle of, 707, 708
Frazer, John W., 593–594
Frederick, Md., 329–330
Frederick County Courthouse, Winchester, Va., 643
Frederick Douglass House National Historic Site, Washington, D.C., 61
Fredericksburg, Battle of, 666–670, *666, 667, 670, 671,* 677
Fredericksburg, Va., 56, 298, 480, 567, 582, 584, 666, 670–672, 688
Fredericksburg and Spotsylvania County Battlefields Memorial National Military Park, Va.:
Chancellorsville unit of, 677–678
Fredericksburg unit of, 670–672
Spotsylvania area and, 686–687
Wilderness unit of, 683–684
Fredericksburg Battlefield Visitor Center, Fredericksburg, Va., 670–671
Fredericksburg National Cemetery, Fredericksburg, Va., 671
Frémont, John C., 260, 399–400, *400,* 406, 410, 652–656, 657, 696

French, Samuel G., 157, 161–163, 169, 172, 188
French, William H., 337, 665
Fritchie, Barbara, 332
Front Royal, Battle of, 640, 643
Fry, Speed, 265
Fuller, John W., 193, 560
Fuller, William A., 131, 132, 133, 161, 180
Fulton Industries, Atlanta, Ga., 198, *207*

Gable, Clark, *194*
Gadsden, James, 108
Gaines, CSS, 16, 19
Gaines's Mill, Battle of, 700, 706
Gainesville, Ala., 27
Galena, Ill., 346–348, *347*
Galena, USS, 715
Gallatin, Tenn., 607
Gallego Flour Mills, Richmond, Va., *735*
Galveston, Tex., 13, 609, 613–615
Gamble Plantation State Historic Site, Ellenton, Fla., 113
Gamble's Hill Park, Richmond, Va., 738
Gano, Richard, 472
Gardner, Alexander, *54, 336, 489, 493,* 688
Gardner, Franklin, 302
Garfield, James A., 264, 579
Garis, Conrad, 273
Garland, Samuel, 334
Garnett, Richard S., 80–81, *496*
Garnett, Robert S., 777, 778
Garrard, Kenner, 166, 179, 182, 184, 191, 198, 200, 221, 222
Garthright House, Va., 704
Gathland State Park, Md., 334
Gault House, Louisville, Ky., 277
Gayoso Hotel, Memphis, Tenn., 554
Geary, John W., 151–152, 155–156, 165, *187,* 188, 240–241, 572–573
General Bragg, CSS, 549
General Earl Van Dorn, CSS, 549, 552
General Grant National Memorial, New York, N.Y., 445
General Lewis Inn, Lewisburg, W.Va., 774, 775
General Order No. 11, 406, 455
General Sterling Price, CSS, 549
General Sumter, CSS, 549
General Sweeny's Museum, Republic, Mo., 417
George Sturgess, 374
Georgetown, S.C., 511
George Washington Birthplace National Monument, Va., 672
Georgia, *128,* 129–243
Georgia, CSS, 240, 242

Georgia Department of Archives and History, Atlanta, Ga., 207
Georgia Military Institute, Marietta, Ga., 177
Georgia Museum of Industry and Trade, Atlanta, Ga., 207
Georgia State Capitol, Atlanta, Ga., *206,* 207
Geronimo, 106, 475
Getty, George W., 647, 680
Gettysburg, Battle of, 163, 246, 340, 477–478, 480, *487, 490, 493, 500*
  Big Round Top in, 491, 496, *496*
  Cemetery Hill in, 488, *490,* 491, *492,* 494, 497, 498, *500,* 501
  Culp's Hill in, 488, *490,* 491, 494–495, 497
  Devil's Den in, *489, 490,* 494
  Evergreen Cemetery and, 488, 500, 501
  first day of, 485–489
  Little Round Top in, *490,* 491, *491,* 492–494, 498
  onset of, 485–486
  Peach Orchard in, *490,* 491, *492,* 494
  Pickett's Charge in, *496, 497,* 498–499, 501, 576, 600
  second day of, 489–497
  third day of, 497–499
  Wheatfield in, *490,* 494
Gettysburg Address, *498,* 500–501
Gettysburg Cyclorama, *497,* 501
Gettysburg National Cemetery, Gettysburg, Pa., 501
Gettysburg National Military Park, Gettysburg, Pa., vii, *499,* 501
Gibbon, John, 495, *496,* 630, *667,* 669, 671, 729–730, 747, *747*
Gibson, St. Pierre, 321
Gilbert, Charles, 268, 269
Gilbert-Alexander House, Washington, Ga., 230
Gillem, Alvan C., 589
Gillmore, Quincy A., 67, 121, 122, 124–125, 235, 506, 508, 515, 519, 520, 522–523, 713
Gist, States Rights, 204
Glasgow, Mo., 409
Glendale (Frayser's Farm), Battle of, 707, 708
Globe Tavern, Battle of, 721, 723, 724
Glorieta, Battle of, 89–94, *91,* 95, 96, 451
Glory (film), 242, 524
Glover House, Marietta, Ga., 177
Golden Gate National Recreation Area, Calif., 82–83
Golding's Farm, Battle of, 706
Goldsborough, Louis M., 421
Gone With the Wind (film), *194,* 207
Gone With the Wind (Mitchell), 210

Goode's Bridge, Va., 741
Gordon, James, 141
Gordon, John B., 129, 197, *197,* 207, 332, 638, *646, 647,* 648, *681,* 682, 725–726, 742–743, 744, 746, 747
Gordon-Lee Mansion, Chickamauga, Ga., 141
Gorgas, Josiah, 230
Gould, Wills, 596
Govan, Daniel, 165–166, 204, 209
Government House, Nassau, Bahamas, 256
Government House, St. Augustine, Fla., 119
Governor Milton, CSS, 121
Governor Moore, 289
Governor's Green, Columbia, S.C., 534
Governor's Mansion, Jackson, Miss., 384
Gowen, George W., 731
Gowen Monument, Petersburg, Va., 731
Grace Episcopal Church, Plymouth, N.C., 424
Grace Episcopal Church, Port Republic, Va., 654
Granbury, Hiram, 165, 166, 601
Grand Army of the Republic Union Monument, Greeneville, Tenn., 590
Grand Coteau, La., 298–299
Grand Gulf, Miss., 376–377, *377*
Grand Gulf Military Monument, Port Gibson, Miss., 377
Granger, Gordon, *15,* 17, 21, 23–24, 138, *138,* 273, 574
Granger, Robert, 3
Granite City, USS, 612
Grant, Julia Dent, 71, 407, 445
Grant, Lemuel P., 197
Grant, Ulysses S., 8–9, 25, 54, 60, 61, 67, 81, 104, 143, 146, 205, 259, 292, 294, 298, 302, 330, 343, 350, 353, 400, *402,* 432, 478, 537, 548, 553, 559, 561, 568, 580, 582, 583, 584, 595, 600, 609, *644,* 651, 657, 667–668, 673, 756
  Alabama operations and, 8–9, 13, 23, 24
  alleged alcoholism of, 372–373, 570–571
  Appomattox Campaign and, 745–749
  Arkansas operations and, 38–40, 42
  Atlanta Campaign and, 144, 145, 150
  at Belmont, 402
  Cairo headquarters of, 345
  at Chattanooga, 572–576, *574*
  Chesnut on, 571

at Cold Harbor, 703
Corinth-Iuka engagement and, 354 357
Crater Battle and, 719–720
Dana on, 372–373
1864 Virginia Campaign and, 679, 679, 702–704, 710, 712–714, 767
First Vicksburg Campaign and, 314, 315, 317, 358–359, 363–364
at Fort Donelson, 540–542, 545
at Fort Henry, 538–540, 544, 545
Galena home of, 344, 347–348
grave of, 445
"Hardscrabble" home of, 407
Johnston's surrender and, 441
Kentucky operations and, 260–261, 262, 263
Lee's surrender to, 212, 440–441, 745–749
Lincoln and, 71, 372, 570–571, 679, 682–683, 731–732, 733
named General-in-Chief, 679
at North Anna, 688–689
Petersburg Campaign and, 716–718, 721, 724, 725, 727, 728, 730, 731–732, 733, 734
Second Vicksburg Campaign and, 39–40, 41, 364–365, 367, 368–369, 372–374, 376–380, 382–383, 385, 386–388, 390–391, 392, 394, 641–643, 645
at Shiloh, 555–558, 556
at Spotsylvania, 684–686, 685, 687, 688
Thomas's Nashville offensive and, 603–605
at Wilderness, 679–683, 681
Grant House, Chattanooga, Tenn., 579
Grant Memorial, Washington, D.C., 54
Grant Park, Atlanta, Ga., 197
Grant's March Through Louisiana—A Tour, 316
"Grant's Tomb," New York, N.Y., 445
Graveyard Hill, Helena, Ark., 42
Graydon, Paddy, 97
Great Britain, 266, 446
    Confederate navy and, 248
    Trent Affair and, 249
    U.S. Civil War and, 245–246
"Great Cavalry Raid," 210–212, 221–222
Great Falls Tavern, Potomac, Md., 341
"Great Locomotive Chase," 131–132, 132, 144, 148, 161, 197
Greeley, Horace, 58
Green, Israel, 781
Green, Tom, 87, 88, 91, 97–98, 296–297, 299, 309, 311, 312, 613
Greenbrier Public Library, Lewisburg, W.Va., 775

Greene, George S., 495
Greene, S. Dana, 755
Greeneville, Tenn., 589–590
Greenhill Cemetery, Martinsburg, W.Va., 784–785
Greenhow, Rose O'Neal, 61, 429
Green-Meldrim House, Savannah, Ga., 241
Green Mount Cemetery, Baltimore, Md., 323
Greenville Expedition, 366
Gregg, David, 496, 499, 500, 635, 660, 661–662, 665, 721, 722, 724
Gregg, John, 382, 383, 710
Gregg, Maxcy, 534
Grenada, Miss., 363–364
Grevemberg House, Franklin, La., 297
Grierson, Benjamin H., 294, 360, 361, 394, 395, 554
Grierson's Raid, 294, 394–395, 554
Grigsby, Warren, 152–153
Groveton, Battle of, 630
Groveton Confederate Cemetery, Manassas Battlefield, Va., 632
Guide to Historic Beaufort, A, 528
Guide to the Campaign & Siege of Vicksburg, A, 386
Guinea Station, Va., 678
Gulf Islands National Seashore, 104, 106, 107
Gurney, William, 519

Hagerstown, Md., 340–341
Hagood, Johnson, 425, 429
Hale Street Inn, Rogersville, Tenn., 591
Hall, Robert H., 88, 89
Halleck, Henry W., 60, 81, 205, 298, 353, 355–356, 357, 538, 548, 556, 568, 611, 666, 668, 679, 696, 715
Hall of Valor, New Market, Va., 651–652
Hallowell, Edward N., 523
Hall's Rifle Works, Harpers Ferry, W.Va., 783
Hamilton, Andrew Jackson, 613
Hamilton House, Dalton, Ga., 151
Hamilton Library Association, Carlisle, Pa., 483
Hampton, Wade, 435, 436, 437, 500, 532, 534, 661, 693, 702, 721, 722
Hampton-Preston Mansion, Columbia, S.C., 534
Hampton Roads Naval Museum, Norfolk, Va., 757
Hancock, Winfield Scott, 81, 82, 492, 494, 497, 680, 681–682, 685–686, 685, 688, 689, 706, 710, 718, 721, 722, 760, 761
Hanging Rock, Battle of, 767
Hanover, Pa., 484–485, 484

Hanover Area Historical Society, Hanover, Pa., 485
Hanover County Parks, Va., 689
Hardee, William J., 11, 129, 148, 150, 154, 156, 158–159, 168, 169, 178, 185–186, 187, 188, 190, 191–192, 195, 199, 201, 203–204, 208, 210, 231, 239, 240, 269, 271, 275, 435, 436–437, 439, 529, 530, 532, 557, 569
Hardee, Willie, 439
Hardin, Martin D., 119
"Hardscrabble" (Grant home), 407
Harper House, Newton Grove, N.C., 439, 440
Harpers Ferry, W.Va., 772, 781–782, 781
Harpers Ferry Cemetery, Harpers Ferry, W.Va., 784
Harpers Ferry National Historical Park, Harpers Ferry, W.Va., 783–784
Harper's Weekly, 247, 454
Harraden, Henry, 220
Harriet Lane, USS, 614
Harris, Clara, 71
Harris House, Spotsylvania, Va., 687
Harrison, Benjamin, 188
Harrison, William Henry, 709
Harrisonburg, Battle of, 652
Harrison House, Franklin, Tenn., 602
Harrison's Creek, Petersburg, Va., 726
Harrogate, Tenn., 594
Hart County Historical Society, Munfordville, Ky., 279
Hartford, USS, 17, 18, 19–21, 22, 63, 287, 289, 301, 302
Hart House, Rich Mountain, W.Va., 778
Hartranft, John F., 726
Hartsfield, Major, 194
Harvest Moon, USS, 238
Hascall, Milo, 169, 202
Hatch, Edward, 604
Hatch, John P., 519, 529
Hatcher's Run, Battle of, 717, 724
Hatchie Bridge action, 554–555
Hatteras, USS, 253
Hatteras Inlet, N.C., 419–420, 524
Hatteras Island Visitor Center, Manteo, N.C., 420
Hawes, Richard, 274–275
Hawkins, John P., 24
Hawkins Zouave Monument, Sharpsburg, Md., 339
Haw's Shop, Battle of, 702, 704
Hay, John, 122
Hayes, Rutherford B., 638, 773
Hay House, Macon, Ga., 225
Hays, Harry T., 492, 494, 496
Hazel Grove, Chancellorsville, Va., 678

Hazen, William B., 165, 179, *223*, 237–238, 569
Hébert, Louis, 32
Helen, Ark., 33, 35, 40–42
Helm, Ben Hardin, 277
Hendley Row, Galveston, Tex., 615
Henricus Historical Park, Henrico, Va., 713
Henry, Guy V., 124
Henry, Joseph, 61
Henry, Judith, 628, 630, 632
Henry, Patrick, 737
Henry Hill, Manassas Battlefield Park, Va., 628–629, 632
Herndon, William, 345
Herold, David, 61, 72, 672
Herrod, John, 167
Herron, Francis J., 36–37, 367
Hessian Barracks, Frederick, Md., 332
Hessian Guardhouse, Carlisle, Pa., 482
Heth, Henry, 485, 486, 487, *487*, 721, 774, 780
Hicks, Stephen G., 263
Higgins, Thomas H., 388
High Bridge, Farmville, Va., 744–745, 746
Hill, Ambrose Powell, 338, 339, 479, 486, 488, 494, 497, 633, 636, 676, 680–681, *681*, 688, 689, 699, 700, 708, 721, 730
   death of, 729, 730
Hill, Benjamin, 207
Hill, Daniel H., 136–137, 334, 335, 336–338, 435, 699, 702, 706
Hill, Joshua, 229
Hillsman Farm, Sailor's Creek, Va., 742, 743, *743*
Hilton Head Island, S.C., 527
Hilton Head Plantation, S.C., 528
Hindman, Thomas C., 35, 36, 37, 41, 134, 247, *247*
Hines, John, 220
Historic Beaufort Foundation, Beaufort, S.C., 528
Historic New Orleans Collection, New Orleans, La., 292
Hobby, A. M., 615
Hobson, Edward H., 274, 282
Hodgenville Courthouse, Hodgenville, Ky., 277
Hog Mountain, Ala., 6
Hoke, Robert F., 423, 425, 429, 438, 704
Holliday Lake State Park, Va., 746
Hollyday House, Washington, N.C., 424
Holly Springs, Miss., 358–359, 364, 368–369
Hollywood Cemetery, Richmond, Va., 739
Holmes, Oliver Wendell, Jr., 67, 338–339

Holmes, Theophilus, 33, 36, 37, 41, 43, 295, 699, 708
Homestead Act (1862), 54
Honey Hill, Battle of, 528–530
Honey Springs, Battle of, 471, 474
Hood, John Bell, 9, 132, 137, *173*, 187, 188, *189*, 199, 200–201, 210, 215, 218, 292, 336, 404, 446, *490*, 492, 543, 544, 572, 599, *599*, 607, 700, 702
   in Atlanta Campaign, 148–149, 150, 154–155, 158–159, 160, 162, 163, 165, 166, 169, 171, 172, 178, 179, 180
   Atlanta evacuation and, 204–205
   at Columbia, 595–596
   Johnston replaced by, 185–186, *189*
   at Jonesboro, 202–203
   at Nashville, 602–605
   at Spring Hill, 597–598
Hooker, Joseph, 151, 154–155, 158–159, 160, *164*, 165, 169, 171, 179, 186, 199, 336, 337, 481, 567, 571, 631, 641, 659, 665, *674*, 690, 709, 761
   Burnside replaced by, 672–673
   at Chancellorsville, 675–678
   at Fredericksburg, *667*, 668–670, 671
   at Ringgold, 142–143
Hoover's Gap, Tenn., 567–568
Horace L. Hunley, CSS, 510, 517
Horseshoe Bend, Battle of, 469
Horse Soldiers, The (film), 395, 554
Hotchkiss, Thomas, 154, 155
Housatonic, USS, 510, 511
Hovey, Alvin, 385
Howard, Oliver O., 144, 149, 154, 155, 159, 161, 165, 172, 178, 179, 186, 188, 199, 200, 203–204, 208, *223*, 237, 436, 437, *438*, 439, 487–488, 530–531, 575, 633, *674*, 676
Huger, Benjamin, 323, 699, 708
Humphrey, Andrew A., 742, 744, 745, 746, 747
Hunley, Horace L., 510
Hunt, Henry, *487*
Hunter, David, 330, 512, 518, 628, 638, 651, 655, 690, 765, 766–767
Hunter, Sherod, 76–77, 78, 81
Hunter-Dawson State Historic Site, New Madrid, Md., 401
Hunt Morgan House, Lexington, Ky., 273
Hupp Hill, Strasburg, Va., 646
Hurlbut, Stephen, 394, 553, 554, 555

Idaho, *448*, 452–453
Illinois, *342*, 344–348
Illinois Memorial, Vicksburg, Miss., *393*
Imboden, John D., 340, 649–650, 655

Imperial, 303
Independence, Mo., 411
Indiana, *342*, 343, 348–349
Indianola, USS, 372
Ingersoll, Robert G., 560, 561
Intelligent Whale, 63–64
Iowa, 449, 450
Iowa Reservation, Chattanooga, Tenn., 579
Iowa Reservation, Rossville, Ga., 141
Irish Bend, Battle of, 296
I Rode with Stonewall (Douglas), 784
Iroquois, USS, 293
Irving Block Prison, Memphis, Tenn., 553
Irwinville, Ga., 220–221
Isaac P. Smith, USS, 518
Island Number 10, Tenn., 261, 401, 537, 545–547
Itasca, 288–289
Iuka, Battle of, 356–357, 358
Iverson, Alfred, 205, 209–210, 222
Ivy Mountain, Battle of, 263, 264

Jackson, Alfred E., 768
Jackson, Andrew, 469, 619
Jackson, Claiborne Fox, 399, 414–415
Jackson, CSS, 213–214
Jackson, Miss., 382–385, *384*
Jackson, Tenn., 559–560, 561
Jackson, Thomas Jonathan "Stonewall," 296, 325, 329, 332, *495*, 595, 625, 634–629, *629*, 636, *639*, 643, 652, 668, 669, 671, 683, 698, 739, 774, 782, 783, 784
   at Antietam, 334–336
   at Cedar Mountain, 657–658
   at Chancellorsville, *674*, 675–678
   at Cross Keys, 653
   death of, 676–677
   equestrian statue of, 632
   at First Kernstown, 637–638
   gravesite of, 766
   Lexington home of, 765–766
   at McDowell, 655–656
   at Port Republic, 653–654
   at Second Manassas, 630–631
   in Seven Days' Battles, 699, 700, 702, 706, 708, 709
   shrine to, 678
   sobriquet of, 628
   Valley Campaign of, 637–638, 640–641, *641*, 652–656
Jackson, William H., 166, 169, 200, 203, 595
Jackson, William L., 775
Jackson County Civil War Museum, Westport, Mo., 413
Jacksonville, Fla., 116–118, 120–123
Jacksonville Maritime Museum, Jacksonville Landing, Fla., 123

Jacksonville Museum of Science and
    History, Jacksonville, Fla., 123
James, Frank, 282, 454
James, Jesse, 408
James Island, Charleston, S.C., 504,
    518, 519
James Robinson House, Manassas
    Battlefield, Va., 632
Jefferson, Thomas, 693
Jefferson, Thomas Garland, *650*
Jefferson Barracks Historical Park, St.
    Louis, Mo., 407
Jefferson Davis Memorial Park,
    Irwinville, Ga., 221
Jefferson Davis State Historic Site,
    Fairview, Ky., 279
Jefferson National Expansion
    Memorial, St. Louis, Mo., 407
Jenkins, Albert, 767–768
Jenkins, Micah, 572–573, 581, 583, 706
Jenkins' Ferry, Ark., 29
Jenkins' Ferry Monument State Park,
    Ark., 49
Jericho Mill, Va., 689
Jetersville, Va., 740–741, *740*
J. M. Chapman, 83
John B. Gordon Hall, Lafayette, Ga., 142
John Neal House, Atlanta, Ga., 207
John's Island, S.C., 518–519
Johnson, Andrew, 53, 72, 115, 328
    home of, 589, 590
Johnson, Bradley T., 326, 480, 780
Johnson, Bushrod R., 137, 606, 728, 742
Johnson, Edward, 494, 641, 656, 686,
    773–774, 779–780
Johnson, Richard W., 201
Johnsonville, Tenn., 543–545
Johnston, Albert Sidney, 80–81, 259,
    261, 282, 355, 357, 541, *555,
    556,* 557, 559
    death of, 557
Johnston, Joseph E., 9, 13, 181, *181,*
    184, 191, 210, 302, 323, 360,
    367, 382, 383, 385, 386, 390,
    391, 435, 531, 566, 600, 619,
    637, 679, 694–695, 705–706,
    725, 739, 746, 760, 762
    Atlanta Campaign and, 132,
    145–146, *145,* 150, 152,
    153–156, 157, 158–161, 163,
    165–167, 169, 171, *173,* 174,
    177–180
    at Bentonville, 436–441
    Hood's replacement of, 185–186,
    189
    surrender of, 440–441
Johnston's River Line, 178–180, 181
John Wesley Methodist Church,
    Lewisburg, W.Va., 775
John Wright Stanley House, New Bern,
    N.C., 427

Jones, Catesby ap Roger, 10–11, 753
Jones, Samuel, 590, 591
Jones, William E., 499, 651, 655, 661
Jones, Willy, 445
Jonesboro, Battle of, 202–204
Jonesboro, Ga., 208–209
Joseph R. Brown State Wayside, Minn.,
    462
Josiah Bell, CSS, 611
J. R. Williams, 472
Juárez, Benito, 248
Judah, 103, 105
Judah, Henry M., 159, 177

Kanawha Canal Locks, Richmond, Va.,
    738
Kansas, *448,* 449–450, 453–454
Kansas-Nebraska Act (1854), 449
Kautz, August V., 712, 723
Kearny, Philip, 621, 625–626, 631, 705,
    709, 761
Kearsage, USS, 63, 254–255, *254,
    257*
Keene, Laura, 71
Kell, John McIntosh, 243, 254, 255
Kelley, Benjamin F., 776
Kelley, David C., 604
Kelly, John H., 165, 602
Kelly's Ford, Battle of, 658–659, *658,*
    663, 665
Kemper, James L., *496*
Kennesaw, Ga., 131–132
Kennesaw Civil War Museum,
    Kennesaw, Ga., 132–133
Kennesaw House, Marietta, Ga., 176,
    176
Kennesaw Mountain, Battle of,
    170–174, *173, 174*
Kennesaw Mountain National
    Battlefield Park, Kennesaw, Ga.,
    170, 174–175
Kentucky, 2, *258,* 259–283
    Confederate cavalry raids into,
    280–283
    1862 campaign in, 266–273
Kentucky Historical Society, Frankfort,
    Ky., 275
Kentucky Military History Museum,
    Frankfort, Ky., 275
Keokuk, USS, 512, 513, 517
Kernstown, First Battle of, 637–638,
    639, 652
Kernstown, Second Battle of, 479,
    638–639, 780
Kershaw, Joseph, 642, 670, 704, 742
Key, Francis Scott, 60, 323, 332
Keystone State, USS, 511
Key West, CSS, 544
Key West, Fla., 113–115
Key West Lighthouse Museum, Key
    West, Fla., 115
Killdeer Mountain, Battle of, 464

Killdeer Mountain Battlefield Historic
    Site, Dickey County, N.Dak.,
    464–465
Kilpatrick, H. Judson, 154, 202, 205,
    209–210, 224–226, 231,
    232–233, 237, 242, 340, 435,
    436, 484, 485, *496,* 499,
    530–531, 533, 635, 636, 662,
    690, 692
King and Queen Court House,
    Walkerton, Va., 693–694
Kingston, Ga., 159–160
Kinney Stockade, Corpus Christi, Tex.,
    616
Kinston, N.C., 425–426
Kirkland, William W., 784
Kittredge, John W., 615–616
Knob Creek Farm, Hodgenville, Ky., 277
Knoxville, Tenn., 143, 571, 580–584,
    592
Kolb, Valentine, 171
Kolb Farm, Battle of, 170–171, 174
Kurtz, Wilbur, *132,* 133
Kurtz Cultural Center, Winchester, Va.,
    644

Lackawanna, USS, 20–21
Lacy House, Fredericksburg, Va., 672
Lafayette, Ga., 142
LaGrange, Oscar, 212
LaGrange, Tenn., 554
Lake Providence, La., 314–315
Lamb, William, 430, 433
Lane, James, 454–455
Lane, James H., *496*
Lanier, Sidney C., 225
Lanier Cottage, Macon, Ga., 225
Latané, William, 699
Laurel Hill, W.Va., 777, 778
Laurel Hill Cemetery, Philadelphia, Pa.,
    694
Law, Evander M., 492, 494, *496,* 572,
    573, 700
Lawler, Michael, 388
Lawrence Massacre, 454–455, *454*
Ledlie, James, 689, 720
Lee, Albert, 309–310
Lee, Fitzhugh, 642, 658, 684, 702–703,
    727, 728, 739, 743, 744, 745, 747
Lee, G. W. "Custis," 742
Lee, Robert E., 9, 13, 21, 25, 56, 116,
    146, 171, 178, 185, 267, 292,
    319, 329, 333, 340, 341, 363,
    404, 435, 462, 478, 537, 567,
    568, 602, 619, 623, 625, 630,
    634, 635, 636, *639,* 640, 641,
    649, 651, 654, 659, 668, *695,*
    697, 699, 702–704, 706, 738,
    757–758, 762–763, 765, 767
    at Antietam, 334–335, 337–338, 339,
    782, 784
    in Appomattox Campaign, 739–743

Lee, Robert E. (*continued*)
  birthplace of, 672
  Brandy Station Battle and, 659–660,
    663
  at Bristoe Station, 632–633
  at Cedar Mountain, 657–658
  at Chancellorsville, *674,* 675–677,
    678
  Fort Stedman assault and, 725–726
  Gettysburg Campaign and, 479,
    480–482, 484, *497*
  gravesite of, 766
  Harpers Ferry raid and, 781–782
  at Malvern Hill, 708–709
  Mine Run Line and, 664–665
  monument to, 739
  at North Anna, 688
  Petersburg Campaign and, 716–717,
    718, 727, 728
  Petersburg sites associated with, 732
  at Port Royal, 525–526
  prewar house of, 621
  Seven Days' Battles and, 708–709
  at Spotsylvania, 684–685
  surrender of, 70, 212, 440–441,
    745–749
  at West Point, 446
  in West Virginia, 772, 778–779
  at Wilderness, 680–681, *681,* 684
Lee, Stephen Dill, 199, 200–201, 203,
    204, 361, 385, 446, 595–596,
    597, 604, 605
Lee, William H. F. "Rooney," 660, *660,*
    661, 662, 723, 740
Lee and Gordon's Mill, Ga., 141, *141*
Lee Chapel, Lexington, Va., 766
Lee Drive, Fredericksburg, Va., 671
Lee House, Richmond, Va., 738
Lee-Jackson Foundation, 656
Lee-Jackson Memorial, Baltimore, Md.,
    323
Lee Memorial Park, Petersburg, Va.,
    732
Leggett, Mortimer, 192
Leigh, Vivian, *194*
Leighton, Ala., 6
Leister, Lydia A., 488, *489*
Leslie's, 247
Letcher, John, 765
Lewis, Joseph H., 151
Lewisburg, Battle of, 774, 775
Lewisburg Visitors Center, Lewisburg,
    W.Va., 775
Lexington, Ky., 273
Lexington, Mo., 410
Lexington, USS, 316, 558
Lexington, Va., 765–766
Lexington Visitor Center, Lexington,
    Va., 765–766
Libby Hill Park, Richmond, Va., 737
Libby Prison, Richmond, Va., 692, 735,
    737

Liberty Gap, Tenn., 568
Lightburn, Joseph, 191
Lilly, Eli, 3
Lincoln, Abraham, 14, 29, 52, 57, 58,
    60, 61, 102, 122, 255, 257, 259,
    275, 294, 303, 332, *345,* 357,
    358, 399–400, 419–420, 432,
    459, 460, 481, 485, 562–563,
    566, 582, 633, 634, 657,
    667–668, 692, 697, 725, 755,
    756, 757, 771
  assassination of, 70–72, 283, 319,
    327, 441, 672, 749
  Baltimore riots and, 321–322
  Cabinet of, 55–56
  Cooper Union speech of, 445
  1864 election and, 122, 205, 307,
    703–704
  Emancipation Proclamation issued
    by, 54, *55,* 56, 307, 339, 565
  Fort Stevens visited by, 67–69
  Gettysburg Address of, *498,* 499–501
  Grant and, 71, 372, 570–571, 679,
    682–683, 731–732, 733
  Hooker's appointment and, 672–673
  "house divided" speech of, 346
  Illinois home of, 344, 345–346
  inaugurations of, 52–54, *54*
  McClellan and, 479, 631–632,
    694–696, 709
  Marx's description of, 246
  political career of, 345–346
  presidency of, 54–56
  Richmond visited by, 731–732, 737,
    738
  Rosecrans described by, *134*
  Sherman's Savannah message to, 241
  Valley campaigns and, 641–642, 652,
    655
Lincoln, Mary Todd, 10, 67, 71, 73,
    273, 277, 346
Lincoln, Robert Todd, 73, 346
Lincoln, Tad, 737
Lincoln administration, 15, 122,
    268–269, 293, 307, 355–356,
    447, 455
  Confederate raiders and, 253–254
  foreign intervention and, 245–246
  French in Mexico and, 609, 613
  prisoner of war policy of, 215
  Trent Affair and, 249
Lincoln-Herndon Law Office,
    Springfield, Ill., 346
Lincoln Home National Historic Site,
    Springfield, Ill., 346
Lincoln Memorial University,
    Harrogate, Tenn., 594
Lincoln Museum, Washington, D.C.,
    73
Lincoln Tomb, Springfield, Ill., 346
Lion of Atlanta (monument), Atlanta,
    Ga., 197

Little Crow, 459, 460, 462
Little Rock, Ark., 29, 35, 41, 42–45, *44*
Little Rock Arsenal, Little Rock, Ark.,
    44–45
Lockett House, Sailor's Creek, Va., 744
Lockridge, Samuel A., 88
Locust Fork, Black Warrior River, Ala.,
    6
Locust Grove, Battle of, 470
Locust Grove, Va., 665
Logan, John A., 154, 171, 172, 179, *191,*
    192, *192,* 193, 194–197, 199,
    201, 203, *223,* 385, 603
Logan, Stephen, 345
London Illustrated News, 247
Long, Eli, 9
Long Bridge, Washington, D.C., 69
Longstreet, James, 83, 129, 136,
    137–138, 140, 151, 207, 230,
    329, 479, 571, 572, 586, 587,
    589, 591–592, 627, 628, 636,
    659, 662, 688, 699, 761
  at Antietam, 334, 335, 337–338
  in Appomattox Campaign, 741–747
  at Fredericksburg, *667,* 668–669, 671
  at Gettysburg, 490–491, *490,* 492,
    494–497
  in Knoxville Campaign, 580–584
  at Sailor's Creek, 741–742, 743
  at Second Manassas, 630–631
  in Seven Days' Battles, 706, 708, 709
  at Suffolk, 762–763
  at Wilderness, 680–682, *681,* 684
Lookout Mountain, Chattanooga,
    Tenn., 570, 573–577, *573,* 574
Loring, William W., 83, 170, 171, 177,
    185, 188, 386
Los Angeles, Calif., 75
Lotz House Museum, Franklin, Tenn.,
    602
Loudoun Valley, Va., 634–635
Louisa, Va., 689, 690
Louisiana, 29, 30, 45, *284,* 285–317
Louisiana, CSS, *286,* 288, 289, 290
Louisiana, USS, 430–431
Louisiana National Guard Military
    History and State Weapons
    Museum, New Orleans, La.,
    291–292
Louisiana Office of State Parks, Baton
    Rouge, La., 317
Louisiana State Museum, New Orleans,
    La., 292
Louisville, Ky., 276–277
Louisville, USS, 552
Lovejoy's Station, Ga., 204–205,
    209–210, 224
Lovell, Mansfield, 288
Lowe, Thaddeus S. C., 58–59, 697
Lowrey, Mark P., 165–166, 203
Lynchburg, Battle of, 651, 763–764
Lynde, Isaac, 84–85

Lyon, Nathaniel, 399, 407, 408, 415–417
Lytle, William H., 271

McArthur, John, 605
McCarthy-Pope House, Clinton, Ga., 228
McCausland, John, 66, 479–480, 765, 767, 780
McCleave, William, 77
McClellan, George B., 60, 178, 247, 266, 287, 329, 339, 343, 355–356, 481, 495, 634, 637–638, 652, 654, 657–658, 716, 762, 772
  at Antietam, 335–338, 337
  Army of the Potomac and, 633, 695, 696
  Burnside's replacement of, 636
  Lincoln and, 479, 631–632, 694–696, 709
  observation balloons and, 58–59
  Peninsula Campaign and, 694–696, 695, 705–707, 715
  at Second Manassas, 631–632
  Seven Days' Battles and, 630, 699, 699, 700, 700, 701–702
  Seven Pines Battle and, 705–706
  at Yorktown, 759–760
McClellan, Henry, 491
McClernand, John A., 39, 314, 358, 365–366, 378–379, 382–383, 385–386, 388, 390, 539, 541
McCollum–Chidester House, Camden, Ark., 48
McCook, Alexander, 67, 133–134, 135, 137, 138, 139, 268, 270–271, 351, 568
McCook, Daniel, 175, 351
McCook, Edward M., 149, 158, 183, 200, 210–212, 221, 351, 570, 587
McCray, T. H., 267
McCulloch, Benjamin, 30, 31–32, 410, 416
McCulloch, Henry E., 316
McDowell, Battle of, 655–656, 774
McDowell, Irvin, 624, 626–629, 627, 631, 638, 652, 657, 706
McGarry, Edward, 452–453
McGavock, John, 601
McGavock, Randal, 601
McIlwaine House, Petersburg, Va., 731
McIntosh, James, 32, 469
McKinley, William, 648, 764, 773
McKissack House, Spring Hill, Tenn., 598
McLaws, Lafayette, 129, 329, 490, 494, 581, 583, 584
McLean, Wilmer, 747, 749
McLean House, Appomattox, Va., 750
McNeil, John, 49

McNeill, Hanse, 642
McNeill Mansion, Moorefield, W.Va., 780
Macon, CSS, 242
Macon, Ga., 224–225
Macon Downtown Welcome Center, Macon, Ga., 225
McPhail's Butte Historic Site, Kidder County, N.Dak., 464
McPherson, James B., 147, 151, 158, 159, 172, 173–174, 184–185, 186, 187, 190–191, 193, 193, 199, 314–315, 366, 372, 378–379, 385, 390, 392–393, 446
  death of, 194–196, 196
  at Raymond, 382–383
  at Resaca, 152–155
McRae, Alexander, 88
Madison, Ga., 229
Maffitt, John Newland, 252
Magnolia Cemetery, Mobile, Ala., 13
Magnolia Spring State Park, Millen, Ga., 233
Magoffin, Beriah, 259
Magruder, John B., 247, 247, 295, 612, 613–614, 699, 759–760
Mahone, William, 689, 720, 721, 723, 731, 742, 743, 745
Mahone House, Petersburg, Va., 731
Malcolm Blue Historic Farm, Aberdeen, N.C., 436
Mallory, Stephen, 103, 751
Malvern Hill, Battle of, 708–709
Manassas, CSS, 287, 288, 289
Manassas, First Battle of, 63, 64, 420–421, 514, 524, 624, 626–630, 627, 629
Manassas, Second Battle of, 267, 462, 625, 630–632, 633, 747
Manassas National Battlefield Park, Va., 632
Manet, Edouard, 254
Maney, George E., 188, 194
Maney, James, 567
Mangas Coloradas, 79
Manhattan, USS, 17
Manigault, Arthur M., 194–195
Mankato, Minn., 461
Mansfield, Joseph, 336, 337
Mansfield (Sabine Cross Roads), Battle of, 308, 310–311, 310, 312
Mansfield State Commemorative Area, Mansfield, La., 312
Manship House, Jackson, Miss., 384
Marais des Cygnes River, Battle of, 412, 413, 456
Marblehead, USS, 518
Marianna, Fla., 107
Marietta, Ga., 175–177
Marietta National Cemetery, Marietta, Ga., 177

Mariners Museum, Newport News, Va., 757, 758
Marion, Battle of, 760–769
Marion, Francis, 118
Marks' Mills, Ark., 29, 47
Marks' Mills Battleground Historic Monument State Park, Jersey, Ark., 49
Marmaduke, John S., 36, 37, 46, 49, 403, 405, 408, 412, 456
Marmiton River, Battle of, 413, 414
Marsh, John S., 459
Marshall, Humphrey, 264, 774
Marshall Farm, Sailor's Creek, Va., 742
Marshall House, Alexandria, Va., 623
Marston, John, 754
Martin, William T., 585, 586, 587
Martin Cheairs House, Spring Hill, Tenn., 598
Martinsburg, W.Va., 784–785
Marx, Karl, 246
Marye's Heights, Fredericksburg, Va., 668, 669, 670, 670, 671, 671, 676, 677
Maryland, 57, 318, 319–341
Maryland Heights, Harpers Ferry, W.Va., 783–784
Maryland Monument to Union Soldiers and Sailors, Baltimore, Md., 323
Maryland State House, Annapolis, Md., 325
Mary Todd Lincoln House, Lexington, Ky., 273
Mason, James M., 249
Mason-Dixon Line, 477
Massaponax Baptist Church, Spotsylvania, Va., 687, 688
Mathew Brady Studio, New York, N.Y., 445
Matthews, Asa C., 472
Matthews Hill, Manassas Battlefield, Va., 632
Maury, Dabney H., 24
Maury, Matthew Fontaine, 248, 602, 739
Maury County Historical Society, 598
Maxcy Gregg House, Columbia, S.C., 534
Maxey, Samuel Bell, 2, 46
Maximilian, emperor of Mexico, 247–248
Meade, George G., 115, 208, 329–330, 444, 478, 481–482, 486, 487, 488, 488, 491, 494, 495, 500, 632–633, 665–666, 667, 669, 671, 679, 680, 683, 687, 688, 692, 702, 703, 710, 719–720, 740, 767
Meade's Station, Va., 719
Meigs, Montgomery, 67, 114

Memminger, Christopher, 503
Memoirs of Service Afloat During the War Between the States (Semmes), *250*
Memorial Fountain, Corpus Christi, Tex., 616
Memphis, Battle of, 315, 552, *552*
Memphis, Tenn., 4, 35, 551–553
Mercedita, USS, 511
Meridian, Miss., 150, 396, 655
Merieult House, New Orleans, La., 292
Merrehope home, Meridian, Miss., 396
Merrick, Robert T., 61
Merrimack, CSS, *see Virginia,* CSS
Merriman House, Corpus Christi, Tex., 616
Merritt, Wesley, *642, 684*
Messersmith's Woods, Chambersburg, Pa., 480
Metacomet, USS, 19
Metarie Cemetery, New Orleans, La., 292
Metro Jackson Convention and Visitors' Bureau, Jackson, Miss., 385
Metropolitan Historical Commission, Nashville, Tenn., 606
Mexico, 245, 246, 313
    France and, 247–248, 298, 308, 609
Miami, USS, 423
Middle Boggy Depot, Battle of, 471–472
Middle Creek, Battle of, 259, 263–264
Middle Tennessee Campaign, 9
Miles, Dixon, 782
Milford Monument, New Ulm, Minn., 461
Milledgeville, Ga., 228–229
Miller, William, 110
Miller Tavern, Gauley Bridge, W.Va., 773
Milliken's Bend, La., 316
Mill Springs, Battle of, 259, 264–266
Mill Springs Battlefield Association, 266
Millwood Ruins, Columbia, S.C., 534
Milroy, Robert H., 641, 656, 773–774, 779
Milwaukee, USS, 24
Mine Creek, Battle of, 413, 456, 457
Mine Run, Va., 664–665
Minnesota, *448,* 449, 450, 459–462
Minnesota, USS, 419, 752, 753–755
Missionary Ridge, Chattanooga, Tenn., 573–576, *574,* 577, *578*
Mississippi, 30, *352,* 353–397
Mississippi, CSS, 288
Mississippi, USS, *300,* 301
Mississippi River Museum, Memphis, Tenn., 553
Mississippi State Historical Museum, Jackson, Miss., 384

Missouri, 30, 33, *398,* 399–417
Missouri Compromise of 1820, 449
Mitchel, Ormsby, 1, 131
Mitchell, Margaret, 210
Mitchell, Robert B., 271
Mobile, Ala., 1, 13–14, 23, 24, 104
Mobile Bay, Battle of, 13, 14–21, *15*
Mobile Infirmary, 14
Modern Greece, 63, 434
Mohican, USS, 242
Monarch, USS, 552
Monitor, USS, 10, 63, 103, 434, 511, 551, 715, *752,* 753–755, 757
Monnett Battle of Westport Fund, Inc., Kansas City, Mo., 413
Monocacy National Battlefield, Frederick, Md., *331,* 333
Monongahela, USS, 20, 301, 610
Monroe, Mich., 343–344
Monroe's Cross Roads, Battle of, 435–436
Montauk, USS, 237
Montgomery, Ala., 11–12, 503
Montgomery, James E., 548–549, 550
Monument to Confederate Women of Maryland, Baltimore, Md., 323
Monument to the Confederate Dead, Baltimore, Md., 323
Moore, Isaiah, 76
Moorefield, Battle of, 780
Morehead City, N.C., 427–428
Morgan, CSS, 16, 19, 24
Morgan, George W., 593
Morgan, James D., 149, 437–438
Morgan, John Hunt, 260, 277, *280,* 562, 563, 566–567, 607
    Cynthiana engagement and, 273–274, 282
    death of, 589–590
    1863 raid of, 343, 348–351
    military career of, 280–282
Morgan City, La., 297
Morgan Monument, Greeneville, Tenn., 590
Morgan-Moore Trail, Green River Lake State Park, Ky., 279
Morgan's Surrender Monument, Ohio, 351
Morning Light, USS, 611
Morris, Charles, 252–253
Morris Island, Charleston, S.C., 503, 504, 513, 515, *520,* 521–524
Mortar Boat No. 16, USS, 548, 549
Morton, James St. Clair, 602–603
Morton, Oliver P., 276–277, 343, 348, *348,* 349
Mosby, John S., 624–625, 642, *644,* 645
Moscow, Ark., 46, 48
Moseley Park, Atlanta, Ga., 201–202
Mossy Creek, Battle of, 585–586, 587
Mott, Greshom R., 686
Mott, Samuel R., 585

Mott House, Columbus, Ga., 214
Mound City, USS, 35, 549
Mound City National Cemetery, Cairo, Ill., 345
Mount Carmel Church, Va., 689
Mount Gilead Methodist Church, Ga., 208
Mount Iser cemetery, Beverly, W.Va., 778
Mount Olivet Cemetery, Frederick, Md., 332
Mount Olivet Cemetery, Hanover, Pa., 485
Mount Olivet Cemetery, Nashville, Tenn., 606
Mount Olivet Cemetery, Washington, D.C., 61
Mount Olivet Church, Pineville, La., 307
Mount Washington, USS, 762
Mouton, Alfred, 296, 310, 312
movies, 82, 132, 787
Mower, Joseph A., *223, 438,* 439, 531–532, 533
Mudd, Samuel A., 72, 115, 328
"Mud March," 670
Mule Shoe salient, Spotsylvania Battlefield, Va., 685–686, 687
Mulligan, James A., 410, 638–639
Mumford, William, 292
Munford, Thomas, 764
Munfordville, Ky., 278–279
Munson's Hill, Fairfax, Va., 624
Murfreesboro, Tenn., 561–562, *561*
    see also Stones River, Battle of
Murray, Eli H., 226, 282
Murray, William M., 321
Museum of Florida's Army, St. Augustine, Fla., 119
Museum of Hilton Head Island, Hilton Head, S.C., 527
Museum of the *Albemarle,* Elizabeth City, N.C., 422
Museum of the Confederacy, Richmond, Va., 738
Museum of the Great Plains, Lawton, Okla., 475
Museum of Western Expansion, St. Louis, Mo., 407
Mustang Island State Park, Tex., 616
Myrtle Grove Cemetery, Rome, Ga., 158

Nahant, USS, 240
Napoleon III, emperor of France, 246
Nashville, Battle of, 538, 602–605
Nashville, CSS, 24, 237, 239
Nashville, Tenn., vii, 2, 4
Nassau, Bahamas, 256
Natchez, Miss., 381
Nathan Bedford Forrest State Historic Area, Eva, Tenn., 545

National Air and Space Museum, Washington, D.C., 59
National Archives, Washington, D.C., 60
National Cemetery, Knoxville, Tenn., 585
National Museum of American Art, Washington, D.C., 60
National Museum of Civil War Medicine, Frederick, Md., 332
National Museum of Health and Medicine, Washington, D.C., 69
National Museum of History and Technology, Washington, D.C., 59
National Museum of Naval Aviation, Pensacola, Fla., 105
National Portrait Gallery, Washington, D.C., 59–60
Natural Bridge, Battle of, 109, 110–111
Natural Bridge State Historic Site, St. Marks, Fla., 110–111, *110*
Natural Resources Department, North Dakota, 465
Naval Academy Museum, Annapolis, Md., 325
Navy Memorial Museum, Washington, D.C., 63–64, 257
Navy Yard, Pensacola, Fla., 105
Nebraska Territory, 449, 450
Negley, James, 134
Negley, John S., 596
Negro Orphanage, New York, N.Y., 445
Nelson, William, 263, 267, 558, 562
   death of, 276–277
Nelson House, Columbia, Tenn., 596
Neptune, CSS, 614
Neuse, CSS, 214, 425–426
Nevada Territory, 75, 81–82, 449, 450
New Bern, N.C., 422, 426–427
Newborn Hall, Martinsburg, W.Va., 784
New Era, USS, 550
New Falls City, 311
New Hope Church, Battle of, 164–165, *164, 167*
New Ironsides, USS, 433, 507, 512–513
New Jersey, *442*
New Johnsonville State Historic Area, New Johnsonville, Tenn., 545
New Madrid, Mo., 49, 401, 546, 548
New Madrid Historical Museum, New Madrid, Tenn., 547
New Manchester, Ga., 180, 198–199, *198*
New Market, Battle of, 649–651, 765
New Market Battlefield Park, New Market, Va., 651–652
New Market Heights, Battle of, 710, 711
New Mexico, *74,* 75, 77, 79, 81, 83–99, 609, 613

New Orleans, La., 285–290, *291,* 293
   French Quarter of, 286, 292
   Garden District of, 292
Newport News, Va., 758
Newport News Park, Newport News, Va., 760–761
New Smyrna Beach, Fla., 119
Newton, John M., 109, 110, 111, 149, 172, *187,* 188
Newtonia, Battles of, 413–414, 456
New Ulm, Minn., 460, 461
New York, *442,* 444–446
New York, N.Y., 444–445, *445*
New York Draft Riots, 444, 445
New York Peace Memorial, Lookout Mountain, Chattanooga, Tenn., 577
Niblo's Tavern, Petersburg, Va., 731
Nichols, Charles H., 61
Nicolay, John, 61
IX Corps, U.S., 65, 334, *487,* 670, 680, 689, 719, 721
XIX Corps, U.S., *62,* 67, 638, *646,* 647, 649
North Anna, Battle of, 654, 688–689
North Carolina, *418,* 419–441
North Carolina Arsenal, Fayetteville, N.C., 436
North Carolina Hospital, Petersburg, Va., 731
North Carolina Monument, Appomattox, Va., 750
North Dakota, *448,* 462–465
Noyes, Henry E., 218

Oak Grove, Battle of, 699–700
Oak Hall Cemetery, Washington, D.C., 61
Oak Hill Cemetery, Lawrence, Kans., 455
Oak Hill Cemetery, Newnan, Ga., 211
Oak Hills, Battle of, *see* Wilson's Creek, Battle of
Oakland Cemetery, Atlanta, Ga., 197–198, *197*
Oaklands mansion, Murfreesboro, Tenn., 567
Oaklawn Manor, La., 297
Oak Ridge Cemetery, Springfield, Ill., 346
Oaks House, Jackson, Miss., 384
Oak Square, Port Gibson, Miss., 380
Oakton, Marietta, Ga., 177
Ocean View, Norfolk, Va., 757
Ocracoke Lighthouse, Cape Hatteras, N.C., 420
O'Hara, Theodore, 275
Ohio, *342, 343,* 349–351
Oklahoma, 30, *466,* 467–475
Okolona, Battle of, 46, 362–363
O'Laughlin, Michael, 72

Old Arsenal Museum, Baton Rouge, La., 294
Old Bayview Cemetery, Corpus Christi, Tex., 616
Old Berea Christian Church, Spotsylvania, Va., 687
Old Blandford Church and Interpretive Center, Petersburg, Va., 731
Old Bricks, Roswell, Ga., 183
Old Buckhead Church, Perkins, Ga., 233
Old Cannonball House and Confederate Museum, Macon, Ga., 225
Old City Cemetery, Lynchburg, Va., 764
Old City Cemetery, Nashville, Tenn., 606
Old City Hall, Frederick, Md., 332
Old Clinton Historical Society, Clinton, Ga., 228
Old Court House, St. Louis, Mo., 407
Old Courthouse Museum, Lynchburg, Va., 764
Old Court House Museum, Vicksburg, Miss., 393–394, *393*
Old Depot Museum, Selma, Ala., 10
Oldest House, St. Augustine, Fla., 119
Old Fort Wayne, Okla., 470, 473
Old Governor's Mansion, Milledgeville, Ga., 228–229
Old Gray Cemetery, Knoxville, Tenn., 585
Old Richmond Academy Building, Augusta, Ga., 232
Old Salem Church, Chancellorsville, Va., 677–678
Old State Capitol, Little Rock, Ark., 44
Old State Capitol, Milledgeville, Ga., 228
Old State Capitol, Springfield, Ill., 346
Old State House, Frankfort, Ky., 275
Old Stone Church, Lewisburg, W.Va., 774, 775
Old Stone Church, Ringgold, Ga., 144
Old Washington Historic State Park, Washington, Ark., 48
Olmstead, Charles H., 235
Olustee, Battle of, 124–127, *124, 704*
Olustee, Fla., 109, 122, 123
Olustee Battlefield State Historic Site, Olustee, Fla., *125,* 127
Opdycke, Emerson, 597, 601, 602
Opequon Creek, Battle of, 643
Opequon Presbyterian Church, Winchester, Va., 639
Opothleyahola, Chief, 468–470
Orchard Knob, Chattanooga, Tenn., 574–575, *574,* 577, 579
Ord, Edward O. C., 320, 356, 357, 359, 390, 555, 624, 710, 714, 727, 741, 744, 746
Oregon, 75, 449, 450

Orton, W., 602
Osage, USS, 24
Osterhaus, Peter J., 32, 313, 379
O'Sullivan, Timothy H., *493, 687,* 688
Our American Cousin, 71
Overton Hill, Nashville, Tenn., 605, 607
Oxford, Miss., 359

Paducah, Ky., 261, 262–263
Page, Richard L., *19,* 21
Palmer, James S., 293, 381
Palmer, John M., 147, 149, 150,
    154–155, 179, 186, 188, 201
Palmer House, Williamsburg, Va., 762
Palmerston, Lord, 246
Palmetto, Ga., 210, 211–212
Palmetto Armory, Columbia, S.C., 534
Palmetto State, CSS, 511
Palmito Ranch, Battle of, 617
Palo Alto Battlefield National Historic
    Site, Brownsville, Tex., 617
Pamplin Park, Petersburg, Va., 730
Parke, John G., 421, 427–428, 586,
    592
Parker, Ely, 749
Parker's Battery, Bermuda Hundred,
    Va., 713
Parker's Cross Roads, Battle of, 560, 561
Parker's Store, Va., 684
Park Hill Mission, Okla., 473
parking, xxviii
Parris Island Museum, Beaufort, S.C.,
    528
Parrott, Robert P., 446
Patapsco, USS, 509, 513
Patrick Cleburne Confederate
    Cemetery, Jonesboro, Ga., 209
Patterson, Robert, 626–627
Paul, Gabriel R., 90
Pawnee, USS, 519
Peach Orchard Hill, Nashville, Tenn.,
    606
Peachtree Creek, Battle of, 184,
    186–187, *187*
Pearce, Nicholas B., 416
Pea Ridge, Battle of, 29, 30–33, *31,* 60,
    400, 474
Pea Ridge National Military Park, Ark.,
    33–34
Peat House Medical Museum,
    Lynchburg, Va., 764
Pecos National Historical Park,
    N.Mex., 95–96
Peebles Farm, Battle of, *717,* 721–722
Pegram, John, 724, 728
Pegram, Willie, 728
Pelham, John, 659, 663, *667,* 669, 671
Pelican Island, Galveston, Tex., 615
Pemberton, John C., 363–364,
    368–369, 375, 376, 383,
    385–388, 390, 391, *392,* 394,
    563

Pemberton, John S., 214
Pender, William D., 486
Pendleton, William, 784
Peninsula Campaign of 1862, 58, 638,
    640, 694–710, 755, 761
    Malvern Hill Battle in, 708–709
    prelude to, 694–696
    Savage's Station Battle in, 707–708
    Seven Pines Battle in, 705–706, 707
    Stuart's ride and, 697–698
    Yorktown engagements in, 759–760
Penn, William, 477
Pennsylvania, *476,* 477–501
Pensacola, Fla., 101, 102–107
Pensacola, USS, 287
Pensacola Historic Museum, Pensacola,
    Fla., 105
Pentagon Barracks, Baton Rouge, La.,
    294
Peralta, Battle of, 96–99
Perkins, George H., 290
Perryville, Battle of, 133, 260, 267,
    268–271, *270, 272,* 537
Perryville Battlefield State Historic
    Park, Perryville, Ky., 272
*Personal Memoirs of Ulysses S. Grant,
    The* (Grant), 445
Peter, W. G., 602
Peters, George Bodley, 598
Peters, Jessie McKissack, 598
Petersburg, Va., vii, 70, 716
Petersburg Campaign, 716–730, *717,
    729*
    Crater Battle in, 719–720
    Five Forks Battle in, 727–728, *729*
    Fort Stedman assault in, 724–726
    Union breakthrough in, 729–730
Petersburg National Battlefield,
    Petersburg, Va., 715, 718–719,
    726
    City Point unit of, 733–734
    Five Forks unit of, 729
Petersburg Visitor Center, Petersburg,
    Va., 731
Petersen, William, 72
Petersen House, Washington, D.C., 60,
    70, 72, 73
Pettigrew, James J., 340, *496,* 576, 600
Philippi, Battle of, 776
Philippoteaux, Paul, *497*
Philips, Pleasant J., 226–227
Phillips, Wendell, 58
Phillips, William A., 470, 471–472
Phoenix, Ariz., 75, 77
Picacho Pass, Battle of, 77–78
Picacho Peak State Park, Ariz., 78
Pickett, George E., 427, *495,* 496, *496,*
    576, 600, 700, 712, 713,
    727–728, 731, 739, 742, 762
Pickett's Mill, Battle of, 165–166
Pickett's Mill State Historic Site, Dallas,
    Ga., 167–168, *168*

Piedmont, Battle of, 651, 654–655
Pierpont, Frances H., 771
Pike, Albert, 30, 32, 33, 467, *473,* 474
    statue of, 60
Pillow, Gideon J., 142, 259, 261, 402,
    541–542
Pine Bluff, Ark., 44, 45, 46
Pineville, La., 306–307
Pineville National Cemetery, Pineville,
    La., 307
Pinkerton, Allan, 52–53, 321, 697
Pinola, 289
Pittsburg, USS, 547
Pittsburg Landing, Battle of, *see* Shiloh,
    Battle of
Pleasant Hill, Battle of, 47, 306, *308,
    309, 310,* 311, 313
Pleasants, Henry, 719
Pleasonton, Alfred, 409, 456, 635,
    659–661, 663
Plum Point Bend, Battle of, 548–549,
    550
Plymouth, N.C., 422–424
Pocahontas, USS, 242, 526
Pocotaligo, S.C., 528, 531
Poe, Orlando M., 588
Poimboef, C. E., 313
Point Lookout, Md., 325–326
Point Lookout State Park, Scotland,
    Md., 326
Poison Spring, Ark., 29, 46
Poison Spring Massacre, 408
Poison Spring Monument State Park,
    Bluff City, Ark., 48
Polignac, Camille, 312
Polk, James K., 596
Polk, Leonidas, 13, 135, 136, *136,* 137,
    153–154, *153,* 155, 158–159,
    160, 185, 259, 261, 269–270,
    292, 357, 396, 557, 566–567, 571
    death of, 169, 170
Polson Cemetery, Grove, Okla., 473
Pope, John, 208, 266, 355, 401, 462,
    464, 546, 547, 625, 630–632,
    633, 657–658, *657*
Poplar Grove National Cemetery,
    Petersburg, Va., 723–724
Port Aransas, Tex., 616
Porter, David Dixon, 39, 41, 45, 103,
    287, 288, 289, 290, 296, 300,
    302, 304–305, 306, 309, 311,
    312, 367–368, 370–374, 376,
    377, 380, 388, 430, 431–433,
    431, 621, 733, 737, 757
Porter, Fitz John, 337, 631, 697,
    699–700, 702, 757, 784
Porter, John L., 757
Porter, William D., 294, 300
Porter House, Portsmouth, Va., 757
Port Gibson, Miss., 377–380, *379, 380*
Port Hudson, La., 42, 299–303, *300,
    301, 302,* 364

Port Hudson National Cemetery, Port Hudson, La., 304
Port Hudson State Commemorative Area, Zachary, La., 303–304
Port Isabel Lighthouse, Tex., 617
Port Republic, Battle of, 653–654
Port Republic Historical Society, Port Republic, Va., 654
Port Royal, S.C., 116, 235, 524–526, *524,* 527, 548
Portsmouth Naval Shipyard Museum, Portsmouth, Va., 757
Potomska, USS, 242
Potter, E. E., 510
Powell, Lewis, *54,* 71, 72
Powell, Samuel, *270,* 271
Powhatan, USS, 103, 505
Prairie DeAnn, Ark., 46, 48
Prairie Grove, Battle of, 29, 34–37, *34, 38*
Prairie Grove Battlefield State Park, Prairie Grove, Ark., 37
Prentiss, Benjamin, 41, 42, 557
Presidio, San Francisco, Calif., 82
Price, Hawkins F., 159
Price, Sterling, 30, 32, 41, 43, 46, 48, 247, *247,* 295, 356, 364, *405,* 456, 459
    1864 Missouri raid of, 404–414, *404, 454*
    at Wilson's Creek, 415–416
Price House, Kingston, Ga., 159–160
Prince Edward Hotel, Farmville, Va., 746
Princeton Court House, Battle of, 773–774
Pritchard, Benjamin D., 220
Proclamation on Amnesty and Reconstruction, 54, 122
Proctor's Creek, Battle of, 714
Provisional Confederate Congess, 10
Pryor, Luke, 3
Putnam, Haldimand, 523
Pyron, Charles S., 87, 89, 90, 92, 93

"Quaker Guns," 624, 695
Quantrill, William C., 277, 282–283, 408, *453,* 454, *454,* 458–459
Quapaw Quarter, Little Rock, Ark., 44
Quarters Number One, Fort Monroe, Va., 757
Queen of the West, USS, *371, 372*

Radical Republicans, 56, 634
Rails to Trails, 3
Rains, Gabriel J., 427
Rains, George W., 230–231
Rains House, New Bern, N.C., 427
Raleigh, CSS, 429
Raleigh, Walter, 422
Ramseur, Stephen, 331
Randall, James Ryder, 319

Randolph County Museum, Beverly, W.Va., 778
Ransom, Thomas, 203
Rappahannock Station, Battle of, 663
Rathbone, Henry, 71, 72
Rattle and Snap, Columbia, Tenn., 596
Rawlins, John A., 347, 348
Ray House, Republic, Mo., *415,* 417
Raymond, Battle of, 382, 383
Read, Abner, 611, 612
Ready, Martha, 566
Reagan, John H., 220, 480–481, 527
Reams Station, Battle of, *717,* 721
Rectortown, Va., 636
Red Oak, Ga., 207–208
Red River Campaign, 15–16, 45, 47, 286, 305, 306, 307–312, 313, 609, 649
Reed's Bridge, Ga., 141
Reily, James, 76
Reno, Jesse L., 61, 65, 81–82, *333,* 334, 421–422
Renwick, James, Jr., 58
Resaca, Battle of, 152–156
Reynolds, Daniel, 152–153
Reynolds, John Fulton, 481, 486, *486,* 487–488, *493,* 631
Reynolds, Joseph J., 579, 778, 779
Rhett, Robert Barnwell, Jr., 515
Rhett, Robert Barnwell, Sr., 515
Rice Museum, Georgetown, S.C., 511
Richard Caswell Memorial, Kinston, N.C., 426
Richard Garrett Place, Port Royal, Va., 672
Richardson, Israel B., 337, *627*
Richmond, Battle of, 267–268, 593
Richmond, USS, 17, 19, 287, 301
Richmond, Va., vii, 11, 60, 70, 619, 734–735, *734, 735, 736*
    "Bread Riot" in, 736
    fall of, 736–737
    Kilpatrick's raid on, 692–693
    Lincoln's visit to, 731–732, 737, 738
Richmond National Battlefield Park, Richmond, Va., 701–702, 704, 709
    Chimborazo Visitor Center of, 737
    Drewry's Bluff unit of, *714,* 715
    Parker's Battery unit of, 713
Richmond National Cemetery, Richmond, Va., 737
Rich Mountain, Battle of, 777–778
Ricketts, James B., 330, 331
Ringgold, Ga., 142–143
Ringgold Gap, Battle of, 142–143, 144
Rio Hill, Battle of, 694
Rippavilla, Spring Hill, Tenn., 598
River Queen, 744, 766
Rivers Bridge, Battle of, 531–532
Rivers Bridge State Park, S.C., 532
Riverside Cemetery, Jackson, Tenn., 561

Roanoke, USS, 752
Roanoke Island, N.C., 420–422
Robert E. Lee Memorial, Arlington, Va., 621
Roberts, Benjamin S., 85, 87, 88–89
Roberts, Thomas L., 79
Robertson, Beverly, 425, 661–662
Robinson, John, *487*
Roche, Theopholie, 182
Rocketts (Confederate Navy Yard), Richmond Va., 737
Rockville, Md., 328
Rocky Face Ridge, Ga., 148–152
Roddey, Philip D., 4–5, 9, 211
Rodes, Robert, 331, 486–487, 488, 643, 663, 785
Rodgers, C.R.P., 118
Rodgers, John, 240
Rodgers, William, 357
Rogersville, Tenn., 591
Rome, Ga., 157–158
Rome Cross Roads, Ga., 156
Romney Expedition, 643
Roosevelt, Theodore, 183, 248
Rose, Thomas E., 735–736
Rosecrans, William S., 5–6, 81, 133–134, *134,* 135, 137, *138,* 139, 141, *141,* 142, 272, 281, 405, 481, 537, 555, 572, 582, 772–773, 776, 777, 778
    Chattanooga occupation and, 567–570
    Corinth-Iuka engagements and, 356–357
    at Stones River, 562–563, *564,* 565–566
    Thomas's replacement of, 571
Rose Hill Cemetery, Columbia, Tenn., 596
Rose Hill Cemetery, Macon, Ga., 225
Rosser, Thomas, 646, 690, 727, 744
Rossville, Ga., 141
Roswell, Ga., 179, 180, 182–183
Rough and Ready, Ga., 203, 208
Round Mountain, Battle of, 468
Royal Navy Dockyard, Bermuda, 256
Royal Victoria Hotel, Nassau, Bahamas, 256
Ruff's Mill, Battle of, 178, 180
Ruger, Thomas H., 600
Rupert, John, 220
Russellville, Tenn., 589
Russia, Imperial, 246
Rust, Albert, 779
Rutherford's Farm, Battle of, 638
Ryan, Abram, 14

Sabine Cross Roads (Mansfield), Battle of, 310–311, *310,* 312
Sabine Lighthouse, Sabine Pass, Tex., 611, 612
Sabine Pass, Tex., 298, 609, 610–612

Sabine Pass Battleground State Historical Park, Sabine Pass, Tex., *611*, 612
Sachem, USS, 612, 615
safety, xxviii
Sailor's Creek, Battle of, 741–743, *743*
Sailor's Creek Battlefield State Park, Sailor's Creek, Va., 743–744, *743*
St. Albans, Vt., 446–447
St. Albans Historical Museum, St. Albans, Vt., 447
St. Augustine, Fla., 118–120
St. Charles Hotel, Cairo, Ill., 345
St. Elizabeths Hospital, Washington, D.C., 61
St. Francis Barracks, St. Augustine, Fla., 119
St. John's College, Annapolis, Md., 325
St. John's Episcopal Church, Ashwood, Tenn., 596
St. John's Episcopal Church, Richmond, Va., 737
St. John's Lutheran Church, Harpers Ferry, W.Va., 784
St. Johns River Lighthouse, Jacksonville, Fla., 123
St. Lawrence, USS, 752
St. Louis, Mo., 406–407
St. Louis, USS, 552
St. Marks, Fla., 101, 108–109
St. Mary's Catholic Church, Burke's Station, Va., 625
St. Mary's Catholic Church, Nashville, Tenn., 606
St. Michael's Church, Charleston, S.C., 517
St. Paul's Church, Petersburg, Va., 732
St. Paul's Church, Richmond, Va., 736, 738
St. Paul's Episcopal Church, Franklin, Tenn., 602
Salineville, Ohio, 351
Saltville, Battles of, 768, 769
Sampson, CSS, 242
San Antonio, Tex., 616
San Augustin Spring, N.Mex., 84, 85
Sand Creek Massacre, 408, 451–452
Sanders, William P., 580, 581, 584
Sandston, Va., 706
Sandusky House, Lynchburg, Va., 764
San Francisco, Calif., 82–83
San Jacinto, USS, 249
San Marcos de Apalache State Historic Site, St. Marks, Fla., 109
Sansom, Emma, 7, 8
Santa Fe, N.Mex., 75, 89, 90, 95
Santa Fe National Cemetery, Santa Fe, N.Mex., 95
Santa Rosa Island, Pensacola, Fla., 104–106

Savage's Station, Battle of, 706, 707–708
Savannah, Ga., 239–242
Savannah History Museum, Savannah, Ga., 241
Savannah Visitors Center, Savannah, Ga., 241
Scales, Alfred M., *496*
Schenck, Robert, 656
Schoepf, Albin, 265, 266
Schofield, John M., 35–36, 144, 147, 149, 154, 158–159, 160, 165, 169, 171, 172, 173, 183, 184, 185, 186, *187*, 190, 191, 195, 197, 201, 203, 208, 223, 414, 425–426, 435, 439–440, 446, 470, 533, 595–598, 599, *599*, 602, 603, 604–605
Schurz, Carl, *487*, 488
Scott, Dred, 407
Scott, George, 110
Scott, John S., 267
Scott, Robert K., 194
Scott, Thomas, 188, 189
Scott, Winfield, 52, 60, 355, 626, 728
Scurry, William R., 87, 90–91, 92, 93–94, 97
Sea King, 255
Sea Rim State Park, Sabine Pass, Tex., 612–613
Sears, Claudius, 162
Seawolf Park, Galveston, Tex., 615
Secessionville, S.C., 512, 518, 521
II Corps, U.S., 495, *496*, 680, 684, 685–686, 705, 718, 721, 722, 726, 727, 742, 744, 745, 746, 747
Seddon, James A., 390, 693
Sedgwick, John, 492, *674,* 675, 677, 680, 682
death of, 684, 686
See/Ward House, Mill Creek, W.Va., 778
Selfridge, Thomas O., *374*
Selma, Ala., 8–11
Selma, CSS, 16, 19, 21
Semmes, Raphael, 13–14, *250,* 251, *252,* 253–255, 320, 614, 765
VII Corps, U.S., 638
Seven Days' Battles, 630, 699–702, 705–710
Seven Pines (Fair Oaks), Battle of, 178, 705–706
XVII Corps, U.S., 171, *173,* 178, 192, 200–201, 224, 314–315, *378,* 385, 390, 396
73rd Pennsylvania Reservation, Chattanooga, Tenn., 578
Seward, William Henry, 55, *55,* 56, 72, 103, 249, 756
Seymour, Truman, 122, 125–126, *520,* 522, 523

Shackelford, James M., 591–592, 593
Shadows-on-the-Teche, New Iberia, La., 298
Sharpsburg, Battle of, *see* Antietam, Battle of
Sharpsburg, Md., 339
Shaw, Robert Gould, *521, 522, 523*
Shelby, Joseph Orville, 44, 46, 49, 247–248, 405, 408–414, 456
Shellman, Mary, 321
Shellman House, Westminster, Md., 321
Shenandoah, CSS, 214, 248, 255–256
Shenandoah Valley, vii
importance of, 637
Jackson's 1862 campaign in, 637–638, 640–641, *641,* 652–656
Sheridan's 1864 campaign in, 637, 641–649, 656–657, 725, 782
Shepherdstown, Battle of, 784
Sheridan, Philip H., 9, 59, 248, 269–270, 446, 474–475, 595, 621, 637, 679, 683, 690, 691, 694, 702, 703, 716–717, 733
in Appomattox Campaign, 740, 741, 744, 746, 747
at Cedar Creek, 646–648, *647*
1864 Valley Campaign of, 637, 641–649, *642,* 656–657, 725, 782
"Ride" of, 648, *648*
at Stones River, 564, *565,* 566
Sherman, Thomas A., 235
Sherman, Thomas W., 525
Sherman, William T., 1, 4, 9, 23, 24, 39, 81, 129, 197, 198, 202, 204, 208, 212, 215, 221, 232, 236, 277, 281, 292, 294, 306, 343, 350, 355, 372, 374, 384, 386, 510, *516,* 519, 537, 538, 543, 545, 553, 557, 571, 584, 595, 655, 679, 733
in Atlanta Campaign, 132, 133, 143–146, *146,* 148, 152–154, 157–161, 163–167, 169, 171–173, *173,* 174, 176, 178–180, 182, 184, 186
at Battle of Atlanta, 190–191, 195
at Bentonville, 437, 439
birthplace of, 351
at Chattanooga, 573, *574,* 575–576, 578
Chickasaw Bayou attack and, 38–39, 368–369
at Ezra Church, 199–201
fall of Savannah and, 240–241
in First Vicksburg Campaign, 314, 315, 358, 360, 362, 363
at Fort McAllister, 237–238
Johnston's surrender to, 440–441
in March to Sea, 223, *223,* 228–229, 425–426, 435

Meridian Campaign and, 396
Red River Campaign and, 308–309
at Resaca, 152–154
in Second Vicksburg Campaign, 364,
367–369, 378, 382–383, 390,
393
statue of, 57
"war is hell" statement of, 205
Sherman Reservation, Chattanooga,
Tenn., 578
Sherman's March to the Sea, 129, 163,
205, 223–243, 396, *502,* 538,
723
Alabama incursion of, 23
Ebenezer Creek disaster and,
233–234
fall of Fort McAllister in, 237–238
fall of Fort Pulaski in, 234–236
fall of Savannah in, 239–242
Federal organization for, 223–224
Griswoldville and, 226–227
Macon and, 224–225
North Carolina and, 425–426,
435–436, 724–725
South Carolina and, 528, 530–533
Waynesboro action and, 232–233
Shields, James, 652–654
Shiloh, Battle of, 280, 355, 359, 537,
538, 555–558, *556*
Shiloh Methodist Church, Shiloh,
Tenn., 559
Shiloh National Military Park, Shiloh,
Tenn., 558–559
Ship Island, Miss., 287–288, 353, 397
Shirley Plantation, Va., 709
Shoup, Francis Asbury, 178
Showalter, Daniel, 81
Shrady, Henry, 54
Shreveport, La., 45, 46, *308,* 313–314
Shriver, Andrew, 321
Shriver, William, 321
Shy, William, 605
Shy's Hill, Nashville, Tenn., 605, 606
Sibley, Henry Hastings, 460, 462–463
Sibley, Henry Hopkins, 76, 78, 81, 83,
85–87, 89–90, 94, 96–98, 613
Sickles, Daniel E., 60, 69, *490,* 491, 492,
494, 675–676
Siege and Battle of Corinth National
Historic Landmark, 555
Sigel, Franz, 31, 33, 414–415, 416,
649–650, 651, 654, 686, 767
Sill, Joshua W., 269, 474–475
Simmons Bluff, S.C., 518
Sioux Memorial, Mankato, Minn.,
461
Sitlington Hill, McDowell, Va., 656
VI Corps, U.S., *62,* 67, 333, 337, 492,
574–575, 638, 645, 646, *646,*
647, 649, *674,* 675, *676,* 677,
680, 683, 684, 685–686, 704,
726, 727, 729, 730, 742, 743

XVI Corps, U.S., 24, 42, 153, 154, 156,
169, 171, *173,* 180, *190,* 191,
193, 203, 209, 396, *430*
Skelly, Johnston H., *495*
Slemmer, Adam, 102–103
Slidell, John, 249, 292
Slocum, Henry, 199, 202–203,
223–224, *223,* 228, 384, 435,
436–437, *438,* 439, 530–531,
533, 633
Slough, John P., 90, 91–94, 96, 97
Smith, Andrew J., 23–24, 305, 306, 311,
359, 360, 361, 405, 407, 604,
605
Smith, Caleb B., *55*
Smith, Charles F., 539, 541
Smith, Edmund Kirby, 27, 45, 46, 47,
220, 260, 267–268, 269,
271–272, 274–275, 276, 280,
281, 295, 309, 311, 313–314,
343, 350, 404, 537, 562, 593,
610
Smith, Giles A., 194, 387
Smith, Gustavus W., 178, 194, 205, 210,
224, 226, 529, 706, 710
Smith, Martin L., 387
Smith, Milo, 227
Smith, Watson, 365
Smith, William F., 572, 703, 713, 718,
761
Smith, William Sooy, 362–363, 396,
550
Smithson, James, 58
Smithsonian Historical Building,
Selma, Ala., 10
Smithsonian Information, Washington,
D.C., 59
Smithsonian Institution, Washington,
D.C., 51, 58–61, *58*
Smyrna, Battle of, 178
Smyrna, Fla., 119
Snyder House, Lawrence, Kans., 455
Snyder's Bluff, Miss., 369
Soldiers' National Cemetery,
Gettysburg, Pa., *498,* 500
Somerwell House, Yorktown, Va., 760
Sorrel, G. Moxley, 684
South Carolina, *502,* 503–535
South Carolina Battleground
Preservation Trust, 521
Southfield, USS, 423
South Fort, Vicksburg, Miss., 375
South Mills, N.C., 422
South Mountain, Battle of, 65, 82,
333–334
South River Meeting House,
Lynchburg, Va., 764
Spain, 103
Spangler, Edman, 72
Spanish Fort, Mobile, Ala., 13, 23–24
Special Order No. 191, 329
Speer House, Lawrence, Kans., 455

Spotsylvania, Battle of, 59, 670,
684–686, *685*
Spotsylvania Confederate Cemetery,
Spotsylvania, Va., 688
Spotsylvania County Museum,
Spotsylvania, Va., 687
Spotsylvania Court House,
Spotsylvania, Va., 687
Spotsylvania Exhibit Shelter,
Spotsylvania Battlefield, Va.,
686
Spotsylvania Visitor Center,
Fredericksburg, Va., 688
Sprague, John W., 196
Sprague, Kate Chase, 56
Spray, 109
Springer Opera House, Columbus, Ga.,
215
Springfield, Ill., 345–346
Spring Hill, Tenn., 597–598, 599, 600
Spring Hill Cemetery, Lynchburg, Va.,
764
Stafford Hall, Va., 672
Stage Coach Inn, Harpers Ferry, W.Va.,
783
Stahl, O. F., 601
Stanford, Leland, 78
Stanley, David S., 204, 597
Stanton, Edwin M., *55,* 56, 61, 73, 372,
551, 568, 652, 657, 682, 696,
709
Star Fort, Winchester, Va., 643
Star of the West, 516, 524
State Capitol, Baton Rouge, La.,
294–295
State House, Columbia, S.C., 533–534
Stately Oaks Plantation, Jonesboro,
Ga., 209
State Museum, Columbia, S.C., 534
Steedman, James B., 604
Steele, Frederick, 24, 41, 42–47, 308,
314, 394
Steele's Bayou Expedition, 367–368
Stembel, Roger N., 549
Stephens, Alexander H., 129, 527,
756
Steuart, George H., 320
Stevens, Isaac I., 66, 518, 625–626
Stevens Battery, USS, 715
Stevenson, Ala., 1–2, 569
Stevenson, Carter L., 83, 178, 180, 575
Stewart, Alexander P., 137, 149, 155,
159, 161, 185, 186, *187,* 188,
190, 193, 200–201, 204, 435,
579, 595, 596, 597, 603, 606
Stirling's Plantation, La., 298
Stone, Charles P., 53, 633–634
Stoneman, George, 8, 23, 166, 169,
179–180, 184, 198, 215,
221–222, 225, 665, 690, 768
Stone Mountain, Ga., 191
Stone Mountain Park, Ga., 195–196

Stones River (Murfreesboro), Battle of, 5, 133, 475, 562–566, *563, 564, 567–568*

Stones River National Battlefield, Murfreesboro, Tenn., *565, 566*

Stonewall, CSS, 248

Stonewall Jackson House, Lexington, Va., 766

Stonewall Jackson Memorial Cemetery, Lexington, Va., 766

Stonewall Jackson Shrine, Guinea Station, Va., 678

Stoughton, Edwin H., 624–625

Stout, Samuel H., 211

Strand, Galveston, Tex., 615

Strasburg, Va., 646

Streight, Abel D., 5–7, 8, 157

Stringham, Silas, 419–420

Strong, George c., 520, 522

Stuart, Flora, 769

Stuart, J.E.B., 328, 340, 394, 446, 477, 478, 563, 624, 625, 633, *644,* 669, *674,* 686, 750, 769
   at Brandy Station, 659–663, *660*
   at Chancellorsville, 675–676
   death of, 684, 691
   at Gettysburg, 491, 492, 496, 499, *500*
   Gettysburg Campaign and, 320–321, 481, 483, 484–485
   gravesite of, 739
   in Loudoun Valley, 634–635
   monument to, 691–692
   in ride around McClellan, 697–698, *698*

Stuart, John T., 345

Stuart, Richard, 672

Sturdivant Hall, Selma, Ala., 10

Sturgis, Samuel S., 334, 360, 417, 585–587

Sudley Church, Manassas Battlefield, Va., 632

Suffolk, Va., 762–763

Sullivans Island, Charleston, S.C., 504, 509–510, 512

Sully, Alfred, 462, 463–464

Sulphur Creek Trestle, Battle of, 3

Sultana, 218

Sumner, Edwin V., 81, 86, 336–337, 666, *667,* 669, 705, 706, 707, 709

Sumter, CSS, 251, 253, 254

Sunnyside mansion, Nashville, Tenn., 606

Sunshine Church, Battle of, 211, 221–222, 225

Supreme Court Building, Washington, D.C., 61

Surratt, Mary, 61, 71, 72, 327

Surratt Tavern, Clinton, Md., 327

Surrender Triangle, Appomattox, Va., 749, 750

Susseratt House, Chambersburg, Pa., 480

Sutherlin, W. T., 765

Swanton house, Decatur, Ga., 196

Sweeney, Joel W., 750

Sweeney, Sam, 750

Sweeny, Thomas, 5, 153, 154–155, 156, 171, 193, 196, 247

Swilling, Jack, 77

Sykes, George, 493, 665, 680, 708

Taliaferro, William, 522

Tallahassee, CSS, 220–221, 251

Talleysville, Va., 699

Tampa, Fla., 101, 112–113

Tannehill State Historic Site, McCalla, Ala., 5

Tanyard Branch Park, Atlanta, Ga., 189

Tatnall, Josiah, 525, 526

Tawah, USS, 544

Taylor, Richard, 2, 26–27, 88, 210, 285, 292, *295,* 298, *308,* 309, 311, 312, 316, 543, *641,* 653, 654
   background of, 295–296

Taylor, Zachary, 295

Tebbs Bend, Battle of, 279, 281

Tecumseh, USS, 17, 18–19, 21, 63

Teel, Travanion T., 88, 95

Tennessee, 30, *536,* 537–607

Tennessee, CSS, 8, 10, 15–16, 18–20, *18,* 21, 64, 423

Tennessee, University of, Knoxville, Tenn., 584

Tennessee Historical Society, 606

Tennessee State Museum, Nashville, Tenn., 606

X Corps, U.S., 710, 711

10th Ohio Volunteer Infantry Camp, Chattanooga, Tenn., 579

Terry, Alfred H., 429, *431,* 432–433, 435

Texas, 307, *608,* 609–619

Thames House, Jonesboro, Ga., 208

Thatcher, Henry K., 24

Thayer, John M., 45–46

Thespian Hall, Boonville, Mo., 409

III Corps, U.S., *490,* 492, 494, 665, 675–676, 678, 705

XIII Corps, U.S., 24, 314, *378,* 385, 390

Thomas, George H., 9, 133–134, 191, 192, 199, 203, 208, 223, 568, 570
   in Atlanta Campaign, 147, 148–149, 150, 158, 165, 169, 179, 185, 186, *187*
   at Chickamauga, 135, *136,* 137–139, *138, 139,* 142
   at Mill Springs, 265–266
   at Missionary Ridge, 575–576
   at Nashville, 603–605
   nom de guerre of, 139
   Rosecrans replaced by, 571

Thomas, Lorenzo, 61

Thomas V. B. Hargis House, Kingston, Ga., 159

Thomas Viaduct, Annapolis Junction, Md., 324

Thompson, Albert, 262

Thompson, M. Jeff, 49, 401, 549, 553

Thoroughfare Gap, Va., 636

Tidewater tour, 756–758

Tigress, 345

Tilghman, Lloyd, 263, 386, 539–540

Tiptonville, Tenn., 547

Todd, George, 454

Todd's Tavern, Spotsylvania, Va., 686

Tomb of the Unknown Soldier of the Confederate States of America, Biloxi, Miss., 397

Tomkins, Sally L., 735

Tom's Brook, Battle of, 646, 648

Toombs, Robert A., 129, 230, 338

Torbert, Alfred, *642,* 645, 690

Totopotomy Creek, Battle of, 702–703

Townsend, George A., 334

Tracey, Edward, 379

Traveler's Rest, Nashville, Tenn., 607

travel symbols, xxviii, xxix

Treasury Building, Washington, D.C., 51, 57–58

Tredegar Iron Works, Richmond, Va., 735, 738

Trent Affair, 249

Trevilian Station, Battle of, 690

Trimble, Isaac R., 320, 323, 576

Trinity, Ala., 4

Trophy Point, West Point, N.Y., 446

Troup Hurt House, Decatur, Ga., 195, 196–197

Trousdale Mansion, Gallatin, Tenn., 607

Tryon Palace, New Bern, N.C., 427

Tuckahoe, Va., 693

Tullahoma, Tenn., 538

Tullie Smith House, Atlanta, Ga., 189

Tunnard, Willie, 391–392

Tunnel Hill, Battle of, 147–148, 150

Tunnel Hill Historical Foundation, Tunnel Hill, Ga., 148

Tupelo, Battle of, 361–362

Tupelo National Battlefield Site, Tupelo, Miss., 361–362

Tupelo Visitors Center, Tupelo, Miss., 360–361, 362

Turchin, John, 572

Turkeytown, Ala., 6

Tuscumbia, Ala., 4–5

Twain, Mark (Samuel L. Clemens), 82

XII Corps, U.S., *490,* 495, 572

XX Corps, U.S., 133, 134, 151, 154–155, *164,* 165, 171, 188, 199, 202–203, 205, 206, 228, 242, *438*

20th Maine Regiment, *491, 493*

XXI Corps, U.S., 133, 134, 135
XXIII Corps, U.S., 165, 169, 171, *173*, 191, 208, 588, 595
XXV Corps, U.S., 737, 747
Twin Lakes State Park, Green Bay, Va., 744
Tybee Museum, Fort Screven, Tybee Island, Ga., 236
Tyler, Daniel, *627*, 628, 785
Tyler, Erastus B., 331, 653
Tyler, Robert C., 212
Tyler, USS, 41, 558

UDC Confederate Monument, Knoxville, Tenn., 584
Ulysses S. Grant Home State Historic Site, Galena, Ill., 347–348
Ulysses S. Grant National Historic Site, St. Louis, Mo., 407
Uncle Ben, CSS, 611, 612
Underground Atlanta, Atlanta, Ga., 206–207
Undine, USS, 544
Union Cemetery, Kansas City, Mo., 413
Union University, Murfreesboro, Tenn., 567
Unionville, Va., 664
United States Army Military History Institute, Carlisle, Pa., 483
United States Army Transportation Museum and Research Library, Newport News, Va., 758
United States Arsenal, St. Louis, Mo., 407
United States Capitol, Washington, D.C., 51, 52–54, 58, 60, 61
United States Colored Troops (USCT), 24, 41, 538, 550, 710
  first combat action of, 316
United States Customs House, New Orleans, La., 292
United States Customs House, Norfolk, Va., 757
United States Military Academy, West Point, N.Y., 446
United States Naval Academy, Annapolis, Md., 324–325
United States Naval Hospital, Portsmouth, Va., 757
United States Sanitary Commission, 445
United States Soldiers' and Airmen's Home, Washington, D.C., 68
University Museums, Oxford, Miss., 359
Upper Sioux Agency State Park, Minn., 461–462
Upton, Emory, 9, *685*, 686
USS *Cairo* Museum, Vicksburg, Miss., 375, 392
Utah Territory, 75, 449, 450

Utoy Church, Atlanta, Ga., 202
Utoy Creek, Battle of, 201

Valentine Museum, Richmond, Va., *738*
Vallandigham, Clement L., 343, 350, 351
Valley Campaign of 1862, 637–638, 640–641, *641*, 652–656
Valley Campaign of 1864, 637, 641–649, 656–657, 725, 782
  "Burning" in, 645
  "Sheridan's Ride" in, 648, *648*
Valverde, Battle of, 85, 87–88, 89
Van Den Corput, Max, 155, 156
Van Derveer, Ferdinand, 139
Vandever, William, 49
Van Dorn, Earl, 5, 30–33, *34*, 35, 38, 356–357, *356*, 358–359, 394, 554–555, 557
  death of, 598
Van Lew, Elizabeth, 737
Van Lew House, Richmond, Va., 737
Varnell House, Varnell, Ga., 144
Varuna, USS, 289–290
Velocity, USS, 611
Vendue House, Nassau, Bahamas, 256
Venus, 544
Vermont, *442*, 446–447
Vest Home, Boonville, Mo., 409
Vicksburg, Miss., 14, 353, *393*
Vicksburg Campaign (First), 286, 358–364
  Brices' Crossroads battle and, 359–360
  Forrest's raid and, 559–560
  "Grant's Canal" and, 314–315, 316
  Holly Springs raid and, 358–359
  Louisiana canal projects and, 314–316, 317
  Okolona battle and, 362–363
  Tupelo battle and, 361–362
Vicksburg Campaign (Second), 39–40, 41, 286, 296, 303, 364–392, *378*, *389*, 568
  Big Black River battle in, 386–387
  Champion Hill battle in, 385–386
  Chickasaw Bayou assault in, 39, 368–369
  Grand Gulf Operation and, 376–377, *378*, 380
  Greenville Expedition in, 366
  Grierson's raid and, 294, 394–395, 554
  May 19 assault in, 387
  May 22 assault in, 388, 390
  naval operations in, 370–372, *373*
  Port Gibson Operation in, 377–380
  Raymond battle and, 382, 383
  Steele's Bayou Expedition in, 367–368, 372
  strategy changes in, 372–375

Vicksburg siege in, 388–390
  Yazoo Pass Expedition in, 365, 368, 372
Vicksburg Circle Tour, Vicksburg, Miss., *352*, 354, *375*
Vicksburg National Cemetery, Vicksburg, Miss., 392
Vicksburg National Military Park, Vicksburg, Miss., 375, 392, 393, *393*
Victoria, queen of England, 246
Vincennes, USS, 287
Vincent, Strong, 493–494
Vinings Hill, Vinings, Ga., 181
Virginia, 57, *618*, 619–769, *620*, *622*, 782
Virginia, CSS, 10, 551, 714–715, 751–757, *752*, 758
Virginia Campaign of 1864, 679–693, 702–705, 710–715, 780
  Bermuda Hundred engagements and, 712–713
  Chaffin's Farm battle and, 710–711
  Cold Harbor battle in, 600, 654, 703
  Drewry's Bluff engagement and, 714–715
  Grant's strategy for, 679
  Kilpatrick's raid and, 692–693
  New Market Heights battle and, 710–711
  North Anna battle in, 688–689
  Spotsylvania battle in, 684–686, *685*
  Totopotomy Creek battle in, 702–703
  Trevilian Station battle in, 690
  Wilderness battle in, 679–683, *681*
  Yellow Tavern battle in, 691
Virginia Historical Society, Richmond, Va., 739
Virginia Military Institute, 649, *650*, 651, 654, 765
Virginia Military Institute Museum, Lexington, Va., 766
Virginia State Capitol, Richmond, Va., 738
Virginia State House, Richmond, Va., 734, *734*

Wabash, USS, 118, 419, 525
Wachusett, USS, 253
Waddell, James I., 255–256
Wade, Jenny, *495*, 497
Wadsworth, James, 682, 696
Wagner, George D., 600
Walcutt, Charles C., 226, 227–228
Walke, Henry, 547
Walker, James G., *573*
Walker, John G., 47, 310, 311, 329
Walker, Norman, 256
Walker, William H. T., 137, 154, 155, 188, 193, 195, 196, *196*, 569

Wallace, Lew, 263, 330–332, *330,* 541, 558
Wallace, W.H.L., 557
Wallace House, Petersburg, Va., 731
Walthall, Edward C., 188, 604, 605
Wangelin, Hugo, 201
Ward, John T., 205, 220–221
Ward, William T., *187,* 188
War Memorial Museum of Virginia, Newport News, Va., 758
War of the Rebellion, The: Official Records of the Union and Confederate Armies, 450
Warren, Gouverneur K., 492–493, 680, 683, 684, *685,* 686, 688, 689, 702, 721, 722, 724, 727, 728
Warren Heritage Society, 643
Warren House, Jonesboro, Ga., 209, *209*
Washburn, C. C., 553
Washburne, Elihu B., 343, 347, 348
Washington, D.C., *see* District of Columbia
Washington, Ga., 230
Washington, George, 679
  Richmond statue of, 738
Washington, N.C., 424
Washington Arsenal, Washington, D.C., 62–63
Washington Confederate Cemetery, Hagerstown, Md., 341
Washington Monument State Park, Md., 334
Washington Navy Yard, Washington, D.C., 63–64
Washington Territory, 75, 449, 450
Washington-Wilkes Historical Museum, Washington, Ga., 230
Watie, Stand, 32, 33, 470–473
Watkins, Louis D., 142
Watt House, Richmond, Va., 701–702
Wauhatchie, Battle of, 572–573, 577
Waynesboro, Battle of, 656–657
Waynesboro, Ga., 231, 232–233
weapons, novel, 303, 388, 510
Weed, Stephen H., *337,* 493
Weehawken, USS, 240, 507, 513
Weeks, Edmund C., 111
Weer, William, 470
Wehner, William, *192*
Weiser, Josiah S., 462
Weitzel, Godfrey, 296
Welles, Gideon, *55,* 56, 103, 512, 524
Wentz, John, 494
West, Joseph R., 78
Westfield, USS, 614, 615
West Martello Tower, Joe Allen Garden Center, Key West, Fla., 114
Westminster, Md., 320–321
West Point, Battle of, 212
West Point Foundry, Cold Spring, N.Y., 446

West Point Museum, West Point, N.Y., 446
West Point (U.S. Military Academy), 446
Westport, Battle of, 412, 413
Westview Cemetery, Atlanta, Ga., 202
West View Cemetery, Dalton, Ga., 151
West Virginia, *770,* 771–785
Wharton, John A., 312
Wheeler, Joseph, 5, 83, 129, 147, 149, 150, 154, 160, 165, 169, 181, 182, 186, *187, 190,* 191, 192, 193, 195, 196, 200, 202, 211, 222, 224–225, 226, 231, 232–233, 234, 269, 280, 435, 436, 527, 531, 543, 563, 570, 571, 579, 580–581, 602
Wheeler Monument, Newnan, Ga., 212
Wheeling Conventions, 771
Whitaker's House, Williamsburg, Va., 761
White, Aaron, 598
White, A. M., 77
White-Force Cottage, Selma, Ala., 10
"White Hall", Spring Hill, Tenn., 598
White Hall State Historic Site, Richmond, Ky., 268
White House, Washington, D.C., 54–57, 58, 60
White House of the Confederacy, Richmond, Va., 734–735, 738
White House Visitor Center, Washington, D.C., 57
White Oak Lake State Park, Bluff City, Ark., 48
White Oak Road, Battle of, 727, 728
White Oak Swamp, Battle of, 707
White River Expedition, 35
Whitestone Battlefield Historic Site, Dickey County, N.Dak., 464–465
Whitestone Hill, Battle of, 463–464
White Sulphur Springs, W.Va., 775
Whitfield-Murray Historical Society, 152
Whiting, William H. C., 433
Whitman, Walt, 672
Whitman-Anderson House, Ringgold, Ga., 143
Whittier, John Greenleaf, 332
Widow Tapp Farm, Wilderness Battlefield, Va., 681, 684
Wilcox, Cadmus M., 83, 677
Wilder, John T., 137, 141, 182, 183, 278, *567,* 568, 569
Wilderness, The, Battle of, 670, 680–683, *681, 682, 683*
Wilderness Church, Chancellorsville, Va., 678
Wilderness Tavern, Wilderness Battlefield, Va., 683

Wilkes, Charles, 249
Willard, Joseph, 61
Willard Hotel, Washington, D.C., 51, 60
Willard Park, "Walk of Cannons," 64
Willett, Charles, 472
William and Mary College, Williamsburg, Va., 762
William P. Clyde, 527
William Presley Gunnell House, Fairfax, Va., 625
Williams, Alpheus S., *187*
Williams, Catherine, 589
Williams, James M., 470–471
Williams, John S., 588
Williams, R. S., 588
Williams, Thomas, 293–294, 315
Williamsburg, Battle of, 761–762
Williamsport, Md., 340–341
Willis, David, 500
Wilmington, N.C., 13, 428–430, 533, 725
Wilson, James H., 1, 8–9, 10, 12, 23, 129, 212–214, 218, 221, 224–225, 365, 394, 595, 597, 600, 604, 605, 606, 717, 723
Wilson, Woodrow, 59
Wilson's Creek, Battle of, 30, 410, 415–417, *415,* 524
Wilson's Creek National Battlefield, Republic, Md., 417
Winchester, First Battle of, 640–641, *641,* 644, 652, 774
Winchester, Second Battle of, *495,* 641, 785
Winchester, Third Battle of, 643, 644
Winder, John H., 218
Winder Building, Washington, D.C., 60
Windsor Plantation, Port Gibson, Miss., 380, *380*
Winnebago, USS, 17
Winslow, John, 254–255, 257
Winstead's Hill, Franklin, Tenn., 602
Winter Quarters State Commemorative Area, Newellton, La., 316–317
Winthrop, Theodore, 759
Wirz, Heinrich "Henry," 61, 218–219
Wisdom, John, 7, 158
Wise, Henry A., 421, 772–773
Wofford, William T., 159, 160
Wood, Charles R., 226
Wood, Thomas J., 137, 574, 579, 604, 605
Wood Lake, Battle of, 460
Wood Lake State Monument, Minn., 461
Woodlawn mansion, Nashville, Tenn., 606
Woodrow Wilson International Center for Scholars, Washington, D.C., 59

Woodruff House, Macon, Ga., 225
"Woodstock Races," 646
Wool, John E., 757
Worden, John L., 103, 754–755
Wornall Home, Kansas City, Mo.,
        413
Wright, Ambrose, 422
Wright, Horatio G., 67, 117, 120, 518,
        526, 638, 641, 645, 647, 703,
        727, 729, 742, 744, 746

Wrightsville, Pa., *483*, 484
Wylie, Andrew, 61
Wyndham, Percy, 662
Wyse Fork, Battle of, 425, 426

Yates, Richard, 347
Yazoo City, Miss., 366–367
Yazoo Pass Expedition, 365
Yellow Bluff Fort State Memorial,
        Jacksonville, Fla., 123

Yellow Tavern, Battle of, 684,
        691
York, Pa., 483–484
Younger, Cole, 454
Younger, Jim, 282

Zion Presbyterian Church, Columbia,
        Tenn., 596
Zollicoffer, Felix, 264–265, 266,
        606